MOON

JAPAN

JONATHAN DEHART

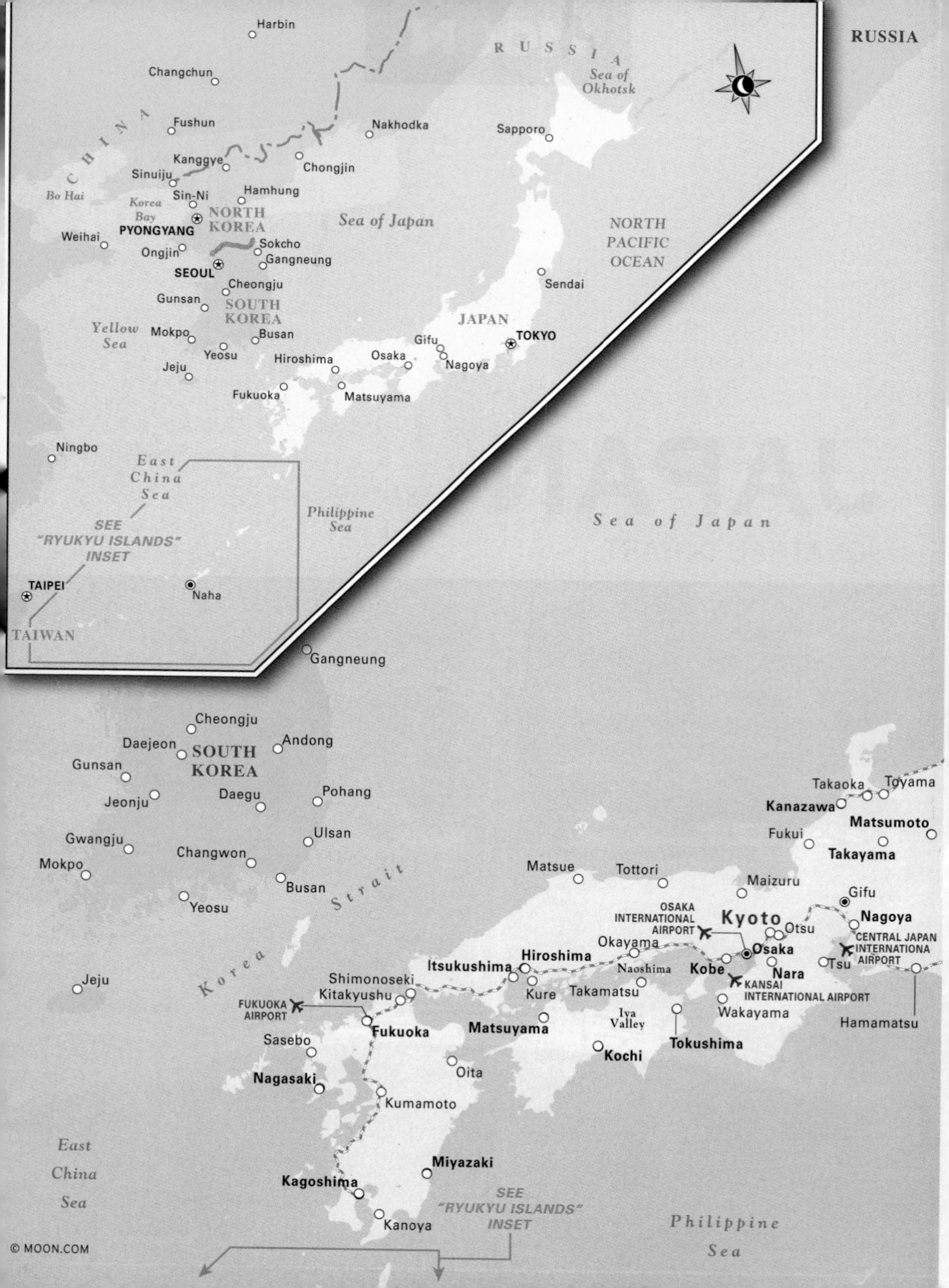

RUSSIA
Harbin
Changchun
CHINA
Fushun
Nakhodka
RUSSIA
Sea of Okhotsk
Sapporo
Kanggye
Chongjin
Sinuiju
Bo Hai
Sin-Ni
Hamhung
Korea Bay
PYONGYANG
NORTH KOREA
Sea of Japan
NORTH PACIFIC OCEAN
Weihai
Ongjin
Sokcho
SEOUL
Gangneung
Cheongju
Sendai
Gunsan
SOUTH KOREA
JAPAN
Yellow Sea
Mokpo
Busan
TOKYO
Yeosu
Gifu
Hiroshima
Osaka
Nagoya
Jeju
Fukuoka
Matsuyama
Ningbo
East China Sea
Philippine Sea
SEE "RYUKYU ISLANDS" INSET
TAIPEI
Naha
TAIWAN
Sea of Japan
Gangneung
Cheongju
Daejeon
SOUTH KOREA
Andong
Gunsan
Jeonju
Daegu
Pohang
Takaoka
Toyama
Kanazawa
Matsumoto
Gwangju
Ulsan
Fukui
Takayama
Mokpo
Changwon
Matsue
Tottori
Busan
Maizuru
Yeosu
Korea Strait
Gifu
OSAKA INTERNATIONAL AIRPORT
Kyoto
Otsu
Nagoya
CENTRAL JAPAN INTERNATIONA AIRPORT
Okayama
Osaka
Hiroshima
Itsukushima
Tsu
Jeju
Shimonoseki
Naoshima
Kobe
Nara
Kitakyushu
Kure
Takamatsu
KANSAI INTERNATIONAL AIRPORT
FUKUOKA AIRPORT
Iya Valley
Wakayama
Hamamatsu
Fukuoka
Matsuyama
Sasebo
Tokushima
Kochi
Oita
Nagasaki
Kumamoto
East China Sea
Miyazaki
Kagoshima
SEE "RYUKYU ISLANDS" INSET
Philippine Sea
Kanoya
© MOON.COM

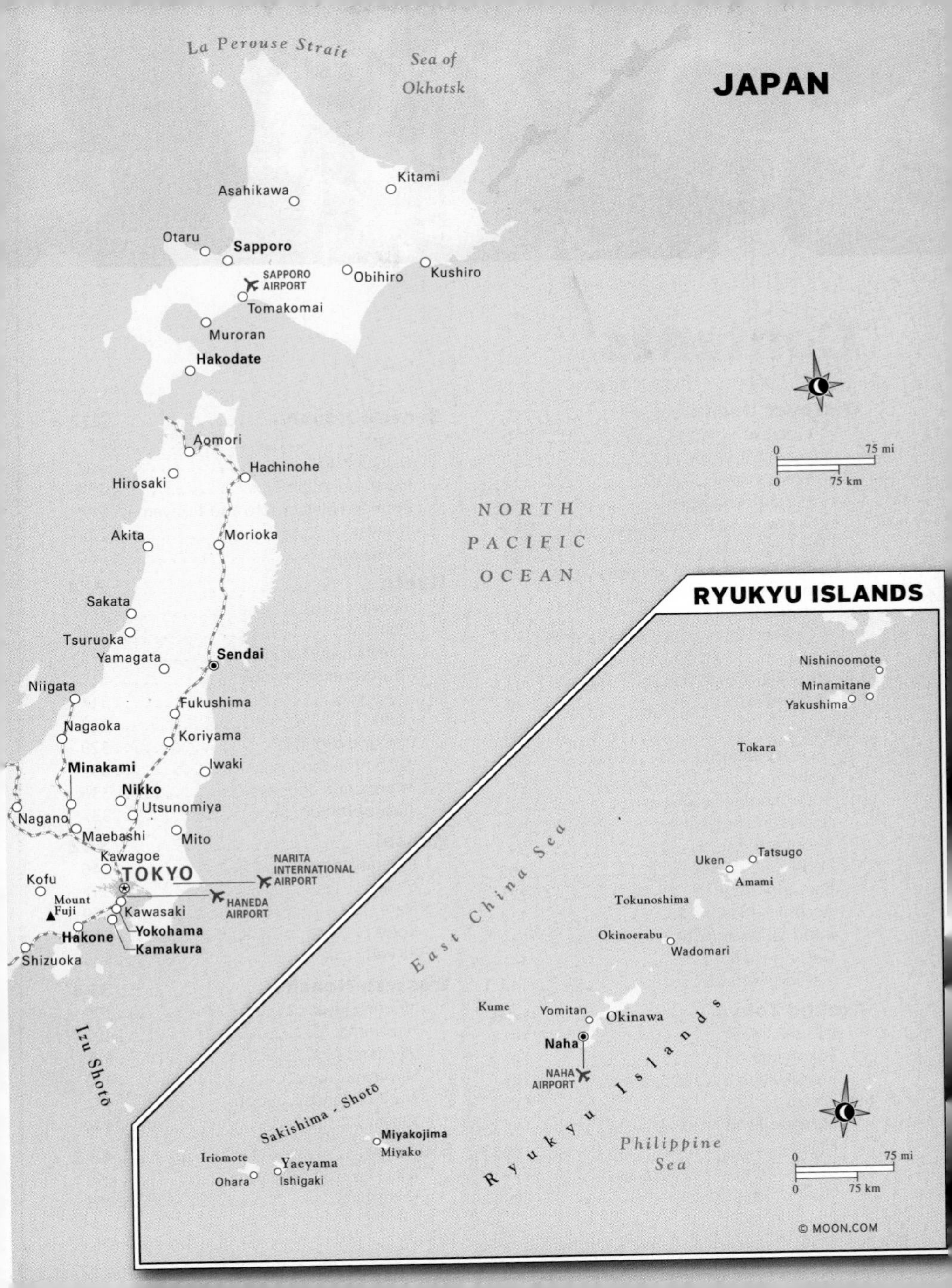

JAPAN

La Perouse Strait
Sea of Okhotsk
Kitami
Asahikawa
Otaru
Sapporo
Obihiro
Kushiro
SAPPORO AIRPORT
Tomakomai
Muroran
Hakodate
Aomori
Hachinohe
Hirosaki
NORTH PACIFIC OCEAN
Akita
Morioka
Sakata
Tsuruoka
Yamagata
Sendai
Niigata
Fukushima
Nagaoka
Koriyama
Iwaki
Minakami
Nikko
Utsunomiya
Nagano
Maebashi
Mito
Kawagoe
TOKYO
NARITA INTERNATIONAL AIRPORT
Kofu
Mount Fuji
HANEDA AIRPORT
Kawasaki
Yokohama
Hakone
Kamakura
Shizuoka
Izu Shotō
0 75 mi
0 75 km

RYUKYU ISLANDS

Nishinoomote
Minamitane
Yakushima
Tokara
East China Sea
Uken
Tatsugo
Amami
Tokunoshima
Okinoerabu
Wadomari
Kume
Yomitan
Okinawa
Naha
NAHA AIRPORT
Ryukyu Islands
Sakishima - Shotō
Miyakojima
Miyako
Iriomote
Yaeyama
Ohara
Ishigaki
Philippine Sea
0 75 mi
0 75 km

Contents

Discover Japan **6**
- 14 Top Experiences 10
- Planning Your Trip 20
  - What's New 21
  - Hanami and Kōyō 24
  - Staying in a Ryokan 28
- The Best of Japan 30
  - Top Temples and Shrines 33
- Japan's Wild North: Tohoku and Hokkaido 35
  - Onsen: Getting into Hot Water in Japan 37
- From Beaches to Volcanoes: Kyushu and Okinawa 39

Tokyo **41**
- Itinerary Ideas 50
- Sights 54
- Entertainment and Events 87
- Sports and Recreation 94
- Shopping 99
- Food 108
- Bars and Nightlife 123
- Accommodations 134
- Information and Services 139
- Getting There 141
- Getting Around 144

Around Tokyo **148**
- Itinerary Ideas 153
- Yokohama 156
- Kamakura 167
- Nikko 177
- Minakami and Around 185
- Hakone 189
- Mount Fuji 199
- Fuji Five Lakes 207

Central Honshu **212**
- Nagoya 217
- Matsumoto 227
- Northern Japan Alps 234
- Between Matsumoto and Takayama 244
- Takayama 251
- Kanazawa 260

Kyoto **274**
- Itinerary Ideas 285
- Sights 289
- Entertainment and Events 313
- Sports and Recreation 315
- Shopping 317
- Food 320
- Bars and Nightlife 329
- Accommodations 332
- Information and Services 336
- Transportation 337

Kansai **342**
- Itinerary Ideas 346
- Osaka 351
- Nara 369
- Kobe 377
- Kii Peninsula 385

Western Honshu **393**
- Itinerary Ideas 399
- Hiroshima 402
- Miyajima 415
- San'yo 420
- The Art Islands 432
- San'in 444

Shikoku **452**
- Takamatsu and Around 458
- Tokushima 463

Iya Valley 470
Matsuyama and Around 476
Kochi 487

Tohoku **494**
Miyagi Prefecture 499
Yamagata Prefecture. 507
Iwate Prefecture 514
Akita and Aomori Prefectures 520

Hokkaido **536**
Itinerary Ideas 541
Sapporo 545
Around Sapporo 557
Hakodate. 569
Daisetsuzan National Park. 576
Eastern Hokkaido 582
Rishiri-Rebun-Sarobetsu National Park. 591

Kyushu **595**
Itinerary Ideas 600
Fukuoka. 605
Nagasaki 624
Central Kyushu 639
Miyazaki Prefecture. 653
Kagoshima 660

Okinawa and the Southwest Islands. **672**
Itinerary Ideas 679
Yakushima. 682
Okinawa-Hontō. 687
Kerama Islands 701
Miyako Islands. 705
Yaeyama Islands 711

Background **721**
The Landscape 721
Plants and Animals 725
History. 729
Government and Economy. 737
People and Culture 740

Essentials **752**
Transportation. 752
Visas and Officialdom 761
Festivals and Events 762
Recreation. 765
Food and Drink 768
Accommodations 771
Conduct and Customs 774
Health and Safety 775
Practical Details. 776
Traveler Advice 781

Resources **784**
Glossary. 784
Japanese Phrasebook 785
Suggested Reading. 793
Internet Resources and Apps 795

Index **797**

List of Maps **808**

Although every effort was made to make sure the information in this book was accurate when going to press, research was impacted by the COVID-19 pandemic and things may have changed since the time of writing. Be sure to confirm specific details, like opening hours, closures, and travel guidelines and restrictions, when making your travel plans. For more detailed information, see page 754.

DISCOVER

Japan

Dusk falls on Shibuya, where trendy Tokyoites amass at the world's busiest crossing. The walk signal turns green and a scramble ensues, resembling a human pinball machine. Meanwhile, in the ancient capital of Kyoto, a geisha's wooden clogs make a distinct clicking sound as she whisks along the cobblestones of Ponto-chō alley.

Tradition and modernity have a unique way of mingling in Japan. Kyoto, and on a slightly smaller scale Kanazawa, on the western coast of Central Honshu, are treasure troves of traditional culture, from temples to tea ceremonies, though the rush of tourists reminds you that the present is never far away. Hypermodern Tokyo and Osaka are urban dream worlds of pop culture and cutting-edge technology, but serene parks, temples, and gardens allow you to find pockets of Zen even in the heart of the urban metropolis.

The food is another study in contrasts. Whether it's a sidewalk ramen stall in Fukuoka, a countryside izakaya (Japanese pub) in a hamlet in the Japan Alps, or a sushi spread in Hokkaido, Japanese cuisine deserves all the praise that it gets. A deep sense of craftsmanship, as well as connoisseurship, informs Japan's

Clockwise from top left: bridge on Okinawa; Hakone Yuryō Onsen; torii of Fushimi Inari-Taisha; Tokyo Bay; lanterns in Hyakumangoku Matsuri; Mount Fuji above Lake Ashi.

fastidious attention to detail in everything from sword-making and distilling whisky to DJ bar sound systems tuned to pin-drop perfection.

Japan's natural wonders exert as much pull as its culture. For a country of its size, the range of terrain is striking—from the sweeping vistas of Hokkaido and the Japan Alps of Central Honshu, to the mist-shrouded peaks of Shikoku and the volcanoes of Kyushu in the south. This landscape means access to hiking and hot springs year-round, and skiing in winter. The string of islands southwest of Kyushu, the largest being Okinawa, add world-class beaches and scuba diving. And when cherry blossoms blanket the entire country every spring, friends throw hanami (flower viewing) parties under the colorful branches.

Above all else, the hospitality of the people—from dark-suited office workers striving to power Japan Inc., to renegade chefs and teens seeking transcendence by dressing like their favorite anime characters—is what makes a trip to Japan special. The Japanese have a history of dusting themselves off and rebuilding after setbacks, from the ashes of World War II to the aftermath of the March 2011 Tohoku earthquake and tsunami. Most recently, the COVID-19 pandemic dealt a blow to Tokyo's Olympics, which were delayed for a year and were the world's first without spectators. Yet, as the haze of the pandemic slowly lifts, there's a buzz of optimism in the air, and Japan is eager to welcome back visitors to fall under its subtle spell.

Clockwise from top left: freshly caught scallops being prepared at a restaurant near Ise; stone statues in Kamakura; dancers in the Kōenji Awa Odori festival; Okayama-jō.

14 TOP EXPERIENCES

1 Crossing through the ancient torii gates of Tokyo's **Meiji Jingū** (page 70) or Kyoto's **Fushimi Inari-Taisha** (page 290).

2 Wandering the sculpted beauty of **Kenroku-en,** one of Japan's most exquisite gardens (page 262).

3 Immersing yourself in Tokyo's nightlife, whether you're bar-hopping in **Shinjuku** (page 131), or sipping Japanese **whisky** in a connoisseur's bar (page 127).

4 Coming face to face with **Mount Fuji,** whether marveling at it from afar (page 202) or climbing it up close (page 200).

5 Savoring **kaiseki ryōri,** a seasonal feast for all the senses that represents Japanese cuisine at its most refined, in its birthplace of Kyoto (page 277).

6 Bedding down for the night in a traditional **ryokan,** feeling the warm welcome of the Japanese hospitality tradition known as omotenashi (page 28).

7 Escaping modern Japan in the **folk villages of Shirakawa-gō and Gokayama,** where thatched-roof farmhouses evoke a fairy-tale scene (page 258).

>>>

8 Tasting the best fried **food in Osaka,** Japan's lively, neon-lit street food capital (page 360).

<<<

9 Taking in world-class art next to sublime seaside panoramas in the picturesque, forward-thinking **Art Islands** (page 432).

>>>

10 Trekking to a temple, whether you're climbing the 1,000 steps of **Yamadera** (page 507) or walking part of the **88-Temple Pilgrimage** (page 464).

11 Dancing and merry-making at a traditional festival; **Awa Odori** in Shikoku (page 465) and **Nebuta Matsuri** in Tohoku (page 532) are two of the best.

12 Soaking in toasty, mineral-rich waters in an **onsen on Kyushu,** which boasts more hot-spring baths than any other island in Japan (page 650).

13 Skiing through fresh powder at **Niseko** (page 560) or one of Hokkaido's other **world-class ski resorts** (page 564).

14 Lounging on the remote beaches of the **Kerama Islands** in Japan's tropical far-south (page 701).

Planning Your Trip

Where to Go

Tokyo

The high-octane capital should be top priority for any first visit to the country. Tokyo is **quintessential modern Japan,** a pop-cultural and economic juggernaut, and base of the national government. The dynamic city is a feast for the senses, with world-class **food, nightlife,** and **shopping.** It's also the most networked **transport hub** in Japan, with two international airports and extensive rail links to the rest of the country.

Around Tokyo

The region surrounding Tokyo offers a number of enticing **side trips** that are perfect if you have limited time. South of Tokyo is Japan's second-largest city, cosmopolitan **Yokohama,** with a buzzing nightlife scene, and the ancient seaside feudal capital of **Kamakura,** with its rich Buddhist heritage. West of there, **Hakone** is a good pick for an **onsen (hot spring)** experience, with Japan's most famous peak, **Mount Fuji,** looming nearby. Northeast of Tokyo is the alpine town of **Nikko,** an ancient center of mountain

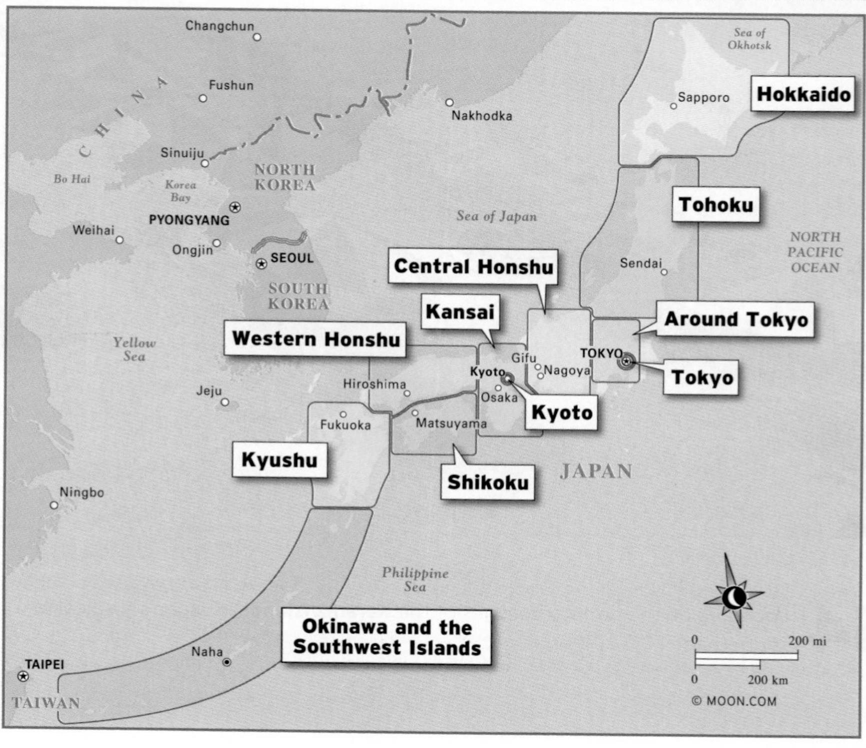

What's New

- Tokyo has a new station on the Yamanote line, **Takanawa Gateway,** which was opened in preparation for the 2020 Summer Olympics. This high-tech hub is staffed by robots that clean and offer guidance, and even an unattended convenience store.
- Both Miyajima's iconic "floating" **torii gate** and **Dōgo Onsen's** historical bathhouse are being revamped. The bathhouse is only partially accessible, while Miyajima's gate can be seen, albeit wrapped in scaffolding.
- Reconstruction works on two iconic castles—**Kumamoto-jō** in the city of its namesake, damaged by an earthquake in 2016; and Naha's **Shuri-jō,** ravaged by a fire in 2019—are ongoing. Both castles can now be viewed in part; Kumamoto's main keep reopened to the public in the summer of 2021, but rebuilding could be ongoing for a few decades in other parts of the mammoth complex. Renovations on Naha's vermillion citadel expected to be done around 2026.
- Nationwide, the impact of the **COVID-19** pandemic has knocked many businesses off balance. Be sure to check the website of a given business, whether it be a shrine, restaurant, or bar, before making the trip.

worship with flamboyant temples, shrines, and mausoleums.

Central Honshu

With the lion's share of the country's highest peaks, the **Japan Alps** offer excellent **hiking** in warmer months and abundant powder for **skiing** and **snowboarding** in winter. Tucked into valleys, rural hamlets oozing rustic charm and historic centers like **Matsumoto** and **Takayama** welcome visitors to their charming townscapes. To the west, beside the Sea of Japan, the city of **Kanazawa** offers a low-key alternative to Kyoto, with its samurai and geisha quarters and dreamy old garden of **Kenroku-en.**

Kyoto

Alongside the modern capital of Tokyo, the ancient capital of Kyoto should be top priority for any first journey to Japan. This is the best place to explore **traditional culture,** to see **geisha,** to try a **tea ceremony,** to **shrine- and temple-hop,** to eat **kaiseki ryori** (haute Japanese cuisine), to stay in a high-end **ryokan,** and to gaze at various styles of **gardens,** from landscape to raked gravel. Step away from the top sights to discover a slower, more local side of the city, beyond the tourist throngs.

Kansai

A great complement to Kyoto, the Kansai region is home to **Osaka,** a fun place to eat, drink, and carouse with legendarily friendly locals. Nearby, the small town of **Nara,** home to the famed **Great Buddha of Tōdai-ji,** is a great place to see traditional Japan, minus Kyoto's crowds. The attractive port city of **Kobe** is known for its high-end beef and jazz, while **Himeji** has Japan's best castle. Farther afield, you'll discover spiritual hot spots like **Kōya-san** and the **Kumano Kodō pilgrimage route.**

Western Honshu

The urbanized, sun-drenched southern coast along the gorgeous **Inland Sea** is home to the vibrant, modern incarnation of **Hiroshima,** as well as the famed "floating" torii shrine gate of **Miyajima's Itsukushima-jinja.** This is juxtaposed against a mellow northern shore on the Sea of Japan side, where the heart of "old Japan" still beats strong. Picturesque historic towns like **Matsue** and the **Izumo Taisha** grand shrine

Ishigaki-jima, one of the Southwest Islands

offer the chance to see a slower, simpler, more local side of Japan free of tourist hype.

Shikoku

Rustic and remote, with a gorgeous coastline and the sparkling **Inland Sea,** one of the world's most beautiful seascapes, to its north, Shikoku is best known for its arduous **88-temple pilgrimage circuit** that runs clockwise around the island and can be done in part or in full. The rugged interior is best explored in the **Iya Valley** region, where vine bridges and hillside hamlets of thatched-roof houses beckon. And in August, **Awa Odori,** Japan's most exciting traditional summer festival, takes place in Tokushima.

Tohoku

Located on the northern end of Honshu, Tohoku is a mountainous region steeped in legend. Here you'll find spiritual **pilgrimage routes,** mountaintop **temples,** stunning natural vistas, hidden **hot springs,** and some of the best **summer festivals** in Japan. It's also the home of the pine-covered islands of **Matsushima.** This is a wonderful region to explore if your goal is to go where the vast majority of tourists don't.

Hokkaido

The hub of Japan's final frontier is the bustling city of **Sapporo,** known for its hearty cuisine. The remainder of the island's inhabitants live in laid-back fishing towns, which serve superb seafood. Beyond the towns, the northernmost main island is awash with unspoiled nature. Come here to experience the wild side of Japan, from world-class **skiing** and **snowboarding** in winter to **hiking, wildflowers,** and **wildlife-spotting** in summer. Not to mention, it's culturally the homeland of Japan's indigenous people, the **Ainu.**

Kyushu

Volcanic, subtropical, and spiritual, Kyushu has deep ties to Shinto myth. It's also where Japan first encountered the West when Portuguese sailors made landfall in 1543. Today you can eat **street food** in **Fukuoka;** stroll through dynamically reborn **Nagasaki;** sip **shōchū** in **Kagoshima;** peer into the caldera of an active

volcano, or relax in an **onsen**—of which there are more here than on any other island in Japan. A trip to Kyushu works well when combined with the emerald isles of Yakushima and Okinawa, Japan's subtropical side.

Okinawa and the Southwest Islands

The long bow of subtropical islands extending southwest from Kyushu toward Taiwan have a culture, diet, and laid-back pace distinct from the rest of Japan. The main transport hub, **Naha,** is located on the main island, **Okinawa-Hontō,** where the region's ties to **World War II** are still visible. **Remote beaches** and **scuba diving** meccas cover the islands to the south. The ancient green **forests** of **Yakushima,** to the north, boast some of the best **hiking** in Japan.

Know Before You Go

When to Go

Most of Japan has four distinct seasons, interspersed by a few rainy periods, though the country's diverse geography means the climate varies. **Spring** (roughly late March through mid-June) and **autumn** (October through early December) are the most pleasant times of year to visit the country. That said, it's a year-round destination, with each season offering its own draw.

SPRING

Spring begins to creep northward from Kyushu around **early to mid-March** and hits most of Honshu soon after. Spring tends to be **cool** (8-24°C/46-75°F in Tokyo)—gradually warming through **April** and **May**—with patches of rain. **Cherry blossoms** start to bloom from around early to mid-March in Kyushu, late March in Tokyo, and around early May in Hokkaido, where

Philosopher's Path

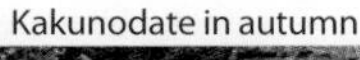

Kakunodate in autumn

Hanami and Kōyō

In Japan, the coming of the **sakura** (cherry blossoms) marks the transition from winter into spring. It is a glorious time to be in the country, underscoring just how much the seasons figure into the nation's psyche. People flock to parks and riversides around the country, sitting under the pink boughs in an annual rite known as **hanami** (flower viewing). In autumn, a more subdued, though equally Japanese pastime known as **kōyō** takes place when the leaves of maples, gingkos, and more blanket the country in an earth-tone palette of red, orange, yellow, tan, and brown.

WHEN TO SEE CHERRY BLOSSOMS AND AUTUMN FOLIAGE

Hanami tends to sweep through Japan's geographical core—Tokyo extending south and west through Kansai and beyond—around the last week of **March** and the first week of **April,** heading north through Tohoku **mid- to late April** and reaching Hokkaido in **late April-early May.**

Peak kōyō runs **mid-November to mid-December** for much of the southern half of Japan, including the Tokyo and Kansai regions and a large swath of southern Kyushu. Expect the leaves to turn from **late September-early November** in higher altitudes. If you're in the mountains of Central Honshu or Tohoku, aim to see the autumnal display from **mid-October-late November** in the lower elevations, or **late September-early November** in the mountains. In Hokkaido, the leaves turn early, from **late September-early October.**

Being in Japan during either season is magical, but be forewarned: These are **peak travel times.** To ensure you're not left with slim pickings for accommodations, or paying maximum yen, plan any travel during these times *early.* Think 9-12 months in advance. Keep in mind that **weekdays** will be less hectic than weekends.

BEST SPOTS

	Hanami	Kōyō
Tokyo	Ueno-kōen (page 95); Yoyogi-kōen (page 95); Inokashira-kōen (page 95)	Shinjuku Gyōen (page 76); Koishikawa Kōrakuen (page 79)

spring temperatures range -1-17°C (30-63°F). Overall, it's a great time to visit.

Except for Hokkaido, most of Japan is wet throughout **June,** during the **tsuyu (rainy season).** Overcast skies with patches of rain and the occasional all-day shower are the norm during this period, though there are plenty of sunny days in between, too.

SUMMER

From **July** through **September** things can be downright **stifling,** with furnace-like temperatures (23-31°C/73-88°F in Tokyo) and high humidity throughout much of the country, save for Hokkaido, which is slightly cooler (14-26°C/57-79°F). While less amenable than spring, the months of July and August can be a fun time to visit the country due to a plethora of vibrant **festivals** held throughout this sweltering period. Among the best are **Fukuoka's Hakata Gion Matsuri** (first half of July), **Kyoto's Gion Matsuri** (most of July, culminating on July 17), **Osaka's Tenjin Matsuri** (July 25), **Aomori's Nebuta Matsuri** (Aug. 2-7), **Akita's Kanto Matsuri** (Aug. 3-6), and **Tokushima's Awa Odori** (Aug. 12-15). If you're visiting the country during any of these bashes, **book accommodations well in advance** (three months or more, to be safe).

	Hanami	Kōyō
Around Tokyo	Tsurugaoka Hachiman-gū shrine, Kamakura (page 169)	Hakone (page 189)
Central Honshu	Matsumoto-jō (page 227); Kenroku-en, Kanazawa (page 262)	Shirakawa-gō (page 258)
Kyoto	The Philosopher's Path (page 301); Heian-jingū (page 298)	Kiyomizu-dera (page 295); Tōfuku-ji (page 294); Jōjakkō-ji (page 310)
Kansai	Osaka-jō (page 353); Himeji-jō (page 381)	Nara-kōen (page 369)
Western Honshu	Hiroshima's Peace Memorial Park (page 406); Miyajima (page 415)	Momijidani-kōen, Miyajima (page 417)
Tohoku	Aoba Castle, Sendai (page 499); Kakunodate (page 526)	Yamadera (page 507); Geibi-kei Gorge (page 515)
Hokkaido	Moerenuma Park, Sapporo (page 549); Goryōkaku Park, Hakodate (page 573)	Daisetsuzan National Park (page 576)
Shikoku	Matsuyama-jō (page 476); Ritsurin-kōen (page 459)	Iya Valley (page 470)
Kyushu	Kumamoto-jō (page 639)	Kurokawa Onsen (page 650); Yufuin (page 650)

AUTUMN

In **September** and **early October**, massive **typhoons** whip through Okinawa, then move northward through Kyushu, Shikoku, and Honshu, but normally stop short of Hokkaido. These storms have been known to wreak havoc on parts of Japan, with torrential rain and even devastating floods on occasion. These extreme cases aside, it's perfectly safe to travel during this time of year. Just be sure to keep an eye on the weather forecast.

Autumn proper starts from around **early October** and lasts through **November** in Tohoku and Hokkaido (fall temperatures range 1-6°C/34-62°F in Sapporo), extending into the first half of **December** for much of Honshu, Shikoku, and Kyushu (10-22°C/50-72°F in Tokyo). This is one of the most pleasant times to visit Japan. As temperatures drop, **blazing foliage** ripples through the country, with November being the high point. Rates for accommodations do spike around this time in scenic places, so **book ahead** if you plan to venture into nature.

WINTER

Winter sets in from **mid-December** through **mid-March**, with temperatures varying significantly across the country (2-12°C/36-54°F in Tokyo, -8-2°C/18-36°F in Sapporo). Okinawa never really gets cold—temperatures range 14-19°C (57-66°F) even in January.

The Sea of Japan side of Honshu is frigid, windy, and snowy, while the Pacific side is cold, dry, and crisp, with clear skies and little snow. Meanwhile, Hokkaido and the western half of Tohoku have some of **the heaviest average snowfalls** on Earth. Legendary powder also accumulates in the Japan Alps. This means great skiing and snowboarding. There are also excellent **winter festivals,** with the huge **Sapporo Snow Festival,** the intimate **Otaru Snow Light Path Festival,** and the dramatic, fiery **Nozawa Onsen Dosojin Matsuri** atop the list.

HANAMI AND OTHER BUSY TIMES

High season in Japan includes **hanami** (cherry blossom viewing) season (roughly late March-early April), the **Golden Week** holidays (April 29-May 5), **Obon** (roughly August 10-17), and the **kōyō** (autumn foliage) craze in November. To avoid crowds, it's best not to visit the country during these periods, as trains, highways, and hotels will overflow with domestic travelers from around the time the cherry blossoms start to bloom, around early to mid-March in Kyushu, late March in Tokyo, and early May in Hokkaido.

SLOWER MONTHS

Less hectic months include **June,** the **dead of summer** (July, August besides Obon, and September), **October,** and **December.** Aside from ski resorts, which do brisk business, the period of **January** through **March** is **low season** for the rest of the country. Deals can be had during any of these off months, especially if you plan several months ahead.

Things generally remain in operation throughout the year, the one exception being the **New Year holidays** (December 29-January 3), when everything but convenience stores, some chain restaurants, and most accommodations (at elevated rates) closes down for the holidays. While experiencing Japan's New Year traditions is one point in favor of visiting over the New Year holidays, it's probably best to come at another time.

Passports and Visas

To enter Japan, you'll need a **passport** valid for the duration of your trip from the date of your arrival in the country. Although you may not be asked to show it, you're legally obligated to have an onward ticket for either a flight or ferry out of Japan for a return trip or a future leg of the journey elsewhere. So have something in hand just in case.

If you're coming from the U.S., Canada, the UK, most European countries, Australia, or New Zealand, you'll be granted a **90-day single-entry visa** on arrival. South African citizens will need to apply for a **90-day tourist visa** at their closest embassy or consulate. For passport holders from the UK, Ireland, and a number of other European countries (Germany, Austria, Switzerland, Lichtenstein), it's possible to extend your visa for another 90 days. This requires a trip to the closest immigration bureau and paying a ¥4,000 fee. For a list of the 68 nations not required to apply for a visa to travel to Japan, visit www.mofa.go.jp/j_info/visit/visa/short/novisa.html.

What to Take

One of the beautiful things about Japan is its well-stocked **convenience stores.** These one-stop shops, selling everything from toiletries and undershirts to bento-box meals and portable phone chargers, umbrellas, cosmetics, and more, are ubiquitous throughout urbanized Japan, making it easy to pick up anything you've forgotten to pack.

Nonetheless, there are a few items you'd be wise to bring. For one: **shoes** that are easy to take on and off (**slip-ons** work best). You'll likely find yourself taking off your shoes much more than you're used to—in someone's home, in a temple, and so on. Also pack any **medications** and accompanying **prescriptions** you may need. Be sure to check Japan's strict laws on medication before traveling with medicine. The **U.S. Embassy** provides helpful information on their website about this matter: https://jp.usembassy.gov/u-s-citizen-services/doctors/importing-medication.

The electrical outlets in Japan are the same shape as those in the United States, so travelers with devices from the UK or Europe may need a plug adapter. The voltage is 100V; many modern electronics are dual voltage, so a converter may not be necessary, but check your devices to be sure.

It also pays to be aware of Japan's love of **gift-giving.** This is especially important if you plan to meet anyone who may invite you to their home. It need not be expensive. Some kind of a sweet snack or beverage that can be shared, a recording of interesting music, or some kind of decorative item would all do. A little gift goes a long way in Japan.

Planning Ahead

There are a few things that need to be in order before you leave for Japan. If you plan to get a **Japan Rail Pass** (www.japanrailpass.net), a great value if you plan on making full use of the country's extensive train network, **you must purchase it before traveling to Japan.** You cannot buy a JR Pass once you are in Japan.

If you're planning to travel to some of the more remote parts of Japan and want to rent a car, make sure you've already gotten your **international driver's license** (IDP, aka international driving permit). To learn more about the process of obtaining an IDP, visit https://internationaldrivingpermit.org, which provides country-by-country information on the process of applying. It doesn't hurt to **book your rental car before your trip** to avoid hassle later.

It also pays to make **reservations** for some meals, attractions, or events, such as a sumo tournament or sporadically held Noh theater performance, a few months in advance. Some **popular attractions,** such as Tokyo's Ghibli Museum and Kyoto's "moss temple" Saihō-ji, only allow a set number of visitors per day; you'll need to book your place at these attractions up to a few months in advance as well. If you're determined to snag a seat at a world-class sushi counter, kaiseki ryōri restaurant, or any other truly **world-famous restaurants,** some of the wait times are shocking. Aim to book seats months in advance.

If your visit coincides with a **festival** or one of the **high seasons,** try to book

shinkansen (bullet train)

Staying in a Ryokan

traditional ryokan

A stay in a traditional Japanese inn (ryokan) offers the chance to experience many classic elements of Japanese comfort—spare traditional interiors, sleeping on a futon on a tatami-mat floor, and haute dining in your room. But perhaps what stands out most is the relaxed pace and impeccable omotenashi (hospitality) at the heart of a ryokan stay.

OMOTENASHI

Translated literally, omote means "public face" and nashi means "nothing." In other words: no pretense; to meet guests' needs wholeheartedly. At its root, this philosophy of hospitality is deeply focused on the anticipation of guests' needs, and the belief that no service task is menial if it is done with a pure heart for the benefit of the customer or guest. This spirit, ubiquitous across Japan, first emerged from the tea ceremony, wherein tea masters prepare the brew in direct view of participants who likewise intently watch the master work. In ryokan, it translates to the sense of ease travelers feel bedding down for the night after a kaiseki feast.

WHAT TO EXPECT

Ryokan vary significantly, from modest family-run countryside pensions to luxe getaways. Some core elements shared by ryokan across the spectrum include simple tatami-mat floors, both private and shared onsen baths, and excellent meals delivered twice daily to your room, from breakfast (Japanese or Western, depending on the inn) to kaiseki spreads for dinner. (Some more modest digs serve meals in common areas.) Furniture will be simple: a low wooden table with floor-cushions to sit on, a futon for sleeping (usually laid out as you eat dinner). And just as you'd imagine: plenty of translucent, paper sliding doors (shoji), and tokonoma (alcoves) containing calligraphy scrolls and vases of flowers.

JAPAN'S BEST RYOKAN

Every traveler to Japan should aim to spend at least one night at a great ryokan. The following list is a good place to start:

- **Ryokana Sawanoya, Tokyo:** A wonderful, family-run, budget ryokan with legendarily helpful staff (page 137).
- **Gōra Kadan, Hakone:** This forest-enshrouded ryokan is justly renowned for delectable kaiseki spreads, incense-laden halls, and superb rooms (page 198).
- **Asadaya, Kanazawa:** An exquisite ryokan full of beautiful artwork, spare Zen-like rooms, and a historic, samurai air (page 272).
- **Yoshida Sansō, Kyoto:** The one-time home of a prince, this ryokan is located on a mountain amidst the temples of Northern Higashiyama (page 334).
- **Edosan, Nara:** Ensconced in Nara-kōen, home to wandering semi-domesticated deer, is this historic ryokan that is hard to resist (page 375).
- **Iwasō Ryokan, Miyajima:** An ideal escape for those who want to experience the sacred isle of Miyajima after the day-trippers return to the mainland (page 419).
- **Tsurunoyu Onsen, Nyūtō Onsen:** An old ryokan awash in rustic charm—dark wood, soft-lantern light, tatami floors, and dinners cooked over an en suite floor hearth (page 524).
- **Hanayura, Noboribetsu Onsen:** This riverside ryokan offers fine seafood spreads and crisp modern rooms (page 568).
- **Chaharu Hanare Dōgo Yumekura, Matsuyama:** A stylish, contemporary ryokan right across the street from the bathhouse that inspired Hayao Miyazaki's *Spirited Away* (page 481).

everything—accommodations, rental car, shinkansen (bullet train) tickets—as far in advance as you can (think three or even six months ahead).

Transportation

GETTING THERE

The vast majority of travelers will arrive in Japan via one of **four main airports:** Tokyo's Narita Airport or Haneda Airport, Osaka's Kansai International Airport, or Nagoya's Chubu Centrair International Airport. It's also possible to enter the country by sea, with **hydrofoils** and **ferries** shuttling daily between **Busan, South Korea,** and **Fukuoka.** Ferries also make the trip between **Shanghai** and both **Osaka** and **Kobe.**

GETTING AROUND

Once you're on the ground, transportation options are profuse, from trains and planes to buses, ferries, and rental cars.

BY TRAIN

Japan's most efficient mode of transport is its **extensive railway** network. You'll be able to get where you're going aboard a train—whether of the **local, rapid,** or **shinkansen** (bullet train) variety—in the vast majority of cases. Traveling short distances within a city or town is also often best done by train, whether aboveground or subway.

If you plan to rely heavily on the rail network, consider buying a **Japan Rail Pass** (www.japanrailpass.net) before your trip. This pass—which offers unlimited trains on the Japan Rail (JR) network nationwide in increments of one, two, and three weeks—is a steal if you maximize it.

BY BUS

Buses are another option for traveling both long distances and just within town. Although less comfortable than trains, buses are sometimes the only means of reaching some **far-flung destinations.** They are also generally **cheaper** than trains, making them a good option if you're on a serious budget and don't mind the journey taking a bit more time.

BY TAXI

Taxis are abundant. That said, fares are **expensive.** They are best used for only **short distances** within a town or city when there's no cheaper means of getting around, when you're in a rush, or if you have money to burn.

BY CAR

A rental car will be invaluable if you're venturing well **off the beaten path.** This is especially the case when traveling in **rural Hokkaido, Tohoku, Shikoku's deep interior,** or some parts of **Kyushu** and **Okinawa.** Trains still run through some parts of these regions, but their frequency and reach can sometimes be frustratingly limited. Driving is on the **left,** like in the UK. If you plan to drive, you must get an **international driving permit (IDP)** before arriving. Visit https://internationaldrivingpermit.org for country-by-country information on the process of applying.

BY AIR

If you're short on time, consider using the country's far-reaching **domestic flight network.** This can prove particularly useful for trips to or from the northern or southern edges of the country, such as **Hokkaido, Kyushu,** or **Okinawa.**

BY BOAT

In terms of experience, taking a **ferry** will add a new dimension to any trip within Japan. If you happen to be traveling between Shikoku and Kyushu, Kyushu and Okinawa, or Honshu and Hokkaido, there are some ferry operators that make overnight journeys. High-speed, jet-propelled **hydrofoils** (aka jet foils) also make shorter journeys (e.g., from Kagoshima to Yakushima, or from Niigata to Sado-ga-shima).

Before hopping on a ferry, consider whether your trip timeline can accommodate a ferry's **slower pace** and whether you're prepared for potential **seasickness.** One advantage is the option to carry a bicycle, motorbike, or rental car on board for an added fee.

The Best of Japan

This two-week itinerary is a good choice for visitors making their first journey to Japan and can be done largely by train (local, express, and bullet train), with a few legs of the trip done by rental car or ferry. It covers the two major "must-visit" cities of Tokyo and Kyoto, and the two important regions in which these cities are located—Kantō, or Greater Tokyo, and Kansai to the south—while also passing through beautifully mountainous Central Honshu, or Chūbu. In Western Honshu, Hiroshima is both a sobering lesson in history and evidence of how resilient humans can be, and nearby Miyajima makes for a beautiful, spiritual day trip. You'll see urban jungles, traditional temples, gorgeous scenery, and fascinating historic sites, and you'll eat very well along the way.

If this itinerary seems a bit ambitious, you could leave off the Japan Alps, or some of the stops in between Kyoto and Hiroshima, and give yourself a buffer day or two in Tokyo and Kyoto. This itinerary starts with your first full day in Japan, so the day you arrive at either Narita or Haneda, just plan on getting to your accommodation and sleeping off some jetlag. It also plans on an open-jaw trip, flying into one of Tokyo's airports and flying out of Kyoto.

Tokyo

For your time in Tokyo, the western districts of Shinjuku or Shibuya or the upscale area around Tokyo Station would each be a good place to base yourself.

DAY 1

Get acquainted with Tokyo's modern side by exploring Shinjuku, Shibuya, and Harajuku. Start at **Meiji Jingū,** Tokyo's most impressive shrine, then wander through the side streets of the sprawling district of **Harajuku,** ground zero for youth fashion in Japan. Proceed down **Omotesandō** and its high-end shops to **Aoyama,** where you'll find the **Nezu Museum's**

Akihabara at night

Shibuya Crossing

collection of premodern Asian art and a wonderful garden. Make your way to **Shibuya,** the beating heart of Japanese youth culture and home to the world's busiest intersection—ascend to the top of **Shibuya Sky** for a bird's-eye view—and finish your night with dinner and drinks at a lively izakaya in trendy **Ebisu.** After you've eaten, go for **cocktails** or to one of the city's many excellent **DJ bars** nearby.

DAY 2

Start the day by exploring the slower, old-school neighborhoods on the east side of town. Begin with a trip to the colorful Buddist temple **Sensō-ji** in **Asakusa,** then head west to **Ueno,** famed for its massive park and the **Tokyo National Museum,** which houses the world's largest collection of Japanese art. Proceed to nearby **Akihabara,** the best spot to glimpse some of Japan's quirky subcultures, chief of them being otaku, a catch-all word for all things geek. End the day with dinner in **Shinjuku,** followed by a bar crawl through **Golden Gai's** drinking dens.

DAY 3

Spend your morning souvenir shopping, perhaps in **Akihabara** for gadgets, quirky items, and things geek, or doing something offbeat that interests you. After lunch, head to the suburb of **Kichijōji,** 15-20 minutes west by train from central Tokyo. Enjoy a visit to **Ghibli Museum,** a quirky ode to anime director Hayao Miyazaki's fictional universe set in the tranquil green space of **Inokashira-kōen.** Make a leisurely trip back to the train, perhaps picking up a coffee and window shopping along the way, then head to the hip enclave of **Shimokitazawa.** Here, you'll find plenty of vintage clothes and atmospheric restaurants, and you can end your night with a drink or even some live music.

Hakone

DAY 4

Leave the mega-city of Tokyo for the hot-spring mecca of **Hakone,** located a few hours by train southwest of Tokyo. Check into a **ryokan** (traditional inn) and spend the day soaking in **onsen baths,** donning a yukata (lightweight kimono), and enjoying Japan's legendary spirit of hospitality (omotenashi)—all with the chance of a view of Mount Fuji if the weather is clear.

The Japan Alps

DAY 5

After breakfast at your ryokan, set out early for the long journey to **Takayama,** a historic town with oodles of charm nestled in the Hida region of the Japan Alps. Aim to be on a train departing Hakone-Yumoto by 9:30am. You'll need to transfer trains in Nagoya, a two-hour journey, where you can grab a bite to eat before hopping onto a limited express train to Takayama (2 hours 20 minutes). Make your way to the **Sanmachi Suji** and enjoy meandering through this district of old wooden lanes for the rest of the afternoon. When dinnertime comes, opt for **Kyōya,** a rustic izakaya serving the town's famed beef, mountain vegetables, and more. At night, enjoy the town's surprisingly lively **nightlife zone.**

DAY 6

Have breakfast at your accommodation before renting a car and setting out for the evocative folk village regions of **Shirakawa-gō** and **Gokayama,** which collectively make up a UNESCO World Heritage site. Your first stop is **Ogimachi.** Soak up the alpine vibes of the wonderfully preserved thatched-roof farmhouses and eat a lunch of regional beef paired with vegetables foraged in the nearby mountains. Then drive north 30 minutes to the more remote folk Gokayama region, arriving first at the village of **Suganuma,** followed by **Ainokura,** perhaps the most atmospheric of all, 15 minutes' drive north of Suganuma. By mid- to late afternoon, drive south to the decidedly urban environs of **Nagoya,** about 2.5 hours to the south, where you'll stay for the night. Try one of Nagoya's sweet and savory specialties for dinner—miso-katsu is a good pick.

house in Ainokura

Arashiyama Bamboo Grove

Kyoto

During your stay in Kyoto, Gion or downtown make convenient bases.

DAY 7

After a good night's sleep, eat breakfast and head to Nagoya Station to hop on a shinkansen bound for Kyoto, a 35-minute ride. Drop off your bags at your accommodation, have some lunch, and spend the afternoon exploring a few of the city's major sights. Consider the hillside temple of **Kiyomizu-dera,** the majestic Pure Land Buddhist temple of **Chion-in,** and maybe **Nijō-jō** castle. In the evening, splurge on a once-in-a-lifetime dinner at a **kaiseki ryōri** restaurant, followed by cocktails or **whisky** at one of Kyoto's refined bars.

DAY 8

Discover Kyoto's less-crowded side on your second day in the city. Head to **Arashiyama's** famous **bamboo grove,** after first exploring the beautiful gardens of neighboring **Tenryū-ji,** and be sure to visit the less-crowded **Ōkōchi Sansō Villa,** once home to a Japanese movie star and famed for its sublime gardens and traditional architecture. The atmospheric temples of **Jōjakkō-ji, Nison-in, Giō-ji,** and **Adashino Nenbutsu-ji** are all within 20 minutes' walk north of the villa, with a fraction of the crowds that visit the grove. Backtrack to the **Katsura-gawa** and have lunch at one of the eateries lining the river. Make your way to **Ryōan-ji** to check out the temple's rock garden and some of the other famous sights in the area, such as the gold-leaf-covered **Kinkaku-ji.** Plan on having dinner in the **Gion district.** Consider seeing a **geisha performance** after dinner, followed by a stroll down the dreamy, lantern-lit alleyway of **Ponto-chō.**

Osaka

DAY 9

In the morning, visit some of the spiritual gems of the **Higashiyama** neighborhood, from important Zen temple **Nanzen-ji** to **Ginkaku-ji,** the silver companion to golden Kinkaku-ji, and the contemplation-inducing

Top Temples and Shrines

Priests and monks have been meditating, chanting, studying, and performing rituals at temples and shrines across Japan for millennia. These spiritual sanctuaries range from humble and rustic to flamboyant and colorful, even plated with gold. In the case of **Shinto,** the form of nature worship native to the archipelago, halls of worship are known as **shrines** (with names that include -jinja, -jingū, -gū, -hongū, Taisha, etc.), while in the case of the imported faith of **Buddhism,** they're known as **temples** (with names that include -tera, -dera, -ji, -in, etc.).

Here are some outstanding examples of the country's religious architecture.

- **Meiji Jingū:** Tokyo's top shrine is set within an expansive swath of green in the heart of the city that makes for a pleasant stroll and reprieve from the din outside (page 70).
- **Fushimi Inari-Taisha:** With a famous walking path lined by thousands of vermillion torii gates, this complex in southeast Kyoto is the head shrine dedicated to Inari, the god of rice (page 290).
- **Kinkaku-ji:** Originally the house of a retired shogun, the upper two floors of this Zen Buddhist temple in Kyoto are coated in gold leaf, inspiring the name "the Golden Pavilion" (page 307).
- **Tōdai-ji:** This temple in Nara is the largest wooden structure on earth, and it's only two-thirds the size of the original. It houses a 15-meter-tall (45-foot-tall) bronze Daibutsu (Great Buddha) (page 372).
- **Okuno-in:** Set amid soaring cedar trees, the cemetery, temple, and mausoleum are full of fierce guardian deities, moss-encrusted stone monuments, and stone lanterns (page 387).

monk at Okuno-in

- **Ise-jingū:** Shinto's holiest shrine, Ise's spell is woven through its sheer simplicity. The shrine has been dismantled and rebuilt every 20 years for the past 1,300 years (page 389).
- **Itsukushima-jinja:** This shrine on the island of Miyajima near Hiroshima is famed for its torii gate that seemingly floats on the Inland Sea during high tide (page 415).
- **Yamadera:** This remote temple complex sprawls over a mountainside in deep Tohoku, reached by a steep path lined by stone lanterns and Buddhist statuary (page 507).

Philosopher's Path. Be sure to check out low-key, moss-drenched **Hōnen-in** when you're in the area. After lunch, make your way to Osaka. Spend some time flaneuring your way through the neon-lit streets of nightlife zones **Shinsaibashi, Amerika-mura,** and **Namba.** For dinner, indulge in a food crawl through **Dōtombori:** options include takoyaki (fried dough balls stuffed with octopus), okonomiyaki (savory pancakes), and kushikatsu (deep-fried skewers of meat, seafood, and veggies).

Kōya-san

DAY 10

Today, make your way to the mountain hermitage of **Kōya-san,** (1-2 hours by train, followed by a 5-minute cable car ride and a 10-minute bus ride). Once you've arrived at the remote mountain hermitage, check into your shukubō (temple lodging), where you'll be based for a night. In the remaining daylight, explore Kōya-san's temples and the atmospheric cemetery of **Okuno-in.** For dinner, eat like a monk with a feast of **shōjin-ryōri** (Buddhist vegetarian fare) at your temple-cum-lodging. If you want to soak up the cemetery at its most otherworldly, consider a second trip after dinner to amble along its paths, which are dimly lit by stone lanterns at night.

Hiroshima and Miyajima

DAY 11

Get an early start and backtrack from Kōya-san to Osaka, where you'll hop on a shinkansen at Shin-Osaka Station bound for Hiroshima (total travel time approximately 4 hours). After arriving in the city and checking into your accommodation, visit Hiroshima's **Peace Park** in the afternoon for a sobering lesson on one of the darkest moments in Japan's history. For dinner, try the city's signature spin on **okonomiyaki,** a delicious savory pancake.

DAY 12

Today, take the JR San'yo line from Hiroshima Station to Miyajimaguchi Station (25 minutes), before walking to the nearby ferry terminal for the 10-minute trip to nearby **Miyajima** and **Itsukushima-jinja,** famed for its "floating" torii shrine gate. After having lunch at one of the island's seaside cafés, consider riding the cable car to the top of **Mount Misen,** then hiking to the peak where you'll discover a series of temples along the way and enjoy phenomenal views of the Inland Sea spreading in all directions. By late afternoon, make your way back to the port to backtrack to Hiroshima by ferry and train (total trip: 30-45 minutes). Back in Hiroshima, take a breather and wash up if you feel the need to rest before dinner, or maybe visit a few of the city's more colorful places to grab a drink.

shōjin-ryōri at Kōya-san

Himeji-jō

Return to Kyoto

DAY 13

Leave Hiroshima early in the morning, taking the shinkansen east to Himeji (1 hour). Visit **Himeji-jō,** easily Japan's best castle. Spend a few hours on its extensive grounds and inside the structure itself, marveling at its construction and scale. But save your appetite for lunch until you've made the journey to Sannomiya Station in **Kobe,** 40 minutes east on the JR line. Treat yourself to the city's melt-in-your-mouth beef. After a leisurely lunch, ride the train north, back to Kyoto (50 minutes), where you can do some souvenir shopping and enjoy dinner at another of the city's elegant eateries.

DAY 14

On your last day in Japan, make your way to **Fushimi Inari Taisha,** one of Japan's most bewitching shrines and a sight that you're sure to remember your whole life. You'll fly out of Kansai International Airport (KIX), roughly 1.5 hours away by train or limousine bus.

Japan's Wild North: Tohoku and Hokkaido

Moving north from Tokyo, through the vast region of Tohoku, the terrain becomes increasingly rugged, while cities and towns feel evermore old-world. This is one of Japan's least-visited regions, making it all the more rewarding. Here, you'll find sparkling seascapes, ancient political centers, samurai heritage, mountaintop temples, pilgrimage trails, remote onsen hideaways, raucous festivals, and some of the deepest snowfalls on earth. Continuing north from Japan's main island of Honshu to Hokkaido, the scenery becomes even wilder. Hokkaido is Japan's last frontier: a vast wilderness, save for its energetic capital of Sapporo and earthy fishing towns dotting its shore. If your aim is to discover Japan's untamed side, this itinerary is for you.

Given that this itinerary involves plenty of time spent walking through nature, it's best suited to the warmer months (roughly May-October), with summer (July-August) being prime time.

Sendai, Matsushima Bay, and Yamadera

DAY 1

Arrive in Sendai from Tokyo by shinkansen (2 hours). After dropping off your bags, you have two options: Option 1: Ride the local Senseki line 40 minutes east to postcard-perfect **Matsushima Bay.** Glide through the lovely waterway in a boat, viewing the array of islands from the water. Back on land, depending on your time and interest, explore some of the nearby historic temples, including standout **Zuigan-ji.** Have lunch near Matsushima-Kaigan Station, then hop back on the Senseki line to Sendai. Option 2: Take the JR Senzan line to **Yamadera** (1 hour). Traipse up to the iconic mountaintop retreat of **Risshaku-ji,** one of the most dramatically placed temples in Japan. Whichever adventure you choose, return to Sendai for dinner of the city's specialty, **gyū-tan** (grilled beef tongue) and a well-deserved night's sleep.

Hiraizumi and Nyūtō Onsen

DAY 2

In the morning, take the train north to Hiraizumi, a once-mighty historical center an easy trip north of Sendai by train via Ichinoseki (average 1 hour, depending on transfers). In Hiraizumi, explore the UNESCO World Heritage jewels of **Chūson-ji,** a temple with a mesmerizing gilt main hall, and **Mōtsū-ji,** a temple with one of Japan's most sublime, and few remaining, Pure Land Buddhist gardens. (Note: If you're feeling tired of temples, as an alternative, consider a visit to **Geibikei Gorge** to be regaled by a boatman on the placid waters of the Satetsu River.) After eating lunch in Hiraizumi, take the train to Tazawa-ko via Morioka (total trip 2.5 hours), then hop on a bus (about 45 minutes) to the secluded onsen hamlet of **Nyūtō Onsen** in time for dinner at your ryokan of choice. After dinner, steep yourself in the hot baths of this legendary onsen, surrounded by natural splendor, before drifting off for a (guaranteed) good night's sleep.

Kakunodate

DAY 3

After breakfast at your ryokan in Nyūtō Onsen and a good morning soak, take the bus back to Tazawa-ko Station, then ride the shinkansen to **Kakunodate** (20 minutes). Stroll through this charming town's **buke yashiki** (samurai quarter), fringed by weeping cherry trees and feudal manors thick with ambiance. Have lunch in this old part of town—its udon noodles are renowned—before returning to Kakunodate Station. Hop on the shinkansen first to Morioka, where you'll transfer shinkansen lines to the one bound for Shin-Hakodate-Hokuto Station (total trip: roughly 3.5 hours), near the port town of **Hakodate,** gateway to Japan's main northern island of Hokkaido. Arriving in Hakodate by around dinnertime, check into your hotel and eat something before retiring for the night.

Hakodate

DAY 4

Begin your day at the **morning market** for a seafood breakfast before hopping on the tram to the east side of town and the star-shaped **Fort Goryōkaku,** the first Western-style fortress built in Japan. Get back on the tram to the west side of town for lunch in the historic **Motomachi** neighborhood and to explore its 19th-centry architecture. Before sunset, hop on the **Mount Hakodate Ropeway** and get in position to see the city's lights flicker, ending the day by heading to dinner on **Daimon Yokōcho,** an alley lined with eateries a quick walk southeast of Hakodate Station.

Matsushima Bay

soup curry

Onsen: Getting into Hot Water in Japan

Few places on earth have elevated bathing to an art as much as Japan. Like eating sushi, glimpsing Mount Fuji, or visiting a shrine, sinking into the hot, rejuvenating waters of an onsen (hot-spring) bath is a singular pleasure that should be high on your list on any trip to Japan. Blessed (or cursed?) with roughly 10 percent of earth's volcanoes, Japan has seemingly infinite pools, where steam wafts, the distinct smell of sulfur lingers, and people flock to steep in the geothermally heated waters.

All told, there are about 3,000 onsen resorts in Japan today, with both indoor and outdoor pools, often looking onto gorgeous natural scenes: mountains, forests, crashing waves. Below are some of the best.

- **Hakone:** This sprawling hot-spring mecca, set amid the natural splendor of Fuji-Hakone-Izu National Park, is the escape of choice for Tokyoites who need a break from the concrete jungle (page 189).
- **Shin-Hotaka Onsen:** Tucked away deep in the mountains east of the town of Takayama, this onsen area is famed for its co-ed bath, Shin-Hotaka-no-yu, set beside a river and surrounded by mountains swathed in forest (page 249).
- **Nyūtō Onsen:** Escape from the modern world at this remote jewel in the depths of Tohoku famed for its milky-white pool and old-school mixed bathing. This is my personal favorite (page 524).

an onsen

- **Kurokawa Onsen:** Located north of the vast caldera of Aso-san, this idyllic onsen village sits in a remote valley in the heart of Kyushu; its well-preserved atmosphere makes it among one of Japan's prettiest onsen towns (page 650).

Tōya-ko and Noboribetsu Onsen

DAY 5

Start your day early, traveling by train northeast for two hours to pristine lake **Tōya-ko.** Stop at the **Volcano Science Museum** to experience a simulated eruption, then take the nearby ropeway to the top of **Usu-zan** for wide-open vistas of Tōya-ko and nearby **Shōwa-shinzan,** Japan's youngest volcano. Follow the **Kompirayama Walking Trail,** which begins near Tōya-ko Visitor Center on the southwest side of the lake, where you'll see glimpses of industrial carnage—apartment blocks, bridges, roads, and more—destroyed when Usu-zan erupted in 2000. After taking in this sobering sight, travel to **Noboribetsu Onsen** to stay overnight at one of the ryokan in this famed hot-spring town.

Sapporo

DAY 6

In the morning, take a 75-minute train ride north to Sapporo, Hokkaido's bustling capital. Begin your exploration of the city at **Hokkaido Jingū,** the island's most important shrine. Have **ramen** or **soup curry** for lunch downtown, then explore the highlights of the city center—the long, central park of **Ōdōri-kōen,** the red-brick, 19th-century **Former Hokkaido Government Office,** and the **Hokkaido University Botanical Garden**—on foot. For another nighttime city view, head to **Mount Moiwa,** southwest of downtown, and ascend by ropeway and cable car. For dinner, try **Genghis Khan** (Mongolian BBQ) and wash it down with **locally brewed beer.** If you've got energy, head to the city's huge entertainment district, **Susukino,** Japan's rowdiest nightlife zone north of Tokyo.

Otaru

DAY 7

Take the train west to the old port town of Otaru and its charming **canal district,** fronted by atmospheric 19th-century warehouses and the **Otaru City Museum.** Continue to **Nichigin-dōri,** once Hokkaido's most important financial district, when Otaru made a mint as a 19th-century herring center. The town is still renowned for its fresh catch, so plan on eating lunch at one of its excellent **sushi** shops. As dusk approaches, get dinner at Otaru's canal-side **brewery** before heading back to Sapporo.

Daisetsuzan National Park

DAY 8

Hop on the train from Sapporo 1.5 hours to **Asahikawa,** the gateway to Daisetsuzan National Park, the largest national park in Japan, with some of its most rugged scenery. Rent a car and drive one hour east to **Asahidake Onsen,** where you'll stay for the night. Take one of the more manageable **hikes** in the Asahidake Onsen area, accessed via the **Daisetsuzan Asahidake Ropeway,** before winding down in the evening with a hot-spring bath in the village.

DAY 9

Drive about two hours northeast to **Sōunkyō Onsen.** Consider hiking to the top of **Mount Kurodake,** with a little help from the **Kurodake Ropeway,** accessed near the Sōunkyō Visitor Center, before staying overnight at the charming hot spring resort.

killer whales near Shiretoko National Park

red-crowned cranes in Hokkaido

Shiretoko National Park

DAY 10

Get an early start and drive roughly four hours east to the southern edge of Shiretoko National Park, which occupies a remote peninsula in northeast Hokkaido. Spend the day exploring the park's wealth of **hiking trails, wildlife-watching** opportunities, and open-air **onsen pools.** Spend the night in the town of **Rausu** on the east coast, a good base for exploring the park.

Kushiro Wetlands

DAY 11

In the morning, drive about three hours southwest to the Kushiro Wetlands, where you can see Hokkaido's famed **red-crowned cranes** in their native habitat. End your trip by driving 45 minutes west of the marshlands to **Kushiro Airport,** from where you can fly to either Sapporo or Tokyo.

From Beaches to Volcanoes: Kyushu and Okinawa

Kyushu is a fantastic representation of classic Japan—volcanos, onsen, great food, and attractive cities—and an appealing alternative to the usual Tokyo and Kyoto itinerary. Meanwhile, Okinawa and the string of islands extending beyond is decidedly un-Japanese: laid-back vibes, white-sand beaches, and a distinct culture and heritage. On this trip, you'll take trains, rental cars, ferries, and planes. It's a great choice if you'd like to discover a balmy, subtropical side of Japan that you may not have realized exists.

Fukuoka

DAY 1

After you've flown from Tokyo to Kyushu's largest metropolis of Fukuoka, begin your journey through Japan's southernmost main island by exploring this thoroughly modern city with a cosmopolitan vibe. Start your day near **Hakata Station,** exploring the city's primary spiritual sights: **Tōchō-ji,** known for its huge wooden Buddha statue, and **Kushida-jinja,** a shrine revered by many as the city's spiritual heart. Visit the **Fukuoka Asian Art Museum,** the **Fukuoka Castle Ruins,** and **Fukuoka City Museum** to dig a bit deeper into the important history of the city and its vibrant present. Head to the rows of **yatai (street food)** stalls along the riverfront on **Nakasu Island** and **Tenjin.**

Nagasaki

DAY 2

Hop on the train for a two-hour ride to Nagasaki. A quick ride on the city's efficient tram network takes you to the sobering **Peace Park,** which commemorates the nuclear bombing of the city during World War II. After leaving the park, head south by tram to the atmospheric district of **Teramachi ("Temple Town")** and visit **Sōfuku-ji,** a temple that demonstrates the clear Chinese influence long felt in the city. The nearby **Chinatown** (Shinchi) will allow you to literally taste China's imprint on the city. Next, head up the **Dutch Slope,** a neighborhood that shows another foreign group's influence. It's lined with 19th-century Western architecture, and is home to **Ōura Cathedral** and **Glover Garden.** Traipse downhill to **Dejima,** an artificial island created to accommodate Dutch traders during the 17th century. For dinner, try **shippoku,** Nagasaki's spin on haute kaiseki ryōri. End the day with a trip to the top of **Inasayama-kōen,** across the bay from downtown, to see the city's lights flicker on.

Kurokawa Onsen

DAY 3

In the morning, rent a car near Nagasaki Station and drive three hours eastward, making your way to the pristine hot spring village of **Kurokawa**

Onsen, set deep in a lush valley in a remote corner of Kumamoto Prefecture, north of the vast caldera of Aso-san. Check into your **ryokan** of choice, don a **yukata** (lightweight kimono), and spend the day vegging out in your room, soaking in your ryokan's tubs, and bath-hopping around the charming town. Eat a lavish dinner at your inn and sleep well.

Aso-san and Kagoshima

DAY 4

After breakfast at the inn and a final morning soak, drive to Aso-san to admire the views across the vast windswept **caldera.** Continue driving south for 3.5 hours to the laid-back city of Kagoshima, where you'll stay for the night. Head over to the pretty gardens of **Sengan-en** and be sure to also visit the nearby **Shoko Shuseikan** factory, where Japan's industrial revolution kicked off. For dinner, try one of Kagoshima's specialties, such as **kurobuta** (black pork) or **shabu-shabu** (hot pot), followed by a proper introduction to the prefecture's beloved beverage of choice, **shōchū.**

Yakushima

DAY 5

Start the day with a brief trip to **Sakurajima** (Japan's very own Vesuvius), crossing the bay by ferry. This active volcano is a daily presence for Kagoshima residents, before whom it belches smoke and ominously looms. Return to downtown Kagoshima for lunch, then head to the ferry terminal again—this time to board the **jet foil** to Yakushima. After arriving in Yakushima, rent a car at Miyanoura Port and drive to your accommodation for the night. Get settled in and rest well—you'll need the energy for the next day.

DAY 6

Wake up early—you will explore the emerald island of Yakushima for the whole day. Drive around the island and explore the beautiful **Ōkonotaki waterfall** or **Yakusugi Land,** a park that makes the island's famed giant Yakusugi trees more accessible, and **Hirauchi Kaichu Onsen,** a hot-spring pool on the south side of the island that can only be accessed at low tide. For something more substantial, consider the 3-4 hour hike through the lush **Shiratani Unsuikyō ravine,** which inspired anime maestro Hayao Miyazaki's masterful film *Princess Mononoke*. Return to your hotel for a good night's sleep.

Naha

DAY 7

Return by jet foil to Kagoshima in the morning. Head to **Kagoshima Airport** and fly to Naha, the capital of Okinawa Prefecture. Plan on eating somewhere with a traditional musical performance of Okinawa's wistful three-stringed instrument, the **sanshin.** Be sure to try Okinawa's potent booze, the spirit known as **awamori.**

Kerama Islands

DAY 8

Today it's all about the beach—take a jet foil to **Zamami-jima,** one of the islands in the Kerama island chain, less than an hour west of Naha, to while away your last day in Japan on **Furuzamami Beach.** As the afternoon wears on, hop on a jet foil from Zamami-jima directly back to **Naha,** where you can prepare for your flight home.

Tokyo

Tokyo is more than a city. Japan's sprawling capital bursts at the seams with a population of 37 million to form the largest metro area on the planet. The dizzying metropolis organically congeals around a cluster of hubs the size of cities themselves, giving Tokyo a labyrinthine quality. With the neon nightscapes of Shinjuku and Shibuya evoking *Blade Runner* in the west, the ancient temples and wooden houses of Ueno and Asakusa in the east, and palpable energy coursing throughout, Tokyo packs a strong sensory punch.

The city's dynamism is inextricably linked to its history of continuous reinvention. Long before its ascent on the world stage, Tokyo was a small fishing hamlet known as Edo, located on the banks of the Sumida River. Its clout began to grow when Tokugawa Ieyasu, founder

Itinerary Ideas 50
Sights 54
Entertainment and Events 87
Sports and Recreation. . 94
Shopping 99
Food 108
Bars and Nightlife 123
Accommodations 134
Information and Services 139
Getting There 141
Getting Around 144

Highlights

Look for ★ to find recommended sights, activities, dining, and lodging.

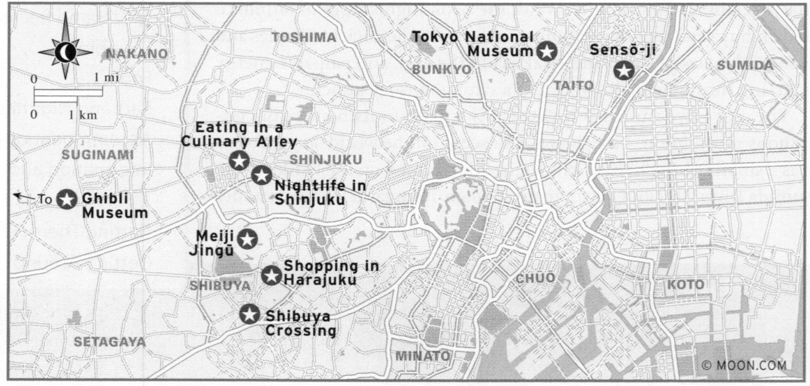

★ **Shibuya Crossing:** Simply crossing the world's busiest pedestrian intersection will leave you gobsmacked by Tokyo's formidable pulse (page 66).

★ **Meiji Jingū:** Surrounded by forest, this majestic Shinto shrine provides an oasis of calm just beyond the fashionable throngs of Harajuku (page 70).

★ **Tokyo National Museum:** If you only have time for one museum in your Tokyo itinerary, make it this one—it holds the world's largest collection of Japanese art (page 79).

★ **Sensō-ji:** Tokyo's most famous temple houses a golden image of the Buddhist Goddess of Mercy (page 83).

★ **Ghibli Museum:** This fantastical museum dedicated to Japan's most beloved anime studio, Studio Ghibli, sits within Inokashira-kōen, one of Tokyo's most appealing parks (page 84).

★ **Shopping in Harajuku:** Ground zero for Japan's colorful youth fashion scene, this neighborhood is full of hip boutiques clustered around the busy thoroughfare of Omotesandō and tucked down a dense tangle of pedestrian-friendly backstreets (page 102).

★ **Eating in a culinary alley:** Take a seat beside locals at a hole-in-the-wall eatery in one of Tokyo's numerous yokochō (culinary alleys) for a meal and an experience you won't forget (page 120).

★ **Nightlife in Shinjuku:** Tokyo's most eclectic nightlife zone offers experiences from robot battles to pub crawls through the tumble-down bars of Golden Gai (page 131).

of the Tokugawa shogunate, chose to base his government in Edo Castle in 1603. By the mid-18th century, Edo's population swelled to 1 million, making it the world's largest city at the time (as it is today).

The city was renamed Tokyo (Eastern Capital) in 1868, when the official capital migrated from Kyoto and the Tokugawa shogunate's rule came to an end. It was this pivotal year when political power returned to the emperor via the Meiji Restoration, and Japan opened up to the world beyond after enforcing a policy of self-isolation for more than 250 years. Tokyoites eagerly lapped up the new influences from abroad, from fashion to philosophy, and the contours of the present city began to take shape.

The capital's culinary offerings are truly world-class, from mom-and-pop ramen shops to lavish sushi spreads. It's the best place in Japan to watch traditional kabuki and Noh theater performances, as well as sumo. The city oozes style, with high-end outposts as well as Harajuku's quirky collection of youth-oriented labels. Tokyo is also home to one of the world's most singular pop culture industries, most visible in the gadget paradise of Akihabara's "Electric Town." Moreover, Tokyo simply works. Compared with other major cities, it's positively spic and span. Well-stocked vending machines and convenience stores are reassuringly never more than a few blocks away. And trains full of dapper commuters rarely miss a beat. While crowds did dwindle during some earlier parts of the COVID-19 pandemic when uncertainty was at its peak, as it wore on, they returned. Aside from the ubiquity of masks in crowded areas, at the time of writing, things have largely returned to normal and the city's buzzing core is once again a dense mass of humanity.

But wander away from any busy station and you'll soon discover a dense network of communities with fiercely maintained traditions, where denizens shop at the neighborhood store and rowdy homegrown festivals mark the passing of time, revealing the city at its most hospitable. Embrace the warm welcome, and enjoy getting lost.

ORIENTATION

Although Tokyo is commonly thought of as a city, it is in fact one of Japan's 47 prefectures. It's divided into 23 special wards, which function as cities themselves. More than 9 million people live in the 23 special wards, and 13 million reside within the prefecture. The greater metropolitan area is home to a whopping 37.8 million, making it the most populous metro area on the planet.

Wherever you are in the city, finding someone fluent in English can be tough. Thankfully, Tokyo residents and police on duty in the city's multitude of koban (police boxes) are legendary for going out of their way to help overseas visitors.

While you wouldn't guess it on the street, Tokyo is a watery realm. All told, upward of 100 rivers and canals flow beneath this concrete jungle, while a handful of broad waterways remain visible: The **Sumida River** drifts southward through the heart of the city, eventually merging with Tokyo Bay, and the **Kanda River** runs eastward from its origin in the central pond of Inokashira-kōen in the western suburb of Kichijōji before spilling into the Sumida River.

Key Railway and Subway Lines

Wrapping your mind around this massive slice of humanity and geography is daunting, but it's helpful to think of Tokyo not in terms of officially drawn lines but rather as a vast collection of neighborhoods that have grown around a matrix of railway stations. The excellent train and subway system can get you within a short walk of just about anywhere in the city. Key among the railway lines are the roughly ovular **JR Yamanote line,** which wraps around the city, and the

Previous: Tokyo Tower; Shibuya Crossing; Meiji Jingū's inner garden.

Tokyo

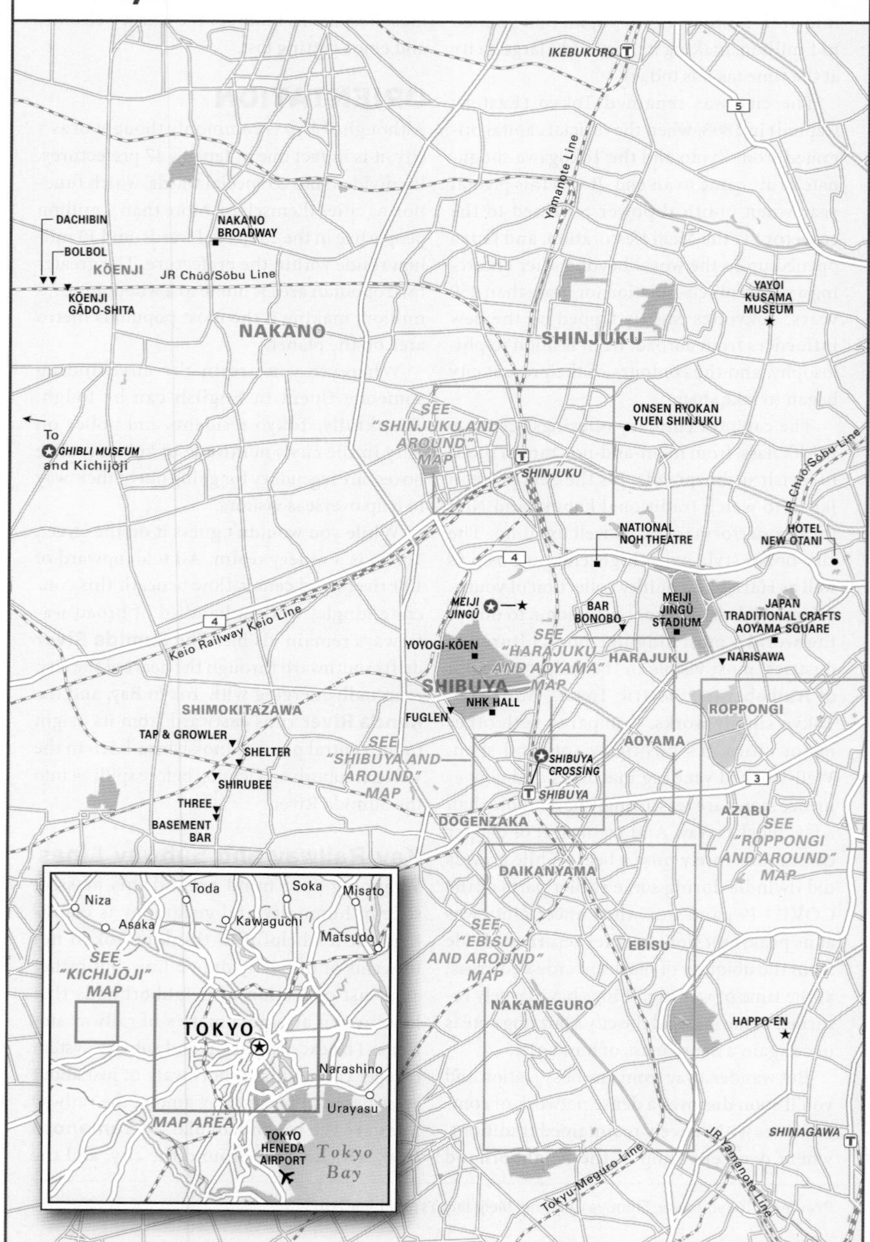
IKEBUKURO
5
Yamanote Line
DACHIBIN
BOLBOL
NAKANO BROADWAY
KŌENJI
JR Chūō/Sōbu Line
KŌENJI GĀDO-SHITA
NAKANO
YAYOI KUSAMA MUSEUM
SHINJUKU
To GHIBLI MUSEUM and Kichijōji
SEE "SHINJUKU AND AROUND" MAP
ONSEN RYOKAN YUEN SHINJUKU
SHINJUKU
JR Chuo/Sobu Line
NATIONAL NOH THEATRE
HOTEL NEW OTANI
4
MEIJI JINGŪ
BAR BONOBO
MEIJI JINGŪ STADIUM
JAPAN TRADITIONAL CRAFTS AOYAMA SQUARE
4
Keio Railway Keio Line
YOYOGI-KŌEN
SEE "HARAJUKU AND AOYAMA" MAP
HARAJUKU
NARISAWA
SHIBUYA
SHIMOKITAZAWA
NHK HALL
ROPPONGI
FUGLEN
TAP & GROWLER
SHELTER
SEE "SHIBUYA AND AROUND" MAP
SHIBUYA CROSSING
AOYAMA
SHIRUBEE
SHIBUYA
3
THREE
BASEMENT BAR
DŌGENZAKA
AZABU
SEE "ROPPONGI AND AROUND" MAP
DAIKANYAMA
Niza
Toda
Soka
Misato
Asaka
Kawaguchi
Matsudo
SEE "KICHIJŌJI" MAP
SEE "EBISU AND AROUND" MAP
EBISU
NAKAMEGURO
HAPPO-EN
TOKYO
Narashino
Urayasu
MAP AREA
TOKYO HENEDA AIRPORT
Tokyo Bay
SHINAGAWA
JR Yamanote Line
Tokyu-Meguro Line

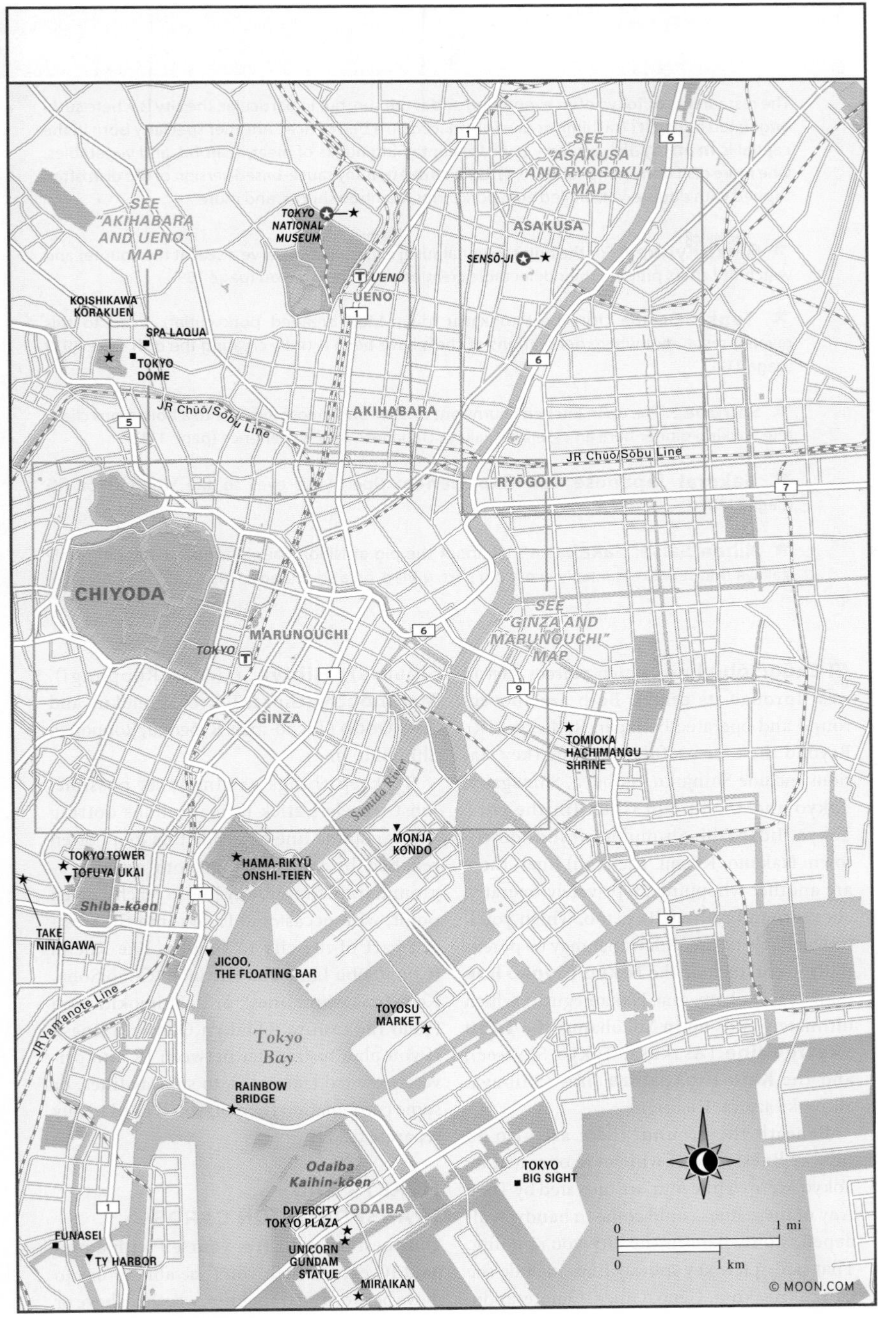
SEE "ASAKUSA AND RYOGOKU" MAP
SEE "AKIHABARA AND UENO" MAP
TOKYO NATIONAL MUSEUM
ASAKUSA
SENSŌ-JI
UENO
UENO
KOISHIKAWA KŌRAKUEN
SPA LAQUA
TOKYO DOME
JR Chūō/Sōbu Line
AKIHABARA
JR Chūō/Sōbu Line
RYŌGOKU
CHIYODA
SEE "GINZA AND MARUNOUCHI" MAP
MARUNOUCHI
TOKYO
GINZA
TOMIOKA HACHIMANGU SHRINE
Sumida River
MONJA KONDO
TOKYO TOWER
TOFUYA UKAI
HAMA-RIKYŪ ONSHI-TEIEN
Shiba-kōen
TAKE NINAGAWA
JICOO, THE FLOATING BAR
JR Yamanote Line
TOYOSU MARKET
Tokyo Bay
RAINBOW BRIDGE
Odaiba Kaihin-kōen
TOKYO BIG SIGHT
DIVERCITY TOKYO PLAZA
ODAIBA
UNICORN GUNDAM STATUE
MIRAIKAN
FUNASEI
TY HARBOR
0
1 mi
0
1 km
© MOON.COM

Best Restaurants

The restaurants of Tokyo offer everything under the sun, but in particular, the city is where sushi originated as **nigiri** (sashimi, or raw fish, placed on a bed of rice). Another specialty born in the capital is **monjayaki,** a savory pancake containing hunks of meat, seafood, and vegetables. One more dish born in the capital is **shoyu ramen,** a soy sauce-based version of the dish often topped with double-yolk boiled egg, pork strips, bamboo shoots, and more.

★ **Ginza Kyubey:** For the quintessential sushi experience, reserve a seat at the counter and watch the chefs prepare their delectable creations right before you (page 109).

★ **Tonki:** For the city's best tonkatsu (deep-fried breaded pork cutlet), head to this revered restaurant where generations of chefs have been artfully creating the dish since 1939 (page 112).

★ **Shirubee:** The open kitchen churns out classics and innovative fare to a boisterous clientele, making dinner here an essential izakaya (Japanese pub) experience (page 113).

★ **Sakurai Japanese Tea Experience:** Open your eyes to the wonders of tea (page 117).

★ **Nihon Saisei Sakaba:** It's all about the pig at Nihon Saisei Sakaba, a standing-only izakaya that serves essentially every pig part, grilled, on a stick (page 118).

JR Chūō/Sōbu line, which pierces east to west through its center. Both are aboveground and operated by Japan Railways (JR). Beyond the ever-useful Yamanote (key stations include Shinjuku, Shibuya, Shinagawa, Tokyo and Ueno) and Chūō (in the core: Tokyo, Iidabashi, Shinjuku; west of downtown: Nakano, Kōenji, Kichijōji) lines, there are another whopping 29 privately operated aboveground railway lines too, which you'll be less likely to use. A few that may be potentially useful include the **Tōkyū Tōyoko line** (Shibuya, Daikanyama, Nakameguro), which ultimately ends up in Yokohama; the **Tōbu Skytree line** (Asakusa, Tokyo Skytree); and the **Keio-Inokashira line** (Shibuya, Shimokitazawa, Kichijōji).

Beneath the ground, there are also 13 subway lines, nine of which are operated by Tokyo Metro while four are operated by Tōei. Any of these lines could come in handy; it all depends on where in the city you're going. That said, a few key subway lines include the **Ginza** (Asakusa, Ueno, Ginza, Omotesandō, Shibuya), **Hibiya** (Ueno, Roppongi), **Marunouchi** (Ginza, Tokyo, Shinjuku), and **Tōei Ōedo** (Tocho-mae, Ryōgoku, Roppongi, Shinjuku) lines.

To keep things as simple as possible, most travelers stick to major hubs dotting the Yamanote line or inside this loop, often reached by transferring from an aboveground train to a subway line to reach a given point, with occasional forays into the western part of the city to suburbs like Kōenji (Chūō/Sōbu Line) and Kichijōji (Chūō/Sōbu, Keio-Inokashira lines), or to Shimokitazawa (Keio Inokashira, Odakyu Odawara lines). If you plan to transfer between JR and privately owned trainlines, to subway lines, or some combination thereof, you'll need to buy separate tickets.

TICKETS AND TRANSPORTATION CARDS

Your best bet is to arm yourself with a prepaid IC card, which you'll be able to use to move between all train lines, whether above or

Best Accommodations

★ **Mandarin Oriental:** Swanky elegance and sweeping views are abundant in this high-rise luxury gem, well located in the heart of the action in Nihonbashi, a brief stroll from the Imperial Palace and Marunouchi's buzz (page 135).

★ **Aman:** Massive yet understated rooms reminiscent of a ryokan (traditional inn), each with a yuzu-infused stone bathtub and outstanding views of the city at night, offer a high-end respite from the city (page 135).

★ **Park Hyatt Tokyo:** This legendary hotel in a prime location amid the skyscrapers of western Shinjuku boasts amazing service, spectacular views of Mount Fuji, and, as seen in the film *Lost in Translation*, one of the most dazzling cocktail bars in the world (page 136).

★ **Ryokan Sawanoya:** This wonderful ryokan in the heart of the charming Yanaka neighborhood includes traditional design elements, cypress bathtubs, and a staff who are eager to assist (page 137).

★ **Asakusa Kokono Club Hotel:** In the heart of Asakusa, this hip boutique hotel is ideally situated for sightseeing in the historic part of town and has a stylish café-bar (page 138).

underground, as well as on public buses, when making purchases in convenience stores, and even at some vending machines, particularly those inside train stations. Note that the JR Pass—recommended—is only valid on trains in the JR network, not on subway or private railway rides.

Ginza and Marunouchi

Starting near **Tokyo Station,** on the eastern side of the Yamanote line, Tokyo's seat of power is Marunouchi and the sprawling green area around the **Imperial Palace,** set in what's known as the **Chiyoda** district, which has marked the geographic heart of the city since the Edo period. South of Tokyo Station is Ginza, its broad avenues lined with luxury **fashion boutiques, department stores,** and upmarket cafés, restaurants, and bars. It's also home to **Kabuki-za,** where most of the city's kabuki plays are staged.

Tokyo Bay Area

Southeast of the central areas of Ginza and Marunouchi, Tokyo Bay was best known as the home of the Tsukiji Fish Market until it closed in 2018. But there's still much to discover here: Across the bay from Tsukiji is **Odaiba,** a human-made island with a number of interesting **museums** and a seaside park, **Odaiba Kaihin-kōen,** that offers some of the best nighttime views of the city.

Roppongi and Around

West of the Tokyo Bay area, within the southern edge of the Yamanote line, a number of cosmopolitan hubs sustain a large share of Tokyo's expat community. Roppongi is at the center of this zone, offering a mix of posh eateries, world-class **art museums,** and one of the city's highest concentrations of **nightlife** (some of it seedy). Nearby, fanning out to the south, east and west, **Azabu** is packed with fine-dining establishments and exclusive shops.

Ebisu and Around

At the southwestern corner of the Yamanote line is upmarket Ebisu, which forms a low-key, sophisticated triangle with neighboring districts **Daikanyama** and **Nakameguro,** chock-full of hip fashion boutiques and excellent options for drinking and dining. There are also a handful of worthwhile **museums** in the area, including the **Tokyo Photographic Art Museum,** Tokyo's largest photography exhibition space.

Shibuya and Around

Continuing clockwise on the Yamanote line from Ebisu, Shibuya is one of the best places to experience Tokyo at full tilt. Stepping into the fray at **Shibuya Crossing** is one of the most intensely urban experiences to be had on earth. The bulk of the action is found in the congested streets of **Center Gai** (the neighborhood's cultural hub) and in the alleys leading away from Shibuya Station, up the hill known as **Dogenzaka.** Just a few stops to the west on the Keio-Inokashira line, more offbeat **Shimokitazawa**—think street art and vintage boutiques—is directly accessible from Shibuya Station.

Harajuku and Aoyama

Just north of Shibuya, Harajuku is hallowed ground, both as the location of **Meiji Jingū,** perhaps the city's grandest shrine, and for youth trends and streetwear. Neighboring Aoyama is a fashion mecca as well, catering to a much more sophisticated and well-heeled class. Architecture buffs will appreciate the hodgepodge of iconic buildings dotting the wide leafy avenue of **Omotesandō**—the Champs-Elysées of Tokyo—which runs through the heart of both neighborhoods. Besides fashion, both areas are home to a number of **museums,** featuring everything from woodblock prints to Buddhist statuary.

Shinjuku and Around

Though Tokyo's historical and geographic heart may lie in the neighborhoods surrounding the Imperial Palace, in many ways its modern heartbeat is the western hub of Shinjuku, once a sleepy suburb. The sheer energy of **Shinjuku Station,** the world's busiest railway terminal, is tremendous. Crowds have dwindled slightly due to the impact of the COVID-19 pandemic, but you'd hardly know it as you pass through the West or East exits, among the most frantic. You'll find a number of the city's nightlife districts here, including **Omoide Yokochō (Memory Lane),** a smoky, raucous pair of lanes tightly packed with small bars and restaurants; **Kabukichō,** Tokyo's largest nightlife zone and home to **Golden Gai,** an iconic collection of tumble-down bars; and lively gay quarter **Shinjuku Ni-chōme.** To the south is **Shinjuku Gyōen,** one of the city's most picturesque parks.

Akihabara and Ueno

On the east side of the Yamanote line's loop, north of Tokyo Station, is the geeked-out zone of Akihabara, devoted almost entirely to supplying the **gadgets** for all manner of quirky hobbies, along with **idol group performances,** cosplay, anime, manga, and more. One stop north is Ueno, a historical and cultural hot spot. The expansive grounds of **Ueno-kōen**—Tokyo's largest park—are home to a number of major museums, from natural history to modern art, with the excellent **Tokyo National Museum** topping the list.

Asakusa and Ryōgoku

North of Ueno, accessible from most of the city only via the Ginza and Toei Asakusa subway lines, Asakusa is Tokyo at its **old-school** best. Like most of the city, much of the area was razed during World War II, but the narrow zigzagging streets, **temples,** aged wooden houses, and shops evoke an earlier time. Across the Sumida River, the neighborhood of Ryōgoku is the nation's foremost center for the ancient sport of **sumo.**

Western Tokyo

There are a few notable areas in Western Tokyo, easily reached from Shinjuku Station along the Chūō line. First is **Nakano,** an otaku (geek culture) haven, and farther west, **Kichijōji** is home to luxuriant **Inokashira-kōen** and the whimsical **Ghibli Museum.** Between Nakano and Kichijōji on the Chūō line, **Kōenji** is one of Tokyo's hotspots for underground music and hip restaurants.

PLANNING YOUR TIME

You can get a good introduction to Tokyo in as little as **two or three days;** this is enough time to see the highlights, and to sample the vast culinary, nightlife, and shopping options. With an additional day or two, you can go a bit off the beaten path and explore the more local side of the city.

Where to Stay

Plan to stay in either **Shibuya** or **Shinjuku** in the west if you want access to the more clamorous, modern side of the city; in the east, the more historic **Ueno** and **Asakusa** are good bases if you like a slower pace. Meanwhile, **Ginza** and **Marunouchi** have a glut of luxury hotels.

Getting Around and Transportation Passes

To get around, you'll be switching between aboveground train lines and the subway system. The most economic and efficient way to transfer between the two is to get a prepaid IC card, such as a **Suica** card (sold at all JR stations) or **PASMO** card (sold at all non-JR stations). Both cards can be used on all rail networks, as well as on public buses, not only within Tokyo but in many other large urban centers nationwide, including Kyoto and Osaka. It's also recommended to get a JR Pass (www.jrailpass.com), which covers all JR lines nationwide, including some shinkansen (bullet train) lines (note that you must purchase your JR Pass before your trip). Train rides between Tokyo's incredible density of transit stations will typically take from 5-30 minutes. Once you're on the ground, you'll end up doing a fair amount of walking; usually, the walk between one train station and the next tends to be about 20-30 minutes, and most sights and restaurants will be within about 15 minutes from the nearest train station.

Opening Hours

In Tokyo **opening times** vary greatly, and many shops, museums, and even restaurants are closed on certain days each week. Some popular sights like **Tokyo Skytree** fill up fast, so it pays to arrive at or just before opening time to beat the rush, or show up from late afternoon on, after crowds have dispersed.

High and Low Seasons

Like the rest of Japan, Tokyo is busiest in **spring** and **autumn,** when gorgeous cherry blossoms bloom in late March or the leaves change color. **Summer** is humid and hot, but it's also a fun time to attend traditional festivals and large music events. As **winter** is off-season, prices for flights and rooms tend to drop.

Advance Reservations

Attractions like the **Ghibli Museum,** as well as many popular restaurants, require bookings weeks or even a month or more in advance. Pre-planning is key, doubly so in light of the impact of **COVID-19.** Some popular attractions have instituted **reservation systems** to control the flow of foot traffic and help prevent the spread of the virus, a practice that may remain in place beyond the pandemic. To be safe, check the website of any given sight, attraction, restaurant, or bar to confirm whether you need to reserve a spot beforehand.

Avoiding Crowds

Given that Tokyo is among the most crowded urban areas on the planet, trying to avoid crowds entirely is a losing battle. Even throughout the COVID-19 pandemic, aside from some uncertain weeks early on when train stations and other busy areas were a smidgen less crowded, at the time of writing, commuters were piling into trains, Shibuya Crossing was still seeing legions traverse through on foot, and cafés, shops, restaurants, and bars were doing brisk business. That said, hand sanitizer and temperature checks at business entrances were entrenched.

Even in Tokyo, though, there are a few things you can do if you want a bit more space: For starters, avoid peak times, like hanami (cherry blossom viewing) season and Golden week (late April through the first week of May). Also consider the timing: Try to visit popular temples and shrines early, just as they open, or near closing time, to avoid the larger crowds in the middle of the day. Popular neighborhoods like Harajuku, Asakusa, and Shibuya will be even more crowded than usual on weekends—on a weekday visit, crowds may be lighter. Consider exploring Tokyo's more local neighborhoods, like Daikanyama, Nakameguro, Kōenji, Kichijōji, Shimokitazawa, and Yanaka, all fantastic areas to get to know on foot.

And finally, a word on trains: Avoid riding them before 10am and between 5pm-8pm on weekdays when commuters are beginning and ending their work days. But don't be shocked if they're crowded at any time of day—it's Tokyo, after all.

Itinerary Ideas

TOKYO ON DAY ONE

Spend your first day getting to know the hip, modern, young side of Tokyo, focusing on the areas of **Harajuku** and its central thoroughfare Omotesandō, along with **Aoyama, Shibuya,** and **Ebisu.** You'll discover Tokyo's top shrine, see cutting-edge architecture, and visit a sleek museum before merging with the masses at the world's busiest pedestrian crossing. You'll also eat great meals and sip tea and creative cocktails.

All the neighborhoods you'll visit are clustered around the southwestern side of town, which makes them easy to travel between: Most are a 20-minute walk apart, though you can opt to take the train instead (usually just one stop).

1 From Harajuku Station, walk 5 minutes down the gravel path behind the station to Tokyo's grandest shrine, **Meiji Jingū.** Explore the expansive green grounds and graceful inner sanctum, its buildings made of cypress wood with copper roofs.

2 After backtracking to the towering torii gate that marks the entrance to the shrine, begin walking down the famous shopping street Omotesandō, taking in architecture and exploring quirky fashion boutiques tucked in backstreets. Stop for an early lunch at **Maisen** (a 1-km/0.6-mi, 15-minute walk from Meiji Jingū), one of the city's better purveyors of tonkatsu (breaded pork cutlet), set in a chicly renovated bathhouse on a Harajuku side street.

3 Continue down Omotesandō another kilometer (0.6 mi, 15 minutes), through the posh Aoyama neighborhood, to the **Nezu Museum.** Explore the collection of East Asian art and religious artifacts inside, then meander through the museum's beautiful garden.

4 Backtrack down Omotesandō toward **Sakurai Japanese Tea Experience,** a 0.7-km (0.5-mi), 10-minute walk. Get to know the ancient tradition of Japanese tea in this modern, stylish tearoom.

5 With your appreciation for the humble tea leaf enhanced, walk southwest (about 1.6 km/1 mi, 20 minutes) to Shibuya Station, where you'll behold the urban maelstrom of **Shibuya Crossing.**

6 Spend a bit of time meandering through the frenzied, pedestrian-only Center Gai area, not far from Shibuya Station, to get a visceral sense of Tokyo's pulse. Stop by **Purikura no Mecca** (less than 5 minutes' walk from the station) to take some self-portraits in one of

the singular photo booths that are all the rage among Japan's youth. (Note that you might not be admitted if you're a guy traveling solo or in a male-only group.)

7 Back on the other side of Shibuya Station, across the thoroughfare of Meiji-dōri (0.5-km/0.3-mi walk east, 10 minutes), take a coffee break—and a step back in time—at **Chatei Hatou,** an excellent old-school kissaten (tea-drinking place).

8 As dinnertime approaches, hop on the JR Yamanote line at Shibuya Station south to the stylish neighborhood of Ebisu, one stop away on the Yamanote line (2 minutes; ¥140). Have dinner in rowdy and boisterous **Ebisu Yokochō,** a covered alleyway 2 minutes' walk northeast of Ebisu Station, filled with no-frills eateries serving grilled meats and vegetables on sticks and in stews, and plenty of booze to wash it all down.

9 If you've got the energy, go for drinks after dinner. **Bar Tram,** a dimly lit bar with a speakeasy vibe known for its absinthe-base cocktails, just a 3-minute walk from Ebisu Yokochō, is a good pick.

TOKYO ON DAY TWO

On Day 2, look back on Tokyo's history, starting with a visit to an ancient temple in **Asakusa** and ending in **Shinjuku,** where nostalgic post-war buildings are juxtaposed with towers draped with neon signs. In between, you can experience the oldest and best collection of classical Japanese art, the **Tokyo National Museum** in **Ueno,** in contrast with the quirky pop-cultural mecca of up-to-the-minute **Akihabara.**

1 Start your day at the famed boisterous temple of **Sensō-ji** in Asakusa, in the older eastern side of town, just north of Asakusa Station.

2 Hop on the Ginza subway line at Asakusa Station and make your way to Ueno Station (5 minutes; 3 stops; ¥170) and **Tokyo National Museum,** a 6-minute (0.5-km/0.3-mi) walk northwest of the station, housing the world's largest collection of Japanese art.

3 Cross Ueno-kōen, Tokyo's largest park, to **Hantei** (about 1-km/0.6-mi, 15-minute walk west) for a lunch of kushiage (battered and deep-fried meat and vegetables on sticks) in a charming Meiji period home.

4 From here, hop on the train at Nezu Station, right outside Hantei. Ride to Nishi-Nippori Station on the Chiyoda subway line (3 minutes; 2 stops; ¥170), then transfer to the Yamanote line to Akihabara Station (7 minutes; 4 stops; ¥160). Spend the next few hours getting lost in Akihabara's warren of quirky pop culture. A good starting point is **Mandarake,** a one-stop shop for everything from anime and manga to vintage figurines and cosplay attire. It's just a 5-minute walk northwest from Akihabara Station.

5 Hop on the JR Sōbu (yellow color-coded) line at Akihabara Station and make your way to Shinjuku (17 minutes; 9 stops; ¥170) as dinnertime approaches. Feast on tempura that doesn't break the bank at **Tempura Tsunahachi,** 2 minutes' walk east of Shinjuku Station.

6 For a mind-blowing spectacle, walk 7 minutes east to **Robot Restaurant** in the neon-drenched red-light district of Kabukichō after dinner. There's no way to easily sum up this epically kitsch, yet technologically stunning, robot showdown.

7 If you're still going strong, follow this up with a bar crawl through Golden Gai. Visitors throng to this former black market to drink their way through a warren of 200 tumbledown bars—each with its own decor, ethos, and regular characters. **Kenzo's Bar** is a great place to start.

Itinerary Ideas

TOKYO AREA

0 2 mi
0 2 km

"DAY TWO" AREA

"LIKE A LOCAL" AREA

"DAY ONE" AREA

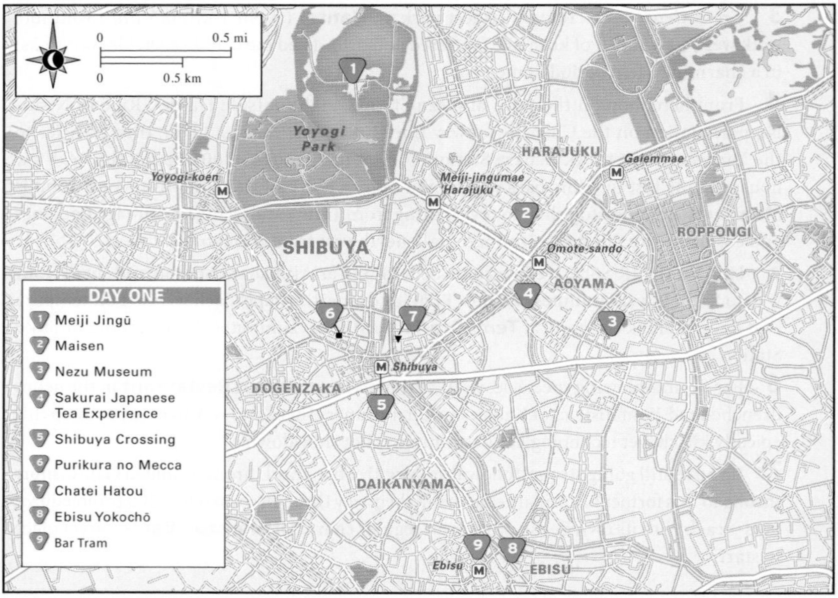

0 0.5 mi
0 0.5 km

Yoyogi Park
Yoyogi-koen
Meiji-jingumae 'Harajuku'
HARAJUKU
Gaiemmae
SHIBUYA
Omote-sando
ROPPONGI
AOYAMA
Shibuya
DOGENZAKA
DAIKANYAMA
Ebisu
EBISU

DAY ONE

1. Meiji Jingū
2. Maisen
3. Nezu Museum
4. Sakurai Japanese Tea Experience
5. Shibuya Crossing
6. Purikura no Mecca
7. Chatei Hatou
8. Ebisu Yokochō
9. Bar Tram

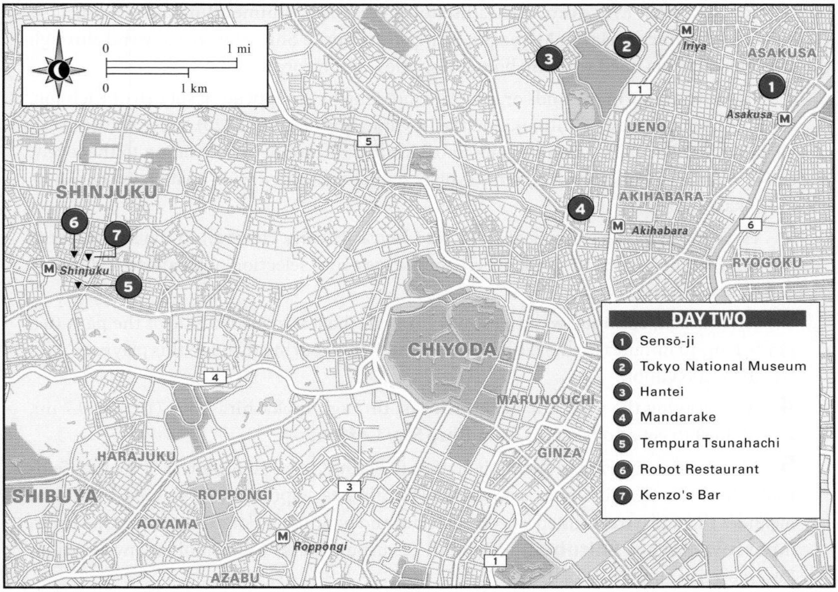
0
1 mi
0
1 km
SHINJUKU
Shinjuku
HARAJUKU
SHIBUYA
AOYAMA
ROPPONGI
Roppongi
AZABU
CHIYODA
MARUNOUCHI
GINZA
UENO
Iriya
ASAKUSA
Asakusa
AKIHABARA
Akihabara
RYOGOKU
DAY TWO
1 Sensō-ji
2 Tokyo National Museum
3 Hantei
4 Mandarake
5 Tempura Tsunahachi
6 Robot Restaurant
7 Kenzo's Bar

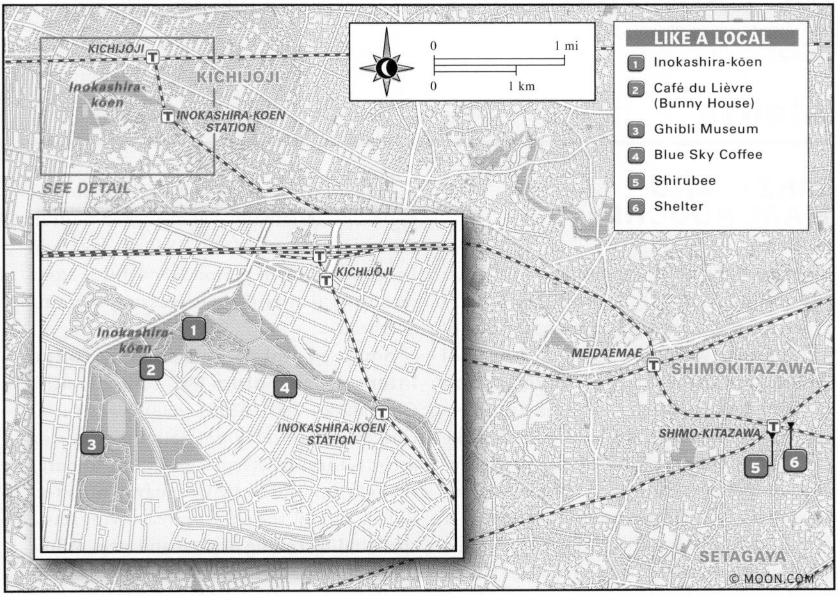
KICHIJOJI
Inokashira-kōen
KICHIJOJI
INOKASHIRA-KOEN STATION
SEE DETAIL
0
1 mi
0
1 km
LIKE A LOCAL
1 Inokashira-kōen
2 Café du Lièvre (Bunny House)
3 Ghibli Museum
4 Blue Sky Coffee
5 Shirubee
6 Shelter
MEIDAEMAE
SHIMOKITAZAWA
SHIMO-KITAZAWA
SETAGAYA
© MOON.COM

TOKYO LIKE A LOCAL

This third itinerary is focused on a few local haunts just west of downtown, namely **Kichijōji** and **Shimokitazawa.** Kichijōji is home to **Inokashira-kōen,** a lovely park with a central pond, and the **Ghibli Museum,** a paradise for lovers of the anime film studio helmed by Oscar-winning director Hayao Miyazaki. In hipster-favorite Shimokitazawa, wend through the scrambled streets lined with hip boutiques, cafés, and record shops.

1 Begin your day in the mid- or even late morning in the appealing suburb of Kichijōji, about 15 minutes west of Shinjuku on the JR Chūō line (6 stops; ¥220). Once you arrive at Kichijōji Station, walk 5 minutes (about 0.3 km/0.2 mi) south of the station to the lovely, leafy grounds of **Inokashira-kōen.** If you're so inclined, rent a swan boat to ply the waters of Inokashira Pond.

2 Have lunch at the whimsical **Café du Lièvre (Bunny House),** to the southwest of the pond on the edge of the park, where they serve a nice selection of Japanese-style curry dishes and crêpes.

3 After lunch, continue walking south through the less-crowded side of the park (0.6 km/0.4 mi, 10 minutes) to the **Ghibli Museum.** Enjoy touring through this playful, artful ode to Studio Ghibli.

4 After leaving the museum, backtrack east through Inokashira-kōen (1.2 km/0.7 mi, 15 minutes) to get a coffee to go from **Blue Sky Coffee.**

5 Make your way back to Kichijōji Station (0.8 km/0.5 mi, 10 minutes). Take the Keio-Inokashira line to Shimokitazawa Station (12 minutes, express train; 4 stops; ¥180) and meander through streets lined by edgy eateries and boutiques. For dinner, eat at the lively, innovative izakaya **Shirubee,** just south (2-minute walk) of Shimokitazawa Station. Reserve a day ahead to be safe.

6 After dinner, check out Shimokitazawa's live music scene at **Shelter,** 5 minutes' walk northeast of Shirubee.

Sights

GINZA AND MARUNOUCHI

銀座, 丸の内

Today, Ginza is synonymous with glitz. It's also conveniently located within easy reach of the buzzing business district of Marunouchi, where you'll find the **Imperial Palace** and the revamped **Tokyo Station** (1-chōme Marunouchi, Chiyoda-ku; www.tokyoinfo.com) building, which evokes the early 20th century with its appealing facade of red brick and stone. Of historic importance, the **Nihonbashi Bridge** (1-1 Nihonbashimuromachi, Chūō-ku), about a 5-minute walk north of Nihonbashi Station, has served as the starting point (marking kilometer zero) for the national network of highways. Originally wooden when built in the early Edo period (1603-1868), today you'll encounter a Meiji period (1868-1912) stone reconstruction, with an expressway running overhead.

South of Tokyo Station, the **Tokyo International Forum** (3-5-1 Marunouchi, Chiyoda-ku; tel. 03/5221-9000; www.t-i-forum.co.jp; 7am-11:30pm daily) is a soaring architectural masterpiece. An ode to natural light envisioned by Uruguayan architect Rafael Viñoly, the ship-like east wing has a spellbinding ceiling of glass and steel. While the building serves primarily as a convention center, it's free to enter for anyone and is worth a quick stop if you're in the area to admire its sky-high ceiling.

Imperial Palace
皇居

1-1 Chiyoda, Chiyoda-ku; tel. 03/3213-1111; https://sankan.kunaicho.go.jp/index.html; free; take Chiyoda line to Ōtemachi Station, exit C13b

Located in the geographic heart of Tokyo, the construction of the Imperial Palace was kicked off by Tokugawa Ieyasu, the first shogun, in 1590. In its heyday, it was the world's largest castle. Today, only the inner circle of the original complex survives. Damaged by fire in 1945, the current palace was rebuilt in 1968. Althought the steel-framed reconstruction is made of concrete, it still looks as you'd expect: sweeping rooflines over white walls, supported by a foundation made from large stones, with a daunting moat crisscrossed by bridges encircling it all. While it commands less attention than the towering original fortress built by Ieyasu must have, the modern-day palace offers respite from the city's hubbub just outside, and the sight of glass-and-steel towers looming nearby offers a striking contrast.

Japan's imperial family resides on the western grounds, which are only open to the public on the emperor's birthday (Feb. 23) and the day after New Year's Day (Jan. 2), when thousands of Japanese try to catch a glimpse of the emperor waving from a palace balcony. The Imperial Household Agency does give two daily **tours** (10am and 1:30pm Tues.-Sat., not held on national holidays; free), each lasting a little more than an hour and delving a bit deeper into the palace grounds. Tours aren't offered during official functions, on public holidays, or during afternoons from late July through August, or December 28-January 4. Spots can be reserved online (http://sankan.kunaicho.go.jp/english/guide/koukyo.html) or by phone as early as a month before you plan to arrive. You can also try your luck and arrive the day of to inquire whether spots are still available; ask at the tour office next to **Kikyo-mon** (Kikyo Gate).

If you decide to forego the tour and explore the grounds on your own, check out the free downloadable **audio guide** (www.kunaicho.go.jp/e-event/app.html). Start in the **Kōkyo-gaien** (www.env.go.jp/garden/kokyogaien), or National Garden, located in the southeastern section of the Imperial Palace grounds. At the western edge of this verdant space, you'll see two iconic bridges. The closer of the two is the **Megane Bridge** ("Eyeglass Bridge");

Imperial Palace

it was given its nickname because it resembles a pair of spectacles when seen reflected in the moat below. Just behind Megane Bridge stands **Nijū Bridge** ("Double Bridge"); its popular name is derived from the fact that it was once a two-level wooden bridge.

EAST GARDEN
皇居東御苑

9am-4pm Tues.-Thurs. and Sat.-Sun. Nov.-Feb., 9am-4:30pm Tues.-Thurs. and Sat.-Sun. Mar.-mid-Apr. and Sept.-Oct., 9am-5pm Tues.-Thurs. and Sat.-Sun. mid-Apr.-Aug.

After either taking a private tour of the palace grounds or capturing a few snapshots in front of these two scenic bridges, proceed to the flawless grounds of the Imperial Palace East Garden. It's a fine example of a Japanese garden, where you can meander along winding paths, over lightly arched bridges, and past stone lanterns, cherry trees, azaleas, and a teahouse. While basking in the pleasant scene, note the stone base of what was once the main tower of Edo Castle, still standing on the lawn. Climb the steps to see the surroundings from atop the remnants of what was once the world's largest keep.

The garden is best entered via **Ote-mon** (Ote Gate), just west of Ōtemachi Station and roughly a 15-minute walk west of Tokyo Station's Marunouchi North Exit. The **Museum of Imperial Collections** (9am-3:45pm Tues.-Thurs. and Sat.-Sun. Nov.-Feb., 9am-4:45pm Tues.-Thurs. and Sat.-Sun. Mar.-mid-Apr. and Sept., 9am-5:45pm Tues.-Thurs. and Sat.-Sun. mid-Apr.-Aug., 9am-4:15pm Oct.; free), just beyond Ote-mon, shows off a small selection of the imperial family's more than 9,000 pieces of Japanese art, though it will be closed through approximately autumn 2023 as a new facility is being built.

Two-hour walking **tours** of the East Garden are offered free of charge by **Tokyo SGG Club,** overseen by the **JNTO Tourist Information Center** (1F Shin Tokyo Bdlg., 3-3-1 Marunouchi, Chiyoda-ku; tel. 03/3201-3331; https://tokyosgg.jp/sp/imperial_palace.html; 1pm Tues.-Thurs. and Sat.-Sun.). To join, arrive at the Tokyo SSG Club's desk at the Tourist Information Center at least 10 minutes before the start of a tour.

National Museum of Modern Art (MOMAT)
国立近代美術館

3-1 Kitanomaru-kōen, Chiyoda-ku; tel. 03/5777-8600; www.momat.go.jp/am; 10am-5pm Tues.-Thurs. and Sun., 10am-8pm Fri.-Sat.; ¥500 adults, ¥250 university and college students, free for high school students and younger; take Tōzai line to Takebashi Station, exit 1b

This massive collection of Japanese art stretches from the turn of the 20th century onward, focusing heavily on the works of modernist Japanese painters, as well as some international artists, with photography, video pieces, sculptures, and more also on show. The key theme illustrated by the artworks being shown is the evolution of modern Japan from the Meiji period (1868-1912) onward. Part of the appeal of visiting the museum is its location beside the walls of the Imperial Palace and its moat, lined with cherry trees that color the area pink in spring; foliage blazes during autumn. Alongside the permanent collection, shown across three floors, the ground floor hosts changing special exhibitions, between which the museum shuts its doors, so check the website to see if an exhibition is ongoing before making the trip.

Yasukuni-jinja
靖国神社

3-1-1 Kudankita, Chiyoda-ku; tel. 03/3261-8326; www.yasukuni.or.jp; 6am-6pm daily Mar.-Oct., 6am-5pm daily Nov.-Feb.; free

About a 15-minute walk northwest from the Imperial Palace grounds, or 7 minutes west of Kudanshita Station, sits Yasukuni-jinja, a shrine that honors Japan's war dead, historically charged due to associations with Japan's World War II sins.

TOKYO BAY AREA
東京湾

Until recently the area's most famous

site was by far the hallowed **Tsukiji Fish Market,** which closed in September 2018. The new market, **Toyosu Market** (6-6-1 Toyosu, Koto-ku; tel. 03/3520-8205; www.toyosu-market.or.jp; 5am-5pm Mon.-Sat., often closed Wed. and other irregular times, hours vary for businesses on site; free), which opened in October 2018, remains the world's largest bazaar of fishmongers, but it's unfortunately a somewhat sterile affair compared to its predecessor in Tsukiji. Though it's safe to give the new market a pass, it is still possible to visit Tsukiji's Outer Market of seafood shops and mom-and-pop sushi counters.

Across the bay lies the hyper urbanized development of **Odaiba.** Linked to the rest of Tokyo by both the scenic **Rainbow Bridge** and the fully automated **Yurikamome New Transit Monorail,** Odaiba is a hodgepodge of family-friendly museums and shopping centers. One of Odaiba's biggest draws is its great views of the city from across the bay.

If you make the trip to Odaiba, pass by the 19.7-meter-tall (65-ft-tall) **Unicorn Gundam Statue** (1-1-10 Aomi, Koto-ku; tel. 03/6380-7800; www.unicorn-gundam-statue.jp; 10am-9pm daily; free), towering over the **DiverCity Tokyo Plaza** (http://mitsui-shopping-park.com/divercity-tokyo). The life-size statue from the anime series *Mobile Suit Gundam* about giant robots "performs" at select times each day when its head moves and eyes light up, and mist wafts through the area as music plays.

Tsukiji Outer Market
築地場外市場

www.tsukiji.or.jp; take Hibiya line to Tsukiji Station, exits 1, 2, or take Ōedo line to Tsukijishijō Station, exit A1

To the chagrin of many foodies and urban anthropologists, the colorful, chaotic inner Tsukiji Fish Market, once the site of legendarily intense morning tuna auctions, closed in fall 2018. The market relocated to a massive, sterile new building, Toyosu Market, southeast of Tsukiji. Though it is possible to get a glimpse of the goings-on in Toyosu, it's probably okay to skip it; thankfully, Tsukiji's outer market, which once spilled into the streets just northeast of the former inner market, has remained in operation. It's perhaps the one place in the world where sushi for breakfast is recommended.

Starting from mid-morning to early afternoon, stalls sell snacks, ranging from oysters to sweet yet savory rolled omelets, alongside sit-down restaurants and shops hawking pottery and kitchenware of excellent quality. The bulk of these stalls are housed in the newly rebuilt **Tsukiji Uogashi** complex (6-26-1 Tsukuji, Chūō-ku; tel. 03/3544-1906; https://uogashi.tsukiji-dainaka.com; 6am-2pm daily). To glean a bit more insight into the fish business and be guided directly to the best spots for nibbles in Tsukiji, check out the highly rated tour of Tsukiji Outer Market run by **Japan Wonder Travel** (https://japanwondertravel.com/products/tokyo-foodrink-tour-tsukiji-fish-market; 3 hours from 8:30am daily; ¥9,500) or the one by **Ninja Food Tours** (www.ninjafoodtours.com/tokyo-food-tours/tsukiji-fish-market; 3 hours from 9am daily; ¥8,800), which also includes a visit to Toyosu Market.

Hama-rikyū Onshi-teien
浜離宮恩賜庭園

1-1 Hama Rikyū-teien, Chūō-ku; tel. 03/3541-0200; www.tokyo-park.or.jp/park/format/index028.html; 9am-5pm (last entry 4:30pm) daily; ¥300; take Ōedo, Yurikamome lines to Shiodome Station, exit 10, or take Ginza, Asakusa lines to Shimbashi Station, Shiodome exit

Like all things with deep roots in Tokyo's past, this calm garden with skyscrapers looming just beyond it has seen its share of radical transformations, including being flattened during World War II. The garden remains in its original location, south of Ginza, right next to the point where the Sumida River mingles with Tokyo Bay. Strolling through the grounds, the space strikes a perfect balance between water and landscape, with numerous native species from hydrangeas to wizened black pines. One pine is said to be 300

Ginza and Marunouchi

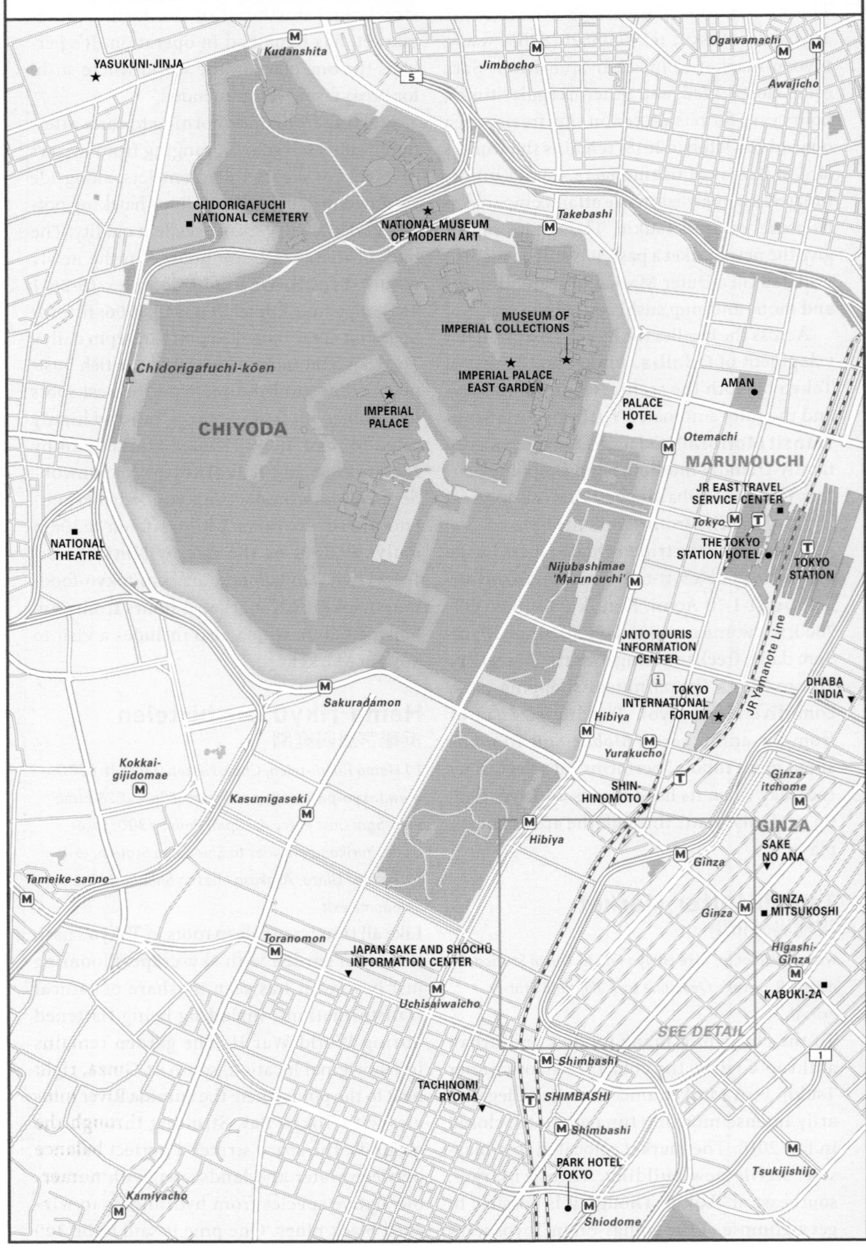

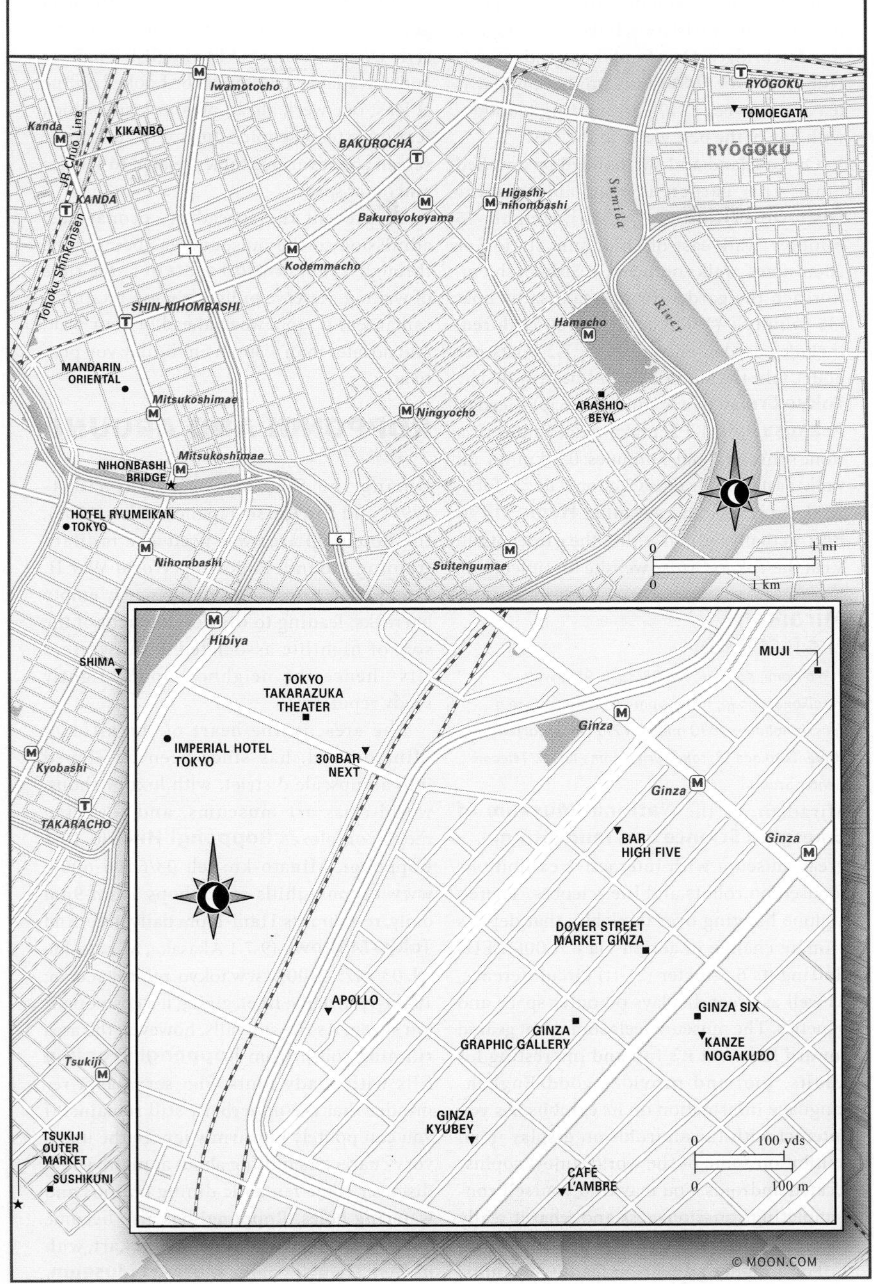
Iwamotocho
Kanda
KIKANBŌ
JR Chūō Line
BAKUROCHĀ
KANDA
Tohoku Shinkansen
Bakuroyokoyama
Higashi-nihombashi
Kodemmacho
SHIN-NIHOMBASHI
MANDARIN ORIENTAL
Mitsukoshimae
Ningyocho
NIHONBASHI BRIDGE
HOTEL RYUMEIKAN TOKYO
Nihombashi
Suitengumae
Hamacho
ARASHIO-BEYA
Sumida River
RYŌGOKU
TOMOEGATA
0 1 mi
0 1 km
Hibiya
SHIMA
TOKYO TAKARAZUKA THEATER
IMPERIAL HOTEL TOKYO
300BAR NEXT
Kyobashi
TAKARACHO
MUJI
Ginza
BAR HIGH FIVE
DOVER STREET MARKET GINZA
APOLLO
GINZA SIX
GINZA GRAPHIC GALLERY
KANZE NOGAKUDO
Tsukiji
GINZA KYUBEY
TSUKIJI OUTER MARKET
SUSHIKUNI
CAFÉ L'AMBRE
0 100 yds
0 100 m
© MOON.COM

years old. Ducks swim in a large central pond that contains two islands, linked by attractive wooden bridges. On one of the islands stands **Nakajima no Ochaya** (9am-4:30pm daily; tea and a sweet ¥740), an inviting teahouse with one of the best views in the city.

On an island and surrounded by a walled moat, this garden is reachable via the **Ōtemon Bridge** (大手門橋), roughly 15 minutes' walk east of Shiodome Station or 20 minutes' walk southeast of Shimbashi; or, to reach the garden from Asakusa by boat (35 minutes; ¥1,040 adults, ¥400 children, includes garden entrance fee; 1-2 boats per hour), take the Sumida River line operated by **Tokyo Cruise** (www.suijobus.co.jp). Head to **Asakusa Pier** (1-1 Hanakawado, Taitō-ku), a stone's throw (about 3 minutes; 0.3-km/0.1-mi walk) east from Asakusa Station (Ginza, Tobu, Asakusa lines), and get off at **Hama-rikyū Pier,** actually located within the garden itself. Visit the Tokyo Cruise website for timetables.

Miraikan

日本科学未来館

2-3-6 Aomi, Koto-ku; tel. 03/3570-9151; www.miraikan.jst.go.jp; 10am-5pm Wed.-Mon., open if Tues. is holiday; ¥630 adults, ¥210 kindergarten students to age 18; take Yurikamome line to Telecom Center Station

Miraikan, or the **National Museum of Emerging Science and Innovation,** is a great museum with interactive exhibitions focused on robots and life sciences. There's a globe hanging over the lobby that depicts climate change in action via 851,000 LEDs dotting its 6.5-meter (21-ft) circumference, as well as great displays on outer space and genetics. The museum feels somewhat geared toward kids, but it's fun and interesting for adults, too, and provides good English-language information on its exhibits. As you interact with the androids on display in an exhibit on some of the world's most sophisticated androids, you may find yourself contemplating consciousness and what it really means to be human.

For a higher admission fee (¥940 adults, ¥310 kindergarten students to age 18), also get access to the museum's planetarium-style Dome Theater GAIA (English language audio available, but it must be booked online at least one week ahead of your visit), which features stereoscopic films on a full-dome screen about various topics related to science and outer space.

To prevent the spread of coronavirus, admission to the museum was being done through a **reservation system** at the time of writing. Reserve online (www.e-tix.jp/miraikan/en) up to a week ahead of your visit, and no later than 4:30pm on the day you plan to go.

ROPPONGI AND AROUND

六本木

During the Sino-Japanese War (1894-1895) and the Russo-Japanese War (1905), the Roppongi area was used as a military training ground. Following World War II, Occupation forces moved into newly empty barracks, leading to the development of the sort of nightlife associated with overseas GIs—hence the neighborhood's slightly seedy reputation.

The area, in the heart of the affluent Minato ward, has since been developed into an upscale district, with luxury shops, world-class art museums, and towering mega-complexes **Roppongi Hills** (6-10-1 Roppongi, Minato-ku; tel. 03/6406-6000; www.roppongihills.com; shops 11am-9pm daily, restaurants 11am-11pm daily; free) and **Tokyo Midtown** (9-7-1 Akasaka, Minato-ku; tel. 03/3475-3100; www.tokyo-midtown.com; 10am-9pm daily; free), giving it a cosmopolitan sheen. As the sun falls, however, the area running south from **Roppongi Crossing** fills with shady touts who serve as a reminder that the underbelly still remains. If you can politely but firmly ignore the unsavory characters milling about at night, you'll discover some fantastic dining options and watering holes. Roppongi has also become Tokyo's main hub for contemporary art, with its "Art Triangle" of the **Mori Art Museum,**

Roppongi and Around

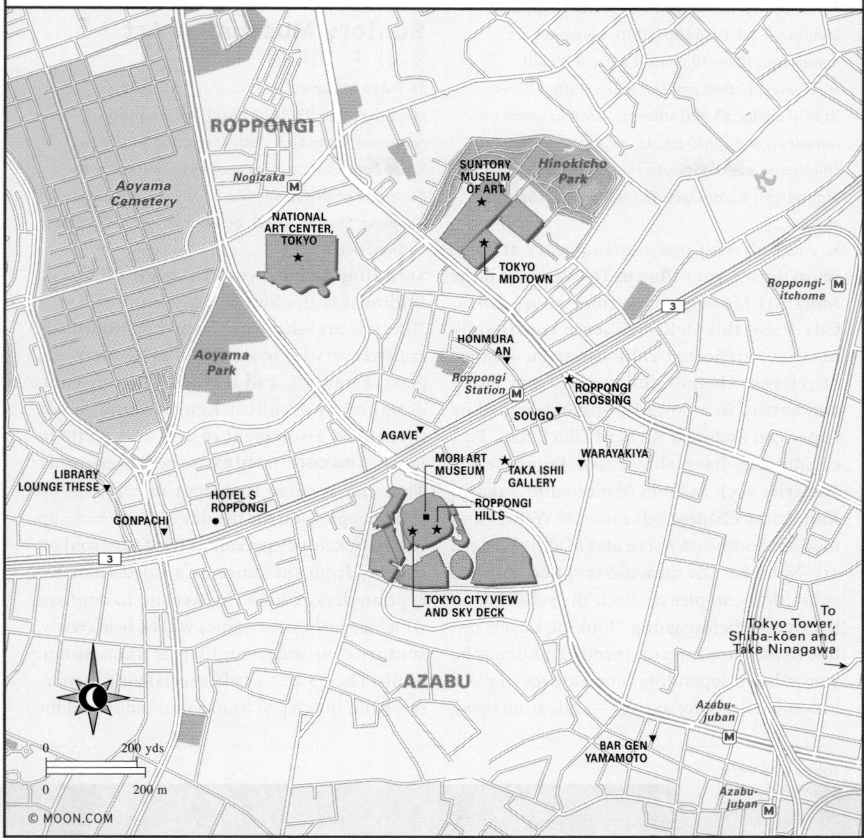

the **Suntory Museum of Art,** and **The National Art Center, Tokyo.**

Close by, roughly 10-15 minutes on foot to the west, south, and east of Roppongi, the posh, slightly rambling greater neighborhood of **Azabu** boasts great restaurants and swanky cocktail bars, minus the unsavory bits. Looming east of Roppongi and Azabu is **Tokyo Tower** in the **Shiba-kōen** area.

Tokyo City View and Sky Deck

東京シティビュー

52F Roppongi Hills Mori Tower; 6-10-1 Roppongi, Minato-ku; tel. 03/6406-6652; https://tcv.roppongihills.com/jp; 10am-10pm (last entry 9:30pm) daily; ¥2,000 adults, ¥1,300 high school and university students, ¥700 ages 4 through junior high school students Mon.-Fri., ¥2,200 adults, ¥1,400 high school and university students, ¥800 ages 4 through junior high school students Sat.-Sun.; take Hibiya line to Roppongi Station, exit 1C, or Ōedo line to Roppongi Station, exit 3

Tokyo City View offers an almost 360-degree view of the city. For an even more unimpeded view, another ¥500 on top of the admission you've already paid allows you to ride an escalator to the rooftop Sky Deck for a view without windows.

Mori Art Museum
森美術館

53F Roppongi Hills Mori Tower; 6-10-1 Roppongi, Minato-ku; tel. 03/6406-6000; www.mori.art.museum/jp; 10am-10pm (last entry 9:30pm) Wed.-Mon., 10am-5pm (last entry 4:30pm) Tues.; ¥1,800 adults, ¥1,200 students, ¥600 children on weekdays, or ¥2,000 adults, ¥1,300 students, ¥700 children on weekends; take Hibiya line to Roppongi Station, exit 1C, or Ōedo line to Roppongi Station, exit 3

If you only visit one contemporary art museum during your time in Tokyo, make it the Mori Art Museum. One floor above Tokyo City View, this stellar museum consistently hosts sophisticated exhibitions on a range of relevant themes and media from Japan and abroad in a fantastic space designed by American architect Richard Gluckman. Past exhibitions have showcased Japanese visionaries such as Aida Makoto and Takashi Murakami, Chinese hell-raiser Ai Weiwei, and modern Southeast Asian and Middle Eastern art. Note that the museum is closed between exhibitions, so please check the schedule on the website before going. Booking tickets online in advance is recommended (and may be compulsory depending on measures in place to combat the coronavirus)—aside from being slightly cheaper than buying tickets on-site, it may also reduce waiting time to enter.

Suntory Museum of Art
サントリー美術館

3F Tokyo Midtown Galleria, 9-7-4 Akasaka, Minato-ku; tel. 03/3479-8600; www.suntory.com/sma; 10am-6pm Wed.-Thurs. and Sun.-Mon., 10am-8pm Fri.-Sat.; fees vary by exhibition; take Ōedo line or Hibiya line (via underground walkway) to Roppongi Station, exit 8, or Chiyoda line to Nogizaka Station, exit 3

Standing at the western edge of Tokyo Midtown is the Suntory Museum of Art, a "lifestyle art" showcase featuring beautifully crafted everyday objects such as lacquerware, glass, ceramics, and textiles. The museum, designed by architect Kengo Kuma, holds the largest assortment of arts and crafts in Japan. **Tea ceremonies** are held every other Thursday at noon, 1pm, 2pm and 3pm for up to 48 people total for the day (¥1,000 each; up to two tickets per person). Tickets are sold on the day from the museum's third-floor reception desk. Check the website to confirm which days the ceremonies will be held (www.suntory.com/sma/rental/teaceremonyroom.html). There's also a **café** specializing in morsels from the city of Kanazawa, renowned for

Tokyo City View

its traditional crafts. The **gift shop** carries exquisitely designed tableware and glassware, some done in the geometric Edo Kiriko style.

The National Art Center, Tokyo
国立新美術館

7-22-2 Roppongi, Minato-ku; tel. 03/5777-8600; www.nact.jp; for exhibitions organized by The National Art Center, Tokyo: 10am-6pm (last entry 5:30pm) Wed.-Thurs. and Sun.-Mon., 10am-8pm (last entry 7:30pm) Fri.-Sat., closed Wed. if Tues. is holiday, for exhibitions organized by artist associations: 10am-6pm (last entry 5:30pm) Wed.-Mon.; fees vary by exhibition; take Ōedo line to Roppongi Station, exits 7, 8

With the biggest exhibition space of any art museum in the country, The National Art Center, Tokyo houses 12 galleries in a striking building designed by the late architect Kurokawa Kisho. Standing in front of the massive structure, the curved green windows of its front wall appear to undulate as it allows natural light to flood the soaring atrium. The museum doesn't have a collection of its own. Instead, it hosts meticulously curated shows ranging from the surrealist mindscapes of Salvador Dalí to the polka-dot infused world of Yayoi Kusama, alongside a host of other exhibitions overseen by various art collectives and associations throughout Japan. The museum also boasts two restaurants, a café, and a stellar gift shop, **Souvenir From Tokyo.**

Tokyo Tower
東京タワー

4-2-8 Shiba-kōen, Minato-ku; tel. 03/3433-5111; www.tokyotower.co.jp; 9am-11pm (last entry 10:30pm) daily; ¥1,200 adults, ¥1,000 16-18 years old, ¥700 junior high and elementary school students, ¥500 ages 4-6; take Ōedo line to Akabanebashi Station, Akabanebashiguchi exit

Finished in 1958, Tokyo Tower was originally intended to commemorate the city's phoenix-like rise after World War II. Its resemblance to the Eiffel Tower is overt, as is the fact that it stands 13 meters taller than its Parisian inspiration. The structure still serves as a radio and television broadcast tower, but the words "tourist trap" are admittedly hard to avoid when thinking of it today. Its extra attractions—a wax museum, an aquarium, and an exhibit dedicated to the anime program *One Piece*—only reinforce this impression. People still flock to it nonetheless, and the white-and-orange behemoth remains one of the most recognizable points in the city's skyline. The observation decks of the Tokyo Metropolitan Government Building, Tokyo Skytree, or Tokyo City View provide more sweeping views. But if you feel the pull of vintage charm, Tokyo Tower still offers thrilling views of the Minato area skyline at night. If you're coming from Roppongi on foot, the tower is about 20 minutes' walk southeast of Roppongi Crossing (intersection of Gaien-higashi Dōri and Roppongi Dōri). You'll see it looming in the distance as you head southeast down Gaien-higashi Dōri.

EBISU AND AROUND
恵比寿

Ebisu is a sophisticated neighborhood, a welcome relief from the chaos of nearby Shibuya to the northwest on the Saikyo line. A mix of locals and expats congregate here to eat and drink at an impressive array of restaurants and drinking dens.

Ebisu has long been associated with food and, more specifically, drink, as its very origin is linked to the founding of a brewery, Yebisu Beer, in the late 1920s. Both neighborhood and brewery are named for the god of prosperity, embodied in a jolly-looking statue next to the train station. **Yebisu Garden Place** (4-20 Ebisu, Shibuya-ku; tel. 03/5423-7111; https://gardenplace.jp; 7am-midnight daily; free), site of the **Museum of Yebisu Beer** (B1F Sapporo Beer Headquarters, Yebisu Garden Place, 4-20-1 Ebisu, Shibuya-ku; tel. 03/5423-7255; www.sapporobeer.jp; 11am-6pm Tues.-Sun., tasting salon last order 5:30pm, closed Tues. if Mon. is holiday), is a city within a city, with a pleasing blend of greenery, shops, and cultural offerings oriented around a spacious central square.

The nearby neighborhoods of **Daikanyama** and **Nakameguro** have a similar vibe, with high-end fashion boutiques and hipster cafés. The mellow streets are worth wandering for the sake of putting yourself in serendipity's way.

Tokyo Photographic Art Museum

東京都写真美術館

Yebisu Garden Place, 1-13-3 Mita, Meguro-ku; tel. 03/3280-0099; https://topmuseum.jp; 10am-6pm Tues.-Sun. (last entry 5:30pm), closed Tues. if Mon. falls on holiday; entry fee varies by exhibition; take Yamanote line to Ebisu station, east exit, or Hibiya line to Ebisu Station, exit 1

Tokyo's premier photography museum, colloquially shortened to **TOP Museum,** is housed in a four-story building toward the back of Yebisu Garden Place. The space boasts a library, studio, research laboratory, film screening hall, and multimedia gallery. Its permanent collection includes works by greats such as Ansel Adams, W. Eugene Smith, and Gustave Le Gray, as well as Japan's own photographic legends, such as Nobuyoshi Araki, Daido Moriyama, Miyako Ishiuchi, Rinko Kawauchi, and Mika Ninagawa, among many others.

A café on the museum's first floor, run by the trendy Maison Ichi bakery in nearby Daikanyama, provides a space to relax with a beverage or light meal after enjoying the visual feast.

Tokyo Metropolitan Teien Art Museum

東京都庭園美術館

5-21-9 Shirokanedai, Minato-ku; tel. 03/3443-0201; www.teien-art-museum.ne.jp; 10am-6pm Tues.-Sun. (last entry 5:30pm); entry fee varies by exhibition, garden only ¥200 adults, ¥160 college students, ¥100 high school and junior high school students; take Yamanote line to Meguro Station, east exit, or Mita, Namboku lines to Shirokanedai Station, exit 1

The Tokyo Metropolitan Teien Art Museum's main draw is the building itself. Completed in 1933, the mansion is a stunning example of art deco architecture, with both a rose garden and a Japanese landscape garden. It was formerly the residence of Emperor Hirohito's uncle, Prince Asaka Yasuhiko, and Princess Nobuko, Emperor Meiji's eighth daughter. Prince Asaka returned from a stint in 1920s Paris, inspired to build a modern home. He enlisted French architect Henri Rapin and glass designer René Lalique, along with a team of Japanese architects, to produce the dazzling result. In 2014, the structures were restored and a new annex was added by artist Sugimoto Hiroshi. A visit to the museum today means exploring the enchanting mansion, with its crystal chandeliers and lush grounds, just as much as seeing whatever exhibition—likely in the decorative arts genre—is taking place at the time.

Happo-en

八芳園

1-1-1 Shirokanedai, Minato-ku; tel. 0570/064-128; www.happo-en.com; 9am-8:30pm daily; free; take Namboku, Mita lines to Shirokanedai Station, exit 2

Happo-en, which means "garden of eight views," is aptly named: It looks beautiful from any angle. Serene paths wind through the beautifully landscaped garden, which has a pond at its heart and is dotted by bonsai trees, some of which are centuries old. A stone lantern said to have been carved by the warrior Taira-no Munekiyo some 800 years ago also stands on the grounds, which were originally the residence of an advisor to the shogun during the early 17th century. The current design was largely realized in the early 20th century by a business magnate who acquired the land and built a Japanese villa, which can still be seen near the garden's entrance. With a large banquet hall on-site, it's no surprise the garden is one of the most popular places in Tokyo for couples to tie the knot. Note that small sections of the garden may be closed off if a wedding is underway.

Muan (tel. 03/3443-3775; www.happo-en.com/banquet/plan_en/detail.php?p=837; 11am-4pm daily), a teahouse, is also tucked away in the garden, offering sets of matcha

Ebisu and Around

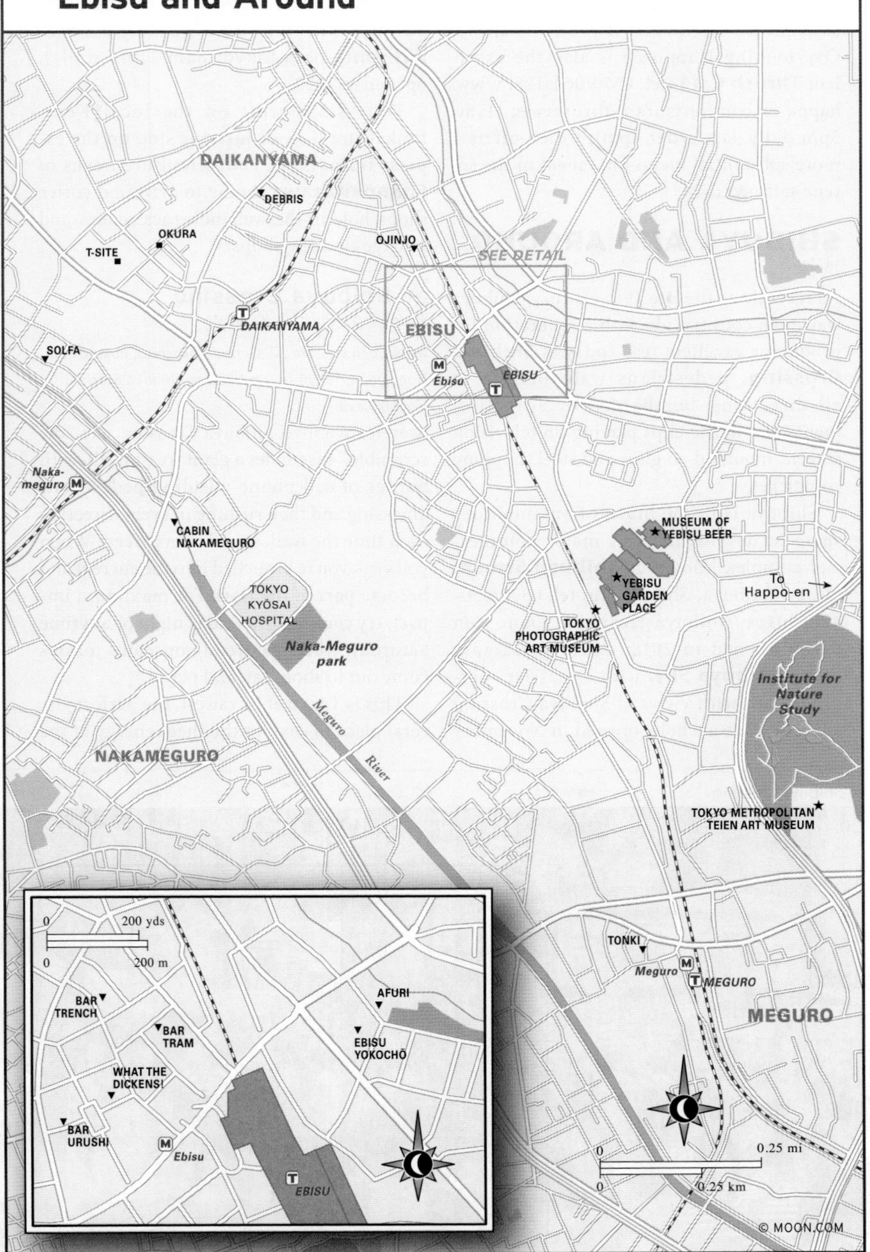

(powdered green tea with a highly caffeinated kick) and Japanese-style sweets, as well as small tea ceremonies if you book ahead. Overlooking Happo-en is also the excellent **Thrush Café** (tel. 0570/064-128; www.happo-en.com/restaurant/thrushcafe; 11am-5pm daily, last order 4pm), which offers a more substantial menu for a meal in the serene setting.

SHIBUYA AND AROUND

渋谷

As recently as the late 19th century, Shibuya was open countryside with a reputation for producing excellent tea. Today at **Shibuya Crossing,** pedestrians walk briskly in all directions, bombarded by advertisements and music clips playing on television screens mounted on glass and steel shopping complexes.

Shibuya is in the midst of an ambitious spate of development: A major commercial complex known as **Shibuya Stream** (3-21-3 Shibuya, Shibuya-ku; tel. 0570/050-428; https://shibuyastream.jp; 10am-9pm daily) opened in 2018, and a skyscraper called **Shibuya Sky,** with a massive rooftop terrace with views of Shibuya Crossing and Tokyo as a whole, opened in November 2019. And a massive new mall with a rooftop park, **Miyashita Park** (6-20-10 Jingūmae, Shibuya-ku; tel. 03/6712-5630; www.miyashita-park.tokyo; 8am-11pm daily), opened in 2020.

Four stops west on the local Keio-Inokashira line, or just one stop on the express train, is the counterculture nexus of **Shimokitazawa,** home to artisanal coffee shops, hole-in-the-wall indie rock venues, and vintage clothing shops.

★ Shibuya Crossing

渋谷スクランブル交差点

www.sibch.tv; take JR, Ginza, Inokashira, Fukutoshin, Hanzōmon, Tōkyū Tōyoko lines to Shibuya Station, Hachikō exit

Seen from above, Shibuya Crossing, aka "the scramble," resembles a giant free-for-all, with hordes of cell phone-wielding pedestrians amassing and then rushing in every direction each time the walk signal turns green. When you visit, you're propelled into the current and become part of the flow. For maximum impact, try coming on a Friday night or anytime Saturday, when the trend-conscious masses come out to shop, eat, and play.

This is Tokyo at its rawest, the perfect visceral place to soak in the sheer energy of the

Shibuya Crossing

Views of Shibuya Crossing

To fully grasp the scale of Shibuya Crossing's foot traffic, head to the hallway linking the JR station to the Keio-Inokashira line on the second floor of the **Shibuya Mark City** commercial complex (1-12-1 Dōgenzaka, Shibuya-ku; tel. 03/3780-6503; www.s-markcity.co.jp; 10am-9pm daily for shops, 11am-11pm daily for restaurants). Windows lining the passageway offer views of the frenzy below. You'll also be able to see the ***Myth of Tomorrow,*** a vivid mural by Tarō Okamoto, dramatically depicting Japan's traumatic relationship with nuclear weapons in its abstractly dread-inducing depiction of the atomic bombing of Hiroshima.

Another good vantage point is **Shibuya Hikarie** (2-21-1 Shibuya, Shibuya-ku; tel. 03/5468-5892; www.hikarie.jp; 11am-8pm daily; free), a complex of boutiques, eateries, and artistic offerings accessible from Shibuya Station's east exit; from the 11th floor, you'll have a view of the spectacle of the fabled Shibuya Scramble, set within a wider view of Shibuya as a whole.

There's also a plexiglass-enclosed viewing platform in **Mag's Park** (1-23-10 Jinnan, Shibuya-ku; tel. 03/3477-5111; https://magnetbyshibuya109.jp/en/mags-park; 10am-9pm daily, last entry 8:30pm; ¥1,000), a rooftop space that opened in 2018 atop the **Magnet by Shibuya 109** department store. Its location on one corner of the scramble gives unimpeded views of the intersection.

Looming highest of them all is **Shibuya Sky,** an open-air, 360-degree rooftop viewing platform.

world's largest metropolis. It's the gateway to a district at the heart of Japanese youth culture, thriving in the teeming streets of Shibuya's **Center Gai;** it's also where you'll find an entry point to **Dogenzaka,** a district bursting at the seams with options for dining and nightlife of every shade, as well as one of Tokyo's most well-known agglomerations of love hotels.

In the frantic square next to the crossing is perhaps Tokyo's most beloved meeting point: **Hachikō Square,** with a bronze statue of the legendarily loyal dog for which it's named. The canine came to meet his master, a professor, at the station as he returned home from work every day, and continued to make his daily trek to Shibuya Station nearly a decade after his master died in 1925.

If you are seriously concerned about crowds in light of COVID-19, it's best not to even bother with Shibuya Crossing. That said, it is notably at its most crowded on weekend afternoons and evenings. Making the trip during the daylight hours of a weekday might give you a slightly less claustrophobic experience. Whenever you choose to visit, just remember that it's the most crowded pedestrian intersection on earth, and the entire point of visiting it is to experience the energy it brings. Finally, consider viewing it from upon high at one of the many viewpoints arrayed around the intersection, such as **Shibuya Sky.**

Shibuya Sky

2-24-12 Shibuya, Shibuya-ku; tel. 03/4221-0229; www.shibuya-scramble-square.com/sky; 10am-10:30pm daily (last entry 9:20pm); tickets purchased online ¥1,800 adults, ¥1,400 junior high and high school students, ¥900 elementary school students, ¥500 children 3-5 years old; tickets purchased in-person ¥2,000 adults, ¥1,600 junior high and high school students, ¥1,000 elementary school students, ¥600 children 3-5 years old; take JR, Ginza, Inokashira, Fukutoshin, Hanzōmon, Tōkyū Tōyoko lines to Shibuya Station, east exit, or in direction of Shibuya Hikarie complex

On the rooftop of a new cloud-scraping complex called Shibuya Scramble Square, at 230 meters (755 ft) aboveground, this observatory, known as Sky Stage, is the highest point in the neighborhood. Besides offering a bird's-eye view of the frantic crossing below, you'll also get sweeping views of Tokyo's sprawl, extending all the way to Mount Fuji on clear days.

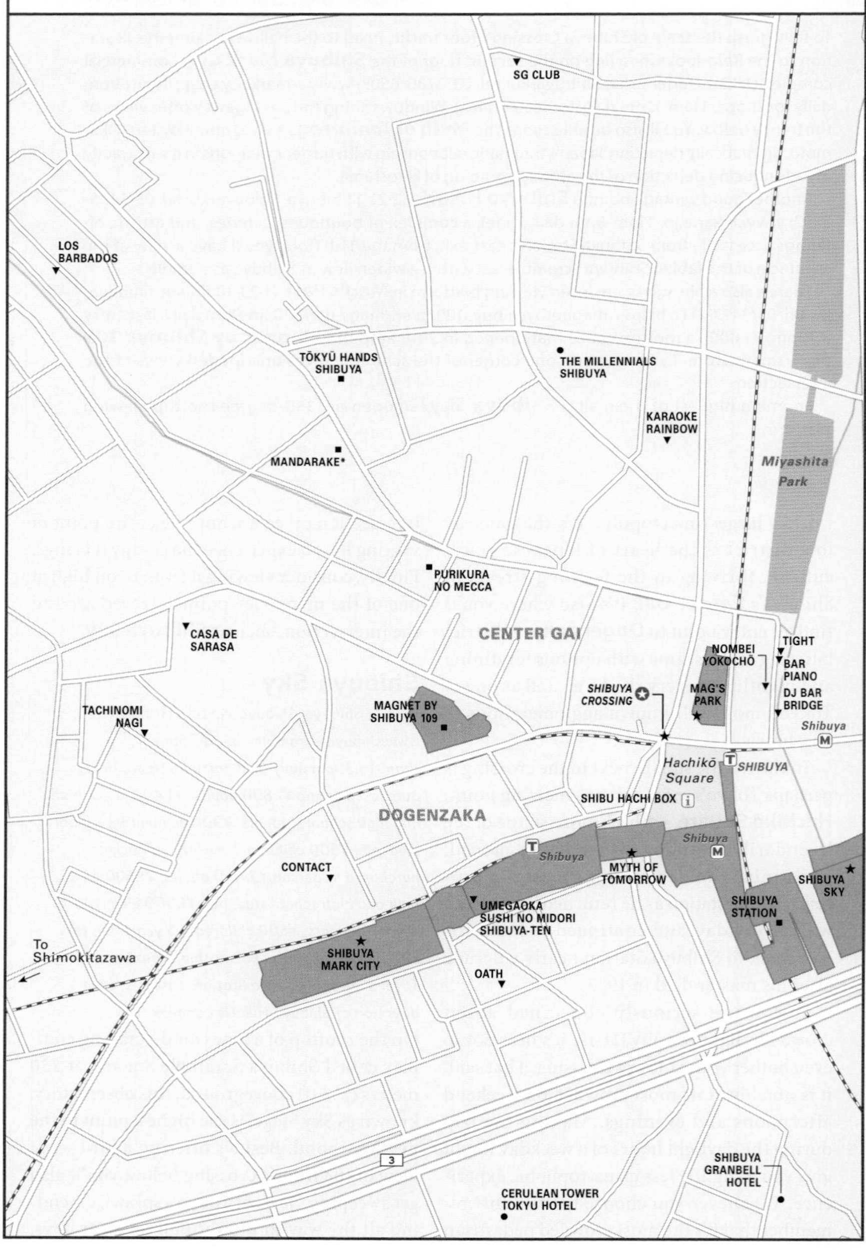
Shibuya and Around
SG CLUB
LOS BARBADOS
TŌKYŪ HANDS SHIBUYA
THE MILLENNIALS SHIBUYA
KARAOKE RAINBOW
MANDARAKE*
Miyashita Park
PURIKURA NO MECCA
CASA DE SARASA
CENTER GAI
NOMBEI YOKOCHŌ
TIGHT
BAR PIANO
DJ BAR BRIDGE
SHIBUYA CROSSING
MAG'S PARK
MAGNET BY SHIBUYA 109
TACHINOMI NAGI
Shibuya
Hachikō Square
SHIBUYA
SHIBU HACHI BOX
DOGENZAKA
Shibuya
Shibuya
MYTH OF TOMORROW
CONTACT
SHIBUYA SKY
UMEGAOKA SUSHI NO MIDORI SHIBUYA-TEN
SHIBUYA STATION
To Shimokitazawa
SHIBUYA MARK CITY
OATH
3
SHIBUYA GRANBELL HOTEL
CERULEAN TOWER TOKYU HOTEL

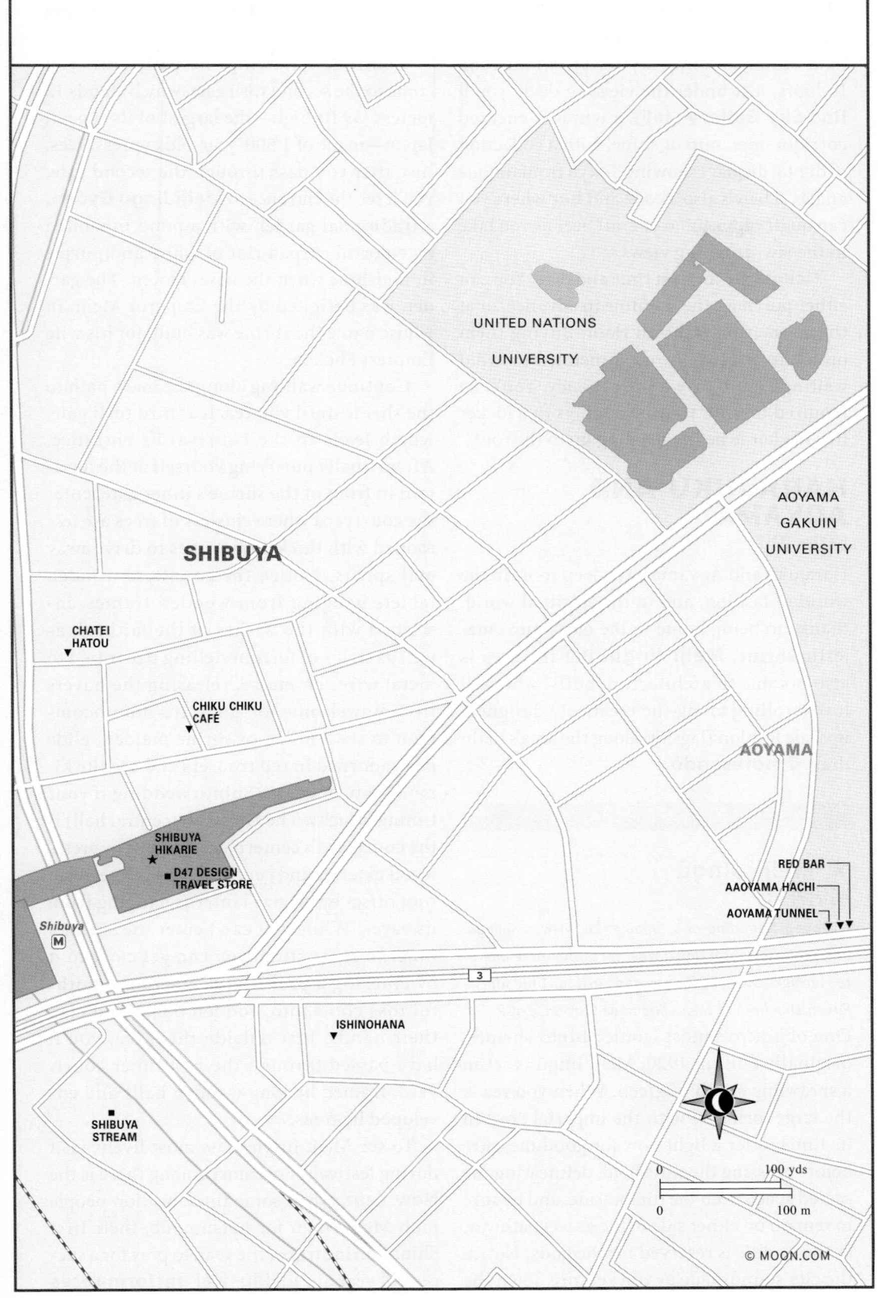
UNITED NATIONS
UNIVERSITY
AOYAMA
GAKUIN
UNIVERSITY
SHIBUYA
CHATEI
HATOU
CHIKU CHIKU
CAFÉ
AOYAMA
SHIBUYA
HIKARIE
D47 DESIGN
TRAVEL STORE
RED BAR
AAOYAMA HACHI
AOYAMA TUNNEL
Shibuya
M
3
ISHINOHANA
SHIBUYA
STREAM
0
100 yds
0
100 m
© MOON.COM

There's a smattering of hammocks, sofas, and, come nighttime, a show of 18 colored light beams shooting skyward from the roof. Indoors, just under the viewing deck, you'll find **Sky Gallery** (46F), a window-encased corridor open rain or shine, with a collection of digital displays showing Tokyo from unique angles. There's also a **café** and **bar** where you can quaff cappuccino or craft beer as you take in the jaw-dropping views.

Tickets are for a set time and date. You can either purchase them online in advance, or at the counter on the 14th floor. Buying them online in advance is recommended to avoid waiting and to save a little money. You'll be required to store your belongings in a locker free of charge before heading up to the roof.

HARAJUKU AND AOYAMA

原宿, 青山

Harajuku and Aoyama have deep roots in the world of fashion, and in the spiritual world, thanks to being home to the city's most majestic shrine, **Meiji Jingū.** But the area is also notable to architecture buffs, who will love strolling along the creatively designed, upscale fashion flagship along the area's main drag, **Omotesandō.**

TOP EXPERIENCE

★ Meiji Jingū

明治神宮

1-1 Yoyogi Kamizono-chō, Shibuya-ku; www.meijijingu.or.jp; sunrise-sunset daily; free; take Yamanote line to Harajuku Station, Omotesandō exit, or Chiyoda, Fukutoshin lines to Meiji-Jingūmae Station, exit 2

One of Tokyo's most iconic Shinto shrines, originally built in 1920, Meiji Jingū is set in a sprawling swath of green. When you reach the large torii gate with the imperial crest in its lintel, offer a light bow for good measure before crossing the threshold, delineating the sacred space from the din outside, and be sure to remain on either side of the gravel pathway, as the middle is reserved for the gods. Notice the city sounds fade as you venture down the shaded trail, deeper into a forest of towering camphor trees.

Continue following the path until you come to the second torii gate, which stands 12 meters (39 ft) high—the largest of its type in Japan—made of 1,500-year-old cypress trees. Just after you pass through the second gate, you'll see the entrance to **Meiji Jingū Gyōen,** a traditional garden with a pond inhabited by colorful carp, a riot of white and purple in mid-June when the irises bloom. The garden was designed by the Emperor Meiji, in whose name the shrine was built, for his wife Empress Shoken.

Continue walking along the main path to the shrine until you reach a third torii gate, which leads to the courtyard's entrance. After ritually purifying yourself at the fountain in front of the shrine's inner gate, enter the courtyard where clusters of trees are festooned with thick straw ropes to drive away evil spirits. Notice the countless wooden tablets hanging from wooden frames, inscribed with the wishes of the faithful, as well as strips of fortune-telling paper tied to metal wires en masse, releasing the buyers from unwelcome fortunes. It's not uncommon to see a miko, or shrine maiden, glide past, adorned in red trousers and a white kimono top, or even a Shinto wedding if your timing is lucky. The **Honden** (central hall) is the courtyard's centerpiece, with its cypress-wood exterior and gently curved copper-clad roof offset by bronze lanterns hanging from its eaves. While you can't enter the shrine's innermost sanctum, you can get close to it by entering a prayer area where the faithful toss coins into wooden boxes and clap their hands. Just outside this area, you'll have passed through the vast inner courtyard, framed by long wooden halls and enveloped by trees.

To see Meiji Jingū at its most lively, visit during festivals. Foremost among these is the **New Year,** when some three million people mob Meiji Jingū for hatsumode, their first Shinto shrine trip of the year, to pray for a successful year ahead. **Musical performances**

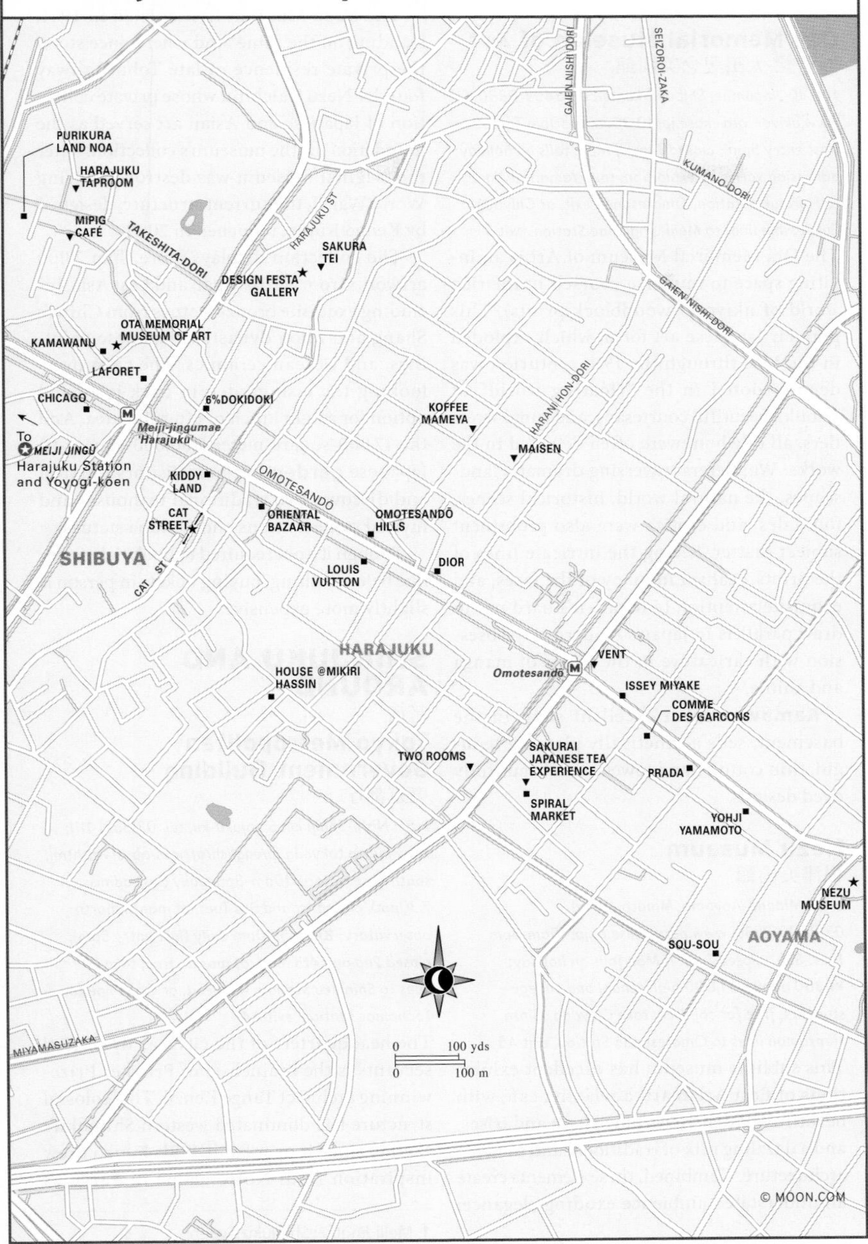
Harajuku and Aoyama
PURIKURA LAND NOA
HARAJUKU TAPROOM
MIPIG CAFÉ
TAKESHITA-DORI
HARAJUKU ST
SAKURA TEI
DESIGN FESTA GALLERY
OTA MEMORIAL MUSEUM OF ART
KAMAWANU
LAFORET
CHICAGO
6%DOKIDOKI
Meiji-jingumae 'Harajuku'
To MEIJI JINGŪ Harajuku Station and Yoyogi-kōen
KIDDY LAND
OMOTESANDO
CAT STREET
ORIENTAL BAZAAR
OMOTESANDŌ HILLS
SHIBUYA
CAT ST
LOUIS VUITTON
DIOR
KOFFEE MAMEYA
MAISEN
HARAJUKU
HOUSE @MIKIRI HASSIN
Omotesandō
VENT
ISSEY MIYAKE
COMME DES GARCONS
TWO ROOMS
SAKURAI JAPANESE TEA EXPERIENCE
SPIRAL MARKET
PRADA
YOHJI YAMAMOTO
NEZU MUSEUM
SOU-SOU
AOYAMA
GAIEN NISHI DORI
SEIZOROI-ZAKA
KUMANO-DORI
GAIEN-NISHI-DORI
HARAMI HON-DORI
MIYAMASUZAKA
0 100 yds
0 100 m
© MOON.COM

and dances are staged in the shrine's courtyard April 29-May 3 and November 1-3.

Ota Memorial Museum of Art
浮世絵 太田記念美術館

1-10-10 Jingūmae, Shibuya-ku; tel. 03/3403/0880; www.ukiyoe-ota-muse.jp; 10:30am-5:30pm Tues.-Sun. (last entry 5pm), closed Tues. if Mon. falls on holiday; admission varies by exhibition; take Yamanote line to Harajuku Station, Omotesandō exit, or Chiyoda, Fukutoshin lines to Meiji-Jingūmae Station, exit 5

The Ota Memorial Museum of Art is an inviting space to immerse yourself in the rich world of ukiyo-e (woodblock prints). This popular Japanese art form, which exploded in the 17th through the 19th centuries, was deeply rooted in the "floating world" of Kabuki, beautiful courtesans, and sumo wrestlers, all of whom were often depicted in the works. Wanderers traversing dramatic landscapes, the natural world, historical scenes, folk tales, and erotica were also prominent subject matter. Seeing the intricate lines of the prints, realism in many of the faces, and exquisite attention to detail, it's hard not to draw parallels to Japan's modern-day obsession with caricature in the forms of manga and anime.

Kamawanu, an excellent shop in the basement, sells aesthetically pleasing tenugui, thin cotton hand towels with beautifully dyed designs.

Nezu Museum
根津美術館

6-5-1 Minami-Aoyama, Minato-ku; tel. 03/3400-2536; www.nezu-muse.or.jp; 10am-5pm Tues.-Sun., closed Tues. if Mon falls on holiday; ¥1,300 adults, ¥1,000 high school and college students, free for children; take Chiyoda, Ginza, Hanzomon lines to Omotesandō Station, exit A5

This sublime museum has excellent exhibitions of East Asian art, a relaxing café with beautiful garden views of wisteria and irises, and a dazzling mix of traditional and modern architecture. Combined, these elements create an understated ambience exuding elegance; you'll sense you've stumbled onto something special.

The Nezu Museum first opened in 1941, standing on the same land where once stood the private residence of late Tobu Railway founder Nezu Kaichiro, whose private collection of Japanese and Asian art served as the foundation for the museum's collection. After the original museum was destroyed during World War II, the current structure, designed by Kengo Kuma, reopened in 2009.

The collection displays more than 7,000 artworks from across Japan and East Asia, including exquisite bronze statues from China's Shang and Zhou dynasties, Japanese paintings, and Korean ceramics. The **café** overlooking the lush garden in back is a good option for a light lunch or afternoon tea. And the 17,000-square-meter (180,000-square-ft) Japanese **garden** beckons visitors to stroll and discover two traditional teahouses and myriad stone lanterns and Buddha statues.

Though it's not required to book tickets online before visiting, buying tickets in person is slightly more expensive.

SHINJUKU AND AROUND
新宿

Tokyo Metropolitan Government Building
東京都庁

2-8-1 Nishi-Shinjuku, Shinjuku-ku; tel. 03/5321-1111; www.metro.tokyo.lg.jp/english/offices/observat.html; south observatory: 10am-8pm daily (last admission 7:30pm), closed 1st and 3rd Tues. of month, north observatory: 10am-5:30pm daily (last entry 5pm), closed 2nd and 4th Mon. of month; free; take JR lines to Shinjuku Station, west exit, or Ōedo line to Tochōmae Station, exit A4

The headquarters of the city's army of civil servants is the brainchild of Pritzker Prize-winning architect Tange Kenzo. This colossal structure has dominated western Shinjuku's skyline since it opened in 1991. Kenzo drew inspiration from Notre Dame in Paris, as

1: Meiji Jingū **2:** Shinjuku Gyōen

1
2

Shinjuku and Around

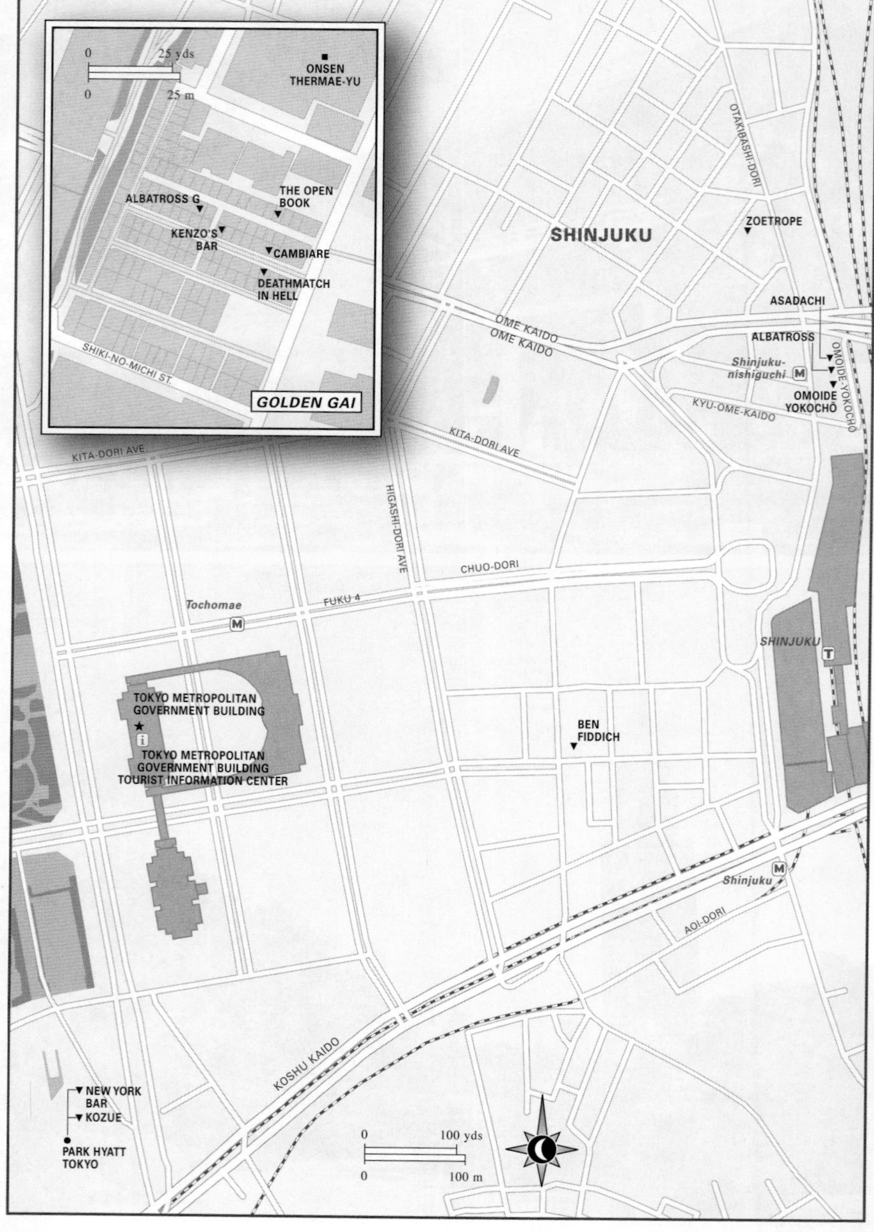

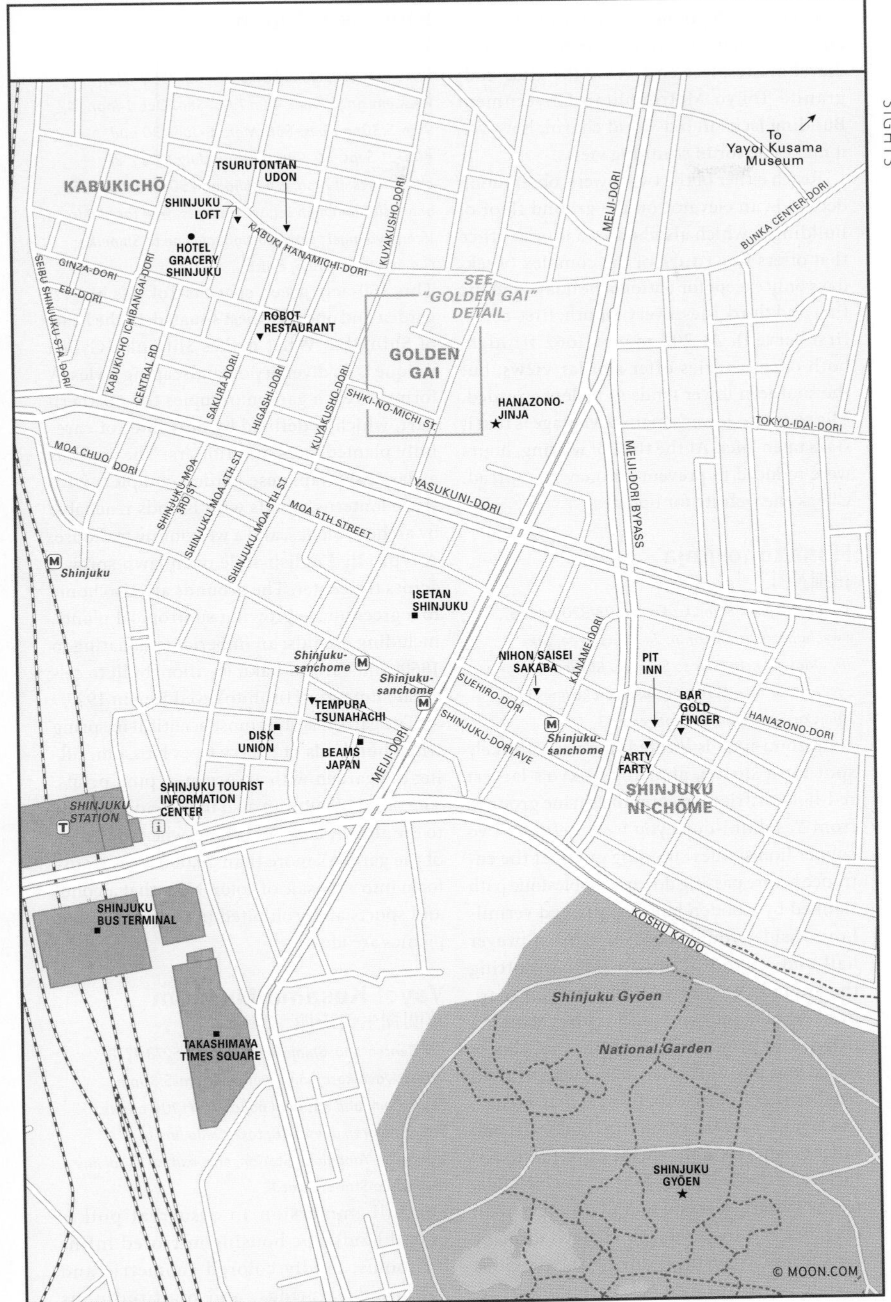
To Yayoi Kusama Museum
KABUKICHŌ
TSURUTONTAN UDON
SHINJUKU LOFT
HOTEL GRACERY SHINJUKU
KABUKI HANAMICHI-DORI
KUYAKUSHO-DORI
MEIJI-DORI
BUNKA CENTER-DORI
GINZA-DORI
EBI-DORI
SEIBU SHINJUKU STA. DORI
KABUKICHO ICHIBANGAI-DORI
CENTRAL RD
SAKURA-DORI
HIGASHI-DORI
ROBOT RESTAURANT
SEE "GOLDEN GAI" DETAIL
GOLDEN GAI
SHIKI-NO-MICHI ST.
HANAZONO-JINJA
TOKYO-IDAI-DORI
MOA CHUO DORI
SHINJUKU MOA 3RD ST
SHINJUKU MOA 4TH ST
SHINJUKU MOA 5TH ST
MOA 5TH STREET
YASUKUNI-DORI
MEIJI-DORI BYPASS
Shinjuku
ISETAN SHINJUKU
Shinjuku-sanchome
NIHON SAISEI SAKABA
KANAME-DORI
PIT INN
BAR GOLD FINGER
HANAZONO-DORI
SUEHIRO-DORI
SHINJUKU-DORI AVE
TEMPURA TSUNAHACHI
DISK UNION
BEAMS JAPAN
ARTY FARTY
SHINJUKU NI-CHŌME
SHINJUKU TOURIST INFORMATION CENTER
SHINJUKU STATION
SHINJUKU BUS TERMINAL
KOSHU KAIDO
Shinjuku Gyōen
National Garden
TAKASHIMAYA TIMES SQUARE
SHINJUKU GYŌEN
© MOON.COM

evidenced in the archetypal twin-tower form, but this is where the similarities to Paris's medieval masterpiece end. What the glass-and-granite Tokyo Metropolitan Government Building lacks in old-world charm, however, it makes up for in stunning views.

Reach either of the two towers' observation decks via an elevator on the ground floor of Building 1, which also houses a tourist office that offers free **tours** of the complex (weekdays only except for national holidays and the first and third Tues. every month; first-come, first-served). At 202 meters (662 ft) high, both observatories offer similar views, but the southern tower tends to be less crowded. The southern tower's main advantage is that it stays open later. At the time of writing, hours were reduced to prevent coronavirus spread. Check the website for updates.

Hanazono-jinja
花園神社

5-17-3 Shinjuku, Shinjuku-ku; tel. 03/3209-5265; www.hanazono-jinja.or.jp; 24 hours; free; take JR, Odakyu, Keio lines to Shinjuku Station, east exit, or take Marunouchi, Shinjuku lines to Shinjuku-Sanchōme Station, exit B3

Hanazono-jinja is located in a very unlikely spot for a shrine, abutting Tokyo's largest red-light district. To enter the shrine grounds from Yasukuni-dōri, you walk between two copper lion statues standing guard at the entrance before passing down a cobblestone path flanked by wooden lanterns painted vermillion. Inside, you'll discover a main prayer hall and a handful of sub-shrines dotting the grounds. Dedicated to the fox god Inari, overseer of money and success, the shrine is a magnet for proprietors of businesses, aboveboard and not, and entertainers who work in neighboring Kabukichō. It's said that yakuza, the Japanese mafia, often run food stalls and other businesses at the shrine's lively festivals, including the **Reitaisai Matsuri,** which falls on the closest weekend to May 28 every year. On January 8, those who purchased talismans for success in business during the previous year line up to toss their old charms into a fire.

Shinjuku Gyōen
新宿御苑

11 Naitomachi, Shinjuku-ku; tel. 03/3350-0151; www.env.go.jp; 9am-4pm Tues.-Sun. Oct. 1-Mar. 14, 9am-5:30pm Tues.-Sun. Mar. 15-June 30 and Aug. 21-Sept. 30, 9am-6:30pm July 1-Aug. 20, closed Tues. if Mon. is a holiday; ¥500 adults, ¥250 university and high school students, free for children 15 and younger; take Marunouchi line to Shinjuku Gyōen-mae Station, exit 1

This 150-acre green space is Tokyo's biggest garden and one of its best situated, in the heart of Shinjuku. What makes Shinjuku Gyōen unique is its diversity of landscaping styles. A formal French garden occupies the northern part, which is defined by neat lines of carefully planted trees and flowers. The south is a classically Japanese garden complete with stone lanterns, ponds with islands reachable by arched bridges, and a welcoming teahouse. A typically English-style open lawn sprawls across the center. The grounds are also home to a greenhouse growing subtropical plants, including orchids; an imperial villa dating to 1869; and Taiwan-kaku Pavilion, built to celebrate Emperor Hirohito's wedding in 1927.

The garden is at its most beautiful in spring when hundreds of cherry trees blossom, filling the garden with an ocean of pink petals. The onset of autumn also injects added color to the already beautiful scene, when the leaves of the garden's more than 20,000 trees transform into a mosaic of color. Note that alcohol and sports are prohibited in the garden, but picnics are ideal.

Yayoi Kusama Museum
草間彌生美術館

107 Benten-chō, Shinjuku-ku; tel. 03/5273-1778; https://yayoikusamamuseum.jp; 11am-5:30pm Thurs.-Sun. and national holidays; ¥1,100 adults, ¥600 children ages 6-18; take Ōedo line to Ushigome-Yanagichō Station, east exit, or Tozai line to Waseda Station, exit 1

For full immersion in a surreal polka-dotted landscape housing mirrored infinity rooms, loudly colored geometric and patterned paintings, and multitudinous phallic sculptures, head to the Yayoi Kusama Museum. The five-story white building full of windows and warm light stands out markedly from the drab apartment blocks surrounding it. The museum hosts two exhibitions per year, drawing on the artist's prodigious body of work. Active since the 1950s, and once a figure in New York City's avant-garde in the 1970s, Kusama, known for her trademark bob-cut red wig, has honed a singular style that has made her one of Japan's most famous contemporary artists. Her work is inspired by the hallucinatory visions of forms superimposed on the world around her, which she's experienced since childhood.

Two floors are dedicated to Kusama's paintings, another floor houses installations for visitors to lose themselves in, and the top floor has a reading room. Tickets must be purchased in advance online; the museum admits ticket holders at six 90-minute time slots daily (11am-12:30pm, noon-1:30pm, 1pm-2:30pm, 2pm-3:30pm, 3pm-4:30pm, 4pm-5:30pm). Tickets are often sold out far in advance. If you plan to visit, book your spot early through the official website.

AKIHABARA AND UENO

秋葉原, 上野

Akihabara has long been associated with commerce, from bicycles and radios during World War II to a flourishing black market that specialized in supplying radios to information-starved civilians in the postwar years. Whether you indulge in one of the obsessions catered to by the neighborhood's myriad niche shops or not, a visit will surely leave you feeling like you've experienced a bona fide slice of Japanese subculture. If you crave a break from all the gadgets, the nearby classical garden of **Koishikawa Kōrakuen** to the west is well worth a detour, too.

To the north are **Ueno-kōen** and **Ueno Station.** West of Ueno you'll discover the laid-back **Yanaka,** a charming neighborhood of mom-and-pop restaurants, shops selling locally made crafts, art galleries, old-school cafés, and a number of serene temples and shrines.

Kanda Myōjin

神田明神

2-16-2 Sotokanda, Chiyoda-ku; tel. 03/3254-0753; www.kandamyoujin.or.jp; 24 hours; free; take Chūō, Sōbu, Marunouchi lines to Ochanomizu Station, exit 1, or Yamanote, Hibiya lines to Akihabara Station, Electric Town exit

It's somewhat counterintuitive that one of Tokyo's oldest shrines, Kanda Myōjin, has become so deeply associated with Akihabara, Tokyo's most technology-crazed neighborhood. Founded in AD 730, the current shrine is in fact a concrete re-creation of the original one. It is dedicated to three gods: Ebisu (god of commerce and fishermen), Daikokuten (guardian of farmers, harvests, and wealth), and Masakado (full name: Taira no Masakado, a guardian deity). Visitors to the shrine typically come to pray for luck in marriage and business.

Passing through the shrine's magnificently carved vermillion gate today, you'll soon discover indicators of its proximity to "Electric Town," such as omamori (amulets purchased for blessing or protection at temples and shrines) to protect electronic gadgets and a glut of ema (wooden prayer plaques) adorned with precise hand-drawn portraits of supplicants' favorite anime and manga characters alongside their prayers. In mid-May during oddly numbered years, the **Kanda Matsuri,** seen as one of Tokyo's top-three festivals, begins at the shrine and then spills out into the area's streets.

Origami Kaikan

おりがみ会館

1-7-14 Yushima, Bunkyō-ku; tel. 03/3811-4025; www.origamikaikan.co.jp; 9:30am-4:30pm Mon.-Sat., closed holidays; free to enter gallery, fees for classes vary; take Chūō, Sōbu, Marunouchi lines to Ochanomizu Station, exit 1

Established in 1859, Origami Kaikan is regarded as the place where the art of origami paper-folding was born. The building houses

Akihabara and Ueno

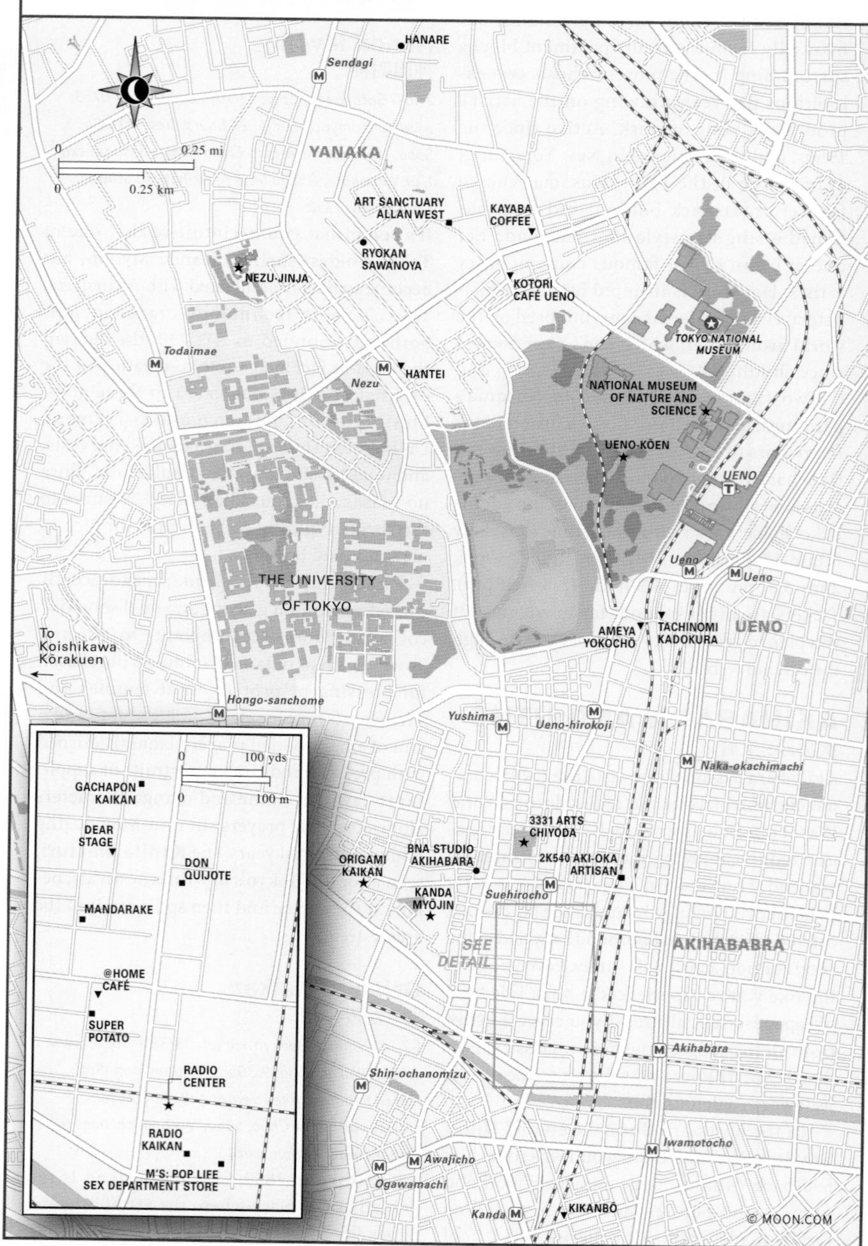

an exhibition space, a workshop where you can see origami paper being created, and a shop devoted to origami papers, books, and more. There are also Japanese-language classes on origami priced according to the class's level of difficulty on any given day.

Koishikawa Kōrakuen

小石川後楽園

1-6-6 Koraku, Bunkyō-ku; tel. 03/3811-3015; www.tokyo-park.or.jp/park/format/index030.html; 9am-5pm daily; ¥300; take Chūō, Sōbu, Ōedo, Tōzai, Namboku, Yurakuchō lines to Iidabashi Station, east exit (JR station) and exit C3 (subway)

West of Akihabara on the Chūō line is the station of Iidabashi, the closest stop to one of Tokyo's most beautiful Japanese-style gardens: Koishikawa Kōrakuen. The origin of this Edo-period garden dates back to 1629, when it was four times as large and the property of Yorifusa Tokugawa, head of the influential Mito Tokugawa clan. The original garden was larger than the current incarnation, but its essence remains. Landscapes from Chinese legend and Japan's natural wonders are re-created in miniature throughout the garden, which erupts in colorful plum blossoms in February and irises in June. The changing color of leaves in autumn is also a draw. The grounds are graced by a lotus pond, small waterways, and bridges, including the famous Full-Moon Bridge (Engetsu-kyo).

★ Tokyo National Museum

東京国立博物館

13-9 Ueno-kōen, Taitō-ku; tel. 03/5777-8600; www.tnm.jp; 9:30am-5pm Tues.-Sun. (last entry 30 minutes before closing), closed on Tues. if Mon. is holiday; ¥1,000 adults, ¥500 college students, free for ages 18 and under; take Yamanote line to Ueno Station, Ueno-kōen exit

At the opulent Tokyo National Museum you'll see the most extensive collection of Japanese art on the planet, including Buddhist sculptures, swords, Noh masks, delicate ceramics, colorful kimonos, and sacred scrolls. All told, there are more than 110,000 pieces in the collection, with around 4,000 items on display at any one time.

The backbone of the collection is in the **Honkan** (Japanese Gallery), a 25-room space that hosts rotating exhibitions of Japanese art and antiquities. The five-floor **Toyokan** on the right exhibits art from China, Korea, Southeast Asia, Central Asia, India, and Egypt; the oft-closed **Hyokeikan,** constructed in 1909 to honor the emperor's wedding, is on the left. Behind the Honkan is the **Heiseikan,** which displays artifacts from prehistoric Japan, occasionally hosts special exhibitions of Japanese art, and houses a gift shop and a few eateries. Behind the Hyoeikan is the newest addition to the museum, the **Gallery of Hōryū-ji Treasures.** This spectacular collection shows off objects from a 7th-century temple built in Nara Prefecture. If you're pressed for time, focus on exploring the Honkan and the Gallery of Hōryū-ji Treasures.

Beyond the galleries, a garden and several teahouses can be found behind the Honkan, but these facilities are only open to the public in spring (mid-Mar.-mid-Apr.), when its cherry trees explode with pink petals, and in autumn (late Oct.-early Dec.), when the leaves become a riot of earth tones. Excellent English signage and free audio tours, including the TNM Art Guide mobile phone application (www.tnm.jp/modules/r_free_page/index.php?id=2010), are available for the museum's main collections, but are not always available for special shows.

To prevent the spread of coronavirus, all visitors must book a ticket ahead of their visit. Tickets go on sale for the following week starting every Friday at noon during the week before. See the official website for details.

National Museum of Nature and Science

国立科学博物館

7-20 Ueno-kōen, Taitō-ku; tel. 03/5777-8600; www.kahaku.go.jp; 9am-5pm Tues.-Thurs. and Sun., 9am-8pm Fri.-Sat. (last entry 30 minutes before closing); ¥630 university students and older, free for

Geek Paradise: Akihabara and Otaku Culture

The district of Akihabara is ground zero for all things geek, or otaku, in Japan. But before geekdom invaded these streets, the area was home to a post-World War II black market where tech-savvy university students known as "radio boys" sold transistor radio parts—often pilfered from the occupation forces—to information-starved citizens. Throughout the 1960s, Akihabara expanded its reach beyond the humble radio and became the premier destination for popular new items like televisions, refrigerators, and washing machines. It was in the mid-1980s that Akihabara exploded into full geek mode.

Today, this is the place to find performances by idol groups—pop music groups composed of teenagers who have been picked, preened, and marketed for mass appeal—cafés where patrons are served coffee by cosplay butlers and maids, and high-rise buildings full of shops selling anime, manga, plastic figurines, video games, and more. Here are some of the best places to get a taste of this unique side of Japanese culture.

RADIO CENTER

1-14-2 Sotokanda, Chiyoda-ku; tel. 03/3251-0614; www.radiocenter.jp; 10am-7pm daily; free; take Yamanote, Chūō-Sōbu, Hibiya lines to Akihabara Station, Electric Town exit

For a glimpse of Akihabara of old, head to the run-down two-floor Radio Center under the Sōbu line train tracks. Here you'll find tumbledown shops peddling parts for all manner of electronic devices, from LEDs and semiconductors to speaker systems and walkie-talkies.

@HOME CAFÉ

3F-7F Mitsuwa Bldg., 1-11-4 Sotokanda, Chiyoda-ku; tel. 03/5207-9779; www.cafe-athome.com; 10am-8pm daily; cover charge ¥770 adults, ¥660 university students, ¥550 high school students, ¥440 junior high and elementary school students

@Home Café is the easiest place to wrap your head around the country's maid café phenomenon. Inside, you're welcomed "home" by the bubbly, attentive waitresses, attired in classic French maid outfits, who speak in high tones, kneel when they take your order, and sketch images like hearts and cats with ketchup or chocolate syrup onto the tops of omelets, waffles, and cappuccinos. Be aware that there is nothing risqué about these establishments. Don't touch, photograph, or attempt to ask for the contact details of the maids, no matter how cutesy they may seem.

high school students and younger; take Yamanote line to Ueno Station, Ueno-kōen exit

From dinosaur bones to a large chunk of a meteorite that fell into China in the 16th century, the National Museum of Nature and Science is the best place to get a glimpse of the natural forces underlying the Japanese archipelago. Spread across two buildings, the Japan Gallery and the Global Gallery, this museum has collections on outer space, evolution, Japan's flora and fauna, and the crucially important role that rice has played in the development of Japan.

Multilingual touch screen displays are conveniently available throughout the museum, along with optional English audio tours (¥300). This is a good rainy-day option for those traveling with kids.

Due to the coronavirus, visitors must book a timed-entry ticket online in advance. Tickets go on sale for a given date 30 days in advance and can be bought for groups of up to five. See the official website for details.

Nezu-jinja
根津神社

1-28-9, Nezu, Bunkyō-ku; tel. 03/3822-0753; www.nedujinja.or.jp; 6am-5pm daily; free; take Chiyoda line to Nezu Station, exit 1

With its long tunnel of red torii gates, koi ponds, some 3,000 azaleas that explode with color in spring, beautiful grounds, and an

DON QUIJOTE

4-3-3-Sotokanda, Chiyoda-ku; tel. 0570/024-511; www.donki.com; 24 hours; take Yamanote, Chūō-Sōbu, Hibiya lines to Akihabara Station, Electric Town exit

Akihabara's branch of Don Quijote, a maze-like chain store selling everything under the sun—gadgets, cosmetics, food, household goods, clothing, over-the-counter medicines—at cheap prices, also hosts daily **performances** (go to http://ticket.akb48-group.com/home/top.php for tickets) by idol group AKB48 in an event space on its top floor.

GACHAPON KAIKAN

3-15-5 Sotokanda, Chiyoda-ku; tel. 03/5209-6020; www.akibagacha.com; 11am-7pm daily; take Yamanote, Chūō-Sōbu, Hibiya lines to Akihabara Station, Electric Town exit

For a glimpse into the wondrous world of gachapon, or toys dispensed in capsules from vending machines, head to the Gachapon Kaikan, where avid collectors zealously part ways with ¥100 coins in their quest for figurines and models of everything from animals to mushrooms.

DEAR STAGE

3-10-9 Sotokanda, Chiyoda-ku; tel. 03/5207-9181; https://dearstage.com; 6pm-10pm Mon.-Fri., 5pm-10pm Sat.-Sun. and holidays; take Yamanote, Chūō-Sōbu, Hibiya lines to Akihabara Station, Electric Town exit

To see idols in the making, check out live music venue Dear Stage. Performances take place in the evenings, when there are also two upper-floor bars staffed by bubbly young women in maid outfits (¥500 per hour). Check the website calendar to confirm start times and more.

INFORMATION AND TOURS

For an English map to help you navigate the delightfully baffling labyrinth of Akihabara, head to **Travel Cube Akihabara Tourist Information Center** (1-13 Kanda Sakuma-chō, Chiyoda-ku; tel. 03/6262-9432; www.facebook.com/OficinadeInformacionTuristicadeAkihabara; noon-5pm daily).

ornate main building reminiscent of the famed Tōshō-gū shrine in Nikko outside Tokyo, Nezu-jinja is one of Tokyo's more beautiful shrines. This shrine is also one of the country's oldest; the main structure dates to 1706, having miraculously survived World War II. In fact, it is said to have stood in Sendagi, just north of the shrine's current location, 1,900 years ago, before being relocated to its current spot to celebrate the fifth shogun Tsunayoshi choosing his nephew Ienobu as his successor.

The shrine can get crowded during spring, but the best thing about Nezu-jinja is its relative lack of popularity, compared to big-name religious sites in the city like Meiji Jingū and Sensō-ji. For these reasons, it's worth going just a bit out of the way to see it, especially if you won't be venturing outside Tokyo.

ASAKUSA AND RYOGOKU

浅草, 両国

Asakusa first emerged as a neighborhood during the early part of the Edo period. The area's location northeast of the shogun's castle was believed to place it in an unlucky direction, according to principles of Chinese geomancy. Thus, Shogun Tokugawa Ieyasu called for the construction of the great temple of **Sensō-ji** in 1590 to keep evil spirits at bay.

Asakusa and Ryogoku

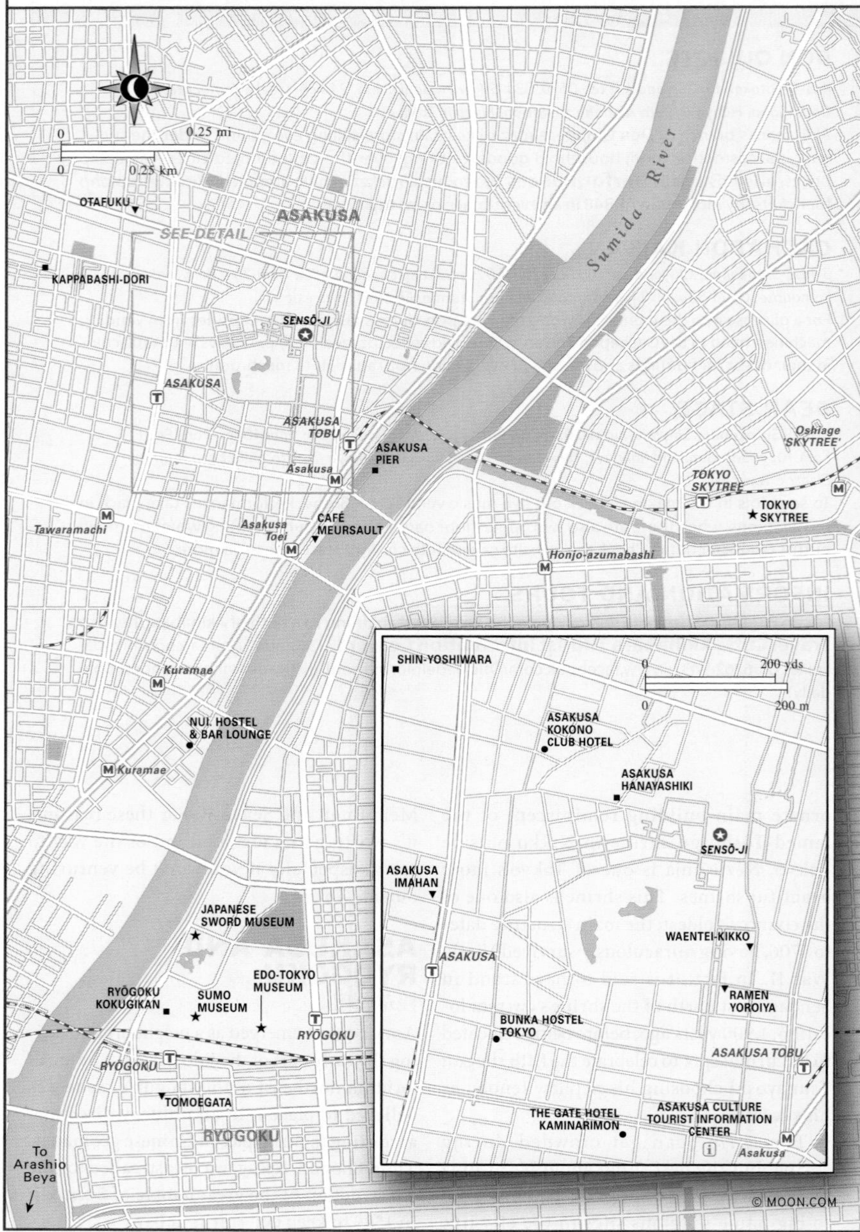

Southeast across the **Sumida River,** the neighborhood of Ryogoku centers around **sumo.**

★ Sensō-ji

浅草寺

2-3-1 Asakusa, Taitō-ku; tel. 03/3842-0181; www.senso-ji.jp; temple grounds always open, main hall 6am-5pm daily Apr.-Sept., 6:30am-5pm Oct.-Mar.; free; take Ginza, Asakusa lines to Asakusa Station, exit 1

Tokyo's oldest temple, Sensō-ji, or Asakusa Kannon, is a testament to the capital's turbulent past. Originally completed in AD 645, the temple is said to have been inspired by two fishermen brothers who miraculously found a golden statue of Kannon, the Buddhist goddess of compassion, wrapped in nets they had cast into the nearby Sumida River. It is said that the golden object still resides in the temple, but it remains hidden from sight.

The temple was mostly razed during World War II, but it has been fully reconstructed. Its current iteration is made of concrete rather than wood, but the atmosphere remains intact. Enter the grounds via the imposing **Kaminari-mon** (Thunder Gate), recognizable by its giant red lantern and flanked by statues of Fujin and Raijin, the rather wrathful-looking deities of wind and thunder. Crossing the threshold, amble along **Nakamise-dōri,** a row of shops and food stalls hawking charms, traditional crafts, and rice crackers and red bean cakes.

At the far end of Nakamise-dōri, where the shops end, stands a second large gate called **Hozo-mon,** and just beyond it is the temple's main hall, **Kannon Hall.** Worshippers gather around a large cauldron to bathe in the smoke, believed to impart good health. If you're inclined, buy a bundle of incense sticks to light and place in the cauldron yourself. Looming to the left of Kannon Hall is a five-story pagoda. And to the east of Kannon Hall is **Asakusa-jinja,** a shrine built in 1649 to commemorate the two fishermen who snagged the golden statue of Kannon almost 1,400 years ago.

With more than 30 million annual visitors, the temple is jam-packed any day of the week. Avoid visiting on weekends, and instead try to go in the late afternoon or after dusk when crowds are thinner.

Tokyo Skytree

東京スカイツリー

1-1-2 Oshiage, Sumida-ku; tel. 03/5302-3470; www.tokyo-skytree.jp; 10am-8pm daily (last entry 7pm); Tembo Deck ¥2,100 Mon.-Fri., ¥2,300 Sat.-Sun. and holidays, Tembo Galleria ¥1,000 Mon.-Fri., ¥1,100 Sat.-Sun. and holidays, combination tickets ¥3,100 Mon.-Fri., ¥3,400 Sat.-Sun.; take Hanzōmon line to Oshiage Station, Tokyo Skytree exit

The world's tallest freestanding tower, Tokyo Skytree rises 634 meters (2,080 ft) above the east bank of the Sumida River. The only human-made structure taller is the 830-meter (2,723-ft) Burj Khalifa in Dubai (which is considered a skyscraper rather than tower). It opened in 2012 to serve as the capital's new and improved television broadcasting tower. The structure itself, a central pillar enmeshed in a giant steel frame, incorporates principles of traditional Japanese and temple architecture in its delicate balance of both convex and concave curves.

But the tower's real draw are the 310 restaurants and shops situated around its base in a complex called **Tokyo Skytree Town,** and the two dizzyingly high observation decks. Reaching these fantastically high perches isn't cheap. A ticket to the **Tembō Deck**—standing 350 meters (1,148 ft) with 360-degree views, a glass-floor paneled section, and a snack bar—sets an adult back ¥2,100 on weekdays (¥2,300 on weekends). Another ¥1,000 on weekdays (¥1,100 on weekends) gives you a combination ticket that sends you via high-speed elevator to the **Tembō Galleria,** which is 100 meters (328 ft) higher and includes a 110-meter-long (360-ft-long) glass floor. Daytime views from either platform are stunning and reach all the way to Mount Fuji when the sky is clear. Arriving just before dusk ensures an awesome view, as the vast blanket of Tokyo's twinkling lights is seemingly endless.

Purchase tickets on the fourth floor, where current wait times are indicated in English. Try showing up in the morning or at night on weekdays to avoid the crowds.

If you're approaching from Asakusa Station and Sensō-ji, Skytree is located about 20 minutes on foot to the east, on the opposite (east) side of the Sumida River.

Japanese Sword Museum
刀剣博物館

1-12-9, Yokoami, Sumida-ku; tel. 03/6284-1000; www.touken.or.jp; 9:30am-5pm Tues.-Sun., closed Tues. if Mon. falls on holiday; ¥1,000 adults, ¥500 students, free for ages 15 and under; take Sōbu, Ōedo lines to Ryogoku Station, west exit (JR station) or exit A1 (subway station)

If you enjoy geeking out on history or samurai cinema, the Japanese Sword Museum is well worth visiting. Its collection of blades came into being thanks to the Ministry of Education's creation of a society and museum dedicated to keeping Japan's rich tradition of sword-making alive after katana seized by U.S. occupation forces were returned to Japan in 1948. Dozens of steel specimens, displaying exceptionally high levels of craftsmanship and decorative flourishes, as well as a large collection of handles and sheaths, are on display with clear English signage. Armor and other artifacts from the Heian and Edo periods are also on show.

From the third floor, step out on the landing to look over the neighboring **Former Yasuda Garden,** which dates to the late 17th century and is free to enter.

If you're approaching on foot from Asakusa's more popular sights, it's about a 20-minute walk south of Sensōji and 30-minute walk south of Tokyo Skytree.

Edo-Tokyo Museum
江戸東京博物館

1-4-1 Yokoami, Sumida-ku; tel. 03/3626-9974; www.edo-tokyo-museum.or.jp; 9:30am-5:30pm Tues.-Sun., closed Tues. if Mon. is a holiday; ¥600 adults, ¥480 college students, ¥300 high school and junior high school students, free for elementary school students and younger; take Ōedo line to Ryogoku Station, exits A3, A4, or Sōbu line, west exit

Visit this museum for an engaging overview of Tokyo's history from feudal days to modern metropolis. Behind an exterior resembling a massive spaceship, the museum illustrates the dramatic ups and downs of the city's past, from the 1923 Great Kanto Earthquake to incineration by American B-29 bombers during World War II. All of this, followed by the dramatic transformation that swept the city during post-World War II "economic miracle," and the subsequent popping of the bubble economy, have molded the city into what it is today. These traumas and transformations are powerfully illustrated through a wide range of displays, including miniature models of entire city districts, a reconstruction of a typical post-World War II apartment, and a hodgepodge of items from daily life, such as vehicles and household objects.

English signs are ubiquitous, and English-speaking volunteer guides are available 10am-3pm daily, reservable on the spot at the sixth-floor Permanent Exhibition Volunteer Guide Reception Center or by phone two weeks in advance. It's also possible to take a self-guided tour with an English-language audio guide, available for a ¥1,000 deposit. Choose your course and leave the museum with a deeper appreciation for the historical journey of the multilayered city around you.

Like the Japanese Sword Museum, it's located a bit of a hike south of Asakusa (25-30 minutes, depending on where you're starting from). Unfortunately, the museum is scheduled to be closed for renovations from 2022 until 2025 or 2026.

WESTERN TOKYO

★ Ghibli Museum
三鷹のジブリ美術館

1-1-83 Shimorenjaku, Mitaka-shi; tel. 0570/05-5777; www.ghibli-museum.jp; 10am-5:30pm Wed.-Mon.;

1: Tokyo National Museum 2: Nezu-jinja 3: Sensō-ji 4: Ghibli Museum

1
2
3
4

Kichijōji

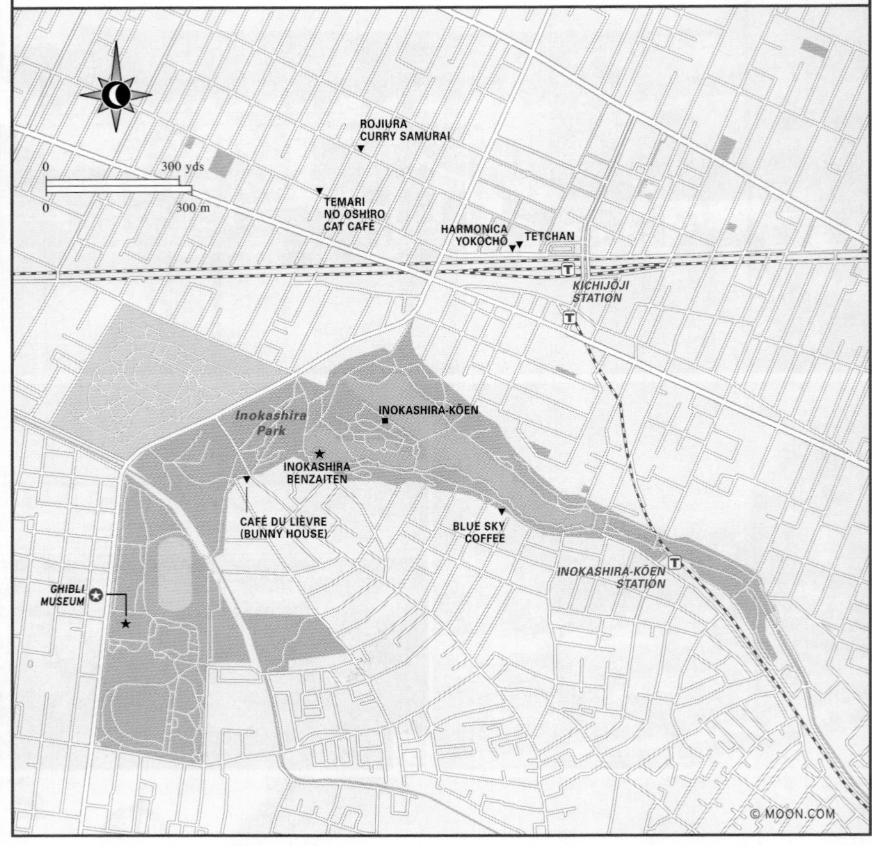

¥1,000 adults, ¥100-700 children; take Chūō line running west from Shinjuku's JR Station to reach both Mitaka Station and Kichijōji Station, which sit beside each other, Chūō, Sōbu lines to Mitaka, south exit, or Kichijōji, park exit

If you're only going to visit one sight outside downtown, make it the Ghibli Museum. Arriving at the whimsical facade of the complex on the edge of the heavily wooded Inokashira-kōen, you'll fittingly feel as if you've just wandered into the imagination of legendary anime director Hayao Miyazaki. It's a must-see for fans of Studio Ghibli and doesn't disappoint even those with only a passing interest. The museum, located west of downtown, is a seamless ode to Miyazaki's vision, which has produced classic films such as *Spirited Away* and *Princess Mononoke*.

The first floor showcases animation techniques, original Ghibli drawings, and a richly illustrated history of the art form; there's also a theater playing short Ghibli flicks that are only viewable at the museum. Special thematic exhibitions, such as the placement of food in Ghibli films, are featured on a rotating basis on the second floor. The rooftop boasts a garden inhabited by Ghibli characters,

Nakano Broadway: An Akihabara Alternative

If you're seeking a less touristy slice of otaku than Akihabara (page 80), consider heading to Nakano Broadway (5-52-15 Nakano, Nakano-ku; https://nakano-broadway.com; store hours vary, roughly noon-8pm), a huge collection of shops hawking otaku goods just north of Nakano Station on the Chūō line, less than 10 minutes from Shinjuku Station. The area has become more popular in recent years, but hasn't yet succumbed to the deluge of duty-free shops catering to the tourists now flooding Akihabara. And at Nakano Broadway, all the shops you would want to see are located under one sprawling roof, rather than scattered around a hectic neighborhood.

- Make a beeline for the flagship **Mandarake** store (page 106), spread across several floors; Mandarake Henya (4F) specializes in vintage collectibles.
- You'll also find four establishments owned by artist **Takashi Murakami,** famous for his collaborations with Louis Vuitton, among other things: pastry shop **Tonari no Kaidako** (2F; https://zingarokk.com/tonarinokaikado/); manga and anime-focused gallery **Animanga Zingaro** (2F; https://zingarokk.com/gallery/animangazingaro/); contemporary art gallery **Hidari Zingaro** (3F; https://zingarokk.com/gallery/hidarizingaro/); and goods shop **Tonari no Zingaro** (4F; https://zingarokk.com/tonarinozingaro/).
- Sing karaoke with maids at **Anison Karaoke Bar Z** (301 No. 2 Sankyō Bldg., 5-57-9 Nakano, Nakano-ku; tel. 03/6454-0790; www.anisonkaraokebar-z.com; 6pm-11:30pm daily), or visit the **Daikaiju Salon** (1F Lions Mansion Nakano, 1-14-16 Arai, Nakano-ku; tel. 03/5942-7382; http://daikaijyu-salon.com; 3pm-11pm Mon.-Fri., 1pm-11pm Sun.), a bar/café revolving around Japan's pantheon of monsters, located about 5 minutes' walk north of Nakano Broadway. Patrons must order at least one food or drink item per hour.

including a towering robot soldier from *Castle in the Sky*, and there's even a giant cat bus brought to life from Miyazaki's hallmark *My Neighbor Totoro,* and both adults and kids can hop aboard.

The museum is extremely popular and limits the number of its daily visitors. Tickets are only valid for the date and time you book and can be purchased up to three months in advance—for example, tickets for October would be sold from July 1. Reserve as early as you can within that timeframe.

Ghibli Museum can be reached either via bus from Mitaka Station (¥320 round-trip, ¥210 one-way; 10 minutes one-way), or a 20-minute walk from Kichijōji Station through leafy **Inokashira Park,** which greatly enhances the experience.

Entertainment and Events

From kabuki and elegant, traditional Noh theater to edgy forms of dance and theater such as butō, Tokyo has a flourishing performance arts scene.

For more information on other Japanese performing arts, go to the **Performing Arts Network Japan** website (www.performingarts.jp/index.html). Another useful resource is the official site of the **Japan Arts Council** (www.ntj.jac.go.jp), where it's also possible to get tickets for performances at Japan's national theaters.

THEATER

Ginza and Marunouchi

KABUKI-ZA

4-12-15 Ginza, Chūō-ku; tel. 03/3545-6800; www.kabukiweb.net; full performance ¥3,000-20,000, one act ¥800-2,000; take Hibiya, Asakusa lines to Higashi-Ginza Station, exit 3

Kabuki-za is the place to see kabuki in Tokyo. The building itself evokes a drama that is decidedly Japanese: the sweeping curves of its roof, pillars dotting its exterior walls, and an arched entryway reminiscent of a shrine over which paper lanterns hang. Even if you don't have time to watch a kabuki performance, pay a visit to this marvelous Ginza landmark.

It's good to be aware that kabuki moves at a slow pace. Showtimes tend to run either from 11am to around 3:30pm or 4:30pm to 9pm. If sitting through a full performance sounds daunting, it's also possible to watch just one act; 90 seats and 60 standing positions at the back of the theater are reserved on the day of each performance for this purpose.

Booking **tickets** is simple thanks to the official English-language website, which offers a clear breakdown of the various plays and showtimes. If you prefer to reserve tickets over the phone, just dial 03/6745-0888. There is usually an English-speaking member of staff available 10am-5pm daily. At the time of writing, tickets could only be booked by phone. Check the theater's official website for any potential updates. For a full performance, it's best to book a few months in advance to snag a good seat. When you reserve your place, be sure to rent a headset if you'd like a running interpretation of the performance in English (¥500 with ¥1,000 refundable deposit for one act, ¥1,000 and personal ID for full performance). And if you plan to see a full performance and think you'll get hungry, bring something to snack on, or perhaps even a bento box meal. On the fifth floor of the complex behind the theater, you'll find a gallery showcasing kabuki-related memorabilia and outfits, and an excellent **café.**

NATIONAL THEATRE

4-1 Hayabusa-chō, Chiyoda-ku; tel. 03/3265-7411; www.ntj.jac.go.jp; ¥3,500-12,800, headsets with English-language interpretation ¥700 with refundable ¥1,000 deposit; take Hanzōmon line to Hanzōmon Station, exit 1

Tokyo's top traditional performance space stages not only kabuki, but also bunraku, a form of theater using oversized puppets that originated in Osaka, as well as gagaku (imperial court music) concerts. Check the website for performance schedules and to reserve tickets in advance.

KANZE NŌGAKUDŌ

Ginza Six B3F, 6-10-1 Ginza, Chūō-ku; tel. 03/6274-6579; www.kanze.net; take Ginza, Hibiya, Marunouchi lines to Ginza Station, exit A3

Found in the third-level basement floor of Ginza Six, this is the new incarnation of the Kanze association, which performed at a renowned theater in Shibuya from 1901 until 2017, when they relocated. In its current home, you can catch performances featuring just the final acts of three Noh plays. This is a good way to receive an enjoyable, not overwhelming introduction to this highbrow form of dance theater, but unfortunately performances at Kanze Nōgakudō are often sold out months in advance, and there is no English-language website for booking tickets.

To see a show, call at least two months in advance to talk with an English speaker; there are a few on staff. Tickets usually start from around ¥4,000, and performances, which last two to three hours, tend to be held on weekend afternoons from 1pm. It's also possible to catch the last act of a play from the unreserved seating section by purchasing a special ticket on the day of a performance (¥3,000).

TOKYO TAKARAZUKA THEATER

1-1-3 Yurakuchō, Chiyoda-ku; tel. 0570/00-5100; https://kageki.hankyu.co.jp; ¥2,500-12,500; take Yamanote line to Yurakuchō Station, or take Chiyoda, Hibiya, Mita lines to Hibiya Station

The Tokyo outpost of the Takarazuka Revue, based in the town of its namesake near Kobe, features all female performers. The performers fit into one of five troupes of around 80 members each—hana (flower), tsuki (moon), yuki (snow), hoshi (star), sora (cosmos)—and

"The Floating World" and Japanese Theater

The performing arts have a rich history in Tokyo, stretching back to the hedonistic ukiyo (floating world) that took shape during the Edo period, in which samurai and sumo wrestlers gathered with geishas in teahouses. This cultural movement, loaded with extravagance, transgression, and ennui, also produced a great deal of art, from poetry and music to painting and woodblock prints known as ukiyo-e.

This was the heyday of kabuki, a traditional form of theater with flamboyant costumes, riveting music, and extravagant stage sets. Today, the art form continues to thrive in the capital, the best place in the country to see it, as well as traditional arts like the more rarefied Noh dance theater, known for its music and poetry.

KABUKI

A kabuki play is visual spectacle above all else: elaborate, billowing costumes of varying hues; dramatic mask-like makeup; a troupe of traditional musicians who provide an evocative soundtrack; elaborate set design including revolving stages and trap doors through which actors appear and disappear; and of course, the fine-tuned gestures, poses, facial expressions, and vocalizations of the highly trained, male-only actors, who command serious presence and occasionally even zip through the air on wires.

When watching kabuki, the audience is often well-heeled and vocal, shouting out in support of their favorite actors at key moments—a practice that had been curtailed at the time of writing due to coronavirus. If you can, try to get a spot near the hanamichi ("flower path"), along which actors make their dramatic entrances and exits and act out key scenes. The stories depicted often involve star-crossed lovers or samurai of yore. **Kabuki-za** is the best place to see kabuki in Tokyo.

NOH

A Noh play is even slower-paced than a kabuki performance. Originating in the 14th century, this stark form of dance theater is a highly standardized art form, largely due to the fact that it was deemed the shogunate's ceremonial art of choice during the Tokugawa Period (1603-1868). This background explains why the origins of Noh are commonly viewed as "higher" than kabuki's "low culture" pedigree.

Today, five troupes continue to perform the austere form of theater, portrayed through slow movements, poetic archaic language, flamboyant costumes, and famously minimal masks. Story lines usually involve incidents from history, literature, legend, and even recent events, and sometimes have a supernatural thread. The shite (main character) wears an array of masks made from Japanese cypress, artfully carved to portray anything from old women to demons and ghosts. These masks evoke a range of emotions and facial expressions. Complementing the actors is a chorus that gives vocal assistance to the lead actor as the story unfolds, as well as a four-piece ensemble that provides a soundtrack of drums and flute. See a Noh performance at the **National Noh Theatre.**

a sixth group of superstars known as senka who rotate in and out of the other five troupes. Think: grand, flamboyant, musical, dance, extravaganza. Check the website for the performance schedule. Arrive at the theater early to get in line, as tickets go fast. Worst case, there are nosebleed seats with slightly obstructed views that tend to be easier to snag.

Harajuku and Aoyama

NATIONAL NOH THEATRE

4-18-1 Sendagaya, Shibuya-ku; tel. 03/3423-1331; www.ntj.jac.go.jp; ¥3,000-5,000; take Sōbu line to Sendagaya Station or Ōedo line to Kokuritsu-kyogijō Station

At the National Noh Theatre, Noh performances are acted out on a beautiful stage crafted from cypress wood. All action takes place on the square wooden stage supported at its four corners by pillars, entered by actors along a bridge that leads into the stage. Noh has a mysterious air that may not be everyone's cup of tea, but it's a singular art form that will prove fascinating for those who like to explore rarefied forms of traditional culture. Shows are sporadic, but when they take place, this is a great venue, as it offers English-language translation on a screen provided at each seat. Check the English-language website for details on show times and prices, which vary by performance, and to book tickets in advance.

ART GALLERIES

Tokyo provides ample choices for gallery-hopping for art lovers. The following galleries stand out for their cutting-edge work by artists both Japanese and international. For extensive gallery listings, exhibition information, and more, **Tokyo Art Beat** (www.tokyoartbeat.com) is an excellent resource. And if you're really keen to dive deep into Tokyo's art world, it's worth looking at the **Grutt Pass** (www.rekibun.or.jp/grutto/english.html), a coupon booklet for more than 70 museums around the city.

Ginza and Marunouchi

GINZA GRAPHIC GALLERY

1F DNP Ginza Bldg., 7-7-2 Ginza, Chūō-ku; tel. 03/3571-5206; www.dnpfcp.jp/gallery/ggg/; 11am-7pm Mon.-Sat.; free; take Ginza, Hibiya, Marunouchi lines to Ginza Station, exit A2

Run by a Japanese printing giant, the Ginza Graphic Gallery focuses on the best in design and graphic arts.

Roppongi and Around

TAKA ISHII GALLERY TOKYO

3F Complex 665, 6-5-24 Roppongi, Minato-ku; tel. 03/6434-7010; www.takaishiigallery.com; noon-6pm Tues.-Sat.; fee varies by exhibition; take Hibiya line to Roppongi Station, exit 3

Taka Ishii Gallery showcases work by big-name Japanese and international photographers. Past exhibits have included Nobuyoshi Araki, Daido Moriyama, and Thomas Demand.

TAKE NINAGAWA

2-12-4 Higashi-Azabu, Minato-ku; tel. 03/5571-5844; www.takeninagawa.com; 11am-7pm Tues.-Sat.; fee varies by exhibition; take Namboku, Ōedo lines to Azabun-Jūban Station, exit 6

This gallery often features pioneering young Japanese artists. The work on display runs the gamut, from drawings and mixed-media paintings to collages, sculptures, and experimental films. Works tend to be built on foundations laid by earlier, post-war experimental Japanese artists and seek to address contemporary issues.

Harajuku and Aoyama

DESIGN FESTA GALLERY

East Bldg.: 3-20-2, West Bldg.: 3-20-18, Jingū-mae, Shibuya-ku; tel. 03/3479-1442; www.designfestagallery.com; 11am-8pm daily; free; take Yamanote line to Harajuku Station, Omotesandō exit, or take Chiyoda, Fukutoshin lines to Meiji-Jingūmae Station, exit 5

Design Festa Gallery is the brainchild of three local artists who had a vision for a dilapidated apartment block in Harajuku's backstreets. Spread across three floors, some of the rooms are overseen by the creators themselves, who rent space from the gallery. The gallery space offers a glimpse into Tokyo's art scene at the young, grass-roots level, and is connected to **Design Festa,** the country's largest art and design fair held twice a year. If you're thirsty or hungry after perusing the eclectic offerings, there's also a funky café and an okonomiyaki (savory pancake) restaurant on-site.

ESPACE LOUIS VUITTON TOKYO

7F Louis Vuitton Omotesandō, 5-7-5 Jingū-mae, Shibuya-ku; tel. 03/5766-1094; www.espacelouisvuittontokyo.com; noon-8pm during exhibitions; free; take Ginza, Hanzomon, Chiyoda lines to Omotesandō Station, A1, or Chiyoda, Fukutoshin lines to Meiji-Jingūmae Station, exit 4

On the seventh floor of the Omotesandō Louis Vuitton store is an airy, well-lit space that has hosted shows by artists from Japan, as well as from Finland, India, the United States, and Brazil.

Akihabara and Ueno

3331 ARTS CHIYODA

6-11-14 Sotokanda, Chiyoda-ku; tel. 03/6803-2441; www.3331.jp; 10am-9pm daily (last entry 8:30pm); fee varies by exhibition; take Ginza line to Suehirocho Station, exit 4, or take Yamanote, Sōbu lines to Akihabara Station, Electric City exit

This experimental art space is housed in a former junior high school. The facility includes private galleries, a large exhibition space, and recording studios, and the schoolyard is now a public park. As with many of Tokyo's galleries, it also has an attractive café and a gift shop stocked with locally created pieces. If you want to feel the pulse of Tokyo's creative world, be sure to pay a visit to this inspired hub.

ART SANCTUARY ALLAN WEST

1-6-17 Yanaka, Taitō-ku; tel. 03/3827-1907; www.allanwest.jp; 1:30pm-4:30pm Mon.-Wed. and Fri.-Sat., 3pm-4:30pm Sun.; take Chiyoda subway line to Nezu Station, then walk 10 minutes northeast

Set in the heart of the charming Yanaka neighborhood, in a beautifully renovated wooden building with handsome sliding doors, exposed beams, and tatami mats throughout, this is the gallery and studio of artist Allan West. Originally hailing from Washington DC, West moved to Tokyo in 1982 to study under master painter Kayama Matazo at Tokyo University of the Arts. Today, he paints brilliantly in the traditional Nihonga style, from prints and scrolls to screens. He is a strict traditionalist, even making his own paint. You can just look or even buy his work. Prices start from as little as ¥5,000 but shoot to upward of ¥5 million from there. It's a great reason to meander into this charming local side of town.

FESTIVALS AND EVENTS

This list of Tokyo events, from celebrations of contemporary art to centuries-old rites, is by no means comprehensive, but covers some of the city's biggest and best. Though all major events and festivals were canceled in 2020 and many were also called off in 2021 due to the coronavirus, hopes are high that they will be reinstated in 2022. Check websites and local restrictions for confirmation.

Spring

ART FAIR TOKYO

Citywide; https://artfairtokyo.com; early Mar.; 1-day pass ¥4,000 for one, ¥6,000 for two

Art Fair Tokyo provides a great chance to dive into Tokyo's art scene, with some 150 galleries participating every March, normally for about a week during the first half of the month. It is a four-day event that requires purchasing a ticket to attend. Participating galleries and museums offer discounted admission for those holding an Art Fair pass.

TOKYO RAINBOW PRIDE

Yoyogi-kōen and around; http://tokyorainbowpride.com; first week of May; free

Thousands suit up in fancy attire for a parade with floats to celebrate LGBTQ pride at Tokyo Rainbow Pride. The parade goes from Yoyogi-kōen toward Shibuya Station. A festival is also held in Yoyogi-kōen.

DESIGN FESTA

Tokyo Big Sight; http://designfesta.com; May, Aug., and Nov.; ¥800 one-day tickets bought in advance, ¥1,000 one-day tickets bought day of entry, ¥1,500 two-day tickets bought in advance, ¥1,800 two-day tickets bought day of entry; take Rinkai line to Kokusai-Tenjijo Station or Yurikamome line to Kokusai-Tenjijo-Seimon Station

Taking place three times a year in May, August, and November, Design Festa is a massive event showcasing the work of the city's newest crop of artists and designers. As the name indicates, it's linked to the Design Festa Gallery in Harajuku. It takes place over a weekend at **Tokyo Big Sight** (3-11-1 Ariake, Kōtō-ku; tel. 03/5530-1111; www.bigsight.jp), a massive exhibition space in Odaiba made of four upside-down pyramids on massive pillars resembling something out of *Star Wars*. There's plenty of food and amenities, but the point is the performances, workshops, and artwork on display.

KANDA MATSURI

Kanda Myōjin and around; closest weekend to May 15 in odd-numbered years; free

Kanda Matsuri is one of Tokyo's three biggest festivals. Thousands flood the streets all the way from Kanda to Nihonbashi and Marunouchi, with hundreds of floats and omikoshi (portable shrines) carried by sweaty participants to the great shrine of **Kanda Myōjin.** It's a spectacle to behold. Held in odd-numbered years, the festival begins Friday afternoon before the weekend closest to May 15 and goes until around early evening. Saturday's festivities begin from around noon and last till late afternoon. Sunday starts around 6am and goes all the way through evening.

SANJA MATSURI

Asakusa-jinja and around; www.asakusajinja.jp/en/sanjamatsuri; third weekend of May; free

The largest festival in Tokyo, drawing a crowd of almost two million, this three-day bash takes place the third weekend of May each year, beginning from Friday afternoon. It celebrates the three founders of Tokyo's most famous Buddhist temple, **Sensō-ji** in Asakusa, which sits next to the Shinto shrine of **Asakusa-jinja,** where the three founders are enshrined. The most visually stunning aspect is about 100 elaborate mikoshi (portable shrines), which symbolically house deities, being paraded through the nearby streets by men and women decked out in Edo-period attire in the hopes of bringing prosperity to the area. The neighborhood around Sensō-ji is overflowing with yatai (food stalls), games, and plenty of locals beating drums, playing bamboo flutes, and milling around in yukata (lightweight kimono). The festivities culminate on Sunday, when three massive mikoshi owned by Asakusa-jinja make their rounds.

ROPPONGI ART NIGHT

Roppongi; www.roppongiartnight.com; last weekend of May; free

During the last weekend of May each year, Roppongi, where three major contemporary art museums are clustered, hosts a two-day overnight event showcasing art, design, film, music, and live performances. Walk through the district, from Roppongi Hills to Tokyo Midtown to The National Art Center, and explore. Stalls selling food and drinks dot the area, too, giving it a lively, even rowdy atmosphere as the night wears on.

Summer

SUMIDAGAWA FIREWORKS

Asakusa; www.sumidagawa-hanabi.com; 7pm last Sat. of July; free

The Sumidagawa Fireworks is Tokyo's largest fireworks show, on the banks of the Sumida River. Crowds of up to one million around Asakusa, the center of the action, are intense, and the displays awesome. To get a good spot, plan on arriving several hours before of the show. Even then, be prepared to jostle for a decent position.

ASAKUSA SAMBA CARNIVAL

Asakusa; www.asakusa-samba.org; last Sat. of Aug. or late Sept.; free

You'd think you were in Brazil at the Asakusa Samba Carnival, a huge celebration with music, floats, and flamboyantly costumed dancers with the requisite tail feathers. The event serves as a reminder of the deep historic ties between Brazil and Japan: Brazil is home to the biggest Japanese diaspora of any country in the world. In celebration, around 20 teams parade down Asakusa's major thoroughfare of Umamichi-dōri, moving past the Kaminarimon gate of Sensō-ji temple in the direction of Tawaramachi. The lively festival draws some 500,000 spectators.

1: Kabuki-za **2:** festival participants carrying an omikoshi (portable shrine) **3:** festival crowd **4:** dancers in Kōenji Awa Odori

1
祥南會
2
3
4

KŌENJI AWA ODORI

Kōenji; www.koenji-awaodori.com; last weekend of Aug.; free

Kōenji Awa Odori is a pulsating, fun, and rowdy festival, by far Tokyo's best awa-odori dance festival. These take place in August during O-bon season, when Buddhist tradition holds that the ancestors return to the world of the living. The festival's roots are actually in Tokushima, Shikoku, where the festival has been going strong for more than 400 years. Each year, more than one million people flock to the suburb of Kōenji to watch troupes of musicians and dancers weave through the neighborhood's streets. This is one of my personal favorites. The street parade begins around 5pm and ends around 8pm or 9pm, although people stick around to eat and drink into the night. All you have to do is ride the Chūō line west of Shinjuku to Kōenji (about 7 minutes); you will be immediately propelled into the action as you exit the station.

Twice-Yearly

TOKYO JAZZ FESTIVAL

Multiple venues; www.tokyo-jazz.com; May or Aug./Sept.; from ¥3,800 depending on seat class and event, free performances also held

Tokyo Jazz Festival brings together a world-class lineup of jazz stars from Japan and abroad for Japan's biggest jazz event. It's definitely recommended for serious devotees of the art. It takes place over a weekend, usually around May or the end of August or early September, mostly in Shibuya and Harajuku, with some outdoor performances in **Yoyogi-kōen** and some indoor performances at **NHK Hall** (2-2-1 Jinnan, Shibuya-ku), among other venues in Shibuya and around (see website). Tickets go on sale starting around late June and sell out relatively fast, so keep an eye on the website if you're keen to attend. Note that there are some free performances in Yoyogi-kōen.

COMIKET

Tokyo Big Sight; www.comiket.co.jp; early Aug., late Dec.; free

This one's for the otaku out there. Comic Market, or Comiket, is Tokyo's largest manga sale, held twice a year, in August and December. Each edition takes place over the course of four days at **Tokyo Big Sight** (3-11-1 Ariake, Kōtō-ku; tel. 03/5530-1111; www.bigsight.jp), which also hosts Design Festa. Hordes of cosplayers and manga fans, with numbers reaching around 200,000, gather for the event, so be prepared for serious crowds.

Sports and Recreation

Tokyo's sights, food, nightlife, and shopping will probably be more than enough to keep you busy during your time in the city, but if you feel the need for some recreation, a number of great parks can be found throughout the city. There's also a classic amusement park, **Asakusa Hanayashiki,** in the heart of the old part of town.

PARKS

Ginza and Marunouchi

CHIDORIGAFUCHI
千鳥ヶ淵

From 2-chōme Kudanminami to 2-chōme Sanbanchō; tel. 03/5211-4243; www.city.chiyoda.lg.jp/shisetsu/koen/chidorigafuchi-ko.html; 24 hours daily; free; take Hanzōmon, Shinjuku, Tōzai lines to Kudanshita Station, exit 2

Just beyond the Imperial Palace, Chidorigafuchi runs along the western side of Hanzo Moat. The park is divided into three sections. The **Chidorigafuchi Greenway,** lined by cherry trees, is one of Tokyo's quintessential hanami (cherry-blossom viewing) spots. It runs south to the **Chidorigafuchi National Cemetery,** burial site of 352,297 unidentified casualties of World War II, including civilians who died from air raids and the atomic bombs dropped on Hiroshima and Nagasaki. South of the cemetery is the park area, **Chidorigafuchi-kōen,** complete with a boathouse where you can rent paddleboats between April and November and ply the palace moat (30 minutes; ¥500, ¥800 during hanami season in spring). During hanami season, when the trees lining the moat explode into a riot of pink, expect considerable wait times for boat rentals and limited space to snap pictures amid the legion of photographers.

Tokyo Bay Area

ODAIBA KAIHIN-KŌEN

お台場海浜公園

1 Daiba, Minato-ku; tel. 03/5500-2455; www.tptc.co.jp/en/c_park/01_02; 24 hours daily; free; take Yurikamome line to Odaiba Kaihin-kōen Station

Across the Rainbow Bridge from the rest of the city, you'll find Odaiba Kaihin-kōen. This seaside park reminds you that Tokyo is in fact a maritime city—something that's easy to forget. Take in some of the best views of Tokyo from across the bay from this 800-meter-long (2,624-ft-long) human-made beach, complete with walking paths, a promenade, and even a Statue of Liberty knockoff. This popular date spot is especially romantic at dusk, as the Rainbow Bridge and city light up and petite cruise boats fill the bay. Windsurfing and kayaking are permitted, and the necessary equipment can be rented at the boathouse next to the beach, but swimming is forbidden.

Shibuya and Around

YOYOGI-KŌEN

代々木公園

2-1 Yoyogi Kamizonocho, Shibuya-ku; www.yoyogipark.info; 24 hours daily; free; take Yamanote line to Harajuku Station, Omotesandō exit; Chiyoda line to Yoyogi-kōen Station, exit 3

Perhaps Tokyo's most popular public park, there are often large weekend festivals held here during spring and summer, and the place is absolutely jam-packed during hanami (cherry-blossom viewing), when the sprawling green space erupts in color as the park's myriad cherry trees blossom. The park is also known as a place for street performers of all kinds, including the famed rockabilly dancers who congregate every Sunday to bust a move to 1950s rock tunes at the park's main entrance near Harajuku Station.

Akihabara and Ueno

UENO-KŌEN

上野公園

5-20 Ueno-kōen, Taitō-ku; tel. 03/3828-5644; www.kensetsu.metro.tokyo.lg.jp/jimusho/toubuk/ueno/index_top.html; 5am-11pm daily; free; take Yamanote line to Ueno Station, Ueno-kōen, Shinobazu exits

This sizable public park is dotted with shrines and temples. It contains Shinobazu Pond, stocked with abundant lotus flowers and waterfowl, and Japan's oldest zoo. Ueno-kōen is also blessed with a large proliferation of cherry trees that burst colorfully to life each spring to make the park one of the city's most popular spots for hanami. The park's real draw is its abundance of museums, with **Tokyo National Museum** (page 79) at the head of the pack.

Western Tokyo

INOKASHIRA-KŌEN

井の頭恩賜公園

1-18-31 Gotenyama, Musashino-shi; www.kensetsu.metro.tokyo.lg.jp/jimusho/seibuk/inokashira/index.html; 24 hours daily; free; take Sōbu, Chūō, Keio-Inokashira lines to Kichijōji Station, Kōen exit

If you want to get outside a bit downtown, Inokashira-kōen is highly recommended. This lovely park is located in the bustling suburb of Kichijōji, which always hovers near the top of any list of Tokyo's most desirable places to call home. The park has a central walking loop that circles a large pond, where you can rent paddle boats shaped like large swans (30 minutes; ¥700 for swan-shaped boats, ¥600 for regular paddle boats and rowboats). On weekends, performers attract crowds and locals sell their wares, from jewelry to photographs

The Lowdown on Sumo

There aren't too many sports more deeply associated with Japan in the popular imagination than sumo. The sport is deeply rooted in ancient Shinto rites meant to entertain the gods in hopes of a good harvest. And in many ways, it remains more ritual than action even today. **Ryogoku,** south of Asakusa and east of Marunouchi, across the Sumida River, is the center of sumo in Tokyo.

If you're lucky enough to attend a match, upon entering the arena, look up. The roof suspended above the ring is the roof of a Shinto shrine. The bulk of the activity taking place under this sacred cover consists of the referees intoning chants and the wrestlers cleansing their mouths with water, throwing salt to symbolically purify the ring (where women are, controversially, not allowed to enter), and repeatedly performing the choreographed show of strength known as shiko, in which they squat, clap their hands, raise each leg, and stamp each foot. The matches themselves sometimes last only seconds, but in rare cases can stretch to around a minute. The first man who leaves the ring or touches its earthen surface with any part of his body but the soles of his feet loses the match. Hence the effort to pack on the pounds by alternating calorie-rich meals with long naps.

Here are the best ways to catch a glimpse into the fascinating world of sumo during your time in Tokyo.

CATCH A MATCH

The best place to see a sumo match is at **Ryogoku Kokugikan** (1-3-28 Yokoami, Sumida-ku; tel. 03/3623-5111; www.sumo.or.jp/kokugikan; take Sōbu line to Ryogoku Station, west exit) in Tokyo. Fifteen-day tournaments are held at this stadium three times a year (Jan., May, and Sept.). The day kicks off around 8am, but it gets interesting around 3pm when the top wrestlers begin to enter the ring. The tournaments usually end around 6pm.

Buy your **tickets** a month in advance (http://sumo.or.jp, http://buysumotickets.com, or http://sumo.pia.jp/en; around ¥4,000-48,000, average ¥18,000 around tournament time). There's also a box office near the station's main entrance that sells a few hundred tickets for nosebleed seats (around ¥2,000) on the day of each match, but you'll need to arrive no later than 5:30am or 6am to have a shot at landing one. You can rent a headset that provides English-language commentary (¥100 with ¥2,000 deposit).

Tournaments are also held in Osaka in March. Advance tickets (book a month beforehand; around ¥2,500-20,000) can be purchased online: http://sumo.or.jp, http://buysumotickets.com, and http://sumo.pia.jp.

WATCH A PRACTICE

If you're not in town during tournament season, it's also possible to watch the wrestlers colliding up close on an intimate visit to a stable, or beya, where asa-keiko (morning practice) can be observed through a window.

and paintings. On an island at the western edge of the park's large pond, you'll find **Inokashira Benzaiten,** a shrine dedicated to Benzaiten, patron of the arts. In the southern part of the park, you'll find the immensely popular **Ghibli Museum** (page 84). There are also some excellent cafés and restaurants in and around Inokashira, so take your time and enjoy this special place.

TOURS

The most rewarding discoveries in Tokyo often come through serendipity and wandering on your own, but sometimes a tour can help unlock facets of the city. Having someone to guide you through Tokyo's labyrinthine food and nightlife options can be particularly helpful; for some recommendations, see pages 108 and 124.

Arashio Beya (2-47-2 Hama-chō, Nihonbashi, Chūō-ku; tel. 03/3666-7646; www.arashio.net/tour_e.html; 7:30am-10am daily Dec.-Feb., Apr.-Jun., Aug.-Oct.; free; take Tōei Shinjuku line to Hamachō Station, exit A2), west across the Sumida River from Ryogoku Kokugikan, accommodates guests who are willing to respect some rules: no talking, filming, flash photography, eating, drinking, or chewing gum. Note that the stable's doors are closed during tournament time as well as one week after each grand tournament. Reservations aren't possible, so it's wise to call the day before sometime between 4pm-8pm to confirm practice will be held the next morning. There's a Japanese-language script on the website, written in romaji (Roman alphabet) with an English translation, that you can use in the call.

There are also sporadically held stable tours with knowledgeable locals offered through the websites **Voyagin** (www.govoyagin.com) and **Magical Trip** (www.magical-trip.com).

EAT CHANKO NABE

The calorie-dense hot pot loaded with vegetables, seafood, and meat is scarfed down by wrestlers daily. Try **Tomoegata** (2-17-6 Ryogoku, Sumida-ku; tel. 03/3632-5600; www.tomoegata.com; 11:30am-3pm, last order 2:30pm, and 5pm-10pm, last order 9pm, Tues.-Fri., 11:30am-3pm, last order 2:30pm, and 4:30pm-10pm, last order 9pm, Sat.-Sun., holidays), located in the heart of sumo territory in Ryogoku. Alternatively, you can get a small bowl of the stuff (¥300) in the basement of the Ryogoku Kokugikan on a tournament day.

LEARN MORE

The **Sumo Museum** (1F Ryogoku Kokugikan, 1-3-28 Yokoami, Sumida-ku; tel. 03/3622-0366; www.sumo.or.jp; 10am-4:30pm Mon.-Fri., sporadically closes to change exhibitions and on national holidays; free) houses memorabilia and woodblock prints related to the sport. It also holds special exhibitions six times a year. Note that the museum closes between special exhibitions and is only open to tournament ticketholders during the grand tournaments held at the Ryogoku Kokugikan three times a year (Jan., May, and Sept.) in Tokyo. Before making the trip, check the museum's schedule online (http://sumo.or.jp/EnSumoMuseum/schedule) to be safe.

At the **Tomioka Hachimangu Shrine** (1-20-3 Tomioka, Koto-ku; tel. 03/3642-1315; www.tomiokahachimangu.or.jp; 24 hours daily; free; take Ōedo, Tōzai lines to Monzen-nakachō Station, exit 1), southeast of Ryogoku Kokugikan, sumo bouts were held for about 100 years during the Edo period. Monuments bearing the names of wrestlers who became yokozuna (grand champions) and ozeki (second-highest rank) dot the grounds. Look to your right as you enter and find the humblingly massive handprints in stone of some sumo superstars. It's also an impressive shrine in its own right.

Walking Tours

For basic walking tours, try the following:

- **Tokyo Metropolitan Government Tours** (www.gotokyo.org/en/guide-services/index.html; average 3 hours; free or only covering costs incurred by guides)
- **Tokyo Systemized Goodwill Guide (SGG) Club** (http://tokyosgg.jp/guide.html; average 1.5-2 hours; free)

Bike Tours

If you're interested in combining a tour with a bike ride, try some of the following providers.

- **Tokyo Bicycle Tours** (www.tokyobicycle-tours.com; 3-6.5 hours; ¥6,000-9,800)
- **Tokyo Great Cycling Tour** (tel. 03/4590-2995; www.tokyocycling.jp; 1.5-6 hours; ¥5,000-13,000 adults, ¥2,500-6,500 ages 12 and under)

BAY CRUISES

Stand at the banks of the Sumida River in Asakusa during the evening and you will most likely see a number of low-slung boats festooned with paper lanterns gliding in both directions on the river. These are traditional houseboats known as **yakatabune.** It's possible to ride one of these crafts up and down the Sumida River, and around the contours of Tokyo Bay, eating and drinking as you go. While the food is hit-or-miss, the views of the city from the water are romantic.

Thoroughly modern compact **cruise boats** also sail the waters around Tokyo. Choosing a cruise provider can be daunting, given the sheer number of them and the language barrier (some do have English-language reservation services). To get a sense for what your options are, visit the website of the **Tokyo Yakatabune Association** (www.yakatabune-kumiai.jp/en/index.php).

FUNASEI

1-16-8 Kita-Shinagawa, Shinagawa-ku; tel. 03/5479-2731; www.funasei.com; 2.5 hours; from ¥10,800 adults, ¥4,000-8,000 children

This yakatabune (traditional houseboat) cruise provider operates six traditional boats and one private charter yacht, seating 20 to 120, depending on the craft. The boats depart from Shinagawa (located south of Ginza and the **Tokyo Tower,** on the west side of Tokyo Bay) and sail northward, up the Sumida River to **Tokyo Skytree** in Asakusa, before returning via **Odaiba.** The meals served on board are Japanese—tempura, sashimi, and more—and booze is unlimited. Note that the liaison by phone is an English-speaking travel agency. Inquire directly with them about cruise schedules and availability.

BASEBALL

An interesting counterpoint to deeply indigenous sumo, the relatively recent import of baseball reveals many of the nation's cultural quirks. Although Tokyo's baseball fans are less fervent than the rabid supporters of Kansai's Hanshin Tigers, the capital boasts two major teams, the **Yomiuri Giants** and **Yakult Swallows.** Stadium capacity was reduced over the course of the coronavirus pandemic, but it has been possible to catch a game for the most part.

TOKYO DOME

1-3-61 Koraku, Bunkyō-ku; tel. 03/5800-9999; www.tokyo-dome.co.jp, tickets sold at www.giants.jp; tickets ¥2,300-6,500; take Marunouchi, Namboku lines to Korakuen Station, exit 1, or JR Chūō, Sōbu to Suidōbashi Station, west exit, or Mita subway line to Suidōbashi Station, exit A5

Home to Japan's winningest team, the Yomiuri Giants, this center in the geographic heart of the city is a great place for the authentic Japanese baseball experience. More popular than Tokyo's second team, the Yakult Swallows, tickets sell out well in advance. Plan and purchase as far ahead as you can.

MEIJI JINGŪ STADIUM

3-1 Kasumigaoka-machi, Shinjuku-ku; tel. 0180/993-589; www.jingu-stadium.com; tickets ¥1,600-5,900; take Ginza line to Gaienmae Station, exit 3

This historic (built in 1926), 37,000-seater stadium is home to the Yakult Swallows. If the Giants are akin to New York's Yankees, the Swallows are the Mets. Nicely located near Aoyama, Harajuku, Shibuya, and Shinjuku, this is a convenient place to experience Japan's true national pastime.

THEME PARKS

Tokyo has its fair share of theme and amusement parks, with **Tokyo Disneyland** and **Tokyo DisneySea,** located just east of town in Chiba Prefecture, firmly atop the list.

ASAKUSA HANAYASHIKI

2-28-1 Asakusa, Taitō-ku; tel. 03/3842-8780; www.hanayashiki.net; 10am-6pm daily; admission ¥500 ages 7-12, ¥1,000 ages 13 and up; free ride pass ¥2,000 ages 6 and younger, ¥2,200 ages 7-12, ¥2,500 ages 13 and up; individual ride ticket ¥100, coupon book of 11 tickets ¥1,000

This old-school amusement park in

Asakusa has been running since 1883. While the park's 20 or so rides won't wow you with thrills, they will certainly inspire a sense of nostalgia. Among them are Japan's oldest rollercoaster, which runs on a steel track, and an old-fashioned haunted house. This is by no means a must-see, but if you feel like doing something offbeat, are traveling with kids, or need a break from temples and shrines, Hanayashiki is a fun option.

ONSEN

Shinjuku

ONSEN THERMAE-YU

1-1-2 Kabukichō, Shinjuku-ku; tel. 03/5285-1726; www.thermae-yu.jp; 11am-9am daily, irregular closings; ¥2,405 Mon.-Fri., ¥1,100 surcharge from midnight-9am daily, ¥880 surcharge on Sat.-Sun. and holidays; take Marunouchi, Fukutoshin, Shinjuku lines to Shinjuku-Sanchōme Station, exit E1, or Chūō, Sōbu lines to Shinjuku Station, east exit

Besides the spic-and-span sex-separated indoor and outdoor pools at this impressive new onsen complex, there are also saunas, a beauty salon, and various exfoliation scrub-downs, as well as a bar, café, and eatery on-site. The water is pumped in daily from Izu Peninsula, southwest of Tokyo. It's a good choice in the heart of Kabukichō. Uncovered tattoos aren't permitted, but coverings can be purchased for ¥300.

Akihabara and Ueno

SPA LAQUA

5-9F Tokyo Dome City, 1-1-1 Kasuga, Bunkyō-ku; tel. 03/5800-9999; www.laqua.jp; 11am-9am daily (last entry 8am); ¥2,900 adults, ¥2,090 children ages 6-17, ¥1,980 surcharge from 1am-6am, ¥550 surcharge Sat.-Sun. and holidays; take Marunouchi line to Kōrakuen Station, exit 2

Real onsen water is piped into the stylish indoor and outdoor pools at this hot-spring complex not far from Koishikawa Korakuen, west of Akihabara, from 1,700 meters (5,577 ft) beneath the earth, said to bestow health benefits such as improved circulation. This huge complex is spread across five floors, which also house facilities for treatments ranging from Thai massages to Korean body exfoliation scrubbing sessions. No tattoos allowed.

Shopping

GINZA AND MARUNOUCHI

銀座, 丸の内

Ginza is home to an array of shops dedicated to high-end fashion and luxury goods, both produced in Japan and overseas. Think world-class brands in sophisticated boutiques and swanky, sprawling emporiums offering an entire city's worth of consumer opulence under one roof.

Fashion

DOVER STREET MARKET GINZA

6-9-5 Ginza, Chūō-ku; tel. 03/6228-5080; http://ginza.doverstreetmarket.com; 11am-8pm daily; take Ginza line to Ginza Station, exit A2

If this seven-floor complex feels like a shopping mall as seen through the eyes of a design renegade with avant-garde sensibilities, that's because it is. Legendary designer Rei Kawakubo, whose label Comme des Garçons exploded onto the world's runways in the 1980s, has revived Ginza's fashion cred with Dover Street Market Ginza, a bleeding-edge, high-concept shopping mall brimming with top-end brands from Japan and overseas.

GINZA SIX

6-10 Ginza, Chūō-ku; http://ginza6.tokyo; 10:30am-8:30pm daily; take Ginza, Hibiya, Marunouchi lines to Ginza Station, exit A3

Ginza's largest shrine to commerce is enormous, with 241 brands under one very exclusive roof. You'll also find an exquisitely designed Tsutaya Books on the sixth floor and even a Noh theater in the basement. Splash out some serious cash and you can even hire a personal stylist to advise you on your shopping spree. And it's not just clothes. If you're in search of that perfect bottle of booze made in Japan (nihonshū, shōchū, whisky, gin), a fantastic choice in this complex is **Imadeya** (B2F Ginza Six; tel. 03/6264-5537; www.imadeya.co.jp/shops/ginza; 10:30am-8:30pm daily).

Souvenirs

MUJI

3-3-5 Ginza, Chūō-ku; tel. 03/3538-1311; https://shop.muji.com/jp/ginza; 11am-9pm daily; take Ginza, Marunouchi, Hibiya subway lines to Ginza Station, exit B4, then walk 3 minutes northeast, or take JR Yamanote line to Yūrakuchō Station, central exit, then walk 5 minutes southeast

This is the seven-floor global flagship of Muji, a brand that has developed a reputation beyond Japan for its classically minimal, affordable, practical, and smartly designed products, from kitchenware and furniture to stationery, clothing, and snacks. There's also a diner and bakery on-site.

EBISU AND AROUND

恵比寿

There's a hip pocket of town located upon a hill between Ebisu and Shibuya called **Daikanyama.** The streets, lined with trendy boutiques and cafés, beg to be strolled. This is one of many places where stylish locals shop.

Fashion

OKURA

20-11 Sarugaku-chō, Shibuya-ku; tel. 03/3461-8511; www.hrm.co.jp/okura; 11:30am-8pm Mon.-Fri., 11am-8:30pm Sat.-Sun. and holidays; take Tōkyū Tōyoko line to Daikanyama Station

Situated on a fashionable street behind T-Site, Okura (オクラ) is a great place to get acquainted with Japan's centuries-old indigo-dyeing tradition. The threads here are all made using old-school indigo-dyeing techniques. A mix of old and modern-style attire are sold, from tabi (split-toed socks) to jackets, jeans, T-shirts, and scarves. The tastefully rustic building that houses the shop is a pleasure to explore, too. As there's no English sign, look out for the squat, traditional-style shopfront, which normally has some indigo-dyed specimen on display out front.

women in yukata shopping in Ginza

Purikura

Purikura, a shortened form of "print club," is a massive industry in Japan, attracting giggling teens en masse to take cutesy photos with friends. They are essentially photo booths, but the photos can be souped up with various digital enhancements. Often located in game centers, purikura booths are popular nationwide, although major cities like Tokyo and Osaka command a particularly large number.

HOW IT WORKS

Many of the booths have a preset theme; for example, a dessert-themed booth may add little digital slices of cake to your photos. Insert money in the slot and step inside. After you've input the settings of your choice—doe eyes and rosy cheeks, perhaps—strike a silly pose and let the camera do its work. After the images have been taken, you'll have the option to do further editing with a stylus in an editing booth outside. Once you've modified your photos to your liking, simply press the "end" button on the screen to print them out. Voilà: a cheap, quirky souvenir.

WHERE TO TRY IT

A few good bets to try out a purikura booth include **Purikura no Mecca** (3F, 29-1 Udagawachō, Shibuya-ku; open 24/7; take JR, Ginza, Inokashira, Fukutoshin, Hanzōmon, Tōkyū Tōyoko lines to Shibuya Station, Hachikō exit) and **Purikura Land Noa** (1-17-5 Jingūmae, Shibuya-ku; tel. 03/3401-7655; 8am-11pm daily; take Yamanote line to Harajuku Station, Takeshita exit) on Takeshita-dōri. Here you'll find collections of purikura booths to snap away to your heart's content. Note that some purikura spots loosely enforce a rule that prohibits men, whether solo or in a group, from entering without at least one woman accompanying them. You'll be less likely to face an issue in an arcade than in a place solely dedicated to the booths.

Bookstores

T-SITE

17-5 Sarugaku-chō; tel. 03/3770-2525; https://store.tsite.jp/daikanyama/; 7am-2am daily; take Tōkyū Tōyoko line to Daikanyama Station

This has to be among the world's coolest bookstores. The design of the complex, which appears to be enmeshed in a knit exterior of countless letter Ts, has won awards for architecture firm Klein Dytham. There's a solid selection of books and magazines on travel, art, architecture, food, and culture, including some in English, and **Anjin,** a chic café and lounge-bar, is on the second floor. It's a great place to chill for a few hours.

SHIBUYA

渋谷

A number of large, eclectic shops carrying quirky lifestyle goods, as well as a number of youth fashion retailers, can be found in Shibuya. Teenybopper fashion emporium **Shibuya 109** (www.shibuya109.jp), housed in an iconic multi-floor tower just west of **Shibuya Crossing,** is the neighborhood's most recognizable fashion landmark. Affordable designer items can be found, too, if you know where to look.

Souvenirs

TŌKYŪ HANDS SHIBUYA

12-18 Udagawachō, Shibuya-ku; 03/5489-5111; https://shibuya.tokyu-hands.co.jp; 10am-9pm daily; take JR, Ginza, Inokashira, Fukutoshin, Hanzōmon, Tōkyū Tōyoko lines to Shibuya Station, Hachikō exit

It's all about household items at Tōkyū Hands Shibuya, from the useful to the downright bizarre. The eight-floor Shibuya branch of this quirky purveyor of miscellaneous goods is Tokyo's largest, with everything from sundry materials for DIY projects to kitchenware shaped like cartoon characters, light fixtures, and more than 400 types of toothbrushes. If you can dream it, Tōkyū Hands likely has it.

D47 DESIGN TRAVEL STORE

8F Shibuya Hikarie, 2-21-1, Shibuya, Shibuya-ku; tel. 03/6427-2301; www.hikarie8.com/d47designtravelstore; noon-8pm Thurs.-Tues.; take Yamanote line to Shibuya Station, east exit

As the name suggests, the D47 Design Travel Store features the unique flavors, arts, and specialties of the 47 prefectures that comprise the Japanese archipelago. Japan may not be a huge country geographically speaking, but a trip to this store will likely impress you with the true extent of its diversity.

★ HARAJUKU AND AOYAMA

原宿, 青山

These neighborhoods are home to the highest concentration of trendsetting shops in the city. Funky Harajuku caters to the young. But if you head down **Omotesandō** toward Aoyama, you'll be dazzled by some of the most bleeding-edge high fashion anywhere, artfully displayed in stunning boutiques. On an even grander scale, **Omotesandō Hills** (4-12-10 Jingūmae, Shibuya-ku; tel. 03/3497-0310; www.omotesandohills.com; 11am-8pm daily) is a sleek, high-end mall built around a cavernous central atrium.

Another great place for urban strolling is the jam-packed pedestrian shopping street of **Takeshita-dōri,** Harajuku at its most youthful and saccharine, directly in front of Harajuku Station's Takeshita exit. Some of the hippest boutiques are located along **Cat Street,** near the intersection of Meiji-dōri and Omotesandō, about a 7-minute walk southeast of Harajuku Station's Omotesandō exit, and in the tangle of backstreets to the north of Omotesandō and east of Meiji-dōri.

Fashion

LAFORET

1-11-6 Jingūmae, Shibuya-ku; tel. 03/3475-0411; www.laforet.ne.jp; 11am-8pm daily; take Yamanote line to Harajuku Station, Omotesandō exit

For a quick introduction to youth fashion trends, come to LaForet in Harajuku. Inside you'll find a smorgasbord of boutiques hawking brightly colored clothes for hip young things, as well as various exhibitions and events. Check out the goth-lolita offerings and local labels Monomania and H>Fractal, all found in the basement, and the legendary, bleeding-edge **GR8** on floor 2.5, incongruously fronted by a traditional garden with stone lanterns and bonsais.

CHICAGO

2F Mansion 31, 6-31-15, Shibuya-ku; tel. 03/6427-5505; www.chicago.co.jp; 11am-8pm daily; take Yamanote line to Harajuku Station, Omotesandō exit

A fixture in Harajuku's always evolving fashion landscape, Chicago has the largest selection of vintage threads of any branch in the chain. The strong suit here is vintage kimonos and lighter cotton versions called yukata, which are sold at prices that won't break the bank.

6%DOKIDOKI

2F TX101 Bldg., 4-28-16 Jingūmae, Shibuya-ku; tel. 03/3479-6116; https://6dokidoki.com; 1pm-6pm Thurs.-Fri., noon-6pm Sat.-Sun. and holidays; take Yamanote line to Harajuku Station, Omotesandō exit

Vivid clothing and accessories, adorned with unicorns, hearts, and ice-cream cones, assault your vision at 6%Dokidoki, which translates to "6% Excitement." It's no shock to learn the shop's founder Sebastian Masuda often works with Kyary Pamyu Pamyu, a J-Pop starlet who is kawaii (cute) incarnate. Come here for the full Harajuku experience. Seeing is believing.

SOU-SOU

1F A-La Croce Bldg., 5-4-24 Minami-Aoyama, Minato-ku; tel. 03/3407-7877; http://sousounetshop.jp; noon-8pm daily; take Ginza, Hanzōmon lines to Omotesandō Station, exit B1

This Kyoto brand injects modern flare into classic Japanese fashions. At its outpost in trendy Aoyama, you'll find a range of excellent souvenir options from cool T-shirts and split-toe trainers to yukata designed with a modern twist.

Japan's Big Three of Fashion

As you walk down Omotesandō, you'll pass architecturally stunning designer shops including **Dior** (5-9-11 Jingūmae, Shibuya-ku; tel. 03/5464-6260; 11am-8pm daily), **Louis Vuitton** (5-7-5 Jingūmae, Shibuya-ku; tel. 0120/264-115; 11am-7pm daily), **Bottega Veneta** (5-1-5 Jingūmae, Shibuya-ku; tel. 03/5962-7630; noon-8pm daily), and **Prada** (5-2-6 Minamiaoyama, Minato-ku; tel. 03/6418-0400; 11am-8pm daily). In addition to these, look out for the flagships of the designers that make up Japan's big three names in fashion when you reach the Aoyama area on the southeastern end of the avenue.

ISSEY MIYAKE

3-18-11 Minami Aoyama, Minato-ku; tel. 03/3423-1408; www.isseymiyake.com; noon-7pm Wed.-Mon.

Crossing the large four-way intersection with Aoyama-dōri, you'll come to the Issey Miyake shop on the first corner on the left. Exploding on the scene in the late 1980s, the designer became famous for his experimental approach, involving fresh uses of fabric, geometric forms, and materials ranging from rough and natural to brightly colored plastic.

COMME DES GARÇONS

5-2-1 Minami Aoyama, Minato-ku; tel. 03/3406-3951; www.comme-des-garcons.com; 11am-8pm daily

Cross the street at the crosswalk and enter the flagship of legendary fashion label Comme des Garçons. Launched in the early 1980s by renowned designer Rei Kawakubo, here you'll find her renegade-chic style on full display. Fashion aside, the striking building, with its dramatic lines and spare interior, is worth a visit in its own right.

YOHJI YAMAMOTO

5-3-6 Minami Aoyama, Minato-ku; tel. 03/3409-6006; www.yohjiyamamoto.co.jp; 11am-8pm daily

Finally, continue up the right side of the street to see the flagship of the third name in Japan's high-fashion trinity, Yohji Yamamoto, who is renowned for his tailoring, which incorporates Japanese techniques onto distinctive black flowing garments.

Souvenirs

ORIENTAL BAZAAR

5-9-13 Jingūmae, Shibuya-ku; tel. 03/3400-3933; www.orientalbazaar.co.jp/en; noon-6pm Sat.-Sun. and holidays; take Yamanote line to Harajuku Station, Omotesandō exit, or Chiyoda, Fukutoshin lines to Meiji-Jingūmae Station, exit 4

Harajuku's Oriental Bazaar is a one-stop souvenir shop with English-speaking staff and reasonable prices. If you have limited time and want to take home a few items, they have it all: origami earrings, sake cup sets, tableware, antiques, yukata, ukiyo-e prints. The store was under renovation at the time of writing, but is set to reopen sometime in 2022.

SPIRAL MARKET AOYAMA

5-6-23 Minamiaoyama, Minato-ku; tel. 03/3498-1171; www.spiral.co.jp; building opens 11am daily, shop closing hours vary; take Ginza, Hanzōmon, Chiyoda lines to Omotesandō Station, exit B1

This arts complex, beautifully designed by Pritzker Prize-winning architect Fumihiko Maki, is built around an ascending spiral at the core of its interior. You'll find shops selling homeware, accessories, stationery, ceramics, and various handmade crafts from around Japan, complemented by an art gallery, café, restaurants, and more.

JAPAN TRADITIONAL CRAFTS AOYAMA SQUARE

1F Akasaka Oji Bldg., 8-1-22 Akasaka, Minato-ku; tel. 03/5785-1301; http://kougeihin.jp; 11am-7pm daily; take Ginza, Hanzōmon lines to Aoyama Itchōme Station, exit 4 north

Another excellent one-stop shop east of Harjuku and Aoyama is Japan Traditional Crafts Aoyama Square, a showcase for

Youth Fashion

Harajuku has been a center of fashion and youth culture since at least the 1990s. Its heyday was well documented in the legendary magazine ***FRUiTS,*** when creativity flourished in the neighborhood's then-pedestrian-only smaller streets. Although recent years have seen *FRUiTS* cease publication (resulting in declarations of the demise of Harajuku as a global fashion hub) and car traffic flowing through those streets that were once youth hangouts, the neighborhood's fashion landscape is far from dead, but rather, in a state of flux.

A host of new fashion leaders are establishing themselves in the scene, such as Peco and Aiba Runa, whose brand **RRR By Sugar Spot Factory** and social media imprint have made her one of Harajuku's new stars. Similarly, new magazines, such as ***Fanatic*** and ***Melt Magazine,*** are popping up. For an easy-to-access look down the rabbit hole that is Japan's fashion subcultural universe, as well as other quirky bits of obscure travel, peruse the blog of writer and TV host **La Carmina** (www.lacarmina.com/blog).

HARAJUKU SUBCULTURES

Although not as prevalent as they once were, many lively fashion subcultures continue to be visible in Harajuku's streets:

- **Cosplay:** "Costume play" is about dressing as an anime, manga, or video game character, and is the most widely recognizable of Harajuku's subcultures.
- **Kawaii:** The "cute" aesthetic extends far beyond the realm of fashion; perhaps no other country has placed such emphasis on the culture of cuteness. The most universally recognizable manifestation of this aesthetic is the iconic character Hello Kitty.
- **Lolita:** Another major trend with roots in Harajuku, this genre sees mostly young women

traditional crafts from all over Japan that receives funding from the government. The crafts incorporate a wide range of materials, from lacquer and textiles to bamboo, metal, ceramics, and glass. Artisans practice their craft in the store, which features their work on a rotating basis. Items sold here are of a uniformly high quality. Check the artist schedule online.

Toys

KIDDY LAND

6-1-9 Jingūmae, Shibuya-ku; tel. 03/3409-3431; www.kiddyland.co.jp/harajuku; 11am-7pm daily; take Yamanote line to Harajuku Station, Omotesandō exit, or Chiyoda, Fukutoshin lines to Meiji-Jingūmae Station, exit 4

Kiddy Land is a monument to toys. The enormous shop is chockablock with characters from Studio Ghibli and Disney films, Doraemon dolls, Godzilla models, Star Wars figures, and Sanrio mascots. If you're buying gifts for kids, this shop ticks all boxes.

SHINJUKU AND AROUND

新宿

While Shinjuku has a hodgepodge of everything, from vinyl records to punk-rock fashion shops, department stores are the defining feature. A number of mammoth electronics stores also dot the area.

Souvenirs

BEAMS JAPAN

3-32-6 Shinjuku, Shinjuku-ku; tel. 03/5368-7300; www.beams.co.jp/global/shop/j; 11am-8pm daily; take Yamanote line to Shinjuku Station, east exit

The Beams Japan flagship carries some of Japan's best designs, from fashion to art and housewares. It also houses a gallery that exhibits works by photographers and artists. If you get hungry while browsing the shop's six floors, head to the basement, where you'll find a restaurant serving Japanese takes on Western staples and curry, as well as a café.

donning knee-high stockings and knee-length skirts with petticoats, sometimes adding a corset or headdress, Victorian-style. There are numerous spins on this style, from **Gothic Lolita** to **Punk Lolita** and beyond.

- **Gyaru:** Based on the English word "gal," the key elements include hair dyed blond or brown, heavy makeup, provocative clothing, and a bit of a devil-may-care attitude to go with it.
- **Visual kei:** The "visual style" trend has roots in a Japanese rock movement akin to glam rock. Young male followers suit up in loud outfits and sport flashy hairstyles and makeup.
- **Fairy kei:** It doesn't get much more saccharine than this: pastel hair bows, decorative stars, babies, angels and polka dots, leg warmers, tights, baggy shirts, oversized glasses, and more. Stop by **Spank!** (4F Nakano Broadway, 5-52-15 Nakano, Nakano-ku; tel. 08/03404-3809; http://spankworld.jp; 12:30pm-7:30pm Thurs.-Tues.), the store that hatched this trend.
- **Dolly kei:** This style is inspired by European fairy tales and religious symbols, filtered through a Harajuku lens.
- **Genderless kei:** A relatively new development, this style draws on flourishes of kawaii to blur the boundaries of gender. Boys have been the predominant force in this movement, which idealizes a slim figure, bright eyes, makeup, expertly coifed hair, painted eyebrows, showy clothing, and plenty of kawaii accoutrements from hats to handbags.
- **Decora:** In this style, accessories, leg warmers, and knee socks are layered over each other to the point of overpowering the rest of an already quirky outfit, funky dental mask and tutu included.

Vinyl Records

DISK UNION SHINJUKU

3-chōme Shinjuku, Shinjuku-ku; tel. differs for each shop; https://diskunion.net; noon-8pm daily

Tokyo is legendary among record collectors—"crate diggers"—as one of the best cities in the world to find vinyl treasure. Sprawling across a tightly knit cluster of five shops, some with up to eight floors, this legendary record shop chain's prominent position in Shinjuku's hectic core covers any genre under the sun. Note that there is a heavy emphasis on the old compact disc here, but there's a decent selection of vinyl, too. To see a map breaking it all down in English, from soul to heavy metal and jazz, visit https://diskunion.net/pdf/shop/e_shop_areamap.pdf.

AKIHABARA AND UENO

秋葉原, 上野

Akihabara is the preeminent place to experience the wonderful and wacky world of otaku culture. Here you'll find all manner of electronic products and parts, multistory complexes filled with anime and manga, video game emporiums, maid and butler cafés, a shocking number of vending machines, and plenty of cosplayers milling about.

Pop Culture

RADIO KAIKAN

1-15-16 Sotokanda, Chiyoda-ku; www.akihabara-radiokaikan.co.jp; 10am-8pm daily; take Yamanote, Sōbu, Hibiya lines to Akihabara Station, Electric Town exit

A 10-story tower to geekdom with deep historical roots, stretching back to the years immediately following the war when radios were a premium item, Radio Kaikan carries a hodgepodge of figurines, dolls, manga, trading cards, and much more. Even if you don't plan to buy anything, it's worth stopping to peruse the merchandise to get a sense of the jaw-dropping extent of the depth and breadth of hobbies catered to in Akihabara.

Top Souvenirs

If you can dream it, you can likely buy it in Tokyo. What follows should give you a starting point for thinking about what to take home from your trip.

lacquerware being painted

FUNKY FASHION

Try **Beams Japan** (page 104) in Shinjuku or any boutique in Harajuku's youth fashion mecca **LaForet** (page 102).

KIMONOS AND YUKATA

Head to **Chicago** (page 102) in Harajuku for vintage options, Jotaro Saito in **Ginza Six** (page 99) for high-end, and **Sou-Sou** (page 102) in Aoyama for traditional items with a contemporary twist.

CRAFT AND DESIGN

For traditional crafts like lacquerware, folding fans, and ceramics, check out **Oriental Bazaar** (page 103) or **Japan Traditional Crafts Aoyama Square** (page 103). For great contemporary design, try **D47 Design Travel Store** (page 102) or **2K540 Aki-Oka Artisan** (page 107).

HOUSEWARES

Tokyo is home to a number of multi-floor "lifestyle goods" emporiums like **Tōkyū Hands Shibuya** (page 101), where everything under the sun is on sale. The famed shopping street **Kappabashi-dōri** (page 107) has a huge selection of knives, kitchenware, and crowd-pleasing fake plastic food samples.

POP CULTURE PICKS

For items like manga and anime merchandise, head to **Mandarake** (page 106). For retro video games, check out **Super Potato** (page 106).

MANDARAKE

3-11-12 Sotokanda, Chiyoda-ku; tel. 03/3252-7007; http://mandarake.co.jp; noon-8pm daily; take Yamanote, Sōbu, Hibiya lines to Akihabara Station, Electric Town exit

Mandarake's eight-floor shop at Akihabara's epicenter has it all: manga, anime, cosplay items, rare art, dolls, doujinshi (a wildly popular genre of self-published manga that's often highly risqué), video games, consoles, vintage figurines and models, card games, and loads of toys. If you don't find what you need at Radio Kaikan, try Mandarake instead.

SUPER POTATO

3F-5F Kitabayashi Bldg., 1-11-2 Sotokanda, Chiyoda-ku; tel. 03/5289-9933; www.superpotato.com/akihabara; 11am-8pm Mon.-Fri., 10am-8pm Sat.-Sun. and holidays; take Yamanote, Sōbu, Hibiya lines to Akihabara Station, Electric Town exit

There may be no better spot for retro video games on earth than the awesomely named Super Potato. This secondhand bazaar of 8- and 16-bit games, from the Super Mario Brothers to Sonic the Hedgehog and Link (The Legend of Zelda), packs a surprisingly powerful nostalgic punch for those who came of age at the dawn of the video game era in the 1980s. Even if you don't buy anything, stopping by this shop is like stepping into a museum dedicated to the heroes and heroines of your lost youth. Be sure to have some coins handy to play a few rounds of old-school arcade games on the fifth floor.

M'S: POP LIFE SEX DEPARTMENT STORE

1-15-13 Sotokanda, Chiyoda-ku; tel. 03/3252-6166; www.ms-online.co.jp; 11am-10pm daily; take Yamanote, Sōbu, Hibiya lines to Akihabara Station, Electric Town exit

It's an open secret that everyone who has spent any amount of time exploring Akihabara's maze of curiosities has snuck into M's: Pop Life Sex Department Store. If nothing else, I'd be remiss not to mention this one for its, ahem, value as a cultural case study. While the name speaks for itself, the sheer scale of the shop and its happy-go-lucky atmosphere are worth marveling at. Its seven floors are overflowing with sex toys, lingerie, costumes, whips, chains, life-sized dolls, DVDs—basically every imaginable product catering to the flesh. And it all feels normalized, with shoppers perusing merchandise as if they're in a sporting goods store.

Souvenirs

2K540 AKI-OKA ARTISAN

5-9 Ueno, Taitō-ku; www.jrtk.jp/2k540; 11am-7pm Thurs.-Tues.; take Yamanote line to Akihabara Station, Akihabara Electric Town exit, Yamanote line to Okachimachi Station, south exit 1, or Ginza line to Suehirocho Station, exit 2

2K540 Aki-Oka Artisan is a unique space under rail tracks that houses a smattering of shops selling both traditional goods and quirkier, more modern items. The eclectic emporium's name derives from its distance from Tokyo Station—2 kilometers and 540 meters (about 1.5 mi)—and its location between Akihabara and Okachimachi. The key thread tying its shops together is the fact that they all sell wares made in Japan, from kaleidoscopes and hats to figurines, sneakers, furniture, and toys. The space also holds occasional hands-on workshops related to traditional crafts.

ASAKUSA AND RYOGOKU

浅草, 両国

True to its locale in the heart of old-school Tokyo, Asakusa is a great place to find traditional crafts and souvenirs that you would associate with Japan. It's also a good place to indulge in a bit of kitsch.

Kitchenware

KAPPABASHI-DŌRI

take Ginza line to Tawaramachi Station, exit 3

A short walk from Sensō-ji brings you to Kappabashi-dōri, a busy road lined with store after store dedicated to the culinary arts. Starting at the corner of Asakusa-dōri and running along Shinbori-dōri, you'll find shops selling tableware, knives, crockery, signage for restaurants, utensils, and more. Some stores worth a look include knife emporiums **Kama-Asa Shoten** (2-24-1 Matsugaya, Taitō-ku; tel. 03/3841-9355; www.kama-asa.co.jp; 10am-5:30pm daily) and **Kamata Hakensha Knife Shop** (2-12-6 Matsugaya, Taitō-ku; tel. 03/3841-4205; www.kap-kam.com; 10am-6pm daily), and shops selling hyperreal plastic food models and other kitchen-related souvenirs of all kinds, such as **Ganso Shokuhin Sample-ya** (3-7-6 Nishiasakusa, Taitō-ku; tel. 0120-17-1839; www.ganso-sample.com; 10am-5:30pm daily). When you spot the huge head of a chef protruding from atop the Niimi building, you'll know you've come to the right place.

Souvenirs

SHIN-YOSHIWARA

102, 3-27-10 Nishiasakusa, Taitō-ku; www.shin-yoshiwara.com; noon-6pm daily; take Ginza line Tawaramachi Station, exit 3

This cheeky souvenir shop is a one-off. Inspired by the carnal essence of Yoshiwara, Edo's legendary red-light district that once stood in the same area, designer Yayoi Okano decided to open Shin-Yoshiwara, a shop that sells traditional items with a sassy twist. Here you'll find Japanese hair ornaments shaped like voluptuous nude women, ceramic dishes etched with two female breasts containing the characters of the shop's name inside them, ukiyo-e style prints depicting tatted-up yakuza at public baths, and more. Okano's sexy merchandise initially received a mixed response from locals, but feelings have slowly warmed and the shop's reputation has grown.

Food

It's not a stretch to say that Tokyo may have the best food on the planet. The level of mastery among chefs, premium ingredients, and sheer number of cooking styles found in Japanese cuisine put the city in a league of its own. Japan's capital boasts more Michelin stars than any other city on earth, to the chagrin of Paris and New York. And where the Big Apple is said to have about 30,000 restaurants, estimates put that number anywhere from 150,000 to 300,000 for Tokyo.

Embarking on a voyage into this vast culinary seventh heaven can be life-changing. Restaurant options run the gamut, from **sushi** and **sashimi** to Japanese-style hot pot dishes **sukiyaki** and **shabu-shabu. Kaiseki** is a multicourse affair that evolved from the tea ceremony, comprising appetizers through a series of dishes that have been grilled, raw, fried, simmered, and steamed, and ending with a light seasonally appropriate dessert.

Okonomiyaki is a savory pancake cooked on a grill in front of you, and then there are meals cooked over an open flame, such as **yakiniku** and **robatayaki.** Noodles, from **ramen** and **udon** to summer favorites **somen** and **soba,** are ubiquitous and served in a staggering variety of broths.

Highly evolved **foreign cuisines** are also readily on offer, from French and Italian to Indian, with chefs routinely going overseas to study their cuisine of choice before coming back to open their own shop and putting twists on the menu.

During the COVID-19 pandemic, restaurants operated at restricted hours and capacities, depending on the state of emergency. When entering, you're often expected to sanitize your hands and get a quick temperature check, as well as wear a mask while not eating.

Food Tours

With more eateries than any city on the planet, it's no surprise that Tokyo is full of food tours. A few operators include:

- **Arigato Japan Food Tours** (https://arigatojapan.co.jp; average 3 hours; from around ¥18,000, includes some food and drinks, private tours available for additional fee)
- **Ninja Food Tours** (www.ninjafoodtours.com; 2-3.5 hours; ¥8,500-10,800, includes some food and drinks)
- **Oishii Food Tours** (www.oishiitours.com; 3.5 hours; ¥12,000-16,500, includes some food and drinks, private tours available for additional fee)

GINZA AND MARUNOUCHI

銀座，丸の内

Izakaya

SAKE NO ANA

3-5-8 Ginza, Chūō-ku; tel. 03/3567-1133; www.sakenoana.com; 11:30am-10pm Mon.-Sat., 11:30am-9pm Sun. and holidays; lunch sets ¥1,050-2,200, dinner courses ¥5,400-6,480; take Ginza, Marunouchi, Hibiya lines to Ginza Station on, A13 exit

Here, the focus is on serving food that goes best with sake. It's a fantastic place to go for a crash course on the Japanese rice-based brew, thanks to an in-house sake sommelier, Sakamoto-san, who is happy to give you a taste-based tour by pairing different varieties with dishes like a natto (fermented soy bean) omelet or deep-fried fugu (puffer fish).

TACHINOMI RYOMA

ALC Bldg. 1F, 2-13-3 Shimbashi; tel. 03/3591-1757; 4:30pm-11:30am Mon.-Thurs., 4:30pm-11pm Fri., 5pm-11pm Sat., closed holidays; ¥4,000; take Yamanote, Ginza, Asakusa lines to Shimbashi Station, Karasumori exit

This welcoming tachinomi (literally: "standing-drinking") in the heart of the salaryman stronghold of Shimbashi, bordering Ginza's southern edge, has an extensive shōchū menu with more than 100 varieties. It's a great place to sample a number of varieties with a booze-friendly menu of choices like karage (fried chicken) and sashimi. The bartenders here really know their stuff and are happy to make suggestions.

SHIN-HINOMOTO

2-4-4 Yūrakuchō, Chiyoda-ku; tel. 03/3214-8021; http://shin-hinomoto.com; 5pm-midnight Mon.-Sat.; courses ¥4,500; take Yamanote, Yūrakuchō lines to Yūrakuchō Station, Hibiya exit

Besides being owned by a Brit, Shin-Hinomoto, aka Andy's Fish, has another twist: It's under the train tracks, so don't be surprised if you feel a rumble each time the Yamanote line rolls overhead. This is a great place to go for the full izakaya experience, complete with cramped quarters, lively customers exclaiming "kanpai" ("cheers") with each round of drinks, and cheap but tasty grub. The menu is heavily weighted toward seafood and is helpfully available in English. As you enter the restaurant, there's a cubby hole lined with vending machines selling booze to the right side of the entrance. The sidewalk here is a favorite place for salarymen to congregate for a canned alcoholic beverage of choice after leaving the office. Reserve a day or two ahead to be safe—by telephone only—especially if you're visiting on the weekend.

Sushi

★ GINZA KYUBEY

8-7-6 Ginza, Chūō-ku; tel. 03/3571-6523; www.kyubey.jp/en; 11:30am-2pm and 5pm-10pm Tues.-Sat.; lunch ¥8,250-30,800, dinner ¥11,000-33,000; take Ginza line to Shimbashi Station, exit 3

Ginza Kyubey is the ideal spot for the full sushi experience. Take a seat at the counter and watch as master chefs work their magic in front of you. Although this place is not cheap, the prices feel commensurate with the ambience and fare. One of the great things about Kyubey is that the atmosphere isn't stuffy, which can sometimes be the case at high-end sushi shops, where a small number of customers sit at one counter as the master does his work, and people converse in hushed tones. By contrast, Kyubey seats more than 17 and has a relatively lively atmosphere, striking the right balance of high quality and friendly ambience. Reservations, made via your hotel concierge, are recommended. If this restaurant is fully booked, try the branch at Hotel New Otani.

Cafés

CAFÉ L'AMBRE

8-10-15 Ginza, Chūō-ku; tel. 03/3571-1551; www.cafedelambre.com; noon-8pm (last order 7:30pm) Mon.-Fri., noon-7pm (last order 6:30pm) Sat.-Sun. and holidays; ¥1,000; take Yamanote line to Shimbashi Station, exit 1

This legendary coffeehouse in the heart of Ginza has been caffeinating the masses since 1948, though its interior looks more recent. Although some old-school Tokyo coffeehouses can be a bit full of themselves, this is a relaxed place for a caffeine hit and conversation. The English-language menu offers more than 30 varieties, including some exotic concoctions. How about coffee with Cognac?

International

DHABA INDIA

Sagami Bldg. 1F, 2-7-9 Yaesu, Chūō-ku; tel. 03/3272-7160; http://dhabaindiatokyo.com; 11:15am-3pm (last order 2:30pm) and 5pm-10pm (last order 9pm) Mon.-Fri., 11:30am-3:30pm (last order 3pm) and 5pm-10pm (last order 9pm) Sat.-Sun. and

Food Underground: Japan's Depachika

A typical Japanese department store (depato) is 5-10 floors high, with women's fashion on the first couple of floors, fashion and sports gear for men on the floors above that, and lifestyle items, stationery, and furniture on the next few floors. Even non-shoppers, however, will appreciate the depato's food offerings: A restaurant floor is at the top, usually providing an impressive range of cuisines, including Italian, Korean, Chinese, and Japanese. Some department stores turn their rooftops into beer gardens in warmer months. But the floor that proves to be the biggest revelation for many is the basement level, where you'll typically find an extensive gourmet food hall known as a depachika. Excellent seasonal produce, sushi, tempura, bento box lunches, tofu, fresh ginger, yakitori, tonkatsu, croquettes, premade salads, sandwiches, cheese, Western and Japanese desserts . . . the list goes on.

For the full depato experience, with an emphasis on the best subterranean food halls, check out the following department stores:

GINZA MITSUKOSHI

4-6-16 Ginza, Chūō-ku; tel. 03/3562-1111; www.mistore.jp/store/ginza.html; 10am-8pm Mon.-Sat., 10am-7:30pm Sun. and last day of holiday periods; take Ginza, Hibiya, Marunouchi lines to Ginza Station, exits A7, A8, A11

Ginza Mitsukoshi has a vast array of decadent culinary options in its sprawling basement food hall. Head to the rooftop garden to eat them.

ISETAN SHINJUKU

3-14-1 Shinjuku, Shinjuku-ku; tel. 03/3352-1111; www.mistore.jp/store/shinjuku.html; 10am-8pm daily; take Marunouchi, Shinjuku, Fukutoshin lines to Shinjuku-Sanchōme Station, exits B3, B4, B5; or Chūō, Sōbu lines to Shinjuku Station, east exit; or Ōedo line to Shinjuku Station, exit 1

Isetan Shinjuku is the flagship of this hip chain. It's renowned for its artistic, attention-grabbing window displays, but the showstopper here is its opulent depachika. There you'll find caviar, giant legs of Iberico ham, Japanese sweets, and a stunning array of booze, from champagne to whisky and nihonshū.

TAKASHIMAYA TIMES SQUARE

5-24-2 Sendagaya, Shibuya-ku; tel. 03/5361-1111; www.takashimaya-global.com/en/stores/shinjuku/; 10am-8pm Sun.-Thurs., 10am-8:30pm Fri.-Sat.; take Chūō, Sōbu lines to Shinjuku Station, South Exit

Takashimaya Times Square has a swanky sensibility, with a glut of luxury brands. Head down to the basement to see how this is applied to food. Take note of the haute bento box meals prepared by the chefs at kaiseki ryōri purveyor Kikunoi. There's a rooftop garden here, too.

holidays; lunch ¥1,200, dinner ¥2,000; take Ginza line to Kyobashi Station, exit 5

Dhaba India is a splendid South Indian restaurant that has it all: chefs recruited straight from Tamil Nadu and Kerala, a soothing ambience thanks to dark blue walls and a turquoise floor, and knockout food. The menu's range is impressive, too, from lemon prawn curry served with delectably thin puri to a mean masala dosa. And perhaps most importantly, the chefs don't tone down the spice to suit local tastes.

Steakhouse

SHIMA

3-5-12 Nihonbashi, Chūō-ku; tel. 03/3271-7889; 6pm-9pm Mon.-Sat.; from around ¥20,000; take Ginza line to Kyobashi Station, exit 6

If you want to go big on one steak meal in Tokyo, Shima is an excellent choice. The immaculately marbled beef, sourced from a Kyoto farm, is phenomenal. Thanks to the warm presence of Chef Oshima Manabu, a Kyoto native, the atmosphere at this discrete basement eatery is friendly, too. Patrons seated at the counter can be heard chatting away with the chefs. It's not cheap, but some Tokyo eateries charge three to four times as much for a similar meal. Reservations required for dinner. Call ahead a few days or more in advance to be safe.

TOKYO BAY AREA

東京湾

Monjayaki

MONJA KONDO

3-12-10 Tsukishima, Chūō-ku; tel. 03/3533-4555; www.monja.gr.jp/kondohonten.html; 5pm-10:30pm Mon.-Fri., 11:30am-10:30pm Sat.-Sun. and holidays; lunch ¥1,500, dinner ¥2,500; take Ōedo line to Tsukishima Station, exit 8

Doing brisk business since 1950, Monja Kondo is said to be Tokyo's first restaurant to serve monjayaki, the Tokyo-born cousin of okonomiyaki, a savory pancake-like dish with stronger ties to Osaka and Hiroshima. The menu boasts a whopping 90 toppings to choose from, and friendly staff are on standby to help you cook your meal at your table's teppanyaki grill.

Sushi

SUSHIKUNI

4-14-15 Tsukiji, Chūō-ku; tel. 03/3545-8234; https://ameblo.jp/sushikuni; 10am-2:30pm and 5pm-7:30pm Thurs.-Tues.; lunch ¥2,000-3,000, dinner ¥5,000-6,000; take Ōedo line to Tsukijishijō Station, exit A1

A stand-out in Tsukiji Outer Market, Sushikuni is known for its kaisen-don, or raw fish served over rice. The specialties here are ikura (salmon roe) and uni (sea urchin roe). Lines do form, but they move relatively fast.

International

TY HARBOR

2-1-3 Higashi-Shinagawa, Shinagawa-ku; tel. 03/5479-4555; www.tysons.jp/tyharbor/en; 11:30am-3pm (last order 2pm) and 5:30pm-11pm (last order 10pm) Mon.-Fri., 11:30am-4pm (last order 3pm) and 5:30pm-11pm (last order 10pm) Sat.-Sun. and holidays; lunch ¥1,400-3,500, dinner ¥1,800-6,200; take Tokyo Monorail or Rinkai line to Tennozu Isle Station, central exit

For a maritime city, Tokyo admittedly has few options for wining and dining with a view of the bay. TY Harbor remedies that. It includes a chic bar serving dark and light California-style beers, and a restaurant serving Western cuisine, from steaks and salads to burgers made with fine cuts of wagyu beef.

ROPPONGI AND AROUND

六本木

Izakaya

GONPACHI

1-13-11 Nishi-Azabu, Minato-ku; tel. 03/5771-0170; https://gonpachi.jp/nishi-azabu/; 11:30am-3:30am (food last order 2:45am, drink last order 3am) daily; lunch ¥1,000-3,500, dinner ¥3,850-9,800; take Ōedo, Hibiya lines to Roppongi Station, exit 2

This towering izakaya is said to be the restaurant that inspired a particularly gory scene in the film *Kill Bill*. Gonpachi has garnered a reputation as a lively spot with a wide-ranging menu of countryside standards like yakitori and grilled fish. Adding to the atmosphere are a soundtrack of the three-stringed shamisen and servers in traditional coats. There is a more upscale sushi restaurant with an open terrace on the third floor as well.

WARAYAKIYA

Roppongi Gordy Bldg. 1F, 6-8-8 Roppongi, Minato-ku; tel. 03/6778-5495; www.dd-holdings.jp/shops/warayakiya/roppongi#; 5pm-5am (last order 4am) Mon.-Sat., 5pm-11pm (last order 10pm) Sun. and holidays; average ¥4,000; take Ōedo, Hibiya lines to Roppongi Station, exit 3

Warayakiya is a great izakaya focused on a grilling method that uses straw instead of charcoal. This style originates from Kochi Prefecture on the Pacific side of Shikoku. With the leaping fire reaching temperatures up to 900°C (1,652°F), it's worth getting a counter seat so you can watch the chefs expertly sear fish, meat, and vegetables to perfection. The seared bonito is a hit, and the place is lively and often packed, so booking ahead is recommended.

Kaiseki

TOFUYA UKAI

4-4-13 Shiba Kōen, Minato-ku; tel. 03/3436-1028; www.ukai.co.jp/english/shiba; 11:45am-3pm and 5pm-7:30pm Mon.-Fri., 11am-7:30pm Sat.-Sun. and holidays; closed third Mon. every month; lunch ¥6,000-8,000, dinner ¥11,000-16,000; take Ōedo line to Akabanebashi Station, Akabanebashiguchi exit

Tofuya Ukai, just a stone's throw from Tokyo Tower, is the best place to taste the wonders of tofu. Impressively, this kaiseki restaurant even makes its own tofu at a shop in the foothills of the Okutama mountain range west of Tokyo. Set amid readily visible gardens with ponds teeming with colorful carp, the restaurant is set within a relocated sake brewery that was originally built in Yamagata Prefecture more than 200 years ago. Staff in kimonos serve up to 500 guests in the wooden complex's 55 tatami-mat private rooms. Book ahead for a seat and to settle on your dining course, which must be determined beforehand.

Soba

HONMURA AN

7-14-18 Roppongi, Minato-ku; tel. 03/5772-6657; www.honmuraantokyo.com; 11:45am-2pm and 5pm-7:30pm Tues.-Sun., closed first and third Tues. of month; lunch ¥1,700, dinner ¥8,300; take Ōedo, Hibiya lines to Roppongi Station, exit 4b

Honmura An elevates the humble buckwheat noodle to an art form. Owner Koichi Kobari returned to Tokyo from New York in 2007 to take over his late father's soba shop, leaving a legion of disappointed fans in his wake. The shop defies the image of soba as being something eaten on the fly or from a bento box, and encourages diners to savor the noodles, which are served both hot and cold. The menu fluctuates by season and is fully bilingual. Prices are shockingly cheap for the quality of the food. A ¥350 seating charge applies at dinner. Reserve over the phone up to a month in advance, then be sure to reconfirm your reservation the day before you are scheduled to dine.

Vegetarian

SOUGO

Roppongi Green Bldg. 3F, 6-1-8 Roppongi, Minato-ku; tel. 03/5414-1133; www.sougo.tokyo; 11:30am-3pm lunch (last order 3pm), 2pm-5pm café time (last order 4pm), 6pm-11:30pm dinner (last order 10pm) Mon.-Sat.; lunch ¥1,500-8,800, café time ¥700-1,500, dinner ¥8,800-13,200; take Ōedo or Hibiya line to Roppongi Station, exit 3

A stellar vegetarian option in a city with limited choices for those who don't eat meat, Sougo has garnered a reputation for its accessible shōjin-ryōri, or vegetarian food eaten by Buddhist monks. It's offered at a price and level of accessibility sadly lacking at most restaurants serving the spiritually inspired cuisine. Bucking tradition, there is an open kitchen fronted by a bar. The menu is seasonal and experimental, and incorporates some nonvegan items such as dashi stock and even cheese. Vegan meals can be ordered a day beforehand.

EBISU AND AROUND

恵比寿

Izakaya

★ TONKI

1-1-2 Shimomeguro, Meguro-ku; tel. 03/3491-9928; www.instagram.com/tonkatsu_tonki/?hl=ja; 4pm-8pm Wed.-Mon., closed third Mon. every month; ¥2,100; take Yamanote line to Meguro Station, west exit

This institution a short walk from Meguro Station has been serving tonkatsu since 1939. The exterior may look plain, but slide open the wooden door, lift the curtain, and you'll enter a surprisingly expansive room with an open kitchen full of diligent chefs at work and surrounded by a counter on three sides. Waits are commonplace, especially for a seat on the first floor, where customers can watch the masterful chefs perform. For quicker seating, choose the second floor. Set meals, including rice, trimmings, and miso soup, are ¥1,900 for both fatty and lean cuts of pork.

OJINJO

2-2-10 Ebusi-nishi, Shibuya-ku; tel. 03/5784-1775; www.facebook.com/OJINJO; 5pm-12:30am Mon.-Fri., 4pm-12:30am Sat.-Sun. and holidays; ¥4,000; take Yamanote line to Ebisu Station, west exit

This lively izakaya hidden down a side street in Ebisu is renowned for the quality and variety of its chūhai, or shōchū mixed with soda and freshly squeezed lemon juice. With a menu containing six spins on the classic izakaya beverage (with crushed ice, mint, etc.), it's a great place to get acquainted with this commonly quaffed cocktail, which is often flavored with other types of fruit juice, such as grapefruit, plum, and more. The shōchū-friendly food menu is likewise diverse, from Okinawa stir-fries and grilled fish to oysters. Reserve a few days in advance to snag a spot.

Ramen

AFURI

1117 Bldg. 1F, 1-1-7 Ebisu; Shibuya-ku; tel. 03/5795-0750; http://afuri.com; 11am-5am daily; ¥1,000; take Yamanote line to Ebisu Station, west exit

Just outside the backdoor of the always-boisterous Ebisu Yokochō, you'll find the flagship of hit ramen shop Afuri. Soup stock here is infused with a mix of chicken, seaweed, and seafood, in varying degrees of fattiness. The most popular variety is shio (salt-based) ramen. I recommend selecting the citrus yuzu-infused shio broth with thick hunks of chashu (pork belly). The thin noodles and surprisingly light broth leave you feeling satisfied without the food coma triggered by some varieties of ramen.

Street Food

EBISU YOKOCHŌ

1-7-4 Ebisu, Shibuya-ku; www.ebisu-yokocho.com; 5pm-late daily; ¥3,000; take JR Yamanote line to Ebisu Station, east exit

Tokyo may lack the cred of a city like Bangkok, but you can find pockets of good, gritty street food. In Ebisu Yokochō, a bustling arcade with a retro feel, small izakaya line a narrow concrete foot path, selling everything from grilled fish and yakitori to yakisoba, even raw horse and whale. Somewhat out of sync with the DIY decor—rickety stools, tables made of beer crates—there are even a few wine bars. It gets rowdy on Friday nights when people meet to wash away the cares of the workweek over frosty pints of beer. While you must order drinks from the store where you're seated, it's possible to order food from other establishments from within the yokochō. At the time of writing, some stores were closing earlier than usual due to coronavirus.

SHIBUYA AND AROUND

渋谷

Izakaya

TACHINOMI NAGI

2-20-7 Dogenzaka, Shibuya-ku; tel. 03/6416-5257; http://tachinomi-nagi.com; 5pm-midnight Mon.-Sat., closed on public holidays; ¥3,000; take JR, Ginza, Inokashira, Fukutoshin, Hanzōmon, Tōkyū Tōyoko lines to Shibuya Station, Hachikō exit

Tucked down a quiet street on Dogenzaka's "love hotel hill," this standing bar—izakaya, really—is a great place to sample nihonshū (commonly known as sake in the west), paired with casual nibbles. It's fronted by a row of bamboo and bottles of the brew it specializes in. In particular, the shop is known for its collection of nihonshū brewed in Fukushima Prefecture. The staff are experts at pairing your booze of choice with food, from sashimi to vegetable medleys to rice dishes. Nihonshū-tasting flights start from a surprisingly reasonable ¥500. Recommended.

★ SHIRUBEE

Pinecrest Kitazawa 1F, 2-18-2 Kitazawa, Setagaya-ku; tel. 03/3413-3785; https://raku-co.com/?page_id=26; 5:30pm-midnight (last food order 11pm, last drink order 11:30pm) daily; ¥4,000; take Keio-Inokashira, Odakyu lines to Shimokitazawa Station, south exit

Shirubee is the place to come for the quintessential izakaya experience. Pull aside the white curtains in front of the door that reads "Izaka-ya-ism," slip off your shoes inside, and take a seat. At the center of the buzzing restaurant is its large open kitchen, where you can see the energetic team of chefs at work.

1

2

3

4

The friendly staff will be happy to help you navigate the diverse menu, also available in English, which features classics such as sashimi, nikujaga (stewed beef with potatoes and onions), and more. These staples are complemented by a number of innovative fusion dishes like cheese tofu and avocado-tuna dip with toast. The simplest (and most recommended) option is the ¥4,000 nomihōdai (all-you-can-drink) plan, which comes with a set meal and lasts 90 minutes. The place gets packed; reservations are recommended.

Sushi

UMEGAOKA SUSHI NO MIDORI SHIBUYA-TEN

4F Mark City East, 1-12-3 Dogenzaka, Shibuya-ku; tel. 03/5458-0002; www.sushinomidori.co.jp/shop.php?name=shibuya; 11am-10pm (last order 9:45pm) Mon.-Sat. and holidays, 11am-10pm (last order 9:30pm) Sun.; courses from ¥1,800, a la carte from ¥50; take JR lines, Tōyoko line, or Ginza, Fukutoshin, Hanzōmon subway lines to Shibuya Station

For cost performance and convenience, this sushi joint is hard to beat. Your choices will range from sea urchin to a whole boiled conger eel. Sushi platters come with green tea and miso soup. Unfortunately, with excellent value comes wait times. If you'd like to avoid the longest wait times, aim to come for a late lunch (around 2:30pm), a late dinner (try 9pm), or during off hours (between the lunch and dinner rush). Also note that the restaurant has eight branches, so have a look at the website and consider another branch to avoid the heaviest crowds.

Cafés

FUGLEN

1-16-11 Tomigaya, Shibuya-ku; tel. 03/3481-0884; www.fuglen.com; 8am-10pm Mon.-Tues., 8am-1am Wed.-Thurs., 8am-2am Fri., 9am-2am Sat., 9am-midnight Sun.; café from ¥250, bar from ¥1,250; take Chiyoda line to Yoyogi-kōen Station, exit 2

A sister cafe to Oslo's fashionable coffee spot of the same name, Fuglen is the central nexus in Tomigaya, an enclave for in-the-know locals on the backside of Shibuya. Although it's firmly on the hipster map, this bar and café has the substance to complement its style. Seating includes a counter, a few tables, and a sofa. They serve excellent coffee and a range of tasty baked goods. From 7pm, they sell well-made cocktails that make for good aperitifs.

CHATEI HATOU

1-15-19 Shibuya, Shibuya-ku; tel. 03/3400-9088; www.instagram.com/hatou_coffee_shibuya/; 11am-11pm daily; ¥1,000; take Yamanote line to Shibuya Station, east exit

With an entrance reminiscent of a lodge in the Alps, Chatei Hatou is a venerable café extolled by serious coffee drinkers the world over, including Blue Bottle Coffee CEO James Freeman. Upon entering, the master selects the cup you'll use from among an eclectic array standing on a shelf behind the counter. A cup from the impressive menu may cost upward of ¥1,500, but if you want a real kissaten experience, it's worth it.

International

LOS BARBADOS

104, 41-26 Udagawachō, Shibuya-ku; tel. 03/3496-7157; www7b.biglobe.ne.jp/~los-barbados; noon-3pm and 6-11pm Mon.-Sat.; plates ¥700-1,100; take JR, Ginza, Inokashira, Fukutoshin, Hanzōmon, Tōkyū Tōyoko lines to Shibuya Station, Hachikō exit

This eight-seat restaurant and bar is an off-the-radar gem in the backstreets of Shibuya, serving surprisingly good African and Middle Eastern fare, including some solid vegetarian options. The cozy space is run by a friendly Japanese couple, Daisuke and Mayumi Uekawa, who developed a passion for the region after spending extended time in central Africa. It's also a bar with a good selection of beer, wine, and rum.

CASA DE SARASA

Shimada Bldg. 2F, 2-25-5 Dogenzaka, Shibuya-ku; tel. 03/5428-6155; www.facebook.com/CasaDeSarasa;

1: Omoide Yokochō 2: yakitori 3: izakaya in Kōenji
4: Sakurai Japanese Tea Experience

Tokyo's Animal Cafés

Tokyo is ground zero for the animal café phenomenon that has swept the globe. What started with the humble cat café—essentially, a café where felines are simply allowed to play, purr, eat, sleep, and strut around as they please—has grown to include a mushrooming menagerie of staggering variety. Today, you can find cafés inhabited by owls, rabbits, dogs, foxes, hedgehogs, snakes, penguins—the list goes on.

A core concern when visiting any animal café is the welfare of its critters. Some things to consider: Are the animals caged? Do they have space to roam? Do they seem at ease? Do they get breaks from customers' attention? Are they well-fed, scrubbed, and groomed? Before visiting, do your research on a given animal café, and on whether a given species may not be well-suited to the experience of being in such an environment. Owl cafés, in particular, have been the subject of animal rights activists' ire for confining the birds and exposing them to excessive contact with people—neither healthy things for birds of prey. Ditto for dogs, which seem overly cooped up in many of the cafés that keep them.

With these ethical concerns in mind, here are some of Tokyo's best animal cafés.

TEMARI NO OSHIRO CAT CAFÉ

Kichijōji Petit Mura, 2-33-2 Kichijōji-Honchō, Musashino-shi; tel. 0422/27-5962; https://temarinooshiro.com; 10am-9pm daily; ¥1,400 before 7pm and ¥1,000 after 7pm Mon.-Fri., ¥1,800 before 7pm and ¥1,200 after 7pm Sat., Sun., and holidays, all prices before tax; take Chūo, Sōbu, Keio-Inokashira lines to Kichijoji Station

Beyond a whimsical facade that gives you the impression you're entering a fairy-tale realm, around 20 felines lounge on platforms, sleep in nooks, and frolic with customers. As a bonus, the cat-shaped sweets are surprisingly good. Children under 10 are not admitted.

KOTORI CAFÉ UENO

1-8-6 Ueno Sakuragi, Taitō-ku; tel. 03/6427-5115; http://kotoricafe.jp; 11am-6pm daily; no cover charge, one-drink minimum; take Chiyoda line to Nezu Station

At this colorful, chirpy café in Ueno, you'll meet a range of avians, from a cockatoo and parrots to canaries and lovebirds. Most of the time the birds are left to flap and sing in peace, but five-minute petting sessions are available for ¥500. During peak time, you may be limited to a one-hour stay.

MIPIG CAFÉ

1F Barubizon, 1-15-4 Jingūmae, Shibuya-ku; tel. 03/6384-5899; https://mipig.cafe; 10am-8pm daily; ¥1,100 per hour, one-drink minimum; take Yamanote line to Harajuku Station, Omotesandō exit, or Chiyoda, Fukutoshin lines to Meiji-Jingūmae Station, exit 2

At this welcoming café in the heart of teenybopper Harajuku, you can play with a breed of cute micro pigs as you quaff coffee. Due to its wild popularity, reservations are required and can be booked ahead through the website (in English).

CHIKU CHIKU CAFÉ

2F Daikyoushibuya Bldg., 1-13-5 Shibuya, Shibuya-ku; tel. 03/6450-6673; https://hedgehoghome.cafe; 1pm-7pm daily; ¥1,300 per 30 minutes, ¥2,400 per 60 minutes; take JR, Ginza, Inokashira, Fukutoshin, Hanzōmon, Tōkyū Tōyoko lines to Shibuya Station, Hachikō exit

This cheerful café ups the cuteness ante once more with hedgehogs. Here you can pet, feed, and photograph the furry little mammals, which have ample room to explore miniature settings made to look like traditional Japanese-style tatami rooms, classrooms, lavatories, and more. Reservations are recommended and can be made in English online.

3pm-10pm daily; ¥3,000; take JR, Ginza, Inokashira, Fukutoshin, Hanzōmon, Tōkyū Tōyoko lines to Shibuya Station, Hachikō exit

Good Mexican food is hard to come by in Japan. Thanks to this restaurant, Tokyoites in need of an authentic taco fix now have relief. The impressive variety of taco fillings ranges from stewed pork with freshly squeezed orange and herb to stir-fried shrimp in garlic oil. There are plenty of sides—cheese-filled battered jalapenos, totopos with guacamole, nachos—and the drink menu is extensive, with a range of Mexican beers and a long list of tequilas. It's a little bit on the pricy side, but the quality and frankly, rarity, of the offerings makes up for it. Recommended.

HARAJUKU AND AOYAMA

原宿, 青山

Okonomiyaki

SAKURA TEI

3-20-1 Jingūmae, Shibuya-ku; tel. 03/3479-0039; www.sakuratei.co.jp/en; 11am-9pm Mon.-Thurs., 11am-10pm Fri.-Sun. and holidays; from ¥1,050; take Yamanote line to Harajuku Station, Takeshita exit

Connected to **Design Festa Gallery** is a bright, lively restaurant called Sakura Tei. While some okonomiyaki joints cook the dish for you, here you do it yourself on a teppanyaki plate at your table. Don't fret; there's a photo guide at each table instructing you how to properly get the job done. The English-language menu includes both okonomiyaki and monjayaki (batter topped with meat, vegetables, and seafood, then cooked to a loose texture resembling a scrambled egg), from classics like pork, kimchi, and seafood medleys, to the experimental, like a carbonara version.

Tonkatsu

MAISEN

4-8-5 Jingūmae, Shibuya-ku; tel. 0120/428-485; https://mai-sen.com; 11am-9pm (last order 8pm) daily; ¥1,680-7,700; take Ginza, Hanzomon, Chiyoda lines to Omotesandō Station, exit A2

Set in what used to be a bathhouse, with soaring ceilings and a small garden in back, Maisen is a popular and excellent tonkatsu restaurant located amid the back lanes of Harajuku. You can choose from a range of pork dishes, from hire katsu (pork filet) to rosu katsu (pork loin). Set meals come with a small dish of pickled radish, rice, and soup.

Cafés

KOFFEE MAMEYA

4-15-3 Jingūmae, Shibuya-ku; tel. 03/5413-9422; www.koffee-mameya.com; 10am-6pm daily; ¥500; take Ginza, Hanzomon lines to Omotesandō Station, exit A2

Koffee Mameya is the new incarnation of once legendary Omotesandō Koffee, which closed in 2015. Fortunately, the same impeccable standards of quality have been maintained. There's no seating at this popular bean specialist, but it's a great place to grab a coffee or espresso to go while exploring Harajuku's backstreets. If you want to purchase beans to brew at home, 15-20 types are available, sourced from five roasteries.

★ SAKURAI JAPANESE TEA EXPERIENCE

Spiral Bldg. 5F, 5-6-23 Minami-Aoyama, Minato-ku; tel. 03/6451-1539; www.sakurai-tea.jp; 11am-10pm Mon.-Fri., 11am-8pm Sat.-Sun.; tea ¥1,850, tasting course ¥4,900; take Ginza, Hanzomon lines to Omotesandō Staion, exit B1

After spending 12 years becoming a master in the realm of tea, Shinya Sakurai finally felt ready to open his exceptional Aoyama café, Sakurai Japanese Tea Experience. This attractive café, which doubles as a chic, innovative tea-ceremony space, is stocked with jars containing tea leaves sourced from around Japan, which Sakurai personally travels to procure. Single varieties are priced at ¥400 each; for the full experience, try a a tasting course of five different varieties (it costs ¥4,900 but is worth it). The range of options is eye-opening, with some tea served with surprising accents, like lime, or infused with spirits. Some tea leaves can be eaten after being prepared. Paired with a traditional Japanese sweet, the combination is exquisite.

International

NARISAWA

2-6-15 Minami Aoyama, Minato-ku; tel. 03/5785-0799; www.narisawa-yoshihiro.com/en/openning.html; noon-3 pm (last order 1pm) and 6pm-10pm (last order 7pm), Tues.-Sat. with other sporadic closings; lunch ¥27,000, dinner ¥32,400; take Ginza, Hanzomon, Ōedo lines to Aoyama-itchōme Station, exit 5

At Narisawa, creativity and attunement to nature are the hallmarks of the culinary creations of pioneering chef Yoshihiro Narisawa. Working away in his immaculate Aoyama kitchen, Narisawa brings a singular sensibility to a host of European cooking techniques—primarily French. He forages his own herbs and adds seasonal touches to every meal. His visually striking creations range from wagyu beef to edible soil, and a range of innovative desserts. The restaurant has an extensive selection of wines and cheeses, too. Reservations for a given month are accepted from the beginning of the month prior through the restaurant's website. In other words, if you want to reserve a table in September, you can reserve from August 1. Be prepared to act promptly when the reservation period officially opens.

SHINJUKU AND AROUND

新宿

Izakaya

★ NIHON SAISEI SAKABA

Marunaka Bldg. 1F, 3-7-3 Shinjuku, Shinjuku-ku; tel. 03/3354-4829; http://ishii-world.jp/nihonsaisei/shinjuku3; 3pm-11pm (last order 10:30pm) Mon.-Sat.; ¥3,000; take Marunouchi, Fukutoshin, Toei Shinjuku lines to Shinjuku San-chōme Station, exit C3

It's all about the pig at Nihon Saisei Sakaba, a standing-only izakaya that serves essentially every pig part, grilled, on a stick. This Shinjuku institution has a friendly, gritty ambience, with smoke wafting into the street where customers stand around makeshift tables made of empty beer crates and drink from frosty mugs. Have a look at the English menu: colon, spleen, womb, even birth canal. Don't worry; there are standard grilled bits, too. For a fun night out with the chance to mingle with fellow customers, this spot is hard to beat.

Kaiseki

KOZUE

Park Hyatt Tokyo 40F, 3-7-1-2 Nishinjuku, Shinjuku-ku; tel. 03/5323-3460; http://restaurants.tokyo.park.hyatt.co.jp/en/koz.html; 11:30am-2:30pm and 5:30pm-10pm; lunch from ¥5,500, dinner from ¥16,500; take Ōedo line to Tochomae Station, exit A4

Kozue serves haute Japanese cuisine with fabulous views on the 40th floor of the Park Hyatt Tokyo. The high-end kaiseki restaurant serves seasonal fare—for instance, fugu in winter, freshly foraged mushrooms in autumn—in artisan-made earthenware, porcelain, and lacquer dishes. Views of the city at night are outstanding year-round, and on clear afternoons you'll be able to see Mount Fuji. It's a spectacular dining experience. Book either online or over the phone a week or more ahead to be on the safe side, and make a special request for a window seat.

Street Food

OMOIDE YOKOCHŌ

1-2 Nishi-Shinjuku, Shinjuku-ku; http://shinjuku-omoide.com; take Yamanote line to Shinjuku Station, west exit

This atmospheric alley, lit by red lanterns and filled with smoke, is packed with small, gritty bars and restaurants serving down-and-dirty fare consisting of animal parts and vegetables cooked over an open flame, washed down with prodigious amounts of booze. It once lacked public restrooms—hence its colloquial name, "Piss Alley." Thankfully, restrooms with dubious levels of privacy are now crammed into one part of the alley. The colorful lanes run alongside the train tracks on the west side of Shinjuku Station, though the area is best reached via a tunnel that cuts under the train tracks near the East Exit. Talk of redevelopment is frequent, but for now the structures still stand in all their dilapidated glory.

As for picking a restaurant, **Asadachi** (1-2-14 Nishi-Shinjuku, Shinjuku-ku; tel. 03/3342-1083; noon-11pm Tues.-Sun.; average ¥3,000) is a lively spot. More mysterious entries on the unconventional menu include exotic fare such as raw pig testicles and grilled salamander; other options include grilled salmon belly, mushrooms, and grated daikon, and boiled trip. Look for the turtle shells hanging over the counter.

And for drinks, try **Albatross** (1-2-11 Nishi-Shinjuku, Shinjuku-ku; tel. 03/5929-8756; www.alba-s.com/#/f3; 5pm-2am Sun.-Thurs., 5pm-5am Fri.-Sat.), a classic watering hole decked out in chandeliers and red velvet that occupies three cramped floors. The top floor is a partially covered rooftop balcony with *Blade Runner*-like views of Shinjuku at night. Note that a ¥300 per person table charge applies.

Tempura

TEMPURA TSUNAHACHI

3-31-8 Shinjuku, Shinjuku-ku; tel. 03/3352-1012; www.tunahachi.co.jp/en; 11am-10:30pm (last order 10pm) daily; lunch from ¥1,540, dinner from ¥2,530; take Yamanote line to Shinjuku Station, south exit

Tempura Tsunahachi is the perfect place to eat excellent tempura that doesn't break the bank. Housed in an old wooden building, the shop has been serving customers from kabuki actors to pro baseball stars since 1923. If you go for lunch, sets start from ¥1,500, which is downright cheap for the level of quality compared to similar spots. Don't be shocked if there's a line out front when it opens for lunch. This is a great, cost-effective option if you're willing to wait.

Udon

TSURUTONTAN UDON

Amimoto Bldg. B1F, 2-26-3 Kabukichō, Shinjuku-ku; tel. 03/5287-2626; www.tsurutontan.co.jp/shop/shinjuku/; 11am-8pm daily; ¥980-1,980; take Yamanote line to Shinjuku Station, east exit

Tsurutontan Udon boasts an expansive menu packed with photos of the numerous creative spins the shop puts on this wheat flour-based noodle dish. It's a good choice for a meal before or after a night out. There are both hot and cold dishes, prepared using both Japanese and overtly Western flavors like carbonara.

AKIHABARA AND UENO

秋葉原，上野

Kushiage

HANTEI

2-12-15 Nezu, Bunkyo-ku; tel. 03/3828-1440; http://hantei.co.jp; 11:30am-2pm and 5pm-9:30pm Tues.-Sun., closed Tues. if Mon. is a holiday; lunch ¥3,200-4,300, dinner from ¥5,000-7,000; take Chiyoda line to Nezu Station, exit 2

Pull back the curtain and step inside Hantei, set in an old three-story wooden building that hints at what the rest of this charming neighborhood once looked like. Kushiage, or deep-fried vegetables, meat, and fish on sticks is the specialty at this old-school restaurant. Lunch courses consist of either 8 or 12 skewers. For dinner, servers bring out six sticks at first, with the option to call for six additional sticks (¥1,500) or three (¥800) at a time. Diners also have the choice of adding either white rice, pickles, and red-bean miso soup, or rice topped with kelp, seaweed, and pickles (¥600).

Ramen

KIKANBŌ

2-10-9 Kajichō, Chiyoda-ku; tel. 03/6206-0239; http://kikanbo.co.jp; 11am-9:30pm Mon.-Sat., 11am-4pm Sun.; ¥1,000; take Chūō, Sōbu lines to Kanda Station, east exit, or walk 8 minutes south of Akihabara Station, Electric Town exit

This restaurant's name translates to "Ogre's iron club," and after experiencing the kick from a bowl of ramen at this well-loved noodle spot, you'll understand why. You'll have to choose your spice level (1 to 5) for kara (chili) and shibi (sansho pepper, akin to the mouth-numbing pepper served in much Sichuan-style Chinese cuisine). The broth is made from a mix of miso, meat, and fish, and the noodles

☆ Tokyo's Culinary Alleys

One of the great experiences of any trip to Tokyo is a visit to the city's atmospheric alleyways known as yokochō, preferably with a twofold agenda: eating grilled meats and swilling back draft beer alongside locals. Smoky, crowded, friendly, sometimes even rowdy, the alleys offer a wonderful way to get up close and personal with Tokyo's earthier and historic side, as well as to make connections with the locals. As an added bonus, you get amazing food at a bargain price. Don't be afraid of the offal. It can be surprisingly good.

A growing trend of new shops opening in some of the city's trendier yokochō has added a buzz around them in recent years. So you've come at a fortunate time. Lucky you, these amazing alleyways are scattered all around the city. Besides **Omoide Yokochō** (page 118), **Kōenji Gādo-shita** (page 123), and **Ebisu Yokochō** (page 113), here are some other culinary alleyways worth visiting:

NOMBEI YOKOCHŌ

1-25-10 Shibuya, Shibuya-ku

"Drunkard's Alley," a 1-minute walk from Shibuya Crossing, is another classic yokochō, firmly on the tourist radar but retaining its old-school atmosphere. To reach it from Shibuya Station's Hachiko exit, cross Shibuya Crossing, turn right and walk under the train tracks, where you'll see the alleyway on your left, lined with hanging lanterns. A few good spots are **Tight** (1-25-10, Shibuya-ku; tel. 03/3499-7668; www.2004-tight.com; 6pm-2am Mon.-Sat.), an appropriately named bar squeezed into a remarkably tiny space, and **Bar Piano** (tel. 03/5467-0258; opening times vary, generally 8pm-late daily), which was visited by the late globe-trotting chef, writer, and food personality Anthony Bourdain.

AMEYA YOKOCHŌ

4-chōme to 6-chōme Ueno, Taitō-ku

This jumble of streets beside and under the elevated train tracks a few minutes' walk south of Ueno Station is known as "Ameyoko" by locals, named for the abundance of candy (ame) that

are topped with hunks of pork and other fixings (bean sprouts, baby corn, optional boiled egg for ¥100). The fiery theme is reinforced by an all-black interior, demon masks hanging from the walls, and taiko (traditional drum) soundtrack. Recommended for those with a penchant for spice, but proceed with caution.

Cafés

KAYABA COFFEE

6-1-29 Yanaka, Taitō-ku; tel. 03/5832-9896; www.facebook.com/kayabacoffee/; 8am-11pm Mon.-Sat., 8am-6pm Sun.; a la carte ¥250-600, lunch sets ¥1,000; take Keihin-Tōhoku, Yamanote, Keisei lines to Nippori Station, north exit, or Chiyoda line to Nezu Station

Housed in a traditional wooden home built in 1916, Kayaba Coffee was founded by Kayaba Inosuke and his wife Kimi in 1938. This charming institution is a stellar example of a kissaten, as Tokyo's retro coffee houses are known. About 5 minutes' walk west of Ueno-kōen, this café is a local landmark with its ambience intact, from the yellow sign out front and retro furniture to the dark wood paneling and brick counter. The menu consists of classic kissaten fare like egg sandwiches and, of course, great coffee. Note that queues do form sometimes, particularly during weekend lunch hours.

ASAKUSA AND RYOGOKU

浅草, 両国

Izakaya

OTAFUKU

1-6-2 Senzoku, Taitō-ku; tel. 03/3871-2521; https://otafuku.ne.jp; 5pm-11pm (last order 10pm) Tues.-Fri.,

was sold here in the postwar years. Ame also denotes "America," as black-market American goods were also hawked in the area after the war. The mostly outdoor market has an indoor mall, where you'll find all manner of cheap clothing and sneakers. Outside, some 500 stalls and hole-in-the-wall eateries make this one of Tokyo's most sprawling and bustling marketplaces. A good starting point is **Tachinomi Kadokura** (Forum Aji Bldg. 1F, 6-13-1 Ueno, Taitō-ku; tel. 03/3832-5335; http://taishoen.co.jp/kadokura; 11am-11pm daily, last order 10:30pm). This no-frills, local bar serves cheap, delicious pub fare: sashimi, a breaded and fried ham cutlet, an omelet with vegetables grilled on a hotplate at your table. It all goes down well with beer. An English menu is available.

Harmonica Yokochō

HARMONICA YOKOCHŌ

1-1-2 Honchō, Musashino-shi; tel. 0422/27-6820; http://hamoyoko.jp/menu/kichijoji_tecchan; 3pm-midnight Mon.-Fri., noon-midnight Sat.-Sun. and holidays; ¥3,000

Harmonica Yokochō is another of Tokyo's culinary alleys in the neighborhood of Kichijōji. It's a friendly local haunt and a fantastic option if you'd like to veer off the tourist trail, and one of its numerous eateries is **Tetchan,** a funky yakitori joint designed by famed architect Kengo Kuma with risqué wall art downstairs. This lively spot has a handful of tables, a long wrap-around bar that looks onto the kitchen, and a few standing tables. The menu includes a tasty range of grilled chicken on skewers, a bit of pork, lamb, and beef, and vegetable side dishes.

4pm-10pm (last order 9pm) Sat.-Sun. and holidays Mar.-Sept., 4pm-11pm (last order 10pm) Tues.-Fri., 4pm-10pm (last order 9pm) Oct.-Feb.; a la carte from ¥110, courses from ¥2,750; take Ginza line to Tawaramachi Station, exit 3, or take Ginza or Asakusa line to Asakusa Station, exit 6

Fitting for this old-school side of town, this shop, entered through a path marked by a large paper lantern and lined by bamboo fencing, has been serving oden for a century. This dish, a classic at Japanese izakayas, consists of a delicate broth made from a dashi (stock) of kombu (kelp), bonito, and soy sauce, within which bob cabbage rolls, eggs, fish cakes, daikon, and a variety of peculiar looking items like shinodamaki (fried tofu containing a concoction of meat, veg, and seafood). The menu, which also includes sundy izakaya staples (sashimi, grilled vegetables, and meat) is hand-scrawled in lovely, flowing calligraphy strokes. There's an extensive sake list too.

Ramen

RAMEN YOROIYA

1-36-7 Asakusa, Taitō-ku; tel. 03/3845-4618; https://yoroiya.jp; 11am-8:30pm Mon.-Fri., 11am-9pm Sat.-Sun. and holidays; ¥1,000; take Ginza or Asakusa line to Asakusa Station, exit 1

The ramen at this Asakusa institution is delicious, and service is fast, friendly, and (mostly) off the tourist track. Ramen Yoroiya specializes in ramen served in a shoyu (soy sauce-based) broth. This style of ramen, usually topped with a double-yolk boiled egg, originated right in the neighborhood. While it's less crowded than many eateries around Sensō-ji, which can be crammed during lunch hours, a queue sometimes forms during peak hours. It moves relatively quickly, but to avoid this, arrive early or in mid-afternoon after the rush passes. An English menu is available.

Kaiseki

WAENTEI-KIKKŌ

2-2-13 Asakusa, Taitō-ku; tel. 03/5828-8833; https://waentei-kikko.com/english; 11:30am-2:30pm and 5:30pm-10:30pm Thurs.-Tues.; lunch ¥2,500-5,000, dinner ¥6,800-10,800; take Ginza or Asakusa line to Asakusa Station, exit 1

Set in an old house near Sensō-ji, Waentei-kikkō has tatami-mat floors, sliding doors framed with translucent paper, dark wooden rafters, and most importantly, four daily performances (12:15pm, 1:30pm, 6:30pm, and 8pm) by Fukui Kodai, one of the restaurant's managers and a master at the three-stringed Tsugaru-shamisen. The restaurant serves seasonal set meals for both lunch and dinner, the former more casual in a bento box and the latter in the form of a kaiseki course. This is a wonderful way to experience traditional Japanese music in an intimate setting. Reservations are recommended.

Shabu-Shabu/Sukiyaki

ASAKUSA IMAHAN

3-1-12 Nishi-Asakusa, Taitō-ku; tel. 03/3841-1114; www.asakusaimahan.co.jp/english; 11:30am-9:30pm (last order 8:30pm) daily; lunch ¥1,870-11,000, dinner ¥8,800-27,500; take Tsukuba Express to Asakusa Station, exit A2, or Ginza line to Tawaramachi Station, exit 3

Take a seat at the Asakusa branch of this butcher-cum-sukiyaki restaurant. Watch as the server places succulent cuts of perfectly marbled wagyu into a soy-based soup in the pot on your table, heated by a flame, with mushrooms, tofu, green onions, and other vegetables. When the dish is cooked just enough, pull out a slice of beef and dip it in the small dish of raw free-range (and perfectly safe) egg. It's pricey but delicious.

Cafés

CAFÉ MEURSAULT

2-1-5 Kaminarimon, Taitō-ku; tel. 03/3843-8008; http://cafe-meursault.com/index.html; 11am-8pm daily; a la carte from ¥300, lunch from ¥1,100, dinner from ¥2,300; take Ginza or Asakusa line to Asakusa Station, exit A2a

Escape Asakusa's buzz at this airy riverside cafe and enjoy the views from its expansive windows, with Tokyo Skytree looming in the backdrop. The menu covers the gamut: coffee, tea, cakes, pasta, quiche, gratin, curry, stew and more.

WESTERN TOKYO

Izakaya

DACHIBIN

3-2-13 Kōenji-Kita, Suginami-ku; tel. 03/3337-1352; www.dachibin.com; 5pm-5am daily; ¥3,000; take Chūō, Sobu lines to Kōenji Station, north exit

Dachibin serves great Okinawan fare made with ingredients sourced from the southern islands, including a healthy list of awamori, their fiery variety of shōchū. The atmosphere is rowdy and inviting, the staff is friendly, and once a month there's a live jam session featuring the sanshin, a three-stringed instrument native to Okinawa. This place has been doing a brisk business for more than three decades.

Soup Curry

ROJIURA CURRY SAMURAI

2-27-2 Kichijōji-Honchō, Musashino-shi; tel. 0422/27-6043; https://samurai-curry.com/shop_kichijoji/; 11:30am-3:30pm and 5:30pm-10:30pm daily; ¥1,500; take Chūō, Keio-Inokashira lines to Kichijōji Station, north exit

Here, you'll find excellent ingredients, from Hokkaido-sourced vegetables to thick cuts of fatty pork, with no additives and a surprisingly spicy kick: This soup curry restaurant with roots in Sapporo is the real deal. The list of customizable options is extensive, from cheese topping to extra helpings of vegetables like burdock root and okra. The sakusaku (crispy) broccoli is amazingly flavorsome. Beware: even at the lower end of the spice spectrum—there are 10 levels—you'll likely be putting out the fire with regular sips of water.

Street Food

KŌENJI GĀDO-SHITA

3-chōme Kōenji-Minami, Suginami-ku; ¥3,000; take Chūō, Sobu lines to Kōenji Station, north exit

Perhaps the most legitimate street food option of Tokyo's vast array of alleyways known as yokochō, Gādo-shita is a hodgepodge of smoky, boisterous bars and restaurants with seating both inside and out, running along the train tracks west of Kōenji Station. It gets rowdy on weekends and is a great place for a night out with locals in one of Tokyo's most bohemian neighborhoods.

International

BOLBOL

2F, 3-2-15 Kōenjikita Suginami; tel. 03/3223-3277; http://bolbol.jp/english.html; 11:30am-3pm and 5pm-10pm Thurs.-Tues.; lunch ¥650-1,000, dinner ¥1,000-4,600; take Chūō, Sobu lines to Kōenji Station, north exit

BolBol offers excellent Persian food and is run by a friendly owner from Iran and his Japanese wife. The atmosphere evokes Iran, from the Persian rugs on the floor to the ornate tableware and instruments hanging on the wall. Try the dinner course, which includes buttered rice, lamb, and chicken on skewers, grilled tomatoes, and pickled vegetables. Combine it with draft beer or wine. If you're so inclined, relax with a hookah after dinner. Belly dance shows that encourage participation from willing audience members are held on Friday and Saturday nights. The showtimes for these performances vary, but are usually from 8pm or later.

Cafés

BLUE SKY COFFEE

4-1-1 Inokashira, Mitaka-shi; http://blueskycoffee.jp; 10am-6pm Thurs.-Tues., closed on some rainy days; ¥250; take Chūō, Sōbu, Keio-Inokashira lines to Kichijōji Station, park exit, or Keio-Inokashira line to Inokashira-kōen Station

Housed in charmingly worn wooden building, this café sits right in the heart of Inokashira-kōen. They brew great coffee using top-notch equipment and sell a smattering of sweets, too. A great spot for a to-go coffee in the park.

CAFÉ DU LIÈVRE (BUNNY HOUSE)

1-19-43 Gotenyama, Musashino-shi; tel. 0422/43-0015; 10:30am-7pm (last order 6pm) daily; ¥1,500; take Chūō, Sōbu, Keio-Inokashira lines to Kichijōji Station, park exit

Set in the forested backside of **Inokashira-kōen,** this charming café with accents of French decor is a great stop for a bite either on the way to or after visiting the nearby **Ghibli Museum.** Using high-quality buckwheat flour sourced from Hokkaido, the restaurant and café whips up tasty galettes with toppings like eggs, pesto, tomatoes, mushrooms, and other veggies. There are also sweet crêpes and a handful of tasty curry-and-rice dishes.

Bars and Nightlife

Befitting a city its size, Tokyo has seemingly infinite options to drink, dance, and mingle once the sun goes down: swanky cocktail bars, thumping clubs, party boats, whisky dens, rambling red-light zones, and venues where indie rockers jam.

For the connoisseur, the capital is a perfect place to get acquainted with Japan's unique alcoholic heritage, from nihonshū to shōchū. It's also home to visionary mixologists who craft cocktails in dreamy hideaways, and masters of malt who helm bars stocked with encyclopedic whisky menus.

Audiophiles will appreciate the city's DJ bars and nightclubs, which are renowned for their exacting standards when it comes to sound, as well as their carefully curated artist lineups. In hipster enclaves like

Shimokitazawa, not far from Shibuya, venues host live performances by indie bands and rowdy punk rockers. If you prefer something with a bit more swing, the city's love of live jazz runs deep, too. Visit **Tokyo Dross** (http://tokyodross.blogspot.jp) for extensive gig listings with an underground bent, from electronic to punk, and **Tokyo Jazz Site** (http://tokyojazzsite.com) to explore the capital's deep jazz scene, from old-school cafés with extraordinary sound systems to underground haunts well off the tourist path.

And in the concrete canyons of **Shinjuku,** the country's largest red-light zone is found in the neon-splashed streets of **Kabukichō.** Here, you can watch a robot battle or drink your way through a maze of pint-sized bars where five is a crowd. A brief stroll away, you'll also find Tokyo's friendly gay district, **Shinjuku Ni-chōme.**

Above all else, exploring Tokyo at night reveals the city with its hair down. Be prepared to make some new friends.

Nightlife Tours

If you're interested in joining a tour down the rabbit hole that is nightlife in Tokyo, here are a few to consider.

- **Backstreet Guides** (https://thebackstreetguides.com; 6 hours, Wed., Fri., Sun.; ¥13,000, includes some food and drinks): Eat yakitori and down drinks in Shibuya and Shinjuku, ending up in the rowdy district of Roppongi.
- **Tokyo Urban Adventures** (www.urbanadventures.com; 2.5-3 hours; ¥11,065, includes snacks, two drinks): Guides lead you through a tour of Shinjuku's endless array of bars and restaurants, with a focus on the red-light district of **Kabukichō** and the drinking dens of **Golden Gai.**
- **"Shibuya Stray Cat"** (www.airbnb.com/experiences/64941; 5 hours; ¥10,000, includes drinks): Go deeper with "Shibuya Stray Cat" Tatsuya, a seasoned journalist and bona fide character who has been drinking and befriending his way through Shibuya's backstreets for decades. His tours veer well off the beaten track.

GINZA AND MARUNOUCHI

銀座, 丸の内

Bars

BAR HIGH FIVE

Efflore Ginza 5 Bldg. B1F, 5-4-15 Ginza, Chūō-ku; tel. 03/3571-5815; www.barhighfive.com; 5pm-1am Mon.-Sat. (last entry 11:30pm); table/cover charge ¥1,000; take Ginza, Marunouchi, Hibiya lines to Ginza Station, exit B5

Located in a basement, amid the Ginza area's glitz, is Bar High Five, with mixologist extraordinaire Hidetsugu Ueno at the helm and a long counter facing an impressive wall of bottles. In addition to world-renowned cocktails, the bar offers a serious selection of scotch and whisky. The owner speaks fluent English, too. This probably won't be the best choice if you're looking to socialize—the atmosphere is a bit buttoned-down and there's a clearly written list of rules (posted in English on the bar's website) that must be upheld by customers. But if you're a keen connoisseur of nuanced drinks, this is among the very best bars in all Asia.

300BAR NEXT

Murasaki Bldg. B1F, 1-2-14 Yūrakuchō, Chiyoda-ku; tel. 03/3593-8300; www.300bar-next.com; 5pm-11pm Mon.-Thurs., 5pm-2am Fri., 3pm-2am Sat., 3pm-11pm Sun. and holidays; take Ginza, Hibiya, Marunouchi lines to Ginza Station, exit C2, or Yamanote, Yūrakuchō lines to Yūrakuchō Station, Hibiya exit

For a budget option in Ginza—yes, you read that right—300Bar Next can't be beat, with all drinks and food costing only ¥300 per item. If you happen to be in Ginza and don't feel like splashing out, this is your best option. The bartenders are friendly and know their drinks (and make a mean mojito), and the crowd is lively and welcoming. It's a fun place to warm up for a big night out.

Sake 101

In Japanese culture, sake is sacred, worthy of gifting to the gods, inseparable from the cycle of the seasons and the rice harvest. What is popularly known as sake overseas is actually called **nihonshū** (literally: "Japanese alcohol") in Japan, where sake denotes all forms of alcohol, from wine and whisky to beer. That said, even in Japan, sake is sometimes used to refer to nihonshū (i.e. "sake bar" or "sake specialist" would tend to imply nihonshū rather than any other type of alcoholic drink). This fermented, rice-based, 15-18% alcohol drink is often served with fine cuisine. **Shōchū** is its fun-loving distilled cousin, more likely to show up at casual gatherings or rowdy izakayas, usually in the 25-30% alcohol range, and made with a laundry list of potential ingredients, from barley to sweet potatoes to fruits.

To go deeper, check out the books *Food Sake Tokyo* by Tokyo-based culinary extraordinaire Yukari Sakamoto, and *The Complete Guide to Japanese Drinks*, an award-winning ode to Japan's drinkable offerings by Stephen Lyman and Chris Bunting. Then, swing by the **Japan Sake and Shōchū Information Center** (1-6-15 Nishishinbashi, Minato-ku; tel. 03/3519-2091; https://japansake.or.jp/sake/en/jss/information-center/; 10am-6pm Mon.-Fri.) for a crash course with one of the sommeliers on staff.

Once you've grasped the basics, here are some of the best spots to drink nihonshū and shōchū in Tokyo.

- **Sake no Ana:** A Ginza restaurant with a fantastic nihonshū and a sommelier on staff with a knack for food pairing (page 108).
- **Tachinomi Nagi:** A friendly standing izakaya (tachinomi) and nihonshū specialist in Shibuya (page 113).
- **Tachinomi Ryoma:** True to its name (tachinomi means "standing bar"), there are 100 types of shōchū here, which you can drink elbow-to-elbow with salarymen (page 109).
- **Ojinjo:** A lively, tightly packed izakaya in upscale Ebisu renowned for its lemon chūhai (shōchū with soda and fresh lemon juice) (page 113).

TOKYO BAY AREA

東京湾

Night Cruise

JICOO, THE FLOATING BAR

1-10-53 Kaigan, Minato-ku; tel. 03/5733-2939; www.jicoofloatingbar.com; 6pm-9pm daily; ¥3,000 entry; take Yurikamome line to Hinode Station; Yamamote, Keihin-Tohoku lines or Tokyo Monorail to Hamamatsucho Station, or Asakusa, Ōedo lines to Daimon Station

This futuristic-looking boat, complete with bar, DJ deck, and multicolored lights, offers nighttime cruises through Tokyo Bay from Hinode Pier to Odaiba, taking in dazzling views of Rainbow Bridge along the way. Jicoo, The Floating Bar, leaves Hinode Pier at 6pm, 7pm, and 8pm on Thursday, Friday, and Saturday nights. The music and vibe on Thursday and Friday nights are mellower, while Saturday nights get a bit rowdier. It's a fun alternative to partying on land and a good way to see Tokyo's lights from the water.

ROPPONGI AND AROUND

六本木

Bars

AGAVE

DM Bldg. B1F, 7-18-11 Roppongi, Minato-ku; tel. 03/3497-0229; http://agave.jp; 6:30pm-2am Mon.-Thurs., 6:30pm-4am Fri.-Sat.; take Hibiya, Ōedo lines to Roppongi Station, exit 2

Frida Kahlo paintings, Zapata posters, and Mexican tunes waft through a room with orange stone walls. There's a humidor full of cigars, and behind the bar an array of some 550 varieties of tequila and mescal. You'd swear you were in Mexico, but Agave is in fact a basement with the ambience of an upscale cantina. It's located near Roppongi's main drag and is seriously committed to the drink derived from the blue-leafed plant after which it's named. Beware that a single pour from the cheaper end of the menu starts at around ¥1,000, while rarer offerings go for upward of ¥9,000.

BAR GEN YAMAMOTO

1-6-4 Azabu-jūban, Minato-ku; tel. 03/6434-0652; http://genyamamoto.jp; 3pm-11pm Tues.-Sun., closed Aug. 18-28; cover charge ¥1,000; take Namboku, Ōedo lines to Azabu-jūban Station, exit 5B

About 5 minutes' walk southeast of the massive Roppongi Hills complex in the affluent neighborhood of Azabu-Juban, you'll find legendary cocktail wizard Gen Yamamoto at work. Bar Gen Yamamoto is a model of simplicity: eight seats at the bar, no soundtrack, minimalist interior. It's just Yamamoto mixing renowned cocktails using seasonal fruits and vegetables from around Japan: lemons and tomatoes from Shikoku, pears from Hokkaido, grapes from Okayama. Rather than measuring everything like a chemist in a lab, he masterfully eyeballs most ingredients in his concoctions. For the full range of flavors, from sweet to savory, try one of the tasting sets of four, six, or seven drinks (¥4,600, ¥6,800, or ¥7,900). It's not cheap, but the quality and craft are phenomenal.

LIBRARY LOUNGE THESE

2-15-12 Nishi-Azabu, Minato-ku; tel. 03/5466-7331; www.these-jp.com/index2.html; 7pm-late daily; cover charge ¥500; take Ōedo, Hibiya lines to Roppongi Station, exit 2

True to its name, you'll find 3,000 tomes filling shelves at this achingly cool, dimly lit reading room, pronounced "teh-zeh." Retro leather sofas, wooden tables, antique lamps, and wood paneling cast their spell. Cocktails are creative and flavorsome—fruit features heavily—and the food menu is surprisingly tasty too.

EBISU AND AROUND
恵比寿

Bars

BAR TRAM

Swing Bldg. 2F, 1-7-13 Ebisu-Nishi, Shibuya-ku; tel. 03/5489-5514; http://small-axe.net/bar-tram; 6:30pm-2am daily; cover charge ¥500; take Yamanote line to Ebisu Station, west exit, or take Hibiya line to Ebisu Station, west exit

Bar Tram and sister bar **Bar Trench** (DIS Bldg., 1-5-8 Ebisu-Nishi, Shibuya-ku; tel. 03/3780-5291; http://small-axe.net/bar-trench; 6pm-1am Mon.-Sat., 6pm-1am Sun. and holidays; cover charge ¥500) specialize in herbal liqueur and absinthe-infused cocktails. Dimly lit atmospheric hideouts with a whiff of 19th-century Paris about them, both bars are a short walk from Ebisu Station, and just around the corner from each other. The bartenders are dressed for the job—white shirt, necktie, vest—of navigating more than 70 varieties of the green fairy at Bar Tram alone. Bar Trench boasts the largest collection of bitters in Japan and has an equally quirky list of cocktail names. Monkey Gland, anyone? Note that both bars' opening hours were shortened at the time of writing to prevent spread of coronavirus. Check the website to see if they have changed.

Clubs

SOLFA

1-20-5 Aobadai, Meguro-ku; tel. 03/6231-9051; www.nakameguro-solfa.com; opening hours vary by event (check calendar on website); fee varies by event; take Tōkyū Tōyoko line to Nakameguro Station, main exit

Located in the hip neighborhood of Nakameguro, one train stop or a 15-minute walk from Ebisu Station, Solfa is a wonderfully intimate nightclub. The dance floor accommodates up to 100 people, and the lounge can squeeze in a bit more. DJs on deck usually play artfully chosen techno and house, with some hip-hop nights, too. If you feel like going to a more discerning club that isn't an

TOP EXPERIENCE

Japan's Award-Winning Whiskies

whisky at Suntory Yamazaki Distillery

"For relaxing times, make it"—Bill Murray dramatically pauses for effect—"Suntory time." Few could have guessed the heights to which Suntory Whisky, and Japanese whisky in general, would soar back in 2003 when Murray's character uttered this classic line in *Lost in Translation*.

First came the "Best of the Best" nod from *Whisky Magazine* to Japanese whisky maker Nikka for its 10-Year Yoichi in 2001. Then, in 2015, *Whisky Bible* declared Suntory's now-legendary Yamazaki Sherry Cask 2013 the world's best whisky. In the ensuing five years, Japanese whisky sales to the U.S. market skyrocketed 1,000%. Awards haven't stopped rolling in since, with makers like Suntory, Nikka, and Chichibu mopping up global prizes. Most recently, Suntory's Hakushu Single Malt 25 Year Old was crowned best single malt in the 2020 World Whisky Awards.

To learn more about Japanese whisky's stratospheric ascent, check out *Japanese Whisky: The Ultimate Guide to the World's Most Desirable Spirit with Tasting Notes from Japan's Leading Whisky Blogger*, by Brian Ashcraft, and *Whisky Rising: The Definitive Guide to the Finest Whiskies and Distillers of Japan*, by Stefan Van Eycken.

Better yet, taste it for yourself in one (or more) of Tokyo's glut of world-class whisky bars, or visit one of the distilleries covered in this book.

TOKYO'S BEST WHISKY BARS

- **Apollo** (B1F, 8-2-15 Ginza, Chūō-ku; tel. 03/6280-6282; https://zy773372.wixsite.com/website-1; 11:30am-10pm daily, last order 9pm, closed 4pm-5pm Mon.-Fri.; ¥1,000 seating charge): This classy spot in Ginza has a deep whisky selection, a Tom Waits soundtrack, and a friendly, erudite bartender.
- **Bar Urushi** (Uchida Bldg. 2F, 1-12-9 Ebisu-nishi, Shibuya-ku; tel. 03/6416-4518; www.bar-urushi-j.com; 7pm-3am Mon.-Sat.): A casual, sophisticated hideout in Ebisu with an affable bartender and an extensive whisky selection.
- **Cabin Nakameguro** (Riverside Terrace 101, 1-10-23 Naka-Meguro, Meguro-ku; tel. 03/6303-2220; www.cabintokyo.com; 7pm-late Mon.-Thurs., 7pm-2am Fri.-Sat., last order 1am, closed on holidays): A great whisky menu in trendy Ebisu.
- **Zoetrope** (3F, 7-10-14 Nishi-Shinjuku, Shinjuku-ku; tel. 03/3363-0162; www.facebook.com/ShotBarZoetrope/; 5pm-midnight Mon.-Fri., 5pm-11:30pm Sat.; ¥1,000 cover charge): A film buff's bar in Shinjuku with more than 300 bottles of domestic whisky.

VISITING A DISTILLERY

By nature, many of Japan's distilleries are out of the way, as they require lots of space for the whisky to age in peace. But there are a few distilleries that may require only a quick train ride off your planned route for your trip, and here are a few of the best:

- **Suntory Yamazaki Distillery:** This distillery just south of Kyoto, on the way to Osaka, is world-renowned (page 330).
- **Nikka Whisky Yoichi Distillery:** Just an hour outside Sapporo and Hokkaido, a trip to this distillery on Japan's northernmost main island is sure to be extra warming (page 560).

overwhelmingly crowded, sweaty affair, this one's for you.

DEBRIS

B1F, 11-12 Daikanyama-chō, Shibuya-ku; tel. 03/6416-4334; https://debrispace.com; 7pm-midnight Mon.-Sat.; take Tōkyū Tōyoko line to Daikanyama Station

Descend the stairs and open the door to this unique space with a speakeasy vibe. Farther inside, the aesthetic is urbanized Asian chic. The eclectic decor was conceived by a team of artists and creators involved in throwing outdoor festivals around Japan, and the space was launched by the crew that organizes Zipang, an annual beachside electronic music festival. Events range from music—the sound system is serious—to occasional film screenings and art shows. Cocktails are creatively made. P.B. Restaurant, serving Chinese food, is attached on the ground floor.

Live Music

WHAT THE DICKENS!

4F, 1-13-3 Ebisu-Nishi, Shibuya-ku; tel. 03/3780-2099; www.whatthedickens.jp; 5pm-midnight Tues.-Sun.; no cover

This foreigner-friendly faux British pub (shepherd's pie and fish-and-chips included) is a favored haunt of Tokyo's expat community and a healthy number of Japanese regulars, too. Local acts jam every evening.

SHIBUYA AND AROUND

渋谷

Bars

ISHINOHANA

B1F, 3-6-2 Shibuya, Shibuya-ku; tel. 03/5485-8405; http://ishinohana.com; 5pm-midnight Mon.-Sat.; cover charge ¥500; take Yamanote line to Shibuya Station, east exit

It's all about seasonality at Ishinohana, evidenced by the owner's obsession with fresh produce at this cocktail den near Shibuya Station. This bar is also thankfully devoid of the pomp on display at some of Ginza's swankier cocktail lounges. There's a menu with myriad takes on the martini and another featuring only infinite variations on the mojito. Exotic fruits and vegetables are injected into classics, alongside a host of cocktails originating from this shop, including the award-winning Claudia, a martini infused with caramel syrup and pineapple juice.

SG CLUB

1-7-8 Jinnan, Shibuya-ku; tel. 03/6427-0204; http://sg-management.jp; 5pm-1am Sun.-Thurs., 5pm-2am Fri.-Sat.; take JR, Ginza, Inokashira, Fukutoshin, Hanzōmon, Tōkyū Tōyoko lines to Shibuya Station, Hachikō exit

This bar has gained serious cred in recent years, coming in at number nine in the 2020 Asia's 50 Best Bars awards. Helmed by fabled bartender Shingo Gokan, this stylish space is spread over two floors: "Guzzle" (ground floor) and "Sip" (downstairs). Guzzle, the more casual of the two, has a 19th-century saloon vibe with subtle Japanese touches, such as menus printed on paper imprinted with kimono designs from the mid-1800s. Sip is dimly lit by Edo-period street lamps, with a jazz soundtrack and industrial decor. Standout cocktails include the Wagyu Mafia Fashioned, made with bourbon, A5 wagyu beef fat, and organic raw honey, and the LOL (aged Scotch, melon, and aged plum liqueur).

TAP & GROWLER

2-33-6 Kitazawa, Setagaya-ku; tel. 03/6416-8767; www.craftbeers.tokyo; 3pm-midnight daily; take Keio-Inokashira, Odakyu lines to Shimokitazawa Station, east exit

Sip some of the finest craft-brewed suds from across Japan beside in-the-know locals at this friendly Shimokitazawa watering hole. There are some 20 taps, and the focus is on domestic breweries. Seating consists of a few small tables, both indoor and al fresco, and some chairs along the counter. Goes well with a trip to the area for dinner and live music.

Clubs

CONTACT

B2F, 2-10-12 Dogenzaka, Shibuya-ku; tel. 03/6427-8107; www.contacttokyo.com; times and fees vary by event; take JR, Ginza, Inokashira, Fukutoshin, Hanzōmon, Tōkyū Tōyoko lines to Shibuya Station, Hachikō exit

Contact is a great choice for discriminating clubbers. There's a clear separation between the dance space and the bar area. A no-drinks policy is in effect on the dance floor, where flashes of lasers and strobes penetrate air cooled by mist machines, all enveloped by a superb sound system. This venue is the latest entry by organizer Global Hearts, who made a mark in Tokyo's electronic music scene with now-closed Yellow and Air. Keep an eye on the website; major international DJs routinely perform.

Karaoke

KARAOKE RAINBOW

Shibuya Modi 8F, 1-21-3 Shibuya, Shibuya-ku; tel. 03/6455-3240; www.karaoke-rainbow.com/pc/shop/shibuya.html; 11am-5am daily; ¥140 per 30 minutes (until 7pm), ¥380 per 30 minutes (after 7pm), first hour free Mon.-Fri. (until 7pm) and Mon.-Thurs. (after 7pm); take JR, Ginza, Inokashira, Fukutoshin, Hanzōmon, Tōkyū Tōyoko lines to Shibuya Station, Hachikō exit

Karaoke Rainbow is a chic karaoke spot in Shibuya with a large English-language catalog of songs. It nicely dodges the garish neon and worn rooms seen in many chains, instead taking its style cues from, say, Brooklyn: art on the walls, plants, streetlamps, and benches in the corridors. Note that while you do get a free hour of crooning before 7pm on Mon.-Fri. and even after 7pm on Mon.-Thurs., you'll still need to buy a drink during the first hour.

DJ Bars

DJ BAR BRIDGE

Parkside Kyodo Bldg. 10F, 1-25-6 Shibuya, Shibuya-ku; tel. 03/6427-6568; https://bridge-shibuya.com; 8pm-5am daily; cover charge ¥1,000 (includes one drink); take JR, Ginza, Inokashira, Fukutoshin, Hanzōmon, Tōkyū Tōyoko lines to Shibuya Station, Hachikō exit

On the 10th floor of a building next to Shibuya Station, DJ Bar Bridge boasts views of the pedestrian scramble below, a friendly crowd, affordable drinks, and a great roster of resident DJs. Most important, its sound system is fantastic. Given its convenient location, this is a great place to begin a night in the area.

OATH

Tosei Bldg. B1F, 1-6-5 Dogenzaka, Shibuya-ku; tel. 03/3461-1225; www.djbar-oath.com; cover charge ¥1,000 (includes one drink); 8pm-5am Mon.-Sat.; take JR, Ginza, Inokashira, Fukutoshin, Hanzōmon, Tōkyū Tōyoko lines to Shibuya Station, Hachikō exit

Descend the stairs and enter this compact club, a vital node in Tokyo's underground scene that hosts performances by a long list of regular local DJs. Opulent chandeliers hang from the ceiling and ornately kitsch mirrors are mounted on the walls. After paying the cover charge, drinks are priced at a reasonable ¥500. But the real draw is the great sound system.

AOYAMA TUNNEL

Aoyama Bldg. B1F, 4-5-9 Shibuya, Shibuya-ku; http://aoyama-tunnel.com; 8pm-5am Tues.-Sat.; cover charge ¥1,000 (includes one drink); take Ginza, Chiyoda, Hanzōmon lines to Omotesandō Station, exit B1, or take JR, Ginza, Inokashira, Fukutoshin, Hanzōmon, Tōkyū Tōyoko lines to Shibuya Station, Hachikō exit

Aoyama Tunnel is the ideal environment for an all-nighter. Cheap drinks, a good DJ list, and stellar sound keep the revelers coming. It's about a 10-minute trek from Shibuya station up a busy main road rammed with traffic, but once you arrive you'll enjoy yourself. For a change of pace, head upstairs to the worn (and storied) multi-floor club of **Aoyama Hachi** (Aoyama Bldg. 1F-4F, 4-5-9 Shibuya, Shibuya-ku; tel. 03/5766-4887; www.aoyama-hachi.net; hours and fee vary by event), or next door on the first floor, the afterhours hot spot **Red Bar** (tel. 03/5888-5847; 8pm-late daily; cover charge ¥1,000, includes one drink), which is bathed in red light as the name suggests, and scope out the vibe.

Nightlife in Kabukichō

Tokyo's largest red-light zone, neon-lit Kabukichō ("Kabuki Town"), occupies 360,000 square meters (89 acres) just north of Yasukuni-dōri.

THE HISTORY

Once known as Tsunohazu, it was a residential zone that was razed during World War II bombing raids. Postwar plans to resurrect the area as a family-friendly entertainment center with a kabuki theater never materialized. Instead, host and hostess bars, strip clubs, soaplands (brothels masquerading as bathhouses), and love hotels proliferated, and the yakuza (Japanese mafia) and Chinese investors moved in. By the 1990s, Kabukichō had become a fuzoku (pink trade) zone, which it remains to this day.

EXPLORING KABUKICHŌ

Despite its seedy reputation, there are security cameras dotting the area and it's a safe place for a stroll if you keep your wits about you and ignore the persistent touts. "Cleanup" efforts are ongoing, as exemplified in the recent opening of the large Toho cinema and shopping complex right in the heart of the action. Definitely go to the unmissable, uncharacterizable Robot Restaurant, but otherwise, just walking around the neighborhood, taking in its atmosphere, and then moving on to Golden Gai is the best way to experience the area.

ROBOT RESTAURANT

Shinjuku Robot Bldg. B2F, 1-7-1 Kabukichō, Shinjuku-ku; tel. 03/3200-5500; www.shinjuku-robot.com; 4pm-11pm daily; ¥8,000; take Shinjuku, Ōedo Marunouchi lines to Shinjuku-Sanchōme Station, exit B3 or E1, or take JR lines to Shinjuku Station, east exit

Robot Restaurant must be experienced to be fully comprehended. But to give an idea, four 90-minute shows happen nightly in a basement in Kabukichō, featuring women in bikinis riding mechanical flame-spewing dragons and towering robots, engaged in a war with a legion of other robots, all set amid a heavily mirrored landscape, drenched in eye-searing neon and with a nonstop din of music and battle sounds (earplugs definitely recommended).

This singular spectacle cost a whopping ¥10 billion to create, which is perhaps reflected in the hefty price of admission. You can book your tickets online in advance, or at the venue. If you opt for the latter, there are often discount vouchers available at tourist information centers and some accommodations that can shave as much as ¥2,000 off the cost of admission. "Restaurant" is a misnomer; the food here is on par with a convenience store bento. Ditto for the drink menu, which extends to canned alcoholic drinks and bottles of tea. This has very much become a "tourist-only" affair, but if you enjoy a zany spectacle, go and leave with your mind blown.

Live Music

SHELTER

Senda Bldg. B1F, 2-6-10 Kitazawa, Setagaya-ku; tel: 03/3466-7430; www.loft-prj.co.jp/SHELTER/index.html; hours and fee vary by event; take Keio-Inokashira, Odakyu lines to Shimokitazawa Station, south exit

Shelter is a compact venue at the center of Shimokitazawa's vibrant rock scene. Domestic and occasional overseas acts jam here nightly. Go early to be sure you get in.

THREE AND BASEMENT BAR

5-18-1 Daizawa, Setagaya-ku; take Keio-Inokashira, Odakyu lines to Shimokitazawa Station, south exit

Three (tel. 03/5486-8804; www.toos.co.jp/3; hours and fee vary by event) and Basement Bar (tel. 03/5481-6366; http://toos.co.jp/basementbar; 6pm-midnight) sit side-by-side in the same building. Basement Bar provides a space for indie rockers to jam on the cheap, and Three does the same, with a lounge for a little class. Rough around the edges, they are vital outposts in Tokyo's indie scene.

HARAJUKU AND AOYAMA
原宿，青山

Bars

HARAJUKU TAPROOM

2F, 1-20-13 Jingūmae, Shibuya-ku; tel. 03/6438-0450; https://bairdbeer.com/ja/taprooms/harajuku; 5pm-midnight Mon.-Fri., noon-midnight Sat.-Sun.; take Yamanote line to Harajuku Station, Takeshita exit

A stone's throw from the youth fashion catwalk of Takeshita-dōri isn't the most likely spot for a craft beer bar to thrive, but Harajuku Taproom, by Baird Brewing, manages to do just that. Its restaurant has an izakaya-inspired menu and serves 15 of Shizuoka Prefecture-based Baird Brewing's fantastic microbrews. On weekends and national holidays, it opens at noon for lunch.

TWO ROOMS

AO Bldg. 5F, 3-11-7 Kita-Aoyama, Minato-ku; tel. 033/498-0002; www.tworooms.jp; 11:30am-2am Mon.-Sat., 11:am-10pm Sun.; take Ginza line to Omotesandō Station, exit B2; or take Fukutoshin line to Kitasandō Station

Two Rooms is a sleekly decorated bar with excellent fish grilled teppanyaki-style, succulent steaks, a motherlode of wine, and a plush outdoor terrace with spectacular views of the city. It's popular as both a sophisticated nightlife spot and a restaurant. On weekends, Two Rooms serves an amazing brunch.

BAR BONOBO

2-23-4 Jingūmae, Shibuya-ku; tel. 03/6804-5542; http://bonobo.jp; hours vary by event (see schedule on website); cover charge ¥1,000 (includes one drink); take Yamanote line to Harajuku Station, Takeshita exit

Bar Bonobo, tucked away on a Harajuku backstreet, is a converted two-story house with a great sound system and friendly vibe. There's a bar on the first floor, a DJ booth upstairs where various music events are held, and a rooftop terrace. A bit off the beaten path, it's worth the detour if you're looking for a laid-back place with a slightly underground feel. Start times vary by night, but the action goes late into the evening.

Clubs

VENT

Festa Omotesandō Bldg. B1F, 3-18-19 Minami-Aoyama, Minato-ku; tel. 03/6804-6652; http://vent-tokyo.net; 11pm-late on nights with events; fee varies; take Ginza, Chiyoda, Hanzomon lines to Omotesandō Station, exit 4

Great DJ lineups and a dance floor with a spectacular sound system are the main selling points at Vent. This newcomer to Tokyo's electronic music scene is located at the corner of Omotesandō and Aoyama Dōri. Its chic interior is minimal and contains a lounge that provides a great place to socialize and drink without being drowned in decibels. These elements tend to attract an aurally savvy crowd who are in-the-know yet friendly. Both local DJs and big names from overseas are routinely scheduled to spin.

TOP EXPERIENCE

★ SHINJUKU AND AROUND
新宿

Tokyo offers a great variety of nightlife, but Shinjuku stands above the crowd in terms of depth and variety. Served by the world's busiest train station, the area is home to **Kabukichō,** the city's biggest red-light district; **Golden Gai,** a warren of more than 200 small bars; and the city's gay quarter centered in **Shinjuku Ni-chōme.**

Bars

BEN FIDDICH

Yamatoya Bldg. 9F, 1-13-7 Nishi-Shinjuku, Shinjuku-ku; tel. 03/6279-4223; www.facebook.com/BarBenfiddich; 5pm-3am Mon., Tues., Thurs., and Sat., 5pm-2am Wed. and Fri., closed holidays; take JR lines to Shinjuku, west exit

At Ben Fiddich there are roots and spices in jars, perfectly sculpted ice cubes, pestles and mortars, and organic mixing ingredients sourced from bar master Hiroyasu

Kayama's family farm in neighboring Saitama Prefecture. What you won't find is a menu; just sit back with an open mind and let the bar master work his magic.

NEW YORK BAR

Park Hyatt, 3-7-1-2 Nishi-Shinjuku, Shinjuku-ku; tel. 03/5323-3458; http://tokyo.park.hyatt.com; 5pm-11pm Sun.-Thurs., 5pm-midnight Fri.-Sat.; ¥2,500 cover charge after 8pm Mon.-Sat., or after 7pm Sun.; take Ōedo line to Tochōmae Station, exit A4

Made famous by Sofia Coppola's film *Lost in Translation,* this bar is a true gem and offers some of the most dazzling views of the city at night. Perched on the 52nd floor of the Park Hyatt Tokyo, in Shinjuku's skyscraper district, New York Bar is the pinnacle of elegance, with its dark wood and floor-to-ceiling windows from which Mount Fuji can be glimpsed on clear days. Here you'll find top-notch cocktails; an array of booze, including the most varieties of wine from the United States in Japan; and excellent steak and pizza.

BAR GOLD FINGER

2-12-11 Shinjuku, Shinjuku-ku; tel. 03/6383-4649; www.goldfingerparty.com; 6pm-2am Sun.-Thurs., 6pm-5am Fri.-Sat.; take Fukutoshin, Marunouchi, Shinjuku lines to Shinjuku Sanchōme Station, exit C8

This bubbly bar is a mainstay in the Shinjuku Ni-chōme area, with revelers sometimes spilling into the street outside. Note that it's women-only on Saturdays.

ARTY FARTY

Kyutei Bldg. 2F, 2-11-7 Shinjuku, Shinjuku-ku; tel. 03/5362-9720; www.arty-farty.net; 8pm-late; take Fukutoshin, Marunouchi, Shinjuku lines to Shinjuku Sanchōme Station, exit C8

Perhaps the most popular of the lot in Ni-chōme, this is a great place to end the night. Note that women are required to come with a gay friend for admission on weekends when the dance floor gets jumping.

Live Music

SHINJUKU PIT INN

B1, 2-12-4 Shinjuku, Shinjuku-ku; tel. 03/3354-2024; www.pit-inn.com/index.html; 2:30pm, 7:30pm; hours and fee vary by event; take Marunouchi line to Shinjuku-Sanchōme Station, exit C5

An eminent jazz spot imbued with history and blessed by a consistently stellar lineup of both Japanese and overseas artists. There are daily matinee and evening shows.

Shinjuku's Kabukichō nightlife district

Pub Crawl Through Golden Gai

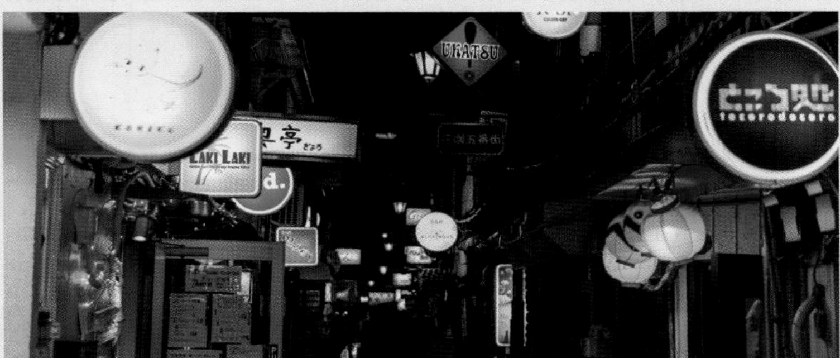

Golden Gai

The endless bars and cramped clubs of Golden Gai make for a perfect pub crawl.

Golden Gai has a rich, bohemian lore, frequented by writers like Japanese literary prize winners Saki Ryūzō and Nakagami Kenji and film directors such as Quentin Tarantino. When in Golden Gai, adhere to some basic rules. First, try to avoid going in groups of more than three. Space is at a premium. Second, confirm whether the bar has a cover charge before entering. Third, be respectful and friendly with the whole bar, and avoid getting rowdy. Fourth, move on to the next bar after a few drinks. The key word is bar *hopping*. Finally, don't smoke or drink in the street, or take photos without permission.

To get there, take the Shinjuku, Ōedo, or Marunouchi line to Shinjuku-Sanchōme Station, exit B3 or E1; or take JR lines to Shinjuku Station, east exit.

- Begin your pub crawl at **Kenzo's Bar** (2F, 1-1-7 Kabukichō, Shinjuku-ku; tel. 090/9847-5563; https://twitter.com/KENZOS_BAR; 8pm-5am daily), a leopard-spot printed bolt-hole with a 1980s soundtrack overseen by the gregarious Kenzo himself, who's adept at easing first-timers into Golden Gai.
- Leaving Kenzo's, turn right and walk to the T-junction, then turn right, and then right again. Walk roughly halfway down this alley until you see **Albatross G** (1-1-7 Kabukichō, Shinjuku-ku; tel. 03/3203-3699; www.alba-s.com; 5pm-2am Sun.-Thurs., 5pm-5am Fri.-Sat.) on the right. This cramped bar has red walls, lots of crystal chandeliers, and friendly bartenders who appeared on the late Anthony Bourdain show *Parts Unknown*.
- When you exit Albatross G, turn right out of the door and walk straight ahead. On your left, toward the end of the alley, you'll come to a large, unmarked wooden door. Slide it open and step inside **The Open Book** (1-1-6 Kabukichō, Shinjuku-ku; tel. 080/4112-0273; www.facebook.com/theopenbook2016; 7pm-midnight daily). This is a great place to get acquainted with the lemon sour (shōchū, soda, and lemon juice), sitting near a wall overflowing with books.
- Upon exiting, turn left and walk to the road ahead. Turn right and then right again down the first lane (the same one Kenzo's Bar is located on). On the right side of the lane, you'll come to **Cambiare** (2F, 1-1-7 Kabukichō, Hanazono Sanban-gai 2F, Shinjuku-ku; https://twitter.com/CambiareB; 6pm-2am Mon.-Thurs., 6pm-5am Fri.-Sat.), a lurid space of reds, blues, yellows, and psychedelic floral patterns.
- End your journey at **Deathmatch in Hell** (1-1-8 Kabukichō, Golden-Gai 3rd street, Shinjuku-ku; tel. 090/2524-5575; www.facebook.com/deathmatchinhell; 8pm-3am Mon.-Sat., closed holidays). Brace yourself. This legendary bar is bursting with horror and sci-fi movie posters, a heavy metal soundtrack, and splatter films playing on TV. The long-haired owner is a bona fide character, and the crowd is fun.

SHINJUKU LOFT

Tatehana Bldg. B2F, 1-12-9 Kabukichō, Shinjuku-ku; tel. 03/5272-0382; www.loft-prj.co.jp; hours and fee vary by event; take Yamanote line to Shinjuku Station, east exit

A stalwart of Tokyo's live music scene. One room hosts the main show and a smaller one near the bar hosts more intimate performances.

Accommodations

When choosing accommodation in Tokyo, the most important factor is convenience. The most popular areas are the zone surrounding Tokyo Station, centered on **Ginza** and **Marunouchi,** and in the western part of the city, **Shinjuku** and **Shibuya.** The draws of these core areas are proximity to the city's best food, shopping, and nightlife. Further, Tokyo, Shibuya, and Shinjuku Stations are on the Yamanote line, which runs in a loop around the city, while Ginza has several subway links (Ginza, Hibiya, Marunouchi lines).

Another area worth considering is the older side of town in the city's northeast, centered on **Ueno** and **Asakusa.** These two neighborhoods have more affordable options and plenty of local character but are also less central.

If you end up staying outside of these core areas, aim to at the very least find a room near a station on the Yamanote loop line, the east-west Chūō/Sōbu line, or a subway station not too far from the city's core, encompassing the area inside the Yamanote line.

GINZA AND MARUNOUCHI

銀座, 丸の内

¥20,000-30,000

HOTEL RYUMEIKAN TOKYO

1-3-22 Yaesu, Chūō-ku; tel. 03/3272-0971; www.ryumeikan-tokyo.jp; ¥24,000 d; take Yamanote line to Tokyo Station, Yaesu North exit

Next to Tokyo Station, Hotel Ryumeikan Tokyo is a branch of the Ryokan Ryumeikan Honten, which has been running since 1899. The rooms are petite but smart, and feature free Wi-Fi access. Helpful staff are ready to assist you in sending your luggage to the airport so you don't have to carry it with you. This is a good option for those wanting an affordable place to sleep, but not much else.

¥30,000-40,000

PARK HOTEL TOKYO

1-7-1 Higashi-Shimbashi, Minato-ku; tel. 03/6252-1111; www.parkhotel-tokyo.com; ¥36,000 d; take Yamanote, Ginza, Asakusa lines to Shimbashi Station, Shiodome exit for JR station, exit 1d for subway station, or take Yurikamome, Ōedo lines to Shiodome Station, exits 7, 8

The Park Hotel Tokyo is a Design Hotel with reasonable rates—not an easy find in Tokyo. The first hotel in the capital launched by Berlin-based Design Hotels, this property in Shiodome boasts a floor with more than 30 rooms, each uniquely painted by Japanese artists. The walls of these special rooms feature contemporary takes on everything from Mount Fuji and the book *Tale of Genji* to samurai and kabuki. The hotel even has pillow consultants on staff and collaborates with pillow-maker Lofty to provide guests with versions that offer maximum rest.

Over ¥40,000

IMPERIAL HOTEL TOKYO

1-1-1 Uchisaiwaicho, Chiyoda-ku; tel. 03/3504-1111; www.imperialhotel.co.jp; ¥47,200 d; take Chiyoda, Hibiya, Mita lines to Hibiya Station, exits A5, A13, or Yamanote, Yūrakuchō lines to Yūrakuchō Station, Hibiya exit

The Imperial Hotel Tokyo has more history coursing through its halls than just about any other hotel in the city. It has been standing on its current site, overlooking the Palace, Hibiya

Park, and Ginza, in some form since 1890. Its second incarnation, which opened (and remained standing) the same day that the 1923 Great Kanto Earthquake struck the capital, was designed by Frank Lloyd Wright. Its current main building opened in 1970 and boasts 13 restaurants and three bars, including the superb Imperial Lounge Aqua and the legendary Old Imperial Bar, originally designed by Frank Lloyd Wright and still graced by the same furniture and motifs. The hotel's proximity to Hibiya, Ginza, and Yūrakuchō Stations ensures easy access to anywhere in the city.

★ MANDARIN ORIENTAL

2-1-1 Nihonbashimuromachi, Chūō-ku; tel. 03/3270-8800; www.mandarinoriental.com/tokyo/nihonbashi/luxury-hotel; from ¥58,000 d; take Ginza, Hanzomon lines to Mitsukoshi-mae Station, or take Chūō line

Perched atop a tower in Nihonbashi, about 10 minutes' walk from Tokyo Station, this hotel offers stunning views at every turn throughout its posh five-star property. Crisp, modern Japanese aesthetics inform the decor, from the soaring lobby to the plush rooms, three Michelin-starred restaurants, bars, and spa. The legendarily friendly staff is always on point and eager to help. Although there's no swimming pool, the large gym is impressive. It's a phenomenal choice if price is no object.

PALACE HOTEL

1-1-1 Marunouchi, Chiyoda-ku; tel. 03/3211-5211; https://en.palacehoteltokyo.com; ¥124,600; take Chiyoda line to Ōtemachi station, exit C13b

The recently revamped historic Palace Hotel is long on views, with its south-facing rooms with balconies—a rare luxury in Tokyo—overlooking the Imperial Palace moat and gardens, with the skyscrapers jutting skyward in the backdrop. The spacious rooms have earth-tone decor that exudes a hushed elegance in harmony with the green space sprawling outside the window. It's also within walking distance of Hibiya Park and the shopping districts of Ginza and Yūrakuchō, and it has phenomenal Japanese and Western food on-site. Cultural events are often held in the lobby to reflect the seasons, such as traditional rice cake-making performances on New Year's Day and cherry blossom events in spring.

★ AMAN

The Ōtemachi Tower, 1-5-6 Ōtemachi, Chiyoda-ku; tel. 03/5224-3333; www.aman.com; ¥100,000-330,000 d; take Marunouchi line to Ōtemachi station, exit A5

Luxury resort giant Aman operates an exclusive hotel on the top six floors of Ōtemachi Tower. The lavish 84-room property is a departure for Aman, being its first in an urban setting. While the brand is a haven for celebrities who want to keep a low profile, this hotel is in the heart of the bustling Ōtemachi business district, only a short walk from Tokyo Station. Friendly, attentive staff are ready to guide you to deluxe facilities, including fine dining, a two-floor spa, a lounge, and a café. The rooms here are massive.

ROPPONGI AND AROUND

六本木

¥20,000-30,000

HOTEL S ROPPONGI

1-11-6 Nishi-Azabu, Minato-ku; tel. 03/5771-2469; http://hr-roppongi.jp; ¥27,045 d; take Hibiya line to Roppongi Station, exit 2

Sleek Japanese aesthetics in many of the rooms and a shared ground-floor lounge with computers, periodicals, and art books give Hotel S Roppongi a sophisticated sheen. The well-designed hotel shares space with serviced apartments and restaurants. The Zen suite comes with a round bathtub made of Hinoki cypress. Located a stone's throw from Nishi-Azabu crossing, a diverse range of eateries and nightlife options are close at hand. The only drawback is that it's about a 10-minute walk from the nearest train station, Roppongi.

SHIBUYA

渋谷

Under ¥10,000

MILLENNIALS SHIBUYA

1-20-13 Jinnan, Shibuya-ku; tel. 03/6824-9410; www.themillennials.jp/shibuya; pods from ¥4,700 with breakfast; take JR lines, Toyoko line, or Ginza, Fukutoshin, Hanzōmon subway lines to Shibuya Station, Hachiko exit, then walk 7 minutes north

Sleep in a "smart pod"—essentially a well-appointed capsule—kitted out with plug and USB socket and comfortable bedding at this chicly minimal hostel. There's a shared workspace and free Wi-Fi throughout, and coffee, breakfast, and beer are all served for free.

¥20,000-30,000

SHIBUYA GRANBELL HOTEL

15-17 Sakuragaoka-cho, Shibuya-ku; tel. 03/5457-2681; www.granbellhotel.jp; ¥21,700 d; take Yamanote line to Shibuya station, south exit

Located just a stone's throw from Shibuya Station, the Shibuya Granbell Hotel is a good option for those on a mid-range budget who want to be near the action. Room design is several cuts above a standard budget hotel, thanks to the involvement of the same company responsible for decking out the fashionable Claska. Think funky pop-art prints adorning curtains, minimalist color schemes, and appliances with a hip edge. Top-floor suites can be booked for longer-term stays. Free Wi-Fi is available in all rooms, which is a good thing given the hotel's popularity among young movers and shakers.

¥30,000-40,000

CERULEAN TOWER TOKYŪ HOTEL

26-1 Sakuragaoka-chō, Shibuya-ku; tel. 03/3476-3000; www.tokyuhotels.co.jp/cerulean-h; doubles from ¥32,000, from ¥35,300 with breakfast; take JR lines, Toyoko line, or Ginza, Fukutoshin, Hanzōmon subway lines to Shibuya Station, west exit, then walk 3 minutes southwest

Occupying floors 19-37, this high-rise hotel has smart, spacious rooms with great views of the city. Bathrooms are well-appointed, there are several restaurants and a bar on-site, and there's a fitness center with a pool. A good pick if you'd like to stay in Shibuya and want something classy.

SHINJUKU AND AROUND

新宿

¥10,000-20,000

ONSEN RYOKAN YUEN SHINJUKU

5-3-18 Shinjuku, Shinjuku-ku; tel. 03/5361-8355; www.uds-hotels.com/yuen/shinjuku; doubles from ¥12,000; take Fukutoshin, Marunouchi or Shinjuku subway lines to Shinjuku San-chōme Station, exit C7, then walk 8 minutes northeast, or take JR lines to Shinjuku Station, east exit, then walk 17 minutes east

Just beyond Shinjuku's hubbub, this modern ryokan has chic, zen-like rooms, some with good views of the surrounding cityscape. All rooms have well-appointed private baths, as well as access to a shared, gender-separated onsen. The rooms are on the petite side but are a great value, given the hotel's location and price point. There's a restaurant on-site serving Japanese food (breakfast: ¥1,800). A good budget pick.

¥20,000-30,000

HOTEL GRACERY SHINJUKU

1-19-1 Kabukichō, Shinjuku-ku; tel. 03/6833-2489; http://shinjuku.gracery.com; ¥25,000 d; take Yamanote line to Shinjuku Station, east exit

The Gracery Shinjuku is for Godzilla fans. A 12-meter (39-ft) statue of the monster bellows and exhales smoke on the hour noon-8pm on the hotel's eighth-floor terrace. Set in the heart of Shinjuku's Kabukichō entertainment district, the 30-floor tower offers guests at the higher levels impressive views of Tokyo—just like the monster would have. The almost 1,000 rooms are small but well designed. For serious fans, there's a room with a statue of the creature inside.

Over ¥40,000

★ PARK HYATT TOKYO

3-7-1-2 Nishi-Shinjuku, Shinjuku-Ku; tel. 03/5322-1234; http://tokyo.park.hyatt.com;

¥144,600 d; take Ōedo line to Tochōmae station, exit A4

Park Hyatt Tokyo is a rock-star hotel that owes much of its fame to Sofia Coppola's 2003 film *Lost in Translation,* starring Bill Murray as jaded action star Bob Harris, fresh in Tokyo to film a whisky commercial. It's hard not to visualize scenes from the movie when passing through the lobby, taking a dip in the pool, or, perhaps most of all, having drinks in the supremely atmospheric New York Bar. Clean lines and minimalist decor imbue the hotel with understated elegance, and Mount Fuji can be glimpsed on clear days.

AKIHABARA AND UENO

秋葉原，上野

¥10,000-20,000

★ RYOKAN SAWANOYA

2-3-11 Yanaka, Taitō-ku; tel. 03/3822-2251; www.sawanoya.com; ¥11,880 d; take Chiyoda line to Nezu Station, exit 1

Ryokan Sawanoya is a great Yanaka-area inn. At this family-run ryokan, the traditional touches are all in place: tatami floors, Japanese-style ceramic and cypress-wood baths (both shared and private in some rooms), paper lanterns, futons in place of beds, and traditional dance performances at select times. The affable owners are happy to help, providing a slew of travel information, local recommendations, and bicycle rentals to guests. What's more, there is English-language information throughout the ryokan, educating guests on such topics as bathing etiquette.

¥20,000-30,000

HANARE

3-10-25 Hagiso, Yanaka, Taitō-ku; tel. 03/5834-7301; http://hanare.hagiso.jp; ¥22,000 d; take Chiyoda line to Sendagi, exit 2

Hanare is a gem in the heart of Yanaka, one of Tokyo's most charming neighborhoods. This ryokan is run by wonderful staff who encourage guests to get out and experience the city. They're always armed with suggestions for the best shrines, public baths, bike rentals, mom-and-pop restaurants, and traditional craft shops. All five rooms have tatami floors, and the bathroom is shared. The inn shares a building with a café, a gift shop, and a gallery.

BNA STUDIO AKIHABARA

6-3-3 Sotokanda, Chiyoda-ku; tel. 03/5846-8876; http://bna-akihabara.com; ¥22,500 d; take Ginza line to Suehirochō Station, or take Yamanote, Chūō-Sōbu, Hibiya lines to Akihabara Station, Electric Town exit

dining with a view at Kozue

This property run by the brilliant Bed & Art Project is an out-of-the-box "art hotel" that is hard to resist. Less than 10 minutes' walk from Akihabara's neon thrum, the studio apartments in this property come with a kitchenette, a washer-dryer, and a well-appointed private bathroom. With names like Athletic Park, Wonder Park, Responder, Hailer, and Zen Garden, each suite is infused with the quirky aesthetics and themes of the artist who designed it: One with blue neon-lit art and a bed behind a chainlink fence; another with a playful, psychedelic motif of dragons and cartoon characters painted across its walls and ceiling. See colorful images of each room on the website. The affable staff are clued in, speak English, and are happy to recommend things around town too. If you're a sucker for unique accommodations and fancy yourself a flâneur or an urban anthropologist, this won't disappoint.

ASAKUSA AND RYOGOKU

浅草, 両国

Under ¥10,000

BUNKA HOSTEL TOKYO

1-13-5 Asakusa, Taitō-ku; tel. 03/5806-3444, http://bunkahostel.jp; ¥2,555 single bunk bed in mixed dorm; take Tsukuba Express to Asakusa Station, exit 4

Bunka Hostel Tokyo appeals to backpackers who want a bit more comfort. Housed in a renovated office building in the heart of Asakusa, the hostel has options ranging from bunk beds to family rooms. It also offers a shared dining room, free Wi-Fi, and an izakaya on the first floor, open to guests and non-guests alike.

NUI. HOSTEL & BAR LOUNGE

2-14-13 Kuramae, Taitō-ku; tel. 03/6240-9854; https://backpackersjapan.co.jp; ¥3,500 single bunk bed in mixed dorm, ¥9,000 twin bunk bed in private room; take Ōedo line to Kuramae Station, exit A7

Nui. Hostel & Bar Lounge is a roughly 15-minute walk from Asakusa, in the trendy district of Kuramae. This is another hostel with all the right touches, including a first-floor bar-café with a nice social buzz. Mixed dorms and doubles share bathrooms and a kitchen, and Wi-Fi is free. Common areas close at midnight.

¥10,000-20,000

★ ASAKUSA KOKONO CLUB HOTEL

2-16-2 Asakusa, Taitō-ku; tel. 03/5830-6533; https://asakusakokonoclub.com; ¥16,000 d; take Ginza line to Asakusa Station, exit A

With design and branding by a Portland-based creative outfit, Asakusa Kokono Club Hotel ticks all the artisanal boxes. On the first floor you'll find a café-bar open to all and serving soy-based snacks, naturally. Single rooms, doubles, and even a penthouse suite ensure that all types of travelers' needs are met. Decor feels more New York studio than old-school Tokyo, but this boutique hideaway is indeed in the middle of Asakusa, the heart of the city's old downtown district.

¥20,000-30,000

THE GATE HOTEL KAMINARIMON

2-16-11, Kaminarimon, Taitō-ku; tel. 03/6263-8233; www.gate-hotel.jp; ¥28,614 d; take Ginza line to Asakusa Station, exit 2

Located just across from Sensō-ji's iconic Kaminarimon Gate, the Gate Hotel Kaminarimon, designed by Shigeru Uchida, whose mastery extends from architectural interiors to furniture and urban planning, offers a stylish option in the heart of old Tokyo. The lobby shares the 13th floor with an eatery specializing in French fusion cuisine. One floor up, there's also a terrace and bar. May-October guests can take an elevator to the rooftop for excellent views of Tokyo Skytree and surroundings. For those seeking a good option in the old part of town, this hotel offers great bang for the buck.

Information and Services

TOURIST INFORMATION

The easiest way to gather information is from your hotel's front desk, but if you're hitting the pavement and need to stop somewhere for additional help, there are a number of tourist information centers scattered around Tokyo. Thankfully, many are located in areas you'll likely pass through as you explore. For a full list of tourist information centers around town, visit https://tokyotouristinfo.com/en. Here are some of the most convenient:

Ginza and Marunouchi

- **JNTO Tourist Information Center** (3-3-1 Marunouchi, Shin-Tokyo Building, Chiyoda-ku; tel. 03/3201-3331; www.jnto.go.jp; 9am-5pm daily; take Chiyoda line to Nijubashimae, exit 1; additional branches at Narita Airport terminals 1 and 2)
- **JR East Travel Service Center** (1-9-1 Marunouchi, Tokyo Station, Chiyoda-ku; www.jreast.co.jp/e/customer_support/service_center_tokyo.html; 7:30am-8:30pm daily; take JR Yamanote line to Tokyo, Marunouchi North exit)

Shibuya

- **Shibu Hachi Box** (2-1 Dōgenzaka, Shibuya-ku; tel. 03/3462-8311; https://tokyotouristinfo.com/en/detail/M0123; 10am-8pm daily; take JR, Ginza, Inokashira, Fukutoshin, Hanzōmon, Tōkyū Tōyoko lines to Shibuya Station, Hachikō exit)

Shinjuku

- **Tokyo Metropolitan Government Building Tourist Information Center** (2-8-1 Nishi-Shinjuku, Shinjuku-ku, Tokyo Metropolitan Government Building 1F; tel. 03/5321-3077; 9:30am-6:30pm daily; take Ōedo line to Tochomae, exit A4)
- **Shinjuku Tourist Information Center** (3-37-2 Shinjuku, Shinjukuku; tel. 03/3344-3160; www.kanko-shinjuku.jp/office/-/index.html; 10am-7pm daily; outside the South East Exit of JR Shinjuku Station)

Asakusa

- **Asakusa Culture Tourist Information Center** (2-18-9 Kaminarimon, Taitō-ku; tel. 03/3842-5566; 9am-8pm daily; take Ginza line to Asakusa, exit 2)

BANKS AND CURRENCY EXCHANGE

ATMs are ubiquitous throughout Tokyo, from convenience stores to banks. To the chagrin of many travelers, however, they often don't cooperate with foreign-issued cards, even when they bear the logos of Visa, MasterCard, American Express, Plus, or any other major card.

For currency exchange, most banks such as **Mizuho, Mitsubishi UFJ,** and **Sumitomo Mitsui** do the job, but only on weekdays 9am-3pm. If you need to exchange currency, it's best to handle it upon arriving at an international airport. You can also exchange money in Marunouchi at **Exchangers** (Shin-Tokyo Bldg. 1F; 3-3-1 Marunouchi, Chiyoda-ku; tel. 03/6269-9466; www.exchangers.co.jp; 10am-6pm Mon.-Fri.).

POSTAL SERVICES

Japan's postal service is efficient and dependable, and Tokyo has local branches in every district, typically open 9am-5pm Monday-Friday and 9am-noon Saturday. Sending packages via airmail to the United States normally takes about one week, while surface deliveries require a month or two.

For the best service, go to any ward's

central post office, which will have English-speaking staff. These larger main branches also tend to have longer hours of operation, such as 9am-9pm on weekdays and 9am-7pm on weekends. Also note that **FedEx** (tel. 0120-003/200 toll free; www.fedex.com) has locations dotted around the city's major business districts. Rates aren't cheap, but this is a reliable way to send a package overseas.

- **Tokyo Central Post Office** (2-7-2 Marunouchi, Chiyoda-ku; tel. 03/3217-5231; open 24 hours; Tokyo Station, Marunouchi South Exit)

INTERNET ACCESS

It's a common complaint that Tokyo has a dearth of Wi-Fi in public spaces like cafés compared with other cities, but the situation is improving. Signal strength varies, but Wi-Fi is available on subway station platforms, in some convenience stores, and even on the streets of some neighborhoods. Many shops and attractions provide Wi-Fi for customers as well. Most hotels provide Wi-Fi for guests, sometimes for a fee, or at least have shared computers in the lobby. There are also Internet cafés, which will have computer booths that you can typically rent in 30-minute or one-hour increments.

Free Wi-Fi Japan (www.flets.com) allows you to connect at various hot spots around Tokyo after registering and getting log-in credentials online or at a tourist center.

PHARMACIES AND MEDICAL SERVICES

For emergency fire and ambulance services, dial 119. Most operators don't speak English, but will transfer you to someone who does. A multilingual service that can connect you to English-speaking doctors of various kinds is the **Tokyo Metropolitan Health and Medical Information Center** (tel. 03/5285-8181; www.himawari.metro.tokyo.jp; 9am-8pm daily). Call the number and request English assistance. They will put you in touch with an operator who can help.

Aside from seeking assistance from one of these services, English-speaking physicians are limited. For emergency room services with English-speaking care, go to **St. Luke's International Hospital** (9-1 Akashi-cho, Chūō-ku; tel. 03/3541-5151; http://hospital.luke.ac.jp; take Hibiya line to Tsukiji, exit 3).

DIPLOMATIC SERVICES

- **U.S. Embassy and Consulate** (1-10-5 Akasaka, Minato-ku; tel. 03/3224-5000; http://jp.usembassy.gov; 8:30am-5:30pm Mon.-Fri.; take Namboku line to Tameike-Sanno, exit 13)
- **Embassy of Canada to Japan** (7-3-38 Akasaka, Minato-ku; tel. 03/5412-6200; www.canadainternational.gc.ca/japan-japon; 9am-5:30pm Mon.-Fri.; take Ginza, Ōedo, Hanzōmon lines to Aoyama-Itchōme Station, exit 4)
- **British Embassy Tokyo** (No. 1 Ichiban-chō, Chiyoda-ku; tel. 03/5211-1100; www.gov.uk/world/organisations/british-embassy-tokyo; 9:30am-4:30pm Mon.-Fri.; take Hanzōmon line to Hanzōmon Station, exit 4)
- **Australian Embassy Tokyo** (2-1-14 Mita, Minato-ku; tel. 03/5232-4111; https://japan.embassy.gov.au; 9am-12:30pm and 1:30pm-5pm Mon.-Fri.; take Ōedo, Nanboku lines to Azabu-jūban Station, exit 2, or take Mita, Asakusa lines to Mita Station, exit A3)
- **New Zealand Embassy, Tokyo** (20-40 Kamiyama-chō, Shibuya-ku; tel. 03/3467-2271; www.mfat.govt.nz/kr/countries-and-regions/asia/japan/new-zealand-embassy/; 9am-5:30pm Mon.-Fri.; take Chiyoda line to Yoyogi-kōen Station, exit 1)
- **South African Embassy in Japan** (Hanzōmon First Building 4F, 1-4 Kojimachi, Chiyoda-ku; tel. 03/3265-3366; www.sajapan.org; 9am-5:30pm Mon.-Fri.; take Hanzōmon line to Hanzōmon Station, exit 3a)

USEFUL WEBSITES

Tokyo Cheapo (www.tokyocheapo.com) is a great resource packed with tips on how to make your yen go further in Tokyo.

TimeOut Tokyo (www.timeout.jp/en/tokyo) offers extensive listings of the best events, restaurants, bars, and more. Check the calendar for events that will be taking place when you're going to be in Tokyo. They also publish a free quarterly print edition.

Savvy Tokyo (https://savvytokyo.com) is a lifestyle website geared toward women living in Japan, operated by the same media outfit that runs Gaijinpot. Another solid resource.

Go Tokyo (www.gotokyo.org/en) offers information on things to do, shopping, transportation, accommodations, and just about anything else you'll need for your time in the capital.

Getting There

AIR

Tokyo is served by **Narita Airport** (tel. 0476-34-8000; www.narita-airport.jp), about 60 kilometers (37 mi) east of the city, and **Haneda Airport** (03/6428-0888; www.tokyo-airport-bldg.co.jp/en), south of the city near the Tokyo Bay. Haneda, Japan's busiest airport, is undeniably more convenient than Narita, but more international flights come and go from the latter.

Whether arriving via Narita or Haneda, if you plan to get to Tokyo by train, it may be worth sending your baggage to your destination in Tokyo via courier service, as navigating the trains with luggage can be challenging. Simply inquire about the nearest **luggage courier service** at an information desk if you don't see one. Signage is clear and in English. Ask the staff at the kiosk about how to send your baggage back to the airport on your return.

From Narita Airport

Narita has three terminals, with **Terminals 1** and **2** handling international flights and **Terminal 3** catering to budget airlines. Be careful to confirm the right terminal for your departing flight; going to the wrong terminal can result in lost time, but don't panic. Free shuttle buses run between the three terminals every 15-30 minutes (7am-9:30pm), departing from the ground floor of each one. If anything is unclear, there are information desks with English-speaking staff all across the airport who can point you in the right direction.

The trip into Tokyo from Narita by bus takes 1.5-2 hours, depending on traffic. By train, it takes 36-80 minutes, depending on your destination.

TRAIN

One of the simplest options for reaching Tokyo from the airport is the **Narita Express,** or **N'EX** (www.jreast.co.jp/e/nex; 7:45am-9:45pm daily; adults ¥3,070-3,250, roughly half for children). The Narita Express runs to a host of stations downtown, including Tokyo (1 hour), Shinjuku, Shibuya, Ikebukuro, and Shinagawa. All seats are reserved and can be purchased at an airport N'EX counter, with trains leaving approximately every 30 minutes. The best deal is the round-trip fare of ¥4,070 for adults, available to foreign travelers (must be used within two weeks).

The **Keisei Skyliner** (www.keisei.co.jp; 7:30am-10pm daily; ¥2,520 one-way) is actually quicker than N'EX, but the destinations are more limited, with half-hourly trains making the roughly 40-minute trip to either Ueno or Nippori station. Tickets must be reserved at the Keisei ticket counter in Terminal 1 or 2. After arriving at either Ueno or Nippori, you'll then have the option of transferring to the JR Yamanote line. The Skyliner & Tokyo Subway Ticket allows travelers to purchase a one-way or return ticket on the Skyliner along with receiving a subway pass for between one and three days. If your destination happens to be in the northeastern part of Tokyo, the Skyliner makes sense, but the N'EX offers easier access to other parts of the city.

For those on a tighter budget, the **Keisei Main line** (6:30am-10:30pm) offers a rapid train every 20 minutes (¥1,050) that takes about 65 minutes to reach Nippori and just over 70 minutes to reach Ueno at the northeastern corner of the JR Yamanote line. This line essentially takes the same path as the Skyliner, but makes extra stops. Another option offered by Keisei is the **Narita Sky Access Express** (5:40am-11pm daily; ¥1,290-1,520), which runs every 40 minutes and follows the same route as the Keisei Main line, but veers southwest at Aoto Station and travels to Nihonbashi Station (59 minutes), Shimbashi (62 minutes), and Shinagawa (72 minutes), all of which are connected to the convenient Ginza line.

BUS

Taking the bus from Narita is straightforward, with tickets sold at counters in the arrivals hall. One of the most popular bus services is the **Airport Limousine Bus** (www.limousinebus.co.jp/en; ¥2,800 adults, ¥1,400 children), which runs at scheduled times to a number of major hotels and major train stations in the capital. The average journey takes around 1.5 hours, or a bit more in heavy traffic. Tickets can be purchased in all terminals, and most staff speak English. This service is particularly good for those staying at a hotel that is directly linked or closer to the Airport Limousine's route.

The **Airport Bus TYO-NRT** (https://tyo-nrt.com/en; ¥1,300) is a good budget option. This service runs every 20 minutes 6am-11pm. Tickets are sold at the service's counter in the arrivals lobby in Terminals 1, 2, and 3. The list of destinations isn't as extensive as it is for the Limousine Bus, but the price is lower, and it does run to Tokyo Station, Sukiyabashi crossing in the heart of Ginza, and Shinonomeshako in Koto-ku, east of Odaiba. Keisei buses also run from Tokyo Station to terminals 2 and 3 from 11pm-6am (¥1,300), though less frequently.

TAXI

Taking a taxi from Narita is, simply put, not economical. But if money is no object, you can take a cab at a fixed rate of ¥19,500-27,500, with a surcharge of 20 percent 10pm-5am, to most places in downtown Tokyo (60-90 minutes). Taxis from the airport can be paid with credit card. To catch a taxi, head to taxi stand no. 15, just outside Terminal 1, south exit S2. For more information, see www.narita-airport.jp/en/access/taxi.

From Haneda Airport

Although the city is closer to Haneda, many of the flights coming into the airport arrive late at night, which means trains into Tokyo may have already stopped running. The good news is that buses run late into the night from Haneda, and taxis are significantly more affordable than from Narita. By bus, the journey is 30-90 minutes, depending on traffic, and by train, it takes as little as 15 minutes.

TRAIN

The trip into Tokyo from Haneda Airport by train is a brief affair, with the **Tokyo Monorail Haneda Airport line** (www.tokyo-monorail.co.jp/english; 5am-midnight daily; ¥500 one-way) running local, rapid, and express service trains between Haneda Airport and JR Hamamatsucho Station on the southeastern side of the JR Yamanote line. Trains run every 5-10 minutes, and the ride to JR Hamamatsucho Station only takes about 15 minutes.

Another option is the **Keikyū Airport Express** (tel. 03/5789-8686; www.haneda-tokyo-access.com/en; 5:30am-midnight; ¥300-500), which stops at Haneda's domestic and international terminals. This train runs several times hourly to Shinagawa Station in about 15 minutes, and then some of the trains continue on along the Toei Asakusa subway line to stations such as Ginza and Asakusa.

Shinagawa is a major hub, linked to the Yamaote line, among others.

BUS

The simplest bus option is the **Airport Limousine Bus** (www.limousinebus.co.jp/en; ¥840-1,150 adults depending on destination, half-price for children). Some of the hubs the bus links to include Shinjuku, Shibuya, Roppongi, and Ginza. Travel times are 20-90 minutes, depending on traffic and the distance of the destination. Late-night buses run to Shinjuku Bus Terminal (12:20am, 1am) and Shibuya Station (12:15am, 12:50am, 2:20am). Note that prices double midnight-5am.

TAXI

It's more reasonable to take a taxi from Haneda than from Narita Airport (though it's still not cheap), with taxis running to some of Tokyo's major hubs for ¥5,600 (to **Ginza**) at the lower end of the scale, up to ¥8,500 (to **Ikebukuro**) at the higher end. Note that a surcharge of 20 percent applies for all rides 10pm-5am. Taxis from the airport can be paid for with a credit card. You can get a taxi at the **first-floor curbside area,** reachable by escalator from the arrival lobby on the second floor (https://tokyo-haneda.com/en/access/taxi/index.html).

TRAIN

Tokyo is by far the most connected city in Japan when it comes to train travel. There are three main train stations in the city that travelers arrive at when traveling by shinkansen (bullet train), which is the simplest, most pleasant, and most efficient way of reaching the city by train.

Tokyo Station is the final station for bullet trains traveling to the capital from all over the country, whether from **Kyoto** (average 2 hours 15 minutes; ¥13,970), **Shin-Osaka** (average 2.5 hours; ¥14,520), or **Hiroshima** (4 hours; ¥19,240). While it's possible to make the trip on a wide range of train types operating at the local level—local, express, rapid, limited express, and so on—in most cases, doing so will increase cost and complexity exponentially, with frequent transfers.

Shinagawa Station, on the south side of downtown, is one stop before Tokyo for bullet trains coming from **Kyoto, Osaka, Hiroshima, Kyushu,** and all other stops to the west. Meanwhile, the hub of **Ueno** on the northeast side of town, which also serves as a shinkansen terminal, receives trains coming from the northeast (**Tohoku** and **Hokkaido**) before they finally reach Tokyo.

Generally speaking, Tokyo Station is a safe bet for your terminus of choice, as the station is also linked to the **Yamanote line,** which runs in a loop around Tokyo's downtown, and the **Chūō** and **Sōbu** lines, which run east-west through the city, as well as the **Marunouchi** subway line. Ueno, serviced by the **Yamanote, Hibiya,** and **Ginza** lines, may be worth considering as your terminus if you're heading into the city's north or east, and Shinagawa, on the **Yamanote** and **Toei Asakusa line,** may be a good pick if you're heading to somewhere in the city's south or west.

BUS

If you're arriving in Tokyo domestically by land, thanks to the **JR Highway Bus** (03/3844-1950; www.jrbuskanto.co.jp) and a few other highway bus companies you can travel between the capital and other major cities around Japan overnight for less than you'd pay for a train ticket. But you get what you pay for, as journeys are significantly longer. Some buses have toilets, while others don't, although all make stops for restroom breaks.

JR Highway Bus terminals in Tokyo are located near the new south exit of **Shinjuku Station** (6:20am-midnight) and the Yaesu South Exit of **Tokyo Station** (6am-12:30am). As there's no easy English-language ticketing website for JR Highway Bus, your best bet is to inquire about tickets directly at the JR ticket window at one of these terminals.

Perhaps the most popular bus route into Tokyo is from **Kyoto,** where JR operates night buses that depart daily, usually from midnight. The trip takes around 7.5 hours and costs ¥9,000-9,500. Another popular trip is from **Osaka,** which takes about 8 hours and costs ¥9,500-10,000.

Among the numerous private bus operators, discount player **Willer Express** (https://willerexpress.com/en) stands out, offering some trips between Tokyo and Kyoto or Osaka for as little as ¥3,000. On the website of **Kosoku Bus** (www.kosokubus.com/en), you'll find bus trips for as little as ¥2,800 (Osaka to Tokyo). The website allows you to search for and purchase tickets in English for a variety of routes and providers around the country. Another good website for booking bus trips across Japan is the handy **Japan Bus Online** (https://japanbusonline.com/en).

Private operators often start and end journeys at terminals elsewhere in Tokyo, beyond the Shinjuku and Tokyo Stations. Just be sure to know how to navigate to or from the departure or arrival point, wherever it is in the city, before setting off. Tokyo is a good jumping-off point for highway bus journeys to elsewhere in the country; to get a sense of the kinds of trips that can be taken from Shinjuku Station's bus terminal, for example, visit http://shinjuku-busterminal.co.jp/en/search.

Car

Renting a car might make sense for some journeys beyond the capital to or from more remote areas that may be less accessible by train. That said, rather than driving all the way to Tokyo from somewhere far-flung, a more likely scenario would be to drop off your rental car at the nearest major train hub, then simply go to Tokyo by rail.

Getting Around

Tokyo has, bar none, one of the best public transport systems of any major global city. Buses, trains, subway lines, and taxis shuttle millions around the city daily. There are also growing numbers of cyclists and plenty of people putting their drivers licenses to use, too. But for the vast majority of travelers, the city's vast network of aboveground trains and subway lines are sufficient for all of their transportation needs.

TRAIN

While Tokyo's train system can feel daunting, don't fret. It's actually not that difficult to navigate once you've grasped a few key things. For starters, the two most important aboveground JR lines (covered by the Japan Rail Pass) for most travelers will be the oval-shaped **Yamanote line** that runs around the core of the city, and the **Chūō line** that shoots directly through the Yamanote line, linking Tokyo's eastern and western suburbs. Key stations on the Yamanote line include **Tokyo, Shinagawa, Shibuya, Shinjuku,** and **Ikebukuro,** while major stations on the Chūō line, from east to west, include **Tokyo, Shinjuku,** and the western suburb of **Mitaka.** Most trains run roughly from around 5am-midnight, with some running a bit later than that.

There are a number of private lines that you may occasionally need to use to reach some more local stations. Some key ones to be aware of include the **Keio-Inokashira line,** which runs between Shibuya and Kichijōji with Shimokitazawa in between; the **Tōkyū Tōyoko line,** linking Shibuya to Daikanyama, Nakameguro, and, much farther along, Yokohama; the **Odakyu line,** which links Shinjuku to Shimokitazawa; and the **Yurikamome line,** which links Odaiba to the rest of downtown across Tokyo Bay.

Tickets

The easiest way to navigate different train and subway lines is by simply getting a **Suica** (www.jreast.co.jp/e) or **PASMO** (www.pasmo.co.jp/visitors/en/) card as soon as you begin to

Day Trips from Tokyo

Destination	Why Go?	Getting There from Tokyo	How Long to Stay
Yokohama (page 156)	cosmopolitan port history, jazz scene, Japan's largest Chinatown, craft beer	Train: 20-40 minutes, ¥280-570	Half-day-one day
Kamakura (page 167)	Zen temples, the Great Buddha, walking trails, seaside views	Train: 45 minutes-1 hour, ¥730-940	One day
Nikko (page 177)	atmospheric temples and shrines, lush forested surrounds	Train: 2-2.5 hours, ¥1,360-2,750	One day-overnight
Hakone (page 189)	onsen hot spring resorts, swanky ryokan, fall foliage, scenic views	Train: 90 minutes, ¥2,330	Overnight
Mount Fuji (page 199)	views of one of the world's most famous mountains, bucket-list hikes, dazzling sunrises and sunsets	Train: 2.5 hours, ¥2,380 Bus: 1.5 hours, ¥2,000	One day-overnight
Fuji Five Lakes (page 207)	great photographs of Mount Fuji, fun and relaxation by Lake Kawaguchi	Train: 2.5 hours, ¥2,500 Bus: 1 hour 40 minutes, ¥2,000	One day-overnight

use Tokyo's public transport system. The Suica card is sold at all JR stations, while PASMO cards can be bought at all non-JR stations, from the city's extensive subway network to all private railway lines. You can purchase both cards at Haneda and Narita airports too. The biggest selling point for either card is that they can both be used across all rail networks, as well as public buses, which makes transferring between various train lines much easier than buying individual tickets for every leg of a given train ride.

To purchase either pass, just find the respective machine (cash only) marked for either PASMO or Suica, located beside all normal ticketing machines next to a station's ticket gate. There will always (mercifully) be an English-language option on these machines. Note that of the total figure charged onto the pass, ¥500 is subtracted from the total balance for the card itself. Whenever you've used up the money you've charged on either card, you can top it up on a PASMO or Suica-stamped machine at any station on the appropriate rail network, in increments of ¥1,000.

There is also a special **PASMO Passport** (www.pasmo.co.jp/visitors/en/buy/) only available to overseas vistors, which works exactly like the standard PASMO, but does not require a ¥500 deposit, so there's no need to return it at the end of your trip. As an added bonus, it comes stamped with kawaii (cute) characters from the Hello Kitty universe and provides discounts at some tourist sites. The **Welcome Suica Card** (www.jreast.co.jp/multi/en/welcomesuica/welcomesuica.html), emblazoned with a sakura (cherry blossom) design, is similarly only for overseas visitors and does virtually the same thing as its PASMO counterpart, but costs an initial ¥2,000 and includes a children's version for kids under 12; the Welcome Suica Card can be purchased with initial charges of ¥1,000 on up. Both cards expire after 28 days, and can be simply kept as a souvenir. You'll need to present your passport to get either version and can only purchase each card at select stations. For more information on the PASMO Passport, including where to buy one and its various benefits, visit www.pasmo.co.jp/visitors/en/buy/. Likewise, all the information you'll need to know to get your hands on a Welcome Suica Card is found at www.jreast.co.jp/multi/en/welcomesuica/welcomesuica.html.

It's also possible to buy paper tickets for these trains as you go. To do this, calculate your price based on the fare chart on the wall above ticket machines at all stations. Generally speaking, single fares within Tokyo for the JR lines range from ¥130 to around ¥390, with fares increasing if you ride beyond the bounds of Tokyo proper. If your route involves transferring to the subway or to other private lines, this will also raise the total fare. There will usually be an English-language station breakdown, but the easiest way to calculate fares is by planning ahead, using the website **Hyperdia** (www.hyperdia.com), which allows you to calculate rail fares anywhere in the country, including aboveground and subway lines, adjusting for date and either the intended time of departure or arrival.

SUBWAY

The city's subway lines are operated by **Tokyo Metro** (www.tokyometro.jp/lang_en/index.html) and **Toei** (www.kotsu.metro.tokyo.jp/eng), both government-run. The fare for one-way journeys is ¥170-320 (¥90-120 for children) for Tokyo Metro lines, and ¥180-320 (¥90-240 for children) for Toei lines. Changing between lines operated by Tokyo Metro and Toei requires a special transfer ticket, which can be slightly complicated for the uninitiated. The easiest way to handle all the tricky transfers between different rail lines is by purchasing either a **Suica** (www.jreast.co.jp/e) from a JR ticket machine or a **PASMO** (www.pasmo.co.jp/visitors/en/) from a Tokyo Metro ticket machine. (The PASMO Passport and Welcome Suice Card also work for this purpose.) The subway runs roughly 5am-midnight.

Of Tokyo's 13 color-coded subway lines, there are a handful that connect to the majority of locations you'll be most likely to visit. These include the **Ginza line,** which stops at Shibuya, Omotesandō, Ginza, Ueno, and Asakusa Stations; the **Marunouchi line** (Shinjuku, Shinjuku-Gyōenmae, Ginza, and Tokyo); the **Hibiya line** (Nakameguro, Ebisu, Roppongi, Ginza, Tsukiji, Akihabara, and Ueno); the **Chiyoda line** (Meiji-jingūmae and Omotesandō); **Hanzōmon line** (Shibuya, Omotesandō, Ōtemachi, and Oshiage); **Fukutoshin line** (Shinjuku Sanchōme, Meiji-jingūmae, and Shibuya); **Toei-Ōedo line** (Roppongi, Tsukijishijō, Ryōgoku, and Ueno-Okachimachi); and **Toei-Shinjuku line** (Shinjuku and Shinjuku Sanchōme). Note that a few subway lines continue on as a separate aboveground line once they reach the terminal stop.

If you'll be using the Tokyo Metro system heavily, it's worth looking into the **Tokyo Metro 24-Hour Ticket** (www.tokyometro.jp/en/ticket/1day/index.html; ¥600 adults, ¥300 children). You can buy this ticket at any Tokyo Metro station and use it for unlimited travel on any Tokyo Metro line. For even greater access, including both the Tokyo Metro and Toei subway lines, there's also the **Common One-Day Ticket for Tokyo Metro & Toei Subway Lines** (www.tokyometro.jp/tst/en/index.html; ¥800 adults, ¥400 children). This ticket allows unlimited travel on all subway lines for one calendar day, either on the day of purchase for a same-day ticket or for any day within six months of the date of purchase for the advance-ticket option.

BUS

Bus stops dot every area of the city, with **Toei** (www.kotsu.metro.tokyo.jp/eng) buses linking every corner. No matter how far you ride, all fare is capped at ¥210 (¥110 for children). Simply hop aboard, drop your money (in coins) into the electronic box next to the driver's seat at the front of the bus, and ride until your intended stop. If you've only got bills on hand, a machine that changes ¥1,000 notes is at the front of every bus, but you won't get any money back if you drop more than the required fare in coins into the box. While buses are plentiful and easy to use, the train and subway networks are so convenient that buses tend only to be necessary in special cases outside the city center where train lines may not reach.

TAXI

Taxis in Tokyo are pricey, usually starting at ¥400-700 for the first 2 kilometers (1.2 mi), after which the fare jumps ¥80-90 for each additional 300-400 meters (1,000-1,300 ft). A surcharge of 20 percent is often applied 10pm-5am. With rates like these, taxis rarely make economic sense unless you're splitting the fare with other passengers and not going too far. That said, they are an option for late-night rides after the train and subway lines stop running. The vast majority accept credit cards, and there are a few taxi companies with English-speaking services, including **MK Taxi** (03/5547-5547; www.tokyomk.com) and **Nihon Kotsu** (03/5755-2336; www.nihon-kotsu.co.jp). For more information on taking taxis in Tokyo, see the website of the **Tokyo-Taxi Hire Association** (www.taxi-tokyo.or.jp).

CAR

Driving a car in Tokyo rarely makes sense due to the tricky network of one-way streets and significant difficulty and expense of parking. The excellent train and subway systems make driving unnecessary.

If you do plan to get around in a car, parking is only had at a premium, starting at ¥100-500 per 30 minutes, to upward of ¥2,800 for 12 hours, or more for 24 hours. The actual parking lots range from self-service lots to underground car parks, often attached to department stores or other large shops, and the very Japanese phenomenon of the parking tower, in which cars are mechanically lifted and lowered by attendants who effectively stack them in shelves.

You can find parking spaces and gauge the rates at www.parkme.com/tokyo-jp-parking. It's ill-advised to try to park beside the street if there is no parking meter present, as police sometimes patrol for illegally parked cars. Also, don't park in the lot of a restaurant or business where you're not actually a customer, which can result in a fine.

Around Tokyo

Itinerary Ideas 153
Yokohama 156
Kamakura. 167
Nikko. 177
Minakami
and Around. 185
Hakone 189
Mount Fuji. 199
Fuji Five Lakes 207

For visitors craving a break from the bustle of Tokyo, Japan's excellent public transport provides easy access to a number of destinations perfectly suited for a day trip or an overnight stay.

Only 30 minutes from Tokyo by train to the south, the cosmopolitan port city of Yokohama offers a fascinating look into Japan's history. Near the scene of Commodore Perry's second arrival in 1854, the city rose as an international port as Japan opened itself to trade. The spirit of international exchange is strongly felt in its expansive Chinatown, too. After dark, the city's burgeoning craft beer and live jazz scenes offer the promise of a great night out.

For a dose of traditional culture and relaxation, head south of Yokohama to the beachside town of Kamakura, Japan's first feudal

Highlights

Look for ★ to find recommended sights, activities, dining, and lodging.

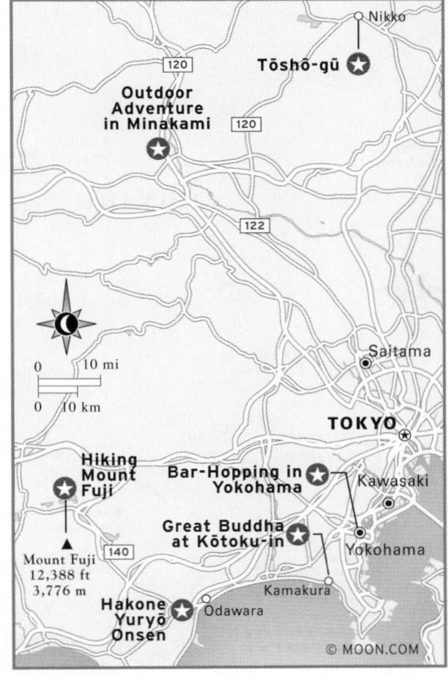

★ **Bar-Hopping in Yokohama:** Yokohama's accessible, low-key nightlife, concentrated in the Kannai, Bashamichi, and Noge neighborhoods, is known for its craft beer and live jazz (page 164).

★ **Great Buddha at Kōtoku-in:** The temple of Kōtoku-in houses the famed bronze Daibutsu (Great Buddha), which stands 11.4 meters (37 ft) tall (page 171).

★ **Tōshō-gū:** Nikko's colorful main shrine, built in the 17th century, is one of the most ornately decorated in Japan (page 179).

★ **Outdoor Adventure in Minakami:** This mountainous region north of Tokyo, pierced by the Tone River, provides ample options for getting outside, from white-water rafting in spring to canyoning in summer (page 185).

★ **Hakone Yuryō Onsen:** In a tranquil forest setting, this onsen features both communal and private baths, as well as a restaurant serving food cooked in a traditional Japanese sunken hearth (page 193).

★ **Hiking Mount Fuji:** Hiking Japan's most sacred peak is a bucket list experience (page 200).

Around Tokyo

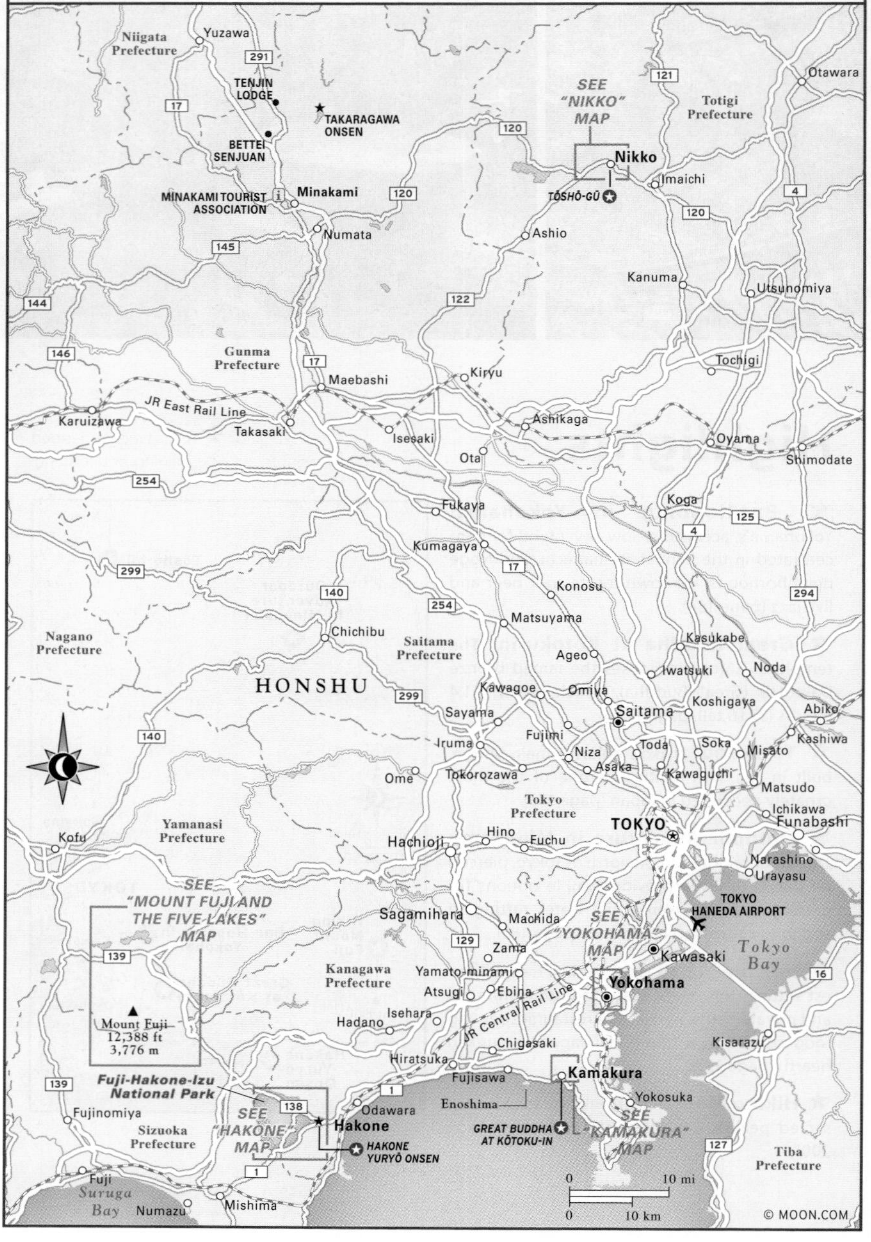

Regional Food Specialties

GYŪ-NABE

Yokohama kitchens gave birth to this fusion dish, popularly known today as sukiyaki, during the cosmopolitan Meiji Period (1868-1912). It's a delectable medley of beef and vegetables simmered in a sweet broth then dipped in raw egg. Try it at **Araiya** (page 164).

YUBA

In Nikko, try yuba (tofu skin), served with noodles, deep-fried, or in gyoza at **Masuda-ya** (page 182).

AMAZAKE

A delicious, surprisingly refreshing infusion made of fermented rice. Try it at **Amazake-Chaya** (page 197).

capital. The earthy town has lovely seaside views and is dotted with temples, including Kōtoku-in, which houses the famed bronze Daibutsu (Great Buddha). The town is surrounded by green hills lined with hiking trails. North of Tokyo, Nikko is home to another collection of temples and shrines set among lofty cedar trees. The mountain town, which gained prominence during the Edo period (1603-1868), is 2.5 hours from the capital by train.

For spectacular views of Mount Fuji, take a train about two hours west of Tokyo to the countryside town of Hakone, nestled in the beautiful Fuji-Hakone-Izu National Park. Here, too, visitors can book a room in a ryokan, peruse art museums in lush outdoor settings, and soak in an onsen. Another place to get your onsen fix within a day trip of Tokyo is Minakami's Takaragawa Onsen (two hours northwest of Tokyo).

Finally, if you want to get up close and personal with Mount Fuji, official climbing season runs from July through August. The Fuji Five Lakes, where you can bask in views of the mountain from the comfort of a hot spring, form an arc around Fuji's base. Lake Kawaguchi in particular is an accessible, pristine vantage point with a wealth of excellent hotels.

ORIENTATION

Nikko, in Tochigi Prefecture, and **Minakami,** in Gunma Prefecture, lie to the north of Tokyo, both about 2.5-3 hours from the capital city by train. Nikko, with its location closer to the Tohoku shinkansen line, is a good stopover for people headed to the northeastern reaches of Japan.

Yokohama and **Kamakura,** both in Kanagawa Prefecture, lie to the south of Tokyo and are within commuting distance from the city. Farther southwest, **Fuji-Hakone-Izu National Park** (富士箱根伊豆国立公園; www.fujihakoneizu.com) covers 1,227 square kilometers (474 square mi) and comprises **Hakone, Fuji Five Lakes,** and **Mount Fuji** itself. The park spreads across parts of three prefectures: Yamanashi, Shizuoka, and Kanagawa.

PLANNING YOUR TIME

If your trip is largely confined to Tokyo, you don't need to go too far to get a well-rounded taste of what Japan has to offer, and all of the destinations covered in this chapter are easily reachable by train from the capital.

Previous: Shin-kyō bridge; Tōshō-gū; private open-air bath at Hakone Yuryō Onsen.

Best Accommodations

★ **Stay Nikkō Guesthouse:** This cozy riverside guesthouse with appealing private rooms and a smattering of villas with mountain views is a great base for exploring Nikko (page 184).

★ **Bettei Senjuan:** This intimate ryokan run by a hospitality dream team boasts phenomenal views of Mount Tanigawa and private open-air baths (page 189).

★ **Fukuzumiro:** This dreamy late-19th-century Hakone gem filled with imaginative woodwork is the perfect place to unplug and recharge (page 197).

★ **Gōra Kadan:** Wander the incense-scented halls, dine on haute cuisine, and soak in a private bath at this premium ryokan in the heart of Hakone (page 198).

Yokohama is only 30 minutes to the south of Tokyo by train, and **Kamakura** is only another 30 minutes south from there. Both cities are easy day trips—neither requires an overnight stay. Yokohama tends to bustle any day of the week, while the pace of Kamakura shifts from relatively sleepy on weekdays to boisterous and crowded on weekends, with beaches filling up from the second half of June through the first half of September. Plan accordingly, avoiding the weekends if possible.

It's possible to visit **Nikko's** temples and shrines, as well as the onsen towns of **Minakami, Hakone,** and the **Mount Fuji** and **Fuji Five Lakes region,** on a long day trip from Tokyo. But to really soak up these places, an overnight stay is recommended; the return trip from any of these destinations is enough to exhaust a seasoned traveler. And considering that all of these destinations are geared toward downtime, rushing back to the hubbub of Tokyo defeats the purpose.

Nikko, with its location closer to the Tohoku shinkansen line, is a good stopover for people headed to the northeastern reaches of Japan. Located between Tokyo and Kyoto, just off the JR Central Rail Line, Yokohama, Kamakura, and Hakone all make good stopovers between these two popular cities.

Keep in mind that many businesses close down quite early in small towns and onsen resorts. It's not uncommon to step out for dinner in the early evening and discover that everything is closed. Be sure to **check the opening hours** on the official website of any restaurant, shop, or attraction before making a trip.

In the higher elevations of Mount Fuji and the surrounding area, winters are very cold, often bringing snow, making late November-March the cheapest time to travel there. That said, climbing Mount Fuji during winter when the mountain is deeply covered in snow requires some serious skills and a guide.

Advance Reservations

Transportation to any of these places can be arranged at the last minute, even day-of. Overnight stays require more planning, as all of these destinations are popular with Japanese urbanites in need of escape (especially Hakone). Try to arrange onsen and ryokan stays as far in advance as possible—even six months or more. As in the rest of Japan, reservations spike around cherry blossom season (early April), when autumn foliage pops (mid-November), and during Golden Week (April 29-May 5) and Obon holidays (mid-August). If you avoid popular onsen during those times, you'll increase the chances of getting your preferred room.

Itinerary Ideas

DAY TRIP TO YOKOHAMA

1 Leave Shibuya Station on the Tōkyū Tōyoko line in the mid-morning, aiming to arrive at Motomachi-Chūkagai Station, in the heart of Chinatown, by around 11am, ahead of the afternoon rush. Eat lunch at **Manchinro Honten,** a 5-minute walk west of the station, and then spend a little time exploring Chinatown's nooks and crannies.

2 Walk about 10 minutes northeast to the harbor to board the **NYK Hikawa Maru,** a ship moored there that was built in the 1930s and has all the period stylings intact.

3 To learn more about Yokohama's long engagement with the West, walk about 10 minutes northwest along the harbor to the **Yokohama Archives of History.**

4 Next, walk 25 minutes northwest to the futuristic Minato Mirai area and visit the quirky **Cupnoodles Museum,** where you can direct the creation of your own one-off cup of noodles yourself for a nominal fee of ¥300.

5 Personalized Cupnoodles in hand, walk 10 minutes southwest across Kokusai Bridge and ascend to the observation deck of **Landmark Tower** for sweeping views over the city and harbor.

6 As dinnertime starts to approach, choose **Araiya** (a 15-minute walk from Landmark Tower, across Kitanaka Bridge), a great spot to try Yokohama's spin on beef hot pot not far from Minato Mirai.

7 In the evening, go on a bar crawl through Yokohama's lively nightlife districts; **Yokohama Bay Brewing Kannai,** 15 minutes south of Araiya on foot, is a great place to start.

DAY TRIP TO KAMAKURA

To get in a full day of temple-hopping, eat breakfast at your hotel in Tokyo and plan to get an early start.

1 Aim to arrive at Kita-Kamakura Station, in the north side of town, around 10am. First, walk about 6 minutes west from the station to the temple of **Jōchi-ji,** where you'll find the trailhead to the Daibutsu Hiking Course. Follow the well-marked course, passing a number of small temples tucked away in the forested hills around the seaside town.

2 You'll know you're at the end of the hiking course when you reach the temple of **Kōtoku-in,** which houses the famed 90-ton Daibutsu, or Great Buddha, statue.

3 Next, walk 10 minutes south to **Hase-dera,** a temple known for its 11-faced, 9-meter-tall (30-ft-tall) wooden visage of Kannon, goddess of mercy.

4 From here, head to nearby **Good Mellows,** a 15-minute walk south, for a satisfying burger.

5 Walk about 10 minutes back toward the temple to Hase Station on the Enoden train line, and ride this local railway to Kamakura Station (4 minutes; ¥200). Take a 10-minute stroll to the end of the famed shopping street of Komachi-dōri, where you'll find the entrance to **Tsurugaoka Hachiman-gū,** a clifftop shrine dedicated to the god of war.

6 For dinner, walk 5 minutes south to try Japan's unique spin on curry at the nostalgic greasy spoon **Caraway Curry House.**

Itinerary Ideas

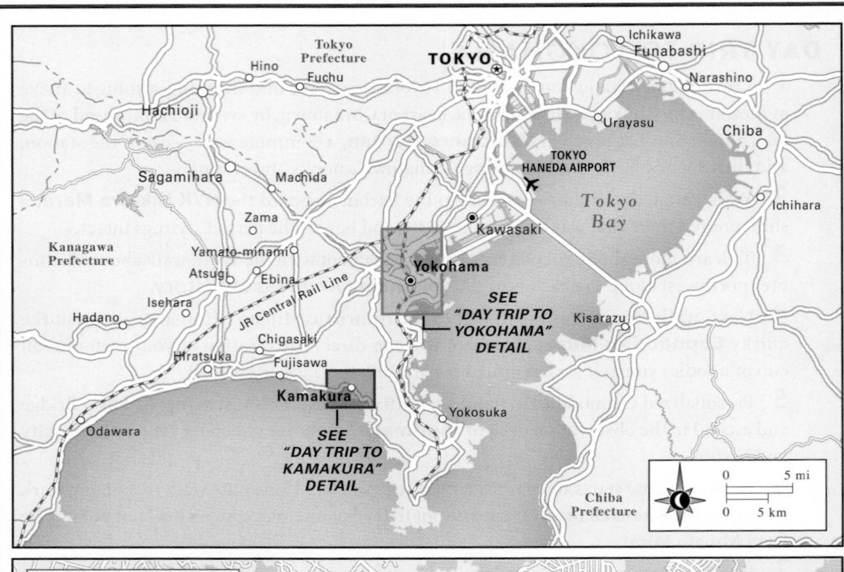

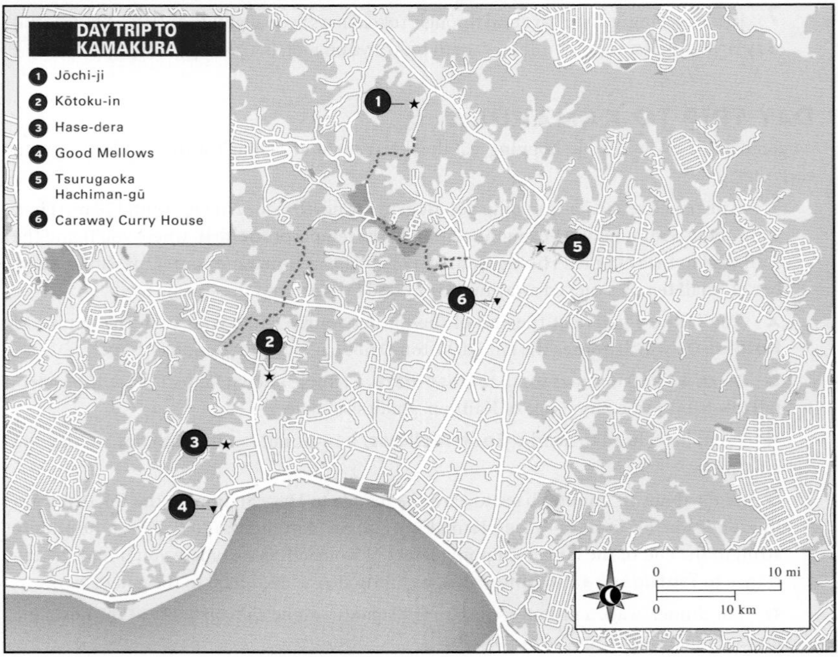

DAY TRIP TO KAMAKURA

1. Jōchi-ji
2. Kōtoku-in
3. Hase-dera
4. Good Mellows
5. Tsurugaoka Hachiman-gū
6. Caraway Curry House

0 10 mi
0 10 km

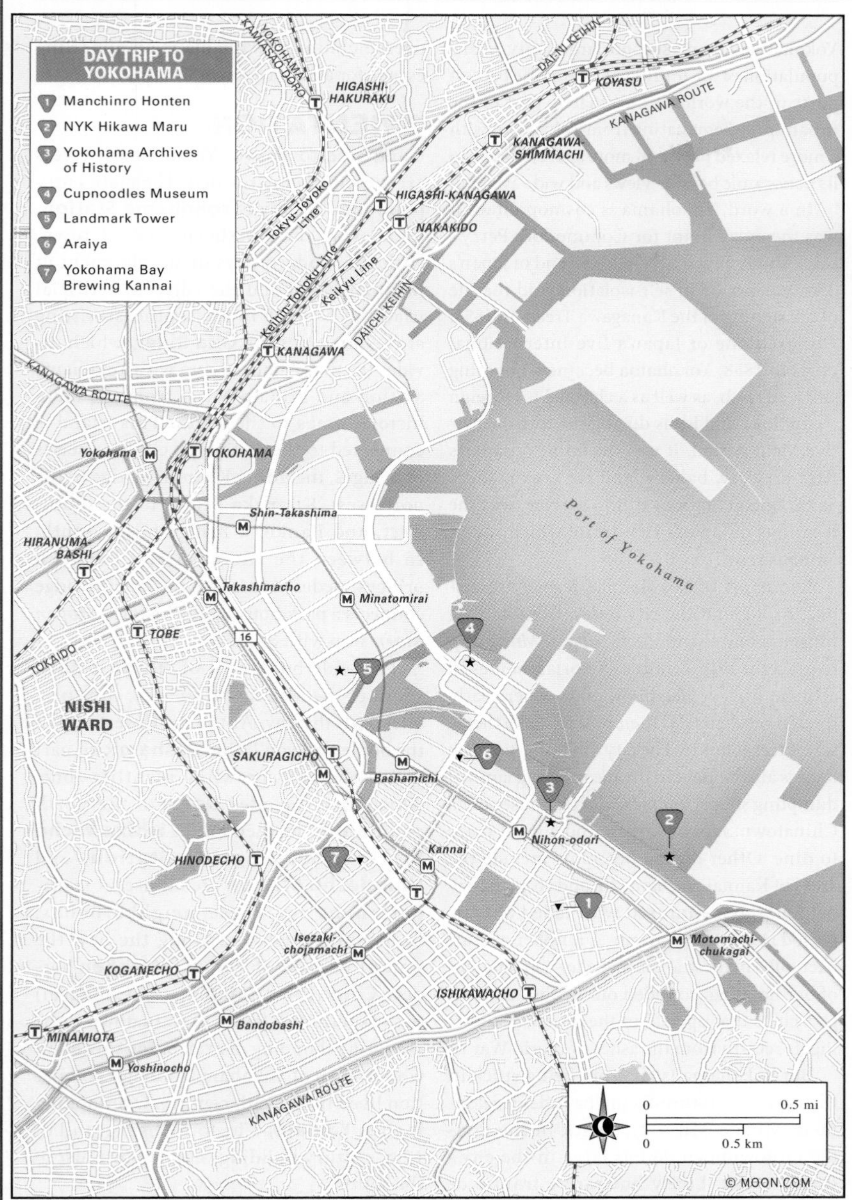
DAY TRIP TO YOKOHAMA
1 Manchinro Honten
2 NYK Hikawa Maru
3 Yokohama Archives of History
4 Cupnoodles Museum
5 Landmark Tower
6 Araiya
7 Yokohama Bay Brewing Kannai
YOKOHAMA KAMIASAO DORI
HIGASHI-HAKURAKU
DAI-NI KEIHIN
KOYASU
KANAGAWA ROUTE
KANAGAWA-SHIMMACHI
HIGASHI-KANAGAWA
NAKAKIDO
Tokyu-Toyoko Line
Keihin-Tohoku Line
Keikyu Line
DAIICHI KEIHIN
KANAGAWA
KANAGAWA ROUTE
Yokohama
YOKOHAMA
Shin-Takashima
Port of Yokohama
HIRANUMA-BASHI
Takashimacho
Minatomirai
TOBE
16
TOKAIDO
NISHI WARD
SAKURAGICHO
Bashamichi
Nihon-odori
HINODECHO
Kannai
Motomachi-chukagai
Isezaki-chojamachi
KOGANECHO
ISHIKAWACHO
Bandobashi
MINAMIOTA
Yoshinocho
KANAGAWA ROUTE
0 0.5 mi
0 0.5 km
© MOON.COM

Yokohama 横浜

Yokohama, Japan's second-largest city with a population of 3.7 million, is one of the biggest ports in the world. It's ultimately part of the urban sprawl emanating from Tokyo, but with a more relaxed pace and more space, thanks to its panoramic bayside views and wide avenues.

In a word, Yokohama is cosmopolitan. It was the entry point for Commodore Perry's black ships, which heralded the end of Japan's 250-year period of self-isolation, and the site of the signing of the Kanagawa Treaty in 1854. Declared one of Japan's five international ports in 1858, Yokohama became a booming silk trade hub, as well as a channel for foreign technology and ideas during the transformative Meiji period. It was the home of Japan's first brewery, bakery, and ice cream shop. Sakuragichō Station, still in service, was the terminus of Japan's first train, which ran to Shinbashi in Tokyo.

Remnants of Yokohama's legacy are visible throughout the city today, from its Port Museum and the moored *Nippon Maru* ship to graceful 19th-century Victorian homes in affluent hillside neighborhoods, where early foreign residents did their best to make themselves feel at home. The city's melting-pot heritage is also evident in the meandering lanes of dumpling shops, temples, and teahouses of its Chinatown, Japan's largest and a great place to dine. Other dining hot spots include the areas of Kannai, Bashamichi, and Noge, boozy neighborhoods infused with faded Shōwa-period (1925-1989) charm. A number of craft beer pubs in these areas make for a great night of bar hopping, rounded out by the excellent jazz clubs that opened in the decades following its rebirth from the ashes of World War II.

But Yokohama is far from being stuck in the past. The future-facing bayside development Minato Mirai 21, smack in the middle of downtown, looms large in the city's image today. Lively but rarely frantic or overwhelming, Yokohama is an appealing escape for an afternoon or evening.

ORIENTATION

Compared to Tokyo, Yokohama's streets are mercifully uncrowded. The main entry point into the city is **Yokohama Station,** located at the northern side of town, with the modern bayside development of **Minato Mirai** and the adjacent artificial island of **Shinkō** to the southeast, sitting at the mouth of the **Ōka River,** which divides the more modern area with Yokohama Station and Minato Mirai from the more historic areas to the south. This island is connected to the rest of the city by a series of bridges, including Kokusai Bridge to the northwest, Kitanaka Bridge to the southwest, and Bankoku Bridge to the south. In between the Kitanaka and Bankoku bridges, pedestrianized Kisa-michi Bridge connects a park housing the historic *Nippon Maru* ship with Shinkō.

The wide boulevard of **Nihon-ōdōri,** south of the Minato Mirai area, runs parallel with the bay. At the northwest end of the boulevard you'll find **Bashamichi,** part of Yokohama's sprawling nightlife zone, which also includes **Noge** to the north and **Kannai** farther south. **Ishikawachō Station, Sakuragichō Station,** and **Hinodechō Station** are all useful transport hubs for these neighborhoods. Continuing eastward along the bay, the waterfront park of **Yamashita-kōen** borders **Chinatown** (Motomachi-Chūkagai) to the southwest. South of Chinatown is the charming shopping district of **Motomachi,** where much of Yokohama's foreign population lived in the 19th century. Overlooking it all is **Yamate,** a historic district full of 19th-century buildings atop a bluff just to the south.

SIGHTS

Minato Mirai and Shinkō

みなとみらい, 新港

Minato Mirai 21 (http://minatomirai21.com) is an ambitious urban development on the bay in downtown Yokohama, with shops, restaurants, museums, hotels, one of Japan's highest observation decks, and even a small amusement park. This "harbor of the future," as its name literally means, is home to most of the structures that make up Yokohama's skyline. As you'll notice from the high perch of Landmark Tower, this development has spilled across a small inlet to the artificial island of Shinkō.

YOKOHAMA PORT MUSEUM AND NIPPON MARU

横浜みなと博物館、帆船日本丸

2-1-1 Minato Mirai, Naka-ku; tel. 045/221-0280; www.nippon-maru.or.jp; 10am-5pm Tues.-Sun., closed on Tues. when Mon. is a holiday; ¥600 adults, ¥300 children; take JR Negishi line, Yokohama Subway line to Sakuragichō Station

To get a sense of Yokohama's role as a center of maritime commerce, visit the Yokohama Port Museum. While the museum may feel slightly dry if you're not a history buff, the accompanying tour of the anchored 1930 ship, the *Nippon Maru*, is worth the price of admission. Originally launched as a training vessel for officers of the merchant marine, the elegant ship was then used for training during World War II, and as a transport ship following the war. Its history comes alive as you amble along the deck and through its halls. At 97 meters (318 ft) long, the ship is quite a sight when its sails are raised.

LANDMARK TOWER

ランドマークタワー

2-2-1 Minato Mirai, Nishi-ku; tel. 045/222-5015; www.yokohama-landmark.jp

The 296-meter-high (971-ft-high) Landmark Tower is worth a visit for its **Sky Garden** (69F The Landmark Tower Yokohama; tel. 045/222-5030; www.yokohama-landmark.jp/skygarden/web/english; 10am-9pm Sun.-Fri., last entry 8:30pm, 10am-10pm Sat. and summer holidays, last entry 9:30pm; ¥1,000 adults, ¥500 elementary and junior high students, ¥800 high school students and over 65, ¥200 children over 4). At 273 meters (895 ft) above the ground, this observation deck is the best place to survey the development, as well as Mount Fuji and Tokyo when the sky is clear. The elevator, which climbs at a speed of 750 meters (2,460 ft) per minute, ensures that the ride to the top is fun, too.

YOKOHAMA MUSEUM OF ART

横浜美術館

3-4-1 Minato Mirai, Nishi-ku; tel. 045/221-0300; http://yokohama.art.museum/eng/index.html; 10am-6pm Fri.-Wed., closed Thurs.; ¥500 adults, ¥300 university and high school students, free for children under 12; take Minato Mirai line to Minato Mirai Station, exit 3

A showcase of contemporary art and photography, the Yokohama Museum of Art is another one of Minato Mirai 21's major draws. The space features Western and Japanese artists, with exhibitions ranging from conservative to groundbreaking (check the schedule). As an added bonus, the building was designed by Pritzker Prize winner Tange Kenzo—something worth appreciating as you pass through the rays of natural light beaming into the courtyard entrance from a soaring skylight. At the time of writing, the museum was closed for renovations and set to reopen in 2023. Check the website for more information.

YOKOHAMA COSMOWORLD

横浜コスモワールド

2-8-1 Shinkō, Naka-ku; tel. 045/641-6591; http://cosmoworld.jp; 11am-9pm Mon.-Fri., 11am-10pm Sat.-Sun.; ¥300-900 for most rides; take Minato Mirai line to Minato Mirai Station, exit 3, or JR Negishi line, Yokohama Subway line to Sakuragichō Station

The most notable point of interest on Shinkō, the artificial island on Yokohama's waterfront, is Yokohama Cosmoworld, a small but lively amusement park famed for the **Cosmo Clock 21,** a Ferris wheel that stands 112.5 meters

Yokohama

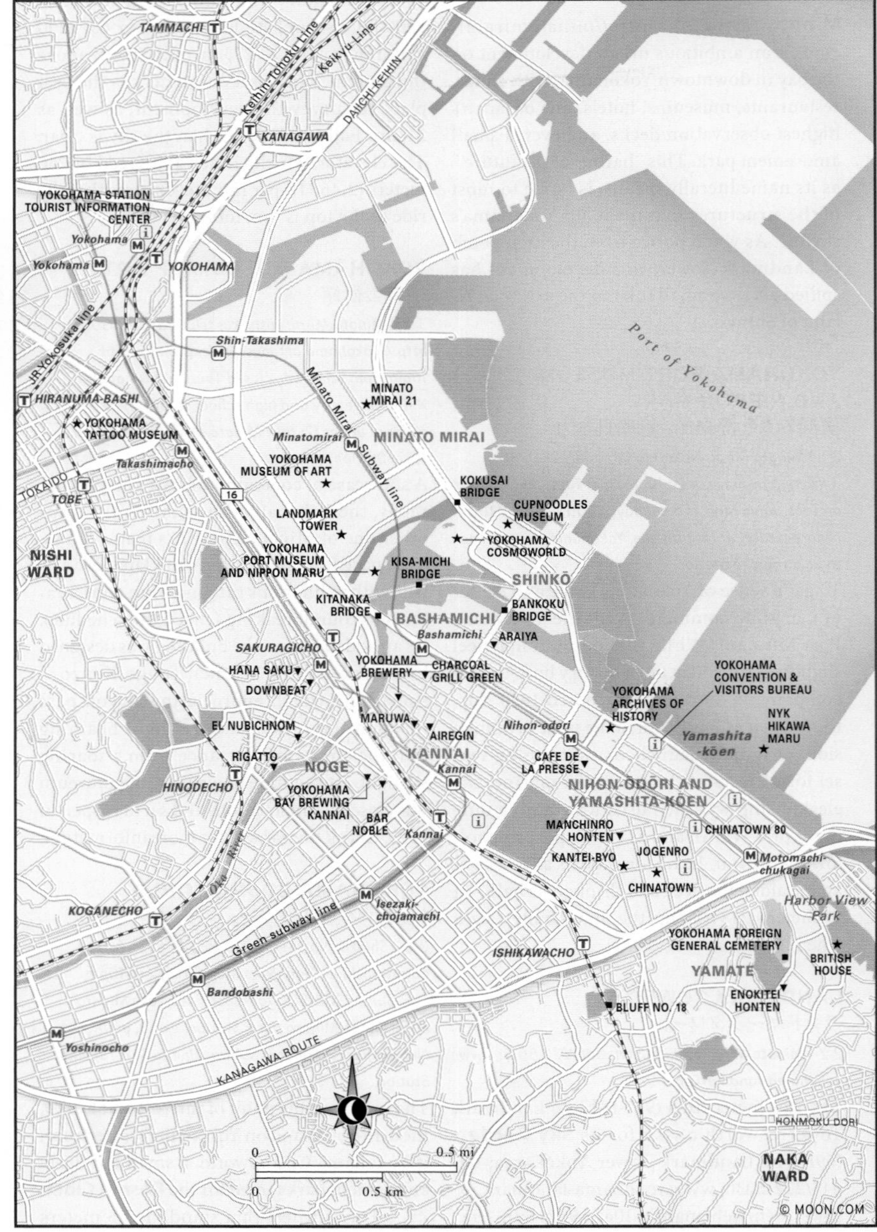

TAMMACHI
Keihin-Tohoku Line
Keikyu Line
DAIICHI KEIHIN
KANAGAWA
YOKOHAMA STATION TOURIST INFORMATION CENTER
Yokohama
Yokohama
YOKOHAMA
JR Yokosuka line
Shin-Takashima
Port of Yokohama
Minato Mirai Subway line
MINATO MIRAI 21
HIRANUMA-BASHI
YOKOHAMA TATTOO MUSEUM
Minatomirai
MINATO MIRAI
Takashimacho
YOKOHAMA MUSEUM OF ART
TOKAIDO
TOBE
16
KOKUSAI BRIDGE
CUPNOODLES MUSEUM
LANDMARK TOWER
YOKOHAMA COSMOWORLD
NISHI WARD
YOKOHAMA PORT MUSEUM AND NIPPON MARU
KISA-MICHI BRIDGE
SHINKŌ
KITANAKA BRIDGE
BASHAMICHI
BANKOKU BRIDGE
Bashamichi
ARAIYA
SAKURAGICHO
HANA SAKU
YOKOHAMA BREWERY
CHARCOAL GRILL GREEN
DOWNBEAT
YOKOHAMA CONVENTION & VISITORS BUREAU
YOKOHAMA ARCHIVES OF HISTORY
MARUWA
AIREGIN
EL NUBICHNOM
Nihon-odori
NYK HIKAWA MARU
Yamashita -kōen
KANNAI
RIGATTO
NOGE
CAFE DE LA PRESSE
Kannai
HINODECHO
YOKOHAMA BAY BREWING KANNAI
NIHON-ŌDŌRI AND YAMASHITA-KŌEN
BAR NOBLE
Kannai
MANCHINRO HONTEN
CHINATOWN 80
KANTEI-BYO
JOGENRO
Motomachi-chukagai
CHINATOWN
Oka River
Green subway line
Isezaki-chojamachi
KOGANECHO
Harbor View Park
YOKOHAMA FOREIGN GENERAL CEMETERY
ISHIKAWACHO
BRITISH HOUSE
YAMATE
Bandobashi
ENOKITEI HONTEN
BLUFF NO. 18
Yoshinocho
KANAGAWA ROUTE
HONMOKU DORI
0
0.5 mi
0
0.5 km
NAKA WARD
© MOON.COM

Irezumi: Japan's Complex Relationship with Tattoos

From ocean waves rolling over an arm to a flamboyant tiger on one's back, Japanese tattoos, or irezumi (literally "insert ink"), are among the most sought-after styles for ink aficionados. But while foreign enthusiasts may clamor for a place under the needle of a great master, the art is weighed down by taboo in Japan—an irony, given its deep history with the art.

DEVELOPING THE STYLE

In the ancient past, Okinawan women tattooed their hands with talismans and shamanic symbols using a blend of ink and the island's very own firewater, awamori. Japan's indigenous Ainu people have an ancient tradition of using soot from the fireside to mark their faces and arms with designs intended to ward off evil spirits and ensure safe passage into the afterlife. The modern tattoo tradition took root on the islands more recently, during the Edo period (1603-1868), in the red-light zones of Edo and Osaka. During this period, the tattoo motifs we think of as "Japanese" today—mythological beasts such as dragons; animals like tigers and koi fish; and images of geisha, samurai, and characters from folklore and religion—began to emerge. The explosion of woodblock prints (ukiyo-e) in the art world grew hand in hand with tattooing.

THE TATTOO TABOO

As the art form grew in popularity, it was promptly banned on the grounds that it caused moral harm. But members of the underclass, from dock workers to firefighters and palanquin bearers, proudly rebelled and got inked in droves. The yakuza (mafia) got inked as well, fueled by the belief that tatting up—painful, permanent—took courage, loyalty, and, as a bonus, disregard for the law. The cost of a full-body tattoo suit came to be viewed as a signifier of financial success. This historical mix of reasons took hold in the public's imagination, and the art form still has never achieved social acceptability. Even today, tattooing remains a very private affair, done discreetly and by appointment only. Most onsen and fitness centers still ban those sporting ink. To learn more, check out *Japanese Tattoos: History, Culture, Design*, by Brian Ashcraft (with Hori Benny).

YOKOHAMA TATTOO MUSEUM

1-11-7 Hiranuma, Nishi-ku; tel. 045/323-1073; www.ne.jp/asahi/tattoo/horiyoshi3/museum.html; noon-6pm Wed.-Mon.; ¥1,000; take Keikyū line for Kanazawa-Bunko to Tobe Station

The Yokohama Tattoo Museum, run by legendary master Horiyoshi III and his wife, is an excellent place to go for a nuanced view of the rich history and impressive level of skill that goes into this art form. The cramped space is positively overflowing with tools of the trade and related memorabilia personally amassed by Horiyoshi himself. Note that the museum is closed on the 1st, 10th, and 20th of every month.

(369 ft) above the crowds and has a massive clock plastered to its side. One rotation on the ride, which was the world's tallest Ferris wheel when it opened, takes 15 minutes and offers stunning views of the city below. It's an ideal attraction if you're traveling with kids.

CUPNOODLES MUSEUM
カップヌードルミュージアム

2-3-4 Shinkō, Naka-ku; tel. 045/345-0918; www.cupnoodles-museum.jp; 10am-6pm Wed.-Mon., closed Wed. if Tues. is holiday; take Minato Mirai line to Minato Mirai Station, exit 3, or JR Negishi line, Yokohama Subway line to Sakuragichō Station

Also in the Shinkō district, the Cupnoodles Museum is a surprisingly inspirational ode to the humble instant meal, a staple among college students worldwide. Following a sleek visual presentation, including anime clips on cup-noodle creator Momofuku Ando's journey toward fast-food superstardom, you can oversee the creation of your own signature noodle variety for a nominal fee (¥300), including the packaging and toppings. With advance reservations, you can even learn to knead your own instant noodles. This is a fun option for those traveling with kids. At the time of writing, the museum was operating on a timed admission system to fight the spread of coronavirus. Check the website for details.

Nihon-ōdōri

日本大通り

Heading south of Minato Mirai and Shinkō brings you to the roughly northeast-southwest avenue of Nihon-ōdōri. This historic thoroughfare was once the heart of Yokohama, reflected in some of the grand architecture seen in the buildings, some of which date to the 19th century.

YOKOHAMA ARCHIVES OF HISTORY

横浜開港資料館

3 Nihon-ōdōri, Naka-ku, Yokohama; tel. 045/201-2100; www.kaikou.city.yokohama.jp/en/index.html; 9:30am-5pm Tues.-Sun., closed Tues. if Mon. is holiday; ¥300 adults, ¥150 children; take Minatomirai line to Nihon-ōdōri Station, exit 3

This one's for the history buffs. If you want to get a sense of what Japan was like when it was first opening up to the wider world after the arrival of Commodore Perry's black ships, the Yokohama Archives of History museum includes more than 200,000 artifacts from that pivotal time, up through the beginning of the Showa period (1926-1989). Maps, newspaper clippings, photographs, prints, models of ships, and more allow you to peer into Yokohama's past.

Adding to the museum's historical significance is the fact that it is situated in the same building where the Treaty of Kanagawa was signed between the shogunate and the US government on March 31, 1854, bringing an end to Japan's 250-year lockdown. One tree in the museum's inner courtyard is supposedly an offspring of the incense tree seen in many sketches of Perry's dramatic arrival at that very spot.

NYK HIKAWA MARU

日本郵船氷川丸

Yamashita-kōen, Naka-ku; tel. 045/641-4362; https://hikawamaru.nyk.com; 10am-5pm Tues.-Sun., closed Tues. if Mon. is holiday; ¥300 adults, ¥100 children; take Minato Mirai line to Motomachi-Chūkagai Station

Another grand vessel from the decadent 1930s, this ship is docked on the east side of Yamashita-kōen. Among the distinguished passengers who traveled across the Pacific aboard the ship in its heyday was Charlie Chaplin. For a small fee, you can roam through its cabins and salons, inspect its engine room, saunter along its deck, and enter its bridge to see where it was commanded.

Chinatown

横浜中華街

As with many port cities, Yokohama is home to a bustling Chinatown. When the city became one of Japan's first ports to welcome foreign trade, many Chinese who were seeking to escape political turmoil found a home here. Today, stores hawk touristy trinkets, lanterns, and tea, but the main draw is some 200 eateries, which generate a steady flow of foot traffic, especially on the weekends.

KANTEI-BYŌ

关帝庙

140 Yamashita-chō, Naka-ku; tel. 045/226-2636; www.yokohama-kanteibyo.com; 9am-7pm daily; free; take Minato Mirai line to Motomachi-Chūkagai Station, or JR Negishi line to Ishikawachō Station

Kantei-byō is a temple dedicated to Guan Yu, a Han war general from China's Three Kingdoms period who is now seen as a guardian of wealth, making the temple a spiritual haven among business owners in the area. Facing the temple's opulent gate, you'll notice the dragons on its roof and the hanging red lanterns. Walk up the first set of steps, lined with stone dragons, past two guardian dogs, and up another staircase to the main hall. Inside, under a ceiling

1: Cupnoodles Museum **2:** Kantei-byō

1

2

Yamate Walk

Begin this 1.8-kilometer (1.1-mi), 35-minute walk through the charming, historic hillside neighborhood known as "the Bluff" by trundling 500 meters (1,640 ft) uphill from Motomachi-Chūkagai Station until you reach the scenic **Harbor View Park** (114 Yamate-chō, Naka-ku; tel. 045/671-3648; 24 hours daily; free), which sits at Yamate's eastern end.

- After admiring the sweeping views of the bustling bay, walk 2 minutes west, heading toward the heart of the neighborhood. Drop into **British House** (115-3 Yamate-chō, Naka-ku; tel. 045/623-7812; www.hama-midorinokyokai.or.jp/yamate-seiyoukan/british-house/#; 9:30am-5pm daily, closed 4th Wed. of month or next day if Wed. falls on holiday; free). This classic house, built in 1937 to serve as the residence of the British consul, is beside a rose garden that blooms April-June, then again in October-November.
- Continue your walk into this formerly well-heeled side of town, once home to a buzzing expat community, by paying your respects at the **Yokohama Foreign General Cemetery** (96 Yamate-chō, Naka-ku; tel. 045/622-1311; www.yfgc-japan.com). Although this graveyard is normally closed, if you happen to be in the area either from February-July or September-December on a Saturday, Sunday, or national holiday, drop by between noon-4pm and give a donation of ¥200-300 to enter the grounds. Whether you enter the cemetery proper or not, there are sweeping views from there over Yokohama's downtown.
- Leaving the cemetery, walk south along Yamate-hondōri for about 3 minutes until you reach **Enokitei Honten** (89-6 Yamate-chō, Naka-ku; tel. 045/623-2288; www.enokitei.co.jp; 11am-7pm (last order 6:30pm) daily; from ¥600; take Keikyū line to Hinodechō Station, then walk 3 minutes east). If you're feeling like dessert, a caffeine break, or even a light lunch, this nostalgic café set in the former home of an American prosecutor sits in the heart of Yamate.
- Continue west along Yamate-hondōri another 10 minutes, then turn right and proceed to **Bluff No. 18** (16 Yamate-chō, Naka-ku; tel. 045/662-6318; www.hama-midorinokyokai.or.jp/yamate-seiyoukan/bluff18; 9:30am-5pm daily, open until 6pm Jul.-Aug., closed 2nd Wed. of month or next day if Wed. falls on national holiday; free), once the home of a local Catholic priest, moved to its current location in 1992.

festooned with myriad shimmering golden ornaments, Guan Yu is powerfully seated at the center, ready to help the finances of the faithful.

If you draw a straight line from Chinatown's main north and south gates, as well as between the main east and west gates, Kantei-byō lies at the intersection of these two lines: Feng Shui is in full effect, maximizing the power of this sacred spot to boost the neighborhood's bottom line.

ENTERTAINMENT AND EVENTS

GREAT JAPAN BEER FESTIVAL YOKOHAMA

www.beertaster.org; usually held on two or three days in mid-Apr. and mid-Sept.; around ¥5,000 for unlimited tasting ticket

This massive beer festival, popularly known as BeerFest Yokohama, attracts the most crowds of any locale to host this annual celebration of all things hoppy. The focus is firmly on Japanese craft beers, although some imports do make an appearance. All told, a few hundred tipples are on tap across the city. Check the website for additional details.

YOKOHAMA JAZZ PROMENADE

tel. 045/211-1510; https://jazzpro.jp; first full weekend of Oct., performances 9am-10pm; one-day ticket ¥5,000 adults, ¥1,000 junior high and high school students, free for primary school students and younger

Japan's biggest jazz festival, Yokohama Jazz Promenade transforms the port city into one giant stage. Jazz bands from Japan and abroad jam in the streets, in the city's numerous jazz clubs, and at large venues like Minatomirai Hall, Yokohama Kannai Hall, and Motomachi's main shopping street, among many others. See the website for a schedule and information about getting tickets.

PARKS

YAMASHITA-KŌEN

山下公園

279 Yamashita-chō, Naka-ku; tel. 045/671-3648; www.city.yokohama.lg.jp/kurashi/machizukuri-kankyo/midori-koen/koen/koen/daihyoteki/kouen008.html; 24 hours daily; free

This bustling park features a broad waterside promenade with open views of the bay, where ships glide by. Within the park, you'll spot a smattering of statuary, ranging from a monument to a Filipino general, an effigy of a girl scout, and even a large head-shaped statue immortalizing the import of Western-style methods of trimming hair to Japan. Most visible of all the park's nearby features is the iconic 1930 ocean liner, the **NYK Hikawa Maru.**

FOOD

Nihon-ōdōri

日本大通り

CAFÉ DE LA PRESSE

Yokohama Media & Communications Center 2f, 11 Nihon-ōdōri, Naka-ku; tel. 045/222-3348; https://alteliebe.co.jp/cafedelapresse/; 10am-8pm Tues.-Sun.; drinks ¥480-900, food ¥800-1,800; take subway Blue line to Nihon-ōdōri, exit 3

A French-style café on tree-lined Nihon-ōdōri, Café de la Presse is located on the second floor of the Yokohama Media & Communications Center. It's good for a pit stop if you're in the area, whether it's for a caffeine hit, a cocktail, or an aperitif. The menu includes a good selection of Western dishes, from quiches and sandwiches to soups and salads, as well as European desserts.

Chinatown

横浜中華街

JOGENRO

191 Yamashita-chō, Naka-ku; tel. 045/641-8888; www.jogen.co.jp/jgr_yokohama; 11:30am-10:30pm Mon.-Thurs. and Sun., 11:30am-11pm Fri.-Sat. and the day before any holiday; ¥1,200-3,500 lunch sets, ¥4,500-20,000 for dinner courses; take Minatomirai line to Motomachi-Chūkagai Station, exit 2

Chinatown's maze of eateries is not solely devoted to Cantonese-style cooking. To shake things up Shanghai-style, try Jogenro. This restaurant sprawls across five floors, each with its own theme. Opulent furniture and decor you'd expect to see in a colonial townhouse in early-20th-century Shanghai evoke the Pearl of the Orient. The menu includes a solid range of soup dumplings, as well as stir-fried and grilled meats, vegetables, noodles, and rice.

MANCHINRO HONTEN

153 Yamashita-chō, Naka-ku; tel. 045/681-4004; https://en.manchinro.com; 11am-10pm daily; ¥1,200-5,500 lunch sets, ¥6,000-21,000 dinner courses; take Minatomirai line to Motomachi-Chūkagai Station, exit 2

This classy spot serves good Cantonese cuisine, made by a chef who trained in Hong Kong and ran a restaurant in Shanghai before relocating to Yokohama. Multicourse feasts are made using local ingredients while remaining loyal to the principles of the Cantonese kitchen. Check out the extensive breakdown of the menu, available in English on the restaurant's website. If the main shop is fully booked, there's a second branch, **Manchinro Tenshinpo** (156 Yamashita-chō, Naka-ku; tel. 045/664-4004; 11am-10pm daily; ¥1,200-3,200 lunch sets, ¥4,200-13,000 dinner courses), just around the corner. This second restaurant is slightly more reasonably priced and more focused on dim sum. Reserve a table online at either restaurant before making the trip for dinner.

Kannai, Bashamichi, and Noge 関内, 馬車道, 野毛

HANA SAKU

2-60 Hanasaki-chō, Naka-ku; tel. 045/325-9215; http://kulakula.info/hanasaku/index.html; 5pm-11:30pm daily; ¥180-880 per plate; take subway Blue line to Sakuragi-chō, south exit 1

An izakaya in Sakuragichō with a minimalist interior of clean lines, wood, and metal, Hana Saku is all about sake. The bartender is happy to introduce patrons to the wonders of sake, from sweet to dry, choosing from more than 20 varieties. The food menu is based on Kyoto-style side-dishes of pickled and cooked vegetables, grilled meats and stews, and creative takes on tofu.

MARUWA

5-61 Sumiyoshichō, Naka-ku; tel. 045/641-0640; 11:30am-2pm and 5:30pm-8pm Mon.-Fri., 11:30am-2pm Sat.; ¥1,000-2,000 lunch, ¥2,000-3,000 dinner; take Minatomirai line to Bashamichi Station, exit 5

For perhaps the best tonkatsu in the city, head to Maruwa in Bashamichi. The shop's no-frills decor and lack of music allow you to fully direct your attention to the delectable breaded cutlets of pork. At lunchtime, be ready for a queue. Arrive around 11:15 to avoid standing in a long line. Alternatively, come for dinner when it's less crowded (though pricier). All meals include miso soup, pickled vegetables, and refillable rice and shredded cabbage.

CHARCOAL GRILL GREEN

6-79 Benten-dōri, Naka-ku; tel. 045/263-8976; www.greenyokohama.com; 11:30am-2pm and 5pm-11:30pm Mon.-Fri., 11:30am-3pm and 5pm-11:30pm Sat.-Sun.; ¥1,400-5,800; take Minatomirai line to Bashamichi Station, exit 3

Charcoal Grill Green is a bistro in the heart of Bashamichi, focused on charcoal-grilled meat (chicken, lamb, steak, duck) and seafood, as well as a good range of salads, soups, and other starters. The drink menu has a good selection of local craft beers and wines from California. This is a good place for either a few bites with drinks or a full meal.

★ ARAIYA

4-23 Kaigan-dōri, Naka-ku; tel. 045/226-5003; www.araiya.co.jp; 11am-2:30pm and 5pm-10pm daily; ¥2,000-5,000 lunch, ¥7,500-12,500 dinner; take Minatomirai line to Bashamichi Station, 6 Akarenga Soko exit

Araiya has a menu of rice bowls topped with strips of beef and sukiyaki, and extensive shabu-shabu courses. But its signature dish, gyū-nabe, consists of lean cuts of beef, leeks, shiitake mushrooms, and thin strands of jelly made from konnyaku (a plant from the taro family). The dish is cooked in a cast-iron pot at the table in a delicately balanced sauce that is both sweet and savory, then dipped in raw egg, and the result is delicious.

RIGATTO

2-39-4 Miyagawa-chō, Naka-ku; tel. 045/253-6116; www.rigatto.jp; 5pm-midnight (last order 11pm) daily; courses from ¥3,000, a la carte ¥380-2,800; take Keikyū line to Hinodechō Station

This chic eatery—its airy wooden interior dimly lit—in the heart of the nightlife action near the Ōka River serves superb Italian fare—salami platters, salads, pizzas, pastas, meat and seafood mains, and more—paired with an extensive Italian wine list. The staff are welcoming, there's an English menu available, and food is made from scratch. Reserve a few days ahead to be safe.

★ BARS AND NIGHTLIFE

If Yokohama's nightlife could be summed up in a few words, they would be "craft beer and jazz." The city's craft beer zone is primarily centered in the neighborhoods of **Kannai** (関内), **Bashamichi** (馬車道), and **Noge** (野毛), all within walking distance of each other. Kannai is in the most southern position of the group, with Bashamichi northeast of there, and Noge is northwest of Kannai, across the Ōka River. The street lined with bars known as **Yoshidamachi** is also wedged into this quarter, between Kannai to the south and Noge to the north. It's possible to walk across the entire area in 10-15 minutes.

YOKOHAMA BAY BREWING KANNAI

2-15 Higashi-dōri, Naka-ku; tel. 045/341-0450; www.yokohamabaybrewing.jp; 4:30pm-11pm Mon.-Fri., 1pm-11pm Sat.-Sun.; take JR Negishi or Blue line to Kannai Station

On the southern edge of the city's craft beer circuit, you'll find the excellent Yokohama Bay Brewing. This shop was opened in 2011 by Suzuki Shinya, trained in the Czech Republic and Germany and formerly the head brewer of Yokohama Brewery. Of the seven or so beers on tap, four or five are carefully selected from local outfits around Japan; the others are Suzuki's creations, always anticipated by his diehard fans. Simple bar nibbles are also on the menu.

YOKOHAMA BREWERY

6-68-1 Sumiyoshi-chō, Naka-ku; tel. 045/641-9901; www.yokohamabeer.com; 11:30am-3pm and 6pm-11pm Mon.-Fri., 11:30am-11pm Sat., 11:30am-9pm Sun.; take Minato Mirai line to Bashamichi Station, exit 3

About 10 minutes' walk north from Yokohama Bay Brewing Kannai, you'll find the city's oldest craft-beer brewery, Yokohama Brewery. Founded in 1995, the brewpub serves a range of pilsners and sweeter Belgian-style beers. Above the brewery is Umaya, a restaurant serving Western and Asian cuisine.

BAR NOBLE

2-7 Yoshida-chō, Naka-ku; tel. 045/243-1673; http://noble-aqua.com; 6pm-1:30am daily; table charge ¥800 per person; take Blue line to Kannai Station, exit 6, JR Negishi line to Kannai Station, Isezakichō exit

If you're feeling like a cocktail, head to Bar Noble, a 1-minute walk around the corner from Yokohama Bay Brewing Kannai. You'll get a whiff of the sort of sophistication emanating from Ginza's swanky cocktail strongholds here, down to the dapper bartenders. Ambient lighting, a Zelkova countertop, and tunes lightly wafting from unseen speakers deepen the spell. With more than 500 types of booze on the shelf, rest assured, the bartenders know how to mix a drink. Try Great Sunrise, the bar's signature cocktail, which won the World Cocktail Championship in November 2011. This deep-yellow concoction is meant to signify the hope of a new day following the March 2011 Tōhoku earthquake and tsunami.

AIREGIN

5-60 Sumiyoshi-chō; tel. 045/641-9191; www.airegin.yokohama; 7pm-10:30pm daily; ¥2,500 cover charge includes one drink; take Blue line to Kannai Station, exit 8

Airegin (Nigeria spelled backward) is a standout in the city's vibrant jazz scene. What is today a live jazz club originally opened as a jazz kissa (jazz café), where patrons listen to jazz records on immaculate sound systems as they sip their brew, in Shinjuku, Tokyo, by a jazz-loving couple in 1969. It later relocated to Yokohama, where it became established as a stalwart in the local scene. This archetypal jazz joint is cozy and smoky, and draws a dedicated crowd of connoisseurs. Look for the large yellow sign on the sidewalk. It's located just down the street (2 minutes' walk) from Yokohama Brewery.

EL NUBICHNOM

1-1 Miyagawa-chō, Naka-ku; tel. 045/231-3626; https://ameblo.jp/el-nubichinom; 5:30pm-10:30pm Mon. and Wed.-Thurs., 5:30pm-11:30pm Fri., 3pm-11:30pm Sat., 3pm-8pm Sun.; take subway Blue line, JR lines to Sakuragichō Station, exit 1

El Nubichnom claims to be the world's smallest craft-beer bar. This standing-only bolthole overlooking the Ōka River is run by a friendly, passionate beer judge named Kajisan. Five or six Japanese craft brews are on tap at any given time, and often include some rare ones. Sizes include 200ml (¥700) and 400ml (¥1,400); prices drop to ¥600 and ¥1,100, respectively, during happy hour (which begins when the bar opens and bizarrely runs until 30 minutes before closing). It's a fun, cramped spot for a drink or two.

Note that the two-story building that houses El Nubichnom is also home to an array of bars. Ascend the staircase on either side of the building to the corridor that runs along the back of the building to find the entrances to all of the second-floor bars.

DOWNBEAT

2F Miyamoto Bldg., 1-43 Hanasaki-chō, Naka-ku; tel. 045/241-6167; www.yokohama-downbeat.com; 4pm-11:30pm Mon.-Sat.; cover charge for some events; take subway Blue line, JR lines to Sakuragichō Station, exit 2

A good place to end the journey through Yokohama's jazz landscape is at one of the best jazz joints in the city. Downbeat is a classic old-school jazz kissa with dim lighting and worn posters plastered on the walls and ceiling. Tunes chosen from a gold mine of some 3,700 records are played through a stellar sound system. It also sometimes hosts live gigs.

INFORMATION AND SERVICES

Good online resources include **Yokohama Seasider** (www.yokohamaseasider.com), with event listings, interviews with locals, and restaurant, café, and bar recommendations; and the **Yokohama Official Visitor's Guide** (www.yokohamajapan.com), with activity recommendations, listings of all kinds, and transportation information.

- **Yokohama Station Tourist Information Center** (2F JR Yokohama Tower, 1-1-1 Minami-saiwai, Nishi-ku; tel. 045/620-9926; 9am-7pm daily; take JR, Tōkyū Tōyoko lines to Yokohama Station, on east-to-west walkway inside station)
- **Yokohama Convention & Visitors Bureau** (Sangyō-Bōeki Center 1F, 2 Yamashita-chō; tel. 045/221-2111; www.welcome.city.yokohama.jp/eng/convention; 9am-5pm Mon.-Fri.; take subway Blue line to Nihon-ōdōri, exit 3)
- **Chinatown 80** (80 Yamashita-chō; tel. 045/681-6022; www.chinatown.or.jp/guide/chinatown80/; 10am-8pm Sun.-Thurs., 10am-9pm Fri.-Sat.; take Minatomirai line to Motomachi-Chūkagai, exit 2).

GETTING THERE

The train ride from Tokyo to Yokohama is easy and surprisingly quick. There are a number of options for getting to Yokohama, but for simplicity's sake I recommend starting your journey from either Shibuya, Shinjuku, Tokyo, or Shinagawa Station.

If you leave from Shibuya Station, take the **Tōkyū Tōyoko Line** straight to **Yokohama Station.** You can catch the express or **limited express train** from Shibuya Station, depositing you at Yokohama Station in as little as 30 minutes. The fares for these faster rides are the same as the local train (¥280 one-way). The Tōkyū Tōyoko Line also continues as the **Minato Mirai Line** to **Motomachi-Chukagai,** the best stop to access Chinatown. If you need to go to a station in downtown Yokohama that is not serviced by express or limited express trains, you can transfer to a local train at Yokohama Station. Also departing from Shibuya Station is the **JR Shonan-Shinjuku Line** (25 minutes; ¥400 one-way), which also leaves from Shinjuku Station (35 minutes; ¥570).

Two other Tokyo hubs with easy access to Yokohama are **Tokyo** (30-40 minutes; ¥480) and **Shinagawa** (20-30 minutes; ¥300). The **JR Tōkaidō line, JR Yokosuka line,** and **JR Keihin-Tohoku line** run from both stations.

GETTING AROUND

Many of Yokohama's sights, clustered around Minato Mirai 21 and the areas of Motomachi and Chinatown, are within walking distance of one another.

The city is served by two easily navigable subway lines, simply called the **Blue** and **Green lines,** which run north-south (¥210-520). There is also the local aboveground **JR Negishi line** that runs through the city. But chances are you won't even need to use these lines. The vast majority of sights you'll likely visit in Yokohama are easily accessed from stops on the Minato Mirai line, which is simply the continuation of the Tōkyū Tōyoko line that runs directly to Yokohama from Shibuya.

In addition to train and subway lines,

there's an **Akai-Kutsu** bus service (www.yokohamajapan.com/information/getting-around-yokohama/akaikutsu.php), which shuttles visitors to popular sights in the Minato Mirai 21, Chinatown, and Motomachi. Buses leave from Sakuragichō Station, located on the Blue subway line and JR Negishi line. A trip on one of these buses costs ¥220 for adults and ¥110 for children ages 11 and under, which you can pay when you get on the bus, and station announcements are made in English.

Kamakura

One hour south of Tokyo by train, Kamakura is the closest place to the capital to deeply experience Japanese Buddhism in its various forms. Located next to the ocean, hemmed in by mountains laced with hiking trails, the city is home to more than 80 temples and shrines. If you're going to make only one trip beyond Tokyo, make it Kamakura.

The vast majority of Kamakura's religious complexes were built during the Kamakura period (1185-1333) by monks who absconded from China during the Song Dynasty, when the climate began to turn against Buddhism. In Japan, on the other hand, the religion was spreading, particularly the Zen school. During this brief period, Japan's first shogun, Minamoto no Yoritomo (1147-1199), chose to base his rather makeshift shogunate here after wresting power from Kyoto, resulting in a temple construction boom.

Modern-day Kamakura has the feeling of a beach town, which it is, with down-to-earth locals, artisan cafés, and restaurants selling health-conscious food. Surfers and sunbathers fill the beaches along the coast heading west to Enoshima, a small island off the coast. Especially on holidays and weekends, the lively shopping street of Komachi-dōri and the town's more popular temples and shrines are thronged with tourists. The town begs to be explored on foot; venture out on the Daibutsu Hiking Course, a pleasant hike that leads southward through the mountains to the iconic Great Buddha statue at the temple of Kōtoku-in.

ORIENTATION

Kamakura's time in the political spotlight was turbulent and brief, but its spiritual legacy is readily visible today, with clusters of temples and a handful of key shrines located throughout the city. The main concentrations can be accessed on foot or by bus from near **Kita-Kamakura Station** in the north; **Kamakura Station** in the city center, where you'll also find the major shopping thoroughfare of **Komachi-dōri;** and **Hase Station** in the southwest, where you'll find the **Great Buddha at Kōtoku-in.** Trails weaving through the hills surrounding the city give you a chance to experience some peace and quiet.

Two of the city's most important Zen temples are **Kenchō-ji** and **Engaku-ji.** In truth, this hardly scratches the surface. If you're keen to temple-hop all day, ask the kind staff at the tourist information center next to Kamakura Station for more information.

Six stops west of Hase Station on the Enoden line is **Enoshima Station,** the gateway (by rail) to the nearby island of **Enoshima,** linked to the mainland by a bridge, with stretches of sandy beachfront flanking its north side.

SIGHTS

Near Kita-Kamakura Station

ENGAKU-JI

円覚寺

409 Yamanouchi; tel. 0467/22-0478; www.engakuji.or.jp/top.html; 8am-4:30pm daily Mar.-Nov., 8am-4pm daily Dec.-Feb.; ¥500 adults, ¥200

Kamakura

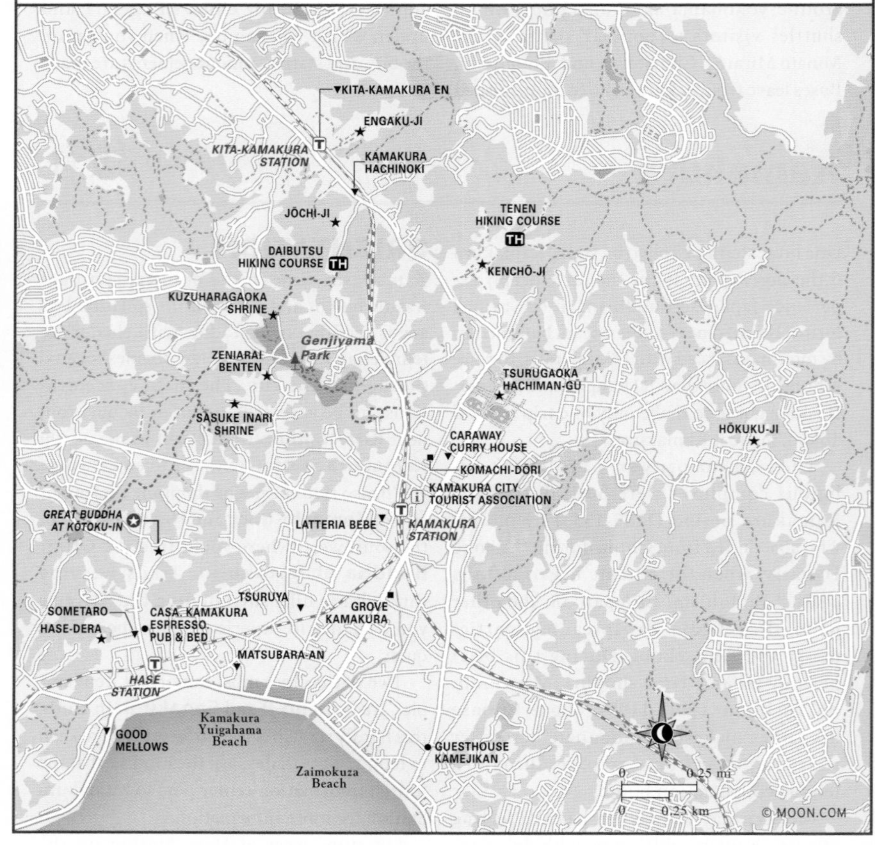

children; take JR Yokosuka line to Kita-Kamakura Station

The biggest of Kamakura's Zen temples, Engaku-ji was founded in 1282 by Hōjō regent Tokimune, with 17 of the complex's original 40 subtemples still standing. The temple's bell, cast in 1301, is Kamakura's biggest, only rung to celebrate the new year.

Attesting to the temple's deep antiquity, the Shozoku-in subtemple showcases some of the best touches of Zen architecture from China's Song Dynasty of any temple in Japan, and even contains a tooth of the Buddha. (Note that this building is not open to the public for most of the year, but can be glimpsed through a gate at other times.) Yasunari Kawabata, the first Japanese writer to win the Nobel Prize for literature, set much of his novel *Thousand Cranes* on the temple's grounds, and legendary film director Yasujiro Ozu is buried in the temple's cemetery.

Before leaving, be sure to relax and sip a tea at the **teahouse** (8am-4:30pm daily Mar.-Nov., 8am-4pm daily Dec.-Feb.) located on the grounds near the large bell. An English menu is available. The temple also holds free zazen (seated meditation) sessions (6am-7am daily, 1:20pm-2:20pm every

Sat., 10am-11am every 2nd and 4th Sun. of month, no sessions Jan. 1-8 and Oct. 1-5). You must show up before a given session starts to join, so be sure to get there with time to spare. Sitting still for an hour is a surprising ordeal for some—be sure you're up to the challenge before setting out.

KENCHŌ-JI

建長寺

8 Yamanouchi; tel. 0467/22-0981; www.kenchoji.com; 8:30am-4:30pm daily; ¥500 adults, ¥200 children; take JR Yokosuka line to Kita-Kamakura Station

Kenchō-ji is Japan's oldest Zen monastery, founded by the Hōjō regent Tokiyori in 1253 and constructed by Rankei Doryu, a Chinese priest who came to spread the message of Zen in Japan. Only 10 buildings now dot the grounds (there were about 49 subtemples and 7 main halls at its peak) but vestiges of greatness remain, from a bell cast in 1255 and classified a National Treasure, to an atmospheric grove of juniper trees as much as 700 years old, said to have sprung from seeds from China and been planted by Rankei himself. Other interesting elements include an effigy of Jizō Bosatsu, guardian of criminals, a grim reminder of the area's use as an execution ground long ago, and a pond shaped like the character for "spirit."

On Friday and Saturday (www.kenchoji.com/zazen; 4:30pm-5:30pm), the temple holds free courses on zazen (seated meditation), open to all, in Japanese. Even if you don't understand the instructions, it's perfectly acceptable to show up and follow visual cues. Arrive about 15 minutes before 4:30pm to join. Brace yourself: you'll need to be able to sit still for more than 30 minutes.

Near Kamakura Station

TSURUGAOKA HACHIMAN-GŪ

鶴岡八幡宮

2-1-31 Yukinoshita; tel. 0467/22-0315; www.hachimangu.or.jp; 5am-8:30pm daily Apr.-Sept., 6am-8:30 daily Oct.-Mar.; free

Given Kamakura's samurai legacy, steeped in power struggle and war, it's appropriate that the first shogun, Minamoto Yoritomo, chose to put the god of war, Hachiman, front and center at the city's largest shrine. Tsurugaoka Hachiman-gū sits at the top of a high bluff, with great views of the city and coast. The design and layout of the shrine were so colored by Minamoto's battle-hardened worldview that even the bridges cutting through the pond on its grounds were meant to symbolize the fissure between the eternally feuding Minamoto and Taira clans.

Be sure to have a look at the marvelous collection of Buddhist statuary held at the **Kamakura National Treasure Museum** (2-1-1 Yukinoshita; tel. 0467/22-0753; www.city.kamakura.kanagawa.jp/kokuhoukan; 9am-4:30pm Tues.-Sun.; adults ¥400, children ¥200; take JR Yokosuka line to Kamakura Station, east exit) behind the pond on the shrine's grounds. The works on display range from wild-eyed temple guardians brandishing swords to beatific, haloed boddhisatvas and jizō, as the oft-bibbed stone statues of the protector of children, travelers, and unborn are known.

HŌKOKU-JI

報国寺

2-7-4 Jomyo-ji; tel. 0467/22-0777; www.houkokuji.or.jp; 9am-4pm daily; ¥300; take bus 23, 24, 36 from Kamakura Station to sixth stop for Jōmyō-ji

Hōkoku-ji, a Rinzai temple built in 1334, is a slight detour, but its atmospheric bamboo grove makes the trip worthwhile. The temple is also home to a raked rock garden, a smattering of Buddhist statuary, and a small teahouse in a pavilion. While you're there, stop at the space with a roof in the grove to sit and slow down with a cup of green tea and a sweet (9am-3:30pm daily; ¥600). While sitting, clearing the mind, and doing nothing may not appeal to all, the temple holds basic Zen seated meditation sessions, or zazen, on Sunday mornings (7:30am-10:30am; free) for those who'd like to add a little Zen to their lives.

Near Hase Station

HASE-DERA

長谷寺

3-11-2 Hase; tel. 0467/22-6300; www.hasedera.jp/en; 8am-5pm daily Mar.-Sept., 6am-5:30pm daily Oct.-Feb.; ¥400 adults, ¥200 children; take Enoshima Dentesu line to Hase Station

At Hase-dera, a veritable storeroom of evocative Buddhist relics, an 11-faced Kannon, the goddess of mercy, with a colorful backstory is the temple's centerpiece. Legend states the statue was one of two carved from a camphor tree found by a monk named Tokudo Shonin in AD 721 in a village called Hase near Nara. While the other statue of the pair now stands in a temple of the same name near Nara, the one in Kamakura is said to have washed ashore on a nearby beach after having been cast into the ocean near Osaka in the faith that it would resurface. Kamakura's Hase-dera was built to commemorate its miraculous discovery.

Along with this multifaced statue of the bodhisattva, 33 other carvings depict Kannon's range of avatars. The complex also houses a sutra library, a bell cast in 1264, and an army of stone jizō statues clad in red bibs encircling a hall dedicated to the guardian of children and travelers. Walk past the jizō and enter the cave beyond, where you'll find a serene candlelit space and exquisite reliefs of Buddha and other sacred figures carved into the walls. Alongside Kōtoku-in, this is one of Kamakura's best temples.

★ GREAT BUDDHA AT KŌTOKU-IN

高徳院

4-2-28 Hase; tel. 0467/22-0703; www.kotoku-in.jp/en; 8am-5:30pm daily Apr.-Sept., 8am-5pm daily Oct.-Mar.; ¥300 adults, ¥150 children; take Enoshima Dentesu line to Hase Station

The 11.3-meter-tall (37-ft-tall), 81-tonne (90-ton) bronze statue of Amida Buddha, the Great Buddha at Kōtoku-in (aka Daibutsu), a temple of the Jōdo (Pure Land) sect, is a symbol of Kamakura itself. Said to be based on the famed gold-encrusted Buddha occupying Tōdai-ji in Nara, the Buddha's calm pose is accentuated by its palms, facing upward in a mudra known as the jobon-josho, believed to maximize potential enlightenment.

This tranquility is impressive given the fact that the Daibutsu, about a 10-minute walk from Hase-dera, has seen its fair share of calamity, from earthquakes to tidal waves and fires. The original sat in a large hall, destroyed by a monumental typhoon that leveled the city in 1494. From that day on, the statue sat in the open air. Besides repairs made to rectify damage dealt by the 1923 Great Kantō earthquake to its base, upon which it sits, and further upkeep done in 1960-1961 and more recently in 2016, the original statue stands intact. Today, it remains seated in blissful meditation—its 1-meter-wide (3.3-ft-wide) eyes half-closed—wearing the same expression of serenity it had when it was cast in 1252. Although temporarily closed at the time of writing to prevent coronavirus spread, it has traditionally been possible to pay an extra ¥20 to enter the statue itself and see the impressive bronzework from the inside; there's even a stairway leading to shoulder-height.

The temple complex itself consists of spacious grounds and a handful of buildings topped with black-tile roofs. More than anything, though, these structures serve as the backdrop for the magnificent statue.

Enoshima

江の島

A short detour from Kamakura's sights will take you to the tiny island of Enoshima. From Kamakura Station, just hop on the laidback Enoshima line and chug your way to Enoshima Station (23 minutes; ¥260). From there, walk 15 minutes south, crossing a bridge from the coast of the mainland to the island. Along the island's main strip, you'll find plenty of stalls serving seafood, cafés, and, hugging its perimeter, eateries with shimmering views. If the sky is clear, you can see Mount Fuji cutting a beautiful profile in the distance.

1: tea at Hōkoku-ji temple **2:** Kenchō-ji **3:** Engaku-ji **4:** Great Buddha at Kōtoku-in

Note that swimming is not allowed on the beaches directly attached to Enoshima itself. However, **Katase Higashihama Beach,** just east of Enoshima on the mainland, fills with sunbathers and swimmers in the scorching summer months.

ENOSHIMA-JINJA

江の島神社

2-3-8 Enoshima; tel. 0466/22-4020; http://enoshimajinja.or.jp; 8:30am-5pm daily; free entrance, ¥200 adults, ¥100 high school and junior high school students to view Benzaiten statue

Once you've reached the island, wander its atmospheric (and often crowded) main thoroughfare toward the main part of this prominent shrine, which is distributed throughout the island in three parts. This holy place is dedicated to Benzaiten, the Japanese incarnation of Sarasvati and goddess of water, knowledge, the arts, and good fortune—hence why some come to wash their money in the shrine's pond. According to legend, Benzaiten created Enoshima, then vanquished a dragon with five heads that was wreaking havoc on the area. The statue of Benzaiten housed here is considered one of the three most venerated in Japan.

ENOSHIMA IWAYA CAVES

江の島岩屋

2 Enoshima; tel. 0466/24-4141; www.facebook.com/enoshimaiwaya; 9am-5pm daily Mar.-Oct., 9am-4pm daily Nov.-Feb.; ¥500 adults, ¥200 junior high and elementary school students

Hollowed by erosion over the millennia, these two caves on the craggy southern side of the island are reached via a stone staircase. The first cave is occupied by Buddhist statuary; the second is devoted to the five-headed dragon that once terrified the residents of the area until it was banished by the goddess Benzaiten.

ENOSHIMA SAMUEL COCKING GARDEN AND SEA CANDLE

江の島サムエル・コッキング苑, 江の島シーキャンドル

2-3-28 Enoshima; tel. 0466/23-2444; https://enoshima-seacandle.com; 9am-8pm daily; ¥800 adults, ¥400 elementary school students, includes garden entry

At the top of the island you'll find this botanical garden of camellias, roses, and more. Named after Samuel Cocking, an English merchant who arrived in Yokohama soon after Japan reopened to the outside world in 1869 and built a villa on the island in 1882, the garden was originally his botanical experiment. For good coastal views, ascend to the viewing deck of the modern construction known as the Sea Candle, a kind of candle-shaped lighthouse. Built with the same materials as the original lighthouse that once stood in Cocking's garden, it stands 59 meters (194 ft) tall. The 360-degree vista from the observation deck is partly hindered by windows, but you can see all the way to Mount Fuji on clear days. Look north and see if you can spot Yokohama's Landmark Tower or even Tokyo SkyTree looming far on the horizon.

SPORTS AND RECREATION

Hiking

Pick up information about other options and maps, or ask questions to the English-speaking staff, at the **Kamakura City Tourist Association**.

DAIBUTSU HIKING COURSE

Distance: *3 km (1.9 mi) one-way*
Time: *1-1.5 hours one-way*
Information and maps: *Kamakura City Tourist Association; www.trip-kamakura.com/img/downloadcontents/map-english.pdf*
Trailhead: *Jōchi-ji*

This hiking course is a great way to explore the city's riches on foot. The route links the temple of **Jōchi-ji** (1402 Yamanouchi; tel. 0467/22-3943; https://jochiji.com/en; 9am-4:30pm daily; ¥200 adults, ¥100 children), located about an 8-minute walk southwest from Kita-Kamakura Station, with the **Daibutsu** (Great Buddha) in the south, passing the atmospheric shrine of **Zeniarai Benten** (2-25-16 Sasuke; tel. 0467/25-1081; 8am-4:30pm daily; free) on the way. You'll also take in **Genjiyama Park** (4-7-1 Ogigayatsu, Kamakura; 24 hours daily; free), the neighboring **Kuzuharagaoka Shrine** (5-9-1 Kajiwara, Kamakura; tel. 0467/45-9002; 24 hours daily; free), and **Sasuke Inari Shrine** (2-22-10 Sasuke; tel. 0467/22-4711; 24 hours daily; free). From the shrine, the hike continues for about 20 more minutes, at which point you'll find yourself at the foot of the temple of Kōtoku-in and its famed Great Buddha.

TENEN HIKING COURSE

Distance: *3.9 km (2.4 mi) one-way*
Time: *1.5-2 hours one way*
Information and maps: *Kamakura City Tourist Association; www.trip-kamakura.com/img/downloadcontents/map-english.pdf*
Trailhead: *Kenchō-ji*

If you are interested in hiking around Kamakura but the Daibutsu Hiking Course seems prohibitively crowded, there are other hiking trails in the hills around Kamakura, including the recommended Tenen Hiking Course, which runs through the hills on the northern edge of town. You'll find the trailhead on the grounds of the temple **Kenchō-ji,** on the north side of town. Here, to the left side of the main hall you'll see the path leads down into a valley. Walk down this path until you reach a large concrete torii gate, and ascend the steep stone steps, lined with protruding-nosed statues of the mythological Tengu. The official start of the Tenen Hiking Course lies just beyond the small rest area at the top of the steps. At the time of writing, the section between the Tenen resthouse and the entrance to **Zuisen-ji** was closed. Before setting out, check www.city.kamakura.kanagawa.jp/visitkamakura/en/routes/index.html for updates.

Beaches

Sunbathers, swimmers, and surfers from the greater Tokyo area flock to the roughly 7 kilometers (4.3 mi) of beaches around Kamakura in the summer. Official swimming season is July-August, when food shacks and various amenities are in operation, and **lifeguards** are on duty 9am-5pm daily. Alcohol, having a barbecue, and smoking are prohibited on the beach; some restaurants near the water serve booze and allow smoking. According to local law, tattoos must be covered on the beach.

YUIGAHAMA BEACH
由比ヶ浜海岸

2-chōme Hase area, Kamakura-shi; https://yuigahama.sos.gr.jp/en; beach open 24 hours daily, official swimming season 9am-5pm daily Jul. 1-Aug. 31; free

Sandy Yuigahama, with its shallow and calm waters, has been popular since the Meiji period. The easy accessibility of this beach makes it popular with families in summer, and it's well-facilitated, with amenities including beach huts, changing rooms, showers, cafés, bars, food shacks, and rental shops for surfboards, wet suits, wakeboards, life jackets, parasols, and more. To the east, separated from Yuigahama by the Nameri River, **Zaimokuza Beach** (材木座海岸; 5-chōme Zaimoku area, Kamakura-shi; http://zaimokuza.net/english; beach open 24 hours daily, official swimming season 9am-5pm daily Jul. 1-Aug. 31; free) is equally popular and with similar amenities. To reach Yuigahama Beach, take the Enoden line to Yuigahama Station, then walk 5 minutes south from there. If you don't mind walking, you can also make your way on foot from Kamakura Station in about 25 minutes. It's also easy to walk between Zaimokuza Beach and Yuigahama.

KATASE HIGASHIHAMA BEACH
片瀬東浜海水浴場

from 3-chōme Koshigoe area, Kamakura-shi in the east, to 1-chōme Katasekaigan, Fujisawa in the west; http://travelenoshima.jp/place/katase_sea.html; beach open 24 hours daily, official swimming season 9am-5pm daily Jul. 1-Aug. 31; free

Extending roughly 1 kilometer (0.6 mi) east to west, facing the northeastern corner of Enoshima, this beach is well known across Japan and has been drawing visitors since the Meiji period. Later, the glut of U.S. troops who sought escape on the beach during the Korean War inspired its nickname of Miami Beach of the East. For better or worse, there's a grain of truth to this moniker. Its clean sand, calm waves, and profuse amenities ensure that this beach is often thronged at summer's sweltering peak. To reach this beach, take the Enoden line to Enoshima Station, then walk 10 minutes south.

FOOD

Near Kita-Kamakura Station

KAMAKURA HACHINOKI

350 Yamanouchi; tel. 0467/23-3723; https://hachinoki-kitakama.jp; 11:30am-2:30pm Mon.-Fri., 11am-3pm Sat.-Sun. and holidays, 5pm-7pm Thurs.-Tues., dinner only by reservation a day early; ¥4,400 lunch, ¥7,700 dinner; take JR lines to Kita-Kamakura Station

Kamakura Hachinoki is a Michelin-starred restaurant serving shōjin ryōri (Buddhist vegetarian cuisine traditionally reserved for Zen monks). Set in an old Japanese house, with tatami mats and exquisite old wooden furniture, the meal is a multicourse banquet. Allow a full evening to properly enjoy it. An English menu is available.

KITA-KAMAKURA EN

501 Yamanouchi; tel. 0467/23-6232; www.kitakamakura-en.com; 11:30am-2pm (last order 1:30pm) lunch, 2pm-5pm teatime, 5pm-8pm dinner Tues.-Sun., reservation required for dinner; ¥5,000 lunch average, ¥10,000 dinner average; take JR lines to Kita-Kamakura Station, west exit

This fantastic family-run kaiseki restaurant overlooks a pond and Zen temple grounds. Kita-Kamakura En is a simple space with an earthy color scheme, free of the stuffy atmosphere often associated with kaiseki. Set courses change with the seasons, and ingredients are sourced from around the country. It's located on the second floor of the ochre building outside Kita-Kamakura Station's main exit. Reserve for dinner a month or more in advance. Alternatively, stop by at teatime if it's fully booked.

Near Kamakura Station

CARAWAY CURRY HOUSE

2-12-20 Komachi; tel. 0467/25-0927; 11:30am-7:30pm Tues.-Sun.; from ¥660; walk 6 minutes northeast from JR Kamakura Station

With its nostalgic interior, kind staff, and reasonably priced hefty portions, this Japanese curry joint really hits the spot. The contents of the curry—chicken, pork, beef, squid, cheese, or egg—are smoothly shredded into a puree-like consistency and served with a side of rice and a salad. Get the small rice if you don't want to leave feeling overstuffed. It's a popular spot and sometimes attracts a queue, which tends to move quickly. A recommended place to try one of Japan's classic comfort foods.

LATTERIA BEBE

11-17 Onarimachi; tel. 0467/81-3440; http://latteria-bebe.com; 11am-9pm Tues.-Sun.; ¥2,000 lunch, ¥3,000 dinner; take JR, Enoden lines to Kamakura Station

Latteria Bebe is an excellent pizzeria owned by two brothers who apprenticed as chefs in Italy (one making pizza, the other cheese). Set in an old wooden house about a 5-minute walk from Kamakura Station, the restaurant has a wood-fire oven and offers on-site cheese workshops where guests make their own mozzarella. The menu includes seasonal ingredients and local seafood. Lunch sets are a good value. Book ahead a few days in advance if possible; otherwise, be prepared to wait. Limited English is spoken.

★ TSURUYA

3-3-27 Yuigahama; tel. 0467/22-0727; http://aquadina.com/kamakura/spot/500/; 11:30am-7pm Wed.-Mon.; average ¥3,000; take Enoden line to Wadazuka Station

It's all about eel at Tsuruya. This Michelin-starred restaurant has been serving a simple menu since 1929 consisting of broiled eel atop rice—either in a stylish wooden box or a bowl—or with rice on the side, delicately flavored with a variety of dipping sauces. The shop has literary associations thanks to the fact that it was frequented by novelist

Kawabata Yasunari, the first Japanese writer to win the Nobel Prize for literature, who lived in the area toward the end of his life. It's advisable to book a few days in advance.

Near Hase Station

SOMETARO

3-12-11 Hase; tel. 0467/22-8694; www.okonomi-sometaro.com; 11:30am-9pm Thurs.-Mon.; ¥1,000; take Enoden line to Hase Station

Sometaro is a great okonomiyaki restaurant where you can cook your own fully customizable savory pancake (toppings include cheese, kimchi, egg, and more) or yakisoba (stir-fried soba noodles) on a hotplate at your table. If you're new to the process, affable staff are happy to help you get the job done.

GOOD MELLOWS

27-39 Sakanoshita; tel. 0467/24-9655; http://goodmellows.jp; 10:30am-6:30pm Wed.-Mon.; ¥1,200; take Enoden line to Hase Station

About a 12-minute walk from Hase-dera, Good Mellows is a great beachside option serving reasonably priced burgers, beers, and the kinds of sides you'd expect to see at a bar stateside (buffalo wings, fries, salads). The burgers can be customized with a range of toppings (pineapple, avocado, bacon, and a slew of cheeses). An English menu is available. The place closes early, so it's a better option for lunch.

MATSUBARA-AN

4-10-3 Yuigahama; tel. 0467/61-3838; http://matsubara-an.com; 11am-10pm (last order 9pm) daily; ¥2,000-3,000 lunch, ¥3,000-4,000 dinner; take Enoden line to Yuigahama Station

Set in an atmospheric old Japanese house, Matsubara-an is a soba restaurant firmly on the foodie map. Guests have a choice between a chic indoor dining area and outdoor seating in a quiet garden. The restaurant makes its own noodles, which it serves both kake (hot) and zaru (cold), along with sides like tempura and sashimi. Lunch sets come with starters like roast duck and veggies with bagna cauda (Italian hot garlic and anchovy) dip. Reserve a few days in advance for dinner; lunch is first-come, first-served.

ACCOMMODATIONS

Kamakura is a comfortable day trip from Tokyo. That said, if you happen to be traveling between Tokyo and Kyoto, or would simply like to slow down, consider staying overnight.

GUESTHOUSE KAMEJIKAN

3-17-21 Zaimokuza; tel. 0467/25-1166; https://kamejikan.com; mixed dorm from ¥3,200, doubles from ¥9,000; take bus no. 12, 40, or 41 from Kamakura Station to Kuhonji bus stop, or walk 25 minutes southeast from Kamakura Station

The name of this languid, renovated wooden home, nearly a century old, appropriately translates to "Turtle Time." Lodging options include a private room for two, a private room for up to four, or a mixed dorm with six beds, all of which share two toilets and one shower. The property sits about 250 meters (820 ft) inland from Zaimokuza Beach. There's also a cozy café and bar on site that operates on weekends (noon-5pm Sat.-Sun.).

CASA. KAMAKURA ESPRESSO. PUB & BED

1-15-5 Hase; tel. 0467/55-9077; www.facebook.com/CASAkamakuraespresso/; double ¥14,200, twin with bunk beds ¥12,000 for two, includes breakfast; take Enoden line to Hase Station, then walk 3 minutes north

This inn in Hase sits right beside the road that leads to Hase-dera, and is about a 7-minute walk north of Yuigahama Beach. There are just two rooms: a double with two twin beds, and another private room with a bunk bed. Each has an en suite toilet and shower. There's also a shared lounge and a café on site where an American-style breakfast is served (included in the price).

INFORMATION AND SERVICES

The city's English-language website (www.city.kamakura.kanagawa.jp/visitkamakura/en/) provides good information about the town's sights, food, shopping, and more. Near the west exit of JR Kamakura Station, there's also a donation-based volunteer tour guide outfit, **Kamakura Welcome Guides** (1-12 Onarimachi; tel. 0467/23-3050; https://kamakurawelcome.guide/en/index.html; 8:30am-5:15pm daily; donations recommended; near west exit of JR Kamakura Station). Your only expense, aside from a recommended donation, will be covering the guides' transport and entrance fees. Reserve online between two weeks and three months ahead of your visit. Finally, for more information on Enoshima, which falls within the boundaries of the city of Fujisawa, check out the **Discover Fujisawa** website (www.fujisawa-kanko.jp).

- **Kamakura City Tourist Association** (1-1-1 Komachi; tel. 0467/22-3350; www.trip-kamakura.com; 9am-5pm daily; outside Kamakura Station's east exit)

GETTING THERE

The **JR Yokosuka line** runs from Tokyo and Shinagawa Stations in Tokyo (1 hour; ¥940), as well as Yokohama Station to Kamakura Station (25 minutes; ¥350). Another option is the **JR Shōnan-Shinjuku line,** which directly links Shinjuku and Shibuya to Kamakura (1 hour; ¥940). To reach Kamakura station on this train, you'll need to transfer at Ofuna, unless you catch a train bound for Zushi.

GETTING AROUND

Kamakura is very walkable, but if you want to save a bit of time, you can get around by taking the train or bus, or even riding a bike.

Train

Aside from the JR lines that connect Kita-Kamakura and Kamakura Stations, the **Enoden (Enoshima Electric Railway) line** is a classic old-school tram that goes from Kamakura Station to Hase, near the Great Buddha, before moving slowly on through the city's coastal neighborhoods and to the island of Enoshima (23 minutes; ¥260 from Kamakura Station).

Bus

There is also a network of city buses leaving from Kamakura Station and connecting to all the main sights. Blue buses are run by **Keikyū** (https://timetablenavi-en.keikyu-bus.co.jp/en/route/dia/landmark); orange by **Enoden** (www.enoden.co.jp/en/bus). These two bus companies tend to share bus stops around town, although they each have a respective terminal stand outside Kamakura Station's east exit. Fares start from ¥180. For a map of town that includes information on bus terminals closest to popular sights and more, visit www.trip-kamakura.com/img/downloadcontents/map-english.pdf.

Finally, the **Kamakura Free Kankyo Tegata** is a special ticket deal that allows you to ride freely on any bus running through the city, as well as most stretches of the Enoden line (www.city.kamakura.kanagawa.jp/visitkamakura/en/access/index.html; ¥570 adults, ¥290 children). These passes can be purchased at tourist information centers in Kamakura Station, near the east exit of Enoden Kamakura Station, at Hase Station, and at a handful of sights around town, including the gift shop at Engaku-ji.

Cycling

While Kamakura is an ideal city to explore on foot, there are options for bicycle rentals for those who would like to cover more terrain. The heart of town is relatively flat, although you may encounter some hills as you pedal inland, toward the low-lying mountains that ring the city. There are no designated cycling routes per se, but traffic tends to be fairly calm and the scale of the town is such that a bicycle can take you everywhere you want to go.

Grove Kamakura (2-1-3 Yuigahama, Kamakura-shi; tel. 0467/23-6667; https://grove-rental.com/; 10am-7pm Fri.-Wed., closed Wed. if Thurs. is national holiday), located about an 8-minute walk from Kamakura Station, rents front-suspension bikes for ¥2,500 and dual suspension bikes for ¥3,000 per day.

Nikko 日光

UNESCO World Heritage site Nikko (Light of the Sun), a mountainous realm located 125 kilometers (78 mi) north of Tokyo, is bisected by the Daiya River and neighbored to the west by the gleaming alpine Lake Chūzen-ji and holy Mount Nantai. Nikko was long believed to be the domain of forest spirits; some shrines in this area date back to the 8th century. This hallowed status inspired Tokugawa Ieyasu (1542-1616), founder of the Tokugawa Shogunate, to have his tomb built there. Ieyasu's grandson, Tokugawa Iemitsu (1604-1651), built the grand mausoleum of Tōshō-gū for his grandfather in 1634, and was later himself enshrined in Nikko at Taiyūinbyō.

During the Meiji period (1868-1912), when Japan began to open up, Nikko became the summer escape of choice among foreign diplomats and merchants escaping the heat of Tokyo. Among these residences was Meiji-no-Yakata, once the grounds of a summer villa owned by American trader F.W. Horn, now filled with swanky restaurants. Even today, Nikko can unfortunately be inundated by crowds. The town is at its most packed on weekends and holidays, particularly from May-October. Your best bet is either to visit on a weekday or stay overnight and get an early start on sightseeing.

ORIENTATION

Nikko is compact, with a population just over 80,000. The town's **heritage area,** where the temples and shrines are all bunched together, is roughly 2 kilometers (1.2 mi) northwest of **downtown,** where you'll find the **JR Nikko** and **Tōbu Nikko Stations.** The gateway to the town's grandiose religious structures is the famed **Shin-kyō,** an arched bridge over the Daiya-gawa river, located about 1.6 kilometers (1 mi) from the town's two main railway stations. You can reach this point either by taking a bus (5 minutes; ¥200) or simply taking the 30-minute walk.

Once you've crossed the famed Shin-kyō, the first major sight you'll come to is the temple of **Rinnō-ji**, followed by **Tōshō-gū.** Another 5-minute walk west of Tōshō-gū brings you to **Futarasan-jinja,** Nikko's most ancient sight, with **Taiyuinbyō Temple,** where Ieyasu's grandson is enshrined, another 15 minutes' walk westward from there.

A worthy detour from Nikko's core sightseeing district is the ethereal ravine known as the **Kanmangafuchi Abyss,** a pathway lined with stone lanterns and stone guardian Jizōstatues along the southern bank of the Daiya-gawa, just about 30 minutes on foot from the town's major cluster of temples and shrines.

SIGHTS

Shin-kyō (Sacred Bridge)

神橋

Kamihatsuishimachi, Nikko; tel. 0288/54-0535; www.shinkyo.net/english; 8am-5pm daily Apr.-Sept., 8am-4pm daily Oct.-mid-Nov., 9am-4pm daily mid-Nov.-Mar.; ¥500 adults, ¥300 high school students, ¥200 junior high and elementary school students; from Nikko Station or Tōbu Nikko Station, take a Tōbu bus to Shin-kyō bus stop

Your survey of Nikko's wonders begins at Shin-kyō (Sacred Bridge), a vermillion arched bridge spanning the banks of the Daiya-gawa. It sits at the entrance to the area of Nikko where most of the temples and shrines are clustered and is actually part of **Futarasan-jinja.** The bridge is said to mark the spot where Shōdō Shōnin, a Buddhist priest who introduced Buddhism to Nikko, crossed the river atop two snakes in AD 766.

Rinnō-ji

輪王寺

2300 Sannai, Nikko; tel. 0288/54-0531; www.rinnoji.or.jp; 8am-5pm Apr.-Oct., 8am-4pm Nov.-Mar.; ¥400 adults and high school students, ¥200 junior high and elementary school students, or ¥900 adults

Nikko

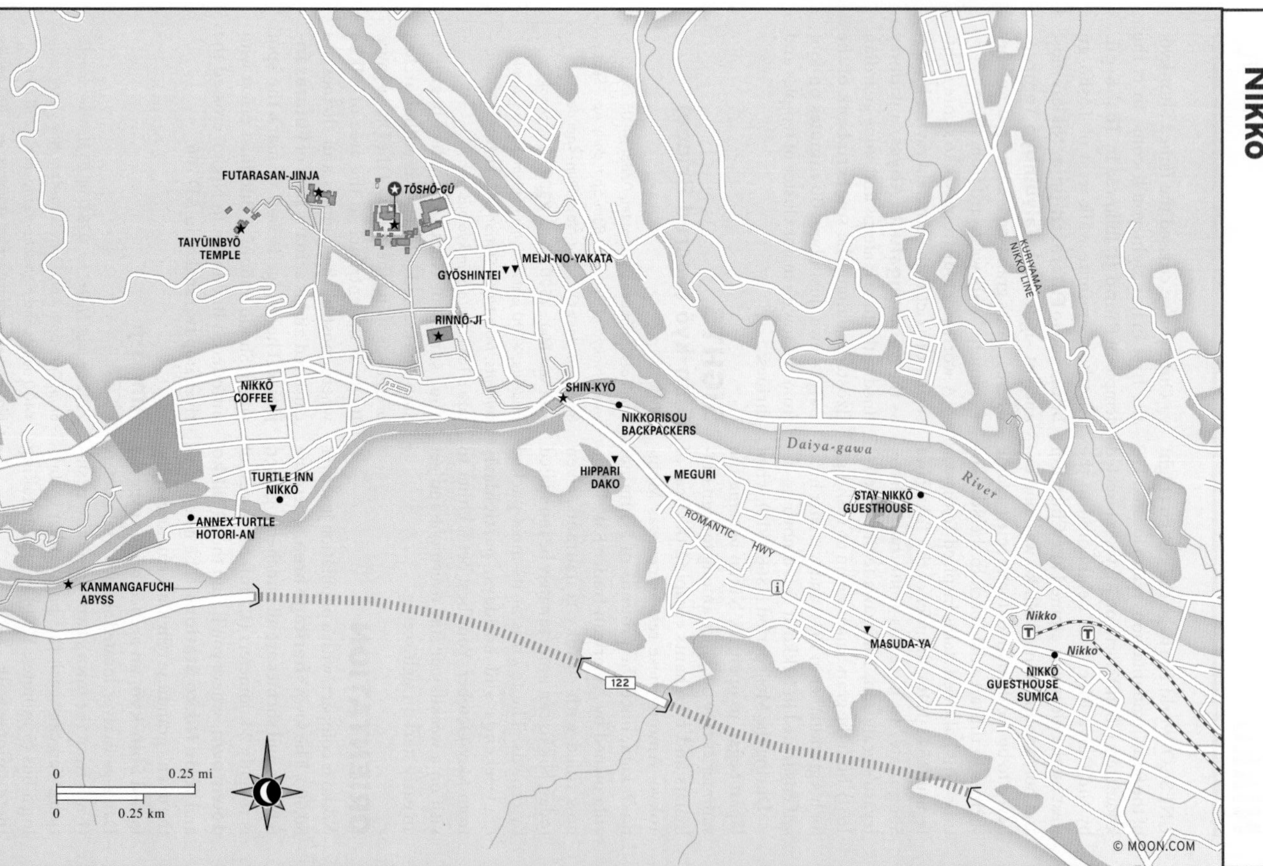
FUTARASAN-JINJA
TŌSHŌ-GŪ
TAIYŪINBYŌ TEMPLE
MEIJI-NO-YAKATA
GYŌSHINTEI
RINNŌ-JI
KURIYAMA-NIKKO LINE
SHIN-KYŌ
NIKKŌ COFFEE
NIKKORISOU BACKPACKERS
Daiya-gawa River
HIPPARI DAKO
MEGURI
TURTLE INN NIKKŌ
STAY NIKKŌ GUESTHOUSE
ANNEX TURTLE HOTORI-AN
ROMANTIC HWY
KANMANGAFUCHI ABYSS
Nikko
Nikko
MASUDA-YA
NIKKŌ GUESTHOUSE SUMICA
122
0
0.25 mi
0
0.25 km
© MOON.COM

and high school students, ¥400 junior high and elementary school students for multi-entry ticket to Taiyūinbyō; take JR Nikko line to Nikko Station and Tōbu Nikko line to Tōbu Nikko Station, then take a Tōbu bus to Nishisando bus stop

After crossing the Daiya-gawa on the backs of two serpents, Shōdō Shōnin went on to found Rinnō-ji, a sprawling temple of the Tendai sect with 1,200 years of history behind it. In the main hall—a striking black, green, and vermillion structure—you'll find three towering figures standing 8 meters (26 ft) tall and representing manifestations of the Buddha, with Senju, the thousand-armed version of Kannon, the goddess of mercy, on the right; Amida Nyorai, the Buddha who guides believers to paradise, in the middle; and Bato-Kannon, the protector of animals, on the left. For an additional fee of ¥300, you can also enter the treasure hall (8am-5pm Apr.-Oct., 8am-4pm Nov.-Mar.), which contains around 6,000 relics linked to the temple, as well as the nearby stroll garden Shōyō-en (8am-5pm Apr.-Oct., 8am-4pm Nov.-Mar.).

North of the main hall is a sub-temple known as Goho-tendo, where the faithful offer up prayers, written on wooden plaques, which are burned and released to the heavens. Three of the Seven Gods of Luck of Chinese folklore are enshrined in Goho-tendo: Daikoku-ten and Bishamon-ten, bestowing wealth and a bountiful harvest, and Benzai-ten, the goddess of the arts. South of the main hall is the abbot's quarters, complete with a beautiful Edo-period garden.

★ Tōshō-gū

東照宮

2301 Sannai, Nikko; tel. 0288/54-0560; www.toshogu.jp/english/; 8am-4:30pm Apr.-Oct., 8am-3:30pm Nov.-Mar.; ¥1,300 adults and high school students, ¥450 junior high and elementary school students for shrine, ¥500 adults, ¥300 high school students, ¥200 junior high and elementary school students for treasure house; take JR Nikko line to Nikko Station and Tōbu Nikko line to Tōbu Nikko Station, then take a Tōbu bus to Nishisando bus stop

Tōsho-gū is a UNESCO World Heritage site and shrine complex originally built in 1617. No expense was spared in the creation of this ostentatious complex, which enshrines Tokugawa Ieyasu, founder of the Tokugawa shogunate.

Make your way up the Omotesandō and walk through the large stone torii gate. Just past the pagoda up a stone staircase is the **Omotemon** shrine gate, flanked by two intimidating deva kings meant to protect the holy site.

In this first square beyond the Omotemon, you'll find a stable housing a white sacred horse. Above the stable door is the iconic panel that has come to symbolize Nikko, which depicts three monkeys—one covering its ears, one its eyes, one its mouth—sending the message of "Hear no evil. See no evil. Speak no evil." The precise origin of this imagery is uncertain, but it's believed that it came to Japan via a Chinese Buddhist monk in the 8th century. At the back of this square is a sutra library, which is closed to the public. The **Nikko Tōshō-gū Museum of Art** (2301 Sannai, Nikko; tel. 0288/54-0560; www.toshogu.jp/shisetsu/bijutsu.html; 9am-5pm Apr.-Oct., 9am-4pm Nov.-Mar.; ¥800 adults, ¥600 high school students, ¥400 junior high and elementary school students) is found at the end of a path that branches off to the right from the courtyard beyond the Omotemon.

Proceeding from this first courtyard, make your way to the second flight of stone stairs. On your right, you'll see a bell tower; on the left, a drum tower and **Yakushi-do,** a temple dedicated to the Buddha's ability to heal sickness, known for the *Crying Dragon* painted on its ceiling. Continue to the top of the stairs where you'll find the mesmerizing 11.3-meter-tall (37-ft-tall) **Yomeimon** (Gate of Sunlight), a National Treasure; so close to perfection was this gate that those who built it inverted the last beam to avoid making the gods jealous.

Across the Yomeimon, to the right is the **Kaguraden,** a space for religious dances and Shinto weddings. On the left is a storage room for portable shrines used in traditional festivals. And on the opposite side of

this courtyard is the gate that leads to the shrine's inner sanctum. This gate, known as the **Karamon** (Chinese Gate), is another opulent National Treasure that leads to the main inner courtyard. After slipping off your shoes, you can enter the main hall and the prayer hall, as far as you may go into Tōshō-gū itself. Deeper into the complex is the inner chamber and innermost chamber, closed to visitors.

Back in the plaza just inside the Yomeimon gate, on the right you'll encounter one more symbol of Nikko, the **Sakashitamon** (Gate of the Sleeping Cat). Cross through this gate bearing the image of a sleeping feline and climb 207 steps to reach Tokugawa Ieyasu's actual tomb. The monument itself is relatively mundane, but the pristine surroundings are worth seeing.

Futarasan-jinja

日光二荒山神社

2307 Sannai, Nikko; tel. 0288/54-0535; www.futarasan.jp; 8am-5pm daily Apr.-Oct., 9am-4pm daily Nov.-Mar.; ¥200 adults, ¥100 children; from Nikko Station or Tōbu Nikko Station, take a Tōbu bus to Nishisando bus stop

The first thing to note about Futarasan-jinja is its age. Founded by Shōdō Shōnin in AD 782, this shrine is the spiritual guardian of Nikko. This feels appropriate, considering that the shrine was built to honor the gods of three sacred mountains surrounding the area: Mount Nantai, Mount Nyoho, and Mount Tarō. The Futarasan-jinja complex next to Tōshō-gū is, in fact, one of three locations, with other shrines including Chugushi-jinja, on the banks of nearby Lake Chūzen-ji, and Oku-miya atop Mount Nantai. Without the pomp of its neighbor, it exudes a sense of calm and relative simplicity.

Entering via a bronze torii gate, you'll discover an ornate gate decorated and carved in much the same way as the Karamon (Chinese Gate) of Tōshō-gū. The same applies to the Haiden (prayer hall), featuring paintings of dragons and lions, beyond the gate. The current incarnation of the Honden (main hall) of the shrine is the oldest structure in Nikko, dating to 1619. Feel your eyes drawn to the room's centerpiece: a 2.7-meter-tall (9-ft-tall) altar adorned with natural scenes of animals and flowers, containing a wooden statue of Tokugawa Iemitsu, grandson of Ieyasu.

1: Futarasan-jinja **2:** Shin-kyō **3:** Tōshō-gū **4:** Rinnō-ji

Taiyūinbyō Temple

大猷院廟

tel. 0288/54-0531; 8am-5pm (last entry 4:30pm) Apr.-Oct., 8am-4pm (last entry 3:30pm) Nov.-Mar.; ¥550 adults and high school students, ¥250 junior high and elementary school students, or ¥900 adults and high school students, ¥400 junior high and elementary school students for multi-entry ticket to Rinnō-ji; take JR Nikko line to Nikko Station and Tōbu Nikko line to Tōbu Nikko Station, then take a Tōbu bus to Nishisando bus stop

This temple is the mausoleum of Tokugawa Iemitsu, third of the Tokugawa shoguns and grandson of Ieyasu. Similar in style and layout to neighboring Tōshō-gū, Iemitsu had Taiyūinbyō built at a slightly smaller scale in deference to his larger-than-life grandfather enshrined next door.

Another difference between the two ornate complexes is that while Tōshō-gū is a shrine, Taiyūinbyō is a temple; more specifically, a sub-temple of Rinnō-ji. It's worth noting that before the Meiji period, there was less effort to draw a clear line between Buddhism and Shintō. The two religions mingled freely, as reflected in many old religious structures like this throughout the country.

Mirroring its grander neighbor, Taiyūinbyō is entered by following a path west of Tōshō-gū until reaching a vermillion gate, through which you encounter a second gate protected by two celestial kings, each holding up one hand and keeping the other down—gestures meant to receive those with pure hearts and repel those without—then, a bell tower on the right and a drum tower on the left. Passing next through the Karamon gate, you come to the prayer hall. Inside, marvel at the pillars and walls adorned with gold lacquer, carvings, and more. Beyond this is the main hall, which can only be observed from outside, and Iemitsu's mausoleum itself.

Taiyūinbyō's visual impact cannot compare with Tōshō-gū, but the overall effect in terms of stillness and the setting within a dense forest of cryptomeria give this smaller complex a special atmosphere all its own.

Kanmangafuchi Abyss

憾満ヶ淵

open 24 hours; free; from Nikko Station or Tōbu Nikko Station, take Tōbu bus to Tamozawa bus stop

To visit a less crowded sight, cross the bridge over the Daiya-gawa to the southern bank of the river, where you'll find a wooded path stretching roughly 100 meters (328 ft) and lined with some 70 moss-encrusted stone statues of Jizō (guardian of children and travelers), adorned with red bibs and crocheted caps. A tradition calls the stone figures lining the path "Bake Jizō" (Ghost Jizō), due to the belief that one always arrives at a different number counting them while walking up the path and then recounting them on the journey back.

Although the walk from Tōshō-gū to the Kanmangafuchi Abyss takes about 30 minutes, or 20 minutes from Shin-kyō, heading west from Shin-kyō along the northern bank of the Daiya-gawa and crossing a bridge from the north to south side of the river on the way, the slight detour is worth it. Imbued with serenity, it's one of the most atmospheric spots in Nikko and a respite from the crowds. If you're not walking from a nearby sight, the path begins after passing through a residential area near the Tamozawa bus stop.

FOOD

Nikko's restaurant options are mostly clustered in the downtown area between JR and Tōbu Nikko Stations and Shin-kyō. There are also a few good options within the prime sightseeing area where all of the famed temples and shrines are located. The offerings extend from locally sourced wagyu beef to meals featuring strips of locally made yuba (tofu skin), a staple in shōjin-ryōri eaten by Buddhist monks.

Downtown

HIPPARI DAKO

1011 Kamihatsuishimachi; tel. 0288/53-2933; www.e-nikko.org/shop_detail1478.shtml; noon-5pm, 6:30pm-9:30pm Mon.-Sat.; from ¥700; from Nikko Station or Tōbu Nikko Station, take a Tōbu bus to Shin-kyō bus stop

Hippari Dako is a greasy-spoon joint with a long history of attracting foreign diners. The copious number of business cards, student ID cards, and random notes scrawled onto scraps of paper plastered all over its walls and ceiling attests to this. Part of its appeal is a cost-effective menu—a rarity in Nikko—of simple items like grilled dumplings, ramen, yakisoba, curry udon (thick wheat-flour noodles), and yakitori.

MEGURI

909-1 Nakahatsuishimachi; tel. 080/9343-0831; https://shizensaryo-meguri.com; 10am-6pm Fri.-Wed.; ¥1,500 average; from Nikko Station or Tōbu Nikko Station, take a Tōbu bus to Shin-kyō bus stop

For a more hip, contemporary, and casual option, Meguri is an excellent vegan restaurant that serves curries, tempura, soups, cakes, and more. The restaurant, run by a friendly young couple, has tatami floor-seating and a mural of birds, flowers, and trees across the ceiling. The dining area is small, and food is sold on a first-come, first-served basis, so show up early if you plan to eat lunch here. Roughly 5 minutes' walk from Shin-kyō; look for a sign outside that says "Oriental Fine Arts."

★ MASUDA-YA

439-2 Ishiyamachi; tel. 0288/54-2151; www.nikko-yuba.com; 11am-3pm Fri.-Wed.; ¥4,290; take JR Nikko line to Nikko Station and Tōbu Nikko line to Tōbu Nikko Station

Masuda-ya is the place in central Nikko to try yuba. These sheets of bean curd are a specialty that was once reserved for royals and priests in Nikko and Kyoto, which are both known for the dish. Set in a cozy space overlooking a Japanese garden, the restaurant serves a kaiseki course with a variety of plates combining yuba with local produce, eggs, trout, pickles, rice, and more. If you're in Nikko, it's worth trying this unique cuisine. Lunch only.

Heritage Area

NIKKŌ COFFEE

3-13 Honchō; tel. 0288/53-2335; http://nikko-coffee.com; 11am-6pm (last order 5pm) Tues.-Sun., closed first and third Tues. every month or next day if Tues. falls on public holiday; ¥600 coffee, ¥1,500 lunch; from Nikko Station or Tōbu Nikko Station, take a Tōbu bus to Nishisando bus stop

Nikko Coffee is set in an old rice store that's been spruced up with antique furniture, exposed rafters, and retro lighting. Tucked down a backstreet, this is a good spot for a caffeine hit, snack, or light lunch, with options like sandwiches, galettes, and curries.

★ MEIJI-NO-YAKATA

2339-1 Sannai; tel. 0288/53-3751; www.meiji-yakata.com; 11am-7:30pm daily Apr.-late Nov., 11:30am-7:30pm daily late Nov.-Mar.; ¥1,760-9,900; from Nikko Station or Tōbu Nikko Station, take Tōbu bus to Nishisando bus stop

Meiji-no-Yakata is an institution. Set in a stone cottage with soaring ceilings and hardwood floors, it was once the home of 19th-century American merchant F.W. Horn, who brought the gramophone to Japan. A short walk from Rinno-ji, this restaurant serves Western fare, from roast lamb to steaks and stews made with locally sourced beef, and fish caught in nearby Lake Chūzen-ji—the very types of dishes being introduced to Japan when Horn called the place home. This is an enjoyable place to dine on the sort of Western-style cooking that emerged during the Meiji era. An English menu is available.

GYŌSHINTEI

2339-1 Sannai; tel. 0288/53-3751; www.meiji-yakata.com; 11am-7pm Fri.-Wed. Apr.-late Nov., 11:30am-7pm Fri.-Wed. late Nov.-Mar.; average ¥4,200; from Nikko Station or Tōbu Nikko Station, take Tōbu bus to Nishisando bus stop

Owned by the same group that runs Meiji-no-Yakata, and located on the same property, Gyōshintei veers away from meat and instead focuses on shōjin ryōri, featuring liberal helpings of local produce and yuba, or tofu skin. Even the soup stock is free of animal products. Tatami-mat-floored rooms, calligraphy scrolls, ikebana arrangements set into alcoves, and views onto a garden dotted with bonsai trees and moss-covered rocks create a calm atmosphere, appropriate for a meal traditionally made for monks. If you crave a little extra protein, the kaiseki courses include a bit of fish.

ACCOMMODATIONS

Under ¥10,000

NIKKŌ GUESTHOUSE SUMICA

5-12 Aioichō; tel. 0288/53-1838; www.nikko-guesthouse.com; ¥3,000 dorm, ¥8,000 double, ¥14,000 private apartment; take JR Nikko line to Nikko Station and Tōbu Nikko line to Tōbu Nikko Station

Located in a nicely revamped house, Nikko Guesthouse Sumica is a chic hostel run by a friendly couple who are eager to make guests feel at home and give suggestions for your journey. Room choices include dorms and tatami-mat doubles. All rooms share a bathroom. Note that the inn enforces an 11pm curfew.

NIKKORISOU BACKPACKERS

1107 Kamihatsuishimachi; tel. 090/8815-3336; http://nikkorisou.com; ¥3,000 dorm, ¥8,000 double; from Nikko Station or Tōbu Nikko Station, take a Tōbu bus to Shin-kyō bus stop

Near Shin-kyō and within easy reach of the main shrine complex of Tōshō-gū, Nikkorisou Backpackers is a laid-back guesthouse with a shared bathroom and dorm rooms, both mixed and female-only, as well as tatami-mat and Western-style doubles. All guests can use a shared kitchen. Bicycles can be rented for ¥500 a day.

¥10,000-20,000

ANNEX TURTLE HOTORI-AN

8-28 Takumichō; tel. 0288/53-3663; www.turtle-nikko.com/hotori-an; ¥15,000 double with bathroom

Near the southwestern edge of the Tōshō-gū area, Annex Turtle Hotori-an is notable for its shared onsen bath overlooking the river. Both Japanese tatami and Western-style rooms with private baths are available. Western-style breakfast can be served in-room upon request. If rooms are all booked, also check at the original **Turtle Inn Nikkō** (2-16 Takumichō; tel. 0288/53-3168; www.turtle-nikko.com/turtle; ¥11,300 double with bathroom), located nearby.

¥20,000-30,000

★ STAY NIKKŌ GUESTHOUSE

2-360-13 Inarimachi; tel. 0288/25-5303; www.staynikko.com; from ¥9,000 for private room for two with shared bathroom inside guesthouse, or from ¥9,600 for villa with private bathroom for two, or from ¥18,800 for villa with private bathroom for three

Set beside the Daiya-gawa river, this friendly guesthouse is set in a refurbished and expanded residence with original design accents intact. There are four private rooms, all of which share a bathroom, and three detached villas with private baths. All sleeping quarters are well-kept, and facilities (shared lounge, bath, toilet, laundry) are clean and up-to-date. Some of the rooms have garden or riverside views. For an additional ¥880, you can add a Japanese-style breakfast (must be reserved at least three days in advance).

INFORMATION AND SERVICES

- **Information Desk, Tōbu Nikko Station** (tel. 0288/54-0864; 8:30am-5pm daily)
- **Nikko Kyōdo Center** (591 Goko-machi; tel. 0288/54-2496; 9am-5pm daily; 15 minutes' walk up the main strip from the JR and Tōbu stations on the left side of the road)

GETTING THERE

Starting from Asakusa Station in **Tokyo,** by far the easiest way to reach Nikko is by taking the **Tōbu Nikko line,** which offers limited-express (tokkyu) trains (1 hour 50 minutes; ¥2,860) roughly twice an hour to Tōbu Nikko Station. Note that the JR Pass is not valid on the Tōbu line, so if you are traveling with a JR Pass, your best bet is to take the **JR Tohoku** shinkansen from either Tokyo or Ueno station to Utsunomiya Station, then transfer to the JR Nikko line for the rest of the journey to JR Nikko Station (1 hour 40 minutes-2 hours; ¥5,270-5,480).

Reaching Nikko from **Kansai** (Osaka, Kyoto) or **Nagoya** involves first going to Tokyo via the Tōkaidō shinkansen, then taking one of the routes from the capital described above. Coming from Shin-Osaka, for example, is roughly a 5-hour journey, costing approximately ¥19,000, depending on which route you take from Tokyo.

GETTING AROUND

The bulk of Nikko's sights are located about a 20-minute walk northwest of both **Tōbu Nikko** and **JR Nikko Stations.** Buses (¥200) that run from both station areas also run to Shin-kyō, Tosho-gu, and all surrounding sights.

It's worth knowing about a few special passes that can save a bit of money on transportation, not only within Nikko but also for the journey to and from Tokyo. The **Nikko City Area Pass** (https://tobutoptours.com/en/nikko-city-area-pass.html; ¥2,040 adults, ¥610 children) covers round-trip train fare between Asakusa and Nikko (excluding limited-express trains) and unlimited local train and bus rides within certain areas of Nikko for two days. The **Nikko All Area Pass** (https://tobutoptours.com/en/nikko-all-area-pass.html; ¥4,600 adults, ¥1,180 children Apr. 20-Nov. 30, ¥4,230 adults, ¥1,060 children Dec. 1-Apr. 19) offers a four-day option that covers round-trip fare between Tokyo and Nikko (limited express not included), as well as more extensive bus travel in the region.

To check fares for other bus trips beyond Nikko's shrine area, consult the Tōbu Bus website (www.tobu-bus.com/en/nikko). And be sure to pick up a clear English-language map—an invaluable resource for visualizing transportation logistics in the area—at either Nikko's JR or Tōbu station.

Minakami and Around 水上

The onsen town of Minakami at Gunma Prefecture's wild northern fringe is perhaps the most well-rounded slice of nature within close range of Tokyo. A little less than two hours from the capital by train and local bus, the area surrounding the town itself is home to 18 onsen pumping volcanically heated water into a plethora of appealing baths, including Takaragawa Onsen, one of Japan's best places to soak.

The area is a known quantity among adventure sports enthusiasts. The beautiful, rugged terrain centers around Mount Tanigawa (1,977 m/6,486 ft), one of Japan's 100 Famous Mountains, with trekking and rock climbing in the warmer months and skiing in winter. The nearby Tone River whips up some of Japan's best white water in spring when snow from the surrounding mountains melts. Opportunities for rafting are abundant from April-June, and for canyoning when it heats up in summer.

ONSEN

Takaragawa Onsen

宝川温泉

1899 Fujiwara; tel. 0278/75-2614; www.takaragawa.com; 9am-5pm daily; ¥2,000 adults, ¥1,500 children, bath towel ¥100, face towel ¥200; take bus heading from Minakami Station toward Takaragawa Onsen (every 1.5 hours), every second or third bus stops directly at Takaragawa Onsen (40 minutes; ¥1,150), while others only go as far as Takaragawa Iriguchi bus stop (30 minutes, ¥1,050), from where you must walk 20 minutes or take courtesy car (no reservation required)

Beside a river flowing through a splendid landscape of forested mountains, Takaragawa Onsen is not only one of Japan's largest outdoor baths, it's one of the most magical. Three large mixed baths and one for women only dot the side of the Takara River, upstream from the Tone River—a breathtaking scene. Recently, the onsen has instated a new policy that requires all guests to wear bathing suits in the mixed area. This is very "un-Japanese," though it may make this a more comfortable onsen for some bathers.

Luxuriating in the steamy pools is likely all you will feel like doing once you've arrived, but the dense forest surrounding the baths is crisscrossed with inviting trails begging to be explored. If you choose to venture out, you'll likely find yourself gravitating back to the baths beside the burbling stream. Close your eyes and ease yourself in. This is what the onsen experience is all about.

★ SPORTS AND RECREATION

A slew of adventure sports tour outfits are active in the Minakami area, thanks to the mountainous terrain and presence of the Tone River. There are excellent English-speaking guides that lead white-water rafting tours on the waterway during spring (Apr.-June), when the rapids pick up, with May being the wildest time. During summer, when the Tone tames a bit and the heat spikes, the attention shifts to canyoning, or traversing canyons by walking, swimming, climbing, and rappelling.

Hiking

Hiking season runs May-October/November, depending on when snow begins to fall. For a detailed hike report, check out the always informative **Hiking In Japan** blog (https://japanhike.wordpress.com/2008/04/09/

mt-tanigawa). Stop by the **Minakami Tourist Association** (page 189) for more information on hikes in the area.

TANIGAWA-DAKE ROPEWAY
谷川岳ロープウェイ

www.tanigawadake-rw.com; tel. 0278/72-3575; 8am-5pm Mon.-Fri. and 7am-5pm Sat.-Sun. and holidays Apr.-Nov., 8:30am-4:40pm daily Dec.-Mar.; ¥1,250 adults, ¥630 children one-way, ¥2,100 adults, ¥1,050 children round-trip

This gondola transports you to the top of the Tenjin-daira ski resort area, located roughly 1,500 meters (4,921 ft) up Mount Tanigawa. A number of hiking trails ranging from easy to grueling start from this point. Even if you don't plan to trek, it's worth boarding one of the gondolas and enjoying the fantastic vista of the dramatic terrain that surrounds Minakami. A bus to the bottom of the ropeway (Ropeway Ekimae bus stop) departs hourly from Minakami Station (20 minutes; ¥750). You can also reach the lower station of the ropeway by taking the train from Minakami Station to Doai Station (8 minutes; ¥240), although these trains run infrequently. From Doai Station, it's a 15-minute walk uphill to the lower station of the ropeway.

MOUNT TANIGAWA

Distance: *9.4 km (5.8 mi) round-trip from lower ropeway station, or 6.4 km (4 mi) from upper ropeway station round-trip*
Time: *10 hours round-trip from lower ropeway station, or 5 hours round-trip starting from upper ropeway station*
Trailhead: *Tanigawa-dake Ropeway lower station (Doaiguchi Station) or Tanigawa-dake Ropeway upper station (Tenjin-daira Station)*
Information and maps: *www.tanigawadake-rw.com/tanigawadake; www.enjoy-minakami.jp/pdf/tanigawadakecourseen.pdf*

Do some research before you try to make the ascent up Mount Tanigawa. It may seem like a straightforward climb, but the peak is tricky and has taken more than 800 lives, dwarfing the number of unfortunate climbers who have died on Everest. There are some good **guides** in the region, but they only speak Japanese (https://mmga.jp). If you're keen to try, you can start either from the service road that runs up the mountain to the left of the **Tanigawa-dake Ropeway** or save yourself the first 600 meters (1,968 ft)—roughly 2.5 hours—of huffing and puffing by riding the gondola and then continuing up the peak from there (recommended).

If you opt for the latter, Mount Tanigawa will be the peak looming to your right at the top of the ropeway. Just follow the trail that starts from that point, which leads to the top. On the way, you'll come to **Kata no Koya** (tel. 090/3347-0802; https://twitter.com/gunmanooyama), a lodge where you can make a pit stop for drinks and food, after just over 2 hours of hiking. Pressing on for another 10 minutes or so, you'll reach **Tomanomimi** (1,963 m/6,440 ft), the first of two peaks that make up Tanigawa-dake. From here, you can either simply turn around and return (about 5.6 km/3.5 mi; 4.5 hours round-trip), or you can press on to Mount Tanigawa's second peak, **Okinomimi** (1,977 m/6,486 ft), following the same trail (6.4 km/4 mi; 5 hours round-trip). This second peak is only a few minutes' walk beyond the first. Unless you are a highly experienced hiker with suitable gear, simply returning from this point is recommended.

Rafting and Canyoning

Among the area's tour providers, here are some that stand out:

- **Canyons** (tel. 0278/722-811; www.canyons.jp) offers half-day (¥9,500) and full-day (¥16,000) rafting trips, including lunch, and canyoning tours (¥4,000-20,000, depending on location and time). They also offer accommodation packages at their Alpine Lodge for those joining a tour (¥4,000 Sun.-Fri., ¥5,000 Sat. and public holidays, includes breakfast).

- **I Love Outdoors** (tel. 0278/72-1337; http://iloveoutdoors.jp) does half-day rafting

1: Takaragawa Onsen **2:** hikers on Mount Tanigawa

expeditions for ¥8,000, half-day canyoning (¥8,000), half-day canoeing-kayaking trips from ¥6,500, and full-day canyoning-kayaking tours (¥12,000 including lunch).

- **H20 Guide Services** (tel. 0278/72-6117; http://h2o-guides.jp) also offers guided rafting (¥8,500 half-day, ¥13,000 full-day including lunch in May only) and canyoning trips (¥8,500).

Skiing and Winter Sports

In winter, Minakami is a destination for powder hounds in search of a fix near Tokyo, with the ski season stretching from December-March.

- Water-sports tour provider **Canyons** excels again here, offering chances to traipse through the snowy landscape with snowshoes (¥6,000 half-day, ¥9,500 full-day) from January-March. Just as it does during summer, Canyons offers accommodation to its winter tour participants at its Alpine Lodge (¥4,000 Sun.-Fri., ¥5,000 Sat. and public holidays, includes breakfast).
- The family-run **Tenjin Lodge** at Mount Tanigawa's base also provides a variety of tours, from backcountry skiing (¥15,000 full-day, ¥5,000 for gear) to snowshoeing (¥7,000 adults, ¥5,000 children under 12). Tenjin Lodge opens its rooms to tour members and nonparticipants alike.
- **H2O Guide Services** (tel. 0278/72-6117; https://h2o-guides.jp/?page_id=3338; ¥40,000 for group of 1-2, ¥51,000 for 3, ¥64,000 for 4) leads private off-piste skiing and snowboarding tours in the Minakami region with a certified guide. Essential equipment rental is available for an extra fee (¥5,500).

ACCOMMODATIONS

Note that there are few food options in the area, and some only operate seasonally. Your best bet is to eat at your ryokan or lodge of choice if you plan to stay overnight. Otherwise, ask for a few recommendations at the tourist information center.

Under ¥10,000

TENJIN LODGE

220-4 Yubiso; tel. 0278/25-3540; www.tenjinlodge.com; ¥6,500 per person for double room; From Tokyo, take Joetsu Shinkansen to Echigo-Yuzawa Station, then take JR Joetsu line to Doai Station, pickup from Minakami Station also available on request

If your aim is to venture into the mountains around Minakami, whether for skiing in winter or trekking during the warmer months, Tenjin Lodge is a great option. This friendly, family-run lodge has Japanese and Western-style rooms and shared male and female bathrooms, and serves up tasty home-cooked breakfasts (¥800) and dinners (¥1,200), from pasta to Southeast Asian and Korean food. Sometimes they also do a good barbecue at the riverside next to the inn (¥2,000). As a bonus, the hosts are passionate about the outdoors and offer a variety of adventure tours in the area, from trekking to skiing.

¥20,000-30,000

TAKARAGAWA ONSEN ŌSENKAKU

1899 Fujiwara; tel. 0278/75-2121; www.takaragawa.com; doubles from around ¥25,000 with two meals and shared bathroom; take bus from Minakami Station to Takaragawa Iriguchi bus stop (30 minutes, ¥1,150), then walk 20 minutes, or take bus (every second or third bus goes to onsen, 40 minutes, ¥1,150)

If you plan to visit the pools at Takaragawa Onsen and feel like extending it for an overnight stay—recommended, given the remoteness—this is the easiest place to do so. This old-school inn, attached to the famed baths, is so close to the river you can hear water gurgling from some of the rooms. Guests have 24-hour access to the onsen baths, which allows you to sneak in a late-night soak after most bathers have gone to sleep. Request in advance for the inn to send a car to pick you up from Minakami Station.

¥30,000-40,000

CANYONS GLAMPING

45 Yubiso; tel. 0278/722-811; https://canyons.jp; from ¥35,000 with breakfast

Canyoning and rafting outfit Canyons offers enticing riverside glamping during summer and early autumn (Jul.-Nov.). The getups range from luxe bell-shaped tents to larger abodes with private decks. BBQ feasts can be had at dinnertime for an additional fee. You don't have to join a canyoning or rafting tour to glamp, but package deals are on offer. Recommended after a day spent in the water.

Over ¥40,000

★ BETTEI SENJUAN

614 Tanigawa; tel. 0278/20-4141; www.senjyuan.jp; from ¥83,000 with two meals; take a taxi from Minakami

Bettei Senjuan is a discrete boutique onsen resort at the foot of Mount Tanigawa. With only 18 exquisite rooms, guests are so well tended to that it's easy to forget others are sharing the inn. The rooms' elegant decor comes in Japanese and Western-style, and each has an expansive private open-air onsen tub with stunning views of the surrounding mountains. Dinner is a multicourse kaiseki affair served in a private dining room. A library with a fireplace is a tempting alternative to the bath during winter. This is the quintessential luxury ryokan experience.

INFORMATION AND SERVICES

- **Minakami Tourist Association** (1744-1 Tsukiyono; tel. 0278/62-0401; http://enjoy-minakami.com/en; 8:30am-5:30pm daily; located next to Jōmō Kōgen Station on the Joetsu shinkansen line, a 25-minute bus ride from Minakami Station)

GETTING THERE AND AROUND

Minakami is best reached from **Tokyo.** Starting from **Ueno Station,** either take the **Joetsu** shinkansen (50 minutes; ¥4,810) or **JR Takasaki line** (1 hour 50 minutes; ¥1,980) via Omiya or Ageo station to **Takasaki,** where you'll change to the Jōetsu line and ride until you reach **Minakami** (1 hour 10 minutes; ¥990). Alternatively, starting at either Tokyo (¥6,020) or Ueno Station (¥5,810), take the Joetsu shinkansen to **Jōmō Kōgen Station.** The trip from either stop takes roughly 1 hour. From Jōmō Kōgen, it's a 25-minute bus ride (¥630) to Minakami.

The area's onsen and other attractions can be accessed by bus or taxi.

Hakone 箱根

Hakone has been known for its wealth of natural beauty, from verdant mountains to a plethora of onsen, since the 16th century. It's said that great samurai warrior Hideyoshi Toyotomi (1537-1598), one of Japan's "three unifiers," treated himself to some R&R in Hakone following the Siege of Odawara in 1590. Located in the heart of **Fuji-Hakone-Izu National Park** (www.fujihakoneizu.com), Hakone's natural splendor and diverse artistic offerings—many of them displayed outdoors—are understandably a draw to busy 21st-century Tokyo-ites too.

The traditional approach to exploring Hakone is to make a loop, completed via a succession of quirky transportation options, from a quaint local train line and a cable car to a ropeway over a dramatically vaporous valley and a galleon-like sightseeing boat on Lake Ashi (Ashi-no-ko), which occupies a caldera and offers stunning views of Mount Fuji looming in the backdrop. While fun, following this well-worn path can feel a bit formulaic. It can pay to follow your own curiosity in Hakone and blaze your own trail. Or, perhaps the simplest plan of all, vegging

Hakone

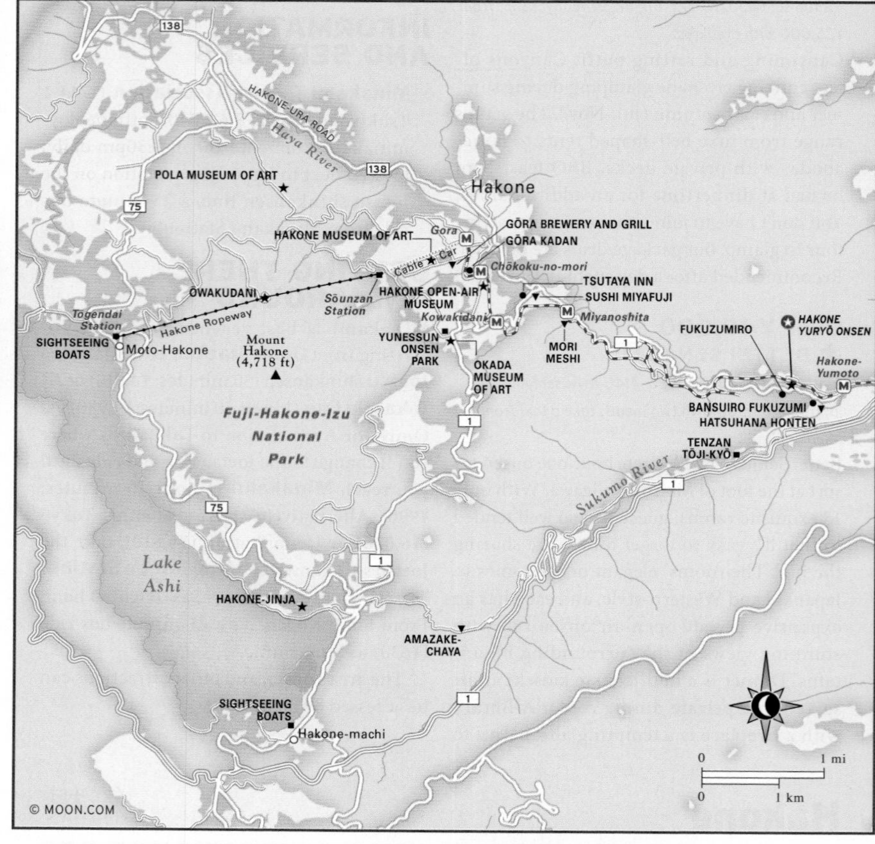

out in an onsen resort and gorging on haute cuisine wearing only a robe and slippers for a few days.

With so many things to do in one place, it's no wonder that Hakone is a destination of choice for day trips and weekend escapes from the capital. The upside of this is that a trip to the area is certain to be a good mix of relaxation and stimulation. The downside is that the place is inundated on weekends, holidays, and in peak season. To minimize the impact of crowds on your experience, come on a weekday and hit the popular spots early in the day.

ORIENTATION

A good way to navigate this area is the **Hakone-Tōzan line,** which starts in the city of **Odawara,** east of Hakone, and winds west almost to the foot of **Mount Hakone.** The first stop of note is **Hakone-Yumoto,** with a wealth of onsen options. Back on the Hakone-Tōzan line, continuing west, you'll come to **Miyanoshita,** a good area to stop for a bite to eat or stay overnight, and **Kowakidani,** where you'll find the stunning Okada Museum of Art and the fun Yunessun Onsen Park. The line's final two stops are **Chōkoku-no-mori,** where you'll find the crowd-pleasing Hakone

Open-Air Museum, and **Gōra,** home to the Hakone Museum of Art and plenty of good ryokan. From there, a cable car links Gōra to **Sōun-zan,** from where hiking trails begin and the **Hakone Ropeway** descends to **Lake Ashi** at Hakone's southwestern edge, hovering above the dramatically volcanic landscape of **Ōwakudani** below.

SIGHTS

Around Kowakidani

OKADA MUSEUM OF ART

岡田美術館

493-1 Kowakudani; tel. 0460/87-3931; www.okada-museum.com/en; 9am-5pm daily; ¥2,800 adults and university students, ¥1,800 children; from Hakone-Yumoto station, take bus to Koakien bus stop

Since it opened in 2013, the Okada Museum of Art has been wowing visitors with its collection of East Asian art, both ancient and modern, from Chinese pottery to Japanese scrolls. Situated on a mountain blanketed in forest, the museum is the creation of casino magnate Kazuo Okada, a self-professed art lover who began to set aside pieces with the express intention to one day open a museum. He succeeded brilliantly. The result is this cutting-edge structure spread over five floors, behind which you'll find a lush stroll garden and laid-back café. There's also a footbath at the entrance where museumgoers can refresh themselves before gawking at the many beautiful artistic specimens in the private collection for the next few hours.

Around Chōkoku-no-mori

THE HAKONE OPEN-AIR MUSEUM

彫刻の森美術館

1121 Ninotarira; tel. 0460/82-1161; www.hakone-oam.or.jp; 9am-5pm daily; ¥1,600 adults, ¥1,200 university and high school students, ¥800 middle school and elementary school students; take electric train to Chōkoku-no-Mori Station

Japan does art in natural settings exceptionally well, and Hakone Open-Air Museum is a superb example. Imagine traipsing through a sculpture garden dotted with works by masters both European and Japanese, from Miró and Rodin to Henry Moore and Taro Okamoto, set against a backdrop of verdant mountains and valleys. You've just pictured this refreshing museum in your mind's eye.

For Picasso fans, there's a pavilion devoted entirely to his work, with some 100 pieces on display from a collection of 319 pieces. Another noteworthy work is the Symphonic Sculpture, a spiral staircase encased by a colorful swirl of glass, leading up to a platform to view the lush natural surroundings.

Those traveling with kids will be relieved to find *Woods of Net,* a sculpture-inspired playground. And if you want to soak and relax after a day spent walking, there's even an outdoor foot bath.

Around Gōra

HAKONE MUSEUM OF ART

箱根美術館

1300 Gōra; tel. 0460/82-2623; www.moaart.or.jp/hakone; 9:30am-4:30pm Fri.-Mon. Apr.-Nov., until 4pm Dec.-Mar., open if Thurs. falls on national holiday; ¥900 adults, ¥400 high school students, free for junior high school students and younger; take Hakone Tozan cable car to Gōra Station

Exquisite Asian pottery and art, a traditional teahouse, and an enigmatic moss garden that crackles with color in autumn are some of the discoveries that await at the Hakone Museum of Art. Built on the collection of art aficionado Okada Mokichi (1882-1955), some of the earthenware pieces date as far back as the Jomon period (13,000-300 BC).

POLA MUSEUM OF ART

ポーラ美術館

1285 Kozukayama; tel. 0460-84-2111; www.polamuseum.or.jp; 9am-5pm daily, ¥1,800 adults, ¥1,300 university and high school students, free for junior high school students and younger; from Gōra Station, take Hakone Tōzan bus for Shissei Kaen to Pola Bijutsukan bus stop

This eye-catching, largely subterranean complex full of windows and light shows off the art collection amassed by the late owner of the POLA skin care and beauty products group, Suzuki Tsuneshi. Discreetly set within a

1
2
3

hillside hidden in a beech forest, where some trees are three centuries old, the museum's collection extends from modern paintings—including Japanese artists like Sugiyama Yasushi and some Western heavy hitters like Picasso, Monet, Renoir, and Cezanne—to surrealists (Dalí), sculptures, Ming Dynasty vases, and glassware delicately crafted mostly by Japanese and European artists. In a word, it's eclectic. Buses bound for the museum depart Gōra Station 4-5 times hourly.

Around Sōun-zan

ŌWAKUDANI

大涌谷

tel. 0460/84-5201; www.kanagawa-park.or.jp/owakudani; cable car 9am-5pm daily Mar.-Nov., 9am-4:15pm daily Dec.-Feb.; ¥1,700 adults, ¥850 children Sōun-zan to Ōwakudani round-trip, covered by Hakone Freepass; from Gōra Station, ride Hakone-Tōzan to Sōun-zan Station, transfer to cable car and ride one stop to Ōwakudani Station

Ride in a cable car over this geologically tortured landscape. Ōwakudani means "Valley of Hell," named for the desolate, steamy valley emitting the strong scent of sulfur that formed 3,000 years ago when Kamiyama erupted, an event that also created the nearby Lake Ashi. If the sulfur fumes get to you, consider that the Japanese government's Ministry of the Environment concluded that the stench ranks among Japan's most prevalent 100 odors. The upshot of all this is that the area is known to turn out tasty onsen tamago: eggs boiled until turning black in the sulfurous springs.

Southern Lake Ashi

HAKONE-JINJA

箱根神社

80-1 Motohakone; tel. 0460/83-7123; http://hakonejinja.or.jp; 8:30am-5pm daily; from Hakone-Yumoto Station, take Hakone Tōzan bus (line H) to Hakone-jinja Iriguchi bus stops

Built in 757, Hakone-jinja is a picturesque shrine on the shore of Lake Ashi; it is at its most dramatic when it's shrouded in mist. To reach the shrine, take the five-minute stroll from the Moto-Hakone boat pier and continue along an ascending path lined by lanterns and marked by an imposing and very photogenic torii gate. Definitely stop by this shrine if you're exploring the Lake Ashi area.

1: Hakone-jinja **2:** sulphur vents of Ōwakudani
3: *Woods of Net,* Hakone Open-Air Museum

ONSEN

Around Hakone-Yumoto

★ HAKONE YURYŌ ONSEN

箱根湯寮

4 Tōnosawa; tel. 0460/85-8411; www.hakoneyuryo.jp/english; 10am-8pm (last entry 6pm) Mon.-Fri., 10am-9pm (last entry 7pm) Sat.-Sun. and holidays; ¥1,500 adults, ¥1,000 children ages 6-12; take shuttle bus from Hakone-Yumoto station, or Hakone-Tōzan line to Tōnosawa Station

For a classic countryside onsen experience within easy reach of Tokyo, Hakone Yuryō Onsen ticks all the boxes. Surrounded by lush, forested hills, the outdoor baths are excellent, with serene views on all sides and baths ranging from large single-sex communal pools to 19 private open-air ones rented for two hours (from ¥8,600). Book a private bath up to a month in advance by phone. Alongside baths, massages are offered in relaxation rooms, and an on-site restaurant serves food cooked over an iori (open hearth).

As is the case with most onsen, if you're sporting any ink you will need to keep it under wraps at the reception desk. Further, the communal baths will not be an option. Conceal what tattoos you have until reaching your reserved private bath, however, and you'll still be able to enjoy the experience.

TENZAN TŌJI-KYŌ

天山湯治郷

208 Yumoto-chaya; tel. 0460/86-4126; www.tenzan.jp; 9am-10pm daily; ¥1,300 adults, ¥650 children; take shuttle bus "B" from Hakone-Yumoto Station

If you're a person with tattoos, this sprawling onsen complex, which doesn't have a policy against tattoos, is your best bet in Hakone. Tenzan Tōji-kyō has indoor and outdoor baths, uniquely designed and surrounded by

The Hakone Loop

Getting around the central area of Hakone, including Mount Hakone and lovely Lake Ashi, is part of the fun of making the trip. The classic way of seeing the region's sights involves a combination of local trains, cable cars, ropeways, buses, and boats. A caveat: While this is the quintessential way to see Hakone, in truth it's a bit cookie-cutter (read: touristy). If there are specific things that appeal to you in the area that don't fit neatly into this route, it may be better to limit the number of things you see and do, while maximizing down time, perhaps soaking in an onsen.

The easiest way to complete the full route is to get a **Hakone Freepass** (www.odakyu.jp/english/passes/hakone), which can be picked up at any train station on the Odakyū line. This pass can either be purchased for a two-day trip from Shinjuku (¥6,100 adults, ¥1,500 children) or Odawara (¥5,000 adults, ¥1,000 children), or as a three-day pass from Shinjuku (¥6,500 adults, ¥1,750 children) or Odawara (¥5,400 adults, ¥1,250 children). For detailed information on where the pass can be bought, visit www.odakyu.jp/english/support/center/.

TRAIN AND CABLE CAR AND ROPEWAY

The Hakone-Tōzan railway, which begins at Odawara, passes through a number of stops near some of the area's best restaurants and museums, ultimately ending up in the heart of Hakone at **Gōra.** From there, most visitors take a 10-minute ride on the Hakone-Tōzan cable car, connected directly to Gōra Station, 1.2 kilometers (0.75 mi) to **Sōun-zan Station** (¥430).

ROPEWAY

At Sōun-zan you have the option of floating over **Ōwakudani** (Great Boiling Valley) aboard the **Hakone Ropeway** (1-15-1 Shiroyama, Odawara; tel. 0460/32-2205; www.hakoneropeway.co.jp/foreign/en; 9am-5pm daily Feb.-Nov., 9am-4:15pm daily Dec.-Jan.; ¥1,700 adults, ¥850 children

lush foliage, set at a range of temperatures, from merely warm to exfoliation-inducing. For maximum relaxation, head to one of the complex's saunas or massage rooms.

Around Kowakidani

YUNESSUN ONSEN PARK

根小涌園ユネッサン

1297 Ninotaira; tel. 0460/82-4126; www.yunessun.com/en; swimwear area 10am-6pm Mon.-Fri., 9am-7pm Sat.-Sun. and holidays, area where swimwear is not permitted 11am-7pm Mon.-Fri., 11am-8pm Sat.-Sun. and holidays; swimwear area ¥2,500 adults, ¥1,400 children; area where swimwear is not permitted ¥1,500 adults, ¥1,000 children, all-area pass ¥3,500 adults, ¥1,800 children; from Gōra, Hakone-machi, or Hakone-Yumoto, take a bus to Kowakien

If you've ever dreamed of dunking yourself in a massive bathtub full of coffee, tea, or something harder like wine, Yunessun Onsen Park gives you that chance. There are also waterslides, mixed open-air baths with sweeping views of nature, and numerous other options for immersing yourself in hot rejuvenating liquid concoctions at this hot spring theme park—bathing suit required.

For a more traditional onsen experience, the adjoining **Mori-no-Yu** offers single-sex, nude (bathing suits are not permitted) bathing both in and outdoors, including tubs under gazebos amid traditional gardens, and private baths that can be rented from ¥3,000 per hour.

And if you want to keep soaking, there are four official hotels connected to the park. Tattoos, no matter how small, are not permitted at Yunessun.

FOOD

Around Hakone-Yumoto

HATSUHANA HONTEN

635 Yumoto; tel. 0460/85-8287; www.hatsuhana.co.jp; 10am-7pm Thurs.-Tues.; ¥1,000-1,600; take Hakone Tōzan railway to Hakone-Yumoto Station

Set in an old wooden building overlooking

Sōun-zan to Ōwakudani round-trip, covered by Hakone Freepass). Gondolas on this line depart about once every minute and carry up to about 18 passengers.

Exiting the infernal valley, proceed along the ropeway to **Tōgendai** on the northeastern shore of the alpine **Lake Ashi.** The entire journey, from Sōun-zan to Tōgendai, takes about 30 minutes (¥1,550 adults, ¥780 children Sōun-zan to Tōgendai one-way, covered by Hakone Freepass).

CRUISE

Head for the dock if you want to take a cruise over the gorgeous Lake Ashi, which offers excellent views of Mount Fuji when the sky is clear (colder months, early morning, and late afternoon are the best times to catcha glimpse of the peak). Cruise boats are operated by **Hakone Sightseeing Boats** (www.hakone-kankosen.co.jp/foreign/en; 9:30am-5:30pm daily Mar. 20-Nov. 30, 10am-4:40pm daily Dec. 1-Mar. 19; 30 minutes; ¥1,200 adults, ¥600 children one-way, ¥2,200 adults, ¥1,100 children round-trip, covered by the Hakone Freepass), and run between **Hakone-machi** and **Moto-Hakone** on the lake's south side, and to Tōgendai on the northern side.

From Moto-Hakone, a great option is to walk to **Hakone-jinja,** a scenic shrine only 5 minutes from town on foot.

BUS

Complete the loop by traveling on the **Hakone Tōzan Bus** (www.hakone-tozanbus.co.jp/english) from Motohakone-ko bus stop back to Hakone-Yumoto, the buzzing gateway to Hakone at the eastern edge of the resort area. The ride takes about 35 minutes and buses depart from every 20-30 minutes (around ¥1,000 depending on route; covered by Hakone Freepass).

the Hayakawa River, Hatsuhana Honten has been serving its distinctive style of soba noodles since 1934. When wheat flour was scarce during World War II, the restaurant's owner tried making the noodles with only buckwheat flour and eggs, then dipping them in mineral-rich sticky yam called jinenjo. An unexpected hit, the recipe survives to this day. Try the original seiro soba, known for its distinctive chewy texture, made without water and dipped in sticky yam.

Miyanoshita

SUSHI MIYAFUJI

310 Miyanoshita; tel. 0460/82-2139; www.miyanoshita.com/miyafuji; 11:30am-2:30pm and 5:30pm-7:30pm Thurs.-Mon.; average ¥2,000; take Hakone Tōzan railway to Miyanoshita Station

Sushi Miyafuji is an old-school family-run sushi joint that brings in fish from the port of Odawara daily. The most popular items on its menu are rice bowls topped with fish, including the aji-don (rice bowl topped with brook trout) and the fisherman's bowl (horse mackerel and squid over rice). Located a five-minute walk up a slope from the historic Fujiya Hotel.

MORI MESHI

404-13 Miyanoshita; tel. 0460/83-8886; https://morimeshi.jp; 11:30am-3pm and 5pm-9pm daily; lunch from ¥1,550, average dinner ¥3,000, dinner courses from ¥3,500; take Tōzan line to Miyanoshita Station

This bistro with a classic, all-wood interior and izakaya vibes sits right outside Miyanoshita Station. It's a great place for a healthy lunch or dinner made with quality ingredients and generous helpings of fresh produce. The menu of tapas-like Japanese dishes includes a mix of salads, oden, sashimi, tempura, Japanese curry, noodles, and more. The staff is friendly and attentive. An English menu is available. Restaurants in the area are often full, so reserve a day ahead or at least earlier the same day to be safe.

1

2

3

Around Gōra

GŌRA BREWERY AND GRILL

1300-72 Gōra; tel. 050/5461-3081; 1pm-9:30pm (last order 8:30pm) daily; lunch ¥3,000, dinner ¥5,000; take Tōzan line to Gōra Station

This stylish brewpub with dark wood paneling, a large tree supporting the vaulted ceiling at the center of the dining space, and a large window behind the bar looking out onto a landscape garden set into a hillside, is a great place for some craft beer and a meal. The grub matches the drink: salads, grilled vegetable platters, sausages, gyoza (fried dumplings), burdock root chips, sautéed shiitake mushrooms, and much more. It's popular, so reserve ahead a day or two to be safe.

Southern Lake Ashi

★ AMAZAKE-CHAYA

395-1 Futoko-yama; tel. 0460/83-6418; www.amasake-chaya.jp; 7am-5:30pm daily; ¥250-750; from Moto-Hakone bus stop or Hakone-Yumoto bus stop, take Hakone Tōzan bus to Amazake Chaya bus stop

From the Moto-Hakone bus stop on the southern shore of Lake Ashi, walk 30 minutes up the cedar-lined Old Hakone Highway—once a segment of the Tōkaidō Highway that linked Edo and Kyoto—until you reach the charming thatched-roof Amazake-Chaya. This 360-year-old teahouse serves the same sweet brew, made from fermented rice (amazake), that it did in Edo days. The drink is imbibed cold, hot, and at room temperature, depending on season, and can have low or no alcohol content, depending on the recipe.

ACCOMMODATIONS

Around Hakone-Yumoto

BANSUIRO FUKUZUMI

643 Yumoto; tel. 0460/85-5531; www.2923.co.jp; doubles ¥45,000 with two meals; take Hakone Tōzan railway to Hakone-Yumoto Station

With a history stretching back to 1625 and old-school ambience intact, Bansuiro Fukuzumi weaves a spell on guests. Rebuilt now several times, the current iteration of this majestic old inn is a product of the Meiji period, when Japanese and Western architectural styles were often blended in experimental ways. Hence, wood, stone, and metal coexist seamlessly in the same building. It was no surprise that this inn—one of Hakone's oldest—was declared an important cultural property in 2002. The cuisine offered is similarly excellent, and there are private onsen baths to boot.

★ FUKUZUMIRO

74 Tōnosawa; tel. 0460/85-5301; www.fukuzumi-ro.com; doubles from ¥52,000 with two meals; from Hakone-Yumoto Station, take Hakone Tōzan railway to Tōnosawa Station

Fukuzumiro is another old-school gem, in business since 1890. Next to the Hayakawa River, the atmospheric property sprawls across three floors with 17 rooms, each with its own unique flourishes. Creativity is built into the ryokan's exquisite woodwork—look for "lucky bat" carvings scattered throughout—and the inn is known as a retreat for writers and artists. Food courses featuring a range of seafood and vegetables are delivered to guests' rooms.

Miyanoshita

TSUTAYA INN

240-1 Sokokura; tel. 0460/83-9580; https://hakone-tsutaya.com; dorm from ¥2,800, doubles with shared bath from ¥13,000; take Tōzan line to Miyanoshita Station, then walk 15 minutes northwest

This freshly revamped ryokan has a great variety of room types—from dorms with bunk beds to spacious suites—and appealing indoor and outdoor onsen baths separated by gender. The staff is energetic and friendly, the design is chic and modern with Japanese touches, and there's a cozy shared kitchen and lounge area too. This is a great mid-range pick.

1: outdoor communal bath at Hakone Yuryō Onsen **2:** private bath at Hakone Yuryō Onsen **3:** entrance to Hakone Yuryō Onsen **4:** irori (sunken hearth) course at Hakone Yuryō Onsen

Around Gōra

★ GŌRA KADAN

1300 Gōra; tel. 0460/82-3331; www.gorakadan.com; from around ¥120,000 with two meals; take Hakone Tōzan railway from Hakone-Yumoto Station to Gōra Station

Gōra Kadan is a legendary ryokan so luxurious, the premium price tag actually feels justified. Top-notch kaiseki cuisine is presented like art in a European-style building, where flower-scented incense infuses the halls. Gorgeous tatami rooms, filled with antiques and separated by sliding rice-paper walls, have private gardens and open-air baths. And, of course, the hospitality is refined to the hilt. No detail is missed, no edges left unsmoothed. Amenities include a pool, spa, and salon. This property is world-class in every sense. If you can manage to book a room—do so as far in advance as possible—this is the Hakone hotel worthy of a serious splurge.

INFORMATION AND SERVICES

There is a **tourist information center** at Hakone-Yumoto Station (706-35 Yumoto Hakone-machi; tel. 0460/85-5700; 9am-5:45pm daily) where you can ask questions of helpful English-speaking staff, and pick up English-language maps and more. Online, **https://hakone-japan.com** provides plenty of information on things to see and do in Hakone.

GETTING THERE

To reach Hakone from Tokyo, take the **Odakyū line** from **Shinjuku Station** to **Hakone-Yumoto Station.** The speedy Romance Car reaches Hakone-Yumoto in 90 minutes (¥2,330), while the kyūkō (express) train will get you there in 2 hours (¥1,220). Note that you may need to change trains at Odawara if you take the cheaper express train.

If you have a JR Pass, you can also take the **JR Tōkaidō shinkansen** (Kodama, Hikari trains only) about 30 minutes to **Odawara Station.** You can then transfer to the local **Hakone-Tōzan line**—not covered by the JR Pass—to access the rest of the Hakone area.

The easiest way to reach Hakone from Kyoto is by taking the **JR Tōkaidō Shinkansen** (Hikari trains only) to **Odawara Station** (2 hours 5 minutes; ¥12,300), then hopping on the Hakone-Tōzan line and traveling west into Hakone proper from there. As is the case with any long-distance journey, there are other potential iterations on this basic route (e.g., taking the Nozomi shinkansen, which is not covered by the JR Pass, to Nagoya, then transferring to the Hikari shinkansen, which is covered by the JR Pass, and riding to Odawara from there). Just be aware that the JR Pass does not cover all shinkansen types, which can complicate and inflate fares if you're traveling with a JR Pass.

Travel Passes

If you're traveling from Tokyo to the Hakone region, the **Hakone Freepass** (www.odakyu.jp/english/passes/hakone; ¥6,100 adults, ¥1,500 children for two-day pass from Shinjuku, or ¥6,500 adults, ¥1,750 children for three-day pass from Shinjuku) includes travel round-trip between Shinjuku and Hakone-Yumoto, and use of the area's various modes of transportation (local train, cable car, Hakone Ropeway, boat). It also allows you to see many of the area's attractions at discounted rates. You can buy the two- or three-day pass at any Odakyū line train station or buy the two-day pass online (www.japan-rail-pass.com/pass-regional/east/hakone-free-pass?ap=j0095g).

If you're combining travel from Tokyo to both Kamakura and Hakone, the **Hakone Kamakura Pass** (www.odakyu.jp/english/passes/hakone_kamakura; ¥7,400 adults, ¥2,250 children) covers your round-trip between Shinjuku, Kamakura, and Hakone, with free access to all Odakyū trains, buses, boats, cable cars, and ropeways around Hakone, as well as the Enoden railway that links Kamakura and Enoshima. The pass also gives you access to many area attractions at discounted rates. Valid for three days, the pass is only available at Shinjuku Station's Odakyū Sightseeing Service Center.

Finally, the **Fuji Hakone Pass** (https://www.odakyu.jp/english/passes/fujihakone) allows you to travel freely for three days within Fuji-Hakone, and receive discounts at more than 90 attractions throughout the area. You have the option to add round-trip train fare from Shinjuku (¥9,340 adults, ¥3,170 children) or, if you happen to be coming from the Lake Kawaguchi area, to begin using the pass from Kawaguchiko Station (¥9,340 adults, ¥3,170 children). You can buy this pass at the Odakyū Sightseeing Service Center in either Shinjuku Station or Kawaguchiko Station.

GETTING AROUND

The local train line servicing the Hakone area is the **Hakone-Tōzan line,** which connects Odawara to Gōra, a one-hour journey, stopping at Hakone-Yumoto, Tōnosawa, Kokakidani, and near the Hakone Open-Air Museum and Okada Museum of Art, among other stations, along the way.

The cheapest way to get around the Hakone Loop is to purchase the **Hakone Freepass** (www.odakyu.jp/english/passes/hakone; ¥6,100 adults, ¥1,500 children for two-day pass from Shinjuku, or ¥6,500 adults, ¥1,750 children for three-day pass from Shinjuku).

Cable Car and Ropeway

From the Hakone-Tōzan line's terminus at Gōra Station, where you'll find the Hakone Art Museum, the classic route includes taking the **Hakone-Tōzan Cable Car** (¥430, covered by Hakone Freepass) from within Gōra Station to Sōun-zan. From here, take the **Hakone Ropeway** (1-15-1 Shiroyama, Odawara; tel. 0460/32-2205; www.hakoneropeway.co.jp/foreign/en; 9am-5pm daily Feb.-Nov., 9am-4:15pm Dec.-Jan.; ¥1,600 adults, ¥800 children Sōun-zan to Ōwakudani round-trip, covered by Hakone Freepass) to Ōwakudani, where plenty of steaming and bubbling volcanic activity is in full view, and then to Tōgendai on the shore of Lake Ashi (¥1,550 adults, ¥780 children Sōun-zan to Tōgendai one-way, covered by Hakone Freepass).

Boat Cruise

Tōgendai is the jumping-off point for a **boat cruise** to Hakone-machi and Moto-Hakone. Cruises are operated by **Hakone Sightseeing Boats** (www.hakone-kankosen.co.jp/foreign/en; 9:30am-5:30pm daily Mar. 20-Nov. 30, 10am-4:40pm daily Dec. 1-Mar. 19, 30 minutes, ¥1,200 adults; ¥600 children one-way, ¥2,200 adults, ¥1,100 children round-trip, covered by Hakone Freepass).

Bus

From Moto-Hakone, return to Hakone-Yumoto by **bus** (35 minutes; around ¥1,000 depending on route, covered by Hakone Freepass). Catch the bus from the Hakone Tōzan Bus Information Center (6 Moto-Hakone; tel. 0460/83-6171; www.hakone-tozanbus.co.jp/english), located about a 15-minute walk southeast of Hakone-jinja.

Mount Fuji 富士山

The Japanese have a word to describe the rush of emotion that ensues in the moments just before the first rays of the sun break over the horizon when viewed from a mountain top: go-raiko. The phrase, roughly meaning "honorable coming of the light," seeks to capture a feeling that is hard to pin down, an innate sense that witnessing the sunrise from a mountain peak is an extraordinary, even spiritual experience. Seeing the sky fill with the colors of dawn followed by sunrise from atop Mount Fuji, Japan's highest peak at 3,776 meters (12,388 ft), is the ultimate way to grasp the essence of go-raiko and to understand why the mountain holds such sway over the national psyche.

Since time immemorial, Mount Fuji has stood as nature's most sacred spot in Japan. The goddess of Mount Fuji, Princess Konohamasakuya—daughter of the mountain god and deity of all volcanoes—is honored at small shrines dotting its slopes. The privilege to climb to the summit was not granted to laypeople until about 150 years ago. Women were not permitted to make the ascent until 1868. Even today, steadfast hikers with mystical leanings approach the mountain only after purifying themselves at Sengen-jinja, a shrine in a dense old-growth forest at the mountain's base. The inner sanctum of Sengen-jinja still stands atop the peak, serving as a reminder of these sacred roots.

Rather than a trickle of holy men, weekend warriors and overseas travelers now crowd the mountain, which is the crowning jewel of **Fuji-Hakone-Izu National Park** (www.fujihakoneizu.com). The summit is flush with the same amenities you'd expect to find in any Japanese town, from 24-hour ramen stalls to a weather station and even a post office. But those who witness sunrise from the summit cannot deny the deeper stirrings felt by seekers who made the same journey centuries ago.

TOP EXPERIENCE

★ HIKING

For most travelers, glimpsing Mount Fuji from afar is enough. But during the official hiking season (July-Aug.), well-established paths beckon to those keen to get up close and personal with the sacred peak. Mount Fuji is one of the most climbed mountains in the world, but don't let the legions of grannies and middle-aged salarymen fool you—the ascent can be arduous. As the old adage goes: "A wise man climbs Fuji once; a fool climbs it twice."

Once you've reached the top, the amenities available may shock you. You can mail a postcard, buy a charm at a shrine, circumnavigate the volcanic crater (a 2-hour walk), and slurp ramen at a food stall perched near the caldera's rim.

Planning Your Hike

Note that temperature differences between the base and summit are as much as 20°C (36°F) in summer. And although Mount Fuji's last eruption was in 1707, its soil still contains a thick layer of granular volcanic ash, prone to shifting as you walk. Wear sturdy boots suited for hiking, a hat that can be fastened to prevent losing it in the wind, sunscreen, gloves, sunglasses, and a headlamp if you're hiking at night. Thick wool socks and waterproof clothes can be a godsend if you get caught in the rain. Be sure to pack sufficient water (3 liters is wise), vitamin-infused drinks, calorific snacks, and a trash bag. In short, prepare for the unexpected.

Depending on where you start and which trail you take, the journey from one of the main fifth stations up the top half of Mount Fuji is usually a 5-6-hour affair. Most begin the journey at night—around 8pm if they're starting from the first station, or 11pm if they're starting from the fifth station—and walk until morning. Another popular way to make the ascent is to start in the afternoon, stay in a hut overnight at the seventh or eighth stage, and then proceed to the summit in the early morning. Walking at either of these times allows hikers to avoid the sun at its peak and to see the sunrise from the top.

Given Fuji's immense popularity, you might find yourself sharing the slopes with loads of hikers, particularly on weekends during the climbing season, with the Obon holidays in mid-August being the busiest time. Foot traffic can be so heavy that queues form at bottlenecks in the trail. Although merging with the crowd is part of the journey, it's helpful to climb on a weekday, preferably in July, and to undertake the majority of the ascent overnight.

Resources packed with Fuji tips include the online guide **Climbing Mount Fuji** (www17.plala.or.jp/climb_fujiyama) and the official **Mount Fuji Climbing website**

Mount Fuji and the Five Lakes

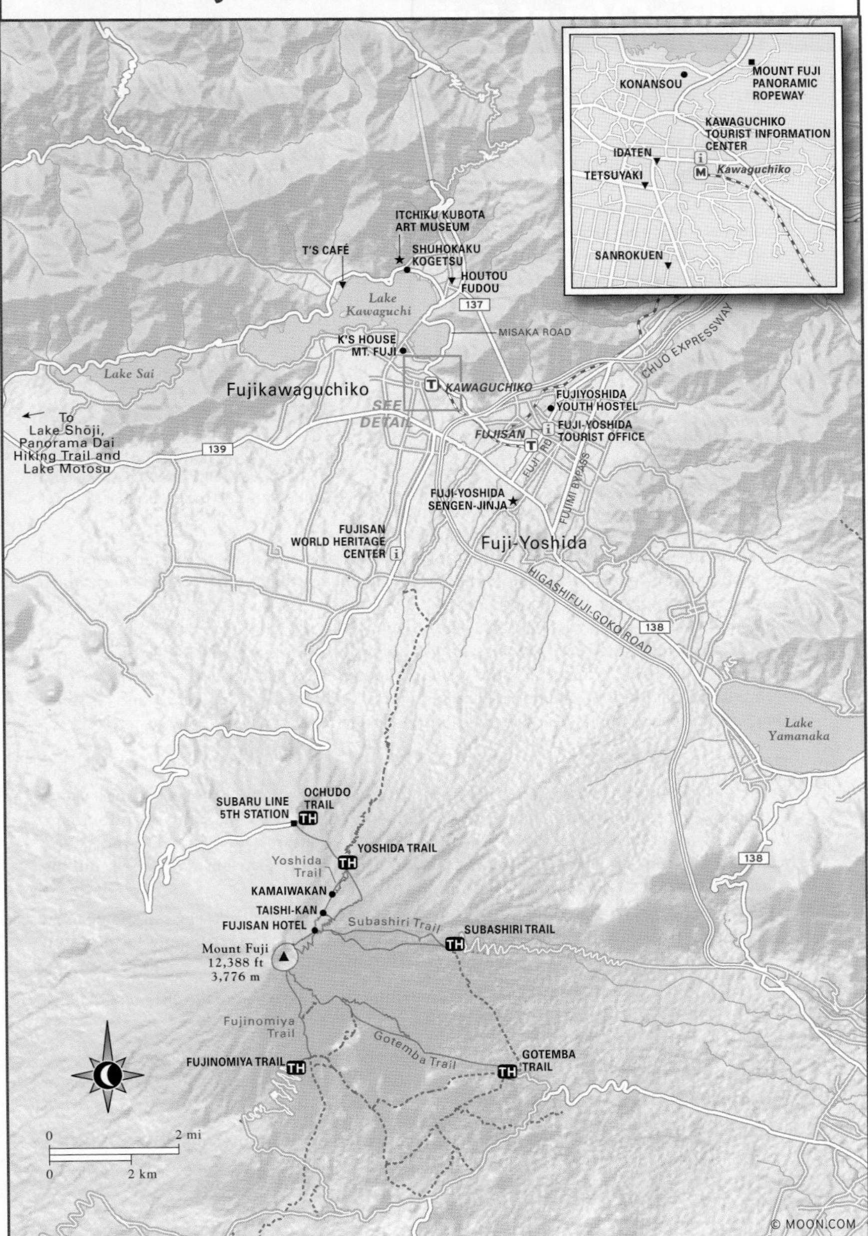

TOP EXPERIENCE

Views of Mount Fuji

Seen from afar, Mount Fuji's symmetry is stunning. Its near-perfect cone, snow-capped most of the year, is easily recognizable whether seen in the background of a 17th-century woodblock print or seen from a bullet train. It's on the ¥1,000 note, is plastered across sento (public bath) walls nationwide, and is a favorite motif in traditional crafts, from exquisitely painted porcelain cups to the scabbards of samurai swords. Its special status as a natural object of such widespread recognition was attested to when it was declared a World Heritage site in 2013—a rare feat for a landform.

Mount Fuji and Lake Yamanaka

A NATIONAL SYMBOL

Since the Heian period (794-1185), Mount Fuji has been the object of poetic admiration, appearing in the 8th-century Manyoshu, Japan's first poetry anthology. During the Edo period (1603-1868), as the seat of political power drifted from Kyoto to Edo (now Tokyo), Mount Fuji's status grew as an increasing number of feudal lords and merchants traversed the country, passing by the increasingly idealized peak. During this time, pilgrims formed associations dedicated to climbing the mountain. Meanwhile, devout lords had small hills built on their property in Edo from which they viewed the summit, not yet obscured by high-rises as it is across most of Tokyo today.

Poems of haiku masters such as Matsuo Basho (1644-1694) paid tribute to the mountain, along with ukiyo-e woodblock prints by masters like Katsushika Hokusai (1760-1849) and Utagawa Hiroshige (1797-1858). In fact, Fuji's snowy summit looms in the background of one of the most recognizable paintings of all time, Hokusai's immortal *Great Wave Off Kanagawa,* and his series *One Hundred Views of Mount Fuji,* which he finished at age 75, is regarded as his masterpiece.

BEST VISTAS

Note that weather around the peak can be fickle. Crisp winter days provide some of the best views, particularly in the morning; the summit is often hidden by clouds in spring, summer, and autumn. While there are no guarantees the weather will cooperate, here are a few of the best spots to try to catch a glimpse of the timeless peak. At the very least, be sure to at least take a peek out the window of the bullet train as you shuttle past the mountain.

- West of Kamakura, the island of **Enoshima** offers some magnificent views of the peak on clear days. Try the observation deck of the lighthouse known as the Sea Candle, located atop the island within the **Samuel Cocking Garden** (page 172).
- In Hakone, the southeast corner of **Lake Ashi** offers splendid views of the distant peak, with **Hakone-jinja** in the foreground (page 193).
- Closer to Mount Fuji itself, the Five Lakes region has some excellent viewing spots. **Lake Kawaguchi** offers some of the best, particularly from its north shore, as does the **Panorama Dai hiking trail** (page 207).
- If you'd like to hike around Mount Fuji, but don't have time to make the summit, the **Ochudo trail** is a good hike for a day trip (page 204).

(www.fujisan-climb.jp). If you're ill equipped to summit the peak and would like to rent gear or attire, check out **Yamarent** (tel. 050/5865-1615; contact by phone 10am-5pm daily; www.yamarent.com), which rents anything you'd realistically need and then some: boots, rainwear, crampons, even avalanche beacons. Have a look at the website first, and then either call or email (via the website) ahead before you make a trip to one of its branches, where an appointment is required.

Safety

Be mindful of your own condition along the way. When you enter the eighth stage, altitude sickness becomes a real concern. If you begin to feel nauseous or uncharacteristically exhausted, don't ignore the warning signs. Turn back if these symptoms arise.

Making the ascent outside of July and August requires legit skills for hiking in icy conditions, and the capacity and gear to handle extremes. Hikers keen to summit Fuji during the off-season should register with local authorities at the **Lake Kawaguchi Tourist Information Center** (3641-1 Funatsu; tel. 0555/72-6700; www.fujisan.ne.jp; 9am-5pm daily) and keep an eye on the weather forecast, respecting the risk involved.

Guides

The best way to stay safe and get the most out of your hike is to hire a guide.

- **Fuji Mountain Guides** (tel. 042/445-0798; www.fujimountainguides.com; ¥48,000 pp for 2-day tours)
- **Discover Japan Tours** (www.discover-japan-tours.com/en; ¥10,000 pp for 2-day tours)

Routes

There are many ways to hike Mount Fuji. The popular **Yoshida trail** runs along the mountain's north face in Yamanashi Prefecture, while the **Subashiri** runs up the eastern face. The less popular **Fujinomiya** and **Gotemba** trails line the south face in Shizuoka Prefecture. Visit www.fujimountainguides.com/uploads/1/5/3/1/15315858/fuji_climbing_map_all4trails.pdf for a map of Fuji's main trails. Each trail is broken into 10 stations, with the fifth being where most climbers start their ascent.

YOSHIDA TRAIL

Distance: *15 km (9 mi) round-trip*
Time: *9-12 hours round-trip*
Information and maps: *Fuji-Yoshida Tourist Office or Fuji Visitor Center; www.japan.travel/en/spot/2328; www.fujimountainguides.com/uploads/1/5/3/1/15315858/yoshida_trail_map.pdf*
Trailhead: *Subaru Fifth Station*

By far the most popular route to the top of Fuji involves starting from the fifth station of the well-trodden Yoshida trail. Known as the **Subaru Line Fifth Station** (aka **Kawaguchi-ko Fifth Station** or **Yoshidaguchi Fifth Station**), this station sits at an elevation of 2,305 meters (7,562 ft) and is by far the most developed of the mountain's fifth stations, including the most mountain huts (20) of all major routes. The ascent takes about 6-7 hours and the descent 3-5 hours. The fifth station can be reached by bus—seat reservations available—from either Kawaguchiko Station or Fujisan Station, operated by **Fujikyū Bus** (tel. 0555/72-6877; http://bus-en.fujikyu.co.jp; 50 minutes, buses start from 6:20am, 1-2 depart hourly; ¥1,570 one-way, ¥2,300 round-trip). For a simplified English explanation of how to take this bus, check out the clear primer at http://bus-en.fujikyu.co.jp/get-on-bus/.

While starting at the fifth station will more than likely be all you need to scratch your Fuji itch, for experience seekers with a slightly masochistic bent, it's entirely possible to climb Fuji the same way that spiritual pilgrims of yore once did. In the town of Fuji-Yoshida, near Lake Kawaguchi at the mountain's eastern base, pilgrims gravitate to **Fuji-Yoshida Sengen-jinja** (aka Kitaguchi Hongū Fuji Sengen-jinja; 5558 Kami-Yoshida; tel. 0555/22-0221; www.sengenjinja.jp; 24 hours daily), a shrine dedicated to the mountain's chief deity,

Princess Konohanasakuya. The Yoshida trail, which goes from the base to the summit, starts from this shrine. Sticklers for tradition swear by this trail, which entails roughly a 12-hour, 19-kilometer (11.8-mi) ascent from base to summit, followed by a descent that takes 3-5 hours.

SUBASHIRI TRAIL

Distance: *14 km (8.75 mi) round-trip*
Time: *10-12 hours round-trip*
Information and maps: *www.japan.travel/en/fuji-guide/mt-fuji-subashiri-trail; www.alltrails.com/trail/japan/shizuoka/mount-fuji-trail-subashiri-trail*
Trailhead: *Subashiri Fifth Station*

On the south face of the mountain, the Subashiri trail begins from the **Subashiri Fifth Station** (1,950 m/6,398 ft) and has relatively well-developed infrastructure with 12 huts along the way. This is the second-best option overall, and is particularly appealing if you happen to be coming from Lake Yamanaka rather than Lake Kawaguchi. It winds through forests and is less crowded, merging with the more accessible, developed, and crowded Yoshida trail from the eighth station onward. The ascent (8 km/5 mi) takes around 7-9 hours, while the descent (6 km/3.75 mi) takes about 3 hours.

To reach Subashiri Fifth Station, take the JR Tokaido line from Tokyo to Kozu (1.25 hours; ¥1,320), then transfer to the JR Gotemba line and ride until Gotemba Station (50 minutes; ¥670). From Gotemba, take the bus to Subashiri Fifth Station (1 hour; ¥1,540 one way, ¥2,060 round trip).

OCHUDO TRAIL

Distance: *7.4 km (4.6 mi) round-trip*
Time: *3-4 hours round-trip*
Information and maps: *www.yamanashi-kankou.jp/kokuritsukoen/en/miryoku/hiking/course2.html; www.fujisan-climb.jp/en/m3oati0000002q40-att/2016Reiho_Climbing_Edition.pdf*
Trailhead: *Subaru Fifth Station*

If you'd like to hike around Mount Fuji without approaching the summit, the Ochudo trail, which begins from the Subaru Fifth Station and moves westward for about 3.7 kilometers (2.3 mi) one-way at a roughly constant elevation, is a good hike for a day trip. This trail is a good choice if you don't want the full, grueling Fuji experience. You'll walk through a sylvan landscape, thick with hemlocks and larch trees, and meadows bright with alpine flowers in summer, and catch glimpses of Fuji's cone, sweeping views of

hiking the Yoshida trail on Mount Fuji

nearby lakes Motosu-ko and Kawaguchi-ko, and see the Southern Alps looming in the distance.

The path first runs to the crater-pocked **Oniwa** area, roughly 1 hour into the hike (2.9 km/1.8 mi). From there, press on for another 40 minutes (0.8 km/0.5 mi), where you'll end in the lush **Okuniwa** nature park area. From Okuniwa, you can either backtrack to the start of the trail or take a bus from the parking lot next to Okuniwa to Kawaguchiko Station (http://bus-en.fujikyu.co.jp/route/detail/id/14/; 40 minutes; ¥1,460).

Be sure to bundle up. Temperatures on the trail tend to be about 15°C (59°F) colder than in Tokyo.

ACCOMMODATIONS

If you're having trouble getting a spot in one of Fuji's mountain huts during climbing season, Fuji Mountain Guides (www.fujimountainguides.com/mountain-hut-reservations.html) offers a reservation service for a nominal fee of ¥1,000.

FUJISAN HOTEL

Yoshida trail, eighth station; tel. 0555/22-0237; www.fujisanhotel.com; from ¥9,250, depending on day and meal option chosen

Fujisan Hotel is a very popular option, given its location at the 3,400-meter (11,154-ft) junction of the Lake Kawaguchi and Subashiri trails. The lodge will hold onto your bag while you walk the final 60 minutes of the path to the summit. Breakfast and dinner are optional. Book two months in advance.

KAMAIWAKAN

Yoshida trail, seventh station; tel. 080/1299-0223; http://kamaiwakan.jpn.org; from ¥9,900, depending on day and meal option

Clean and revamped, Kamaiwakan is a good option at 2,790 meters (9,153 ft) with free Wi-Fi and two optional meals. Some English is spoken. Book two months ahead.

TAISHIKAN

Yoshida trail, eighth station; tel. 0555/22-1947; www.mfi.or.jp/w3/home0/taisikan; from ¥10,000, depending on day

Taishikan is a tried-and-true mountain hut for Fuji hikers. It sleeps 350 hikers in sleeping bags. Two meals (including vegetarian and halal on request) are included in the price. Checkout time is 5am. Soft drinks and snacks are sold. Some English is spoken. Book two months in advance.

INFORMATION AND SERVICES

- **Fuji-Yoshida Tourist Office** (2-3-6 Kamiyoshida, Fujiyoshida; tel. 0555/22-7000; https://fujiyoshida.net/spot/54; 9am-5pm daily; next to Fuji-Yoshia/Fujisan Station)
- **Lake Kawaguchi Tourist Information Center** (3641-1 Funatsu, Fujikawaguchiko; tel. 0555/72-6700; www.fujisan.ne.jp; 9am-5pm daily)
- **Fujisan World Heritage Center** (6663-1 Funatsu, Fujiwaguchiko; tel. 0555/72-0259; www.fujisan-whc.jp/en/index.html; 8:30am-6pm daily late July-Sept., 9am-4pm daily Dec.-Feb., 9am-5pm daily rest of year; on the north face of the mountain, south of Lake Kawaguchi)

GETTING THERE

Straddling the border of Yamanashi and Shizuoka Prefectures, Mount Fuji is within easy reach of Tokyo by bus or train. The main transit hubs for accessing the Mount Fuji area include the town of **Fuji-Yoshida** and **Lake Kawaguchi,** which are served by buses and trains from Tokyo.

Train

To come via train, starting from **Shinjuku,** take the **Chūō line** west to **Otsuki.** The limited express (tokkyū) train takes 1 hour 10 minutes (¥2,360), while the regular (futsū) train takes about 1 hour 30 minutes (¥1,340) and may require a transfer at Takao Station. From Otsuki, transfer to the **Fuji Kyūkō** to Fuji-Yoshida (Fujisan Station; 50 minutes; ¥1,040). Note that the JR Pass covers the leg of the trip up to Otsuki, but does not cover the Fuji Kyūkō line.

Bus

If you'd rather take a bus—in some ways the simpler option—buses operated by **Keiō Dentetsu** (tel. 03/5376-2222; http://highway-buses.jp; ¥2,000 adults, ¥1,000 children) and **Fujikyū Express** (http://bus-en.fujikyu.co.jp/highway; ¥2,000 adults, ¥1,000 children) depart once or twice hourly from the **Shinjuku Highway Bus Terminal** (Shinjuku Station west exit; https://highway-buses.jp/terminal/shinjuku.php) and run to both Fuji-Yoshida (Fujisan Station) and Kawaguchiko Station. Both journeys take just under two hours. **Fujikyū** (http://bus-en.fujikyu.co.jp/highway) and **JR Kanto Bus** (www.jrbuskanto.co.jp.e.wn.hp.transer.com) also operate buses between Yaesu South Exit of Tokyo Station and Kawaguchiko Station (2 hours; ¥2,000 one-way), as well as from the Mark City shopping complex attached to Shibuya Station to both Kawaguchiko Station and Fujisan Station (2-2.5 hours, depending on traffic; ¥2,000 adults, ¥1,000 children one-way).

Finally, **Keiō Dentetsu** also runs buses directly to the mountain's fifth station from Shinjuku Highway Bus Terminal (tel. 03/5376-2222; http://highway-buses.jp; ¥2,950 adults, ¥1,480 children one-way). Note that you must reserve a seat in advance.

If you're coming from Kyoto, board the **Tōkaidō shinkansen Kodama line** and ride to **Mishima Station** (2 hours 40 minutes; ¥11,310). From the south exit of Mishima Station, catch a **Fujikyūkō bus** (http://bus-en.fujikyu.co.jp/highway) to Kawaguchiko Station. This last leg of the journey takes anywhere from 1.5 to more than 2 hours, depending on road conditions, and costs ¥2,300 one-way (¥1,150 children).

To reserve a seat online with minimum fuss for any of the above routes, visit the website of **Japan Bus Online** (https://japanbusonline.com/en) or **Willer Express** (https://willerexpress.com/en).

GETTING AROUND

Once you've arrived in either the hub of Fuji-Yoshida (Fujisan Station) or Kawaguchiko Station, buses operated by **Fujikyū Bus** (tel. 0555/72-6877; http://bus-en.fujikyu.co.jp) connect to the five lakes and other area attractions.

To get farther up the mountain by bus, you can travel about one hour from either Kawaguchiko Station or Fujisan Station to the **Subaru Fifth Station** (¥1,570 one-way, ¥2,300 round-trip). During the official climbing season, buses run to the fifth station 7am-8pm, and return 8am-9pm. They run much less frequently throughout the rest of the year—roughly 9am-3pm. For more details about timetables and fares, see the **Fujikyū Yamanashi** website (http://bus-en.fujikyu.co.jp/route/). All buses running to the fifth station operate from mid-April to early December. As these buses are essentially local, there's no reservation system. Plan on showing up and buying a ticket on the same day in person. Find detailed English instructions at http://bus-en.fujikyu.co.jp/get-on-bus.

Fuji Five Lakes

富士五湖

Five lakes surrounding the iconic peak teem with visitors, particularly in summer, reaching fever pitch during climbing season. **Lake Yamanaka** is a favorite for water-sports lovers, while **Lake Sai** is a good place to camp and, in summer, to swim. **Lake Shōji,** the smallest of the five, and **Lake Motosu,** famed for its appearance on the ¥1,000 note, are both west of Lake Sai. Farther from Tokyo than the other three lakes, they offer fewer amenities and don't warrant a detour for those with limited time. **Lake Kawaguchi,** on the north face of the mountain, is the most developed and easy to access from Tokyo, and therefore the one covered here.

Along with the neighboring town of Fuji-Yoshida, the town surrounding Lake Kawaguchi, known as **Fujikawaguchiko,** makes for a good overnight stay before or after climbing Fuji. Of the five lakes at the base of the revered volcano, Kawaguchi is the one worth a stop for those on a short trip, due to its easy access from Tokyo and its well-developed infrastructure. The town is teeming with onsen resorts, most offering unobstructed views of Fuji, which looms to the south. The southern shore is admittedly touristy and can become jammed with visitors during summer. But the lake's east side and less-developed northern shore offer spectacular views of the mountain and are home to a few museums worth visiting. Lake Kawaguchi is a great choice if you want to appreciate Fuji at a distance, preferably while lounging around a ryokan clad in a yukata or soaking in an onsen tub.

SIGHTS

Itchiku Kubota Art Museum

2255 Kawaguchi; tel. 0555/76-8811; www.itchiku-museum.com; 9:30am-5:30pm Wed.-Mon. Apr.-Nov., 10am-4:30pm Wed.-Mon. Dec.-Mar., closed Wed. if holiday falls on Tues., open daily Oct.-Nov.; ¥1,600 adults, ¥900 college and high school students, ¥400 junior high and elementary students; from Kawaguchiko Station take Kawaguchiko bus (Kawaguchiko line) to Itchiku Kubota Art Museum bus stop

In Kawaguchi, the Itchiku Kubota Art Museum showcases textiles woven by master artist Kubota Itchiku (1917-2003), who elevated the kimono to stunning heights. The museum itself is housed in a pyramidal building and presents Kubota's stunning vision in the artwork called Symphony of Light, containing 80 kimonos, of which 30 are shown at any one time. Each hefty garment in this work is three to four times heavier than a normal kimono and incorporates dyeing techniques dating to the 14th-17th centuries. There's a café with a glass beads gallery on site (coffee or tea ¥500), as well as a garden with a teahouse on the grounds (10am-2:30pm daily; tea ¥1,000, tea with sweets sets ¥1,300-2,500).

HIKING

MOUNT FUJI PANORAMIC ROPEWAY

1163-1 Azagawa; tel. 0555/72-0363; www.mtfujiropeway.jp; 9:30am-4pm (last descent 4:20pm) Mon.-Fri., 9:30am-4pm (last descent 5:20pm) Sat.-Sun. and holidays; ¥500 adults, ¥250 children one-way, ¥900 adults, ¥450 children round-trip

At the southeastern edge of Lake Kawaguchi, the Mount Fuji Panoramic Ropeway will transport you 1,104 meters (3,622 ft) up to a viewing deck with superb views of Mount Fuji. You won't get views of Japan's most famous peak better than this.

PANORAMA DAI HIKING TRAIL

Distance: *14.1 km (8.8 mi) round-trip*
Time: *6.5 hours round-trip*
Information and maps: *https://nowrongturnsblog.wordpress.com/2017/05/10/itinerary-for-an-unforgettable-trip-to-mt-fuji*
Trailhead: *Panorama-dai-shita bus stop*

Traveling westward from Lake Kawaguchi

1
2

by car (30 minutes) or bus (40 minutes), start hiking from the northwestern shore of Lake Shoji along the Panorama Dai hiking trail. After following the moderately difficult path for about 1 hour, you'll reach a breathtaking lookout point (elevation 1,325 m/4,347 ft) directly facing Fuji. Note that the signage is almost entirely in Japanese—just look for the boards indicating the Panorama Dai (パノラマ台) and stick to the path, which entails walking roughly 45 minutes uphill to a junction, then veering left and forging on for another 15 minutes to the lookout point.

A caveat: Buses running between Kawaguchi-ko Station and Panorama Dai Shita bus stop are very sporadic (Blue line bus, 4-5 daily; ¥1,040 one-way from Kawaguchi-ko Station). I would only recommend this trip if you have a rental car. Also note that there are numerous locations called "Panorama Dai" in the region. If you're using Google Maps, instead search for the GPS coordinates 35°29'25.9"N 138°36'09.3"E; there's a small parking lot next to the bus stop. The trailhead is right across the street. Alternatively, search for the Yamadaya Hotel in Google Maps. The trailhead is about 200 m (656 ft), or a 3-minute walk south, from there.

FOOD

T'S CAFÉ

Ridge E 1F, 1477-1 Ōishi; tel. 0555/25-7055; www.takeda-shokuhin.co.jp/ts_cafe.html; 10am-6pm daily in summer, 10:30am-5pm daily in winter; average ¥1,000; take Fuji Kyūkō line to Kawaguchiko Station, then take Kawaguchiko "retro bus" (Kawaguchiko line) to Kawaguchiko Natural Living Center bus stop

Tucked away in Fuji Ōishi Hanaterrace—a cluster of shops next to Ōishi Park dedicated to locally produced foods and goods—T's Café offers a reasonably priced menu of drinks, snacks, light meals, and ice cream, all made using locally sourced ingredients. Views of lavender fields and Mount Fuji are an added bonus. This is a good pick if you're on the lake's north shore.

TETSUYAKI

3486-1 Funatsu; tel. 070/4075-1683; https://tetsuyaki.business.site; 11:30am-2pm and 5pm-9:30pm daily; average ¥1,000; take Fuji Kyūkō line to Kawaguchiko Station

Two minutes' walk from Kawaguchiko Station, Tetsuyaki offers good, greasy-spoon options on a budget-friendly menu. You'll find chicken and rice dishes, steak and fries, okonomiyaki, ginger pork, and booze. It's a good option if you're searching for a bite after dark, as many restaurants close early around town.

IDATEN

3486-4 Funatsu; tel. 0555/73-9218; http://ida-ten.jp; 11am-1am (last order midnight) Wed.-Mon.; average ¥1,000; take Fuji Kyūkō line to Kawaguchiko Station

Generous portions of tempura are the focus of the menu at Idaten. Sit in a counter seat for a view of the kitchen, where you can see the chefs at work. Optional sets include rice, miso soup, and udon. An English menu is available. This is a good choice if you're on the south side of the lake, near Kawaguchiko Station.

HOUTOU FUDOU

707 Kawaguchi; tel. 0210/41-0457; www.houtou-fudou.jp/index.html; 11am-7pm daily; average ¥1,100; take Fuji Kyūkō line to Kawaguchiko Station, then take Kawaguchiko "retro bus" (Kawaguchiko line) to Kawaguchiko Music Forest bus stop

Houtou Fudou, on the eastern shore of the lake, is a good restaurant to sample houtou, a dish that includes flat noodles akin to udon in a bowl of miso-based stew and vegetables. This dish is a specialty of Yamanashi Prefecture and a local favorite. Along with houtou, the menu also includes soba noodles, minced tuna with rice, basashi (raw horse meat), and inari sushi (sweetened tofu pouches stuffed with sushi rice). Call ahead if you plan to visit the store after 4pm on a weekday.

1: Lake Kawaguchi from the top of the Mount Fuji Panoramic Ropeway **2:** passengers boarding the ropeway car

★ SANROKUEN

3370-1 Funatsu; tel. 0555/73-1000; 11am-7:30pm Fri.-Wed.; ¥2,160-4,320; take Fuji Kyūkō line to Kawaguchiko Station

A 15-minute walk from Kawaguchiko Station, Sanrokuen is an atmospheric restaurant set in a thatched-roof house, built 150 years ago. Guests sit on the floor around a sunken hearth and slow-grill five-course sets of meat, fish, vegetables, and tofu on spears over an open charcoal pit. While rainbow trout, duck, pork, beef, and a variety of delicious local vegetables feature heavily on the menu, some items are not your everyday fare. Barbecued jellyfish, anyone? This is a good choice for a unique, homey meal with friendly hosts. It's wise to book a week or more in advance to ensure a seat. English is spoken.

ACCOMMODATIONS

K'S HOUSE MT. FUJI

6713-108 Funatsu; tel. 0555/83-5556; https://kshouse.jp/fuji-e/index.html; from ¥2,500 dorm, from ¥3,600 private room for 2 without bathroom, from ¥4,400 private room for 2 with bathroom; take Fuji Kyūkō line to Kawaguchiko Station

Popular among backpackers and hikers who are in town to climb Mount Fuji, K's House Mt. Fuji offers clean, cozy Japanese-style private rooms with tatami-mat floors and dorm-style rooms, including some that are female-only, at reasonable rates. Guests have access to a shared lounge and kitchen, and the hostel is close to a convenience store, a supermarket, and a few eateries. It's located only a three-minute walk from the south side of the lake. This is a solid budget option for those seeking to meet fellow travelers.

FUJIYOSHIDA YOUTH HOSTEL

3-6-51 Shimoyoshida, Fujiyoshidashi; tel. 0555/22-0533; ¥3,800 dorm; take JR Chūō line to Otsuki Station, and then take Fuji Kyūkō railway to Shimoyoshida Station

Given that its no-frills rooms are private, the name Fujiyoshida Youth Hostel is a bit of a misnomer. Guests share a clean bathroom and sleep on futons on tatami-mat floors in the six rooms of this tiny inn, which is a Japanese-style home run by a family who lives on the first floor. The owners are extremely hospitable and are happy to help with local recommendations. This is a solid budget option in the town of Fuji-Yoshida, away from the more touristy Lake Kawaguchi. Breakfast is available for an additional ¥600.

KONANSOU

4020-2 Funatsu; tel. 0555/72-2166; www.konansou.com; ¥42,000 with two meals; take Fuji Kyūkō line to Kawaguchiko Station

Konansou is a ryokan with modern Japanese and Western-style rooms, some with private outdoor bathtubs, at the southeastern corner of Lake Kawaguchi. There are fantastic views of Mount Fuji and the lake throughout the hotel. Alongside gender-separated indoor and outdoor public onsen baths, there is a rooftop garden with an onsen footbath and private onsen baths that can be reserved in 50-minute increments. Guests can opt for a breakfast buffet and dinner plan comprising kaiseki fare, either eaten in the restaurant or delivered to the room.

SHUHOKAKU KOGETSU

2312 Kawaguchi; tel. 0555/76-8888; www.kogetu.com; ¥47,000 with two meals; pickup from Kawaguchiko Station available for guests

The biggest draw at this plush onsen ryokan is the stunning view of Fuji, seen from both the men's and women's open-air pools. On the northern shore of Lake Kawaguchi, this luxury spot has all the bells and whistles—top-notch hospitality, kaiseki meals made with the finest seasonal ingredients, and large, well-appointed Japanese-style rooms with views of the lake and peak looming beyond. There's also a stunning garden and a private lakeside beach. If you've got the cash, this is a worthy splurge.

INFORMATION AND SERVICES

- **Lake Kawaguchi Tourist Information Center** (3641-1 Funatsu, Fujikawaguchiko; tel. 0555/72-6700; www.fujisan.ne.jp; 9am-5pm daily; just outside Kawaguchiko Station)

GETTING THERE AND AROUND

As Kawaguchiko Station is one of the major gateways to Mount Fuji itself, making a trip to Lake Kawaguchi, which is next to Kawaguchiko Station, means taking the same route you would if you were traveling to Mount Fuji, as described above. This applies to both train and bus routes.

If you're coming from Tokyo by train, take the Chūō line limited express train (1 hour; ¥2,360) or the regular train (1 hour 30 minutes; ¥1,340; may require transfer at Takao Station) west from Shinjuku Station to Otsuki. When you've reached Otsuki, change trains to the Fuji Kyūkō line and ride until Kawaguchiko Station (1 hour; ¥1,170). Note that the JR Pass does not cover rides on the Fuji Kyūkō line.

Traveling from Tokyo by bus, either take one of the buses operated by **Keiō Dentetsu** (tel. 03/5376-2222; http://highway-buses.jp; ¥2,000 adults, ¥1,000 children) or **Fujikyū Express** (http://bus-en.fujikyu.co.jp/highway; ¥2,000 adults, ¥1,000 children), both running once or twice hourly, from the Shinjuku Highway Bus Terminal (Shinjuku Station west exit; https://highway-buses.jp/terminal/shinjuku.php) to Kawaguchiko Station. The trip takes roughly 1 hour 40 minutes. Alternatively, ride a bus operated by **Fujikyū** (http://bus-en.fujikyu.co.jp/highway) or **JR Kanto Bus** (www.jrbuskanto.co.jp.e.wn.hp.transer.com) from Tokyo Station's Yaesu South exit to Kawaguchiko Station (2 hours; ¥2,000 one-way). Fujikyū runs another route that starts from near the Mark City commercial complex linked to Shibuya Station and runs to Kawaguchiko Station (2-2.5 hours, depending on traffic; ¥2,000 adults, ¥1,000 children one-way).

Likewise, if you are coming to Lake Kawaguchi from Kansai (Osaka, Kyoto), or a closer hub, such as Nagoya, you would follow the same route described above to reach Mount Fuji from the west. The simplest way is by taking the Tōkaidō shinkansen **Kodama line** from Kyoto to **Mishima Station** (2 hours 40 minutes; ¥11,310). Near Mishima Station's south exit, ride a **Fujikyū bus** (http://bus-en.fujikyu.co.jp/highway) to **Kawaguchiko Station** (1.5-2 hours depending on road conditions; ¥2,300 adults, ¥1,150 children).

Central Honshu

Nagoya 217
Matsumoto 227
Northern Japan Alps . . . 234
Between Matsumoto and
Takayama. 244
Takayama. 251
Kanazawa. 260

The geographical center of Japan, Central Honshu (sometimes called Chūbu), draws visitors with its access to the Japan Alps, a vast chain of mountain ranges that cuts through the center of Honshu; its proliferation of onsen (hot spring baths); and its abundance of well-preserved historic towns. The most popular of the region's many storied cities is Kanazawa, home to charming teahouses, a former samurai quarter, and Kenroku-en, one of Japan's finest gardens.

In the mountains that spread across the region's interior, small cities offer a glimpse of a more traditional way of life. Takayama boasts a well-preserved merchants' quarter, crisscrossed by streams, along with Hida-no-Sato, a cluster of thatched-roof houses rebuilt to evoke Japan's

Highlights

Look for ★ to find recommended sights, activities, dining, and lodging.

★ **Matsumoto-jō:** The country's oldest wooden castle, nicknamed "Crow Castle" for its iconic black walls, Matsumoto-jō is an immaculate representation of a classical Japanese fortress (page 227).

★ **Walking Japan's Medieval Highway:** Ramble along a rural section of Japan's famed medieval highway, the Nakasendō, between the well-preserved Edo-period (1603-1868) towns of Tsumago and Magome (page 228).

★ **Hiking in Kamikōchi:** This highland valley offers some of the most breathtaking alpine scenery in all of Japan. Rivers course through verdant forests, and onsen offer relaxation to weary hikers (page 246).

★ **Sanmachi Suji:** Takayama's well-preserved riverside merchant's quarter lures you into its many museums, galleries, shops, and eateries (page 251).

★ **Folk Villages of Central Honshu:** These mountain villages of A-frame, thatch-roofed farmhouses conjure the archetypal image of bucolic bliss, and dramatically display the rhythm of the seasons (page 258).

★ **Kenroku-en:** Kanazawa's famed castle garden is widely regarded as one of the country's best designed landscapes (page 262).

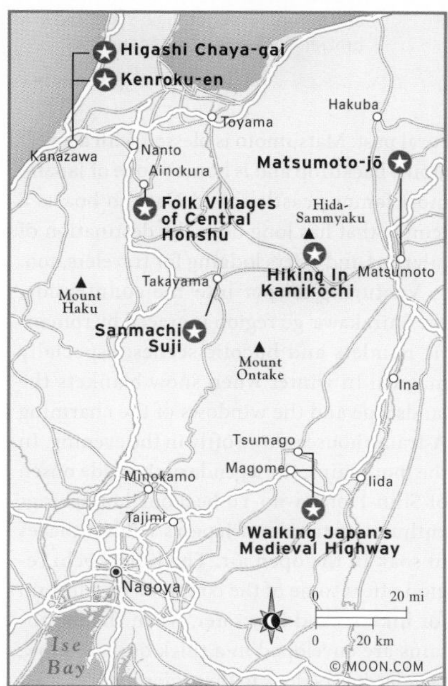

★ **Higashi Chaya-gai:** The myriad teahouses lining the cobblestone paths of Kanazawa's geisha district offer an evocative glimpse of the past (page 266).

Regional Food Specialties

The industrial city of **Nagoya** is known for dishes liberally slathered in sauce and sweetened flavors. Meanwhile, the decidedly more rural town of **Takayama**'s contribution to the region's cuisine is its locally sourced beef, known as **hida-gyū,** which ensures you'll find no shortage of good burger joints in town. Local chefs also take advantage of the profusion of **sansai,** or vegetables growing in the surrounding mountains.

NAGOYA

- **Hitsumabushi:** A prime example of Nagoya's sweetened cuisine, hitsumabushi is thinly sliced saltwater eel flavored with soy-based sauce atop a bed of rice. Try it at **Atsuta Horaiken Honten** (page 224).
- **Miso-nikomi udon:** Nagoya-style thick udon noodles in a viscous miso broth. Try it at **Yamamotoya Honten (Meieki)** (page 224).
- **Miso-katsu:** Breaded and deep-fried cuts of fatty pork in a sweetened miso-based sauce. Try it at **Yabaton Honten** (page 224).

TAKAYAMA

Sold at shops around town, **mitarashi-dango,** or balls made of rice cake dipped in soy, are put on skewers and slowly toasted.

- **Hoba-miso:** This dish from Takayama takes advantage of locally sourced beef (Hida-gyū) and mountain vegetables, slathered in a dollop of miso paste and then cooked over a charcoal brazier. Try it at **Kyōya** (page 256).

rural past. Matsumoto is blessed with a lovely alpine backdrop and is home to one of Japan's most famous castles. And Nagano boasts a temple that has long been the destination of pilgrims and offers lodging for travelers, too.

Venturing deeper into the countryside, the Shirakawa-gō region is graced by romantic hamlets and bucolic scenes, especially magical in winter when snow blankets the landscape and the windows of the charming A-frame houses glow softly in the evening. In the mountains, the legendary riverside onsen of Shin-Hotaka-no-Yu beckons hot-springs enthusiasts to one of Japan's wildest places to soak in the open air. The Kamikōchi region offers some of the country's best terrain for hikers. And in winter, when the mountains are enveloped in a thick quilt of snow, powder-lovers flock to the region's world-class ski slopes.

Meanwhile, in the south, the mercantile city of Nagoya is a convenient, no-frills transit hub, with rich culinary options injecting a bit of flavor. Hop aboard a local train bound for the Kiso Valley for a change of scenery. This alpine pass, dotted by atmospheric towns that once stood along the medieval Kyoto-Tokyo highway known as the Nakasendō, is best experienced on foot, traipsing between the old post towns of Tsumago and Magome against a backdrop of rolling peaks.

ORIENTATION

Central Honshu is Japan's vast heartland, sandwiched between Greater Tokyo, known as Kanto, to the east, and the nation's similarly sprawling historic heart in Kansai (Kyoto, Osaka, and around) to the west. Aichi Prefecture—home to **Nagoya,** the region's largest city with a population of

Previous: Higashi Chaya-gai; the folk village of Ainokura; Matsumoto-jō.

Best Accommodations

★ **Sumiyoshi-ya:** This nostalgic, rustic ryokan is a wonderful place to immerse yourself in the quintessential hot-spring village of Nozawa Onsen (page 239).

★ **Backcountry Lodge Hakuba:** Run by a friendly couple, this homey lodge is a relaxed place to base yourself in the Hakuba Valley, and to kick back and read by the fire after a day on the slopes (page 243).

★ **Flatt's:** Slow down to savor ocean views, ingenious meals, and genuine warmth at this charming bed-and-breakfast run by a gregarious Australian chef and his local wife on the quiet eastern shore of the Nōto Peninsula (page 269).

★ **Asadaya:** With brilliant service, Edo-period chic, and exquisite cuisine, this is the finest ryokan in Kanazawa (page 272).

2.3 million—sprawls along the southwestern Pacific coast, bordered on the north by landlocked Gifu Prefecture. The prefectures of Fukui and Ishikawa, home to the historic town of **Kanazawa,** make up the Japan Sea side. Meanwhile, Nagano Prefecture commands a large swath of Central Honshu's rugged core.

The primary feature of Central Honshu is its abundance of mountains. A series of ranges, collectively called the **Japan Alps,** run through the center of the region, tapering off near both the Pacific and the Japan Sea coasts. This craggy interior can be easily accessed from the greater Tokyo area, Nagoya in the south, or Kanazawa in the north. The towns of **Takayama,** located in Gifu Prefecture, and **Matsumoto** and **Nagano,** both in Nagano Prefecture, are the main hubs in the Alps region. Located roughly between Takayama and Kanazawa, the **Shirakawa-gō** and nearby **Gokayama** regions are collectively a UNESCO World Heritage site made famous by the tranquil folk villages fit for a fairy tale.

PLANNING YOUR TIME

How long you'll want to devote to Central Honshu will depend on whether you plan to explore its mountainous interior or simply head to one of the region's coastal hubs. It's best viewed as a place to spend two or three days exploring some of Japan's natural beauty—hiking in the warmer months or skiing in winter—as you shuttle between greater Tokyo (Kanto) and Kansai. That said, if you don't plan to visit Kansai's historical gems, Kyoto and Nara, a day or two in **Kanazawa** provides a good dose of traditional Japan.

Although it's easy to access from Tokyo and Kansai's major hubs, thanks to its large shinkansen (bullet train) station, **Nagoya** is best viewed as a transit point and less as a base. If you're heading into the mountains, it pays to stop in one of the region's provincial hubs, like **Takayama** or **Matsumoto,** good bases for exploring the surrounding countryside, taking a day hike, or seeing the thatched-roof houses of **Shirakawa-gō** and **Gokayama.** The city of **Nagano,** home of **Zenkō-ji** temple, is an entry point to a cluster of rustic, secluded onsen, and hiking or winter sports options. Between Nagoya and Nagano, the **Nakasendō**, popularly known as "Japan's medieval highway," is a great place for a lovely walk, and it pays to savor the experience with an overnight stay in either town.

Getting Around

When it comes to accessing this vast region,

Central Honshu

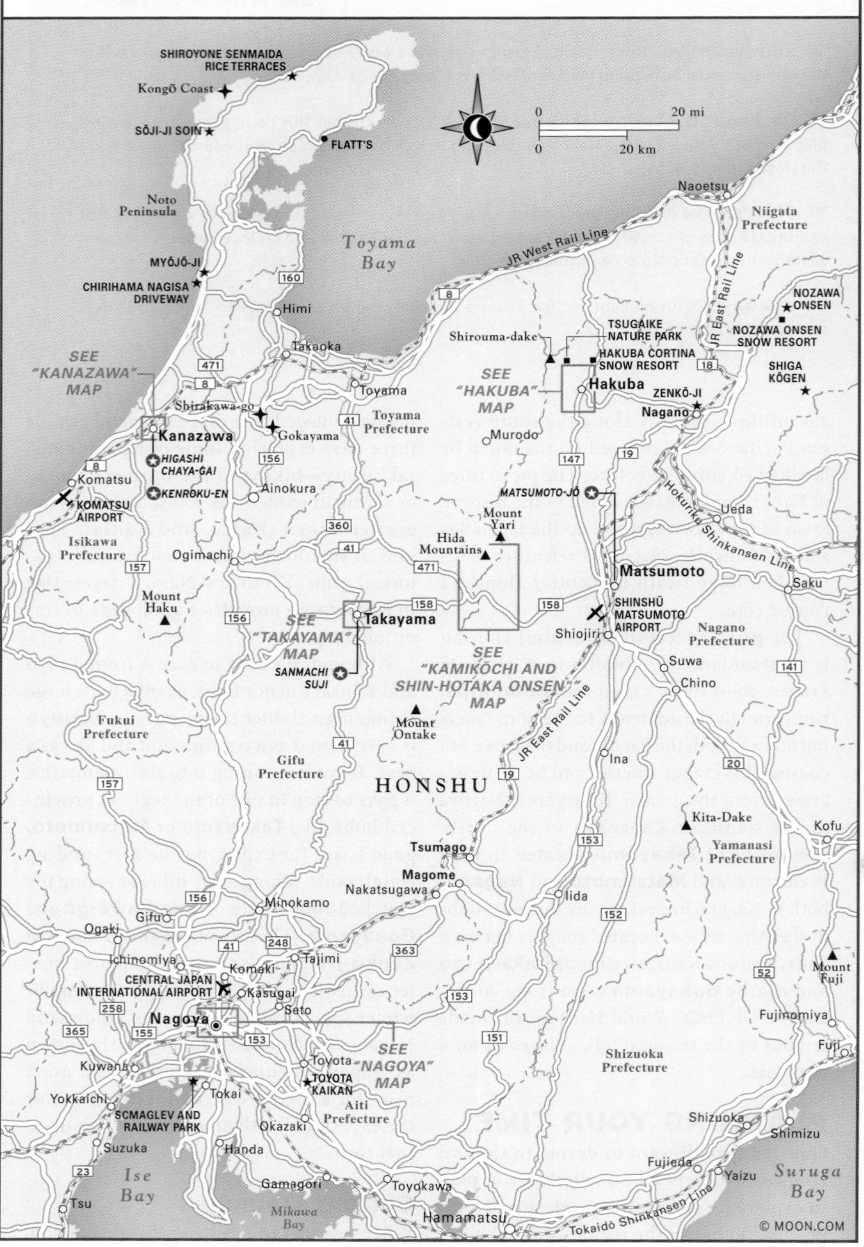

CENTRAL HONSHU

Nagoya is a convenient entry point if you're approaching from the south, given its position on the shinkansen line. Other stations in the region with shinkansen links include Nagano, Kanazawa, and Toyama. To reach Matsumoto and Takayama, local and in some cases faster limited express trains are available. Penetrating deeper into the mountains, to ski towns like **Hakuba**, **Nozawa Onsen**, and **Shiga Kōgen**, the mountaineer's realm of **Kamikōchi**, the folk villages of Shirakawa-gō and Gokayama, or remote hot-spring escape of **Shin-Hotaka-no-Yu Onsen** requires first taking a local or express train to a point, then driving or taking a bus for the rest of the way.

When to Go

The mountains running through the middle of the region heavily influence the weather, especially in winter. In winter, while the Pacific side is relatively dry and sunny (but cold), the Japan Sea side gets a heavy dump of snow. There are excellent resorts for **skiing** and **snowboarding** throughout the Alps. Book rooms a few months in advance for popular ski resorts like **Hakuba, Nozawa Onsen,** and **Shiga Kōgen.** Similarly, accommodations book up fast for some of the bigger **festivals** in the region, such as the Takayama Matsuri, and during the popular **autumn leaves** viewing season that peaks in November.

Nagoya 名古屋

Nagoya, Japan's fourth-largest city with a population of 2.3 million, has the unenviable distinction of being considered boring. This bad rap can be traced to the 1980s when the TV star and comedian Tamori, in his trademark black sunglasses, began to knock the city as a middling place lacking zest, sophistication, or distinguishing traits of any kind. The city's image took another hit in 2016 when its own residents rated it among the least desirable destinations of eight cities across Japan, in a variety of categories. Ouch.

One thing to keep in mind is that vast swaths of Nagoya were reduced to rubble during World War II, wiping out most traces of historical charm that may once have graced its streets. The city's manufacturing might—it was a major producer of Japan's legendary Zero fighter planes—made it a prime target for Allied bombers, and a gray cityscape arose from the ashes. But if you find yourself here, don't despair: you'll likely be pleasantly surprised. Its diverse range of attractions—including a reconstructed castle, one of Shinto's holiest shrines, museums showcasing feudal treasures of the mighty Tokugawa family, the heritage of automotive giant Toyota, and a stellar look at Japan's rich history with trains—as well as its down-to-earth residents, green downtown, and local dishes that pair well with beer will engage and satiate you.

The city's sturdy mercantile backbone is reflected in some of its better-known attractions, such as the Toyota Commemorative Museum of Industry and Technology and the SCMaglev and Railway Park, a hit with children and train geeks. Stellar museums and parks, important spiritual sites, and a reproduction castle are also scattered around the city. Given its convenient location between Kanto and Kansai and accessibility by shinkansen, Nagoya is an ideal jumping-off point for journeys into the Japan Alps.

ORIENTATION

The bulk of the city's attractions are spread across **downtown,** fanning out eastward from **Nagoya Station.** Noritake no Mori (a garden on the grounds of a former ceramics factory) and the Toyota Commemorative Museum of Industry and Technology are just north of the station. The rebuilt fortress of Nagoya-jō looms in the north-central side of downtown, while Tokugawa-en garden and

Nagoya

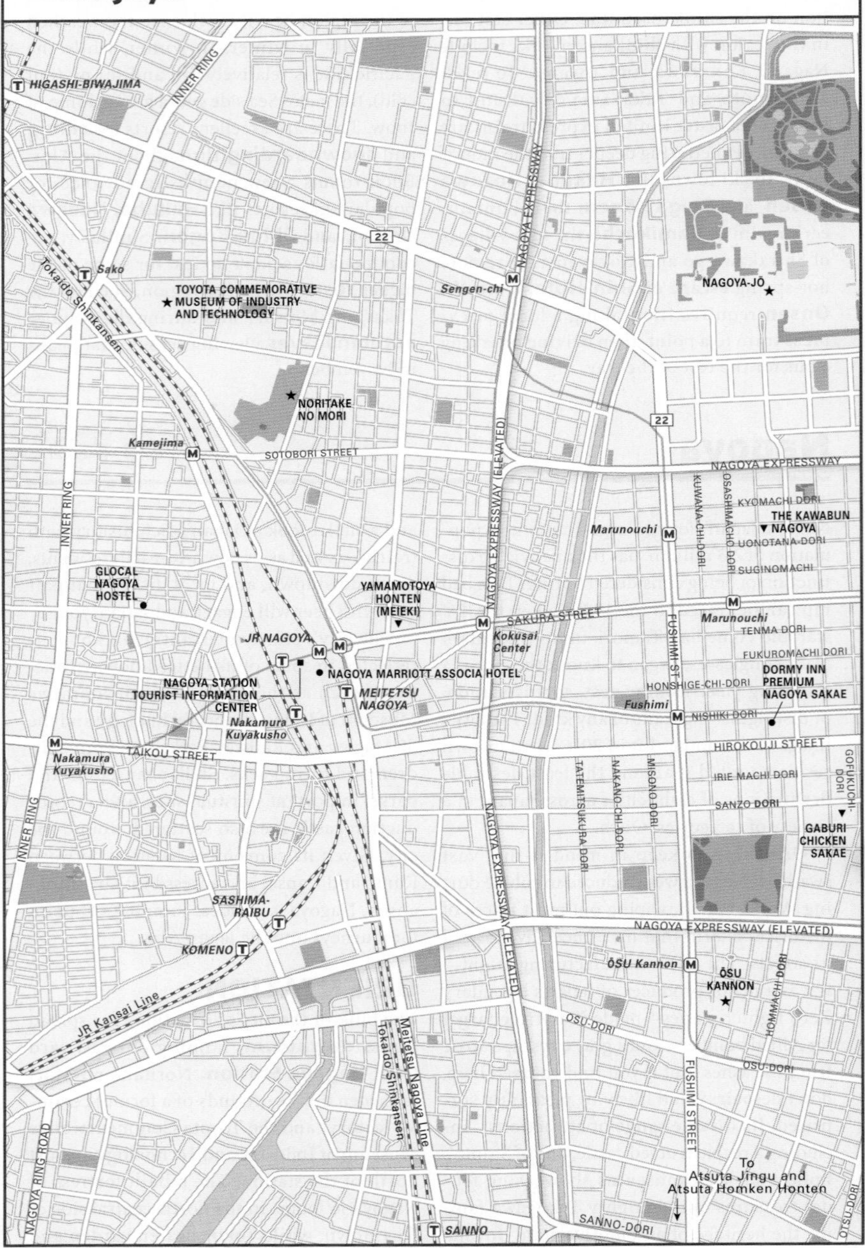

HIGASHI-BIWAJIMA
INNER RING
NAGOYA EXPRESSWAY
22
Sako
Tokaido Shinkansen
TOYOTA COMMEMORATIVE MUSEUM OF INDUSTRY AND TECHNOLOGY
Sengen-chi
NAGOYA-JŌ
NORITAKE NO MORI
Kamejima
SOTOBORI STREET
NAGOYA EXPRESSWAY (ELEVATED)
KUWANA-CHI-DORI
OSASHIMACHO DORI
KYOMACHI DORI
THE KAWABUN NAGOYA
UONOTANA-DORI
SUGINOMACHI
Marunouchi
GLOCAL NAGOYA HOSTEL
YAMAMOTOYA HONTEN (MEIEKI)
SAKURA STREET
Kokusai Center
TENMA DORI
FUKUROMACHI DORI
JR NAGOYA
NAGOYA MARRIOTT ASSOCIA HOTEL
NAGOYA STATION TOURIST INFORMATION CENTER
MEITETSU NAGOYA
Nakamura Kuyakusho
HONSHIGE-CHI-DORI
DORMY INN PREMIUM NAGOYA SAKAE
Fushimi
NISHIKI DORI
FUSHIMI ST
HIROKOUJI STREET
TAIKOU STREET
TATEMITSUKURA DORI
NAKANO-CHI-DORI
MISONO-DORI
IRIE MACHI DORI
GOFUKUCHI-DORI
SANZO DORI
GABURI CHICKEN SAKAE
SASHIMA-RAIBU
KOMENO
ŌSU Kannon
ŌSU KANNON
HOMMACHI DORI
JR Kansai Line
OSU-DORI
Meitetsu Nagoya Line
FUSHIMI STREET
NAGOYA RING ROAD
To Atsuta Jingu and Atsuta Homken Honten
SANNO-DORI
SANNO

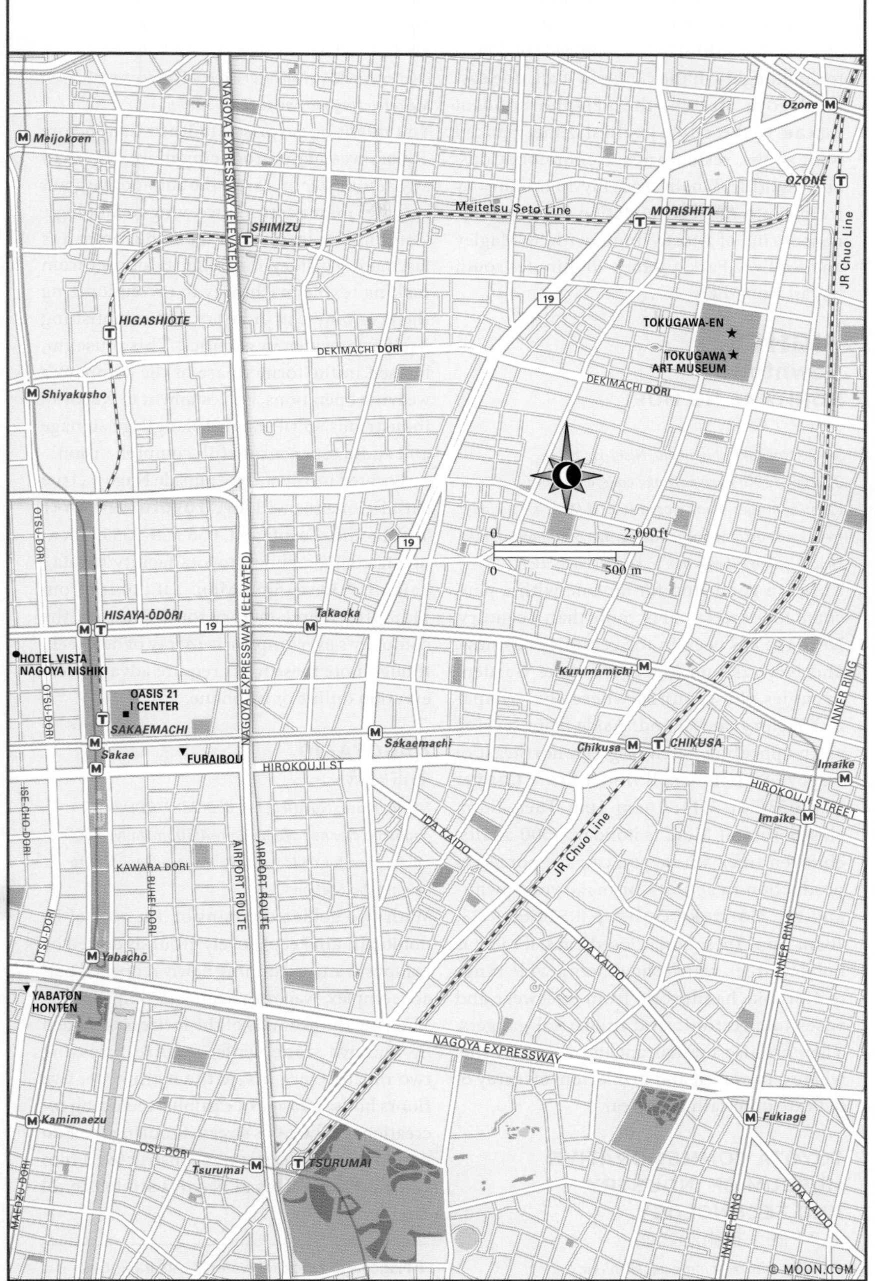
Meijokoen
Ozone
OZONE
Meitetsu Seto Line
MORISHITA
SHIMIZU
NAGOYA EXPRESSWAY (ELEVATED)
JR Chuo Line
HIGASHIOTE
19
TOKUGAWA-EN
TOKUGAWA ART MUSEUM
DEKIMACHI DORI
Shiyakusho
OTSU-DORI
0
2,000 ft
0
500 m
HISAYA-ŌDŌRI
Takaoka
HOTEL VISTA NAGOYA NISHIKI
Kurumamichi
OASIS 21 I CENTER
SAKAEMACHI
Sakaemachi
Sakae
FURAIBOU
HIROKOUJI ST
Chikusa
CHIKUSA
Imaike
HIROKOUJI STREET
INNER RING
ISE-CHO-DORI
IDA KAIDO
KAWARA DORI
BUHEI DORI
AIRPORT ROUTE
Yabachō
YABATON HONTEN
NAGOYA EXPRESSWAY
Kamimaezu
Fukiage
OSU-DORI
Tsurumai
TSURUMAI
MAEDZU-DORI
© MOON.COM

the Tokugawa Art Museum sit in the northeast. The hallowed temple of Ōsu Kannon attracts the faithful to the south side of downtown. Roughly in the center of it all, due east of Nagoya Station, the neighborhood of **Sakae** is the city's liveliest zone, packed with shops, restaurants, accommodations, and nightlife. Finally, roughly 10 minutes by train south of Nagoya Station is the prominent shrine of Atsuta Jingū, with SCMaglev and Railway Park another 40 minutes south by rail from there.

SIGHTS

Downtown

NORITAKE NO MORI

ノリタケの森

3-1-36 Noritake-shinmachi, Nishi-ku; tel. 052/561-7290; www.noritake.co.jp/eng/mori; 10am-6pm Tues.-Sun., closed Tues. if Mon. is a holiday; free (some attractions inside garden cost money); take Higashiyama subway line to Kamejima Station

This is a good stop for anyone with a penchant for porcelain. For more than a century, Noritake has been in the ceramics business, and Noritake no Mori (Noritake Garden) occupies the grounds where the company's factory once stood. Aside from serving as an appealing patch of green northeast of Nagoya Station, you'll find a **Craft Center** (tel. 052/561-7114; 10am-5pm Tues.-Sun., closed Tues. if Mon. is holiday; ¥500 adults, children free), where you can see porcelain production in action—or make your own—and the **Noritake Gallery** (052/562-9811; 10am-6pm Tues.-Sun., closed Tues. if Mon. is holiday; free), which showcases a wide range of Noritake handiwork, from tablewear and vases to electronic and industrial gadgets. There are also a restaurant and a **café** on-site, where patrons eat and drink from an array of delicate porcelain tablewear.

TOYOTA COMMEMORATIVE MUSEUM OF INDUSTRY AND TECHNOLOGY

トヨタ産業技術記念館

4-1-35 Noritake-shinmachi, Nishi-ku; tel. 052/551-6115; www.tcmit.org; 9:30am-5pm Tues.-Sat., closed Tues. if Mon. is holiday; ¥500 adults, ¥300 high school and junior high school students, ¥200 elementary school students; take Meitetsu Nagoya line to Sako Station

You might be surprised to learn that, before Toyota was mass-producing more cars than any automaker on earth, the automotive giant actually manufactured weaving technology. Come here to learn more about the company's fascinating history, including its journey from making textile machinery to revolutionizing the economy-car industry and establishing itself as a leader in robotics. This museum, housed in the former base of the company's weaving operations, is a testament to Nagoya's industrious spirit. English-language signage and audio tours ensure full comprehension.

Located in Toyota city outside Nagoya, true car aficionados will love **Toyota Kaikan** (1 Toyota-chō, Toyota; tel. 0565/29-3355; www.toyota.co.jp/en/about_toyota/facility/toyota_kaikan; 9:30am-5pm Mon.-Sat., tours from 11am; free). Free factory tours show off the company's ever-impressive array of new tech, though note these tours require advance reservation online or by phone.

NAGOYA-JŌ

名古屋城

1-1 Honmaru, Naka-ku; tel. 052/231-1700; www.nagoyajo.city.nagoya.jp; 9am-4:30pm daily; ¥500 adults, free for children; take Meijo subway line to Shiyakusho Station

With two golden dolphins on the roof of its donjon (main keep), lovely grounds dotted by teahouses and a stunning newly reopened palace complex, Nagoya-jō cuts a striking profile. Entering the grounds of the fortress, shielded by massive stone walls, requires crossing two moats. Once inside the main keep, five floors house a range of exhibits, including recreations of the city's streetlife during the Edo period when the castle was constructed. From the top floor, vistas of Nagoya stretch in all directions.

1: Nagoya-jō **2:** Tokugawa-en **3:** Atsuta Jingū

1
2
3

The castle's legacy underlines Nagoya's historical importance. No less than Oda Nobunaga (1534-1582), the great warrior famed for unifying half of Japan's provinces; Toyotoi Hideyoshi (1536-1598), who completed the mammoth task begun by his predecessor Oda; and Tokugawa Ieyasu (1543-1616), who founded the mighty Tokugawa shogunate that reigned throughout the Edo period (1603-1868), were all born in the area. It was the last of these three towering figures, Tokugawa, who called for the construction of Nagoya-jō in 1609, to serve as the base of the Owari branch of the Tokugawa family.

The castle has been undergoing ambitious redevelopment. The palace, **Honmaru Goten,** also on the grounds, reopened to visitors in June 2018, after a lengthy renovation using time-honored materials and techniques. With its elegant entrance, immaculate tatami rooms, and beautifully painted sliding doors, the building is one of the best examples of classical Shoin architecture in the country.

TOKUGAWA ART MUSEUM
徳川美術館

1017 Tokugawa-chō, Higashi-ku; tel. 052/935-6262; www.tokugawa-art-museum.jp; 10am-5pm Tues.-Sun., closed Tues. if Mon. is holiday; ¥1,400 adults, ¥700 university and high school students, ¥500 junior high and elementary school students; take JR Chūō line to Ozone, or Meguru loop bus to stop 11

To glean some sense of the power wielded by the Owari branch of Tokugawa Ieyasu's lineage, which was based in Nagoya, be sure to visit this excellent museum. Built on the grounds where the Owari family once resided, the museum contains some 10,000 precious artifacts possessed by the Owari line of the Tokugawa family.

Six exhibition halls showcase armor and weapons of war, a re-created teahouse with exquisite utensils, household items that would have once been found in the reception chambers and living quarters of a palace, a Noh theater with a collection of haunting masks, and perhaps most impressive of all, a scroll of *The Tale of Genji* dating to the 12th century. The scroll is only exhibited briefly each year to preserve the delicate parchment, but videos revealing its intricate details stand ready at other times.

If you check out the Tokugawa Art Museum, be sure to stop at the lovely garden next door, **Tokugawa-en** (1001 Tokugawa-chō, Higashi-ku; tel. 052/935-8988; www.tokugawaen.aichi.jp; 9:30am-5:30pm Tues.-Sun., closed Tues. if Mon. is holiday; ¥300 adults; take JR Chūō line to Ozone, or Meguru loop bus to stop 11). It's at its most resplendent in spring, when peonies (mid- to late April) and irises (late May to early June) bloom, and in autumn when foliage turns fiery red, bright yellow, and earthy brown. The Tokugawa family donated the garden to the city in 1931, but it was subsequently decimated by Allied bombs in 1945. Restored in 2001 and reopened in 2004, today the garden is beautifully landscaped, complete with bodies of water crisscrossed by bridges, meandering footpaths, and a waterfall. This is a great place to slow down and contemplate how the ruling class once lived.

ŌSU KANNON
大須観音

2-21-47 Ōsu, Naka-ku; tel. 052/231-6525; www.osu-kannon.jp; 24 hours a day; free; take Tsurumai subway line to Ōsu Kannon Station

Within this popular temple stands a wooden statue of Kannon, Buddhist goddess of mercy, sculpted by Kobo Daishi (aka Kūkai), founder of the Shingon school of Buddhism and one of Japan's most important spiritual figures. Originally built in Gifu Prefecture, north of Nagoya, this popular hall of worship was moved to its current location by Tokugawa Ieyasu in the early 17th century. Although originally built at the end of the Kamakura Period (1192-1333), its current incarnation was born in 1970. Despite the relative youth of the structure, beneath its main hall is a library that holds some 15,000 ancient texts, including what is considered the oldest copy of the kojiki, a handwritten chronicle of Japan's mythical history.

Just next to the temple, you'll find the **Ōsu Shopping Street,** a covered shopping area crammed with hundreds of cafés, restaurants, and shops hawking all manner of goods, from geeky paraphernalia to cheap threads.

South of Downtown

ATSUTA JINGŪ

熱田神宮

1-1-1 Jingū, Atsuta-ku; tel. 052/671-4151; www.atsutajingu.or.jp; 24 hours a day; free; take Meitetsu Nagoya line to Jingū-mae Station, or Meijo subway line to Jingū-nishi Station

This shrine, tucked away in a leafy grove in the south of Nagoya, 6 minutes by train from Meitetsu Nagoya Station, is among the most important sites in Shinto, as it is said to house the sacred sword known as **Kusanagi,** which legend says was bestowed upon the royal family by Amaterasu Omikami, the sun goddess herself, Shinto's chief deity. Along with the mirror (symbolizing wisdom and held in Ise Jingū) and the jewel (embodying the virtue of benevolence and kept at the Imperial Palace in Tokyo), the sword at Atsuta Jingū (denoting valor) is one of the three Imperial Regalia of Japan. These "Three Sacred Treasures" have been presented to Japan's emperors over the millennia by Shinto priests upon coronation, and are said to be divine gifts. These relics are so steeped in mystery, so guarded, only a few souls have ever laid eyes on them. The shrine buildings are modeled on the style of Ise Jingū—Shinto's holiest site, located about 100 kilometers (62 mi) south in Mie Prefecture—resembling a storehouse with a raised floor and gabled roof. Similar to Ise's evasive mirror, the sacred sword within the inner sanctum of Atsuta Jingū is never put on public display. In truth, the sword's existence is now a matter of faith, akin to legendary King Arthur's fabled Excalibur.

SCMAGLEV AND RAILWAY PARK

リニア・鉄道館　～夢と想い出のミュージアム～

3-2-2 Kinjofuto, Minato-ku; tel. 052/389-6100; http://museum.jr-central.co.jp; 10am-5:30pm Wed.-Mon., closed Wed. if Tues. is holiday; ¥1,000 adults, ¥500 children, shinkansen simulator ¥500; take Aonami line from Nagoya Station to Kinjofuto Station

Train geeks, rejoice. The entire history of Japan's sophisticated engagement with train technology is explored in this excellent museum, from early steam locomotives and the iconic bullet train (shinkansen) to futuristic, lighting-fast maglev trains that approach speeds of almost 600 kilometers (373 mi) per hour. A massive, elaborate miniature train set runs through an exceedingly realistic diorama of Japan's major train hubs. Elsewhere, almost 40 actual train cars can be examined, up close, from below, and from the inside. Simulators let you experience what it's like to be at the controls, to open and close doors for passengers, or to be at the helm of a shinkansen. (Note that you'll need to reserve a spot to try any of the simulators, which cost anywhere from ¥100-500 per turn, 45 minutes in advance.)

There's a strong educational component geared toward kids throughout, and an English-language audio guide can be rented for ¥500. This is a highly recommended stop if you have a keen interest in trains.

FOOD

Downtown

GABURI CHICKEN SAKAE

3-12-11 Sakae, Naka-ku; tel. 052/262-8739; https://gabuchiki.com/shop/#!/l/-/-/1010; 5pm-3am Mon.-Sat., 4pm-3am Sat., 4pm-midnight Sun. and holidays; dishes ¥350-990; 10-minute walk from the Sakae subway station

While Furaibou is a good place for a sit-down meal, Gaburi is a fun, boisterous fried-chicken spot with a cheaper, booze-friendly menu. Drink options are weighted toward various spins on the highball (whisky-soda), mixed with lemon, cola, and more. In the heart of the nightlife zone, Sakae, this is a fun place for a bite before a big night out.

YAMAMOTOYA HONTEN (MEIEKI)

1st Horiuchi Bldg. B1F, 3-25-9 Meieki; tel. 052/565-0278; http://yamamotoyahonten.co.jp; 11am-10pm daily; ¥700-1,600; take JR lines to Nagoya Station

A local specialty, the thick udon here, miso-nikomi udon, is served in a heavy, flavorful miso broth. Unlike a lot of Japanese fare, it's not subtle, but this is part of its appeal for many foreign palates. Options to go with the noodles include tempura, oysters, locally raised chicken, and kuro-buta (black pork), as the intensely flavorsome variety of Berkshire Pork that originated in the English countryside is known in Japan.

★ YABATON HONTEN

3-6-18 Ōsu, Naka-ku; tel. 052/252-8810; www.yabaton.com; 11am-9pm daily; ¥1,300-1,900; take Meijo line to Yabachō Station

With a logo featuring a portly pig, the chain's signature dish is clear: miso-katsu (juicy pork, breaded and deep-fried, then slathered in sweet, savory miso sauce, and served with shredded cabbage). In business since 1947, this restaurant is most noted for pushing this dish into Japan's culinary consciousness.

FURAIBOU

Gourmet Bldg. Aeri 1F, 4-5-8 Sakae, 1F Airy Bldg., Naka-ku; tel. 052/241-8016; www.furaibou.com; 5pm-midnight Mon.-Thurs., 5pm-1am Fri.-Sat.; ¥3,000-4,000 average; take Higashiyama and Meijo lines to Sakae Station

This restaurant serves another down-and-dirty Nagoya specialty that will feel somewhat like home for many Western travelers: chicken wings (tebasaki). Nagoya's take on the classic beer food is deep-fried and basted in a sweet, lightly spicy sauce, with a pinch of sesame and seasoning. The menu also extends to sashimi, noodles, and more. Note that it can get smoky at times.

THE KAWABUN NAGOYA

2-12-30 Marunouchi, Naka-ku; tel. 052/222-0020; www.thekawabunnagoya.com; lunch 11am-2pm Mon. and Wed.-Fri. except holidays, dinner 5:30pm-10pm Mon. and Wed.-Fri., 6:30pm-10pm Sat.-Sun. and holidays; lunch ¥1,200-5,000, dinner ¥4,500-10,000; take Sakuradōri, Tsurumai lines to Marunouchi Station

Housed in a traditional home boasting views onto a lovely garden with a pond, this classy restaurant serves great Italian food. It's ideal for families, couples, or groups who want a quality meal in elegant surroundings, with chic furniture and subdued lighting. The seasonal Italian menu includes pasta, salmon, and steak. Lunch sets are a good value. Sumptuous multicourse dinners are complemented by an extensive wine list. To be safe, reserve a day or more ahead for dinner.

Around Nagoya

★ ATSUTA HORAIKEN HONTEN

503 Godo-chō, Atsuta-ku; tel. 052/671-8686; www.houraiken.com/honten; 11:30am-2pm and 4:30pm-8:30pm Thurs.-Tues., closed every 2nd and 4th Thurs.; dishes ¥550-950, set meals ¥2,500-5,500; take Meijo subway line to Temmachō Station

Hitsumabushi, or thinly cut eel drizzled in a soy-based sauce and served over rice (¥3,600), has been served to patrons in this vaunted restaurant's tatami-floored rooms since 1873. Add scallion, wasabi, and seaweed for extra zing. There's also an a la carte menu and various other set meals beyond eel (assorted tempura and more). It draws a crowd, particularly in summer, so you may have to wait for a seat. A recommended local favorite. The restaurant is about 10 minutes' walk south of Atsuta Jingū, which is about 10 minutes by train from Nagoya Station and 20 minutes by train from most points downtown.

ACCOMMODATIONS

Under ¥10,000

GLOCAL NAGOYA BACKPACKERS HOSTEL

1-21-3 Noritake, Nakamura-ku; tel. 052/446-4694; www.facebook.com/hostelnagoya; dorms ¥3,200, private ¥12,500; 10-minute walk west of JR Nagoya Station

This hip hostel has a café-bar, where fellow

Pachinko

Luridly bright, smoky, deafening, and utterly inscrutable to the uninitiated, pachinko is one of Japan's more mystifying pastimes. For sheer shock value, step inside of one of the pachinko parlors you'll undoubtedly come across during your trip. Myriad silver ball bearings ricochet through a pinball-like glass box filled with a variety of obstacles and carefully arranged brass pins. Bored salarymen and office ladies sit before the machines for hours on end.

PACHINKO'S HISTORY

Since the first commercial pachinko parlor opened in Nagoya in 1948, the garish establishments have popped up like mushrooms around the country. Today, the pachinko industry is massive, with more revenue than all gambling in Las Vegas, Macau, and Singapore combined. Gambling is illegal in Japan, but pachinko found a loophole: If a player hits a jackpot, a flood of the small silver orbs fills a tray that they can exchange for prizes at an on-site gift shop. These prizes can then be exchanged for money at a separate window outside the parlor. These cash-exchange windows evade the law by nominally separating the prizes from the parlors themselves. Previously run by the yakuza (mafia), they are now tightly regulated.

Some 80 percent of all pachinko parlors are owned by ethnic Koreans, who, despite being born in Japan, are still considered foreign residents. The community, known as zainichi, is often subject to discrimination, and pachinko is their largest economic foothold in Japan. The randomness of the game is brilliantly used as a metaphor for the vagaries of fate in Korean-American author Min Jin Lee's novel *Pachinko,* which traces four generations of a Korean family from pre-World War II Japanese-occupied Korea to a zainichi neighborhood in Osaka, where one generation of the fictional family runs a parlor of its own.

HOW TO PLAY

To play, insert money or a prepaid card into the desired machine to receive a throng of tiny silver balls. Next, pull a lever to release a stream of the balls through the machine's maze. If one of the spheres released manages to ping a specific spot, the player gets a chance to receive more balls to play again. The more balls you've got, the higher your chance of winning. Most machines have a digital screen that plays short animations to escalate tension as a potential jackpot looms. To emerge victorious, players must trigger three matching symbols or numbers on the screen. Varying levels of wins are possible, depending on how many times the player manages to align these numbers, facing increasingly challenging odds as they pull the lever.

travelers and locals congregate, and friendly English-speaking staff who are keen to introduce you to their city. Each dorm room sleeps four people, and one floor is women-only. All rooms share showers and toilets, which are grouped on one floor. There's also a shared kitchen and lounge, and coin laundry. A fantastic choice for budget travelers who want to socialize.

¥10,000-20,000

HOTEL VISTA NAGOYA NISHIKI

3-3-15 Nishiki, Naka-ku; tel. 052/951-8333; https://nagoya-nishiki.hotel-vista.jp/ja; from ¥10,080 d with breakfast; take Meijo or Sakuradōri subway line to Hisaya-ōdōri Station

Situated amid the buzz of Sakae's north side, this modern hotel has compact, well-maintained rooms with spacious bathrooms. Staff at the front desk speak English and are happy to help. A breakfast buffet is available.

DORMY INN PREMIUM NAGOYA SAKAE

2-20-1 Nishiki, Naka-ku; tel. 052/231-5489; www.hotespa.net; ¥12,000 d with breakfast; take Higashiyama and Tsurumai lines to Fushimi Station

This sharp hotel is a great pick if you're

planning to spend real time in the entertainment district of Sakae, which is walkable from the hotel. This branch is a cut above the norm when it comes to ambience compared to most Dormy Inn properties, and its rooms are petite but clean. It also has an appealing shared bath on-site to complement the small yet well-appointed en-suite bathrooms.

¥30,000-40,000

NAGOYA MARRIOTT ASSOCIA HOTEL

JR Central Towers Office, 1-1-4 Meieki, Nakamura-ku; tel. 052/584-1111; www.marriott.com; ¥30,000 d (room only), ¥35,500 (with breakfast); in the JR Central Towers, right above JR Nagoya Takashimaya Department Store and JR Nagoya Station

Perhaps the city's most luxurious digs, this hotel stands above Nagoya Station, offering stellar vistas over the city. The decor has a European flair, rooms are airy and plush, and nine restaurants are on-site. There's a fitness center with a fabulous pool, the service is stellar, and the concierge is ready at hand to assist with anything. If you're seeking convenience and amenities, this is arguably the best choice in town. If you're traveling off-season or reserve well in advance, reasonable deals can be discovered.

INFORMATION AND SERVICES

For online resources, go to the **Nagoya Pocket Guide** website (www.nagoyapocketguide.com) for food and nightlife listings, as well as transport information. **Nagoya-Info** (www.nagoya-info.jp) provides a good breakdown of things to see, do, and eat, including helpful brochures available for download. Check the local English zine **Nagmag** (https://nagmag.jp) for event listings and recommendations for food, nightlife, and more.

- **Nagoya Station Tourist Information Center** (1-1-4 Meieki, Nakamura-ku; tel. 052/541-4301; 8:30am-7pm daily; on Central Concourse of JR Nagoya Station)
- **Oasis 21 i Center** (Oasis 21 B1F, 1-11-1 Higashisakura, Higashi-ku; tel. 052/963-5252; 10am-8pm daily; on the basement floor of the towering Oasis 21 complex linked to Sakae Station)

GETTING THERE

Train

Towering over the western side of downtown, the mammoth complex housing **JR Nagoya Station** contains rambling department stores and food courts. The station is served by the **shinkansen;** other **JR lines;** the **Kintetsu line,** which leads southwest into Mie Prefecture and the Kii Peninsula; and the **Meitetsu line,** which runs north to Inuyama. The six lines of the city's subway network also pass through the station, and a large bus terminal sits out front.

The shinkansen links Nagoya to Japan's main hubs, including **Tokyo** (1 hour 45 minutes; ¥11,300), **Shin-Osaka** (50 minutes; ¥6,680), **Kyoto** (35 minutes; ¥5,910), **Hiroshima** (2 hours 15 minutes; ¥14,430), and beyond. The JR Chūō line's Shinano limited express runs north to **JR Matsumoto Station** (2 hours 10 minutes; ¥6140) and **JR Nagano Station** (3 hours 15 minutes; ¥7,460). To reach **JR Takayama Station,** take the Hida limited express on the JR Takayama line (2 hours 30 minutes; ¥6,140).

If you've got a little time before your next connection, note that **Sky Promenade** (4-7-1 Meieki; tel. 052/527-8877; www.midland-square.com; ¥750 adults, ¥500 children; 11am-9:30pm daily), one of Japan's highest viewing platforms without a roof, covers floors 44-46 of the Midland Square complex, rising above the station.

Air

If you're coming to Nagoya from most points on Honshu, taking a train is likely your best bet. This is especially true if you've got a JR pass. But if you're coming from abroad, it's worth checking flights. Nagoya's main airport is **Central Japan International Airport** (tel. 056/938-1195; www.centrair.jp), much calmer than Tokyo's airports, and very conveniently located. Around 30 international flights from Asia, North America, and Europe, and domestic flights to about 20 locations across Japan, come through this airport.

Chūbu Centrair, as it's often called, sits on an artificial island about 40 kilometers (25 mi) south of downtown in the bay of Ise-wan. It's become something of a draw for locals with its collection of restaurants and its onsen **Fū-no-yu** (tel. 0569/38-7070; www.centrair.jp/interest/visit/relax/bath.html; ¥1,030 adults, ¥620 elementary school students, ¥210 children age 6 and under; 8am-10pm daily). To reach downtown, take the speedy **Meitetsu Airport Line** to Nagoya Station (28 minutes, ¥1,230).

GETTING AROUND

Transit passes, sold at ticket counters and windows, allow unlimited travel for a day on both the subway system and bus network (¥850 adults, ¥430 children under 12). On weekends, public holidays, and the 8th of each month, prices drop (¥600 adults, ¥300 children under 12).

Subway

Nagoya is well-connected belowground, with six subway lines (¥200-330). One-day passes for unlimited subway travel can be purchased at ticket counters or machines across the city (¥740 adults, ¥370 children under 12). The yellow color-coded **Higashiyama line** and red **Sakura-dōri lines** are particularly useful, as they thread through downtown's core areas such as Sakae and the neighborhood surrounding Ōsu Kannon.

Bus

A far-reaching bus system serves Nagoya, with the **Me-guru** (www.nagoya-info.jp/en/routebus; single rides ¥210 adults, ¥100 children; one-day pass ¥500 adults, ¥250 children) doing a one-way circuit around the city's core sites. These buses run at roughly 30-60-minute intervals 9:30am-5pm Tuesday through Sunday.

Matsumoto 松本

The attractive town of Matsumoto is most famous for its iconic black castle. But wander away from the moat into downtown and you'll soon sense an air of sophistication. **Nawate-dōri** and **Nakamachi** are pleasant streets for a stroll, with classic shopfronts that have been reborn in the modern age as trendy cafés, eateries, galleries, and shops selling various crafts. There are also a few worthwhile art museums.

But the city's true draw is its access to the mountains. The old castle town is set in a valley surrounded by some of the highest peaks in the Japan Alps, a few of which are more than 3,000 meters (almost 10,000 ft) high. Stepping off the train at Matsumoto Station, the air feels different—fresh, vital—and the mountains beckon. The city makes for a great jumping-off point for a jaunt into the Northern Alps, with easy access to great hiking in Kamikōchi and the remote Shin-Hotaka-no-Yu onsen.

SIGHTS

★ Matsumoto-jō

松本城

4-1 Marunōchi; tel. 0263/32-2902; www.matsumoto-castle.jp; 8:30am-5pm daily, until 6pm during Ō-bon and Golden Week holidays (last admission 30 minutes before closing); ¥610 adults, ¥420 children; walk 15 minutes northeast of Matsumoto Station, or take northern course of "Town Sneaker" bus to Matsumoto-jō bus stop from Matsumoto Station

Matsumoto-jō is among Japan's most stunning castles. Japan's oldest wooden castle, it has been given the status of National Treasure. Set on an expansive plain in the heart of

☆ Walking Japan's Medieval Highway

The old Nakasendō (中山道) highway used to stretch from Kyoto to Edo. In the heart of the Kiso Valley, located roughly 100 kilometers (62 mi) northeast of Nagoya and 160 kilometers (99 mi) southwest of Nagano city, is a preserved, 7.8-kilometer (4.8-mi) stretch, between the old post towns of **Magome** (馬籠; https://kiso-magome.com) and **Tsumago** (妻籠; https://tsumago.jp), essentially pit stops on the highways running all around the country during the Edo period.

The well-marked trail, with its verdant mountain views, can still be traversed on foot in the same way that wanderers did during feudal times, in about three hours moving at a steady pace. It's best to begin the journey in Magome and end in Tsumago, as this direction is more downhill, though the first leg of the hike suggests otherwise. A **bus** runs a few times daily between the two towns in both directions (30 minutes; ¥600), stopping at Magome Pass.

WALKING THE TRAIL

Before heading out, be sure to forward your luggage to your destination. Deposit your luggage at the **Tourist Information Center** in Magome (4300-1 Magome, Nakatsugawa; tel. 0573/69-2336; 8:30am-5pm daily) or Tsumago (2159-2 Azuma, Nagiso-machi; tel. 0264/57-3123; 8:30am-5pm daily) between 8:30am and 11:30am—any time from mid-March through November—and arrange with staff to send your bags on. You can pick them up on the other side of the trail any time after 1pm on the same day.

- Enjoy the smooth stone footpath that runs through the heart of **Magome,** and past the well-groomed greenery sprouting up beside the path and fronting the classic wooden shop fronts that are ubiquitous in the charming town.
- The clearest example of Magome's post-town past is its still-standing **Honjin** (本陣) (9am-5pm daily Apr.-Nov., 9am-4pm Dec.-Mar., closed Wed. Dec.-Feb.; ¥500), now known as the **Tōson Memorial Museum** (藤村記念館; http://toson.jp). This structure was once the main inn for officials and dignitaries passing through in feudal times. In contrast, the **Wakihonjin Museum** (馬籠脇本陣史料館) (9am-5pm daily Mar. 2-Dec. 24; ¥300) was where those from the middle and lower rungs of the social ladder were permitted to bed up.
- Stop at **Hillbilly Coffee Company** (4278 Magome, Nakatsugawa; www.facebook.com/iamhilbillycoffee; 8am-5pm daily; drinks from ¥500) to fuel up before you hit the medieval highway.
- As you leave Magome, you'll find yourself walking over cobblestones along some stretches of the hike and asphalt in others, as the path plods steadily uphill to Magome Pass (801 m/2,628 ft), before gliding down toward **Tsumago.**
- Tsumago's ambience is thick with history: Cars are banned on the main road of the historic district during daylight hours, and there are no wires hanging overhead. Like in Mangome, the feudal **Honjin** (9am-5pm daily; ¥300, ¥700 combination ticket for Honjin, Wakihonjin, and Rekishi Shiryokan) and **Wakihonjin** (9am-5pm daily; ¥600, ¥700 combination ticket) remain in place.
- Assuming you've worked up an appetite, **Keiseian** (5438-1 Magome, Nakatsugawa; tel.

Matsumoto, the imposing black fortress—its color inspiring the nickname Karasujō, or "Crow Castle"—is impressive and stately. The main keep is accompanied by three turrets, along with a freshly renovated pavilion. Built in stages, the complex as it stands today was largely completed by 1635.

Defensive flourishes include small windows for the arrows of archers to fly through and openings in the floor through which stones could be dropped on invaders. The original wooden exterior of the castle extends throughout six floors, with stunning panoramas of Matsumoto and the surrounding mountains to be had from the top level of the keep. If you happen to be in the city in

Nakasendō highway

0573/69-2311; www.takenet.or.jp/~keiseian; 11:30am-2:30pm daily; from ¥900) is the place to drop in for soba. All noodles are made from scratch. Order the tororo soba, made with yamaimo (grated yam).

SPENDING THE NIGHT

To fully appreciate the Nakasendō, stay overnight at a local ryokan. In Magome, try **Tajimaya** (4266 Magome, Nakatsugawa; tel. 0264/69-2048; www.kiso-tajimaya.com; from ¥9,200 pp with two meals). In Tsumago, **Ryokan Fujioto** (858-1 Tsumago Azuma, Nagiso-machi, Kiso-gun; tel. 0264/57-3009; www.tsumago-fujioto.jp; ¥12,500 pp with two meals) or **Takimi No Ie** (4689-447 Tsumago Azuma, Nagiso; tel. 0264/58-2165; www.takiminoie.com; ¥29,400 pp with two meals) are recommended.

GETTING THERE

To reach Magome, head to Nakatsugawa, which is linked by the Shinano limited express to both Nagoya (via Nakatsugawa Station on the JR Chūō line; 50 minutes; ¥2,820) and Matsumoto (1 hour 15 minutes; ¥4,090). From **Nakatsugawa Station,** hourly buses run to Magome (30 minutes; ¥560) from bus platform 3. Buses also shuttle from Magome and Tsumago five times per day (25 minutes; ¥600). To reach Tsumago from Nagoya (1 hour 20 minutes; ¥3,160), take the Shinano limited express to Nakatsugawa, then transfer to the JR Chūō local line for the last 20 minutes of the journey to JR Nagiso Station. From Matsumoto, take the JR Chūō local line directly to Nagiso (2 hours; ¥1,490). Once you've reached Nagiso Station, take a bus into Tsumago (10 minutes; ¥270).

mid-April, a profusion of cherry trees bloom around the castle, their pink petals contrasting brilliantly with the black structure.

Free guided English-language tours of the castle are provided by the **Alps Language Service Association** (www.npo-alsa.com/home-en). Reserve online at least two weeks in advance. Plan on spending an hour or two exploring the castle, depending on your interest.

Matsumoto City Museum of Art

松本市美術館

4-2-22 Chūō; tel. 0263/39-7400; www.matsumoto-artmuse.jp; 9am-5pm Tues.-Sun., closed

Japanese Castles 101

Ensconced on mammoth stone foundations, built many stories high with enormous timber planks, painted white or black on the outside and dimly lit on the inside, and topped by gently sweeping roofs, Japanese castles cut a striking profile. Here's what you need to know to get the most out of your visit to Matsumoto-jō or one of Japan's other stunning fortresses.

Matsumoto-jō

HISTORY AND CASTLE TYPES

During the turbulent **Sengoku (Warring States) Period,** roughly from the mid-15th-early 17th centuries, the country was divided between a number of small independent fiefdoms that were locked in a seemingly endless squabble for power. The nearly constant state of war necessitated the building of hilltop fortifications known as **yamajiro** ("mountain castles"), solely for defense.

As Japan became more unified, castles known as **hirayamajiro** ("flatland mountain castles") were built on hilltops and used for administrative affairs more than defense. By the time Tokugawa Ieyasu (1543-1616) brought all of Japan under one central power with the dawn of the Edo period (1603-1868), castles known as **hirajiro** ("flatland castles") were simply built on flat land, as their overtly martial roots faded.

With the **Meiji Restoration** of 1868 and the dawn of the modern age, many of these magnificent complexes were razed following a government decree that sought to do away with the reminders of the country's feudal past. Others still were bombed to smithereens during **World War II.** Today, only 12 castles retain their original keeps, while a slew of others are concrete reconstructions.

THE CASTLE LAYOUT

A classic Japanese castle layout revolved around concentric rings, with the **homaru** ("main circle") at the heart and containing the **tenshukaku,** or main keep or castle tower, usually between two and five stories high; surrounded by the **ninomaru** ("second circle"), where the nobles often lived; in turn surrounded by the **sannomaru** ("third circle"). The outer reaches of a castle consist of a series of moats and walls, punctuated by strategically placed guard towers known as **yagura** and heavily fortified entrance gates.

JAPAN'S BEST CASTLES

- **Matsumoto-jō:** One of Japan's 12 remaining original castles, this stunning, black hirajiro ("flatland castle") stands on the plains of Matsumoto, its black exterior contrasting sharply with the Japan Alps looming in the backdrop (page 227).
- **Himeji-jō:** Hovering at the edge of modern-day Himeji, "White Heron Castle" is Japan's most remarkable castle, thanks to its sprawling, immaculate grounds, sheer size, and incredible condition considering that it's another one of the country's 12 originals still standing (page 381).
- **Matsuyama-jō:** This handsome white fortress sprawling across a lofty hilltop above the city of Matsuyama is one of Japan's greatest original examples of a yamajiro ("mountaintop castle"), ensuring superb vistas of the city and Inland Sea below (page 476).

Tues. if Mon. is holiday; ¥410 adults, ¥200 university and high school students; 15-minute walk east of Matsumoto Station

This stylish exhibition space doesn't hide the fact that Matsumoto is the hometown of internationally renowned avant-garde artist Yayoi Kusama, famed for her infinity-inspired mirror installations and iconic polka-dotted dreamscapes. One section of the museum is dedicated specifically to her work, but Kusama's work is not the only thing on show. Other sections of the museum host revolving exhibitions, with an inclination toward domestic artists either with ties to or inspiration from Matsumoto and around.

FESTIVALS

MATSUMOTO-JŌ TAIKO MATSURI
松本城太鼓祭り

Matsumoto-jō grounds; last weekend of July; free

During the last weekend of July every year, some of Japan's best taiko, or traditional drum, troupes converge on Matsumoto to beat hearty rhythms with hefty batons. Their high-energy performances against the stunning backdrop of one of Japan's most pristine original castles make for an impressive introduction to Japan's rich tradition of percussion.

TAKIGI NOH MATSURI
薪能祭り

Matsumoto-jō grounds; tel. 0263/32-2902; 5pm-8pm Aug. 8; free

Although usually performed on a spartan, indoor stage made of cypress, a special Noh performance is held once every August in Matsumoto-jō's inner garden. Starting before dusk, the first part of the performance is visible by daylight. After sunset, the stage is illuminated by the soft glow of lanterns. The content of the dialog—sung and spoken in rarefied, archaic language—will be lost on both foreign and (most) Japanese audience members. But the air is alive with myth. Further, the slapstick interludes known as kyogen ("crazy talk") breaking up the sections of heady Noh provide the same sort of relief to today's audiences as they did in feudal days.

FOOD

Soba

★ KOBAYASHI SOBA

3-3-20 Ōte; tel. 0263/32-1298; www.kobayashi-soba.co.jp; 11am-8pm daily; soba ¥1,000-2,500, set meals ¥2,200-7,700; just off the Nawate-dōri shopping street

This fantastic soba restaurant boasts toppings like burdock root, mountain vegetables, herring, and even basashi (horse sashimi). The kamo (duck with warm dipping sauce) option is recommended. After placing your order, you'll receive an elegant piece of tableware with spring onion, a fresh stick of wasabi, and daikon. Use the grater to shred the wasabi and daikon and wait for your noodles to arrive. After eating, try a cup of soba yu, which is nutrient-dense water in which soba noodles have been boiled. You'll find the restaurant in a classy traditional building with modern accents beside Yohashira Shrine. Recommended.

Izakaya

ITOYA

2-10-16 Chūō; tel. 0263/32-3826; http://nakamachi-street.com/shop/itouya; 5:30pm-11pm Wed.-Sat., 5:30pm-10pm Sun.; dishes ¥300-1,500; 10-minute walk northeast of JR Matsumoto Station

This small izakaya sits amid the old storehouses on historic Nakamachi Street on the south side of the river. The menu offers a good range of oden—vegetables, fish cakes, tofu, and eggs boiled in a soy- and kelp-infused dashi broth—and small dishes made with locally sourced ingredients like mushrooms and vegetables foraged in the nearby mountains. The warm, kimono-clad host speaks some English and knows her sake. An English menu is available. All guests dine at a 10-seat wooden countertop.

Ramen

MENSHŌ SAKURA

1-20-26 Chūō; tel. 0263/34-1050; 11:30am-3pm and 5:30-10pm daily; ramen from ¥850; 10-minute walk northeast of JR Matsumoto Station

If you're a fan of ramen served in a hearty

miso broth, you'll love this spot. The gyoza (fried pork dumplings) are also excellent—try them with chopped spring onion, chili, and mayo for a refreshing twist. It gets busy during peak hours, sometimes attracting a queue. Look for the charming white townhouse across the street from the Richmond Hotel.

International

DOON SHOKUDO INDOYAMA

4-6-18 Ōte; tel. 0263/34-3103; www.facebook.com/Doon-shokudo-indoyama-460214724171580; 11am-7:30pm Mon.-Sat.; average ¥1,200; 10-minute walk east of Matsumoto-jō

This cozy, family-run restaurant does a few curries—vegetarian and meat (chicken, keema)—and does them exceedingly well. Owners Ashish and his Japanese wife are exceptionally welcoming. The bargain-priced food tastes home-cooked, which makes sense considering Ashish learned to cook from his mother in Dehradun. Recommended.

Cafés and Light Bites

THE STORYHOUSE CAFÉ

1-5-29 Josei; tel. 080/4355-6283; www.facebook.com/thestoryhousecafe; 8am-4:30pm daily; drinks from ¥250, food from ¥500; 8-minute walk west of Matsumoto-jō

This charming café, run by friendly, bilingual owners, serves great coffee, desserts, baked goods, light lunches (including good bagel sandwiches), and even a couple of vegan options. Besides a few tables, there's a comfy sofa and a few musical instruments, and even a kid's area, making it a good choice if you're traveling with children. This is a solid spot for breakfast, a pit-stop, or a light lunch.

ACCOMMODATIONS

Under ¥10,000

NUNOYA RYOKAN

3-5-7 Chūō; tel. 0263/32-0545; www.mcci.or.jp/www/nunoya/; ¥4,500 pp; 15-minute walk northeast of JR Matsumoto Station

Housed in a well-preserved storehouse just off the atmospheric Nakamachi Street, this classic ryokan, built in the 1920s, has eight well-appointed tatami rooms—tastefully furnished with antique furniture and the odd scroll painting or tea bowl—a shared bath, kitchen, and lounge. The cheerful English-speaking host is happy to help with making restaurant reservations or recommendations around town. It's within walking distance of most of the town's major sights and is surrounded by good food options. Note that no meals are served. Also, you'll have to go to a nearby café for a Wi-Fi connection.

RYOKAN MARUMO

3 Chōme-3-10 Chūō; tel. 0263/32-0115; www.avis.ne.jp/~marumo/index-j.html; ¥5,000 s, ¥10,000 d, breakfast ¥1,000; 13-minute walk northeast of JR Matsumoto Station

This aged, Meiji-period ryokan, neighboring the Nunoya and set in a white storehouse, sits beside the river on Nakamachi Street. You'll find private tatami rooms with shared baths, a café on-site serving good breakfasts and coffee throughout the day, a compact private bamboo garden, and dark wood throughout. It's in a great location and has plenty of ambience.

¥10,000-20,000

MATSUMOTO MARUNOUCHI HOTEL

3-5-15 Ōte; tel. 0263/35-4500; www.matsumoto-marunouchi.com; ¥15,000 d; 5-minute walk south of the castle

Located in a lively part of downtown surrounded by restaurants, this smart modern hotel offers chic, spotless rooms, some of which (the suites) are a bit more spacious than the norm for Japan. The stylish en-suite bathrooms are well-appointed. Staff are helpful, and there's a concierge to help with local tips and making dinner reservations. There's also a good breakfast buffet. For the quality, the price is a bargain.

HOTEL KAGETSU

4-8-9 Ōte; tel. 0263/32-0114; www.hotel-kagetsu.jp; ¥16,270 d without breakfast, ¥20,240 d with breakfast; 5-minute walk east of the castle

This classy hotel with a slightly European touch is tucked down a nice quiet street. There's an on-site café and restaurant serving good Western fare, an indoor gender-separated onsen, and clean and spacious (if mildly dated) en-suite rooms with dark wood furnishings—both Western and tatami. Extras include a Bluetooth speaker and handy phone. Shuttle service from JR Matsumoto Station is available on request.

INFORMATION AND SERVICES

Find the excellent **Matsumoto Tourist Information Center** (1-1-1 Fukashi; tel. 0263/32-2814; 9am-5:45pm daily) in Matsumoto Station. There's another branch a few minutes' walk south of Matsumoto-jō on Daimyō-chō-dōri (3-8-13 Ōte; tel. 0263/39-7176; 9am-5:45pm daily). Online, visit https://visitmatsumoto.com for a good introduction to the town and surrounding area.

GETTING THERE

Train

While it's not served by the shinkansen, **JR Matsumoto Station** can be reached directly by limited express train from Shinjuku Station in **Tokyo** (2.5 hours; ¥6,500), **Nagoya** (2 hours; ¥6,230), and **Nagano** (50 minutes; ¥3,040). To come from Kanazawa, you'll need to first take the shinkansen to Nagano, then transfer to the limited express. And from **Kyoto,** you'll need to make the journey to Nagoya, then change to the limited express.

Bus

Underneath the ESPA building just across the street from Matsumoto Station's east side is the **Matsumoto Bus Terminal** (1-2-30 Fukashi; tel. 0263/32-0910). This is the hub that links Matsumoto to a few other cities around Honshu. **Tokyo, Nagoya,** and **Osaka** are served by **Alpico** (www.alpico.co.jp), while **Nōhi Bus** (www.nouhibus.co.jp) shuttles between Matsumoto and **Takayama.**

Air

Flights arrive daily from **Fukuoka** (1.5 hours; ¥26,000) and **Sapporo** (1 hour 40 minutes; ¥22,000) to Matsumoto's **Shinshū Matsumoto Airport** (tel. 0263/57-8818; www.matsumoto-airport.co.jp). All arriving passengers have the option to take a bus to Matsumoto, about 10 kilometers (6 mi) north of the airport (25 minutes; ¥600).

GETTING AROUND

Once you're in the downtown and castle area, getting around Matsumoto **on foot** is a breeze. The train station is located just under a 20-minute walk (1.3 km) south of the castle. Free **bicycles** are available at eight locations around town; inquire at the Tourist Information Center for more details. Another option is the **Town Sneaker minibus system** (https://visitmatsumoto.com/en/guide/buses#townsneaker; ¥200 per ride, ¥500 one-day pass). The buses follow four circuits around town, starting from the Matsumoto Bus Terminal, opposite Matsumoto Station's east (Castle) exit in the ESPA complex.

Northern Japan Alps 北アルプス

The Japan Alps are a cluster of ranges in the center of Honshu, namely, the Hida, Kiso, and Akaishi. The Hida range, also known as the Northern Alps, runs through Gunma, Nagano, Niigata, and Toyama Prefectures; the Kiso is clustered in Nagano Prefecture; and Akaishi range sprawls across Nagano, Yamanashi, and Shizuoka. While they can't claim Mount Fuji, the Alps boast the bulk of Japan's highest peaks, with a number of summits above 3,000 meters (9,843 ft).

Among the Japanese, Nagano Prefecture (also home to Matsumoto in the south) is synonymous with mountains. It's known for its wealth of onsen and world-class ski resorts. Japanese mountaineering began in Nagano, where Walter Weston, a British preacher and polymath, launched Japan's first alpine club in 1905. At peak times, trekkers crowd Nagano's most popular trails.

Slow and serene, **Nagano** is the capital of the mountainous prefecture. Today, most visitors either come to see the grand temple of **Zenkō-ji,** which offers lodging to pilgrims and adventurous travelers alike, or stop en route at one of the remote onsen villages or picturesque ski resorts located within driving distance. In the far northern part of the Alps, the ski town of **Hakuba** is one of Japan's top winter sports destinations for serious powder hounds.

Before heading into the remoter parts of this region, be sure to stock up on food and drinks. Though many accommodations serve meals, there are few other options for food in the mountains.

NAGANO
長野

Although perhaps most famous for hosting the 1998 Winter Olympics, whose facilities still dot the town, looking further back into Nagano's history, the eponymous capital of Nagano Prefecture grew around the famed temple of Zenkō-ji. This temple, located about 30 minutes' walk (or 10 minutes by bus) north of Nagano Station and surrounding business district, is the town's main draw and is a great place to experience an overnight temple stay. Nagano's accessibility from Tokyo via the Hokuriku Shinkansen line also makes it a convenient gateway to the surrounding Japan Alps region.

Sights

ZENKŌ-JI
善光寺

491 Motoyoshi-chō; tel. 026/234-3591; www.zenkoji.jp; about 1 hour before dawn-4:30pm Apr.-Oct., closes 4pm Dec.-Feb., closes 4:15pm Mar. and Nov.; grounds free, inner sanctum and history museum ¥500 adults, ¥200 students in grades 10-12, ¥50 students through 9th grade

Zenkō-ji has been a beacon to seekers of all stripes since it was founded in the 7th century. The temple's appeal is universal: belonging to no specific sect, it has for centuries accepted women both as participants and priests.

Much of the temple's power emanates from a sacred statue, **Ikkō-Sanzon Amida Nyorai,** which remains hidden from even the emperor's gaze. This visage dates to 552 and is said to be the first Buddhist icon to reach Japan's shores. Although the original is never unveiled, a replica is brought forth every seven years and made public from April to mid-May in the **Gokaichō Matsuri.** The next showing is expected from April 3 to June 29, 2022, extending the normal exhibition time by a month to prevent overcrowding amid the ongoing coronavirus pandemic.

The current incarnation of the temple's main hall dates to 1707. You can enter the ornate building, which houses an elaborate altar, as well as a pitch-black subterranean corridor containing a key, affixed to a wall, that is said to bestow salvation on all those who manage to touch it. Also included in the cost of admission is a history museum housed in a pagoda behind the main hall with an array of statues depicting various Buddhas and bodhisattvas. The temple is located 1.5 kilometers (1 mi) from Nagano Station.

Accommodations

Given Zenkō-ji's history of openness, it's no surprise that the temple is surrounded by a large area of shukubō, or temple lodgings. There are 39 different accommodations all clustered on the street in front of Zenkō-ji.

FUCHINOBO

462 Motoyoshi-chō; tel. 026/232-3669; https://fuchinobo.or.jp; ¥12,000 pp with two meals

A good bet is Fuchinobo, inside the Zenkō-ji grounds. Staying here allows you to slow down, eat vegetarian cuisine (shōjin ryōri) like a monk, and attend morning prayers. Information on shukubō in Nagano is sparse online, but Fuchinobo can be booked through the ryokan reservation website Japanese Guesthouses (www.japaneseguesthouses.com).

Information and Services

Online, head to www.go-nagano.net for great information on the town and prefecture as a whole.

- **Nagano Tourist Information Center** (Nagano Station; tel. 026/226-5626; http://en.nagano-cvb.or.jp; 9am-7pm daily Apr.-Oct., 9am-6pm daily Nov.-Mar.)

Getting There and Around

Nagano Station is a stop on the Hokuriku Shinkansen line, which links directly to **Tokyo** (1 hour 45 minutes; ¥8,400) and **Kanazawa** (1 hour 10 minutes; ¥9,160). **Matsumoto** is accessible by the Shinano limited express (50 minutes; ¥3,040), which also runs to **Nagoya** (3 hours; ¥7,530).

Buses run to and from a number of ski resorts and onsen towns, from Hakuba to Nozawa Onsen, as well as other hubs, such as Matsumoto, Tokyo, and Kyoto, all from the **Nagano BT Bus Stop** (178-2 Okadamachi, Nakagosho; tel. 026/228-1155; www.nagano-bt.co.jp), about 10 minutes' walk west of Nagano Station's Zenkō-ji exit on the clearly indicated thoroughfare Terminal-dōri.

If you want to rent a car—a good option for exploring the countryside—there's an **Eki Rent-a-Car** (tel. 026/227-8500; www.ekiren.co.jp) just to the left, outside the Zenkō-ji exit, and a **Toyota Rent-A-Car** (1275-12 Minami Ishidōchō, Minaminagano; tel. 026/228-0100; https://rent.toyota.co.jp) 6 minutes' walk northwest of the same exit.

NOZAWA ONSEN

野沢温泉

With 13 community-owned onsen, relief for sore muscles is ready at hand in the wistful village of Nozawa Onsen. Although its prime time is winter, when skiers flock to the nearby slopes, this small town is a good escape any time of year. Alongside the public pools, ryokan are also arrayed around town, each with its private onsen.

The best part is, the 13 community-owned baths dotting the village are all free (6am-11pm daily), although a small donation to help with maintenance is welcome. Just drop a few coins into the boxes mounted on the outside of each pool's door. Each has its own mineral fusion and temperature, with some so scalding that only hard-boiled veterans, mostly local, dare enter. For the best experience, wander the atmospheric lanes and try as many baths as you can.

If you prefer to choose just one pool, make it **Ō-yu** (大湯; 9328 Toyosato; tel. 026/985-3155; donation suggested), which can be found inside a lovely wooden building in the heart of town. Before you slip into any of the pools, gingerly check the temperature; some are alarmingly hot, ranging from 40°C (104°F) at the lower end up to a scorching 90°C (194°F) for the daredevils out there.

Skiing in Central Honshu

Just the mention of skiing destinations like Nagano Prefecture conjures up images of world-class ski resorts, such as those that hosted the Winter Olympics. Listed here are some of the area's best ski resorts.

SHIGA KŌGEN

志賀高原

Hasuike, Yamanouchi; www.shigakogen-ski.com; 8:30am-4:30pm Dec.-Apr.; 1-day lift pass ¥5,000 adults, ¥4,200 seniors and students, ¥2,500 children

The Shiga Kōgen Ski Area is massive, with a whopping 51 lifts and 80 runs, many of which were used in the 1998 Winter Olympics. Receiving 12 meters (39 ft) of snow every winter, 21 separate ski areas cater to all skill levels. The **Haisuke area** is a good bet if you're a beginner or traveling with kids. For a full range of resorts, search for Shiga Kōgen at www.snowjapan.com or www.powderhounds.com/Japan.aspx.

Shiga Kōgen Tourist Association is next to the Haisuke bus stop (7148 Hirao, Hasuike; tel. 0269/34-2404; www.shigakogen.gr.jp), run by helpful English-speaking staff. **Hotel Shirakabaso** (7148 Hasuike, Yamanouchi; tel. 0269/34-3311; www.shirakaba.co.jp; from ¥25,300 d with 2 meals) is a cozy ryokan with clean, simple rooms; both indoor and outdoor onsen; nutritious, filling meals; and ski equipment rentals.

To get here, take a Nagaden Shiga Kōgen Express bus from Nagano Station (www.nagadenbus.co.jp; 1 hour 10 minutes; ¥1,800) to Shiga Kōgen Yamanoeki bus stop, from where other points within the Shiga Kōgen Ski Area can be reached via other local buses. These buses depart roughly once per hour from Nagano Station during winter but are less frequent in the warmer months.

NOZAWA ONSEN SNOW RESORT

野沢温泉スキー場

7653 Toyosato, Nozawaonsen-mura, Shimotakai-gun; tel. 0269/85-3166; https://en.nozawaski.com; 8:30am-4:30pm Dec.-Apr.; 1-day lift ticket ¥4,800 adults, ¥2,200 children under 15, ¥3,700 seniors over 60

These ski slopes are a great alternative to the runs in the region's more widely known resorts. The legendary soft snow and ample onsen make it a wonderful place for powder lovers to get their fix and rest their weary bones. There are 21 lifts and runs catering to all ability levels. There's also a half-pipe if you're partial to a snowboard. Ample English-language information in print and on boards around town make your visit easier.

Coming from Tokyo, take the Hokuriku shinkansen to Iiyama (1 hour 50 minutes; ¥8,830), transfer to the Nozawa Onsen Liner bus to Nozawa Onsen bus stop (25 minutes; ¥600). From Nagano, take the JR Iiyama line to Togari-Nozawa-Onsen Station (1 hour; ¥710), then take the local bus to Nozawa Onsen (20 minutes; ¥310). Or take the "snow shuttle" bus straight from Narita or Haneda

Festivals

DŌSOJIN MATSURI (NOZAWA FIRE FESTIVAL)

道祖神祭り

Nozawa Onsen; https://nozawa-onsen.com/nozawa-fire-festival; Jan. 15; free

In Japan it's believed that the ages of 25 and 42 are unlucky for men. Since 1863, locals of the small village of Nozawa Onsen have been fending off evil spirits and asking for the growth and health of all first-born sons in incendiary fashion. Considered one of Japan's top three fire festivals, the proceedings in Nozawa Onsen resemble all-out war.

Every January 15, the 25- and 42-year-old men of the town fight with the rest of the village men in a literal flame battle. First, some 100 villagers build a towering wooden shrine, which, after being blessed by a Shinto priest, is defended at its base by the 25-year-olds, while

Nozawa Onsen Snow Resort

Airport during winter (www.naganosnowshuttle.com). The ski resort is located right up the mountain from the town of Nozawa Onsen itself.

HAKUBA VALLEY

白馬渓谷

It's possible to access all 10 ski resorts around the valley with the **Hakuba Valley Ticket** (www.hakubavalley.com/en/ticket). A 1-day pass costs ¥6,000. Among the resorts, **Happō-One Ski Resort** (Kitaazumi-gun, Hakuba-mura; tel. 0261/72-2715; www.happo-one.jp; Dec.-Apr.; 1-day lift ticket ¥5,200), **Hakuba 47 Winter Sports Park & Hakuba Goryū Ski Resort** (24196-47 Kamishiro, Hakuba-mura; tel. 0261/75-3533; www.hakuba47.co.jp; Dec.-Apr.; 1-day lift ticket ¥5,000); and **Hakuba Cortina Snow Resort** (12860-1 Chikuniotsu, Otari; tel. 0261/82-2236; www.hakubacortina.jp/ski; Dec.-Apr.; 1-day lift ticket ¥4,000) are standouts.

Hakuba is best reached from JR Matsumoto Station, from where you'll need to take the JR Ōito line to JR Hakuba Station (1 hour; limited express Azusa ¥2,140, limited express Shinano ¥3,040). If you're coming from Nagano, you can take a bus operated by Alpico (www.alpico.co.jp/en/; 1 hour 10 minutes; ¥1,600), which also departs from the West Exit of Shinjuku Station in Tokyo (5 hours; ¥4,850). The same "snow shuttle" that runs to Nozawa Onsen from Narita and Haneda Airport in winter also runs to Hakuba. See the website for more details (222.naganosnowshuttle.com).

the 42-year-olds guard the top. Encroaching hordes wielding torches descend on the structure with the goal of burning it to the ground. Throughout the event, participants and spectators alike are primed with a continuous flow of sake by—no joke—the local fire department. The defenders and attackers take the fight seriously. It's not uncommon to see participants whose faces are covered in soot and fresh wounds oozing blood.

The guardsmen have no real chance of successfully defending the tower: The 25-year-olds have nothing but pine boughs to swat at the flames, while the 42-year-olds "protect" the shrine by dropping a steady supply of kindling down to the base. Ultimately, the fire wins out and the structure is consumed in a blazing inferno. Bad luck purged, the village returns to its sleepy status quo. The festival has become a popular spectacle, so book accommodations a few months ahead.

Food

NAPPA CAFE

8661-1 Toyosato; tel. 080/1250-7878; http://nappa-cafe.com; 10am-5pm (lunch served 11am-2pm) daily; ¥500-1,000

With walls plastered in retro-cute and cat-themed decor, this cozy spot, also known as 78 Cafe, is run by friendly owners. The menu includes excellent coffee and chai, and a range of dishes like curry, croque monsieur, and salad, as well as desserts. About 2 minutes' walk north of Ō-yu. An English menu is available.

LIBUSHI

9347 Toyosato; tel. 080/6930-3992; http://libushi.com; 4pm-11pm daily Dec.-Apr., 4pm-11pm Fri.-Sun. May-Nov.; ¥650-1,200

This little artisan brewpub adjacent to Ō-yu serves a great range of beers from 10 taps. They brew in-house with water flowing under the town and occasionally serve the odd rare beer from elsewhere. A good spot to unwind after a day on the slopes. They open sporadically during the warmer months, so call ahead before making the trip.

GENKI BURGER

9534 Toyosato; tel. 050/5532-7945; www.genkiburger.com; 7:30am-10pm daily Dec. 1-Mar. 17, noon-10pm daily Mar. 18-Apr. 1; ¥850-1,400

With its English menu and crowd-pleasing classics, there's no hiding the fact that this burger joint, situated about a 1-minute walk southwest of Ō-yu, caters heavily to the foreign contingent. But sometimes only a burger will do. The menu is diverse, with plenty of toppings—red cheddar cheese, avocado, egg, bacon, cream cheese, jalapenos, chunky mushrooms, and more—and the loaded fries (cheese, spring onion, and more) are hard to resist.

JUNTOS MEXICAN

9256-1 Toyosato; tel. 090/9951-8700; www.facebook.com/juntosmexican; 4pm-11pm daily Dec.-mid Mar., 6pm-11pm Tues.-Sun. mid-Mar.-early May and Nov., 6pm-11pm weekends and public holidays Jul.-Aug., hours vary Sept.-Oct.; ¥1,500-3,000

Take a break from Japanese fare and get your taco fix at this implausibly located cantina. The menu includes very decent tacos, burritos, churros, margaritas, and more. Portions are modest and you'll pay a premium, but consider it the cost of eating Mexican grub in the remote mountains of Japan. Located about 4 minutes' walk west of Ō-yu. English menu available.

Accommodations

For more information on accommodations, see the local booking website **Stay Nozawa** (www.staynozawa.com).

PEANUTS HOUSE KUMAKUMA

4403-1 Toyosato; tel. 090/2317-1660; http://p-kumakuma.sakura.ne.jp; ¥11,400 d with two meals

Located about 7 minutes' walk south of Ō-yu in the heart of town and 10 minutes' stroll to the main gondola that leads to the top of the slopes, this conveniently located guesthouse is a great pick. It offers clean Japanese-style rooms with a shared bathroom, tasty home-cooked breakfast, and (with two day's advanced reservation) dinner. The welcoming hosts speak some English, too.

KAIYA NOZAWA

9695-1 Toyosato; tel. 0269/85-3474; www.nozawaholidays.com/properties/kaiya; ¥6,500 dorms, ¥15,000 d with shared bathroom, ¥19,000 d with private bathroom, ¥22,000 studio apartment for two adults

This freshly renovated guesthouse has an appealing mix of stylish Western and Japanese-style rooms, one of which has a private bathroom. There's also a full studio apartment, with a kitchen, bathroom, and living space. There's a communal lounge with a fireplace that serves as a nice spot to socialize in comfort on cold days. All rates include a hearty breakfast to fuel you up before a day on the slopes. The friendly staff, both Japanese and foreign, are happy to help. It's an 8-minute walk southwest of Ō-yu and only 5 minutes west of the slopes.

★ SUMIYOSI-YA

8713 Toyosato; tel. 0269/85-2005; https://sumiyosiya.co.jp; ¥24,200 d pp with 2 meals

This historic ryokan offers a diverse selection of 15 rooms, ranging from wooden floors with beds to tatami-and-futon affairs. Of the rooms, four have bathtubs. All rooms have access to the ryokan's stunning, gender-separated communal hot-springs pools, both outdoors and indoors. The indoor pools are graced with windows containing colorfully tinted panes. The meals are excellent, as is the service. Most staff speak some English. This inn offers the quintessential onsen-ryokan experience. Highly recommended.

Information and Services

Note that the town's online tourism portal provides a contact form (https://booking.nozawakanko.jp) for visitors to request assistance with things like room reservations.

- **Nozawa Onsen Visitor Center** (9780-4 Toyosato, Nozawaonsen-mura; tel. 0269/85-3155; http://nozawakanko.jp; 8:30am-5:30pm daily)

Getting There and Around

From **Tokyo,** take the Hokuriku shinkansen to Iiyama (1 hour 50 minutes; ¥8,830), then transfer to the Nozawa Onsen Liner bus and take that to the **Nozawa Onsen stop** (25 minutes, ¥600). From Nagano, you can take the JR Iiyama line to **Togari-Nozawa-Onsen Station** (1 hour; ¥710). From there, the center of Nozawa Onsen is a bus ride away (20 minutes; ¥310). Thorough English instructions on reaching the hamlet by bus can be seen at https://en.nozawaski.com/access/coming-train-bus/. If you're landing in Japan and plan to head to Nozawa Onsen just to hit the slopes, during ski season **"snow shuttle" buses** run directly from Narita and Haneda airport. See www.naganosnowshuttle.com for details.

There's no need to have your own car here. Although it's remote, most of the ski resorts are easy to access with public transport thanks to their popularity.

HAKUBA

白馬

With a total of 10 ski resorts, Hakuba is a winter sports mecca spread across a valley in the heart of the Northern Alps's highest section, with many peaks in the area topping 3,000 meters (9,842 ft). In the warmer months, avid hikers flock to the area. Year round, a proliferation of onsen baths provide relaxation and relief for skiers' and hikers' sore muscles. With relatively easy access from both Tokyo and Kansai, Hakuba makes for an appealing escape for those with limited time to explore Japan's vast alpine riches.

Hiking

Thanks to its easy access to some of the Alps' loftiest peaks, Hakuba is a wonderland for hikers. Though it does get crowded, these trails are less full than those at Kamikōchi. **Tsugaike Nature Park** is a great option for those seeking a manageable walk in lovely surroundings. Summiting Shirouma-dake, the region's tallest peak, however, is a real challenge.

You might also want to inquire about a guided expedition at **Evergreen Outdoor** (4377 Hokujō; outdoor center; tel. 0261/72-5150; www.evergreen-hakuba.com). They offer a ski school (Dec.-Mar.; from ¥9,000 per day) and backcountry outings (Apr.-Nov.; from ¥4,000 for half-day). Excursions include half-day tours and multiday expeditions for hiking (Apr.-Nov.), climbing (Apr.-Nov.), mountain biking (Apr.-Nov.), backcountry trekking (Apr.-Nov.), canoeing (with fireflies in July and August; Jun.-Sept.), canyoning (Jul.-Sept.), rafting (Apr.-Oct.), kayaking (May-Nov.), and snowshoeing (Dec.-Apr.).

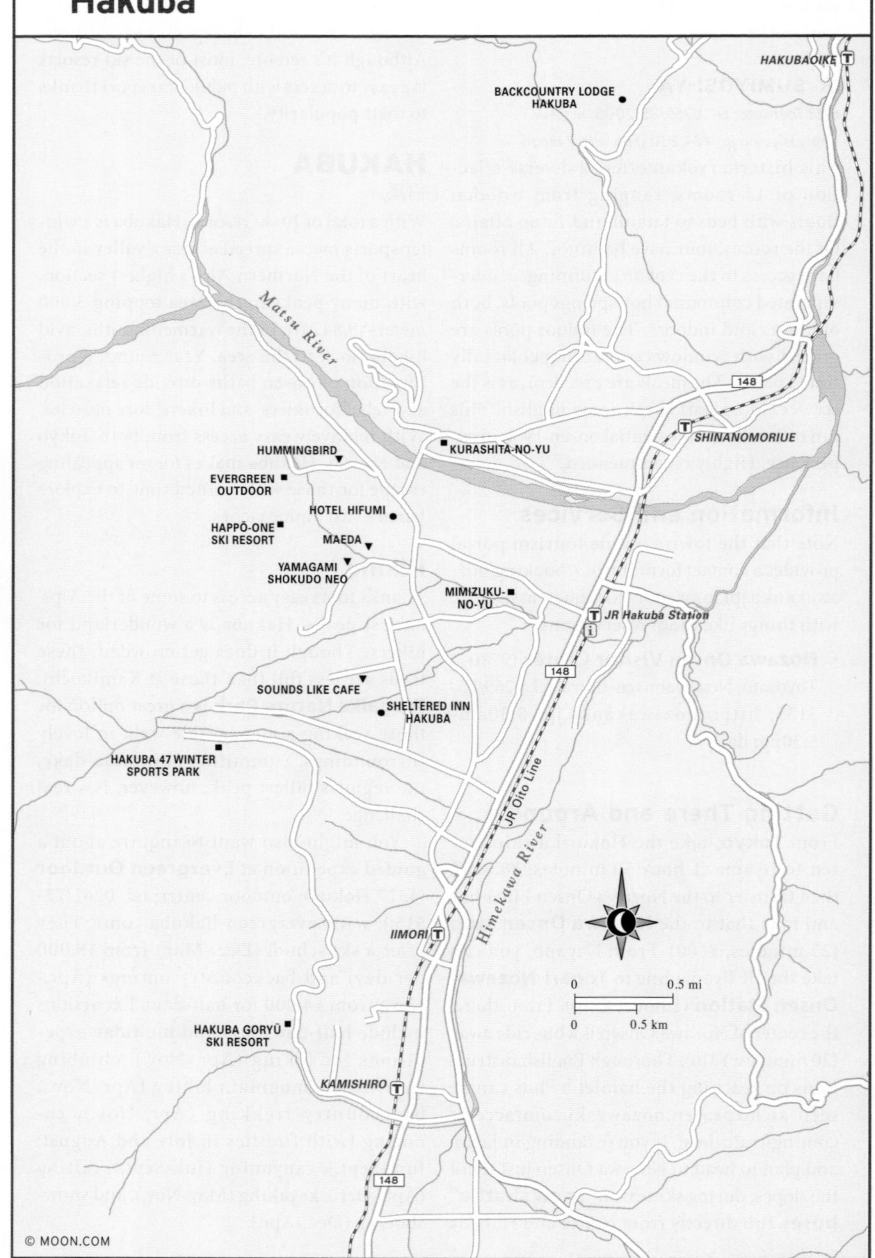
Hakuba
HAKUBAOIKE
BACKCOUNTRY LODGE HAKUBA
Matsu River
148
SHINANOMORIUE
KURASHITA-NO-YU
HUMMINGBIRD
EVERGREEN OUTDOOR
HOTEL HIFUMI
HAPPŌ-ONE SKI RESORT
MAEDA
YAMAGAMI SHOKUDO NEO
MIMIZUKU-NO-YU
JR Hakuba Station
SOUNDS LIKE CAFE
SHELTERED INN HAKUBA
HAKUBA 47 WINTER SPORTS PARK
JR Oito Line
Himekawa River
IIMORI
0
0.5 mi
0.5 km
HAKUBA GORYŪ SKI RESORT
KAMISHIRO
© MOON.COM

TSUGAIKE NATURE PARK

Distance: *5.5 km (3.4 mi)*

Time: *4 hours*

Trailhead: *Tsugaike Ropeway (gondola, followed by a cable car)*

Information and maps: *June-Oct.; adults ¥300, children ¥250; https://sizenen.otarimura.com*

If you're looking for a gorgeous hike that's not overly taxing, Tsugaike Nature Park is ideal, as you'll travel part of the way by gondola (departs from the nearby Tsuhaike Kogen bus stop) and cable car along the aptly named Panorama Way (26 minutes one-way; ¥3,600 adults, ¥2,050 children round-trip). Traipse through a lush highland (elevation: 1,900 m/6,233 ft), surrounded by soaring peaks and dotted by large patches of clinging snow until early summer, and wildflowers from mid-June to mid-August. Starting in mid-September, the leaves blaze with autumn colors. When you reach the observation platform, you'll see Shirouma-dake glistening in the distance.

Daytime temperatures are warm but dip at night. Take a fleece jacket, a sturdy pair of shoes, a hat, and sunglasses. With a hiking time of about 4 hours, it's not necessary to carry too much—just water and a few snacks. Because most of the trail is wooden boardwalk, this route is a particularly good option if you're traveling with kids or simply want to enjoy the views in comfort. The "Getting Here" section of the park's website provides clear instructions on how to reach the park from both Shinjuku Station in Tokyo or Nagano Station.

SHIROUMA-DAKE

Distance: *7.4 km (4.6 mi)*

Time: *5 hours to summit*

Trailhead: *beside Sarukuraso Lodge (Hokujō, Kitaazumi-gun, tel. 0261/72-4709)*

Information and maps: *June-Nov.; free; www.japan-guide.com/blog/peaks/170904.html*

The best hike in the Hakuba region is Shirouma-dake (White Horse Peak), the area's tallest peak at 2,932 meters (9,619 ft), with a 1,700-meter (5,577-ft) elevation gain; it's one of Japan's only peaks that has snowfields year-round. There are wildflowers blooming in summer and breathtaking vistas from every angle, but don't underestimate the terrain: the mountain is notorious for landslides and falling boulders. It's best not to attempt summiting Shirouma-dake in squally weather or spring, when avalanches are common. The best time to make the hike is from June-October. Before setting off, share your trekking plan with Sarukura Lodge, which

trekking in Hakuba

can be reached by car or bus from JR Hakuba Station in 20-30 minutes. If taking a bus, catch the one bound for Sarukura and get off at the last stop (¥1,000).

Wear full-blown hiking boots and waterproof clothing if the forecast says rain. If conditions are clear, a fleece top or medium-weight coat will do. Buy a pair of cheap crampons at the lodge so you're well prepared for the snowfield, and bring plenty of water and food. A hat and sunglasses are a good call, too.

The ascent starts on a gravel road, which runs past an artificial waterfall before phasing into a more traditional trail. When you reach two mountain huts and a neighboring campground, you'll know that you're about to enter the **Daisekkei** (Great Snowfield). This is the place to get serious. Put on your crampons, don a helmet (if you have one), and start to make your way upward, through the immense valley of snow. The bulk of the hike takes place in this snowy section of the mountain.

You'll know you're about to reach the summit when you exit the snowy expanse and come to **Hakuba Sansō Lodge** (tel. 0261/72-2002; www.hakuba-sanso.co.jp; ¥10,000 adults, ¥7,000 children 12 and up, ¥2,000 children under 12, prices are per person with 2 meals), beside a campground. The unfortunate reality is that conditions atop Shiroumadake tend to be cloudy. But if it happens to be clear, the views are stunning. It's possible to stay the night at the mountain lodge and witness the glorious sunrise the next morning.

On your descent from Hakuba Yarigatake, after about 1.5 hours of lumbering downhill, you'll come to **Hakuba Yari Onsen** (¥1,000). This hot spring bath is among the highest in all the land at 2,100 meters (6,889 ft), and the views from its outdoor pool are just as dramatic as you'd imagine. After enjoying a soak, it's another 2-4 hours to complete the loop and reach the Sarukura Lodge trailhead.

Onsen

The entire Hakuba Valley is brimming with onsen baths. You can find a comprehensive list on the Hakuba Tourism website (http://hakubatourism.jp/hotsprings). The following are two of the best and most accessible ones.

MIMIZUKU-NO-YU
みみずくの湯

5480-1 Kitajō Happo-guchi, Hakuba-mura; tel. 0261/72-6542; http://hakuba-happo-onsen.jp/mimizukunoyu; 10am-9:30pm daily, last entry 9pm; ¥600 adults, ¥300 children; 12-minute walk or a few minutes' drive west of Hakuba Station

At this old-school onsen, located between Hakuba Station and the slopes of Happō-One, the baths are divided by gender and include both indoor and rotenburo (outdoor) options. It's open year-round and offers arguably the best views of the Alps of all the onsen around Hakuba. There's also a room with massage chairs if you feel like even more relaxation after exiting the bath.

KURASHITA-NO-YU
倉下の湯

9549-8 Hokujō, Hakuba-mura; tel. 0261/72-7989; www.kurashitanoyu.com; 10am-9:30pm daily Dec.-Mar.; ¥600 adults, ¥300 children; 30-minute walk west of Shinano-Moriue Station (one stop from Hakuba on Oito line)

Another rotenburo with good mountain views, Kurashita-no-yu is located about 40 minutes' walk northeast of Happō-One, making it a convenient option after a day on the slopes at Hakuba's biggest resort. Its interior is bare-bones and rustic, but the waters here are known to be among the most mineral-rich in Hakuba.

Food

MAEDA

5054 Hokujō, Hakuba-mura; tel. 0261/72-2295; 11am-9pm daily; ¥700-1,350; 30-minute walk west of Hakuba Station, on the eastern edge of the Happō-One resort

This family-run noodle shop is a good choice for lunch. Other items on the menu include tasty karage (fried chicken), tempura, and more. There are tables with chairs and a tatami-floor seating area. Cash only. It fills up sometimes during peak hours. If you arrive when it's busy, put your name in and wait. An English menu is available.

YAMAGAMI SHOKUDO NEO

4086 Hokujō, Hakuba-mura; tel. 0261/72-8228; http://yamagami-hakuba.main.jp; 6pm-9pm daily; gyoza from ¥390, barbecue ¥420-3,900, noodles ¥750-1,800; 30-minute walk west of Hakuba Station, 2-minute walk south of Maeda

This joint serves gyoza (pan-fried pork dumplings), ramen, yakiniku (barbecue), and other hearty fare, best washed down with a mug of ice-cold beer. An English menu is available. It's laid-back at lunchtime but fills up at dinner. Service is efficient, if slightly brusque. Reserve ahead to avoid being turned away or forced to wait. Situated just east of the Happō-One resort.

HUMMINGBIRD

4715-1 Hokujō Wadano, Hakuba-mura; tel. 0261/72-7788; 6pm-9pm daily; ¥1,000-3,800; 10-minute walk east of Evergreen Outdoor Center, or a few km northeast of Hakuba Happō-One resort

This cozy, family-run restaurant is set in a highly inviting home. The generous couple who run it serve a nicely varied menu with stews, meat loaf, and sauteed chicken, pork, and salmon. The ingredients are seasonal and crisp. It's a highly popular spot, so call ahead to book a table a day or more in advance to avoid disappointment.

SOUNDS LIKE CAFÉ

3020-504 Hokujō, Hakuba-mura; tel. 0261/72-2040; www.sounds-like-cafe.com; 8am-5:30pm (last food order 5pm) Sat.-Wed.; breakfast from ¥900, lunch from ¥1,050, coffee from ¥350, dessert from ¥400; 30-minute walk southwest of Hakuba Station, with the Hakuba 47 ski area to the southwest and the Happō-One resort to the northwest

This great little café serves fantastic coffee, cake, breakfast items (muffins, eggs benedict, and more), burgers, and sandwiches. Service is friendly, and the all-wooden interior and laid-back atmosphere make it an inviting place to while away a few hours if you need a break from the slopes. Given its early closing hours, it's best chosen for breakfast or lunch.

Accommodations

Accommodations in Hakuba fill up fast and can be frustratingly hard to book. Thankfully, the choices are seemingly endless. For an extensive list of potential lodgings, check out the websites **Snowbeds Travel** (www.skijapantravel.com) and **Destination Hakuba** (https://hakubatravel.com).

★ BACKCOUNTRY LODGE HAKUBA

14718-174 Hokujō, Hakuba-mura; tel. 050/3497-9595; http://backcountry-hakuba.com; ¥20,000 d with breakfast; complimentary shuttle from JR Hakuba Station and Hakuba Happō Bus Center

This stylish bed-and-breakfast wins massive points for hospitality. Nestled in a forest and run by a friendly American and Japanese couple, this inviting hideaway offers clean, airy rooms that are tastefully decorated. The hosts are happy to share their local wisdom and make great meals. There are two homey lounges—one with a fireplace—and various other nooks and crannies to relax in. A hearty breakfast is included. For dinner, the hosts are happy to recommend local dinner options and even give guests a lift to local eateries. It's located toward the north of the Hakuba Valley, between the Iwatake and Tsugaike ski areas. Free shuttle to and from JR Hakuba Station and Hakuba Happō Bus Center is available upon request. A fantastic base for exploring Hakuba.

HOTEL HIFUMI

4998 Happo, Hakuba-mura; tel. 0261/72-8411; ht
www.hakubahifumi.jp; average ¥50,000 d wi
two meals; complimentary shuttle from J
*Station and Hakuba Happō Bus Cente*se rooms
This stylish ryokan has swan floors, and
with a mix of tatami and of the rooms
various modern tou For those that
have private ou s can be reserved
don't, shared guests. Two commu-
hourly for outdoor) are accessible
nal po

to both genders within specified hourly time slots. Japanese-style breakfast and exquisite kaiseki dinners are served. It's conveniently located near the Happō-One gondola. There are only 10 rooms, so reserve as far in advance as possible.

SHELTERED INN HAKUBA

836-66 Hokujō, Hakuba-mura, Kitaazumi-gun; tel. 0261/85-2088; https://shelteredinnhakuba.com; ¥100,000 d with breakfast; free shuttle to and from JR Hakuba Station and Hakuba Happō Bus Center

This clean, cozy lodge is well-located close to restaurants and the slopes of both Happō-One and Hakuba 47. This completely self-contained, private property is essentially a house run by warm, genuine, foreign staff who know the area intimately and are happy to share their knowledge and shuttle you around town. The relatively high price tag is reflected in the fact that you'll be getting the entire property to yourself, which makes it particularly good if you're traveling in a group—it sleeps up to 15 across eight rooms. All private rooms are nicely decorated and well-appointed, sharing four Western-style bathrooms, a kitchen, and an inviting lounge with cushy sofas and a large flat-screen TV. There are also laundry facilities on-site and complimentary Western breakfast (fruit, toast, cereal). Only operates during ski season. There's a minimum stay of two nights and no guests under age 13 are permitted. Recommended.

Information and Services

Excellent online resources include the **Hakuba Valley** website (http://hakubavalley.com/en) and **Hakuba Connect** (www.hakubaconnect.com), which offer information on ski runs, restaurants, nightlife, and gondola schedules.

- **Tourism Information Center** (in front of JR Hakuba Station at Snow Peak Land Station Hakuba; 5497 Hokujō, Hakuba-mura; tel. 0261/85-4210; www.snowpeak.co.jp/landstation/hakuba/; 9am-5pm daily)

Getting There and Around

The best way to reach **JR Hakuba Station,** at the heart of the valley, is aboard a limited express train on the JR Ōito line from JR Matsumoto Station (1 hour; limited express Azusa ¥2,140, limited express Shinano ¥3,040).

By bus, you'll have more options. **Alpico** (https://www.alpico.co.jp/en/) runs shuttles between **Nagano** and Hakuba (1 hour 10 minutes; ¥1,600), and even links to Tokyo's Shinjuku Station Nishi-guchi (5 hours; ¥4,850).

And if your aim is to be gliding through fresh powder the day you touch down in Japan, there's a **"snow shuttle"** that runs to and from the slopes directly from the airports in both Narita and Haneda. See the website (www.naganosnowshuttle.com) for details.

Between Matsumoto and Takayama

K

Tally halfway between the towns of bath and Matsumoto, the free, open-air best hi -Hotaka-no-Yu is one of the a soak in most otherworldly spots for mountain r n the opposite side of the legendary poo rises to the east of the region offers son ificent **Kamikōchi** tas in all Japan. t hiking and vis-

KAMIKŌCHI

上高地

Kamikōchi is Japan's answer to the Yosemite Valley or Patagonia. At an elevation of about 1,500 meters (4,921 ft), this highland plateau extends about 15 kilometers (9.3 mi) through the Azusa River Valley, a landscape of soaring peaks, pristine rivers, expansive marshes, crystal-clear lakes, ponds, and primordial

Kamikōchi and Shin-Hotaka Onsen

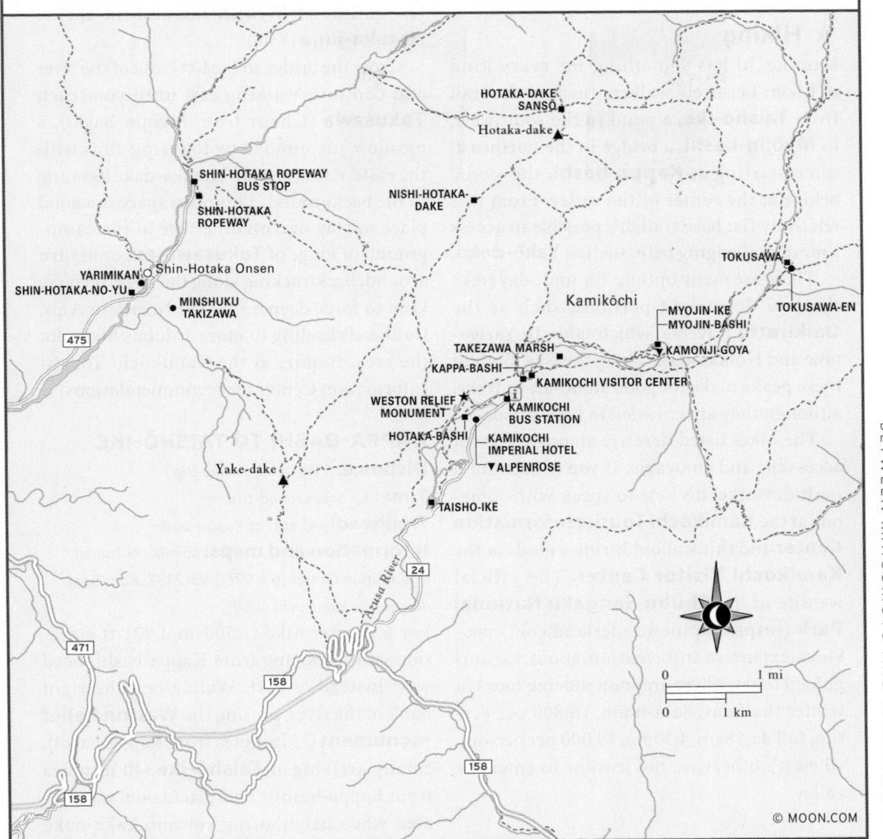

forests teeming with deer, foxes, troops of monkeys, and the occasional bear. Notable peaks surrounding the valley include the volcanic Yake-dake (2,455 m/8,054 ft) and Oku-Hotaka-dake (3,190 m/10,465 ft), the highest in all the Northern Alps.

In many ways, Kamikōchi is the spiritual and historical heart of Japanese mountaineering. Victorian archaeologist and Renaissance man William Gowland (1842-1922) first called these mountains the "Japanese Alps." Reverend Walter Weston (1861-1940), an intrepid British missionary, published his journal *Mountaineering and Exploration in the Japanese Alps,* documenting his explorations of the area and drumming up Japanese interest in exploring their rich alpine heritage.

Kamikōchi is open from late April through mid-November, though snowshoeing is possible in winter. Peak times are mid-July through the end of August, and October, when the leaves blaze orange, red, and copper. To avoid the rush, try to come mid-week or plan to stay overnight in the valley so you have a chance to explore the area before and after the day-trippers descend. The average temperature in the Kamikōchi area is about 5°C (9°F) cooler than outside the valley: You'll thank yourself for bringing a jacket.

★ Hiking

Kamikōchi has something for every kind of hiker. Leisurely walkers flock to the trail from **Taishō-ike,** a pond in the southwest, to **Myōjin-bashi,** a bridge in the northeast, often starting at **Kappa-bashi,** the iconic bridge at the center of the valley. From this relatively flat base trail, it's possible to access a more challenging path, such as **Yake-dake.**

There are many options for multiday treks that are downright perilous, such as the **Daikiretto** traverse, which takes in Yarigatake and Hotaka-dake along the way. Both of these peaks make for good stand-alone treks, although they are crowded in high season.

The hikes listed here are among the most accessible and enjoyable. If you're keen for a multiday hike, it's best to speak with someone at the **Kamikōchi Tourist Information Center** and think about hiring a guide at the **Kamikōchi Visitor Center.** The official website of the **Chūbu-Sangaku National Park** (https://alpinewonderland.com) provides extensive information about various guided tours. There are snowshoeing tours in winter (half day, 8am-noon, ¥6,800 per person; full day, 8am-4:30pm, ¥9,000 per person), when it's otherwise not feasible to enter the valley.

KAPPA-BASHI TO TOKUSAWA

Distance: *13.4 km (8.3 mi) round-trip*
Time: *4 hours round-trip*
Trailhead: *just east of Kappa-bashi*
Information and maps: *Kamikōchi Tourist Information Center (tel. 0260/95-2433; 8am-5pm daily; www.kamikochi.or.jp)*

This easy day hike (1,500-m/4,921-ft elevation gain) begins at **Kappa-bashi** and runs east along the Azusa River. It's possible to hike along either bank: The right bank leads past lovely views of **Takezawa Marsh.** From the marsh, continue walking east along the right bank of the river, until you reach the **Myōjin-bashi** bridge (1 hour from Kappa-bashi). Next to this bridge you'll find the tranquil pond **Myōjin-ike** and the shrine **Hotaka-jinja** (¥300).

Cross the bridge to the left bank of the river and continue walking east until you reach **Tokusawa** (1 hour from Myōjin-bashi), a meadow surrounded by towering elms with the eastern face of Mae-Hotaka-dake looming in the background. This open space is a good place to stay overnight, either in the campground or lodge of **Tokusawa-en,** or to turn around, backtracking along the river. If you're keen to forge deeper into the Northern Alps, trailheads leading to more arduous hikes dot the area. Inquire at the Kamikōchi Tourist Information Center for recommendations.

KAPPA-BASHI TO TAISHŌ-IKE

Distance: *6 km (4 mi) round-trip*
Time: *1.5 hours round-trip*
Trailhead: *just east of Kappa-bashi*
Information and maps: *Kamikōchi Tourist Information Center (tel. 0260/95-2433; 8am-5pm daily; www.kamikochi.or.jp)*

For a shorter hike (1,500-m/4,921-ft elevation gain), starting from Kappa-bashi, head west instead of east. Walk along the right bank of the river, passing the **Weston Relief monument** (15 minutes from Kappa-bashi), finally arriving at **Taishō-ike** (40 minutes from Kappa-bashi). This placid pool was created when neighboring volcano Yake-dake erupted in 1915, blocking the Azusa River. Even today, rotted trees remain rooted in the soil that now forms the bottom of the pond.

For a more strenuous hike, you can walk to the top of nearby volcano Yake-dake (2,455 m/8,054 ft; 13 km/8 mi round-trip from Hotaka-bashi, 5.5. hours round-trip). From the Weston Relief, you'll reach Hotaka-bashi (about 20 minutes' walk), where you'll follow a paved road and veer left. You'll come to the trailhead for Yake-dake after about 10 minutes.

1: Azusa River running beneath Kappa-bashi
2: hikers in Kamikōchi

1
2

KAMIKŌCHI TO SHIN-HOTAKA

Distance: *9 km (4.3 mi)*
Time: *4 hours one way*
Trailhead: *Next to Hotaka-bashi (35-minute walk from Kappa-bashi)*
Information and maps: *Kamikōchi Tourist Information Center (tel. 0260/95-2433; 8am-5pm daily; www.kamikochi.or.jp)*

It's possible to hike from Kamikōchi to **Nishi-Hotaka-guchi** (2,156-m/7,073-ft elevation gain), the upper terminus of the Shin-Hotaka Ropeway. This hike has stunning views throughout, and you have the option of taking the ropeway down the other side of the mountain to Shin-Hotaka Onsen, provided you arrange for your luggage to be sent there before setting off.

To make this trip, take the same route you would to walk toward Taishō-ike, following the trailhead with a wooden gate located near **Hotaka-bashi;** it is clearly marked for **Nishi-hotaka-dake.** It's a steep, 3-hour climb to the **Hotaka-dake Sansō** mountain hut; from here, push on for another hour to Nishi-Hotaka-guchi, the top station of the Shin-Hotaka Ropeway.

Food

KAMONJI-GOYA

4469-1 Azumino Kamikōchi; tel. 0263/95-2418; www.kamonjigoya.wordpress.com; 8:30am-4pm daily; ¥500-1,600

Just beside the placid waters of Myōjin-ike, this historic, cabin-like restaurant whips up celebrated iwana (river trout) lunch sets. Caught nearby, the fish is then cooked over hot charcoal in an irori (sunken hearth). Diners sit at hefty wooden tables and benches, alfresco, tucking into the eatery's famed dish. The menu also includes a smattering of oden (vegetables and fish cake stewed in soy- and kelp-infused broth), among other items.

ALPENROSE

Kamikōchi Imperial Hotel 1F, Azumino Kamikōchi; tel. 0263/95-2001; www.imperialhotel.co.jp/e/kamikochi/restaurant/alpenrose; lunch 11am-2:30pm daily; ¥2,000-3,000

This restaurant pays homage to the European mountaineering associations with the area. This is the casual culinary arm of the Kamikōchi Imperial Hotel, in which the restaurant is located, serving a delicious range of western dishes a la carte. The biggest hit is hashed beef, soft-cooked eggs, and a rice-stuffed omelet covered in the Imperial's signature demi-glace. Ingredients sourced from the nearby mountains figure heavily on the menu. Reservations are not accepted during lunchtime, and dinner (5:30pm-8pm daily; ¥8,000-10,000) is only available for hotel guests.

Accommodations

In addition to the following recommended options, Kamikōchi has an extensive list of places to stay (www.kamikochi.org/plan/accommodation), ranging from plush hotels and humble bed-and-breakfasts to beautiful campsites. During the warmer months, lodgings are known to book up, so reserve a few months ahead if possible. And if your place of choice is full, don't fret; there's likely an appealing alternative.

TOKUSAWA-EN

tel. 0260/95-2508; www.tokusawaen.com; May-Oct.; camping ¥500, ¥13,500 dorm (with 2 meals), ¥17,000 private room (with 2 meals)

Kamikōchi's busier junctions feel like Tokyo's Shinjuku Station compared to this serene campsite and lodge found deeper within the park. You can camp or stay in one of the shared or private Japanese-style rooms at the appealing lodge. Filling meals are served in a large dining room. It's possible to rent a tent and bedding if you don't have your own, but you'll have to reserve in advance (¥7,500 for 3- to 4-person tent, ¥2,000 sleeping bag, ¥500 blanket, ¥400 sleeping mat).

KAMIKŌCHI IMPERIAL HOTEL

Azumino Kamikōchi; 0260/95-2001; www.imperialhotel.co.jp; ¥21,000 pp

In business since 1933, this sumptuous lodge brilliantly fuses luxurious accents with the beautiful natural surroundings. The interior is reminiscent of a chalet in the Alps, and the cooking is fittingly European. All elements are stellar, from the impeccable service to the top-notch bar. If you've got the means, it's a good place to indulge. It's often booked up a year or more in advance. If you want to snag a room, make the attempt as early as the inkling strikes.

Information and Services

Stop at the **Tourist Information Center** (tel. 0260/95-2433; 8am-5pm daily; www.kamikochi.or.jp) in the Kamikōchi bus station and buy the trusty English-language *Kamikōchi Pocket Guide*, which contains good maps of the area's trails. To glimpse the full extent of Kamikōchi's hiking possibilities, see the Trekking section of the Kamikōchi website (www.kamikochi.org/plan/trekking).

To pick up some English-language materials on the natural history, flora and fauna, and lay of the land, walk a bit past Kappa-bashi to the **Kamikōchi Visitor Center** (tel. 0260/95-2606; 8am-5pm daily), where you may be able to join a guided hike.

Getting There and Around

Coming from Matsumoto Station, take the **Matsumoto Electric Railway** to Shin-Shimashima Station (30 minutes; ¥700). From there, **buses** run to Kamikōchi (1 hour 15 minutes; ¥2,100). **Direct buses** also run all the way from Matsumoto (2 hours; ¥2,700 one-way, ¥4,800 return) or Takayama via Hirayu Onsen (www.nouhibus.co.jp/route_bus/kamikochi-line-en; 1 hour 25 minutes; ¥2,250).

Getting around with your own **car** is a wise move, particularly with an English GPS navigation setup. However, it'll only get you as far as the Sawando area, located next to National Route 158 en route to Naka-no-yu, closer to Matsumoto, or the Hirayu area, closer to Takayama. Driving from Matsumoto, take National Route 158 to Sawando Parking Area, which is searchable on Google Maps. From Takayama, take National Route 158 to Hirayu Parking Area, which is also searchable on Google Maps. You can **park** in either lot (¥600 per day), then take a **shuttle bus** for the remainder of the journey into the park (25 minutes; ¥1,000 one-way, ¥1,800 return). If you can stomach the fare, a **taxi** costs upward of ¥4,000. Speaking of which, reserve your return bus fare as soon as you arrive so that you're not stranded as dusk falls, at which point a taxi will be your only option.

SHIN-HOTAKA ONSEN

新穂高温泉

One of five hamlets in the alpine, hot-springs retreat of Okuhida (deep Hida) Onsen-gō, Shin-Hotaka Onsen is a hidden village blessed with an abundance of rotenburo (outdoor baths). While the other four onsen towns—namely Hirayu Onsen, Fukuji Onsen, Shin-Hirayu Onsen, and Tochio Onsen—have their charms, Shin-Hotaka is the most remote and dramatic.

This realm of steamy pools and mountainside vistas is a destination for powder hounds and trekkers in need of a break from modern life. It's not cheap, but a night at one of the ryokan here will be among the most relaxing you'll ever have.

Alongside its abundance of hot springs, the town is known for the **Shin-Hotaka Ropeway,** which glides toward the nearby peak Nishi-Hotake-dake and offers breathtaking views. If you're prepared for the journey, it's possible to trundle from the cable car station on the summit of Nishi-Hotake-dake to Kamikōchi on the opposite side of the mountain in three hours.

Onsen

SHIN-HOTAKA-NO-YU

新穂高の湯

Okuhida Onsengō Kansaka; tel. 0578/89-2614 (Okuhida Onsen-gō Sightseeing Information Center); https://shinhotaka.com/place/486/; 8am-6pm daily late Apr.-Oct.; free

This public riverside rotenburo (open-air bath) is, awkwardly, visible from a nearby bridge. Moreover, it's a mixed-gender pool. But none of this stops adventurous onsen connoisseurs from stripping down and sinking in. If you're not shy, give it a try and you'll be rewarded. The sound of the river resonates in the bathing area, while pebbles covering the floor of the pool massage the soles of your feet. Mountains covered in spindly foliage rise from both riverbanks. Before you enter the pool, just be sure to enter through the correct-gendered changing room, and use a small privacy towel while walking outside the pool for courtesy's sake.

NAKAZAKI SANSŌ OKUHIDA-NO-YU
中崎山荘 奥飛騨の湯

710 Okuhida Onsen-gō Kansaka; tel. 0578/89-2021; www.okuhida.or.jp/roten_catalog/detail?id=3311; 8am-8pm daily; ¥900 adults, ¥450 children

This recently renovated complex is conveniently located a quick walk downhill from the Shin-Hotaka Ropeway. This makes it a particularly appealing option for those seeking a bath before or after zipping up the mountain. The mountainside view from the indoor pool is spectacular, and the milky waters are packed with minerals too. Unlike the exhibitionists' mecca of Shin-Hotaka-no-yu just downhill, the baths here are separated by sex and well-concealed from passersby; this is a good thing for privacy, but the view from the outdoor bath is slightly obscured as a result.

Sports and Recreation

SHIN-HOTAKA ROPEWAY
新穂高ロープウェイ

710-58 Okuhida Onsen-gō Kansaka; tel. 0578/89-2552; www.shinhotaka-ropeway.jp; 8:30am-4:30pm daily; ¥1,700 adults, ¥850 children one-way, ¥3,000 adults, ¥1,500 children round-trip

The longest ropeway in Asia, Shin-Hotaka Ropeway offers phenomenal views of the Northern Alps. As you climb up the Hotake Mountain Range, the verdant Okuhida Onsen-gō region ripples through the landscape below. You'll be transported in two double-decker cars more than 800 ear-popping meters (2,624 ft) up to a viewing platform at 2,156 meters (7,073 ft), where you'll be greeted with a sweeping panorama of the Northern Alps.

If you make this trip between late June and the end of September, a hiking trail will likely be open from this viewing deck. The well-marked trail allows hikers to descend about 1.5 hours to a mountain hut called Hotaka-dake Sansō, situated on the ridge. From there, you can continue trailing downward for another 2.5 hours to the nature lovers' utopia of **Kamikōchi,** a highland valley on the other side of the mountains (about 3 hours).

Accommodations

MINSHUKU TAKIZAWA

261 Nakao, Okuhida Onsen-gō; tel. 0578/89-2705; www.okuhida.com; ¥25,920 d with two meals

This authentic onsen-ryokan offers spacious tatami rooms with en-suite toilets. There are four onsen baths—two indoors, two open-air—all of which are private. The gourmet meals are beautifully presented and taste a cut above what you'd expect for the price. The ever-helpful host Takizawa-san extends a warm greeting to all guests. Free shuttle pickup and drop-off at the Shin-Hotaka Ropeway—10 minutes' drive north—are available upon request.

YARIMIKAN

587 Okuhida Onsen-gō Kansaka; tel. 0578/89-2808; www.yarimikan.com; average ¥40,000 d with two meals

This immaculate riverside inn, set in an old, relocated manor house with its ambience intact, has two indoor baths and a whopping eight open-air baths fringing the banks of the Kamata-gawa (both gender-separated and mixed), a few of which can be reserved for private use. For staying guests, baths are open around the clock. They're open to day-trippers 10am-2pm (¥500). There are 16 rooms, including a mix of Japanese and Western. All rooms have a private toilet; one has a private indoor tub, and two have private outdoor tubs. Service is stellar and the kaiseki meals are sublime. Splurge-worthy.

Getting There and Around

You can reach Shin-Hotaka from Takayama by **bus** (1.5 hours; ¥2,200; www.nouhibus.co.jp/route_bus/shinhotaka-line-en/), passing Hirayu Onsen on the way. Take the bus all the way to the last stop, Shin-Hotaka Ropeway.

That said, this onsen is legitimately remote and having your own **car** is by far the best way to explore these parts. To reach Shin-Hotaka Onsen village by car from Takayama, take Prefectural Route 458 east out of town, then continue east on National Route 158 to National Route 471. Drive north on National Route 471 towards Kamioka/Shinhodaka, then veer east on Prefectural Route 475 for the remainder of the drive along the northern bank of the Takahara River. The total trip is about 1 hour 15 minutes long. From Matsumoto, take National Route 158 westward to National Route 471, where you'll veer north and follow the same route for the rest of the trip that you would if you were coming from Takayama. The journey from Matsumoto is about 1 hour 40 minutes.

Takayama 高山

Takayama is an amiable mountain town that wears its history well. The streets of its charming old section—which runs along the murmuring Miyagawa river, crisscrossed by a series of traditional red bridges—are home to museums, crafts shops, eateries, and family-run inns. Shrines and temples, connected by a range of footpaths, make for an inviting stroll in the hills just beyond downtown. For such a small city, there's a surprisingly decent nightlife zone too.

Often called by its fuller name of Hida-Takayama (Hida being the name of the mountain range that runs through this region), Takayama's biggest claim to fame is the visually impressive Takayama Matsuri, a festival held in spring and autumn every year. Towering floats are paraded on wheels through the old part of town to the accompaniment of traditional music.

The city rose to prominence in the 17th century when it became known as a reliable source of high-grade timber—no small thing in a country where traditional architecture was entirely based on wood. This fostered a local culture of brilliant carpenters, who in turn ushered great riches into the city, which was brought under the control of the shogunate in what was then Edo (modern-day Tokyo).

Today, the town's history and local character are well-preserved, and Takayama can be enjoyably explored on foot. The word is unfortunately out and tourists do flock to the town, but the magic remains. Either as an entry point into the Japan Alps or as a standalone destination, if you're going to make it to just one town in Central Honshu's vast mountainous interior, make it Takayama.

SIGHTS

★ Sanmachi Suji

三町筋

10-minute walk east of JR Takayama Station on eastern bank of Miyagawa

Takayama's merchant class has long made a mint. Nowhere is this more evident than in the old quarter of Sanmachi Suji. This old business district is concentrated around three streets (namely Sannomachi, Ninomachi, and Ichinomachi), which run east to west along the north side of the Miyagawa, a river coursing through the center of town that is crisscrossed by picturesque red bridges. The district has admittedly succumbed to full-blown, touristic euphoria and gets very crowded, but its charm remains intact.

To appreciate the ambience of this lovely old town, go for a leisurely stroll along these streets and take in the lovely wooden gates and windows fronted by the narrow wooden slats characteristic of traditional Japanese

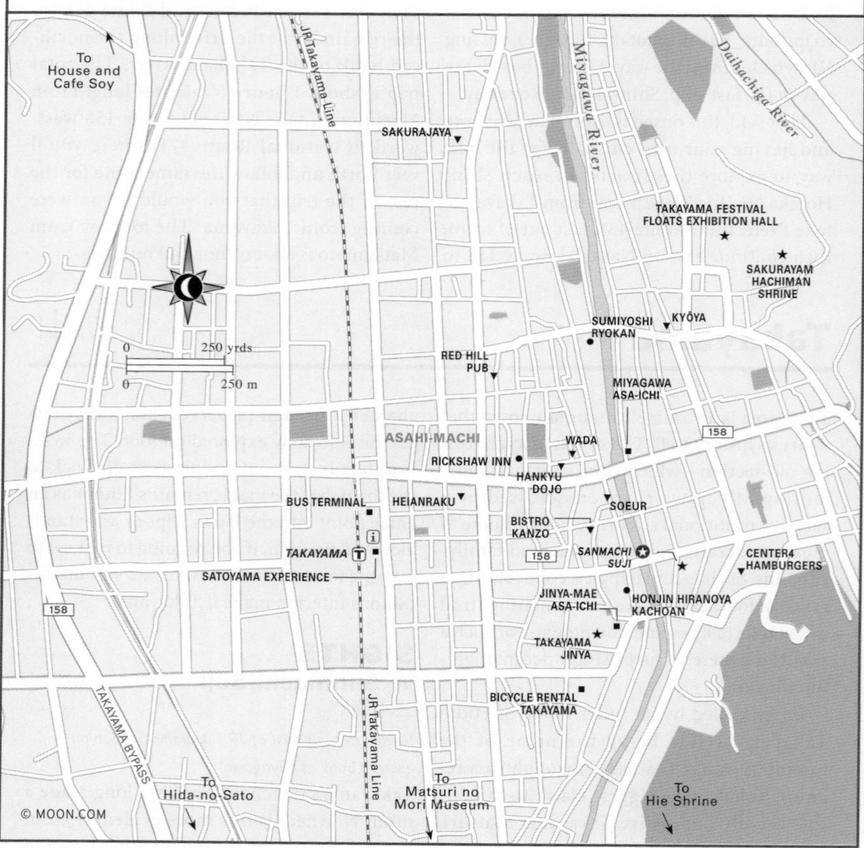

architecture. Within this pedestrian dream you'll find a host of sake breweries, cafés, shops selling traditional wooden crafts, and lovely old homes. Note that most of the neighborhood businesses are open 9am-5pm on most days.

TAKAYAMA SHŌWA MUSEUM
高山昭和館

6 Shimōichino-machi; tel. 0577/33-7836; www.takayama-showakan.com; 9am-6pm daily; ¥800 high school students and older, ¥500 junior high school students, ¥300 elementary school students; 12-minute walk northeast of JR Takayama Station

One of the more colorful stops in the Sanmachi Suji area, the Takayama Shōwa Museum reveals a joyous glimpse of what life was like in Japan during the Shōwa Period (1926-1989), with special attention given to the postwar years of the 1950s and 1960s. Western visitors may be surprised to see just how much some of the starlets, superheroes, fashion trends, and household items in Japan bear resemblance to the era of the space race and Lucille Ball. The postwar zeitgeist was global.

Plastic figurines and metal toys, outsized radios, bicycles with long, curved (now-vintage) handlebars, posters of singers with perfectly coiffed hair who laid the foundation of what would become the mammoth J-Pop music biz: Curios hang from the ceiling, crowding shelves of faux barber and electronics shops alongside juke boxes, early television sets, and more. This museum gives you a fun glimpse into Japan's buoyant rise from the ashes of World War II, when the country had just begun to rebuild its sense of nationhood and there was widespread hope for a brighter future.

Takayama Jinya

高山陣屋

1-5 Hachiken-machi; tel. 0577/32-0643; https://jinya.gifu.jp; 8:45am-5pm Mar.-Jul. and Sept.-Oct., 8:45am-6pm Aug., 8:45am-4:30pm Nov.-Feb.; ¥430 adults, free for under 18; 9-minute walk southeast of JR Takayama Station

About five minutes' walk southwest of the Sanmachi Suji area, just across the Miyagawa river, this rambling one-story building is the last-standing prefectural office left over from the Edo period. Constructed in 1816, the building was used by the local government as recently as 1969. The well-preserved building is essentially empty, but offers views onto a spacious garden. The kitchen and granary offer interesting perspectives on old food preparation and storage methods. On a darker note, exhibits in the interrogation room reveal the ways torture was used in feudal days to extract information from those unlucky enough to have been brought in for questioning. There's English-language signage throughout.

FESTIVALS

TAKAYAMA MATSURI

高山祭り

Takayama's old town, centered on Sanmachi Suji area; www.hida.jp/english/festivalsandevents/4000105.html; Apr. 14-15, Oct. 9-10; free

Considered one of Japan's three most visually stunning festivals (alongside Kyoto's Gion Matsuri and the Chichibu Yomatsuri), the Takayama Matsuri is a wonderful display of the town's brilliant knack for craftsmanship. Twice yearly, in spring and autumn, throngs gather in the heart of the old town to witness a dozen towering floats strutted through the streets. The spring half of the event, known as the Sannō Matsuri, is held in the southern section of the old town where the **Hie (aka: Sannō) Shrine** (156 Shiroyama; tel. 0577/32-0520; https://hiejinja.com; 8:30am-4:30pm daily) is located. The autumn edition, known as the Hachiman Matsuri, fills the streets a bit to the north, closer to the associated **Sakurayama Hachiman Shrine** (178 Sakuramachi; tel. 0577/32-0240; www.hidahachimangu.jp; 9am-5pm daily).

The parades take place during the mornings and afternoons of all festival days. If the weather takes a sour turn, the floats are kept dry within their respective storehouses around town, where they can still be viewed. The biggest thrill comes in the evenings, when the colorfully decked-out floats roll through town ridden by mechanical dolls. Floats are convoyed by locals dressed in traditional attire, who strum, sing, and hammer out heartfelt songs from the past. The festival is immensely popular, so it's wise to reserve accommodations three months or more in advance.

If you're not fortunate enough to be here during festival time, the **Takayama Festival Floats Exhibition Hall** (178 Sakura-machi; tel. 0577/32-5100; www.hidahachimangu.jp; 8:30am-5pm Mar.-Nov., 9am-4:30pm Dec.-Feb.; ¥820) displays a few of the floats, while the **Matsuri no Mori Museum** (1111 Chishima-machi; tel. 0577/37-1000; www.togeihida.co.jp; 9am-5pm daily; ¥1,000) offers a more in-depth look, though it's a detour from downtown.

TOURS

SATOYAMA EXPERIENCE

Takayama tour desk (i-café Takayama, 1-22-2 Shōwamachi, Takayama; tel. 0577/62-8180); https://satoyama-experience.com

For an authentic glimpse into the soul of the

1

2

3

Hida region, you won't be disappointed by the well-regarded cultural and outdoor experiences provided by this excellent tour outfit staffed by friendly, English-speaking guides. Explore the surrounding countryside, from its towns to its natural beauty, by bicycle or on foot. You can even don snowshoes during winter, or join a cooking class or culinary tour. For details, check the website or stop at one of their inviting tour desks, located around the Takayama region.

SHOPPING

The area starting from Sanmachi-dōri in the south up to Yasugawa-dōri two blocks to the north has a glut of **antique shops.** This is a good place to search for a piece of lacquerware or something artfully made of wood. There are more great shops selling crafts old and new throughout the town.

Two open-air **morning markets** are held in Takayama, each offering its own range of goods and flavor. These markets are a good place to mingle with local vendors and to pick up a few locally made snacks, and perhaps a small token, such as one of the ubiquitous saru-bobo (baby monkey) folk-dolls.

- At the **Jinya-mae Asa-ichi** (陣屋前朝市; 1-5 Hachiken-machi; tel. 0577/32-3333; www.jinya-asaichi.jp; 6am-noon daily; 10 minutes' walk southeast of JR Takayama Station), local produce is sold in front of the Takayama Jinya complex.
- The other, **Miyagawa Asa-ichi** (宮川朝市; Shimosannomachi; tel. 0577/35-3145; www.asaichi.net; 7am-noon daily; 10 minutes' walk northeast of JR Takayama Station), is largely focused on arts and crafts. This one is set up along the east bank of the Miyagawa, occupying the stretch between the bridges of Kaji-bashi in the south to Yayoi-bashi in the north.

1: Sanmachi Suji historic district **2:** decorative festival float **3:** crowd at Takayama Matsuri

FOOD

In Takayama you'll find a refreshingly vibrant restaurant scene, offering everything from countryside cooking to inventive fusion fare.

International

HEIANRAKU

6-7-2 Tenman-machi; tel. 0577/32-3078; https://heianraku.com; 11:30am-1pm and 5:30pm-8pm Wed.-Mon.; ¥740-1,500; 7-minute walk northeast of JR Takayama Station

This inviting, home-cooked restaurant offers a mix of Chinese, Japanese—including delicious gyoza (fried pork dumplings)—and vegetarian fare made with liberal helpings of locally foraged mountain vegetables. There's enough space for about a dozen at a time, with seating on tatami mats and at the counter. The staff give a warm welcome, and an English menu makes ordering a cinch. A great spot for either lunch or dinner.

BISTRO KANZO

46 Uramachi; tel. 0577/34-2363; www.bistro-kanzo.com; 11:30am-2pm and 5pm-9pm Thurs.-Tues.; lunch ¥1,500-6,000, dinner ¥3,900-8,800; 7-minute walk east of JR Takayama Station

This chic bistro in the heart of downtown puts a French spin on local ingredients. Tender slabs of Hida-gyū feature prominently, alongside a range of seafood and beautiful desserts. The chef at the helm has a knack for presentation, routinely serving food that looks as artistic as it is delicious. The staff are friendly and helpful, and the prices are surprisingly reasonable in light of the caliber of the top-notch fare. An English menu is available. Reserve a few days or more in advance.

★ SAKURAJAYA

3-84-13 Sowamachi; tel. 0577/57-7565; 11:30am-2pm and 6pm-10pm Thurs.-Tues.; average dinner ¥4,000-5,000; 20-minute walk north of JR Takayama Station on the west side of the Miyagawa

Serving up an intriguing fusion of German and Japanese food, this restaurant sits in a quiet residential area in the north of town. The menu reflects the chef and owner's long sojourn in Europe, combined with his love of using locally sourced ingredients. The menu includes fried chicken salad, duck sashimi, fried tofu, corn and mushroom tempura, roast Hida-gyū, baguette, and fried waffle-cut potatoes. Simply put, it's one of the most unique places to dine in town. Reserve a few days ahead and request a seat at the bar to watch the master at work. An English menu is available.

Burgers

CENTER4 HAMBURGERS

94 Kamiichino-machi; tel. 0577/36-4527; http://tiger-center4.com; 11am-2:30pm and 6pm-9:30pm Thurs.-Tues.; ¥760-1,340; 13-minute walk east of JR Takayama Station

This fantastic hamburger joint is overflowing with nostalgic bric-a-brac and loads of charm. The local couple who run it serve excellent burgers made from Hida-gyū, as the prized local beef is known, with a generous range of toppings. There's even liver pâté. The menu also includes sandwiches (BLT, club, vegetarian), salads, clam chowder, and delicious milkshakes. Recommended.

Izakaya

WADA

23 Asahi-machi; tel. 0577/33-4850; 5pm-1am Mon.-Thurs. and Sun., 5pm-2am Fri.-Sat.; dishes ¥370-600, ¥3,000 average per person; 10 minutes on foot, northeast of JR Takayama Station on the west side of the Miyagawa

Come to this atmospheric local haunt if you'd like to veer off the tourist trail. You'll find dark wood beams, diners washing skewers of fried goodness down with beer, and friendly chefs shouting back and forth behind the counter. The menu is delicious and varied: grilled meat on sticks, sashimi, tempura, tofu dishes, grilled eggplant basted in miso paste, and much more. There's an extensive drinks menu too. Although it's largely off the radar for foreign visitors, some staff speak English and there's an English menu, too. Highly recommended.

★ KYŌYA

1-77 Oshin-machi; tel. 0577/34-7660; www.kyoya-hida.jp; 11am-9:30pm Wed.-Mon.; dishes from ¥450, set meals ¥1,200, full-courses from ¥3,500; 15-minute walk northeast of JR Takayama Station

This cozy restaurant's all-wood interior, vaulted ceiling, and mix of rustic tables and tatami seating conjure a farmhouse vibe. The focus here is on local favorites like tender Hida-gyū beef and vegetables barbecued at the table, and hoba-miso (vegetables such as leeks and shiitake mushrooms mixed with miso paste and grilled on a magnolia leaf). This restaurant provides charming ambience, wonderful service, and fabulous food at a reasonable price. It sits next to a river on the north side of town. Look for the white building with a traditional roofline beside a bridge. Barrels of sake and bags of rice are perched above the entrance.

Cafés and Light Bites

SOEUR

2-35 Honmachi; tel. 0577/35-2001; https://soeur.hida-ch.com; 10:30am-6:30pm Wed.-Mon.; from ¥450; 10-minute walk east of JR Takayama Station, just west of the Miyagawa as you head toward the Sanmachi Suji area

This bright riverside café serves tasty baked goods, sandwiches, coffee, and a range of teas. Its back wall is a floor-to-ceiling window overlooking the Miyagawa, with the old town across the river. It's got a relaxing jazz soundtrack and free Wi-Fi too.

BARS AND NIGHTLIFE

For a small town, Takayama has a surprising number of lively little watering holes. Most of the after-hours action takes place in the **Asahi-machi** neighborhood, about 10 minutes' walk northeast of JR Takayama Station and west of the Miyagawa.

RED HILL PUB

2-4 Sowachō; tel. 0577/33-8139; https://redhilltakayama.wordpress.com; 7pm-midnight daily; 10-minute walk northeast of Takayama Station, on the west side of the Miyagawa

This chilled-out, low-lit bar brims with funky decor. Run by a cheerful English-speaking host with great taste in music, it's a magnet for friendly locals and travelers alike. Alongside bar standards, including good cocktails, there's an eclectic range of tasty nibbles.

HANKYU DOJO

11 Asahi-machi; tel. 090/1234-5959; www.hankyudojo.com; 7pm-10pm daily; 8-minute walk northeast of JR Takayama Station

There's nothing quite like firing some arrows when you're fresh off a pub crawl. This little archery range routinely has tipsy Robin Hood wannabes lining up for a chance to try for a bull's-eye. The jovial staff gives a crash course to the novice archers. Safety first. A quiver of 10 arrows will set you back ¥300.

ACCOMMODATIONS

Under ¥10,000

SUMIYOSHI RYOKAN

4-21 Hommachi; tel. 050/3160-9558; http://sumiyoshi-ryokan.com; ¥6,000 d with shared bath (¥10,000 with two meals), ¥9,000 d with private bath (¥13,000 with two meals); 15-minute walk northeast of JR Takayama Station

Packed with curios, this riverside ryokan oozes Meiji-era charm and boasts a prime location on the west bank of the Miyagawa, a stone's throw from the old town. All rooms have tatami floors and a liberal dose of antique charm. The kind owners are eager to please and serve excellent meals for an additional charge. One room has an en-suite bathroom, while the others share an appealing bath. Recommended.

RICKSHAW INN

54 Suehiro-machi; tel. 0577/32-2890; www.rickshawinn.com; ¥4,200 single with shared bathroom, ¥8,000 twin with shared bathroom, ¥11,900 twin with private bathroom, breakfast ¥500; 10-minute walk northeast of Takayama Station at the southern end of the entertainment district

This popular inn offers a range of room styles, from Western with en-suite bathrooms to tatami suites with shared or private baths. The helpful owners speak English and are happy to share their local expertise. There's an appealing shared lounge and kitchen, as well as laundry facilities. One of the larger rooms has a private kitchenette, while another sleeping up to six has a private lounge.

¥10,000-20,000

HOUSE AND CAFÉ SOY

365 Kamigiri-machi; tel. 0577/62-9005; www.hidatakayama-soy.com; ¥17,140 d; 15-minute drive north of JR Takayama Station

This beautiful, family-run inn is set in a century-old country home. Fully up-to-date creature comforts have been added while maintaining the original aesthetic, wood beams and all. There are three spacious rooms: two with tatami floors, futons, and detached, private toilet and shower; the other with a wooden floor, beds, a private workspace, and a private bathroom. The first floor has an inviting lounge with large windows, plenty of cushy chairs, and a fireplace. There's also an on-site café, serving drinks (from ¥550) and lunches (from ¥1,000). A great breakfast is included (either Western or Japanese). The warm hosts speak English and bend over backward to make your stay as comfortable as possible. Car pickup from JR Takayama Station is available on advance request. There's also a bus stop nearby. Recommended.

¥30,000-40,000

HONJIN HIRANOYA KACHOAN

1-34 Hon-machi; tel. 0577/34-1234; https://ssl.honjinhiranoya.com; from ¥18,360 pp with two meals; 9-minute walk east of JR Takayama Station

This elegant, high-end ryokan is an excellent choice for a serious splurge. There are phenomenal meals, 28 immaculate traditional rooms with plush private bathrooms as well as shared gender-separated onsen baths, wonderfully attentive English-speaking staff who glide through the corridors in kimonos, and car pickup from the station, which is only about 10 minutes away on foot. Just slip into one of the 800 yukata on offer and luxuriate for a night or two. Nearby, the same ryokan

TOP EXPERIENCE

☆ Folk Villages of Central Honshu

Shirakawa-gō

Not far from Takayama, you can visit villages filled with homes built in the gassho-zukuri style, which roughly translates to "built like hands joined in prayer." The Shirakawa-gō and Gokayama regions both boast UNESCO World Heritage for their communities of traditional houses, some of which are more than 250 years old. While these hamlets may look like the setting for a fairy tale, the unique roofs were built to withstand the enormous weight put upon them by upwards of 10 meters (32 ft) of snow that blankets the region every winter.

Within the Shirakawa-gō region, the village of **Ogimachi** is the most popular for day-trippers. Slightly more remote, the Gokayama region is home to less-visited hamlets like **Suganuma** and **Ainokura.** One of the most memorable overnight stays on offer in Japan can be had at one of the gasshō-zukuri farmhouses found throughout these picturesque villages. These rooms fill up fast, so it's best to be flexible and book as far in advance as you can. Check out the **Japan Guest Houses** website (www.japaneseguesthouses.com) and the website of the **Shirakawa-gō Tourist Association** (https://shirakawa-go.gr.jp/en/staytypes/gassho), which offer reservation services.

If you don't have time to stay the night, the **Hida-no-Sato Folk Village** (1-590 Kamiokamoto-machi, Takayama; tel. 0577/34-4711; www.hidanosato-tpo.jp; 8:30am-5pm daily; ¥700) is only a slight detour from downtown Takayama. About 30 minutes' walk west of Takayama Station, this open-air grouping of some 30 buildings—from houses to storehouses and logging huts—dates to the Edo period but were moved from the nearby Shirakawa-gō region to their current location in 1971.

SHIRAKAWA-GŌ 白川郷

Ogimachi, the premier village in the Shirakawa-gō region where you'll find its sprawling collection of UNESCO World Heritage registered homes built in the gasshō-zukuri style, is a community of about 600 residents. Within this idyllic scene, you'll find 114 thatched-roof farmhouses, many of them open to the public. If you want to stay here, good picks include:

- The nicely decorated **Furusato** (588 Ogimachi; tel. 057/696-1033; https://shirakawago-furusato.business.site; ¥17,600 pp with two meals), run by an English-speaking owner.
- The expansive riverside **Magōemon** (360 Ogimachi; tel. 057/696-1167; https://shirakawa-go.gr.jp/stay/39/; ¥13,000 pp with two meals).
- **Kōemon** (456 Ogimachi; tel. 057/696-1446; www.shirakawago-kataribe.com; ¥10,000 pp with meals), an old-school gem run by a helpful English-speaking owner.

The best way to get here is by driving yourself. Take the Tokai-Hokuriku expressway from Takayama until you reach Ogimachi, roughly 45 minutes one-way. Alternatively, **Nōhi Bus** (tel. 0577/32-1688; www.nouhibus.co.jp) offers daily trips between Takayama and Ogimachi (¥2,470 one-way, ¥4,420 round-trip), and Kanazawa and Ogimachi (1.5 hours; ¥1,850 one-way, ¥3,290 round-trip). The Shirakawa-gō official website has an English-language page that gives thorough directions for getting here and beyond (http://ml.shirakawa-go.org/en/access/).

GOKAYAMA 五箇山

Though harder to reach, the isolated villages in the Gokayama region, especially **Suganuma** (菅沼) and **Ainokura** (相倉) are incredibly atmospheric. The nine farmhouses of Suganuma rise from the verdant landscape like a mirage from a few centuries back. Twenty gasshō-zukuri farmhouses make up Ainokura, some of them converted into museums and inns.

To sleep in Ainokura, try:

- **Goyomon** (438 Ainokura; tel. 0763/66-2154; ¥21,000 d with two meals), a friendly family-run place.
- **Yomoshirō** (395 Ainokura; tel. 0763/66-2377; ¥11,000 pp with two meals), a four-room affair run by a friendly owner with a penchant for playing a percussion instrument called the sasara, commonly used in folk music.
- **Nakaya** (231 Ainokura; tel. 0763/66-22457; www1.tst.ne.jp/snakaya/index.html; ¥10,500 pp with two meals), where guests dine around a cozy irori (sunken, open fireplace).

shrine in Ainokura

To reach the Gokayama area from Takayama, take the Tokai-Hokuriku expressway to the Gokayama exit, from which Suganuma can be reached in just a few minutes; Ainokura is an additional 15-minute drive. Alternatively, if you're first stopping at Ogimachi, take the more scenic route 156 north to Gokayama. This road will first bring you to Suganuma, roughly 15 kilometers (9 mi) north of Ogimachi, followed by Ainokura, another 9 kilometers (6 mi) north of Suganuma. It's also possible to reach Ainokura by **bus**, operated by **Kaetsunou Bus** (tel. 076/234-0123; www.kaetsunou.co.jp) from Shirakawa-gō Bus Terminal in Ogimachi six times daily (45 minutes; ¥1,300).

also runs the less pricy, though also striking, **Bekkan Annexe** (www.honjinhiranoya.co.jp). Check the website for details.

INFORMATION AND SERVICES

For information about the greater Hida region online, go to www.hida-kankou.jp.

- **Hida tourist information center** (5-51 Hanasato-machi, just outside Takayama Station; tel. 0577/32-5328; www.hida.jp; 8:30am-7pm Apr.-Nov., 8:30am-5:30pm Dec.-Mar.)

GETTING THERE

Train

Sitting at the west side of town, **Takayama Station** is served by the JR Takayama line, which runs south to **Nagoya** (2 hours 45 minutes; ¥6,230) and north to **Toyama** (1.5 hours; ¥3,560). Depending on where you're coming from, you can approach from either direction, with Nagoya linked to **Kyoto** and **Osaka** to the west and **Tokyo** to the east, and Toyama being directly linked by the (almost) brand-spanking-new Hokuriku shinkansen line to Tokyo in the east.

Bus

Nōhi Bus (www.nouhibus.co.jp; tel. 0577/32-1688) operates from a highway **bus terminal** next to Takayama Station. Buses run to and from Shinjuku Station in **Tokyo** (5.5 hours; ¥6,690), **Matsumoto** (2.5 hours; ¥3,190), **Kanazawa** (2 hours 15 minutes; ¥3,600), **Nagoya** (2.5 hours; ¥2,980), **Kyoto** (4 hours 15 minutes; ¥4,200), and **Osaka** (5.5 hours; ¥4,700), among others.

If you plan to venture farther into the countryside and don't want to bother with buses, there's a **Toyota Rent-A-Car** across the street from Takayama Station (5-20 Hanasato-machi; tel. 0577/36-6110; www.trl-gifu.co.jp; 8am-8pm daily).

GETTING AROUND

Takayama is highly **walkable,** with the downtown area surrounding Sanmachi Suji about 10 minutes east of JR Takayama Station on foot. If you'd prefer to pedal your way around town, **Bicycle Rental Takayama** (1-77 Hachiken-machi; tel. 080/4771-7562; http://craftharvest.html.xdomain.jp; 8am-6pm daily; ¥500 half-day, ¥800 full day) offers well-maintained bikes and is run by friendly staff who are happy to answer questions. It's located about 10 minutes southeast of Takayama Station, or 3 minutes on foot south of Takayama Jinya at the south edge of the old part of town.

Kanazawa 金沢

Many towns in Japan are called "Little Kyoto," but Kanazawa is most deserving. Its wealth of historical sights and charm can be traced to its past status as the base of the mighty Maeda samurai clan. During the Edo period, this feudal superpower ruled over the Hokuriku region, encompassing modern-day Fukui, Ishikawa, Toyama, and Niigata prefectures. Largely thanks to the region's abundant rice production, the clan's wealth and might were second only to the shogunate-founding Tokugawa clan itself.

Around this significant seat of feudal power arose a great city of cobblestone streets, geisha districts lined with teahouses, a samurai quarter, a bustling market, a castle, and one of Japan's loveliest landscape gardens, Kenroku-en. Like Kyoto, Kanazawa's historic treasures are well-preserved, as it escaped bombing during World War II. Today, the city of 450,000 is the capital of Ishikawa Prefecture. In addition to its feudal-era charm, it also boasts an energetic fish market and an excellent contemporary art museum.

Kanazawa

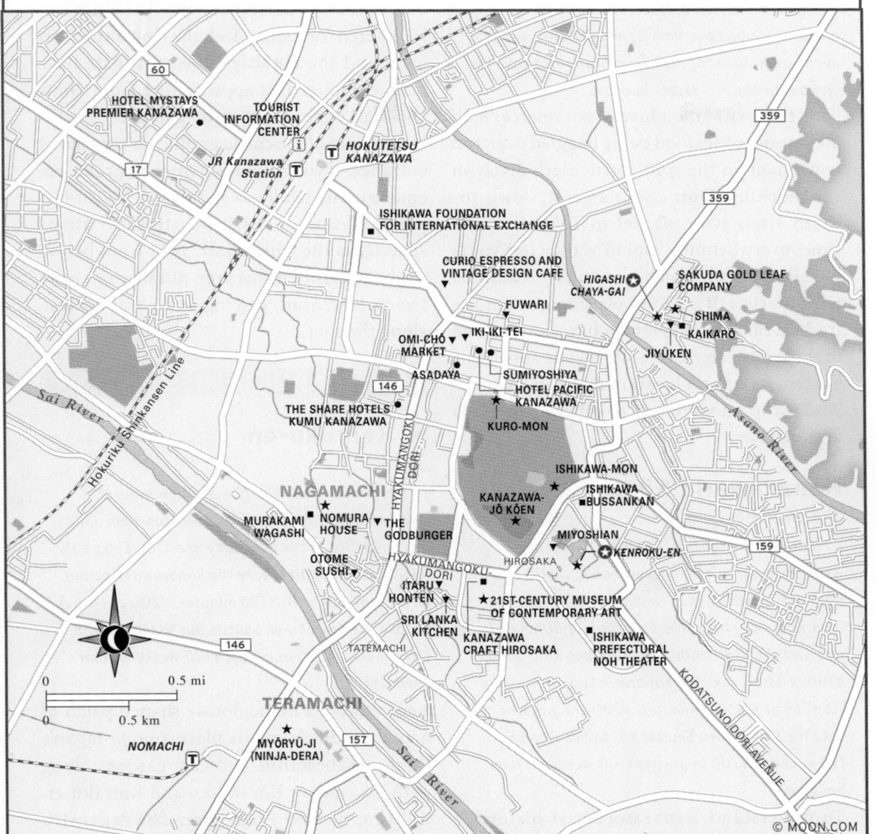

It's possible to see Kanazawa's top sights in an afternoon, but spending one or two nights will give you a chance to take it all in.

ORIENTATION

Most of the attractions in Kanazawa are in the area stretching between Kanazawa Station and the Katamachi and Kōrinbō shopping areas, about 2-3 kilometers to the south, with the **Asano-gawa** river bordering the city center to the north. Make your way about a kilometer southeast on the major thoroughfare running from Kanazawa Station and you'll arrive at the **Omi-chō seafood market; Kanazawa-jō Kōen** castle and the dazzling **Kenroku-en** landscape garden are just beyond. The historic **Nagamachi** samurai district is just to the west, and to the south (across the city's other main waterway, the **Sai-gawa**), the Teramachi temple district is home to the quirky "Ninja Temple" **Myōryū-ji.** The **Higashi Chaya-gai** geisha district is approximately 2 kilometers (1 mi) southeast of Kanazawa Station, northeast of Kanazawa-jō Kōen, on the eastern bank of the Asano-gawa.

SIGHTS

Omi-chō Market

50 Kamiomichō; tel. 076/231-1462; https://ohmicho-ichiba.com; 9am-5pm daily; free; walk 15 minutes southeast of Kanazawa Station, or take the city bus to Musashigatsuji bus stop

This fish market is a hive of commerce, with all manner of seafood being haggled over and consumed on the spot. Particularly lively in the morning, Omi-chō is a great, down-to-earth alternative market to Tokyo's sometimes overwhelming Tsukiji Market or Kyoto's Nishiki Market, which is routinely crammed with tourists. It's a good place to gawk at the freshest catches and perhaps have lunch at one of the many eateries on-site if your appetite is stirred. Its central location makes it a worthwhile stop on your way to other attractions around town.

Kanazawa-jō Kōen
金沢城公園

1-1 Marunouchi; tel. 076/234-3800; www.pref.ishikawa.jp/siro-niwa/kanazawajou/e; castle 9am-4:30pm daily year-round, park grounds 5am-6pm daily Mar.-mid-Oct., 6am-4:30pm daily mid-Oct.-Feb.; grounds free, buildings ¥310 adults, ¥100 children; take the Kanazawa Loop Bus to bus stop LL9 or RL8 (20 minutes, ¥200 one way), or take the Kenroku-en Shuttle Bus to bus stop S8 (20 minutes, ¥200 one-way; ¥100 weekends and holidays)

To understand Kanazawa's vast historical wealth, a trip to Kanazawa-jō Kōen is in order. This park encircles what remains of the resplendent white castle that was once the base of the mighty Maeda Clan. From 1583 until the end of the Edo period, this powerful family ruled the fiefdom of Kaga, the second largest and richest of all domains during the long period of Tokugawa rule. Ravaged by fire over the centuries, most recently in 1881, the only original structures left standing are two storehouses and the **Ishikawa-mon** gate, which faces the northern edge of Kenroku-en. The main keep was incinerated in 1602 and never reconstructed.

That said, a drawn-out process of rebuilding the various structures of the fortress is underway. So far a pair of reconstructed turrets connected by a narrow storehouse (which can be entered for a small fee), the **Kahoku-mon** gate, and the **Hashizume-mon** gate have been completed. If approaching from Omi-chō Market, the **Kuro-mon** gate at the northwest corner of the castle grounds is the closest entrance. If you're coming from Kenroku-en, enter via the Ishikawa-mon gate. A visit just before closing, at dusk, is particularly atmospheric, as the white castle is lit from below, while a slightly unnerving number of crows swarm overhead, cawing and congregating along the roof.

TOP EXPERIENCE

★ Kenroku-en
兼六園

1-1 Marunouchi; tel. 076/234-3800; www.pref.ishikawa.jp/siro-niwa/kenrokuen/e; 7am-6pm daily Mar.-mid-Oct., 8am-5pm daily mid-Oct.-Feb.; ¥310 adults, ¥100 children; take the Kanazawa Loop Bus to bus stop LL9 or RL8 (20 minutes, ¥200 one-way), or take the Kenroku-en Shuttle Bus to bus stop S8 (20 minutes, ¥200 one-way; ¥100 weekends and holidays)

Kenroku-en, a meticulously shaped patch of green, easily claims its place among Japan's three most beautiful landscape gardens, along with Okayama's Kōraku-en and Kairaku-en in Mito, Ibaraki Prefecture. The expansive grounds are dotted with ponds, streams, an artificial waterfall, fountains, flowers, various trees, teahouses, stone lanterns, winding paths up and over hills, and lovely views of the city below.

Originally the exterior garden of Kanazawa-jō, the castle where the powerful Maeda clan once resided, the garden has been open to the public since 1871. Unlike most landscape gardens, which often feel like nature in bite-sized miniature, these extensive grounds take a bit of time to explore properly. Hidden nooks abound throughout the

1: Kenroku-en **2:** Nagamachi **3:** Kanazawa-jō Kōen

sprawling open terrain. The ponds, waterfalls, and streams are fed by a complex system built in 1632 that deftly redirects water from a far-away river. Ancient trees, weather-beaten stones, and moss-encrusted lanterns are ubiquitous throughout the grounds.

Seasonality is another key element of Kenroku-en's beauty. Winter—not usually a time you'd associate with viewing a garden—presents a starkly beautiful scene, as a thick blanket of snow covers the long limbs of trees and stone lanterns that dot the garden. As winter comes to an end, mid-February brings plum blossoms, which remain on the trees until end of March, after which the garden's numerous cherry trees pop with pink petals around mid-April. Summer is primarily a time of deep green, while autumn colors bring a pleasing mix of earthy and fiery tones when the garden's abundant maple foliage starts to turn. No matter the season, it's enjoyable to slow down and enjoy a tea and sweet at one of the garden's teahouses.

21st-Century Museum of Contemporary Art, Kanazawa
金沢21世紀美術館

1-2-1 Hirosaka; tel. 076/220-2800; www.kanazawa21.jp; 10am-6pm Tues.-Thurs. and Sun., 10am-8pm Fri.-Sat.; price varies by exhibition; take the city bus from Kanazawa Station to Hirosaka bus stop (10 minutes, ¥200) or the Kanazawa Loop Bus to bus stop RL9 or LL8 (20 minutes, ¥200)

Kanazawa's attractions aren't limited to the feudal era. Just south of Kanazawa-jō Kōen, the 21st-Century Museum of Contemporary Art, Kanazawa shows modern art from Japan and abroad, and the massive circular building that houses the exhibitions is a work of art itself. The slightly baffling lack of a clear entrance or exit is part of the fun: Various doors exist around the round structure—take your pick. There are usually a few paid exhibitions to choose from, as well as a few free permanent installations; the most popular by far is the social media-friendly *Swimming Pool* by Argentine artist Leandro Erlich. Looking down into this "pool" from above is free. To go "underwater" to look up and see the blurry outlines of people standing above the distorted glass display overhead, you'll need to pay a fee. Check out the exhibition schedule to see what catches your interest.

Nagamachi
長町

Ambling through the narrow cobblestone lanes of Nagamachi, bear in mind that this was once the domain of Kanazawa's burgeoning samurai class. In feudal times, the elite warriors convened behind the numerous private gates, plotting, carousing, and meditating. Today, as you weave through these pedestrian-only streets framed by classically low rooflines and twisting pine boughs reaching overhead, you can pass through a few of the private entrances to see what lies behind the fortified earthen walls. This would have been unthinkable to commoners in the Edo period (1603-1868) when samurai influence was at its peak. You'll note two canals, or moats, enclosing the neighborhood. One of these waterways, which supplied water to the castle, was built as early as the late 16th century.

The streets themselves ooze ambience, but to get a glimpse of life behind the scenes, head to the **Nomura House** (武家屋敷跡野村家; 1-3-32 Nagamachi; tel. 076/221-3553; www.nomurake.com; 8:30am-5pm daily Apr.-Sept., 8:30am-4:30pm daily Oct.-Mar.; ¥550 adults, ¥400 high school students, ¥250 junior high and elementary school students; from Kanazawa Station take any city bus from bus stop 7-11 to Korinbo bus stop (10 minutes, ¥200), or from Omi-chō Market walk 15 minutes southwest, or walk 20 minutes west of Kanazawa-jō Kōen), once home to a prominent samurai family. This renovated home boasts a lovely garden with a pond stocked with fat, colorful koi.

To reach this area, take the city bus from JR Kanazawa Station (Kenroku-en Exit) to Korinbō bus stop (10 minutes; ¥200), then walk about five minutes south.

Japan's Most Beautiful Gardens

Gazing onto a spare kare-sansui (dry landscape) garden at a Zen temple—raked gravel, enigmatically placed shards of misshapen rock caked in tufts of moss—or while seated before the watery, lush realm of a landscape garden, centered on a pond surrounded by shrubs, trees, stone lanterns, and sacred statuary, often dotting a hill rising beyond, you'll likely feel a transcendent calm take hold. Wandering through a stroll garden, a similar experience occurs as you slowly cross arched bridges over streams of colorful koi (carp), meander along winding paths, and stop at a pavilion to rest and reflect.

Shukkei-en

There's a common underlying theme shared by Japanese gardens of all types: They are meticulously formed, down to the smallest detail, with nothing left to chance. The experience of viewing, or meandering through, a great Japanese garden offers a potent glimpse into the deep intentionality of the culture, its spiritual worldview, its love of nature, and its view of humanity's relationship to it. Japanese gardens invite us to contemplate, slow down—an experience that should not be missed on any trip to Japan.

The list of great Japanese gardens is long, with Kenroku-en safely ensconced among the best. Here are a few others to seek out.

- **Kōraku-en:** Located in Okayama, Kōraku-en is another of the top gardens in all of Japan, an expansive green space laced with walking paths and streams all wrapped around a central pond (page 429).
- **Hama-rikyū Onshi-teien:** In Tokyo, centrally located Hama-rikyū Onshi-teien is a striking contrast to the skyscrapers surrounding it (page 57).
- **Shinjuku Gyōen:** Perhaps the capital's most famous garden, Shinjuku Gyōen has a few different types of green spaces within (page 76).
- **Ōkōchi Sansō:** In Kyoto, my top pick is this tranquil garden just beyond Arashiyama's bamboo grove (page 311).
- **Isui-en:** Tōdai-ji temple looms in the background of this garden in Nara (page 373).
- **Shukkei-en:** Shrunken valleys, mountains, and forest are represented by the careful landscaping in this garden in Hiroshima (page 409).
- **Ritsurin-kōen:** Wandering Takamatsu's rambling Ritsurin-kōen feels akin to navigating a coniferous maze (page 459).
- **Sengan-en:** This subtropical garden in Kagoshima takes the concept of borrowed scenery to another level, with the smoldering volcano Sakurajima looming on the horizon across a bay (page 662).

Teramachi
寺町

Teramachi (literally: Temple Town) is a neighborhood brimming with temples in the south of town, across the Sai-gawa, about 15 minutes by bus from Kanazawa Station. What little historical ambience is left in the area is a bit underwhelming, except for Myōryū-ji (Oddly Built Temple, aka Ninja-dera, or Ninja Temple). If you're on the southern side of town and feel like a stroll, you can make the trip on foot from the Katamachi area (10 minutes), Kōrinbō (15 minutes), or even Kenroku-en (25 minutes).

MYŌRYŪ-JI (NINJA-DERA)
妙立寺

1-2-12 Nomachi; tel. 076/241-0888; www.myouryuji.or.jp; 9am-4pm Mon.-Fri., 9am-4:30pm Sat.-Sun. and holidays; ¥1,000 adults, ¥700 children; take the left loop of the Kanazawa Loop Bus to Hirokoji bus stop (LL5), then walk 4 minutes south

Like most structures of historical import in Kanazawa, Ninja-dera was built by the Maeda Clan. Although it looks like a temple, it doubled as a secret outpost where agents could hide and escape to warn Kanazawa-jō of approaching invaders.

Some of the temple's ingenious devices include tunnels said to be linked to underground passages that lead all the way to Kanazawa-jō, hidden chambers, booby traps, and confusingly arrayed sets of stairs and passageways meant to throw off would-be intruders. This clever defensive approach was developed in response to the Tokugawa Shogunate's stringent building codes, meant to prevent regional fiefdoms from gaining the military upper hand. Among the regulations was the stipulation that a temple could be no taller than three stories. Once you pass through the main chamber of Ninja-dera, however, you'll discover that the structure is in fact four stories. If you count hidden subterranean levels, this number jumps to seven. The seppuku room is a self-locking chamber specifically designed to give a lord a secret place to commit ritual suicide rather than face capture, before setting the entire temple ablaze with a flame kept burning in the room.

A helpful English-language pamphlet also does a good job of introducing the singular temple.

★ Higashi Chaya-gai
東茶屋街

Located northeast of Kanazawa-jō and Kenroku-en, across the Asano-gawa, you'll

Higashi Chaya-gai

find Higashi Chaya-gai, an atmospheric district built in 1820 that's still the haunt of the occasional geisha. Wooden teahouse exteriors are fronted by wooden lattices, and old gaslight lamps line the pedestrianized streets. A weeping cherry tree presides over a busy point where geisha once met with clients and today young couples wearing yukata stroll with ice-cream cones. Amble the streets and follow your curiosity where it leads. The main thoroughfare runs east to west for about 150 meters (490 ft), then splits off into cobblestone alleys to the north and south.

As you stroll, keep your eyes open for two former geisha houses now open to the public, **Shima** and **Kaikarō.** While most of the neighborhood's distinctive two-story shopfronts now house modern shops, restaurants, and cafés serving treats sprinkled with locally made gold-leaf flakes, these two teahouses remain untouched. The neighborhood's other nooks and crannies are especially alluring after dusk when the shopfronts are gently lit by paper lanterns, evoking the district's prime two centuries ago.

To reach the district, take Kanazawa Loop Bus (Right Loop) from JR Kanazawa Station (10 minutes; ¥200) to RL4 bus stop, near the western edge of the area.

SHIMA

志摩

1-13-21 Higashiyama; tel. 076/252-5675; www.ochaya-shima.com; 9am-6pm daily; ¥500 adults, ¥300 children age 16 and under

If you feel the urge to see where the geisha working in the district's numerous teahouses once lived, visit the two-story former geisha residence known as Shima. This building, constructed in 1820 and officially designated an Important Cultural Property by the Japanese government, is strewn with implements of the geisha trade, including an array of impeccably lacquered and bejeweled combs. It's worth going in for a peak into a genuine geisha's residence if this side of the culture intrigues you.

ENTERTAINMENT AND EVENTS

Performing Arts

ISHIKAWA PREFECTURAL NOH THEATER

4-18-3 Ishibiki; tel. 076/264-2598; https://noh-theater.jp; 9am-5pm (last entry 4:30pm) Tues.-Sun.; price varies by performance; take the Hokuriku Railroad bus from bus stop no. 7 at Kanazawa Station Kenrokuen (East) Gate to Dewamachi bus stop

Kanazawa is among the best places in Japan to see the beautifully arcane spectacle of Noh drama. This theater, constructed of cypress and topped with a roof resembling a Shinto shrine, hosts hour-long performances with breaks for kyogen (comedic intermissions) on Saturday evenings during summer. There are day-long performances once monthly throughout the rest of the year. Inquire far in advance of your trip with the city's tourist information center for more details and to find out your chances of catching one of the sporadic performances. Even if you're not keen to see a performance, you can pop in to admire the stage as long as there are no rehearsals taking place that day. It's a 3-minute walk from the Dewamachi bus stop, about 3 minutes' walk from Kenroku-en's Zuishinzakaguchi entrance, or about 15 minutes on foot from the Kōrinbō area.

KAIKARŌ

1-14-8 Higashiyama; tel. 076/253-0591; www.kaikaro.jp; 10am-5pm daily to tour residence; ¥750 adults, ¥500 high school students and younger to tour residence; take Kanazawa Loop Bus (Right Loop) from JR Kanazawa Station (10 minutes; ¥200) to RL4 bus stop

Here you can experience full geisha entertainment with a kaiseki (multicourse meal) in Higashi Chaya-gai. The price is on a sliding scale, depending on the number of diners, but for a group of 10, the cost is ¥28,000 per person, excluding drinks, for the company of three geisha and a full-course spread. Check the website and inquire by phone for details.

Festivals

KAGATOBI DEZOMESHIKI
加賀鳶出初式

Kanazawa Castle, 1-1 Marunouchi; tel. 076/234-3800; https://experience-kanazawa.com/events/dezomeshiki.html; Jan. 6; free

With the nation's traditional architecture being built almost entirely of wood, the role of the firefighter looms large in Japan's history. In the dead of winter every year, scantily clothed firefighters perform acrobatic feats linked to ancient firefighting maneuvers, precariously perched on bamboo ladders in front of Kanazawa Castle.

HYAKUMANGOKU MATSURI
百万石祭

http://100mangoku.net; early June; free

The city's biggest festival, spanning three days in early June each year, commemorates Kanazawa's founding by Lord Maeda Toshiie on June 14, 1583. A procession of locals in 16th-century attire marches through the streets, a special tea ceremony is held in a variety of styles, Noh is performed in the ethereal glow of torch light, 1,500 floating lanterns drift down the lazy Asano-gawa, and thousands of youngsters advance through the streets bearing red lanterns and beating taiko drums. The main event of the festival, the Hyakumangoku parade, takes place on the first Saturday of June, and the other events are held on the day prior and the day after.

SHOPPING

Kanazawa's shopping options are geared toward traditional arts and crafts. The highest density of sprawling department stores is found in the Kōrinbō and Katamachi neighborhoods, particularly along the bustling **Hyakumangoku-dōri** thoroughfare that runs north-south to the west of Kanazawa-jō Koen. For a discerning selection of artfully made local items—including gold leaf, intricately painted Kutani pottery, and roughly hewn ceramics—head to the **Hirosaka** shopping street, which runs east-west, between Kōrinbō and Kenroku-en, along the southern edge of Kanazawa-jō Koen. If you're after something hip or offbeat, try some of the boutiques along the **Tatemachi** shopping street, a short walk southwest of the 21st Century Museum of Contemporary Art.

Around Kenroku-en

KANAZAWA CRAFT HIROSAKA

1-2-25 Hirosaka; tel. 076/265-3320; www.crafts-hirosaka.jp; 10am-6pm Tues.-Sun., closed Tues. if Mon. is a holiday; take city bus from Kanazawa Station to Hirosaka bus stop (10 minutes; ¥200) or the Kanazawa Loop Bus to bus stop RL9 or LL8 (20 minutes; ¥200)

This elegant shop sells a plethora of refined regional arts and crafts under one roof. This is a great place to find a striking conversation piece to take home with you. It's located next to the north side of the 21st Century Museum of Contemporary Art.

ISHIKAWA BUSSANKAN

2-20 Kenrokumachi; tel. 076/222-7788; https://kanazawa-kankou.jp; 9:30am-5:50pm Mon.-Fri. and 8:50am-5:50pm Sat.-Sun. and holidays Mar.-May, 8:50am-5:50pm daily Jun.-Oct., 9:50am-5:50pm Wed.-Mon. Dec.-Feb.; take city bus from Kanazawa Station to Kenrokuen-shita/Kanazawa-jō bus stop (20 minutes; ¥200)

This four-story shop sells reasonably priced traditional arts, crafts, and snacks in a laid-back setting. On the basement level, there are displays on taiko drums and sweets production. Workshops held on the third floor teach guests about crafts from making drums and confections to applying gold leaf and glass etching.

Nagamachi

MURAKAMI WAGASHI

2-3-32 Nagamachi; tel. 076/264-4223; www.wagashi-murakami.com; 9:15am-5pm daily; around the corner from the Nomura House in the heart of the Nagamachi samurai district

This historic shop is the best place in town to find colorful, exquisitely packaged wagashi (traditional Japanese sweets), made in the shapes of flowers, fish, rabbits, and

Noto Peninsula Road Trip

North of Kanazawa, the Noto Peninsula (能登半島) protrudes some 100 kilometers (62 mi) into the Sea of Japan. The dramatic coastline is dotted by fishing hamlets, craggy cliffs, quiet beaches, and rustic shrines and temples. It makes for a very appealing day trip from Kanazawa. The climax is the dramatic Shiroyone Senmaida Rice Terraces; if you return from here, the total drive takes about 5.5 hours (260 km/161 mi). If you go all the way to the northern tip of the peninsula, the journey takes around 7 hours (300 km/186 mi).

To properly explore this rugged stretch of oceanfront, rent a car in Kanazawa—an English GPS system is a lifesaver—then head north.

Shiroyone Senmaida Rice Terraces

- Begin by driving up the Noto-Satoyama Kaidō (Expressway) along the west coast of Noto, passing along the **Chirihama Nagisa Driveway,** an 8-kilometer (5-mi) stretch of sand about 40 kilometers (65 mi) north of Kanazawa that's a beach-party zone in summer.

- Continue north along the Noto-Satoyama Expressway until it meets route 249. **Myōjō-ji** (Yo-1 Takidanimachi, Hakui-shi; tel. 0767/27-1226; http://myojoji-noto.jp; 8am-5pm daily Apr.-Oct., 8am-4:30pm daily Nov.-Mar.; ¥500 adults, ¥300 junior high and elementary students), a 1.2-kilometer (0.7-mi) detour off of 249, is an important temple of the Nichiren Buddhist sect, constructed in 1294. The temple's most prominent building is the five-story pagoda, which can be seen from a distance.

- Continue north along the stretch of coastline between Fukūrako and Sekinohana. This spectacular shoreline is known as the **Kongō Coast.** Soak up the vista of the gnarled rock formations along this jagged section of beach. For this stretch of the drive, use routes 36 and 49; it will take an extra 10 minutes, but it hugs the coast and offers a more scenic ride than 249.

- From Sekinohana, merge back onto 249 and continue north 14.3 kilometers (8.9 mi) to **Sōji-ji Soin** (1-18 Monzen, Monzen-machi, Wajima-shi; tel. 0768/42-0005; https://noto-soin.jp; ¥400), an atmospheric Zen temple with a history stretching back to 1321. The temple accepts staying guests who can participate in monks' regimented daily activities such as zazen (seated meditation), morning prayers, and feasting on shōjin-ryōri (Buddhist vegetarian cuisine). A night with two meals costs ¥6,500 per person. You can join a guided zazen session (¥1,000, including temple admission) or eat a monk's meal without staying overnight (¥2,500-3,500).

- Continue along route 249 until reaching the **Shiroyone Senmaida Rice Terraces** (99-5 Shiroyone-machi, Wajima-shi; tel. 0768/23-1146; http://senmaida.wajima-kankou.jp; 24 hours daily; free). Some 2,000 highly photogenic, terraced rice fields lead like vast steps down to the Sea of Japan.

After coming this far you may want to ease more into Noto-time at ★ **Flatt's** (27-26-3 Yanami, Noto-chō; tel. 0768/62-1900, http://flatt.jp, ¥16,500 pp for a room with two meals), a wonderful bed-and-breakfast located near route 249 on the eastern side of the peninsula, a 62.6-kilometer (38.9-mi) drive from the Shiroyone Senmaida Rice Terraces. The B&B is run by an Australian chef and his Japanese wife. Aside from cozy rooms with oceanside views, the food is stellar: Japanese for breakfast, Italian with a twist for dinner. All meals for non-staying guests must be booked at least one day in advance. Accommodations must be booked by phone.

more. Made with ingredients like mochi (rice cake), azuki (red-bean paste), and sesame, the confections here, many packaged to take home, are much more subtle than most Western sweets, best paired with a cup of green tea.

Higashi Chaya-gai

SAKUDA GOLD LEAF COMPANY

1-3-27 Higashiyama; tel. 076/251-6777; https://goldleaf-sakuda.jp; 8:30am-6pm daily; take Kanazawa Loop Bus (Right Loop) from JR Kanazawa Station (10 minutes; ¥200) to RL4 bus stop

Come to this fun shop for anything gilded: chopsticks, folding fans, owl figurines, gold-flecked tea sets, and more. And if you're a golfer, you can even get gold-leaf-coated golf balls. It's a short walk north of the main entrance to the Higashi Chaya-gai district.

FOOD

Around Omi-chō Market

IKI-IKI-TEI

Omicho Ichiba-kan 1F, 88 Aokusa-machi; tel. 076/222-2621; 7:00am-5:00pm (until all food is sold) Fri.-Wed.; from ¥1,000; on a corner near the market entrance closest to Kanazawa Station

This little joint in Omi-chō Market is routinely elbow-to-elbow with diners eating fish sourced from stalls nearby. They serve great set meals and donburi (rice bowls) of both sushi and sashimi. If you're visiting in the morning, try to arrive as soon as the shop opens for a sushi breakfast. Otherwise, be prepared to queue or place an order and wander the market while you wait.

CURIO ESPRESSO AND VINTAGE DESIGN CAFÉ

1-13 Yasuecho; tel. 076/231-5543; www.facebook.com/CurioEspresso; 8am-5pm Mon. and Wed.-Fri., 9am-5pm Sat., 9am-3pm Sun.; ¥1,000-2,000; 5-minute walk north of Omi-chō Market

Discerning coffee drinkers, head to this stylish café for a caffeine hit. The menu includes an extensive range of brews, from espressos to flat-whites, alongside a good range of sandwiches that make for a good light breakfast or lunch. The amiable staff is happy to make local recommendations too.

FUWARI

2-6-57 Owari-chō; tel. 076/207-3417; www.facebook.com/fuwari.ip; 5pm-11pm Tues., Thurs., and Sun., 5pm-1am Fri.-Sat.; ¥4,000 average; 3-minute walk northeast of Omi-chō Market

This stylish restaurant, housed in an atmospheric wooden building, is another great spot to sample local seafood, from grilled to raw. Also on the menu (English version available) are beef, tempura, yakitori, and vegetable medleys. The experience is highly visual, with dishes beautifully presented on artfully made tableware. The service is friendly and attentive, and the drinks menu is extensive. Highly recommended. Reserve a day or more in advance.

Higashi Chaya-gai

JIYŪKEN

1-6-6 Higashiyama; tel. 076/252-1996; www.jiyuken.com; lunch 11:30am-3pm Wed.-Mon., dinner 5pm-9pm Mon.-Fri. and 4:30pm-9pm Sat.-Sun. and holidays, closed 3rd Mon. of month; ¥720-1,855; take Kanazawa Loop Bus (Right Loop) from JR Kanazawa Station (10 minutes; ¥200) to RL4 bus stop

Near the entrance to the Higashi Chaya-gai district, and set amid dessert shops and teahouses, this faintly nostalgic diner serves classics from Japan's yoshoku repertoire. This style of cooking was born when Western influence flooded into Japan during the Meiji period (1868-1912). Dishes include "hamburg" (beef patty), omuraisu (omelet stuffed with ketchup-infused rice), and all manner of vegetables, meat, and seafood breaded and fried, from tonkatsu to korokke (croquette). It fills up at lunchtime, so you may have to wait for a bit. There's an English menu, and some of the staff speak English.

Around Kenroku-en

MIYOSHIAN

1-11 Kenroku-machi; tel. 076/221-0127; http://miyoshian.net; 9:30am-4:30pm Thurs.-Tues., closed irregularly; tea sets ¥700, bento set lunches

¥1,500-3,000; 4-minute walk south of the entrance at the north of the garden

An atmospheric spot in Kenroku-en for a potent cup of matcha (green tea) and a sweet, or for a bento box lunch of local dishes. It sits beside a serene backdrop of a waterfall and pond. Tatami-floor seating only.

SRI LANKA KITCHEN

3-6 Kakinokibatake; tel. 076/223-6255; https://srilankacurrykanazawa.wordpress.com; 11:30am-2:30pm and 6pm-10pm daily; lunch ¥780-1,480, dinner ¥2,000-3,000, a la carte from ¥300; 5-minute walk west of the 21st-Century Museum of Contemporary Art, on same street as Itaru Honten

This Sri Lankan joint is a great place for a break from Japanese cuisine. It serves excellent vegetarian and meat-based curries, and a broad menu extending to vegan fare. For a great lunch, try the set served on a banana leaf (¥1,280). In the evening, try one of the bang-up dinner courses. The menu is in Japanese, but the friendly staff speak English.

ITARU HONTEN

3-8 Kakinokibatake; tel. 076/221-4194; www.itaru.ne.jp; 5:30pm-11:30pm Mon.-Sat.; plates from ¥300, courses ¥3,000-6,000; 5-minute walk west of the 21st Century Museum of Contemporary Art

For a boisterous izakaya (pub) experience, this popular local spot fits the bill. Patrons sit along an L-shaped counter facing the open kitchen where the chefs chop, mix, sear, and season a creative selection of dishes. Food is heavily weighted toward seafood, from sushi and sashimi platters to fish served in stews or basted and grilled. There are also non-seafood items on the menu, as well as an extensive sake list. Reserve a day or more ahead if you can.

Nagamachi

THE GODBURGER

2-12-10 Korinbo; tel. 076/205-2925; www.instagram.com/the_godburger/; noon-4pm and 6pm-10pm Thurs.-Tues.; ¥1,000-2,000; take the city bus from JR Kanazawa Station (Kenroku-en Exit) to Korinbō bus stop (10 minutes; ¥200)

This trendy modern burger shop, run by friendly staff, sits beside a stream just east of Nagamachi's samurai residences. There's a good range of toppings—chili beans, avocado, bacon, fried egg—as well as a veggie burger option. This is a good place for a delicious, casual meal on the go between Kenroku-en and Nagamachi or Kanazawa Castle, or if you just feel like a burger and fries.

★ OTOME SUSHI

4-10 Kigura-machi; tel. 076/231-7447; lunch noon-2pm daily, dinner seatings at 5pm and 7pm Mon.-Tues. and Thurs.-Sat.; lunch from ¥10,000, dinner from ¥18,000 (sushi); shop is tucked down a side street and lacks English signage, so arrival by taxi is recommended

If you're keen to splurge on sushi, you won't go wrong at this high-end specialist near the Nagamachi samurai quarter. With access to exceptional fish and a meticulous master who grew up around the docks, this sushi joint ticks all the boxes. Relax into its wooden interior—counter seats and a private room are available—and get acquainted with the region's oceanic bounty. The deep sake selection features labels from within the region. There's no English menu, but the staff speak limited English and do their best to guide you through the meal. The bill will reflect the quality, so budget accordingly. Reserve a few weeks or more in advance either by phone or via the reservation website Table All (www.tableall.com/restaurant/89).

ACCOMMODATIONS

Under ¥10,000

HOTEL PACIFIC KANAZAWA

46 Jikkenmachi; tel. 076/264-3201; www.hotel-pacific.jp; ¥5,000 s, ¥8,000 d; 3-minute walk southeast of Omi-chō Market

Set in a prime location, this clean, current hotel has a chic little café on the first floor, amiable bilingual staff, and 31 trim, well-appointed rooms (both tatami and Western) with tiny en suite showers. Bicycles can be rented for an additional charge.

HOTEL MYSTAYS PREMIER KANAZAWA

2-13-5 Hirooka; tel. 076/290-5255; www.mystays.com/en/hotel/kanazawa/mystays-premier-kanazawa; ¥8,000 d; on the western side of JR Kanazawa Station, 5-minute walk

This smart, modern hotel has sprawling rooms by Japanese budget-hotel standards, each with a desk, seating area, and a bit of floor space left over. Amenities include a fitness room, a nicely balanced breakfast buffet, and a café beside the entrance. The English-speaking staff are warm and happy to help. Pound for pound, this is one of the city's best values.

¥10,000-20,000

SUMIYOSHIYA

54 Jikken-machi; tel. 076/221-0157; https://sumiyoshiya-ryokan.com; ¥12,400 d without meals, ¥14,400 d with breakfast, ¥22,000 d with two meals; 18-minute walk southeast of Kanazawa Station, or take city bus to Musashigatsuji bus stop and walk 5 minutes southeast

Pristine tatami rooms, warm English-speaking staff, and reasonable rates make this mid-range ryokan just north of Kanazawa Castle Park and east of Omi-chō Market a great place to stay without breaking the bank. The hotel serves both Japanese and Western breakfasts, and exquisite Japanese dinner spreads. Some rooms have private baths and toilets, while others have private toilets but share a bath. There are also free bicycle rentals.

THE SHARE HOTELS KUMU KANAZAWA

2-40 Kamitsutsumi-chō; tel. 076/282-9600; www.thesharehotels.com/kumu; from ¥15,400 d; 10-minute walk east of the Nagamachi samurai quarter on Route 157

This fresh, modern hotel has a café on the first floor and a chic, artsy interior. Rooms include both dorms and spacious private rooms, many with tatami platform lounge areas with floor cushions for seats. The optional breakfast buffet includes good Western-style basics (eggs, sausage, baked goods). There's a rooftop balcony with good views of the surrounding area and bicycles for rent for staying guests. This hotel has a slightly grown-up vibe, so you may want to stay somewhere else if you're traveling with kids.

Over ¥40,000

★ ASADAYA

23 Jikken-machi; tel. 076/231-2228; www.asadaya.co.jp; single ¥65,000 pp, doubles ¥46,000 pp; 3-minute walk southeast of Omi-chō Market

In business for more than 140 years, this is Kanazawa's top ryokan. It offers only four guest rooms, and you can rest assured that Japan's legendary spirit of omotenashi (service as an art form) is alive and well here. With antique screens depicting mystical landscapes, flower arrangements tucked into alcoves, and tatami floors throughout, the ambience is akin to the set of a samurai movie. Three of the rooms have en suite baths. The other one gets first dibs on the shared family bathing facilities. The immaculate kaiseki meals are presented on gorgeous tableware and made with locally sourced, seasonal ingredients. If you've got the cash to splurge, this is the best place in town to do so. Book as far in advance as possible to get one of the few rooms.

INFORMATION AND SERVICES

For an up-to-date rundown on things to see and do, and places to eat and drink, be sure to pick up a copy of the English tourist zine ***Eye on Kanazawa*** (http://eyeon.jp). The free paper, accompanied by a good website, is carried at the Tourist Information Center in Kanazawa Station and other pickup points around town.

- **Tourist Information Center** (Kanazawa Station; tel. 076/232-6200; www.kanazawa-tourism.com; 8:30am-8pm daily)
- **Ishikawa Foundation for International Exchange** (1-5-3 Honmachi; tel. 076/262-5931; www.ifie.or.jp; 8:30am-8pm Mon.-Fri., 8:30am-5pm Sat.-Sun.; 6 minutes' walk southeast of Kanazawa Station)

GETTING THERE

Train

In 2015, the grand, expansive new **Kanazawa Station** opened on the western side of town to serve the then newly launched Hokuriku shinkansen line. This train line has shortened the trip from **Tokyo** (2.5 hours; ¥14,320) by a full hour, making Kanazawa easier to reach than ever before. Coming from **Nagoya,** Shirasagi limited express trains zip to Kanazawa (3 hours; ¥7,530), while Thunderbird limited express trains run between Kanazawa and **Shin-Osaka Station** (2 hours 40 minutes; ¥7,850), passing **Kyoto** en route (2 hours 15 minutes; ¥7,100).

Air

Komatsu Airport (tel. 076/121-9803; www.komatsuairport.jp), located about 30 kilometers (18.6 mi) southwest of Kanazawa, services flights from around Japan and a few other Asian hubs, including **Seoul** and **Shanghai.** Hourly buses run between the airport and **Kanazawa Station** (www.hokutetsu.co.jp; 50 minutes; ¥1,130), stopping in the Katamachi area in the heart of Kanazawa on the way.

Bus

JR Highway Bus (www.kousokubus.net/JpnBus/en) operates routes between Kanazawa and **Tokyo, Osaka,** and **Kyoto,** among other cities. It's possible to travel to and from Nagoya by highway bus through **Hokutetsu Kankō** (tel. 076/237-5115; www.hokutetsu.co.jp). The same operator, along with **Nōhi Bus** (www.nouhibus.co.jp), also services **Takayama,** via Gokayama and Shirakawa-gō. See the relevant websites for detailed routes, timetables, and fares. Highway buses arrive and depart from the bus terminal outside JR Kanazawa Station's east exit.

Car

There are numerous car rental agencies around Kanazawa Station. A good bet is **Toyota Rent-A-Car** (2-15-1 Honmachi; tel. 076/223-0100; https://rent.toyota.co.jp), located about 4 minutes' walk southeast of Kanazawa Station, next to Hotel Nikko Kanazawa. If you plan to venture into the countryside around Kanazawa—to the Noto Peninsula, for example—a car will be necessary.

GETTING AROUND

Compact Kanazawa is a great **walking** city. Most of the sights are concentrated around the central districts of Katamachi and Kōrinbō—both within about 15 minutes' walk of Kanazawa Station—or a bit farther north in the Higashi Chaya-gai district. There is a city-run bicycle rental system known as **Machi-nori** (www.machi-nori.jp), but it's unfortunately a bit of a headache to figure out, and the bicycles are best suited to those with smaller frames.

Bus

Buses leave from the **terminal** next to the station's east exit. Any bus leaving from bus stop nos. 7, 8, or 9 will get you downtown (¥200), and from there it's easy to get around on foot. The **Kanazawa Loop Bus** (www.hokutetsu.co.jp/en/en_round; 8:30am-6pm daily; ¥500 adults, ¥250 children) does a circuit around the city, starting from **Kanazawa Station.** One route moves clockwise, the other counter-clockwise. It passes through the Nagamachi samurai district in the west, veers south to the Ninja Temple, and makes various stops in the area surrounding Kenroku-en in the heart of town and the teahouse district of Higashi Chaya-gai in the north.

Kyoto 京都

Itinerary Ideas 285
Sights 289
Entertainment and Events 313
Sports and Recreation 315
Shopping 317
Food 320
Bars and Nightlife 329
Accommodations 332
Information and Services 336
Transportation 337

The ancient Japanese capital hardly needs an introduction. It provides the source material for the vision many hold of Japan: geisha, tea ceremony, and more than 1,400 temples and shrines. With more than 12 centuries of heritage, Kyoto is inarguably one of the world's most culturally rich cities. In many ways, it is traditional Japan boiled down to its essence, where its history, spiritual life, aesthetics, ambience, and culinary genius coalesce. But there's plenty of modernity and industriousness here, too. It's the ideal complement to Tokyo for any first-time trip to the country.

Kyoto was Japan's capital for almost a millennium. Besides the Kamakura period (1185-1333), when the temporary feudal government moved its political base to Kamakura, the emperor ruled from

Highlights

Look for ★ to find recommended sights, activities, dining, and lodging.

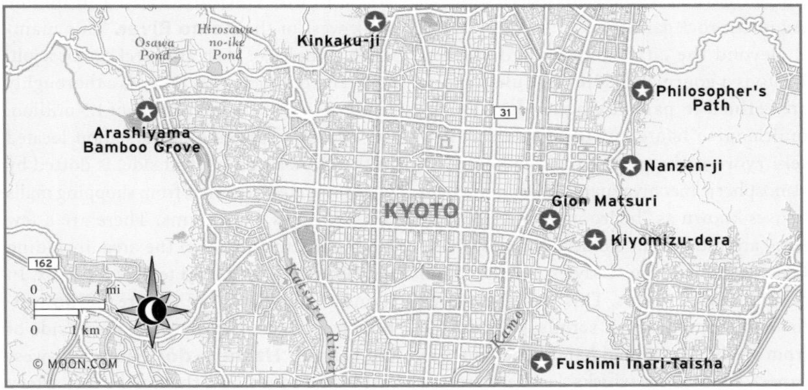

★ **Fushimi Inari-Taisha:** At Kyoto's must-see Shinto shrine, the main complex is merely the prelude to a long mountain trail lined with 10,000 vivid torii gates (page 290).

★ **Kiyomizu-dera:** This temple sits imposingly atop a hill in the Southern Higashiyama district, affording sweeping views (page 295).

★ **Nanzen-ji:** One of Kyoto's grandest temples, it's surrounded by gardens, an aqueduct, and a hilly trail that leads to a sacred grotto (page 299).

★ **Philosopher's Path:** Seek tranquility with a walk along this contemplative, flower-lined pedestrian path (page 301).

★ **Kinkaku-ji:** The upper two floors of this famed pavilion, once the retirement villa of a shogun and now a temple of the Rinzai sect of Zen Buddhism, are gold-plated—an homage to the extravagance of Kyoto's aristocratic past (page 307).

★ **Arashiyama Bamboo Grove:** This magical bamboo grove is the perfect place for an otherworldly stroll (page 311).

★ **Gion Matsuri:** One of Japan's biggest festivals commemorates a purification ritual aimed at appeasing the gods of fire, earthquakes, and floods (page 313).

Kyoto between 794 and 1868. The foundations of Japanese traditional culture and aesthetics, especially the austerity and restraint of Zen Buddhism, were laid by the aristocracy here in the Heian period (794-1185). Over its long history, Kyoto was struck by fires and wars, but was mercifully spared bombing raids during WWII due to its extraordinary historical and cultural value.

At its heart, Kyoto is a city of temples. "Kyoto and Zen go together like love and Paris," wrote scholar and scribe John Dougill in the insightful and beautifully photographed *Zen Gardens and Temples of Kyoto.* Monks practice zazen (seated meditation) in rooms adorned with brushstrokes of flowing calligraphy and paintings of misty landscapes and serpentine dragons. They eat elaborate vegetarian feasts (shōjin ryōri) and gaze at the simple lines and symbolically placed stones of enigmatic rock gardens.

Beyond the city's temples and shrines, Kyoto is a gourmand's dream. Culinary arts are refined to painstaking levels, with the multicourse haute cuisine known as kaiseki ryōri at the pinnacle, often served in atmospheric machiya (narrow wooden townhouses known as "bedrooms for eels") scattered around the city's oldest districts. Kyoto is also home to Japan's heaviest concentration of traditional artisans. This is the best place to shop for calligraphy scrolls, goods made from washi (traditional handmade Japanese paper), bamboo tea whisks, lacquerware, tea and sweets, textiles from kimono to yukata (lightweight summer kimono), and a variety of other accoutrements, from folding fans to the sorts of elegant hairpins worn by geisha.

ORIENTATION

Kyoto is laid out in a refreshingly simple grid pattern, and the main boulevards and some small side streets are often mercifully named, especially in the city center. This makes navigating the city easy. A series of main thoroughfares run east-west through the city, numbered from north to south in ascending order (e.g., Ichijō for "First Avenue," Sanjō for "Third Avenue," etc.). The streets running north-south through the city and intersecting these broad east-west avenues are likewise often named (e.g., Kawaramachi-dōri, Senbon-dōri, etc.). The **Kamo River** also runs north-south through the city and serves as a geographic marker, with the culturally and historically rich neighborhoods of **Gion** and **Higashiyama** east of the river and **downtown** and the rest of Kyoto to the west. Looming to the east of the whole city, abutting the Higashiyama district, is the Higashiyama mountain range.

Kyoto Station Area

Virtually all visitors to Kyoto will first arrive at **Kyoto Station,** located a 10-minute walk west of the **Kamo River.** This mammoth complex of glass and steel can be a jolt, a visceral reminder that Kyoto is a thoroughly modern city with a population of 1.5 million. The cityscape surrounding the station, located in the city's south-central side, is dotted by drab concrete structures, from shopping malls to electronics emporiums. There are a few more attractive sights in the area, including the **Higashi Hongan-ji** temple complex. In terms of major roads in the area, **Shiokoji-dōri** runs east-west along the north side of the station, **Hachijo-dōri** runs east-west just to the south, and the north-west artery of **Karasuma-dōri** runs north of the station all the way up into downtown and the central part of the city.

Southeast Kyoto

Moving beyond the Kyoto Station area, the city's history remains preserved in bronze, bamboo, and wood, tucked down atmospheric, dense lanes around the edges of town. Beginning in Southeast Kyoto, located roughly 30 minutes' walk southeast of

---

Previous: Arashiyama Bamboo Grove; stone fox at Fushimi Inari-Taisha; Gion Matsuri parade.

TOP EXPERIENCE

Kaiseki Ryōri

summertime kaiseki cuisine

Kaiseki ryōri is essentially Japanese fine dining, one of the world's most aesthetically sophisticated and beautiful cuisines, and Kyoto is the place to eat it. This rarefied style of cooking initially emerged as a complement to the tea ceremony, meant to be served before sipping the bitter green brew. Kaiseki embodies everything Japan does right in the kitchen, from selecting the very best, exquisitely fresh seasonal ingredients to artful presentation in elegant tablewear.

WHAT TO EXPECT

A typical kaiseki meal consists of five or more dishes, served in a very specific order, often beginning with an aperitif such as a small cup of nihonshū (rice wine) and a small appetizer, followed by soup, sashimi, and individual dishes that are, respectively, boiled, grilled, deep-fried, steamed, and served in a vinegar-based sauce. Finally, a light dessert, often fresh fruit or wagashi (Japanese sweets), which are themselves another Kyoto specialty. The preparation methods are simple: Rather than adding new layers of taste with seasoning or sauce, kaiseki chefs are masters of letting the natural flavors of the ingredients speak for themselves.

Beyond the food, a staunch emphasis on hospitality (omotenashi) and the aesthetic dimension of the meal—involving gorgeous ceramic tableware and careful placement of individual courses—elevate a kaiseki meal to a multisensory experience. Unsurprisingly, this doesn't come cheap: Expect to pay more than ¥20,000 for a full kaiseki meal. Note that reservations must be made at least a few weeks or a month ahead for any kaiseki meal.

WHERE TO TRY IT

- **Kikunoi Honten,** a stalwart in the heart of the Southern Higashiyama near Kōdai-ji and Maruyama-kōen (page 321).
- **Kappo Yamashita,** a laid-back restaurant with casual countertop seating in front of a kitchen run by gregarious chefs (page 324).
- **Shoraian,** an atmospheric restaurant that has a tofu-focused menu and is housed in a formerly private residence overlooking a river (page 328).

Best Accommodations

★ **Hotel Granvia:** This clean, modern hotel, literally in the Kyoto Station building, wins big points for convenience (page 332).

★ **Sowaka:** This chic property, brilliantly located in Gion, provides the traditional ryokan experience with a 21st-century sheen (page 333).

★ **Yoshida Sansō:** This discreet luxury ryokan, close to nature in a quiet part of Northern Higashiyama near Ginkaku-ji, remains slightly off the radar (page 334).

★ **The Millennials Kyoto:** This sleek capsule hotel, with a shared lounge and workspace, is a great choice for young travelers on the go (page 334).

★ **Ace Hotel Kyoto:** This decidedly un-Kyoto-like hotel features hip design, artisan coffee, Californian cooking, and colorful artwork, all in a gorgeous complex renovated and designed by "starchitect" Kengo Kuma (page 335).

★ **Ritz-Carlton Kyoto:** The Ritz offers a fantastic mix of luxury and convenience in the city center, with stellar amenities and a renowned kaiseki restaurant (page 336).

Kyoto Station, the major draw of this district is the spellbinding shrine complex of **Fushimi Inari-Taisha,** famed for its tunnel of vermillion torii gates that winds over a mountain trail. The splendid **Tōfuku-ji** temple complex is also located in the area, about 10 minutes' walk north of Fushimi Inari-Taisha.

To access this rich district, take the **JR Nara line** from Kyoto Station to **Tōfukuji Station** (for Tōfuku-ji) or **Inari Station** (for Fushimi Inari-Taisha). It's also possible to walk from Kyoto Station to Tōfuku-ji (25 minutes) or from Fushimi Inari-Taisha (40 minutes), or make either journey quicker by traveling on a bicycle.

Southern Higashiyama

To the north is the southern edge of the large district of Higashiyama, which occupies most of the eastern half of the city. Southern Higashiyama's best-known sight is the crowd-pleasing temple complex of **Kiyomizu-dera.** Other notable spots in the area include the temple of **Sanjūsangen-dō,** which houses roughly 1,000 effigies of Kannon, Buddhism's goddess of mercy, and the huge complex of **Chion-in,** the head temple of the Jōdo school of Pure Land Buddhism.

The busy thoroughfare of **Shichijo-dōri** runs east-west along the southern edge of the area, with east-west **Sanjō-dōri** hemming in the northern edge. The **Higashiyama mountains** lie to the east. The crowded pedestrian thoroughfare of **Sannen-zaka,** which runs uphill to Kiyomizu-dera, is also found in this district. The easiest way to reach the area is via the **Karasuma subway line** from Kyoto Station, exiting at **Karasuma-Oike Station** and transferring to the **Tōzai line** to **Higashiyama Station.** From here, the district spreads out to the south.

Gion

About 5 minutes' walk southwest of Chion-in, **Yasaka-jinja** is the important shrine presiding over the district of Gion, the city's main entertainment district, along the eastern bank of the Kamo River. This area originally developed into an entertainment hub to cater to the earthly needs of the pilgrims who came to visit the grand Yasaka-jinja, and today, it remains the best part of the city to see **kabuki performances,** glimpse geisha flitting over

Kyoto Area

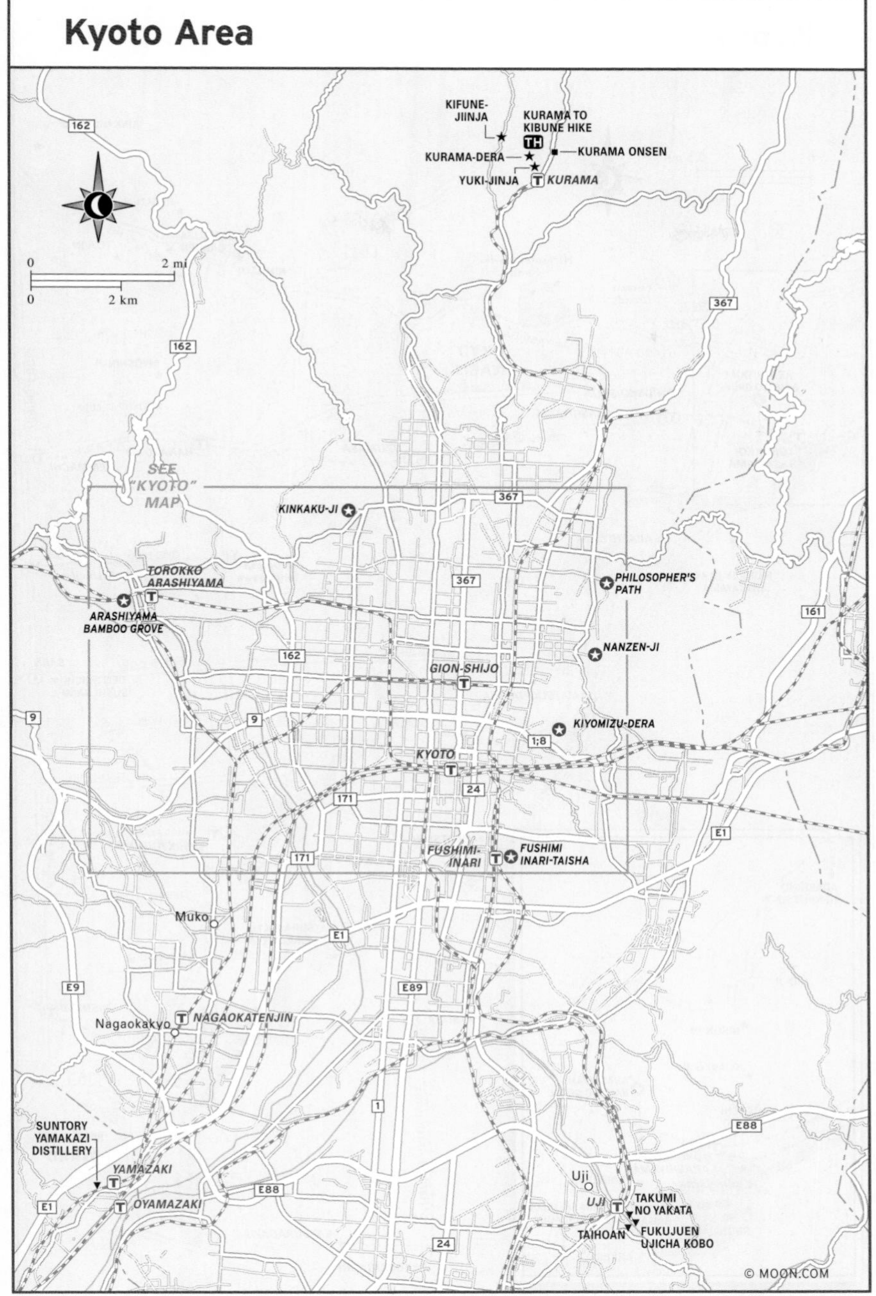

162
KIFUNE-JIINJA
KURAMA TO KIBUNE HIKE
TH
KURAMA-DERA
KURAMA ONSEN
YUKI-JINJA
KURAMA
0
2 mi
0
2 km
367
162
SEE "KYOTO" MAP
367
KINKAKU-JI
TOROKKO ARASHIYAMA
ARASHIYAMA BAMBOO GROVE
367
PHILOSOPHER'S PATH
161
162
NANZEN-JI
GION-SHIJO
9
9
KIYOMIZU-DERA
1;8
KYOTO
24
171
E1
171
FUSHIMI-INARI
FUSHIMI INARI-TAISHA
Muko
E1
E9
E89
NAGAOKATENJIN
Nagaokakyo
1
E88
SUNTORY YAMAKAZI DISTILLERY
YAMAZAKI
E88
Uji
E1
OYAMAZAKI
UJI
TAKUMI NO YAKATA
TAIHOAN
FUKUJUEN UJICHA KOBO
24
© MOON.COM

Kyoto

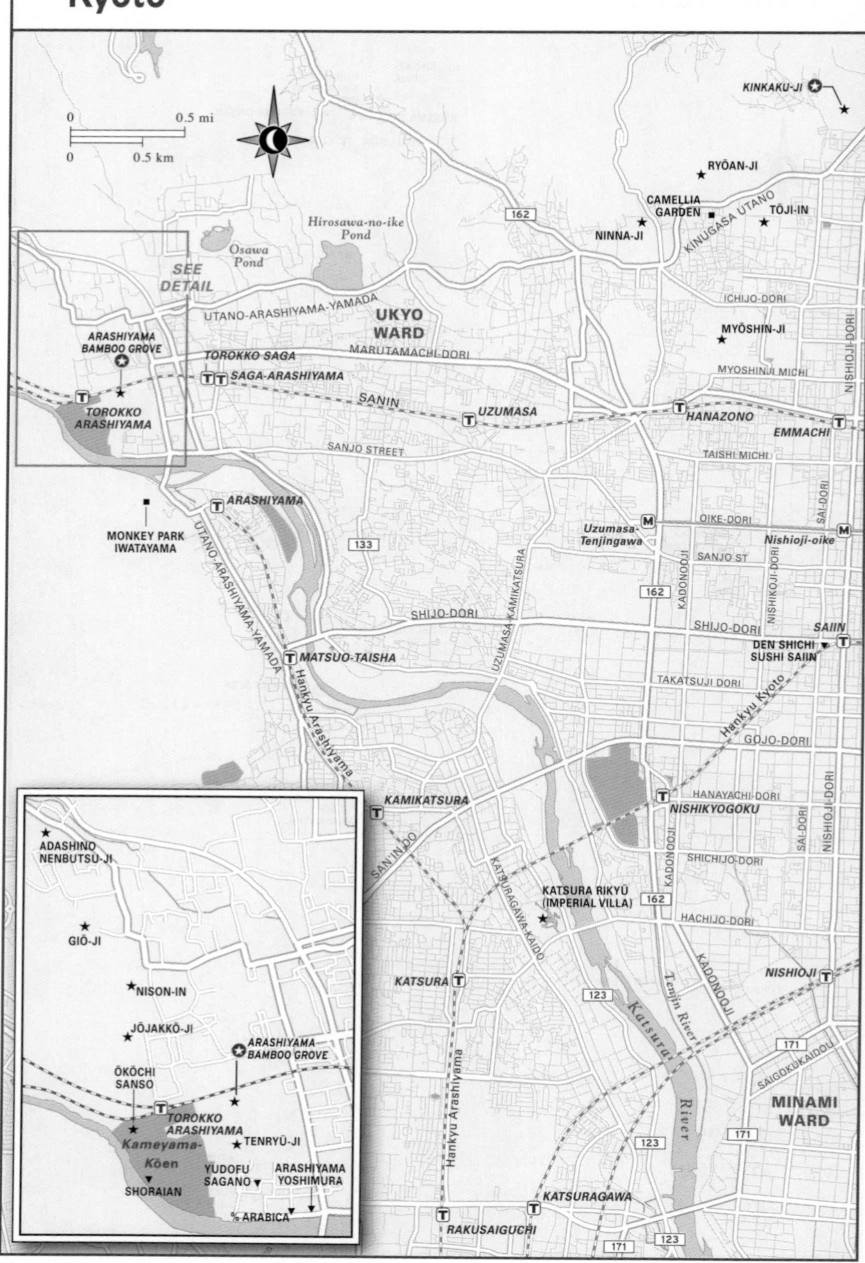

0 0.5 mi
0 0.5 km
KINKAKU-JI
RYŌAN-JI
CAMELLIA GARDEN
KINUGASA UTANO
TŌJI-IN
NINNA-JI
162
Hirosawa-no-ike Pond
Osawa Pond
SEE DETAIL
UTANO-ARASHIYAMA-YAMADA
UKYO WARD
ICHIJO-DORI
MYŌSHIN-JI
ARASHIYAMA BAMBOO GROVE
TOROKKO SAGA
MARUTAMACHI-DORI
SAGA-ARASHIYAMA
MYOSHINJI MICHI
NISHIOJI-DORI
SANIN
TOROKKO ARASHIYAMA
UZUMASA
HANAZONO
EMMACHI
SANJO STREET
TAISHI MICHI
SAI-DORI
ARASHIYAMA
MONKEY PARK IWATAYAMA
OIKE-DORI
Uzumasa-Tenjingawa
Nishioji-oike
133
SANJO ST
UTANO-ARASHIYAMA-YAMADA
UZUMASA-KAMIKATSURA
KADONOOJI
NISHIKOJI-DORI
162
SHIJO-DORI
SHIJO-DORI
SAIIN
DEN SHICHI SUSHI SAIIN
MATSUO-TAISHA
Hankyu Arashiyama
TAKATSUJI DORI
Hankyu Kyoto
GOJO-DORI
KAMIKATSURA
HANAYACHI-DORI
NISHIKYOGOKU
SAN'IN DO
SHICHIJO-DORI
KATSURAGAWA-KAIDO
KATSURA RIKYŪ (IMPERIAL VILLA)
162
HACHIJO-DORI
KATSURA
NISHIOJI
KADONOOJI
123
Tenjin River
Katsura River
171
SAIGOKUKAIDOU
MINAMI WARD
Hankyu Arashiyama
171
123
KATSURAGAWA
RAKUSAIGUCHI
123
171
ADASHINO NENBUTSU-JI
GIŌ-JI
NISON-IN
JŌJAKKŌ-JI
ARASHIYAMA BAMBOO GROVE
ŌKŌCHI SANSO
TOROKKO ARASHIYAMA
TENRYŪ-JI
Kameyama-Kōen
YUDOFU SAGANO
ARASHIYAMA YOSHIMURA
SHORAIAN
% ARABICA

KYOTO

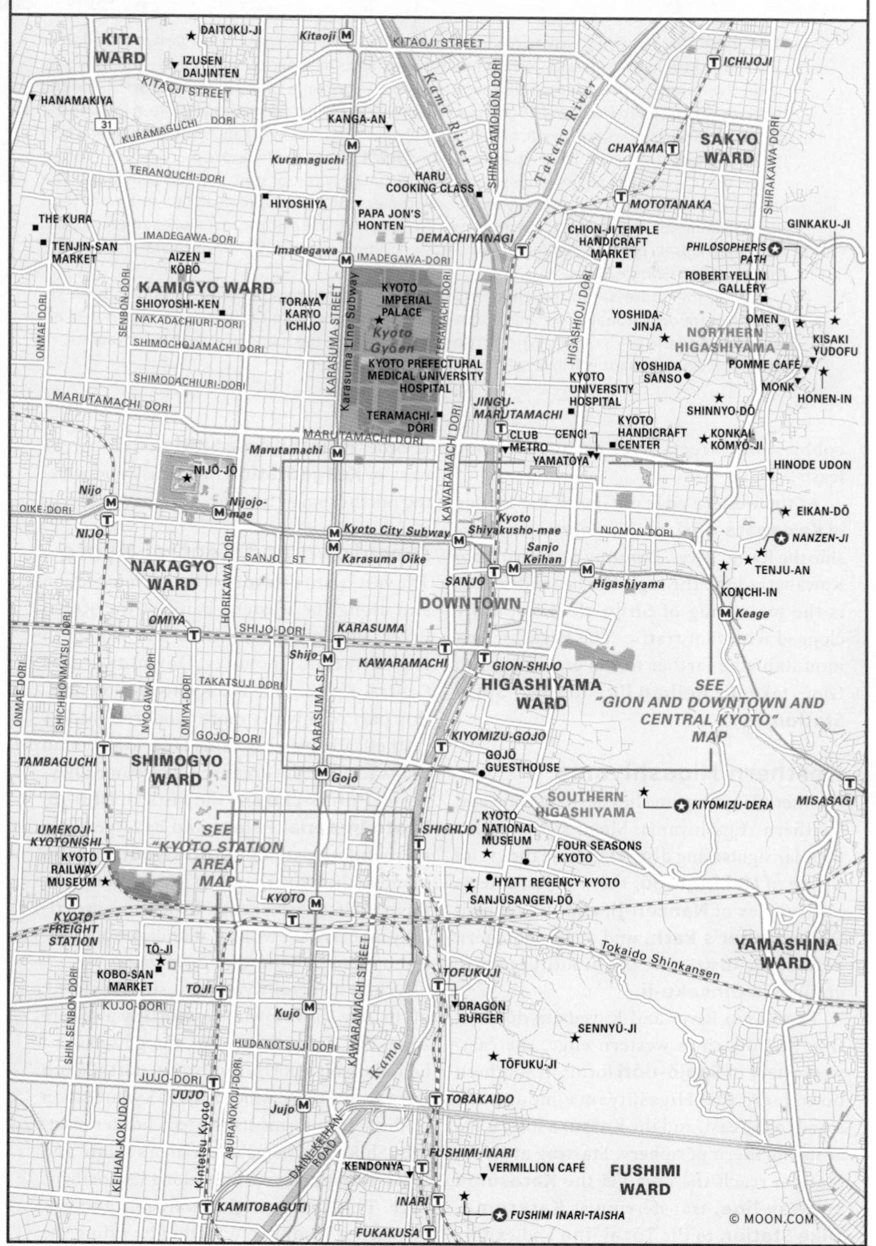

KITA WARD
DAITOKU-JI
IZUSEN DAIJINTEN
Kitaoji
KITAOJI STREET
HANAMAKIYA
KURAMAGUCHI DORI
KANGA-AN
Kamo River
SHIMOGAMOHON DORI
Takano River
ICHIJOJI
CHAYAMA
SAKYO WARD
Kuramaguchi
TERANOUCHI-DORI
HARU COOKING CLASS
HIYOSHIYA
PAPA JON'S HONTEN
MOTOTANAKA
SHIRAKAWA DORI
THE KURA
TENJIN-SAN MARKET
IMADEGAWA-DORI
AIZEN KŌBŌ
Imadegawa
DEMACHIYANAGI
CHION-JI TEMPLE HANDICRAFT MARKET
GINKAKU-JI
PHILOSOPHER'S PATH
KAMIGYO WARD
SHIOYOSHI-KEN
TORAYA KARYO ICHIJO
KYOTO IMPERIAL PALACE
Kyoto Gyoen
ROBERT YELLIN GALLERY
NAKADACHIURI-DORI
SHIMOCHOJAMACHI DORI
SHIMODACHIURI-DORI
KYOTO PREFECTURAL MEDICAL UNIVERSITY HOSPITAL
YOSHIDA-JINJA
NORTHERN HIGASHIYAMA
OMEN
KISAKI YUDOFU
YOSHIDA SANSO
POMME CAFÉ
MONK
HONEN-IN
KYOTO UNIVERSITY HOSPITAL
SHINNYO-DŌ
MARUTAMACHI DORI
TERAMACHI-DŌRI
JINGU-MARUTAMACHI
CLUB METRO
CENCI
KYOTO HANDICRAFT CENTER
KONKAI-KŌMYŌ-JI
Marutamachi
YAMATOYA
HINODE UDON
NIJŌ-JŌ
Nijo
Nijojo-mae
OIKE-DORI
NIJO
EIKAN-DŌ
Kyoto City Subway
Kyoto Shiyakusho-mae
NIOMON-DORI
NANZEN-JI
SANJO ST
Karasuma Oike
Sanjo Keihan
TENJU-AN
NAKAGYO WARD
SANJO
Higashiyama
KONCHI-IN
DOWNTOWN
Keage
OMIYA
SHIJO-DORI
KARASUMA
Shijo
KAWARAMACHI
GION-SHIJO
HIGASHIYAMA WARD
SEE "GION AND DOWNTOWN AND CENTRAL KYOTO" MAP
TAKATSUJI DORI
GOJO-DORI
KIYOMIZU-GOJO
TAMBAGUCHI
SHIMOGYO WARD
GOJŌ GUESTHOUSE
Gojo
MISASAGI
SOUTHERN HIGASHIYAMA
KIYOMIZU-DERA
SEE "KYOTO STATION AREA" MAP
UMEKOJI-KYOTONISHI
KYOTO NATIONAL MUSEUM
SHICHIJO
FOUR SEASONS KYOTO
KYOTO RAILWAY MUSEUM
HYATT REGENCY KYOTO
SANJŪSANGEN-DŌ
KYOTO
KYOTO FREIGHT STATION
YAMASHINA WARD
Tokaido Shinkansen
TŌ-JI
KOBO-SAN MARKET
TOJI
TOFUKUJI
KUJO-DORI
Kujo
DRAGON BURGER
SENNYŪ-JI
HUDANOTSUJI DORI
TŌFUKU-JI
Kamo
JUJO-DORI
JUJO
TOBAKAIDO
Jujo
FUSHIMI-INARI
KENDONYA
VERMILLION CAFÉ
FUSHIMI WARD
DAINI-KEIHAN ROAD
INARI
KAMITOBAGUTI
FUSHIMI INARI-TAISHA
FUKAKUSA
Kintetsu Kyoto
KEIHAN-KOKUDO
ABURANOKOJI DORI
SHIN SENBON DORI
KAWARAMACHI STREET
KARASUMA ST
KARASUMA STREET
Karasuma Line Subway
KAWARAMACHI DORI
TERAMACHI DORI
HIGASHIOJI DORI
HORIKAWA DORI
SENBON-DORI
ONMAE DORI
SHICHIHONMATSU DORI
NYOGAWA DORI
OMIYA-DORI
31

A Word on Addresses in Kyoto

Though Kyoto is relatively easy to navigate compared to other large cities in Japan, the address system is a little quirky. In addition to the usual elements in Japanese addresses—the building name, the number of a business, apartment, or house ("-gō" or 号), the area ("-chō" or 町), the city ("-shi" or 市), the ward ("-ku" or 区), and postal code (〒)—Kyoto addresses also often include the name of the nearest access road (often, but not always "-dōri" or 通り) and the cardinal direction ("iri" or 入) from the access road where you'll find the address you're seeking.

This twist, rooted in an ancient system, is unfortunately out of sync with Google Maps. The easiest way around this is to simply input only the essentials—city (e.g., Kyoto-shi), ward (e.g., Higashiyama-ku), and area (e.g., Shimokawara-chō), and leave out the rest. For example, to find the famed kaiseki ryōri restaurant Kikunoi Honten, simply input "459 Shimokawara-chō Higashiyama-ku" into Google Maps.

Most of the addresses in this chapter are written in this simplified way, although some do include extra directional information that could prove helpful to taxi drivers or locals well acquainted with the city's quirks. When in doubt, simply type the name of a temple, restaurant, or hotel, and Google Maps will likely already have it in the system.

cobblestone streets, and eat multicourse feasts.

At the western edge of Gion is the avenue of **Kawabata-dōri,** running north-south beside the Kamo River. Running eastward from Kawabata-dōri, through the heart of Gion, is the main drag of **Shijo-dōri,** typically clogged with foot traffic. The Higashiyama mountains lie farther to the east. To get to Gion, take the **Keihan line** to **Gion-Shijō Station.**

Northern Higashiyama

Northern Higashiyama lies north of Gion and Southern Higashiyama. Major sights in this popular sightseeing district include the grand shrine of **Heian-jingū,** the wonderful temple complex of **Nanzen-ji,** and the vaunted **Philosopher's Path,** and at the northern edge of the district lie the beautiful temple grounds of **Ginkaku-ji.**

The Kamo River and Kawabata-dōri define this district's western edge, the east-west artery of **Sanjō-dōri** forms its southern boundary, the Higashiyama mountains stand to the east, and the **Katsura Rikyū** sits at its northern periphery. Starting at Kyoto Station, reach the area via the **Karasuma subway line,** transferring at **Karasuma-Oike Station** to the **Tōzai line** and exiting at either **Higashiyama Station** in the area's west, or **Keage Station** in the east, and walking north from either one.

Downtown and Central Kyoto

The vast swath of town north of Kyoto Station and along the western bank of the Kamo River, sitting opposite Gion and Northern Higashiyama, includes Downtown and Central Kyoto. Like the Kyoto Station area, this part of town is more modern and less aesthetically pleasing. This large area's main sights include the dreamy cobblestone alleyway of **Ponto-chō** and the castle of **Nijō-jō. Kyoto Imperial Palace** and its large, leafy surrounding park of **Kyoto Gyōen** are also found in this broad swath of town. Otherwise, this part of town makes up for its more generically modern face with an abundance of excellent options to wine, dine, and shop.

While Central Kyoto is a sizable chunk of the city, downtown is essentially a square zone. The Kamo River runs along its eastern boundary on a north-south axis; north-south **Karasuma-dōri,** which runs to Kyoto Station in the south, forms its western border; east-west Shijo-dōri hems in the area's south; and **Oike-dōri** runs east-west along its northern edge. This area is highly walkable and can be reached from Kyoto Station by riding the

Karasuma subway line to **Shijo Station** near the southwest corner of the downtown area, or to **Karasuma-Oike Station** in the neighborhood's northwest corner.

Northwest Kyoto

Moving west of Downtown and Central Kyoto, the district of Northwest Kyoto is another major sightseeing area, despite its slightly farther-flung position. A few standout sights in the area include the famously gilt temple of **Kinkaku-ji** and the iconic Zen temple of **Ryōan-ji,** known for its classic rock garden. Nearby, the less thronged temple complex of **Myōshin-ji** also begs to be explored.

This vast area lies north of east-west avenue **Imadegawa-dōri** and west of north-south oriented **Senbon-dōri.** Mountains define its northern and western boundaries. To reach the area from Kyoto Station, take the **JR San-in line** to **Hanazono Station,** a short walk south of the temple of Myōshin-ji, from where it's possible to walk or cycle north to Ryōan-ji (25 minutes) and then Kinkaku-ji (20 minutes). The area's main sights are spread out north of there.

Arashiyama

In the far west of town, Arashiyama is among Kyoto's most crowded areas. Running through the heart of the district is the area's ethereal **bamboo grove,** with the temple of **Tenryū-ji** sitting near the south end and the dreamy house and gardens of the **Ōkōchi Sansō villa** occupying a lofty spot above the area, affording great views of the city.

Arashiyama is located about 30 minutes by train from Kyoto Station, along the **Katsura River,** which flows along the southern edge of the district, and near the base of the Arashiyama mountain range. The **Tōgetsu-kyō bridge** spans the Katsura River, and an unnamed main drag lined with touristy shops and cafés runs on a north-south axis to the east of the bamboo grove and the rest of the area's attractions. Take the **JR Sagano/San-in line** from Kyoto Station to **Saga-Arashiyama Station,** from where most of the area's sights are about 10 minutes' walk to the southwest.

Around Kyoto

Around Kyoto, there are a few appealing escapes in the mountains surrounding town. You'll find **hiking trails** in the mountains bordering the town to the east, north, and northwest, which run to atmospheric temples that only attract a fraction of the crowds seen in town. Nearby sits one of Kyoto's top onsen, **Kurama Onsen.** South of Kyoto are some great places to try two quintessential Japanese beverages: in the southeast, **Uji** is surrounded by tea fields and is a prime spot to try the brew; in the southwest, **Suntory Yamazaki Distillery** is home to whiskies regularly named the best in the world.

PLANNING YOUR TIME

Like most of Japan, Kyoto is a highly seasonal destination. In **spring** (Mar.-May), an explosion of cherry blossoms bathes the city in a soft pink glow. In **autumn** (late Oct.-Nov.), foliage bursts into shades of red, orange, yellow, and brown. If you don't mind sharing the city with large tour groups and other international travelers, these times of year are popular for a reason.

The off-seasons are the stuffy days of **summer** (June-Aug.)—note that June is on average the rainiest month of the year—and **winter** (Dec.-Feb.), which is cold and sometimes snowy but not overly harsh, with temperature ranges of 1-11°C (34-52°F). If you don't mind sticky weather, summer offers long, glorious evenings that provide ideal conditions for strolling along the burbling Kamo River.

Even with only one day, you'll be able to see a handful of the city's key temples and shrines, which are clustered mainly around the Southern Higashiyama area and west of the city in the famous district of Arashiyama. But ideally, you'll have two to five days to explore the city. While areas around the edges of town are magical—Arashiyama and the Southeast come to mind—they aren't

Avoiding Kyoto's Crowds

Kyoto's treasures are well-known—and extremely crowded. Its most popular sights (including Fushimi Inari-Taisha, Kiyomizu-dera, Ginkaku-ji, Nijō-jō, Ryōan-ji, Kinkaku-ji, and the Arashiyama's bamboo grove) host almost Disneyland-level throngs. The famous landmarks are still amazing, crowds aside, but given how popular Kyoto has become, having genuinely good offbeat alternatives to escape the crowds is very important. There are strategies for escaping the crowds throughout this chapter, but here are a few general suggestions.

- **Avoid peak seasons** (late Mar.-early Apr. and Nov., and the Obon holidays of mid-Aug.).
- **Visit attractions at off-peak times** (before 8am or after 4pm on weekdays). Some standouts like Fushimi Inari-Taisha and the Arashiyama Bamboo Grove are open 24/7; you can enjoy them almost alone if you're willing to visit at certain hours.
- Seek out **lesser-known gems;** most of Kyoto's busiest sites have stunning, less-crowded options just a short walk away.
- Finally, dare to **veer off the beaten path** to discover charming shops, antique wooden townhouses, and local shrines well off the radar.

convenient for accessing restaurants or other sights. For maximum convenience, the areas around Kyoto Station and downtown can't be beat. To strike a balance between (more) ambiance and (slightly less) convenience, Gion and Higashiyama are good bets.

It's easy to be overwhelmed by the sheer number of Buddhist temples—Zen and otherwise—throughout Kyoto. Highlights include the Zen temples of **Nanzen-ji** and **Gingaku-ji,** the famed rock garden of **Ryōan-ji,** the gold-plated **Kinkaku-ji** (Golden Pavilion), and **Kiyomizu-dera,** perched high above the city with stunning views. As for Shinto shrines, the one must-see is **Fushimi Inari-Taisha** with its hiking trail lined with more than 10,000 vivid torii, as the red gates seen at Shinto shrines are called. An equally striking sight is Arashiyama's magical **bamboo grove** on the outskirts of the city. When planning your time, one thing to keep in mind is the reality that you simply can't see everything, so you'll have to prioritize carefully. Avoid temple fatigue by exploring the city's **performance arts,** going on a **day trip, shopping** downtown, and having a **kaiseki ryōri** feast.

Itinerary Ideas

KYOTO ON DAY ONE

On this first day, you'll explore the buzzing east side of town, from **Southern Higashiyama** to **Southeast Kyoto.** Some of Kyoto's most famous sights are found along this route, which can be followed mostly **on foot.** There are also a few off-the-radar stops for balance.

1 Plan to start at **Chion-in,** arriving by 9am. Ascend the imposing stone steps that lead up to this vast temple complex, the "Vatican of Pure Land Buddhism."

2 Continue on foot another 5 minutes through the leafy park of Maruyama-kōen, stopping at **Yasaka-jinja.** This handsome shrine sits perched atop an incline overlooking the commercial district of Gion.

3 Walk just over 15 minutes to the magnificent hilltop temple of **Kiyomizu-dera.** On the way, you'll walk along Sannen-zaka, an iconic though very touristy cobblestone street with shops selling kitschy souvenirs and soft-serve ice cream.

4 Walk downhill via Chawan-zaka and continue west toward the Kamo River until you reach Kiyomizu-Gojō Station. Take the Keihan line to Tōfuku-ji Station (4 minutes). Eat lunch at **Dragon Burger,** just outside the station.

5 After you've fueled up, walk 5 minutes to **Tōfuku-ji.** This relatively uncrowded temple, set within a forest, has a sublime garden.

6 Walk 12 minutes south to **Fushimi Inari-Taisha** and spend the remainder of the afternoon walking along the atmospheric mountain path of Kyoto's most etherial shrine, lined with vermillion gates.

7 After your day of exploration, return to your accommodation to freshen up for haute kaiseki fare at the vaunted **Kikunoi Honten.**

8 After dinner, take a nighttime stroll through **Ponto-chō** alley, soaking up the old-school ambience cast by the light of lanterns gently illuminating the cobblestone path.

9 If you're feeling like a nightcap, for something a little off the beaten path, the cocktails at **Bar Rocking Chair** are wonderful. It's a 10-minute walk southwest of Ponto-chō.

KYOTO ON DAY TWO

On your second day, you'll discover the western district of **Arashiyama** and the city's northwest, where many of its greatest hits are found.

1 Begin the day in the district of Arashiyama, west of the city, stopping by **Tenryū-ji,** a temple that was originally built to soothe the angry spirit of an emperor betrayed.

2 Next, proceed through the otherworldly path of the **Arashiyama Bamboo Grove,** just north of Tenryū-ji.

3 Climb the steps at the end of the path that leads through the grove to the **Ōkōchi Sansō** villa. Peruse the gardens of this classic home and enjoy a green tea with a sweet snack at the end of your tour.

4 For lunch, backtrack through the bamboo grove to **Arashiyama Yoshimura,** 15 minutes' walk southeast of the villa. It's a popular soba restaurant beside the Katsura River.

5 Make your way to the northwest side of downtown to visit **Ryōan-ji.** To reach it, take

Itinerary Ideas

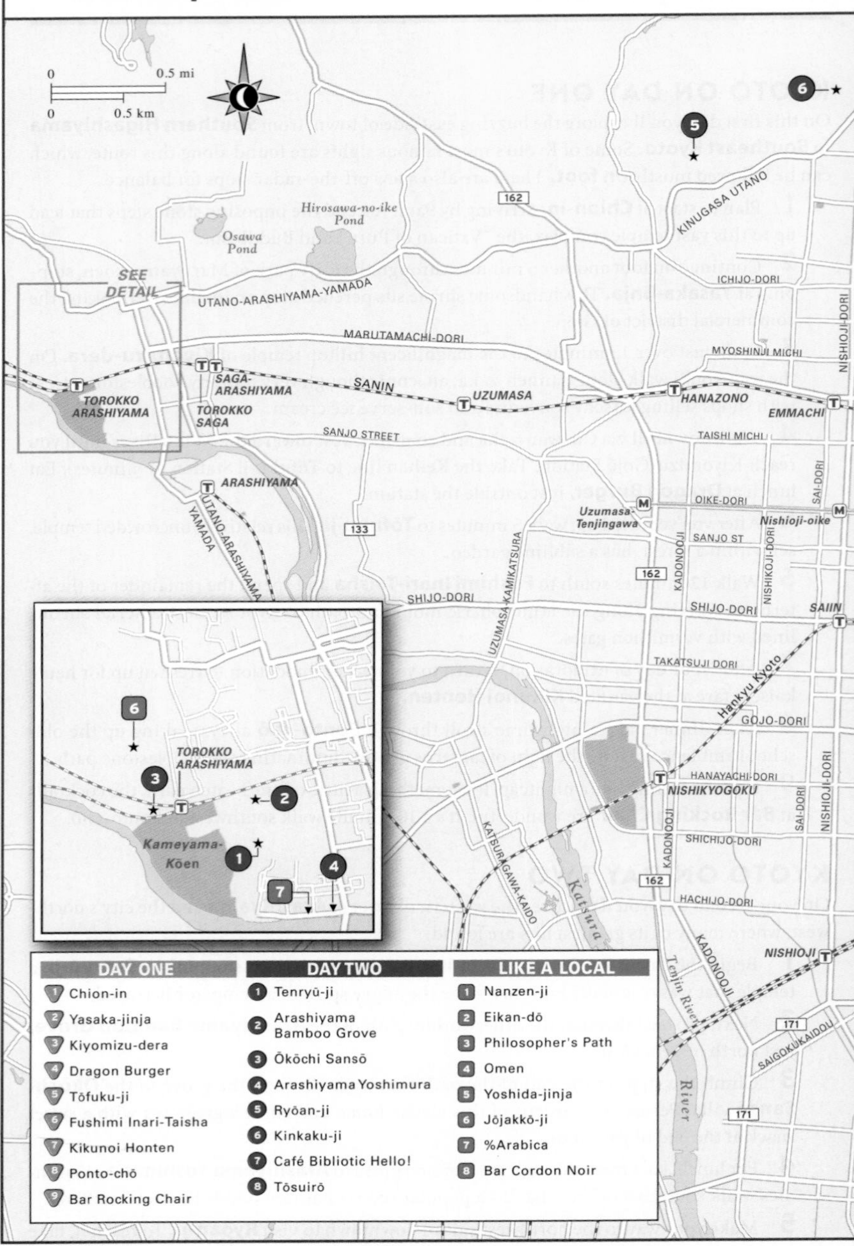

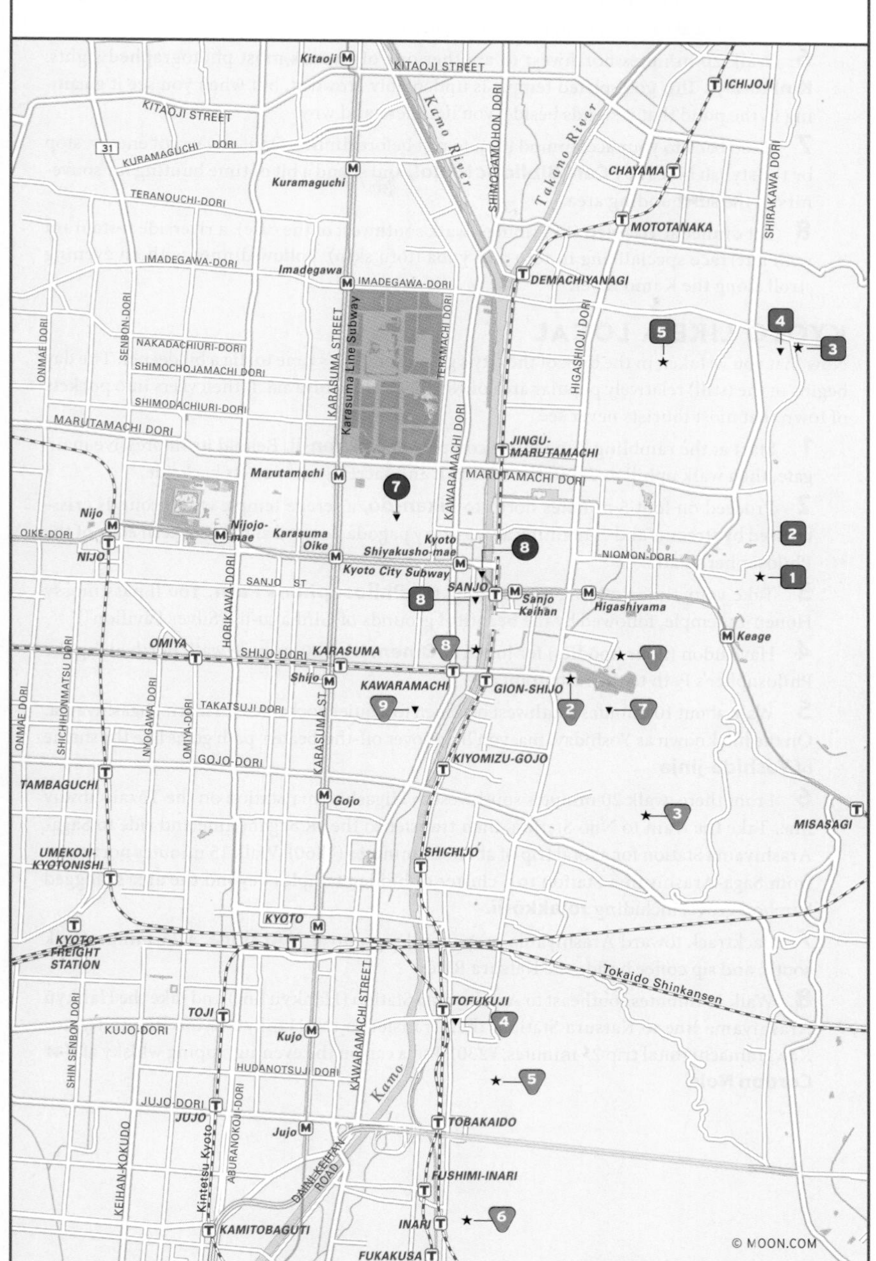

KYOTO ITINERARY IDEAS

the Randen Arashiyama tram line from Arashiyama Station to Katabiranotsuji Station, then transfer to the Randen Kitano tram line to Ryōan-ji Station. The enigmatic raked gravel garden at this Zen temple is world famous.

6 Walk 20 minutes northwest to another one of Kyoto's most photographed sights: **Kinkaku-ji.** This gold-plated temple is undeniably crowded, but when you see it gleaming in the pond that it stands beside, you'll understand why.

7 Head back to your accommodation to rest before dinner. Or, if you've got energy, stop by the stylish hideaway **Café Bibliotic Hello!,** and spend a bit of time hunting for souvenirs in the surrounding area.

8 Eat dinner at **Tōsuirō** (15 minutes' walk southwest of the café), a riverside restaurant with a terrace specializing in tofu and yuba (tofu skin). Follow dinner with an evening stroll along the Kamo River.

KYOTO LIKE A LOCAL

Now that you've taken in the bulk of the city's greatest hits, it's time to dig a bit deeper. The day begins in the (still) relatively popular area of Northern Higashiyama. It then veers into pockets of town that most tourists never see.

1 Start at the rambling Zen temple complex of **Nanzen-ji.** Behold its impressive main gate, then walk uphill and find the waterfall and sacred grotto on its backside.

2 Proceed on foot 5 minutes north to **Eikan-dō,** a serene temple with grounds crisscrossed by streams and containing a two-story pagoda, located at the southern edge of the Philosopher's Path.

3 Take your time ambling north along the **Philosopher's Path.** You'll pass mossy Hōnen-in temple, followed by the beautiful grounds of Ginkaku-ji ("Silver Pavilion").

4 Have udon (flour noodles) for lunch at **Omen.** It's a 20-minute walk north along the Philosopher's Path to the restaurant.

5 Walk about 10 minutes southwest of Omen to a quiet pocket of Northern Higashiyama. On the hill known as Yoshidayama, you'll discover off-the-beaten-path gems like the shrine of **Yoshida-jinja.**

6 From there, walk 20 minutes southwest to Higashiyama Station on the Tōzai subway line. Take the train to Nijō Station, then transfer to the JR Sagano line and ride to Saga-Arashiyama Station for a total trip of about 25 minutes (¥460). Walk 15 minutes northwest from Saga-Arashiyama Station to a cluster of hidden temples beyond the area's clogged bamboo grove, including **Jōjakkō-ji.**

7 Backtrack toward Arashiyama proper and regroup at **%Arabica,** a 25-minute walk south, and sip coffee beside the Katsura River.

8 Walk 10 minutes southeast to Arashiyama Station (Hankyū line) and take the Hankyū Arashiyama line to Katsura Station, then transfer to the Hankyū Kyoto line to Kyoto-Kawaramachi (total trip 25 minutes; ¥230). Put a cap on the evening sipping whisky at **Bar Cordon Noir.**

Sights

KYOTO STATION AREA

Aside from a few temples hiding inside this slice of decidedly modern Japan, Kyoto's treasures lie in the districts beyond. View the station area as a means to an end: the city's entry and exit point, and a place to handle logistics and shopping.

Kyoto Tower
京都タワー

Karasuma-dōri, Shichijō-sagaru, Shimogyō-ku; tel. 075/361-3215; www.kyoto-tower.co.jp; 9am-9pm daily; ¥800 adults, ¥650 high school students, ¥550 elementary and junior high school students, ¥150 children over 3; take JR lines to Kyoto Station, Karasuma central exit

Five minutes' walk north of Kyoto Station, you'll encounter an eyesore of a monument that Japanologist and author Alex Kerr once called "a stake through the heart of the city." Behold, 131-meter (430-ft) Kyoto Tower, built in 1963. You'll want to move outward toward the more historic districts, but it is true that there are great vistas from the viewing deck up top.

Higashi Hongan-ji
東本願寺

Karasuma-dōri, Shichijō-agaru, Shimogyō-ku; tel. 075/371-9181; www.higashihonganji.or.jp; 5:50am-5:30pm daily Mar.-Oct., 6:20am-4:30pm daily Nov.-Feb.; free; from Kyoto Station, take the Karasuma central exit

A short walk north from Kyoto Tower, up the main north-south artery of Karasuma-dōri, you'll find a stunning sight that is thankfully much more in line with what you'd expect to see in Kyoto: Higashi Hongan-ji. The main hall of this temple is one of the largest wooden structures on the planet. Unfortunately, you can't glimpse much beyond the facade of this complex, which is closed to the public. But the buildings themselves still induce a sense of awe, with both their scale and their elaborate gold-plated flourishes. They're by far the most splendid glimpse of Kyoto's illustrious past in the area surrounding the station.

Kyoto Railway Museum
京都鉄道博物館

Kankiji-chō, Shimogyō-ku; tel. 0570/080-462; www.kyotorailwaymuseum.jp; 10am-5:30pm Thurs.-Tues.; ¥1,200 adults, ¥1,000 university and high school students, ¥500 junior high and elementary students, ¥200 children over three; walk 20 minutes west of JR Kyoto Station, or take bus no. 205 or 208 from JR Kyoto Station to Umekoji-kōen-mae stop, or bus no. 104 or 110 to Umekōji-kōen/Kyoto Railway Museum-mae stop

If you're looking for a great rainy-day option, or you simply want a break from temple-hopping, head to the Kyoto Railway Museum. A hit with kids and train lovers, this museum traces train history from the steam engine all the way through to the bullet train. Old bullet-train models, commuter trains from days past, and even steam locomotives are on display. It's also possible to hop aboard a steam locomotive and go for a short ride (¥300 adults, ¥100 children).

Tō-ji
東寺

1 Kujō-chō, Minami-ku; tel. 075/691-3325; www.toji.or.jp; 8:30am-5pm daily Mar. 20-Sept. 19, 8:30am-4pm daily Sept. 20-Mar. 19; grounds free, kondo, kodo, and treasure hall ¥500, pagoda (9am-4pm only) ¥800; take the Kintetsu line to Tō-ji Station

Thanks to its towering pagoda, Tō-ji is one of the more visually prominent temples in the Kyoto Station area. Located southwest of the station, this wooden spire rises from a small sea of gloomy apartment blocks as a reminder that the heart of tradition still beats here, too. The best time to visit—perhaps the main reason—is its **Kōbō-san market,** held on the

Kyoto Station Area

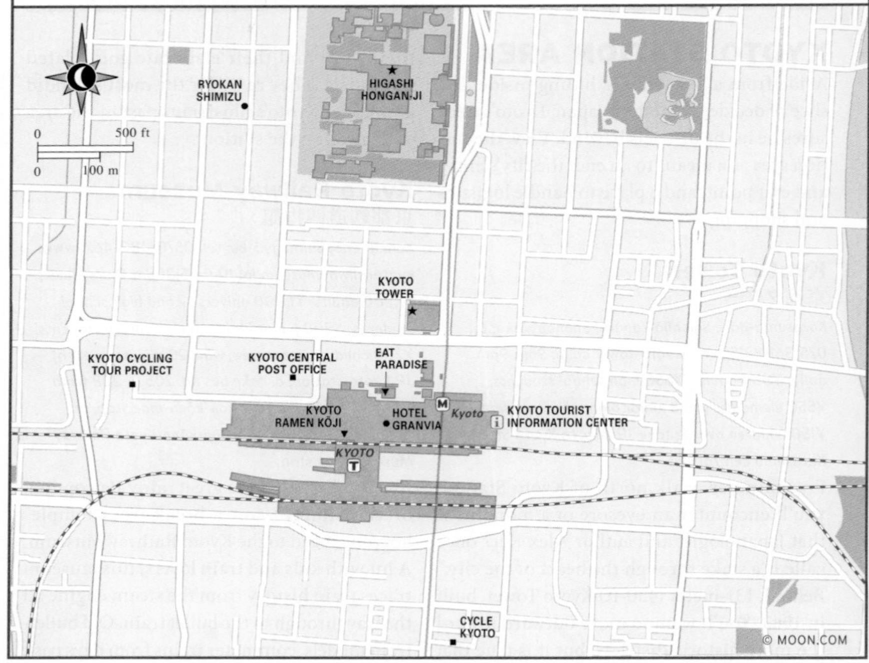

21st of every month, an excellent stop if you're keen to visit a flea market.

SOUTHEAST KYOTO

Southeast Kyoto is dense in noteworthy sights, and slightly less crowded than Southern Higashiyama, to its north.

TOP EXPERIENCE

★ Fushimi Inari-Taisha

伏見稲荷大社

68 Yabunouchi-chō, Fukakusa, Fushimi-ku; tel. 075/561-1551; http://inari.jp; dawn to dusk daily; free; take JR Nara Line to Inari Station, or Keihan Railway line to Fushimi-Inari Station

If you only have time to visit one Shinto shrine during your stay in Kyoto, make it Fushimi Inari-Taisha. It is the head shrine for 40,000 shrines throughout Japan that are dedicated to Inari, the kami (god) of fertility, rice, sake, and prosperity.

Easily one of the most arresting sights in Kyoto, the bewitching complex spreads across a mountain, where more than 10,000 vermillion torii gates envelop a 4-kilometer (2.5-mi) path through heavily wooded terrain. The complex consists of five shrines, numerous mausoleums, and altars where devotees leave open cartons of sake as offerings. Hundreds of stone foxes with granary keys in their mouths stand watch; foxes are mystical animals in the Japanese tradition, with the power to possess human beings by entering via the fingernails. Spiritual possession aside, if you're on the path as the sun begins to fall, the slightly eerie atmosphere may spook even the staunchest skeptic.

1: Tō-ji pagoda **2:** Fushimi Inari-Taisha

1
2
十五年十月吉日建之
成二十四年十一月吉日建之
成十四年十一月吉日建之
平成二十年六月吉日建之
平成十四年七月吉日建之
平成二十五年十月吉日建之
平成十八年十一月吉日建之
川県川崎市中原区小杉町二の二〇五
有限会社 松宮興業 代表取締役 松宮芳行
ラクーン 代表 園田建二
はりたけモータープール 椋本きみ子 行俊
富士市久沢二、九、九〇 青木俊雄・健一郎
香川県観音寺市豊浜町 富田桂太郎・二枝・宗宏・直子
東京都江東区大島九ノ一ノ五 さくら紙工株式会社
滋賀県東近江市 有大橋三省堂 大橋慶之
大阪府 山中宏晃 利恭
東京都足立区中央本町 株式会社 孫八

Gion and Downtown and Central Kyoto

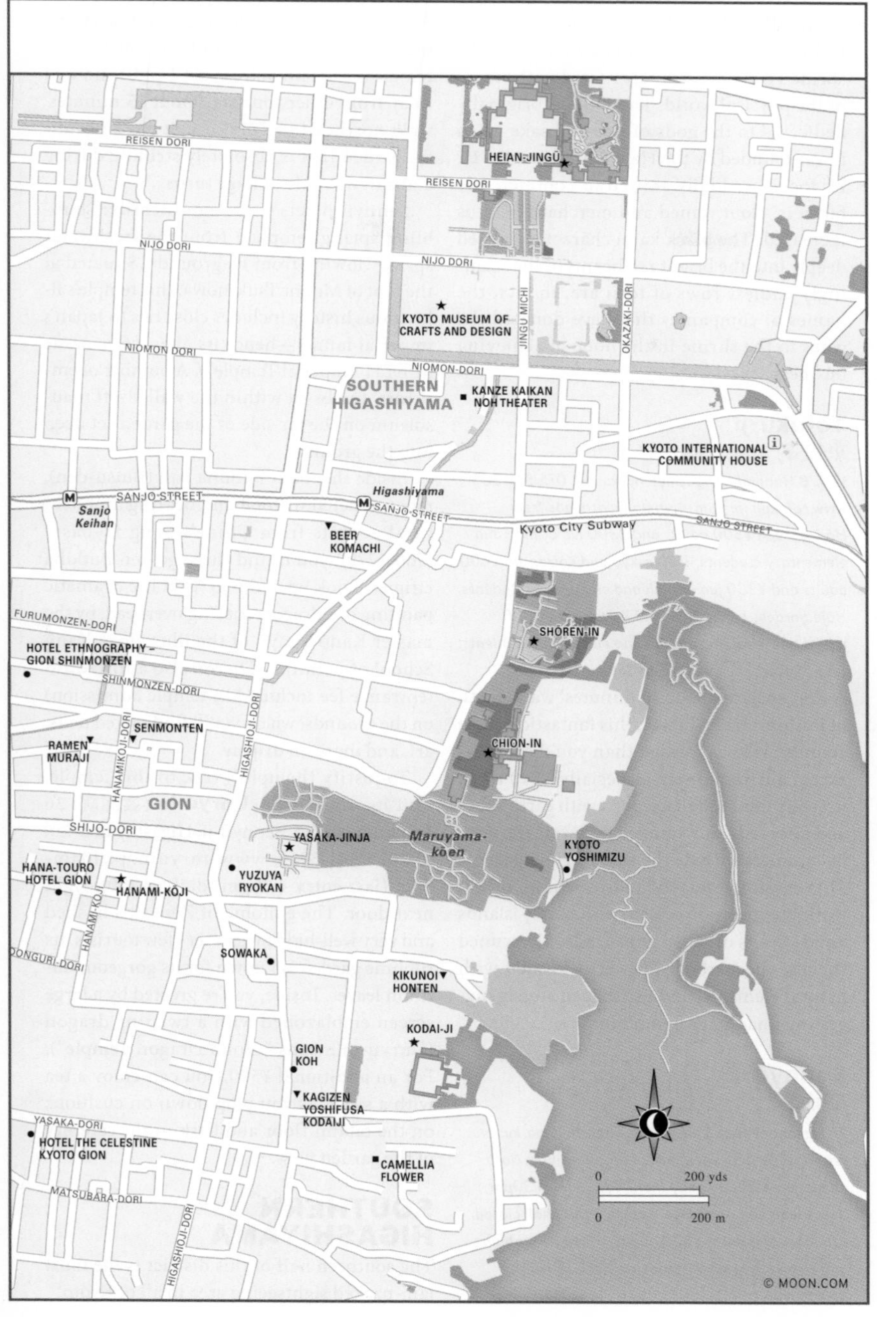
REISEN DORI
HEIAN-JINGŪ
REISEN DORI
NIJO DORI
NIJO DORI
KYOTO MUSEUM OF CRAFTS AND DESIGN
JINGU MICHI
OKAZAKI-DORI
NIOMON DORI
NIOMON-DORI
SOUTHERN HIGASHIYAMA
KANZE KAIKAN NOH THEATER
KYOTO INTERNATIONAL COMMUNITY HOUSE
SANJO STREET
Sanjo Keihan
Higashiyama
SANJO STREET
BEER KOMACHI
Kyoto City Subway
SANJO STREET
FURUMONZEN-DORI
HOTEL ETHNOGRAPHY - GION SHINMONZEN
SHŌREN-IN
SHINMONZEN-DORI
SENMONTEN
RAMEN MURAJI
HANAMIKOJI-DORI
HIGASHIOJI-DORI
CHION-IN
GION
SHIJO-DORI
YASAKA-JINJA
Maruyama-kōen
KYOTO YOSHIMIZU
HANA-TOURO HOTEL GION
HANAMI-KŌJI
YUZUYA RYOKAN
HANAMI-KOJI
DONGURI-DORI
SOWAKA
KIKUNOI HONTEN
KODAI-JI
GION KOH
KAGIZEN YOSHIFUSA KODAIJI
YASAKA-DORI
HOTEL THE CELESTINE KYOTO GION
CAMELLIA FLOWER
0
200 yds
0
200 m
MATSUBARA-DORI
HIGASHIOJI-DORI
© MOON.COM

Ambling through the tunnel of red may feel ethereal, but the chief concerns of the shrine's deity are strongly rooted in the cares of the physical world. The site was originally dedicated to the gods of rice and sake when it was founded by the Hata family in AD 711. Its focus gradually shifted to commerce as farmers' clout waned and merchants' status increased. The black kanji characters etched deeply into the bright red beams of the seemingly endless rows of torii are, in fact, the names of companies that have donated the gates to the shrine in the hope of achieving business success.

Tōfuku-ji
東福寺

15-778 Honmahi, Higashiyama-ku; tel. 075/561-0087; www.tofukuji.jp; 9am-4pm daily; grounds free, Hōjō garden ¥500 adults and ¥300 junior high and elementary students, Tsūten-kyō and Kaizan-dō ¥600 adults and ¥300 junior high and elementary students, Hōjō garden, Tsūten-kyō, and Kaizan-dō ¥1,000 adults and ¥500 junior high and elementary students; take JR Nara, Keihan lines to Tōfuku-ji Station

A Zen enclave about 20 minutes' walk north of Fushimi Inari-Taisha, this fantastic temple complex is less crowded than you'd expect—except during autumn (especially Nov.) when its justly famous foliage pops with earth tones and fiery reds. Surrounded by a wall, the temple grounds include the superb Hōjō garden. This carefully shaped landscape is an otherworldly expression of Zen, with mossy islands amid oceans of raked gravel, adroitly pruned shrubs, checkerboard patterns formed with natural elements, and misshapen stones suggesting imaginary mountains.

Sennyū-ji
泉涌寺

27 Yamanouchi-chō, Sennyū-ji, Higashiyama-ku; tel. 075/561-1551; www.mitera.org; 9am-5pm (last admission 4:30pm) daily Mar.-Nov., 9am-4:30pm (last admission 4pm) Dec.-Feb., treasure hall closed 4th Mon. of month; ¥500 adults, ¥300 junior high and elementary school students; take JR Nara, Keihan lines to Tōfuku-ji Station

After jostling through the camera-wielding masses at nearby Fushimi Inari-Taisha, this temple is a breath of fresh air. Uphill and well away from other tourists, about 15 minutes' walk northeast of Tōfuku-ji, it has a beautiful garden that is absolutely striking during autumn when the foliage turns.

Sennyū-ji gets its name (literally: "bubbling spring temple") from the freshwater spring flowing from its grounds. Situated at the foot of Mount Tsukinowa, this temple's illustrious history includes close ties to Japan's imperial family—hence its alternative name Mitera ("Imperial Temple"). A number of emperors' tombs sit within the walled-off mausoleum on the far side of the garden set deep into the grounds.

Inside the main Buddha hall (Butsu-den), reconstructed in 1668 and bearing architectural accents from China's Song Dynasty (960-1279), you'll find three golden Buddha effigies. Look up and marvel at the dramatic painting of a dragon, soaring overhead, by the master Kanō Tanyū of the illustrious Kano School of painting. There's also a **museum** (entrance fee included in temple admission) on the grounds, where you'll find sacred texts, art, and more on display.

To justify the uphill trek to this temple, visit its sub-temple, **Unryū-in** (雲龍院; 36 Yamanouchicho, Sennyū-ji, Higashiyama-ku; tel. 075/541-3916; www.unryuin.jp; 10am-5pm (last entry 4:30pm) daily; ¥400), right next door. The epitome of Zen, this hushed and very well-hidden gem sees few tourists. Its sublime garden is known for its gorgeous autumn leaves. Inside, you're greeted by a large screen emblazoned with a twisting dragon (Unryū-in means "Cloud Dragon Temple"). For an additional ¥500, you can enjoy a tea with a sweet as you plop down on cushions on the tatami floor and bask in the serenity of the garden view.

SOUTHERN HIGASHIYAMA

The southern half of this district is the most jam-packed sightseeing area in all of Kyoto.

Sanjūsangen-dō
三十三間堂

657 Sanjusangendoma wari-cho, Higashiyama-ku; tel. 075/561-0467; http://sanjusangendo.jp; 8am-5pm daily Apr.-Nov. 15, 9am-4pm daily Nov. 16-Mar.; ¥600 adults, ¥400 high school and junior high school students, ¥300 children; from Kyoto Station, take Kyoto City Bus 100 or 206 to Sanjūsangen-dō-mae bus stop, or Keihan line to Shichijō Station, exit 2

Inside Sanjūsangen-dō you'll find a surreal sight: around 1,000 statues of Kannon, the Buddhist goddess of mercy, standing like ethereal sentinels. (Strictly speaking, Kannon is not a goddess, but a bodhisattva, or an enlightened one who has voluntarily delayed entering nirvana to save others trapped in the wheel of suffering, or life, death, and rebirth.) At the center of these gold-plated beings is the thousand-armed Kannon, known as Senjū Kannon. Highly recommended at any time of year, and the fact that the treasures here are all under a roof make it a great choice for a rainy day.

Kyoto National Museum
京都国立博物館

527 Chaya-machi, Higashiyama-ku; tel. 075/525-2473; www.kyohaku.go.jp; 9:30am-6pm Tues.-Thurs. and Sun., 9:30am-8pm Fri.-Sat., closed Tues. when Mon. is holiday; fee varies by exhibition; from Kyoto Station, take Kyoto City Bus 100 or 206 to Sanjūsangen-dō-mae bus stop, or Keihan line to Shichijō Station

Just across the street from Sanjūsangen-dō, you'll find Kyoto National Museum. Although the permanent collection is a little halfhearted, the museum often hosts stellar temporary exhibitions featuring some of the Japanese greats, such as the Edo-period woodblock print master Hiroshige. All information is clearly presented in bilingual displays. Like its neighbor Sanjūsangen-dō, the museum is also an excellent rainy-day option.

★ Kiyomizu-dera
清水寺

1-294 Kiyomizu, Higashiyama-ku; tel. 075/551-1234; www.kiyomizudera.or.jp; 6am-6pm daily (closing time varies by season); ¥400 adults, ¥200 junior high and elementary students; from Kyoto Station, take Kyoto City Bus 100 or 206 to Gojō-zaka or Kiyomizu-michi bus stop

Perched above the sight-dense district of Southern Higashiyama, Kiyomizu-dera is one of Kyoto's most iconic temples. Look beyond the crowds and you'll see a fantastic temple that offers sweeping views of the city below. If you happen to be at Kiyomizu-dera when the

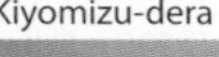
Kiyomizu-dera

cherry blossoms are in bloom—ill-advised if you can't stand crowds—the nighttime illumination of the trees surrounding the temple is spectacular.

Coming from Higashi Ōji-dōri, proceed up either Matsubara-dōri or the Chawan-zaka ("Teapot Lane"), via **Gōjō-zaka,** to the temple's main gate. Before entering the temple's main hall, keep your eyes open for **Zuigu-dō,** a separate hall on the temple's grounds with a hidden cave beneath it called the **Tainai-meguri.** The building itself is located to the left of the staircase leading up to the main temple. After paying ¥100 and removing your shoes, make your way down the stairs and through the pitch-black grotto, navigating with only the help of a rope. This sacred subterranean space symbolizes the womb of Daizuigu Bosatsu, a female bodhisattva believed to have the power to grant wishes. Inside, there's a stone that is said to have the power to grant any wish.

After making your wish, continue to **Jishu-jinja,** a matchmaking shrine on the backside of the temple's grounds where you may see young students trying their luck at walking 18 meters (59 ft) between two stone pillars in the shrine's grounds with their eyes closed. If successful, the feat is believed to bring about luck in romance. From here, continue to wander the complex, exploring its various temples, subtemples, rituals, and faithful masses.

Chion-in
知恩院

400 Rinka-chō, Higashiyama-ku; tel. 075/531-2111; www.chion-in.or.jp; 9am-4:30pm daily; outer grounds free, ¥500 adults, ¥250 junior high and elementary school students for all inner buildings and gardens; take Tōzai line to Higashiyama Station, or Kyoto City Bus 206 to Chion-in-mae bus stop

Located just north of Yasaka-jinja and Maruyama-kōen, and about 8 minutes' walk north of Kōdai-ji, this massive temple is known as the "Vatican of Pure Land Buddhism." Besides being the head temple of the Jōdo sect of this branch of Buddhism, the sheer scale of the complex is reminiscent of its Roman Catholic counterpart.

The sweeping front staircase was used in the film *The Last Samurai.* It also makes an appearance in *Lost in Translation.* There's very impressive joinery on display in the large Sanmon gate, the biggest in the country. After passing through the gate, ascend the stairs to the temple's main grounds, centered on an expansive courtyard laced with stone paths.

It's free to enter the Miei-dō (main hall), which houses an effigy of Hōnen, the priest who founded the Jōdo sect, and the neighboring Amida-dō, in which you'll see a magnificent visage of the Amida Buddha ("Amida" is the Japanese version of the Sanskrit word for "Infinite Light"). Amida Buddha is the principle Buddha of the Pure Land sect, and is believed to have fashioned an afterlife paradise where anyone is welcome who faithfully chants Amida's name. You'll need to pay admission to venture farther inside.

Deeper within the temple precincts, alongside more buildings, you'll discover two gardens: **Yūzen-en** (9am-4pm daily; ¥300 adults, ¥150 children), a rock garden with a pond that sits southeast of the Sanmon gate, and **Hōjō-en** (9am-3:50pm; ¥400 adults, ¥200 children), a classic landscape garden dating to the mid-17th century that lies east of the temple's main hall. You can also pay to enter both gardens at a discounted rate (¥500 adults, ¥250 children).

Shōren-in
青蓮院

69-1 Sanjōbōchō, Awataguchi, Higashiyama-ku; tel. 075/561-2345; www.shorenin.com; 9am-5pm daily; ¥500 adults, ¥400 junior high and high school students, ¥200 elementary school students; take Tōzai line to Higashiyama Station, or Kyoto City Bus 5, 46, or 100 to Jingū-michi bus stop

This is a hidden gem in the truest sense: Now a temple, it was originally built as villa for an abbot of the Tendai School of Buddhism. The temple also had longstanding ties to the imperial family: an empress temporarily called it home in the 18th century after a fire.

The first building you'll enter brings you to the tatami-floored Kachoden (drawing room). Here, you'll find sliding doors with paintings of natural scenes and court life, opening onto an exquisite garden centered on a pond filled with colorful koi. Wooden boardwalks link this building to other structures in the complex, including the Shijokodō, or compact main hall. After viewing the garden from within the drawing room, meander along the snaking path that laces it. It passes by a lovely **teahouse** (¥1,000, includes green tea and sweet; only open select days throughout year; for details, go to www.shorenin.com/english/tea), a shrine, and through an atmospheric bamboo grove. The grounds are lit up at night during spring and autumn (for details, go to www.shorenin.com/english/night). This is a recommended, largely crowd-free stop near Chion-in, from where it's about 5 minutes' walk north.

Kōdai-ji
高台寺

526 Shimokawara-chō, Higashiyama-ku; tel. 075/561-9966; https://www.kodaiji.com/e_index.html; 9am-5:30pm daily; ¥600 adults, ¥250 high school and junior high school students, free for children; take Kyoto City Bus 206 to Higashiyama Yasui bus stop

This Rinzai sect temple features exemplary gardens (raked-gravel and landscape). The main hall was once lacquered and graced with gilt designs, although the current incarnation is a simpler affair built in 1912. The grounds are illuminated in spring and autumn, conjuring a dreamy landscape (for details, visit https://www.kodaiji.com/e_illumi.html).

The temple was originally built in 1606 in honor of Toyotoi Hideyoshi, one of Japan's three "great unifiers," who is honored along with his wife Nene in a mausoleum that sits atop a hill behind the main temple complex. The temple's interior contains plenty of flamboyance thanks to the financial backing of Tokugawa Ieyasu, who followed Hideyoshi as the founder of the Tokugawa shogunate. There are two teahouses on the grounds, reached via a path that runs through a bamboo grove. The construction of one of these teahouses was overseen by none other than Sen no Rikyū, creator of the tea ceremony.

It's located between Kiyomizu-dera, which lies about 20 minutes' walk south, and Yasaka-jinja, 8 minutes' walk to the northwest. This temple is passed over by most tourists, making it a great place to go to escape the crowds of the area.

GION
祇園

To soak up the ambience of Kyoto's entertainment district, take a stroll down the cobblestone lane of **Hanami-kōji,** starting from the south side of Shijō-dōri, as dusk falls and the lanterns that hang in front of the wooden shopfronts flicker. Without an appointment to see a geisha performance or dine at a kaiseki restaurant, there's little in the way of casual entertainment here, but you can enjoy the area by simply meandering through its lanes and breathing in the air of sophistication.

Yasaka-jinja
八坂神社

625 Gion-machi Kitagawa, Higashiyama-ku; tel. 075/561-6155; www.yasaka-jinja.or.jp; 24 hours daily; free; take Keihan line to Gion-Shijō, exit 6, or Kyoto City Bus 206 to Gion bus stop

In the heart of Gion, Yasaka-jinja is a grand shrine that is best known for hosting Kyoto's epic summerly **Gion Matsuri.** Despite its location in the heart of Kyoto's entertainment district, Yasaka-jinja is a dignified spiritual center. It's hard to miss, given its location in the heart of the southern half of Higashiyama, the city's most dense sightseeing district, and the steady flow of faithful who come for weddings, or to pray or make a New Year's Day request to the gods for a good year ahead. Religious proceedings aside, the shrine is a great place to stroll in serenity. It backs onto the excellent Maruyama-kōen, and at night it is lit by the soft glow of hanging lanterns.

Geisha

If you find yourself in Kyoto's Gion district in the mid-evening, a geisha in training, known as a maiko, may float past. This district, dating to the 16th century, remains one of the best places to spot one. These nostalgic entertainment quarters, called hanamachi (flower towns), are the traditional stomping grounds of the increasingly rare geisha (person of the arts), or geiko (child of the arts), as they're known in Kyoto.

Carried along by high-set geta, as her elevated wooden sandals are known, a maiko is easily recognized by her thick white makeup, charcoal-painted eyebrows, and deep-red lower lip. She is draped in an exquisite, flowery kimono tied with an elongated obi (belt) left to dangle from her waist as she walks.

TRAINING AND WORK

A common misconception is that geisha are prostitutes. Historically, some geisha would enter contractual relationships with wealthy patrons who would pay for their companionship, which would include a romantic dimension. The woman would often use the money earned to pay off her debt to her okiya, the matriarchal school where she spent five to six years acquiring her substantial talents: traditional dance, playing instruments such as the three-stringed shamisen, as well as singing and engaging in wide-ranging conversation.

Before World War II, some 80,000 geisha worked in hanamachi across Japan; today, a mere 1,000 work in this trade. In their heyday, geisha in training would enter an okiya as early as six years old. Today, the situation is more fluid, with geisha living where they want, dating whom they want, and entering—at the earliest—at 15 (the age when compulsory education is completed in Japan).

ENTERTAINMENT AND EVENTS

To be entertained by geisha, you more or less need to know somebody. They mostly flit to and from exclusive parties at secretive inns, high-end restaurants, and in members-only teahouses. But if you happen to spot a geisha in the street, don't interrupt her. She's a highly trained professional who is likely on her way to an appointment. The best places to catch a glimpse of a geisha or maiko in this candid way are **Ponto-chō** and **Gion** in Kyoto and **Ginza** in Tokyo.

- **Festivals:** Geisha often dance at public performances, staged to coincide with cherry

NORTHERN HIGASHIYAMA

Northern Higashiyama has an abundance of spiritual sights, atmospheric paths, and gardens. It's also a bit less crowded than the neighboring districts.

Kyoto Museum of Crafts and Design

B1F Miyako Messe Bldg., 9-1 Okazaki Seishoji-chō, Sakyō-ku; tel. 075/762-2670; https://kmtc.jp; 9am-5pm (last admission 4:30pm) daily; free; take Tōzai subway line to Higashiyama Station

A solid rainy-day option is this museum near Heian-jingū that shows off Kyoto's wide range of traditional crafts under one roof. It's commonly referred to as the Fureaikan. You'll find sterling examples of woodworking, basket weaving, textiles, metalwork, lacquerware, gold-leaf work, and more. To find this nicely curated—and importantly, free—museum, enter the gray Miyako Messe building, then ride the escalator to the first basement floor. English signage throughout.

Heian-jingū
平安神宮

97 Nishitennō-chō, Okazaki, Sakyō-ku; tel. 075/761-0221; www.heianjingu.or.jp; 6:30am-5:30pm daily Feb. 15-Mar. 14 and Oct., 6am-6pm daily Mar. 15-Sept. 30, 6am-5pm daily Nov. 1-Feb. 14; shrine grounds free, garden ¥600 adults, ¥300 children; from Kyoto Station, take Kyoto City Bus 5 to

maiko in Kyoto

blossom season and autumn foliage in Kyoto. The most popular dances include **Miyako Odori** (held throughout Apr.), **Kyō Odori** (first three Suns. in Apr.), **Kitano Odori** (daily Apr. 15-25), **Kamogawa Odori** (daily May 1-24), and **Gion Odori** (daily Nov. 1-10). Ask your hotel concierge if your visit coincides with one of these occasions, and to help land tickets if it does.

- **Private experiences:** If you're determined to experience an evening with geisha, some pricey options do exist. Check out the varied geisha experiences provided by **Maikoya** (https://mai-ko.com/geisha); the offerings of **Chris Rowthorn Tours** (www.chrisrowthorn.com/kyoto-geisha-tours), an outfit with deep ties to hard-to-access geisha houses; or **Gion Hatanaka** (www.gionhatanaka.jp/maiko/english/about.html), a Gion ryokan that hosts regular geisha dinners.

Okazaki-kōen/Bijutsukan bus stop, or Tōzai subway line to Higashiyama Station

In the heart of the Northern Higashiyama area, you'll find an imposing shrine known as Heian-jungū. Constructed in 1895 in honor of Kyoto's 1,100th birthday, it's a replica—5/8 in scale—of the city's ancient Heian Palace, where the earliest emperors resided. The shrine is a good place to begin a journey through this culturally rich neighborhood.

The approach to the shrine is unique in that the vermillion torii gate that marks its first entrance stands nearly 25 meters above the road that leads to the shrine, which sits in a park called Okazaki-kōen. After passing through the park, you'll find the shrine at the northern end of Jingū-michi, where it meets Nijō-dōri, running east to west.

Inside the main three-doored gate is an expansive gravel-covered space that fronts the main hall of the shrine. Near the entrance, amulets and talismans are sold by shrine maidens from windows, and myriad hanging wooden plaques are scrawled with visitors' wishes. Toward the back of the complex, locals approach the main altar to offer prayers.

Beyond the shrine's main building there's a garden that can be entered for a fee, but is fine to skip, as better ones await nearby.

★ Nanzen-ji
南禅寺

86 Fukuchi-chō, Nanzen-ji, Sakyō-ku; tel.

1
2
3
4

075/771-0365; www.nanzen.net; 8:40am-5pm daily Mar.-Nov., 8:40am-4:30pm daily Dec.-Feb.; grounds free, Hōjō garden ¥600 adults, ¥500 high school students, ¥400 junior high and elementary school students, San-mon gate viewing platform ¥600 adults, ¥500 high school students, ¥400 junior high and elementary school students; take Tōzai subway line to Keage Station

A personal favorite, Nanzen-ji is a magical temple complex that sprawls over a large area in Northern Higashiyama. Its grounds invite roaming and its paths lead up into the hills surrounding this lush site, transporting those who walk them to a hidden grotto and a smattering of subtemples with pristine gardens that most visitors to the site pass by. This 13th-century temple is the head temple of a strain of the Rinzai sect of Zen Buddhism.

As you approach the temple grounds, take note of a couple of atmospheric, often missed subtemples: **Konchi-in** (86-12 Fukuchi-chō, Nanzen-ji, Sakyō-ku; tel. 075/771-3511; 8:30am-5pm daily Mar.-Nov., 8:30am-4:30pm daily Dec.-Feb.; ¥400 adults, ¥300 high school students, ¥200 junior high and elementary school students) and **Tenju-an** (86-8 Fukuchi-chō, Nanzen-ji, Sakyō-ku; tel. 075/771-0744; 9am-5pm daily Mar.-mid-Nov., 9am-4:30pm mid-Nov.-Feb.; ¥500 adults, ¥300 children). Both boast sublime gardens that are only visited by a fraction of the crowd streaming into Nanzen-ji. The entrance to Konchi-in is located on the right side of the road leading up to Nanzen-ji, about 40 meters (130 ft) before you come to the main gate to the Nanzen-ji complex. Proceed past the public restrooms on the right, and just beyond them, roughly parallel with the southern edge of Nanzen-ji's lofty San-mon Gate, you'll see the entrance to Tenju-an.

After soaking up the calm ambience at these two subtemples, explore Nanzen-ji's grounds at a contemplative pace. Note the aqueduct running through the grounds—a Meiji-period (1868-1912) construction once used to transport goods and water between Kyoto and Lake Biwa northeast of the city. Facing the aqueduct from the temple's main grounds, up a stone staircase, is the subtemple **Nanzen-in** and its Hōjō garden. Follow the path leading uphill to the right, walking beside the canal as you go, for a great view of the city below.

If you cross under the canal from the main temple grounds and, instead, take a hard left, following the road beside the stream, you'll reach a stone stairway that leads into the hills. Walk to the top—about 200 meters (656 ft) behind the temple grounds—where you'll discover **Okuno-in,** a sacred space containing a waterfall and a hidden grotto.

1: Nanzen-ji 2: Heian-jingū 3: Ginkaku-ji 4: Philosopher's Path

★ Philosopher's Path
哲学の道

Strolling the Philosopher's Path, the inspiration for its name—Tetsugaku-no-michi in Japanese—will be evident. This pathway runs beside a canal that directs a gentle stream of water through one of the city's most tranquil neighborhoods, and the combination of the water and greenery is the ideal place for a contemplative stroll. This is exactly what Kyoto University philosophy professor Nishida Kitaro—who inspired the name of this path—did whenever he grew weary of trying to untangle some question and craved reconnection with his senses and the outside world.

The path winds past a host of atmospheric temples and shrines, some of them with stellar gardens. Rather than having a set agenda, I recommend ambling at your own pace and stopping at any that may catch your eye. In the spirit of its namesake, stroll the path with an open mind and see where your intuition leads. You'll see a wide range of foliage, including cherry trees that burst with color during hanami season. (Note that the path is thronged in springtime. Avoid visiting during daylight hours during the hanami rush. Instead, go after dusk when the trees are lit up for a few hours.)

This path begins in the south from about 100 meters (300 ft) north of the temple of

Eikan-dō and ends at the foot of the approach to **Ginkaku-ji** in the north, for a total distance of about 1.8 kilometers (1.1 mi). It takes about 30 minutes to walk at a leisurely pace, not accounting for stops at sights along the way.

Ginkaku-ji
銀閣寺

2 Ginkaku-ji-chō, Sakyō-ku; tel. 075/771-5725; www.shokoku-ji.jp/en/ginkakuji/; 8:30am-5pm daily Mar.-Nov., 9am-4:30pm daily Dec.-Feb.; ¥500 adults, ¥300 junior high and elementary school students; take Kyoto City Bus 5 or 17 to Ginkaku-ji-michi bus stop

Ginkaku-ji, or the "Silver Pavilion," is a stunning temple complex with superb gardens and rambling halls. Built in 1482, it was originally the retirement villa of shogun Ashikaga Yoshimasa. Yoshimasa was the grandson of Ashikaga Yoshimitsu, who a few decades prior had built Kinkaku-ji (the Golden Pavilion) on the other side of town. It was repurposed into a Zen temple following Yoshimasa's death in 1490.

Located near the northern end of the Philosopher's Path, the grounds of Ginkaku-ji are classically Zen. On one hand, there's an intensely green, moss-covered garden. Contrasting this is a separate dry-gravel garden complete with a miniature representation of Mount Fuji. A still pond surrounded by gnarled pine trees frames the beautiful main hall, which is decidedly more rustic than the temple's gold-plated counterpart, Kinkaku-ji, across town.

Simply exploring the grounds via a circular loop and meandering through the buildings' dark wooden corridors makes a visit to Ginkaku-ji worthwhile. But be sure to also walk the path that leads up a hill behind the complex, affording a sweeping vista of the grounds and the surrounding area below.

For better or worse, Ginkaku-ji is one of Kyoto's most popular spots. Aim to visit either just as it opens, or within an hour of closing to avoid the picture-snapping masses.

Eikan-dō
永観堂

48 Eikandō-chō, Sakyō-ku; tel. 075/761-0007; www.eikando.or.jp; 9am-5pm (last entry 4pm) daily, special hours during evening in autumn; ¥600 adults, ¥400 children; take Tōzai line to Keage Station, or Kyoto City Bus 5 to Nanzenji-Eikandō-michi bus stop

This tranquil Jōdo (Pure Lane) sect temple is 7 minutes' walk north from Nanzen-ji. It serves as the southern end of the Philosopher's Path and is famed for its autumn foliage, particularly its fiery maples. Originally the villa of a court noble during the Heian period (794-1185), it was converted into a temple originally known as Zenrin-ji. Its popularly used name of Eikan-dō is derived from an 11th-century priest named Eikan.

Its buildings, containing attractively painted sliding doors and linked by wooden walkways, sit beside a serene garden, crisscrossed by tiny streams that run into a pond with an island in the middle where a petite shrine stands. Standing above the grounds on a hill is the two-story Tahoto Pagoda, which has a square base and a rounded second level. Climb the stairs to this structure and enjoy views over the temple grounds and city beyond.

Note that the cost of entry is raised during autumn, when the grounds are illuminated at night (second half of Nov.; ¥1,000 daytime, ¥600 nighttime). Be forewarned: The crowds are intense when the leaves turn, particularly in November. During other times of year, however, the temple is an appealing escape from selfie-stick-toting masses who congregate at many of the other more famous temples around town.

Hōnen-in
法然院

30 Goshonodan-chō, Shishigatani, Sakyō-ku; tel. 075/771-2420; www.honen-in.jp; 6am-4pm daily; free; take Kyoto City Bus 5 or 17 to Ginkaku-ji-michi bus stop

A hushed temple founded in 1680 just off the Philosopher's Path, tucked away in a lush grove dotted by pools of water, Hōnen-in is

Northern Higashiyama's Less Crowded Side

The quieter side of Northern Higashiyama is best seen on a hill known as **Yoshidayama,** about 25 minutes' walk northwest of Nanzen-ji, or 20 minutes west of the northern edge of the Philosopher's Path. Simply strolling through the grounds through these three sights (for free) will work its magic.

KONKAI-KŌMYŌ-JI

金戒光明寺

121 Kurodani-chō, Sakyō-ku; tel. 075/771-2204; www.kurodani.jp/en; 9am-4pm daily; grounds free, garden ¥600 (Nov.-early Dec. only)

Known for its atmospheric **Kurodani Garden,** this gem of a temple is ensconced on the southern side of Yoshidayama. To find it, walk west on Marutamachi-dōri. Walk about 200 meters (650 ft), then curl into the alley located just past on your right. Follow the alley, then at the end walk up the stairs, which lead to the temple. It's free to enter the main hall and walk through its grounds, where you'll find a pagoda and a graveyard. To enter the garden tucked away behind the temple you must pay ¥600 throughout November and into the first week of December when autumn leaves have peaked.

Shinnyo-dō

SHINNYO-DŌ

真如堂

82 Shinnyo-chō, Jōdoji, Sakyō-ku; tel. 075/771-0915; https://shin-nyo-do.jp; 9am-4pm daily; grounds free, ¥500 main hall and inner garden, ¥1,000 during special periods of Mar. and Nov.-early Dec.

A brilliant place to see autumn foliage with a fraction of the crowds, this temple of the Tendai sect is about 5 minutes' walk uphill from Konkai-Kōmyō-ji (aka Kurodani). Established in 984, razed in the Onin War (1467-1477), and finally rebuilt and relocated to its current location in 1693, its grounds include a main hall with a gilt canopy, sacred statues, paintings that alternate every half-year (one depicting the scene of Buddha's death, the other a mandala representing the Buddhist Pure Land), a three-storied pagoda, and an inner garden.

YOSHIDA-JINJA

吉田神社

30 Kaguraoka-chō, Yoshida, Sakyō-ku; tel. 075/771-3788; www.yoshidajinja.com; 9am-5pm daily; free

Standing above both temples is the secluded hilltop shrine of Yoshida-jinja, which was originally built by nobleman Fujiwara no Yamakage in 859 to ward off evil spirits from what was then the ancient capital of Heian-kyō. The shrine grounds contain one main hall (Hongū) and 10 other sub-shrines, dedicated to an array of kami (gods): one guarding from evil, one bringing good fortune, another boosting scholarship, and so on. The shrine is known for its annual **Setsubun Festival** (Feb. 2-4), the end of winter on the traditional calendar. Attendees throw soybeans at someone suited up in an oni (demon) costume while chanting "Fuku wa uchi! Oni wa soto!" ("Happiness come in! Demons go out!"). Sticklers will also eat the same number of soybeans as their age to protect from illness in the coming year.

about 10 minutes' walk south of jam-packed Ginkaku-ji. The thatched-roof entrance gate, blanketed in moss, is approached via a leafy path, creating a magical atmosphere. Upon entering, walk between two sculpted rectangular mounds of sand, over a pond, and past raked-gravel gardens to a hidden grotto. The main temple, which houses a black statue of Amida Buddha, can only be entered from April 1-7 and November 1-7. There's also a gallery on-site that hosts local art exhibitions. This is a worthwhile stop off the Philosopher's Path that is mercifully free of crowds.

DOWNTOWN AND CENTRAL KYOTO

Roughly in Kyoto's geographical heart, downtown is a convenient place to shop, eat, go out in the evening, and sleep.

Ponto-chō

先斗町

If you've ever seen a photograph of a cobblestone alley in Kyoto—festooned with softly glowing red lanterns and flanked by dark wooden shopfronts with doors obscured by curtains—chances are the street in the image was Ponto-chō.

This pedestrian-only street is a sight in itself and evokes the quiet refinement of old Kyoto perhaps better than any other lane in the city. Running along the west bank of the Kamo River, Ponto-chō extends from just south of Sanjō Station (Tōzai subway line, Keihan line) at its northern edge to bustling Shijō-dōri, near both Gion-Shijō Station (Keihan line) and Kawaramachi Station (Hankyū line) at its southern end.

For maximum impact, visit Ponto-chō after the sun sets, when the paper lanterns flicker and well-heeled patrons make their way into one of the alley's exclusive eateries and bars.

Kyoto Imperial Palace

京都御所

3 Kyoto Gyōen, Kamigyō-ku; tel. 075/211-1215; https://sankan.kunaicho.go.jp/guide/kyoto.html; 9am-4:30pm (last entry 3:50) Tues.-Sun., closed Tues. if Mon. falls on national holiday Mar.-Sept., 9am-4pm (last entry 3:20) Tues.-Sun., closed Tues. if Mon. falls on national holiday Oct.-Feb.; free; take Karasuma subway line to Imadegawa Station

Ensconced in the center of a large park, the Gosho, as it's known in Japanese, is the Imperial family's home away from their current home in Tokyo. It's the site various ceremonies infused with much pomp, including the ascension of each new emperor to the throne. Originally constructed in 794, the current complex was built in 1855, following numerous incarnations made necessary by fires. Surrounded by a wall and laced with gravel pathways, the palace does retain Japanese accents—low, sweeping rooflines, a mostly wooden shell—but it's otherwise quite modern. If you're a history buff and would like to see the emperor's old primary residence, it's worth a stop. You can either follow a simple route with English language signage or join a free group **tour** in English (1 hour; 10am and 2pm) by showing up at the Kunaicho (Imperial Household Office). Be sure to bring your passport, which is necessary to join one of the tours.

Nijō-jō

二条城

541 Nijōjō-chō, Nijō-dōri, Horikawa Nishi-iru, Nakagyō-ku; tel. 075/841-0096; http://nijo-jocastle.city.kyoto.lg.jp/?lang=en; 8:45am-5pm (last entry 4pm), Ninomaru Palace closed Tues. Dec.-Jan. and Jul.-Aug., closed Dec. 26-Jan. 4; ¥620 adults, free for junior high school students and younger for Nijō-jō only, ¥1,030 adults, ¥350 high and junior high school students, ¥200 elementary school students for Nijō-jō and Ninomaru Palace; take Tōzai line to Nijō-jō-mae Station

This imposing castle compound—surrounded by stunning gardens and towering stone walls—is the city's most visible demonstration of the power that the military elite held over the emperor during the feudal Edo period (1603-1867).

Construction of the majestic complex began in 1603. It was intended to serve as the

Kyoto home of the first shogun, Tokugawa Ieyasu, and was completed 23 years later by Ieyasu's grandson Iemitsu, who also built a five-story keep. When the Edo period came to a close in 1867 and power was restored to the emperor, the castle was then used as an imperial palace for a time, until it was donated to the city.

The castle can roughly be split into four sections: the outer walls and moats, two inner layers of defenses that encircle the complex—the Honmaru, or main ring of defense, and the secondary layer, or Ninomaru—and a smattering of attractive classical gardens. The Honmaru is not usually open to the public, but the Ninomaru area is.

Be sure to visit the **Ninomaru Palace.** Inside you'll discover some of the defensive tricks employed by the shoguns to subvert would-be assassins, such as the legendary "nightingale floors" that squeaked in a way that vaguely resembles a bird call to warn of any attempted sneak attack. The palace is also covered in artistic flourishes, from floridly adorned ceilings to handsomely painted sliding doors, reflecting the opulent tastes of the shoguns. Outside the palace, be sure to meander through **Seiryū-en,** a beautiful landscape garden.

This castle stands at the center of the ancient capital, a stellar example of Japanese castle architecture and one of the city's most popular sites. Avoid going during the middle of the day when the site is flooded with visitors. Try to arrive just as it opens to beat the rush.

Kyoto International Manga Museum

京都国際マンガミュージアム

Karasuma-dōri, Oike-agaru, Nakagyō-ku; tel. 075/254-7414; www.kyotomm.jp/en; 10am-6pm Thurs.-Mon., closed Fri. when Thurs. is holiday; ¥900 adults, ¥200 junior high and high school students, ¥100 elementary school students; take Karasuma, Tōzai lines to Karasuma Oike Station

For hardcore manga fans, this place is pretty special. It's essentially a massive library of manga. It's housed in a former school building and boasts an impressive 300,000 individual volumes, which can be freely read for the price of admission. There are also (mostly bilingual) exhibitions on the history of manga and how it's drawn. Storytellers known as kamishibai, who essentially read a story from a scroll of images, sporadically perform onsite; the kamishibai tradition began long ago with monks who used drawings on scrolls to teach the basics of Buddhism to peasants who couldn't read. An essential stop for manga fans and a good rainy-day option for anyone.

Kyoto Samurai and Ninja Museum with Experience

侍体験、ニンジャ体験 | サムライ忍者ミュージアム京都

Teramachi Utanokoji Bldg. 2F, 292 Higashidaimonji-chō, Nakagyō-ku; tel. 075/585-5410; https://mai-ko.com/samurai/; 10:30am-8pm daily; ¥2,500 adults, ¥2,200 children; take Hankyū line to Kawaramachi Station, or Karasuma line to Shijō Station

This "experience-based museum" gives a fun look into the iconic yet obscure world of Japan's warriors and assassins of yore, the samurai and ninja. It begins with a guided tour (in English) through a varied collection of armor and weaponry, peppered with plenty of history and lore. You'll then suit up in samurai kit and learn to sheath and unsheath a katana, then fire arrows with a bow, before donning an all-black getup, flinging ninja stars, and puffing darts from an assassin's blowgun. On irregular days, you may also have a chance to see a sword demo by a bona fide samurai descendent. A sure hit if you're traveling with kids, although adults enjoy discovering their inner warrior too. Walk-ins are permitted, but it's popular. Reserve ahead through the English-language website to avoid being forced to join a queue.

NORTHWEST KYOTO

More out of the way than other areas of the city, Northwest Kyoto is nonetheless home to a handful of significant temples. Besides heavy hitters like **Kinkaku-ji** in all its gilt

glory, and **Ryōan-ji**, famed for its rock garden, there are a number of quieter gems like the serene temple compounds of **Myōshin-ji** and **Daitoku-ji.** East of the temples is **Kyoto Botanical Gardens** (Shimogamohangi-chō, Sakyō-ku; tel. 075/701-0141; www.pref.kyoto.jp/plant/; gardens 9am-5pm (last entry 4pm) daily, conservatory 10am-4pm (last entry 3:30pm) daily; ¥200 adults, ¥150 high school students, ¥80 elementary and junior high school students, additional ¥200 for conservatory; take Karasuma subway line to Kitayama Station, exit 3), a pristine natural space brimming with bamboo, cherry trees, hydrangeas, peonies, plum trees, lotus flowers bobbing in ponds, and more.

Ryōan-ji
龍安寺

13 Goryōnoshitamachi, Ryōan-ji, Ukyō-ku; tel. 075/463-2216; www.ryoanji.jp; 8am-5pm daily Mar.-Nov., 8:30am-4:30pm daily Dec.-Feb.; ¥500 adults, ¥300 junior high and elementary school students; take Kyoto City Bus 59 to Ryōan-ji-mae bus stop, or Keifuku Kitano line from Arashiyama to Ryōan-ji Station

The raked-gravel garden in the grounds of Ryōan-ji, with 15 rocks placed just so, is in many ways the embodiment of what most people think of when they hear the words "Zen garden." As with Ginkaku-ji, Ryōan-ji was once a villa, lived in by an aristocrat during the Heian period (794-1185). It became a temple of Zen Buddhism's Rinzai sect in 1450.

The origins of the temple's iconic rock garden are less clear. Though the precise meaning of the garden is an enigma, various stabs have been taken at theories on its meaning, from islands in the ocean to a tiger carrying her cubs across a pond to infinity. One interesting point: Viewed from any angle, one rock will always be concealed from view.

Aside from this spiritual statement made in gravel, the head priest's former quarters (Hōjō) and the old kitchen (kuri) still stand. Take a peek at the compact gardens behind the Hōjō, as well as the beautifully painted sliding doors inside the Hōjō's tatami rooms.

To have a fighting chance of pondering the famed rock garden when it's not being mobbed by visitors, aim to arrive either just after the temple opens, or within an hour of closing.

★ Kinkaku-ji
金閣寺

1 Kinkaku-ji-chō, Kita-ku; tel. 075/461-0013; www.shokoku-ji.jp/en/kinkakuji; 9am-5pm daily; ¥400 adults, ¥300 junior high and elementary school students; from Kyoto Station, take Kyoto City Bus 205 to Kinkaku-ji-mae bus stop, or Kyoto City Bus 12 from Sanjō-Keihan Station (Tōzai line) to Kinkakuji-michi bus stop

Easily Kyoto's most recognizable temple, Kinkaku-ji cuts a striking profile, particularly on a sunny day. Its upper two stories are famously covered in gold, giving the site an ethereal glint and causing a mirage-like reflection to form in the pond surrounding its base. This Zen temple was originally built to serve as the villa of shogun Ashikaga Yoshimitsu, whose grandson built Ginkaku-ji in the northeast of town. The site was converted into a temple in 1408 upon Yoshimitsu's death.

Surrounded by greenery and fronted by a pond, Kinkaku-ji's design reflects the opulent Kitayama aristocratic culture at its height. The first floor was built in the style of a Heian-period palace—pillars made of timber, plaster walls painted white. The second floor is in the style of a samurai residence with statues of Kannon, the Buddhist goddess of compassion, and Four Heavenly Kings, mythological guardians of the four cardinal directions. The third floor is designed like a Zen Hall in the Chinese style. The roof is topped by a phoenix made of, yes, gold.

The grounds also include the former head priest's residence, or Hōjō, which can only be seen from outside, and a series of gardens that remain as they were when Yoshimitsu once strolled through them. If you see other visitors tossing ¥1 coins onto a statue—with a small

1: Nijō-jō **2:** Ryōan-ji **3:** Kinkaku-ji

Northwest Kyoto's Less Crowded Side

Check out these two temples if you want to get away from the crowds:

NINNA-JI
仁和寺

33 Omurōuchi, Ukyō-ku; tel. 075/461-1155; www.ninnaji.jp/en; 9am-5pm daily Mar.-Nov., 9am-4:30pm daily Dec.-Feb.; grounds free, admission to Goten ¥500 adults, ¥300 junior high and elementary school students; take Kyoto City Bus 59 from Sanjō Keihan Station (Tōzai line), or Keifuku Kitano line from Arashiyama to Omuro-Ninna-ji Station

A 15-minute walk northwest of Myōshin-ji, this ancient temple (founded in 888) at the base of the mountains north of town is a good place to escape the crowds of Ryōan-ji and Kinkaku-ji. A UNESCO World Heritage Site with a handsome five-story pagoda, its gardens are perfectly suited to a meditative ramble. Be sure to visit the **Goten,** where the head priest once resided. Surrounding this building on the southeastern corner of the compound are idyllic gardens centered on ponds, bridges, a variety of trees and shrubs, and raked gravel.

Around mid-April, when the Omuro cherry tree blossoms, is the one time the temple gets crowded; admission also increases to ¥600.

TŌJI-IN
等持院

63 Tōji-in Kita-machi, Kita-ku; tel. 075/461-5786; https://toujiin.jp; 9am-5pm daily; ¥500 adults, ¥300 children; take Keifuku Kitano line to Tōji-in Station

About 20 minutes' walk east of Ninna-ji, this temple is another good off-the-radar option. Founded by Shogun Ashikaga Takauji in 1341, with the present structures dating to 1818, the real star at this temple is its garden. The serene space contains two notable ponds: one shaped like the character for the word shin or kokoro (心), which means "heart" or "mind," and one that resembles a lotus blossom. There's also a superb teahouse on-site that was built in 1457, brilliantly exhibiting the wabi-sabi (shabby-chic plus Zen) aesthetic of the tea ceremony.

fortune on the ground surrounding it—this is your chance to try to toss a few of your own. If you can throw a coin directly into the statue's lap, you'll be blessed with good luck.

As you exit the grounds, you'll pass a teahouse, some shops selling trinkets, and a small subtemple that contains a statue of one of the Five Wisdom Kings that is believed may have been carved by Kobo Daishi (774-835), a monk and scholar of legendary proportions, and founder of the Shingon school of Buddhism.

As with many of Kyoto's top sights, it's worth trying to avoid going at the most popular times: midday any day of the week, and all day on weekends. Opening time on Monday or Tuesday mornings is a good time to visit.

Myōshin-ji
妙心寺

64 Myōshin-ji-chō, Hanazono, Ukyō-ku; tel. 075/461-5226; www.myoshinji.or.jp/english; 9:10am-11:40am (entry permitted every 20 minutes), 12:30pm (entry permitted once), 1pm-4:40pm (entry permitted every 20 minutes) daily, closed sporadically; ¥700 adults, ¥400 junior high and elementary school students; take JR Sagano San-in line to Hanazono Station, or Kyoto City Bus 62, 63, 65 or 66 from Sanjō Keihan Station (Tōzai line) to Myōshin-ji-mae bus stop

This sprawling Zen Buddhist complex of the Rinzai sect is just south of Myōshin-ji Station on the Kitano line. The grounds are peppered with subtemples as well as a wonderful garden. Myōshin-ji is also notable for its zazen (seated meditation) classes (for prices and times, go to www.myoshinji.or.jp/english/zen/info.html).

The temple complex was founded in 1337, originally as a villa for an abdicated emperor, and was later converted into a temple. Today, there are nearly 50 subtemples, most of which are closed to the public with four open year-round. The bulk of the major structures are grouped around the southern gate. Whether you enter from the north or south, wandering through the lanes that thread through the compound will leave you feeling enchanted.

Within the temple of Myōshin-ji itself, stop by **Hattō Hall,** where a huge painting of a dragon is emblazoned across its ceiling. Note that this building can only be entered on a guided tour (30 minutes, Japanese language only). The subtemple of **Taizo-in** (9am-5pm daily; ¥500) is renowned for its stunning garden centered on a pond.

Two other subtemples within the complex that can be entered by the public are **Keishunin** (9am-5pm daily; ¥400), which has some alluring stroll gardens, and **Daishinin** (9am-5pm daily; ¥300), where you'll find a meditative rock garden.

Daitoku-ji
大徳寺

53 Daitoku-ji-chō, Murasakino, Kita-ku; tel. 075/491-0019; http://zen.rinnou.net/head_temples/07daitoku.html; main temple and grounds 24 hours, subtemples various hours; free to enter complex, subtemples charge separate admission fees; take Karasuma line to Kitaōji Station

In some ways similar to Myōshin-ji, this sprawling, walled temple compound is one of Kyoto's prime Zen centers. This oasis of calm has some of the best rock gardens in Kyoto, minus the throngs of Ryōan-ji. It's also home to **Izusen Daijinten,** a restaurant that is the best place to dine like a monk in Kyoto.

Enter through the main gate, located at the east side of the complex, then proceed to explore four magical subtemples with gardens: **Ryōgen-in** (9am-4:30pm daily; ¥350), **Zuihō-in** (9am-5pm daily; ¥400), **Kōtō-in** (9am-4:30pm daily; ¥500) and **Daisen-in** (https://daisen-in.net; 9am-5pm daily; ¥400). Daitoku-ji itself, after which the entire compound is named, is not open to the public.

Check out Ryōgen-in's raked-gravel garden (thought to be Japan's smallest) and moss garden, and don't miss Zuihō-in's stunning rock garden, designed in the 1960s by Shigemori Mirei. This is a fantastic alternative to the popular Ryōan-ji. Kōtō-in's inner temple grounds are home to a garden and a humble tearoom designed by Sen no Rikyū, founder of the tea ceremony. Daisen-in boasts two spectacular dry landscape gardens considered to be among Japan's most iconic examples of this quintessential element of Zen culture, but note that there's a very strict no-photography policy.

ARASHIYAMA
嵐山

West of Kyoto proper, Arashiyama is dense with sights, centered around the atmospheric **Arashiyama Bamboo Grove.** The main unnamed thoroughfare running through the area that connects to the **Tōgetsu-kyō bridge,** which spans the Katsura River, is a tourist trap, to be passed over for the treasures beyond.

Tenryū-ji
天龍寺

68 Susukinobaba-chō, Saga Tenryū-ji, Ukyo-ku; tel. 075/881-1235; www.tenryuji.com; 8:30am-5:30pm daily Mar. 21-Oct.20, 8:30am-5pm daily Oct. 21-Mar. 20; Hōjō garden ¥500 adults and high school students, ¥300 junior high and elementary school students, garden and buildings ¥800 adults and high school students, ¥600 junior high and elementary school students; take JR Sagano line to Saga-Arashiyama Station, or Hankyū line to Arashiyama Station

The best place to begin your exploration of Arashiyama is Tenryū-ji. This important temple—the base of the Rinzai school of Zen Buddhism—has a wonderful garden beside the area's famed bamboo grove, a stunning example of the old Chinese gardening principle of drawing on "borrowed scenery."

Arashiyama's Less Crowded Side

Although it may be hard to believe after a trip to the bamboo grove, a few pockets of Arashiyama remain surprisingly uncrowded. The simplest way to explore the area's lesser-known temples is to turn right at the T-junction at the western end of the path that leads through the area's thronged bamboo grove, near the entrance to Ōkōchi Sansō. After that, walk straight ahead and pass the pond on your left. From here, it's possible to take a lovely 25-minute walk (one-way) passing through a rural area of rice paddies and residences, where you'll find some enchanting smaller temples well away from the crowds, including (in south-north order):

JŌJAKKŌ-JI

常寂光寺

3 Saga Ogurayama, Ukyō-ku; tel. 075/861-0435; www.jojakko-ji.or.jp; 9am-5pm daily; ¥500

This discreet temple is a good place to come for some peace and quiet. Its mossy grounds contain a pagoda and lots of trees. If you're going to pay admission to one of these temples, make it this one.

NISON-IN

二尊院

27 Monzenchōjin-chō, Saga Nison-in, Ukyō-ku; tel. 075/861-0687; 9am-5pm (last entry 4:30pm) daily; ¥500 adults, free for ages 12 and under

About 3 minutes' walk north of Jōjakkō-ji, Nison-in offers a similar experience. Leisurely strolling its grounds has a calming effect.

GIŌ-JI

祇王寺

32 Kozaka-chō, Saga Toriimoto, Ukyō-ku; tel. 075/861-3574; www.giouji.or.jp; 9am-5pm daily; ¥300 adults, ¥100 students

A 4-minute walk north from Nison-in, Giō-ji has a petite main hall topped by a thatched roof and a moss garden on its grounds.

ADASHINO NENBUTSU-JI

化野念仏寺

17 Adashino-chō, Sagatoriimoto, Ukyō-ku; tel. 075/861-2221; www.nenbutsuji.jp; 9am-4:30pm daily Mar.-Nov., 9am-3:30pm daily Dec.-Feb.; ¥500 adults, ¥400 high school and junior high school students, free for elementary school students and younger

This temple has some 8,000 stone effigies commemorating those who have died without any surviving kin. From here, it's a 40-minute walk southeast back to Arashiyama Station on the Keifuku line.

This temple was built 1339-1345 by shogun Ashikaga Takauji (1305-1358), in the hopes of appeasing the angry spirit of Emperor Go-Daigo. Takauji had once been Go-Daigo's ally, but later turned on him in his attempt to gain control of Japan. The original complex contained as many as 150 buildings, which have been ravaged by fire many times through the centuries; the ones that stand today were built during the Meiji period.

The garden, however, remains largely as it was when it was first designed by famed garden master Muso Soseki (1275-1331), the first head priest of the temple. Centered on an expansive pond surrounded by manicured pines and misshapen rocks, a bamboo-covered slope rises into the distance. The story goes that the garden was meant to reflect a Chinese myth about a koi (carp) that made its way up a waterfall and transformed into a dragon. Stones rising from the pond, which teems with koi, stretch up a hill strewn with large stones, said to resemble the legendary waterfall.

Begin your tour of the temple by slipping off your shoes and exploring the interior of the main hall, or Hōjō (9am-5pm daily Mar. 21-Oct. 20, 9am-4:30pm daily Oct. 21-Mar. 20; ¥500), then meander through the garden. Drift toward the north gate of the temple complex, which deposits you right in the thick of the area's iconic bamboo grove.

★ Arashiyama Bamboo Grove
嵯峨野の竹林

Arashiyama, Ukyō-ku; 24 hours; free; take JR Sagano (San-in) line to Saga-Arashiyama Station, or Hankyū line to Arashiyama Station

Strolling through the Arashiyama Bamboo Grove feels like passing into another realm, where shoots reach skyward and extend in all directions with no other competing forms of vegetation in view. The real magic of this grove must be experienced firsthand: It doesn't always fully translate to photographs. You can almost imagine two martial artists lithely leaping between the supple sprouts—the largest being up to 40 meters (131 ft) in height and 35 cm (18 in) in diameter—evoking the famous scene from *Crouching Tiger, Hidden Dragon*. There is an almost eerie glow to the light in this singular forest, which takes on an increasingly ethereal glow as dusk begins to fall.

I recommend entering this enchanted realm after first exploring Tenryū-ji. You'll find yourself in the midst of the bamboo as soon as you pass through the north gate of the temple. Once you pass through the gate, turn left and simply walk straight up the mountain path. The grove works its magic most intensely as you reach its final section, which terminates at the entrance to the alluring **Ōkōchi Sansō** villa.

Ōkōchi Sansō
大河内山荘

8 Tabuchiyama-chō, Saga Ogurayama, Ukyō-ku; tel. 075/872-2233; 9am-5pm daily; ¥1,000 adults and high school students, ¥500 junior high and elementary school students; take Hankyū line to Arashiyama Station, or JR Sagano line to Saga-Arashiyama Station

On the far side of the bamboo forest, you'll discover the highlight of Arashiyama: a dreamy mountaintop villa known as Ōkōchi Sansō. Like many of Kyoto's beautiful places, Ōkōchi Sansō was once the home of a figure of ample means, namely the movie star Ōkōchi Denjirō (1898-1962), famous for his roles in

Arashiyama Bamboo Grove

dramas set during the Edo period. This site is a bit of a walk from the nearest station through the area's iconic bamboo forest, but that's part of the fun.

When you reach the top of the famed bamboo grove, forge ahead to the ticket window at the start of a footpath leading up a slope before making your way toward the magnificent garden above. Simply follow the arrows indicating the order in which to explore the grounds, winding through dense tunnels of foliage and past a swath of earth overtaken by a verdant blanket of moss, revealing glimpses of downtown Kyoto spreading out in the distance below, as well as a mystical mountain vista seen from the other side of the peak.

As you move through the grounds, also take time to savor the beautiful villa itself—built in a traditional Japanese residential style—as well as a serene teahouse oozing rustic charm. You can't enter either of these structures, but you can take a break at a modern teahouse that you come to at the end of the walking route. Here, hand over your entrance ticket to the kindly staff in exchange for a sweet and a warm cup of matcha.

Katsura Rikyū (Imperial Villa)
桂離宮

Katsura-Misono, Nishikyō-ku; tel. 075/211-1215; http://sankan.kunaicho.go.jp/english/guide/katsura.html; by appointment (tours offered hourly 9am-4pm Tues.-Sun., not offered Tues. if Mon. is holiday); ¥1,000 adults, free for ages 12-17; take Hankyū line to Katsura Station

Roughly 6 kilometers (3.7 mi) southeast of Arashiyama's main drag and 5 kilometers (3.1 mi) west of Kyoto Station in the rather drab suburban neighborhood of Katsura, this villa was built on a plot of land gifted by Shogun Toyotomi Hideyoshi, one of Japan's "three great unifiers," to a prince named Hachijō Toshihito. It's a stellar example of a traditional villa, boasting four teahouses and an exquisite garden. Visiting requires joining a 40-minute **tour** (English audio guides available; English tours offered at 10am, 11am, 2pm, and 3pm), held several times daily (except Mon.) through the grounds, looping around the pond at the center of the stroll garden. Buildings can't be entered and photos can only be shot from certain places.

To reserve a spot on one of the tours, you must apply in person—be sure to take your passport—at the **Imperial Household Office** (tel. 075/211-1215; 8:40am-5pm Tues.-Sun., closed Tues. if Mon. is holiday), located inside **Kyoto Gyōen.** There are also limited places up for grabs on the Imperial Household Agency's website (http://sankan.kunaicho.go.jp/order/index_EN.html), but they tend to get taken fast.

Saihō-ji
西芳寺

56 Matsuo Jingatani-chō, Nishikyō-ku; tel. 075/391-3631; http://saihoji-kokedera.com; by appointment; ¥3,000; walk 2 minutes from Kokedera Suzumushidera bus stop (from Kyoto Station, take Kyoto City Bus 73), or take Kyoto City Bus 63 or 73 from Arashiyama to Kokedera Suzumushidera bus stop

This atmospheric temple, popularly known as Kokedera ("Moss Temple"), is famed, as this name suggests, for its lush moss garden. The entire complex is awash in emerald hues from some 120 varieties of moss. Before proceeding to the garden, all guests must first chant and write out a sutra (Buddhist scripture). Just follow the lead of the monk and the brush strokes of Japanese visitors seated around you.

All visits must be booked in advance via post, but the effort is worth it. Note that the temple accepts reservations up to two months before the date of a desired visit and requires a minimum of up to three weeks' notice for those coming from overseas. Go to http://saihoji-kokedera.com/en/reservation.html for detailed application instructions.

Entertainment and Events

THEATER

While it may not match the scope of Tokyo's performing arts scene, Kyoto is a good place to catch traditional theater performances, from flamboyant kabuki to enigmatic Noh. On the avant-garde side of things, the city is home to Japan's only theater dedicated solely to the grotesque, mesmerizing style of modern dance known as butoh. And of course, Kyoto is the best place in the country to see geisha perform seasonal dances or entertain over a meal or tea (page 298).

MINAMI-ZA

198 Nakano-chō, Shijō-dōri, Yamato-oji nishiiru, Higashiyama-ku; tel. 075/561-1155; www.kabukiweb.net/theatres/minamiza; performances from ¥5,000; take Keihan line to Gion-Shijō Station, exit 6

The premier theater for kabuki in Kyoto is Minami-za, an imposing building at the corner of Kawabata-dōri and Shijō-dōri. If kabuki intrigues you, it's possible to sit in for a few acts rather than watch an entire play, which can last upward of four hours. English audio guides are available. Tickets can either be bought at the box office or online at www.kabukiweb.net. Ask your hotel concierge for help if you're unsure whether a performance is scheduled during your stay.

KANZE KAIKAN NOH THEATER

44 Enshoji-chō, Okazaki, Sakyō-ku; tel. 075/771-6114; www.kyoto-kanze.jp; performances from ¥2,000; take Tōzai subway line to Higashiyama Station, exit 1

The other form of traditional theater with a presence in Kyoto is the more refined—and enigmatic—Noh. The best place to watch this slow-paced, restrained artform is at the Kanze Kaikan Noh Theater. Performances on the stunning cedar-wood marvel of a stage are mainly held on holidays and weekends. Your best bet is to ask your hotel concierge whether a performance will take place during your stay, then for help with securing tickets.

BUTOH KAN

123 Tsukinuke-chō, Nakagyō-ku; tel. 075/257-2125; www.butohkan.jp; ¥4,200; take Karasuma or Tōzai line to Karasuma Oike Station, exit 6

For a truly avant-garde dance experience, this theater run by legendary dancer Ima Tenko is the only space dedicated solely to the starkly emotive dance style known as butoh, which has made waves in the dance world since its birth in the late 1950s. It somehow feels fitting that this provocative performance art—raw, primal, erotic, grotesque—should find a home in an Edo period storehouse in the heart of ancient Kyoto, bastion of Japan's most traditional of arts, which butoh haughtily subverts. And with just enough seating for eight, the line between dancer and audience is thin indeed. At the time of writing, the theater had indefinitely stopped performances due to the coronavirus pandemic, but is intent to resume. Visit the website and contact the theater to check on the status of potential upcoming performances.

FESTIVALS

★ GION MATSURI

Gion; www.gionmatsuri.jp/manu/manual.html; throughout July; free

One of Japan's most iconic festivals, centering on the shrine of Yasaka-jinja, Kyoto's Gion Matsuri takes place each year during the sweltering month of July. The highlight is a parade of truly astounding floats pushed through Gion by revelers in traditional garb. Known as omikoshi, the floats are up to 25 meters (82 ft) tall and weigh up to 10 tonnes (12 tons). Up to 30 of them slowly proceed along Shijō-dōri, representing individual neighborhoods scattered around the city.

The festival dates back to the 9th century, originally a purification ritual to appease what were believed to be the angry gods responsible for fires, earthquakes, floods, pestilence, and plague. In 869, Emperor Seiwa ordered a mass prayer and ritual at Yasaka-jinja to appease the god of the shrine. It was officially made an annual event in 970. By the Edo period, extravagant touches added by the merchant class had made it an occasion devoted to the peacocking of wealth.

Today, the festival culminates July 14-17, when Kyoto's city center is blocked off to traffic and residents mill about in yukata, drinking beer and nibbling on grub from food stalls. The city is decorated with flowers and flags, and lit by hanging lanterns. The yamaboko junkō (grand procession of floats) occurs July 17 and 24. The city's accommodations are booked well in advance of the festival, so book as far ahead as possible.

DAIMON-JI GOZAN OKURIBI

Five mountains surrounding city (viewable from downtown); Aug. 16; free

Another iconic Kyoto summer festival, the Daimon-ji Gozan Okuribi, begins at 8pm on August 16 every year, an occasion to bid farewell to deceased spirits believed to visit the living during the holiday of Obon, celebrated in mid-August in Kyoto. Blazing fires in the shape of Chinese characters are lit and left to burn for about 40 minutes on the slopes of five mountains surrounding the city. The most famous one burns atop Daimon-ji-yama, a mountain looming over the northeastern side of the city. The best spot to view the blaze is from the Kamo River, between Sanjō-dōri in the south and Imadegawa-dōri in the north (best accessed via Sanjō Station, Tōzai subway line).

Gion Matsuri float

Sports and Recreation

PARKS

Kyoto is home to some serenely beautiful parks. Whether you're in the city during hanami season, want to spot wildlife, or simply want to have a picnic, there are plenty of good options.

MARUYAMA-KŌEN

Maruyama-chō, Higashiyama-ku; tel. 075-561-1350; https://kyoto-maruyama-park.jp; 24 hours; free; from Kyoto Station, take Kyoto City Bus 100 or 206 to Gion bus stop, or Keihan line to Gion-Shijō Station, exit 1

Perhaps the city's most popular park, smack in the middle of Higashiyama, behind Yasaka-jinja. It features a pond, burbling brooks, and an array of cherry trees. Thronged during hanami season, the rest of the year it's ideal for a picnic or stroll.

KYOTO GYŌEN

Kyoto Gyōen, Kamigyō-ku; tel. 075/211-6348; www.env.go.jp/garden/kyotogyoen/; 24 hours daily; free; take Karasuma subway line to Imadegawa Station or Marutamachi Station

Kyoto Gyōen is another downtown oasis. Set in the center of town, the grounds of the former **Kyoto Imperial Palace** are the geographic heart of the city. It's another famed hanami spot, renowned for its beautiful collection of weeping cherry trees. It's a great place to meander on foot or sit down for a picnic with the former imperial palace looming beyond.

MONKEY PARK IWATAYAMA

8 Genrokuzan-chō, Arashiyama, Ukyō-ku; tel. 075/872-0950; www.monkeypark.jp; 9am-4:30pm daily (last entry 4pm); ¥550 adults, ¥250 ages 15 and under; take JR Sagano line to Saga-Arashiyama Station, or Hankyū line to Arashiyama (transfer at Katsura Station)

For something wilder, there's Monkey Park Iwatayama in the west of the city. While it's certainly not a completely natural jungle out there, the Japanese macaques on this site in Arashiyama are essentially just going about their business. This is a good place to observe them close up. They're free to play and jump about, while the humans are enclosed.

KAMEYAMA-KŌEN

Saga Kamenō-chō, Ukyō-ku; tel. 075/701-0101; 24 hours daily; free; take JR Sagano line to Saga Arashiyama Station, or Hankyū line to Arashiyama Station

Across the Katsura River from the Iwatayama Monkey Park, this oasis of calm offers a refreshing escape from the crowds of the area. While there aren't as many as you'll see at Iwatayama, monkeys do hang around here, too. There are also sweeping views of the river gorge and much of Arashiyama below. To reach the park, simply turn left and walk uphill when you reach the T junction at the western end of Arashiyama's famed bamboo grove.

CYCLING

Kyoto is a fantastic city for cycling. In a basin ringed by mountains, downtown is mostly flat. Its clean grid pattern, wide boulevards, and relatively tame traffic also make navigation easy. For a wide range of detailed cycling itineraries, visit www.cyclekyoto.com/popular-cycling-routes.

KAMO RIVER CYCLING PATH

Cycling distance: *16 km (9.9 mi) round-trip*
Cycling time: *about 2 hours round-trip*
Trailhead: *Kyoto Station*
Information and maps: *www.insidekyoto.com/cycling-kyoto*

A popular and easy cycling route is biking northward on the walking/cycling path that runs along the Kamo River. There are numerous staircases, typically beside bridges, that lead down to a path that runs along both sides of the river. You'll need to actually carry your bicycle down these stairs in most places, although you may spot ramps in some locations.

While simply riding along the river is pleasant in itself, there are many potential trips you can also make from the riverside path. For example, when you reach Sanjō-dōri, ascend to the street and cycle northeast into Northern Higashiyama. Head for Nanzen-ji, then from there, pedal north to Ginkaku-ji, via the Philosopher's Path. This trip takes about two hours from Kyoto Station, depending on your speed.

CYCLE KYOTO

7 Higashikujō, Nishi Sannōchō, Minami-ku; tel. 090/9165-7168; www.cyclekyoto.net; tours ¥7,000-12,000 pp; Kyoto Station Hachijō, east exit

While you may prefer to explore on your own, there are also some great cycling tours available. The most reputable agency is Cycle Kyoto. Alongside group tours of the city's north and south, it's also possible to arrange family tours (¥40,000), private tours (¥45,000-85,000), and custom tours (price varies; inquire for details).

KYOTO CYCLING TOUR PROJECT

552-13 Higashi-Aburanokoji-chō, Aburanokoji-dōri, Shiokoji-sagaru; tel. 075/354-3636; www.kctp.net; 9am-6pm daily; from ¥1,000 for standard bicycles, from ¥2,300 for electrically assisted bikes; Kyoto Station, central exit

The most reliable rental shop in town is Kyoto Cycling Tour Project, which rents a variety of bicycles, including mountain bikes, city bikes, children's bikes, and more. Call the head office, where the staff speak English, to ask about availability. After riding around for the day, you can drop off your bike at one of the outfit's five terminals spread around the city.

HIKING

KURAMA TO KIBUNE HIKE

Distance: *5.2 km (3.2 mi) one-way*
Time: *1.5 hours one-way*
Trailhead: *Kurama Station*
Information and maps: *www.insidekyoto.com/kurama-to-kibune-hike; https://patrickcolgan.net/2017/01/15/hike-kibune-kurama*

This easy-to-access hike is set in the mountains north of town, combining spirituality and a stunning natural setting in a route that goes up and over Mount Kurama, between two mountain hamlets. Reached by train (about 30 minutes from downtown), the villages of Kurama and Kibune are well away from the masses; it's possible to walk between them in about 1.5 hours. To reach the starting point of the hike, Kurama Station, hop on the Eizan line at Demachiyanagi Station, which is the northern terminus of the Keihan line, then ride to Kurama Station (30 minutes; ¥420).

To get started, exit Kurama Station and walk by the large statue of the bright-red noggin of the mythical, improbably long-nosed Tengu (a prominent creature in Japanese folklore). Turn left onto Kurama's main thoroughfare, which leads to a set of stairs. Climb them and follow the path up Mount Kurama for about 10 minutes. You'll recognize the first sight of note, **Yuki-jinja** (1073 Kuramahonmachi, Sakyō-ku; tel. 075/741-1670; www.yukijinjya.jp; 24 hours daily; free) by the giant cedar tree at its entrance (instead of a vermilion torii gate). This is the guardian shrine of Kurama village.

Push on from Yuki-jinja and after about 5 more minutes of walking you'll come to the temple of **Kurama-dera** (1074 Kurama Honmachi, Sakyō-ku; tel. 075/741-2003; www.kuramadera.or.jp; 9am-4:30pm daily; free), which stands near the top of Mount Kurama. From here, the trail to Kibune is pretty clearly marked. Once you make it to Kibune, the one must-visit sight is **Kifune-jinja** (180 Kuramakibune-chō, Sakyō-ku; tel. 075/741-2016; http://kifunejinja.jp; 9am-5pm daily; free), a shrine approached via an ethereal stone staircase flanked by red lanterns.

There's also a fantastic mountain onsen with both indoor and outdoor pools at **Kurama Onsen** (520 Kuramahonmachi, Sakyō-ku; tel. 075/741-2131; www.kurama-onsen.co.jp; 11am-8pm, last admission 7pm, daily; ¥2,500 adults, ¥1,600 ages 4-12 for full use of facilities, ¥1,000 adults, ¥700 ages 4-12 for open-air baths only). Note that it's also possible to walk this route in reverse if you'd like to take a dip in the hot spring baths of Kurama Onsen after a hike. Kurama Onsen is about 12 minutes' walk north of Kurama Station, set beside the burbling Anba River. There's Japanese fare served on-site at the onsen's restaurant (www.kurama-onsen.co.jp/plan01_e/index.html).

From Kibune, you can either return to Kurama Station or board the train at Kibuneguchi Station, also on the Eizan line, to Demachiyanagi Station, where you can transfer to the Keihan line and head downtown.

COOKING CLASSES

HARU COOKING CLASS

166-32 Shimogamo Miyazaki-chō, Sakyō-ku; www.kyoto-cooking-class.com; classes start from 2pm; from ¥6,900; take Eizan, Keihan Main lines to Demachiyanagi Station

At Haru Cooking Class, you can join bilingual cooking instructor and Kyoto food insider Taro at his home in the north of the city. Taro is well versed in both vegetarian and non-vegetarian cuisine, and he offers guided tours of the rambling realm of local food that is Nishiki Market. Lessons typically last up to four hours.

Shopping

KYOTO STATION AREA

Flea Markets

KŌBŌ-SAN MARKET

1 Kujō-chō, Minami-ku; tel. 075/691-3325; www.toji.or.jp; 8:30am-5pm (last entry 4:30pm) 21st of the month Mar.-Aug., 8:30am-4pm (last entry 3:30pm) 21st of the month Sept.-Feb.; free; take Kintetsu line to Tō-ji Station

On the 21st of every month, a great flea market known as the Kōbō-san Market is held at the temple of Tō-ji, southwest of JR Kyoto Station. Go in the morning before the good stuff is picked over.

GION

In the heart of Gion, the two parallel streets of **Furumonzen-dōri** and **Shinmonzen-dōri** are chock-full of businesses selling traditional Japanese art. You'll find landscape paintings, Buddhist sculptures, teapots and implements, and scrolls. It's a fairly pricey area to shop, but if you mean business and could potentially buy something, the sellers welcome foreign customers. To get to these two streets, take the Tōzai subway line or Keihan line to Sanjō Keihan Station, exit 2.

NORTHERN HIGASHIYAMA

Traditional Goods and Souvenirs

KYOTO HANDICRAFT CENTER

21 Shōgoin Entomi-chō, Sakyō-ku; tel. 075/761-8001; www.kyotohandicraftcenter.com; 10am-7pm daily; take Kyoto City Bus 206 to Kumano-jinja-mae bus stop, or take Keihan line to Jingu Marutamachi Station

Kyoto Handicraft Center is the best one-stop souvenir shop in the city. Yukata, ceramics, accessories, jewelry, woodblock prints, and more are available.

Ceramics

ROBERT YELLIN GALLERY

Ginkakuji-mae-chō 39, Sakyō-ku; tel. 075/708-5581; http://japanesepottery.com; take Kyoto City Bus 5 or 17 to Ginkaku-ji-michi bus stop

A stone's throw from Ginkaku-ji, you'll find one of Kyoto's best ceramics shops: the Robert Yellin Gallery. The gallery is set in a beautiful traditional home, complete with a landscape garden. Yellin is an American expat based in Kyoto who has a masterful grasp on the Japanese yakimono (ceramics; literally "fired thing") tradition, and

Top Souvenirs: Omamori

If you discreetly glance around at the cell phones, purses, or bags of the people around you in Japan, chances are you'll notice colorful handmade pouches dangling by white woven cords. These pouches are amulets, or talismans, known as omamori: small ornaments sold at shrines and temples generally believed to bring protection or good luck to the owner. Rectangular ones contain words penned on thin strips of wood or paper inside. Others come in a variety of shapes, from foxes to bells and gourds.

HISTORY AND SIGNIFICANCE

The belief in omamori stems from the idea that Shinto charms contain a sprinkling of the power of a kami (god) that is housed in the shrine, combined with Buddhism's amulet culture, readily visible throughout other parts of Asia (for example, in the ubiquitous tiny Buddha statues seen swinging from the rearview mirrors of Bangkok taxis). Although Shinto shrine maidens known as miko were once responsible for crafting omamori, today they are largely produced in factories and blessed by priests upon arrival at shrines and temples where they're sold.

BUYING AN OMAMORI

You don't need to be a devotee to respectfully buy and keep an omamori. If you choose to pick one up, just be sure you handle it with the same amount of respect you would any religious object. While there's big business in souvenir shops hawking cutesy omamori featuring manga characters like Hello Kitty, some religious groups don't regard them as being authentic. A final note: Whatever kind of omamori you choose, resist the urge to loosen the straps and see what's inside! Opening the pouch is believed to drain the talisman of its power.

has amassed an eye-popping collection to prove it. To avoid sticker shock, have a look at the online gallery on the official website to get a sense of how much a quality piece can potentially cost. Note that there are no official hours, but Robert is a friendly host who welcomes visitors. Your best bet is to call or email ahead and confirm he's not out with clients or visiting kilns when you plan to visit. Otherwise, knock on the door if the gate is open and he'll be happy to greet you if he's there. Have a look at the access map, available on the website, before making the trip.

DOWNTOWN AND CENTRAL KYOTO

You'll find two grand department stores downtown: **Daimaru** (79 Tachiuri Nishimachi, Shijō-dōri, Takakura Nishi-iru, Shimogyō-ku; tel. 075/211-8111; www.daimaru.co.jp; 10am-8pm daily) and **Takashimaya** (52 Shinchō, Shijō-dōri, Kawaramachi Nishi-iru, Shimogyō-ku; tel. 075/221-8811; www.takashimaya.co.jp; 10am-8pm daily). Both have a staggering selection of international brands and offer world-class service, along with stellar food floors in their basements. Stop by either one to browse and discover the phenomenon that is the Japanese department store. Take the Hankyū line to Karasuma Station, or the Karasuma subway line to Shijō Station. Both stores are within walking distance from there.

Shopping Districts

NISHIKI MARKET

www.kyoto-nishiki.or.jp; 9am-5pm daily; take Hankyū line to Kawaramachi Station or Karasuma Station, or Karasuma line to Shijō Station

One block to the north of Shijō-dōri, running parallel to the busy thoroughfare, Nishiki Market is an extensive smorgasbord of local edibles. Whether you aim to buy something or not, the covered pedestrian thoroughfare is a sight to behold.

EBISUGAWA-DŌRI

take Karasuma subway line to Muratamachi Station

This street two blocks south of Marutamachi-dōri that runs westward from Teramachi-dōri is the best place in the city to pick up a piece of antique furniture, such as a tansu (antique chest).

TERAMACHI-DŌRI

about 10 minutes' walk east of Muratamachi Station

Another great shopping street for old Japanese items, Teramachi-dōri is the (north-south) street you'll come to when you reach the eastern end of Ebisugawa-dōri. It's heaving with shops selling Japanese antiques, tea ceremony implements, painted scrolls, and more. Consider coming to Teramachi-dōri after a stroll to Ebisugawa-dōri.

Traditional Goods and Souvenirs

KYŪKYODŌ

520 Shimohonnōjimae-chō, Teramachi-dōri, Aneyakōji-agaru, Nakagyō-ku; tel. 075/231-0510; www.kyukyodo.co.jp; 10am-6pm Mon.-Sat.; take Tōzai subway line to Kyoto Shiyakusho-mae Station

For the best place to buy an assortment of traditional items related to the arts, from artsy stationery and calligraphy brushes to incense, an item with great history in the city's myriad Buddhist temples, head to Kyūkyodō. A great pick if your time is limited and you want to find anything you'd realistically desire under one roof.

MORITA WASHI

1F Kajinoha Building, 298 Ogisakaya-chō, Higashinotoin-dōri, Bukkoji-agaru, Shimogyō-ku; tel. 075/341-1419; www.wagami.jp; 10am-6pm Mon.-Fri., 10am-5pm Sat.; take Karasuma subway line to Shijō Station, or Hankyū line to Karasuma Station

The best place in the city to see art made of traditionally handmade paper—a craft with deep roots in Kyoto.

MIYAWAKI BAISEN-AN

80-3 Daikoku-chō, Rokkaku-dōri, Tominokōji, Higashi-iru, Nakagyō-ku; tel. 075/221-0181; www.baisenan.co.jp; 9am-6pm daily; take Kurasuma or Tōzai subway line to Karasuma-Oike Station

Another traditional item that says "Kyoto" is the folding fan. For a superb selection, go to Miyawaki Baisen-an. This fan specialist has been in business since 1823.

Nishiki Market

SHOYEIDO KYOTO MAIN STORE

Karasuma Nijō, Nakagyō-ku; tel. 075/212-5590; www.shoyeido.co.jp; 9am-6pm daily; take Karasuma, Tōzai lines to Karasuma Oike Station, exit 1

It's a bit on the formal side, but if you're intent on getting ahold of high-grade incense—conjure the aroma that hits your nostrils when you step foot in a temple—this is one of the best stores in Kyoto.

Kitchenware and Food

ARITSUGU

219 Kajiya-chō, Nishikikoji-dōri, Gokomachi Nishi-iru, Nakagyō-ku; tel. 075/221-1091; www.kyoto-nishiki.or.jp/stores/aritsugu; 10am-5pm daily; take Hankyū line to Kawaramachi Station

The best place to buy traditional Japanese kitchen knives, Aritsugu, is housed in Nishiki Market.

ZŌHIKO

719-1 Yohojimae-chō, Teramachi-dōri, Nijō-agaru, Nishigawa, Nakagyō-ku; tel. 075/229-6625; www.zohiko.co.jp; 10am-6pm daily; take Tōzai subway line to Kyoto Shiyakusho-mae Station

If you dine at a kaiseki restaurant, something that will leap out at you as much as the flavor is the visual power of the feast. Lacquerware is a major reason for this. To see an excellent selection of this classic Japanese craft, go to Zōhiko. This shop sometimes closes on random days, so be sure to call ahead.

IPPŌDŌ

52 Tokiwagi-chō, Teramachi-dōri, Nijō-agaru, Nakagyō-ku; tel. 075/211-4018; www.ippodo-tea.co.jp; 9am-6pm daily; take Tōzai subway line to Kyoto Shiyakusho-mae Station

After sampling some of the different brews available at any number of the city's teahouses, you might be tempted to take home some high-grade tea. Ippōdō has the best selection of teas in the city.

Food

Kyoto is most known for its painstakingly prepared, beautifully presented style of haute cuisine known as **kaiseki ryōri,** which evolved to complement the tea ceremony. But this only scratches the surface. Other dishes and cooking styles with a strong presence in the ancient capital include **shōjin-ryōri,** a vegetarian form of cooking used to nourish Buddhist monks; stellar soba and udon noodles; and **traditional desserts** made with ingredients like azuki red bean paste, rice cake, and arrowroot noodles, perhaps paired with the city's endless supply of high-grade **matcha** (green tea).

It's advisable to make restaurant bookings a few days in advance for dinners, especially during busy seasons.

KYOTO STATION AREA

Ramen

KYOTO RAMEN KŌJI

10F Kyoto Station Building, Higashi Shiokoji-chō, Shiokoji-sagaru, Shimogyō-ku; tel. 075/361-4401; www.kyoto-ramen-koji.com; 11am-10pm daily; ¥1,000

If you're in or near Kyoto Station and need a quick, cheap meal on the go, Kyoto Ramen Kōji is a good bet, with eight styles from all corners of Japan. To reach here, turn so that you're facing north toward Kyoto Tower while you're under Kyoto Station's main soaring atrium. Look to your left and you'll see a number of escalators. Follow them to the 10th floor. From this lofty perch, turn left and you'll see the hall of ramen before you.

Cafés and Light Bites

EAT PARADISE

11F Kyoto Station Building, Higashi Shiokoji-chō, Shiokoji-sagaru, Shimogyō-ku; tel. 075/352-1111; www.mistore.jp/store/kyoto/restaurant_search.html; 11am-10pm daily; ¥1,500

If you're not a noodle aficionado, don't fret. There's also a food court with more variety on the 11th floor of Kyoto Station: Eat Paradise. The restaurants here, ranging from Japanese (tempura, tonkatsu) to Italian, are appropriate when you're in the mood for a proper meal before hopping on the shinkansen or striking out for a day of sightseeing. To reach this food court, simply take the escalators one floor higher than where Kyoto Ramen Kōji is located and walk to the left until you reach the restaurants. Many restaurants here have English-language menus. Just pick the one that strikes your fancy.

SOUTHEAST KYOTO

Udon

KENDONYA

41 Fukakusa, Ichinotsubochō, Fushimi-ku; tel. 075/641-1330; https://kendonya.com; 11am-6pm Thurs.-Tues., random closing one day per month; ¥1,000; take JR Nara line to Inari Station

A worthwhile udon (flour noodle) restaurant about 5 minutes' walk from Fushimi Inari-Taisha, this shop serves a form of chewy al dente udon known as koshi in a flavorsome soup. The staff are bubbly, creating a welcoming atmosphere.

Cafés and Light Bites

VERMILLION CAFÉ

5-31 Kaidoguchi-cho Fukakusa, Fushimi-ku; tel. 075/644-7989; www.vermillioncafe.com; 9am-5pm daily; ¥1,000; take JR Nara line to Inari Station

A stone's throw from the army of fox statues and tunnel of vermillion torii gates snaking through the mountain where Fushimi Inari-Taisha stands, you'll find the aptly named Vermillion Café. This cozy café is located in the shrine area's backstreets and has a terrace overlooking a pond on the shrine's sprawling grounds. Excellent coffee and tasty baked goods are prepared on-site. This café is recommended for a great pit stop or a sit-down lunch.

International

DRAGON BURGER

13-243 Hommachi, Higashiyama-ku; tel. 075/525-5611; https://dragon-burger.com; 10am-11pm daily; from ¥1,020; take Keihan, JR Nara lines to Tōfuku-ji Station

Sometimes you just need a burger. Toppings range from wasabi and blue cheese to tsukemono (pickled vegetables), for which Kyoto is famed. Sets come with a side salad, fries, and a drink, and buns are made with domestically sourced ingredients. It's a good spot for a lunch or casual dinner near Tōfuku-ji or Fushima Inari-Taisha.

GION

Kaiseki

★ KIKUNOI HONTEN

459 Shimokawara-chō, Shimokawara-dōri, Yasakatoriimae-sagaru, Higashiyama-ku; tel. 075/561-0015; http://kikunoi.jp; noon-1pm (last order 12:30pm) and 5pm-8pm (last order 7:30pm) Wed.-Mon.; lunch ¥25,000 and up, dinner ¥30,500 and up; take Keihan line to Gion-Shijō Station

For a stunning example of a kaiseki feast, you won't be disappointed at Kikunoi Honten. Serving refined fare since it opened in 1912, Kikunoi is now run by Yoshihiro Murata, a third-generation chef. Located near Maruyama-kōen in the heart of Gion, Kyoto's historic entertainment quarter, this restaurant changes its menu and the decor with the seasons. To get a spot at the table, speak with the staff or concierge of your accommodations at least one month prior.

Japanese

SENMONTEN

380-3 Kiyomoto-chō, Higashi-gawa, Hanamikoji Shimbashi kudaru, Higashiyama-ku; tel. 075/531-2733; 6pm-2am Mon.-Sat.; from ¥530; take the Keihan line to Gion-Shijō Station, then walk 7 minutes

Fried dumplings (gyoza) and beer: If this sounds good and you're not overly concerned about caloric intake or a balanced diet, you can't go wrong with Senmonten. There's nothing else on the menu, and that's fine. The gyoza, served in batches of 20, are crispy outside and stuffed with juicy pork and scallions.

Ramen

RAMEN MURAJI

373-3 Kiyomotocho, Higashiyama-ku; tel. 075/744-1144; http://ramen-muraji.jp/en; 11:30am-3pm and 5pm-10pm dinner Mon.-Sat., 11:30am-8pm Sun. and public holidays; ¥850; take the Keihan line to Gion-Shijō Station, then walk 5 minutes

Ramen Muraji serves a mean bowl of ramen in a creamy broth made from chicken bones left to boil for hours then tossed with bamboo strips and chicken. Add an egg to make it more filling. Housed in a classic machiya-style building that's been tastefully spruced up and decorated, it's tucked down a cobblestone alley in Gion next to a canal. There's unfortunately no English sign, so keep an eye out for the white curtains in front of the entrance. An English-language menu is available.

Sushi

CHIDORITEI

203 Rokken-chō, Donguri-dori Yamato-oji Nishi-iru, Higashiyama-ku; tel. 075/561-1907; www7b.biglobe.ne.jp/~chidoritei/index.html; 11am-8pm Fri.-Wed.; ¥2,000; take Keihan line to Gion-Shijō Station

Being landlocked, Kyoto isn't known for sushi, but the city does serve a variety based on seasoned, marinated mackerel. The best place to try this is Chidoritei, a cozy family-run joint that also serves good chirashi bowls (sashimi over rice) and eel.

Cafés and Light Bites

★ KAGIZEN YOSHIFUSA KŌDAI-JI

Kōdai-ji Omote-mon-mae Agaru, Higashi-yama-ku; tel. 075/525-0011; www.kagizen.co.jp; 9am-6pm (last order 5:45pm) Thurs.-Tues.; ¥1,000; take Keihan line to Gion-Shijō Station, or Hankyū line to Kawaramachi Station

Any traveler with a sweet tooth take note: Kagizen Yoshifusa Kōdai-ji is one of the city's most venerated traditional dessert cafés. The shop's most popular branch is right on Shijō-dōri in the heart of Gion. I prefer the Kōdai-ji branch in Southern Higashiyama; it's a calm place to sample traditional sweets, such as azuki red bean paste-stuffed pastries and arrowroot noodles dipped in black sugar, washed down with bitter matcha tea. This location is close enough to the bustling shopping streets leading uphill toward Kiyomizu-dera without being in the thick of it.

NORTHERN HIGASHIYAMA

Udon

HINODE UDON

36 Kitanobo-chō, Nanzen-ji, Sakyō-ku; tel. 075/751-9251; 11am-3pm Tues.-Sat.; from ¥750; take Tōzai subway line to Keage Station, exit 2

A fantastic udon restaurant near the Philosopher's Path, this cozy family-owned shop is famous for its noodles served in flavorsome curry. The menu also includes more traditional udon, as well as soba noodle dishes. A great pick if you're feeling famished around the southern end of the Philosopher's Path, near Nanzen-ji and Eikan-dō. Queues do sometimes form but tend to move relatively fast. An English menu is available.

★ OMEN

74 Jōdo-ji, Ishibashi-chō, Sakyō-ku; tel. 075/771-8994; www.omen.co.jp; 11am-9pm (last order 8pm) daily; ¥1,200; take Kyoto City Bus no. 5 to Ginkakuji-michi

The formula is simple at Omen. A generous portion of seven varieties of vegetables are served along with white wheat-flour noodles (udon)—either hot or cold—with soup and a liberal hit of sesame (to be used as seasoning) on the side. Mix the vegetables into the soup and dunk the noodles. Delicious. This is a great choice for a meal when you're in the vicinity of Ginkaku-ji. You'll have a choice of sitting at the counter, at a separate table, or on a tatami floor.

International

CENCI

44-7 Entomi-chō, Shōgoin, Sakyō-ku; tel. 075/708-5307; https://cenci-kyoto.com; lunch noon-3pm (last order 12:30pm), dinner 6pm-10:30pm (last order 7:30pm) Tues.-Sun., irregular closings on Sun.; lunch from ¥6,000, dinner from ¥12,000; take Keihan line to Jingu-Marutamachi Station, exit 4

This first-rate Italian eatery is one of the city's new "it" restaurants. As you pass through the tunnel, built with bricks made from the soil dug up from the site on which it stands, you emerge into a singular space that is faintly European, yet also Japanese. This reflects the menu. With Kyoto-born chef Ken Sakamoto at the helm, the kitchen rustles up fantastic Italian fare with a distinctly local twist, from ayu (sweetfish) instead of anchovies in the bagna càuda to liberal use of Japanese ingredients like buckwheat and yuzu. Produce is locally sourced—mushrooms and root vegetables foraged in the mountains nearby—and dishes are beautifully presented on smart tableware crafted by Japanese artisans. Reserve as far ahead as you can. Inform the restaurant in advance if you're traveling with children under the age of 10.

★ MONK

147 Jōdo-ji Shimominamida-chō, Sakyō-ku; tel. 075/748-1154; https://restaurant-monk.com; 5pm-8:30pm Tues.-Sat.; set course ¥10,000; take Kyoto City Bus no. 5 to Ginkakuji-michi

This intimate, 15-seat eatery puts a local twist on Italian cooking. Romantically set beside the Philosopher's Path, its atmosphere is casual yet refined, with a prominent wood-fired pizza oven in the open kitchen. Ingredients are sourced from farms in the mountains outside Kyoto and markets around town daily to craft a slow seven-course meal cooked by flame and built around items like mackerel, mozzarella, wild boar, and duck, liberally infused with a colorful medley of organic vegetables from turnips and daikon to beetroot. The pièce de résistance is the pizza—chef Yoshihiro Imai has written a recipe book on the dish—made with the best organic flour Japan has to offer. Reservations (essential) can be made online two months in advance.

Cafés and Light Bites

YAMATOYA

25 Sanno-chō, Shōgoin, Sakyō-ku; tel. 075/761-7685; www.jazz-yamatoya.com; noon-11pm Thurs.-Tues., closed second Tues. of month; from ¥650; take Keihan line to Jingu-Marutamachi Station, exit 4

This jazz café is the stuff of legend. It's been going strong for five decades, and the elegant interior of this cozy joint has dark wood furniture, stone walls, antique lamps, and a corner of floor-to-ceiling shelves overflowing with vinyl. But what really grabs you are the perfect tunes wafting through the stellar audio system. The coffee is top-notch, too. Recommended. Cash only.

DOWNTOWN AND CENTRAL KYOTO

Kaiseki

GUILO GUILO HITOSHINA

420-7 Namba-chō, Nishikiyamachi-dōri-Matsubara-sagaru, Shimogyō-ku; tel. 075/343-7070; 5:30pm-11pm daily, closed last Mon. of month; dinner from ¥4,000; take Keihan line to Kiyomizu-Gojō Station, exit 3

At this chic, fun riverside restaurant in a two-story revamped warehouse, trendy young chefs in a tiny open kitchen whip up shockingly affordable kaiseki courses with a modern twist. The menu leans heavily toward simple, affordable, seasonal seafood and vegetables, with some curveballs like gyoza (dumplings) stuffed with broad beans, pea mousse, and caramel imbued with roasted green tea. Don't come here for a traditional feast; do come if you'd like to see the young, modern face of kaiseki without breaking the bank. The place gets packed, so reserve a month or more in advance. Cash only.

KAPPO YAMASHITA

491-3 Kami Korikicho, Nakagyō-ku; tel. 075/256-4506; 11:30am-1:30pm and 5pm-10pm Tues.-Sun.; lunch ¥5,000, dinner ¥15,000; take Tōzai line to Kyoto Shiyakusho-mae Station

In a culinary tradition as focused on refinement as kaiseki, Kappo Yamashita stands out for its down-to-earth atmosphere. The friendly chefs here are known to engage in banter with customers who sit at the counter—kappo means "counter style"—to watch them at work. The staff are also happy to field questions about the menu.

Tempura

MIZUKI

Kamogawa Nijō-Ōhashi Hotori, Nakagyō-ku; tel. 075/746-5555; www.ritzcarlton.com/en/hotels/japan/kyoto/dining/kaiseki-mizuki; 11:30am-2pm (last order 2pm) and 5:30pm-9pm (last order 8pm) Thurs.-Mon.; lunch from ¥9,000, dinner from ¥12,000; take Tōzai line to Kyoto Shiyakusho-Mae Station

The best tempura in Kyoto is arguably served at a large granite counter in the decidedly modern, luxurious setting of the Ritz-Carlton Kyoto; the atmosphere is sleek, in an elegant dining room with tableware made by artists. Diners at a large granite counter are treated by tempura maestro Chef Fujimoto, who has earned a Michelin star for his delicate seasonal and local creations, made with safflower oil instead of the heavier sesame oil used in most Tokyo kitchens. Alternatively, the hotel's innovative chefs also serve a kaiseki menu in the restaurant's main dining area. They aim to hit the principles of go-mi (five flavors), go-shyoku (five colors), and go-ho (five cooking methods).

Ramen

NAMAE NO NAI RAMENYA

CEO Mokuyachō Bldg. B1F, 534-31 Ebisu-chō, Nakagyō-ku; www.takakura-nijo.jp; 11:30am-3pm and 6pm-10pm Mon.-Fri., 11:30am-3pm and 6pm-9pm Sat.-Sun. and holidays; ¥1,000; take Tōzai line to Kyoto Shiyakusho-mae Station

Kyoto has a penchant for hiding good things, like this "ramen shop with no name," as the name translates. The stock is made from chicken and fish, and contains fresh vegetables and chunks of meat. Motsu (offal) and curry-based broth are also available. The springy noodles, resembling soba, are either served in the bowl or to the side (tsukemen). For a kick, an array of spices—Japanese sansho pepper, chili pepper, black pepper, garam masala—sit in beautifully crafted wooden drawers. You'll know you've found the shop

soba and tempura

when you come to the staircase, over which hangs a sign indicating the business on each floor of the building, save for the basement level. Downstairs, the door has a single lamp on the wall beside it. Recommended.

INOICHI

1F, 528 Ebisuno-chō, Ebisuterasu, Shimogyō-ku; tel. 075/353-7413; https://ramen-restaurant-1526.business.site; 11:30am-2pm and 5:30pm-10pm Tues.-Sun.; ¥1,200; take Hankyū line to Kawaramachi Station

Inoichi serves ramen with white (lighter) or black (fuller) soy sauce for your broth. Bamboo shoots and a delicious "red egg" marinated in soy sauce fill out the bowl, with the light yet robustly flavored broth being made with a mix of dried fish and kelp. If you don't mind waiting in the line that often forms outside, there's an English menu.

Soba

HONKE OWARIYA

322 Niomontsukinuke-chō, Nakagyō-ku; tel. 075/231-3446; https://honke-owariya.co.jp; 11am-4pm (last order 2:30pm) daily; from ¥880; take Karasuma or Tōzai subway line to Karasuma Oike Station, exit 1

This soba shop is an institution. Set in a historic building that embodies the classic Kyoto aesthetic, just south of the Kyoto Imperial Palace Park, this shop makes arguably the city's best soba noodles. It is the soba pick of choice for the imperial family when they come to town. The menu ranges from spare bowls of the buckwheat strands to filling sets with a slew of toppings: grated daikon, nori, leeks, wasabi, shrimp tempura, shiitake mushrooms, sesame seeds, and more. Friendly warning: Prepare to wait 15-30 minutes or more at peak lunchtime hours.

Vegetarian

MUMOKUTEKI CAFÉ

2F Human Forum Building, 261 Shikibu-chō, Nakagyō-ku; tel. 075/213-7733; http://mumokuteki.com; 11:30am-10pm daily; from ¥1,000; take Hankyū line to Kawaramachi Station

If you're in search of a vegetarian or vegan restaurant downtown, head to the airy, elegant Mumokuteki Café. There's a clearly labeled menu (English available) that breaks down the ingredients in each dish. Options include set meals, a salad bar, and a good selection of items that can be ordered a la carte. Avoid the lunch rush by coming early or mid-afternoon.

AIN SOPH. JOURNEY KYOTO

538-6 Nakano-chō, Shinkyogoku-dōri Shijō-agaru, Nakagyō-ku; tel. 075/251-1876; www.ain-soph.jp/journeykyoto; noon-8pm (last order 7pm) Mon.-Fri. and Sun., noon-9pm (last order 8pm) Sat.; from ¥1,000; take Hankyū line to Kawaramachi Station, exit 9

This elegant restaurant on a pedestrian lane downtown serves good vegan fare: vegan burgers topped with coconut cheese, tofu omelets, spinach curry, and surprisingly convincing desserts (vegan pancakes, soy ice cream, chocolate gateau, faux New York cheesecake).

★ TŌSUIRŌ

517-3 Kamiosaka-chō, Sanjō-agaru, Kiyamachi-dōri, Nakagyō-ku; tel. 075/251-1600; http://tousuiro.com; 11:30am-3pm (last order 2pm) and 5pm-10pm (last order 9pm) Mon.-Sat., 11:45am-3pm (last order 2pm) and 5pm-9:30pm (last order 8:30pm) Sun. and holidays; lunch from ¥4,000, dinner from ¥5,800; take Hankyū line to Kawaramachi Station

Tōsuirō is a great place to explore the wonders of tofu and yuba—and surprising wonders they are. Multicourse meals consist of small variations in cooking method. Assorted sashimi brings a different element to the table. When the weather is warm, book ahead to get a seat on the veranda overlooking the Kamo River—a quintessential Kyoto experience.

International

SAMA SAMA

532 Kamiosaka-chō, Kiyamachi, Sanjō-agaru, Nakagyō-ku; tel. 075/241-4100; www.facebook.com/SamaSama0214; 6pm-2am Tues.-Sun.; ¥200 cover charge, dishes from ¥850; take Keihan line to Sanjō Station

Uji and Japanese Tea: A Primer

Tea has been imbibed in Japan since the 8th century, when it arrived from China. The small town of Uji, just south of Kyoto and home to the famed **Byōdō-in** temple (116 Uji-Renge, Uji-shi; tel. 0774/21-2861; www.byodoin.or.jp; grounds 8:30am-5:30pm, last entry 5:15pm, daily, Phoenix Hall 9:30am-4:10pm daily, temple museum 9am-5pm, last entry 4:45pm, daily; ¥600 adults, ¥400 high school and junior high school students, ¥300 elementary school students), seen on the back of the 10-yen coin, has deep ties to Japan's rich tea culture, particularly celebrated for green tea, which has been grown in the surrounding mountains since the 12th century.

BACKGROUND

In the Nara period (710-794), Buddhist priests and aristocrats began to quaff tea, which had then only recently been brought to Japan from China. By the Muromachi period (1333-1573), tea had trickled down to the masses. Tea drinking was infused with Zen sensibilities, and a detailed set of movements and social protocols began to grow around the simple act. These behaviors gradually became what we know today as the sadō or cha-no-yu (the way of tea), which is fully expressed in the act of the tea ceremony, or chaji.

Fast-forward to the present. Today, tea is ubiquitous in Japan, with some popular types including ryokucha (green tea), which can also be roasted (hōjicha) and combined with roasted brown rice (genmaicha); matcha (powdered green tea); and jasmine-cha.

TASTING TEA IN UJI

There are some wonderful opportunities to taste and learn about tea in Uji, which is just 20-30 minutes from Kyoto on the JR Nara line to JR Uji Station (¥240). Trains on the Keihan main line also run from downtown Kyoto (including Gion-shijō, Sanjō, and Demachiyanagi Stations) to Keihan Uji Station (¥310-400). Note that some Keihan express trains traveling south from Kyoto to Uji may require a transfer to a Keihan local train at Chushojima.

Takumi no Yakata

17-1 Mataburi, Uji-shi; tel. 0774/23-0888; www.ujicha.or.jp; 11am-5pm (last order 4:30pm) Thurs.-Tues.; tasting sets from ¥800; Keihan Uji Station or JR Uji Station

Learn to brew your own tea with certified expert instruction at this teahouse beside the Uji River.

Fukujuen Ujicha Kobo

10 Yamada, Uji-shi; tel. 050/3152-2930; www.ujikoubou.com; 10am-5pm (last order 4:30pm at teahouse) Tues.-Sun.; workshops from ¥2,000; Keihan Uji Station or JR Uji Station

Come here for a range of hands-on tea workshops. You'll learn to grind tea leaves, whisk the powder you've created, and then quaff the resulting brew. Walk-ins are welcome. There's also a café on site that serves a variety of teas.

Taihoan

2 Togawa, Uji-shi; tel. 0774/23-3334; www.city.uji.kyoto.jp/site/uji-kankou/7035.html; 10am-4pm daily, closed Dec. 21-Jan.9; from ¥1,000; Keihan Uji Station or JR Uji Station

Come to this city-run traditional teahouse, a stone's throw from Byōdō-in, for a remarkably affordable tea ceremony. A member of staff will kindly guide you in proper etiquette.

A non-Japanese choice for spicing things up is Sama Sama. The kitchen at this cozy Indonesian restaurant and bar whips up a diverse menu of omelets, and rice dishes with lots of chicken and fish. The Balinese owner is friendly and makes guests comfortable with a bit of conversation. Guests sit on floor cushions, creating a very laid-back atmosphere.

MUGHAL

2F Airu Takeshima Bldg., Kiyamachi-dōri Oike agaru, Nakagyō-ku; tel. 075/241-3777; www.kyoto-mughal.com; noon-3pm (last order 2:30pm) and 5pm-11pm (last order 10pm) Wed.-Mon.; lunch from ¥1,000, dinner from ¥2,850; take Tōzai subway line to Kyoto Shiyakusho-mae, exit 3

As you eat your way through numerous rice,

a tea ceremony

TASTING TEA IN KYOTO

While a full-scale tea ceremony lasts up to four hours—from the preceding kaiseki feast to the ceremony itself—it's possible to experience a shortened version that simply consists of drinking one kind of matcha accompanied by a small sweet. To experience this Zen ritual in Kyoto in a relaxed yet refined setting, try **Camellia,** which has two locations. Book a spot on their website.

Camellia Flower

349-12 Masuya-chō, Higashiyama-ku; tel. 075/525-3238; www.tea-kyoto.com/experience/flower; 10am-6pm daily; shared tea ceremony ¥3,000 adults, ¥1,500 children ages 7-12, free for children under 6, private tea ceremony ¥6,000 ages 12 and up for group of 2 or more, free for children under 6; take Kyoto City Bus 206 to Higashiyama Yasui bus stop

The bilingual woman who performs the 45-minute ceremonies here is informative and has a knack for putting guests at ease.

Camellia Garden

18 Ryōan-ji Ikenoshita-chō, Ukyō-ku; tel. 070/5656-7808; www.tea-kyoto.com/experience/garden; 11am-6pm Mon.-Sat.; ¥8,000 per person for group of 2 or more, free for children under 6 years old; take Kyoto City Bus 59 to Ryōan-ji-mae bus stop, or Keifuku Kitano line from Arashiyama to Ryōan-ji Station

Set in an old house with a lovely garden, this branch is also run by a charming bilingual woman with a masterful grasp on the art of tea. The dreamy setting and slightly longer time given for each session (1 hour) justifies the slightly higher price tag.

noodle, tofu, and fish-based meals, you might start to crave something different. Mughal, a spacious Indian restaurant beside the Kamo River near the northeast corner of downtown, offers a nice alternative. The excellent menu is mostly north Indian: curries, tandoori dishes, biryanis, and more.

Cafés and Light Bites

PAPA JON'S HONTEN

642-4 Shokokuji-chō, Karasuma-dōri, Kamidachiuri higashi-iru, Kamigyō-ku; tel. 075/415-2655; www.papajons.net; 10:30am-8pm daily; lunch ¥1,000, dessert from ¥350; take Kurasuma subway line to Imadegawa Station

If you're near Imadegawa Station north

of Kyoto Imperial Palace Park, Papa Jon's Honten is a good place for lunch—curry, quiche, sandwiches—or a coffee break with a slice of their famed cheesecake.

CAFÉ BIBLIOTIC HELLO!

650 Seimei-chō, Nijō-dōri, Yanaginobanba higashi-iru, Nakagyō-ku; tel. 075/231-8625; http://cafe-hello.jp; 11:30am-midnight daily; ¥1,000; take Tōzai line to Kyoto Shiyakusho-mae Station

With serious points for atmosphere—excellent lighting, exposed-brick walls lined with books, a globe lit from within—is the awesomely named Café Bibliotic Hello!. It's an appealing place to while away a few hours over a coffee, smoothie, or light meal with a book or laptop in hip surroundings. Just look for the red-brick exterior fronted by large banana plants.

TORAYA KARYO ICHIJO

400 Hirohashidono-chō, Karasuma-Nishi-iru, Ichijo-dōri, Kamigyō-ku; tel. 075/441-3113; https://global.toraya-group.co.jp/pages/kyoto-ichijo-store; 10am-6pm daily (last order 5:30pm), closed last Mon. every month; from ¥1,000; take the Karasuma line to Imadegawa Station, exit 6

Set beside Kyoto Imperial Palace, Toraya is an elegant place to sample a traditional sweet (think: rice cake stuffed with red bean paste) and a cup of matcha green tea—in summer, try it iced—while gazing onto a beautiful garden.

NORTHWEST KYOTO

Soba

HANAMAKIYA

17-2 Kinugasa Gochonouchi-chō, Kita-ku; tel. 075/464-4499; https://hanamakiya.gorp.jp; 11:30am-7pm Fri.-Wed., irregular holidays; from ¥950; a few minutes' walk east of Kinkaku-ji's grounds

There is a surprising dearth of restaurants around Kinkaku-ji, but thankfully there's Hanamakiya for a quick, filling lunch at a good value. The restaurant serves handmade soba noodles, tempura, unagi-don (grilled eel over rice), and more. Seating is on tatami floors around low tables. It's busy at peak times, but queues move fast. An English menu is available.

Vegetarian

★ IZUSEN DAIJINTEN

4 Daitoku-chō, Murasakino, Kita-ku; tel. 075/491-6665; http://kyoto-izusen.com; 11am-4pm daily; from ¥3,500; from Kyoto Station, take Kyoto City Bus no. 204, 205, or 206 to Daitoku-ji bus stop

On the grounds of the atmospheric Daitoku-ji temple complex, Izusen Daijinten offers one of Kyoto's best shōjin-ryōri experiences. Great Buddhist vegan fare is served in a series of dishes that keep coming, one after the other. Surprisingly diverse in flavor—pleasing even non-vegans—the dishes are beautiful to look at, too. You can sit in a garden attached to the restaurant in good weather. Be sure to wander the vast temple grounds after you eat—highly recommended.

ARASHIYAMA

Kaiseki

★ SHORAIAN

Sagameno-chō, Ukyō-ku; tel. 075/861-0123; www.shoraian.com; 11am-5pm Mon.-Thurs., 11am-8pm Fri.-Sun. and holidays; lunch from ¥4,180, dinner from ¥6,930; take Hankyū line to Arashiyama, or JR Sagano line to Saga-Arashiyama Station

For a unique kaiseki experience in a more natural setting, try Shoraian. Set in the hills of Arashiyama, overlooking the Katsura River, the restaurant is housed in an old private residence. Climb a stone stairway through the forest, go inside, and sit down on a tatami floor. The service is outstanding, making guests feel like they're dining at someone's home. The menu consists of set courses that are heavily tofu-based and surprisingly affordable by kaiseki standards. Reservations for dinner Fri.-Sun. and on holidays are required and must be made before 5pm on the day prior. That said, booking ahead a few weeks or even a month is wise to ensure a spot. Reservations aren't required for lunch, although booking a week or more in advance is recommended. Its location outside the city and its affordability make this a superb introduction to kaiseki.

Soba

ARASHIYAMA YOSHIMURA

3 Saga-Tenryū-ji, Susukinobaba-chō, Ukyō-ku; tel. 075/863-5700; http://yoshimura-gr.com; 11am-5pm daily; from ¥1,300; take Hankyū line to Arashiyama station

Arashiyama Yoshimura is a local soba shop that sells soba (hot or cold) lunch sets with various side dishes. Located a few minutes' walk from the temple of Tenryū-ji, this popular restaurant has a nice view of the Hozu River rushing by outside. This is a good pick for a lunch before setting off on foot to explore the sights of the area. Note that it often attracts a queue, so try to avoid peak hours if you don't like to wait.

Vegetarian

YUDOFU SAGANO

45 Saga-Tenryū-ji, Susukinobaba-chō; tel. 075/871-6946; www.kyoto-sagano.jp; tel. 075/871-6946; 11am-7pm daily; courses from ¥4,000; take JR Sagano line to Saga-Arashiyama Station

For a more casual tofu-based meal, another option in Arashiyama is Yudofu Sagano. The specialty here is simmered pieces of hot tofu known as yudo, served with side dishes of mountain vegetables, tempura, and more.

Cafés and Light Bites

%ARABICA

3-47, Saga-Tenryū-ji, Susukinobaba-chō, Ukyō-ku; tel. 075/748-0057; https://arabica.coffee, 8am-6pm daily; from ¥500; take Hankyū line to Arashiyama station

Just down the road from Arashiyama Yoshimura, you'll find %Arabica. This hip café, overlooking the Hozu River, serves artisanal coffee and makes for an ideal pit stop before or after exploring the area's sights. There's not much in the way of seating, but the area makes takeaway an appealing alternative.

Bars and Nightlife

If you'd like to get acquainted with the city's breweries, check out **Kampai Sake Tours** (tel. 080/7045-8365; https://kampaisake-tours.com/tour/kyoto-sake; 3 hours; 2pm-5pm Wed.-Sun.; ¥6,900).

SOUTHERN HIGASHIYAMA

BEER KOMACHI

444 Hachiken-chō, Higashiyama-ku; tel. 075/746-6152; www.facebook.com/beerkomachi/; 5pm-11pm Mon. and Wed.-Fri., 3pm-11pm Sat.-Sun.; take Tōzai subway line to Higashiyama Station

Beer Komachi is a friendly, laid-back spot to sample a range of Japan's craft beer offerings, with usually around seven types on tap. This spot also serves good nibbles, from beer-battered chicken to deep-fried blowfish.

NORTHERN HIGASHIYAMA

CLUB METRO

B1F Ebisu Building, 82 Shimotsutsumichō, Kawabata-dōrii, Marutamachi-sagaru, Sakyō-ku; tel. 075/752-4765; www.metro.ne.jp; 8pm-3am daily; fees vary by event; take Keihan line to Jingū-Marutamachi Station

Club Metro is a longstanding venue with a penchant for catering to a wide range of musical tastes, from big-name DJs to indie rockers and even art exhibitions. With room for about 250 people, the space has an intimate feel. Events change nightly, so check the calendar online before making the trip.

Suntory Yamazaki Distillery and Japan's Award-Winning Whisky

tasting at the Suntory Yamazaki Distillery

Japan's renowned spirit of craftsmanship, knack for detail, and fresh, flavorsome groundwater have all contributed to the country's success in the world of whisky. Aficionados credit the nation's four seasons with adding extra layers of texture to barrel casks that sit aging for years.

Japan's first domestically distilled malt whisky was bottled in 1924 at Suntory Yamazaki Distillery (5-2-1 Yamazaki, Shimamoto, Mishima District, Osaka Prefecture; tel. 075/962-1423; www.suntory.com/factory/yamazaki; 9:30am-5pm daily, sporadic closings) in Osaka Prefecture, between Osaka and Kyoto. Their **Yamazaki 12 Years single malt** was the first Japanese whisky to win a gold medal at the International Spirits Challenge in 2003. The success has snowballed from there, with Suntory's **Hibiki** taking the Best Blended Whisky in the World prize for the fourth time at the World Whiskies Awards in 2016. At the 2017 awards, Japan made the strongest showing of any country, snagging three prizes: World's Best Single Cask Single Malt (Chichibu Whisky Matsuri 2017); World's Best Blended (Hibiki 21 Year Old); and World's Best Grain (Fuji-Gotemba Distillery Single Grain 25 Year Old Small Batch).

If you visit Suntory Yamazaki Distillery, you can walk through on your own, with bilingual exhibits at an on-site **museum** about the history of the label, and sample the goods at a paid **tasting counter** (10am-4:30pm). Or, pay for a guided, behind-the-scenes **distillery tour** (80-100 minutes; ¥1,000-2,000) in English; **reserve ahead** at www.suntory.com/factory/yamazaki/info. To get here, take the JR Kyoto line to Yamazaki Station (30 minutes from Osaka Station, ¥460; 15 minutes from Kyoto Station, ¥220), then walk 10 minutes west.

DOWNTOWN AND CENTRAL KYOTO

SOUR

607-19 Uradera-chō, Nakagyō-ku; tel. 075/231-0778; https://sour.jp; 3pm-midnight daily; take Hankyū line to Kyoto-Kawaramachi Station, exit 2

This chic, cramped standing bar offers a range of "sours," made with shochū, tonic, and infused with a range of fresh fruits. Staff are a bit unengaged, but the mixed crowd is friendly. A good spot to start an evening if you're feeling social.

BEE'S KNEES

1F Matsuya Bldg., 364 Kamiya-chō, Agaru, Kiyamachi, Nakagyō-ku; tel. 075/585-5595; https://

bees-knees-kyoto.jp; 6pm-1am (last order 12:30am) Mon.-Thurs., 6pm-2am (last order 1:30am) Fri.-Sat.; take Hankyū line to Kyoto-Kawaramachi Station, exit 1A, or Keihan line to Gion-Shijō Station, exit 4

Push open the door to "The Book Store," pull aside the black curtain, and enter this dimly lit space, which evokes a serious cocktail den. Friendly young bartenders in bowler hats mix drinks with ingredients like honey and citrus to mask the scent of the gin that delivers the punch. Prohibition-era black-and-white photos hang in golden frames on the walls, and 1990s hip-hop permeates the air. The cocktails are all beautifully garnished, and some come with dry ice for dramatic effect.

ROCKING BAR ING

2F Royal Bldg., Nishikiyamachi-dōri, Takoyakushi-agaru, Nakagyō-ku; tel. 075/255-5087; www.kyotoingbar.com; 7pm-2am Sun.-Thurs., 7pm-5am Fri.-Sat.; take Hankyū line to Kyoto-Kawaramachi Station, exit 1A, or Keihan line to Sanjō Station, exit 6

If you like rock 'n' roll, this popular bar ticks the right boxes: guitars and Rolling Stones posters on the walls and tunes drift through the air, as a friendly international crowd swills cheap drinks and eats pub fare.

L'ESCAMOTEUR BAR

138-9 Saito-chō, Saiseki-dōri, Shijō-sagaru, Shimogyō-ku; tel. 075/708-8511; 8pm-2am Tues.-Sun.; take Keihan line to Gion-Shijō Station, or Hankyū line to Kawaramachi Station

For a cocktail, L'Escamoteur Bar is a known quantity. Bartenders wearing bowler hats and bow ties mix great cocktails, some of which look like magic potions. This fun and friendly bar is strewn with curios and has an air of enchantment.

BAR CORDON NOIR

3F Matsushimaya Building, 121 Ishiya-chō, Nakagyō-ku; tel. 075/212-3288; 7pm-3am daily; cover charge ¥500; take Tōzai subway line to Sanjō Station

Whisky aficionados, take note of this compact bar. It's not cheap, but the range of bottles is truly impressive, most of them either limited-edition or aged at least 17 years. The bartenders are friendly and highly knowledgeable, and cigars are sold.

URBANGUILD

3F New Kyoto Building, 181-2 Kiyamachi, Sanjō-shita, Nakagyō-ku; tel. 075/212-1125; www.urbanguild.net; 6:30pm-1am daily; fee varies by event; take Tōzai subway line to Sanjō Station

Urbanguild is the best place to catch a glimpse of Kyoto's underground scene. A bit of decay and a DIY spirit are on display, with an antique chandelier and furniture made from recovered wood. Think punk, avant-garde theater, noise, and experimental electronic music. Check the website's events page to see what's on and for the cover charge.

BAR ROCKING CHAIR

434-2 Tachibana-chō, Gokomachi-dōri, Bukkoji-sagaru, Shimogyō-ku; tel. 075/496-8679; www.bar-rockingchair.jp; 5pm-2am (last order 1am) Wed.-Mon.; take Hankyū line to Kawaramachi Station

Bar Rocking Chair is a serious cocktail den. Bartender and owner Kenji Tsubokura is a renowned mixologist who uses homegrown ingredients in his flavorsome creations. A great pick for laid-back drinks in a classy, unstuffy atmosphere.

SHOOTING BAR M4

3F TN Building, 452 Matsugae-chō, Nakagyō-ku; tel. 080/5350-0556; https://m4-kyoto.jimdo.com; 5pm-midnight daily; take Tōzai subway line to Sanjō Station

At Shooting Bar M4 you'll find friendly staff, affordable drinks, and a BB gun shooting range. What more can you ask for?

SAKE BAR YORAMU

35-1 Matsuya-chō, Nijō-dōri, Higashinotoin, Higashi-iru, Nakagyō-ku; tel. 075/213-1512; www.sakebar-yoramu.com; 6pm-midnight Wed.-Sat.; from ¥1,600; take Tōzai or Karasuma subway line to Karasuma-Oike Station

Make your way to Sake Bar Yoramu for a great introduction and sake-tasting course. Owned by an Israeli sake enthusiast, the bar is a cramped but friendly spot to glean a bit more insight into the joys of Japan's most iconic drink. Friendly forewarning: Yoram—his real name—takes the brew very seriously and has developed a reputation as an agitator due to the way he dispenses his opinions on the brew. If you go with an open mind and don't mind getting schooled in his own heretical tradition, you'll likely leave with a much more nuanced appreciation for sake—particularly of the aged variety.

Accommodations

KYOTO STATION AREA

¥10,000-20,000

RYOKAN SHIMIZU

644 Kagiya-cho, Shichijō-dōri, Wakamiya agaru, Shimogyō-ku; tel. 075/371-5538; www.kyoto-shimizu.net; ¥13,000d with private bath; 5-minute walk from JR Kyoto Station's Karasuma central gate

Ryokan Shimizu is a great budget ryokan. There are no luxurious meals or landscape garden views, but the rooms are clean, and both English-speaking staff and friendly fellow travelers are happy to swap information. If you're content sleeping in a futon on a tatami floor, and proximity to Kyoto Station is important to you, this hotel is a good bet. Bicycle rentals are available (¥700 per day). Note that there is a midnight curfew.

¥30,000-40,000

★ HOTEL GRANVIA

JR Kyoto Station, Central Exit, Karasuma-dōri, Shiokōji-sagaru, Shimogyō-ku; tel. 075/344-8888; www.granviakyoto.com; ¥35,000 d

Hotel Granvia has well-appointed rooms with chic decor. The hotel is literally in the JR Kyoto Station building, offering direct access to transport links. The views over the city (or train tracks) are notable, too.

SOUTHERN HIGASHIYAMA

¥10,000-20,000

KYOTO YOSHIMIZU

Maruyama-kōen, Bentendoue, Higashiyama-ku; tel. 075/551-3995; http://yoshimizu.com; ¥15,000 d; 10-minute walk from Gion bus stop

Set behind Maruyama-kōen, Kyoto Yoshimizu scores points for its tranquil setting beyond the city's thrum. The inn is set in a traditional-style ryokan building but has both Western-style and Japanese-style rooms. Breakfast is included.

Over ¥40,000

HYATT REGENCY KYOTO

664-2 Sanjūsangen-dō-mawari, Higashiyama-ku; tel. 075/541-1234; www.hyatt.com; ¥55,700 d; take Keihan line to Shichijō Station

The Hyatt Regency Kyoto is a fantastic hotel with luxury trimmings at a relatively reasonable price. In the southern edge of Higashiyama, the hotel has helpful staff and chic, spacious rooms, each with room service a touch screen away.

GION

Under ¥10,000

GION KOH

475 Shimokawara-chō, Higashiyama-ku; tel. 075/561-0125; http://gion-koh.com;from ¥7,300 d; take Keihan line to Gion-Shijō Station, exit 1

This charming guesthouse tucked down a quiet sidestreet near Kōdai-ji is a great choice if you're on a budget and want to stay in a place with some ambiance. There's a mix of Western (wooden floors, beds) and Japanese-style (tatami, futon) rooms—some sharing a bathroom, others with their own—an interior courtyard, and a shared kitchen. It's a little bit far from the nearest station, so either be ready for a bit of a walk with your luggage or simply catch a taxi from the station.

¥10,000-20,000

HOTEL ETHNOGRAPHY - GION SHINMONZEN

219-2 Nishinochō, Shinmonzen, Yamato Ōji Hirashi-iru, Higashiyama-ku; tel. 075/708-7858; www.hotel-ethnography.com; rooms from ¥18,000; take Keihan line to Gion-Shijō Station, exit 7

Hotel Ethnography - Gion Shinmonzen is a boutique hotel a short walk from the east bank of the Kamo River. The interior is minimalist with tasteful Japanese accents, including local arts and crafts. Some rooms even look out onto private gardens. Friendly English-speaking staff are on call to help you navigate the city. Fantastic value.

¥30,000-40,000

OLD KYOTO

536-12 Komatsu-chō, Higashiyama-ku; tel. 075/533-7775; www.oldkyoto.com; suites from ¥22,000 per night; take Keihan line to Gion-Shijō Station, exit 1

There are three charming machiya in the southeastern corner of Gion run by an aesthetically minded restoration organization called Old Kyoto. Up to four people can occupy the Gion House, Indigo House, or Amber House at any one time, with a requirement of at least five nights' stay. Spruced up retro Japanese-style interiors are complemented by fully modernized creature comforts, including decked-out kitchens and laundry facilities. Considering the space and amenities, as well as the charm and location, these homes are excellent affordable alternatives to the city's hotels.

HOTEL THE CELESTINE KYOTO GION

572 Komatsu-chō, Yasaka-dōri, Higashiōji-nishi-iru, Higashiyama-ku; tel. 075/532-3111; www.celestinehotels.jp; from ¥33,580 d; take Keihan line to Gion-Shijō Station, exit 1

Hotel The Celestine Kyoto Gion is brand-new and sits in a sweet spot right in the heart of Gion. If you're seeking an excellent option at the higher end of the mid-range, and convenience is a priority, this hotel is highly recommended. En-suite bathrooms are complemented by gender-separated public baths, and an on-site restaurant whips up Japanese and Western offerings. The rooms are sleek and amply sized, and the hotel's location is excellent.

HANA-TOURO HOTEL GION

555 Komatsuchō, Higashiyama-ku; tel. 075/525-8100; https://hanatourohotelgion.jphotel.site; from ¥38,000 d; take Keihan line to Gion-Shijō Station, exit 7

Hana-Touro Hotel Gion is a sleek new boutique hotel smack in the middle of Kyoto's old geisha quarter. The rooms are modern, stylish, and clean, with balconies and wooden bathtubs. There's a rooftop terrace and a restaurant serving Japanese fare, and the front desk can assist with anything from attending geisha performances to renting bikes and kimonos.

Over ¥40,000

YUZUYA RYOKAN

Yasaka-jinja Minami-tonari, Gion-machi, Higashiyama-ku; tel. 075/533-6369; http://yuzuyaryokan.com; from ¥60,000 d; take Keihan line to Gion-Shijō, exit 7

Yuzuya Ryokan is a sophisticated ryokan located right on Higashiōji-dōri, a stone's throw from Yasaka-jinja. The inn, discretely tucked away up a stairway right off the main drag, oozes refinement once you step inside. There's a charming garden for a relaxing stroll, excellent meals, wooden tubs in the rooms, and highly attuned staff. It's also very convenient, with downtown a mere 10-minute walk away and the sights of Southern Higashiyama arrayed all around it.

★ SOWAKA

480 Kiyoi-chō, Higashiyama-ku; tel. 075/541-5323; https://sowaka.com; from ¥70,000 d; take Keihan line to Gion-Shijō Station, exit 7

The name of this lush boutique property, an impeccably made-over century-old teahouse in an atmospheric pocket of Gion, translates to "well being." Approaching via a path lined with trees, guests enter a serene realm of wooden passages, hushed rooms with tatami floors, and shoji paper-screen doors guarding windows that open onto an inner garden. Rooms are spacious, with comfortable beds and luxuriant wooden bathtubs ideal for a soak and a mixture of antique and modern decor. At the beautiful restaurant, sumptuous Japanese fare is served for dinner, with breakfast available in either Japanese or Western style. Friendly, savvy staff in kimono are ready at hand to help, and know the city deeply.

NORTHERN HIGASHIYAMA

Over ¥40,000

★ YOSHIDA SANSŌ

59-1 Yoshida Shimōji-chō, Sakyō-ku; tel. 075/771-6125; www.yoshidasanso.com; from ¥123,000 d with breakfast; take a taxi from Kyoto Station (20 minutes), or Kyoto City Bus no. 5 to Ginkaku-ji Michi bus stop and walk 15 minutes

Yoshida Sansō has a whiff of secrecy and history about it. In a quiet corner of the city near Ginkaku-ji, on the summit of Mount Yoshida, this classic old ryokan was originally built during the Shōwa Period (1926-1989)—seen in the architectural blend revealing inspiration from both East and West—to serve as the home of a prince, Higashi-Fushimi, who was the uncle of Japanese Emperor Akihito. There's an atmosphere of elegant wear on the surfaces of this hideaway. A short walk from Northern Higashiyama's temple circuit, as well as a network of hiking trails, Yoshida Sansō is a ryokan set apart.

DOWNTOWN AND CENTRAL KYOTO

Under ¥10,000

HOSTEL LEN KYOTO KAWARAMACHI

709-3 Uematsu-chō, Shimogyo-ku; tel. 075/361-1177; https://backpackersjapan.co.jp/kyotohostel; mixed dorms from ¥2,600, private rooms from ¥3,500 pp; take Keihan line to Kiyomizu-Gojō Station, or Hankyū line to Kawaramachi Station, exit 4

With a café, bar, and restaurant on-site, this trendy hostel is a popular choice for young, stylish travelers looking to mingle. It's near the west bank of the Kamo River, a stone's throw from downtown, making it a good base. Room types range from dorms (mixed, female only) to private rooms—all with shared bath. There's also a shared kitchen and a library.

★ THE MILLENNIALS KYOTO

235 Yamazaki-chō, Nakagyō-ku; tel. 050/3164-0760; www.themillennials.jp; single capsules from ¥4,300, adjoining capsules from ¥8,300; take Tōzai subway line to Sanjō Station, exit 6

The Millennials Kyoto is a hip "smart pod" (capsule hotel) aimed, as the name suggests, at young professionals on the go. Each "pod," just big enough to crawl in and comfortably crash, has a plug and USB socket, and its own iPod touch. There's a shared lounge, a shared workspace, and amenities including free Wi-Fi, free breakfast and coffee, and even free beer. Restrooms, showers, laundry facilities, and lavatories are all shared. If you're looking to mingle and don't mind sleeping in a capsule, this is a stylish option in a central location.

¥10,000-20,000

CROSS HOTEL

71-1 Daikoku-chō, Kawaramachi-dōri Sanjō sagaru, Nakagyō-ku; tel. 075/231-8831; www.crosshotel.com/kyoto; from ¥14,000 d with breakfast; take Keihan line to Sanjō Station or Tōzai subway line to Sanjō Keihan Station, exit 6

This chic, modern hotel smack in the heart of downtown is a great mid-range pick. The rooms are bright and clean, and while not massive, are larger than many similarly priced options. The bathrooms are well-appointed and roomy, with separated bath and toilet. The cheery staff are happy to help, and there's an appealing lounge with free coffee, as well as a bar. Breakfast is very decent, but you can safely pass on dinner.

¥20,000-30,000

SOLARIA NISHITETSU HOTEL KYOTO PREMIER SANJŌ

509 Kamiosaka-chō, Kiyamachi-dōri Sanjō-agaru, Nakagyō-ku; tel. 075/708-5757; http://solaria-kyoto.nishitetsu-hotels.com; ¥26,000 d; take Tōzai subway line to Kyoto Shiyakusho-Mae Station

Solaria Nishitetsu Hotel Kyoto Premier Sanjō opened in 2016 and is one of the city's best values. With a boutique feel, the property is smack in the middle of downtown, right next to the Kamo River. It commands stellar views of the river as well as the Higashiyama Mountains looming to the east. Rooms are well appointed, surprisingly chic for the price, and quiet. The staff are friendly and speak English. A solid balance at a reasonable price.

¥30,000-40,0000

★ ACE HOTEL KYOTO

245-2 Kurumaya-chō, Nakagyō-ku; tel. 075/229-9000; https://acehotel.com/kyoto/; ¥30,000 d; take Karasuma, Tōzai lines to Karasuma Oike Station

Housed within a classic 1926 modernist brick facade, this boutique hotel is the first in Asia from the bleeding-edge cool, U.S.-based Ace Hotel chain. Smack in the middle of town, directly linked to Karasuma Oike Station, it gives the city massive hipster cred. "Starchitect" Kengo Kuma, whose modernist spin on architectural renovations can be seen throughout urban Japan, made over the original brick building, and also oversaw an additional building infused with the clean, angular lines he is known for. The rooms have a homey atmosphere with turntables, stacks of vinyl records, bold maximalist paintings, and outsized windows. There's also a coffee roaster with Portland roots in the lobby; restaurants serving Italian, Mexican, and U.S. fare; a rooftop bar; and a 24-hour gym. In-the-know staff are friendly and happy to help.

Over ¥40,000

AOI HOTEL KYOTO

Reception at 145-1 Tenno-chō, Shimogyō-ku; tel. 075/354-7770; www.kyoto-stay.jp; from ¥42,000 d with breakfast; take Hankyū line to Kawaramachi Station to reach reception

Aoi Hotel Kyoto is a great value. It has an excellent concierge service, and spacious rooms that are more akin to small studio apartments than to hotel rooms, with Japanese flourishes, including painted screens and flower arrangements. The hotel is right next to the Kamo River in the heart of downtown, within walking distance of heaps of good food options, nightlife, and a number of sights. Each room has ample amenities, including its own washer and dryer.

KINMATA

Gokomachi, Shijō-agaru, Nakagyō-ku; tel. 075/221-1039; www.kinmata.com; from ¥45,000 pp with 2 meals; take Hankyū line to Kawaramachi Station

Founded in 1801, this institution is both a high-end ryokan with seven Japanese-style rooms and a bastion of kaiseki dining (lunch ¥6,000-16,000, dinner ¥13,000-35,000). The ryokan rooms look the part: wooden interiors, opening onto an inner garden, tatami floors, and screens made of reed and paper. The restaurant is overseen by Chef Haraju Ukai, a seventh-generation culinary wizard. Classic, old-school, and exquisite.

HIIRAGIYA

Nakahakusan-chō, Fuyachō, Aneyakōji-agaru, Nakagyō-ku; tel. 075/221-1136; www.hiiragiya.co.jp; ¥36,000-90,000 pp with two meals; take Tōzai subway line to Kyoto Shiyakusho-mae Station, exit 8

While the vaunted Tawaraya ryokan across the road may be steeped in more mystique, the Hiiragiya is on par with its renowned neighbor and is, relatively speaking, easier to book. From the outside, the inn looks exactly like you'd expect: earthen walls separate it from the street, with foliage poking over the top and black tiles on the roof. Inside, hushed tatami-mat rooms with sliding paper doors look onto private landscape gardens. Exquisite kaiseki ryōri meals are de rigueur, as is impeccable service. In a surprise twist, there is not only an old classic wing, but also a shiny modern one, offering a range of room types. Unlike at many of Kyoto's elite ryokan, the staff here is accustomed to hosting visitors from abroad. To book a room, you'll need to submit a request online (in English) through the official website.

★ RITZ-CARLTON KYOTO

Kamogawa Nijō-Ōhashi-hotori, Nakagyō-ku; tel. 075/746-5555; www.ritzcarlton.com; from around ¥115,000; take Tōzai subway line to Kyoto Shiyakusho-mae Station

For an ideal balance of extravagance and convenience, the Ritz-Carlton Kyoto reigns supreme. It's right next to the western bank of the Kamo River in the center of the city, a bit north of the major artery of Nijō-dōri. It comes with all the sumptuous amenities you'd expect from this global luxury juggernaut. It also houses a fantastic kaiseki ryōri restaurant. Perhaps its biggest trait worthy of mention is that it blends in seamlessly with Kyoto's low-rise skyline.

Information and Services

TOURIST INFORMATION

Kyoto Travel Guide (www.kyoto.travel) is a great English-language resource online. The site introduces Kyoto's cuisine, culture, sights, neighborhoods, travel agents, and more. The **Deep Kyoto** (www.deepkyoto.com) blog unearths some of the city's hidden gems, from cafés to art exhibits. For inspiration both visual and written, head to the lush website of **Kyoto Journal** (https://kyotojournal.org), an award-winning nonprofit quarterly that's been going strong from the city since 1987. The staunchly independent magazine covers all of Asia but remains deeply rooted in its home, Kyoto. **Inside Kyoto** (www.insidekyoto.com) is another great resource. Be sure to pick up a copy of the **Kyoto Visitor's Guide** (www.kyotoguide.com) at the visitor center for a good rundown of sights, events, restaurants, and lodgings.

- **Kyoto Tourist Information Center** (2F Kyoto Station Building; tel. 075/343-0548; https://ja.kyoto.travel/information/; 8:30am-7pm daily)
- **Kyoto International Community House** (2-1 Torii-chō, Awataguchi, Sakyō-ku; tel. 075/752-3010; www.kcif.or.jp; 9am-9pm Tues.-Sun)

POSTAL SERVICES

- **Kyoto Central Post Office** (843-12 Higashishiokoji-chō, Shimogyō-ku; tel. 0570/943-790; https://map.japanpost.jp/p/search/dtl/300144089000/; 9am-7pm Mon.-Fri., 9am-6pm Sat.-Sun.)

PHARMACIES AND MEDICAL SERVICES

Pharmacies (yakyoku) are plentiful; simply look for the internationally recognizable red cross symbol out front. Call **AMDA International Medical Information Center**'s Osaka branch (tel. 06/4395-0555; http://amda-imic.com/oldpage/english/E-index.html; 9am-5pm Mon.-Fri.) for medical advice in the Kansai region, including Kyoto. The English-speaking operators are happy to help you navigate the Japanese medical system, referring you to doctors, hospitals, and so on.

- **Kyoto University Hospital** (54 Shōgoin Kawahara-chō, Sakyō-ku; tel. 075/751-3111; www.kuhp.kyoto-u.ac.jp; 8:15am-11am Mon.-Fri. reception), located just east of the Kamo River in Northern Higashiyama. English-speaking assistance and quality of care are ensured here.
- **Kyoto Prefectural Medical University Hospital** (Kawaramachi-Hirokoji, Kajii-chō, Kamigyō-ku; tel. 075/251-5111; www.kpu-m.ac.jp; 8:45am-11am reception Mon.-Fri.)

Transportation

GETTING THERE

If you're traveling to Kyoto from within Japan, the shinkansen (bullet train) is your best bet, particularly if you have a JR Pass. If you're coming from overseas and Kyoto is your first or only stop, there are also three airports within relatively easy reach, although none of them are actually in the city.

Air

The nearest flight hub to Kyoto is **Osaka International Airport** (tel. 06/6856-6781; www.osaka-airport.co.jp), also known as Itami Airport. Located roughly 50 minutes from the city by limousine bus, this hub is, despite its name, primarily a stop on domestic routes. But if you see a good flight deal that connects to the airport from another international airport in the country, don't hesitate. Some airlines offer connecting flights via Tokyo's Narita Airport.

Osaka Airport Transport (tel. 06/6844-1124; www.okkbus.co.jp; 50 minutes; ¥1,340 adults, ¥670 children) offers limousine bus services from the airport to Kyoto Station and vice versa. Tickets can be purchased from machines outside the arrivals area.

You can also fly directly to Osaka's **Kansai International Airport** (KIX; tel. 072/455-2500; www.kansai-airport.or.jp). Access to Kyoto is by express train via the **JR Haruka Airport Express** (80 minutes, ¥3,430). Note that this route is covered by the JR Pass. You can take the JR Airport Rapid train to Osaka Station, then transfer to a special rapid train on the JR Kyoto Line to Kyoto Station (1 hour 40 minutes; ¥1,910). Finally, if you have a JR Pass, you can even consider flying into **Central Japan International Airport** (tel. 0569/38-1195; www.centrair.jp) in Nagoya. Although the distance between the two cities is 129 kilometers (80 mi), the journey by bullet train from Nagoya to Kyoto—covered by the JR pass—is a mere 35 minutes (¥5,910).

Flights from either Narita or Haneda Airport to Kansai International Airport or Osaka International Airport take about 1.5 hours and start from around ¥10,000 on budget airlines. Just be aware that you'll have to also pay for ground transport to Kyoto (bus, taxi, train) from the airport, and further, that travel times grow longer than taking the train with airport check-ins and ground transport.

Train

By far, the easiest way to reach Kyoto from Japan's other major transport hubs is the shinkansen (bullet train); from **Tokyo,** Nozomi trains (140 minutes; ¥14,170 reserved seat) and Hikari trains (160 minutes; ¥13,850 reserved seat) make the journey. Note that the JR Pass does not cover Nozomi trains.

From **Hiroshima,** take the Sakura shinkansen to Shin-Kobe Station, where you'll transfer to the Hikari shinkansen and travel the rest of the way to Kyoto Station (total trip: 1 hour 50 minutes; ¥11,300). Alternatively, if you're not using a JR Pass and don't mind paying out of pocket, you can also hop on the Nozomi shinkansen and travel directly from Hiroshima Station to Kyoto Station (1 hour 40 minutes; ¥11,620).

From **Kobe,** take the Hikari shinkansen (30 minutes; ¥3,390), which departs from Shin-Kobe Station and is covered by the JR Pass. A second option is the **Hankyu Kyoto/Kobe line,** which links Kobe-Sannomiya Station and Karasuma Station in downtown Kyoto with a transfer at Juso Station (70 minutes; ¥630).

Bus

Buses between **Tokyo** and Kyoto take 7-8 hours one-way. **Willer Express** (http://willerexpress.com, fares from ¥4,000) is one of the best-known operators, with fares from around ¥4,000. Compare fares and book tickets via their website, **Japan Bus Online** (https://

Day Trips from Kyoto

Destination	Why Go?	Getting There from Kyoto	How Long to Stay
Osaka (page 351)	garish lights, greasy food, and fun; savory okonomiyaki pancakes; dough balls stuffed with octopus (takoyaki)	Train: 15-45 minutes, ¥570-2,660	One day
Nara (page 369)	Tōdai-ji, the world's largest wooden structure, with the Great Buddha; Nara-kōen, a sprawling park with legions of deer; escaping the crowds	Train: 35 minutes-1 hour, ¥720-1,160	One day
Kobe (page 377)	19th-century European-style architecture; urban walks; slower pace; Kobe beef; a buzzing jazz scene	Train: 30 minutes-1 hour, ¥1,100-3,190	Half day
Himeji (page 381)	the best surviving example of a feudal castle in Japan	Train: 55 minutes-1 hour 40 minutes, ¥2,310-5,170	Half day
Okayama (page 428)	Kōraku-en, considered one of Japan's top three gardens, with a black castle looming nearby	Train: 1 hour, ¥7,790	Half day
Kurashiki (page 426)	Edo-period townscape, a dreamy canal	Train: 1 hour 15 minutes, ¥8,120	Half day
The Art Islands (page 432)	unconventional spaces designed by cutting-edge architects, natural beauty, world-class artwork	Train and ferry: 2 hours, ¥8,650	Overnight-a long weekend
Onomichi (page 420)	a classic Japanese port, temples that beg to be explored on foot	Train: 1.5 hours, ¥9,220	Half day
Shimanami Kaidō (page 424)	a scenic, six-island bicycle journey leading over roads and bridges	Ferry and bicycle: from Onomichi Port, 10-40 minutes; ¥70-1,200	One day-overnight

japanbusonline.com), or **Kosoku Bus** (www.kosokubus.com).

Car

It rarely makes sense to drive to Kyoto unless you happen to be traveling through Japan by car already and it's your only means of transport. The toll fees are not particularly cheap, reaching about ¥10,000 one-way. If you do happen to arrive in Kyoto in a rental car, visit www.parkme.com/kyoto-jp-parking to search for available **parking** spaces, rates, and more. Do not attempt to park along any random stretch of road, or in the lot of a business where you are not a paying customer, no matter how free a given space may look. Doing so could result in a fine.

GETTING AROUND

Kyoto's public transport network leaves a bit to be desired, at least compared to Tokyo. There are only two subway lines, but aboveground trains also connect disparate parts of town, and Kyoto's easily navigable streets are ideally suited for getting around by bus, taxi, or better yet, on a bicycle or your own two feet.

As with anywhere in Japan, **prepaid IC cards** bought from ticket machines in both JR and non-JR railways stations (Suica cards, Pasmo cards, etc.) can be used across various transport networks in the city, from buses to the subway system. The local IC card variant purchased through JR stations in Kyoto is the Icoca. There's a special type of Icoca for foreign visitors called the **Kansai One Pass** (https://kansaionepass.com/kf_pr/kf_pr_en.html; ¥3,000), which offers the functionality of the Icoca, plus discounts at some tourist attractions around the Kansai region. After the initial ¥3,000 is used up, you can recharge the pass up to ¥20,000. For an English-language **map** of the city's train and subway system, visit www.jrpass.com/maps/map_kyoto_metro.pdf.

The city's streets can become crowded; jams are frequent during hanami season in late March-early April, as well as during the height of the kōyō (autumn leaves) season in November. Stick to subways and trains, or get around on a bicycle or on foot during these times to avoid getting stuck in a traffic jam.

Subway

Kyoto has an efficient if limited subway system, with the **Karasuma line** running north-south and the **Tōzai line** running east-west. The Karasuma line is named after the city's main north-south artery, Karasuma-dōri, under which the subway runs. Sights near the Karasuma line include Daitoku-ji and Kyoto Imperial Palace. At Karasuma-Oike Station, the Karasuma line crosses with the Tōzai line, bringing you within easy reach of Nijō-jō in the west and Gion and southern Higashiyama in the east.

Single journeys on the subway start from ¥210 (¥110 children). One-day unlimited subway passes (¥800 adults, ¥400 children) are sold at the Kyoto City Bus & Subway Information Center and at subway station ticket windows and through ticket machines. The Kyoto Subway & Bus Pass allows you to hop on both subway lines and buses an unlimited number of times for one day (¥1,100 adults, ¥550 children). You can pick up one of these passes at the Kyoto City Bus & Subway Information Center, at any commuter pass sales counter, or at the ticket window of any subway station. This pass doesn't cover rides on any of the aboveground train lines.

Train

Trains run by JR and a number of private operators serve Kyoto. The subway and bus systems provide more direct access to various sights and corners of the city, but a few areas—particularly the southeast around Tōfoku-ji and Fushimi Inari-Taisha (**JR Nara line**), and the sight-rich area of Arashiyama in the west (Sagano line)—are conveniently reached by train. The **Keifuku line** (aka **Randen line**) is essentially a sightseeing train that links Arashiyama in the west to the area in the city's northwest near Kinkaku-ji and Ryōan-ji.

Bus

Originating from Kyoto Station, the green-striped **Kyoto City Bus** and red-striped **Kyoto Bus** companies serve different sections of the city. The bus system can be difficult to navigate, but it does have an extended reach, so buses can be useful when you need to reach sights that are not easily accessed by subway or train, are too far to reach by bicycle, or are too expensive to go by taxi.

Northwest Kyoto—home to sights like Ryōan-ji and Kinkaku-ji—is one part of the city that may call for a journey by bus. Likewise, sights dotting the area around Gingaku-ji in **Northern Higashiyama** are also best served by bus. That said, even these parts of town can be reached by train if you're willing to walk up to 10-30 minutes from the nearest station.

If you don't mind spending a bit of time puzzling out timetables and routes and you plan to use the bus system a lot, it's worth investing in a special bus pass (¥700 adults, ¥350 children), sold at the **Kyoto City Bus & Subway Information Center** (tel. 075/371-4474; 7:30am-7:30pm), found just outside the central exit of Kyoto Station, or any other bus or subway ticket counter. Activate your pass by inserting it into the slot in the payment machine next to the driver's seat of all buses as you exit. The one-day bus pass covers unlimited rides on both Kyoto City Bus and Kyoto Bus routes for a day. If you plan to get around by bus, remember to pick up an English-language bus map (Bus Navi: Kyoto City Bus Sightseeing Map) at the Kyoto Bus Information Center or at any tourist information center around town.

To take a single journey, enter through the back door and pay upon exiting via the front of the bus. Fares within the city are generally a flat ¥230 (¥120 children ages 6-12, free for children under 6), but go up for longer distances. Fares can be paid either with coins or any one of the types of IC cards available in Japan.

As its name suggests, the **K'Loop** (tel. 075/661-1234; http://kloop.jp; ¥500 adults one-day, ¥200 children one-day, 9am-6pm Mon.-Fri. call center) sightseeing bus makes a loop around the city, hitting a number of highlights (Kiyomizu-dera, Ginkaku-ji, Kinkaku-ji, Nijō-jō, etc.). Note that it only operates on Sat., Sun., and holidays.

Bicycle

Kyoto feels tailor-made for cycling. Its mostly flat, grid-pattern streets and the path-lined Kamo River burbling through the eastern half of town beg to be explored by bicycle. Many major sights have designated bicycle parking lots. Orderly traffic and a glut of bicycle rental shops make this an even more appealing proposition.

Before hiring a bicycle from a specialized rental shop, check to see if your accommodation happens to provide bike rentals for guests. Daily rentals typically cost ¥1,000-1,500 for standard city bikes, while paying around ¥2,000 will often get you an electrically assisted one, which can come in handy if you plan to go into any of the hillier districts dotting the eastern edges of town. **Cycle Kyoto** and **Kyoto Cycling Tour Project** are reliable rental options. For extensive rental shop listings, visit https://kyoto-bicycle.com/en/rental_search.

A few more thoughts to consider before pedaling through Kyoto's streets: It's illegal to park your bike outside of a bicycle parking area. Illegally parked bicycles are routinely picked up in city-run sweeps. If your bicycle is gone after you've left it on a stretch of sidewalk outside a café or leaning against some random building, it's quite likely been impounded. If you experience this unfortunate fate, look for a paper affixed somewhere near where you parked your bicycle and use the map on it to make your way to where it's being kept. You'll typically pay ¥2,000 to get your bike back.

To avoid this fate, stick to parking your bike only in specifically designated bicycle lots outside major sights and train or bus stations. Or, leave it at one of the large parking lots found around town. A good example is the

Kyoto Wings lot, found north of Daimaru department store in the heart of downtown, near the intersection of Takoyakushi-dōri and Higashinotoin-dōri. You can leave your bike here for ¥150 per day. For an extensive list of bicycle parking lots, which will keep you on the right side of the law, view the **map** at the bottom of this page: www.cyclekyoto.com/bicycle-parking.

Be aware that there are certain stretches of downtown Kyoto where it's illegal to ride a bicycle. For a detailed breakdown of exactly where you should not ride a bicycle, go to www.cyclekyoto.com/areas-to-avoid.

Taxi

Taking taxis is normally not advisable for those on a budget in Japan. Kyoto bucks this trend. The city is blessed with an overabundance of taxis, and relatively short distances between sights ensures that most fares won't climb much above a few thousand yen. They typically start from around ¥650, then climb ¥80 every 300-400 meters. Thanks to Kyoto's thriving tourism industry, most drivers speak a smattering of English. There's a stand in front of the **Kyoto Century Hotel,** just outside Kyoto Station's central exit, to the right, specifically reserved for English-friendly cabs.

Kansai 関西

Itinerary Ideas 346
Osaka 351
Nara 369
Kobe 377
Kii Peninsula 385

Japan is full of contradictions. Its modern heart is, without a doubt, in Tokyo. Go deeper into the past, however, and Kansai is the cultural birthplace of the nation. This dichotomy is felt in daily life, with reality TV shows and books expounding on subtle differences in customs between the politically, economically, and pop-culturally mightier pole of Kantō (Greater Tokyo) and the historically rich region of Kansai a few hours by shinkansen (bullet train) to the west. There's very much a Kansai-Kantō rivalry in Japan (think New York versus Los Angeles), with Kansai denizens—of whom there are about 22 million—known for their fierce local pride.

Kansai takes up a coast-to-coast chunk of the bottom third of Honshu, Japan's largest island. Kyoto is in Kansai, but the nearby

Highlights

Look for ★ to find recommended sights, activities, dining, and lodging.

★ **Dōtombori:** Eat yourself into a state of ruin on this famed food street, where fried, greasy goodies are sold by the plate, bowl, and skewer (page 364).

★ **Tōdai-ji:** The Buddhist temple known as Tōdai-ji, one of the largest wooden structures in the world, contains an awe inspiring 15-meter (49-ft) bronze statue of Buddha (page 372).

★ **Himeji-jō:** This soaring white fortress is an architectural reminder of a time when Japan was under the rule of ruthless feudal lords (page 381).

★ **Kōya-san:** Many of the Buddhist temples sprawling across this sacred mountain in Wakayama Prefecture accept overnight guests (page 385).

★ **Ise-jingū:** This majestic shrine, ritually dismantled and rebuilt every two decades for centuries, is Shinto's holiest site (page 389).

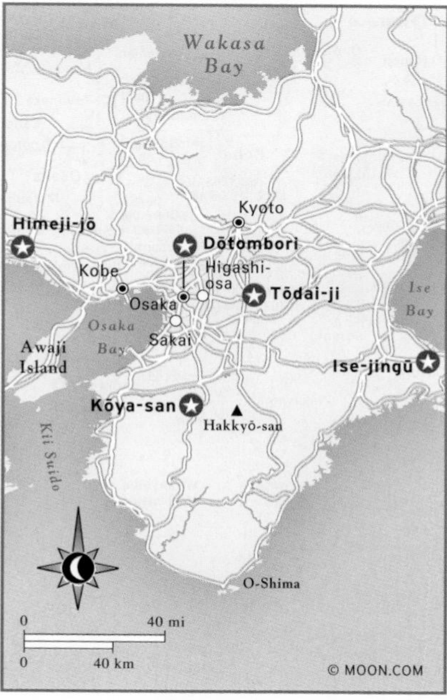

Kansai

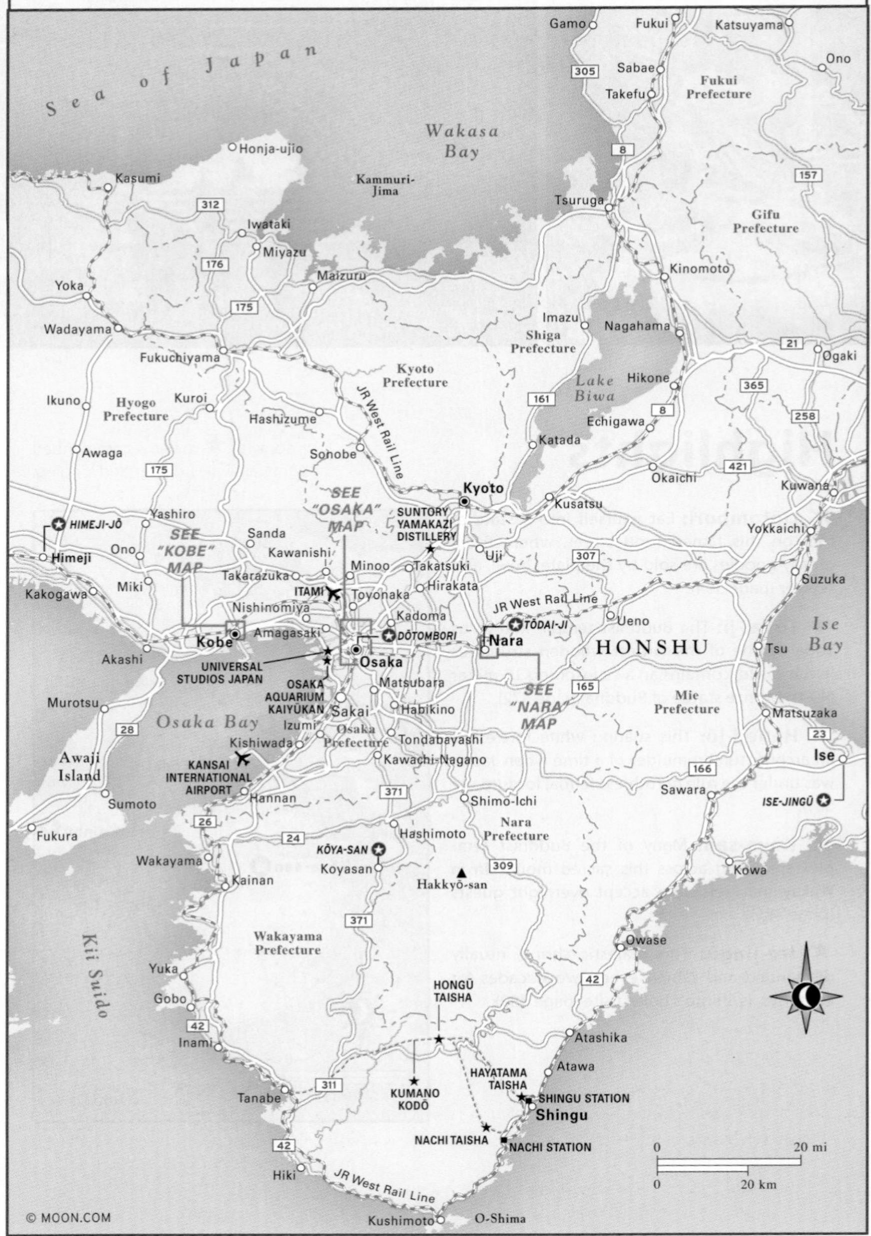
Sea of Japan
Wakasa Bay
Kammuri-Jima
Gamo
Fukui
Katsuyama
Ono
Sabae
Takefu
Fukui Prefecture
Honja-ujio
Kasumi
Iwataki
Miyazu
Maizuru
Yoka
Wadayama
Fukuchiyama
Tsuruga
Gifu Prefecture
Kinomoto
Imazu
Nagahama
Shiga Prefecture
Ogaki
Kyoto Prefecture
JR West Rail Line
Lake Biwa
Hikone
Ikuno
Hyogo Prefecture
Kuroi
Hashizume
Echigawa
Awaga
Sonobe
Katada
Okaichi
Kuwana
Kyoto
Kusatsu
SEE "OSAKA" MAP
SUNTORY YAMAKAZI DISTILLERY
HIMEJI-JŌ
Yashiro
SEE "KOBE" MAP
Sanda
Yokkaichi
Himeji
Ono
Kawanishi
Uji
Takarazuka
Minoo
Takatsuki
Suzuka
Miki
Hirakata
Kakogawa
ITAMI
Toyonaka
JR West Rail Line
Nishinomiya
Kadoma
Ueno
Ise Bay
TŌDAI-JI
Kobe
Amagasaki
DŌTOMBORI
Nara
HONSHU
Tsu
Akashi
Osaka
UNIVERSAL STUDIOS JAPAN
OSAKA AQUARIUM KAIYŪKAN
Matsubara
SEE "NARA" MAP
Murotsu
Sakai
Habikino
Mie Prefecture
Osaka Bay
Izumi
Osaka Prefecture
Matsuzaka
Kishiwada
Tondabayashi
Awaji Island
KANSAI INTERNATIONAL AIRPORT
Kawachi-Nagano
Ise
Sawara
Hannan
Sumoto
Shimo-Ichi
ISE-JINGŪ
Fukura
Hashimoto
Nara Prefecture
KŌYA-SAN
Wakayama
Koyasan
Hakkyō-san
Kowa
Kainan
Kii Suido
Wakayama Prefecture
Owase
Yuka
Gobo
HONGŪ TAISHA
Inami
Atashika
Atawa
HAYATAMA TAISHA
KUMANO KODŌ
Tanabe
SHINGU STATION
Shingu
NACHI TAISHA
NACHI STATION
Hiki
JR West Rail Line
Kushimoto
O-Shima
0
20 mi
0
20 km
305
8
157
312
176
175
21
365
161
8
258
175
421
307
165
28
23
166
371
26
24
309
371
42
42
311
42

Regional Food Specialties

OSAKA STREET FOOD

Osaka is known worldwide for its unparalleled **street food**—much of it cheap, greasy, fried, and completely delicious (page 360).

KOBE BEEF

For many people, the port city of Kobe brings to mind only one thing: **steak** (page 383).

cities of Osaka, Kobe, and Nara to the south make up the region's core, and are all within a short train ride of the ancient capital. A few short jaunts around the area will add a dash of zest to the rarefied offerings of Kyoto.

The urban nucleus of the region, Osaka is a garish, boisterous, smaller-scale alternative to Tokyo. The city is famous for its decadent dishes, such as takoyaki (fried octopus dumplings) and okonomiyaki, a savory pancake stuffed with cabbage, meat, or seafood, and topped with all manner of sauces, fish flakes, mayonnaise, and more.

To the west of Osaka, about 30 minutes by train, Kobe is a sophisticated city set between green hills and the Inland Sea. Much more pleasing to the eye than Osaka, Kobe invites visitors to become urban explorers. Farther west, the city of Himeji is home to what is perhaps Japan's most recognizable castle, the soaring white fortress of Himeji-jō.

To look deeper into the region's past, turn to Nara, Japan's first permanent capital. A half-hour express train ride south of Kyoto and about an hour east of Osaka by train, Nara's main draw is Nara-kōen, a large park inhabited by some 1,200 deer, and home to Tōdai-ji, a wooden temple with an awe-inspiring statue of Buddha.

Equally (if not more) impressive reminders of Kansai's spiritual roots are found in the Kii Peninsula, south of Osaka. Here, the mountaintop of Kōya-san is a repository of Buddhist temples, brimming with on-site temple lodgings. In the southern heart of the peninsula, the millennium-old pilgrimage route known as the Kumano Kodō runs over dramatically mountainous terrain. And in the eastern part of the peninsula, you'll find Shinto's holiest of holies, Ise-jingū, dating to the 3rd century.

ORIENTATION

With the mountainous region of Central Honshu to the east, Western Honshu to the west, and the island of Shikoku to the southwest, Kansai accounts for a large part of the western core of Honshu.

On the eastern edge of Kansai is **Mie Prefecture,** home to Japan's holiest site, Ise-jingū, in the small seaside town of the shrine's namesake. Landlocked **Nara Prefecture,** home to Japan's ancient capital of the same name, lies to Mie's west. Moving southwest from Nara, **Wakayama Prefecture** is home to the mountaintop Buddhist center of Kōya-san, the mystical Kumano Kodō pilgrimage route, and beautifully rugged southern and western coastlines. Just north of Wakayama is **Osaka Prefecture,** home to the eponymous, food-obsessed city and undoubtedly the region's modern heart. Finally, west of Kyoto and Osaka is **Hyogo Prefecture;** its largest urban center is **Kobe.** A brief train ride west of Kobe, **Himeji** is home to Japan's most recognizable castle, the majestic white fortress of Himeji-jo.

Previous: Dōtombori canal; Okuno-in at Kōya-san; Ise-jingū.

Best Accommodations

★ **Intercontinental Osaka:** Perhaps Osaka's best hotel, the Intercontinental is top-notch in all respects, from the views and dining to its prime location (page 366).

★ **Edosan:** A night at this atmospheric, family-owned inn, enshrouded by trees and visited by Nara-kōen's wandering deer, is an irresistibly contemplative escape (page 375).

★ **Nara Hotel:** Luminaries like Albert Einstein and the Dalai Lama have slept at this historic property and wandered through its enchanting grounds (page 376).

★ **Oriental Hotel:** One of Japan's first hotels, this rebuilt waterfront tower offers a first-rate experience and stunning views of Kobe's appealing cityscape (page 384).

★ **Ekō-in:** Get a taste of the monk's life at Kōya-san firsthand at this excellent temple lodging, located a brief stroll from the magical Okuno-in cemetery (page 388).

PLANNING YOUR TIME

Most destinations in Kansai are best viewed as add-ons to Kyoto, given their proximity to the ancient capital. Otherwise, if you have time to spare, consider spending a few nights in a particular city or historical or cultural spot if it interests you.

Plan to spend anywhere from a half day to two days in each of Kansai's main hubs. **Osaka** and **Nara** work as day trips, or you could visit Osaka just for dinner and drinks. Osaka also makes a good base for exploring the region, conveniently near **Nara,** as well as **Kobe** and **Himeji,** only about 30-40 minutes apart by train—you could even see both in one long day. If you have more time, Kobe is a pleasing place to stay the night, heading to Himeji the next day.

How long to spend on the spiritually loaded Kii Peninsula depends on the individual. **Kōya-san** deserves one night—staying in temple lodgings—with time to explore the misty mountainscape on foot. The **Kumano Kodō** region can be a day trip, an overnight jaunt, or a much lengthier multiday trek. **Ise-jingū,** on the eastern side of the peninsula, calls for a day of exploration. It's Shinto's holiest site, after all.

Itinerary Ideas

A WEEKEND IN OSAKA AND NARA

Day One: Osaka

1 Start your day in Osaka getting a view of the city from above with a trip to **Umeda Sky Building** in the city's Kita (north) side, which opens at 10am.

2 Eat excellent okonomiyaki for lunch at **Kiji,** in Umeda Sky Building's basement.

3 Hop on the Midō-suji line at Umeda Station and ride south to Shinsaibashi, the northern gateway to the city's Minami (south) side (6 minutes; ¥230). Grab a coffee at **Lilo Coffee Roasters.**

4 Walk a few blocks south toward **Triangle Park** in the heart of youth culture mecca Amerika-mura. Spend your afternoon here and in the stylish nearby Horie district a couple of blocks southwest, people-watching and popping into shops.

5 Continue south to the Dōtombori-gawa canal. Walk along the river's northern bank until you reach **Ebisu-bashi,** the famous bridge at the heart of Dōtombori, an 8-minute walk southeast of Triangle Park. Join the throngs taking selfies in front of the famous Glico "running man" billboard.

6 Cross the bridge and enter the famed Dōtombori arcade proper. As dusk sets, this strip becomes a surreal, neon-soaked realm. Be sure to stop by **Hōzen-ji** (2 minutes southwest of Ebisu-bashi), an enigmatic temple in the heart of a consumerist frenzy.

7 Eat dinner in Dōtombori. Your choices are endless, but trying deep-fried delights at the Dōtombori branch of **Ganso Kushikatsu Daruma** is a good place to start. It's just north of Hōzen-ji on Dōtombori-gawa.

8 If you still have energy, explore Minami's nightlife. In Amerika-mura, back near Triangle Park, try **Bar Nayuta** for a good cocktail. It's a 10-minute walk northwest of Ganso Kushikatsu Daruma.

Day Two: Nara

1 Aim to arrive at either JR Nara Station or Kintetsu-Nara Station around 10am. Head about 2 kilometers (1.2 mi) east to **Tōdai-ji,** housing one of Japan's most awesome sights, the giant bronze Diabutsu statue.

3 Walk about 15 minutes south to **Le Case** for lunch. They serve great quiche.

4 Continue south from the restaurant to **Kasuga Taisha,** Nara's most important shrine, set in a forest teeming with deer.

5 Gradually make your way west, crossing through the center of Nara-kōen. After walking about 20 minutes, you'll exit the west side of the park and find yourself back at **Kōfuku-ji;** look for its looming pagoda, and spend some time strolling the grounds.

6 For dinner, try the excellent izakaya **Kura,** 5 minutes' walk south of Kōfuku-ji.

HIMEJI AND KOBE IN ONE DAY

1 Start your day in Himeji, aiming to arrive at stunning **Himeji-jō** by 10am—the earlier the better to dodge the crowds.

2 After exploring what is perhaps Japan's most beautiful castle, hop on the JR Special Rapid Service train from JR Himeji Station to Sannomiya Station (40 minutes; ¥990), Kobe's bustling core, where you'll be spoiled for choice of lunch spots. **Grill Jūjiya,** about 6 minutes' walk south of Sannomiya Station, serves nostalgic Western food with a Japanese twist.

3 Hop back on the Seishin-Yamate subway line from Sannomiya Station to Shin-Kobe Station (2 minutes; ¥210) and walk north. You'll find yourself at the foot of a forested slope. Walk along the steep path for about 400 meters (1,312 ft) until you reach the sublime **Nunobiki Falls,** which have inspired poets and artists for centuries.

4 Backtrack toward Shin-Kobe Station, walking 20 minutes or so southwest to the historic hilltop neighborhood of **Kitano-chō.** Amble through this upscale hillside neighborhood, dotted by elegant Western-style ijinkan ("foreigner's houses") that were once lived in by Kobe's well-heeled early foreign transplants.

5 Treat yourself to Kobe beef for dinner at **Steak Aoyama,** 15 minutes further south.

6 Finish off the evening by catching a live show at legendary live jazz joint **Sone.** It's a 10-minute walk northeast of Steak Aoyama.

Osaka and Nara Itinerary Ideas

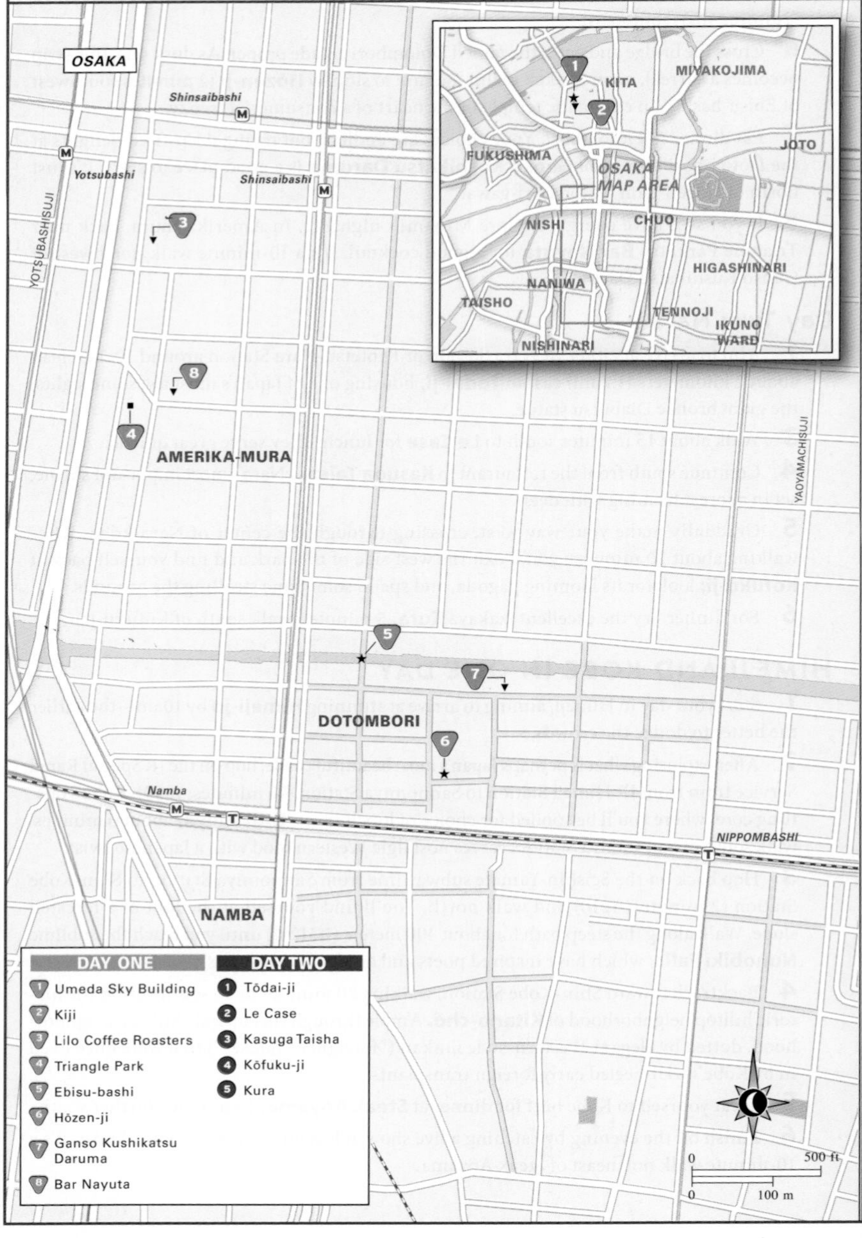

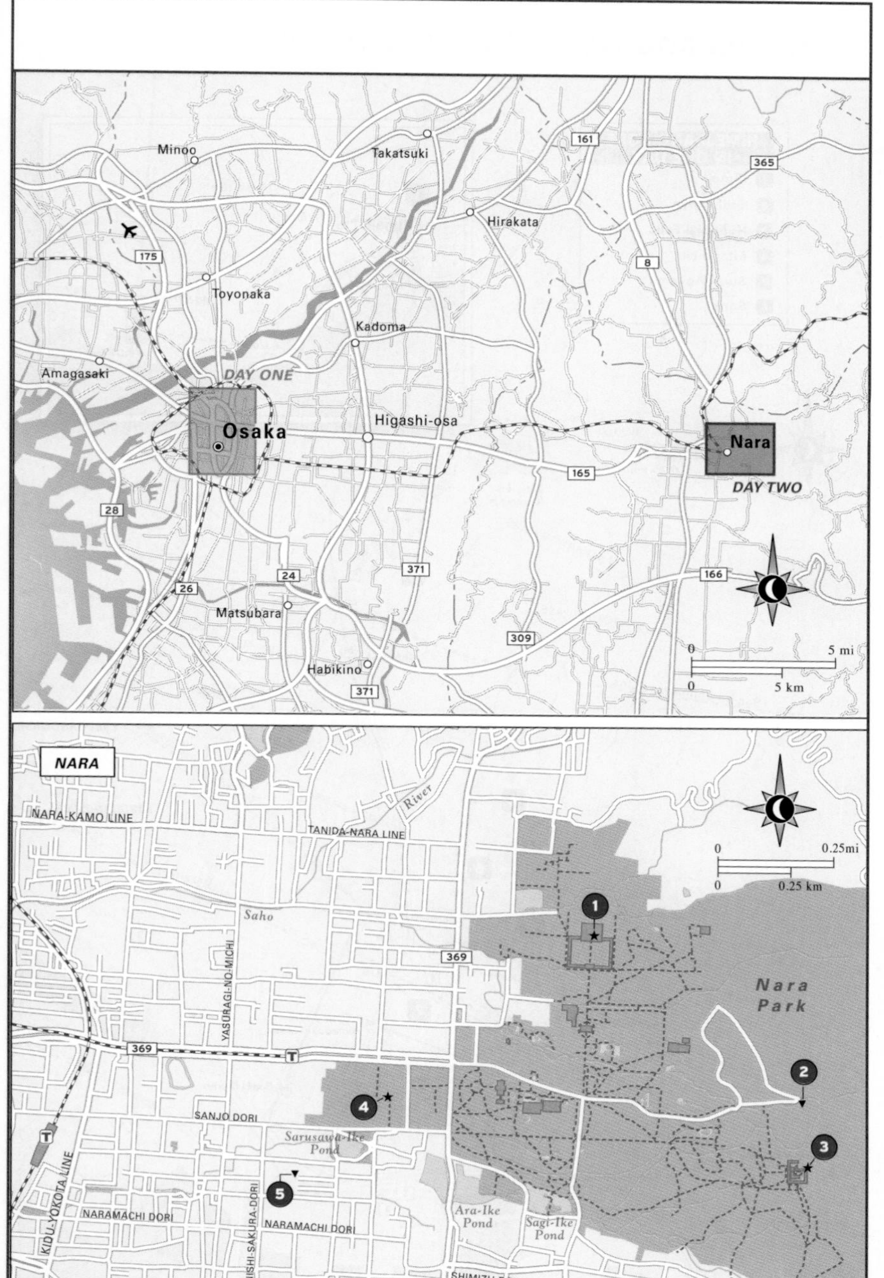
Minoo
Takatsuki
161
365
Hirakata
175
8
Toyonaka
Kadoma
Amagasaki
DAY ONE
Osaka
Higashi-osa
Nara
165
DAY TWO
28
24
371
166
26
Matsubara
309
Habikino
371
0
5 mi
0
5 km
NARA
River
NARA-KAMO LINE
TANIDA-NARA LINE
0
0.25mi
0
0.25 km
Saho
1
369
YASURAGI-NO-MICHI
Nara
Park
369
2
4
SANJO DORI
Sarusawa-Ike
Pond
3
KIDU-YOKOTA LINE
5
NARAMACHI DORI
KONISHI-SAKURA-DORI
NARAMACHI DORI
Ara-Ike
Pond
Sagi-Ike
Pond
SHIMIZU DORI
© MOON.COM

Himeji and Kobe Itinerary Ideas

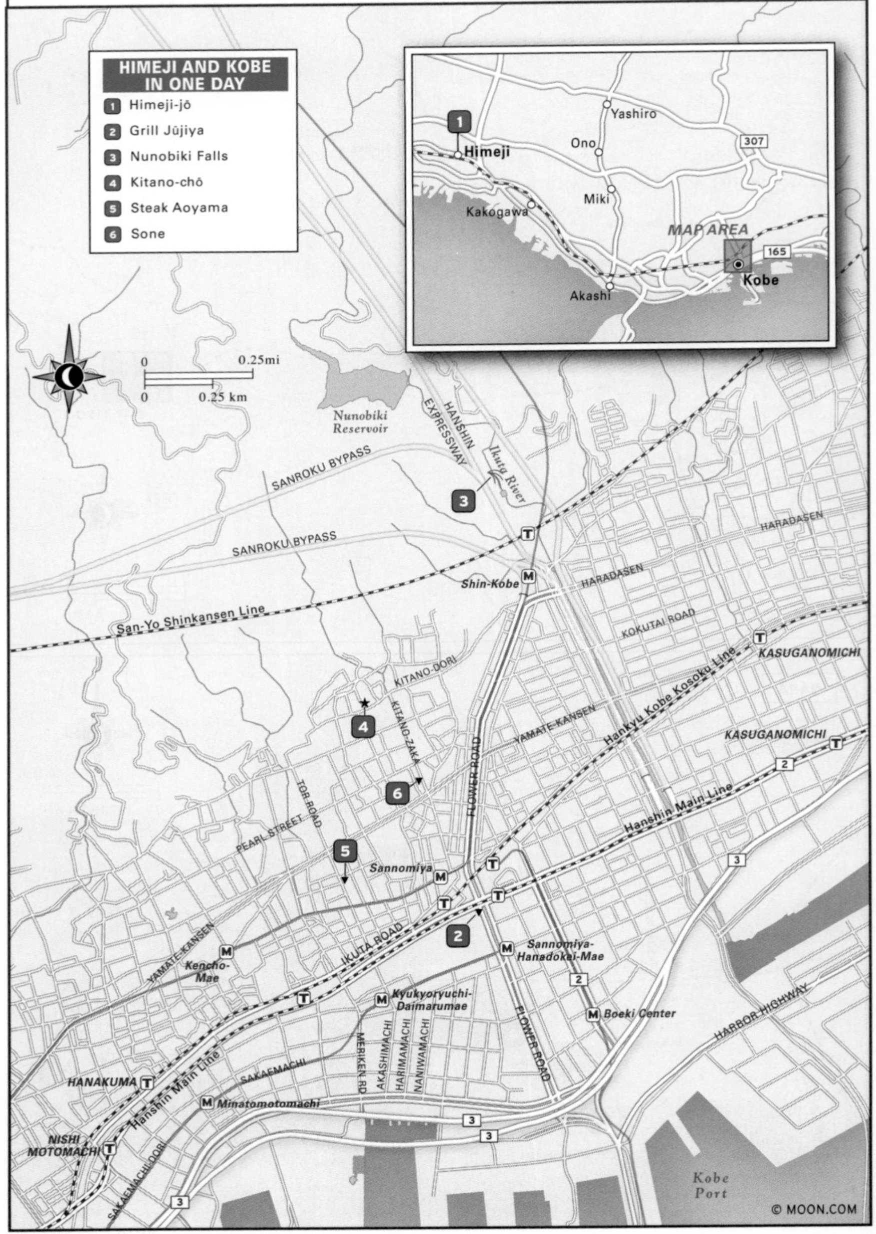

Osaka 大阪

A concrete jungle in the truest sense, Osaka can't claim to be pretty. But it exerts a strange kind of magnetism, emanating from Osaka-jō in the center of town, vast shopping arcades and entertainment centers in the south, and the bay on the west side of town where you'll find Universal Studios Japan and a massive aquarium. The beating heart of the city is in the area surrounding the large canal, Dōtombori-gawa, running through the south side of town, the domain of an army of street-food vendors, rowdy bars, and loudly dressed, disarmingly friendly locals who know how to have a good time.

Japan's third-largest city, Osaka is fundamentally a place of commerce that has been the region's economic core since the Edo period (1603-1868). Shunning pleasantries, the greeting shared by dyed-in-the-wool Osakans is "mōkari makka?" ("making any money?"). The cash does indeed flow into this bustling city, with Panasonic and Sharp among the commercial giants based here. Among its many monikers, Osaka has been called the City of Water and the City of 1,000 Bridges, alluding to the network of rivers crisscrossing the city that has long served as the circulatory system for shipping goods in and out of this vast commercial organism.

Despite its reputation as a place for earning, Osaka remains notably cheaper than Tokyo or Kyoto. Instead of breaking the bank at a high-end sushi counter in Ginza or slowly savoring a rarefied kaiseki feast in a Kyoto townhouse, in Osaka you'll more likely be standing in a street eating fried balls of battered octopus on a stick while kicking back a beer.

Similarly, Osaka's entertainment is of the earthy variety. Since rakugo (humorous storytelling) was born in the city in the Edo period, the city has been the center of Japan's comedy scene, from slapstick to saucy. All told, the city's food, drinking dens, and earthy locals add up to a fun, colorful escape from Kyoto when the temples all start to look the same. Beyond this, Osaka is an exciting city in its own right and begs to be experienced by insatiable urban explorers and gourmands with a taste for the deep-fried side of life.

ORIENTATION

The easiest way to get the lay of the land in Osaka is to think of it on a north-south axis. Buttoned-down **Kita** (north) Osaka encompasses the vast business district of Umeda, as well as Osaka and Shin-Osaka stations. The fun, chaotic image most associated with Osaka comes from the flashy **Minami** (south) side of town. Here, the vast shopping and entertainment districts of **Shinsaibashi, Dōtombori, Namba,** and **Amerika-mura** exude a hedonistic air. Shops and cafés rule the daylight hours, while food, drink, and entertainment in all its forms take center stage at night.

Osaka is split by many rivers. The Ō River runs just past the northwestern corner of the grounds of **Osaka-jō.** Boats congregate along this stretch of water during the city's great summertime bash, the Tenjin Matsuri. Meanwhile, the concrete-canalled **Dōtombori River** runs through the heart of the pedestrian district of the same name in the south side of town.

SIGHTS

Kita

UMEDA SKY BUILDING
梅田スカイビル

1-1-88 Ōyodonaka, Kita-ku; tel. 06/6440-3855 (for Kuchu Teien); www.kuchu-teien.com; 9:30am-9pm (last entry 8:30pm) daily; ¥1,500 adults, ¥700 children ages 4-12; 10-minute walk northwest from JR Osaka Station's north central gate, or 10-minute walk west from Umeda Station

One of Osaka's most impressive buildings, the Umeda Sky Building was once declared to be the "triumphal arch of the future." It certainly

Osaka

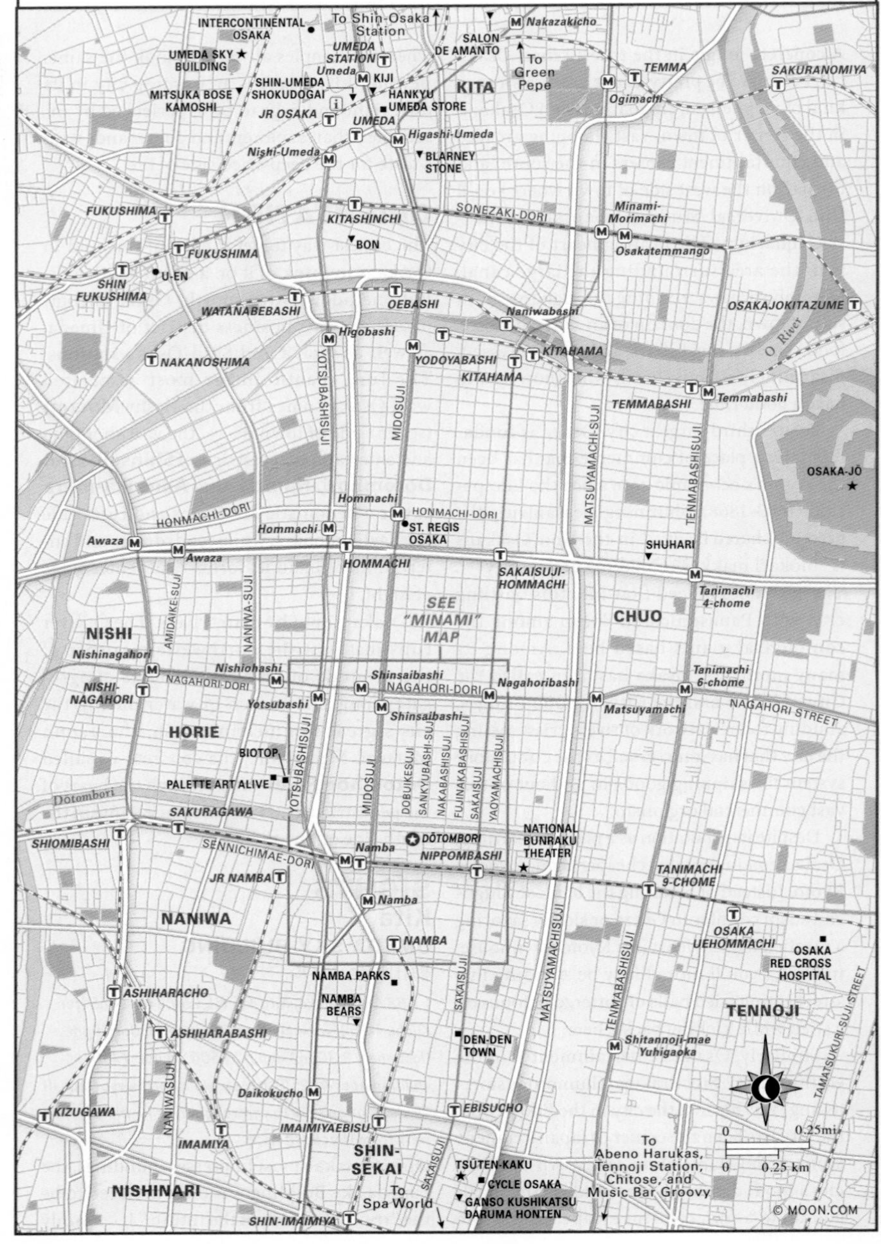
INTERCONTINENTAL OSAKA
To Shin-Osaka Station
Nakazakicho
UMEDA SKY BUILDING
UMEDA STATION
Umeda
KIJI
SALON DE AMANTO
To Green Pepe
TEMMA
SAKURANOMIYA
MITSUKA BOSE KAMOSHI
SHIN-UMEDA SHOKUDOGAI
HANKYU UMEDA STORE
KITA
Ogimachi
JR OSAKA
UMEDA
Higashi-Umeda
Nishi-Umeda
BLARNEY STONE
FUKUSHIMA
KITASHINCHI
SONEZAKI-DORI
Minami-Morimachi
BON
FUKUSHIMA
Osakatemmango
SHIN FUKUSHIMA
U-EN
WATANABEBASHI
OEBASHI
Naniwabashi
OSAKAJOKITAZUME
Higobashi
NAKANOSHIMA
YODOYABASHI
KITAHAMA
KITAHAMA
O River
TEMMABASHI
Temmabashi
YOTSUBASHISUJI
MIDOSUJI
MATSUYAMACHI-SUJI
TENMABASHISUJI
OSAKA-JŌ
Hommachi
HONMACHI-DORI
HONMACHI-DORI
Hommachi
ST. REGIS OSAKA
Awaza
Awaza
HOMMACHI
SAKAISUJI-HOMMACHI
SHUHARI
Tanimachi 4-chome
AMIDAIKE-SUJI
NANIWA-SUJI
SEE "MINAMI" MAP
CHUO
NISHI
Nishinagahori
Nishiohashi
Shinsaibashi
Nagahoribashi
Tanimachi 6-chome
NISHI-NAGAHORI
NAGAHORI-DORI
NAGAHORI-DORI
Yotsubashi
Matsuyamachi
NAGAHORI STREET
Shinsaibashi
HORIE
BIOTOP
PALETTE ART ALIVE
YOTSUBASHISUJI
MIDOSUJI
DOBUIKESUJI
SANKYUBASHI-SUJI
NAKABASHISUJI
FUJINAKABASHISUJI
SAKAISUJI
YAOYAMACHISUJI
Dōtombori
SAKURAGAWA
SHIOMIBASHI
DŌTOMBORI
NATIONAL BUNRAKU THEATER
SENNICHIMAE-DORI
Namba
NIPPOMBASHI
JR NAMBA
TANIMACHI 9-CHOME
Namba
NANIWA
OSAKA UEHOMMACHI
NAMBA
OSAKA RED CROSS HOSPITAL
NAMBA PARKS
MATSUYAMACHISUJI
TENMABASHISUJI
ASHIHARACHO
NAMBA BEARS
SAKAISUJI
TENNOJI
ASHIHARABASHI
DEN-DEN TOWN
Shitannoji-mae Yuhigaoka
TAMATSUKURI-SUJI STREET
NANIWASUJI
Daikokucho
KIZUGAWA
EBISUCHO
IMAIMIYAEBISU
IMAMIYA
SHIN-SEKAI
To Abeno Harukas, Tennoji Station, Chitose, and Music Bar Groovy
0 0.25 mi
0 0.25 km
SAKAISUJI
TSŪTEN-KAKU
CYCLE OSAKA
NISHINARI
To Spa World
GANSO KUSHIKATSU DARUMA HONTEN
SHIN-IMAIMIYA
© MOON.COM

has a futuristic layout, with a "floating garden" called the **Kuchu Teien** ("Garden in the Sky") on the 39th-41st floors. Come for striking views of the mammoth cityscape, with both outdoor and indoor observatories. Try visiting during the evening when the city becomes a vast sea of lights. Buy tickets to the Kuchu Teien on the ticket counter on the 39th floor. You can reach the building either aboveground or via a well-marked underground walkway.

OSAKA-JŌ
大坂城

1-1 Osaka-jō, Chūō-ku; tel. 06/6941-3044; www.osakacastle.net; 9am-5pm (last entry 4:30pm) daily; grounds free, inside keep ¥600 adults, free for children under 15; take Tanimachi or Chūō subway line to Tanimachi 4-Chōme Station, or JR Loop line to Osaka-jō-kōen Station

The warlord Toyotomi Hideyoshi, Japan's great unifier of the 16th century, directed 100,000 laborers to construct his imposing castle, Osaka-jō. Even today, it looms over the eastern side of the city, dramatically illuminated at night.

Originally completed in 1583, the castle was soon after sacked by the forces of Tokugawa Ieyasu, the first shogun of the Tokugawa Shogunate, in 1614. Ieyasu simply rebuilt it block by block, ensuring its fortitude with even larger stones, each weighing up to 100 tonnes (110 tons), studding its wall. In 1931, citizens raised money to reconstruct the main tower. After being razed by bombing during World War II, the main structure was later refurbished in 1995. Thirteen structures from the 17th-century version built by Ieyasu remain in place. Even the concrete reproductions have enough visual oomph to make the castle one of Osaka's biggest draws.

The complex towers over a 106-hectare (262-acre) park that comes vividly alive in spring with the cherry blossoms. It's an excellent place to stroll or have a picnic. Inside the castle, there are displays on the lower floors with information about Osaka's history, the castle, and original builder Hideyoshi, and on the top floor, there's an observation deck looking over the eastern side of the city.

Minami

Less a place to take in sights than a neighborhood to people-watch and gawk at seemingly endless shopping arcades bathed in neon lights, Minami rewards aimless strolling.

EBISU-BASHI

1-6 Dōtonbori, Chūō-ku; 24 hours daily; free

This bridge straddling the Dōtombori-gawa is ground zero for Osaka's Minami (south) side. Tourists jostle for a spot in front of candy maker Glico's **Running Man** neon billboard hovering in the backdrop, and the area's famed deep-fried food zone starts from the south side of the bridge. Come here to feel the city's thrum and gawp at the neon light dancing in the intensely urbanized waterway below.

HŌZEN-JI
法善寺

1-2-16 Namba, Chūō-ku; tel. 06/6211-4152; http://houzenji.jp; 24 hours; free; take Midōsuji, Yotsubashi, Sennichimae subway lines to Namba Station, exit B-16

Walk two blocks south of the main culinary thoroughfare to a small atmospheric lane known as **Hozenji Yokochō,** where you'll find Hōzen-ji, a temple frequented by those working in the mizu shōbai ("water trade"), as the sensual realm of nightlife is known. Peek inside the temple to see the moss-encrusted statue of the esoteric Buddhist deity Fudō Myō-ō.

TSŪTEN-KAKU
通天閣

1-18-6 Ebisu-higashi, Naniwa-ku; tel. 06/6641-9555; www.tsutenkaku.co.jp; 8:30am-9:30pm (last entry 9:05pm) daily; ¥900 adults, ¥400 junior high school and elementary school students, free for children under 5; take Sakai-suji subway line to Ebisu-chō Station, exit 3, or take Midō-suji subway line to Dōbutsuen-mae Station, exit 5

Minami

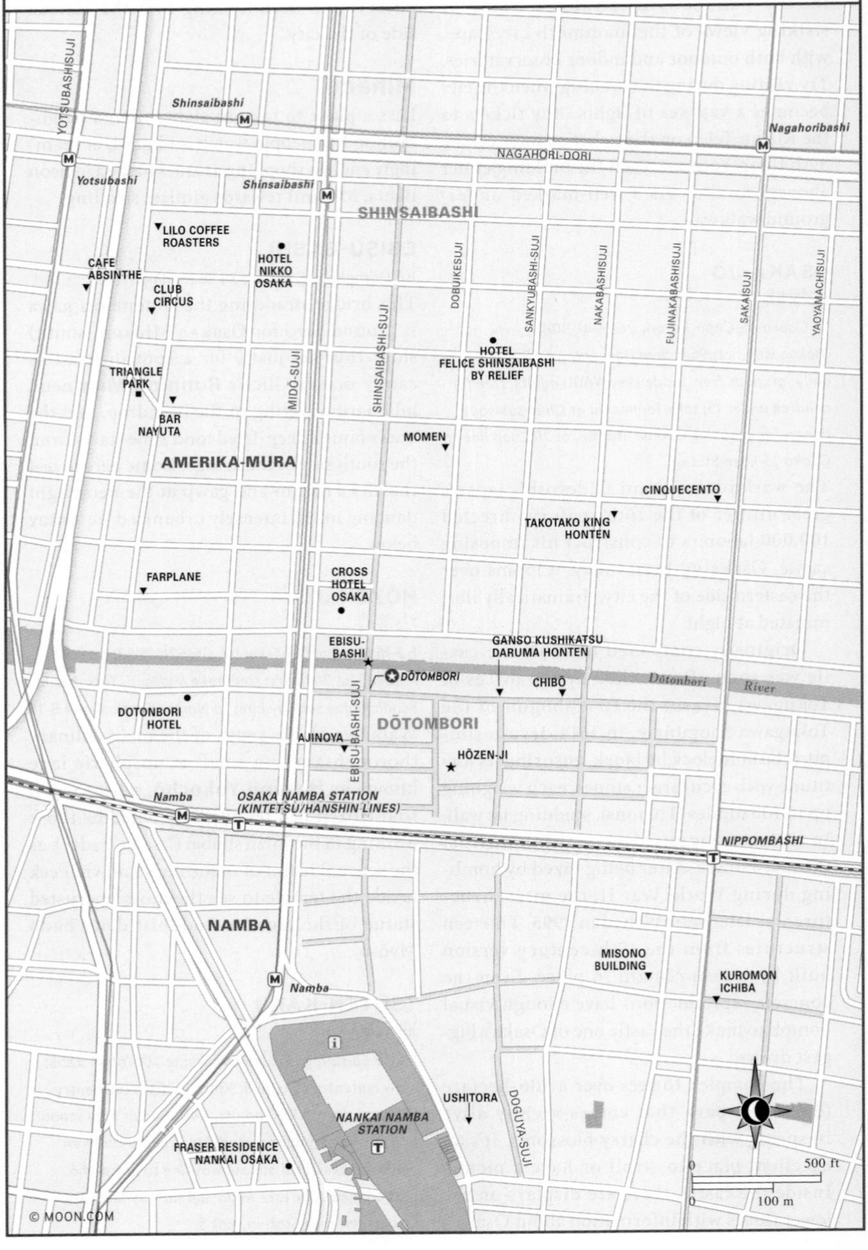

Shinsaibashi
Nagahoribashi
NAGAHORI-DORI
Yotsubashi
Shinsaibashi
SHINSAIBASHI
YOTSUBASHISUJI
LILO COFFEE ROASTERS
HOTEL NIKKO OSAKA
CAFE ABSINTHE
CLUB CIRCUS
DOBUIKESUJI
SANKYUBASHI-SUJI
NAKABASHISUJI
FUJINAKABASHISUJI
SAKAISUJI
YAOYAMACHISUJI
MIDO-SUJI
SHINSAIBASHI-SUJI
HOTEL FELICE SHINSAIBASHI BY RELIEF
TRIANGLE PARK
BAR NAYUTA
MOMEN
AMERIKA-MURA
CINQUECENTO
TAKOTAKO KING HONTEN
FARPLANE
CROSS HOTEL OSAKA
EBISU-BASHI
GANSO KUSHIKATSU DARUMA HONTEN
DŌTOMBORI
CHIBŌ
Dōtonbori River
DOTONBORI HOTEL
DŌTOMBORI
AJINOYA
EBISU-BASHI-SUJI
HŌZEN-JI
Namba
OSAKA NAMBA STATION (KINTETSU/HANSHIN LINES)
NIPPOMBASHI
NAMBA
MISONO BUILDING
KUROMON ICHIBA
Namba
USHITORA
DOGUYA-SUJI
NANKAI NAMBA STATION
FRASER RESIDENCE NANKAI OSAKA
0
500 ft
0
100 m

At 103 meters (338 ft) tall, this nostalgia-inducing tower stands in the heart of the tumbledown zone of Shin-Sekai, a mix of Paris and Coney Island. Originally built in 1912, it was once the second tallest tower in all of Asia at a mere 63 meters (207 ft). After being damaged by fire during World War II, it was rebuilt in 1956. Today, it has a fifth-floor viewing deck at 91 meters (299 ft) and an open-air one above that. An admitted eyesore, it is nonetheless a symbol of Osaka, similar in spirit to Tokyo Tower, which was also built by architect Tachū Naitō. Be forewarned: A show employing a captive monkey is sometimes held in the entrance area. If you feel squeamish about such spectacles, consider viewing the tower from the outside, and skip the observation deck.

ABENO HARUKAS
あべのハルカス

1-1-43 Abenosuji, Abeno-ku; tel. 06/6621-0300; www.abenoharukas-300.jp/en/observatory/; 10am-9pm (last entry 8:30pm) daily; ¥1,500 adults, ¥1,200 ages 12-17, ¥700 ages 6-11, ¥500 ages 4-5; take Midō-suji, Tanimachi subway lines or JR Loop line to Tennō-ji Station, or take Kintetsu Minami Osaka line to Osaka-Abenobashi Station

A southern answer to the Umeda Sky Building in the city's north, the towering Abeno Harukas complex is Japan's tallest skyscraper at 300 meters (984 ft) and houses Osaka's highest observation deck, Harukas 300. Designed by Argentine-American architect Cesar Pelli of Petronas Towers fame, this hulking monolith in the southern hub of Tennō-ji is at the center of an urban renaissance sweeping through what was previously considered a dingy, dated side of town, giving the name Harukas ("clear up" or "brighten") added meaning. Another good choice for jaw-dropping views.

The lower portion of the vast complex houses the **Kintetsu department store** (B2-14th floor; https://abenoharukas.d-kintetsu.co.jp; 10am-8pm daily), Japan's largest, with three stories of restaurants (12th-14th floors; 10am-11pm daily).

Osaka Bay Area

OSAKA AQUARIUM KAIYŪKAN
海遊館

1-1-10 Kaigan-dōri, Minato-ku; tel. 06/6576-5501; www.kaiyukan.com; 10am-8pm (last entry 7pm) daily; ¥2,400 adults, ¥1,200 ages 7-15, ¥600 ages 4-6, free for ages 3 and under; take Chūō subway line to Osakako Station

This excellent aquarium shows off the wildly diverse sea life of the Pacific Ring of Fire, from Antarctica and the Arctic to Monterey Bay in California, the Gulf of Panama, the Ecuadorian jungle, the Great Barrier Reef, and more. It is one of the world's largest aquariums, and its centerpiece is a massive tank large enough to accommodate a whale shark. Other residents of this impressive complex include bizarre jellyfish, penguins, manta rays, sea lions, coralfish, and many more.

At the time of writing, the aquarium was only admitting visitors on a timed admission basis. All tickets must be bought online up to five days in advance and can only be used to enter at the set date and time. Should its entrance policy return to normal, visit on a weekday morning or evening to avoid the crowds.

ENTERTAINMENT AND EVENTS

Bunraku

If you're going to watch one traditional performance in Osaka, make it bunraku. This singular form of puppet theater involves fully visible puppeteers dressed all in black, controlling the nearly life-size puppets onstage. The art form, listed as UNESCO World Intangible Cultural Heritage, was not born in Osaka but has thrived more in the city than anywhere else. The outsized puppets depict tales set in the pleasure quarters of old, where dramas played out among merchants and members of the sensually loaded mizu shōbai (water trade).

NATIONAL BUNRAKU THEATER

1-12-10 Nipponbashi, Chūō-ku; tel. 06/6212-2531; www.ntj.jac.go.jp; from ¥2,400 for full

1
2
3
4
木場
木場 若中

performances, from ¥500 for single acts; take Sakai-suji subway line to Nipponbashi, exit 7

To learn more about this unique form of theater, or to see a performance, go to the National Bunraku Theater. Similar to kabuki, the length of bunraku performances can test your endurance, with some clocking in at more than four hours. If that sounds like too much, non-reserved tickets for single acts are also available. If you want to sit through an entire play, reserve as far in advance as possible. Check the website for the performance schedule.

Festivals

TENJIN MATSURI

天神祭

Tenmangū shrine and Ō River; www.tenjinmatsuri.com; July 24-25; free

Along with Tokyo's Kanda Matsuri and Kyoto's Gion Matsuri, Osaka's Tenjin Matsuri is one of Japan's blowout festivals. Taking place every July 24-25, practically all of the city participates in this massive festival—dedicated to Sugawara Michizane, the God of learning—with a history that stretches back to the 10th century. The proceedings begin the morning of the 24th at Osaka Tenmangū (2-1-8 Tenjinbashi, Kita-ku; tel. 06/6353-0025; https://osakatemmangu.or.jp; take JR Tōzai-Gakkentoshi line to Osakatemmangu Station, or take Sakaisuji or Tanimachi line to Minami-Morimachi Station), located on the north side of town about 25 minutes' walk southeast of JR Osaka Station.

Following a ritual and prayers for the city's peace and prosperity at Tenmangū on the first day, the festival reaches a crescendo on the second day when (starting from around 3:30pm) locals wearing traditional garb pull opulent portable shrines the size of cars, known as mikoshi, from Tenmangū through the surrounding streets, then proceed to glide through the Ō River in swarms of boats. The evening ends with a huge fireworks show along the Ō River.

1: Osaka-jō **2:** Umeda Sky Building **3:** Osaka Aquarium Kaiyūkan **4:** Tenjin Matsuri

KISHIWADA DANJIRI MATSURI

岸和田だんじり祭

1-10 Miyamoto-chō, Kishidawashi; tel. 072/423-2121; https://osaka-info.jp/en/page/kishiwada-danjiri-festival; 6am-10pm Sat.-Sun. of third weekend in Sept.; free

In the Kishiwada Danjiri Matsuri, scores of locals tug around 35 massive wooden floats called danjiri, weighing up to 3,000 kg (6,613 lbs), through the streets west of Kishiwada Station in far southern Osaka (reached via Nankai line from Namba Station in 25 minutes; ¥490). The floats, which resemble religious architecture, are ridden by revelers wearing white headbands and colorfully woven traditional threads. The festival always falls on the weekend preceeding a national holiday known as Respect for the Aged Day (third Mon. of Sept.). Visit www.city.kishiwada.osaka.jp/site/danjiri/danjiri-map.html for a map of the route that the floats typically take through the town's streets.

SPORTS AND RECREATION

SPA WORLD

3-4-24 Ebisu-higashi, Naniwa-ku; tel. 06/6631-0001; www.spaworld.co.jp; 10am-8:45pm daily, closing hours vary for some bathing areas; ¥1,500 junior high school students and older, ¥1,000 age 12 and under for onsen and swimming areas; take Midōsuji, Sakai-suji subway lines to Dobutsuen-mae Station, or take Nankai, JR Loop lines to Shin-Imamiya Station

At the southern end of Shin-Sekai is this rambling smorgasbord of bathing options. Supplied with water drawn from deep within the earth, there are floors for European- (4th floor, with towel) and Asian- (6th floor, nude) style bathing, which alternate monthly by gender (only women can access Asian zone, while only men can access European zone in even-numbered months). Beyond onsen (hot-spring) pools, there are areas for swimming (8th floor; ¥600 bathing suit rental), and for an additional fee you can access 8 types of ganban-yoku (stone sauna) options in a range of styles from around the world, from the Turkish hamam to the Russian banya (3rd floor; ¥800 adults 10am-8:30pm Mon.-Fri., ¥1,000 adults 10am-8:30pm Sat.-Sun. and holidays). Pay a bit more and you'll also have access to water slides, a game room, and a few on-site restaurants. For a full list of options and prices, visit https://www.spaworld.co.jp/english/info/ryokin/. If you arrive between midnight-5am or extend your stay during this window of time, you'll be charged an additional ¥1,450.

SHOPPING

Kita

On the north (Kita) side of town, the shopping options are mostly concentrated in **Umeda,** where department stores and chains of every stripe abound. The hip, artsy enclave of **Nakazaki-chō** on the east side of the JR Kyoto line tracks is filled with indie boutiques, stylish cafés, and bars set in retro Shōwa period (1926-1989) buildings draped in vines that somehow managed to evade bombing during World War II. If you linger until the evening, alternative types congregate at the watering holes around the area. The area rewards wandering. It's 5 minutes' walk east of Hankyū-Umeda Station, or 5 minutes' walk west of Nakazaki-chō Station (Tanimachi subway line).

GREEN PEPE

3-1-12 Nakazaki, Kita-ku; tel. 06/6359-5133; www.greenpepe3104.com; noon-7pm Wed.-Mon

In Nakazaki-chō, check out Green Pepe, a quirky purveyor of vintage clothing and antique miscellany that is very in keeping with the ethos of the neighborhood.

HANKYŪ UMEDA STORE

8-7 Kakuda-chō, Kita-ku; tel. 06/6361-1381; www.hankyu-dept.co.jp/fl/english/honten; 10am-8pm Sun.-Thurs., 10am-9pm Fri.-Sat., 11am-10pm restaurant floors

This is the best department store in town. As the flagship of the Hankyū department store chain, this monument to high-end commerce is suitably chic both in its atmosphere and offerings. Alongside pricey, stylish attire and a seemingly endless range of goods for home and life, there's a cavernous basement food hall and two restaurant floors on the 12th-13th floors. It occupies the building above Umeda Hankyū Station.

Minami

In the south side of Osaka, **Amerika-mura** (http://americamura.jp/en) is a rough approximation to Tokyo's Harajuku. This maze of lanes brims with shops selling streetwear, vintage threads, and hip-hop attire marketed to the city's fashion-conscious youth. Literally meaning America Village, the neighborhood has been a mecca for the city's 20-somethings for decades. To get here, take Midō-suji subway line to Shinsaibashi Station, exit 7.

SHINSAIBASHI-SUJI

East of Midōsuji, from Shinsaibashi Station in north to Dōtombori in the south; hurs vary by shop; take Midōsuji subway line to Shinsaibashi Station, exit 5

This seemingly neverending covered walkway, situated east of and running parallel to the major north-south artery of Midōsuji, is lined with shops of every kind: groceries, cosmetics, bookstores, cheap threads, cafés. In truth, it's mostly notable for its bustle rather than its shops. Walk down it on your way from Shinsaibashi Station to Dōtombori to people-watch and check the city's pulse.

DOGUYA-SUJI

14-5 Nanbasennichimae, Chūō-ku; tel. 06/6633-1423; https://doguyasuji.or.jp; hours vary by shop; take Midōsuji, Yotsubashi, Sennichimae subway lines to Namba Station, exit E-3, or Nakai line to Namba Station, south exit

This pedestrian emporium's name literally translates to "Kitchenware Street," which sums it up. Pick up things for the kitchen here, from cookery and sushi-shaped magnets for the fridge to high-grade knives. The shops are generally open daily from around 10am-6pm. The street runs north-south, parallel to

Namba Station, which is a few minutes' walk west.

DEN-DEN TOWN

4-12 Nipponbashi, Naniwa-ku; tel. 06/6655-1717; www.denden-town.or.jp; hours vary by shop; take Sakai-suji, Sen-Nichimae subway lines to Nippombashi Station, exit 5, or Sakaisuji line to Ebisu-chō Station, or Nakai line to Namba Station, south exit

Roughly 10 minutes' walk south of both Doguya-suji and Kuromon-Ichiba lies a shopping district where you'll find gadgets and various accoutrements of geekdom. If you're visiting Tokyo, then a trip to Akihabara will more than have these things covered. But if you're only going to be in Osaka and want to peruse cameras, electronics, computer parts, and pop-cultural artifacts (manga zines, anime figurines, cosplay outfits, retro video games, and more), then this is your place.

FOOD

Kita

Kita's eateries are concentrated around Osaka and Umeda Stations. One zone worth knowing about is **Shin-Umeda Shokudogai,** an atmospheric, rowdy network of restaurants under the train tracks of JR Osaka Station. There are also dining options in the area around Umeda Sky Building, about 15 minutes' walk west of Osaka and Umeda Stations; in the hip youth zone of Nakazaki-chō, about 15 minutes' walk east Osaka and Umeda Stations; on the tightknit streets of Kitashinchi, about 10 minutes' walk south of Osaka and Umeda Stations; and in the Tanimachi area next to Osaka-jō.

MITSUKA BOSE KAMOSHI

1-2-16 Ōyodominami, Kita-ku; tel. 06/6442-1005; https://mitsukabose.com; 6pm-9pm (last order 8:30pm) Tues.-Fri., 11:30am-2:30pm and 6:30pm-9pm Sat. and holidays, 11:30am-2:30pm Sun.; ¥1,000; take the JR line to JR Osaka Station's central north gate

Mitsuka Bose Kamoshi is the best spot to try miso-based ramen, with soup stock options including squid ink and burnt miso. It's located right next to the Umeda Sky Building.

SHUHARI

1-3-20 Tokiwa-machi, Chūō-ku; tel. 06/6944-8808; http://shuhari.main.jp; 11:30am-3pm (last order 2:30pm) and 5:30pm-9:30pm daily; average ¥1,000; take the Tanimachi subway line to Temmabashi Station, exit 2

If you've worked up an appetite after exploring Osaka-jō, Shuhari is a good spot for lunch. Located in Tanimachi 4-chōme near the park around Osaka-jō, this restaurant has a nice menu of soba sets served with tempura and fresh wasabi.

KIJI

9-20 Kakuda-chō, Kita-ku; tel. 06/6361-5804, 11:30am-9:30pm Mon.-Sat.; ¥1,500; take Midōsuji subway line to Umeda Station, exit 6

For okonomiyaki on the north side of town, head to Kiji, a great okonomiyaki set in the second floor of a building in the tightly packed Shinumeda Shokudogai restaurant district located between JR Osaka Station and Hankyū Umeda Station. There's another branch 12 minutes' walk to the west in the first basement floor of the Umeda Sky Building (Umeda Sky Bldg. B1F, 1-1-90 Ōyodonaka, Kita-ku; tel. 06/6440-5970; 11:30am-9:30pm Fri.-Wed.). This is a great pick if you plan to ascend to the rooftop for sweeping views.

BON

Merry Center Bldg. B1F, 1-3-16 Dojima, Kita-ku; tel. 06/6344-0400; www.kitchen-dan.jp; 6pm-12:30am daily; from ¥15,000; take Yotsuhashi-suji subway line or JR Tōzai line to Kitashinchi Station, exit 11-5

Deep-fried goodies on skewers (kushikatsu) await at Bon, an expert shop in Kita-Shinchi, just south of JR Osaka and Umeda stations. This is the place to go for this local favorite in a refined setting. Reservations are recommended. In case it's booked out, the website contains a full list of branches in Osaka and beyond (in Japanese).

TOP EXPERIENCE

"Eat Yourself to Ruin"

A stereotype exists across Japan that Osakans have a devil-may-care attitude toward indulging in earthly pleasures. Of all the seven deadly sins, gluttony, or at least something approaching it, tops the city's list. A jaunty attitude toward culinary excess has a long tradition in Osaka, which was historically referred to as "Japan's Kitchen." There's even a word for draining one's financial resources in the pursuit of scarfing down all the deep-fried goodies the city has to offer: kuidaore ("ku-ee-dao-rei"). After a night spent tipsily stumbling between rickety ramen stands and smoky yakitori (grilled, skewered chicken) joints, the risk of succumbing to kuidaore (literally: "eating oneself to ruin") becomes a distinct possibility. Here's a small sample of what you'll find:

takoyaki

- **Takoyaki:** Fried balls of dough stuffed with chunks of octopus tentacle. **Takotako King Honten,** situated in the heart of Shinsaibashi, is a fun, friendly place to indulge in the dish over beers (page 361).
- **Okonomiyaki:** Savory pancakes sizzling on an open griddle are stuffed with cabbage, meat, and seafood, and often topped with sweet sauce, bonito flakes, and mayonnaise. In Namba, **Ajinoya** (page 363) is a well-loved purveyor of this dish. Further south, amiable chefs at **Chitose** (page 363) hold court around a cramped griddle.
- **Kushikatsu:** All manner of things on sticks—lotus root, sausage, eggplant, pork belly, mushroom—are dipped in panko, egg, and flour, then deep-fried in a vat of boiling oil until crispy on the outside. For something refined, head to elegant **Bon** (page 359). If you prefer greasy authenticity, **Ganso Kushikatsu Daruma Honten** (page 361) in the entertainment district of Shin-Sekai is said to be where this deep-fried favorite was born.
- **Kappō-ryōri:** In essence, this means kaiseki minus the fuss, with diners sitting directly at the counter to banter with the chef who serves up beautifully presented courses made from the finest seasonal ingredients. **Momen,** tucked away in an alley in Shinsaibashi, is a solid pick (page 363).

For a guide into Osaka's culinary madness, try food-focused tour outfit **Ninja Food Tours** (www.ninjafoodtours.com; from ¥9,500 including dinner and two drinks) or **Backstreet Osaka Tours** (https://backstreetosakatours.com; tours from ¥6,500), which offer greasy spoon "soul food" tours and treks through the city's deep back alleys.

Minami

In Minami, **Dōtombori** canal is a quintessential part of a visit to the city. Although there are other purveyors of Osaka's signature dishes elsewhere in the city, there's something special about savoring them in this bright, bustling strip. Out of all the tacky signs demanding your attention (and yen), some of the shops really deliver on their promises.

Eating along this neon-splashed canal is fundamental to any introduction to Osaka, but for some, the crowds and kitsch may be too much. If you prefer somewhere a little more subdued and authentic, there are loads of other great restaurants nearby. To get to the canal, take the Midōsuji, Yotsubashi, or Sennichimae subway lines to Namba Station, exit 14.

KUROMON ICHIBA

2-4-1 Nipponbashi, Chūō-ku; tel. 06/6631-0007; https://kuromon.com/jp; hours vary by shop; take Sakai-suji, Sen-Nichimae subway lines to Nippombashi Station, exit 10

About 6 minutes' walk east of Doguya-suji, you'll find Osaka's largest food market. This covered walkway contains some 170 shops hawking culinary items of every type, from skewers of grilled meat and noodles to fresh fruits, vegetables, and fish. The market is inundated with tourists from around 10am, so aim to visit by around 9am.

If you'd like to sample something at the market, quaff a paper cup of rich, flavorsome soy milk from **Takahashi Shokuhin** (1-21-31 Nipponbashi, Chūō-ku; tel. 06/6641-4548; https://kuromon.com/en/takahashi-shokuhin; 8am-5pm Mon.-Sat.; ¥70). To reach this vendor, established in 1925, walk straight out of Nippombashi Station, exit 10, and take the first left. Takahashi Shokuhin will be on the right side of the first block of shops. From here, wander through the market, following your inspiration, and take in the atmosphere.

★ GANSO KUSHIKATSU DARUMA HONTEN

2-3-9 Ebisu-Higashi, Naniwa-ku; tel. 06/6645-7056; www.kushikatsu-daruma.com; 11am-10:30pm daily; single skewers from ¥110; take Midō-suji subway line to Dōbutsuen-mae, exit 5

If you prefer to eat kushikatsu right on Dōtombori, the Daruma shop there does a fine job. But to experience this dish in the gritty surroundings of its glorious origins, head farther south to Ganso Kushikatsu Daruma Honten. Set in the aged commercial development of Shin-Sekai, this shop claims to be where the dish originated.

GANSO KUSHIKATSU DARUMA, DŌTOMBORI

1-6-8 Dōtombori, Chūō-ku; tel. 06/6213-8101; www.kushikatu-daruma.com; 11:30am-10:30pm daily; single skewers from ¥110, average meal ¥2,000; take Midōsuji, Yotsubashi, Sennichimae subway lines to Namba Station, exit 14

Head here for excellent kushikatsu right on the main strip just a few doors down from Chibō.

LILO COFFEE ROASTERS

1-10-28 Nishi-Shinsaibashi, Chūō-ku; tel. 06/6227-8666; https://coffee.liloinveve.com; 11am-11pm daily; average ¥500; take Midō-suji subway line to Shinsaibashi Station, exit 8

With its cozy patio and streetside seating, and baristas who know their stuff, this narrow, minimalist café is the place to go for a proper cup of coffee to fuel your stroll through Amerika-mura. A variety of beans are on offer, from single-origin to blends, in a range of roasts. They also sell light nibbles like croissants and hot dogs and have a few beers on tap.

★ TAKOTAKO KING HONTEN

2-4-25 Higashishinsaibashi, Chūō-ku; tel. 06/6213-0098; https://takotakoking.com/honten.html; 6pm-4am daily; ¥400-1,000; take Midō-suji subway line to Shinsaibashi, exit 6

This is a great spot to indulge in one of Osaka's signature greasy-spoon dishes, takoyaki (fried balls of dough stuffed with octopus), away from the throngs of Dōtombori. This friendly local institution draws a crowd, especially on weekends, with its mix of affordable, delicious food made on the spot (takoyaki, okonomiyaki, and more), drinks, and lively ambience. There's both seating inside and on the sidewalk, and a takeout window. If this location is too crowded, there's an equally good branch 2 minutes' walk west on the same side of the same street (2-8-28 Higashishinsaibashi, Chūō-ku; tel. 06/6212-0079; https://takotakoking.com/honnishiten.html; 6pm-3am daily).

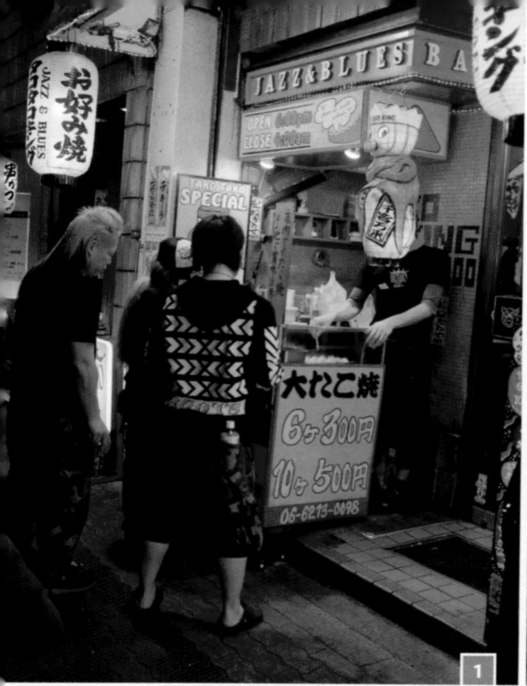
お好み焼
JAZZ & BLUES
JAZZ&BLUES BA
OPEN 6:00pm
CLOSE 6:00am
TAKO TAKO
SPECIAL
大たこ焼
6ヶ300円
10ヶ500円
06-6213-0098

1

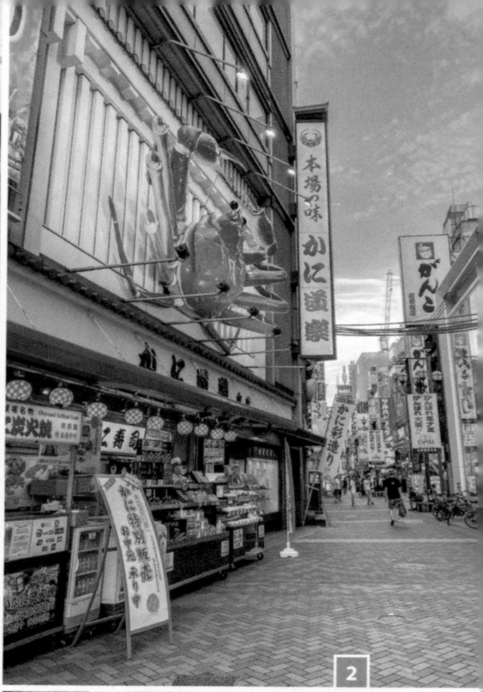
本場の味
かに道楽
がんこ
かに特別販売

2

づぼらや
3F/4F
TAX FREE
薬
がんこ寿司
EDION

3

4

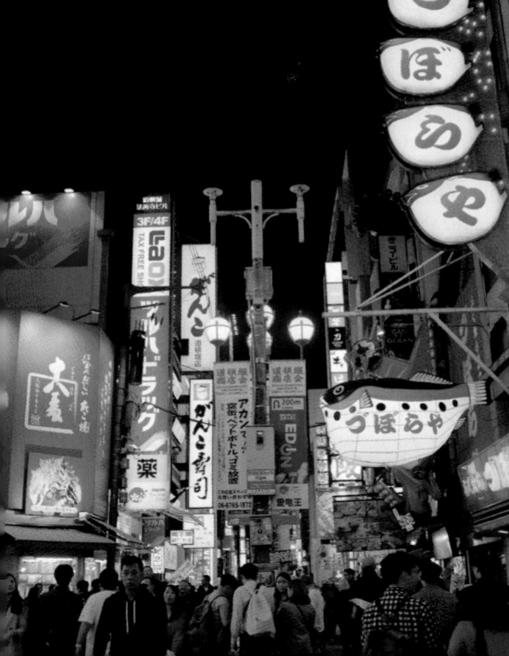

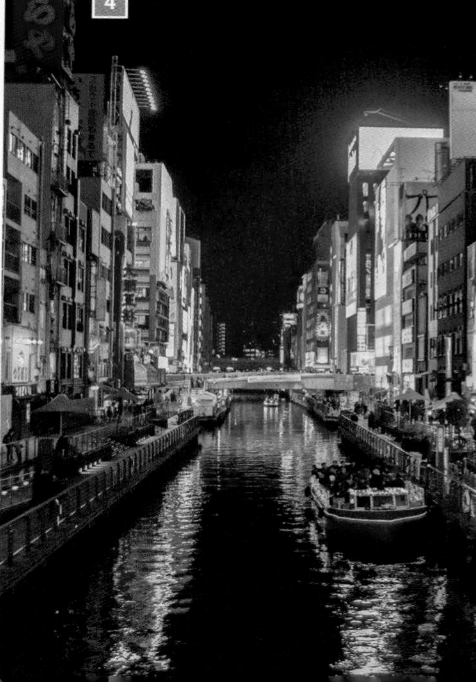

CHITOSE

1-11-10 Taishi, Nishinari-ku; tel. 066/631-6002; www.bunjin.com/chitose; 11:30am-7pm Thurs.-Tues.; from ¥800; Dōbutsuen-mae Station

If authenticity is what you're after, it's hard to beat this okonomiyaki spot set on a sidestreet in a colorful corner of town that's seen better days. This legendary greasy spoon is run by cheerful staff who are happy to chat with customers in English. The interior looks like it hasn't been updated since the 1950s, with just a few solid tables and a couple of countertop seats. The chef works his magic just a few feet away.

CAFE ABSINTHE

1-2-27 Kitahorie, Nishi-ku; tel. 066/534-6635; www.absinthe-jp.com/cafe-absinthe; noon-1am daily; dishes from ¥900; Yotsubashi Station

Tired of deep-fried batter? This chic café, restaurant, and bar offers a nice balance of Middle Eastern and Mediterranean fare: salads, tapas, falafel, hummus, pizzas, couscous, mussaka, kebabs, and more. By day, fresh juices, teas, coffee, and smoothies are on offer, with cocktails served at night when a nice buzz settles in. Shisha is available, too, if you're so inclined. It's located just west of Amerika-mura, beside a bustling street that runs beneath an expressway.

CHIBŌ

1-5-5 Dōtombori, Chūō-ku; tel. 06/6212-2211; www.chibo.com; 11am-1am (last order midnight) Mon.-Sat., 11am-midnight (last order 11pm) Sun.; from ¥900; take Midōsuji, Yotsubashi, Sennichimae subway lines to Namba Station, exit 14

For great okonomiyaki right next to the canal, try Chibō. There's often a queue, but it moves fast.

★ AJINOYA

1-7-16 Namba, Chūō-ku; tel. 06/6211-0713; http://ajinoya-okonomiyaki.com; noon-10:45pm Tues.-Fri., 11:30am-10:45pm Sat.-Sun.; lunch from ¥1,000, dinner from ¥2,000; take Midōsuji, Yotsubashi, Sennichimae subway lines to Namba Station, exit 14

Just a few blocks south of Dōtombori, Ajinoya serves fantastic okonomiyaki. If the line for the nearby more touristy Chibō is discouragingly long, take heart. The service is speedy and the quality of the food is excellent.

USHITORA

15-19 Nanba Sennichimae, Chūō-ku; tel. 066/632-7830; 4pm-9pm daily; ¥3,000; Namba Station, exit E9

This dimly lit standing bar, or tachinomi, occupies an inviting spot near the entry point into the backstreets of Namba. The menu consists of eclectic izakaya fare, from sashimi spreads to fried fusions, changing sporadically. If you feel like an evening of urban adventure, begin at Ushitora, then follow your inspiration.

★ MOMEN

2-1-3 Shinsaibashi, Chūō-ku; tel. 06/6211-2793; 6pm-10pm Mon.-Fri.; from ¥15,000; take Midō-suji subway line to Shinsaibashi Station, exit 6

If all the deep-fried fare begins to fatigue, remember that Osaka does have a refined side. Momen is an excellent kappō-ryōri—essentially kaiseki served more casually at a countertop—restaurant in Shinsaibashi, where patrons sit bantering with the chefs as they whip up seasonally inspired creations with top-notch ingredients. The restaurant seats only nine, so reserve at least a few weeks in advance, if not earlier. Also note that the restaurant only accepts cash.

BARS AND NIGHTLIFE

Osaka is a fun city at night, with most of the action taking place in the southern half of the city. Cocktail bars, dance clubs, and live music are abundant in the bustling streets of Shinsaibashi and Namba.

1: Takotako King Honten **2:** crab restaurant on Dōtombori **3:** fugu restaurant on Dōtombori **4:** Dōtombori canal

Minami's Nightlife Zones

Minami, the southern part of Osaka, contains its garish, neon-lit nightlife districts. For the purposes of this book, it encompasses the large swath between **Shinsaibashi Station** in the north down to **Tennō-ji Station,** roughly 4 kilometers (2.5 mi) southwest. Hemming all of this in at the northern border is the major east-west thoroughfare of **Nagahori-dōri,** which is bisected by the north-south artery of **Midō-suji.**

SHINSAIBASHI
心斎橋

Calm by day, this neighborhood along the north bank of the Dōtombori-gawa shows its real face when the sun sets and its warren of bars, hostess clubs, and restaurants comes to life. On any given evening, touts in flamboyant attire stand on their appointed corners, while hostesses in cocktail dresses stride briskly to clubs where they banter with businessmen using corporate expense accounts to cover lavishly priced drinks. Also roaming these streets are groups of 20-somethings on pub crawls and clubbers heading to the city's best music venues.

AMERIKA-MURA
アメリカ村

An enclave of tattoo parlors, love hotels, and shops hawking everything from curios to street fashion occupies a number of blocks just west of the major aboveground traffic artery of Midōsuji, on the north side of the canal that runs through Dōtombori a handful of blocks to the south. The neighborhood takes its name from the brisk business selling U.S.-made goods in this area in the postwar years.

There are no sights here, per se, but it's an interesting place to wander and see what flavor of the month the pierced, hair-dyed youth of Osaka are into. There are also lots of bars and restaurants dotting the area. Particularly at night, the central **Triangle Park** is a popular hangout spot. Behold the faux Statue of Liberty perched atop a drab apartment block.

★ DŌTOMBORI
道頓堀

Named after the Dōtombori-gawa canal running through it, this is where the bulk of the eating and partying takes place. Of the numerous bridges and walkways on the canal, the most famous

Kita

BLARNEY STONE

6F Sonezaki Center Bldg., 2-10-16 Sonezaki, Kita-ku; tel. 06/6364-2001; https://the-blarney-stone.com; 5pm-1am Sun.-Thurs., 5pm-3am Fri.-Sat.; take Midō-suji or Tanimachi subway line to Higshi Umeda Station, exit 7

Blarney Stone is a good spot in the northern half of the city to mix with expats and locals over a pint or two. This faux Irish pub is especially lively during the after-work hours.

Minami

CINQUECENTO

2-1-10 Higashi-Shinsaibashi, Chūō-ku; tel. 06/6213-6788; www.osakacinquecento.com; 8pm-5am daily; take Sakai-suji subway line to Nipponbashi, exit 2

Cinquecento is a lively martini bar with a reasonably priced menu (all drinks ¥500—cinquecento means 500 in Italian). It's a fun place to mingle with locals and expats before or after hitting the local clubs. Alongside domestic standards, a handful of other Japanese microbrews flow from 10 taps.

is **Ebisu-bashi,** which offers the best vantage point of the iconic Glico Running Man billboard. While this area is touristy, you owe it to yourself to indulge in some takoyaki while perusing Osaka at its most brash.

NAMBA

難波

This sprawling district, brimming with restaurants, shops, and nightlife options, fans southward from Dōtombori. Just walk south on any of the streets that run from Dōtombori's pedestrian promenade, such as the frenetic covered shopping street of **Ebisu-bashi-suji.** You'll find the temple of **Hōzen-ji** here, as well as **Doguya-suji** ("Kitchenware Street") and a clutch of restaurants and bars.

SHIN-SEKAI

新世界

Farther south, get a sense of how the city imagined the future around the turn of the 20th century. Shin-Sekai ("New World") is a rundown entertainment area dotted by gritty restaurants, garish pachinko parlors, dive bars, and old-timers playing mah-jongg. The centerpiece is the 103-meter-tall (338-ft-tall) **Tsūten-kaku,** a retro steel tower bearing a heavy dose of neon. Get dinner at one of the famed kushikatsu restaurants, though keep to the main area: To the west and south are a homeless encampment and a red-light district.

Via JR, take the Loop Line to Shin-Imamiya Station; via subway, hop on the Sakai-suji line bound for Tengachaya and get off at Ebisucho; or, if you're taking the Midō-suji line, go to Dōbutsuen-mae.

TENNŌ-JI

天王寺

About 15 minutes' walk southeast of Shin-Sekai, Tennō-ji Station has become a fashionable hub thanks to the March 2014 opening of the mammoth **Abeno Harukas** tower, looming over the area around Tennō-ji Station. It's the tallest building in Japan, and the observation deck is a great chance to get as high off the ground as possible.

BAR NAYUTA

Mario Bldg. 5F, 1-6-17 Nishi-Shinsaibashi, Chūō-ku; tel. 06/6210-3615; http://bar-nayuta.com; 5pm-3am daily; take Midō-suji subway line to Shinsaibashi Station, exit 7

For great cocktails in a classic speakeasy atmosphere, head to Bar Nayuta. The man behind the bar, Hiro, is a master mixologist who puts a unique spin on his drinks. This is an excellent choice if you're seeking a place with a whiff of refinement. The bar is a little tricky to find. The elevator to the fifth floor is at the end of a corridor leading in from the street that runs along the left side of the building that houses the Cook Jeans shop on the first floor.

MISONO BUILDING

2-3-9 Sennichimae, Chūō-ku; hours vary; take Sakai-suji subway line to Nipponbashi Station, exit 5

For adventurous nightlife connoisseurs with a penchant for slightly grittier surroundings, head to Namba's iconic Misono Building. The second floor of this dilapidated building is crammed with old bars that stay open into the wee hours. Choose the quirky facade that most strikes your fancy, then bar hop from there. Beyond the bars, **Misono Universe** (tel. 06/6641-8733; http://universe.osaka) is a cavernous club and live house sprawling across the basement floor.

CIRCUS

Nakanishi Bldg. 2F, 1-8-16 Nishi-Shinsaibashi; tel. 06/6241-3822; http://circus-osaka.com; 11pm-late Fri.-Sat. nights and special events; take Midō-suji subway line to Shinsaibashi Station, exit 7

If you're seeking a club that takes its electronic music seriously, Circus is the best place in Osaka. The crowd goes more for the music than to see or be seen. An added bonus: the dance floor is non-smoking.

FARPLANE

East Village Bldg. 3F, 2-8-19 Nishi-Shinsaibashi, Chūō-ku; tel. 06/6211-6012; https://farplane.jp; 8pm-late daily; cover charges vary for special events; take Midō-suji subway line to Shinsaibashi Station, exit 8

For something outré, the appropriately named Farplane cannot be beat. This fetish bar with velvet-draped ceilings, chandeliers, and edgy posters on the walls grew out of what was once a shop selling sexy attire. Today, the city's weirdos flock to the space, run by bartenders in kinky outfits. It hosts occasional events like the monthly Creamy Banana Burlesque show and its annual Farplane Night (http://farplane.jp/farplane-night).

NAMBA BEARS

New Japan Namba Bldg. B1F, 3-14-5 Nambanaka, Naniwa-ku; tel. 06/6649-5564; http://namba-bears.main.jp; hours vary by event; take Midōsuji, Yotsubashi, Sennichimae subway lines to Namba Station, exit 4

If your musical taste leans toward rock, head to Namba Bears. DIY in spirit, the compact, bare-bones space hosts indie bands and punk rockers, providing sustenance to the city's underground scene. Bring your own booze.

ACCOMMODATIONS

Kita

U-EN

2-9-23 Fukushima, Fukushima-ku; tel. 06/7503-4394; www.hostelosaka.com; ¥2,800 dorm bed, ¥6,600 d; take Hanshin main line to Shin-Fukushima Station, exit 2

U-en is a stylish hostel set in an old, renovated townhouse in the north of town. There are both Japanese-style private rooms and dorm beds. Flashes of traditional design—tatami floors, paper-screen doors—give it just the right amount of style. This is a great choice if you're on a tight budget.

★ INTERCONTINENTAL OSAKA

3-60 Ofuka-chō, Kita-ku; tel. 06/6374-5700; www.ihg.com; ¥48,000 d; take JR lines to Osaka Station or the Hankyū line to Umeda Station

A stone's throw from both JR Osaka Station and Umeda Station, the Intercontinental Osaka has all the amenities of a five-star hotel and is easily one of the city's best. This property is in an excellent location, with fantastic views and great restaurants on-site. Highly recommended.

Minami

DOTONBORI HOTEL

2-3-25 Dōtombori, Chūō-ku; tel. 06/6213-9040; http://dotonbori-h.co.jp; ¥12,000 d; take Midōsuji, Yotsubashi, Sennichimae subway lines to Namba Station, exit 25

Beyond its quirky exterior fronted by pillars shaped like large human faces perched atop pairs of legs, Dotonbori Hotel is a solid, no-frills option in the center of Dōtombori. It's clean, modern, and convenient, and friendly staff are ready to help. This is a good pick for value, and a Japanese and Western-style breakfast buffet is available for an additional fee.

CROSS HOTEL OSAKA

2-5-15 Shinsaibashisuji, Chūō-ku; tel. 06/6213-8281; www.crosshotel.com; ¥17,000 d; take Midōsuji, Yotsubashi, Sennichimae subway lines to Namba Station, exit 14

Cross Hotel Osaka is only a few minutes' walk from Dōtombori, Shinsaibashi, and Amerika-mura, putting street food, nightlife, and funky boutiques within easy reach. Rooms here are smart and clean, and the bathrooms are spacious compared to hotels in the same price range. It also has a bar and a few restaurants.

HOTEL NIKKŌ OSAKA

1-3-3 Nishi-Shinsaibashi, Chūō-ku; tel. 06/6244-1111; www.hno.co.jp; ¥24,000 d; take Midō-suji subway line to Shinsaibashi Station, exit 8

The Hotel Nikkō Osaka is a great pick if you want to stay near the heart of the action in Minami with a whiff of luxury. The hotel's quality breakfast spread, on-site dining options, and clean, stylish rooms put it a cut above the more budget-conscious options in the area. Its location directly above Shinsaibashi Station offers fantastic access to the attractions in the south part of the city.

FRASER RESIDENCE NANKAI OSAKA

1-17-11 Nambanaka, Naniwa-ku; tel. 06/6635-7111; https://osaka.frasershospitality.com; from ¥27,000; take Namba Nankai line to Namba Nakai Station

If you prefer to feel "at home" in a hotel, check out Fraser Residence Nankai Osaka. Aside from being in the thick of the action in Namba, what sets Fraser Residence apart is that its rooms resemble apartments. This makes the hotel an especially appealing option for those who are traveling with kids or staying longer-term.

ST. REGIS OSAKA

3-6-12 Honmachi, Chūō-ku; tel. 06/6258-3333; www.marriott.co.jp/hotels/travel/osaxr-the-st-regis-osaka/; ¥55,000 d; take Chūō subway line to Honmachi Station, exit 3

Starting from its 12th-floor lobby, St. Regis Osaka exudes chic design sense throughout its 160-room property. Located on the prestigious Midō-suji shopping artery, this classy hotel has an outdoor Japanese garden and haute restaurants on-site (French, Italian). This is an excellent pick if you want to travel in style.

INFORMATION AND SERVICES

Tourist Information

For information on how to connect to one of some 5,000 free Wi-Fi points around the city, see http://ofw-oer.com/en.

These city-run centers have a good selection of English-language maps, brochures, and friendly bilingual staff who are happy to help you handle trip logistics, including booking accommodations:

- **Tourist Information Osaka** (tel. 06/6131-4550; https://osaka-info.jp/en/spot/tourist-information-osaka/; 9am-6pm daily for tourist office, 9am-5:30pm daily for phone inquiries; located in front of the central ticket gate of JR Osaka Station)
- **Tourist Information Namba** (first floor of Nankai Namba Station; tel. 06/6131-4550; https://osaka-info.jp/en/spot/tourist-information-namba/; 9am-6pm daily for tourist office, 9am-5:30pm daily for phone inquiries)

Medical Services

The **Osaka Call Center** (http://ofw-oer.com/call/en; 24 hours daily) offers free English-language medical support, reachable directly through the website. To call, dial 06/6131-4550 (9am-5:30pm daily). For extensive online medical listings in English, visit www.mfis.pref.osaka.jp/omfo/fo_toppage.aspx?lang=en.

- **Japanese Red Cross Osaka Hospital** (5-30 Fudegasaki-chō, Tennō-ji-ku; tel. 06/6774-5111; www.osaka-med.jrc.or.jp/english/; 24 hours daily; take Kintetsu line to Osaka-Uehonmachi Station)
- **Ohkita Medical Clinic** (Umeda Square Bldg. 4F, 1-12-17 Umeda, Kita-ku; tel. 06/6344-0380; www.ookita.com; 9:30am-1pm and 4pm-7:30pm daily; take JR lines to Osaka Station, south-central exit)
- **Yasugi Clinic** (1-75 Ikeda-chō, Osaka-fu, tel. 06/6353-0505; http://yasugi-clinic.com; 9am-11:45am Mon.-Sat., 4:30pm-6:45pm Mon., Wed.-Fri.; take Osaka loop line to Tenma Station).
- **Nakamura Clinic** (NKM Bldg. 1F, 4-10-15 Daido, Tennō-ji-ku; tel. 06/6771-0266; http://nkcl.net/en/; 9am-1pm and 3pm-6pm Mon.-Tues. and Thurs.-Fri., 9am-1pm Sat.;

near Terada-chō Station on the Osaka Loop line one stop from Tennō-ji Station)

Diplomatic Services

- **U.S. Consulate General Osaka** (2-11-5 Nishitenma, Kita-ku; tel. 06/6315-5900; https://jp.usembassy.gov; 9am-5pm Mon.-Fri.; take Midō-suji subway line to Yodoyabashi Station, exit 1)

GETTING THERE

Air

Osaka is served by two airports. The larger of the two is **Kansai International Airport** (www.kansai-airport.or.jp), or KIX, located about 50 kilometers (31 mi) southwest of town. **Itami Airport** (www.osaka-airport.co.jp) is located about 12 kilometers (7 mi) northwest of the city. Though sometimes referred to as "Osaka International Airport," Itami only hosts domestic flights.

FROM KANSAI INTERNATIONAL AIRPORT

To shuttle back and forth between KIX and downtown, most convenient is the twice-hourly **Nankai Rapid Limited Express** train (7am-10pm daily; ¥1,430), or "Rapi:t," which takes you from the airport to Namba Nakai Station (40 minutes) in the heart of the Namba district in the Minami (south) side of the city. Another train running twice an hour is the **JR Kansai Airport Express Haruka** (6:30am-10pm), which runs to both Tennō-ji (35 minutes; ¥1,710) on the south side of downtown, and Shin-Osaka (45 minutes; ¥2,330) in the north. Note that the Haruka trains only run select times of day. If you arrive at a time when Haruka trains are not running, simply hop on the regularly running JR Kansai Airport Rapid train to Tennō-ji (55 minutes; ¥1,080) or JR Osaka Station (1 hour 10 minutes; ¥1,210). While one of these trains is generally the best way to go, there's also a limousine service called **KATE** (www.kate.co.jp) that runs between KIX and Osaka Station (1 hour, depending on traffic; ¥1,600). Worst case, you can hail a taxi, although this isn't recommended as fares to Namba in the city's south start from around ¥14,000 and climb as you go north.

FROM ITAMI AIRPORT

Traveling between Itami and downtown is done either by **Osaka Airport Limousine** (www.okkbus.co.jp) or **Osaka Monorail.** The former runs to Osaka Station (25 minutes; ¥650) in the city's north and Namba Station (35 minutes, ¥650) in the south. The latter runs to Senri-Chūō Station (12 minutes; ¥340), where you can transfer to the Hankyū Senri line, which runs to Osaka Station, with connections to the rest of the city's train and subway lines.

Train

Coming from Tokyo (3 hours; ¥14,400) or Kyoto (15 minutes; ¥2,860) the **Tōkaidō-San'yō shinkansen** stops at **Shin-Osaka Station.** If you have a JR Pass, simply hop on any shinkansen other than Nozomi or Mizuo trains, which aren't covered by the pass.

Otherwise, take the **JR Kyoto line** from Kyoto Station to Osaka Station (30 minutes; ¥570), the **Hankyū Kyoto line** from Kyoto-Kawaramachi Station in downtown Kyoto to Osaka-Umeda Station (Hankyū line) in Osaka's northern Umeda district (45 minutes; ¥400), or the **Keihan Main line** to Yodoyabashi Station in the center of Osaka (linked to the Midō-suji subway line) from Gion-Shijō (50 minutes; ¥920) and Sanjō (50 minutes; ¥920) Stations in the heart of Kyoto.

Bus

If you don't mind taking the bus, it will save you a few thousand yen. Willer (www.willerexpress.com) runs buses to and from **Tokyo, Hiroshima, Hakata** (Fukuoka), and has a center on the first floor of the east tower of the Umeda Sky Building (Tower East 1F, 1-1-88 Ōyodo-naka, Kita-ku; https://willerexpress.com/en/wbt-umeda; 6:30am-11pm daily, 6:30am-2pm on third Thurs. of month). Operating out of the JR Osaka Station

Highway Bus Terminal, just outside JR Osaka Station's north-central concourse, **JR West Highway Bus** (www.nishinihonjrbus.co.jp) operates along similar routes.

GETTING AROUND

Once you're on the ground in Kita (Umeda), the Osaka-jō area, or in the core of the rambling Minami area (Shinsaibashi, Amerikamura, Dōtobori, Namba), you'll find Osaka an enjoyable city to explore on foot. However, when shuttling between Kita and Minami, or to Minami's southernmost districts, you'll want to make use of the **subway** system. Although Osaka does have an aboveground train network, its subway system is much more useful.

Out of eight subway lines, you'll most likely only need the red-coded **Midōsuji line.** This line starts from Shin-Osaka in the north and runs southward through the business and entertainment zone of Umeda near Osaka Station, the entertainment districts of Shinsaibashi and Namba, and the relaxed southern hub of Tennō-ji. Trains depart every 3-5 minutes and run from early morning until around midnight, with single journeys costing from ¥180-380.

Nara 奈良

Nara has a lot to be proud of. This small city of about 360,000 can rightly claim to be the birthplace of Japanese culture as we know it. Founded in 710 and initially named Heijōkyō, or "citadel of peace," it was the first capital of Japan until 794, when the new nation's political center migrated to Kyoto. During its brief period as the nation's capital, religious, artistic, and architectural influences from China found fertile ground, and Japanese Buddhism emerged from the city.

Remnants of this eventful history are everywhere, with myriad temples and gardens scattered throughout the city. In the sprawling green space of Nara-kōen, you'll find a throng of docile deer in search of a handout and the towering temple of Tōdai-ji, housing one of Japan's most iconic sights, the Great Buddha, a statue standing 16 meters (53 ft) tall.

Beyond the grounds of Nara-kōen, a cluster of temples in the west side of town are also a draw, including Horyū-ji, which contains the world's oldest wooden buildings. You can head to **Naramachi,** fanning out from the southwestern edge of Nara-kōen a brief stroll from the city's main railway hubs, where Edo-period ambience oozes from the narrow roads lined by old, whitewashed wooden buildings that now house a variety of restaurants, cafés, shops, and galleries. Overlooking it all is gently sloping **Mount Wakakusayama,** topped by a large grassy vantage point, standing at the north side of Nara-kōen. Also known as Mount Mikasa, it's more hill than mountain, at 342 meters (1,122 ft) high.

SIGHTS

Nara-kōen
奈良公園

tel. 0742/22-0375; 24 hours daily; free; take Kintetsu line to Kintetsu Nara Station, or take JR Nara, Yamatoji, Sakurai lines to JR Nara Station

Stretching from downtown Nara in the west to the hills at the eastern edge of town, Nara-kōen is an expansive leafy space dotted with important religious sites, crisscrossed by paths and ponds full of colorful koi (carp).

The prized citizens of this green expanse are around 1,500 semi-wild deer, believed to be couriers of the gods in Shinto. Today they are doted on by visitors who feed them with deer crackers (shika senbei; ¥150), sold in the park. Forget Bambi—the deer here can become surprisingly aggressive in their quest for crackers. Don't be surprised if you're besieged as soon as you open a pack. It's best not to allow small children to feed them.

Nara

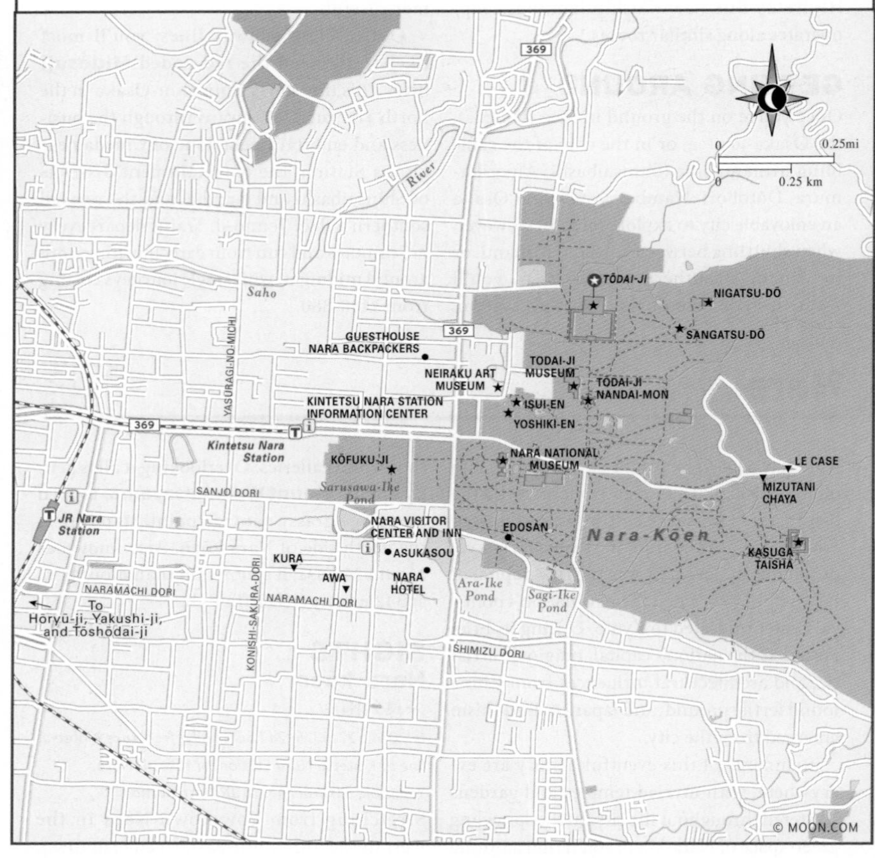

Kōfuku-ji

興福寺

48 Noborioji-chō; tel. 0742/22-7755; www.kohfukuji.com; grounds 24 hours daily, Golden Hall 9am-5pm (last entry 4:45pm) daily; grounds free, treasure hall ¥700 adults, ¥600 high school and junior high school students, ¥300 elementary school students; take the Kintetsu line to Kintetsu Nara Station

Begin your exploration of Nara-kōen's Buddhist treasures at Kōfuku-ji, an illustrious temple complex with a lofty five-level pagoda and a more modest three-story one in the west side of the park. Built in 669, it was relocated to Nara-kōen when the fledgling nation's capital moved to Nara in 710. In its heyday, it had some 175 structures; over the centuries, many of the buildings succumbed to fires and fighting between rival factions of the Fujiwara clan's temple-raised warrior monks, or invasions from the Taira clan. Although Shogun Minamoto Yoritomo (1147-1199) had the complex rebuilt, many of its structures burned again in 1717.

Though the treasure hall does house some compelling Buddhist images, and the

1: a woman selling snacks for the deer at Nara-kōen **2:** Tōdai-ji

1

2

octagonal Tōkondō (East Golden Hall) is populated by impressive Buddha statues, I recommend just strolling through the atmospheric grounds for free.

Nara National Museum
奈良国立博物館

50 Noboriōji-chō; tel. 050/5542-8600; www.narahaku.go.jp; 9:30am-5pm (last entry 4:30pm) Tues.-Sun.; ¥700 adults, ¥350 university students, free for high school students and younger; take Kintetsu line to Kintetsu Nara Station

Just east of Kōfuku-ji is this excellent museum, with a wide array of Buddhist statuary, paintings, calligraphy, and other art, stretching from the 7th century to the Edo period, and quality English signage throughout. The informative illustrated guide "Viewing Buddhist Sculptures" (¥500) will help you understand the symbolism in Buddhist art.

Kasuga Taisha
春日大社

160 Kasugano-chō; tel. 0742/22-7788; www.kasugataisha.or.jp; 6am-6pm daily Apr.-Sept.; 6:30am-5pm daily Oct.-Mar.; free; take Kintetsu line to Kintetsu Nara Station

In the southeast corner of Nara-kōen, Kasuga-Taisha is the most important Shinto shrine in the city. There's a honden (main hall) and a haiden (prayer hall), but the real magic is found by meandering along the paths on the shrine's grounds and exploring its subshrines. This is one of the most worthwhile stops in the park.

While it's free to wander through the shrine's rambling, lantern-fringed paths and see its 12 subshrines, for an extra fee (¥500 adults, ¥300 university and high school students, ¥200 junior high and elementary school students) you can also enter the **Kasuga Taisha Museum,** where prized relics are arrayed, and get a glimpse of its inner sanctum. Since the Great Tohoku Earthquake struck the northeastern coast of Honshu in March 2011, a group of priests has been leading the faithful in morning prayers each day for the protection and peace of Japan. To witness this ceremony, which is open to the public, head to the Naoraiden (Ceremonial Hall) at 8:50am.

★ Tōdai-ji
東大寺

406-1 Zōshi-chō; tel. 0742/22-5511; www.todaiji.or.jp; 7:30am-5:30pm daily Apr.-Oct., 8am-5pm daily Nov.-Mar. for Daibutsu-den, 9:30am-5:30pm daily Apr.-Oct., 9:30am-5pm daily Nov.-Mar. for Tōdai-ji Museum; ¥600 junior high school students and older, ¥300 elementary school students for Daibutsu-den, ¥600 junior high school students and older, ¥300 elementary school students for Tōdai-ji Museum, ¥1,000 junior high school students and older, ¥400 elementary school students for Daibutsu-den and Tōdai-ji Museum joint pass; take Kintetsu line to Kintetsu Nara Station

Northwest of Kasuga Taisha, Tōdai-ji is the centerpiece of Nara-kōen. This magnificent wooden temple houses the giant bronze Daibutsu statue. If you're only going to see one sight in Nara, make it Tōdai-ji's Great Buddha.

Emperor Shomu (701-758) directed the building of the temple for the sole purpose of hosting the towering bronze Vairocana, the cosmic Buddha from whom all worlds and beings are believed to emanate. Shomu held a ceremony for the unveiling of the statue; gifts from visiting monks from China and India are on display in the Nara National Museum today. The original structure was set ablaze during the wars that ultimately brought the Heian period to a close in 1185.

Approach the temple via the **Tōdai-ji Nandai-mon,** or Great South Gate, flanked by two fierce, muscular statues of Niō, a divine Buddhist guardian. These dramatic wooden sentinels stand 8 meters (26 ft) tall.

About 200 meters (656 ft) to the north is the **Daibutsu-den** (Great Buddha Hall), the world's largest wooden building and the home of the Daibutsu statue. Despite measuring 57 meters (187 ft) in width, 50 meters (164 ft) in depth, and 48 meters (157 ft) in height, the current structure, built in 1709, is only two-thirds the size of the original. The octagonal bronze lantern in front of the main hall dates to the 8th century. The spectacular Daibutsu statue weighs 500 tonnes (550 tons)—103 kilograms (290 lbs) of it gold—stands 16 meters (53 ft) tall, and exudes an uncanny sense of calm.

After basking in the presence of the Great Buddha, ascend a staircase to **Nigatsu-dō,** a subtemple atop a hill about 300 meters (984 ft) east of Tōdai-ji. The interior of this small structure is only glimpsed by elite priests, but you will be able to take in the stunning views over Nara from the veranda. Two minutes south, the oldest structure in the Tōdai-ji complex, **Sangatsu-dō,** houses a towering Kannon statue and more than a dozen other figures from the Nara Period.

Isui-en and Yoshiki-en
依水園, 吉城園

74 Suimon-chō; tel. 0742/25-0781; https://isuien.or.jp; 9:30am-4:30pm (last entry 4pm) Wed.-Mon. Jun.-Mar., 9:30am-5pm (last entry 4:30pm) Wed.-Mon. Apr.-May; ¥1,200 adults, ¥500 college students and high school students, ¥300 junior high and elementary school students; take the Kintetsu line to Kintetsu Nara Station, then walk 15 minutes

Isui-en has all the makings of an ideal landscape garden: abundant flowering plants and trees, a pond, and winding pathways. Access to the neighboring **Neiraku Art Museum,** which houses a collection of bronzes and ceramics from China and Korea, is included in the garden's admission fee. If you're taken enough by the scene to appreciate it while sitting on a tatami floor, there's a teahouse (cup of green tea and a sweet, ¥850). The view of Tōdai-ji's Nandai-mon (Great South Gate) in the backdrop is worth the cost of admission. Foreigners get in free to the garden next door, Yoshiki-en.

Western Nara

As if the impressive structures around Nara-kōen weren't enough, some temples of great historical import sit just west of town, with roots stretching back to the 7th and 8th centuries, when Buddhism was just being transplanted to Japanese soil. Take a half-day to explore these gems if you have extra time in Nara and want to dodge crowds.

HŌRYŪ-JI
法隆寺

1-1 Hōryūji Sannai, Ikaruga-chō; tel. 0745/75-2555; www.horyuji.or.jp; 8am-5pm daily late Feb.-early Nov., 8am-4:30pm daily early Nov.-late Feb.; ¥1,500 adults, ¥750 ages 12 and under

This sprawling complex was founded in 607 by Prince Shotoku (574-622), credited with drafting Japan's first constitution. The temple's Chūmon (Central Gate) is flanked by Japan's oldest effigies of Kongo Rikishi, the fearsome pair of deities seen at temples throughout Japan. In fact, some of the original structures on the complex are among the world's oldest surviving wooden constructions. The recently built Gallery of Temple Treasures houses a vast wealth of paintings, relics, statues, and more, and the Yumendono (Hall of Dreams) houses other treasures.

From JR Nara Station, take the Yamatoji line to Hōryū-ji Station (12 minutes; ¥220), then hop on bus 72 (8 minutes; ¥190) to Hōryū-ji Sandō, or simply walk north from Hōryū-ji Station for 20 minutes. To return to Nara, take bus 97 from Hōryū-ji-mae bus stop.

YAKUSHI-JI
薬師寺

457 Nishinokyo-chō; tel. 0742/33-6001; www.yakushiji.or.jp/en; 8:30am-5pm (last entry 4:30pm) daily; adults ¥1,100, high school and junior high students ¥700, elementary school students ¥300

The temple of Yakushi-ji is another of the oldest temples in Japan, built by Emperor Tenmu in 680 in hopes for the healing of his sick wife. The temple's sole surviving original structure is the East Pagoda, renovated in mid-2020. The rest of the buildings date to the 13th century or are modern reconstructions, but the real treasures are found within.

To reach Yakushi-ji from Hōryū-ji, take bus 97 from Hōryū-ji-mae (bus stand 2) to Yakushi-ji Higashiguchi (40 minutes). If you're coming directly from Kintetsu Nara Station, take the Kintetsu Nara line to Yamato-Saidaiji Station, then transfer to the Kintetsu Kashihara line and ride until Nishinokyō Station (25 minutes; ¥260). The temple is about a 1-minute walk southeast from there.

TŌSHŌDAI-JI
唐招提寺

13-46 Gojō-chō, Nara; tel. 0742/33-7900; www.toshodaiji.jp; 8:30am-5pm (last entry 4:30pm) daily; ¥1,000 adults, ¥400 high school and junior high school students, ¥200 elementary school students

Walk north from Yakushi-ji for about 10 minutes to reach Tōshōdai-ji, the youngest of the three temples, constructed in 759 by a visiting Chinese priest named Ganjin (Jian Zhen). Today, a wooden statue of the roving priest is brought before into the temple's Miedō (Founder's Hall) for a few days in early June, to commemorate his death (June 6). At any time of year, however, you can glimpse the 5-meter-tall (16-ft-tall) effigy of Kannon (Goddess of Mercy), complete with what are said to be 1,000 arms, towering within the main hall, or Kondō. The grounds are also laced with leafy footpaths.

To directly reach Tōshōdai-ji from Kintetsu Nara Station, take the Kintetsu Nara line to Nishinokyō Station (15 minutes; ¥260), then walk 500 meters (1,640 ft) north. Alternatively, take bus 78 from JR Nara Station (bus stand 6; 20 minutes; ¥260) or Kintetsu Nara Station (bus stand 8; 20 minutes; ¥260) to the Tōshōdai-ji bus stop. When returning to Nara, you must depart from the Tōshōdai-ji Higashiguchi bus stop on bus 77 or 97.

FESTIVALS

WAKAKUSAYAMA YAMAYAKI
若草山山焼き

At the base of Mount Wakakusayama, next to Nara-kōen; www3.pref.nara.jp/yamayaki/; around 5pm-evening fourth Sat. of Jan.; walk about 15 minutes east of Tōdai-ji and Kasuga Taisha

On the fourth Saturday of each January, fireworks are launched in town, and then the slope of Mount Wakakusayama is lit ablaze in this fiery festival. The action heats up from about 5pm, when a procession of locals light their torches at a shrine in town, then proceed to the foot of Mount Wakakusayama to set the grass blanketing the slope on fire (in a safe, contained manner, of course!). The festival has been going on for centuries, though its origins remain a mystery.

SHUNI-E
修二会

Nigatsu-dō; from sunset on Mar. 1-14; walk 10 minutes west uphill from Tōdai-ji's main temple complex

This festival sees monks stand along the veranda of Nigatsu-dō, a subtemple of Tōdai-ji, from where they fling embers from around 10 huge flaming bundles of kindling onto a crowd of onlookers below. This is a 1,250-year-old ritual intended to spiritually cleanse the repentant recipients of the raining cinders. The ritual begins on each day of the period at around 6:30pm. Aim to arrive a few hours early if you want a good spot from which to receive the purifying sparks. On the 12th and 13th nights, around 1:30am-2:30am, priests ceremonially draw curative water (omizutori, or drawing water), said to only fill a nearby well at that time every year. Following the water drawing, a ritual known as Dattan is performed until about 3:30am inside Nigatsu-dō, involving the waving of torches, ringing of bells, and playing of horns.

FOOD

Nara-kōen

MIZUTANI CHAYA

30 Kasugano-chō; tel. 0742/22-0627; 10am-4pm Thurs.-Tues.; from ¥600; take Kintetsu line to Kintetsu Nara Station, then walk 25 minutes

Charming Mizutani Chaya is housed in a thatched-roof building and set in a grove of trees between Kasuga Taisha and Nigatsu-dō, the hillside subtemple of Tōdai-ji. Alongside teahouse staples, the restaurant also serves rice dishes and bowls of udon with various toppings. It's nice, simple food with a classic ambience.

LE CASE

158 Kasugano-chō; tel. 0742/26-8707; http://quicheteria-lecase.com; 10am-5pm Wed.-Mon. (last order 4pm), closed second and fourth Mon. every month; from around ¥1,500; take the Kintetsu line to Kintetsu Nara Station, then walk 25 minutes

A great choice for a meal while you're tramping between Nara-kōen's sights is Le Case. This eatery between Todai-ji and Kasuga-Taisha serves French fare, including quiche (its specialty), as well as cheesecake. Given the dearth of restaurants in this part of town, this is highly recommended if you're hungry in the park.

Naramachi

WAKAKUSA CURRY

38-1 Mochiidono-chō; tel. 0742/24-8022; www.wakakusacurry.jp; 11am-3:45pm (last order 3:15pm) and 5pm-9pm (last order 8pm) Thurs.-Tues.; ¥700-1,290; take the Kintetsu line to Kintetsu Nara Station, exit 2

This curry joint in the midst of Naramachi serves tasty curry and rice, from chicken and lamb curry to vegetarian and more. There are plenty of toppings, from cheese to breaded-and-fried pork cutlets. You can choose your spice level (0-25), too. A great place for lunch before or after traipsing through Nara-kōen.

AWA

1 Shonami-chō; tel. 0742/24-5699; www.kiyosumi.jp/naramachiten; 11:30am-3pm (last entry 2pm) and 5:30pm-10pm (last entry 9pm) Wed.-Mon.; lunch from ¥2,900, dinner from ¥3,900; take the Kintetsu line to Kintetsu Nara Station, exit 2

This atmospheric restaurant is set in a restored townhouse in the heart of Naramachi. One seating area looks onto a garden, another has the aesthetic of a timeworn kura, or traditional storehouse, and another has tatami floors. The menu is based on locally grown organic produce, grains including millet, local beef, and sake brewed nearby. Meals are beautiful collections of small dishes presented in kaiseki fashion. Reservations are required. Aim to book a week or more in advance.

KURA

16 Komyoin-chō; tel. 0742/22-8771; 5pm-9:30pm daily; dinner from ¥4,000; take the Kintetsu line to Kintetsu Nara Station, exit 2

In the old-school section of downtown known as Naramachi, Kura is an izakaya that serves good food, from yakitori to fried pork cutlets and oden (vegetables and fishcake left simmered in broth and served with spicy mustard). Given that booze is a vital component here, this place may be best suited to dinner rather than lunch. Set in a white-walled building, the interior is composed of aged wood with a wraparound countertop. At first glance, it may look slightly intimidating, but step inside and the friendly staff will offer an English-language menu.

ACCOMMODATIONS

Nara-kōen

GUESTHOUSE NARA BACKPACKERS

31 Yurugi-chō; tel. 0742/22-4557; www.nara-backpackers.com; ¥2,400 dorm rooms, doubles from ¥5,800; take the Kintetsu line to Kintetsu Nara Station, exit 1

Guesthouse Nara Backpackers is perhaps Nara's best budget accommodation option. Set in the 90-year-old former home of a tea master, this hostel has many original design flourishes intact, such as its original glass windows, and some of the rooms look out onto a garden. Rooms range from mixed dorms and female-only dorms to a selection of private rooms. There's also a shared lounge and kitchen (7am-11pm). The hostel does not accept guests younger than 10 years old. All guests share a common bath where towels can be rented and toiletries can be bought. Rental bikes are also on offer. Room rates drop with longer stays.

★ EDOSAN

1167 Takabatake-chō; tel. 0742/26-2662; www.edosan.jp; from ¥24,200 pp regular plan with dinner (plus ¥3,300 for dinner upgrade), from ¥29,700 pp with special dinner plan; take the Kintetsu line to Kintetsu Nara Station, exit 2

This dreamy ryokan set in the heart of Nara-kōen has deer ambling its grounds. Still run by the family who founded a restaurant here in 1907, the inn prides itself on its exquisitely presented kaiseki cuisine. Each room is named after a musical instrument, a specimen of which can be found within (dora for the "gong" room, taiko for the "drum" room, etc.). A number of creative luminaries have stayed at the inn, from writers and kabuki actors to painters and fashion designers. A highly atmospheric place to stay, dine, and disconnect from the modern world for a night.

Naramachi

ASUKASOU

1113-3 Takabatake-chō; tel. 0742/26-2538; www.asukasou.com; from around ¥30,000 d with breakfast; take Kintetsu line to Kintetsu Nara Station, exit 2

For ease of access to the main sights of Nara-kōen, Asukasou is a great pick. It's located in Naramachi just a few minutes' walk from the southwest corner of Nara-kōen, and there's a Japanese restaurant on-site and a rooftop open-air onsen bath that can be reserved. Some rooms have futons on tatami floors, while others have beds.

★ NARA HOTEL

1096 Takabatake-chō; tel. 0742/26-3300; www.narahotel.co.jp; from around ¥33,500 d with breakfast; take Kintetsu line to Kintetsu Nara Station, exit 2

If you like the idea of staying in a truly historic hotel and don't mind parting ways with hard-earned cash, try the Nara Hotel. In business since 1909, this hotel's distinctive architecture is a fusion of Japanese and Western design. The rooms are expansive, the service top-notch, the grounds immaculate, and the on-site dining first-rate. Even the Dalai Lama and Albert Einstein bedded down at Nara Hotel when they passed through.

INFORMATION AND SERVICES

There are a few good tourist information centers with abundant English-language materials near both the main JR and Kintetsu stations.

- **JR Nara Station Information Center** (just outside the east exit of JR Nara Station; tel. 0742/27-2223; www.narashikanko.or.jp; 9am-9pm daily)
- **Kintetsu Nara Station Information Center** (near exit 3 of Kintetsu Nara Station; tel. 0742/24-4858; 9am-6pm daily)
- **Nara Visitor Center and Inn** (3 Iken-chō, near Nara-kōen; attached to the Sarusawa Inn; tel. 0742/81-7461; www.sarusawa.nara.jp; 8am-9pm daily)

A good downloadable guide with loads of suggestions, from food to historical sights, can be found at www.visitnara.jp.

GETTING THERE

To reach **JR Nara Station** from Osaka, take the JR Kansai line from Namba Station (45 minutes; ¥570) in the south side of Osaka. From **Osaka-Namba Station**, you can take the Kintetsu Nara line to **Kintetsu Nara Station** (40 minutes; ¥570). From JR Osaka Station, you can take the JR Yamatoji line to JR Nara Station as well (55 minutes; ¥810). Several rapid trains run along this route hourly and stop at Tennō-ji Station in Osaka's Minami (south) en route (Tennō-ji to Nara: 35 minutes; ¥470). Another option is to take the JR Nara line from Shin-Osaka Station to JR Nara Station (55 minutes; ¥940).

Coming from **Kyoto Station,** take the Kintetsu line to Kintetsu Nara Station (35-45 minutes; ¥1,160) or take the JR Nara line to JR Nara Station (45 minutes-1 hour 15 minutes; ¥720). From **Hiroshima,** first ride the shinkansen to Shin-Osaka Station (Sakura trains, 1 hour 40 minutes; ¥10,420), then transfer to the JR Nara line and ride the rest of the way to JR Nara Station (55 minutes; ¥940).

It's also possible to arrive in Nara directly from both of Kansai's main regional airports.

From **Kansai International Airport** (KIX), there's an hourly limousine run by **Nara Kōtsū** (www.narakotsu.co.jp). The ride takes 60-90 minutes and costs ¥2,100 for adults (¥1,050 children). Hourly Nara Kōtsū buses also make the 1-hour journey from Osaka Itami Airport (¥1,510 adults, ¥760 children).

GETTING AROUND

The easiest way to get around much of Nara is **on foot,** but there are two **buses** that run in a loop around the main sights, with bus 1 running counterclockwise and bus 2 running clockwise (www.narakotsu.co.jp/language/en/sightseeing_bus/; runs every 10 minutes; ¥220 flat fee for single journey). When venturing farther afield to the temples west of town, make use of the Yamatoji line, Kintetsu Nara line, or the city's bus network.

There's a **bus information center** (www.narakotsu.co.jp/language/en/stop/#jr_i_cen; 8:30am-5pm daily) on the second floor of JR Nara Station, right beside the ticket gate, and another (8:30am-5pm daily) on the first floor of the Nara Line House building across from Kintetsu Nara Station. Inquire about **day passes** at either one (1-day passes for central Nara ¥500 adults, ¥250 children, for wider area, including Hōryū-ji, ¥1,000 adults, ¥500 children).

Kobe 神戸

Kobe ("God's Door") is situated on a slope that leads from the peak of Mount Rokko, looming to the north of the city, down toward the bay on the Inland Sea, where small islands are dotted by forests and fishing hamlets. Kobe has long been an important maritime center, having opened up to foreign trade during the Meiji Restoration (1868-1912). Beyond trade, the city became a conduit to the world beyond and was the first place in Japan to have a cinema or host jazz musicians. In a word, Kobe is cosmopolitan.

Mirroring its larger sibling near Tokyo, Yokohama, the city's mercantile past also led to the creation of a bustling Chinatown centered in the area of Nankinmachi (named after the city of Nanjing). Victorian architecture is still on display in the affluent neighborhood of Kitano-chō, once home to many members of the city's foreign traders and diplomats. The modern hub of **Sannomiya,** a short walk downhill toward the bay, is the city's modern heart. Excellent restaurants, ample shopping, and nightlife with a nice buzz are the draws of this neighborhood.

Though all indicators suggest that Kobe is thriving, in January 1995 the city was hit by a 6.9-magnitude quake that left 6,400 dead, 40,000 injured, and 100,000 homes along with much of the infrastructure in ruins. Thankfully, the city bounced back and its streets hum with life. The city still retains its global orientation with an expat population of around 50,000 and a host of multinational firms based here, particularly concentrated on manmade Rokko Island.

With many of Kobe's desirable neighborhoods within walking distance of each other, the city is an ideal place to stroll in search of a good café, a well-made meal, or perhaps a drink, while taking in views of the seaside in the distance.

ORIENTATION

Shin-Kobe Station, and next to it, the entrance to the path that leads uphill to **Nunobiki Falls and Herb Garden,** are at the northern edge of the areas covered here. Trundling about 10 minutes downhill to the southwest, you'll reach the neighborhood of **Kitano-chō,** perched on a hillside at the north end of downtown. Continuing downhill from Kitano-chō for another 15 minutes brings you to **Ikuta Jinja** and the bustle of **Sannomiya.** Fifteen minutes west, you'll pass through one of the most happening parts

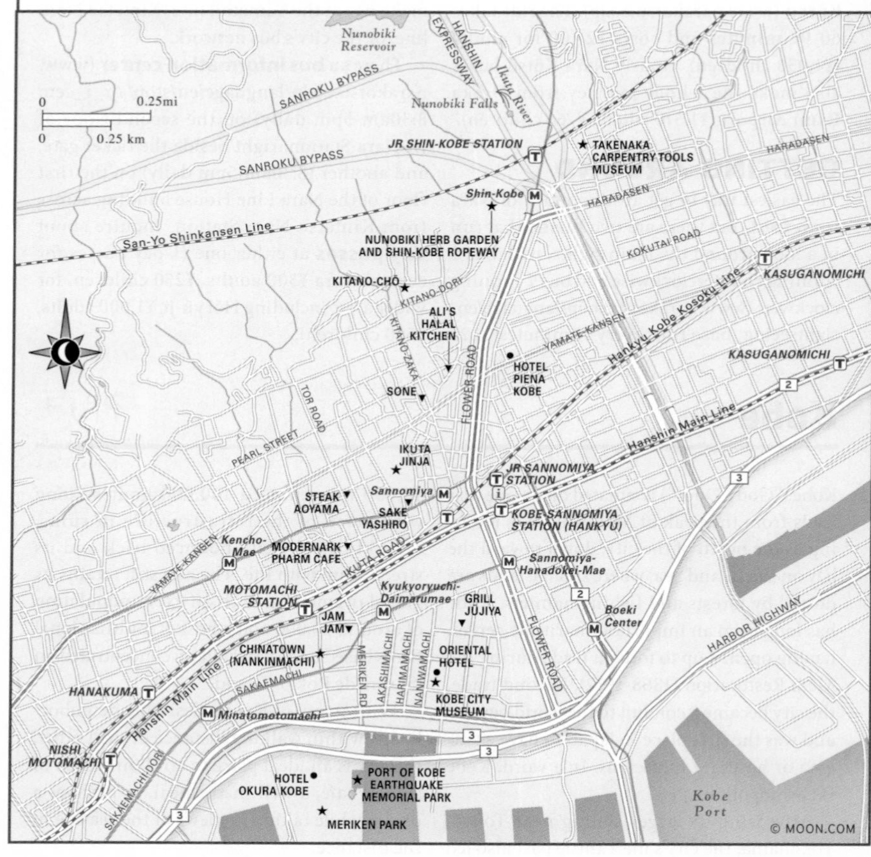

of town and end up in Chinatown. From there, **Kobe City Museum** is about 7 minutes' walk east, while **Meriken Park** and **Port of Kobe Earthquake Memorial Park** are 15-20 minutes' stroll to the south.

SIGHTS

Light on sights, Kobe is more of a place for a stroll. Be sure to spend some time in **Kitano-chō,** filled with the charming 19th-century Western-style brick residences of diplomats and merchants. Its atmospheric streets wind past cafés and bistros, and shops selling art, crafts, and fashion. The kitschy shops and food offerings of Kobe's **Chinatown** (Nankinmachi), illuminated by red lanterns at night, can seem a bit tired and overpriced, but it's a fun place to wander.

Nunobiki Herb Gardens and Ropeway

布引ハーブ園，神戸布引ロープウェー

1-4-3 Kitano-chō, Chūō-ku; tel. 078/271-1160; www.kobeherb.com; herb garden only ¥200, Kobe Nunobiki Ropeway ¥950 one-way/¥1,500 round-trip, both including herb garden admission; take Seishin-Yamate line to Shin-Kobe Station

Not far from Shin-Kobe Station, a stone

path leads 400 meters (1,312 ft) up a mountain where you'll find the strikingly pristine Nunobiki Falls, the serene Nunobiki Herb Garden, and zipping over it all, the Shin-Kobe Ropeway. You can either walk or ride the ropeway to the top and return down either way, too. The first leg of a walk up the mountain leads to **Nunobiki Falls** (24 hours; free; about 20 minutes from the bottom). Long the object of reverence and artistic inspiration, the falls vividly illustrate just how close to nature Kobe is.

Another 20 minutes' walk uphill from the falls is the **Nunobiki Herb Garden** (10am-5pm Mon.-Fri., 10am-8:30pm Sat.-Sun. and holidays, only viewing platform is open after 5pm). This sculpted green space has lavender fields, glasshouses full of tropical blossoms, a café, and a viewing platform. The top station of the **Shin-Kobe Ropeway** (9:30am-5:15pm Mon.-Fri. and 9:30am-8:30pm Sat.-Sun. and holidays Mar. 20-Jul. 19 and Sept. 1-Nov. 30, 9:30am-8:30pm daily Jul. 20-Aug. 31, 9:30am-5pm daily Dec. 1-Mar. 19) lies just beyond the upper entrance to the herb garden, which is roughly 30 minutes' walk uphill from the lower entrance to the garden.You can access the trail that leads to Nunobiki Falls and beyond by exiting from the ground floor of Shin-Kobe Station, turning left, and walking beneath the station to the beginning of the path. To access the lower station of the Shin-Kobe Ropeway, walk about 10 minutes southwest of Shin-Kobe Station.

Takenaka Carpentry Tools Museum

7-5-1 Kumochi-chō, Chūō-ku; tel. 078/242-0216; www.dougukan.jp; 9:30am-4:30pm (last entry 4pm) Tues.-Sun., closed Tues. when Mon. is a holiday; ¥700 adults, ¥500 age 65 and over, university and high school students, free for junior high and elementary school students

For a captivating glimpse into the world of Japanese carpentry, head to Kobe's stunning Takenaka Carpentry Tools Museum, which does a phenomenal job of elucidating what could potentially be construed as a dry topic. It's located a stone's throw from Shin-Kobe Station. Pick up a free English-language audio guide that sheds light on the deep history, techniques, and masterful craftsmanship inherent in Japan's carpentry tradition, which relies on complex joinery and shuns the use of nails, from intricate latticework to large-scale temple architecture.

Ikuta Jinja
生田神社

1-2-1 Shimo-Yamate-dōri; tel. 078/321-3851; 7am-dusk daily; free; take the JR line to Sannomiya Station

Ikuta Jinja is a surprisingly old shrine in the heart of Kobe's Sannomiya area. It's remained standing through generations of war from the earliest days of the nation, World War II bombing raids, and even more recently, the 1995 earthquake that reduced much of the city to rubble. Some dating puts the shrine's age at up to 18 centuries. Less a spectacular sight than it is a pocket of calm in the midst of the bustle, it's a nice place for a breather as you walk through downtown.

Kobe City Museum
神戸市立博物館

24 Kyōmachi; tel. 078/391-0035; www.kobecitymuseum.jp; 9:30am-5:30pm (last entry 5pm) Tues.-Thurs. and Sun., 9:30am-7:30pm (last entry 7pm) Fri.-Sat.; ¥300 adults, ¥200 university students, free for high school students and younger, up to ¥1,000 special exhibits; take the JR line to Sannomiya Station

Housed in a Greek revival-style building dating from the pre-World War II years, the Kobe City Museum does a good job of documenting the history of the city's interactions with the west. The displays incorporate art and relics from the 19th century on, revealing the ways that Western culture gradually became part of the fabric of the city, from fashion to technology. An interesting example of this cross-cultural exchange is seen in the "Southern Barbarian" school of art, which emerged after Jesuit missionaries began to train Japanese artists in painting techniques from the West. There's sufficient English-language signage throughout.

Meriken Park
メリケンパーク

2-2 Hatoba-chō, Chūō-ku; tel. 078/304-2500; www.feel-kobe.jp; 24 hours daily; free; take Kaigan subway line to Minato Motomachi, or JR or Hanshin line to Motomachi Station

This harborside park is home to a few of the city's most popular sights, one being the **Kobe Maritime Museum** (2-2 Hatoba-chō, Chūō-ku; tel. 078/327-8983; www.kobe-maritime-museum.com; 10am-6pm, last entry 5:30pm, Tues.-Sun.; ¥900 adults, ¥400 elementary school, junior high school, and high school students), easily recognizable with its white sailboat-shaped roofline. This museum contains displays on shipbuilding, cruise ships, the inner workings of ports, and well-made faux ships, including the types that plied Japan's waters during feudal days, but English information is limited.

Looming over the park and serving as an emblem of the city is the iconic hourglass-shaped **Kobe Port Tower** (5-5 Hatoba-chō, Chūō-ku; tel. 078/291-6751; www.kobe-port-tower.com; 9am-9pm, last entry 8:30pm, daily Mar.-Nov., 9am-7pm, last entry 6:30pm, daily Dec.-Feb.; ¥700 adults, ¥300 children). There's a 360-degree viewing deck atop the 108-meter-high (354-ft-high) spire, offering good views of the city and surrounding harbor, with the lush mountains hemming in the city beyond.

Note that it's possible to buy a combination ticket that gives access to both the museum and the tower's observation deck (¥1,300 adults, ¥550 children).

About 10 minutes' walk west of Meriken Park, **Harborland** (1-chōme Higashikawasaki-chō, Chūō-ku; tel. 078/360-3639; www.harborland.co.jp; 10am-9pm daily) is an entertainment and commercial complex on the waterfront.

Port of Kobe Earthquake Memorial Park
神戸港震災メモリアルパーク

24 hours; free; take the Kaigan subway line to Minato Motomachi, or the JR or Hanshin line to Motomachi Station

In this park in the harbor area, a cluster of displays with a video in English retell the fateful events of the morning of January 17, 1995, when the 6.9-magnitude Great Hanshin Earthquake rocked the city, killing more than 6,000 people and knocking down some 300,000 buildings. The most telling display is a section of the harbor left as it was immediately following the quake: the concrete tilted and partly submerged in water, with lampposts pointing in unnatural angles.

FESTIVALS

KOBE JAZZ STREET FESTIVAL

Various locations around town, starting from north side of Hankyū-Kobe Sannomiya Station; www.kobejazzstreet.gr.jp; noon-5pm Sat.-Sun. during first half of Oct.; ¥4,600 1-day pass, ¥8,700 2-day pass

True to its cosmopolitan roots, Kobe is said to be the birthplace of Japan's first jazz group, the Laughing Stars, which formed in the city in 1923. After World War II, jazz giants like Louis Armstrong and Duke Ellington also jammed in the emergent jazz hub. Given its importance as a commercial port, Kobe's already international district of Kitano was fertile ground for a postwar jazz explosion. Today, the heart of the city's jazz scene still beats strong. Check the website for dates and times.

FOOD

GRILL JŪJIYA

96 Strong Bldg. 1F, Edo-chō, Chūō-ku; tel. 078/331-5455; www.grill-jujiya.com; 11am-8pm (last order 7:30pm) Mon.-Sat.; from ¥850; JR Sannomiya Station

Harkening back to Kobe's deep historic ties with the West, the interior of this eatery, founded in 1933, evokes a mid-20th-century diner. The menu consists of Japanese spins on Western fare, a style of cooking known as

☆ Himeji-jō 姫路城

68 Honmachi; tel. 079/285-1146; www.city.himeji.lg.jp/castle/index.html; 9am-5pm (last entry 4pm) daily Sept.-late Apr., 9am-6pm (last entry 5pm) daily late Apr.-Aug.; ¥1,000 adults, ¥300 high school students and younger

In the sleepy city of Himeji, home to some 500,000 people, you'll find the most stellar surviving example of a castle in all of Japan. "White Heron Castle," as it is also known, describes well Himeji-jō. Refined and nearly unconquerable, this luminous white fortress atop a hill is hands-down the most stunning citadel in Japan. Aside from being a brilliant example of Japanese castle architecture, it is one of the few original structures left intact—a miracle in itself, considering that Himeji was razed by Allied bombers during World War II.

Himeji-jō

Built by warlord Toyotomi Hideyoshi in 1581, the trusty stronghold was expanded in the 16th century by Ikeda Terumasa, shogun Tokugawa Ieyasu's son-in-law. It served as the home and fortress of almost 50 lords until 1868, when the Meiji Restoration brought Japan's feudal era to an end and ushered in the modern age. Renovated in 2015, it looks as good as new.

The castle's main five-story keep and a few smaller ones are all surrounded by moats and stone walls with defensive openings for arrows, bullets, boiling oil, or water to be sent the enemy's way. The castle's ceramic roof tiles are believed to impart supernatural protection upon the fortress. Some of them are onigawara ("ogre tiles"), which bear the visages of ogres believed to fend off evil spirits and misfortune. Between the castle's various buildings, well-landscaped grounds full of flowering plants and well-sculpted trees also make for an appealing stroll.

If you have time and want to extend your visit in Himeji by an hour or two, cross the castle's western moat and enter **Kōkō-en** (9am-6pm, last entry 5:30, daily May-Aug., 9am-5pm, last entry 4:30, daily Sept.-Apr.; ¥310 adults, ¥150 high school students and younger, ¥1,050 adults, ¥360 high school students and younger with Himeji-jō combination ticket). These reconstructed samurai homes and gardens are thick with feudal-period ambience—a recommended addition to your exploration of the castle.

GETTING THERE

Visiting Himeji-jō is best approached as a jaunt from nearby Kobe, Osaka, Nara, or Kyoto, or as a stop on a longer westward journey to Okayama or Hiroshima aboard the San'yō shinkansen.

Himeji Station is a straight shot on the JR Tōkaidō line from **Kobe** (40 minutes; ¥990). From **Kyoto Station,** take the Super Hakuto limited express (90 minutes; ¥4,260) or Hikari shinkansen (55 minutes; ¥5,370). And from **Shin-Osaka Station,** take the Kodama, Sakura, or Hikari shinkansen (30-45 minutes; ¥3,810) or the JR special rapid train from **Osaka Station** (1 hour 10 minutes; ¥1,520). From **Hiroshima,** Sakura shinkansen trains run directly to Himeji Station (1 hour 10 minutes; ¥8,440).

To reach the castle, exit the north side of JR Himeji Station and **walk** 25 minutes north along Ōtemae-dōri. Alternatively, you can take advantage of the city's local bus network, run by **Shinki Bus** (www.shinkibus.co.jp). Buses depart directly in front of JR Himeji Station's north exit. Bus fares, including for the trip from Himeji Station to Himeji-jō, start from ¥100. For detailed routes and fares, visit www.himeji-kanko.jp/files_foreign/pdf/transportation_guide.pdf.

yōshoku: omuraisu (omelet stuffed with rice), beef stew, ham and egg sandwich, and hayashi rice (demi-glace sauce slathered over beef hash and onions served over rice). A thoroughly modern complement: There's also a nice selection of craft beer from Osaka.

MODERNARK PHARM CAFE

3-11-15 Kitanagasa-dōri; tel. 078/391-3060; http://modernark-cafe.chronicle.co.jp; 11:30am-10pm daily; food from ¥950, drinks from ¥500; take JR Tōkaidō line or Hanshin main line to Motomachi Station

Kobe also has a good range of healthier food options. For quality vegetarian fare in a laid-back café, Modernark Pharm Cafe is a good bet. The menu includes a vegetarian platter, bean burrito, various baked goods, organic beers, teas, juices, coffee, and more. Located north of Motomachi Station in the heart of downtown.

ALI'S HALAL KITCHEN

1-20-14 Nakayamatedōri, Chūō-ku; tel. 078/891-3322; www.aliskitchen.jp; 11am-10pm daily; lunch sets ¥750-1,500, dinner courses ¥2,500-5,000; take JR Kobe, Hankyū-Kobe, Hanshin Main, Port Island lines to Sannomiya Station

The owner and chef at this cozy halal spot whips up excellent Pakistani and north Indian food, from tandoori prawn to mutton masala to biryani. There's also a nice range of Middle Eastern fare, such as fattoush, a type of Lebanese salad containing cucumbers and tomatoes, and kabsa (basmati rice with a mix of meat and veg). A great pick if you're feeling like something different. It's also an interesting place to get a glimpse of the city's thriving South Asian community.

★ STEAK AOYAMA

2-14-5 Nakayamate-dōri, Chūō-ku; tel. 078/391-4858; www.steakaoyama.com; noon-2:30pm and 5pm-9pm Thurs.-Tues.; lunch from ¥1,760, dinner from ¥3,080; take Hankyu Kobe, JR Tokaido, Seishin Yamate subway line to Sannomiya Station, east exit 3

For an affordable Kobe beef experience, you can't go wrong with Steak Aoyama. This family-owned restaurant, serving succulent slabs of meat since 1963, is the stuff of local culinary legend. Its masterful chef makes pleasant conversation with guests without resorting to cheesy teppanyaki grill sideshows. Set meals come with soup, locally prepped vegetables, tofu, and dessert, all complemented by a great wine selection. To snag one of the eight seats offered in four rounds of meals per day, book at least a month, if not two, in advance via phone or the restaurant's Facebook page.

KOBE TANRYŪ SANNOMIYA-TEN

Ikuta Shindō Bldg. 1F, 1-10-9 Kitanagasa-dōri, Chūō-ku; tel. 078/391-2922; www.koubegyuu.com/shop/tanryu-sannomiya/; 11am-3:30pm (last order 3pm) and 5pm-10pm (last order 9:30pm) daily; average lunch from ¥8,000, average dinner from ¥12,000; take Seishin-Yamate subway line to Sannomiya Station, west exit 1

In-the-know locals head to this classy teppanyaki joint for the city's famously well-marbled meat. The beef, cooked on the countertop griddle in front of you, comes with grilled vegetables, soup, rice (garlic optional), and dessert. Excellent lobster, abalone, prawn, and more are also prepared a la carte. Ask for your hotel concierge to reserve ahead to be safe.

BARS AND NIGHTLIFE

When it comes to nightlife, Kobe is best known for its jazz haunts. East of downtown, the city is also home to a thriving sake brewing district, **Nada**, with some 40 breweries. If you'd like to get acquainted with the city's breweries and do some tasting during daylight hours, before a night of jazz perhaps, check out **Kampai Sake Tours** (tel. 080/7045-8365; https://kampaisaketours.com/tour/sake-kobe; 3.5 hours; 1:30pm-5pm Tues.-Sun.; ¥7,700).

SONE

1-24-10 Nakayamate-dōri, Chūō-ku; tel. 078/221-2055; http://kobe-sone.com; 5pm-midnight daily; ¥1,140 cover, meals from around ¥2,500; take Hankyu Kobe, JR Tokaido, or Seishin Yamate subway line to Sannomiya Station, east exit 8

Kobe has a long association with jazz, and

Kobe Beef

Kobe beef

Rare indeed does a slab of meat have such a household name that simply uttering it, anywhere from New York to Paris, will invoke an air of reverence. Even rarer is a cut of beef so famous that it's more recognizable to many than the city after which it is named. Such is the power of Kobe beef. A taste will convince the hardest skeptic: Beyond well-marbled, it has fat so soft that it actually melts in your mouth.

BACKGROUND

The legendary quality of Japanese beef can be traced back to the 1880s, when several European cattle breeds were brought to Japan and mixed with breeds native to the islands. Four strains emerged that remain the backbone of Japan's beef industry even today. While Kobe beef is indeed delicious, there are equally great strains of beef in Matsusaka, Mie Prefecture, northwest of Ise; Sendai and Hokkaido up north; and Miyazaki, down south in Kyushu. A mere 3,000 head of a breed of Tajima cattle, as the famed breed raised in Hyōgo Prefecture is known, are officially recognized as the source of bona fide Kobe beef. These legendary cows are fattened up on a choice diet of grass, dried pasture forage, and supplements, and even occasionally massaged, although their troughs are not filled with beer, nor are the bovines serenaded with classical music.

WHERE TO TRY IT

To taste what all the fuss is about, there's no better way than eating it in the place of its origin. Try **Steak Aoyama** (page 382). A small cut at the cheap end of the scale will set you back around ¥7,000, while choicer steaks cost upward of ¥20,000. You may find more reasonable prices during lunchtime—typically from around ¥2,000 at the cheaper end.

Sone is the best place to experience the rhythm of the city. This live house—pronounced "so-nay"—has been hosting gigs for the musically discerning since it held its first spontaneous jam session in 1969. Even today, the venue gets hopping during its four nightly performances and is regarded as Kobe's preeminent jazz den. Recommended for serious jazz aficionados. Performances start at 6:50pm.

JAM JAM

B1, 1-7-2 Motomachi; tel. 078/331-0876; https://jam-jam-jazz-club.business.site; noon-11pm daily; take JR Kobe, Hanshin lines to Motomachi Station

This subterrannean jazz bar has a phenomenal sound system and two separate seating areas: one for those who want to listen in peace, and another for those who want to talk quietly. The drinks are good and the soundtrack sets a perfectly laid-back mood. Enjoy the tunes and note that no song requests are taken.

SAKE YASHIRO

Fujiya Bldg. 1F, 1-1-5 Shimoyamate-dōri, Chūō-ku; tel. 078/334-7339; 4pm-11:30pm daily; take the Hankyu Kobe line, JR Tokaido line, or Seishin Yamate subway line to Sannomiya Station

Kobe's Nada district in the east part of the city is one of Japan's biggest producers of sake (rice wine), supplying about one-third of the country's stock. A great place to try some is at the laid-back bar of Sake Yashiro, a stone's throw from Ikuta Jinja. The bar's extensive, seasonal menu includes nibbles as well as

90-plus varieties of sake from around Japan, with about half of them coming from Kobe. This is a great place for an introduction to the world of sake.

ACCOMMODATIONS

HOTEL PIENA KOBE

4-20-5 Ninomiya-chō, Chūō-ku; tel. 078/241-1010; www.piena.co.jp; ¥13,000 d; take Hankyu Kobe, JR Tokaido, or Seishin Yamate subway line to Sannomiya Station

If you're looking for a clean, centrally located hotel in a mid-range budget, Hotel Piena Kobe is a cut above. Although they look slightly tired, the Western-style rooms are a good size compared to many mid-level hotels in the city and have touches of chic design. There's a good breakfast buffet, too.

HOTEL OKURA KOBE

2-1 Hatoba-chō, Chūō-ku; tel. 078/333-0111; www.kobe.hotelokura.co.jp; ¥26,400 d; take Kaigan subway line to Minato Motomachi, or JR or Hanshin line to Motomachi Station

For something a bit more luxurious, situated beside Meriken Park, the rooms in this 35-story tower are well-equipped and comfortable, with many boasting great views of the city and harbor. Staff are helpful and the dining room serves a good breakfast, too. The hotel shuttles guests from Kobe Sannomiya Station by bus for free.

★ ORIENTAL HOTEL

25 Kyōmachi, Chūō-ku; tel. 078/326-1500; www.orientalhotel.jp; ¥39,000 d; take Hankyu Kobe, JR Tokaido, or Seishin Yamate subway line to Sannomiya Station

The Oriental Hotel is a graceful property closely linked to Kobe's cosmopolitan past. Although it was rebuilt following the Great Hanshin Earthquake of 1995, the hotel still retains a sense of history as one of Japan's first hotels, having originally opened in 1870. Friendly, bilingual staff, well-appointed rooms with plush furnishings and great views, and elegant on-site dining make it one of the best places to stay in the city. Room rates appear steep on the hotel's website, but look at various booking sites and you may find a good deal.

INFORMATION AND SERVICES

- **Kobe Information Center** (8 Kumoi-dōri, Chūō-ku; tel. 078/241-1050; http://hello-kobe.com; 9am-7pm daily)

GETTING THERE

Air

Arriving via **Kansai International Airport,** the **limousine bus** to Kobe is more comfortable than the longer train journey via Osaka. The bus journey (75 minutes; ¥2,000 adults, ¥1,000 children) ends right at **Sannomiya Station** in the heart of downtown Kobe. Buy bus tickets on the spot at the airport; just follow the signs for the bus limousine in the arrivals hall.

If you're flying into **Osaka Itami Airport,** the **limousine bus** is also the way to go. This ride, to Sannomiya Station, takes 40 minutes and costs ¥1,070 per person (¥540 adults). From the smaller **Kobe Airport,** which only handles domestic flights, take the **Portliner** (20 minutes; ¥340) to Sannomiya Station. Buy tickets on-site in the arrivals hall in both airports.

Train

If you're traveling to Kobe via shinkansen—whether on the Sanyō or Tōkaidō line—you'll arrive at **Shin-Kobe Station,** slightly north of downtown. Transfer to the Seishin-Yamate line to travel south from Shin-Kobe Station to the more central **Sannomiya Station** (8 minutes; ¥210).

Coming from Osaka Station, you can easily arrive at Sannomiya Station in less than 30 minutes. If you're using a JR Pass, take the JR Kobe Line (22 minutes; ¥410 without JR Pass). Another option is the private Hankyū Kobe line, which runs from Hankyū Umeda Station in Osaka to **Hankyū Kobe-Sannomiya Station** (30 minutes; ¥320).

From Kyoto, you can take the Super Hakuto

limited express directly to Sannomiya Station (50 minutes; ¥2,620), which only makes sense if you're traveling with a JR Pass due to the cost. Alternatively, first travel to Osaka and change trains to either the JR Kobe line at Osaka Station, or the Hankyū Kobe line at Umeda Station.

From Hiroshima Station, ride the shinkansen to Shin-Kobe Station (1 hour 20 minutes; ¥10,200), then transfer to the city's subway or other local train lines to reach Sannomiya or elsewhere from there.

Bus

Like Osaka, Kobe can be reached from a number of stations in Tokyo or Yokohama on a highway bus. The trip takes about 8.5 hours and fares start from ¥5,800. Check **Willer Express** (http://willerexpress.com) for details. Willer Express also offers bus journeys from **Hiroshima** to Kobe (6 hours; from ¥3,000).

GETTING AROUND

Train

Kobe's relatively small scale means short walk-times between most places and the nearest train station, making its **train network** the easiest way to get around. It's only about a 25-minute walk between Kitano-chō in the north and Chinatown in the south. There are also three aboveground lines and two subway lines running through the city.

Starting from Sannomiya Station in the east, the **JR, Hanshin,** and **Hankyū lines** run westward across the city. The Seishin-Yamate subway line runs north from **Sannomiya Station** to **Shin-Kobe Station,** and from there all the way up to **Tanigami Station.** The Kaigan subway line runs from **Sannomiya-Hanadokeimae Station** southward through downtown toward the bay, where a handful of other stations are located.

For a **map** of the city's train lines, visit www.westjr.co.jp/global/en/timetable/pdf/map_kobe.pdf. Subway fares start from ¥210; all aboveground lines start from ¥130. Purchase tickets from machines near the ticket gates at any station.

Bus

Beyond the rail network, there's also the **City Loop bus** (https://kobecityloop.jp; ¥260 adults, ¥130 children under 12 for single ride; ¥680 adults, ¥340 children under 12 for one-day pass). The green buses with a retro flair loop the city's most touristed areas, including Sannomiya, Meriken Park, Harborland, and Kitano-chō. The easiest place to hop onto one of these buses is at the stop on the north side of Sannomiya Station. Pay for a single journey at the machine next to the driver's seat as you exit the bus. If you plan to use a one-day pass, buy one at the **Kobe Information Center** outside JR Sannomiya Station's east exit.

Kii Peninsula 紀伊半島

Stretching across southern Kansai is a wild, spiritually rich swath of terrain—the Kii Peninsula, Honshu's largest. At its heart, the mystical Buddhist center of Kōya-san sprawls across a mountaintop, south of which a series of pilgrimage routes known collectively as the Kumano Kodō connects a circuit of shrines set in dense alpine forest. To the east in neighboring Mie Prefecture is Ise-jingū, a relatively unadorned spiritual mecca of vast importance; it is considered the holiest site in all of Shinto. Visiting the Kii Peninsula region will give you a nature fix as well as a spiritual one: an antidote to the concrete urban centers to the north.

★ KŌYA-SAN

高野山

Moss-encrusted lanterns, misty forest, and a host of storied temples and mausoleums

1

2

3

4

await at Kōya-san, one of the holiest, most atmospheric places in Japanese Buddhism. Established by Kōbō Daishi (aka Kūkai, 774-835) as the headquarters of the still vital sect of esoteric Shingon Buddhism in 826, this dense network of monasteries sits beside a mystically charged graveyard, towering cedar trees, and myriad statues of red-bibbed jizō (guardian of children and travelers) sprawling across a verdant plateau at an elevation of about 1,005 meters (3,300 ft), deep in the mountains.

To experience the full power of Kōya-san, plan to stay for one night. Aim to arrive in the early or mid-afternoon, check into your lodging, and then after dinner, head to the cemetery of Okuno-in at nighttime to the sound of crickets—or cicadas in summer—with only the soft glow of stone lanterns lining the path. The effect is magical. Strike off early the next morning to explore Okuno-in again—this time as the rays of the sun gently infuse the forest with soft light in the often-misty morning. The earlier and closer to dawn the better. After this, return to the town section of Kōya-san. Here, visit the Danjō Garan temple complex, including stops at Kongōbu-ji and Tokugawa Ieyasu's mausoleum in town.

Sights

DANJŌ GARAN
壇上伽藍

grounds 24 hours, buildings 8:30am-5pm daily; grounds free, ¥500 admission to each structure

Kōya-san is roughly divided into the Danjō Garan, or simply Garan, temple precinct (with eight temples and pagodas in all), the surrounding small town dotted by temples and temple residences (shokubo) in the west, and the heavily forested cemetery of **Okuno-in** (24 hours; free) in the east. Its immense cultural value has landed it firmly on UNESCO's World Heritage list. Among the Garan's standouts are **Kondō Hall**, a ceremonial temple that enshrines the Medicine Buddha (Yakushi Nyōrai), and **Konpon Daitō Pagoda**, housing a towering effigy of the Cosmic Buddha, or Vairocana in Sanskrit (Dainichi Nyōrai in Japanese), and a singular 3D mandala formed by painted pillars and statues arrayed within.

KONGŌBU-JI
金剛峯寺

.132 Kōya-san; tel. 0736/56-2011; 8:30-5pm daily; ¥500

Highlights of the western section include the temple complex of Kongōbu-ji, the HQ of the Shingon Buddhist sect known for its range of beautifully painted, sliding fusama doors. Also among the sights in the western half of town are the various structures of the Danjō Garan complex, as well as the **mausoleum of the clan of Tokugawa Ieyasu** (682 Kōya-san; tel. 0736/56-2011; 8:30am-5pm daily; ¥200), founder of the Tokugawa shogunate.

MAUSOLEUM OF KŪKAI
弘法大師御廟

tel. 0736/56-2002; 24 hours; free

The main draw of the Okuno-in area is the mausoleum of Kūkai, standing grandly in the back of a deep forest of enormous cedar trees, dotted by some 100,000 gravestones and stone lanterns. Also of interest in the cemetery is the mausoleum of warlord Toyotomi Hideyoshi (1537-1598), the brilliant general and samurai who played a prominent role in unifying Japan. The mausoleum of Kūkai is more accurately a temple. Its ceiling is lined with seemingly infinite rows of suspended lanterns. Around the backside of the mausoleum, incense wafts from sticks planted in large bronze cauldrons, and chanting pilgrims wear conical straw hats and carry walking sticks.

Accommodations

One of the best ways to see behind the scenes of temple life in Japan is by staying at one of the lodgings known as shukubō. It's similar to the experience of staying at a ryokan, but at breakfast and dinner, guests are served

1: private room at Kōya-san **2:** shōjin-ryōri at Joki-in **3:** lanterns, gates, and gravesites at Okuno-in **4:** inner shrine area, Ise-jingū

shōjin-ryōri, a refined form of strictly vegetarian cuisine eaten by monks, consisting of elements like rice, soup, vegetable tempura, pickled greens, tofu, tea, and perhaps a single cherry for a light finishing note. You also have the chance to rise at dawn to meditate, transcribe a sutra, chant, help spruce up the grounds, or witness a goma (fire ceremony), in which a monk tosses grains, oil, incense, flowers, water, and rice into a fire, suggesting the transformation of ignorance to wisdom.

KŌYA-SAN GUEST HOUSE KOKUU

49-43 Kōya-san; tel. 0736/26-7216; http://koyasanguesthouse.com; ¥3,600 for capsule, ¥6,200 for double bed in private room for one person, ¥9,200 for double bed in private room for two people

Kōya-san Guest House Kokuu is a budget-conscious yet stylish hostel with both capsules and private rooms. It's located about 6 minutes' walk from Okuno-in. While there is food on offer, it's not shōjin-ryōri (monk's vegetarian fare). Instead, it's Western breakfast and curry from India and Thailand for dinner (both reasonably priced). The helpful hosts are friendly and speak English. Note that toiletries cost a small amount extra—see the website for prices.

★ EKŌ-IN

497 Kōya-san; tel. 0736/56-2514; www.ekoin.jp; from ¥12,000 pp with meals

This well-loved temple lodging is a short walk west of Okuno-in, making it a prime spot for exploring Kōya-san. Known for its interesting nighttime tours of the sprawling cemetery, the inn also has clean, well-maintained rooms—some with private bath, others shared—and the English-speaking monks who run the operation are gracious hosts. There's a lovely garden on-site and a shared onsen bath (sex separated), and guided meditation sessions are on offer.

JOKI-IN

365 Kōya-san; tel. 0736/56-2321; https://jokiin.jp; from ¥12,000 pp with two meals

On the west side, close to Kongōbu-ji, Joki-in is a great low-key shukubō run by friendly English-speaking staff. It has both private and shared rooms, and is conveniently located between Kongōbu-ji and Danjō Garan. The dinners are served privately to the rooms, while breakfast is eaten communally. This is a good choice if your aim is to avoid the more crowded shukubō around town.

FUDO-IN

456 Kōya-san; tel. 0736/56-2414, https://fudouin.or.jp; from ¥16,000 pp with two meals

In the center of town, Fudo-in is an excellent pick with spacious rooms. It's roughly in the middle between Okuno-in in the east and Kongōbu-ji in the west. The temple's biggest draw is its position away from the road, which makes it an exceptionally quiet place. The grounds are beautiful and the monks on staff are eager to serve guests.

Information and Services

Online, to dig deeper into some of Kōya-san's intricacies, as well as practicalities, visit www.koyasan.or.jp.

- **Kōya-san Shukubō Assocation** (600 Kōya-san, Kōya-chō; tel. 0736/56-2616; http://shukubo.net; 8:30am-5pm Mar.-Dec., 9am-5pm Jan.-Feb.; next to the bus stop for Senjūin-bashi)

Getting There and Around

The easiest way to reach Kōya-san by **train** is by taking the Nakai line from Namba Station in Osaka (1 hour 30 minutes-1 hour 45 minutes, ¥890-1,410). Note that you may need to change trains at Hashimoto Station, depending on the particular train you board. Disembark at **Gokuraku-bashi Station** and take the **cable car** five minutes to the top of Kōya-san, the mountain itself. The ¥390 charge for the cable car ride is covered in the cost of the train ticket.

Exiting the lift, buses will be waiting to whisk you into town, about 2.5 kilometers (1.5 mi) away. Once you're in town, all sights of note are within a radius of about 4 kilometers

(2.5 mi), making the area an appealing place to discover **on foot.** There are also **buses** that shuttle to and from the main sights. You can also save a little money by traveling to Kōya-san via the JR line, but the route involves multiple transfers.

If you want to get there quickly and you don't mind spending a little extra for the limited express (tokkyū) train, note that the **Kōya-san World Heritage Ticket** (www.nankaikoya.jp/en/stations/ticket.html; ¥3,400) offers discounts on some of Kōya-san's sights, and on round-trip travel to Osaka. If you opt for the limited express train, which costs ¥2,110 one-way, then it's a no-brainer to get this special ticket. Pick one up in advance at the ticket counter in Namba Station.

ISE

伊勢

Arriving in Ise, you could be forgiven for thinking that the town—home to Shinto's holiest shrine—is a bit mundane. Truth be told, it is. Aside from the neighboring town of Toba's claim to fame as the first place in the world to successfully culture pearls, not much draws visitors to this remote corner of Japan. However, proceed to Ise's dense cedar groves, where the Gekū (outer) and Naikū (inner) shrines await, and the town's subtly spiritual atmosphere becomes palpable.

Sights

★ ISE-JINGŪ

伊勢神宮

www.isejingu.or.jp; free

Shinto's holiest shrine, Ise-jingū is ancient, yet continuously renewed: It is symbolically torn down and rebuilt every 20 years using cypress wood felled in the Kiso Mountains of Japan's Central Alps. This ancient rite was last conducted in 2013, the 62nd time. The leftover wood from each previous version of the shrine is whisked away to be used at other shrines around the country. While the exteriors of the shrine buildings can be at least partly glimpsed from the outside, the inner precincts are only accessible to the emperor and a handful of elite priests.

Above all else, Ise-jingū is a stronghold of secrets. Housed in the innermost section of the sacred complex is a bronze mirror believed to have been given to the emperor by the sun goddess Amaterasu-Omikami herself, from whom the Japanese imperial line is said to have emerged. This sacred object—one of the three Imperial regalia, along with sacred beads housed in Tokyo's Imperial Palace and the sacred sword held in Nagoya's Atsuta-jingū—has been shrouded in a thick layer of cloth since the 3rd century and has never even been seen by the emperor himself.

Despite this layer of secrecy, visiting Ise-jingū is a powerful experience. The shrine is divided into **Gekū** (Outer; sunrise-sunset; free) and **Naikū** (Inner; sunrise-sunset; free) areas. Spaced 6 kilometers (4 mi) apart, the two parts of the complex are set amid thickly forested hills crisscrossed by gently running streams. Gekū, which is approached via a path lined by immense cryptomeria trees and three immense torii gates, is dedicated to Toyouke-Omikami (goddess of the harvest, hearth, and home). Naikū, which is approached by crossing the Isuzu-gawa by walking over the Uji-bashi bridge, is presided over by Amaterasu, mythical progenitor of the Imperial family. The shrine buildings themselves are relatively humble in appearance, akin to ancient granaries, with decorative beams extending from the highest point of the thatched rooftops. The inner precincts are hidden from view by wooden fences.

Note that photography and smoking are strictly banned in the inner precincts of the shrine. Be sure to pick up the English-language booklet and map available at the small information booth next to the entrance of both Gekū and Naikū.

SENGŪKAN

せんぐう館

126-1 Maeno, Toyokawa-chō; tel. 0596/22-6263; www.sengukan.jp; 9am-4:30pm (last entry 4pm

Kumano Kodō 熊野古道

If Kōya-san is the Buddhist heart of the Kii Peninsula, the pilgrimage circuit known as Kumano Kodō that runs through the rugged south of the region is its partly Shinto sibling. For more than a millennium, pilgrims, emperors, and priests have flocked to the region. The religious roots of these four pilgrimage routes, together designated a UNESCO World Heritage Site, are a syncretic blend of Japan's two main faiths. This ease with mystic mixing gives the Kumano Kodō region a revered status among followers of the syncretic spiritual path known as Shugendō, followed by mountain-traipsing monks known as the yamabushi.

The best point of entry into the Kumano Kodō region is the town of **Tanabe,** located in southwestern Wakayama Prefecture (2 hours 25 minutes via Kuroshio limited express train on the JR Kinokuni line from Shin-Osaka Station to Kii-Tanabe station; ¥5,370). Reaching the bulk of the sights requires taking a bus from Tanabe to **Hongū** (bus stop 2; 2 hours; ¥2,060), though a rental car is another good option (**JR Rent-a-Car** just outside Kii-Tanabe Station, 1-24 Minato, Tanabe-shi; tel. 0739-26-0939; www.ekiren.co.jp; 9am-6pm daily).

THE KUMANO SANZAN

Although the Kumano Kodō covers a vast region of subshrines and hallowed terrain, for a more casual visitor there are three main shrines, referred to as the Kumano Sanzan.

- At the nexus of the four paths of the Kumano Kodō is **Hongū Taisha** (本宮大社; tel. 0735/42-0009; www.hongutaisha.jp; shrine office 8am-5pm daily, treasure hall 9am-4pm daily; grounds free, treasure hall ¥300 adults, ¥100 ages 12-15), located deep in the mountains of the peninsula atop a verdant, rocky spine. Tanabe to Hongū (bus stop 2, 2 hours; ¥2,060) also passes through the main onsen towns of the area, including Yunomine. To reach Hongū Taisha, get off at the Hongu Taisha-mae Bus Stop; it's a short walk from there.
- To the southeast, **Nachi Taisha** (那智大社; 1 Nachi-san, Nachikatsuura; tel. 0735/55-0321; www.kumanonachitaisha.or.jp; grounds 24 hours, shrine office and Nachi-no-taki waterfall viewing platform 7am-4:30pm daily, treasure hall 8am-4pm daily; grounds free, treasure hall ¥300 adults, ¥200 ages 6-15, Nachi-no-taki waterfall viewing platform ¥300) sits in front of Japan's highest waterfall, Nachi-no-taki, a picturesque 133-meter-high (436-ft-high) waterfall that inspired the building of the shrine, where the Pacific is also in sight. The Nachi area can be reached by bus from Nachi Station (20 minutes; ¥490), accessed from Kii-Tanabe Station via the Kinokuni line bound for Shingū (2 hours 20 minutes, ¥1,690 local; 1 hour 40 minutes, ¥3,210 limited express) and from Kii-Katsuura Station (30 minutes; ¥630) by bus, departing roughly every 45 minutes from either station. Just take the bus until Nachi-san bus stop, near the base of the shrine's grounds, and make your way about 10 minutes uphill on foot from there.
- On the eastern coast of Wakayama Prefecture, north of Nachi Taisha, is **Hayatama Taisha** (速玉大社; 1-1 Kamihonmachi, Shingū; tel. 0735/22-2533; http://kumanohayatama.jp; 8am-5pm daily shrine grounds, 9am-4pm daily treasure house; shrine free, treasure house ¥500), the terminus of the pilgrimage route. This prehistoric shrine is said to house the kami (god)

daily), closed second and fourth Tues. every month or Wed. if Tues. falls on national holiday; ¥300

For a good breakdown of the ceremonial rebuilding of the shrine that takes place every 20 years, be sure to stop by the Sengūkan. This museum on the grounds of the Gekū contains visual displays depicting the process of shrine renewal, as well as a model of the Gekū's premises at a 1:20 scale. There's also a life-size replica of the Goshōden to satisfy the curiosity of visitors who are barred from entering the real one.

Food

The town becomes very sleepy at night, which could be good or bad, depending on what

who oversees the rhythms of nature and all lifeforms. Either take a bus from Nachi Station (40 minutes; ¥580) or Shingū Station (5 minutes; ¥200), from where you can also walk to the shrine in 15 minutes. To reach Shingū Station from Kii-Tanabe Station, take the JR Kinokuni line (2 hours 50 minutes, ¥1,980 local; 2 hours, ¥3,930 limited express). You can also make the journey straight from Shin-Osaka (4 hours 35 minutes, ¥7,350 limited express) or Nagoya (1 hour 50 minutes, ¥7,530 limited express).

along the Kumano Kodō

PLANNING YOUR PILGRIMAGE

It's possible to access one or all of these three main shrines via a combination of bus and train, but the more orthodox (and adventurous) may prefer to see a section of the trails on foot. The most popular trail is the **Nakahechi route** (56 km/35 mi). To trod a more manageable version of this well-worn pilgrim's path, take the bus bound for Ryūjin from Kii-Tanabe Station and ride until the Hosshinmon-oji bus stop, near the trailhead of a path that leads to the holiest of the three main shrines, Hongū Taisha. If you plan to embark on this jaunt, stop by the Tanabe City Kumano Tourism Bureau before setting out to pick up maps and ask for pointers.

WHERE TO STAY

The path to Hongū Taisha leads to **Yunomine Onsen** (湯の峰温泉), a wonderful place to soak and stay for a night. Standout places to bathe and rest include **Tsubo-yu Onsen** (www.hongu.jp/en/onsen/yunomine/tsuboyu/; 6am-10pm daily, last entry 9:30pm; ¥780 adults, ¥470 children under 12), and **Ryokan Yoshino-ya** (359 Yunomine; tel. 073/542-0101; www.yunomine.com; from ¥11,000 pp with 2 meals).

MORE INFORMATION

The **Tanabe City Kumano Tourism Bureau** (1-20 Minato, Tanabe-shi; tel. 0739/34-5599; 9am-5pm Mon.-Fri.), located on the second floor of JR Kii-Tanabe Station on the Kisei line, goes above and beyond the call of duty to help foreign visitors, as does the **Kumano Hongū Heritage Center** (100-1 Hongū; tel.0735/42-0751; 9am-5pm daily; free), which doubles as a museum. Online, the Tanabe City Kumano Tourism Bureau's official website (www.tb-kumano.jp) addresses logistical concerns like bus timetables and offers extensive resources from rundowns on activities in the region to lodging and food.

you're seeking. If this appeals to you, spending one night in Ise can be a good way to catch your breath.

AKAFUKU

26 Ujinakanokiri-chō; tel. 0596/22-7000; www.akafuku.co.jp/store/5139; 9am-5pm daily; ¥290-550

With 300 years of history, the akafuku mocha (pounded-rice cake covered in red bean paste) served here is famous.

BUTASUTE GEKUMAETEN

1-1-33 Iwabuchi; tel. 050/5485-2517; https://butasutegekumae.gorp.jp; lunch 11am-3pm (last order 2:30pm), dinner 5pm-9pm (last order 8pm) Fri.-Wed.; ¥900-2,800

Gyūdon (beef atop rice) is the specialty here. Portions are good and the quality of beef is high. They also sell menchi katsu (croquette filled with minced beef), which are ideal for a bite on the go. This location is 7 minutes' walk southwest of Iseshi Station, heading toward Gekū. There's another branch near Naikū (52 Ujinakanokiri-chō; tel. 0596/23-8802; 11am-6pm Apr.-Sept., 11am-5pm Oct.-Mar.), which tends to get more crowded.

Accommodations

ISE GUESTHOUSE KAZAMI

1-6-36 Fukiage, Ise; tel. 0596/63-9170; www.ise-guesthouse.com; mixed dorms ¥4,200, private room singles ¥9,000, ¥10,000 d

Freshly reopened after extensive renovations in autumn 2018, with exposed timber throughout, and clean, cozy rooms, this is Ise's best budget accommodation. There's a shared lounge, kitchen, and laundry facilities. All rooms share a bathroom, too. The guesthouse is a social place and occasionally hosts music events. It's only a few minutes' walk south of Iseshi Station. Bicycle rentals are available (¥500 per day). Note that a separate modest fee is also charged for toiletries.

HOSHIDEKAN

2-15-2 Kawasaki; tel. 0596/28-2377; www.hoshidekan.jp; ¥6,500 s, ¥12,800 d with breakfast

For something on the quiet northern side of Iseshi Station, away from the tourists, this spacious ryokan with a leafy courtyard at its core is a good pick. There are 10 Japanese-style rooms that share bathroom and toilet facilities. The staff are helpful and speak English. Bicycle rentals are available (¥300 per day). It's 15 minutes' walk northeast of Iseshi Station.

Information and Services

For information in English about the Ise area online, visit https://ise-kanko.jp.

- **Ise Tourist Information Center** (Iseshi Station; tel. 0596/65-6091; 9am-5:30pm daily)

Getting There and Around

You can get to Ise by taking either the JR or Kintetsu line from Nagoya, Kyoto, Osaka, or Nara to **Iseshi Station,** about 10 minutes' walk from the outer shrine. The closest option from among these four is the Kintetsu line limited express (tokkyū) from Kintetsu-Nagoya Station (1 hour 25 minutes; ¥2,810). If you have a JR pass and you're coming from either Kyoto or Osaka, it's easiest to take the shinkansen to Nagoya, then travel from there.

If you don't have a JR pass and you're coming from **Kyoto,** take either the express (kyūkō) or limited express (tokkyū) train on the Kintetsu line to Yamatoyagi, then transfer to the limited express to Iseshi Station (2 hours 20 minutes-2 hours 40 minutes, ¥3,390-3,690). To arrive via **Osaka** without a JR Pass, take the Osaka Loop line bound for Tennō-ji to Tsuruhashi Station, then transfer to the Kintetsu line, preferably paying the additional fee for the limited express, which will get you to Iseshi Station (1 hour 40 minutes; ¥3,170).

Begin your exploration at Gekū by **walking** 10 minutes from Iseshi Station down the main avenue of Gekū-sandō, which leads directly to the Outer shrine's entrance. Proceed to the Goshōden, or main hall, about 10 minutes past the shrine's entrance. To reach Naikū, hop on the bus from the stop in front of Gekū (15 minutes; ¥440). Alternatively, ride bus 51 or 55 to Naikū-mae bus stop from Iseshi-eki-mae bus stop just south of the south exit of Iseshi Station, or simply hail a taxi from Iseshi Station (about ¥2,000). Return to Iseshi Station from Naikū by bus from Naikū-mae bus stop near Naikū.

Western Honshu

Long ago, Western Honshu—also known as

Chūgoku ("middle country")—was the geographical heartland of nascent Japan. The imperial family was based in Kyoto to the east, the large island of Kyushu defined the western edge, and anything east of Kyoto was terra incognita. Tokyo was not yet a dream.

Today, this region is defined by its San'yo (southern) and San'in (northern) coasts. Making a circuit around the coasts dramatically illustrates Japan's most fundamental dichotomy: While the northern San'in side is quieter and more steeped in tradition, the faster-paced southern San'yo coast presents a modern face and is conveniently served by bullet train.

The region's top destination is Hiroshima, a city on the southern

Itinerary Ideas 399
Hiroshima 402
Miyajima 415
San'yo 420
The Art Islands 432
San'in 444

Highlights

Look for ★ to find recommended sights, activities, dining, and lodging.

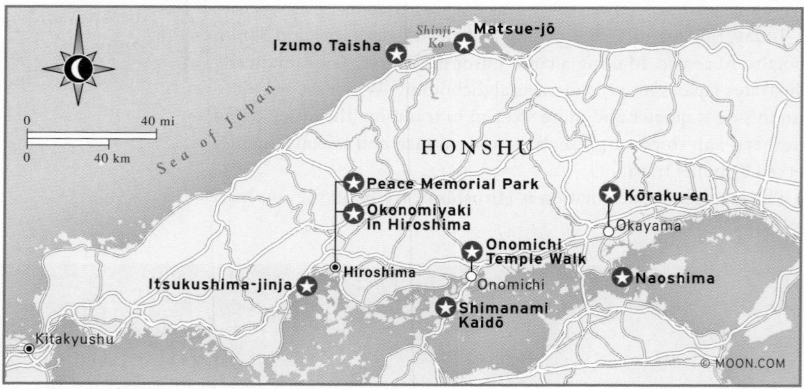

★ **Peace Memorial Park:** Pay your respects to Hiroshima's harrowing past with a visit to its sobering collection of atomic bomb monuments (page 406).

★ **Okonomiyaki in Hiroshima:** Most associate the savory pancake known as okonomiyaki with Osaka, but Hiroshima has its own spin on the dish (page 411).

★ **Itsukushima-jinja:** Take in one of Japan's quintessential views, the "floating" vermillion torii gate of Miyajima (page 415).

★ **Onomichi Temple Walk:** This hilly route meanders above the idyllic port town of its namesake, taking in 25 historic temples and offering gorgeous views of the Inland Sea below (page 420).

★ **Shimanami Kaidō:** Cross the sparkling Inland Sea by bicycle, following a series of bridges over a string of isles between Honshu and Shikoku (page 424).

★ **Kōraku-en:** Wander this sprawling landscape garden and see why it safely claims a spot among Japan's top three gardens (page 429).

★ **Naoshima:** Take a ferry to this idyllic island for its rustic charm and bohemian ethos as much as for its collection of world-class art museums (page 432).

★ **Matsue-jō:** Explore one of Japan's most atmospheric, original castles, surrounded by an imposing moat (page 444).

★ **Izumo Taisha:** Visit this grand shrine, to which all kami (gods) retreat for a divine council during the 10th lunar month every year (page 448).

(San'yo) coast whose destruction by atomic bomb during World War II left a scar that will never fully heal. But its energetic modern incarnation is an inspiring testament to the power of the human spirit. Nearby, the island of Miyajima is famed for the "floating" torii gate of Itsukushima-jinja, one of the most photogenic shrines in Japan. Though the fabled gate is currently wrapped in scaffolding for maintenance and may remain so for another 4-5 years, and renovation works are underway around a portion of the shrine near its western gate until December 2022, what remains accessible of the shrine itself, and the mountainous island on which it stands, are beautiful as ever.

Heading east of Hiroshima on the San'yo coast, the classic port town of Onomichi effortlessly enchants. Beyond the fishing boats docked in the harbor and mom-and-pop sushi shops, a mountainside strewn with temples and guarded by an army of casts rises sharply behind downtown. From here, a 70-kilometer (43-mi) scenic route known as the Shimaniami Kaidō crosses six islands linked by some of the world's longest suspension bridges, ending up on the northwest corner of Shikoku. To fully experience the magic of this route, make the journey on two wheels for what is surely one of the world's prettiest bicycle trips. Next, Kurashiki is famed for its canal district that oozes Edo-period charm, followed by Okayama Prefecture, known for its sublime garden Kōraku-en, overseen by a castle.

These towns face the beautiful Seto Naikai (Inland Sea), a narrow body of water bounded by Honshu to the north, Shikoku to the south, and Kyushu to the west. It's dotted with islands, the most accessible being the three "art islands"—Naoshima, Teshima, and Inujima—whose world-class museums and public artworks were developed to revitalize the quaint villages on their shores.

While most travelers stick to exploring San'yō, the more rural, weather-beaten northern shore (San'in) casts an enchanting spell. Here, the prefectures of Tottori and Shimane are among Japan's least visited. At times, you'll feel like you've got the place to yourself as you visit the 50-meter-high (164-ft-high) sand dunes of Tottori, one of the most alien landscapes in Japan; charming, historic towns like Matsue, famed for its lovely castle; and nearby Izumo, home to one of Shinto's oldest and holiest shrines, Izumo Taisha.

ORIENTATION

The region between Kansai and Hiroshima is part of **Chūgoku,** which takes up the southernmost tip of Honshu, Japan's main island. It's bordered by Kyushu to the west and the Inland Sea and Shikoku to the south, and is often divided into its more heavily populated southern coast (**San'yo,** or "sunny side of the mountains"), and the rural northern coast (**San'in,** or "in the shadow of the mountains"), facing the frothy **Sea of Japan.**

San'yo
山陽

Approaching from elsewhere in Honshu, which means coming from the east, the first place most travelers come to in Western Honshu is the city of **Okayama,** a shinkansen (bullet train) stop only 25 minutes' ride west of Himeji and 35 minutes' ride west of Kobe. Also in Okayama Prefecture is the historic town of **Kurashiki,** known for its charming canals, about 20 kilometers (12.4 mi) west of Okayama. This is also the main jumping off point for the **Art Islands** of the Inland Sea; you'll need to first head south from Okayama to Chayamachi where you'll transfer trains and continue on to Uno Port (total journey time 50 minutes), from where you can get a 20-minute ferry to Naoshima, the islands' main gateway.

Moving west into Hiroshima Prefecture, the first town of note you'll come to here is the

Previous: Shimanami Kaidō; Atomic Bomb Dome in Peace Memorial Park; okonomiyaki, Hiroshima style.

Western Honshu

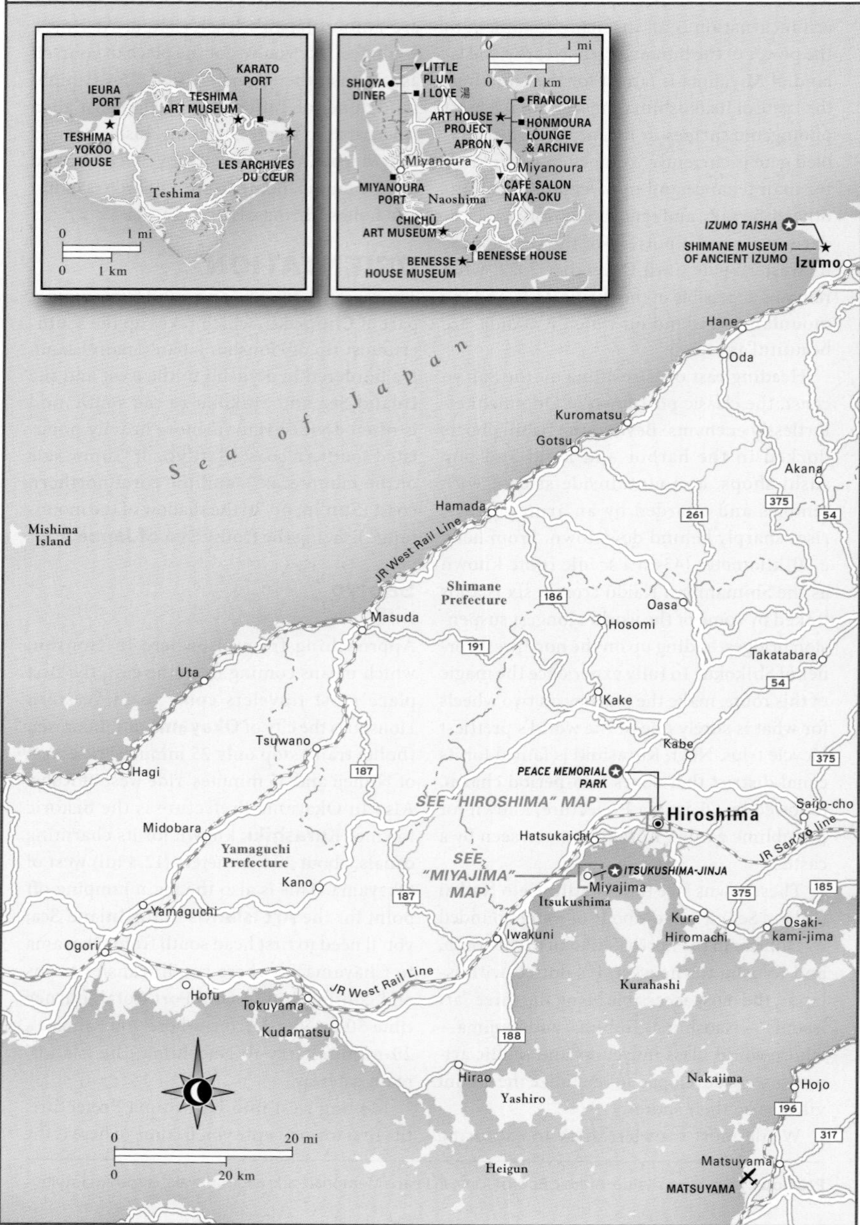

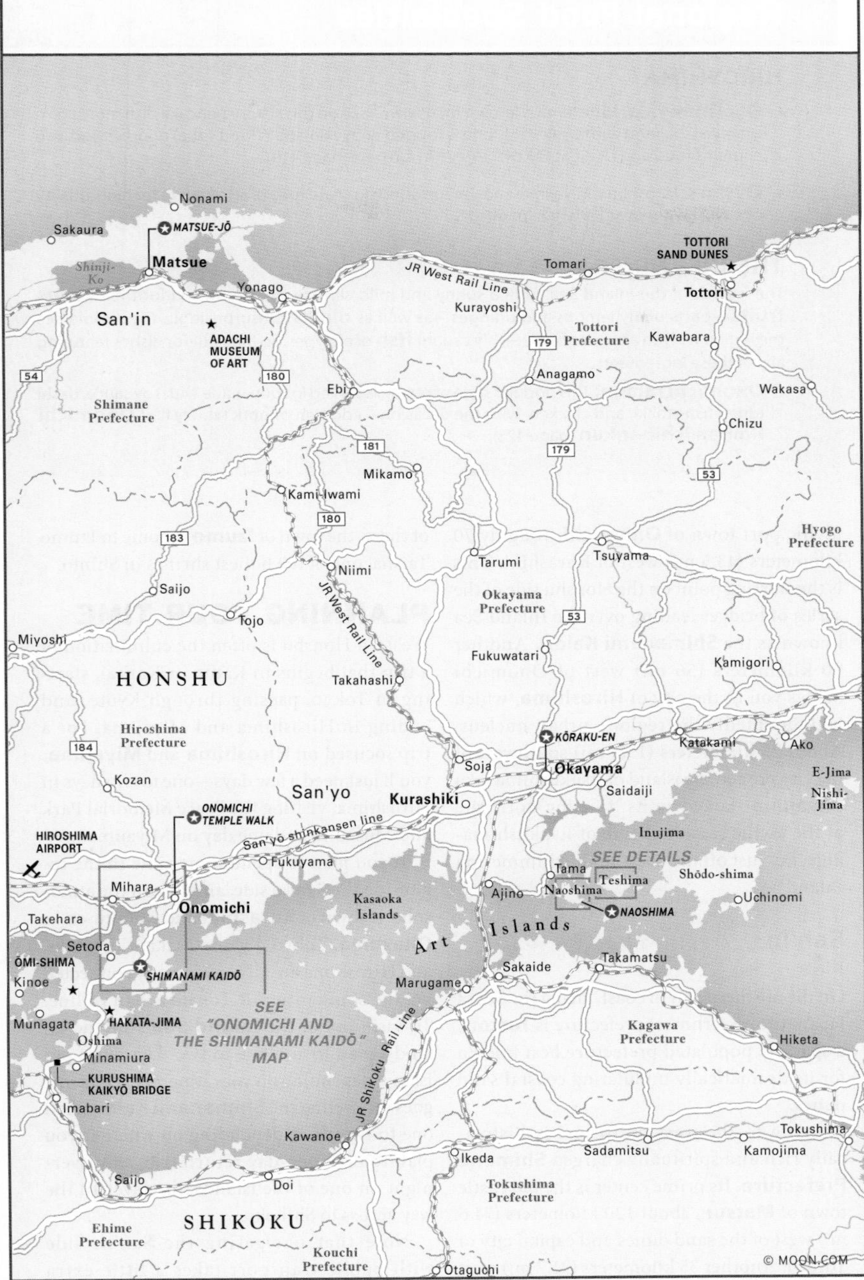
Nonami
Sakaura
MATSUE-JŌ
Shinji-Ko
Matsue
Yonago
JR West Rail Line
Tomari
TOTTORI SAND DUNES
Tottori
San'in
ADACHI MUSEUM OF ART
Kurayoshi
Tottori Prefecture
179
Kawabara
54
180
Anagamo
Ebi
Wakasa
Shimane Prefecture
Chizu
181
179
Mikamo
53
Kami-Iwami
180
183
Hyogo Prefecture
Tarumi
Tsuyama
Niimi
JR West Rail Line
Saijo
Okayama Prefecture
Tojo
53
Miyoshi
Fukuwatari
Kamigori
HONSHU
Takahashi
Hiroshima Prefecture
184
KŌRAKU-EN
Katakami
Ako
Soja
Okayama
Kozan
San'yo
Kurashiki
Saidaiji
E-Jima
Nishi-Jima
ONOMICHI TEMPLE WALK
HIROSHIMA AIRPORT
San'yo shinkansen line
Inujima
Fukuyama
SEE DETAILS
Tama
Teshima
Shōdo-shima
Mihara
Ajino
Naoshima
Onomichi
Kasaoka Islands
NAOSHIMA
Uchinomi
Takehara
Islands
Art
Setoda
Takamatsu
ŌMI-SHIMA
SHIMANAMI KAIDŌ
Sakaide
Kinoe
Marugame
SEE "ONOMICHI AND THE SHIMANAMI KAIDŌ" MAP
Munagata
HAKATA-JIMA
Oshima
Kagawa Prefecture
Hiketa
Minamiura
KURUSHIMA KAIKYŌ BRIDGE
JR Shikoku Rail Line
Imabari
Tokushima
Kawanoe
Sadamitsu
Kamojima
Ikeda
Saijo
Doi
Tokushima Prefecture
SHIKOKU
Ehime Prefecture
Kouchi Prefecture
Otaguchi
© MOON.COM

Regional Food Specialties

HIROSHIMA

- **Okonomiyaki:** Hiroshima is known for its own take on this savory pancake dish more commonly associated with Osaka; this one is topped with yaki-soba (fried soba) noodles and also contains fried egg. Try it at **Okonomiyaki Lopez** (page 410).
- **Oysters:** Hiroshima, Miyajima, and the surrounding seascape are also known for high-quality oysters. Try them at **Kakiya** (page 418).

THE INLAND SEA

The islands of the Inland Sea, with a sunny and mild climate, are renowned for their **citrus fruits**—particularly lemons and oranges—as well as **olives.** Unsurprisingly, the sea blesses the region with an abundance of freshly caught **fish** of all types. So look out for dishes featuring any of these ingredients.

- **Onomichi ramen:** This popular style of ramen is served in soup made with soy sauce, dashi (dried fish stock), and chicken, with the occasional addition of pork fat. Try it at **Onomichi Ramen Ichibankan** (page 423).

idyllic port town of **Onomichi,** roughly 70 kilometers (43.5 mi) west of Kurashiki. This is the starting point on the Honshu side of the series of bridges leading over the Inland Sea known as the **Shimanami Kaidō.** Another 90 kilometers (56 mi) west of Onomichi brings you to the city of **Hiroshima,** which is undoubtedly the region's urban nucleus. About 25 kilometers (15.5 mi) southwest of the city proper, the island of Itsukushima (aka **Miyajima**), famed for its "floating" torii gate of the idyllic seaside shrine of Itsukushima-jinja, lies just off the coast in the shimmering Inland Sea.

San'in
山陰

On the northern San'in coast, facing the Sea of Japan, the easternmost prefecture is **Tottori,** a sparsely populated prefecture best known for its dramatically undulating coastal sand dunes.

Lying to the west of Tottori is historically rich and spiritually charged **Shimane Prefecture.** Its prime center is the old castle town of **Matsue,** about 120 kilometers (74.6 mi) west of the sand dunes and capital city of Tottori. Another 35 kilometers (21.7 mi) west of there, the town of **Izumo** is home to Izumo Taisha, one of the holiest shrines in Shinto.

PLANNING YOUR TIME

Western Honshu is often the culmination of a trip that begins in Kanto or Kansai, starting in Tokyo, passing through Kyoto, and ending in Hiroshima and Miyajima. For a trip focused on **Hiroshima** and **Miyajima,** you'll just need a few days—one to two days in Hiroshima, visiting the Peace Memorial Park and Museum, and one day on Miyajima.

If you plan to spend more time in the region, on the San'yo side, aim to visit the atmospheric town of **Kurashiki** and Kōraku-en in **Okayama.** Tokyo, Kyoto, Osaka, Kurashiki, and Hiroshima are all conveniently connected via the shinkansen JR Tōkaidō- San'yo line. To visit any of the **Inland Sea's** idyllic islands, plan to add one to two days extra per island, depending on your itinerary. The same goes for cycling the **Shimanami Kaidō:** Add one to two days, depending on whether you plan to do a one-day return trip, stay overnight on one of the islands, or travel all the way across to Shikoku.

Note that navigating the San'in side with public transport takes a little extra

Best Accommodations

★ **Iwasō Ryokan:** This historic ryokan in Miyajima is surrounded by maple trees that become a kaleidoscope of color in fall (page 419).

★ **Ryokan Kurashiki:** With top-end meals and plush rooms, this old-school ryokan is the best place to stay in Kurashiki's atmospheric old town (page 428).

★ **Benesse House:** Sleep amid the works of world-famous artists at Naoshima's luxury museum-cum-hotel, which offers sweeping views of the Inland Sea (page 437).

★ **Minamikan:** Enjoy Matsue in style at this swank ryokan with a mix of traditional and modern rooms, many with lakeside views of Shinji-ko (page 447).

coordination and planning; tour this area in a rental car if possible, and prioritize **Matsue** for its castle and **Izumo** for its ancient Shinto Shrine.

San'yo is one of the sunniest parts of Japan; temperatures drop in winter (Dec.-Feb.) to as low as 2°C (36°F), but rarely dip below freezing. San'in has similar weather throughout most of the year, with the exception of winter, when snow covers the landscape and temperatures can fall to freezing. As with most parts of Japan, be sure to book accommodations well ahead for April-May or October-November, when cherry blossoms and fall foliage, respectively, add color to the landscape. Booking accommodations far in advance is good advice all year round on the Art Islands, which tend to book up fast.

Itinerary Ideas

TWO DAYS IN HIROSHIMA AND MIYAJIMA

Day One

1 Start your day in Hiroshima at **Peace Memorial Park.** Pay your respects at the memorials strewn throughout this serene place, viewing the sobering Atomic Bomb Dome, prayerfully ringing the Peace Bell, and giving the emotive displays of the Peace Memorial Museum your full attention. Take your time and let the gravity of the city's past sink in.

2 For lunch, return to Hiroshima's bustling present and make your way to nearby greasy spoon **Okkundo** for some comforting, tasty noodles, roughly 7 minutes' walk east across the Motoyasu River.

3 Fueled up, walk to nearby Chūden-mae tram stop (3 minutes' walk east). Ride the tram line (numbers 3 or 7) to Kamiyachō-nishi tram stop (7 minutes; ¥190), then walk 10 minutes north to **Hiroshima Castle.** Amble through the castle grounds and get close to the reconstructed keep for a photo.

4 From the castle grounds, walk 10 minutes east to **Shukkei-en.** Wander the winding paths and enjoy discovering the numerous views of this nicely shaped landscape

Hiroshima Itinerary Ideas

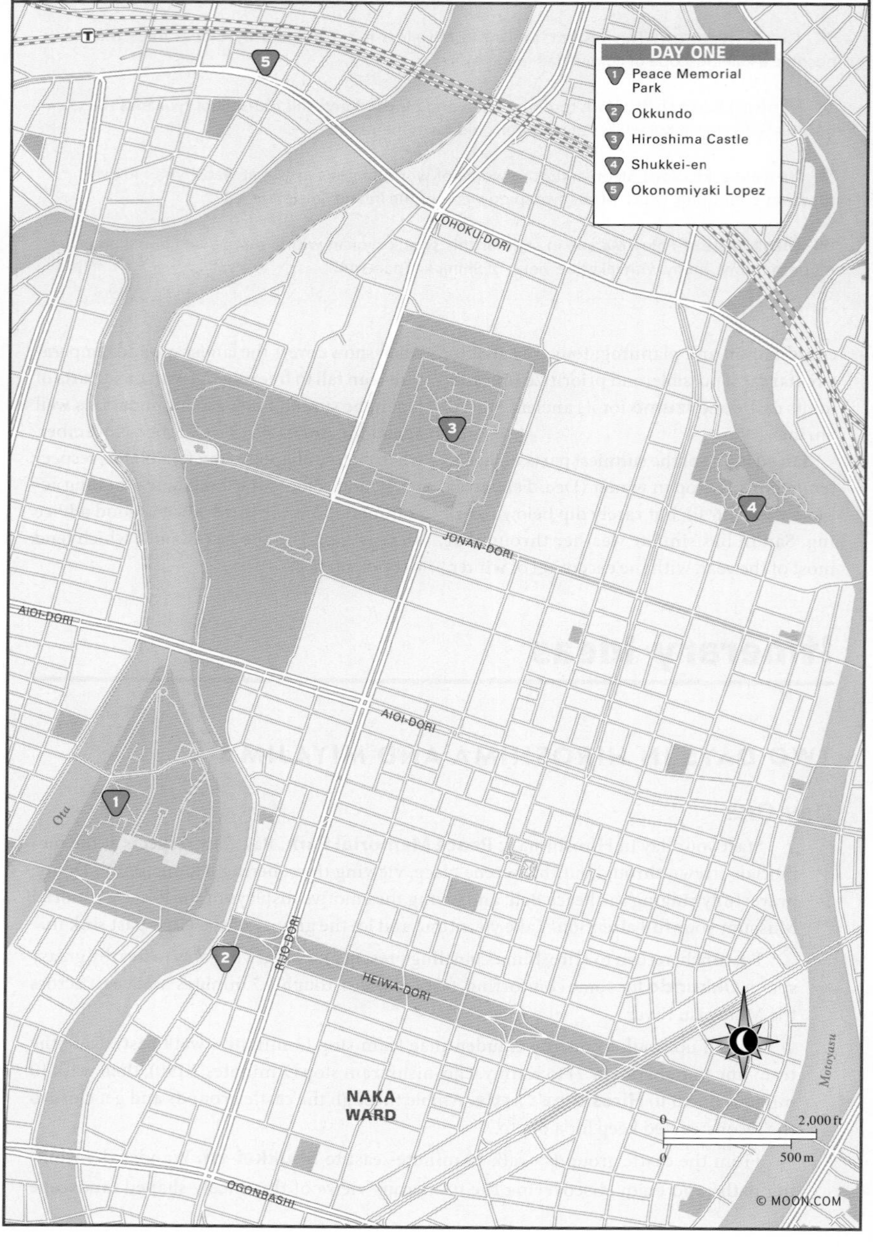

DAY ONE

1. Peace Memorial Park
2. Okkundo
3. Hiroshima Castle
4. Shukkei-en
5. Okonomiyaki Lopez

JOHOKU-DORI

JONAN-DORI

AIOI-DORI

AIOI-DORI

Ota

RIJO-DORI

HEIWA-DORI

Motoyasu

NAKA WARD

0 2,000 ft

0 500 m

OGONBASHI

Miyajima Itinerary Ideas

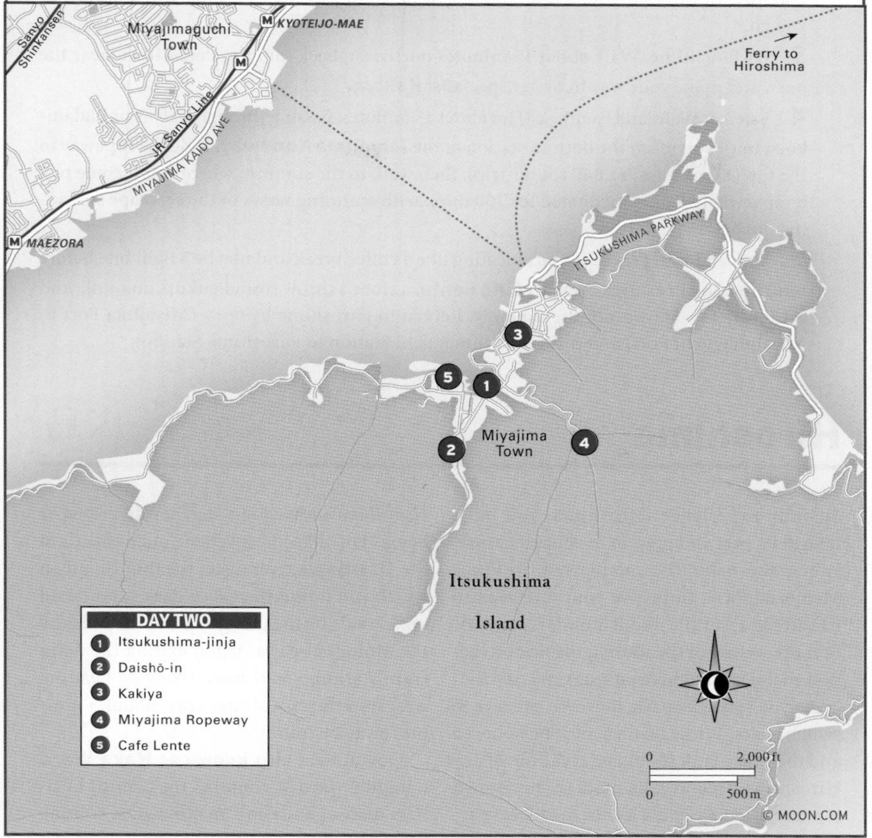

garden—nature in miniature—which incredibly sprang back to life soon after it was razed by the A-bomb.

5 Continue on foot to Hiroshima Station, 6 minutes to the east. Take the JR Kabe line to Yokogawa Station (5 minutes; ¥150). Walk 7 minutes east to **Okonomiyaki Lopez.** This unlikely institution, run by a Guatemalan chef and his Japanese wife, serves fantastic okonomiyaki, Hiroshima-style, complemented by a nice range of Latin-American appetizers.

Day Two

1 Strike out for the sacred isle of Miyajima in the morning. Alighting on the hallowed island, make your way on foot down the shore, passing deer and large stone lanterns as you go, for about 10 minutes to **Itsukushima-jinja.** Although the iconic "floating" shrine gate is currently wrapped in scaffolding for maintenance work, the seaside shrine is still a bewitching place.

2 Miyajima contains other holy sites beyond Itsukushima-jinja. To discover one that many visitors miss, walk inland (south) and uphill for about 10 minutes until you reach **Daishō-in.** Climb the stone staircase that leads to the temple, spinning prayer wheels as you go.

3 It's lunchtime. Walk about 15 minutes northeast, back into the sleepy town near the port, and make your way to oyster specialist **Kakiya.**

4 Sated, walk inland (southeast) for about 15 minutes, passing through leafy Momijidani-kōen until you reach the bottom station of the **Miyajima Ropeway.** Ride the ropeway to the top (15 minutes; ¥1,840 round-trip), then walk to the summit, where you'll come to a temple where Kūkai meditated for 100 days, with stunning views of the seascape spreading out below.

5 Descend to sea level. If you're feeling like a coffee break and maybe a light bite before returning to Hiroshima, head to **Cafe Lente,** a stone's throw from Itsukushima-jinja and a 15-minute walk west of the ropeway. Return to Hiroshima by ferry (Miyajima Port to Miyajimaguchi Port) and train (Miyajimaguchi Station to Hiroshima Station).

Hiroshima 広島

To fully experience Hiroshima, you must take in its past and present in equal measure. When you make the somber trip to Peace Memorial Park, fully give your attention to its call for a world without atomic weaponry. Feel the weight of the unimaginable destruction that occurred here on August 6, 1945.

As you leave the park, however, prepare to switch gears. While history must be honored and the Peace Park should be at the top of any Hiroshima itinerary, its modern downtown is a revelation. Friendly locals, broad leafy avenues, a buzzing restaurant scene, and lively nightlife beckon you to enjoy the city as it lives and breathes today. Some of Hiroshima's sights have also been rebuilt, including its castle and the Shukkei-en landscape garden.

To properly take all this in, avoid treating Hiroshima like a whistle-stop. Instead, plan to stay for a night. Few cities in the world offer such a poignant message on the human ability to overcome tragedy and bring about rebirth.

ORIENTATION

Hiroshima is relatively compact, with almost everything you'll be seeking just west of **Hiroshima Station.** The city, which *Hiroshima* author John Hershey described as being "fan-shaped," covers six main islands in the **Ōta-gawa** river delta; the thin island on which you'll find the Peace Park is bordered on one side by the Ōta-gawa and the other by the Motoyasu-gawa. Upon exiting the main train station, you'll most likely be heading west into the city's inner core, about 5 minutes away by tram.

Downtown, also known as **Naka Ward** ("middle ward"), contains the central business district and most major sights. Among them, the garden of **Shukkei-en** lies about 7 minutes' walk west of Hiroshima Station, with **Hiroshima Castle** situated another 10 minutes farther west. **Peace Memorial Park** is about 20 minutes' walk southwest of the castle. The bulk of the city's best restaurants, accommodations, and nightlife also lie within this area. North and west of downtown lies **Nishi-ku** ("west ward"), while **Minami-ku** ("south ward") encompasses the area south and southeast of Hiroshima Station, and includes the **Mazda Zoom Zoom Stadium.**

The city's main thoroughfare is **Hon-dōri,**

1: Itsukushima-jinja **2:** seafood meal

1

2

Hiroshima

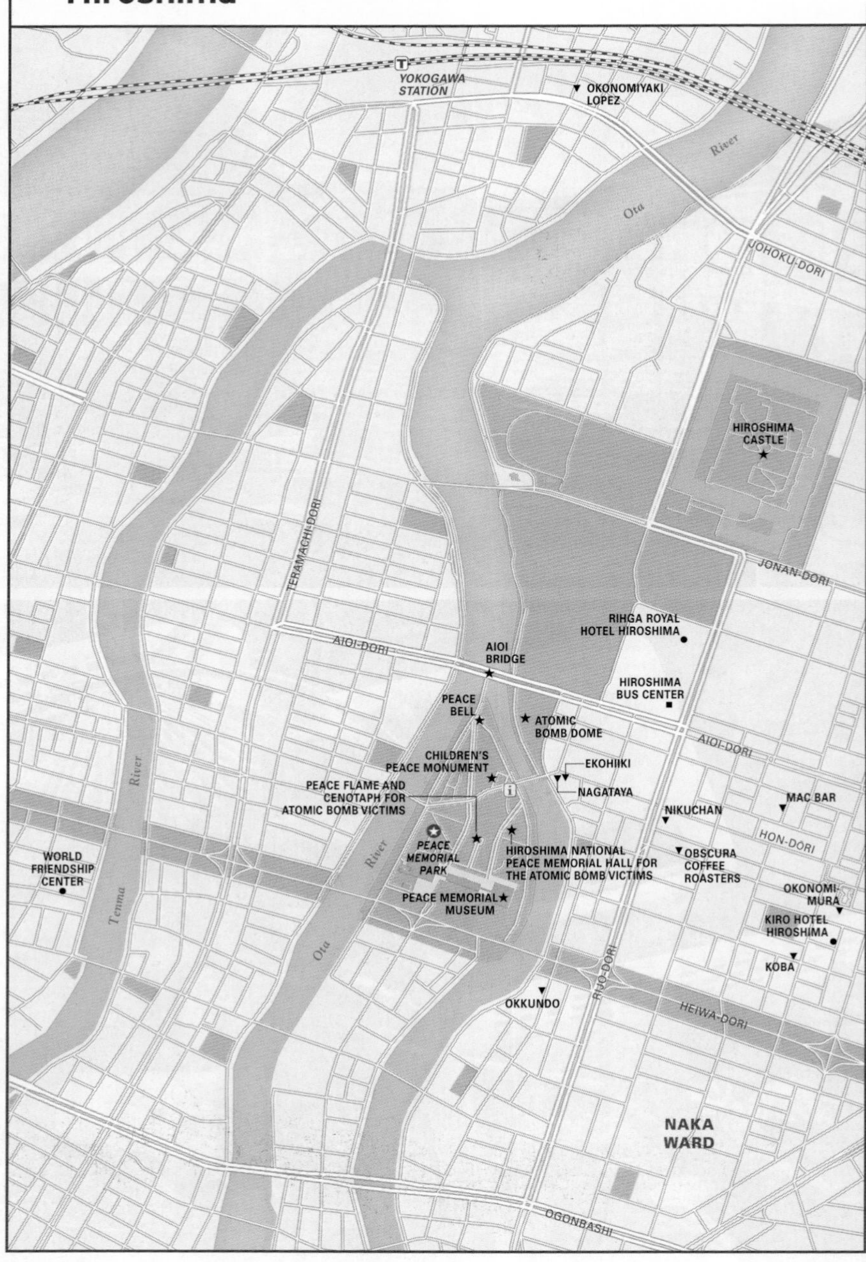
YOKOGAWA STATION
OKONOMIYAKI LOPEZ
Ota River
JOHOKU-DORI
HIROSHIMA CASTLE
TERAMACHI-DORI
JONAN-DORI
RIHGA ROYAL HOTEL HIROSHIMA
AIOI-DORI
AIOI BRIDGE
HIROSHIMA BUS CENTER
PEACE BELL
ATOMIC BOMB DOME
AIOI-DORI
CHILDREN'S PEACE MONUMENT
EKOHIIKI
NAGATAYA
PEACE FLAME AND CENOTAPH FOR ATOMIC BOMB VICTIMS
MAC BAR
NIKUCHAN
HON-DORI
Tenma River
Ota River
PEACE MEMORIAL PARK
HIROSHIMA NATIONAL PEACE MEMORIAL HALL FOR THE ATOMIC BOMB VICTIMS
OBSCURA COFFEE ROASTERS
WORLD FRIENDSHIP CENTER
PEACE MEMORIAL MUSEUM
OKONOMI-MURA
KIRO HOTEL HIROSHIMA
KOBA
RIJO-DORI
OKKUNDO
HEIWA-DORI
NAKA WARD
OGONBASHI

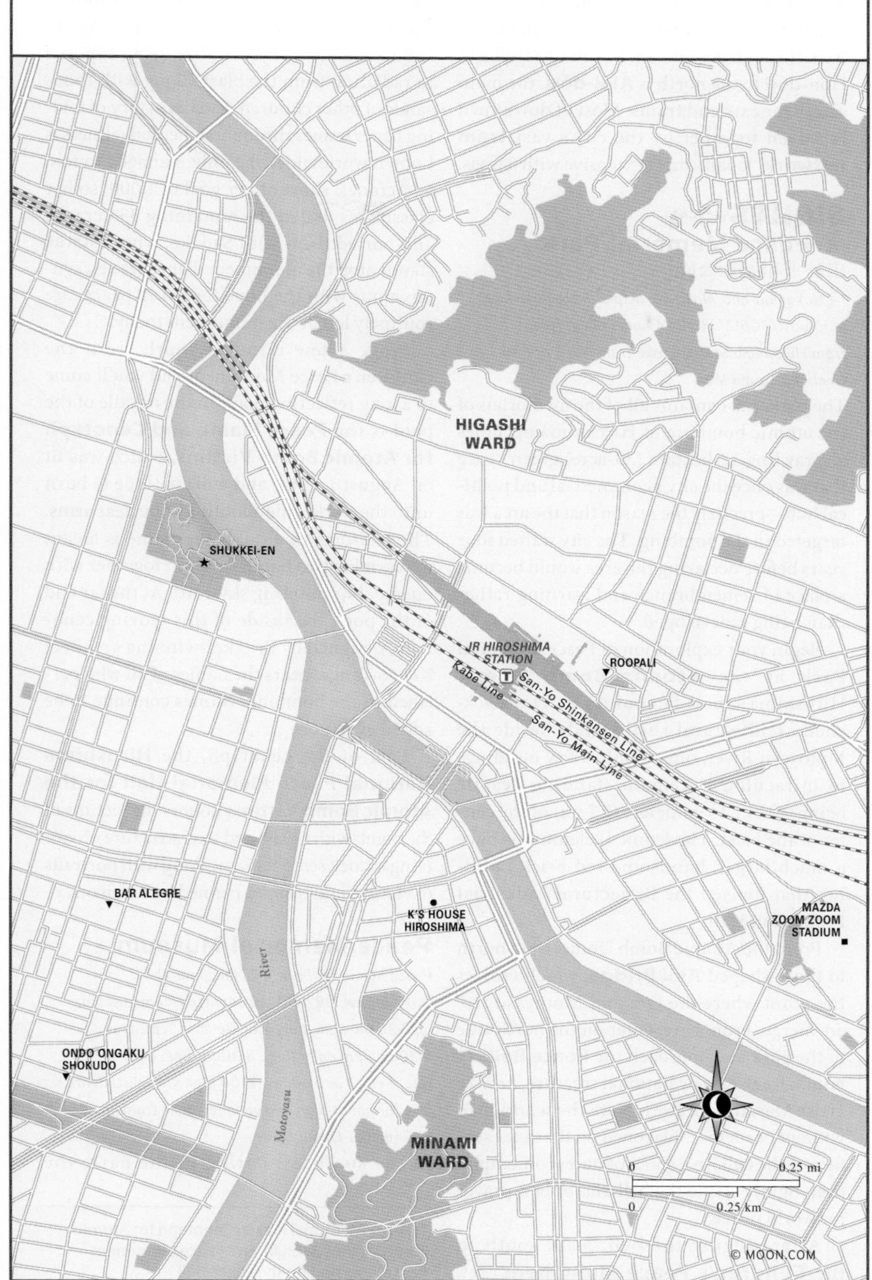

HIGASHI WARD
SHUKKEI-EN
JR HIROSHIMA STATION
ROOPALI
Kabe Line
San-Yo Shinkansen Line
San-Yo Main Line
BAR ALEGRE
K'S HOUSE HIROSHIMA
MAZDA ZOOM ZOOM STADIUM
Motoyasu River
ONDO ONGAKU SHOKUDO
MINAMI WARD
0
0.25 mi
0
0.25 km
© MOON.COM

a covered pedestrian arcade that runs 0.6 kilometers (0.4 mi) east from Peace Memorial Park through downtown. Running parallel to Hon-dōri to the north is **Aioi-dōri,** the main artery for cars and trams. Most of downtown is woven together by the city's vast **tram network,** Japan's most extensive with 8 lines.

SIGHTS

★ Peace Memorial Park
広島平和記念公園

1-1 Nakajima-chō, Naka-ku; https://hiroshima-navi.or.jp/post/006127.html; 24 hours daily; free; from Hiroshima Station, take tram line 2 or 6 to Genbaku-Domu Mae

The park that contains all of the memorials of the atomic bombing of Hiroshima occupies a sprawling 12-hectare (30-acre) green space that was once the city's commercial and political hub—precisely the reason that the area was targeted in the bombing. The city waited four years before declaring the area would become a place of remembrance and learning rather than being redeveloped.

Begin your exploration of Peace Memorial Park at the **Atomic Bomb Dome,** Hiroshima's most famous sight. The blackened architectural shell stands beside the Motoyasu River, one of only a few buildings to miraculously remain standing despite being within 2 kilometers (1.2 mi) of the center of the blast. The iconic skeleton was once a much larger, handsome red-brick building that housed the Prefectural Industrial Promotion Hall.

From the Atomic Bomb Dome, walk north to the T-shaped **Aioi Bridge,** which crosses the point where the Ōta and Motoyasu rivers merge. From here, enter on the north side of the park and approach the **Peace Bell** (24 hours; free), cast by national treasure, bronze artist Masahiko Katori. Note the world map without borders emblazoned on the outer surface of the bell. In a spirit of quiet contemplation, lightly strike the bell and offer a prayer for world peace.

After ringing the bell, walk south to the **Children's Peace Monument** (tel. 082/242-7831; 24 hours; free) dedicated to Sadako Sasaki, a young girl who died at age 12 from leukemia, 10 years after being exposed to radiation from the blast, along with thousands of other children. Sadako's story of folding paper cranes throughout her long illness is known worldwide. She only managed to fold 644 cranes, short of her goal of 1,000, so her classmates folded the remaining 356 cranes and buried them with Sadako, whose statue stands atop the monument. Paper cranes, synonymous with the hope for world peace, are routinely left at the monument today.

Walk a few minutes south from the Children's Peace Monument and you'll come to a long reflecting pool. In the middle of the pool is the **Peace Flame and Cenotaph for Atomic Bomb Victims,** which was lit on August 1, 1964, and will continue to burn until the worldwide abolition of nuclear arms. The platform that holds the flame is meant to resemble two hands brought together with open palms pointing skyward. At the far end of the pool, the inside of this moving cenotaph, designed by Pritzker-winning architect Kenzo Tange, bears the names of all who perished in the bombing. Names continue to be added even now.

East of the cenotaph, the **Hiroshima National Peace Memorial Hall for the Atomic Bomb Victims** honors the victims of the bomb with a glass and steel structure resembling a clock set to 8:15am, along with portraits of victims and tributes penned by survivors.

Peace Memorial Museum

Peace Memorial Park, 1-2 Nakajima-chō, Naka-ku; tel. 082/241-4004; http://hpmmuseum.jp; 8:30am-6pm daily Mar.-Jul and Sept.-Nov., 8:30am-7pm daily Aug., 8:30am-5pm daily Dec.-Feb.; ¥200 adults, ¥100 high school students, free for junior high and younger; take tram line 2 or 6 to Genbaku-Domu Mae

In the southeast corner of the park, the

1: Peace Memorial Park **2:** Cenotaph for Atomic Bomb Victims **3:** Children's Peace Monument **4:** students ringing the Peace Bell

1

2

3

4

August 6, 1945

At 8:15am on the fateful day of August 6, 1945, the skies were clear. Just as Hiroshima was waking up, a rotund capsule named *Little Boy* was dropped over the city by a U.S. bomber plane called the *Enola Gay*. The bombers aimed for the T-shaped Aioi Bridge, which crosses the Ōta and Motoyasu rivers. This bridge—rebuilt and now bustling with traffic—stands just north of the Atomic Bomb Dome in Peace Memorial Park, near the hypocenter of the blast. In an instant, a blinding, incinerating flash consumed the sky and half the city was flattened. The other half soon went up in flames.

THE IMPACT

Thousands upon thousands died in an instant, while thousands of brutally charred victims sought relief by throwing themselves into the Motoyasu River, swelling the waterway with corpses. Those who survived the first wave of horrors would soon contend with lethal drops of "black rain," pregnant with radioactive fallout. All told, some 140,000 died in the world's first nuclear bomb attack.

WHY WAS HIROSHIMA TARGETED?

Hiroshima had the unfortunate distinction of being an ideal target for the bomb. For starters, the U.S. military sought a city with a downtown core that measured more than 4.5 kilometers (3 mi) around. Hiroshima was on a short list that also included Niigata, Kokura, and Nagasaki. Hiroshima's grim fate was sealed partly due to the fact that U.S. forces did not think any American prisoners of war were being kept in the city.

COMMEMORATING THE BOMBING

On each anniversary of the city's decimation, around 50,000 people fill Peace Memorial Park. Alongside locals and travelers, foreign dignitaries and ambassadors amass to hear speeches and pleas for world peace. The day's proceedings begin at 8:15am, when temple bells chime, sirens wail, and all citizens observe a somber moment of silence to honor those who perished in the blast and its aftermath. In the evening, 10,000 floating lanterns are released onto the Motoyasu River. Seeing myriad floating lights, gently flowing past the Atomic Bomb Dome, is an undeniably haunting, ethereal sight.

Peace Memorial Museum opened in 1955. It powerfully communicates the horrors of atomic weaponry and makes a compelling case for a world without nuclear arms. Exhibits explain the events that led to the horrific bombing and display documentation, photographs, and personal effects that belonged to the victims. Some of the images are graphic, such as those showing the burns suffered by the people on the ground. Be prepared for an affecting, emotional experience.

Hiroshima Castle
広島城

21-1 Motomachi, Naka-ku; tel. 082/221-7512; www.rijo-castle.jp; 9am-6pm (last entry 5:30pm) daily Mar.-Nov., 9am-5pm (last entry 4:30pm) daily Dec.-Feb.; grounds free, main keep ¥370 adults, ¥180 high school students, free for junior high school students and younger; take tram lines 1, 2, or 6 to Kamiyachō-nishi or Kamiya-chō-higashi

"Carp Castle," as it's popularly known, was originally built in 1589 by the powerful feudal lord Mori Terumoto. It's located smack in the middle of town, rather than looming on a hill, hinting at its pragmatic function as an economic and political center. Although the castle was only partly dismantled when a number of fortresses around the country were completely taken down following the Meiji Restoration of 1868, what remained was sadly blown to smithereens by the atomic bomb. A concrete reproduction was built in 1958, with an exterior partly made of wood, along with a few structures of the ninomaru (second circle of defense).

Entering from either the south or east, on the grounds you'll find a smattering of ruins and a shrine where romantic hopefuls pray for luck in love. Inside the five-story keep, there are displays (with limited English) outlining the history of the castle and the city, and on Japanese castles more broadly. At minimum, meander through the leafy grounds and take a quick look at the castle's handsome wooden exterior for free if you're already in the area (say, walking from the Peace Park to the garden of Shukkei-en). You can pass on paying to see its sterile, modern interior, unless you're keen to glimpse the vistas from the top. Thanks to its downtown location, the views of the castle's impressive moat, bridges, and the cityscape below are worth the charge of admission.

The castle's nickname was inspired by the old name for the region, Koi-no-ura ("Carp Sea Shore"). Naturally, a multitude of colorful koi now swims in the moat around the castle. And the hometown baseball club is known as the Hiroshima Carp.

Shukkei-en
縮景園

2-11 Kaminoborichō, Naka-ku; tel. 082/221-3620; http://shukkeien.jp; 9am-6pm daily Apr.-Sept., 9am-5pm daily Oct.-Mar.; ¥260 adults, ¥150 high school students, ¥100 junior high and elementary school students; from Hiroshima Station, take tram line 9 to Shukkeien-mae stop, or walk 8 minutes northwest to the garden from JR Hiroshima Station or 10 minutes east to the garden from Hiroshima castle

Shukkei-en roughly translates to "contracted view garden," and it lives up to its name, emulating peaks, woodlands, islands, and valleys in miniature form. Paths wind through these natural scenes with ease, just as Lord Asano Nagaakira had in mind when he appointed tea master Ueda Soko to create a green escape for him in 1620. The garden was all but flattened in 1945, but some vegetation miraculously flourished the year after the bombing, and the natural space was eventually revived. Today, its striking layout, with a variety of alluring footpaths, plum and cherry blossoms, teahouses, and island-studded pond, make it one of the city's loveliest spots.

ENTERTAINMENT AND EVENTS

Festivals and Events

TŌKASAN YUKATA FESTIVAL
とうかさん大祭

Chūō-dōri and around; www.toukasan.jp; noon-11pm for three days starting first Fri. of June; free

The streets of downtown fill with denizens in yukata (lightweight cotton kimonos) during this lively annual festival. Expect to see yatai (street food stalls), carnival-type games, dancing, beating on taiko drums, and more.

PEACE MEMORIAL AND PEACE MESSAGE LANTERN FLOATING CEREMONIES

Peace Memorial Park; www.city.hiroshima.lg.jp/site/english/115509.html; 8am-9am and 6pm-9pm Aug. 6; free

On the morning of August 6, officials give speeches imploring for world peace, the Peace Bell and temple bells are rung, sirens are sounded, and one minute of silence is observed out of respect for those who died at 8:15am in 1945. Seating begins at 6:30am. Arrive *early* if you want to get a spot. In the evening, a more casual, visually moving tribute is paid when people release lanterns into the Motoyasu River to console the souls of the victims of the bombing. Make your way to the river at dusk to witness this poignant sight.

Baseball

MAZDA ZOOM ZOOM STADIUM

2-3-1 Minami-Kaniya, Minami-ku; tel. 082/568-2777; www.mazdastadium.jp; from JR Hiroshima Station, walk 12 minutes southeast

They may not have the same clout nationally as Tokyo's Yomiuri Giants or Kansai's Hanshin Tigers, but Hiroshima's hometown baseball team, the Carp, have a fierce following. Visit www.japanball.com to see the schedule in English, and inquire at one of the tourist information centers in JR Hiroshima

Station about getting **tickets,** which start from around ¥2,000.

FOOD

Okonomiyaki

★ OKONOMIYAKI LOPEZ

1-7-13 Kusunoki-chō, Nishi-ku; tel. 082/232-5277; 11:30am-2pm Tues. and Fri., 4:30pm-11pm Mon.-Fri.; from ¥650; take JR San'yo line to Yokogawa Station

This okonomiyaki institution is run by Guatemalan-born chef Fernando Lopez and his Japanese wife Makiko. Lopez has lived here for more than two decades and learned from okonomiyaki maestro Ogawa Hiroki. The friendly husband-wife team engage in lighthearted conversation while adroitly flipping okonomiyaki that's among the best in the city. Portions are generous.

OKONOMI-MURA

2F-4F, 5-13 Shintenchi, Naka-ku; tel. 082/241-2210; www.okonomimura.jp; 11am-2am daily; from ¥800-1,300; take tram lines 1, 2, or 6 to the Ebisu-chō tram stop

It's firmly on the tourist track, but this is a great place to enter the world of okonomiyaki. Some 25 stalls serve up the city's signature dish in this cramped, boisterous "Okonomiyaki Village" spread across the second through fourth floors of the building. This place hops late at night, but it's good any time of day. Among the glut of purveyors, **Hasshō** on the second floor stands out.

NAGATAYA

Shigeishi Bldg. 1F, 1-7-19 Ōtemachi, Naka-ku; tel. 082/247-0787; http://nagataya-okonomi.com; 11am-8:30pm Wed.-Mon., closed second and fourth Wed. every month; ¥750-1,500; take Astram line or tram line 1, 3, or 7 to Hon-dōri tram stop

This spacious okonomiyaki spot with nostalgic atmosphere sits right beside Peace Memorial Park, making it a great place to try this dish after a visit to the park. Toppings range from garlic and oysters to squid and vegetarian. Seating includes both a countertop with grill-side views and booths. All tabletops have inbuilt griddles to keep your food piping hot. Be aware that queues do form at peak times. Aim to eat a late lunch or early dinner to avoid the rush.

Oysters

EKOHIIKI

1-7-20 Ōtemachi, Naka-ku; tel. 082/545-3655; http://ekohiiki.com; 11:30am-2pm and 5pm-11pm Tues.-Sun.; plates from ¥480-3,300, set meals ¥1,000-3,300; take Astram line or tram line 1, 3, or 7 to Hon-dōri tram stop

This restaurant just east of Peace Memorial Park is a great place to sample the city's famed oysters. The consistently plump, juicy oysters are prepared any way you like: raw, grilled, deep-fried, and more. There's also a good range of side dishes, from chicken wings to sashimi, and a diverse alcohol selection, too. Service is friendly, and there's a good English-language menu.

Noodles

OKKUNDO

Sansan Bldg. 3-3-3 Ōtemachi, Naka-ku; tel. 082/246-1377; www.powerland.co.jp; 11am-11pm daily; ¥520-1,060; take tram line 1, 3, or 7 to Chūden-mae tram stop

Serving up generous helpings of mazemen—flavorful noodles mixed with a light sauce topped with soft-boiled egg, leek, roast pork, and more—this shop is a good option if you've had your fill of okonomiyaki and seafood. There's also a good side menu of items like gyoza (fried dumplings) and onion rings, too. It feels like a hole in the wall, but the service is friendly.

International

ROOPALI

14-32 Wakakusa-chō, Higashi-ku; tel. 082/264-1333; www.roopali.jp; 11am-2:30pm and 5pm-9:30pm daily; lunch ¥720-1,300, dinner a la carte ¥1,200-2,000, set meals ¥1,880-3,500; 6 minutes' walk east of JR Hiroshima Station's north exit

A meal at this Indian restaurant is a good way to spice things up. The menu includes a nice range of curries, and its lunch sets are very good value. Its bright decor and sign bearing

☆ Okonomiyaki in Hiroshima

There's a rivalry between Osaka and Hiroshima over which city whips up the best okonomiyaki. The name of this hearty dish, which roughly translates to "how you like it cooked," is apt. This pancake-like concoction became famous throughout Japan after World War II, when various ingredients were in short supply. Creative chefs had to "use their noodle" to make something tasty with whatever was at hand, and okonomiyaki was born.

okonomiyaki, Hiroshima style

OSAKA- VS. HIROSHIMA-STYLE

Osaka chefs start with a filling, doughy batter, with grated Japanese yam and shredded cabbage, which is poured directly onto a griddle. Various toppings (pork, shrimp, seafood, kimchi, and so on) are then added, and a healthy slathering of sweet and savory sauce, mayonnaise, powderized seaweed, and bonito flakes are then spread across the top. By contrast, chefs in Hiroshima add each ingredient in a distinct layer, starting with the batter, composed of wheat or Japanese yam; then adding noodles, a distinctly-Hiroshima item; followed by various toppings (cabbage, tempura scraps, pork, seafood, green onions, bean sprouts, egg, and more). The thing is then repeatedly flipped, until the final, noodle-infused pancake, topped by the obligatory sweet-savory sauce, mayonnaise, and bonito flakes, lands on your plate.

WHERE TO TRY IT

Although Osaka claims to be the birthplace of the dish, some say that making it Hiroshima-style requires more skill. This means fewer self-service okonomiyaki joints in the city, compared to Osaka, where they are common. Still, all told, Hiroshima is said to have more than 2,000 purveyors of the flavorsome comfort food.

- A fun, albeit somewhat touristy, place to try the dish is at **Okonomi-mura,** where okonomiyaki shops cover three floors (page 410).
- For good okonomiyaki near Hiroshima Peace Park, head for the well-loved **Nagataya** (page 410).
- For a truly unique spin, **Okonomiyaki Lopez** is run by a kind Guatemalan chef who was trained by a local okonomiyaki wizard (page 410).

the visages of Krishna and Ganesh make it easy to spot.

Cafés

OBSCURA COFFEE ROASTERS

3-28 Fukuro-machi, Naka-ku; tel. 082/249-7543; https://obscura-coffee.com; 9am-8pm daily; ¥290-570; take the Astram line or tram line 1, 3, or 7 to Hon-dōri tram stop

Originally launched in Tokyo, this café chain was founded by three coffee lovers from Hiroshima. For a quick pick-me-up or pastry, this artisanal café is a great bet. The minimalist interior is offset by rugs and wooden furniture. If you're seeking a calm break, it fits the bill nicely, but might not be the place to go with young kids. Note that there's a 45-minute limit for sitting at the café.

BARS AND NIGHTLIFE

While not as raucous as, say, Tokyo or Osaka, Hiroshima does have a nice buzz when the sun goes down. Don't expect mind-blowing spectacles or to party until sunrise, but on a good night you'll likely find yourself making some new friends and might be surprised by how late you stay out. Most of the action is concentrated around the **Nagarekawa** area in Naka Ward, just east of Chūō-dōri and north of Heiwa Ōdōri (Peace Boulevard), but bleeds into the area west of Chūō-dōri and beyond. For more extensive listings, check out the nightlife section of expat-run website **Get Hiroshima** (https://gethiroshima.com/category/nightlife/bars/).

MAC BAR

Borabora Bldg. 3F, 3-4 Tatemachi, Naka-ku; tel. 082/243-0343; www.facebook.com/pages/Mac-Bar/845730498970349; 6pm-late daily; take tram lines 1, 2, 6, or 9 to Tatemachi tram stop

If you like classic rock and want a mellow evening out with a 40s-and-up crowd, this is your place. Tucked away in a nondescript building, this is the third incarnation of this local institution, which has been in business for more than four decades. With its remarkable CD collection and solid sound system, it's a laid-back spot for a drink.

BAR ALEGRE

Cony Bldg. 3F, 1-32 Horikawa-chō, Naka-ku; tel. 082/545-5295; www.facebook.com/alegre.hiroshima; 7pm-2am Mon.-Sat.; ¥500 cover charge; take trams 1, 2, or 6 to Ebisu-chō tram stop

The talented mixologists at this cozy bar make serious craft cocktails. The bar is well-stocked and the atmosphere evokes a speakeasy. It's a great place to go if you want something sophisticated but not fussy.

KOBA

Rego Bldg. 3F, 1-4 Naka-machi, Naka-ku; tel. 082/249-6556; www.facebook.com/Koba-211406912214710; 6pm-2am Thurs.-Tues.; take trams 1, 3, 7 to Fukuromachi tram stop

This heavy-metal bar's affable owner Bom-san makes instant friends with his customers (currency notes from around the world dangling above the bar attest to just how many friends he's made). The soundtrack leans heavy, with occasional live performances. The drinks are good and reasonably priced, and Bom-san is handy in the kitchen, too. The bar is a little tricky to find: Walk down the corridor next to the Stussy shop (1F Diamond Namiki Bldg., 1–3 Naka-machi, Naka-ku), then walk upstairs.

ONDO ONGAKU SHOKUDO

Ondo Onsen Bldg. B1, 6-3 Tanaka-machi, Naka-ku; tel. 082/245-9563; www.ongakushokudoondo.com; 6pm-3am daily; take trams 1, 2, 6 to Ebisu-chō tram stop

This cozy basement-level music bar and restaurant is tucked beneath a public bath, Ondo Onsen, on the south side of Hiroshima's sprawling Nagarekawa nightlife zone. Alongside a serious sound system—Ongaku means "music"—the owners whip up good home-cooked fare—Shokudo means "canteen." There's a respectable collection of vinyl behind the bar, extending to reggae, jazz, and soul, and the bar hosts occasional live shows on weekends. A relaxed spot to mingle with a crowd who is friendly yet in-the-know.

ACCOMMODATIONS

Given that most of Hiroshima's points of interest are centrally located, the heart of downtown (Naka-ku) is the most convenient place to base yourself.

Under ¥10,000

K'S HOUSE HIROSHIMA

1-8-9 Matoba-chō, Minami-ku; tel. 082/568-7244; https://kshouse.jp; dorms from ¥2,600, double with en-suite bath from ¥3,950; take tram line 1, 2, 5, or 6 to the Matobachō tram stop

Located an 8-minute walk southwest of Hiroshima Station, this hostel has mixed dorm rooms, private tatami rooms, and rooms for two. All rooms share a bathroom, lounge, kitchen, and laundry facilities. This is a good place to meet fellow travelers and exchange tips, and it's an affordable, convenient home base.

¥10,000-20,000

KIRO HOTEL HIROSHIMA

3-21 Mikawa-chō, Naka-ku; tel. 082/545-9160; www.thesharehotels.com/kiro; from ¥12,000 d; take tram lines 1, 2, 6, 9 to Hatchobori tram stop

This stylish new hotel in the heart of the action, yet tucked down a side street, is a great mid-range choice. It offers a bit more space than most hotels at a similar price point. There's an on-site restaurant, a shared kitchen and lounge, and free Wi-Fi throughout. The design sense is simple and modern, and the staff are friendly, young, and hip. Compared to many petite "unit baths," the separated toilet-bath-style bathrooms are well-stocked and large. Great bang for your buck in a very convenient location.

RIHGA ROYAL HOTEL HIROSHIMA

6-78 Motomachi, Naka-ku; tel. 082/502-1121; www.rihga.co.jp/hiroshima; ¥15,000 d; take Astram line to Kencho-mae Station

The rooms at this classy hotel are spacious, and many boast fantastic views. It's conveniently located between the castle to the north and Peace Park to the south, and the friendly concierge is happy to assist with restaurant bookings and more. There's an on-site restaurant, a rooftop bar, an indoor pool, a fitness center, laundry services on offer, and more, making this a recommended upper-mid-range pick.

INFORMATION AND SERVICES

Tourist Information

For information online, from restaurant and nightlife listings to transportation breakdowns, check out the helpful websites **Visit Hiroshima** (http://visithiroshima.net) and **Hiroshima Navi** (www.hiroshima-navi.or.jp). It's possible to use free Wi-Fi in 30-minute blocks of time for an unlimited period of time anywhere a "Hiroshima Free Wi-Fi" sticker is placed. You must first register with either your email address or a social media account. These Wi-Fi points are typically found at major tourist spots. For more information, visit www.hiroshima-navi.or.jp/en/information/service/wifi/.

- **Hiroshima Station Tourist Information Centers** (three locations: one next to the ticket gate for shinkansen bullet train arrivals and departures at the north side of the station, one next to the north exit, and one next to the south exit; tel. 082/263-5120; 6am-midnight daily)
- **Hiroshima Peace Memorial Park Rest House** (1-1 Nakajima-machi, Naka-ku; tel. 082/247-6738; www.hiroshima-resthouse.jp; 8:30am-7pm daily Aug., 8:30am-6pm daily Mar.-July and Sept.-Nov., 8:30am-5pm daily Dec.-Feb.; on the northeast side of Peace Memorial Park beside the Motoyasu-bashi bridge)

Postal Services

- **Hiroshima Central Post Office** (1-4-1 Kokutaiji-machi, Naka-ku; tel. 0570/004-356; 9am-7pm Mon.-Fri., 9am-5pm Sat., 9am-12:30pm Sun. and public holidays)

GETTING THERE

Train

On the east side of downtown, **Hiroshima Station** is served by the shinkansen, running to and from **Tokyo** (Nozomi shinkansen 4 hours, ¥19,440; Hikari shinkansen 5 hours 15 minutes, ¥18,910), **Shin-Osaka** (Sakura shinkansen 1.5 hours, ¥10,420), and **Kyoto** (Nozomi shinkansen 1 hour 40 minutes, ¥11,620; Hikari shinkansen with transfer to Sakura Shinkansen at Shin-Kobe Station 2 hours 5 minutes, ¥11,300) in the east, and **Fukuoka** (Hakata Station; Nozomi shinkansen 1 hour, ¥9,310; Sakura shinkansen 1 hour 5 minutes, ¥9,100) in the west. Local trains on the JR San'yo line also stop at the station, with the train route beginning from Himeji in the east and heading westward to Honshu's far western fringe.

Air

Both international and domestic flights serve **Hiroshima Airport** (tel. 0848/86-8151;

www.hij.airport.jp), about 45 kilometers (28 mi) east of downtown. Overseas routes include Dalian and Shanghai in China, as well as Hong Kong, Taipei, and Seoul; while domestic links include Okinawa (1 hour 45 minutes; ¥20,000) and Sendai (1 hour 45 minutes; ¥20,000). **Shuttle buses** connect the airport to Hiroshima Station (50 minutes; 8:20am-9:40pm from the airport to downtown, 6am-7:20pm from Hiroshima Station to airport; ¥1,370). If you've got a JR rail pass, it will most likely prove more effective to travel to Hiroshima by train, unless you're coming from overseas or somewhere particularly far-flung within Japan, such as Okinawa.

Bus

Hiroshima is well-connected by highways, with buses heading to the city from around Japan. Some buses use **Hiroshima Bus Center** (6-27 Motomachi, Naka-ku; www.h-buscenter.com), accessed via the third floor of the Sogō Department Store in the heart of downtown. One-way trips between Tokyo and Hiroshima range from ¥6,000-13,000 depending on timing and the type (read: comfort level) of a given bus (about 13 hours). Buses also run between Kyoto and Hiroshima (7 hours; ¥3,200-4,200). **Willer Express** (https://willerexpress.com/en) is a good provider. Search for tickets at **Japan Bus Online** (https://japanbusonline.com/en).

Ferry

High-speed boats to Miyajima (30 minutes; ¥1,900) are run by **Setonaikai Kisen Ferry** (tel. 082/253-1212; www.setonaikaikisen.co.jp) and arrive at and depart from **Hiroshima Port Ujina Passenger Terminal** (1-13-26 Ujinakaigan, Minami-ku; tel. 082/253-6907), which is located south of downtown and accessible by Ujina-bound tram lines 1, 3, and 5 (all ¥190). You can also take a ferry operated by **Aqua Net Ferry** (tel. 082/240-5955; www.aqua-net-h.co.jp; 8:30am-5:10pm daily) straight to and from a terminal on the other side of the Ōta River from Peace Memorial Park (45 minutes; ¥2,200 one-way, ¥4,000 return).

GETTING AROUND

Hiroshima's scale makes it ideal to explore **on foot.** That said, some sights are just far enough that you may want to hop on the city's efficient tram network or avail yourself of a tour bus.

Tram

Hiroshima is well-served by the handy **Hiroden tram network** (www.hiroden.co.jp; single ride ¥190, one-day pass ¥700, one-day pass with Matsudai ferry to Miyajima ¥900), which has a total of eight lines. Trams 2 and 6 are particularly useful, linking the area around Peace Memorial Park. To take a single ride, board from the back and deposit your fare in the machine beside the driver's seat when you exit from the front. Passes can be bought at the tram terminal in Hiroshima Station.

Tour Bus

The city's meipurū-pu **Sightseeing Loop Bus** (www.chugoku-jrbus.co.jp; single ride ¥200, one-day pass ¥400) traces two color-coded routes (orange and green) around town, both starting from the north side of the station near the shinkansen concourse. The orange route passes by the Shukkei-en landscape garden, the castle, and some museums, while the green bus takes in temples dotting the north side of town. Both link to Peace Memorial Park. JR pass holders can ride both buses for free.

Miyajima 宮島

The island of Miyajima (officially named Itsukushima) may not be a household name in the West, but the scene of the vermillion torii gate rising directly from the sea at the shrine of Itsukushima-jinja is widely hailed as one of Japan's three best views. Beyond this famously "floating" shrine gate, the island is defined by low-lying mountains dotted by temples and laced with good walking trails up Mount Misen, where you'll find a cluster of temples and shrines.

Similar to Nara-kōen, Miyajima is also known for its population of alarmingly tame deer, whose heads are topped with tiny horns. Don't be surprised if they walk right up to you, and don't feed them unless you want to be mobbed.

Miyajima is easily visited on a day trip from Hiroshima, less than an hour away. But if you'd like to avoid the crowds and soak up its ethereal atmosphere, consider staying overnight. After dusk falls, stone lanterns flicker beside the sea, and the famed shrine gate cuts a striking profile during the evening.

Sights

★ ITSUKUSHIMA-JINJA
厳島神社

1-1 Miyajima-chō, Hatsukaichi; tel. 0829/44-2020; www.itsukushimajinja.jp; 6:30am-5:30pm daily Jan.-Feb. and mid-Oct.-Nov., 6:30am-6pm daily Mar.-mid-Oct., 6:30am-5pm Dec.; shrine ¥300 adults, ¥200 high school students, ¥100 junior high and elementary school students , treasure hall ¥300 adults, ¥200 high school students, ¥100 junior high and elementary school students, combination ticket ¥500 adults, ¥300 high school students, ¥150 junior high and elementary school students; walk 10 minutes southwest from Itsukushima ferry terminal

Fringed by verdant hills and tucked into a small inlet of the Inland Sea, in which it is partly submerged, this shrine and its "floating" torii gate are among the most recognizable Shinto shrine complexes. It's made of camphor-tree wood, known to keep from rotting. Unfortunately, the iconic gate was wrapped in scaffolding at the time of writing, and it remains unclear how long it will stay that way. A priest I asked about it said it could be as long as 3-4 years. Structures elsewhere in the complex include a main hall, prayer hall, and Noh theater stage, linked by a series of boardwalks.

Although the shrine was originally founded as early as the 6th century, it was rebuilt in 1168 by then Heike clan leader Taira no Kiyomori, who selected the site to be the location of his family shrine. The Noh stage next to the shrine was constructed in 1680. Its peculiar construction can be attributed to the belief that the island is hallowed ground. Traditionally, only the priestly class were permitted on the island and were required to approach by boat.

To see the shrine and its famed gate "floating," arrive at high tide. Inquire at the ferry terminal for a tide forecast. If you stick around for sunset, the gate and shrine are lit up until 11pm: a magical sight best appreciated on a leisurely walk, preferably from your local ryokan during an overnight stay on the holy island. The shrine is arguably at its most bewitching at night; though it's not open, the complex is nicely lit, the approach bathed in soft light by large stone lanterns. Sauntering along the coastal path leading to the shrine after the day-trippers have left leaves a deep impact. Another time to appreciate the shrine is by arriving *before* the day-trippers, anytime from when it opens at 6:30am until around 8am, when tour groups start to trickle in.

The sprawling shrine complex of **Senjōkaku** (8:30am-4:30pm daily; ¥100 adults, ¥50 junior high and elementary school students) (the name means "hall of 1,000 mats") stands atop a hill just north of Itsukushima-jinja. Built in 1587, the shrine

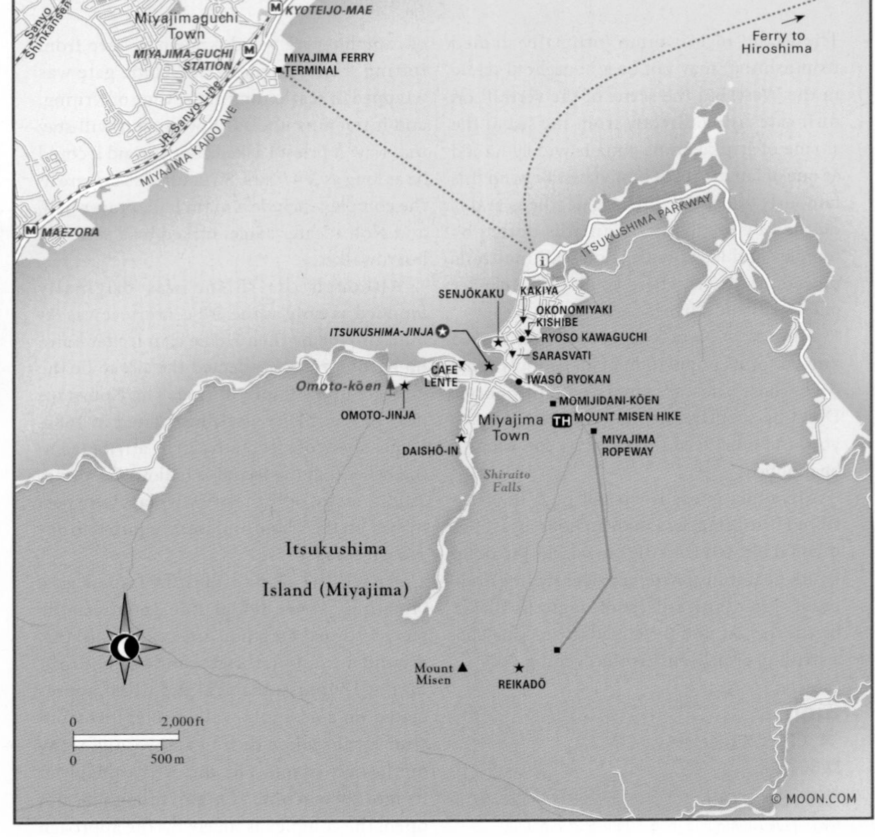

was commissioned by Toyotomi Hideyoshi. Alongside the complex stands a five-story pagoda that was built in 1407. The complex wasn't finished by the time Toyotomi died in 1598, and the next ruler to take the reins, Tokugawa Ieyasu, didn't follow through. The shrine remains incomplete, as reflected in the lack of an official front gate.

DAISHŌ-IN

大聖院

210 Miyajima-chō, Hatsukaichi; tel. 0829/44-0111; https://daisho-in.com; 8am-5pm daily; free; walk 20 minutes southwest from Itsukushima ferry terminal

About 10 minutes' walk south of Itsukushima-jinja, sitting at the foot of heavily wooded Mount Misen, this intriguing temple is worth seeing if you plan to hike up or down the mountain. It is one of the most important in the Shingon sect, founded by Kōbō Daishi (aka Kūkai), who called for the building of the temple in 806.

At the temple, you can see prayer wheels, a cave festooned with lanterns that feature images depicting the 88 pilgrimage stops of the famed Shikoku pilgrimage, 500 statues of a disciple of Amida Nyorai (Buddha of Infinite Light) named Rakan, an 11-headed effigy of

Kannon (Goddess of Mercy), a mandala sand painting done by visiting Tibetan monks, and more.

To accelerate your own Buddhist scholarship, reach out and spin the prayer wheels bearing the inscriptions of sutras (scriptures) as you walk up the temple's main staircase, said to be equal to reading their content, and bestowing the blessing contained therein.

Parks

MOMIJIDANI-KŌEN

Miyajima-chō, Hatsukaichi; www.miyajima.or.jp/english/spot/spot_momiji.html; 24 hours daily; free; 20-minute walk south of Itsukushima ferry terminal

Momijidani-kōen sits at the foot of Mount Misen, the island's highest peak at 535 meters (1,755 ft). It's justly known for its autumn foliage. Bisected by a stream, spanned by arched bridges, and lined by stone lanterns, with tame deer roaming freely, it's near the **ropeway** that takes you within a 30-minute walk of the summit of Mount Misen.

Hiking

MIYAJIMA ROPEWAY

www.miyajima-ropeway.info; 9am-4pm (last descent 4:30pm) daily; ¥1,010 one-way/¥1,840 round-trip adults, ¥510 one-way/¥920 round-trip children

If you'd rather not work up a sweat getting to the top of Mount Misen, simply hop on the (recommended) Miyajima Ropeway to the top. The lower ropeway station is about 10 minutes' walk from Momijidani-kōen, from where the ride to the upper station, with a transfer midway at **Kayatani Station,** takes about 15 minutes. From there, it's another 30-minute hike uphill to the summit. If you've got time, and are a glutton for punishment, you can trundle up the verdant peak on foot.

MOUNT MISEN

Distance: *2.5 km (1.5 mi) one-way*
Time: *1.5-2 hours one-way*
Trailhead: *Momijidani-kōen*
Information and Maps: *www.miyajima.or.jp/english/course/course_tozan3.html; www.miyajima.or.jp/english/map/map_misen.html*

Mount Misen offers phenomenal views of the Inland Sea, stretching to Hiroshima and even as far away as Shikoku on cloudless days. You can hike to the top, passing through thick forest, where a temple marks the spot where Kūkai meditated for 100 days. A flame housed at the **Reikadō** (Hall of the Spiritual Flame) was lit by Kūkai and has been continuously burning for 1,200 years. The Peace Flame at Hiroshima's Peace Park was lit with this fire.

Itsukushima-jinja

To reach the summit of Mount Misen, one option is to start in Momijidani-kōen. This is the shortest yet steepest trail to the top of the peak. There are also two other trails, one that starts behind **Daishō-in** temple (2.6 km/1.6 mi; 1.5-2 hours), which is the least strenuous of the lot and arguably boasts the prettiest views; and the third starts at **Omoto-kōen**, a park behind **Omote-jinja** (10 Miyajima-chō, Hatsukaichi; tel. 0829/44-2020; www.hiroshima-jinjacho.jp/month01; 24 hours daily; free), a shrine located about 7 minutes' walk west of Itsukushima-jinja (3.4 km/2.1 mi; 2-2.5 hours), the longest and least crowded climb of the three. The **Miyajima Tourist Association** has information on all the routes online in English.

You'll likely find yourself panting if you hike to the top. Easier is to take the **Miyajima Ropeway** up, then trundle down one of the three trails on your return.

Festival

MIYAJIMA WATER FIREWORKS FESTIVAL

宮島水中花火大会

tel. 0829/44-2011; https://visithiroshima.net/things_to_do/seasonal_events/summer/miyajima_water_fireworks_festival.html; 7:40pm-8:40pm second to last Sat. of Aug.; free

Some 300,000 spectators, many dressed in yukata, throng to Miyajima and the adjacent coastline of Honshu to watch this spectacular fireworks festival every summer. Some 5,000 fireworks burst over the water between the island and the mainland. Special ferries shuttle between the mainland and the island until around midnight to account for the crowds making their way back to Hiroshima. A good strategy is to take the train one stop toward Iwakuni, then transfer to the next Hiroshima-bound train to beat some of the crowds to the train. Note that the festival has been postponed by a week or canceled due to rain some years.

Food

★ CAFE LENTE

1167-3 Miyajima-chō, Hatsukaichi-shi; tel. 0829/44-1204; https://lente-miyajima.business.site; 11am-5pm Fri.-Mon.; drinks from ¥500, dishes from ¥800; walk 7 minutes west of Itsukushima-jinja

This is a chic little oasis with nearly floor-to-ceiling windows that offer great views of the pine-studded shore and iconic floating torii gate beyond. They serve good coffee, tea, desserts, and a smattering of light, healthy meals.

SARASVATI

407 Miyajima-chō, Hatsukaichi-shi; tel. 0829/44-2266; https://itsuki-miyajima.com/shop/sarasvati; 8:30am-7pm daily; drinks from ¥550, sandwich sets ¥990; walk 2 minutes east of Itsukushima-jinja

This stylish café a stone's throw from the shrine serves great coffee, tea, and desserts. It's located in the midst of the tourist buzz but is a good place to escape the crowds.

OKONOMIYAKI KISHIBE

483-2 Miyajima-chō, Hatsukaichi-shi; tel. 0829/44-0002; 11am-2pm and 5pm-9pm Sat.-Sun., 5pm-9pm Mon.-Wed.; average ¥1,000; walk 4 minutes northeast of Itsukushima-jinja

Like oysters, okonomiyaki is as good on the island as it is on the neighboring mainland. If you haven't had your fill in Hiroshima, this mom-and-pop shop serves Hiroshima-style okonomiyaki as well as ramen. This is a good place for a homey meal.

★ KAKIYA

539 Miyajima-chō, Hatsukaichi-shi; tel. 0829/44-2747; www.kaki-ya.jp; 10am until oysters are sold out daily; ¥1,200-3,000; walk 5 minutes northeast of Itsukushima-jinja

If you haven't already sampled oysters in Hiroshima, or if you want more, this is a great spot to try them in their various guises (deep-fried, raw, grilled) in the heart of the island's small town.

Accommodations

Staying overnight on Miyajima is a great

way to experience the island's subtle charms that are often missed amid the crowds of day-trippers. If you have the time and budget, there are some wonderful traditional lodgings tucked away in the island's small village.

RYOSO KAWAGUCHI

469 Miyajima-chō, Hatsukaichi-shi; tel. 0829/44-0018; http://ryoso-kawaguchi.jp; from ¥14,850 d with breakfast and dinner; walk 3 minutes east of Itsukushima-jinja

This welcoming inn, tucked away in the heart of the village east of the shrine, is a great mid-range pick. The guesthouse itself is quite old but well-maintained, with private rooms sharing two private onsen (hot spring) tubs (one for couples, one for singles). The host is warm and helpful, and the meals (breakfast and dinner) are tasty and filling. Recommended.

★ IWASŌ RYOKAN

345-1 Minamimachi, Miyajima-chō, Hatsukaichi-shi; tel. 0829/44-2233; www.iwaso.com; ¥25,300-58,300 pp with breakfast and dinner; walk 4 minutes southeast of Itsukushima-jinja, heading toward Momijidani-kōen

This renowned high-end ryokan has history and a magical ambience. In business since 1854, the property is divided into three wings with a handful of cottages. Some rooms use a shared bathroom. All rooms have access to a shared onsen. Two lavish meals are served daily to the exquisite tatami rooms. It's located about 15 minutes' walk east of the Miyajima-sanbashi Pier. There's also an optional courtesy shuttle bus pickup from the pier. You'll have to reserve six months or more in advance to snag a room in autumn, when the leafy gorge behind the property explodes with red, orange, and yellow.

Information and Services

- **Tourist Information Booth** (in the ferry terminal; tel. 0829/44-2011; www.miyajima.or.jp; 9am-6pm daily)

Getting There and Around

Miyajima is accessible by ferry from **Miyajima-guchi Station,** a stop on the JR San'yo line, about 20 kilometers (12 mi) southwest of Hiroshima (30 minutes; ¥420). From Miyajima-guchi's **ferry terminal,** two companies operate ferries to and from Miyajima: **JR** (tel. 0829/56-2045; www.jr-miyajimaferry.co.jp; departures from Miyajima-guchi 6:25am-10:42pm daily) and **Matsudai** (tel. 0829/44-2171; www.miyajima-matsudai.co.jp; departures from Miyajima-guchi 7:15am-8:35pm daily). Note that while both operators charge the same fare (10 minutes; ¥180 adults, ¥90 children one-way), you can ride the JR ferry for free if you have a JR pass.

If you'd like to zip straight to the island from Hiroshima's core, hydrofoil operator **Setonaikai Kisen** (tel. 082/253-1212; www.setonaikaikisen.co.jp; 30 min.; departures from Ujina Port 9:25am-4:25pm Mon.-Fri., 8:25am-4:25pm Sat.-Sun.; ¥1,900 one-way) serves Hiroshima's **Ujina Port,** which can be reached from downtown via tram numbers 1, 3, and 5 (20 minutes; ¥190).

Aqua Net Ferry (tel. 082/240-5955; www.aqua-net-h.co.jp; departures from Peace Memorial Park 8:30am-5:10pm daily) whisks away passengers directly from Peace Memorial Park (45 minutes; ¥2,200 one-way, ¥4,000 return). You'll find the dock on the opposite side of the Ōta-gawa river from the Peace Memorial Park.

While **taxis** do trundle through the island's quiet lanes, plan to explore Miyajima **on foot.** All sights of interest are within a comfortable stroll from each other.

San'yo

山陽

Approaching "the sunny side of the mountains," as San'yo translates, from points west, you'll come first to old-school Onomichi, a quintessential port town with a small, temple-studded mountain rising behind downtown patrolled by an army of cats. This inviting town is also the gateway to the Shimanami Kaidō, a 60-kilometer (37-mi) cycling route that links Honshu to Shikoku via six islands. Farther east, the town of Kurashiki is celebrated for its romantic canal where boats once transported rice and other goods to and from the former mercantile hub. Nearby, the city of Okayama is known for its sublime Kōraku-en garden. South of Okayama and Kurashiki, the Art Islands of Naoshima, Teshima, and Inujima draw art lovers and anyone who wants to slow down in beautiful surrounds.

ONOMICHI

尾道

This seaside town is full of retro storefronts, traditional homes, and aging fishing boats floating in the harbor. A vintage shopping arcade houses a mélange of old and new: classic kissaten (old-fashioned coffee shops), bakeries, trendy fashion boutiques, and art galleries. In temple-studded neighborhoods spread across the slopes behind the town, an army of cats makes itself at home. Many films, including Yasujirō Ozu's timeless masterpiece *Tokyo Story*, and TV dramas have been shot in Onomichi, which has also produced its fair share of auteurs. This artistic cred makes sense as you stroll around town and up through the hills behind it. Rather than ticking off boxes of sights, Onomichi feels ready-made to wander and follow where inspiration leads.

To take in the spiritual side of the town, there's the temple walk. If you're of a more literary bent, there's also a path marked by poetry-inscribed stones that intersects the temple walk and pays homage to literary figures who were inspired by the town, haiku master Matsuo Bashō among them. Onomichi also serves as the starting point of the Shimanami Kaidō, a 70-kilometer (43-mi) series of bridges across the Inland Sea that links Honshu and Shikoku. This scenic journey can be made by car or bicycle and traverses a string of rural islands en route.

Hiking

★ TEMPLE WALK

Distance: *2.5 km (1.6 mi) one-way*

Time: *1-3 hours (depending on time spent at temples)*

Trailhead: *North of first bridge that goes over train tracks east of Onomichi Station*

Information and maps: *Tourist Information center (1-1 Higashigosho-chō)*

This famed walking route leads to 25 temples, which were built using donations from well-heeled merchants during the town's heyday as a major port city. Aside from some spectacular architecture, the walk offers stunning views of the Inland Sea.

Senkō-ji (千光寺; 15-1 Higashitsuchido-chō; tel. 0848/23-2310; www.senkouji.jp; 9am-5pm daily), said to have been built by Kōbō Daishi (aka Kūkai) in 806, is the most iconic temple. This complex sits below a park that is reachable by ropeway and offers fantastic views of the city and sea below. Another notable temple is **Jodo-ji** (浄土寺; 20-28 Higashikubo-chō; tel. 0848/37-2361; https://ermjp.com/j/temple; 9am-4pm daily), the last one on the walk; it is said to have been built in the early 7th century, making it the oldest on the route. The temple has a two-story pagoda and lovely garden, both of which are officially designated National Treasures by the Agency for Cultural Affairs. If you prefer to go straight to the town's highest viewing platform without breaking a sweat, hop on the **Senkō-ji Mountain Ropeway** (tel. 084/822-4900; http://onomichibus.jp/ropeway; 9am-5:15pm

Onomichi and the Shimanami Kaidō

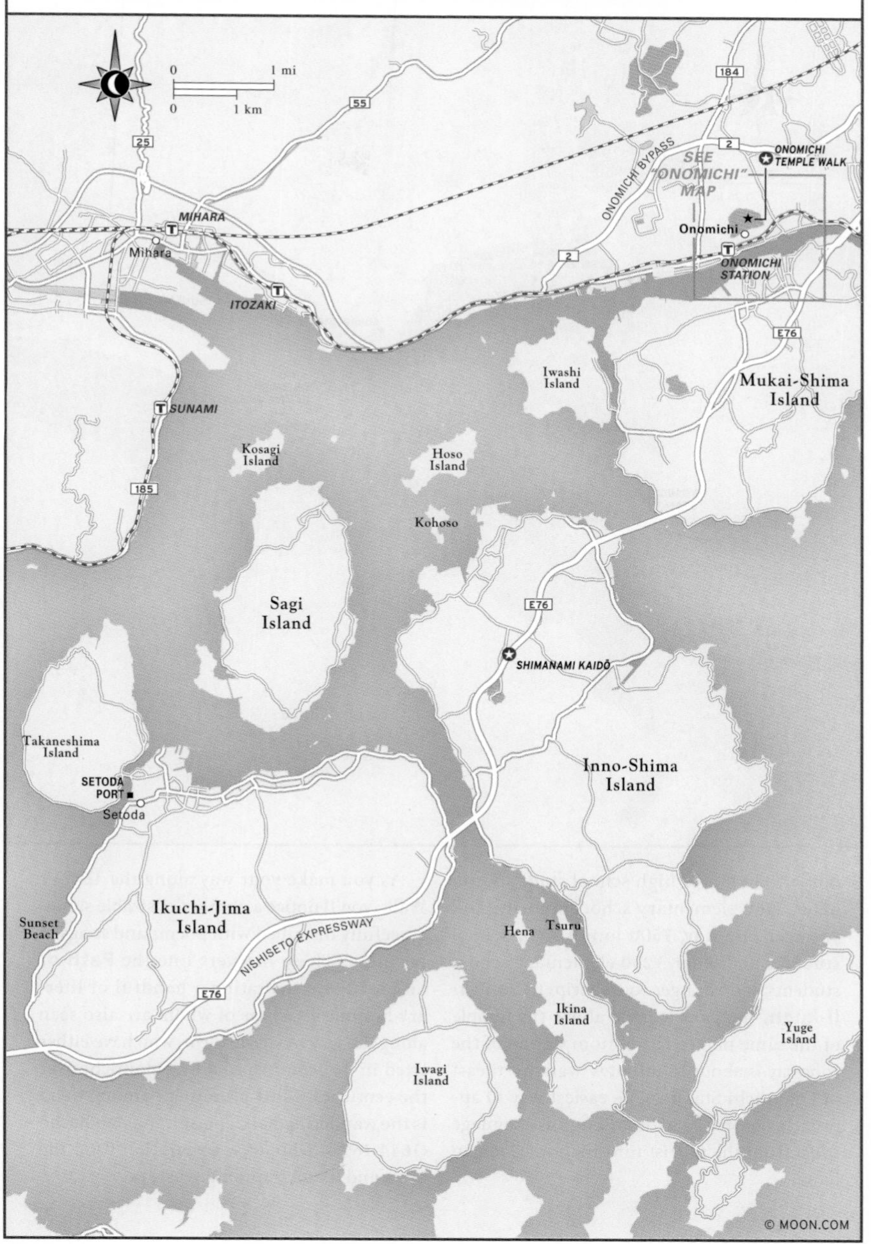

Onomichi

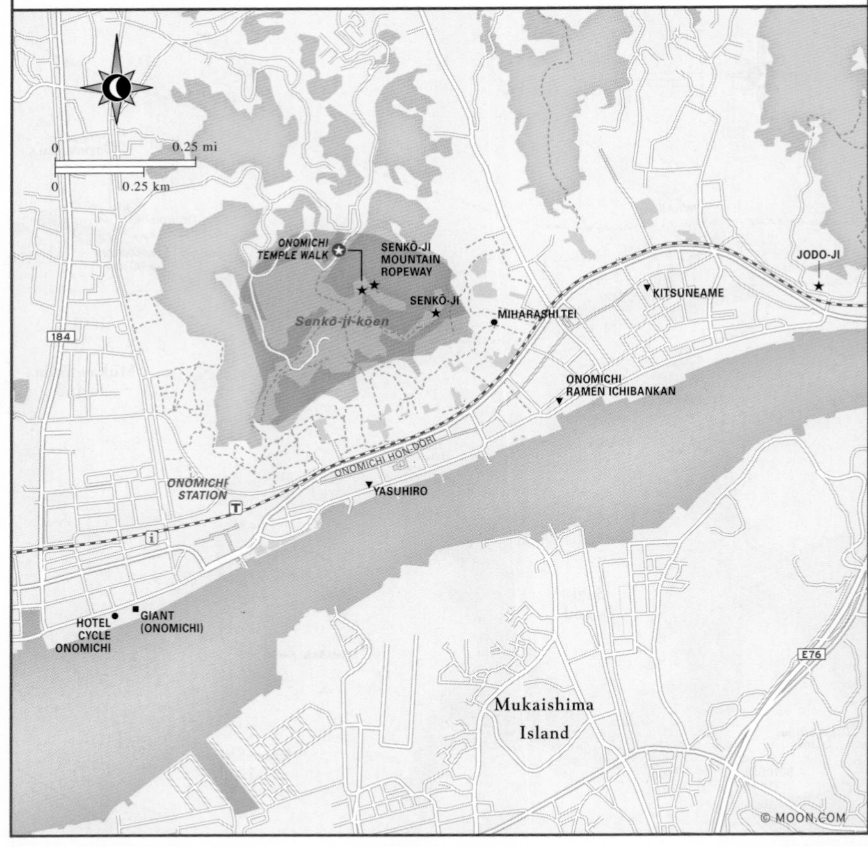

daily; ¥320 junior high school students and older, ¥160 elementary school students and younger one-way, ¥500 junior high school students and older, ¥250 elementary school students and younger round-trip) to **Senkō-ji-kōen,** the park located above the temple of the same name. The bottom station of the ropeway is about 15 minutes' walk northeast of Onomichi Station. The easiest way to approach the trek is with an English-language **map** from the tourist information center in hand.

As you make your way along the Temple Walk, you'll notice a number of sizable stones gracefully inscribed with poems and songs in Japanese. These markers line the **Path of Literature,** celebrating a handful of literary luminaries, some of whom are also seen along the way in statue form, who have either lived in or been inspired by Onomichi over the centuries. Most prominent among them is the wandering haiku master Matsuo Bashō (1644-1694), who drew inspiration from the town and its surrounding seascape.

Shopping

ONOMICHI HON-DŌRI

3-17 Higashigosho-chō; tel. 0848/23-5001; https://onomichi-hondoori.jp; street open 24 hours daily, shop hours vary

Many Japanese towns have covered pedestrian shopping streets known as shōtengai running through their downtowns. Today, most shōtengai are lined by chain stores where mom-and-pop stores once did brisk business. Onomichi Hon-dōri, however, retains its roots as a thriving piece of the local economy and has its mid-20th-century ambiance fully intact. The street's western edge begins about 4 minutes' walk east of Onomichi Station and continues eastward, through the center of downtown for 1.2 kilometers (0.7 mi), making it a particularly rambling example of this classic style of shopping arcade. Be sure to wander along this retro time capsule to admire the nostalgic shop fronts and weave in and out of the lanes that branch off from it. Rather than set out for a particular shop, just wander down this street, stop anywhere that catches your eye, and enjoy getting a little bit lost.

Food

KITSUNEAME

2-11-17 Kubo; www.facebook.com/kituneame; 9am-11am (last order 10am) and noon-6pm (last order 5pm) Fri.-Mon.; from ¥600; walk 18 minutes northeast of Onomichi Station

Tucked down a side street that branches off of the town's nostalgic Hondōri shōtengai (covered shopping street), this hushed old-school café is a classic example of a kissaten: dark wood tables, chandeliers, lights behind stained-glass windows. The menu includes items like parfait, French toast, simple pasta dishes, and basic Japanese set meals. Look for the white sign with two foxes under an umbrella and the cafe's name (キツネ雨) under a sign simply saying "Coffee" on the outside.

ONOMICHI RAMEN ICHIBANKAN

2-9-26 Tsuchidō; tel. 0848/21-1119; www.f-ichibankan.com; 11am-7pm Sat.-Thurs.; average ¥1,000; walk 13 minutes northeast of Onomichi Station

In a town famed for its ramen, this shop is among the most accessible places to eat the town's signature spin on the dish. Springy medium-size noodles are served in a hearty broth made from soy sauce, dashi (fish stock), and chicken, enriched by fatty cuts of pork. Side items like gyoza (fried dumplings), fried rice, and karage (fried chicken) are also served.

YASUHIRO

1-10-12 Tsuchidō; tel. 0848/22-5639; https://yasuhiro.co4.jp; 11:30am-2pm and 5pm-9pm (last order 8:30pm) Tues.-Sun., closed on Tues. if Mon. is a holiday; lunch sets from ¥1,700, dinner courses from ¥5,500; walk 6 minutes east of Onomichi Station

This mom-and-pop sushi shop near the waterfront has been in business for upward of five decades. The menu includes a good range of rice bowls, sushi platters, tempura, set meals, and more. The quality of the fish used has garnered a loyal following. Lunchtime prices are more affordable. There's a good English-language menu on the website.

Accommodations

Onomichi is a peaceful place for an overnight stay, either while traveling between Kyoto or elsewhere in Kansai and Hiroshima, or before or after a jaunt on the Shimanami Kaidō. For a full list of accommodations, visit www.ononavi.com/accommodations.

MIHARASHI TEI

15-7 Higashitsuchido-chō; tel. 0848/23-3864; http://miharashi.onomichisaisei.com; dorms from ¥3,000, private rooms from ¥7,500 pp

Ensconced on a cliff near Senkō-ji temple, this inn occupies a once-abandoned hilltop villa built a century ago during the town's saen ("tea culture") boom, when well-heeled residents built vast residences geared toward drinking tea with guests. It fell into disrepair until an extensive renovation project was launched in 2015. There are both dorms (mixed and women-only) and private rooms, all with tatami-mat floors, futon bedding, and shared bathrooms. A caveat: It's located about

☆ Cycling the Inland Sea

Extending southward from Onomichi, a route known as the **Shimanami Kaidō** (Shimanami Sea Route) links six picturesque islands via nine massive bridges, terminating in the town of Imabari in northwest Shikoku's Ehime Prefecture. The roadway takes in sublime stretches of the Inland Sea and reveals snapshots of bucolic island life, as well as more industrialized areas. Though this route makes for a spectacular scenic drive (roughly 60 km/37 mi; 1 hour; one-way tolls add up to about ¥5,000), an even more breathtaking way to enjoy it, when the weather cooperates, is by bicycle. Whether you cycle part or all of it, it's sure to be memorable.

ISLANDS AND BRIDGES

The islands crossed on the Shimanami Kaidō, from north to south, are **Mukai-shima, Inno-shima, Ikuchi-jima, Ōmi-shima, Hakata-jima,** and **Ōshima,** and the bridges that link them are engineering marvels. The **Tatara Bridge,** which spans Ikuchi-jima and Ōmi-shima, has the fourth-longest main span of any cable-stayed bridge in the world, with a center span of 890 meters (2,920 ft) and a total length of 1,480 meters (4,855 ft). Bridging Ōshima and Imabari, the **Kurushima Kaikyōu Bridge** is one of the world's longest suspension bridges at a staggering 4 kilometers (2.5 mi) long. Tolls for cyclists have been waived on the bridges for some time, although there's a chance they could be in effect in the future (up to ¥200 per bridge).

THE ROUTE

The recommended Shimanami Kaidō cycling course is well marked. If you want to cycle all the way from Onomichi to **Imabari** on Shikoku, the 70-kilometer (43-mi) trip takes about 8 hours without pit stops. Many cyclists prefer to spend a night on one of the islands, **Ikuchi-jima** being a prime spot. Others go partway, and then take the ferry back to Onomichi.

Starting in Onomichi, you'll first need to hop on a **ferry** from **Onomichi Ekimae Port** (9-1 Higashigosho-chō), a short walk from JR Onomichi Station to nearby **Mukai-shima** (Setouchi Cruising; tel. 0865/62-2856; www.s-cruise.jp; ¥70-110 pp with bicycle)—the bridge linking Onomichi to Mukai-shima doesn't allow pedestrians or cyclists. From Mukai-shima, you can pedal all the way to Imabari. Note that **Setoda Port** on Ikuchi-jima, roughly 2 hours by bicycle (30 km/18.6 mi) from the port on Mukai-shima, is the farthest point from Onomichi that can be reached by ferry (40 minutes; ¥1,300 adults, ¥650 children; boats depart every hour or two); this is an important consideration if you plan to return to Onomichi by ferry on the same day (last ferry 6:30pm). You'll need to pay up to an additional ¥300, depending on the route, to bring a bicycle on the ferry.

RENTING A BIKE

You can rent a bicycle and pick up a map of the route at a variety of **bicycle terminals** in Onomichi, a short walk toward the waterfront from the main train station, and on some of the islands (¥2,000 per day, plus ¥1,100 deposit, refundable if bicycle is returned to same terminal). Electrically assisted bicycles are on offer at some of these terminals (up to 6 hours; ¥2,500 per day, ¥1,100 deposit; must be returned to same terminal), as are tandem bicycles (¥3,000 per day, ¥1,100 deposit; must be returned to same terminal). **Reserving a bicycle online** is recommended during high season and must be done at least a week in advance. For a full list of terminals or to reserve a bicycle in advance, visit http://shimanami-cycle.or.jp/rental/english.

cyclists on the Shimanami Kaidō

If you prefer a fancier steed and don't mind paying a premium, **Giant** (https://bicyclerental.jp/en; from ¥4,000 per day) has rental outlets in both Onomichi and Imabari. Advance reservation and an extra ¥3,300 is required if you want to drop off one of Giant's road bikes at a non-Giant terminal, which is only permitted with road bicycles. As with regular bicycles, you can reserve online with Giant.

CYCLING TIPS

Be sure to always **stay on the left side of the road** and avoid hogging the lane. Set out with enough **cash** for your needs, as the small mom-and-pop businesses, from izakaya to ryokan, likely won't take other forms of payment. Finally, if you plan to stay overnight in a ryokan on any of the islands, **arrive by 5pm** so you are in time for dinner. Besides being disappointing, missing a meal in your inn could leave you without many options once the sun goes down, as shops close early on the islands.

You can leave your luggage in a locker at most bicycle terminals if you plan to return the same day, or forward your luggage with **Kuro Neko** (www.kuronekoyamato.co.jp; from ¥1,000), which sends packages overnight to and from select convenience stores. Catering specifically to the Shimanami Kaidō, **Sagawa Express** (www.sagawa-exp.co.jp/stc/english/) sends luggage between participating hotels in both Onomichi and Imabari.

MORE INFORMATION

For general information on the route, including a downloadable English **map,** visit https://shimanami-cycle.or.jp/go-shimanami/. Another helpful free resource, which includes information on bicycle rentals, accommodation across the islands, maps, and summaries of things to do is this downloadable **guide:** https://shimanami-cycle.or.jp/cycling/assets/pdf/shimap-en.pdf. And of course, the friendly **tourist information office** in Onomichi can also provide any information you need, as well as help with booking accommodations on the islands.

20 minutes' walk from Onomichi Station and involves a climb up some 370 stone steps, so take a taxi from the station if you're arriving with heavy luggage. Direct the taxi driver to Senkō-ji, as you can't drive directly to the inn, then walk 10 minutes downhill from there. Children under 6 are not permitted, and you must check in before 10pm.

HOTEL CYCLE ONOMICHI

Onomichi U2 complex, 6-15 Nishigosho-chō; tel. 0848/21-0550; www.onomichi-u2.com; twins from around ¥22,000

About 9 minutes' walk west of Onomichi Station on the waterfront, this modish hotel is set within a large complex called Onomichi U2, which used to serve as a warehouse. The rooms are all twins (deluxe size available), with a minimalist design sense and well-stocked, spacious bathrooms. The U2 complex also houses restaurants, cafés, shops, and a **Giant** store offering bicycle rentals.

Information and Services

Visit the town's official tourism portal, **Ononavi** (www.ononavi.com), which offers food, accommodation, sight and activity listings, and a number of sample itineraries for exploring the town.

- **Tourist information counter** (Onomichi Station, 1-1 Higashigosho-chō; tel. 0848/20-0005; www.ononavi.com; 9am-6pm daily)

Getting There and Around

Onomichi's core centers around **Onomichi Station,** which is served by local trains on the **JR San'yo line.** Coming from Hiroshima, you can take the Nozomi shinkansen to Fukuyama (not covered by the JR Pass), then transfer to the local JR San'yo line bound for Mihara (1 hour; ¥5,580). If you're traveling without a JR Pass, take the Kodama shinkansen from Hiroshima to Mihara, then transfer to the JR San'yo line (1 hour 25 minutes; ¥3,810). Coming from the east, you can take the JR San'yo line directly from both Kurashiki (1 hour 5 minutes; ¥1,170) and Okayama (1 hour 25 minutes; ¥1,340), from where you can also take the Sakura shinkansen to Fukuyama (covered by JR Pass), then transfer to the JR San'yo line from there (45 minutes; ¥3,630).

Once you've arrived in Onomichi, the easiest way to get around is **on foot.**

KURASHIKI

倉敷

Continuing east along the San'yo coast, the "Kura" ("storehouse") in Kurashiki relates to the fact that this quaint townscape was one replete with storehouses full of rice during the Edo period (1603-1868). The charming canal that runs through the center of downtown Kurashiki was one of the arteries used to transport rice to port. Today, Kurashiki attracts a bustling tourist trade. The most scenic part of the canal district is the **Bikan Historical Quarter,** spanned by stone bridges and fringed by hanging willow branches.

Starting at the canal's northern end at the Ōhara Museum of Art, slowly amble beside the canal and take in the old-world ambience conjured by the white-plaster storefronts and black-tile roofs. A number of small museums with collections of folk crafts and old-fashioned toys are housed in some of the storehouses, along with cafés, restaurants, and boutiques. Also atmospheric, Kurashiki's **Ivy Square** is a former spinning mill whose ivy-covered brick buildings now house restaurants, small museums, and a hotel.

The Bikan neighborhood is located about 10 minutes' walk southeast of JR Kurashiki Station. Though the town can easily be seen in a day, it can get packed in the afternoon. To experience its subtler magic, try to stay for a night at one of the town's many charming ryokan. After the tourists depart, take a long stroll along the canal and you'll be mesmerized by the soft light from the street lamps dancing in the water. A caveat: If you choose to visit Kurashiki, avoid arriving on a Monday, when many of the town's shops close.

Sights

ŌHARA MUSEUM OF ART

大原美術館

1-1-15 Chūō; tel. 086/422-0005; www.ohara.or.jp; 9am-5pm (last admission 4:30pm) Tues.-Sun.; ¥1,500 adults, ¥500 students; walk 12 minutes southeast of Kurashiki Station

If you've traveled in Paris or visited some of New York's fantastic museums of Western art, this charming complex in Kurashiki may slightly underwhelm. But this was the first museum in Japan dedicated to Western art, founded in 1930. Local textile tycoon Ōhara Magosaburō (1880-1943) and local artist Kojima Torajirō (1881-1929) teamed up to assemble a collection of works by artists including Picasso, Gauguin, Modigliani, Matisse, Rodin, El Greco, Pollock, Warhol, and more. Even a canvas containing some of Monet's immortal water lilies resides here, apparently purchased directly from the French Impressionist himself. The Western art is concentrated in the **Main Gallery.** The museum is spread across three buildings that sit side-by-side along the canal.

For a change of pace, two buildings adjacent to the Main Gallery house the museum's **Craft Art Gallery,** which displays Japanese works from woodblock prints to pottery, while the **Asiatic Art Gallery** exhibits antiquities from China and from countries as far away as Egypt. The museum has instituted a list of coronavirus-related precautions and rules, outlined on its website.

Food

KURASHIKI COFFEE-KAN

4-1 Hon-machi; tel. 086/424-5516; www.kurashiki-coffeekan.com; 10am-5pm daily; ¥580-1,400; walk 13 minutes southeast of Kurashiki Station

In this 19th-century building with a warm interior—exposed brick, dark-wood countertop, exposed wooden beams—the brew is high-grade, with prices to match. The menu only includes coffee, both hot and iced, so this is just a spot to take a quiet break from the crowds. When the weather's nice, there's an atmospheric inner courtyard with outdoor seating. Look for the arched doorway, fronted by a red iron gate facing the canal.

MIYAKE SHOTEN

3-11 Hon-machi; tel. 086/426-4600; www.miyakeshouten.com; 11:30am-5pm (last order 4:30pm) Sat.-Sun. holidays, 11:30am-4pm (last order 3:30pm) Mon.-Fri.; set meals ¥1,045-1,650, desserts ¥550-1,155; walk 13 minutes southeast of Kurashiki Station

This shop serves one main dish and does it well: Japanese-style vegetable curry over brown rice. The set meals include side dishes of pickled vegetables. The menu also includes coffee and desserts. The ambience is cozy and classic: wood beams and furniture, fusama (sliding doors), and a mixture of seating at tables and on the floor. It's tucked behind a classic storefront with a white noren bearing the restaurant's name. This is a good spot for a healthy lunch, situated on a street running parallel to the canal.

★ TAKADAYA

11-36 Hon-machi; tel. 086/425-9262; www3.kct.ne.jp/~takataya_ikunoya/index.htm; 5pm-10pm (last order 9:30pm) Tues.-Sun.; skewers and plates ¥130-715, courses ¥4,400; walk 15 minutes southeast of Kurashiki Station

This cozy restaurant oozes retro charm, sporting a storehouse facade and an interior of dark wood, dim lighting, and plenty of crumbling beer posters. The menu includes all forms of meat on skewers, alongside varied side dishes of vegetables, tofu, rice, and more. There's a good list of cocktails on offer as well. There's seating at tables, in tatami rooms, and at the counter. An English menu is available. Look for the blue noren (curtain). It's about 4 minutes' walk from Ōhara Museum of Art. Recommended.

Accommodations

NAGI KURASHIKI HOTEL & LOUNGE

1-14-3 Achi; tel. 050/5210-8506; https://nagi-kurashiki.com; from ¥13,500 s with breakfast, from ¥27,000 d with breakfast; 1-minute walk south from JR Kurashiki Station

This chic, brand-new boutique hotel right in front of JR Kurashiki Station is a comfortable and exceedingly convenient choice if access to the train station is important to you. It's about 12 minutes' walk from the Bikan historic district, but that's just fine since the hotel provides free bicycles for guests. The hotel's eight artfully designed rooms are spacious, easy on the eyes, and have well-stocked private bathrooms. A continental breakfast is included, and the friendly English-speaking staff provides concierge services.

★ RYOKAN KURASHIKI

4-1 Honmachi; tel. 086/422-0730; www.ryokan-kurashiki.jp; average ¥45,000 pp with 2 meals; 15-minute walk southeast from JR Kurashiki Station

Right next to Kurashiki Coffee-kan, this luxurious time capsule is the finest accommodation in town. The buildings were once storehouses for sugar and rice. Each room has a Western-style bedroom, private bathroom, and tatami-floor lounge, plus tastefully chosen artwork, calligraphy, flower arrangements, and antique furniture. The kimono-clad staff are supremely attentive and speak some English. Meals served are of the haute kaiseki (multicourse) variety, featuring locally caught seafood and seasonal ingredients. If you want to splurge, this is the best place to do so in Kurashiki.

Information and Services

Visit the **Kurashiki Sightseeing Web** (www.kurashiki-tabi.jp) for information on what to see and where to shop, eat, and sleep.

- **Kurashiki City Plaza Information Center** (1-7-2 Achi; tel. 086/424-1220; 9am-6pm daily; just outside Kurashiki Station).
- **Bikan Tourist Information Center** (1-4-8 Chūō; tel. 086/422-0542; 9am-6pm daily)

Getting There and Around

Kurashiki Station is on the JR San'yo line, southwest of **Okayama Station** (15-20 minutes; ¥330) and east of **Onomichi** (1 hour; ¥1,170). About 10 kilometers (6.2 mi) southwest of Kurashiki Station is **Shin-Kurashiki,** a stop on the shinkansen line that is directly accessible from **Hiroshima** to the west, but only by Kodama trains (50 minutes; ¥5,370).

Given that Shin-Kurashiki Station is only accessible by Kodama shinkansen trains, it's easiest to reach Kurashiki via Okayama Station instead. Okayama Station can be accessed directly by shinkansen from **Hiroshima Station** (40 minutes; from ¥6,140), **Shin-Osaka Station** (45-80 minutes; ¥6,140-6,350, depending on shinkansen type), and from **Kyoto Station** (1-1.5 hours; ¥7,670-7,990 depending on shinkansen type; some itineraries may call for transfer to different shinkansen train type at Shin-Osaka or Fukuyama; note that Nozomi shinkansen trains are not covered by JR Pass, while Hikari, Sakura, and Kodama trains are). From Okayama Station, just take the JR San'yo line to Kurashiki Station (15-20 minutes; ¥330).

Once you're in Kurashiki, exploring the narrow back lanes and lazy canal **on foot** is the only way to go.

OKAYAMA

岡山

Okayama is a compact city with friendly denizens and a mostly sunny sky. The city is most famous for its landscape garden Kōraku-en, a sprawling green space that was originally commissioned in 1687 by local lord Ikeda Tsunamasa and completed in 1700. It was originally used to entertain and host well-heeled guests during Japan's feudal heyday, when the garden could only be reached by aristocrats crossing the river by boat. The public was only permitted to enter on special occasions until 1884, when its doors were flung open. Alongside typical elements of a classic shūyū (stroll garden), such as walking paths, streams, and a hilltop meant for surveying the scene, Kōraku-en is also notable for its atypically expansive lawns and even an archery range.

Beyond its sublime garden, Okayama is a pleasant city for a stroll. Surrounding Okayama Station, which sits in the western side of downtown, the main east-west thoroughfare of Momotarō Ōdōri divides the town into northern and southern halves straight from Okayama Station in the west to Okayama-jō in the east. The Asahi River is another feature of the city's layout. This wide waterway runs north-south along the eastern edge of downtown, with Kōraku-en actually occupying a large sand bar on this river and Okayama-jō standing beside its western bank, separated from the famed garden by the flowing water. Walking paths line this river, and wide sidewalks can be found throughout much of downtown, making Okayama a good place for a flaneur.

More often than not, Okayama is approached as a brief stop and a convenient transport hub, serving as both a shinkansen stop and the station to transfer to the only railway line that links Honshu to Shikoku. Though it can be seen in a day, Okayama is a pleasant place to spend the night. There's a nice buzz in the air in the area near the city's main train station in the evening.

Sights

★ KŌRAKU-EN

後楽園

1-5 Kōraku-en, Kita-ku; tel. 086/272-1148; https://okayama-korakuen.jp; 7:30am-6pm (last admission 5:45pm) daily Mar. 20-Sept. 30, 8am-5pm (last admission 4:45pm) daily Oct. 1-Mar.19; ¥400, combined admission to castle ¥560, combined admission to Okayama Prefectural Museum ¥520 for ages 15 and over, free for under age 15

Long considered one of Japan's top three gardens, alongside Mito's Kairaku-en and Kanazawa's Kenroku-en, Kōraku-en straddles the Asahi River. It was originally built in 1700 by local lord Ikeda Tsunamasa, whose former home, **Okayama-jō** (2-3-1 Marunouchi; tel. 086/225-2096; https://okayama-kanko.net/ujo; 9am-5:30pm daily, closed until Nov. 2022 for renovation; ¥300 adults; ¥120 children 6-14), sits beside the lush landscape garden. It's a black fortress (nicknamed "crow castle"), with white and gold fish ornaments curling upward on the corners of its eaves. If you're most interested in seeing it from the outside, the view from the garden suffices.

The garden was opened to the public in 1884, following the dawn of the Meiji era. Although floods in 1934 and World War II bombing marred the grounds, they have been returned to their former state. The main structure on the grounds is the reconstructed **Enyo-tei House,** once a living quarters for the local lord. There are also a series of open-air pavilions, a large central pond, streams and smaller pools of water inhabited by colorful koi, and a few secluded teahouses. Groves of plum, cherry, apricot, and maple trees, flowers from azaleas to rhododendrons, and a tea field draw the eye, while shrines and a Noh stage add a dose of culture. There's a crane aviary, too. Cherry blossom season in spring and the coming of autumn foliage are popular times to visit the grounds, but they're expansive enough never to feel thronged.

The gardens occupy 14 hectares (2.5 acres), which should take you a few hours to explore, depending on how much you stop to soak in the views and snap photos. Meander along the paths, admiring the wide range of viewpoints from bridges, rest houses, and atop the prominent hill. Kōraku-en's layout is wonderfully open: You can see most of the garden from almost anywhere you look.

The garden is about 25-30 minutes' walk northeast of Okayama Station. You can also take the Higashiyama tram line to Shiroshita stop (10 minutes; ¥100), from where the castle is about 10 minutes' walk east and the garden's main gate is 10 minutes' walk northeast (via the large bridge). Alternatively, catch the bus that runs several times hourly from Okayama Station bus stop 1 to Kōrakuen-mae bus stop (15 minutes; ¥100), which puts you directly in front of the garden's main gate.

Food

TORIYOSHI

5-8 Honmachi, Kita-ku; tel. 086/233-1969; 4pm-midnight daily; ¥250-850 per plate; walk 3 minutes east of Okayama Station

This boisterous izakaya is a great place to drink and eat with locals. The menu includes staples like yakitori (grilled chicken on skewers), side salads, grilled fish, sashimi, and more. Come here if you want to supplement your dinner with a steady flow of booze (beer, sake, whisky soda, etc.) and mingle with friendly locals. An English menu is available.

OKABE

1-10-1 Omote-chō; tel. 086/222-1404; http://tofudokoro-okabe.com/shokujidokoro; 11:30am-2pm Mon.-Wed. and Fri.-Sat.; ¥900-990; take the Higashiyama tram line to Kencho-dōri tram stop

This homey tofu-focused lunch spot is a good option before or after visiting Kōraku-en. There are just three set meals on offer: deep-fried tofu, tofu skin over rice, and the assorted Okabe original set. The food is reasonably priced and tasty. Note that the food is not vegan, as some fish stock is used in the preparation. An English-language menu with pictures is available.

ICHIRIN SHUZO

2-16 Honmachi, Kita-ku; tel. 086/231-0690; www.ichirinshuzo.com; 5pm-midnight Mon.-Sat., open Sun. and closed Mon. if Mon. falls on holiday; ¥428-1,200 per dish, courses ¥3,000-4,000; walk 3 minutes east of Okayama Station

Across the street from Toriyoshi, this seafood izakaya is a popular spot serving creative seafood concoctions and more, from fermented soybeans atop squid sashimi to salted mackerel and black pepper-infused pork spare ribs. It gets busy, especially on the weekends, so reserve ahead to be safe.

J'S EN

2-10-11 Hokan-chō, Kita-ku; tel. 086/251-0088; http://js-kitchen.jp; 4pm-midnight (last order 11:30pm) daily, 11:30am-2pm (last order 1:30pm) Sat.-Sun. and holidays; lunch sets ¥1,100-3,090, dinner average ¥4,000-5,000; walk 10 minutes northwest of Okayama Station

This friendly Korean barbecue (yakiniku) joint is an excellent place to sample Okayama beef. The meat is balanced by a healthy range of salads, cabbage, soups, and more. The welcoming staff go out of their way to help. Reserve a day in advance if you can.

Kōraku-en

Peach Boy Momotarō

Okayama Prefecture, along with Kagawa Prefecture on Shikoku, are said to be where Momotarō, one of Japan's most beloved folk heroes, sprang from a peach, and then grew up to save his homeland from marauding ogres. Momotarō—literally "Peach Tarō"—holds special status in Japan's rich mythology, along with other heroes and monsters from Astro Boy to Godzilla. You won't have to look far in this region to see his cherubic face plastered on buses, billboards, and manhole covers.

THE LEGEND

Our hero was said to have been discovered by chance when the peach in which he descended to earth was plucked from a river by a childless elderly woman, who was washing clothes as the fruit bobbed by. When she and her husband went to eat the fruit, out popped Momotarō. After the kindly older couple raised the boy, he embarked on his hero's journey by venturing to a faraway island to fight a band of three-eyed ogres that plundered the locals' wealth and even ate villagers. Along the way, Momotarō teamed up with a dog who could talk, a pheasant, and a monkey. Together, the motley crew routed the ogres in their lair on a distant isle. They reclaimed the loot previously stolen by the demons and took the chief ogre hostage. Everyone lived happily ever after.

WHERE TO SEE MOMOTARŌ

You'll see Momotarō and peach motifs all throughout Okayama, from the hero's visage emblazoned on peach-flavored confectionary packaging to peach-shaped trinkets. A prominent **statue** of the beloved peach-boy is right outside the east exit of Okayama Station, gazing into the distance with his dog, pheasant, and monkey companions. As you walk around town, keep your eyes open and you'll soon grow familiar with his boyish countenance.

If you have time, interest, and want to dig deeper into the nuts and bolts of the legend itself, check out the English-language website **Momotarō Ura** (https://momotaro-ura.jp/en/), which provides Momotarō-related itineraries (https://momotaro-ura.jp/en/course/list/) and information on a number of spots around the region with ties to the story (https://momotaro-ura.jp/en/point/map/).

Accommodations

TORII-KUGURU GUESTHOUSE AND LOUNGE

4-7-15 Hōkan-chō, Kita-ku; tel. 086/250-2629; http://toriikuguru.com; private singles ¥4,500, private doubles ¥8,000; walk 13 minutes northwest of Okayama Station

This laid-back, welcoming guesthouse, in an old-school shopping district on the quieter side of town, is a great option for those traveling on a tight budget. The interior is clean and bright with wood floors, tasteful lighting, and shared bathrooms. Uniquely, the guesthouse is situated in Nawate, a petite complex that also includes a lounge and bar. You'll know you've found it when you reach the torii gate left over from a shrine that once stood on the plot next to the reception desk.

KŌRAKU HOTEL

5-1 Heiwa-chō, Kita-ku; tel. 086/221-7111; https://hotel.kooraku.co.jp; from ¥7,500 d room only, from ¥10,320 with breakfast; walk 5 minutes east of Okayama Station

This clean, bright mid-range hotel has airy, modern rooms with well-appointed bathrooms. The common areas are stylish with a boutique vibe, and there's a restaurant serving Japanese fare on the second floor. The breakfast plan is optional. This is a good mid-priced option in the heart of the entertainment district.

Information and Services

Online, the official **Explore Okayama** website (www.okayama-japan.jp/en) is a useful resource.

- **Momotarō Tourist Information Center** (east exit of Okayama station, in the underground shopping complex; tel. 086/222-2912; www.okayama-kanko.net; 9am-8pm daily)

Getting There and Around

Okayama Station sits on the western side of downtown, roughly 25 minutes' walk from Kōraku-en, which sits on the eastern side of downtown, alongside the Asahi River and Okayama-jō. Its position on the shinkansen line and local JR San'yo line makes Okayama easily accessible by rail. Coming from the east, a number of major hubs are accessible via shinkansen: **Shin-Osaka** (50 minutes; ¥6,140), **Kyoto** (1 hour 10 minutes; ¥7,880; requires transfer at Shin-Osaka, Shin-Kobe, or Himeji when traveling on shinkansen not covered by JR Pass), and **Tokyo** (4-4.5 hours; ¥17,130; requires transfer at Shin-Osaka or Shin-Kobe when traveling on shinkansen not covered by JR Pass). Lying to the west is **Hiroshima** (40 minutes; ¥6,230). Remember that the JR Pass does not cover Nozomi trains.

Okayama is a very **walkable** city, but to cut down on walking time, hop on the efficient **tram network** (all rides within downtown ¥100). The Higashiyama line runs all the way up the main thoroughfare of Momotarō Ōdōri to the gently flowing Asahi-gawa near both the garden and castle. Another good way to get around is on two wheels. There are many **bicycle** rental shops scattered around the east side of the station. Try **Eki Rinkun** (1-2 Ekimotomachi, Kita-ku; tel. 086/223-7081; www.ekiren.com/ekirinkun; 7am-9pm daily; ¥400 per day).

The Art Islands

TOP EXPERIENCE

Gliding through the blue-green expanse of the Inland Sea south of the San'yo coast, approaching any one of the thousands of alluring islands in this waterway, boats tethered to weather-beaten docks bob on gentle waves. Fishermen empty barnacle-encrusted fishing nets of their daily catch. Squid hang to dry on wires in the open air like garments on clotheslines. In town, octogenarian aunties run corner stores and greasy-spoon restaurants, while stray cats prowl nearby for scraps.

The island of **Naoshima** in particular has become a jewel of the Inland Sea, combining beautiful natural surroundings, a fabulous design sense, and a forward-looking spirit of artistic experimentation. Easily accessed from Uno Station on Honshu, a sleepy stop on the JR Uno line about 22 kilometers (13.7 mi) southeast of Kurashiki and 21 kilometers (13 mi) south of Okayama, Naoshima is a must-visit for any trip to the area. Beyond offering a deep-dive into contemporary art, the island's communities are charming, authentic, slow-paced, and mellow, and the seaside views are stunning.

The artistic development of Naoshima has set something larger in motion in the region. Nearby, the tiny, art-studded islands of **Teshima** and **Inujima** are brilliantly following Naoshima's lead. But venture a bit farther out to sea and you'll discover a constellation of quieter isles that radiate a distinct charm at once magnetic and subtle. Experiencing this slower, unsung side of Japan firsthand is the Inland Sea's greatest draw. You'll be amply rewarded with solitude and feel as if you've taken a trip back in time if you hop on a ferry bound for some of the sea's lesser-known gems, like **Shōdo-shima, Shiraishi-jima,** and **Manabe-shima.**

★ NAOSHIMA

直島

Roughly 7.8 square kilometers (3 square mi), with a population of around 3,300, this sublime isle is awash with art, mostly due to Benesse Art Site Naoshima (http://

benesse-artsite.jp), funded by the educational publishing company Benesse Corporation. Soichiro Fukutake, the former chairman of Benesse, is a native of nearby Okayama and a keen patron of the arts. Since 1992, when the Benesse House Museum opened as a boutique hotel-cum-museum where guests are permitted to roam unfettered until 11pm, Naoshima has been transformed from a dwindling fishing community into an immersive, world-class art hub. As the island's profile rose, other creatives came to launch cafés, bed-and-breakfasts, and restaurants.

The minimalist structures in this area that were created by Pritzker Prize-winning architect Tadao Ando are works of art themselves, not to mention the outdoor sculptures dotting the landscape, and works by Claude Monet and David Hockney scattered around the island's museums.

If you time your visit carefully, you can visit Naoshima on a day trip. But consider staying on the island for a night. After the legion of day-trippers depart, quiet falls across the island and Naoshima returns to its slower native rhythm. A caveat: Avoid visiting on Monday, when most museums are closed. If Monday happens to be a holiday, things close on Tuesday instead.

Orientation

Naoshima can be reached via two ferry ports: the more popular **Miyanoura Port** on the west side of the island, and **Honmura Port** in the east. Ferries run between Miyanoura and Takamatsu in Shikoku's northeast, Uno on Honshu, and Ieura Port on the tiny isle of Inujima, another roughly 25 kilometers (15.5 mi) northeast of Naoshima. Miyanoura has a well-stocked information center, a number of food and accommodation options, and several bicycle rental shops. Honmura also has a range of restaurants, inns, and, significantly, is the location of the **Art House Project,** a premier art installation strewn throughout the nearby village. The rest of the island's major museums are clustered along the southern side of the island, southeast of Miyanoura and southwest of Honmura. These include **Benesse House Museum** and **Chichū Art Museum.**

Buses shuttle once or twice hourly between Miyanoura Ferry Terminal to Honmura, on to Tsutsujiso bus stop, which is near Benesse House and the **Chichū Art Museum.** But the most appealing way to see the island when the weather cooperates is by **bike.**

Sights

ART HOUSE PROJECT
家プロジェクト

Various locations in Honmura; http://benesse-artsite.jp/en/art/arthouse.html; 10am-4:30pm Tues.-Sun., closed Tues. when Mon. is holiday; ¥1,050 multi-site admission, ¥420 admission to single site; take a bus from Miyanoura Port to Honmura (¥100), or walk 3 minutes' west from Honmura pier

The Art House Project in the traditional community of Honmura, on the island's east side, presents a series of conceptual artworks incorporated into unassuming old structures dotting the village. Art lovers find these works by following a walking route like a treasure hunt, with map in hand. The traditional buildings in which they appear range from homes and workshops to a shrine and a temple. The works are eclectic: LED lights illuminating a pool of water inside a home, underground chambers in hillsides looking onto glass staircases emerging up through the surface of the earth, a two-story Statue of Liberty replica jutting up through a former dentist's home, and more.

Honmura is a good place to visit during the morning or early afternoon. That way, you can combine your art walk here with a stop at one of the area's homey cafés or restaurants, serving fresh, healthy nosh. For more information on the individual artists and their creations spread around the village, and to purchase a ticket to enter the various sites of the Art House Project, stop by the **Honmura Lounge** (850-2 Naoshima; tel. 087/840-8273; http://benesse-artsite.jp/en/art/arthouse.html; 10am-4:30pm Tues.-Sun., closed Tues.

when Mon. is public holiday), located near the town's main bus stop.

KUSAMA'S *YELLOW PUMPKIN*

24 hours daily; free; 1-minute walk west of Tsutsujiso bus stop

On the walk from Tsutsujiso bus stop to Benesse House, you'll also pass Yayoi Kusama's famed *Yellow Pumpkin* seaside sculpture—if it's been restored to form by the time of your trip, that is. The iconic sculpture was unfortunately damaged by a typhoon in the summer of 2021 and was removed from the site for repair with no clear date for its return at the time of writing. Kusama, known for her eye-catching bob-cut red wig, has created an intensely colorful, polka-dot-infused artistic universe, ranging from large geometric paintings and sculptures to her deeply immersive "infinity room" installations. This polka-dotted giant yellow squash sits on a short pier near the Tsutsujiso bus stop and contrasts brilliantly with the sea beyond.

BENESSE HOUSE MUSEUM
ベネッセハウス ミュージアム

Gotanchi, Naoshima; tel. 087/892-3223; https://benesse-artsite.jp/en/art/benessehouse-museum.html; 8am-9pm (last entry 8pm) daily; ¥1,300 adults, free for ages 15 and under; take a bus from Miyanoura Port, via Honmura, to the Tsutsujiso bus stop

This well-known complex doubles as a museum and high-end accommodation. It's the jewel in Benesse Corporation's crown, designed by architectural giant Tadao Ando. The sprawling property on the south side of the island includes a museum, a building called the Oval, a park, and a beach.

Beyond art featured in the rooms and museum—David Hockney, Gerhard Richter, Hiroshi Sugimoto—the grounds are dotted by outdoor pieces that suit the surroundings, such as Yayoi Kusama's avant-garde take on a giant pumpkin. Guests can peruse the museum's collection 24/7. The views over the Inland Sea from the hill outside the museum are phenomenal at any time of day, but the sunsets are especially stunning.

At the time of writing, the museum had reduced its hours to 10am-6pm in an effort to curb the spread of coronavirus. If you'd like to avoid the 10-minute walk from the Tsutsujiso bus stop, there's a free shuttle (3 minutes) that also stops at Chichū Art Museum (7 minutes).

CHICHŪ ART MUSEUM
地中美術館

3449-1 Naoshima; tel. 087/892-3755; http://benesse-artsite.jp/en/art/chichu.html; 10am-6pm (last entry 5pm) Tues.-Sun. Mar.-Sept., 10am-5pm (last entry 4pm) Tues.-Sun. Oct.-Feb.; ¥2,100 adults, free for ages 15 and under; take the bus from Miyanoura Port, via Honmura, to the Tsutsujiso bus stop, then walk (30 minutes) or take the free shuttle bus (10 minutes), or walk east from Miyanoura Port (35 minutes) or cycle over (10 minutes)

This museum is a mind-bending, almost completely subterranean complex lit mostly by natural light filtered through skylights of various shapes and sizes. This is one of Naoshima's highlights, one of many structures designed by all-star architect Tadao Ando. Natural light changes throughout the day in a seamless dance with the artworks on display. The collection is not huge, but it includes heavy hitters like Claude Monet and Walter De Maria. On Friday and Saturday evenings, the "Open Sky Night Program" is held, in which the sunset can be viewed from within the subterranean space.

Tickets must be reserved in advance to enter the museum. Visit the museum's official webpage to find a link to the English-language online reservation system. You can reserve even a day before visiting, but reserve a week or more ahead to be safe. You must leave any luggage or cameras in one of the lockers provided at the ticket center.

1: *Inland Sea Driftwood Circle* and *River Avon Mud Circles by the Inland Sea* installations by artist Richard Long at Benesse House **2:** sunset on Naoshima **3:** Art House Project **4:** Benesse House

Spas and Relaxation

I LOVE 湯 ("I LOVE YU")

2252-2 Naoshima; tel. 087/892-2626; http://benesse-artsite.jp/en/art/naoshimasento.html; 1pm-9pm Tues.-Sun., closed Tues. if Mon. is holiday; ¥660 adults, ¥310 children ages 2-15, free for ages 2 and under; walk 4 minutes east of Miyanoura Port on the island's west side

For an experience beyond ogling art, why not bathe in it? I Love Yu (*Yu* meaning "hot water") is a funky sento (bath house) designed by artist Shinro Ohtake, whose quirky spin on the neighborhood bath is a natural fit on the island. In place of the de rigueur mural of Mount Fuji, you'll find a life-size elephant walking overhead; white tiles emblazoned with blue undersea visions of divers, jellyfish, and octopuses on the walls; and a ceiling made of vivid stained glass.

Events

SETOUCHI TRIENNALE

https://setouchi-artfest.jp; 3-season passport to most art sites ¥4,800 adults, ¥3,000 ages 16-18, free for ages 15 and under, single-season passport ¥4,000 adults, ¥2,500 ages 16-18, free for ages 15 and under

This massive happening features performances (dance, music, drama) and visual spectacles. Taking place every three years on Naoshima and an array of other islands in the Inland Sea, the proceedings are generally broken into seasonal programs in spring, summer, and autumn, with the next one scheduled for 2022. The website has thorough English-language information on everything from the event, the islands involved, ferry links, and more. If you intend to catch this world-famous arts and culture event, book your accommodation as far in advance as you can—six months ahead or more. If you have trouble landing a room, check out potential options around Takamatsu on Shikoku or Uno in Okayama Prefecture.

Food

Naoshima's restaurants and cafés tend to close on the early side. Plan your mealtimes carefully and be sure a given restaurant is open before making the trip.

★ CAFÉ SALON NAKA-OKU

1167 Honmura; tel. 087/892-3887; https://cafesalon-naka-oku.jimdofree.com; 11:30am-3pm (last order 2:40pm) and 5:30pm-9pm (last order 8:30pm) Wed.-Mon., some irregular closings; set lunches ¥650-800, ¥480-980 per dish; 8-minute walk southwest from Honmura Port

Much of Naoshima shuts down on Monday, giving this inviting café added cache. Its nicely aged wooden interior and home-cooked menu of classics like karage (fried chicken), omuraisu (omelet stuffed with fried rice), Japanese-style curry rice, and cakes are a winning combination. There's also a good selection of booze if you want a drink in the evening. It's at the top of a hill on the backside of the village of Honmura, away from the bustle.

APRON CAFÉ

777 Naoshima-chō Ichien; tel. 090/7540-0010; www.facebook.com/aproncafe.naoshima; 11am-4pm Tues.-Sun.; ¥1,100-1,580; near the Ando Museum down one of the footpaths that snake through inner Honmura

This bright, friendly café in the heart of Honmura is a great place for a healthy lunch. Stylish furniture, potted plants, art on the walls, and a chilled-out soundtrack create a relaxed vibe. The inventive lunch plates contain many small dishes: organic salads with fresh herbs, quiche packed with local produce, multigrain and black rice, cheese gratin, quinoa, vegetable curry, and scones made with cranberry and coconut.

SHIOYA DINER

2227 Naoshima; tel. 087/892-3290; www.facebook.com/Shioya-Diner-437280336290995; 11:30am-2:30pm and 5pm-9pm (last order 8:30pm) daily; ¥1,280-2,280; walk 4 minutes inland from the port, around the corner from I Love Yu bathhouse

As advertised, this is a diner in the classic sense, and the retro decor and soundtrack straddling rockabilly and oldies reinforces this. Run by a friendly Japanese couple smitten by Americana, it's homey and funky, with just the right amount of kitsch. The menu includes comfort foods like chicken breast and mashed potatoes, tacos, hot dogs, burgers, and fries, plus there's beer on tap and Corona in the bottle. This is a great place to dine on the Miyanoura Port (west side) of the island, particularly if you're feeling like a break from Japanese fare.

Accommodations

If you can manage to snag a room on the island, be prepared for a surprisingly quiet night. The whole island closes down by around 7pm, save for a convenience store each in Honmura and Miyanoura, and a smattering of vending machines. That said, experiencing the island minus the tourist hordes is a revelation. You'll feel as if you could be on any one of the myriad sleepy isles dotting the Inland Sea.

Naoshima's lodgings are often fully booked, so be sure to conduct an exhaustive search (www.naoshima.net/stay). If the island's lodgings are full, aim to stay either on Honshu or Shikoku near either ferry port. It's simple to shuttle between Naoshima and Uno (Honshu) or Takamatsu (Shikoku) for a day trip or two.

UNO PORT INN

1-4-4 Chikko, Tamano; tel. 0863/21-2729; http://unoportinn.com; ¥11,800 d; take the JR Uno line to Uno Station

With a cozy café on-site serving nibbles and coffee, English-speaking staff, and petite, clean rooms (both Western and Japanese-style), this welcoming inn near the port on the Honshu side is a good place to stay for a night either before or after a trip to Naoshima. All rooms—each with a unique Japanese cinema-inspired theme—have a private bathroom, with most of them accessed through separate doors at the end of the hallway on each floor. Free Wi-Fi and laundry facilities are available.

FRANCOILE

953-2 Sonota, Naoshima-chō; tel. 090/4375-1979; www.francoile.com; ¥19,000 d; 6-minute walk west from Honmura Port

On the Honmura side, this bed-and-breakfast is a great place to stay for a night. There are just two rooms in this modern, well-decorated lodging on the backside of the village. Both rooms have good lighting, spacious private bathrooms, and two twin beds. There's also a café (2pm-5pm Tues.-Thurs. and Sat.-Sun.) on the first floor serving good pour-over coffee and muffins. The place is run by a young Japanese couple with an amazing sense of hospitality, one of whom speaks great English. With only two rooms, peace and quiet are a given. But it also means you'll need to reserve well in advance. Recommended.

★ BENESSE HOUSE

Gotanchi, Naoshima; tel. 087/892-3223; http://benesse-artsite.jp/en/stay/benessehouse; from ¥37,000 d; take bus from Miyanoura Port, via Honmura, to Tsutsujiso bus stop, then walk 12 minutes west or take free shuttle bus

In the island's museum-studded south, this luxury property has rooms spanning four sites, all of which sit near the museum at the center of the Benesse art empire. All four complexes are paragons of the art gallery-cum-hotel concept. These include the beachside Benesse House Park and Beach, with its spa and library; the museum itself, which can be wandered by guests after hours; and the most-expensive Oval, which is perched on a hill above the museum and reached by monorail. The rooms are stylish yet minimal—televisions are notably absent—and feature artwork that belongs in the museum's private collection. If you have the means, this is the most luxurious, visually stunning accommodation on the island. Book as far in advance as you can.

Information and Services

Online, visit the official **Naoshima tourism portal** (https://naoshima.net/en/).

- **Naoshima Tourism Association** (inside Miyanoura ferry terminal; tel. 087/892-2299; 9am-6pm daily)
- **Honmura Lounge & Archive** (850-2 Naoshima; tel. 087/840-8273; 9:30am-4:30pm Tues.-Sun.)

Getting There

You can reach Naoshima by **ferry** from both Honshu and Shikoku. If you're coming from **Okayama Station** (Honshu), you'll need to take the Marine Liner (13 minutes; ¥770) or the JR Seto-Ohashi line (22 minutes; ¥240) to **Chayamachi Station.** Both lines are covered by the JR Pass. At Chayamachi Station, transfer to the JR Uno Port line (30 minutes; ¥330) to **Uno Station,** then walk 3 minutes south to **Uno Port** where you'll catch a ferry (20 minutes; ¥300 adults, ¥150 children). Note that ferries bound for **Miyanoura Port** on the south side of Naoshima depart from Uno Port once or twice hourly, while those running to **Honmura Port** on the north side of Naoshima leave five times per day. For a full ferry timetable to and from Naoshima, and additional information on how to reach these ports, visit http://benesse-artsite.jp/en/access.

From **Takamatsu** on Shikoku, you can catch a ferry directly from Takamatsu Port (1 hour; ¥520), which is a few minutes' walk from JR Takamatsu Station.

Getting Around

Your best options for getting around Naoshima are either by **bus** or **bicycle. Buses** shuttle once or twice hourly (all rides ¥100) from Miyanoura Ferry Terminal to Honmura (10 minutes), on to Tsutsujiso bus stop (15 minutes), with Benesse House about 10 minutes' walk west from there.

There are loads of bicycle **rental shops** (single-speed from ¥300, multi-speed from ¥500, electrically assisted from ¥1,100) around the port in Miyanoura, as well as a few shops in Honmura, but be forewarned: The bicycles are often all booked very early in the day. If you want to rent a bicycle, plan on showing up at either port around 8:30am, or making a reservation. For a list of rental shops on the island, including information on which ones allow advanced reservations, visit www.naoshima.net/en/access/rental. The island is hilly in parts, so an electrically assisted bicycle is a good option if you can manage to snag one. It's also possible to explore the island on foot, but the hills are a bit daunting, and the distances can add up.

TESHIMA
豊島

Of Naoshima's two sister islands, Teshima and Inojima, Teshima is the larger and more popular, sitting between Shōdo-shima to the east and Naoshima to the west. The thinly populated green isle, which is the second largest in the Inland Sea after Shōdo-shima, is dotted by three fishing villages and swathed in citrus trees.

Since it has emerged as one of the leading lights of the Inland Sea's art scene in recent years, Teshima serves as one of the main venues of the Setouchi Triennale. This is a dazzling success story when considering the fact that the island was at the center of a scandal involving the dumping of hundreds of thousands of tons of toxic waste near its western coast in the 1980s, for which cleanup was finished in 2017.

Compared to Naoshima, which runs on tourism, Teshima still has the feeling of a living, breathing fishing community. Besides striking, conceptual artworks set amid a lovely natural environment, you'll also find terraced rice fields, weather-beaten coastline, and a forested interior. The relatively smaller number of tourists, at least compared to Naoshima, gives you the chance to slow down and relax.

Plan on spending a half day or full day exploring Teshima, depending on how slowly you want to go. To enjoy the island to its fullest, rent an electrically assisted bicycle at Ieura Port in the island's northwest, then pedal through the rural landscape. If you can't manage to get an electric bike, a standard bicycle will suffice. But be forewarned the island is quite hilly in parts. If you've got a full day, it's also possible to walk.

Sights

TESHIMA YOKOO HOUSE

豊島横尾館

2359 Teshimaieura; tel. 0879/68-3555; http://benesse-artsite.jp/en/art/teshima-yokoohouse.html; 10am-5pm (last entry 4:30pm) Wed.-Mon. Mar.-Oct., 10am-4pm (last entry 3:30pm) Wed.-Mon. Nov., 10am-4pm (last entry 3:30pm) Fri.-Mon. Dec.-Feb.; ¥520

Built inside a traditional house near Ieura Port, the Teshima Yokoo House complex was designed by architect Nagayama Yuko. The house showcases works on life and death by the artist Yokoo Tadanori, after whom it is named. Outside, a classical Japanese rock garden strewn with multicolored rocks and mosaic tiles was built by locals. Inside, carp swim through a pond under a plexiglass floor. Inside an attached tower with mirrored floor and ceiling, the 14-meter-tall (46-ft-tall) walls are plastered with nearly 1,000 waterfall postcards. Look up or down for a simulated glimpse of infinity. Even the bathrooms' chrome interiors are disorienting.

TESHIMA ART MUSEUM

豊島美術館

607 Karato; tel. 0879/68-3555; http://benesse-artsite.jp/en/art/teshima-artmuseum.html; 10am-5pm (last entry 4:30pm) Wed.-Mon. Mar.-Oct., 10am-4pm (last entry 3:30pm) Wed.-Mon. Nov., 10am-4pm (last entry 3:30pm) Fri.-Mon. Dec.-Feb.; ¥1,570

This mesmerizing water-droplet-shaped structure sits beside a rice terrace on a hill. A joint collaboration by artist Naito Rei and architect Nishizawa Ryūe, this shell is punctuated by openings in the ceiling that reveal the sky and lush backdrop of the island's verdant topography. To enter, you must take off your shoes. Inside, look down and observe the captivating rivulets of water that periodically spring from the floor and dance around the space. This is a place to slow down and observe the beauty of the island itself, which is the true star of this exhibit. Attached, there's a glass-roofed café that maintains the same hours as the museum.

At the time of writing, the museum was requiring advance reservations to combat the spread of coronavirus. Check the website for the current admission policy and to book a ticket if needed.

Teshima Art Museum

LES ARCHIVES DU CŒUR

2801-1 Karato, Teshima, Tonosho-chō; tel. 0879/68-3555; http://benesse-artsite.jp/en/art/boltanski.html; 10am-5pm (last entry 4:30pm) Wed.-Mon. Mar.-Oct., 10am-4pm (last entry 3:30pm) Wed.-Mon. Nov., 10am-4pm (last entry 3:30pm) Fri.-Mon. Dec.-Feb.; ¥520

Come here to hear a singular archive of heartbeats recorded around the globe that are piped through a mesmerizing sound system in a special darkened room. You can also record, register, and get a CD of your own heartbeat for ¥1,570.

Food

Eateries on Teshima close early, so plan ahead. For a full list of the island's scant eateries, visit https://teshima-navi.jp/en/restaurants/.

TESHIMA NO MADO

2458-2 Ieura, Teshima, Tonosho-chō; teshimanomado@gmail.com, www.teshimanomado.com; 10am-5:30pm Wed.-Mon.; average ¥1,000

Five minutes' walk inland from Ieura Port and next to Teshima Yokoo House, this café occupies a renovated building made with tin sheets that was once a seaweed-processing workshop. The menu includes good coffee and bread, respectively roasted and baked in-house; light meals (curry and rice dishes, salads, and more); and desserts.

SHIMA KITCHEN

1061 Karato, Teshima, Tonosho-chō; tel. 0879/68-3771; www.shimakitchen.com; 11am-3:30pm (lunch until 2pm, café until 3:30pm) Sat.-Mon. and holidays; from ¥1,200

About 12 minutes' walk south of Teshima Art Museum, this restaurant is set in a formerly abandoned house redesigned and refurbished into a restaurant and art space by architect Abe Ryo in 2010 as part of the Setouchi Triennale. Today, it's run by locals who have trained under chefs from a four-star hotel in Tokyo to whip up a healthy menu of dishes such as curry and rice, fish, vegetable medleys, and desserts. Ingredients are gathered from around the island, from rice and produce to fruits, olives, and fish caught offshore. There are tables with floor cushions arrayed around a wooden veranda, and occasional events are hosted on the large open terrace, which is a great place to socialize with other diners.

UMI NO RESTAURANT

525-1 Ieura, Teshima, Tonosho-chō; tel. 0879/68-3677; https://il-grano.jp/umi/; 11am-4:30pm (last order 4pm), lunch until 3pm, irregular closings; dinner courses (from 6pm daily Mar.-Nov., 5pm daily Dec.-Feb.) also available with at least 2 days' advance reservation, irregular holidays; lunch ¥3,000, dinner course ¥8,800

About 15 minutes' walk east from Ieura Port, this stylish beachside eatery set in a minimalist white structure serves Italian cuisine made with local ingredients, from produce to fish. The pies are made in a wood-fired Neapolitan pizza oven, and seating is available both inside and on an open-air terrace that overlooks the sea. The restaurant's schedule is patchy, so check the calendar on the English-language website to be sure it's open before planning to dine here.

Accommodations

Teshima has limited accommodation options, but if you inquire in advance, you may be able to secure a room at one of the island's inns, which range from family-owned minshuku to chic private residences. Visit https://teshima-navi.jp/en/accommodation for a full list of options.

Information and Services

Online, check out the island's tourism portal, **Teshima Tourism Navi** (https://teshima-navi.jp/en).

- **Tourist information desk** (Ieura Port Ferry Terminal; 9am-5pm Wed.-Mon.; tel. 087/968-3135)

Getting There

On Teshima, the main ports are **Ieura** on the northwest shore and **Karato** in the northeast. Ferries run between Ieura and **Miyanoura** on

Naoshima (22 minutes; ¥630 adults, ¥320 children) and **Uno** on Honshu (40 minutes; ¥780 adults, ¥390 children); some continue on to **Karato** (1 hour; ¥1,050 adults, ¥530 children from Uno; or 15 minutes, ¥300 adults, ¥150 children from Ieura).

If you're coming directly from Uno, take either the Marine Liner (13 minutes; ¥770) or the JR Seto-Ohashi line (22 minutes; ¥240) to **Chayamachi Station,** then transfer to the JR Uno Port line to Uno Station (30 minutes; ¥330), then walk 3 minutes to Uno Port. Ferries run from Uno to Ieura on Teshima every 1-2 hours. Separately, ferries sailing from **Tonosho** on Shōdo-shima sail to both Karato (20 minutes; ¥490 adults, ¥250 children) and Ieura (35 minutes; ¥780 adults, ¥390 children). Note that some of these ferries do not run every day. For a full ferry timetable to and from Teshima, visit http://benesse-artsite.jp/en/access.

Getting Around

On Teshima, sporadic **buses** (¥200 adults, ¥100 children) run between Ieura and Karato, stopping at sights including the Teshima Art Museum along the way. See the schedule online at https://benesse-artsite.jp/en/uploads/access/map_201903.pdf. Alternatively, and recommended, rent a **bicycle** at the port in Ieura or Karato (standard ¥500 per day, electric ¥1,000 four hours, ¥100 each additional hour). Given the hilliness of the island's terrain, it's worth paying a bit extra for an electrically powered bicycle.

INUJIMA

犬島

This diminutive island (literally "Dog Island") lies to the north of Naoshima and Teshima, closer to Okayama. Here you'll find more galleries with stunning seaside vistas, but Inujima's backstory is rather more industrial. The small isle was the source of large granite blocks used in castle construction during Japan's feudal heyday, before turning to refining copper in the early 20th century—a short-lived boom due to a steep drop in prices for the metal. The ruins of the island's once bustling refinery now serve as the basis for its largest attraction, the Seirensho Art Museum.

Unlike Teshima and Naoshima, Inujima lacks public transport and is best explored on foot. Its manageable scale and rustic setting make it an appealing, offbeat option if you've already seen Naoshima and Teshima or would like to explore on foot in a relatively uncrowded environment. You can smoothly see the island in a half day.

From December 1, 2020, Inujima's art sites are only open Friday-Monday from March-November (open Tues. when Mon. is national holiday; otherwise, open on national holidays and closed the following day). From December-February, the island's art sites are completely shuttered. Check for updates on the official website of Benesse Art Site Naoshima (https://benesse-artsite.jp/en/), which also includes information for Inujima, before planning a trip.

Sights

SEIRENSHO ART MUSEUM

精錬所美術館

327-4 Inujima; tel. 086/947-1112; http://benesse-artsite.jp/en/art/seirensho.html; 9am-4:30pm (last entry 4pm) Fri.-Mon. Mar.-Nov., open Tues. when Mon. falls on holiday, closed Dec.-Feb.; ¥2,100, including admission to Inujima Art House Project and Seaside Inujima Gallery

The top sight on Inujima, much less visited even than Teshima, is the dreamlike, highly interactive Seirensho Art Museum. Built around the shell of a former copper refinery, this museum explores environmental crises and the contradictory nature of modernization in Japan through the artwork of Yanagi Yukinori. Among the materials Yanagi used to create the works housed in the museum are the remnants of the house once lived in by Mishima Yukio, a controversial, conflicted literary figure who is widely considered one of the most important Japanese novelists of the 20th century. It's worth noting that the architect Sambuichi Hiroshi had the museum built according to strict eco-friendly standards, using locally sourced granite and waste left over from the process of smelting copper. Plan your lunchtime around your visit to the museum: The attached café serves great lunches made with ingredients sourced from the island.

INUJIMA ART HOUSE PROJECT

Various locations around island; tel. 086/947-1112; http://benesse-artsite.jp/en/art/inujima-arthouse.html; 9am-4:30pm (last entry 4pm) Fri.-Mon. Mar.-Nov., open Tues. when Mon. falls on holiday, closed Dec.-Feb.; ¥2,100 including admission to Seirensho Art Museum and Seaside Inujima Gallery

The island's 50 or so inhabitants have fully embraced the "art island" concept, which has overtaken the main village in the form of five "art houses" and a few installations. As with the Seirensho Art Museum, the island's past and locally available materials figure heavily in the works on display. A good example is Asai Yusuke's installation *Listen to the Voices of Yesterday Like the Voices of Ancient Times*, which is built on the spot where a stonecutter's home once stood, using stone and other materials collected around the island, juxtaposed with images of plants and animals reminiscent of ancient cave paintings scrawled across the ground.

Food

Restaurants and cafés on Inujima close early on days they are open for business, and close on days when ferries do not run to the island, or when the main art sites are closed.

TREES INUJIMA

324 Inujima; tel. 086/947-1988; www.trees-rest.jp; 11am-3pm Wed.-Mon., otherwise closed on days when ferry does not run and other irregular holidays; ¥1,000

This restaurant, set in a wooden building by the water, has indoor seating and an open-air deck that is ideal for warm, sunny days. The simple menu consists of chicken curry and rice, salad made with local vegetables, and pudding made in-house. Try the craft beer brewed on the island (¥600).

UKI CAFE

293-2 Inujima; tel. 086/947-0877; www.facebook.com/Ukicafe; 10am-5pm Wed.-Mon. Mar.-Nov.; ¥1,000

This cozy restaurant set in a traditional wooden home has tatami-floor seating at low tables. The menu consists of good salads and pasta dishes made with local ingredients, from vegetables to octopus caught nearby. It's a good pick for lunch or an early dinner.

Information and Services

- **Inujima Ticket Center** (327-4 Inujima; tel. 086/947-1112; 9am-5pm Wed.-Mon. Mar.-Nov., closed Dec.-Feb.)

Getting There and Around

Inujima's one main port is on the northeast corner of the island. Ferries connect the island to **Miyanoura** on Naoshima (55 minutes; ¥1,880 adults, ¥940 children), via **Ieura** on Teshima (25 minutes; ¥1,250 adults, ¥630 children), and Okayama's **Hoden port** (10 minutes; ¥400 adults, ¥200 children). To reach Hoden port by train, take the JR Ako line from Okayama Station to Saidaiji Station (20 minutes; ¥240; 2 trains per hour), then transfer to a bus and ride to Nishi-Hoden (東宝伝) bus stop (1 hour; ¥540; 3-4 buses daily). Hoden port is about 2 minutes on foot south of there. Three buses also run between Okayama Station and near Hoden port (50 minutes; ¥760; daily during Setouchi Triennale, otherwise Sat. and Sun. only). Be aware that not all of these ferries run every day, with limited capacity in winter, among other times. For a full ferry timetable to and from Inujima, and additional information on how to reach these ports, visit http://benesse-artsite.jp/en/access.

Once on Inujima, it's possible to see all of its main sights **on foot** in about three hours.

The Inland Sea's Quieter Side

Naoshima and the other creative hubs nearby on Inujima and Teshima are undeniably the most accessible—and consequently, crowded—places to experience this gorgeous swath of sea. Other islands beckon from just beyond the tourist trail for those who yearn to experience the Inland Sea's charm at a much more intimate level, less impacted by the encroachment of mass tourism. Here are a few of the best slivers of land to get a taste of this simpler way of life.

SHŌDO-SHIMA

小豆島

To sink deeply into the Inland Sea's island time and immerse yourself in the local rhythms, the climatically mild Shōdo-shima, east of Teshima, is a good starting point. Here you'll find olive groves, citrus trees, walking trails, soaring cliffs, and lovely seascapes. Visit www.town.shodoshima.lg.jp for information about activities on the island and detailed access information.

While a day trip to Shōdo-shima is possible, an overnight stay will allow you to fully soak up the laid-back pace. A great spot to do this is the **Sen Guesthouse** (687-15 Tanoura Otsu; tel. 0879/61-9980; www.senguesthouse.com; ¥12,000 d with shared bathrooms, dorms ¥3,400). Run by a friendly English-speaking couple, this property has a private beach, balcony with seaside views, shared kitchen, and more. Another good option on the island is the **Shōdo-shima Olive Youth Hostel** (1072 Nishi-mura, Uchinomi-chō; tel. 0879/82-6161; www.jyh.gr.jp/shoudo; dorms ¥3,650).

Standard ferries run from Okayama's Uno Port to Tonosho Port in Shōdo-shima's west, stopping en route at Teshima's Ieura Port and Karato Port (8 ferries daily; 6:45am-7:30pm; 1 hour 30 minutes; ¥1,260 adults, ¥630 children standard ferry). If you're coming from Teshima, you can hop aboard a ferry to Tonosho following this same route at Ieura Port in the island's northwest (¥780 adults, ¥390 children) or Karato Port in the northeast (¥490 adults, ¥250 children). From Takamatsu in Shikoku's northeast, direct ferries depart for Tonosho (2-3 per hour; 6:25am-1:40pm; 1 hour; ¥700 adults, ¥350 children standard ferry, ¥1,190 adults, ¥600 children high-speed ferry).

KASAOKA ISLANDS

笠岡諸島

Farther west, the Kasaoka Islands also make for a great escape. Accessed from Kasaoka Port, located 5 minutes' walk from JR Kasaoka Station which is about 45 minutes by local train on the JR San'yo line from Okayama (¥760) and 30 minutes from Kurashiki (¥500), two of the most charming islands are **Shiraishi-jima** (www.kasaoka-kankou.jp/en/island/shiraishijima) and **Manabe-shima** (www.kasaoka-kankou.jp/en/island/manabeshima/), one of Japan's famed "cat islands," where felines rule the roost. Ferries run from Kasaoka Port to both Shiraishi-jima (4 times daily each for standard ferries and high-speed ferries; 7:25am-5:50pm; 35 minutes standard ferry, 22 minutes high-speed boat; ¥660 standard ferry, ¥1,150 high-speed ferry) and Manabe-shima (4 times daily each for standard ferries and high-speed ferries; 7:25am-5:50pm; 1 hour 12 minutes standard ferry, 44 minutes high-speed ferry; ¥1,020 standard ferry, ¥1,760 high-speed ferry). All fares for children elementary school age and younger are half-price.

Both islands make for a pleasant day trip, but the **Shiraishi Island International Villa** (tel. 086/256-2535; www.international-villa.or.jp; ¥3,600 pp, plus ¥500 single occupancy) is a great place for a serene overnight stay. The International Villa's staff are happy to recommend points of interest on either island, such as the mini-version of Shikoku's 88-temple pilgrimage spread across Shiraishi-jima, or discuss food options. (Stock up on snacks on the mainland before making the trip.) If you're on Shiraishi-jima during the warmer months, swing by the beachside **Moooo! Bar** (www.shiraishiisland.com/home/restaurants-and-bar/mooo-bar/; late morning-evening daily July-Aug., weekends only June and Sept.), run by expat Amy Chavez (http://amyonasia.com), who has deep ties to the local community. It's a great place to sip a cocktail in the summer heat or watch the sunset. Manabe-shima is best visited as a day trip from Shiraishi-jima. For access information on both islands, go to www.kasaoka-kankou.jp/en/access.

San'in 山陰

Travelers to the somewhat remote northern coast of Western Honshu, which sits in "the shadow side of the mountains" that bisect the region from east to west, will discover a quieter, slower side of Japan than the more developed southern coast. Dramatically rolling beside the Sea of Japan, Tottori Prefecture's singular sand dunes mark the eastern edge of the region. Moving west, Shimane Prefecture is home to the lovely castle town of Matsue and the spiritual power spot of Izumo, blessed with one of Japan's most important shrines.

MATSUE

松江

Nicknamed the "water city," Matsue is sandwiched between the salt lake of Nakaumi in the east and Shinji-ko in the west, with the river Ōhashi-gawa running between these two lakes and bisecting the city into northern and southern districts.

The bulk of compact Matsue's sights are located on the north bank of the Ōhashi-gawa. There, you'll find a pristine original black castle and the former **samurai quarter,** lined by a number of well-preserved samurai residences, hidden behind white plaster and wood-paneled walls. It was in this neighborhood where writer Lafcadio Hearn (1850-1904), the West's earliest great interpreter of things Japanese, first lived and fell under the spell of his adopted nation in 1890-1891.

Matsue can easily be seen in a day, and used as a base for exploring regional attractions like the grand shrine of Izumo Taisha and the Adachi Museum of Art, with its superb landscape garden.

Sights

★ MATSUE-JŌ

松江城

1-5 Tono-machi; tel. 0852/21-4030; www.matsue-castle.jp; 7am-7:30pm daily Apr.-Sept., 8:30am-5pm daily Oct.-Mar.; ¥680 adults (¥470 with foreign passport), ¥290 junior high and elementary school students (¥200 with foreign passport); walk 30 minutes north of Matsue Station, or take the Lake Line bus from Matsue Station to Ōte-mae bus stop (10 minutes; ¥200)

This black castle, constructed with pine timber in 1611, is one of Japan's most atmospheric and well preserved. Local lord Yoshiharu Horio (1542-1611) had the fortress built in 1611. Sitting atop a hill overlooking Matsue, the groaning main tower stands 30 meters (98 ft) tall, second in height among Japan's 12 remaining original castles.

Matsue-jō miraculously withstood the Edo period (1603-1868) and the anti-feudal wave of dismantling that ensued following the Meiji Restoration (1868), as well as centuries of earthquakes and fire. Walk through the subdued, pine-studded grounds, across its moat, and through its heavily fortified outer walls, and feel the subtle air of mystery surrounding the darkened citadel. The requisite display of samurai armor and weaponry is exhibited on the first few floors. Each level reveals more expansive vistas of Matsue and the surrounding countryside, extending as far as Mount Daisen on clear days. If you're visiting Matsue, the castle is a must-see.

To reach the castle, walk 30 minutes northwest of JR Matsue Station, crossing the Ōhashi River on the way. Alternatively, take the Lakeline bus from terminal seven in front of Matsue Station to the Ōte-mae bus stop (13 minutes, ¥150 one way).

ADACHI MUSEUM OF ART

足立美術館

320 Furukawa-chō, Yasugi; tel. 0854/28-7111; www.adachi-museum.or.jp; 9am-5:30pm daily Apr.-Sept., 9am-5pm daily Oct.-Mar.; ¥2,300 adults, ¥1,800 university students, ¥1,000 high school students, ¥500 junior high and elementary school students; from Matsue Station, take JR San'in line to Yasugi

Station (25 minutes; ¥420), then take museum shuttle bus (20 minutes; free)

Truth be told, the main draw of this museum is not so much its art collection, amassed by local businessman Adachi Zenkō (1899-1991), but its sublime gardens. The museum's collection consists of more than 1,000 paintings by 20th-century Japanese artists, including Yokoyama Taikan (1868-1958), a painter who played a seminal role in establishing the modern Nihonga movement. Founded in 1980 and located 20 kilometers (12.4 mi) southeast of Matsue in the town of Yasugi (25 minutes from Matsue by train), the museum claims the top slot year after year in polls on Japan's top gardens.

Adachi is divided into six separate gardens, each one as fastidiously laid out as the next. Every element is perfectly in its place, from the patterns raked into gravel to the placement of orbed shrubs with the mountains rising up beyond the garden.

Unlike most formal gardens, this one can only be appreciated from afar. Following an indoor trail of sorts, you pass through passageways walled only by glass on one or both sides, taking in views of the Moss Garden, the Dry Landscape Garden, the Kikaku Waterfall, the Garden of Juryū-an, the Pond Garden, and the White Gravel and Pine Garden. As you proceed through the museum's various stages, you'll take in views of Japanese art dating from the 1870s until today.

Most people visit the museum and its gardens on a day trip from Matsue. Regardless of whether you're stopping in the old castle town to the west, Adachi's collection and remarkable landscape are worth the trip.

Food

CAFE BAR E.A.D

E.A.D Bldg., 36 Suetsugu Hon-machi; tel. 0852/28-3130; 9pm-1am Wed.-Mon.; www.facebook.com/eadcafe; ¥300-900 per dish; around the corner from Kawakyō

Sitting beside the Ōhashi River, near the eastern edge of Shinji-ko, this café and bar is a good place to eat a casual late-night dinner or unwind over a few drinks. When it's warm, you can also kick back on the rooftop terrace, where the restaurant sometimes holds BBQs and concerts. The food menu includes good pizza and curry with rice.

YAKUMO-AN

308 Kitahori-chō; tel. 0852/22-2400; www.yakumoan.jp; 11am-1:30pm Mon.-Fri., 10am-2pm Sat.-Sun.; ¥700-1,150

Just beyond the moat on the north side of the castle, next to the Buke Yashiki samurai house, this soba joint serves good set lunches. With its garden and pond filled with colorful carp, the historic building reflects the atmospheric surroundings. Service is good and friendly. There's no English menu, but pictures give a clear indicator of what you're ordering. The kamo (duck) soup is delicious. Also on the menu, warigo includes three stacked lacquer bowls of soba, into which you pour dashi (soup stock), then add seaweed flecks. A queue often forms during the lunch rush, but it moves relatively fast. Incidentally, famed expatriate writer Lafcadio Hearn lived just a few doors down.

★ KAWAKYŌ

65 Suetsugu Hon-machi; tel. 0852/22-1312; 6pm-10:30pm Mon.-Sat.; ¥800-1,575, courses from ¥3,500; walk 20 minutes north of JR Matsue Station

This friendly, family-run restaurant serves up the touted "seven delicacies" of nearby lake Shinji-ko. Among these dishes are a standout called hosho-yaki, a style of cooking suzuki (sea bass) by swathing it in washi (traditional paper) and slow-baking it over heated coals, and broiled unagi (freshwater eel) that's been basted in soy sauce. The daughter of the charming family speaks English well, and there's an English menu too. This is a great place to pair your meal with locally produced sake, as well. Reserve at least a few days in advance. Highly recommended.

Accommodations

Extensive accommodation listings in English

1

2

are available at www.visit-matsue.com/info/lodging.

RYOKAN TERAZUYA

60-3 Tenjin-machi; tel. 0852/21-3480; www.mable.ne.jp/~terazuya; room only ¥4,600 pp, room with breakfast ¥5,300 pp, room with breakfast and dinner ¥9,100 pp; walk 10 minutes southwest of Matsue Station

This inviting family-run ryokan is a great option if you're traveling on a budget. The simple, clean tatami rooms all have futons instead of beds, air-conditioning, and a shared bathroom. The friendly couple who run the inn speak a smattering of English. Note that there's a curfew of 10pm. If you can accept this doors-closing policy and work with the shared bathroom, it's an excellent place to stay. The owners provide complimentary pickup from the train station.

★ MINAMIKAN

14 Suetsugu Hon-machi; tel; 0852/21-5131; www.minami-g.co.jp/minamikan; ¥55,750 d with two meals; walk 17 minutes from Matsue Station

This plush ryokan is Matsue's best hotel. In business for well over a century and renovated in 2007, the lavish property sits at the eastern edge of Shinji-ko, which it overlooks. The aesthetic is distinctly classical, from the beautiful garden of white gravel dotted by stone lanterns and pine trees to the tatami rooms of varying grades (and prices): some more Western, others strictly classic. The simpler rooms are tatami-mat affairs. At the upper end, rooms come with en-suite cypress onsen bathtubs fronted by lake-facing windows. The entire property is non-smoking. It's located a stone's throw from the popular local restaurant Kawakyō.

Information and Services

There's a friendly **tourist information center** just in front of the north exit of Matsue Station (665 Asahi-machi; tel. 0852/21-4034; www.kankou-matsue.jp; 8:30am-6pm daily). English-speaking staff are happy to give advice on sights and transportation. There's also free Wi-Fi on-site.

For a good online guide to Matsue and to Shimane Prefecture as a whole—encompassing Izumo and the Oki Islands—visit Shimane's helpful English website at www.kankou-shimane.com/en.

Getting There

Matsue is best reached by train. The closest shinkansen stop is actually in **Okayama;** you can reach Matsue from Okayama Station via the **Yakumo limited express train** (2 hours 40 minutes; ¥6,140), or by **local train** via Niimi and then Yonago, taking the JR Hakubi line from Okayama to Niimi, then transferring to another section of the JR Hakubi line to Yonago, where you'll then transfer to the JR San'in line, which you'll ride until Matsue (5-10 hours depending on time between transfers; ¥3,410). Given the exceptionally long time it takes to travel by local train, the limited express, covered by the JR pass, is an attractive option.

Matsue Station is on the JR San'in line, which runs from Tottori in the east, continuing west along the Sea of Japan coast. From Tottori, which lies to the east of Matsue, take the Tottori-Liner to Yonago, then transfer to either the Yakumo limited express (2.5 hours; ¥3,600) or the Aqua-Liner (3 hours, ¥2,310) and ride the rest of the way to Matsue. Alternatively, take the local JR San'in line to Yonago, where you'll transfer to the next stretch of the same line bound for Izumo-shi and ride the rest of the way to Matsue (3 hours; ¥2,310). You can cut the time required for this journey by hopping on the **Super Matsukaze limited express,** which goes directly from Tottori to Matsue (1 hour 25 minutes; ¥4,700). Coming from Izumo in the west, take either the local JR San'in line (45 minutes; ¥590) or the Yakumo limited express (25 minutes; ¥1,880) from Izumo-shi Station to Matsue Station. The limited express trains are good options for holders of the JR pass.

Taking the train is the most comfortable,

1: Matsue-jō **2:** Izumo Taisha

efficient way of reaching Matsue, but there is a **bus terminal** next to Matsue Station. Visit the website of the **Chūgoku JR Bus Company** (www.chugoku-jrbus.co.jp) for detailed routes, timetables, and fares. Alternatively, visit **Japan Bus Online** (https://japanbusonline.com/en), which aggregates a number of providers' routes nationwide.

Getting Around

Matsue is a very **walkable** city. It's about 30 minutes on foot from Matsue Station to the castle.

The **Lake Line** bus follows a circuit around town, stopping at the castle and neighboring samurai quarter (www.visit-matsue.com/info/moving; 8:40am-6:48pm daily Mar.-Nov., 8:40am-4:58pm Dec.-Feb.; single ride ¥200 adults, ¥100 children, day pass ¥500 adults, ¥250 children). Buses depart every 20 minutes, and riding the full route takes about 50 minutes.

Another great way to explore Matsue is on two wheels. **Bicycle rentals** are available outside both Matsue Station and Matsue Shinji-ko Onsen Station. A good bet is **Eki Rent-a-Cycle** (483-5 Asahi-machi; tel. 0852/23-8880; 9am-5pm daily), located just outside the south exit of Matsue Station. Note that this outfit rents cars, too, in case you want to venture farther afield.

IZUMO
出雲

The charming town of Izumo, located about a half-hour train ride west of Matsue on the pastoral San'in coast, is primarily known for its myth-infused grand shrine, Izumo Taisha. After Ise Jingu, Izumo Taisha is Shinto's second-holiest shrine and is believed to be its oldest. The main deity enshrined at this sprawling complex is the god of marriage and relationships, Ōkuninushi. Beside the shrine, the Shimane Museum of Ancient Izumo illuminates the region's primeval past, as well as the construction and gradual evolution of this monumentally important shrine. With its compact size, Izumo is an easy day trip from Matsue.

Sights

★ IZUMO TAISHA
出雲大社

195 Kizukihigashi, Taisha-chō; tel. 0853/53-3100; www.izumooyashiro.or.jp; 6:30am-8pm daily; free; walk 5 minutes north of Izumotaisha-mae Station (Ichibata Densa-Taisha line)

Izumo Taisha is Japan's oldest Shinto shrine, and second only to Ise-jingu in cultural importance. Its history stretches back so far into antiquity that the founding of the shrine is almost indistinguishable from the beginnings of Japan itself. It's mentioned in the 8th-century *Kojiki,* Japan's earliest penned chronicle, which tells us that it dates at least as far back as the early part of that century.

The setting is lovely, with verdant mountains hovering in the background just beyond the grounds. On the approach to the shrine, walk along either side of a long avenue lined by pine trees, but whatever you do, don't walk in the middle: This walkway is reserved for the gods.

The main hall, constructed in 1744, is 23.8 meters (78 ft) tall. Until that time, it was rebuilt semi-regularly, much like Ise-jingu still is today. In ancient times, it was the largest wooden structure in Japan, but was scaled down by half with each successive rebuilding, starting in the 13th century. At its highest point, the main hall was said to have been as tall as 48 meters (157.5 ft). The main hall's most distinguishing feature today is the 7.6-meter-long (25-ft-long), five-ton shimenawa (braided straw rope) festooned above the main entrance. As in the shrine's counterpart in Ise, it's forbidden for commoners to enter the inner sanctum, which sits tucked away behind towering fences.

The shrine's principle deity is Ōkuninushi ("Great Land Master"), the god of marriage and fortune and, legend tells us, the creator of Japan's geographical contours and onetime ruler of Izumo. Worshippers visiting the shrine clap their hands four times instead of two, as is customary in Shinto, when summoning Ōkuninushi. Two claps are reserved for themselves, and the other two for their hoped-for or current partner. In addition to praying for success in marriage, if you can manage to chuck a ¥5 piece and lodge it into the mammoth rope overhanging the entrance—no small feat—it's said that you'll be blessed with good fortune and your marriage will be relatively smooth sailing. It's worth a shot!

The shrine is located more than 9 kilometers (5.6 mi) northwest of Izumo-shi Station. To reach the shrine, catch a bus in front of Izumo-shi Station at stop number one (25 minutes ¥520 one way). Buses leave about twice hourly. Alternatively, take the local Ichibata railway line from Izumo-shi Station to Izumo Taisa-mae Station (20 minutes, ¥490 one way). The shrine is about 10 minutes' walk north of there.

SHIMANE MUSEUM OF ANCIENT IZUMO
島根県立古代出雲歴史博物館

99-4 Kizukihigashi, Taisha-chō; tel. 0853/53-8600; www.izm.ed.jp; 9am-6pm daily Mar.-Oct., 9am-5pm daily Nov.-Feb., closed third Tues. of month; ¥310 adults, ¥200 university students, ¥100 high/junior high/elementary school students; walk 10 minutes north of Izumo Taisha-mae Station (Ichibata Densa-Taisha line)

Sitting on the right side of the main gate to Izumo Taisha, this museum illuminates Izumo's rich history. Bronze bells and swords unearthed in the area date back to the Yayoi period (300 BC-AD 300). The focus of the museum, however, is on the shrine: its evolution over time and the myths attached to it, including the great annual Kamiari Festival, in which Japan's 8 million deities meet in Izumo for a week during the 10th lunar month.

One relic of note is a gigantic pillar that measures a full meter (3.3 ft) in circumference. The discovery of pillars of such mammoth proportions, among other evidence, has led to speculation that the main hall may have been as tall as 48 meters (157.5 ft) at its peak. Models illustrate how this top-heavy construction might have looked. From the displays, it's easy to see why it is said to have collapsed under its own weight five times between the 11th and 13th centuries.

Festivals

KAMIARI-SAI
神在祭

Seven days (11-17) of the 10th lunar month

According to legend, Ōkuninushi relinquished control of Izumo to the lineage of Amaterasu (sun goddess) in exchange for the founding of a grand shrine for him. Every year during the 10th lunar month, which is usually November, all 8 million gods and goddesses convene in Izumo to determine the fates of mortals during the year to come. This month is called Kamiarizuki ("month with gods") in Izumo, but Kannazuki ("month without gods") throughout the rest of Japan. The shrine hosts the annual Kamiari Festival during that week. When the gods crowd into Izumo, they stay in the two long buildings that sit along both sides of the complex.

The proceedings are marked with bonfires on the beach and other rituals. During this special month, Izumo Taisha becomes a special place of pilgrimage for marriage-hopefuls. If you're already attached, however, be careful not to come together; it's said that Okuninushi is displeased by those who show up with their partner without first consulting him. As fun as a joint trip to the shrine during Kannazuki may sound, don't tempt fate!

Food

ARAKIYA

409-2 Kizuki-higashi, Taisha-chō; tel. 0853/53-2352; www.izumo-kankou.gr.jp/1640; 11am-5pm Thurs.-Tues., closed Thurs. if Wed. falls on holiday; set meals ¥810-1,490; walk 5 minutes south of Izumo Taisha bus stop, or 10 minutes northwest of Izumo Taisha-mae Station on the Ichibata Densha-Taisha railway line

Housed in a traditional building, this restaurant serves great soba warigo style, stacked in three lacquerware boxes. Just pour the soup stock over the noodles and add the seaweed flakes, grated daikon, and chopped green onions. The kamo (duck) option is also delicious. A picture menu makes ordering easy. While it has a solid local following and sometimes attracts a slight queue, this restaurant is outside the more bustling tourist zone.

TONKI

1266-2 Tsukane, Imaichi-chō; tel. 0853/21-4395; 5pm-11pm Tues.-Sun.; ¥1,100-2,000 set meals; walk 8 minutes north of Izumo-shi Station

This restaurant has the broad menu of an izakaya, but is known for its tonkatsu (fried, breaded pork cutlet). The easiest thing to do is order a tonkatsu teishoku (set meal). There's no English menu, but there are photos. Of the seven types of pork to choose from, the main two worth trying are hire (lean, tenderloin) and rousu (fatty, loin). If you feel like something else, the menu extends to sashimi, various grilled meat dishes, and other nibbles.

Information and Services

If you're arriving via Izumo-shi Station, stop by the **tourist information office** located in the station (tel. 0853/30-6015; 9am-5pm daily). Near Izumo Taisha-mae Station, proceed a few minutes north along the main road that leads to the shrine grounds and you'll find a helpful **tourist information center** on the right side of the street (780-4 Kizukiminami; tel. 0853/53-2298; 9am-5pm daily).

Online, the **Visit Izumo** website (www.izumo-kankou.gr.jp/english) provides plenty of good local intel, from a primer on the region's history and sights off the beaten path to a list of eateries in town.

Getting There and Around

To reach Izumo Taisha from nearby **Matsue,** you can take the JR San'in line from Matsue Station to **Izumo-shi Station** (45 minutes; ¥590), then transfer to the old-school Ichibata line and ride until **Izumo Taisha-mae Station** (30 minutes; ¥500).

Alternatively, you can hop on a **local bus** from Matsue Station to **Matsue Shinji-ko Onsen Station,** which sits at the northeast corner of lake Shinji-ko. From there, you can hop on the Ichibata Kita-Matsue line bound for Dentetsu Izumoshi to Kawato, where you'll transfer to the Ichibata Taisha line bound for Izumo Taisha-mae and ride for the rest of the trip to Izumo Taisha-mae Station (1 hour 5 minutes; ¥820).

From Izumo Taisha-mae Station, the grounds of Izumo Taisha are about 10 minutes' **walk** north.

Tottori Sand Dunes

Tottori Sand Dunes

Tottori is Japan's most sparsely populated prefecture, a tiny sliver of land populated by warm-hearted locals with a singular claim to fame: massive hills of sand. The sakyū (dunes) sprawl across more than 30 square kilometers (12 square mi). The dunes are part of the San'in Kaigan National Park, a wild stretch of shoreline that runs from the city of Tottori in the west to Kyoto Prefecture in the east.

This unlikely simulacrum of the Sahara is located about 5 kilometers (3.1 mi) north of town. The massive dunes were created over millennia, as sands from the **Sendai-gawa River** were pushed out to sea, only to be brought back to shore by the **Sea of Japan**'s currents. This process of redistribution is ongoing, and the coast of Tottori is always in flux. You can either gaze seaward from atop the dunes or walk along the beachfront. Tour providers in the sand dunes' area offer everything from paragliding and sandboarding to yoga sessions on the dunes and cycling with bikes with special tires that don't get bogged down in the terrain. In the Uradome area, you'll also find sea kayaking outfits. To learn more about the activities available, visit Tottori's **tourist information portal** (www.tottori-tour.jp/en), where you'll also find food listings for the area, access information, and more.

Near the east side of the dunes, the **Tottori Sand Museum** (2083-17 Yūyama, Fukube-chō; tel. 0857/20-2231; www.sand-museum.jp; 9am-4pm Mon.-Fri., 9am-5pm Sat.-Sun. and public holidays; ¥600 university students and older, ¥500 high/junior high/elementary school students, free for younger than elementary school students) houses massive, intricate sand sculptures, created by artists from all corners of the world. Be sure to check the museum's website to confirm whether it's open during your planned visit. It's located at the eastern edge of the dunes near the intersection of routes 265 and 319.

GETTING THERE AND AROUND

Buses from **Tottori Station** run to the **Sakyū Center,** a worn complex atop the dunes with an observation deck and a tacky souvenir shop. From here you can gaze seaward from on high, then either walk down to the beachfront or take a chairlift down. Alternatively, you can take a bus to **Sakyū Kaikan,** which will put you right next to the eastern side of the dunes. To reach Tottori Station from JR Matsue Station, take the limited express train (1 hour 35 minutes; ¥4,500) or JR San'in line, sometimes requiring a transfer to the Tottori-Liner train at Yonago (2 hours 30 minutes; ¥2,310). From JR Izumo-shi Station, take the Limited Express Super Matsukaze train straight to JR Tottori Station (1 hour 50 minutes; ¥5,170), or if you're in less of a hurry, board the Aqua-Liner train to Yonago, then transfer to the JR San'in line for the rest of the journey to JR Tottori Station (3 hour 30 minutes; ¥2,640).

Shikoku 四国

Takamatsu and Around 458
Tokushima............. 463
Iya Valley 470
Matsuyama and Around 476
Kochi 487

The smallest and least populated of Japan's four main islands, Shikoku has always felt removed from the Japanese mainland. It's much easier to access now, thanks to a series of bridges linking Honshu with Shikoku's northern coast, but a sense of otherness pervades the island nonetheless. Its deep mountainous interior has limited public transportation, and its dramatic coastline rolls on seemingly without end.

The island's northern coast is bordered by one of the world's loveliest seascapes, the Seto Naikai (Inland Sea), a calm, blue expanse often compared to Greece's Aegean Sea. In the east, in the city of Tokushima, colorfully clad dancers bring the streets to life at the electrifying Awa Odori dance festival at the sweltering peak of summer each year.

Highlights

Look for ★ to find recommended sights, activities, dining, and lodging.

★ **Ritsurin-kōen:** Wander through tunnels of boughs and over arched bridges in this pine-studded garden wonderland (page 459).

★ **Konpira-san:** Climb the dizzying staircase of stone to the mountaintop shrine dedicated to the divine protector of mariners, basking in stunning vistas from the top (page 462).

★ **88-Temple Pilgrimage:** While walking the entire 1,200-kilometer (750-mi) circuit is a Herculean task, traipsing at least some of the way that Kōbō Daishi, the founder of Shingon Buddhism, once trod, is an unforgettable experience, both earthy and enlightening (page 464).

★ **Awa Odori:** Join the dancing throngs of merrymakers in yukata (lightweight kimonos) at Japan's quintessential summer festival in balmy Tokushima (page 465).

★ **Kazura-bashi:** A careful walk across this famed vine bridge is an unforgettable stop in the Iya Valley, where you'll find some of Japan's wildest terrain (page 470).

★ **Dōgo Onsen:** Bathe in the antique onsen that helped inspire anime maestro Hayao Miyazaki's dreamy bathhouse of the gods, seen in his masterpiece *Spirited Away* (page 477).

Regional Food Specialties

SANUKI UDON

The island of Shikoku is known for the quality of its udon, and this is its most famous variety: wheat noodles eaten cold with dipping sauce or in a hot soup. Toppings include grated daikon, green onion, bonito flakes, and more. Try it at **Udon Honjin Yamadaya Sanuki Honten** (page 460).

HONETSUKI-DORI

A specialty of Kagawa in the island's northeast is this style of crispy, fried chicken, intensely seasoned with salt and pepper. Try it at **Ranmaru** (page 460).

TOKUSHIMA-STYLE RAMEN

In Tokushima's spin on ramen, the noodles are served in a heavy broth made from soy sauce and pork bones, topped with pork ribs, green onions, bean sprouts, and a raw egg that cooks in the soup. Try it at **Menō** (page 466).

KATSUO

The southern prefecture of Kochi has a reputation for this dish, bonito seared until golden outside but rare inside. The dish is then served with ginger, leek, garlic, citrusy ponzu, soy dipping sauce, and more. Try it at **Myojinmaru** (page 490).

TAIMESHI

Shikoku's northwestern Ehime Prefecture is known for red snapper dipped in raw egg, served with sweetened rice. Try it at **Daikokuya** (page 480).

Heading inland, in the rugged Iya Valley, deep ravines are crossed by bridges made from thick vines, with white-water rapids rushing below. Here, hamlets cling to vanishing ways of life, now slowly being revived thanks to staunch preservation.

In balmy Kochi Prefecture, sprawling across the island's vast subtropical south, palm trees, citrus fruit, great beaches, fun-loving locals, and Shikoku's other rowdy dance festival, the Yosakoi Matsuri, make for an intoxicating mix. And in western Ehime Prefecture, Matsuyama is home to a superb castle and the vaunted Dōgo Onsen, straight out of a fantastical Studio Ghibli film.

The island's most epic journey is its 88-Temples Pilgrimage Route, for which we have native son Kōbō Daishi (774-835), or Kūkai, founder of the sect of Shingon Buddhism, to thank. Stretching 1,400 kilometers (870 mi), it takes about 40 days to walk, as countless pilgrims have done in the past. These days, many undertake the journey in the comfort of a bus or car, but completing even a section of the epic journey on your own two feet can be transformative.

ORIENTATION

Shikoku may be the smallest of Japan's four main islands, but it's not exactly bite-sized at 225 kilometers (140 mi) long east to west, and anywhere from 50 kilometers (31 mi) to 150 kilometers (93 mi) wide. Honshu lies to the north, across the Inland Sea, and east, across the Kii Strait. Kyushu lies to the southwest, across the Bungo Strait.

Shikoku translates to "four provinces"; moving clockwise from Shikoku's northeast,

Previous: Ritsurin-kōen; Kazura-bashi bridge in Iya Valley; Awa Odori.

Best Accommodations

★ **Chiiori:** This thatched-roof home is a dreamlike escape from modernity on the steep slopes of the Iya Valley (page 474).

★ **Chaharu Hanare Dōgo Yumekura:** A stone's throw from the historic bathhouse of Dōgo Onsen, this chic, up-to-the-minute ryokan offers guests premium service, exquisite meals, and inviting en suite baths (page 481).

★ **Hotel Cocoro.Kura:** This smart property set in a renovated home in the heart of Uchiko's historic district has spacious rooms, a private garden, and plenty of old-world charm (page 484).

★ **Nipponia Hotel:** Scattered around Ōzu's historic castle area, this "decentralized hotel" offers a range of boutique guest rooms in refurbished historic residences, overseen by a passionate team eager to ensure your stay in their charming town is memorable (page 485).

Kagawa Prefecture, with its urban center of **Takamatsu,** is the most urbanized of the four and the most connected to the rest of Japan. Just south of Kagawa, occupying the eastern-central section of the island, is **Tokushima Prefecture,** a great entry point to the island's wild interior, including the **Iya Valley.** Along its southern edge flows the Yoshino River, a white-water-rafting mecca that also forms the northern border of **Kochi Prefecture** (formerly Tosa).

Kochi encompasses the southern half of the island. This thinly populated prefecture brims with thickly forested mountains and wild stretches of coast. The prefectural capital city, **Kochi,** is a lively, subtropical town on an alluvial plain blessed by mild winters and agricultural abundance. Rounding out the island, northwestern **Ehime Prefecture** (once called Iyo) borders Kochi to the south and both Kagawa and Tokushima to the east. Its main city and capital is **Matsuyama,** home to the famed **Dōgo Onsen,** Japan's first hot-spring inn. **Ishizuchi-san,** Shikoku's tallest mountain at 1,982 meters (6,503 feet), is also found in Ehime.

In 1988, the **Seto-Chūō Expressway** was completed, linking Shikoku's northeast coast to Okayama Prefecture in Western Honshu via six long bridges. A decade later came the **Kobe-Awaji-Naruto Expressway,** linking Kobe on Honshu with Naruto on Shikoku's northeastern coast via the rather large island of Awaji-shima. This route includes the world's longest suspension bridge, the Akashi-Kaikyō Bridge. Finally, the **Nishiseto Expressway,** commonly referred to as the **Shimanami Kaidō** (page 424), was finished in 1999, bridging the gap between Onomichi in Hiroshima Prefecture and Imabari in Ehime Prefecture. It's the only bridge of the three that can be traversed by bicycle or on foot. But most visitors arrive from Honshu via Okayama by train, a lovely ride over the Inland Sea in its own right.

PLANNING YOUR TIME

Despite its relatively small size, there is a lot to discover on Shikoku, which can make for an enticing addition to any trip through Western Honshu, but it deserves deep exploration on its own. A jaunt through the **northern half** of the island calls for about five days. Plan to add another 2-3 days if you include **Kochi** in your itinerary. One could easily spend 10-12 days on the island and still find more to discover.

The island is blessed with **warmer weather** than most of Honshu: a long, pleasant spring, hot muggy summers,

Shikoku

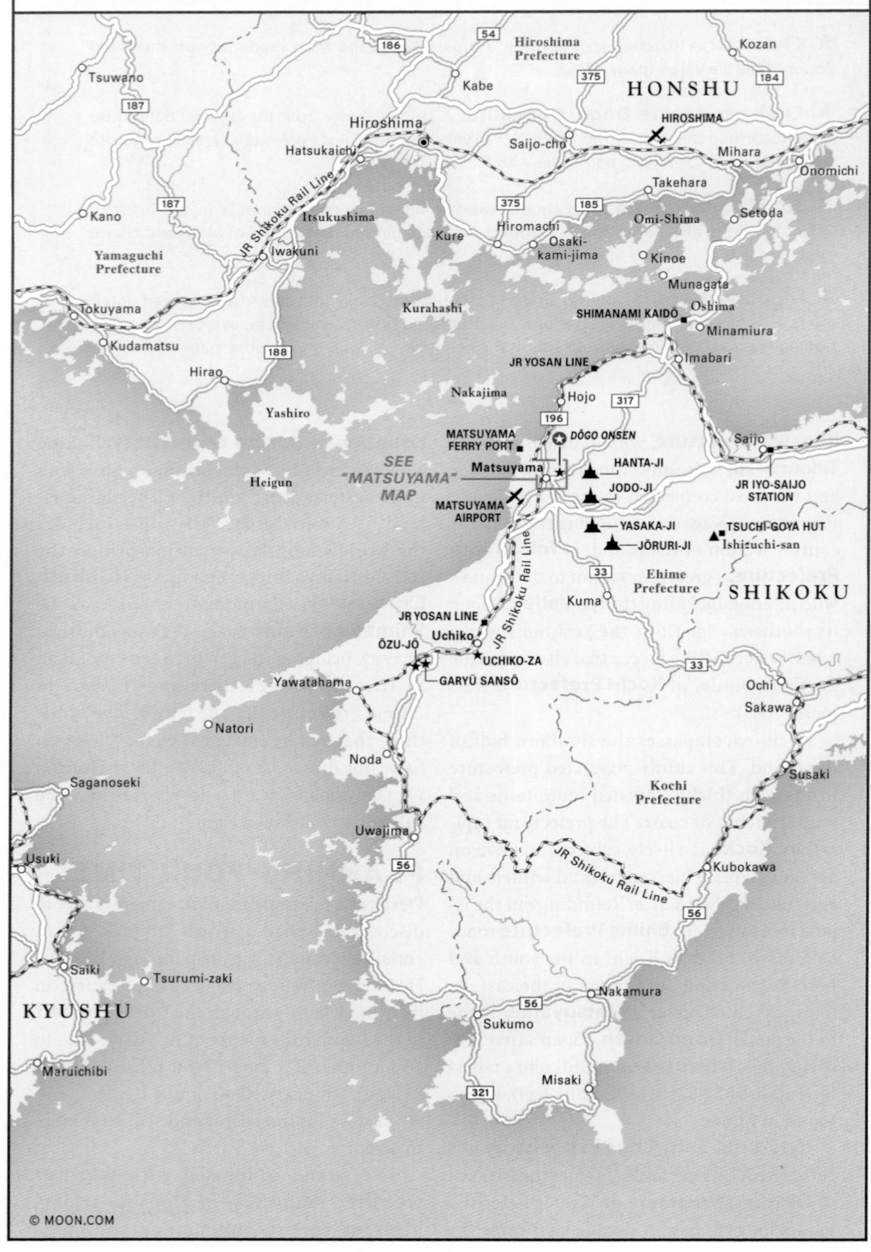

Hiroshima Prefecture
HONSHU
Tsuwano
Kabe
Kozan
Hiroshima
HIROSHIMA
Hatsukaichi
Saijo-cho
Mihara
Onomichi
JR Shikoku Rail Line
Kano
Itsukushima
Takehara
Kure
Hiromachi
Osaki-kami-jima
Omi-Shima
Setoda
Yamaguchi Prefecture
Iwakuni
Kinoe
Munagata
Tokuyama
Kurahashi
SHIMANAMI KAIDŌ
Oshima
Minamiura
Kudamatsu
JR YOSAN LINE
Imabari
Hirao
Nakajima
Hojo
Yashiro
MATSUYAMA FERRY PORT
DŌGO ONSEN
Saijo
SEE "MATSUYAMA" MAP
Matsuyama
HANTA-JI
Heigun
JODO-JI
JR IYO-SAIJO STATION
MATSUYAMA AIRPORT
YASAKA-JI
TSUCHI-GOYA HUT
JŌRURI-JI
Ishizuchi-san
Ehime Prefecture
SHIKOKU
Kuma
JR YOSAN LINE
Uchiko
ŌZU-JŌ
UCHIKO-ZA
GARYŪ SANSŌ
Yawatahama
Ochi
Sakawa
Natori
Noda
Susaki
Saganoseki
Kochi Prefecture
Uwajima
Usuki
Kubokawa
Saiki
Tsurumi-zaki
Nakamura
KYUSHU
Sukumo
Maruichibi
Misaki
54
186
375
184
187
187
375
185
188
317
196
33
33
56
56
56
321

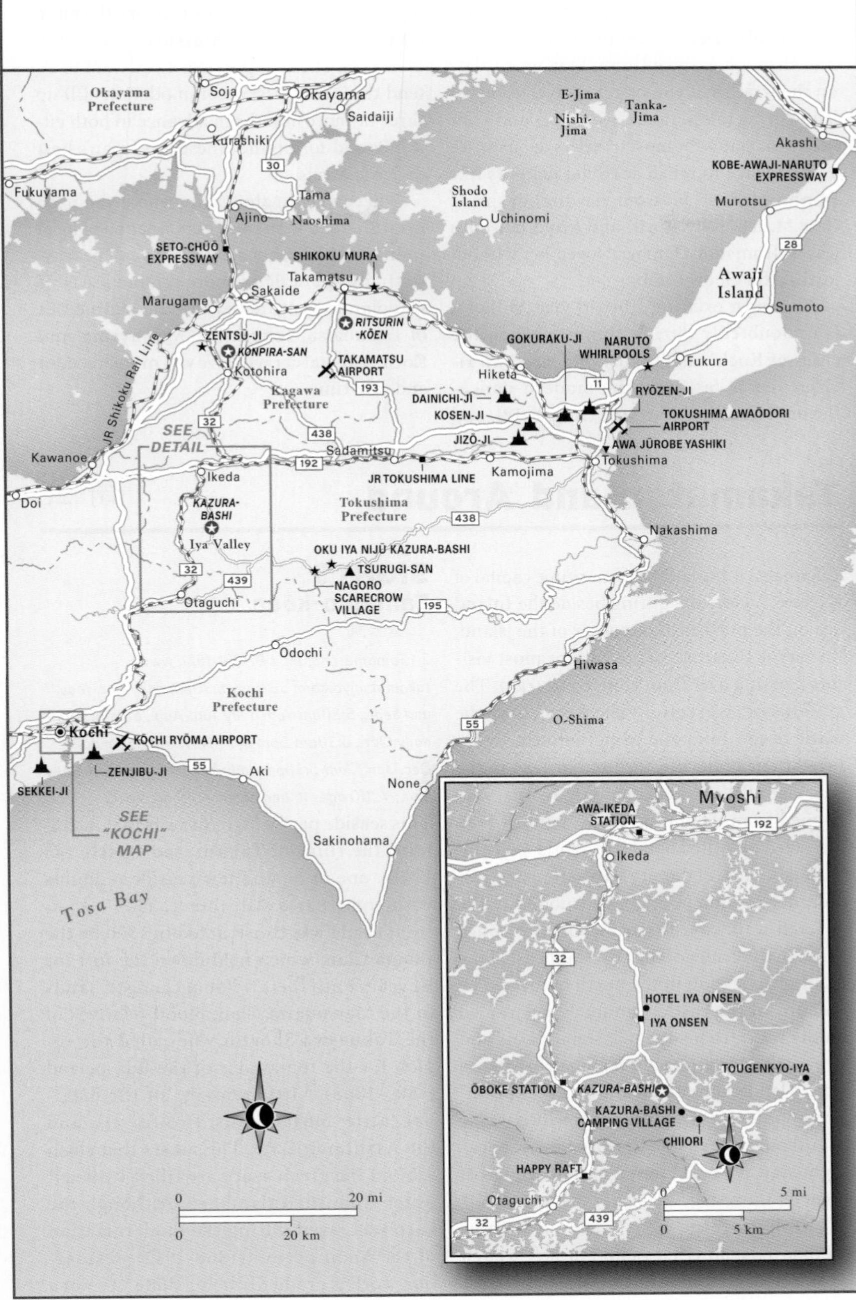
Okayama Prefecture
Soja
Okayama
Saidaiji
E-Jima
Nishi-Jima
Tanka-Jima
Akashi
KOBE-AWAJI-NARUTO EXPRESSWAY
Kurashiki
30
Fukuyama
Tama
Shodo Island
Ajino
Naoshima
Uchinomi
Murotsu
SETO-CHŪŌ EXPRESSWAY
SHIKOKU MURA
28
Takamatsu
Awaji Island
Marugame
Sakaide
Sumoto
RITSURIN -KŌEN
ZENTSŪ-JI
KONPIRA-SAN
GOKURAKU-JI
NARUTO WHIRLPOOLS
TAKAMATSU AIRPORT
Kotohira
Hiketa
Fukura
193
11
RYŌZEN-JI
Kagawa Prefecture
DAINICHI-JI
JR Shikoku Rail Line
32
KOSEN-JI
TOKUSHIMA AWAŌDORI AIRPORT
SEE DETAIL
438
JIZŌ-JI
AWA JŪROBE YASHIKI
Sadamitsu
Kawanoe
192
Tokushima
Ikeda
JR TOKUSHIMA LINE
Kamojima
Doi
KAZURA-BASHI
Tokushima Prefecture
438
Nakashima
Iya Valley
OKU IYA NIJŪ KAZURA-BASHI
TSURUGI-SAN
32
439
NAGORO SCARECROW VILLAGE
Otaguchi
195
Odochi
Hiwasa
Kochi Prefecture
55
O-Shima
Kochi
KŌCHI RYŌMA AIRPORT
55
ZENJIBU-JI
SEKKEI-JI
Aki
None
SEE "KOCHI" MAP
Sakinohama
Tosa Bay
0
20 mi
0
20 km
Myoshi
AWA-IKEDA STATION
192
Ikeda
32
HOTEL IYA ONSEN
IYA ONSEN
TOUGENKYO-IYA
ŌBOKE STATION
KAZURA-BASHI
KAZURA-BASHI CAMPING VILLAGE
CHIIORI
HAPPY RAFT
Otaguchi
0
5 mi
32
439
0
5 km

pleasant autumns, and relatively tame winters. **Typhoons** are common in late summer through early autumn. Stay up-to-date on the weather if you plan to travel to the island during this period. Given the island's off-the-radar status for most travelers to Japan, it's a great place to relish seasonal delights like **hanami** (cherry blossom viewing) in spring (late March-early April) and **kōyō** (autumn leaves) from mid-October-November without jostling for elbow room.

The most exciting time to visit Shikoku is undoubtedly during summer, when the cities of Kochi and Tokushima host two riotous dance festivals: the modern-dance-flavored **Yosakoi Matsuri** (Aug. 9-12), and my personal favorite of any matsuri, the more traditional **Awa Odori Matsuri** (Aug. 12-15). Plan as far ahead as possible if you want to attend these festivals; accommodations fill up three or more months in advance in both cities. Pound for pound, these are Japan's best dance festivals.

You can get to almost anywhere you need to on Shikoku with some combination of local trains and buses, but connections can be frustratingly sporadic in more remote areas. If you plan to venture beyond the main cities of Takamatsu, Tokushima, Matsuyama, and Kochi, a rental car will give you more freedom and save time.

Takamatsu and Around 高松

Takamatsu is the laid-back maritime capital of Kagawa Prefecture. Sitting beside the Inland Sea on the northeastern corner of the island, the city is the first port of call for most visitors crossing over from Honshu by train. The city's history is eventfully checkered, from the battle of the Taira and Minamoto clans that raged in neighboring Yashima in 1185 to the later rise of Warlord Chikamasa Ikoma, who reigned from the hilltop castle, built in 1588 but razed by Allied bombs in World War II.

Today, most of the city's action—cafés, restaurants, fashion boutiques—is found in the covered walkways that run north to south through the center of the city, southeast of the main train station in the north of town. The remains of the castle—uniquely positioned on the waterfront—include some moats and stray walls. More intact is its Ritsurin-kōen, a superb landscape garden known for its profusion of pine trees twisting every which way.

Although the city makes for a pleasant one-night stay, it's best viewed as a jumping-off point for the rest of Shikoku or the "art island" of Naoshima (page 432). Nearby, **Kotohira** is home to Japan's first kabuki theater, as well as one of its grandest shrines, Konpira-san.

SIGHTS

Tamamo-kōen

玉藻公園

2-1 Tamamo-chō; tel. 087/851-1521; www.takamatsujyo.com; 5:30am-6:30pm daily Apr.-May and Sept., 5:30am-7pm daily Jun.-Aug., 6am-5:30pm daily Oct., 6:30am-5pm daily Nov., 7am-5pm daily Dec.-Jan., 7am-5:30pm daily Feb., 6:30am-6pm daily Mar.; ¥200 ages 16 and older, ¥100 ages 6-15

This seaside park's main draw is that it contains the ruins of **Takamatsu Castle** (高松城), one of Japan's few seaside redoubts with some parts still intact. This ocean-front castle was constructed in 1590 by the Ikoma Clan, which held down the fort for 54 years until their fiefdom changed hands to the Matsudaira Clan, blood relatives of the Tokugawa Shogun who ruled the region for the remainder of the Edo period (1603-1868). Little remains of the original castle: moats, walls, two turrets, and the Asahimon Gate. The moats that slosh around the green space are filled with salt water from the Inland Sea. Although the keep was razed during the modernization of the Meiji period (1868-1912), restoration work is gradually being done. It's not a must-see, but the rare position next to the waterfront is unique.

★ Ritsurin-kōen

栗林公園

1-20-16 Ritsurin-kōen; tel. 087/833-7411; www.my-kagawa.jp/ritsuringarden; dusk to dawn daily; ¥410

Though not technically part of the trio considered Japan's top landscape gardens (Mito's Kairaku-en; Kanazawa's Kenroku-en, page 262; and Okayama's Kōraku-en, page 429), Ritsurin is of the same caliber. Planted, expanded, and pruned for more than a century by a succession of Takamatsu's feudal lords starting in the 17th century, this 750,000-square-meter (75-acre) green space—Japan's largest dedicated garden—deserves at least two hours of wandering.

Divided into south and north sections, the garden began to take shape in the mid-1620s at the hand of Takatoshi Ikoma, once the feudal lord of Sanuki (modern-day Kagawa). The grounds were inherited next by Yorishige Matsudaira, who was later appointed lord of the Takamatsu domain in 1642. The Matsudaira clan continued to expand the grounds until it finally reached its full dimensions in 1754. It served as the Matsudaira family's private escape until opening to the public in 1875, following the Meiji Restoration (1868). It was declared a National Treasure in 1953.

There are arched wooden bridges, almost 30,000 trees, long winding paths through tunnels of pine branches, artificial hills, teahouses, a manmade waterfall, and several lakes teeming with colorful koi (carp). Be sure also to stop by **Kikugestu-tei** (9am-4pm daily), a lovely teahouse perched beside the South Lake, for a green tea and a sweet—you can buy a combination ticket at either of the garden's two entrances for the gardens and the teahouse.

Located about 2.5 kilometers (1.5 mi) south of JR Takamatsu Station in the center of Takamatsu, the garden can be reached on foot (35 minutes) or via taxi (about 5 minutes; ¥700); travel south along Chūō-dōri until you reach the East Gate, which serves as the main entry point. Alternatively, you can take the JR line from Takamatsu Station to Ritsurin-kōen Kita-guchi Station, which is a short walk from the garden's North Gate (5 minutes; 2-3 times hourly; ¥210). Another option is taking the Kotohira Line from Takamatsu-Chikko Station to Ritsurinkoen Station (7 minutes;

Ritsurin-kōen

4 trains per hour; ¥190). Pick up an English-language map at either entrance and meander. English audio guides are also available for ¥200.

Shikoku Mura
四国村

91 Yashima Nakamachi; tel. 087/843-3111; www.shikokumura.or.jp; 8:30am-6pm daily Apr.-Oct., 8:30am-5:30pm daily Nov.-Mar.; ¥1,000 adults, ¥600 high school students, ¥400 junior high school and elementary school students; from JR Takamatsu Station, take the JR Kōtoku line to Yashima Station (15 minutes, ¥220)

This open-air museum at the foot of the Yashima Plateau, east of downtown Takamatsu, features traditional thatched-roof homes from the island's interior mountainsides, storehouses, and cabins from fishing hamlets. Activities include workshops for making products like soy sauce and pressing sugarcane, and even a kabuki theater that periodically hosts plays. There's good English-language signage throughout. The hillside grounds are worth checking out if you don't plan to venture deeper into the island's core, particularly the lush Iya Valley.

FOOD

OFUKURO

1F Hamada Enterprise Bldg., 1-11-12 Kawaramachi; tel. 087/831-0822; www.facebook.com/ofukuromiso/; 5pm-11pm Mon.-Sat.; dishes from ¥300; from Takamatsu-Chikko Station, take Kotoden Kotohira or Kotoden Nagao line to Kawaramachi Station, then walk 5 minutes northwest

For something healthier, Ofukuro is a great place to dig into a well-balanced set meal. You'll find various fish dishes, combined with a generous range of vegetable side dishes, a salad, and miso soup served with a variety of garnishes. This cozy restaurant, run by friendly staff, is located on a street lined with shops. If you have trouble finding it, just ask around, as it's a local favorite. An English menu is available.

UDON HONJIN YAMADAYA SANUKI HONTEN

3186 Mure, Mure-chō; tel. 087/845-6522; www.yamada-ya.com; 10am-8pm daily; ¥800-1,150

Near Shikoku Mura is this excellent purveyor of sanuki udon, a thick style of noodle made from wheat flour and originating in Kagawa, and arguably Shikoku's most famous contribution to the nation's menu. Set in a historic mansion registered as a cultural property, this homey shop offers an experience as much as a meal. I recommend trying udon with crispy tempura (battered and fried vegetables and shrimp) or with pork (niku udon).

★ RANMARU

7-4 Daikumachi; tel. 050/5484-1897; https://ranmaru-takamatsu.gorp.jp; 6pm-1am (last order 11pm) daily; ¥1,000; from Takamatsu-Chikko Station, take Kotoden Nagao line to Kataharamachi Station, then walk 5 minutes southwest

Most people think of silky sanuki udon noodles at the mention of Kagawa. But the truth is, the prefecture is just as crazed about chicken. Chicken served sanuki style, known as honetsuki-dori (fried bone-in chicken), involves slathering the chicken in copious amounts of garlic, oil, and salt and cooking it like a steak. The flavorful meat is surprisingly tough and requires the use of kitchen shears to scissor through it. It goes best with ice-cold beer. Ranmaru, a greasy spoon with a 1960s-era interior, is a lively local favorite for this hearty dish. There's often a queue, but a shorter one than at some of the other sanuki chicken joints in the area.

ACCOMMODATIONS

¥10,000-20,000

DAIWA ROYNET HOTEL TAKAMATSU

8-23 Marugamemachi; tel. 087/811-7855; www.daiwaroynet.jp/takamatsu; ¥10,400 d; take the Kotoden Nagao line or the Kotoden Kotohira line from Takamatsu-Chikko Station, about 7 minutes' walk from JR Takamatsu Station, to Kawaramachi Station, and the hotel is 7 minutes' walk from there

Located smack in the middle of the city's

main shopping and entertainment zone, this modern hotel with pleasant service has well-appointed, compact rooms with free Wi-Fi throughout. A restaurant serving a Western- and Japanese-style breakfast is also available on-site, as are bicycle rentals and coin laundry facilities.

FAV HOTEL TAKAMATSU

2-4-20 Shiogami-chō; tel. 087/802-5775; https://takamatsu.fav-hotels.com; ¥13,200 d; take the Kotoden Nagao line or the Kotoden Kotohira line from Takamatsu-Chikko Station, about 7 minutes' walk from JR Takamatsu Station, to Kawaramachi Station (5 minutes, ¥190), and the hotel is 7 minutes' walk from there

Located near the downtown, this stylish new hotel has well-appointed, spacious rooms, some with kitchenettes and laundry machines. The rooms come in a variety of sizes, accommodating up to six guests in some, making it a good choice for families. The staff are ready to lend a helping hand.

INFORMATION AND SERVICES

Online, **Takamatsu Life** (http://takamatsu-life.com) features listings of entertainment and events, local activities, and more.

- **Tourist Information Center** (first floor of JR Takamatsu Station; 1-20, Hamanochō; tel. 087/826-0170; www.my-kagawa.jp/point/2486; 9am-8pm daily)
- **I-PAL Kagawa** (1-11-63 Banchō; tel. 087/837-5908; www.i-pal.or.jp; 9am-4pm Tues.-Sun.; 15-minute walk south of Takamatsu Station)

GETTING THERE

Train

Most people arrive in Takamatsu by train. If you're coming from Honshu, it's possible to go directly to the city from **Okayama** (55 minutes; ¥2,080). From within Shikoku, it's possible to take trains directly from **Matsuyama** (2.5 hours; ¥6,490), **Tokushima** (1 hour 5 minutes; ¥3,400), and **Kochi** (2 hours 20 minutes; ¥5,720). As long as you're coming via a **JR line** from any of these cities, the JR Pass will cover the fare.

Bus

It's also possible to arrive in Takamatsu on a night bus from **Tokyo** (10 hours; ¥10,000 one-way, ¥19,000 return), as well as from **Kōbe, Osaka,** and a number of cities within **Shikoku.** Buses arrive and depart near **JR Takamatsu Station.** Check the website of the highway bus operator **Willer** (http://willerexpress.com) or bus booking service **Japan Bus Online** (https://japanbusonline.com/en) for full timetables and rates.

Boat

If you'd rather enjoy views of the Inland Sea as you make your way to Shikoku, it's also possible to take a ferry from **Kōbe** (4.5 hours; ¥1,990 one-way, ¥3,390 return adults, ¥990 one-way, ¥1,690 return ages 6-11, plus ¥300 on Sat., Sun. and national holidays). Ferries dock about a 10-minute shuttle bus ride (free) to the east of JR Takamatsu Station at the **Jumbo Ferry Takamatsu** docks (5-12-1 Asahimachi; tel. 087/811-6688). This ferry also stops at **Shodoshima** (1 hour from Takamatsu) en route. For details, check the **Japan Ferry** website (https://ferry.co.jp).

Another ferry network, **Shikoku Kisen** (www.shikokukisen.com), links Takamatsu to **Naoshima** (1 hour). Ferries coming from or going to Shodoshima, Naoshima, or Uno leave and arrive from **Sunport Ferry Port** (8-22 Sunport; tel. 087/822-4383; www.shikokuferry.com), a short walk northeast of JR Takamatsu Station.

Air

If you prefer to fly, there are daily flights to **Takamatsu Airport** (Konanchooka; tel. 087/814-3355; www.takamatsu-airport.com) from Tokyo's **Haneda** and **Narita** airports (1 hour 25 minutes; average ¥15,000), as well as from **Naha,** Okinawa (2 hours; from ¥20,000). Admittedly, flying to Takamatsu is not the most economical option. Although

JAL (Japan Airlines) and ANA (All Nippon Airways) fly to Takamatsu from Tokyo, the budget carrier **Jetstar Japan** offers much cheaper deals. Internationally, there are limited flights between Takamatsu and regional cities like Seoul, Taipei, Shanghai, and Hong Kong.

Takamatsu Airport is located about 40 minutes from downtown, about 16 kilometers (10 mi) south of the city. You can take a **bus** (¥780; www.kotoden.co.jp/publichtm/bus/limousine/index-en.html) or **taxi** (¥5,000) into downtown.

GETTING AROUND

Once you're in the city, Takamatsu is laid out on a straightforward grid pattern. This makes the city easy to navigate. You can negotiate most of the downtown **on foot,** but the show-stopping sight of Ritsurin-kōen is farther from town. To save on travel time, there's also a good local train network known as **Kotoden.** These trains run to the eastern suburb of Yashima and south to the town of Kotohira. The easiest place to hop on this line is at the **Takamatsu Chikkō-Station,** located next to Tamamo-kōen about 4 minutes' walk east of JR Takamatsu Station. Meanwhile, the **JR Tokushima** line links Takamatsu and Tokushima. Unlike the Kotoden line, it has the added bonus of being covered by the JR Pass.

If you want to rent a car to venture further into Shikoku, the ever-trusty **Toyota Rent-a-Car** (10-21 Nishinomaruchō; tel. 087/851-0100; www.r-higashishikoku.jp/shop/takamatsu.php; 8am-8pm daily) operates an office about 2 minutes' walk southeast of JR Takamatsu Station.

★ KONPIRA-SAN

こんぴらさん

892-1 Kotohira-chō; tel. 0877/75-2121; www.konpira.or.jp; 9am-5pm (last entry 4:30pm) daily; Hōmutsu-kan ¥800, Shoin ¥800

Soon after exiting the main train station of Kotohira, a seaside suburb of Takamatsu, signs of seafaring begin to rise up around you. A few minutes down the main street from the station's main exit, you'll come to a large wooden tower with a stone base and a giant lantern at its top. This was once Japan's tallest lighthouse.

In keeping with Kotohira's connections to seafaring, Konpira-san, or **Kotohira-gu** (金刀比羅宮), is not only one of Shinto's holiest sites, it's a shrine devoted solely to the protection of sailors. The complex sprawls

path to the top of Konpira-san

up the slopes of Zozu-san (Elephant Head Mountain) on the western outskirts of town. Reaching the main shrine is no light matter. Walking up a path lined by a multitude of stone lanterns, you'll climb 785 steps before you reach the main hall, where you'll be rewarded with stunning views of the town and distant peaks on the horizon. On the way up, you'll pass several stop-off points where there are various subshrines and small museums exhibiting kabuki and Noh masks, painted screens, and other more peculiar items. Among them: a huge golden propeller, massive anchors, a white horse in a stable for the shrine's god to ride, and at the top, memorabilia from the high seas. In the Ema Hall, you'll find photos of commercial ships, battleships, and even spaceships and astronauts, extending the shrine's powers of protection into the interstellar orbit.

If you're a glutton for punishment and want to see the entire complex, push on for another 583 steps past the main hall until you reach the Okusha (inner shrine). However much of the path you plan to walk, be sure to wear comfortable footwear. The walk to the main hall takes about 45 minutes from the foot of the mountain, and from there it's an additional 45 minutes to the inner shrine.

Getting There

You can arrive in Kotohira by either the JR line or Kotoden line. Coming from Takamatsu, the JR trains depart from JR Takamatsu Station once hourly (1 hour; ¥850 one-way). Less frequent Shimanto limited express trains make the same journey (35 minutes; ¥2,000). JR Kotohira Station is located about 10 minutes' walk northeast of the heart of town, toward Konpira-san. From JR Kotohira Station or Kotoden Kotohira Station, either walk 15 minutes to base of the steps that lead to the shrine, or call ahead (tel. 0877/73-2221) to reserve a spot on a bus that departs from in front of the JR station and drops off passengers about halfway to the main hall.

Tokushima 徳島市

Located on the eastern coast of Shikoku, positioned at the mouth of the Yoshinagawa river, Tokushima is synonymous with the raucous Awa Odori dance festival that takes the affable city by storm each August. Dancing aside, the city is a fun place in its own right with a surprisingly lively nightlife district, **Sakaemachi,** and nice riverside promenades. Bizan-san, a mountain accessible by cable car, looms beyond the south side of the city, offering panoramic views. It's also possible to hop on a boat and cruise the city's extensive waterways.

Tokushima can easily be seen in a day. Unless you're headed to the city's legendary summer shindig, plan to pass through, en route to the Iya Valley or Kochi.

SIGHTS

Awa Odori Kaikan
阿波おどり会館

2-20 Shinmachibashi; tel. 088/611-1611; www.awaodori-kaikan.jp; 9am-5pm daily, closed second Wed. of Feb., Jun., and Oct.; ¥300; walk 12 minutes southwest of JR Tokushima Station

While there's no substitute for the real thing, if you visit Tokushima outside of festival time, this building contains a gift shop, a third-floor museum dedicated to the festival, and a hall that hosts dances by professional troupes several times daily (¥800). The most impressive performance is held at 8pm nightly (¥1,000). In keeping with the spirit of the festival, full participation is encouraged, so you may just end up learning how to do the city's signature dance.

TOP EXPERIENCE

☆ Kōbō Daishi and the 88-Temple Pilgrimage

Kūkai, known posthumously as Kōbō Daishi (774-835), may be pound-for-pound the most important figure in the history of Japanese religion. Starting in 804, Kūkai embarked on a two-year journey into the heart of Buddhism's deepest teachings in China. Kūkai returned to Japan having mastered Sanskrit and Chinese, calligraphy, and poetry, and began wandering the wilds of Shikoku, ending amid the rocky cliffs of Cape Muroto in the far southeast of Kochi Prefecture, where he is said to have reached enlightenment.

THE ROUTE

Since Kōbō Daishi (aka Kūkai) established the 1,200-year-old, 1,400-kilometer (870-mi) route known as the 88-Temple Pilgrimage, the motives for undertaking the journey are as varied as the pilgrims who make it, from atonement for past misdeeds to praying for health and success, all the way up to striving for enlightenment. Each temple along the route is said to symbolize a craving, or sin, thought to plague humankind. Over mountains and along rugged coastline, all told, walking the loop clockwise around Shikoku takes around two months, walking around 25 kilometers (15.5 mi) daily.

HOW TO SPOT A PILGRIM

An ohenro-san, as a pilgrim who walks this pilgrimage (henro) route is known, is traditionally outfitted in a white vest called a **hakui,** with a conical **sugegasa** hat of woven straw. Completing the getup are prayer beads strung around the wrists and a **zudabukuro** bag slung over the shoulder, used for toting candles, incense, and their **nōkyōchō** (book for collecting stamps at each temple). Another important item is the **kongozue** (wooden staff), which symbolizes Kūkai. It has a bell on top meant to deter wild animals and keep one in the present moment with its light jingle. The bottom end is respectfully washed at night, symbolically cleaning Kūkai's feet, and must never be etched with a knife or used when walking across a bridge (as Kūkai is said to have once slept under a bridge).

PLANNING YOUR PILGRIMAGE

Today, those who drive, cycle, ride a bus, or take the train far outnumber the purists who walk the whole thing. For pilgrims with less time on their hands who still want to try some of the route on foot, it's perfectly acceptable to walk a short leg of the circuit, and a few popular options for shorter segments are covered throughout this chapter.

However much of the circuit you undertake, wear cushy shoes meant for running or walking, and thick socks, and bring a first-aid kit. Plan to hike in April-May or October-November. Winter tends to be frigid, while summer is sweltering. Good books for planning the journey include the ***Shikoku Japan 88 Route Guide*** (https://henro.co/route-guide-book), which can also be bought at Ryōzen-ji (no. 1), and the free e-book ***Shikoku Pilgrimage: A Guide for Non-Japanese*** (http://henro88map.com/pdf/Henro-ENG.pdf). Online, check out the introductory guide provided by **Shikoku Tours** (www.shikokutours.com/shikoku-pilgrimage), a great travel outfit focused on the island that also offers tours.

KŪKAI'S BIRTHPLACE

One satisfying stop for would-be pilgrims who are short on time is Kūkai's birthplace in Shikoku, **Zentsū-ji** (3-3-1 Zentsūji-chō; tel. 0877/62-0111; www.zentsuji.com; always open; free), temple no. 75 on the 88-temple circuit, a brief trip north of Kotohira. It's home to a five-story pagoda and the Golden Hall—housing a statue of Amida Buddha, the main celestial Buddha of the Pure Land sect—and to the Mie-dō, said to be where Kūkai received his first bath. To reach Zentsū-ji, take the JR Dosan line from Kotohira Station to Zentsūji Station (5 minutes; ¥210), then walk just under 20 minutes southwest.

On the fifth floor of the Awa Odori Kaikan, you'll find the lower station of the **Bizan Ropeway** (眉山ロープウェ; tel. 088/652-3617; 9am-5:30pm daily Nov.-Mar., 9am-9pm daily Apr.-Oct.; ¥620 one-way, ¥1,030 return adults, ¥300 one-way, ¥510 return elementary school students; walk 12 minutes southwest of JR Tokushima Station). After seeing and, perhaps, joining a dance performance, ride to the top of Mount Bizan for a nice panorama of the city below.

Chūō-kōen

1 Jōnai; www.city.tokushima.tokushima.jp/shisetsu/park/chuo.html; 24 hours; free

Tokushima's best green space, Chūō-kōen (Central Park) is a great place to unwind. You'll find the remnants of the city's former castle, a museum dedicated to it, and a lovely landscape garden dating from the 16th century. More specifically, the **Tokushima Castle Museum** (1-8 Jōnai; tel. 088/656-2525; www.city.tokushima.tokushima.jp/johaku; 9:30am-5pm Tues.-Sun; ¥300) has a model of the former castle and various artifacts from the lords who once ruled from the city. And the **Senshūkaku-teien** (additional ¥50 with castle museum ticket), located beside the museum, has ponds, stone bridges, and perfectly sculpted shrubs. This park isn't a must-see, but it is a nice place to unplug.

ENTERTAINMENT AND EVENTS

TOP EXPERIENCE

★ AWA ODORI
阿波おどり

www.awaodori.tokushima.jp; Aug. 12-15

"The dancing fool and the watching fool are both fools, so why not dance?" There could be no better tagline for Tokushima's—and Japan's—summer dance festival par excellence.

The Awa Odori Matsuri takes place during Obon, Japan's festival of the dead, when everyone traditionally returns to their hometown to honor their ancestors; it's as much a fête as a remembrance of those who have passed. The formula is simple: don geta (wooden sandals) and a vivid yukata, and follow the lead of those around you, dancing in unison. Some of the pros wear a combination of happi, or shortened yukata, worn with shorts or pants, and a headband or taco-shaped straw hat. Dance troupes known as ren range from groups created just before the festival to seasoned pros who practice all year. Slowly step along to the rhythm of the taiko drums, accompanied by the three-stringed shamisen and bamboo flutes, and wave your hands as gracefully as you can.

Every August, 1 million revelers flock to the city to participate in the Awa Odori. All of downtown is blocked off to traffic evenings during the event, and from 6pm to 10:30pm, troupes of dancers are seen at practically every turn. You'll notice that the dancers tend to stick to the old-school, down-tempo two-step format earlier in the evening. But as dusk falls, the vibe intensifies until the party finally quiets down around 11pm.

If you plan to attend, book accommodations at least three months in advance—the earlier the better. If you have an interest in joining an official dance troupe, contact the **Tokushima International Association** (www.tia81.com), which assembles a ragtag group to dance in one of the officially designated zones on one of the nights.

AWA JŪROBE YASHIKI
阿波十郎兵衛屋敷

184 Miyajima Motoura, Kawauchi-chō; tel. 088/665-2202; http://joruri.info/jurobe; 9:30am-5pm daily Sept.-June, 9:30am-6pm daily July-Aug.; ¥410 adults, ¥310 university and high school students, ¥200 junior high and elementary school students

Farmers in the rural Tokushima area have a centuries-old tradition of putting on community puppet shows. Head to this historic building, once lived in by Bandō Jūrobe, a local samurai who handed himself over to be executed so that his master's name would remain untainted. The tale of Jūrobe's plight inspired the puppet play *Keisei Awa no Naruto*, first performed in 1768. Every day a group of puppeteers, clad in black from head to toe, kneel behind the large puppets and control them in plain view of the audience. All of this takes place to a soundtrack of vocals and the three-stringed shamisen.

SPORTS AND RECREATION

HYŌTANJIMA BOAT TOUR

tel. 088/621-5232; www.city.tokushima.tokushima.jp/kankou/taiken/hyoutanjima.html; 11am-4pm (last boarding 3:40pm) daily Sept.-Jun., 11am-4pm (last departure 3:40pm) and 5pm-8pm (last departure 7:40pm) daily Jul.-Aug. 31, 9am-10pm (last departure 9:45pm) Aug. 12-15; ¥300 adults, ¥150 junior high school students and younger; walk about 10 minutes' south of Tokushima Station

Tokushima is a town of rivers, with the Shinmachi and Suketo rivers chief among them. The island-like area between these two rivers is known as Hyōtanjima (Gourd-shaped Island). One of the city's lesser-known attractions is an affordable boat tour that begins near the Ryōgoku Bridge in the Shinmachi Riverside Park and motors around Hyotanjima (about 30 minutes). It's a fun, budget-conscious way to see the heart of the city. Boats run about every 40 minutes.

FOOD

KARLITO'S BB MEX

1F Nishiyama Bldg., 2-38 Tomidamachi; tel. 088/600-8107; https://karlhammot7.wixsite.com/karlitosbbmex; 6pm-late daily; dishes from ¥450

Who would have thought you could get tasty Mexican food in Tokushima? Karlito's whips up tacos, burritos, quesadillas, chimichangas, and more. There's a good selection of Mexican beers and tequilas, and a decent cocktail menu too. Funky decor and a lively crowd of locals and expats make it a fun place for a few drinks and nibbles. The friendly staff speak some English and are happy to make various recommendations around town.

MENŌ

1F Asahi Bldg., 3-6 Terashima Honchō Higashi; tel. 088/623-4116; http://7-men.com; 10am-9pm daily Apr. 16-May 31, 11am-midnight daily Jun.-Apr. 15; from ¥550

A greasy spoon a short walk from JR Tokushima Station, this is the best-known shop in town for Tokushima's signature ramen, topped with stir-fried pork belly, green onions, bean sprouts, and sometimes raw egg,

dancers in Awa Odori

88-Temple Pilgrimage Route: Temples No. 1-5

Temples Visited: Ryōzen-ji, Gokuraku-ji, Konsen-ji, Dainichi-ji, and Jizō-ji (Temples no. 1 through no. 5)
Distance/Time: 11 km/7 mi, 2.5 hours one-way (15 km/9.3 mi; 3 hours one-way including time walking to and from train stations)
Getting There: Take the JR Kotoku line from Tokushima Station to Bandō Station (20 minutes; ¥260), then walk 15 minutes to Ryōzen-ji. At the end of the walk, head from Jizō-ji to Itano Station (50 minutes), two stops west of Bandō Station on the JR Kotoku line, 4 kilometers (2.5 mi) northeast of temple no. 5.

This popular section of the trail not far from Tokushima is a logical choice for many, as **Ryōzen-ji** (126 Higashitsukahana, Oasa-chō, Naruto; tel. 088/689-1111; https://88shikokuhenro.jp/en/jikuwazan-ichijyouin-ryozenji/; 7am-5pm; free), located near Naruto of whirlpool fame, is the route's starting point. Many pilgrims vow to walk the entire circuit here, then return to offer thanks after completing the loop.

Beyond Ryōzen-ji, **Gokuraku-ji** (Danōe 12, Hinoki Oasa-chō, Naruto; tel. 088/689-1112; https://88shikokuhenro.jp/en/nisshouzan-muryoujyuin-gokurakuji/; 7am-5pm daily; free) stands beside a dairy farm in the Sanuki Mountains' foothills. At **Kosen-ji** (Kameyamashita-66 Otera, Itano; tel. 088/672-1087; https://88shikokuhenro.jp/en/kikouzan-shakain-konsenji/; 7am-5pm; free), Kūkai is said to have thumped the ground with his staff to bring forth a golden stream of water (hence the temple's name: "Golden Well Temple"). Pressing on to **Dainichi-ji** (Iuchi-28, Itano-chō; tel. 088/672-1225; https://dainichiji-temple.com; 7am-5pm daily; free), which stands in a valley near Tokushima city, and just south of there, the large **Jizō-ji** (Hayashihigashi 5, Rahan, Itano-chō; tel. 088/672-4111; https://88shikokuhenro.jp/en/mujinzan-shougonin-jizoji/; 7am-5pm daily; free) complex rewards those who finish the walk with its rambling grounds.

While the walk from start to end takes about 3 hours, including the time spent walking to and from the train stations at either end of the trek, this doesn't account for time spent exploring each temple. Plan to expand this time an additional few hours, depending on how leisurely you want to proceed. If you'd prefer a slightly less ambitious walk, you can simply follow the same route, but end the trip at temple no. 3, Konsen-ji; Itano Station is only 10 minutes' walk southwest from there (total journey 4.7 km/2.9 mi; 1 hour one-way).

and served in a rich brown broth made with pork bones and soy sauce. If you've got the appetite, order a bowl of white rice and pour the remaining soup over it after finishing the noodles. Many locals swear by this heavy finishing move. Select what you want based on the pictures on the ticket machine out front, insert the money required, and hold on to your tickets until you're seated. There's often a queue, but it tends to move fast.

YAKINIKU ORENCHI

1F Daisan Bldg. 2, 1-59 Sakaemachi; tel. 088/655-0691; http://0691.web.fc2.com; 6pm-1am Mon.-Sat.; dishes from ¥300, course ¥4,000

This yaki-niku (grilled meat) restaurant in the heart of the Sakaemachi entertainment district is a good choice for a hearty meal either before a night out, or late-night after visiting the bars. Put cuts of locally sourced beef on the grill at your table, let them sizzle, and combine with trimmings—kimchi, salads, rice—of your choice. Look for the door with a window shaped like an electric guitar.

BARS AND NIGHTLIFE

INGRID'S INTERNATIONAL MUSIC BAR

2-7-1 Sakaemachi; tel. 088/626-0067; www.facebook.com/ingridsinternationalmusicbar; 8:30pm-late Tues.-Sun.

Going strong for two decades, this jovial

bar is run by the warm, charming Filipina proprietor Ingrid. A steady flow of locals and expats makes this one of the city's more hopping spots at night, especially on the weekend. You'll find cozy couches, a wide selection of booze, and free karaoke; in fact, the whole bar can, in theory, join in thanks to a slew of wireless mics and four television screens on the walls to display the scrolling lyrics.

ACCOMMODATIONS

HOTEL SUNROUTE TOKUSHIMA

1-5-1 Motomachi; tel. 088/653-8111; https://en.sunroute.jp; from ¥10,000 d

Just a stone's throw from the main station, this hotel offers reasonably priced rooms that are simple but stylish enough. Bathrooms are well-appointed, and free Wi-Fi is available throughout. There are three restaurants on-site.

DAIWA ROYNET HOTEL TOKUSHIMA EKI-MAE

3-8 Terashima Honchō Higashi; tel. 088/611-8455; www.daiwaroynet.jp/tokushimaekimae; ¥10,500 d with breakfast

This hotel, close to the train station, has clean, comfortable rooms that are more spacious than most Japanese business hotels: a good balance of convenience, comfort, and a reasonable price tag. There's a breakfast buffet with a range of Western and Japanese dishes.

AGNES HOTEL

1-28 Terashima Honchō Nishi; tel. 088/626-2222; www.agneshotel.jp; ¥12,000 d with breakfast

Located just across the street from JR Takamatsu Station, the Agnes Hotel has cozy, though minimal, rooms. Staff at the reception desk are notably friendly and helpful. There's an eatery that functions as a café by day and a chic restaurant by night, and a bakery that serves delightful pastries made in-house. Note that there are no rooms with double beds—only twins.

INFORMATION AND SERVICES

Online, Tokushima Prefecture runs the excellent **Discover Tokushima** tourism portal (https://discovertokushima.net).

- **Tokushima International Strategies Center** (Clement Plaza 6F, next to JR Tokushima Station, 1-61 Terashimahonchō Nishi; tel. 088/656-3303; www.topia.ne.jp; 10am-6pm daily)

GETTING THERE

Train

JR Tokushima Station is located more or less in the center of the city, just south of Chūō-kōen and the remains of the castle ruins. Coming from **Tokyo** (6 hours; ¥20,490 one-way) or **Osaka** (3.5 hours; ¥10,740 one-way), you can simply take the shinkansen to Okayama, then transfer to a rapid train to Takamatsu and take a local or limited express train to Tokushima from there. Or, you can take a limited express train directly from **Okayama** to Tokushima. Within Shikoku, you can directly reach Tokushima by train from **Awa-Ikeda** in the Iya Valley region (1 hour 15 minutes; ¥3,590); **Matsuyama** (4 hours; ¥9,860), transferring at Takamatsu; or from **Kochi** (2.5 hours; ¥6,160), transferring at Awa-Ikeda.

Bus

If you prefer to take a bus, you can make the long journey from **Tokyo** (9 hours; from ¥7,500 one-way) or **Osaka** (2.5 hours; about ¥4,000). It's also possible to travel by highway bus from most of **Shikoku's** major towns and cities. To learn more about bus options, check out **Tokushima Bus** (tel. 088/622-1826; www.tokubus.co.jp), **Shikoku Kotsu Bus** (tel. 088/372-1231; www.yonkoh.co.jp) and **JR Shikoku Bus** (tel. 088/602-1090; https://www.jr-shikokubus.co.jp).

Air

While not the cheapest route, you can also access the city by plane. **Tokushima Awaōdori Airport** (16-2 Asahino, Matsushige; tel.

Naruto Whirlpools

About 13 kilometers (8 mi) north of Tokushima city, Naruto is a scenic town clinging to a craggy peninsula overlooking a peculiar natural phenomenon: cavernous whirlpools that form underneath the nearby Ō-Naruto Bridge. The whirlpools are a worthwhile day trip from Tokushima if you time it right. These forces of nature are created when an enormous volume of water is pushed through the slender strait between Naruto and the neighboring island of Awaji-shima during high and low tide. On a good, frothy day, the whirlpools are a sight to behold.

You can witness this phenomenon either from the glass-bottom **Uzu-no-Michi Promenade** (772-0053 Naruto Park; tel. 088/683-6262; www.uzunomichi.jp; 9am-6pm, last entry 5:30pm, daily Mar.-Sept., 9am-5pm, last entry 4:30pm, daily Oct.-Feb., 8am-7pm, last entry 6:30pm, Golden Week and summer holidays of Jul.-mid-Aug.; ¥510 adults, ¥410 junior high and high school students, ¥260 elementary school students) below the O-Naruto Bridge, or from the deck of a tour boat operated by **Naruto Kankō Kisen** (264-1 Oge, Tosadomariura; tel. 088/687-0101; www.uzusio.com; 9am-4:20pm daily; rides ¥1,800-2,400 adults, ¥900-1,200 elementary school students). See the website for details, including the best times of day to see the whirlpools.

In truth, the whirlpools are hard to predict. There's a chance you could make the trip and not see much of a swirl. But if the timing is right—new moon and full moon days are prime—the pools swell to 20 meters (65 ft) across.

GETTING THERE

The easiest way to reach Naruto if you're coming from Tokushima is with your own **car.** It's about 30 minutes' drive via the Yoshinogawa Bypass and Route 11. Otherwise, you can take a **bus** from Tokushima Station to the Uzu-no-michi bus stop (1 hour 15 minutes; ¥710 one-way). From there, the boat dock from which to access the whirlpools is about 8 minutes **on foot.** Alternatively, you can take a **train** on the JR Naruto line from Tokushima to JR Naruto Station (35 minutes; ¥360). From Naruto Station, take either a **bus** or **taxi** to Uzu-no-michi bus stop and walk to the seaside from there. From JR Naruto Station, take a bus to Naruto Park (20 minutes; ¥310).

088/699-2831; www.tokushima-airport.co.jp) services daily flights from Fukuoka (1 hour; ¥10,000) and Tokyo (1 hour 15 minutes; ¥15,000). Note that flight prices are sky-high during the summertime Awa Odori Matsuri. You can reach **JR Tokushima Station** from the airport by **bus** (30 minutes; ¥600 one-way).

GETTING AROUND

JR Tokushima Station is more or less in the center of downtown, accessible on foot to the many food and entertainment options arrayed throughout the Sakaemachi district and along the banks of the Shinmachi-gawa.

That said, having a car is recommended for exploring the surrounding area. **JR Rent-a-Car** (1-4-2 Terashimahon-chō Nishi; tel. 088/622-1014; www.ekiren.co.jp; 9am-7pm daily) is right in front of JR Tokushima Station. If you're flying into town, **Toyota Rent-a-Car** (15-10 Asahino, Toyohisa Matsuhige-chō; tel. 088/699-6606; https://rent.toyota.co.jp; 8am-8pm daily) is located at the airport. Cars can be booked out surprisingly far ahead, especially during peak season. Reserve your car online as far in advance as possible.

Iya Valley

祖谷渓

Entering the misty Iya Valley ("Ancestor Valley") and the neighboring Ōboke Gorge in Tokushima's deep, rugged west feels akin to entering some sort of lost world. Dangling vine bridges cross rushing rivers, with lush mountains shooting skyward on each side. Smoke rises from fairy-tale houses clustered in small settlements scattered across the rugged valley walls.

The Iya Valley is often divided into **Nishi Iya** (West Iya) and **Oku Iya** (Inner Iya), or Higashi Iya (East Iya). Given the remoteness of the terrain, it's no surprise that in 1185 the vanquished soldiers from the defeated Heike (aka Taira) clan found refuge in this remote swath of wilderness after losing on the battlefield at Yashima, near Takamatsu, to the Minamoto clan. Some of these conquered fighters stayed on and made the valley home, propagating hamlets that are now only glimpsed in fleeting remnants. Apart from precarious mountain roads and a one-man train car transporting the odd passenger, little has changed in the valley since then.

It's more than bucolic bliss. The section of the nearby Yoshino-gawa near the Awa-Ikeda train station is home to Japan's best stretch of white water rapids, in the Ōboke and Kōbōke gorges, through which the frothy Yoshino River flows. Iya Onsen, deeper into the valley itself, is a good place to soak in calmer—and warmer—waters. Tsurugi-san, east of the valley proper, makes for a great hike.

SIGHTS

Nishi Iya (West Iya)

★ KAZURA-BASHI

かずら橋

162-2 Nishi Iya Yamamura Zentoku, Miyoshi-shi; tel. 0883/76-0877; https://miyoshi-tourism.jp/spot/iyanokazurabashi/; sunrise-sunset daily; ¥550 junior high school students and older, ¥350 elementary school students; take a bus from Ōboke Station (20 minutes, 4-8 buses per day, ¥670)

This vine bridge is perhaps Iya's most recognizable spot. Although the bridge can get crowded at times, it's still an incredible sight.

This type of bridge, made of thick vines growing wild in the surrounding mountains, was once a necessity for valley dwellers to transport goods from one side of the valley to the other. Legend holds that Kōbō Daishi had the first such bridge built. According to another version of the story, survivors from the vanquished Heike clan built the bridges after fleeing into the depths of the valley with the intention of being able to destroy them in a hurry if their enemies approached. At one time, there were 13 of these bridges spanning the valley. Today, only three remain, and this is the most popular.

Crossing the 45-meter-long (148-ft-long) bridge is surprisingly unnerving. Thankfully, the only danger here is succumbing to a mild fear of heights. The river can be seen through the uneven slats, 14 meters (46 ft) below, but the bridge is secure. It's been shored up with steel cables, concealed by the vines, and is rebuilt every three years.

Across the bridge, back on terra firma, turn left and walk down the road that runs alongside the river to your left. You'll soon come to a lovely waterfall pouring over the mountainside on the right, and a series of covered rest areas and staircases that lead down to the river on the left. Continuing down this same road will eventually bring you to a lovely riverside campsite.

On your way to Kazura-bashi on Route 32 (9 km/5.5 mi north), keep your eye out for one of the most accessible viewpoints from which to admire the region. The viewpoint is shared with a statue known as the **Manikin Peeing**

1: Ōboke Gorge and Yoshino River **2:** rafting the Yoshino River **3:** food provided by a rafting company **4:** rafting the Yoshino River

1

2

3

4

Boy, who is appropriately peeing from the edge of a precipitous 200-meter-high (656-ft-high) cliff.

Oku Iya (Inner Iya)

NAGORO SCARECROW VILLAGE
名頃かかしの里

www.iyatime.com/nagoro-scarecrow-village

Passing the village of Ochiai as you drive along Route 439, deep into Oku Iya, you'll eventually begin noticing figures standing along the roadside and sitting under bus stop shelters. These figures are not human, but are hauntingly lifelike scarecrows (kakashi). Welcome to Nagoro, a hamlet that's come to be known as Scarecrow Village, or the Village of the Dolls. All told, around 350 of these dolls sit on porches and behind windows, stand beside bicycles, sit as "students" in the now-closed local school, work in the fields, perform roadwork, and fish in the river.

These hauntingly lifelike dolls are the brainchild of artist Ayano Tsukimi, who grew up in Nagoro and returned more than a decade ago. Tsukimi was shocked by how empty Nagoro had become in her absence and was struck with the idea of addressing the loneliness by crafting dolls and placing them in various poses around town. Adding to the poignant nature of this deeply personal effort, the first doll she ever made was meant to resemble her father. Many of the other dolls are designed to look like past residents.

Her project has not been commercialized in any way. The dolls simply fill the town, turning the village into an unlikely stop for travelers. To reach the hamlet, which is easy to miss, it's best to take a taxi or drive yourself, using a GPS for good measure.

OKU IYA NIJŪ KAZURA-BASHI
奥祖谷二重かずら橋

620 Higashi Iya Sugeoi, Miyoshi; tel. 0883/76-0877; https://miyoshi-tourism.jp/spot/okuiyanijukazurabashi/; 8am-5pm daily Apr.-Jun. and Oct.-Nov., 7:30am-6pm daily Jul.-Sept.; ¥550 adults, ¥350 elementary school students; take a bus from Awa-Ikeda Station to Kubo bus stop (2 hours, 4 buses per day, ¥1,790), then transfer to bus bound for Nijū Kazura-bashi or Tsurugi-san (30 minutes, 2 buses per day, ¥430)

Deeper into the inner side of Iya, 3.5 kilometers (2 mi) past Nagoro on Route 439, two more vine bridges come into view on the right side of the road. Compared to Kazura-bashi in Nishi Iya, these two vine bridges feel like they're in the middle of nowhere. Fewer people make it this far into the valley.

The higher, slightly more daunting of the two is known as the Otto no Hashi (husband bridge), while the slightly shorter one is the Tsuma no Hashi (wife bridge). Nearby, there's also a wooden vehicle that glides along a system of ropes known as the yaen (wild monkey), from which you pull yourself across the river using your own strength.

There's a **campsite** on the far side of the river, a **gift shop** serving a peculiar array of ice-cream flavors (soba, anyone?), and a few places to access the riverside. If you've got your own wheels or the patience to use the limited public transport needed to get to this faraway corner of Japan, it's a great escape far beyond where most travelers go. Note that buses only run to Nijū Kazura-bashi bus stop on weekends from April-November, and daily during the peak seasons of Golden Week (late Apr.-early May), summer holidays (mid-Jul.-Aug.), and during autumn when the leaves blaze (Oct.-early Nov.).

SPORTS AND RECREATION

Hiking

TSURUGI-SAN

Distance: *5 km (3 mi)*

Time: *3 hours round-trip*

Trailhead: *Near Mi-no-Koshi bus stop (near lower chairlift station)*

Information and maps: *http://best-hike-japan.com/hiking/mt-tsurugi-tsurugi-san; https://japanhike.wordpress.com/2008/04/26/tsurugisan; www.shikokutours.com/shikoku-walks/Shikoku-Walks/Mt-Tsurugi*

Tsurugi-san, located at the eastern edge of the Iya region, is the island's second-tallest mountain (1,955 m/6,414 ft). The smooth-edged outline of the mountain is often contrasted with jagged Ishizuchi-san, the loftier peak in Ehime Prefecture. Adding an element of mystique to the summit, the sword of the vanquished Heike emperor was purportedly laid to rest in the earth of the expansive plain atop the peak, known as Heike-no-baba, inspiring the nickname "Sword Peak."

To reach the top, you can ride a chairlift that whisks passengers to a stop 30 minutes' walk from the top. It's also possible to hike from a trailhead located near the Mi-no-Koshi bus stop (2 hours one-way). To reach this bus stop, take the bus from Awa-Ikeda Station to Kubo bus stop (2 hours, 4 buses per day, ¥1,790), then hop on another bus bound for Tsurugi-san and ride until the final stop (50 minutes, 2 buses per day, ¥1,380). Note that buses only run to Mi-no-Koshi on weekends from April-November, and daily during Golden Week (late Apr.-early May), during summer holidays from mid-July through August, and when the autumn foliage turns (Oct.-early Nov.). Given the logistics, it's best to only plan on hiking this mountain if you've got your own wheels. The mountain is a magnet for pilgrims, and at the top, you'll find a shrine, huts, and a series of wooden walkways that lead to superb vistas of the entire region.

Unfortunately, the top of Tsurugi-san has a disconcerting amount of concrete, a weather tower, and other signs of development. To enjoy better views without so many dreary reminders of modern life, hike in the direction of the Jirōgyū Pass, then make the ascent to the nearby peak of **Jirōgyū** (1,929 m/6,328 ft). From Jirōgyū, trace your steps back to the Mi-no-Koshi bus stop.

White Water Rafting

The bluish-green stretch of the **Yoshino River** that flows through the **Ōboke** and **Kōbōke** gorges, surrounded by stunning scenery, is widely considered to have the best rapids for white water rafting in Japan.

HAPPY RAFT

221-1 Ikadagi; tel. 0887/75-0500; www.happyraft.com; Mar.-Nov. tours; half day from ¥6,000, full day from ¥11,000

Of the slew of rafting outfits operating in the Yoshino River area, Happy Raft, based near Tosa Iwahara Station, is at the top of the game. Their bilingual river guides have vast experience working and rafting on the best rivers around the world, from New Zealand and the American West to Nepal. The river hits a certain sweet spot due to the fact that it's just difficult enough to be exciting without being notably dangerous, with many rapids in the Class III and IV range.

Happy Raft's guides know the quirks of the terrain, such as the best outcrops from which to jump into deep pools and the safest spots to just horse around. If you'd rather get wet while scuttling along the gorge walls, they conduct canyoning tours, and, back on land, trekking tours too. Check the website for up-to-date offerings, and if you'd like to stay overnight, they run a handful of cozy, bare-bones guesthouses overlooking the Yoshino River valley.

Onsen

IYA ONSEN

367-2 Matsuo Matsumoto; tel. 0883/75-2311; www.iyaonsen.co.jp; 7:30am-6pm (last entry 5pm non-staying guests); bathing and cable car ¥1,700 adults, ¥900 children

If you go to the effort of reaching this remote pocket of misty mountains, be sure to stop at Iya Onsen. This excellent hot spring—the valley's one and only—is reached via a cable car that zips from Hotel Iya Onsen down to indoor and outdoor pools beside the Iya River below. The Heike clan is said to have plunged into these steamy pools after retreating in defeat at the hands of the Minamoto clan in the 12th century. This is a fantastic spot to soak year-round, but the views really pop in spring and autumn. If you've got time, stick around for an excellent meal at the hotel's restaurant, or better yet, stay for a night. Hotel Iya Onsen is located on Route 32, near the Peeing Boy statue.

FOOD AND ACCOMMODATIONS

Iya doesn't offer much in the way of restaurants, but most of the hotels in the region prepare meals for guests. Rice wasn't historically as plentiful here as in the rest of Japan due to the difficulty of cultivating it on the region's steep hillsides, so traditionally, a meal in Iya is likely to consist of grains, tubers, venison, and boar. As for staying, there are appealing options from swanky onsen resorts and guesthouses to restored thatched-roof farmhouses and places to camp. The Chiiori Project, launched in the 1970s by American author, art collector, and Japanologist Alex Kerr, aims to restore traditional houses dotting the lush Iya Valley and promotes sustainable tourism deeply rooted in the valley community.

TOUGENKYO-IYA

142 Higashi Iya, Ochiai, Miyoshi; tel. 0883/88-2540; www.tougenkyo-iya.jp; from ¥11,500 pp d without meals, cheaper with larger groups, catered meals ¥3,200 pp

A cluster of similarly stunning houses, overseen by the Chiiori Alliance & Trust (est. 2005), can be found deeper within the Iya Valley at the "Shangri-la" mountain hamlet of Tougenkyo-Iya. Here you'll find eight charming renovated farmhouses with painstakingly maintained thatched roofs, tucked away deep in a remote gully. Meals are available upon request. For ¥15,000 per group, you can get a home-cooked dinner made by a local aunty.

HOTEL IYA ONSEN

367-28 Matsuo Matsumoto, Ikeda-chō; tel. 0883/75-2311; www.iyaonsen.co.jp; from ¥15,000 pp with meals

It's not cheap, but this hotel is worth every yen. This onsen ryokan is located in Nishi Iya and backs directly onto the valley. Meals are fantastic, rooms are spacious, and onsen options include both indoor and outdoor baths, with the latter sitting almost next to the river at the base of the valley. The hotel is adept at accommodating foreign guests, and most staff speak English. If you're going to splurge on lodgings on any leg of a Shikoku journey, you won't be disappointed by doing so here.

★ CHIIORI

209 Higashi Iya, Miyoshi; tel. 0883/88-5290; www.chiiori.org; ¥19,250 pp d without meals, cheaper with larger groups, meals ¥3,200 pp

Documented in the beautifully written memoir *Lost Japan*, Kerr bought Chiiori (House of the Flute) in a ramshackle state in 1971 and proceeded to renovate the home slowly, with locals' help, to its current gorgeous state. It has an immaculate kitchen and bathroom with cypress bathtub, beautiful antiques carefully arranged, a floor hearth, calligraphy scrolls, shoji (paper screens), and of course, stunning valley views. Catered dinners with ingredients from around the valley can be had if you request in advance.

KAZURA-BASHI CAMPING VILLAGE

233 Nishiiyayamamura Kanjo, Miyoshi; tel. 090/1571-5258; check-in 9am-5pm Wed.-Mon. Apr.-Nov.; tent sites from ¥1,000, tents from ¥1,030, bungalows (up to 4 guests) from ¥5,200 per night

After crossing Kazura-bashi, turn left and walk 0.5 kilometers (0.3 mi) upstream, and you'll come to Kazura-bashi Camping Village. This spot is bare-bones, but it's a wonderful place to camp, or sleep in a bungalow, for a night. There are free showers and a good barbecue area, and cooking equipment, tents, and bedding can be rented. Have someone who can speak Japanese call ahead on your behalf to make a reservation, including specifying anything you may want to rent.

INFORMATION AND SERVICES

A great online resource for the region is **Iya Time** (www.iyatime.com), covering everything from things to see and do to small cafés and farmhouse lodgings in the Iya Valley, Ikeda, and Ōboke and Koboke gorge areas.

- **Miyoshi Tourist Information Center** (1810-18 Sarada, Ikeda-chō, next to Awa-Ikeda Station; tel. 0883/76-0877; https://tic.jnto.go.jp/eng/detail.php?id=1269; 9am-6pm daily)

- **Lapis Ōboke** (1553-1 Kamimyo, Yamashiro-chō; tel. 0883/84-1489; https://miyoshi-tourism.jp/en/spot/restareaoboke-lapisoboke/; 9am-5pm daily Mar.-Nov., 9am-5pm Wed.-Mon. Dec.-Feb.; 20 minutes' walk north of Ōboke Station beside Route 32)

GETTING THERE

Car

Your best bet is having your own wheels. Though Awa-Ikeda Station and Ōboke Station are accessible on the JR Shikoku Line, the main sights and accommodations stretch to the east, with limited public transport options. From **Takamatsu,** the center of the valley is a 2-hour-15-minute drive south (100 km/62 mi); from **Tokushima,** it's also a 2-hour-15-minute drive to the west (130 km/80 mi). Coming from the west, it's a 2-hour-45-minute drive east from **Matsuyama** (160 km/100 mi) and a 1-hour-45-minute drive northeast from **Kochi** (85 km/52 mi).

Train

Awa-Ikeda Station and **Ōboke Station** are the main entry points to the region by train. Both of these stations, on the **JR Dosan** line, lie between **Okayama** (1 hour 15 minutes; ¥3,860 one-way to Awa-Ikeda) on Honshu to the north, and **Kochi** (50 minutes; ¥3,230 one-way to Ōboke) to the south. It's also possible to reach Awa-Ikeda from either **Takamatsu,** sometimes requiring a transfer at Utazu (1 hour 15 minutes; ¥3,400 one-way), or directly from **Tokushima** (local train 2 hours, ¥1,660 one-way; limited express 1 hour 15 minutes, ¥3,590 one-way).

Bus

If you're coming from Osaka, you also have the option of taking a highway bus operated by **Shikoku Kotsu Bus** (tel. 0883/72-1231; www.yonkoh.co.jp) from Hankyū Umeda Station to the **Awa-Ikeda bus terminal** (4 hours; ¥4,750 one-way, ¥8,600 round-trip).

GETTING AROUND

Once you're in the valley region, there are sporadic public buses that run from **Ōboke Station** into Nishi Iya's core sights, such as Kazura-bashi. Outside of winter, limited buses run as far east as Tsurugi-san.

If you're not averse to spending a fair chunk of change—about ¥4,000 to Kazura-bashi, for example—Ōboke Station is a good place to catch a **taxi.** Have a station attendant call the taxi company (tel. 0883/87-2017) if none roll up after you've been waiting in front of the station for a bit.

Still, the best option for getting around the Iya Valley on your own schedule is to rent a car. If you haven't rented a car in Tokushima, Takamatsu, Kochi, or Matsuyama, about 30 minutes' walk north of Ōboke Station (a brief walk from the information center at Lapis Ōboke), you'll come to a small car rental outfit, run by a restaurant called **Mannaka** (1520 Yamashiro-chō Nishi; tel. 0883/84-1211; www.mannaka.co.jp; 9am-5pm). At ¥5,000 for 3 hours and ¥9,000 for 24 hours, it's a good deal.

Matsuyama and Around 松山

Capital of Ehime Prefecture and Shikoku's largest city with a population of 450,000, Matsuyama is loaded with history. You wouldn't necessarily sense this upon exiting its main train station, however, as drab buildings line the streets fanning out in all directions, largely the result of bombing during World War II. But forge ahead, past the immediate station area, and the city's gems soon come into view.

Chief among them is Matsuyama-jō, an impressive original castle perched atop a hill overlooking the city. Just southeast of the castle, the city's welcoming locals come to the lively area surrounding the **Ōkaidō** shopping arcade to eat, drink, and shop. The other major point of interest is legendary Dōgo Onsen, northeast of downtown, where Japan's first onsen ryokan, inspiration for the bathhouse in Miyazaki's movie *Spirited Away,* proudly occupies a prominent corner. Beyond the famed bathhouse, there's a vast, fading red-light district that makes for an interesting after-hours stroll for a particular sort of armchair anthropologist.

Matsuyama also likes to brandish its literary credentials. Natume Sōseki (1867-1916)—author of classics including *I Am a Cat* and *Kokoro*, and widely regarded as the godfather of modern Japanese literature—taught English in the city before devoting himself to writing full-time. Although the often-melancholic scribe's *Botchan* lightly skewers many aspects of life in Matsuyama during the tumultuous Meiji Restoration (1868), it didn't stop the city from erecting the **Botchan Wind-up Clock** in his honor at the entrance to the long arcade that runs through the Dōgo Onsen neighborhood, with figures of characters from the novel appearing at each new hour. Sōseki's one-time roommate in the city, the tragically short-lived haiku poet Masaoka Shiki (1867-1902), also boosts the city's literary cred.

Matsuyama moves at a leisurely pace. While it's certainly possible to see the city's major attractions in a day, an overnight stay allows you to explore without feeling rushed. It's also possible to use Matsuyama as a base if you plan to venture farther into Ehime's south, perhaps to the historic town of Uchiko and the castle town of Ōzu; or to the island's highest point, Ishizuchi-san, an hour-and-a-half drive east.

SIGHTS

Matsuyama-jō
松山城

1 Marunouchi; tel. 089/921-4873; www.matsuyamajo.jp; 9am-5pm daily Feb.-Jul. and Sept.-Nov., 9am-5:30pm daily Aug., 9am-4:30pm daily Dec.-Jan.; ¥520 adults, ¥160 elementary school students

Looming above Matsuyama, atop the steep hill of Katsuyama, this white fortress has been added to, renovated, and in the case of the main keep, rebuilt after a lightning strike in 1784. The overall impact of entering the grounds is of stepping into one of Japan's best-preserved castles with some of the most dramatic vistas to boot.

The construction of the complex we see the remnants of in Matsuyama today began in 1602, when feudal lord Katō Yoshiakira envisioned a stronghold on the hill overlooking the city. Only 26 years later, Katō moved north to Aizu, and in 1635, the Matsudaira clan, relatives of the ruling Tokugawa regime in Edo, moved in. The Matsudaira lords stayed on as rulers of the region until 1868, when the Meiji Restoration brought Japan's feudal age to an end.

The classic fortress is replete with dark corridors, steep rickety stairs, and openings from which arrows and large rocks were once shot and hurled at would-be invaders. The highest floor has sweeping views of Matsuyama rolling toward the Inland Sea.

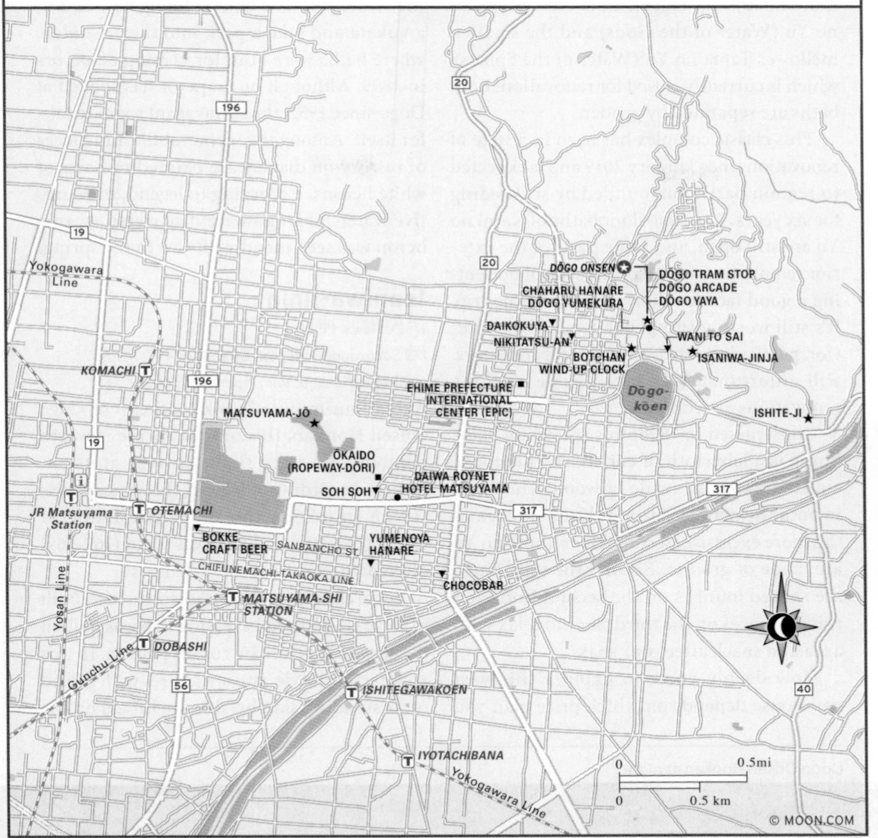

To get here, take tram line 5 from JR Matsuyama Station to the Okaido tram stop (8 minutes; ¥170). From Okaido, walk north 5 minutes along Katsuyama's eastern side to the **ropeway/chairlift station** (8:30am-5:30pm daily Feb.-Jul. and Sept.-Nov., 8:30am-6pm daily Aug., 8:30am-5pm daily Dec.-Jan.; ¥270 one-way, ¥520 round-trip), or walk the 15 minutes to the summit via the path from the lower ropeway station.

★ Dōgo Onsen

道後温泉

5-6 Dōgo-yunomachi; tel. 089/921-5141; https://dogo.jp; 6am-10pm, Kami no Yu 6am-11pm (last entry 10:30pm); ¥420 ages 12 and older, ¥160 ages 2-11; take tram line 5 from JR Matsuyama Station or tram line 3 from Matsuyama-shi Station to Dōgo Onsen Station, then walk 4 minutes

This iconic complex, widely considered Japan's first onsen bathhouse, is famed among fans of legendary anime director Hayao Miyazaki due to its links with his animated masterpiece *Spirited Away*. Miyazaki famously drew inspiration from this venerable complex when envisioning the film's fantastical spirit-run bathhouse. Occupying a large block and dominating a corner about four minutes' walk northeast of the Dōgo tram stop, this archetypal onsen complex has two indoor baths: the bigger, more crowded Kami no Yu (Water of the Gods) and the smaller, mellower Tama no Yu (Water of the Spirits), which is currently closed for renovation. Both baths are separated by gender.

This classic complex has been in a state of renovation since January 2019 and is expected to remain partly surrounded by scaffolding for six years. The first-floor baths of Kami no Yu are still open, and some parts of the exterior remain uncovered for the sake of presenting a good face for those who make the trip. It's still worth visiting, but some of the interior, particularly the second and third floors, will unfortunately be inaccessible until the renovations are complete.

Constructed in 1894, this sprawling bathhouse is a labyrinth of corridors, chambers, and staircases, all made of wood. The baths in both the main, first-floor Kami no Yu and the more exclusive, second-floor Tama no Yu are made of granite. Beyond the tubs, there are shared lounges on the second floor and private spaces on the third floor to relax with a tea and snack after your soak.

How deeply you can explore this vast bathhouse depends on which price plan you choose upon entering (and what's not being renovated at the time). At the higher end of the scale, you'll be able to lounge around in a yukata and take a peek into the Yushiden, where baths were built for visiting emperors in 1899. Although no emperor has soaked at Dōgo since 1952, the extravagant room speaks for itself. Among the memorabilia and pieces of history on display are painted mosaics of white herons. According to legend, the curative waters of Dōgo were discovered when a heron was seen mending its leg in the spring.

Isaniwa-jinja
伊佐爾波神社

173 Sakuradani-chō; tel. 089/947-7447; https://isaniwa.official.jp; 9am-5pm daily; free

About four minutes' walk southeast of Dōgo Onsen Honkan, this unique shrine is worth climbing the steep flight of steps at its entrance. According to legend, the atmospheric shrine stands on the site where Emperor Chuai (149-200) and Empress Jingū (169-269) often bathed in the primordial past.

For architecture geeks: This structure, built in 1667, is a National Treasure and was built in the atypical hachiman-zukuri pattern. In this architectural style, two structures with gabled roofs standing side-by-side are linked on the

Dōgo Onsen Honkan at night

side without gables. This layout creates the appearance of two separate buildings, although there is in fact only one.

Ishite-ji

石手寺

2-9-21 Ishite; tel. 089/977-0870; www.88shikokuhenro.jp/ehime/51ishiteji; 24 hours daily; free

If you're up for a slightly longer stroll, about 15 minutes' walk east of the Shiki Memorial Museum you'll come to Ishite-ji (Stone Hand Temple), the city's most important (and quirky) temple; it's number 51 on the island's 88-temple circuit. Its peculiar name is linked to a legend in which a fading local lord, unable to reach Kōbō Daishi, perished with a stone in his hand. As the story goes, he was later reborn still clutching it.

Trundling down a stone pathway lined by wooden stalls hawking amulets, fortunes on strips of paper, and other suitably spiritual trappings, you soon reach the **Niomon Gate,** a National Treasure. Passing through the opulent entry and emerging into the temple's expansive grounds, you'll find a three-tiered pagoda, numerous statues, halls, buildings filled with paintings of various deities, a giant bronze bell, praying pilgrims kitted out in white outfits and conical hats, and an army of prowling cats.

Perhaps most intriguing is the golden inner temple, accessed via a cavernous passageway filled with statuary and murals that burrows some 200 meters (656 ft) through the earth behind the main hall. Exiting the other side, you'll come to a statue of the emaciated historical Buddha, pre-enlightenment, and a towering effigy of Kōbō Daishi on a hill behind this hidden, inner sanctum. If you've got time, Ishite-ji is a worthwhile detour from Dōgo. If you stop by, try the grilled mochi (rice cake) sold on the grounds.

PARKS

DŌGO-KŌEN

1 Dōgo-kōen; tel. 089/941-1480; www.dogokouen.jp/dogokouen/gaiyou.html; open 24 hours; free; take tram bound for Dōgo Onsen to Dōgo-kōen tram stop, then walk 2 minutes east

On the site where Yuzuki Castle once stood, this green space about 5 minutes' walk south of Dōgo Onsen Honkan is a known quantity in Japan for its abundance of cherry trees that create a pink wonderland during hanami season every spring. Of the former castle, the only remains are the moats and some of the earthworks created to support the redoubt, which occupied the space for about 250 years, from the early 14th century to the second half of the 16th century. Some samurai homes have also been reconstructed. It's worth visiting for a stroll, an escape, or to have a picnic under the pink branches if you happen to be in the city in spring.

FOOD

Matsuyama is blessed with a lovely seaside location. Its mild climate results in a bounty of produce and the assurance of a regular fresh catch. Among its well-known local dishes is taimeshi, or rice mixed with sea bream.

SOH SOH

3-2-10 Ōkaido; tel. 070/5510-7568; http://greenlabel-group.com/sohsoh/shop#ropeway; 11:30am-10pm (last order 9pm) Sun.-Fri.; from ¥1,500

Soh Soh is a nationwide chain with a legion of fans attracted to its balanced meals, which include a healthy dose of vegetables, and notably modest portions of meat and fish—in essence, nouvelle Japanese fare. The chic ambience is pleasant, too.

YUMENOYA HANARE

Yoshida Bldg. 1F, 3-1-14 Sanbanchō; tel. 089/932-3939; www.dreamthanks.com/; 6pm-midnight daily, irregular holidays; average dinner ¥3,200

If you're looking for an izakaya to provide a healthy flow of booze to go with the food, and feel torn by the city's bewildering number of choices, you won't go wrong here. The dishes are a fusion twist, drawing from Japan and the West, with ingredients sourced locally. Servers are friendly

88-Temple Pilgrimage Route: Temples No. 46-51

Temples Visited: Jōruri-ji, Yasaka-ji, Sairin-ji, Jodo-ji, Hanta-ji, and Ishite-ji (Temples no. 46 through no. 51)
Distance, Time: 27 km/17 mi, 2 hours 45 minutes one-way (14.4 km/8.9 mi; 3 hours one-way including time walking to Dōgo Onsen at the end)
Getting There: From Matsuyama City Station, take the Iyo Railway's Yokogawara line bound for Yokogawara to Takanoko Station (13 minutes; ¥260). From there, take a local bus bound for Tanba, getting off at the Jōruri-ji-mae bus stop.

This section of the 88-Temple Pilgrimage Route begins not far from Matsuyama, and even passes through the city, ending up at Ishite-ji before continuing north. You'll start at **Jōruri-ji** (no. 46; 282 Jōruri-machi; tel. 089/963-0279; https://88shikokuhenro.jp/en/iozan-yojyuin-jyoruriji/; 7am-5pm daily; free), enveloped by a forest of juniper trees said to be a millennium old, with an inviting garden and a lotus pond. Nearby, **Yasaka-ji** (no. 47; 773 Joruri-machi; 089/963-0271; https://88shikokuhenro.jp/en/kumanozan-myokenin-yasakaji/; 7am-5pm daily; free) is a colorful sight, with its greenish copper rooftop and array of red flags flapping on the grounds, as well as its large graveyard with views of Matsuyama, a subterranean tunnel brimming with some 8,000 ceramic Amida Buddha figurines placed there by pilgrims, passages representing Buddhist heaven and hell, and a pond teeming with vivid carp.

From here, the riverside temple of **Sairin-ji** (no. 48; 1007 Takai-machi; tel. 089/975-0319; https://88shikokuhenro.jp/en/seiryuzan-anyoin-sairinji/; 7am-5pm daily; free) offers good views of Ishizuchi-san looming in the distance, as does **Jodo-ji** (no. 49; 1198 Takanoko-machi; tel. 089/975-1730; https://88shikokuhenro.jp/en/sairinzan-sanzoin-jyodoji/; 8am-5pm daily; free), with its rustic air, atmospheric graveyard, bamboo grove, and viewing platform with vistas of the Inland Sea beyond. **Hanta-ji** (no. 50; 32 Hatadera-machi; tel. 089/975-0910; https://88shikokuhenro.jp/en/higashiyama-rurikoin-hantaji/; 7am-5pm daily; free), once favored by the Imperial family in Kyoto, has Chinese scenes painted on the ceiling of its bell tower and offers superb views of Matsuyama and the Inland Sea. Finally, you'll reach quirky **Ishite-ji** (no. 51; 2-9-21 Ishite; tel. 089/977-0870; www.nehan.net/sp/indexenglishi.html; 24 hours; free), not far from Matsuyama's Dōgo Onsen, only about 20 minutes' walk to the west.

The walk itself takes a total of about 3 hours, but plan to spend up to another few hours lingering at the temples. If you don't want to visit all six temples, you can stop at no. 49 (Jodo-ji), then walk 7 minutes west to Kume Station (total journey: 8.8 km/5.5 mi; 1 hour 50 minutes one-way). From Kume, hop on the Iyo Tetsudo Yokogawara line and ride to Matsuyama-shi Station (11 minutes; ¥250), putting you right in central Matsuyama.

and speak enough English to help you navigate the menu.

★ NIKITATSU-AN

3-18 Dogokitamachi; tel. 089/924-6617; www.dogobeer.jp/nikitatsu-restaurant; 11am-9:30pm Tues.-Sun., closed Tues. if Mon. falls on holiday, closed first Tues. of month; lunch courses from ¥1,430, dinner courses from ¥3,300

Nikitatsu is actually a sake brewer. Beside the shop that sells the highly regarded drink, you'll find a restaurant set in a garden villa. From the dark-wood interior, diners enjoy tranquil views of the greenery just outside, as servers shuffle between tables in traditional garb. The menu includes a simple selection of set courses—fish, meat, and vegetables with rice, seasoned by soy sauce and fish broth—that goes down well with sake from next door.

★ DAIKOKUYA

8-21 Dogokitamachi; tel. 089/925-5005; www.daikokuya-udon.co.jp; 11am-10pm daily; udon and rice dishes from ¥820, multicourse meals ¥1,550-4,680

While taimeshi is sometimes served as sea

bream sashimi atop rice, Daikokuya mixes the two elements together in an iron pot called a kama and whips up a dish known as tai no kama meishi (sea bream kettle rice). This is the dish to go for. Beyond this, the menu makes heavy use of seasonal ingredients. The noodles are great too—not too soft, not too firm.

BARS AND NIGHTLIFE

The bulk of Matsuyama's nightlife is concentrated along three parallel streets that run east to west: Ichibanchō, Nibanchō, and Sanbanchō. The airy, covered arcade known as Ōkaido cuts through the middle of these three strips, running north to south. This swath of downtown spreads southward from the southern base of the large hill that Matsuyama-jō stands on, and roughly 20 minutes' walk northeast of Matsuyama-shi Station. The Dōgo area also has its share of nightlife, some of it on the seedier side.

BOKKE CRAFT BEER

5-6 Minami-horibata; tel. 088/906-8349; www.facebook.com/people/BOKKE/100063871140046/; 5pm-midnight Mon.-Sat.

If you're a craft beer fan, this is your place in Matsuyama. There's a broad spectrum of Japanese microbrews on tap in this smartly designed space with seating both in- and out-of-doors. The menu also includes a good range of savory nibbles. It's a good place to socialize on weekends.

WANI TO SAI

1-39 Dōgo-yunomachi; tel. 080/3319-2765; www.facebook.com/wanitosai; 6pm-late daily

It would be safe to call this hideaway in Dōgo the city's most bohemian haunt. Wani to Sai (Alligator and Rhinoceros) has a peculiar circus theme—philistine art, sundry oddities, and marionettes—which is the direct product of the proprietor's life experience. He went to Italy to study fresco painting, only to redirect his efforts into making marionettes. His project today is running this fun dive bar, serving cocktails, European beers, Japanese comfort foods like ramen and yaki-niku donburi (rice topped with grilled meat), and more. It's located near the base of the stairs that lead to Isaniwa-jinja.

CHOCOBAR

1F First Kisuke Bldg., 2-6-2 Sambanchō; tel. 089/933-2039; www.facebook.com/chocobar2013/; 7pm-late daily

This lively shot bar is popular with locals and expats looking to tie one on to a hip-hop soundtrack. Sitting on a busy street corner, the place can get packed on weekends, with crowds spilling onto the sidewalk outside. There are hookahs too, if that's your thing.

ACCOMMODATIONS

DAIWA ROYNET HOTEL MATSUYAMA

2-6-5 Ichibanchō; tel. 089/913-1355; www.daiwaroynet.jp/matsuyama; ¥10,760 d with breakfast

This neat, modern hotel is smack in the middle of the city. The rooms here are reasonably spacious and come with large bathrooms. English-speaking staff are happy to answer questions. There's a breakfast buffet, as well as a restaurant serving Asian cuisine throughout the day. It's a great pick for convenience and value.

DŌGO YAYA

6-1 Dōgo-takōchō; tel. 089/907-1181; www.yayahotel.jp; ¥12,000 d

A great mid-range option near Dōgo Onsen, this hotel has a distinctly Japanese aesthetic, with shoji (paper screen) doors and windows veiled behind wooden slats—a sleek, modern touch. The rooms are compact but well-appointed with good bathrooms, and the friendly staff are welcoming. Guests are eligible for a discount at Dōgo Onsen. A breakfast buffet is available.

★ CHAHARU HANARE DŌGO YUMEKURA

4-5 Yuzukichō, Dōgo; tel. 089/931-1180; www.yume-kura.jp; from ¥15,400 pp for twin room without breakfast and dinner, from ¥17,600 pp for twin room with breakfast and dinner

Flawless service is provided by friendly staff at this luxe, modern ryokan, located across the road from Dōgo Onsen Honkan. The spacious rooms have private baths filled with local onsen water. There's no public bath in the hotel itself, but guests receive coupons to soak in Dōgo Onsen Honkan, right across the street. Excellent dinner and breakfast spreads are served in private dining rooms. Amenities down to the toiletries, robes, and towels are top-notch. If you can afford to splurge, this boutique ryokan, with only seven rooms, is an excellent choice.

INFORMATION AND SERVICES

Tourist information centers are located in **JR Matsuyama Station** (tel. 089/931-3914; 8:30am-8:30pm daily) and another next to the Botchan Wind-up Clock outside the **Dōgo Onsen tram stop** (tel. 089/921-3708; 8:30am-7pm daily). Online, check out the city's official tourism portal, **Matsuyama Sightseeing** (https://en.matsuyama-sightseeing.com/). **Team Camellia** (https://matsuyamavolunteerguide.jimdo.com) offers free English-language tours of some of the city's main sights.

- **Ehime Prefecture International Center** (EPIC) (1-1 Dōgo Ichiman; tel. 089/917-5678; www.epic.or.jp; 8:30am-5pm Mon.-Sat., three-minute walk from the Minami-machi tram stop on tram lines 3 and 5)

GETTING THERE

Train

Matsuyama's two main train stations are **JR Matsuyama Station,** located west of the city's heart at Matsuyama-jō, and south of the castle, **Matsuyama-shi Station,** the main hub of the local Iyotetsu line. You can reach Matsuyama by limited express train on the **JR Yosan** line from **Takamatsu,** sometimes requiring a transfer at Tadotsu Station (2.5 hours; ¥6,490), or by a limited express train directly from **Okayama** on Honshu (3 hours, ¥7,150).

Bus

You can take a highway bus between Matsuyama's main **bus stop,** located directly in front of JR Matsuyama Station, and most major cities around Shikoku. Longer bus routes also run between Matsuyama and **Osaka** (5.5 hours) and **Tokyo** (12 hours). For timetables, routes, and fares, see the websites of **Japan Bus Online** (https://japanbusonline.com/en) and **Willer Express** (https://willerexpress.com/en/).

Boat

It's possible to make the trip to Matsuyama over the Inland Sea from **Hiroshima** (1 hour 15 minutes, ¥7,800 by hydrofoil; 2 hours 40 minutes, ¥4,500 by standard ferry). For details, check the website of ferry and hydrofoil operator **Setonaikai Kisen** (tel. 082/253-1212; www.setonaikaikisen.co.jp; 7am-9pm daily). These ferries depart from **Hiroshima Port Ujina Passenger Terminal** (1-13-26 Ujinakaigan, Minami-ku; tel. 082/253-1212) and arrive at **Matsuyama Tourist Port Terminal** (5-2259-1 Takahama-machi; tel. 089/953-1003; www.kankoko.com/english/; 4am-11pm daily), located roughly 10 kilometers (6.2 mi) northwest of downtown Matsuyama.

Air

It's possible to fly from any of Fukuoka (45 minutes; ¥10,000) and Tokyo (1 hour 35 minutes; ¥15,000), and from Seoul and Shanghai, to and from **Matsuyama Airport** (2731 Minami Yoshidamachi; tel. 089/972-5600; www.matsuyama-airport.co.jp), located just west of town and easily reachable by a **bus** that runs twice hourly to and from the main bus station in front of JR Matsuyama Station (15 minutes; ¥630).

GETTING AROUND

Most points of interest are found somewhere between the castle mount of Katsuyama and

Dōgo Onsen, northeast of the city. The best way to shuttle between them is either **on foot** or aboard the city's smoothly operating **tram** network.

Tram

Matsuyama's main transport feature is its classic trams, with five lines in total. Loop **lines 1** (clockwise) and **2** (counterclockwise) run around the large hill, Katsuyama, atop which Matsuyama-jō stands. **Line 3** links Matsuyama-shi Station, on the local Iyotetsu train line, to Dōgo Onsen. **Line 5** (number 4 is skipped over) goes from JR Matsuyama Station to Dōgo Onsen. **Line 6** runs between Matsuyama-shi Station and the Honmachi 6 tram stop north of Matsuyama-jō.

To ride the tram, simply hop on via the back door and pay a flat ¥170 when you exit via the front door wherever you get off. You can also buy a **one-day pass** (¥700 adults, ¥350 children) for unlimited tram rides at the **Iyotetsu Ticket Center,** located at Matsuyama City Station, or at any station on the Iyotetsu line. See the official website (http://www.iyotetsu.co.jp) for more details.

UCHIKO

内子町

The historic town of Uchiko, about 40 kilometers (25 mi) southwest of Matsuyama, makes for a good day trip from the city. Uchiko became rich during the early 20th century thanks to a thriving wax industry. The remnants of that period of its past make Uchiko a great place to step back in time to the Taishō-era (1912-1926) and imagine daily life then from the perspective of the elite.

Centered in the historic Yōkaichi district, the townscape is a mix of grand old homes once occupied by well-heeled denizens, from wax moguls to the founder of the still-thriving beer giant Asahi. Many of the abodes in the **Yōkaichi Historic District** feature immaculate gardens and sprawling courtyards. All told, some 90 homes, once built by the town's wealthy merchant class, line this 1.5-kilometer-long (1-mi-long) street.

Sights

UCHIKO-ZA

内子座

2102 Uchiko; tel. 0893/44-2840; www.we-love-uchiko.jp/spot_center/spot_c2/; 9am-4:30pm daily; ¥400; walk 7 minutes northeast of Uchiko Station

This old-school kabuki theater is a beautiful structure dating to 1916 that was spruced up in the mid-1980s. It's still in use and hosts the occasional performance of kabuki or bunraku puppet theater. It's possible to go behind the scenes and under the stage to see how the magic is created through trapdoors, hidden passages, and a revolving stage. Have a Japanese speaker call ahead to inquire about upcoming performances.

KAMIHAGA RESIDENCE

上芳我邸

Kamihaga Residence: 2696 Uchiko; tel. 0893/44-2771; www.we-love-uchiko.jp/spot_center/spot_c3; 9am-4:30pm daily; ¥500; 20 minutes' walk northeast of Uchiko Station

Of the various old homes that can be entered in the Yōkaichi Historic District, visit this one, a museum set in the grand old home and former workshop of the Kamihaga family, who were among the town's most influential wax producers. Inside the home is a museum that explores the town's once-booming wax industry. The home is also a fantastic example of an affluent Meiji-period residence; painted screens and exquisite pottery grace elegant rooms with tatami floors, alongside Western design accents, which were just coming into vogue when the home was built.

Shopping

ŌMORI WA-RŌSOKU

大森和ろうそく

2214 Uchiko; tel. 0893/43-0385; https://omoriwarosoku.jp; 9am-5pm Wed.-Thurs. and Sat.-Mon.; free

After exploring the atmospheric kabuki theater, backtrack to the main street that you walked along from the station. Turn right and continue walking northeast, away from the station. When you reach a four-way intersection with a bank in front of you, turn left and walk straight for two minutes. You'll come to this small shop selling candles on the left side of the road. Pull aside the noren (curtains) decorated with candle motifs and step inside. This is Uchiko's last candle workshop, where all work is still done the old-fashioned way: by hand. Watch the artisans at work and, if you feel inspired, purchase a few of the candles for which the town is known.

Food and Accommodations

ZUM SCHWARZEN KEILER

204-1 Shiromawari, Uchiko; tel. 0893/57-9066; https://peraichi.com/landing_pages/view/keiler2013; 5pm-9:30pm (last order 8:30pm) Thurs.-Tues.; dinner courses from ¥2,500

If you're feeling like mixing it up and taking a break from Japanese fare, you're in luck. This restaurant, run by a German expat and his Japanese wife, serves a hearty range of sausages, schnitzels, pretzels, and other things you'd expect from Deutschland. There's a nice range of German beer and wine too.

★ HOTEL COCORO.KURA

1949 Uchiko; tel. 0893/44-5735; www.uchi-cocoro.com/eng/yado/cocoro/; ¥12,000 pp with breakfast

Café by day, boutique inn by night, this unique lodging is a great option set in an old storehouse in the Yōkaichi area. This property accommodates up to two groups per night. There's a private garden behind the building here, too. The rooms have a stylish spin, with clean minimal lines and a slightly more modern Japanese aesthetic. As an added bonus, each room has a pristine wooden tub for a soak. If it's booked out, check the website (www.uchi-cocoro.com/eng/), which features three similar properties also set in renovated historic buildings in the old town.

Information and Services

Online, check out **Uchikogenic** (https://uchikogenic.com/en/), an English-language travel guide to the city, with listings for lodgings, restaurants, and more.

- **Tourist information center** (324 Uchiko, next to Uchiko Station; tel. 089/343-1450)
- **Uchikochō Visitor Center** (2020 Uchiko; tel. 0893/44-3790; 9am-5:30pm Fri.-Wed., 10 minutes northeast of Uchiko Station)

Getting There

The easiest way to reach Uchiko and Ōzu is by **train** from **Matsuyama.** Uchiko is about 25 minutes south of Matsuyama on a limited express train (¥2,260).

ŌZU

大洲市

About 10 minutes by train west of Uchiko, the small town of Ōzu arose as a castle town during the Edo period (1603-1868). By the Meiji period (1868-1912), moneyed merchants' houses infused a nice blend of historical strata into the city's architecture. One Meiji-period residence worth a trip is just east of town: Garyū Sansō. This thatched-roof villa is graced by an exquisite garden and a pavilion overlooking the Hiji-kawa river. The town's most unique characteristic point is its ukai (cormorant fishing) demonstrations that take place in this river from June 1-September 20 each year. This is one of the best places to see this singular fishing technique in action.

Sights

ŌZU-JŌ

903 Ōzu; tel. 0893/24-1146; www.ozucastle.jp; 9am-5pm (last entry 4:30pm) daily; ¥550 adults, ¥220 junior high school students and younger, joint ticket with Garyū Sansō ¥880 adults, ¥330 junior high school students and younger

With a history stretching back to the 14th century, this diminutive castle has been refurbished numerous times, most recently in 2004. Traditional building methods and materials were used, imbuing it with authenticity. Climb to the top and look out over the lovely countryside scene and the Hiji-kawa River.

The castle is about 25 minutes' walk south of JR Iyo-Ōzu Station. You'll pass over the Hiji-kawa on the way. Alternatively, you can take a taxi (5 minutes; about ¥900).

Cormorant Fishing in Ōzu

Some 1,300 years ago, fishermen developed the technique of ukai, a peculiar fishing method with cormorants, large black birds that dive into rivers to hunt for ayu (sweet freshwater fish). Traditionally dressed fishermen board long, narrow wooden boats with lanterns hanging from the front to attract ayu. Birds, with ropes tied around their long necks like leashes to prevent larger fish from being swallowed, swoop into the water to catch up to a half-dozen fish at a time. Unconsumed fish are collected by the fishermen.

Ōzu no Ukai (649-1 Ōzu; tel. 0893/57-6655; www.visitehimejapan.com/en/see-and-do/6718; 7pm daily Jun.-Sept.; ¥7,000 junior high school students and older, ¥4,500 elementary school students) gives demonstrations, which last about half an hour; ukai season stretches roughly from early June through September. Reserve at least a day ahead.

GARYŪ SANSŌ

411-2 Ōzu; tel. 0893/24-3759; www.garyusanso.jp; 9am-5pm (last entry 4:30pm) daily; ¥550 adults, ¥220 junior high school students and younger, joint ticket with Ōzu-jō ¥880 adults, ¥330 junior high school students and younger

Fifteen minutes' walk east of the castle, this thatched-roof teahouse and garden is in a tranquil spot with views of the Hiji-kawa below. You'll pass through Ōzu's quaint old town on the way to reach this aesthetically refined villa, which required four years and a whopping 9,000 craftsmen to complete it in 1907. The grounds are equally alluring. If you make the trip to Ōzu, a visit to Garyū Sansō is a more moving experience than the town's castle.

Food and Accommodations

★ NIPPONIA HOTEL

Reception: 378 Ōzu; tel. 0120/210-289; www.ozucastle.com; from ¥18,634 pp with dinner

Following the concept of a "decentralized hotel," this newly opened set of properties near the Hiji-kawa river is ensconced in Ōzu's old town. All told, 11 inviting guest rooms, very much in the boutique vein with stylish Japanese accents, are arrayed in a variety of renovated historic properties—think: former residences of feudal lords—throughout the beautifully preserved neighborhood. All rooms have amply sized private baths with cypress tubs. Aside from the sleeping quarters, there's a shared reception desk, and **Le Un** (888 Ōzu; 11:30am-3pm and 5:30pm-10pm daily; lunch courses from ¥1,800, dinner courses from ¥3,200), a restaurant serving French-inspired cuisine with a local twist. The friendly staff, noted for their local expertise, are ready at hand to provide concierge services. It's worthy of a splurge.

Information and Services

For a deeper glimpse with an English-speaking guide who can offer broader historical context, **Feel Ōzu** (https://feel.visitozu.com; 2-6 people; from 2.5 hours; from ¥7,000) gives excellent walking tours centered on the town's gems.

- **Tourist Information Center** (inside Iyo-Ōzu Station; tel. 0893/57-9161; 9am-6:30pm daily)
- **Ōzu Kankō Total Information Center** (649-1 Ōzu; tel. 0893/57-6655; 9am-5pm daily; https://jp.visitozu.com)

Getting There

Ōzu, best accessed via **Iyo-Ōzu Station,** is about 15 minutes farther south of **Uchiko** (¥260) by local train and 10 minutes by express train (¥1,510). The station is located a 25-minute walk north of Ozū-jo.

ISHIZUCHI-SAN

The highest mountain in western Japan at 1,982 meters (6,502 ft), Ishizuchi-san is a pointed, hammer-shaped peak and one of

Japan's 100 Famous Mountains. Like Tsurugi-san, it's also a pilgrimage destination and makes for a challenging hike. Traditionally, women are forbidden from climbing the peak on July 1 when a mountain opening ceremony is held. There are numerous shrines dedicated to mountain deities as you make your way up.

ISHIZUCHI-SAN SUMMIT HIKE

Distance: *7.2 km (4.5 mi) round-trip from upper station of Shimotani cable car; 9.2 km (5.7 mi) round-trip from Tsuchi-goya Hut*

Time: *6-7 hours round-trip (from upper station of Shimotani cable car); 5-6 hours round-trip (from Tsuchi-goya Hut)*

Trailhead: *upper station (Sancho-Jojū) of Ishizuchi Tōzan Ropeway (north side of mountain); Tsuchi Goya Hut (south side of mountain)*

Information and maps: *www.ishizuchisankei.com/en/climbing/; English-language map available online: www.ishizuchi.com/web/wp-content/uploads/2014/10/102a1bab9c7e6d293bd4432da75530ff.pdf; https://japanhike.wordpress.com/2008/06/12/mt-ishizuchi; www.shikokutours.com/shikoku-walks/Shikoku-Walks/Mt-Ishizuchi; https://hikesinjapan.yamakei-online.com/course/119.php*

You can hike from the top of a cable car line that begins from **Shimotani** cable car station, located near **Nishi-no-kawa** bus stop on the north side of the mountain (tel. 0897/59-0331; www.ishizuchi.com; 8am-6pm Jul.-Aug., irregular hours at other times of year; ¥1,030 one-way, ¥1,950 round-trip). The cable car whisks passengers from an elevation of 455-1,300 meters (1,493-4,265 ft). From the upper station of **Sancho-Jōju**, it's a 6- to 7-hour hike round-trip. A less grueling trail begins at **Tsuchi-goya Hut** (1,500 m/4,921 ft) on the south side of the mountain. The round-trip hike on this trail takes 5-6 hours.

Whichever path you choose, the trails merge eventually and the path becomes increasingly steep as you approach the summit. At **Misen** (1,974 m/6,476 ft), you'll discover **Ishizuchi-jinja**, likely to be thronged with pilgrims, and you'll be rewarded with dramatic views stretching from the nearby mountains all the way to the Inland Sea. The **Ishizuchi-san Summit Hut** (tel. 080/1998-4591; http://ishizuchisan.jp/sansou/index2.htm; ¥8,700 pp with two meals) is open from May through October. This lodge accommodates up to 50 in a large, simple shared space. If you don't mind roughing it for the night and enjoy a bit of camaraderie, this is a good option. Reservations must be made by phone or email at least 10 days in advance.

From here, you can clamber up the final jagged section of the mountain known as **Tengudake** (1,982 m/6,502 ft). Note that some sections of this final leg of the ascent require the use of chains drilled into rock faces. Thankfully, stairs are also available for those with less of a taste for adventure.

Getting There

The trailhead for both the Sancho-Jōju and Tsuchi-goya routes can be reached directly by car. Coming from Matsuyama, to reach the lower cable car station of **Shimotani,** take the Matsuyama Expressway to the parking lot in front of Sancho-Jōju, the upper cable car station of the Ishizuchi-Tōzan Ropeway (61.7 km/38.3 mi; 1 hour 15 minutes). To reach the **Tsuchi-goya** trailhead by car, take National Route 33, then Prefectural Road 12 to Tsuchigoya parking lot (83.4 km/51.8 mi; 2 hours). Driving to either route, use your rental car's inbuilt GPS, set to English, to ensure you remain on course to your destination.

If you're limited to public transport, making it to Tsuchi-goya is complicated by the fact that buses only run on holidays and weekends. **Setouchi Bus** (tel. 0898/23-3450; www.setouchibus.co.jp; ¥1,000 one-way) runs four buses daily between JR Iyo-Saijo Station, accessible from JR Matsuyama Station via the Shiokaze limited express train (1 hour; ¥3,590), and the Shimotani cable car station (for bus timetable: www.ishizuchi.com/company; 50 minutes; ¥1,020 adults, ¥510 children). That said, given the challenge with reaching the top, it's best to pass on Ishizuchi-san if you don't have a car or have limited time.

Kochi

高知市

There's a subtropical vibe in sun-kissed Kochi's air. As you exit the main station, palm trees line the boulevards, gregarious locals banter in a carefree tone, and just south of downtown, Katsurahama Beach stands at the foot of cliffs renowned for being a prime spot to moon-gaze. These bluffs were once frequented by the city's favorite son, legendary samurai and political revolutionary Sakamoto Ryōma, a pivotal figure in advancing the Meiji Restoration of 1868. Sakamoto is hard to miss with his scowling visage glaring from so many billboards and shop signs around town, including from the **Sakamoto Ryoma Statue** (Urado, Kochi; tel. 088/823-9457; www.city.kochi.kochi.jp/site/kanko/ryomazou.html; 24 hours; free) looming over Katsurahama.

Downtown, a townscape punctuated by rivers, is centered around a well-preserved, original castle. There's a vibrant dining scene, heavily featuring katsuo no tataki (flame-broiled bonito), as well as a smattering of lively nightlife, mostly condensed in the Obiyamachi district, which spreads eastward from the southeastern corner of Kochi-kōen park and the castle that stands atop it. These draws make the city of Kochi a good base for a day or two of exploration, eating, and drinking in the city if you're not rushed.

Kochi's colors are most visible during the spirited Yosakoi Matsuri in August, hands-down the best time to visit. The festival features a range of modern dance troupes frolicking in the streets and on stages to music ranging from hip-hop to traditional scores and high-speed anime soundtracks. This decidedly colorful, modern take on the summer dance matsuri is in many ways an ideal complement to neighboring Tokushima's more historically grounded, though also lively, Awa Odori festival. Both bashes attract huge crowds, so book accommodation well in advance.

SIGHTS

Kochi-jō

高知城

1-2-1 Marunouchi; tel. 088/824-5701; http://kochipark.jp/kochijyo; 9am-5pm daily; ¥420 ages 18 and older, free for ages 18 and younger; take tram bound for Sambashi-dōri 5-chōme from Kochieki-mae tram stop to Harimaya-bashi, then transfer to tram bound for Ino and ride to Kochijō-mae tram stop (8 minutes, ¥200), or walk from JR Kochi Station (20 minutes)

This stout castle in the center of town is one of Japan's 12 citadels still standing in original form since the end of the feudal era in 1868, when the Meiji Restoration swept the country. First completed in 1611, the current incarnation largely dates from 1748, after a rebuilding effort that followed a fire.

After passing the moat, make your way up through the grounds of **Kochi-kōen** (1-2-1 Marunouchi; tel. 088/824-5701; https://kochipark.jp/kochijyo/; open 24 hours; free) and enter the castle proper. You'll sense its age when you see its lived-in chambers, deep stairwells, and commanding watchtower. Uniquely, the main keep doubled as a residence for the lords of the Yamauchi clan who reigned over what was then Tōsa (Kochi today) during the feudal era. From the top floor of the main tower, you'll be rewarded with excellent views of the city fanning out in all directions below.

Godai-san

五台山

A rewarding side-trip from downtown Kochi, the peak of Godai-san, named after a mountain in China by visiting monks, boasts temple number 31 on the circuit of 88—Chikurin-ji—as well as the lovely Makino Botanical Garden, an expansive green space with walking paths, a greenhouse, and more. The mountain is also a great place to take in views of the city and Katsurahama Beach. To reach Godai-san, take

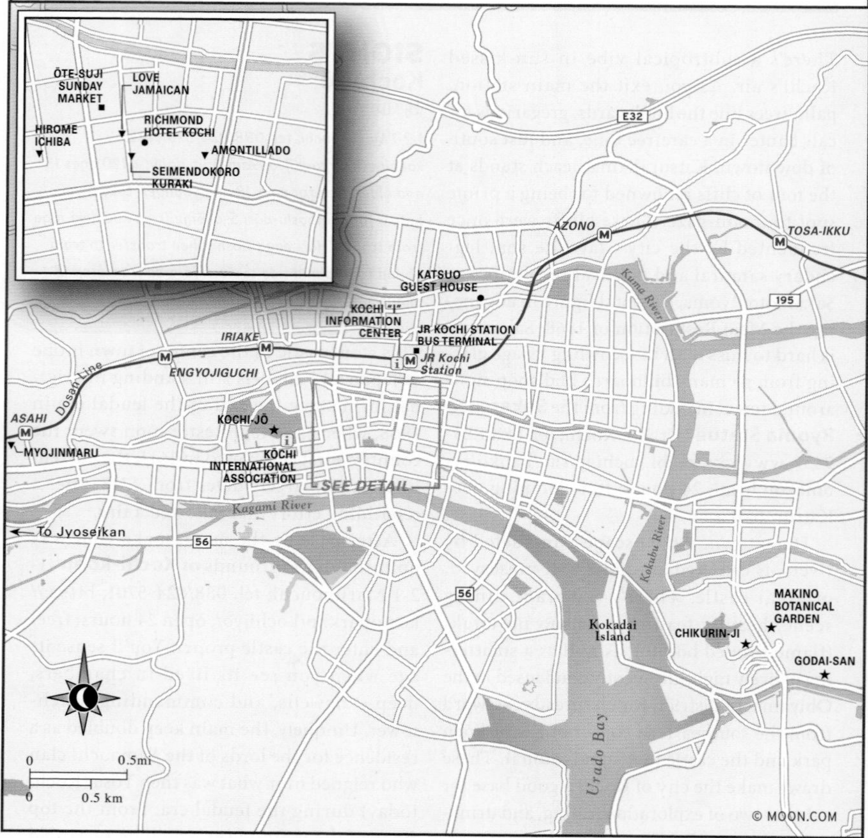

the My Yu Bus from JR Kochi Station (25 minutes, ¥600 for day pass). Alternatively, take a taxi from JR Kochi Station to Godai-san (20 minutes, about ¥1,500).

CHIKURIN-JI

竹林寺

3577 Godai-san; tel. 088/882-3085; www.chikurinji.com; 8am-5pm daily for main hall, 8:30am-5pm daily for garden and treasure hall; ¥400 adults, ¥200 high school students, ¥150 junior high school students, ¥100 elementary school students

Founded in 724 by a monk visiting from China, this temple (no. 31 on the circuit of 88) has scholarly associations, venerating Manjusri, a bodhisattva of wisdom. As such, it attracts not only pilgrims but also a steady flow of students hoping for high marks on exams. A five-tiered pagoda, a tranquil garden, and a host of buildings dot the grounds. Inside its treasure hall are scrolls and various statuary with a decidedly Indian touch. The temple's spacious grounds are especially lovely in spring and autumn.

MAKINO BOTANICAL GARDEN

牧野植物園

4200-6 Godai-san; tel. 088/882-2601; www.makino.

88-Temple Pilgrimage Route: Temples No. 31-33

Temples Visited: Chikurin-ji (no. 31), Zenjibu-ji (no. 32), and Sekkei-ji (no. 33)
Distance, Time: 14.4 km/8.9 mi, 3 hours 30 minutes one-way
Getting There: Take the My Yu Bus from JR Kochi Station (25 minutes; ¥600 for day pass) to Chikurin-ji, situated on the lofty hill in Kochi city's limits known as Godai-san, then walk from there.

pilgrim at Zenjibu-ji

Just east of central Kochi, **Chikurin-ji** (no. 31; 3577 Godai-san; tel. 088/882-3085; www.chikurinji.com; 8am-5pm daily for main hall, 8:30am-5pm daily for garden and treasure hall; ¥400 adults, ¥200 high school students, ¥150 junior high school students, ¥100 elementary school students) is approached via a stone staircase and mossy path, but its name ("Bamboo Forest Temple") is something of a misnomer, given the swath of broad-leaf and pine trees blanketing Godai-san. Continuing along this particularly scenic stretch, the path to **Zenjibu-ji** (no. 32; 3084 Tochi, Nankoku; tel. 088/865-8430; https://88shikokuhenro.jp/en/hachiyouzan-gumonjiin-zenjibuji/; 7am-5pm daily; free) takes in sweeping views of the beach of Katsurahama.

Sekkei-ji (no. 33; 857-3 Nagahama; tel. 088/837-2233; https://88shikokuhenro.jp/en/kofukuzan-kofukuin-sekkeiji/; 7am-5pm daily; free), in a suburb of Kochi city, is one of only three Zen temples on the circuit. This was the ancestral temple of the Chosokabe clan, which unified Shikoku under feudal lord Chōsokabe Motochika (1539-1599). To reach Sekkei-ji, you'll need to take a free ferry ride (5 minutes) from Tanezaki Ferry Port (1-2-20 Marunouchi, Kochi; tel. 088/823-9892; www.pref.kochi.lg.jp/soshiki/170701/keneitosen.html; 6am-9pm daily), 1 hour 15 minutes' walk southwest (6.1 km/3.8 mi) from Zenjibu-ji, to Nagahama Port, from where Sekkei-ji is 20 minutes' walk west. To return to Kochi's city center, walk 5 minutes northeast of Sekkei-ji to Nagahama bus stop and catch a bus to Harimaya-bashi bus stop in Kochi's downtown (once hourly; 20 minutes; ¥440).

For a detailed rundown of how to undertake the latter stages of this journey, including the ferry journey and bus ride back into Kochi proper, visit https://visitkochijapan.com/en/activities/10478, scroll down the page, and click on "Henro Trail Guide (31st-33rd)_page 14-19" and "Henro Trail Guide (31st-33rd)_page 20-23".

or.jp; 9am-5pm daily; ¥730 adults, free for high school students and younger

Located a pleasant 20-minute walk east of Chikurin-ji, this lush zone bears the family name of a prominent Kochi-born botanist, Dr. Makino Tomitaro (1862-1957). Walk among 3,000 species of plant-life in 6 hectares (14.8 acres) of outdoor gardens and in a large greenhouse, and learn about Dr. Makino's contributions to science at the on-site museum.

FESTIVALS AND EVENTS

YOSAKOI ODORI MATSURI
よさこい祭

Aug. 9-12

Kochi's flamboyant, kinetic Yosakoi Matsuri is one of the 10 largest festivals in Japan, and the energy level doesn't disappoint. Consecutive waves of dance troupes dressed in colorful costumes—many of them being playful twists on traditional forms—jump, shout, and groove through the city's downtown streets, fill covered shopping arcades, and perform in parks, on stages next to the castle, and various other locations. The atmosphere is fun and loud. Revelers spill into local restaurants and bars after the dancing stops, and street food stalls hum with energy into the night.

The best days are Aug. 10-11. This festival has a more modern flavor than Tokushima's **Awa Odori,** which is held immediately following Kochi's big bash on August 12-15. The two festivals complement one another perfectly. If you can swing it, consider attending both. Just be sure to book accommodations as far in advance as possible to account for the inevitable crowds.

SHOPPING

ŌTE-SUJI SUNDAY MARKET

1.3-km (0.8-mi) stretch of Ōte-suji; 5am-6pm Sun. Apr.-Sept., 5:30am-5pm Oct.-Mar.

For more than three centuries, a street bazaar has buzzed on Sundays along Ōte-suji, the street leading to the Ōte-mon gate of Kochi-jō. Nearly 500 stalls hawk everything from local fruits and vegetables to flowers, wooden crafts, and daily sundries. The atmosphere is friendly and boisterous. It makes a great introduction to the lively spirit of Kochi.

FOOD

★ HIROME ICHIBA

2-3-1 Obiyamachi; tel. 088/822-5287; http://hirome.co.jp; 10am-11pm Mon.-Sat. and holidays, 9am-10pm Sun., open times of individual restaurants vary

Boisterous, sprawling, and brimming with variety, this indoor food court shares space with a market that serves a bit of everything Japanese. Near the castle downtown, at the end of the Obiyamachi covered arcade, this is a good place for a cheap, casual meal. After buying your dish and beverage of choice, find an empty seat at any of the large wooden tables. This is a good place to strike up a conversation over a few drinks too, particularly on the weekends.

SEIMENDOKORO KURAKI

1-10-12 Obiyamachi; tel. 088/871-4059; 11am-3:45pm and 5:30pm-11:45pm daily, until 1:45am Sat.; ¥1,000

This popular ramen joint near the Obiyamachi shopping arcade serves its noodles in either pork- or chicken-based soup, with an infusion of soy sauce (miso) or salt (shio), as well as a dose of fish powder. The noodles are then topped with vegetables and pieces of either chicken or pork. If you crave something different, there's also a beef motsu (tripe, offal) option, and also tsukemen, which presents the noodles on the side of a rich broth for dipping. This is a popular choice among the late-night crowd, so don't be surprised if there's a queue if you show up after hours.

★ MYOJINMARU

1-1-2 Motomachi, 1F Yachiyo Bldg.; tel. 088/820-6505; https://myojinhomachi.owst.jp; 5pm-11:30pm (last order 11pm) daily; courses from ¥3,500

This is an excellent place to sample Kochi's local specialty, katsuo tataki (lightly seared bonito), in a relaxed setting. This dish is often served with garlic, ginger, onions, and various herbs. Cozy and elegant with soft lighting, this branch of the restaurant is a laid-back alternative to the one next to Hirome Ichiba, which is often thronged with tourists. Nonetheless, it's still popular, so reserve ahead a few days or more to be safe.

BARS AND NIGHTLIFE

AMONTILLADO

1-1-17 Obiyamachi; tel. 088/875-0599; www.facebook.com/irishpubamo; 5pm-1am Mon.-Thurs., 5pm-2am Fri.-Sat., 5pm-midnight Sun.

Even in Japan, sometimes you just need a pint. Come in here for a glass of Kilkenny or Guinness, and a chance to chat with friendly locals. There's live music on some nights, too. Happy hour is 5pm-7pm daily.

1: roofline of Kochi-jō **2:** Hirome Ichiba **3:** katsuo tataki (seared bonito) at Hirome Ichiba **4:** Yosakoi Odori Matsuri dancers

1
2
明神丸
3
4

LOVE JAMAICAN

9-1 Ōte-suji; tel. 090/8973-4736; www.facebook.com/pages/Lovejamaican/222934694390072; 10pm-late daily

This lively club is a good place to mingle with young locals on a dance floor. As the name suggests, the music leans reggae, with hip-hop sometimes added to the mix.

ACCOMMODATIONS

KATSUO GUEST HOUSE

4-7-28 Hijima-chō; tel. 070/5352-1167; http://katuo-gh.com; mixed dorm ¥2,800 pp, private rooms ¥3,800 pp

For a hostel just north of downtown, this cheerful, family-run guesthouse has a number of playfully themed dorm rooms with a mix of futons and bunk beds. There's also a shared kitchen, bathroom, and showers. Wi-Fi is available throughout. Located about 15 minutes' walk northeast of Kochi Station.

RICHMOND HOTEL KOCHI

1-9-4 Obiyamachi; tel. 088/820-1122; https://richmondhotel.jp/kochi/; ¥6,900 d; walk 5 minutes from the Hasuikemachi-dōri tram stop, or walk 13 minutes southwest of Kochi Station

Well located in the heart of downtown, this business hotel has well-appointed, clean rooms sized slightly above average. Prices are reasonable, with a decent breakfast provided. The hotel is attached to the Obiyamachi shopping arcade, which means plenty of restaurants, cafés, and nightlife are all around.

JYOSEIKAN

2-5-34 Kamimachi; tel. 088/875-0111; www.jyoseikan.co.jp/; from ¥20,100 pp d with breakfast, from ¥35,800 pp d with breakfast and dinner; take tram from Kochieki-mae tram stop to Harimayabashi tram stop, then transfer to the Ino line and ride to Kamimachi 1-chōme tram stop, or take a taxi (about 10 minutes; about ¥1,500)

Located right beside Harimayabashi tram stop, about 10 minutes' walk southwest of the castle, this elegant, historic ryokan is a cut above most in town. In fact, the emperor routinely sleeps here when passing through. There's a mix of Western and Japanese-style rooms, all with well-appointed bathrooms. There's a bar, a restaurant, a shared lounge, and a sauna on-site. A good continental and Japanese-style breakfast buffet is included, with an optional Japanese-style feast served to your room for an extra fee. Staff are cheerful, and guests are welcome to use free bicycles to explore the city. It's a good pick if you'd like to indulge a bit.

INFORMATION AND SERVICES

- **Kochi "i" Information Center** (2-10-17 Kitahonmachi; tel. 088/826-3337; http://visitkochijapan.com; 8:30am-6pm daily, in front of the south exit at JR Kochi Station)
- **Kochi International Association** (2F Marunouchi Bldg., 4-1-37 Honmachi; tel. 088/875-0022; www.kochi-kia.or.jp; 8:30am-5:15pm Mon.-Sat., closed Sat. in Aug., across the street from the southeast corner of the castle grounds)

GETTING THERE

Train

JR Kochi Station, located in the north part of the city, is on the **Dosan** line. To travel between Kochi and **Matsuyama,** it's best to go via **Tadotsu Station** (4 hours 15 minutes; ¥10,850).

To travel from Kochi to **Tokushima,** take the Limited Express Nanpu train north to Awa-Ikeda and transfer to the JR Tokushima line (3 hours; ¥5,160) or the Limited Express Tsurugi-san (2.5 hours; ¥6,160). To reach Takamatsu Station, take the Dosan line north, transferring at Utazu Station (2.5 hours; ¥5,380), or take the Limited Express Shimanto train directly (2 hours 20 minutes; ¥5,720). It's possible to travel directly between Kochi and **Okayama** on Honshu via the Limited Express Nanpu train, too (2 hours 40 minutes; ¥6,270).

Bus

You can take a highway bus to or from Kochi

and most of Shikoku's major towns and beyond. Buses arrive and depart from **JR Kochi Station Bus Terminal,** just north of JR Kochi Station. See the websites of **Japan Bus Online** (https://japanbusonline.com/en) and **Willer Express** (https://willerexpress.com/en/) for details, routes, and fares.

Air

Domestic flights from Tokyo (1 hour 30 minutes; ¥15,000), Nagoya (1 hour 5 minutes; ¥12,000), Osaka (45 minutes; ¥11,000), Kobe (45 minutes; ¥8,000), and Fukuoka (50 minutes; ¥17,000 land daily at **Kochi Ryōma Airport** (www.kochiap.co.jp). It's located about a 40-minute **bus** ride east of JR Kochi Station (¥740).

GETTING AROUND

If you plan to visit only the castle and core downtown area, you'll be able to manage **on foot.** But if you plan to travel to Godai-san Beach, you'll definitely want to make use of the city's **tram** and **bus** networks.

Tram

There are two tram lines in Kochi. The **Sanbashi line** runs north to south from just outside the south exit of JR Kochi Station to the port in the south, while the **Ino line** runs east to west. They intersect at Harimaya-bashi in the center of town. All rides cost a flat fee of ¥200. To ride the tram, simply enter via the back side and take one ticket from the machine. When you reach your destination, drop your fare into the box beside the driver's seat as you exit from the front. If you need to switch to the other tram line, request a norikae-ken (transfer ticket) from the driver as you exit.

Bus

To reach Godai-san, you'll need to take the **My-Yu Bus.** The buses run on a loop that starts and ends at the **bus terminal** just outside the north exit of JR Kochi Station. A one-day pass for the return trip is ¥600. A one-day unlimited pass is ¥1,000 and a two-day pass is ¥1,600. Pick up a pass and get information on the bus schedule from the **Kochi "i" Information Center** at Tosa Terrace just in front of the south exit of JR Kochi Station. If you're a foreign tourist, you can get a 50 percent discount if you show your ID when buying the pass.

Tohoku 東北

Miyagi Prefecture 499
Yamagata Prefecture . . . 507
Iwate Prefecture 514
Akita and Aomori Prefectures 520

Tohoku is old Japan at its best, a land where treasures lie hidden in a rugged landscape of windswept coastline, primeval forests, and impenetrable mountain ranges. The region's climate fluctuates between sweltering summers and severe winters, when some of the heaviest snowfalls on earth, carried by harsh Siberian winds, pile up on the western side of Tohoku's colossal rocky spine.

A wellspring of myth, Tohoku is a place where aquatic monsters await those who stray too close to rural riverbanks, demons visit village homes to frighten children into good behavior every New Year, and shapeshifting fox spirits morph into femme fatales.

Once known as Michinoku (The Interior Road), the region was vividly described by the wandering haiku poet Matsuo Bashō

Highlights

Look for ★ to find recommended sights, activities, dining, and lodging.

★ **Matsushima Bay:** This rugged bay, immortalized by haiku poet Matsuo Bashō during his 17th-century pilgrimage across the region, is dotted by 260 pine-tree-covered islands (page 504).

★ **Yamadera:** Pilgrims who make the steep hike up 1,015 stone steps to this Buddhist temple complex clinging to a mountainside are rewarded with breathtaking views (page 507).

★ **Zaō-san:** This volcano is host to some of Japan's best skiing, and is famed for its "snow monsters" (page 508).

★ **Nyūtō Onsen:** Feel like you're in the romantic Japan of days gone by at this cluster of rustic hot springs resorts (page 524).

★ **Osore-zan:** "Mount Dread," believed to mark the entrance to Buddhist Hell, is a windswept volcanic landscape at Honshu's northern edge (page 531).

★ **Aomori Nebuta Matsuri:** Featuring dancers and illuminated floats in Aomori's streets, this legendary festival is held every August (page 532).

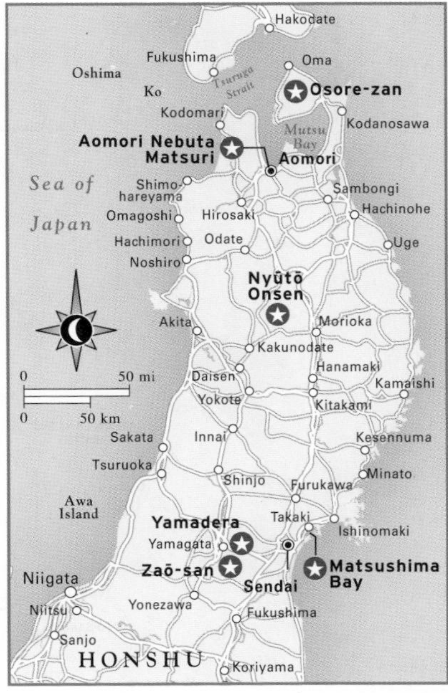

Tohoku

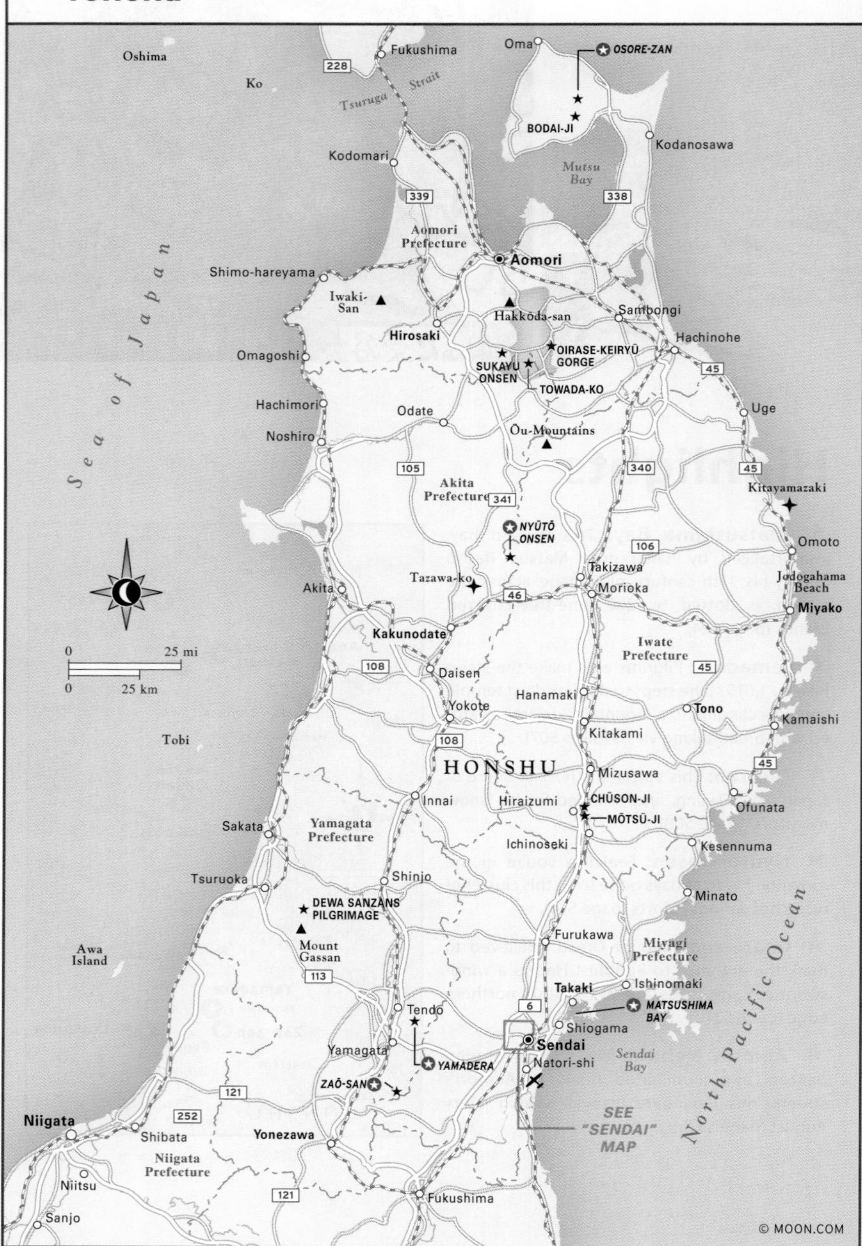
Oshima
Ko
Fukushima
228
Tsuruga Strait
Oma
OSORE-ZAN
BODAI-JI
Kodanosawa
Mutsu Bay
Kodomari
339
338
Aomori Prefecture
Aomori
Sea of Japan
Shimo-hareyama
Iwaki-San
Hakkoda-san
Sambongi
Hirosaki
Hachinohe
Omagoshi
SUKAYU ONSEN
OIRASE-KEIRYŪ GORGE
TOWADA-KO
45
Hachimori
Odate
Uge
Noshiro
Ōu-Mountains
105
340
45
Akita Prefecture
341
Kitayamazaki
NYŪTŌ ONSEN
106
Omoto
Takizawa
Jodogahama Beach
Tazawa-ko
Akita
46
Morioka
Miyako
Kakunodate
Iwate Prefecture
0
25 mi
25 km
108
Daisen
45
Hanamaki
Yokote
Tono
Kamaishi
Kitakami
Tobi
108
HONSHU
45
Mizusawa
Innai
Hiraizumi
CHŪSON-JI
MŌTSŪ-JI
Ofunata
Sakata
Yamagata Prefecture
Ichinoseki
Kesennuma
Tsuruoka
Shinjo
Minato
DEWA SANZANS PILGRIMAGE
Mount Gassan
Furukawa
Miyagi Prefecture
Awa Island
113
Takaki
Ishinomaki
6
MATSUSHIMA BAY
Tendo
Shiogama
Sendai
Yamagata
Natori-shi
YAMADERA
Sendai Bay
ZAŌ-SAN
North Pacific Ocean
121
252
SEE "SENDAI" MAP
Niigata
Shibata
Yonezawa
Niigata Prefecture
Niitsu
121
Fukushima
Sanjo
© MOON.COM
TOHOKU

Regional Food Specialties

SENDAI

- **Gyūtan:** Grilled beef tongue is a Tohoku classic, renowned in the city of Sendai. Try it at **Kaku** (page 502).
- **Seri nabe:** This duck-and-vegetable medley is packed with fortifying properties for cold winters, yet is light enough to be enjoyed in the warmer months too. Try it at **Wabisuke** (page 502).

AKITA PREFECTURE

- **Inaniwa udon:** Akita Prefecture is famed for its Inaniwa udon, a thinner variety of udon than what is usually served around Japan. Try it at **Kosendō** (page 527).

(1644-1694) in his immortal collection of verse, *The Narrow Road to the Deep North*. In Bashō's day, a number of mighty towns, from Hiraizumi to Kakunodate and Hirosaki, were home to castles run by powerful clans, whose power waned with the coming of modern Japan. The remains of this history can still be seen today. Complementing these links to the past are a handful of pleasant, modern cities, with bustling Sendai—an ideal gateway to the region—at the head of the pack.

In more recent times, Tohoku's image was altered dramatically following the March 2011 9.0-magnitude earthquake and tsunami that devastated large swaths of Iwate, Miyagi, and Fukushima Prefectures. (Fukushima's Pacific coastline has gained unfortunate name recognition for the ongoing nuclear meltdown triggered by the disaster.) As the region continues to regain its footing, visitors are welcomed with open arms. But for the time being, this underappreciated side of Japan remains delightfully off the radar.

The region's summer festivals, especially Aomori Nebuta Matsuri in the far north, can fairly be ranked among Japan's best, and the region's poetic landscape is fully on display in Miyagi Prefecture's Matsushima Bay. In the mountainous interior, the mountaintop temple complex at Yamadera, the pilgrimage route of Dewa Sanzan, and Osore-zan, believed to be an ethereal gateway to the other side, magnetically draw seekers. Running through this landscape are towns like Kakunodate and Hirosaki, where streets and structures harken back to Japan's feudal days. And deep in alpine forests, you'll find some of the most magical onsen pools in all Japan.

ORIENTATION

Honshu's wild north, Tohoku ("northeast"), sprawls across six prefectures for a total land area of roughly 67,000 square kilometers (26,000 square mi).

Miyagi Prefecture is the gateway to Tohoku for many travelers; it contains Tohoku's largest city, **Sendai,** which can be reached from Tokyo in around 90 minutes by shinkansen, as well as **Matsushima Bay.** Moving west, **Yamagata Prefecture,** where you can find the temple complex of **Yamadera** and the holy mountains of **Dewa Sanzan,** borders the Sea of Japan. **Zaō-san,** a picturesque volcano, straddles the border of Miyagi and Yamagata Prefectures.

Tohoku's Sanriku coastline, famed for its dramatic rock forms at Jōdogahama and sweeping cliffs at Kitayamazaki, begins along Miyagi's Pacific coastline and stretches northward into **Iwate Prefecture,** which is home

Previous: Kakunodate; snow on Zaō-san; Aomori Nebuta Matsuri.

Best Accommodations

★ **Miyamaso Takamiya:** This four-century-old ryokan has it all: curative onsen baths, haute cuisine, and easy access to spectacular ski slopes (page 513).

★ **Tsurunoyu Onsen:** This rustic ryokan in the Nyūtō Onsen area, known for its milky white waters, is home to one of the most picture-perfect onsen pools in all of Japan (page 524).

★ **Ishiba Ryokan:** With a few centuries of history behind it, this welcoming inn looks onto a serene garden, with Hirosaki Castle just a brief stroll away (page 530).

to the historic town of **Hiraizumi** and **Tōno. Morioka,** the capital of Iwate Prefecture with a population just shy of 300,000, is a straight shot on the shinkansen, 2.5 hours north of Tokyo. Moving west, on the Sea of Japan side, the pastoral landscape of **Akita Prefecture** is known for its summer festivals, onsen, and rice.

North of Iwate, the weather-beaten coastline of **Aomori Prefecture** extends from the Pacific in the east to the Tsugaru Strait in the north, dividing Honshu from Hokkaido, with the Sea of Japan lying to the west. Aomori is known for its ancient castle town of **Hirosaki,** the Aomori Nebuta Matsuri, and the volcanic landscape of **Osore-zan.**

PLANNING YOUR TIME

If you're keen to explore one of Japan's least visited, most rewarding regions, plan to allow anywhere from **three days** to **a week or more,** especially given the effort required to reach some of the most magical spots. A foray into Tohoku works best as a multiday excursion from Tokyo, a leg of a journey to or from Hokkaido, or as a stand-alone trip.

Visiting Tohoku involves considerable **train travel.** Two shinkansen lines link Tokyo to the region. The **Tohoku line** runs northeast to Sendai before continuing on to the transit hubs of Morioka and Shin-Aomori. Separate regional shinkansen lines provide direct access to Yamagata and Akita. Local train lines also branch off the shinkansen tracks to provide links to regional towns.

Tohoku's largest city, **Sendai,** serves as a good base for day trips to **Matsushima Bay** and **Yamadera.** The **Zaō Onsen** area offers excellent skiing in winter, hiking in the warmer months, and onsen resorts year-round. In neighboring Yamagata Prefecture, the three holy mountains of **Dewa Sanzan** make for a great day hike.

Back on the Tohoku shinkansen (bullet train), the historically rich towns of **Hiraizumi,** onsen town **Tazawa-ko,** and samurai town **Kakunodate** can all be explored in about a day each, though you might be tempted to stay a night or two if you feel like slowing down and enjoying the countryside. **Aomori Prefecture** rewards those intrepid enough to forge into Tohoku's northern edge, with the ancient castle town of **Hirosaki** and the desolately beautiful volcanic landscape of **Osore-zan** beckoning seekers of the mysteries of the afterlife.

If you'll be driving in the region, it's worth looking into the **Tohoku Express Pass** (www.go-etc.jp/english/expressway/index.html), which allows for unlimited use of Tohoku's expressways. Having your own wheels comes in handy if you're visiting particularly remote areas, such as Dewa Sanzan, Nyūtō Onsen, or Osore-zan, where public transport links are limited.

High and Low Seasons

More so than in most parts of Japan, time of year is key in Tohoku, which is most magical during **winter,** when skiers shred through some of the world's best snow before retiring to secluded hot springs, though note that areas like Dewa Sanzan will be harder if not impossible to access. In **summer,** Tohoku's mountains are crisscrossed by excellent hiking trails, and in its cities and towns, festivals reveal the region's wild side. Though the region is delightfully off the tourist track for much of the year, popular **onsen resorts** book up fast in winter, as do hotels during popular summer **festivals.**

Miyagi Prefecture 宮城県

Only 90 minutes away from Tokyo by train, Miyagi Prefecture, in Tohoku's southeastern corner, couldn't feel further away. Sendai is Tohoku's largest metropolis and the capital of Miyagi Prefecture, with a population of more than 1 million—tiny compared to the capital's megalopolis. Many people arrive in Sendai only to continue immediately east to Matsushima Bay, one of Japan's most famous scenic sights: a deep blue body of water dotted with dozens of islands placed just so that have been the source of countless haikus. But if you dig deeper beneath Sendai's urban sheen, you'll discover Tohoku's rural core and welcoming people. A smile and openness go a long way here.

SENDAI
仙台

Sendai is laid out in a grid with numerous tree-lined boulevards and abundant parks, earning it the nickname "City of Trees." Its history is deeply entwined with the once great Date clan (pronounced dah-tay), and Sendai still bears the fingerprints of its founder, the dynamic feudal lord Date Masamune (aka the "one-eyed dragon"). His fearsome nickname refers to the story that he plucked out his own right eye after being struck by smallpox as a youth.

Tohoku thrived for some 270 years, with the Date clan at the helm, but its influence waned following the Meiji Restoration. Mostly razed in World War II bombing raids, Sendai has few historical sites today, though the ruins of Aoba Castle are worth visiting. More recently, the city was front and center when the devastating earthquake and tsunami struck the east coast of northern Honshu in March 2011, but Sendai is miraculously back on its feet. Public transport networks, which took a heavy blow, are all in working order and there are no visible signs of the disaster in the city center.

The best time to visit Sendai is early August during the famous annual Tanabata Matsuri, when the city's locals, and throngs of visitors, amass downtown to wander through covered shopping streets overhung with huge colorful streamers. Whatever time of year you find yourself in Sendai, it's a convenient base for making trips elsewhere in the region. Be sure to eat grilled gyūtan (beef tongue), the local dish. And if you're in town for a night, take a stroll through the city's entertainment district, Kokubunchō, the largest nightlife zone between Tokyo and Sapporo.

Sights

AOBA CASTLE
青葉城

1 Kawauchi, Aoba-ku; tel. 022/222-0218; www.sendaimiyagidc.jp/en/sendai_castle/; 9am-5pm daily Apr.-Oct., 9am-4pm daily Nov.-Mar., closed on days after national holidays; ¥700; from Sendai Station, take the Loople Sendai bus (¥260) to bus stop 6 (castle grounds), or take Tōzai subway line to International Center Station, then walk 15 minutes south

Although the ruins of its outer walls and a lone guard tower are the only remains of the mighty fortress that once served as the early-17th-century headquarters of Date Masamune, a visit to Mount Aoba and Aoba Castle offers sweeping views of the cityscape below.

Sendai

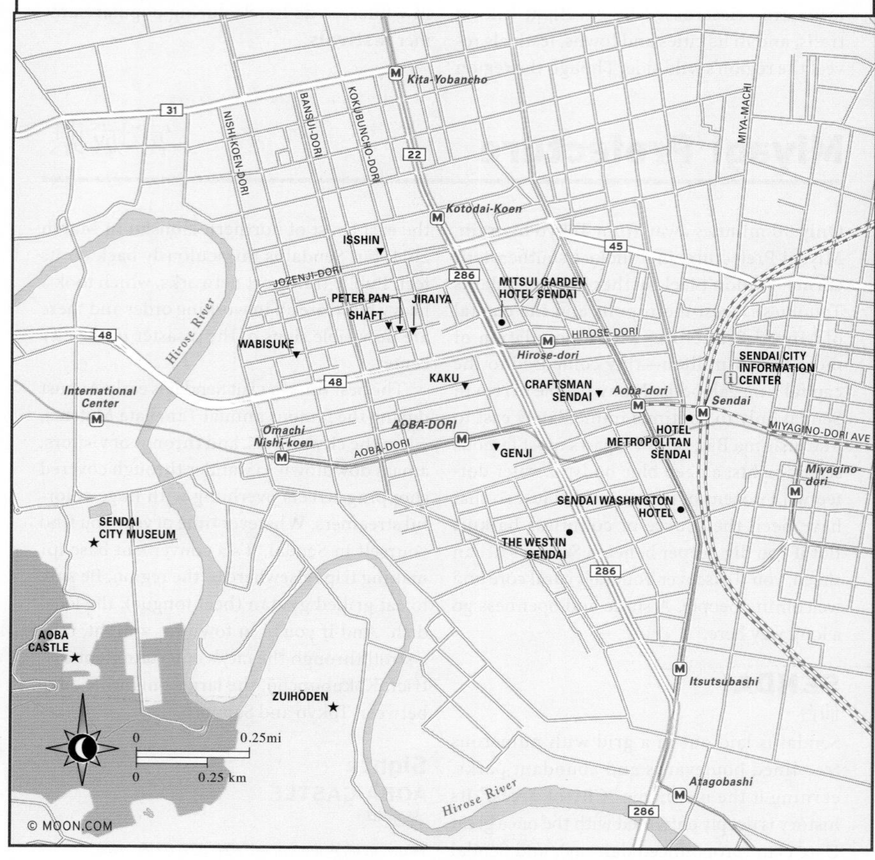

Built in 1600, the stronghold that once loomed above Sendai was ravaged by fire in 1882 and further decimated by bombing toward the end of World War II. Alongside the remnants, a statue of Date dynamically mounted on a horse and kitted out in armor proudly stands on the grounds. If Date's helmet looks familiar, it's likely because it inspired Darth Vader's helmet in *Star Wars*.

Within the grounds you'll also find a museum that recaps the citadel's glory days through models, artifacts, and a brief film in Japanese (English headsets available).

SENDAI CITY MUSEUM
仙台市博物館

26 Kawauchi, Aoba-ku; tel. 022/225-3074; www.city.sendai.jp/museum/museum/; 9am-4:45pm Tues.-Sun.; ¥460 adults, ¥230 high school students, ¥110 elementary and junior high school students; from Sendai Station, take the Loople Sendai bus (¥260) to bus stop 5

The Sendai City Museum is a good place for history buffs to get a samurai fix. An array of gear once used by the warrior class, from helmets and armor to weaponry—much of it donated by the Date family—fills this well-designed complex. In addition to the trappings of war, the collection also includes Edo-period costumes and artwork. There's even an interactive section for kids. If you're going to Aoba Castle, it's a pleasant 15-minute walk to the museum.

ZUIHŌDEN
瑞鳳殿

23-2 Otamayashita, Aoba-ku; tel. 022/262-6250; www.zuihoden.com; 9am-4:50pm (last entry 4:30pm) daily Feb.-Nov., 9am-4:20pm (last entry 4pm) daily Dec.-Jan.; ¥550 adults, ¥400 high school students, ¥200 elementary and junior high school students; from Sendai Station, take the Loople Sendai bus (¥260) to bus stop 4

Razed during World War II, the reconstructed mausoleum of Date Masamune, Zuihōden, faithfully captures the essence of the original, built in 1637, and is a textbook example of the florid architectural characteristics of the Momoyama period (1568-1600), overloaded with red, blue, orange, and gold and carvings of birds and dragons. Date's elaborate crypt is surrounded by the graves of Date's retainers (who committed ritual suicide when their lord died), as well as the final resting places of the second and third lords in the Date line. It's about a 25-minute walk from the Sendai City Museum.

Festivals

TANABATA MATSURI
七夕まつり

various locations downtown; www.sendaitanabata.com/en; 10am-9pm Aug. 6-8; free

It's all about love at the Tanabata Matsuri (Star Festival), one of Tohoku's biggest summer festivals, which revolves around the story of two star-crossed lovers, Princess Orihime (embodied by the star Vega) and the simple country boy Hikoboshi (embodied by Altair). The festival marks the time they are able to meet once a year, barring the interference of clouds.

Sendai's version of the event on August 6-8 elevates pageantry to an art. Kicking off the festivities from around 7pm on August 5, upward of 15,000 fireworks are launched in Nishi-kōen on the west side of town. On the following day, streamers inscribed with flowery verses are hung from doors, flapping in the breeze. Large multihued balls, filled with spices and herbs, hang from the ceilings of covered pedestrian arcades, warding off demons. The streets fill with sentimental revelers who are encouraged to (literally) wish upon a star by writing out their desires on paper strips known as tanzaku, which are then affixed to bamboo strewn throughout the city, and to freely reveal their bottled-up feelings.

detail of Zuihōden

JOZENJI STREETJAZZ FESTIVAL
定禅寺ストリートジャズフェスティバル

various locations downtown; www.j-streetjazz.com; second weekend of Sept., hours vary by performance; free

Buskers from across Japan jam in Sendai's downtown, drawing hundreds of thousands to the city center for this impressively free festival. Performances take place in the downtown area in parks, shopping arcades, and beyond, rain or shine. If jazz isn't your thing, there are also performances of other musical genres, from Latin and pop to rock and gospel. The festival is very popular, so you'll have to book your accommodation far in advance (six months or more to be safe).

Food

★ KAKU

3-8-14 Ichibanchō, Aoba-ku; tel. 022/268-7067; http://gyutankaku.in; 11:30am-2:30pm (last order 2pm) and 5pm-10:30pm (last order 9:30pm) daily; ¥1,700; take Nanboku line to Kotodaikoen Station, south exit 2

Sendai's most famous dish is its gyūtan. Ask any local where to go and they'll vote for Kaku, where you can get boiled and grilled beef tongue, served with oxtail soup and crispy pickled cucumbers and cabbage. The menu has photos that make it easy to choose, despite the lack of English. The dish goes well with beer or sake. Note that Kaku allows smoking.

GENJI

2-4-8 Ichibancho, Aoba-ku; tel. 022/222-8485; 4:30pm-10pm Tues.-Sat., ¥2,500; take Tozai line to Aoba-dōri Ichibancho Station, exit 1

For a classic greasy-spoon izakaya, this small dark tavern is tucked down a side street and gets rowdy, thanks in part to its loyal following and the seating arrangement that hugs the counter. The menu is a good mix of Japanese-style pub food—small plates of sashimi, oden (boiled eggs, fishcakes, daikon in a soy-flavored broth)—and plenty of sake and beer.

WABISUKE

6-16 Tachimachi, Aoba-ku; tel. 022/217-8455; http://wabisuke.style.coocan.jp; 5pm-11pm (last order 10pm) Mon.-Fri., 5pm-10pm (last order 9pm) Sat.-Sun.; ¥4,500; take Tozai line to Ochonishikoen Station, east exit 1

One more dish that Sendai can claim as its own is seri nabe, a style of hot pot that combines duck, tofu, greens, mushrooms, and herbs in a light soup stock made from kelp and bonito flakes. Wabisuke does it best. The flavors are rich but subtle. Traditionally a winter dish, seri nabe can be eaten any time of year thanks to its light soup stock.

JIRAIYA

2-1-15 Kokubun-chō, Aoba-ku; tel. 022/261-2164; www.jiraiya.com; 5pm-11pm Mon.-Fri., 5pm-10:30pm Sat., last order one hour before closing; courses from ¥6,600; take Nanboku line to Kotodaikoen Station, south exit 2

Jiraiya has a reputation for serving the fresh local catch, grilled over an open fire, and pairing it well with local sake. The specialty is kinki (deep water rockfish), skewered whole on a stick and finished off with soup made from the fish's head and bones. Look for the oversized red paper lantern. Reserve at least a day in advance, especially on weekends.

ISSHIN

B1F Jozenji Hills, 3-3-1 Kokubunchō, Aoba-ku; tel. 022/261-9888; 5pm-midnight Mon.-Sat.; ¥8,000; take Nanboku line to Kotodaikoen Station, exit 2

Isshin is famed across Japan among izakaya (pub) buffs for its meticulous attention to getting food just right. The menu makes good use of local, seasonal ingredients. Complementing the food is an impressive sake menu, which mainly stocks labels from Miyagi Prefecture. There is a ¥1,500 entrance fee, but the dish that comes with the fee is almost meal-size.

Bars and Nightlife

Sendai is home to Tohoku's biggest entertainment zone, with the bulk of the action taking place in the neon-soaked district of Kokubun-chō. This grid of streets extends roughly from the streets of Hirose-dōri in the south to Jozenji-dōri in the north. Look past the glut of "pink" (Japan's version of "red-light") establishments, and you'll find some good spots.

PETER PAN

2-6-1 Kokubun-chō, Aoba-ku; tel. 022/264-1742; http://peterpan-rock.com; 3pm-midnight Tues.-Sun.; ¥500 cover charge after 6pm; take Nanboku line to Hirose-dōri Station, west exit 5

Cafe by day, rock 'n' roll bar by night, this welcoming spot is manned by a father-son duo who delight patrons with the diverse assortment of vinyl, ranging from classic rock to alternative.

CRAFTSMAN SENDAI

1F 2-2-38 Chūō, Aoba-ku; tel. 022/797-8431; https://craftsman-sendai.com; 11:30am-1am daily; take Senseki line to Aoba-dōri Station, exit 1

This modish craft beer bar has around 30 craft brews on tap, rotating sporadically, from ales to IPAs. Most of the suds are from Japan, with a few American options and a nice list of New World wines too. If you're hungry, you can pair your booze with Italian and French tapas or other bar eats rustled up by chefs who use ingredients sourced from around Tohoku.

SHAFT

Sankei 18 Bldg. 1F, 2-7-22 Kokubunchō, Aoba-ku; tel. 022/722-5651; www.clubshaft.com; hours vary by event; cover charge varies by event; take Nanboku line to Hirose-dōri Station, west exit 2

This intimate nightclub has a good sound system, offers affordable drinks, and draws a young, friendly crowd. Events range from techno DJs to live digeridoo sessions. Check the website to see what's on before making the trip.

Accommodations

MITSUI GARDEN HOTEL SENDAI

2-4-6 Honcho, Aoba-ku; tel. 022/214-1131; www.gardenhotels.co.jp; ¥8,000 d; take Nanboku line to Hirose-dōri Station, west exit 1

Like many hotels in Sendai, the Mitsui Garden Hotel Sendai is a great value. The reception desk is on the seventh floor, and the rooms all have large picture windows offering views of the streets below. The rooms are compact but well-appointed, and the free Wi-Fi is strong. For a short stay, this hotel has everything you need.

SENDAI WASHINGTON HOTEL

4-10-8 Chuo, Aoba-ku; tel. 022/745-2222; http://sendai.washington-hotels.jp; ¥13,000 d; from JR Sendai Station, take west exit 1

The Sendai Washington Hotel, just southwest of the station, offers reasonably priced rooms and convenience. It also has a restaurant serving a menu based around local ingredients.

HOTEL METROPOLITAN SENDAI

1-1-1 Chūō, Aoba-ku; tel. 022/268-2525; https://east-sendai.metropolitan.jp; ¥16,000 d room only, ¥20,000 with breakfast

The stylish Hotel Metropolitan Sendai serves breakfast that is made using locally sourced ingredients and served in a dining room with a great view of the city. But the main selling point is the fact that it's directly connected to JR Sendai Station.

THE WESTIN SENDAI

1-9-1 Ichibancho, Aoba-ku; tel. 022/722-1234; www.westin.com; ¥22,000 d; take Tozai line to Aoba-dōri Ichibancho Station, south exit 1

For a five-star experience without a five-star price tag, stay at the Westin Sendai. You'll find chic rooms, good dining, and stellar views of the city and surroundings.

Information and Services

- **Sendai City Information Center** (second floor of JR Sendai Station; tel. 022/222-4069; www.sentabi.jp; 8:30am-7pm)

Getting There

From **Tokyo,** the **JR Tohoku** shinkansen runs to Sendai in about 2 hours (¥11,200 or included with JR pass). To the north, the next major hub on the train is **Morioka,** a

Rebuilding After the 2011 Earthquake and Tsunami

On March 11, 2011, at 2:46pm, a 9.0-magnitude earthquake struck from under the Pacific off the eastern coast of Tohoku. The fourth most powerful quake in recorded history, it could even be felt in Osaka.

Much greater destruction was left by the tsunami that followed. Some 30 minutes after the rumbling subsided, a succession of waves up to 15 meters (50 ft) high thundered into the coastlines of Fukushima, Miyagi, and Iwate Prefectures, wiping out entire communities, tossing fishing boats around like toys, and taking more than 15,000 lives, with a few thousand more unaccounted for. It's estimated as many as 470,000 became refugees following the disaster. In a word, the human cost was immense. Economically, the damage amounted to a staggering estimated $300 billion.

Although the process of recovery was relatively speedy in Sendai, where everything feels very much like business as usual, the pace of renewal in the surrounding coastal region lags as small seaside communities continue to rebuild more than a decade on. And of course, there is the ongoing crisis triggered by the meltdown of the Fukushima Dai-ichi nuclear power plant. A 20-kilometer (12-mi) exclusion zone surrounds the plant, and cleanup efforts, involving the removal and disposal of extremely radioactive spent nuclear fuel, will last indefinitely. The upshot of this catastrophe is that the Japanese are more engaged in the nuclear debate than ever before, and the push toward green energy solutions is gaining traction.

40-minute ride on the JR Tohoku shinkansen (¥6,670).

Sendai also has a domestic airport, which connects to Tokyo, Sapporo, Osaka, and Hiroshima, among other cities. To reach **JR Sendai Station** from **Sendai Airport** (tel. 022/382-0080; www.sendai-airport.co.jp), take the **Sendai Kūkō Access line,** which departs three times hourly (30 minutes; ¥650).

Taiheyo Ferry (tel. 022/263-9877; www.taiheiyo-ferry.co.jp) also runs between Sendai and **Tomakomai,** near Shikotsu-ko in Hokkaido, up north. Check the website for timetables and fares.

Finally, if you have rented a **car,** the **Tohoku Expressway** links Tokyo and Sendai (5 hours; 370 km/230 mi) before continuing north through Morioka and Aomori. If you prefer to take a **bus,** check out **Willer Express** (tel. 050/5805-0383; http://willerexpress.com), which has buses running from Tokyo to Sendai in 5.5 hours from about ¥2,500.

Getting Around

Sendai's downtown core is relatively compact and easy to get around **on foot,** with streets laid out on the same grid pattern envisioned by Date Masamune when he had Aoba Castle built. The city does have two **subway** lines, the Tōzai line running east to west, and the Namboku line running north to south, with tickets costing ¥200-350. Aside from the Tōzai line's International Center Station, located near Aoba Castle, these lines don't have stations close to any tourist sites, although they might be useful for reaching your hotel.

A more useful mode of transport within the city is the **Loople Sendai** (http://loople-sendai.jp) bus, which runs in a clockwise loop around town. Among its stops are Zuihōden, Sendai City Museum, and Aoba Castle. The loop takes an hour and leaves Sendai Station every 20-30 minutes (9am-4pm; one-day pass ¥600, single ticket ¥260).

★ MATSUSHIMA BAY
松島湾

Matsushima; https://visitmiyagi.com/areas/matsushima-bay; from Sendai Station, take Senseki line to Matsushima-Kaigan Station, then walk 6 minutes northeast to Matsushima Pier, or take

Senseki line to Hon-Shiogama Station, then walk 10 minutes east to Shiogama Pier

Few places in Japan have as many historical associations with beauty as Matsushima Bay, considered one of Japan's three most scenic spots (along with Miyajima, page 415, near Hiroshima, and Amanohashidate, on the Japan Sea coast of Kyoto Prefecture). Famously celebrated in the poetry of haiku master Matsuo Bashō, who was said to be left speechless by the scene in 1689, this misty stretch of water is dotted with some 260 tiny islands topped by twisted pine trees. These same islands, centuries later, shielded the communities along the bay from the brunt of the destruction caused by the March 2011 earthquake and tsunami that ravaged large swathes of Tohoku's coast.

Seen from above, the bay resembles a miniature landscape garden, its islands akin to well-placed rocks or clusters of shrubs. Many of these small spits of land are ascribed personalities and special properties. It may be a stretch, but the tiny rock formation of **Niojima** is said to look like a sculpture of a Deva King. **Sagijima** (Heron Island) is said to look like the bird of its namesake taking flight. **Kabutojima** appears to be the helmet of a warrior floating above the waters. And passing through the tiny opening, known as **Chomei-ana,** at the bottom of a craggy islet is said to bring longevity.

A number of architectural gems also surround the bay, thanks in part to the efforts of feudal lord Date Masamune. If you have time, plan to spend a few hours at these sights before or after your cruise.

Sights

ZUIGAN-JI

瑞巌寺

91 Chōnai; tel. 022/354-2023; www.zuiganji.or.jp; 8:30am-5pm (last entry 4:30pm) Apr.-Sept., closes 30-90 minutes earlier in Oct.-Mar.; ¥700 adults, ¥400 children 15 years and under; take the Senseki line to Matsushima-Kaigan Station, then walk 10 minutes north

Established as a sanctuary for meditation in AD 828 by a priest named Jikaku Daishi (aka Ennin) of the Tendai sect, Zuigan-ji was transformed into a Zen temple during the militaristic Kamakura Period (1192-1333). Date Masamune ordered the complex to be rebuilt in 1606, hiring an army of artists and craftsmen for the job.

Designated a national treasure, Zuigan-ji is one of Tohoku's best Zen Buddhist temples. Approach the main hall via a cedar-lined

view over Matsushima Bay

path. Inside, you'll discover that Zuigan-ji has some unique features, among them a watchtower and nightingale floors, which make a chirping sound akin to the bird after which they are named to alert of any stealthily approaching enemy. These floors, known as uguisubari ("bush warbler guard watch"), are often found in castles that were once resided in by lords wary of the potential threat of stealthy ninja invaders. These wooden surfaces produce their trademark acoustic effect via nails underneath the floorboards that scrape against strategically placed metal clamps when they are walked on. The fine examples of Edo-period religious architecture that make up this complex were recently renovated. English-speaking guides are on-site on the first, third, and fourth Sunday each month from 10am to 3pm.

ENTSŪ-IN

円通院

67 Chōnai; tel. 022/354-3206; www.entuuin.or.jp; 8:30am-5pm daily Apr.-late Oct., 8:30am-4:30pm daily late Oct.-Nov., 9am-4pm daily Dec.-Mar.; ¥300 adults, ¥150 high school students, ¥100 junior high and elementary school students; take the Senseki line to Matsushima-Kaigan Station, then walk 5 minutes north

Next to Zuigan-ji and about six minutes' walk north from Matsushima Kaigan Station, Entsū-in was constructed in 1646 as the mausoleum of Date Mitsumune, the son of lord Date Terumune, who died at the young age of 19. The temple may not be as famous as its neighbor, but its gardens, which include a mossy landscape garden with a heart-shaped pond and a cedar grove, make it rewarding to visit.

Although the temple is dedicated to Kannon, the Buddhist goddess of mercy, there are a slew of peculiar icons peppered throughout the mausoleum, such as crosses, hearts, spades, diamonds, and clubs, and the first known depiction in Japanese art of a rose. These notably Western flourishes are no surprise, as the Date clan was known to have a keen interest in Christianity and the West.

GODAI-DŌ

五大堂

111 Chōnai; tel. 022/354-2023; https://zuiganji.or.jp/?page_id=7977; 8am-5pm daily; free; walk 1 minute northeast of Matsushima Pier

An icon of Matsushima Bay, this compact temple stands on a tiny island next to Matsushima Pier, reached from the mainland via two bridges. Originally built in 807, the current structure is a reconstruction built in 1604 by Date Masamune, the prominent lord who once wielded great power from his base in Sendai. Inside the hall there are a collection of statues only unveiled to the outside world once every 33 years—the next showing won't be until 2039. What you can see are the 12 animals of the Chinese zodiac etched into the temple's outside walls. The main draw of making a stop at this landmark, however, is the lovely views of the bay from its grounds.

Boat Tours

Perhaps the best way to see Matsushima is by boat. **Ferries** run by several operators depart on the hour (10am-4pm daily, until 3pm in winter; ¥1,500 adults, ¥750 elementary school students one-way) from **Matsushima Pier** (98-1 Chōnai; tel. 022/354-2233; www.matsushima.or.jp; walk 7 minutes northeast from Matsushima-kaigan Station) and **Shiogama Pier** (1-4-1 Minatomachi, Shiogama; tel. 022/365-3611; http://shiogama.co.jp/marinegate; walk 10 minutes east of Hon-Shiogama Station); tours last approximately 50 minutes. From April-October, boats also run from Matsushima Pier into the quieter side of the bay, known as **Oku-Matsushima.** These longer tours last more than 1.5 hours and cost ¥2,900.

Information and Services

- **Tourist Information Center** (Matsushima-kaigan Station; tel. 022/354-2263; www.matsushima-kanko.com; 9:30am-4:30pm Mon.-Fri.; 8:30am-5pm Sat.-Sun.)

Getting There and Around

From **Sendai,** take the **JR Senseki** line from JR Sendai Station to **Matsushima-kaigan Station** (40 minutes; ¥410), which is the easiest gateway to the area with all major temples and Matsushima Pier within a 10-minute walk, or to **Hon-Shiogama Station** (30 minutes; ¥320), which is a bit too far to stroll to the area's main temples but is 10 minutes' walk west of Shiogama Pier. To drive from Sendai (27 km/17 mi; 35 minutes), take the **Sanriku Expressway,** which links to Matsushima.

Yamagata Prefecture 山形県

Journey to Yamagata Prefecture, just to the west of Miyagi Prefecture, and you'll start to get a real sense of what Tohoku is all about, from mountain scenes straight out of a painting, to the exemplary ski and onsen resort that is Zaō-san, to the region's deep spiritual roots, dramatically visible in the temple complex of Yamadera or on the Dewa Sanzan pilgrimage.

TOP EXPERIENCE

★ YAMADERA

山寺

Yamadera 4456-1; tel. 023/695-2843; www.rissyakuji.jp; 8am-5pm daily; ¥300 adults, ¥200 junior high school students, ¥100 elementary school students

Yamadera ("Mountain Temple") is one of the most scenic religious sites in all of Japan. The largest temple complex of the Tendai Buddhist sect in Tohoku, it is located in a dramatic spot, clinging to a series of ledges on the face of verdant Mount Hoju. Ascending a steep stone staircase through an enchanted forest dotted by Buddhist statues and stone lanterns, you're rewarded with stunning views of a river valley below and mountains in every direction, as far as the eye can see. If you're only going to visit one temple in Tohoku, make it this one.

Although colloquially known as Yamadera, the official name of this ancient, atmospheric temple is **Risshaku-ji** (立石寺). The journey to this lofty cluster of pavilions and temples—more than 30 structures in all—makes you feel like you've been transported to another realm.

Eminent Buddhist priest Jikaku Daishi, popularly known as Ennin, led an expedition to bring the light of Buddhism to the north in 860, carrying a sacred flame that still burns today in **Konpon Chūdō,** Yamadera's main hall at the base of Mount Hoju. This is the oldest surviving structure in the complex, rebuilt numerous times over the centuries, with the current structure dating to 1356. Only the temple at Mount Hiei in Kyoto is more important to the Tendai sect of Buddhism.

Veering to the left of Konpon Chūdō, you'll pass a statue of Bashō. Across from the statue, on the other side of the path, is a small **treasure hall** (tel. 023/695-2002; 9am-5pm daily Apr.-Nov.; ¥200 adults, ¥100 children), built in 1976 to house some of the temple's holiest artifacts.

The vertical journey to the lofty temples for which the complex is best known begins at the **San-mon** gate, where you pay an admission fee to enter the bulk of the complex. From this point, you must climb 1,015 stone steps; the hike takes about 30 minutes. Buddhist statues dot the hills and a multitude of weathered stone lanterns line the path.

You'll know you're nearing the top when you come to the 19th-century **Nio-mon** gate, a relatively recent addition to the complex. Up another short staircase, you'll see a slew of temples clinging to craggy outcrops of rock and superb views of the landscape below. The large temple straight ahead is **Okuno-in,** in front of which is one of the largest stone lanterns in all of Japan. A path veering to the left leads you to **Kaisan-dō,** Ennin's mausoleum, and just to its left, **Nokyo-dō,** a tiny pavilion once used for copying sutras, or Buddhist scripture, coated in red lacquer hanging onto the edge of a cliff.

For maximum impact, proceed to **Godai-dō,** a sheltered wooden terrace built in the 17th century and suspended from a cliff that offers a panoramic vista of the small hamlet below, pierced by a river, and endless rows of peaks beyond.

There isn't much in the way of dining options around Yamadera Station, but **Enzou** (4273-1 Yamadera; tel. 050/5485-6748; https://t280307.gorp.jp; 11am-3pm, last order 2:30pm daily; ¥1,500 average), 1-minute walk north of the station, serves filling soba noodle sets, tempura, desserts, and coffee during lunch hours, and has an English menu. There are also a few mom-and-pop shops on the approach to Risshaku-ji. If you'd prefer to bring your own snacks, stock up at a convenience store in Sendai, or eat a filling meal before you make the trip.

Getting There and Around

If you're coming from **Sendai** in the east, take the **JR Senzan** line for about an hour (¥840) to **Yamadera Station.** If you're coming from **Yamagata** in the west, you'll also take the JR Senzan line for about 20 minutes (¥240).

The base of the mountain is five minutes' **walk** from the train station. Take note of the **public restroom** on the road leading toward the river after you exit the station. There aren't any bathroom facilities once you reach the temple complex. Cross the river, then turn right at the T-intersection. The trail that leads to Risshaku-ji is on the left-side of that road.

★ ZAŌ-SAN

蔵王山

Zaō-san (Mount Zaō) is a picturesque volcano straddling the border of Yamagata and Miyagi Prefecture, offering the ideal setting for a range of outdoor activities year-round. In winter, Zaō Onsen Ski Resort, famed for its frozen, powder-encrusted trees playfully known as "snow monsters," draws serious powder hounds to its slopes. In summer, Okama Crater at the mountain's summit is a fantastic trekking destination. And at any time of the year, the village of Zaō Onsen beckons visitors to its ancient sulfuric onsen baths, which offer an ideal place to escape from the frantic modern world and relax in nature.

Hiking

Zaō-san is laced with hiking trails, ranging from 30-minute strolls to half-day journeys. The most popular route involves traipsing across the summit and taking in stellar views of the Okama Crater. Go online for a basic map of Zaō-san's trails, as they connect to the **Zaō Ropeway.** The ropeway puts the summit a simple, pleasurable ride away.

ZAŌ ROPEWAY

229-3 Zaō Onsen; tel. 023/694-9518; http://zaoropeway.co.jp

There are two main stretches of the ropeway:

- The **Zaō Sanroku Line** (8:30am-5pm daily Apr.-Dec. 10, 8:15am-4:45pm daily Dec. 11-Mar.; ¥800 one-way, ¥1,500 round-trip adults, ¥400 one-way, ¥800 round-trip children), which starts at Zaō Sanroku Station (855 m/2,805 ft), is located about 10 minutes' walk southeast of the Zaō Onsen Bus Terminal and ends at Juhyō Kogen Station (1,331 m/4,367 ft).
- The **Sanchō Line** (8:30am-5pm daily Apr.-Dec. 10; 8:30am-4:30pm daily Dec. 11-Mar.; ¥1,500 one-way, ¥3,000 round-trip adults, ¥800 one-way, ¥1,500 round-trip children) starts from Juhyō Kogen Station and glides up to Jizō Sanchō Station (1,661 m/5,449 ft), where most hikers begin their exploration of the mountain on foot.

In addition to the Zaō Sanroku Line, there's also the separate, less extensive **Zaō Chūō Ropeway** (940-1 Zaō Onsen; tel. 023/694-9168; http://zaochuoropeway.co.jp; 8:30am-5pm daily Apr.-Oct., 8:30am-4pm daily Nov.-Dec. 20; ¥800 one-way, ¥1,500

1: Kaisan-dō and Nokyo-dō in winter **2:** statue in the snow at Yamadera **3:** Okama Crater lake on Zaō-san **4:** Zaō-san skiing

1
2
3
4

The Dewa Sanzan Pilgrimage

Dewa Sanzan, or "Three Mountains of Dewa," is an ancient pilgrimage destination deep in the mountains of Yamagata Prefecture. These three mountains became known among spiritual seekers 1,400 years ago when Prince Hachiko declared them a sacred site.

Dewa Sanzan is at the core of a syncretic folk religion that blends Buddhism and Shinto known as **Shugendō.** Those who are adept in Shugendō, known as **yamabushi,** roam and live off the land, seeking enlightenment through long journeys on foot. Only a small fraction of practicing yamabushi today are full-fledged monks, but there is a growing trend toward weekend warriors who head for the mountains when they've got the chance and even suit up in full kit: straw sandals, rosary beads, and robes. Headgear ranges from conical to pillbox-shaped, meant to double as protection and a cup for drinking. Some wield flutes, small hand-drums, or an iconic conch-shell trumpet.

Haguro-san (羽黒山), **Gas-san** (月山), and **Yudono-san** (湯殿山) represent birth, death, and rebirth, respectively, and are meant to be traveled in that order. They can be visited individually, but if you plan to hike the entire circuit, allow a minimum of two days and nights, and book accommodations before reaching Tsuruoka, the closest transit hub to the pilgrimage path.

PRACTICAL INFORMATION

Note that travel in the area around Dewa Sanzan is treacherous during winter. To avoid unnecessary complications, it's best to visit between April-October. Wear sturdy hiking boots and waterproof outerwear (pants, jacket). When you're in Tokyo or another urban hub (Tsuruoka will do), pick up a bit more food and water than you may expect to need, as well as bug spray and a bear bell. Before venturing to any of the three mountains, it's best to stop at Tsuruoka's **Tourist Information Center** (1-34 Suehiro-machi; tel. 0235/25-7678; 10am-5pm daily), a good place to pick up supplies, right outside Tsuruoka JR Station.

A number of tour operators give you the chance to take part in this unique, life-affirming walk; contact **Yamabushido** (https://yamabushido.jp), **Travel Tohoku** (www.traveltohoku.co.jp), or **Oku Japan** (www.okujapan.com) to learn more. Another handy online resource is The Dewa Sanzan (https://dewasanzan.com), which offers practical tips, itineraries, and more.

WHERE TO STAY

If you want to stay overnight, bare-bones ★ **Saikan** (7 Tōge; tel. 0235/62-2357; ¥8,400), a small annex of the shrine atop Haguro-san, offers shukubō (temple lodging) with tatami floor

round-trip adults; ¥400 one-way, ¥750 round-trip children). This line runs from Onsen Station in the heart of Zaō Onsen's town area to Torikabuto Station (1,387 m/4,550 ft), set atop the neighboring peak of Torikabuto.

OKAMA CRATER HIKE

御釜

Distance: *2.2 km (1.4 mi) one-way to Kumano-dake; 4 km (2.5 mi) one-way to Kattadake*

Time: *1 hour to Kumano-dake; 90 minutes to Kattadake*

Trailhead: *Zaō Jizō Sanchō Station (upper terminus of Zaō Ropeway)*

Information and maps: *Zaō Onsen bus terminal (http://zaoropeway.co.jp)*

At 1,841 meters (6,040 ft) high, Zaō-san is one of the loftier peaks in Tohoku. At its center, the indigo-blue **Okama** is a crater lake named for its visual similarity to a pot. The cooking analogy is apt: Zaō-san is a recently active volcano. Exercise caution and check on conditions before attempting to make the trek to its summit; the area surrounding the crater is closed in winter, but it makes for a spectacular hike during the warmer months. You can begin a hike to the mountain's summit by riding the ropeway

and futon and a lunch served Buddhist style: vegetarian fare known as shōjin ryōri, featuring locally foraged vegetables. Book a few months in advance for an undeniably singular experience. If Saikan is all booked up, try **Daishinbo** (95 Tōge; tel. 0235/62-2372; 9,000), another fantastic temple lodging on Haguro-san. This 350-year-old inn has a public bath and a lovely garden, and meals of shōjin ryōri are served here, too. Atop the second peak, **Gas-san Summit Hut** tel. 090/8781-7731; www5c.biglobe.ne.jp/~gassan/index.html/#top; ¥9,000 with 2 meals) is a bare-bones, although staffed, summit hut a short walk from the shrine at the peak. **Yudono-san Sanrōsho** (7 Rokujuri-yama, Tamugimata; tel. 0235/54-6131; www.yudonosan-stay.com; May-Oct.; ¥8,950 with 2 meals) provides spent pilgrims a place to crash at the end of the journey, monks' vegetarian cuisine, and hot bath included.

five-storied pagoda on Haguro-san

GETTING THERE

Dewa Sanzan is reached via **Tsuruoka station.** From **Tokyo,** take the JR Joetsu shinkansen to **Niigata** (2 hours; ¥10,570), then transfer to the limited express to Tsuruoka, (2 hours; ¥4,450). Coming from JR Sendai Station, take the shinkansen first to Akita (2 hours 15 minutes), then transfer to the limited express Inaho 14 train and ride until Tsuruoka (1 hour 50 minutes) for a total cost of ¥14,430. Both trips are covered by the JR Pass.

Shonai Kutsu (www.shonaikotsu.jp) runs overnight buses between Tokyo and Tsuruoka (8 hours, ¥7,540 one-way; ¥13,570 round-trip). Once in Tsuruoka, **buses** run from JR Tsuruoka Station to Haguro-san's base (40 minutes; ¥820) and summit (one hour; ¥1,190), or to the eighth station of Gas-san (¥1,580). Services to Gas-san run daily in July-August, and on weekends only until mid-September. Yudono-san is only accessible via public transport on weekends during the hiking months, when three buses go to and from Haguro-san and the trailhead at the base of Yudono-san (1 hour; ¥1,500).

You can also **rent a car** in Tsuruoka and drive; inquire at the Tourist Information Center next to JR Tsuruoka Station about rental car options, which are readily available in town.

to its top station and then walking the rest of the way.

After taking the Zaō Ropeway to the terminus at **Zaō Jizō Sanchō Station**, follow the path that leads to the right, southeastward toward **Jizō-san** (1,736 m/5,695 ft), the mountain's third-highest peak, and **Kumano-dake,** the highest at 1,841 meters (6,040 ft). To reach Kumano-dake, you'll need to walk for about an hour over fairly rocky terrain. Along the way, you'll pass Buddhist statuary discretely dotting the landscape, which becomes increasingly volcanic as you approach the top; there you'll enjoy fantastic views of Okama Crater lying to the southeast. From there, you can press on for another 40 minutes or so to **Katta-dake** (1,758 m/5,768 ft), Zaō-san's second-highest peak looming beyond the southern edge of the cobalt waters of Okama Crater.

Skiing

ZAŌ ONSEN SKI RESORT

tel. 023/694-9328; www.zao-spa.or.jp/english/; ¥3,500-5,500 one-day lift ticket (price varies by season)

One of the best places to ski in Japan, the Zaō Onsen Ski Resort is famed for its juhyō, or "snow monsters," trees encased in ice and snow. At the upper reaches of this ski resort, you can ski and snowboard past these "beasts," which often seem to take on lives of their own. The best time to see them is mid-February through early March, when things are fully frozen.

The snow here is soft, deep, and powdery, making it optimal for skiers. Snowboarders also flock to the resort, but there are many places where the runs temporarily plateau, which can be a tad frustrating for those on boards.

Starting from the top of the resort, the run down the mountain is 10 kilometers (6 mi) long. More than 30 ski lifts, as well as a series of gondolas and ropeways, help people move between runs, which include a large number of beginner and intermediate courses, as well as a few daunting runs for those who are more experienced. Stunning vistas of Yamagata's surrounding mountains, extending in every direction, enhance the experience, as does the proximity to Zaō Onsen near the bottom of the ski area.

There are a number of ski rental shops and schools around the base of the ski lift area, most of them renting ski and snowboarding equipment from around ¥4,000 per day.

Onsen

This hot spring village, 880 meters (2,625 ft) up the face of Mount Zaō, is the ideal place to rest and unwind after a day of hiking in the warmer months, or skiing in winter. The water is highly acidic, with PH levels approaching 1, evident from the pungent scent of sulfur in the air. There are old-school communal tubs and a range of more modern pools to choose from.

Some old-school options include:

- **Shinzaemon-no-yu** (905 Zaō Onsen, Kawamae; tel. 023/693-1212; 10am-6:30pm Mon.-Fri., 10am-9:30pm Sat.-Sun.; ¥700). Note that it closes sporadically on Wednesday, generally once a month.
- **Kawarayu Public Bath** (6am-10pm daily; ¥200) is another public bath that's worth a trip, in that it's open daily and is the cheapest of the lot.
- There's also a fantastic large gender-separated outdoor bath, **Zaō Onsen Dai-rotemburo** (853-3 Zaō Onsen; tel. 023/694-9417; www.jupeer-zao.com/roten/; 6pm-7pm daily May-Oct., 6am-6pm daily late-Apr. and early Nov.-mid-Nov.; ¥600 ages 13 and older, ¥350 ages 1-12), which sits beside a mountain river. This is the best pool in town, but it's unfortunately closed late November to mid-April.

Food

For more extensive English-language food listings in the Zaō Onsen area, visit www.zao-spa.or.jp/english/foods/.

SANGORO

Zaō Onsen Chuo Kogen Gerende; tel. 023/694-9330; http://sangoro.co.jp/restaurant.html; ¥1,300-2,500; in between the top stations of Zaō Sky Cable (10-minute walk) and Zaō Chūō Ropeway (15-minute walk)

If you're feeling like a lighter mix of Japanese- and Western-style classics, head for the café and restaurant housed within the ski lodge **Forest Inn Sangoro,** which can only be accessed via Zaō Sky Cable or Zaō Chūō Ropeway. The menu ranges from pizza and clam chowder to curry and udon noodles. The cozy interior revolves around a circular counter with a fireplace in the center.

ROBATA

42-5 Zaō Onsen; tel. 023/694-9565; 11am-11pm Fri.-Wed.; ¥3,000; from JR Yamagata Station, take bus to Zaō Onsen bus stop; from there, it's a 3-minute walk

Serving Genghis Khan (Mongolian barbecue), Robata is a hit in Zaō Onsen, particularly in winter. Customers grill lamb, pumpkins, cabbage, and sundry other veggies on hot plates at the table.

Accommodations

For a thorough English rundown on accommodations in the Zaō Onsen area, visit www.zao-spa.or.jp/english/stay/.

ZAŌ SUNRISE

832 Zaō Onsen; tel. 023/694-9055; www.sunrise-zao.com/#hotel; ¥7,000

For a no-frills guesthouse that sits literally right at the bottom of a ski run, a few minutes' walk from the lower station of a ski lift, Zaō Sunrise is good if you're on a tight budget and don't mind sharing a bathroom or sleeping on a futon. The owner is a very laid-back, friendly guy who speaks English and is happy to assist you with getting settled in and renting skis.

MEITOYA SOU

48 Zaō Onsen; tel. 023/666-6531; www.meitoya.com; ¥15,000 with breakfast; from JR Yamagata Station, take bus to Zaō Onsen bus stop; from there, walk to the center of the Zaō Onsen village area

Meitoya Sou is a traditional Japanese-style inn that was remodeled in 2017. The rooms are a combination of Japanese- and Western-style. Each has a private toilet and basin, but only some have private full bathrooms. There is an indoor and outdoor onsen bath. Japanese-style breakfast is available.

★ MIYAMASO TAKAMIYA

54 Zaō Onsen; tel. 023/694-9333; www.zao.co.jp/takamiya; ¥35,000; from JR Yamagata Station, take bus to Zaō Onsen bus stop; from there, walk to the center of the Zaō Onsen village area

Established in 1716, Miyamaso Takamiya wears its history well. The hotel has even hosted the imperial family. With nine indoor and outdoor onsen baths, and a restaurant serving kaiseki (traditional multicourse meals) with famous Yamagata beef, guests don't want for much. It's a 10-minute walk to the ropeway station. Dark wood, soft lighting, and Japanese-style rooms with tatami floors complete the picture.

Information and Services

- **Tourist Information Center** (Zaō Onsen bus terminal; 708-1 Zaō Onsen; tel. 023/694-9328; www.zao-spa.or.jp/english/)

Getting There and Around

From **Tokyo,** take the **Yamagata** shinkansen to Yamagata Station (2.5 hours; ¥11,000); from **Sendai,** take the **JR Senzan** line to JR Yamagata Station (1.5 hours; ¥1,140 one-way); trains depart hourly. From there, you can reach Zaō Onsen via a **bus** that departs hourly (40 minutes; ¥1,000 adults, ¥500 children under 12) from bus stand #1. The train ride is covered by the JR Pass, but the bus is not.

During the ski season, you can travel by highway bus from the **JR Shinjuku Station Highway Bus Terminal** (http://shinjuku-busterminal.co.jp; 6am-11:30pm daily) in **Tokyo.** The bus ticket office is located near the JR Shinjuku Station New South Exit. The overnight trip takes about 8 hours and costs ¥4,500 (¥8,000 round-trip). The trip back to Tokyo runs during the day. Similarly, a round-trip bus travels once a day between **Sendai** and Zaō Onsen during ski season. The trip takes a little over an hour and a half (¥1,600). Inquire at the ticket window in **JR Sendai Station** for details.

The gateway to the onsen area is Zaō Onsen Bus Terminal, which is the terminus of the bus route from JR Yamagata Station. From this bus station, it's a 5-minute walk east to the lower station of Zaō Chūō Ropeway and a 15-minute walk northeast to the lower station of Zaō Sky Cable. The lower station for the main Zaō Ropeway is about 10 minutes' walk southeast of Zaō Onsen Bus Terminal. From these three ropeways, some 25 slopes and courses can be accessed. Local buses also shuttle between the lower stations of Zaō Chūō Ropeway and Zaō Ropeway. For a detailed English-language map of the resort's numerous ski runs, check out www.zao-spa.or.jp/english/ski/.

Iwate Prefecture 岩手県

To the north of Sendai and Miyagi Prefecture, Iwate Prefecture rewards those who venture this far into Tohoku with pristine landscapes, well-preserved samurai history in Hiraizumi, and deep stores of local mystery and lore in the town of Tōno. Those with the luxury of time won't regret discovering the picturesque Sanriku Coast, whose 300 kilometers (186 mi) of remote beaches and cliffs are the perfect antidote to the more hectic pace of Japanese cities.

HIRAIZUMI
平泉

Once the northern foothold of the mighty Fujiwara clan, Japan's most powerful family during the Heian Period (794-1185), Hiraizumi briefly rivaled Kyoto in cultural and mercantile prowess, thanks to its thriving trade in gold bullion. During its heyday, Hiraizumi was a boomtown where wayward children of noble birth and insubordinate military types were sent to keep the rough-and-tumble northern wilds under control.

During the 12th century, the Fujiwara lords poured vast wealth into the building of villas, pagodas, and shrines around the city, an attempt to create a Buddhist paradise on earth. But Hiraizumi's time in the sun was short-lived. The great northern center would ultimately succumb to treachery and court intrigue, but today, a few reminders of its former greatness are on display, earning the town's sites UNESCO World Heritage status in 2011. There's the captivating Chūson-ji temple complex, famed for the entirely gilt interior of its main hall, and the transcendent garden behind the temple of Mōtsū-ji.

Any trip to Hiraizumi is incomplete without making a detour east of town to Geibi-kei (Geibi Gorge). Here you can drift downriver on a boat steered by a good-natured boatman who regales passengers with traditional songs and tales. It's all in Japanese, but it's good fun. And if you happen to be in town during the first five days of May, the Fujiwara Spring Festival features locals dressed in period costume, a parade, and Noh theater performances on Chūson-ji's classic outdoor stage.

Sights

CHŪSON-JI
中尊寺

202 Koromonoseki; tel. 0191/46-2211; www.chusonji.or.jp; 8:30am-5pm daily Mar.-Nov. 3, 8:30am-4:30pm daily Nov. 4-Feb.; ¥800 adults, ¥500 high school students, ¥300 junior high school students, ¥200 elementary school students; from Hiraizumi Station, take regular bus from bus stand 1 (5 minutes), Hiraizumi Loop Bus (20-30 minutes), or walk about 20 minutes northwest

The approach to the stunning temple Chūson-ji leads you along a path set in a thick cedar forest. Founded in 850 by the wandering priest Ennin, who also founded Risshaku-ji at Yamadera, the complex grew to include dozens of buildings and flourishes thanks to investment by the Fujiwara clan in the 12th century. In 1337, the temple was sadly ravaged by a fire that destroyed all but two buildings, the **Konjiki-dō** ("Golden Pavilion") and **Kyōzō**, or sutra repository.

The first building you encounter on your way into this rambling complex is the main hall. Toward the back of the path you'll also encounter an outdoor Noh stage. The Konjiki-dō is by far the most famous building in Hiraizumi, or in Tohoku for that matter. From the outside, you see a white shell of a building. But step inside and you'll be dazzled by a mausoleum, built in 1124, entirely covered in gold. This extravagant building enshrines four generations of the Fujiwara clan and actually contains the mummies of its first three lords. Behind the Konjiki-dō, you'll also find the Kyōzō sutra hall, which was actually built 16 years before the Konjiki-dō.

For a sense of Hiraizumi's former glory,

follow the path next to the entry to Konjiki-dō until you'll reach the **Sankōzō**. This treasure hall features fans, jewelry, garments, Buddhist statuary, sacred scrolls, and other personal effects from the Fuijiwara clan.

MŌTSŪ-JI
毛越寺

58 Osawa; tel. 0191/46-2331; www.motsuji.or.jp; 8:30am-5pm daily Mar. 5-Nov. 4, 8:30am-4:30pm daily Nov. 5-Mar. 4; ¥700 adults, ¥400 high school students, ¥200 junior high and elementary school students; from Hiraizumi Station, take Hiraizumi Loop Bus (3 minutes) or walk 10 minutes west

After Chūson-ji, if you see only one more temple during your time in Hiraizumi, head to Mōtsū-ji. Like its gilt cousin, this temple was also founded by Ennin. Alas, Mōtsū-ji suffered a similar fate to its once opulent neighbor, succumbing to a succession of sieges and fires. Thankfully, not all was lost.

A few structures remain, including a treasure hall that's worth a look. As you walk through the site, signposts indicate where temple structures once stood. Mōtsū-ji's magic is revealed when you stroll through its garden, one of Japan's last remaining Pure Land gardens. This style of landscaping, aimed at manifesting an earthly vision of Buddhist paradise, was popular during the Heian Period. The garden is meant to evoke a sense of expansiveness and beauty.

Sports and Recreation

GEIBI-KEI (GEIBI GORGE)
猊鼻渓

467 Nagasaka Azamachi, Higashiyama-chō, Ichinoseki-shi; tel. 0191/47-2341; www.geibikei.co.jp; 8:30am-4:30pm daily Apr.-Aug., 8:30am-4pm daily Sept.-Nov. 10, 8:30am-3:30pm daily Nov. 11-Nov. 20, 9:30am-3pm daily Nov. 21-Nov. 30, 10am-2pm daily Dec.-Mar.; ¥1,800 adults, ¥900 elementary school students, ¥200 ages 3 and older; from Hiraizumi Station, take JR Tohoku line to Ichinoseki, then transfer to JR Ofunato line and ride to Geibikei Station (55 minutes; ¥580); or, take bus from Hiraizumi Station (35 minutes; 4 daily Apr.-Nov.; ¥500)

Flat-bottomed boats glide about 2 kilometers (1.2 mi) down the lazy Satetsu River in this picturesque gorge, located about 15 kilometers (9.3 mi) east of Hiraizumi. Limestone cliffs more than 50 meters (164 ft) tall bound the gorge, which is named after a rock formation resembling the nose of a lion. The gorge is particularly beautiful in autumn. During winter, passengers are kept relatively warm by sitting around kotatsu (low heated tables) on the crafts.

The boats, operated by bargepole, accommodate up to a few dozen passengers. The boat also stops so passengers can walk for about 20 minutes deeper into the gorge for a glimpse of the rock resembling a lion's snout. While you're on shore, you can also pay ¥100 for five "lucky stones" known as undama, signifying various themes (love, money, health, etc.), which you can attempt to throw into a hole in the rock beside the lion's nose. If your aim is good, it's said that you'll be blessed in the area of life signified by the stone you've thrown. On the way back to the port, the boatman regales the passengers with a folk song, which can be hauntingly beautiful as it echoes through the chasm. The full experience lasts about 90 minutes.

Festivals

FUJIWARA FESTIVAL
藤原まつり

Hiraizumi town center, Chūson-ji; contact tourist information center for details; May 1-5, Nov. 1-3; free

Once in spring and again in fall, Hiraizumi hosts a festival that brings back to life the town's glory days in the Heian period (794-1185). The festival takes its name after the Fujiwara clan, which was at the helm when Hiraizumi rose to prominence.

The spring edition of the festival reaches its climax May 3, when locals in period garb parade through downtown. This spectacle commemorates Minamoto no Yoshitsune, brother of Minamoto Yoritomo, who fled to Hiraizumi from Kyoto in search of asylum in the mid-12th century after his father was killed in battle by the Taira clan. The role of Yoshitsune is always played by a fresh young heartthrob each year, ensuring the attendance of a gaggle of female admirers. Various games, dances, and a memorial service to honor the Fujiwara clan also take place during the festival.

In autumn, the Fujiwara lords are again honored. There's also a parade of children in kimono, a Noh play on the stage at Chūson-ji, and various traditional dances. Another draw coinciding with the autumn edition of the festival is the brilliant foliage that will have reached the town and its surroundings by then.

Food and Accommodations

For a full list of Hiraizumi's accommodation options, visit https://hiraizumi.or.jp/en/archive/stay/index.html.

SOBADOKORO YOSHIIE

43 Koromonoseki; tel. 0191/46-4369; 10:30am-3pm daily; from ¥880; walk about 22 minutes northwest of Hiraizumi Station

Set in an old-school building, this soba restaurant serves buckwheat noodles in various guises (cold, in hot soup, or in disconcerting quantities of tiny bowlfuls as wanko-soba). All meals come with a nice spread of vegetable side dishes, chopped green onions, and dipping sauce (for noodles not served in soup). A good choice if you've worked up an appetite either before or after visiting Chūson-ji, which is about 3 minutes' walk uphill to the north.

CAFE SEKIMIYA

36-1 Suzusawa; tel. 0191/34-4030; 11:30am-2:30pm and 5:30pm-9pm Mon.-Sat., closed third Mon. of month; lunch ¥1,000-2,000, dinner ¥2,000-3,000; walk 7 minutes northwest of Hiraizumi Station

This cozy café serves well-rounded Western meals, from soup and quiche to pasta and grilled fish and meat dishes. The stylish interior is nicely lit with dark wood furniture, doors, and beams.

MINPAKU HIRAIZUMI

117-17 Hiraizumi Shirayama; tel. 0191/48-5866; ¥6,000 pp with breakfast; walk 7 minutes west of Hiraizumi Station

This inviting B&B has two nicely appointed tatami-mat rooms, a hot tub, and a comfortable lounge area. It's run by a warm elderly couple who whip up a nice Japanese-style breakfast for guests. It's located between Hiraizumi Station and Mōtsū-ji. It's very popular, so book as far as possible in advance.

Information and Services

To dig deeper into Hirazumi, check out the website of the **Hiraizumi Tourism Association** (www.hiraizumi.or.jp).

- **Tourist Information Center** (61-7 Izumiya, outside JR Hiraizumi Station; tel. 019/146-2110; 8:30am-5pm daily)
- **Hiraizumi Cultural Heritage Center** (44 Hanadate; tel. 0191/46-4012; 9am-5pm daily; 15-minute walk northwest of Hiraizumi Station on the way to Chūson-ji)

Getting There

If you begin this journey from **Sendai,** take the **JR Tohoku** shinkansen to Ichinoseki, then transfer to the **JR Tohoku Main Line** for the remainder of the trip (40 minutes; ¥4,020). Or, take the local JR Tohoku line (1 hour 15 minutes; ¥1,670) directly to Hiraizumi.

Coming from **Tokyo,** take the JR Tohoku shinkansen to Ichinoseki Station (2-2.5 hours; ¥13,000). From Ichinoseki, transfer to the JR Tohoku Main Line, which links to Hiraizumi (8 minutes; ¥200). The entire trip is covered with a JR Pass.

From **Morioka** in the north, take the JR Tohoku shinkansen to Kitakami (20 minutes). Then transfer to the JR Tohoku line and ride the rest of the way to Hiraizumi (30 minutes). The entire trip costs ¥3,950. The local JR Tohoku line also makes the journey (1.5 hours; ¥1,490).

If you're driving, the **Tohoku Expressway** runs from Tokyo and Sendai in the south, through Hiraizumi, up to Morioka and

Aomori in the north. The journey from Tokyo to Hiraizumi is about 5 hours 30 minutes (450 km/280 mi), while the trip from Sendai takes about 1 hour 30 minutes (90 km/56 mi).

Getting Around

Hiraizumi is compact and easy to navigate on foot. The town's popular sights are within 20 minutes' walk from Hiraizumi Station. The bulk of Hiraizumi's sights, including Mōtsū-ji and Chūson-ji, can also be reached by riding the **Hiraizumi "Run Run" Loop Bus.** It departs from **Hiraizumi Station,** makes a loop around town in 15-30 minutes, then returns to Hiraziumi Station. A single ride costs ¥150, and an unlimited day pass is ¥400.

TŌNO

遠野

Set amid rice paddies and encircled by verdant undulating mountains, Tōno is a hamlet in the heart of Iwate Prefecture with deep ties to Japanese folklore. Featured in *Legends of Tōno*, a collection of mythical tales released in 1910 by Yanagita Kunio, the town's most famous residents are supernatural, with the troll-like river-dwelling kappa, believed to snatch children who stray too close to the water, atop the list. Venture into the countryside around Tōno, preferably on a bicycle (you can rent one from the Tourist Information Center), to discover spots that will give you a backdrop to imagine Tōno's mythology and history.

Sights

Start your journey into another time at the **Tōno Municipal Museum** (3-9 Higashidate-chō; tel. 0198/62-2340; 9am-5pm daily; ¥310), which offers an overview of Yanagita's tome and features displays on village life from centuries past. Nearby, you'll also find **Tōno Folktale Museum** (2-11 Chūō-dōri; tel. 0198/62-7887; www.city.tono.iwate.jp/index.cfm/48,23855,166,html; 9am-5pm daily; ¥310), which is housed in the former ryokan where Yanagita penned his work.

DENSHŌEN

6-5-1 Tsuchibuchi; tel. 0198/62-8655; www.densyoen.jp; 9am-5pm daily Apr.-Dec., 9am-4pm daily Jan.-Mar.; ¥320 adults, ¥220 children ages 7-18; 5 km/3.1 mi east of downtown Tōno

From downtown Tōno, head into the surrounding countryside to Denshōen, a folk village that offers glimpses into the legends, crafts, and traditional skills of the area. It features some 1,000 Oshira-sama dolls, made from mulberry wood and traditionally worshipped as agricultural spirits. There's also a soba restaurant on-site. To reach this folk village from downtown Tōno, ride your bicycle for about 15 minutes heading northeast on Route 340 for about 5 kilometers (3.1 mi).

JŌKEN-JI

7-50 Tsuchibuchi, Tsuchibuchi-chō; tel. 0198/62-1333; open 24/7; free

From Denshōen, cycle southeast a few minutes (about 0.6 km/0.4 mi) to Jōken-ji, a temple that is associated with the kappa, the legendary river-dwelling monster. Note the stone kappa guardian dog statue located on the left side of the temple grounds. Behind the temple, you'll find the Kappabuchi pool, believed to be the home of the river spirit.

FUKUSEN-JI

7-57 Matsuzaki-chō Komagi; tel. 0198/62-3822; 8am-5pm daily Apr.-Dec.; ¥300 adults, ¥250 junior high and high school students, ¥200 elementary school students

Leaving Jōken-ji, pedal north for 2.1 kilometers (1.3 mi) along Route 160 to Fukusen-ji, a temple that sprawls over a verdant mountain slope. A number of substantial halls are featured, along with a five-story pagoda, and Japan's largest wooden sculpture of Kannon, the goddess of mercy.

Food and Accommodations

TŌNO BREWING TAPROOM

10-15 Chūō-dōri; tel. 0198/66-3990; http://tonobrewing.com; hours vary, check website for monthly schedule; from ¥550

Alongside great brews, they serve tasty nibbles

The Sanriku Coast 三陸海岸

The 300-kilometer (186-mi) Sanriku Coast, on Iwate's Pacific shore, is wild, windswept, and rocky, its clifftops peppered with twisted pines and gnarled rock forms that are continuously pounded by surf, most famously at Jodogahama Beach and the cliffs of Kitayamazaki. This untamed natural beauty has made the Sanriku Coast a popular destination since the 19th century. Today, it is part of the **Sanriku Reconstruction National Park,** created in the wake of the March 11, 2011, earthquake and tsunami that devastated Tohoku's coastline. If you're traveling through Tohoku, this remote coast makes for a fantastic drive or overnight stay if you want to get away from the bustle of modern Japan.

JODOGAHAMA BEACH

浄土ヶ浜

"Pure Land Beach" lies just beyond the coastal city of Miyako in the south of Iwate Prefecture. Its name aptly evokes the Buddhist paradise: a promenade strewn with white pebbles, inlets split by craggy outcrops of rock, and calm, clear waters safely nestled within a cove, fronted by giant shards of rock that protect it from the open sea. The paradisiacal associations were cemented in Japan's popular imagination by poet and fairytale scribe Kenji Miyazawa (1896-1933). Its views are gorgeous year-round, although summertime draws crowds of sunbathers and swimmers. If you happen to visit then, there are basic amenities, including changing rooms, showers, and toilets. Here are some other places to stop by to make the most of your trip:

- Boats depart from **Jodogahama Marine House** (32-32-4 Hitachihama-chō, Miyako; tel. 0193/63-1327; www.j-marine.com; 8:30am-5pm daily Mar.-Nov.; 20 minutes; ¥1,500; 15 minutes' walk, 5 minutes' drive from Jodogahama Visitor Center) to whisk passengers around the weathered cove and into the famed **Blue Grotto,** a cave carved into the shoreline so named for its cobalt-hued water. The Marine House doubles as a seafood restaurant (plates from ¥250), if you're feeling peckish.
- If you'd like to stay for a night, **The Park Hotel Jodogahama** (32-32-4 Hitachihama-chō, Miyako; tel. 0193/62-2321; www.jodo-ph.jp; ¥24,000 d with two meals) is a good pick right next to the bay.
- **Jodogahama Visitor Center** (32-69 Hitachihama-chō, Miyako; tel. 0193/65-1690; https://jodogahama-vc.jp; 8am-6pm daily Apr.-Oct., 9am-5pm daily Nov.-Mar.) offers information on activities and a small museum about the coast.

KITAYAMAZAKI

北山崎

Roughly 60 kilometers (37 mi) north of Jodogahama, an 8-kilometer (5-mi) series of precipitous cliffs plummet 201 meters (660 ft) to the water at Kitayamazaki. The "Alps of the Sea" are blanketed in pine trees and laced with walking paths that lead to sweeping vistas of the Pacific. Listed below

such as curry rice dishes, sausages, fried chicken, salads, and more.

★ TONOYA YO

2-14 Zaimokuchō; tel. 0198/62-7557; http://tonoya-yo.com; dinner served once daily from 7pm; courses ¥4,000-14,000

This restaurant and B&B is housed in an atmospheric former rice storehouse, eight minutes' walk from Tōno Station. Word has begun getting around about this singular institution, run by a Tōno native named Yotaro, whose adroitness in the kitchen shines through in his highly polished meals infused with the spirit of kaiseki. Yotaro's secret weapon is doburoku, an unrefined counterpart to nihonshū (aka sake) that has been brewed, moonshine-style, across rural

are some of the best places to take in the scene, whether you want to hop on a boat excursion or dine with a view.

- **Kitayamazaki Observatory** (24 hours; free) is a clifftop park where you'll find a series of viewpoints with superb panoramas, a staircase that descends to the sea (no swimming), and a few no-frills holes-in-the-wall serving simple seafood meals.
- For a more proper meal, the chef at **L'auréole Tanohata** (309-5 Aketo, Tanohata; tel. 080/9014-9000; http://laureole7.com; 12pm-2pm and 6pm-8pm daily; lunch from ¥3,000, dinner from ¥4,500), near the southern section of the cliffs, whips up great French food, and the views can't be beat.
- If you'd like to stay overnight in the area, **Hotel Ragaso** (60-1 Raga, Tanohata; tel. 0194/33-2611; www.ragaso.jp; ¥26,400 d with two meals) is a clean, simple hotel with Japanese-style rooms and shared indoor onsen baths about 20 minutes' walk, or four minutes' drive, northeast of Tanohata Station. The staff are happy to help arrange activities in the area.
- At **Kitayamazaki Visitor Center** (129-10 Kitayamazaki, Tanohata; tel. 0194/33-3248; www.vill.tanohata.iwate.jp/kankou/see/kitayamazaki.html; 9am-5pm daily Mar.-Nov., 9am-4pm daily Dec.-Feb.), you can learn about various activities in the area, such as sightseeing cruises (50 minutes; ¥1,500) that leave from a local port near Shimanokoshi Station about 7 kilometers (4.3 mi) south of the cliffs.

GETTING THERE

Coming from Tokyo, take the shinkansen to Morioka (2.5 hours), then transfer to either the Rias line or JR Yamada line and ride until Miyako Station (4.5-5 hours total trip time; ¥16,240). If you're taking the train from Sendai, first ride the shinkansen to Morioka (40 minutes), then switch to the Rias or JR Yamada line (3-3.5 hours total trip time; ¥8,550). Buses operated by Iwate Kenpoku Bus leave Miyako Station for Jodogahama Visitor Center (twice hourly; 15 minutes; ¥180), from where the beach is about 15 minutes' walk. If you'd like to avoid the walk, shuttle buses go between the visitor center and the beach twice hourly during summertime. Some of the buses from Miyako Station go all the way to the bus stop at Oku-Jodogahama (20 minutes; ¥230), right next to the beach. That said, your most convenient option is to rent a car at one of the outlets just outside Miyako Station, from which the Jodogahama Visitor Center is only about 10 minutes' drive east (4.2 km/2.6 mi). Driving from Sendai, follow the Sanriku Expressway north for 245 kilometers (152.2 mi) until you reach Jodogahama Visitor Center (3 hours 30 minutes).

Combining the trip with a stop at Kitayamazaki, you can simply drive one hour northward on Prefectural Route 45, which roughly follows the coast (60 km/37 mi); as with visiting Jodogahama, having a rental car is the superior option. You'll have much more freedom, and you'll cut the hassle factor inherent in relying on the region's patchy public transport.

Japan since the days of yore. This brew is white and foamy, with sweet and acidic accents, and Yotaro has a fantastic lineup that he serves before the meal arrives. Reserve at least a few months in advance. You can also rent out the Tonoya Yo storehouse for up to seven people (5-7 guests ¥16,000 pp, includes 2 meals).

KURANOYA

3-145-136 Kokoji, Matsuzaki-chō; tel. 0198/60-1360; www.kuranoya-tono.com; ¥6,800 s, ¥12,600 d

This wonderful B&B is run by a warm English-speaking couple. The Japanese-style rooms are clean and comfortable, with either a bathtub or shower, and the delicious home-cooked meals are made with local, seasonal ingredients (breakfast included for all rates, dinner ¥1,000).

Information and Services

Helpful staff at the **Tourist Information Center** (across the street from Tōno Station; tel. 0198/62-1333; www.tonojikan.jp; 9am-5pm Mon.-Fri.; bicycles ¥1,000 per day) can tell you about the combination ticket (¥1,170), or **Shinai Kanko Kyotsuken,** which allows you to enter five sites of your choice.

Getting There and Around

Take the **JR Tohoku** shinkansen to Shin-Hanamaki Station from **Tokyo** (3 hours; ¥13,870) or from **Sendai** (1 hour; ¥5,810). From there, change to the local **JR Kamaishi** line (45 minutes; ¥1,280). From **Hiraizumi,** take the JR Tohoku line to Hanamaki (45 minutes), then transfer to the JR Kamaishi line (1 hour; ¥1,660).

There's a **JR Rent-a-Car** (5-8 Shinkokuchō; tel. 0198/63-2515; www.ekiren.co.jp; 8:30am-5pm daily; ¥5,940-14,580 per day) office across the street from the train station.

Akita and Aomori Prefectures 秋田, 青森県

Until recently, Honshu's northernmost prefecture, Aomori (https://www.en-aomori.com), was a wild and enigmatic land. Its interior is split down the middle by the soaring Ōu Mountains, while the rugged Tsugaru Peninsula in the northwest and the windswept Shimokita Peninsula in the northeast surround Mutsu Bay as they jut into the storm-torn Tsugaru Strait that separates Honshu from Hokkaido to the north.

Today, **Aomori** is a proud and lively port city, acting as the prefecture's capital from where it sits on the southern shore of Mutsu Bay. Although the city doesn't have as many sights as the castle town of **Hirosaki** to the south, it hosts one of Japan's greatest summertime festivals, the Nebuta Matsuri, in which towering illuminated floats depicting figures and myths are transported through streets packed with revelers.

South of Aomori and east of Hirosaki, the volcanic peak of Hakkōda-san, famous for its autumn foliage and deep winter snows, the deep, dark-blue waters of lake Towada-ko, and the stunning nearby Oirase-keiryū gorge all comprise the northern part of **Towada-Hachimantai National Park.** The southern section of the park contains the fantastic Nyūtō Onsen; the samurai town of Kakunodate is just south of there. Technically in Akita Prefecture, south of Aomori Prefecture, Nyūtō Onsen and Kakunodate are best visited together.

To glimpse the old Aomori, shrouded in mystery, head for Osore-zan deep in the heart of the Shimokita Peninsula in the prefecture's faraway northeast. Here, the world's northernmost wild monkeys stay warm in onsen pools, and blind mediums at Osore-zan (Mount Dread) make contact with the dead.

TOWADA-HACHIMANTAI NATIONAL PARK
十和田八幡平国立公園

Northern Tohoku's splendor is beautifully encapsulated in Towada-Hachimantai National Park, blessed with virgin beech forests, cobalt-blue caldera lakes, secret onsen pools, and volcanic mountains laced with hiking trails, ski slopes, and forests that pop with some of Japan's deepest colors in fall. Importantly, it's also very off the radar and attracts a fraction of the crowds who flock to the Japan Alps in Honshu's central core.

This 855-square-kilometer (330-square-mi) realm straddles Iwate,

Akita, and Aomori Prefectures in Honshu's far north, divided between two separate parts, roughly 55 kilometers (34 mi) apart. The northern section in Aomori Prefecture is centered on Lake Towada and the Hakkōda-san group of mountains, drawing hikers in the warmer months and powder hounds in winter, and Oirase-Keiryū gorge, famous for its beautiful autumn leaves. The southern Hachimantai side, sprawling across a good chunk of northern Iwate and Akita Prefectures, boasts gorgeous volcanic landscapes with peaks like Mount Iwate, Mount Hachimantai, and Mount Akita-Komagatake, and is also home to some of Japan's most atmospheric hot-spring villages such as Nyūtō Onsen. Be aware that many facilities in the park are closed from November-April.

Sights

TOWADA-KO

十和田湖

The biggest caldera lake on the island of Honshu and the fourth-largest lake in all of Japan, this pristine alpine lake was formed millions of years ago when a volcano collapsed into itself. Pine-topped islands, deep-blue water, rugged peninsulas, and scattered temples and shrines along its 52-kilometer (32-mi) shoreline complete the near-perfect picture. The best way to see this vast lake is to board one of the sightseeing boats that depart hourly from the small town of **Yasumiya,** one of the lake's only settlements with amenities. There is a circular boat trip, starting and ending at Yasumiya, which explores the southern section of the lake (1 trip hourly; 50 minutes, www.toutetsu.co.jp/ship/pamphlet/english.pdf; ¥1,400 adults, ¥700 children), and a one-way trip from Yasumiya to Nenokuchi on the eastern shore (50 minutes; ¥1,400). Boat trips run from 8am-4pm and are in operation from around late April until early November.

Alternatively, you can drive around the lake, preferably with a rental car picked up in Aomori City to the north (via Route 103 from Aomori City), then stopping at the various viewpoints that dot the road that winds around the lake, before returning north to the Oirase-Keiryū stream or Hakkōda-san area to stay at one of the onsen villages or hike. JR buses also make the trip from Aomori Station to Yasumiya (3 hours; ¥3,090). Limited local buses shuttle between Yasumiya and Nenokuchi, before proceeding northeast along the Oirase-Keiryū stream to points north like Tsuta Onsen, Sukayu Onsen, and Hakkōda Ropeway. These buses only operate from mid-April to early November.

Hiking

Despite being well off the beaten path, Towada-Hachimantai National Park draws a healthy trickle of hikers in summer, culminating in legions brandishing cameras and tripods during autumn when some of Japan's most gorgeous fall colors ripple through the forests and mountains around the lake. Two spots with a heavy dose of autumnal glory are the lush Oirase-Keiryū Gorge, which flows northward from the northeastern corner of the lake, and the Hakkōda Mountains, centered on the peak of Hakkōda-san, roughly 55 kilometers (34 mi), or 1 hour 15 minutes' drive, northeast of the lake. Experienced hikers can embark on the 11.6-kilometer (7.2-mi) **Hakkōda Loop** (www.alltrails.com/trail/japan/aomori/hakkoda-mountains-loop), but you should only consider undertaking it if you're experienced, and have appropriate footwear and all essentials at hand.

HAKKŌDA-SAN HIKE

Distance: *11.6 km (7.2 mi)*

Time: *approx. 5 hours*

Trailhead: *Sanchō-kōen Station (top station of Hakkōda Ropeway)*

Information and maps: *https://hikesinjapan.yamakei-online.com/course/163.php*

The Hakkōda Mountains, popularly and collectively known as Hakkōda-san, are a group of peaks that loom at the northern edge of the Ōu Mountains, a parent range that stretches from Aomori Prefecture in the far north, southward for 500 kilometers (311 mi). Among Honshu's northernmost volcanic peaks, the Hakkōda-san group tops out at 1,585 meters (5,200 ft) at their highest point. Trails on the mountains wind through wetlands, marshes, and around lakes, making for fantastic hiking from May through autumn, when colors start to pop in late September before reaching their peak in late October.

There are several ways to hike among these beautiful peaks, but perhaps the most pleasing route starts from the top of **Hakkōda Ropeway** (1-12 Kansuizawa, Arakawa; tel. 017/738-0343; www.hakkoda-ropeway.jp; 9am-4:20pm daily Mar.-early Nov., 9am-3:40pm daily mid-Nov.-Feb.; ¥1,250 adults, ¥450 children one-way, ¥2,000 adults, ¥700 children return), which whisks you a distance of about 2.5 kilometers (1.6 mi), or 650 meters (2,132 ft) higher, up Mount Tamoyachi-dake (1,324 m/4,343 ft) to Sanchō-kōen Station. You'll start by walking through pine forest and wetlands to a new path that continues about 45 minutes to **Mount Akakura-dake** (赤倉岳), followed 15 minutes later to **Mount Ido-dake** (井戸岳). You'll descend past a volcanic crater (on your right) to the **Mount Ō-dake Refuge** (大岳鞍部避難小屋), a mountain hut beside a pond that is intended for use by those approaching the summit of its namesake.

Here, you have the option of ascending to the top of Ō-dake. It's about 30 minutes' slog up the wooden stairs that run up through a pine belt beyond the mountain hut. The trip back to the hut takes roughly 20 minutes. From the hut, continue your descent through a forest for roughly 45 minutes until you reach the Kenashitai marshlands. Continue down the mountain for about another 50 minutes, through a beech forest, going straight at the next fork in the path and following the trail to where it ends, at the parking lot behind **Sukayu Onsen**—journey complete.

To reach Hakkōda Ropeway, your best bet will be to drive yourself (via Route 103 from Aomori City), due to the region's infrequent buses. That said, from JR Aomori Station, you can also take a bus from just outside the station to Hakkōda Ropeway bus stop (1 hour; ¥1,120). This same bus also stops at Sukayu Onsen (1 hour 10 minutes; ¥1,340 from JR Aomori Station), meaning the trip (both ways) between Hakkōda Ropeway and Sukayu Onsen bus stops is only 10 minutes (¥240). Be aware that these buses only run mid-April-early November.

OIRASE-KEIRYŪ GORGE
奥入瀬渓流

Distance: *approx. 14 km (8.7 mi)*
Time: *approx. 4 hours*
Trailhead: *Nenokuchi*
Information and maps: *http://towadako.or.jp/en/wp-content/themes/towadakoen/pdf/en_map_oirase.pdf; http://towadako.or.jp/en/walking-map/oirase-gorge-nenokouchi/*

The area around Towada-ko is known for having some of the most beautiful autumn foliage in Japan. A particularly dazzling scene unfolds in late September and runs through October when the leaves explode with earthy tones and fiery reds along the Oirase-keiryū, a stunning gorge through which the sole tributary of the lake flows towards the Pacific.

You don't need to come to this stream in autumn to be moved by its beauty. Waterfalls cascade over the walls of the gorge, while caves and ravines dot this scenic stretch. Starting from Nenokuchi, on the lake's northeastern shore, there is a 14-kilometer (8.7-mi), well-marked and mostly flat walking trail running along the gorge from Nenokuchi to the village of Yakeyama. Of this trail, the first 9-kilometer (5.6-mi) section, which leads to Ishigedo, is the most scenic and takes about 2.5 hours to walk one way. Some stop at Ishigedo and hop on the bus back to Nenokuchi or north to Yakeyama, another 5-kilometer (3.1-mi), 1-hour walk north from there. Note that it's also possible to walk the path in reverse, starting from Yakeyama and ending at Nenokuchi.

The proximity of Route 102 means traffic sounds sometimes do reach the trail, and you'll sometimes need to follow alongside of or cross the road, so be aware of traffic. And, particularly during autumn, the place can get crowded. As with reaching Towada-ko or the Hakkōda-san area, your best bet for reaching any section of this Oirase-Keiryū stream path is renting a car (via Route 103 from Aomori City) and driving to either end of it, walking from there, then returning to where you've parked (either at Nenokuchi, Ishigedo, or Yakeyama) on one of the local buses running along Route 102. Alternatively, take a bus from outside Aomori Station to Yakeyama (2 hours; ¥2,300), at the northern end of the walking path, or Nenokuchi (2.5 hours; ¥3,140), at the southern edge, then walking from there. Note that these JR buses only run to the region from mid-April through early November.

Skiing

The mountains of the Hakkōda-san area are renowned for their heavy dump of snow come winter—17 meters (56 ft) of snowfall on average each year. Hakkōda-san is one of the only places in Japan where "snow monsters" form when trees freeze encased in monstrous amounts of snow. While word has gotten out and queues do now form around of **Hakkōda Ropeway** (1-12 Kansuizawa, Arakawa; tel. 017/738-0343; www.hakkoda-ropeway.jp; 9am-4:20pm daily Mar.-early Nov., 9am-3:40pm daily mid-Nov.-Feb.; ¥1,250 adults, ¥450 children one-way, ¥2,000 adults, ¥700 children return) on busy weekends, this was once a truly hidden gem among powder fiends, due to its phenomenal powdery snowfall. It's not recommended for newbies, but if you're a serious backcountry skier or snowboarder and love deep powder, these resorts are an excellent wintery realm well off most travelers' radars.

Hakkōda International Ski Resort (1-34 Kansuizawa, Arakawa; tel. 017/738-8591; www.hakkouda-p.com/cn21/pg110.html; 9am-4pm daily late Nov.-early Apr.; ¥3,200 4-hour pass, ¥3,800 1-day pass, equipment rentals ¥4,200 per day) is hallowed ground for a certain stripe powder hound who craves off-piste terrain. This ski zone is not a resort in the traditional sense, but more a creative usage that deposits riders at a nexus of backcountry terrain. Officially, there are three groomed runs and two ungroomed ones, including the experts-only Forest Course, which weaves in and out of the tree line. Note that there are a variety of other similarly wild off-piste ski zones scattered around the region. To learn more about them, check out https://hakkoda-ski.com.

Onsen

Deep-woods onsen are hidden away throughout Towada-Hachimantai National Park. In the north is Sukayu Onsen, while Nyūtō Onsen, one of Japan's very best hot-spring hideaways, is to the south in the wild Akita Prefecture.

SUKAYU ONSEN

50 Minamiarakawayama, Arakawa; tel. 017/738-6400; https://www.sukayu.jp; 7am-6pm (last entry 5:30pm) daily day bathing, 8am-9am and 8pm-9pm women only; day bathing ¥1,000 adults, ¥500 elementary school students, ¥8,360 pp d with 2 meals for staying guests

This antique onsen ryokan, supplied by waters from a hot spring in use for three centuries, is famed for its konyoku (mixed bathing) Hiba Sennin Buro (1,000 Person Bath), said to be large enough for said number of bathers. Although the practice continues to this day, some modern mores have infiltrated this policy: all guests are now required to wear strategically positioned privacy towels. There are also separate, less spacious baths for men and women (9am-5pm, last entry 4:30pm), should you prefer to avoid entering the mix. All of the baths are open to both day-trippers and overnight guests.

The cavernous, indoor bathing space is all dark beech wood and steam, evoking the ambiance of a bathhouse in an Edo period woodblock print. The water itself is divided into four tubs of varying temperatures, and its overarching characteristic is its acidic quality that—be forewarned—burns the eyes on contact and lets off a notable whiff of sulphur. The attached ryokan offers basic, cozy Japanese-style rooms (futons, tatami floors), a casual restaurant, and an on-site café with plenty of wood-beamed charm. Given its location on the western base of Hakkōda-san, this onsen ryokan is a great place for a soak or even a peaceful overnight stay after a hike or a day skiing on the mountain.

To access the onsen, either drive a rented car south of **Aomori Station** (Routes 4 and 103 toward Hakkōda and Towada-ko; approx. 60-minute drive) or take the JR Bus from JR Aomori Station to **Sukayu Onsen-mae bus stop** (1 hour 20 minutes; ¥1,360). This bus doesn't operate from mid-November through mid-April.

★ NYŪTŌ ONSEN
乳頭温泉

Nyūtō Onsen ("nipple hot spring") is a cluster of onsen ryokan tucked away in the mountains of Akita Prefecture, within the southern Hachimantai portion of Towada-Hachimantai National Park. The onsen's suggestive name was inspired by the cloudy tint of the water running under the ground in the area, said to resemble, ahem, milk. The baths are not the private property of the inns; rather, non-overnight guests are permitted to use them during select hours for a fee. Mixed bathing is permitted in many of them—with privacy towel, of course—though gender-segregated baths are also available.

Some of the best baths include **Tsurunoyu Onsen** (50 Kokuyurin, Sendatsui-zawa; tel. 0187/46-2139; www.tsurunoyu.com; ¥9,830-19,950 pp with meals, ¥1,100 heating fee charged during winter; get off at the **Arupa Komakusa bus stop,** 35 minutes on the bus from Tazawa-ko Station) and **Taenoyu** (2-1 Komagatake; tel. 0187/46-2740; www.taenoyu.com; ¥18,000-23,500 with 2 meals; 10:30am-2:50pm, last entry 2pm Wed.-Mon., ¥800 adults, ¥400 elementary school students and younger for shared bath, 10:30am-2:50pm, last entry 2pm Wed.-Mon., ¥3,300 private bath for non-staying guests, reservations required; take the bus from **Tazawa-ko Station** until **Taenoyu-mae bus stop**).

The **Yumeguri Pass** (https://glocalpromo.wixsite.com/nyutoonsen-extrainfo/hot-spring-pass; ¥1,800) gives guests unlimited access to the baths at all seven ryokan, as well as access to the **Yumeguri-go shuttle bus**. Pick it up at the help desk of any of the area's ryokan. Local **buses** run hourly to the Nyūtō Onsen area from **Tazawa-ko Station,** accessible by shinkansen from **Tokyo** (3 hours; ¥16,470) and **Sendai** (1.5 hours; ¥8,360).

Food and Accommodations

Food options are limited in the region, aside from a smattering of restaurants around Towada-ko's scant villages, Yakeyama beside the Oirase-Keiryū stream, and around the upper and lower stations of the Hakkōda Ropeway. Your best bet will be to simply book a meal plan at one of the area's hotels or ryokan.

GURILAND NIDOM CAFÉ

123-1 Utarabe, Towada-ko; tel. 080/6010-5151; www.facebook.com/nidomcafe/; 11am-5pm daily Apr. 20-Nov. 20; average ¥1,000

This woodsy yet stylish café beside the lake serves light, simple meals (think: BBQ, slices of pie, coffee, etc.). Alongside normal seating, there are hammocks if you prefer to kick back and swing. Various water sports and nature tours are run from the café as well (kayaking in summer, snowshoeing in winter, etc.; all require advanced booking). For a detailed list of options, with prices (from ¥3,000 pp), visit http://guriland.jp/en/towadaguesthouse_en.html.

HAKKŌDA SANSŌ

1-61 Kansuizawa, Arakawa; tel. 017/728-1512; www.hakkoda-sanso.com; ¥8,000 dorm, ¥10,000 double with 2 meals

This no-frills ski lodge sits beside the lower station of Hakkōda Ropeway, making it a convenient pick for those coming to carve through the powder come winter if you don't want to shuttle back and forth between the

1: the famed "milky" water of Tsurunoyu Onsen **2:** torii at Tazawa-ko **3:** Tsurunoyu Onsen complex **4:** Tsurunoyu Onsen in fall

1
2
3
4

slopes and, say, a nearby onsen ryokan. There are dorms with bunk beds with a shared indoor bath and toilet set-up, and private rooms with en suite baths. Two meals are served.

OIRASE KEIRYŪ HOTEL

231 Tochikubo, Oirase; tel. 0176/74-2121; https://hoshinoresorts.com/ja/hotels/oirasekeiryu/; from ¥35,000 d with 2 meals

For luxury deep in the great outdoors, this swish property operated by Hoshino Resorts ticks all the right boxes: stylish modern Japanese-style rooms with tastefully chosen earth tones, wooden onsen tubs plopped beside the burbling Oirase-Keiryū itself, and an airy restaurant on the second floor with a soaring, vaulted ceiling, central fireplace, and massive windows looking out onto the surrounding forest.

Information and Services

Visit the official website of Towada-Hachimantai National Park (www.env.go.jp/en/nature/nps/park/towada/index.html) and Aomori Prefecture's official sightseeing portal, Aptinet (www.en-aomori.com) to dig deeper.

- **Towada Visitor Center** (486 Aza-Towadakohan, Yasumiya, on Towada-ko's south shore; tel. 0176/75-1015; www.env.go.jp/park/towada/guide/towadavc/index.html; 9am-4:30pm Thurs.-Tues.)
- **Oirase Stream Museum** (183 Tochikubo, Okuse; tel. 0176/74-1233; https://oirase-towada.jp; 9am-5:30pm daily mid-Apr.-mid-Nov., 9am-4:30pm daily late Nov.-early Apr.)
- **Tazawa-ko Tourist Information Center** (68 Osaka, Tazawa-ko Obonai; tel. 0187/43-2111; 8:30am-5:15pm daily)

Getting There

The long journey to the northern half of Towada-Hachimantai National Park, from Hakkōda-san in the north to Towada-ko in the south, is best made through the city of Aomori. If you can swing it, rent a car in Aomori City—it will make your journey much freer and easier. Try **Toyota Rent-a-Car** (104-79 Takama, Ishie, tel. 782-0100, http://rent.toyota.co.jp, 8am-10pm daily) near the west exit of Shin-Aomori Station.

With your own wheels, you'll simply follow Route 103 south toward Hakkōda-san, the Oirase-Keiryū stream, and Towada-ko beyond (67 km/41.6 mi; 1 hour 45 minutes). Note that many roads around the region are closed from late November-April, but the road from Aomori to Hakkōda-san remains open for those headed for the ski slopes.

If renting a car isn't an option, limited public buses are operated by JR from both Shin-Aomori and Aomori Stations, following the same southward path. See www.jr-bustohoku.co.jp for bus route details and schedules. From Aomori Station, some of the stops include Hakkōda Ropeway at Ropeway Eki-mae bus stop (1 hour; ¥1,120), Sukayu Onsen (1 hour 10 minutes; ¥1,360), Yakeyama (2 hours; ¥2,320), and JR Bus Towada-ko Station in the village of Yasumiya (3 hours; ¥3,090).

Getting Around

Once you're in the Towada-Hachimantai region, having a car makes things a cinch. Otherwise, you'll be getting around on the sporadic local bus network that runs from mid-April through early November between Shin-Aomori and Aomori Stations in the north, Yasumiya in the south, and all points in between (Hakkōda-san, Oirase-Keiryū stream, etc.).

KAKUNODATE

角館

Kakunodate is an archetypal samurai town. The castle may have vanished during the early days of the Edo period, but a cluster of samurai residences, among the best preserved in all of Japan, remain. Founded in 1620 by Ashina Yoshikatsu of the Satake clan, this charming town evokes the past, most notably in its samurai district, or buke yashiki, located about 20 minutes' walk from Kakunodate Station.

If you find yourself in Kakunodate during cherry blossom season, which runs from late April to early May, consider yourself blessed. This is one of Tohoku's most stunning spots to view the pink blossoms. The town boasts some 300 weeping cherry trees, of which more than 150 are designated National Natural Treasures.

Sights

BUKE YASHIKI

Atmospheric gated homes, craft shops, and wooden storehouses line the streets of Kakunodate's samurai district, inspiring the nickname "Little Kyoto." Of the six residences open to the public, two stand out: the rambling, atmospheric **Aoyagi House,** where you'll find the **Aoyagi Samurai Manor Museum** (3 Omotemachi; tel. 0187/54-3257; www.samuraiworld.com; 9am-5pm daily, until 4:30pm in winter; ¥500 adults, ¥300 junior high and high school students, ¥200 elementary students); and **Ishiguro House** (1 Omotemachi; tel. 0187/55-1496; 9am-5pm daily, ¥500 adults, ¥300 children), with its striking garden and finely preserved stockroom.

ANDŌ JOZO MISO

27 Shimo-Shinmachi; tel. 0187/53-2008; 11am-5pm daily; free

South of the samurai residences and about 15 minutes' walk from Kakunodate Station, you'll also discover an old merchants' district with a few atmospheric storehouses still intact. It's worth visiting Andō Jozo Miso, a nicely preserved brick storehouse built in 1891. This brewery has been producing miso and soy sauce since the 18th century, and it shows. Sample some of their delicately flavored pickled vegetables or sip on miso soup in the café.

Food and Accommodations

★ KOSENDŌ

9 Higashi Katsuraku-chō; tel. 0187/53-2902; 11am-3:30pm daily; from ¥1,050

This well-loved purveyor of udon noodles is housed in a wooden schoolhouse two-and-a-half centuries old, smack in the middle of the samurai district. Seating is split between long wooden tables with benches and tatami-mat floors strewn with cushions around low wooden tables. The noodles, served in the local Inaniwa style, come with a range of toppings—mushrooms, spring onions, bamboo shoots, eggplant, egg, and basil leaves

gate to a samurai manor in Kakunodate

deep-fried into a crisp tempura finish. The menu includes some rice-based dishes, too. A recommended place for a locally inspired lunch in atmospheric surroundings.

NISHINOMIYAKE

11-1 Kami-chō, Tamachi; tel. 0187/52-2438; http://nishinomiyake.jp; 10am-5pm daily; from ¥1,080

Set in a stylishly refurbished samurai kura (storehouse), this restaurant and café has plenty of dark wood, exposed beams, and a main hall with vaulted ceiling. The menu is focused on Japanese set meals, hot-pot, Western-inspired dishes, and a good mix of coffee, tea, and small desserts. An adjacent shop features accessories and handicrafts made by local artisans. Conveniently located about 8 minutes' walk west of Kakunodate Station, en route to the historic district.

WANOI KAKUNODATE

11-1 Kami-chō, Tamachi; tel. 0187/53-2774; https://familio-folkloro.com/wa-no-i/kakunodate/en/; from ¥31,500 d without breakfast, from ¥35,100 d with breakfast

This unique property is housed in two stylishly revamped storehouses that were once the property of an illustrious local samurai family. The Nishinomiyake Bushigura, which sleeps up to six guests, is named after the Nishinomiya samurai clan, who once owned the land where the hotel now stands. Exposed wooden beams, katana and samurai armor on display, and more evoke the samurai heyday. Nearby, the Nishinomiyake Gakkogura ("pickling storehouse"), which sleeps up to four guests, is appropriately decorated with the types of tools used to make them—even the bathtub resembles an old-school pickle barrel. Both storehouses have traditional irori floor hearths, where guests are served breakfast spreads made with local rice and miso for an extra charge. Beds are comfortable, amenities generous, and bathrooms luxurious.

Information and Services

For a well-organized English portal covering everything from food and accommodations to activities in and around Kakunodate, visit the **Samurai Akita** website (https://tazawako-kakunodate.com/en/).

- **Tourist Information Center** (394-2 Kamisugasawa, in front of Kakunodate Station; tel. 0187/54-2700; 9am-6pm Sat.-Thurs., 9am-5:30pm Fri.)

Getting There and Around

The shinkansen runs to **Kakunodate Station** from **Tokyo** (3 hours; ¥17,150) and from **Sendai** (1.75 hours; ¥9,120). Trips from the Nyūtō Onsen area require going back to Tazawa-ko. Coming from nearby Nyūtō Onsen, first take the local bus to **Tazawa-ko Station** (50 minutes; ¥840), then ride the Tazawa-ko local train line from Tazawa-ko Station to Kakunodate Station (25 minutes, ¥320; or 15 minutes, ¥1,390 by shinkansen). Simplest of all, with a rental car you can drive northeast from Nyūtō Onsen to Kakunodate, (45 minutes; 38 km/24 mi).

HIROSAKI

弘前

The name Hirosaki evokes many images and ideas, from the popular belief that it's home to some of Japan's most beautiful women to its splendid cherry blossoms. This old castle town was once the cultural and political heart of the Tsugaru region, as the western half of Aomori Prefecture was known during the Edo period. Navigating the maze-like streets that wind slowly toward the castle grounds provides a visceral reminder of the town's former political importance. One is forced to weave patiently through the former samurai quarter in the same muddled way laid out by the city's creators to slow down advancing enemy troops.

Partly thanks to the fact that Hirosaki was spared the firebombing raids that leveled so many Japanese cities in World War II, today the city feels a little neglected in parts, but its large number of Edo-period buildings, the castle, and the lovely surrounding countryside add up to a beautiful provincial city worth exploring for a day, preferably by bicycle (bikes can be rented from the Hirosaki tourist center).

Sights

HIROSAKI CASTLE
弘前城

1 Shimoshiroganechō; tel. 0172/33-8739; 9am-5pm daily Apr. 1-Nov. 23; ¥320 adults, ¥100 children; from JR Hirosaki Station, take Dotemachi Loop Bus to Shiyakusho-mae bus stop

Set in **Hirosaki-kōen** (www.hirosakipark.jp/en/), a lovely park west of Hirosaki Station, Hirosaki Castle is on the petite side, but what remains is genuine. Originally built in 1611 by Lord Tamenobu Tsugaru, the first iteration of the castle was slightly grander, with a five-story keep that burned to the ground after it was struck by lightning in 1627. The three-story keep standing today was constructed in 1810. Elsewhere, three moats, a smattering of turrets, and some gates—the Kamenoko-mon on the north side being a fine example—were either rebuilt or remain from the original structure.

While the castle is an attractive sight, the real stars of the park are 2,500 stunning cherry trees. In late April and early May, a profusion of pink petals form canopies and tunnels, and delicately float on the waters of the moats, creating one of Japan's most famous hanami spots. It makes sense to start your tour of Hirosaki in this park, as the bulk of the city's sights can be reached on foot from here.

NEPUTA MURA
ねぷた村

61 Kamenokomachi; tel. 0172/39-1511; www.neputamura.com; 9am-5pm daily; ¥550 adults, ¥350 high school and junior high school students, ¥220 elementary school students; from JR Hirosaki Station, take Dotemachi Loop Bus to Bunka Center bus stop

Located near the northeast corner of Hirosaki-kōen, Neputa Mura, or Neputa Village, is a good place to get a sense of Hirosaki's local culture, particularly the iconic summer festival known as the **Neputa Matsuri,** held in Hirosaki and Aomori. Inside the dimly lit museum you'll find towering floats, lit from within and covered by paintings of fearsome warriors, striking women, mythological figures, and more. If you're unable to attend the real festival, getting up close to these stunning floats is the next best thing.

There are also displays and exhibitions on local arts and crafts, such as making wooden kokeshi dolls, as well as performances on the Tsugaru shamisen, a three-stringed instrument that emits a twang when plucked, often at blazing speeds; and sporadic demonstrations of a beat-down on a rotund taiko drum.

Festivals

HIROSAKI CASTLE SNOW LANTERN FESTIVAL
弘前城雪燈籠祭

Hirosaki-kōen; www.hirosaki-kanko.or.jp/en/edit.html?id=snow%20lantern%20festival; 9am-9pm, illumination from 4:30pm, second Fri. of Feb. through following Mon.; free

In an event that is locally known as the **Hirosaki Yuki-doro Matsuri,** the town's denizens make good use of the heavy dump of snow their town receives each winter. In early February, the town builds some 200 lanterns and 300 tiny igloos, illuminated from within by candlelight, from snow throughout the park surrounding Hirosaki Castle. It's hard to deny the magic of the wintry scene.

HIROSAKI NEPUTA MATSURI
ねぷた祭

Around Hirosaki Castle, Dotemachi shopping street, around Hirosaki Station; tel. 0172/37-5501; www.hirosaki-kanko.or.jp/en/edit.html?id=edit11; from 7pm Aug. 1-6, from 10am on Aug. 7; free

Some 80 fan-shaped floats featuring scowling samurai, fair maidens, and mythological figures are paraded through town alongside locals dressed in traditional attire who beat massive taiko drums and play bamboo flutes. Hirosaki's Neputa Matsuri is intimately connected to the larger **Aomori Nebuta Matsuri,** held around the same time in Aomori city. The intensity of the festival in Aomori city is associated with preparing for battle. By contrast, the more low-key festival in Hirosaki is said to mark the victors' return from combat, with some of the art on the floats showing grizzly skirmish scenes.

Food and Accommodations

★ KADARE YOKOCHŌ

2-1 Hyakkoku-machi; tel. 0172/38-2256; http://kadare.info; 3pm-11pm daily

There are eight small eateries on the first floor of this building, akin to an indoor culinary alley. Food ranges from Indian and yakitori to crepes and some excellent grilled seafood. You can sit anywhere in the space and freely order from any of the restaurants. Most of the shops have an English-language menu. The restaurants effectively function as bars, making it a great place to dine, carouse with locals, and maybe make some new friends.

AIYA

2-7-3 Tomita; tel. 0172/32-1529; www.shibutanikazuo.com/aiya; 5pm-11pm daily; ¥3,000; walk 15 minutes west from JR Hirosaki Station

If you find yourself in Hirosaki at dinnertime, head to Aiya. At 7pm and 9pm every night, there is a thrilling jam session on the Tsugaru jamisen, a three-stringed instrument with deep historical and soulful ties to the Hirosaki region. The musicians, who play with great dexterity and speed, are members of the family that owns and runs the restaurant. Sometimes multiple generations take to the stage in one evening.

★ ISHIBA RYOKAN

55 Mototera-machi; tel. 0172/32-9118; www.ishibaryokan.com; ¥4,950 pp with shared bath/toilet, ¥6,050 pp with en suite bath/toilet, breakfast ¥880

This charming inn is set in an old, creaky building with lots of dark wood dating to the 1800s. It has clean, expansive tatami rooms, and the older couple who own and run the place are friendly and eager to assist. Its location, only a few minutes' walk east of Hirosaki Castle's grounds, is hard to beat for access to exploring the historic side of town. Perhaps its biggest draw is the calming garden seen from most of the rooms. Pickup from Hirosaki Station is possible with advanced request. Rental bicycles are also available.

DORMY INN HIROSAKI

71-1 Hon-machi; tel. 0172/37-5489; www.hotespa.net/hotels/hirosaki; ¥10,500 d

Reasonably priced, clean, decent-sized

Hirosaki Neputa Matsuri festival float

rooms, very helpful staff, and both an indoor and open-air onsen bath on the rooftop make this a good budget option. Bowls of ramen are served free of charge to guests at night (9pm-11pm daily). It's a bit far from the station on foot (25 minutes' walk west), but the hotel provides a free shuttle bus. It's about 10 minutes' walk southeast of the Hirosaki Castle grounds, with most of the town's other attractions also within walking distance.

Information and Services

- **Hirosaki City Tourist Information Center** (JR Hirosaki Station; tel. 0172/26-3600; 8:45am-6pm daily)
- **Hirosaki Municipal Tourist Center** (2-1 Shimoshirogane-machi; tel. 0172/37-5501; www.hirosaki-kanko.or.jp/en/; 9am-6pm)

Getting There and Around

To reach Hirosaki, take the **JR Ōu** line from **Aomori** (45 minutes; ¥670). If you're traveling from anywhere south of Aomori—**Morioka, Sendai, Tokyo,** and so on—you'll first need to make the trip to Shin-Aomori Station via the **JR Tohoku** shinkansen, then transfer to the JR Ōu line for the remainder of the trip.

If you happen to be coming from **Hokkaido,** note that eight ferries run daily between Hakodate in southern Hokkaido and Aomori (4 hours; from ¥2,200). For details, ask at the ticket counter in the **Tsugaru Kaikyō Ferry Hakodate Terminal** (3-19-2 Minato-chō; tel. 0138/43-4545; www.tsugarukaikyo.co.jp/terminal/hakodate), where the ferries depart on the Hokkaido side.

Thanks to the Seikan Tunnel, which runs under the Tsugaru Strait, separating Honshu from **Hokkaido,** it's also possible to take the Hokkaido shinkansen from Shin-Hakodate-Hokuto Station to Shin-Aomori (1 hour 45 minutes; ¥8,300). From Shin-Aomori, transfer to the JR Ōu line, which runs directly to Hirosaki.

★ OSORE-ZAN (MOUNT DREAD)

恐山

One of Japan's three most sacred peaks, along with Kōya-san in Wakayama Prefecture and Hie-zan in Kyoto, Osore-zan is the northernmost of the lot, looming over the remote Shimokita Peninsula in the north of Aomori Prefecture. The mountain was discovered more than a millennium ago by a Buddhist priest seeking a hallowed peak bearing a likeness to the otherworldly realm of purgatory as envisioned by Buddhism.

The name Osore-zan literally means "Mount Dread." This is appropriate, given that it's believed to be sacred to the spirits of the dead. The desolate landscape does a good job of evoking dread, with signs of volcanic activity bubbling to the surface of the gray, windswept terrain. Jets of steam and hot water routinely spout from openings in the earth, and throughout the mountain there is a thick odor of sulfur.

Sights

BODAI-JI

菩提寺

3-2 Usoriyama, Tanabu, Mutsu-shi; tel. 0175/22-3825; http://kankousan.com/kankou/aomori/osorezan; 6am-6pm daily May-Oct.; ¥500 adults, ¥200 junior high and elementary school students

Similar to the three holy mountains of Dewa-Sanzan, Osore-zan is laden with Buddhist symbolism and is said to feature elements of the realm souls must pass through en route to the afterlife. At the peak of the mountain you'll find Bodai-ji, a temple with a clear focus on Jizō, the guardian of children. Near this holy place is Usori-ko—a lake with excessively blue water due to its toxically high sulfur content, which is believed to embody the Sanzu no Kawa, a mythical river akin to the ancient Greeks' River Styx that must be crossed to reach the afterlife.

It is believed that the souls of unborn infants and dead youngsters stack pebbles on the bottom of this "river" to help them walk across it, but demons seek to topple the stone

TOP EXPERIENCE

☆ Aomori Nebuta Matsuri ねぶた祭

various locations in downtown Aomori; www.nebuta.or.jp; Aug. 2-7; sidewalk seating free, reserved seating ¥3,000, on sale from about one month before festival

Every August in the prefectural capital of Aomori city, locals parade some two dozen large, luminous papier-mâché lanterns through heaving streets, reaching a crescendo the night of August 5. The ornate floats, measuring 5 meters (16.4 ft) tall, 9 meters (29.5 ft) wide, and 7 meters (23 ft) deep, depict samurai warriors, kabuki actors, mythical figures, animals, and more. Revelers fill the streets wearing colorful, lightweight summer kimonos (yukata) nibbling on summer fare—yakitori, grilled corn—and downing beers. It's easily one of Japan's best festivals and attracts people from across the country.

HISTORY OF THE FESTIVAL

No one really knows how the Nebuta Matsuri came about. Some say it's a regional variant of the Tanabata Matsuri, for which Sendai is most famous. More colorfully, others point to the account of Sakanoue-no-Tamuramaro, a 9th-century warrior and imperial commander who led troops in a campaign to conquer the far north. According to legend, Tamuramaro placed massive lanterns, similar to those mimicked in the Nebuta Matsuri today, as bait to draw curious enemy combatants to the imperial camp.

THE FLOATS

The imposing floats are painstakingly made with washi paper wrapped around wire frames by teams of nebutashi (Nebuta masters) who envision, design, and create these labor-intensive works of art year-round. Surrounding the floats, an army of haneto dancers in colorful traditional garb chant, jump, and gyrate through the streets to a soundtrack provided by bayashi bands. The spirited music drives the event, with taiko drums setting the rhythm, flutes piping a melody, and handheld cymbals adding accentuating flashes. If you'd like to enter the fray, it's possible to join the festival as a haneto dancer. See the festival's official website for details on how to become a haneto, rent an outfit (¥4,000), and more.

FOOD AND ACCOMMODATIONS

To stay in Aomori during the festival, book accommodations six months in advance. For a fuller list of accommodations in the city, visit www.en-aomori.com/category/accommodations.

piles to divert the souls of the young from reaching paradise. Thankfully, ever-present guardian Jizō—represented in the stone statues seen throughout the mountain—watch over these souls and keep the evil spirits at bay. Colorful toy pinwheels and piles of stones are laid throughout the landscape by parents whose children have passed on, in the hopes of assisting them in crossing. Feel free to add more stones to any of the piles to help the souls make their way.

After making the journey to this far-flung holy spot, feel free to avail yourself of the rustic hot springs found on the temple grounds.

Festivals

OSORE-ZAN TAISAI 恐山大祭

Bodai-ji; www.en-aomori.com/culture-043.html; Jul. 20-24, Oct. 9-11

It's no surprise that Osore-zan is believed to be an ideal space to commune with the dead. People keen to reach the other side flock to the mountain for the Osore-zan Taisai festival at Bodai-ji twice yearly—July 20-24 and October 9-11—when the mountain becomes a gathering point for blind mediums called Itako, who ritually purify themselves for three months prior. During the two days on

- ★ **Tsugaru Joppari Isariya Sakaba** (2-5-14 Honchō; tel. 017/722-3443; http://marutomisuisan.jpn.com/isariya-tugaru; 5pm-midnight daily; dishes ¥590-1,890; walk 15 minutes southeast of Aomori Station): Come here for the atmospheric room, delicious food, and sake brewed in Aomori. At 7pm nightly, a musician in traditional garb strums a banjo-like jamisen and sings folk songs. Book a few days in advance to be sure you get a seat.
- **Cafe Marron** (2-6-7 Yasukata; tel. 017/722-4575; 7am-8pm Thurs.-Tues.; drinks from ¥400, dishes ¥250-880): This old-school café, infused with 1950s ambience, serves good coffee and reasonably priced bites and desserts.
- **Hotel JAL City Aomori** (2-4-12 Yasukata; tel. 017/732-2580; www.aomori-jalcity.co.jp; ¥13,000 d with breakfast): This business hotel with clean, stylish rooms is 7 minutes' walk east of Aomori Station and offers a Japanese-style breakfast buffet.

Aomori Nebuta Matsuri

- **Daiwa Roynet Hotel Aomori** (1-11-16 Shinmachi; tel. 017/732-7380; www.daiwaroynet.jp/aomori/; ¥14,400 d with breakfast): This clean, modern hotel offers well-appointed rooms and spacious bathrooms. It's a 7 minute-walk southeast from Aomori Station.

GETTING THERE

To reach Aomori, take the JR Tohoku shinkansen (Hayabusa train; seat reservation required) to Shin-Aomori Station from **Tokyo** (3.5 hours; ¥17,150) or **Sendai** (1.5 hours; ¥11,420), then transfer to the JR Ōu line and make the short journey to **Aomori Station** (6 minutes; ¥190), which is the gateway to downtown. Coming from **Hirosaki**, you can take the JR Ōu line (50 minutes; ¥670) directly to Aomori Station.

the mountain, these highly trained spiritual messengers, seen toting mulberry-wood dolls believed to serve as conductors for sending and receiving psychic communiques, enter deeply into the trance state needed to do their job. Smaller numbers of Itako can sometimes be found on the mountain at other times of the year.

Food and Accommodations

The Shimokita Peninsula is best treated as a day trip from Aomori City, Hirosaki, or Towada-ko region, where you'll have better pickings when it comes to food and accommodations. That said, there are decent, basic options in the area around Shimokita Station. For slightly more exhaustive food and hotel listings in the area, visit http://mutsu-kanko.jp/en/taberu_01.html and http://mutsu-kanko.jp/en/stayichiran.html.

EKIMAE SYOKUDO

5-45 Shimokita-chō, Mutsu-shi; tel. 0175/22-0860; 11am-2:30pm and 5:30pm-8pm Fri.-Wed.; average ¥1,000

For sheer convenience, consider this simple eatery right across the street from

Shimokita Station. It serves hearty set meals of ramen, tonkatsu, curry rice, and the like. While it can't claim to be gourmet, it scores points for having an English menu.

SHUKUBO KISSHOKAKU

3-2 Usoriyama, Tanabu, Mutsu-shi; tel. 0175/22-3826; https://osorezan.or.jp/?page_id=216; ¥12,000 pp with 2 meals

If you're spending a night on the peninsula, you might as well stay on the desolate mountain itself, in the shukubo (temple lodging) of Bodai-ji. The rooms are basic, but huge by Japanese standards, and two shōjin ryōri (vegetarian Buddhist) meals (dinner and breakfast) are served in the communal dining hall. There are onsen baths on the grounds for guests, who have the option of participating in morning prayers (reservation required). You'll need to have a Japanese person reserve over the phone for you, as there's no website to book ahead, let alone one in English. They're used to accommodating the odd, intrepid foreign guest, though. Like the temple itself, the lodgings are only open from May-October.

Information and Services

- **Tourist Information Center** (4-3 Shimokita-machi, Mutsu-shi; tel. 0175/34-9095; www.mutsu-kanko.jp/en/info_center.html; 9am-7pm daily; next to Shimokita Station)

Getting There and Around

Osore-zan is admittedly a difficult place to reach. Its remoteness is part of its appeal, but it definitely takes some planning to pull off a trip here without headache. While it's certainly possible to reach Osore-zan using public transportation, if you're coming from Aomori or Hirosaki and you're able to **drive,** this is by far the smoothest option. The drive from **Aomori** takes 2 hours (115 km/72 mi); the drive from **Hirosaki** takes about 2 hours 45 minutes (160 km/99 mi).

If driving isn't an option, allow lots of time to arrive and be sure to have all of the transfers between different train lines, buses, and so on very clearly mapped out before setting off. Coming from **Aomori,** take the Aoimori Railway (not to be confused with "Aomori") and ride 45 minutes to **Noheji** (¥1,040). If

Osore-zan

you're coming from **Hirosaki,** take the JR Ōu line to Aomori, then transfer to the Aoimori Railway and take it until Noheji (1.5 hours; ¥1,710).

Once you've reached Noheji, transfer to the **JR Ōminato line** and ride about 50 minutes to Shimokita Station (¥1,140). Now you're finally deep in the Shimokita Peninsula, where you'll find the elusive Osore-zan. Exit Shimokita Station and move next to the **Mutsu Bus Terminal,** about 3 kilometers (2 mi) northeast of Shimokita Station. You can reach Mutsu Bus Terminal either by walking (37 minutes), by taxi (about 8 minutes; approximately ¥1,000), or by local bus (departs every 40 minutes; 23 minutes; ¥190), which you can take from Toshokan-mae bus stop, about 10 minutes' walk northwest of Shimokita Station, across the Tanabu River. From Mutsu Bus Terminal, catch the bus to Osore-zan (45 minutes; ¥810). Four or five buses depart Mutsu Bus Terminal from bus stand #1 daily May-October. Buses don't run to Osore-zan November-April due to inclement weather.

Hokkaido 北海道

Itinerary Ideas 541
Sapporo 545
Around Sapporo 557
Hakodate 569
Daisetsuzan National Park 576
Eastern Hokkaido 582
Rishiri-Rebun-Sarobetsu National Park 591

Relaxed people, wide-open spaces, and an abundance of nature characterize Japan's northernmost main island of Hokkaido, which, despite being Japan's largest prefecture, only accounts for 5 percent of its population. In many ways, Hokkaido is Japan's final frontier. Those who are drawn to the island come largely seeking adventure.

The last major island in the country to be developed, Hokkaido has a history that in some ways mirrors that of the American West, complete with 19th-century settlers intent on blazing new trails. Also calling to mind North America's Wild West, Hokkaido is home to Japan's original inhabitants, the Ainu, whose customs and culture were sadly pushed to the fringes by the encroachment of modern life.

Highlights

Look for ★ to find recommended sights, activities, dining, and lodging.

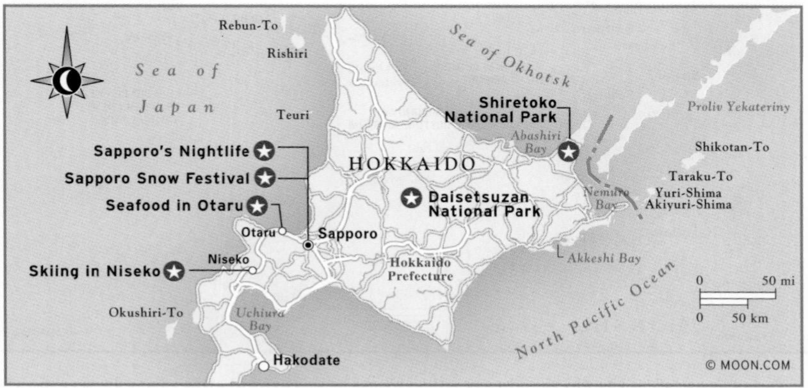

★ **Sapporo Snow Festival:** Teams of artists carve intricate statues in ice and build massive snow sculptures as large as buildings, drawing thousands of visitors to Sapporo every February (page 549).

★ **Sapporo's Nightlife:** The Sapporo neighborhood of Susukino boasts 4,000 bars, restaurants, and clubs, making it the largest nightlife zone north of the capital and one of the biggest in all of Japan (page 553).

★ **Seafood in Otaru:** The picturesque port of Otaru, historically a center for herring fishing, remains a major destination for seafood lovers (page 558).

★ **Skiing in Niseko:** The best places to ski in Hokkaido, Niseko's four resorts are a known quantity among devoted powder hounds worldwide (page 561).

★ **Daisetsuzan National Park:** Options for hiking and onsen abound in Japan's largest national park (page 576).

★ **Shiretoko National Park:** This vast wilderness and UNESCO World Heritage Site is known by the Ainu as "the end of the world" (page 587).

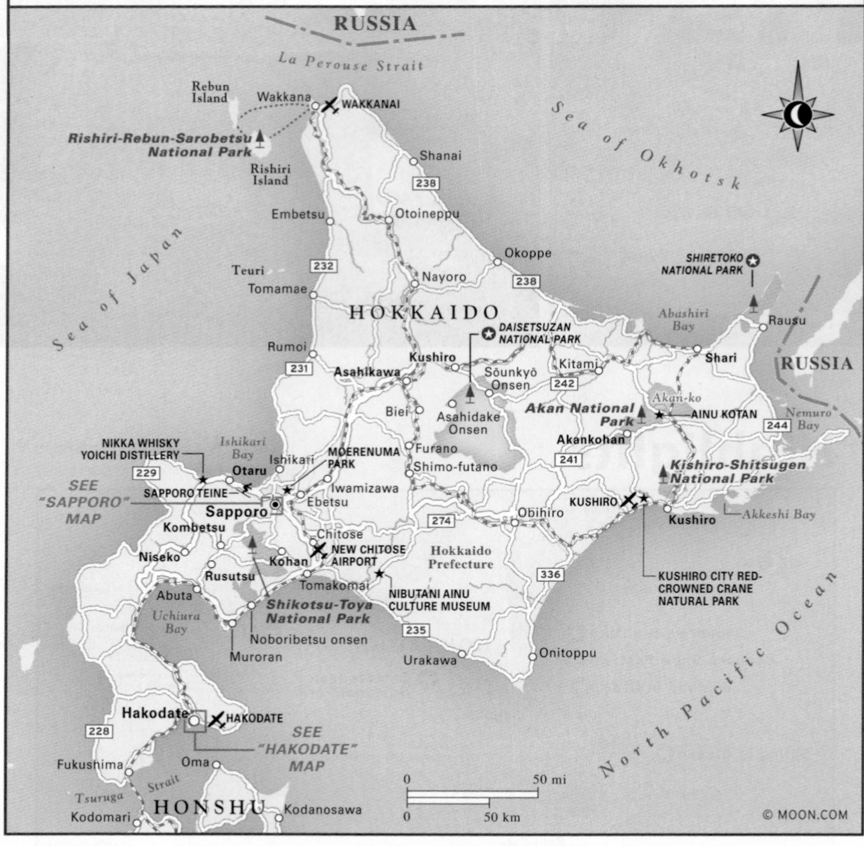

Today, most of Hokkaido remains as wild as ever. The architecture seen in its scant cities and towns reveals an urban history that is decidedly modern compared to the rest of the nation. This is not the Japan of grand temple complexes or ancient Shinto rites. Here, the cultural markers were largely set from the 19th century on.

Most visitors access the island via the port town of Hakodate by train or through Sapporo by plane. In Sapporo, travelers eat their way through the city's hearty food scene and explore the lively nightlife of the Susukino area. In winter, the impressive Sapporo Snow Festival also draws a crowd. Craft beer flows from taps in the nearby cities of Hakodate, which charms guests with its 19th-century ambience, and Otaru, known for fresh seafood.

Beyond the urbanized southwest, visitors are drawn to Hokkaido's onsen (hot spring baths) and expansive national parks. In the

Previous: hiking in Daisetsuzan National Park; Sapporo Snow Festival sculpture; seafood at an Otaru market.

Regional Food Specialties

- **Beer:** Sapporo, and to a lesser extent Otaru, have thriving beer scenes, with Sapporo's eponymous beer brand being the island's most prominent brew. Try it at **Sapporo Beer Garden and Museum** (page 549).
- **Seafood:** Hokkaido is particularly known for its seafood, with crab being king. Try it at **Isezushi** (page 559).
- **Genghis Khan:** Among Hokkaido's iconic cold-weather dishes is this, the local name for Mongolian barbecue. This DIY meal, ubiquitous in Sapporo, consists of lamb and onion cooked on dome-shaped grills resembling a battle helmet. Try it at **Daruma** (page 551).
- **Miso ramen:** The local flavor of ramen is served in a flavorsome miso-based broth. Try it at **Shingen** (page 550).
- **Soup curry:** A curry-flavored soup packed with tender meat (commonly pork or chicken) and loads of vegetables (eggplant, lotus root, pumpkin, etc.). Try it at **Suage+** (page 551).
- **Ainu cuisine:** The island's original native menu, made in the kitchens of the indigenous Ainu, is heavy on local flavors. Think freshly caught salmon, venison, and mountains foraged in the island's wild interior. Try it at **Poronno** (page 585).

warmer months, when wildflowers erupt in vivid colors across much of the island, this region offers fantastic hiking opportunities. And during the long, snowy winters, ski resorts beckon powder lovers. Brown bears, red-crowned cranes, and abundant marine life along the coast also make the island an excellent choice for wildlife enthusiasts. For a truly unique cultural experience, head to the Lake Akan area in the remote northeast. This region is home to a sizable number of Japan's indigenous Ainu people, who have managed to preserve their traditional ways.

ORIENTATION

Japan's northernmost main island, with Russia's far east looming to the north, Hokkaido is vast by Japanese standards at 83,423 square kilometers (32,210 sq mi), making it the country's second-largest island after Honshu. As a visitor, it may make sense to divide this large area into four main zones: Southern Hokkaido, Central Hokkaido, Eastern Hokkaido, and remote Northern Hokkaido.

The main city in Southern Hokkaido is **Hakodate,** the first port of call for those traveling to the island from Honshu across the Tsugaru Strait, by shinkansen (bullet train) or ferry.

Moving north, the **Central Hokkaido** region is by far the island's most populated and influential (politically and economically) today. This is largely thanks to **Sapporo,** the island's capital and its largest (Japan's fifth-largest) metropolis. The port town of **Otaru,** 35 kilometers (22 mi) northwest of Sapporo, is one of the other main towns of the region. The interior is also home to **Shikotsu-Tōya National Park,** a wonderland of lakes and volcanoes; the famed hot-spring village of **Noboribetsu Onsen;** and the standout ski resorts of **Niseko** and **Rusutsu,** only about 20 kilometers (12 mi) apart.

East of greater Sapporo is Hokkaido's second-largest city, Asahikawa, which sits on the western edge of the vast **Daisetsuzan National Park.** Located essentially in the geographic center of the island, this massive swath of nature is Japan's largest national park. Also in the island's heartland are the towns of **Biei** and **Furano,** which are awash in wildflowers in summer.

Heading eastward from Daisetsuzan, a hint of the pioneer spirit persists in the salty fishing towns of **Eastern Hokkaido.** This part of

Best Accommodations

★ **Aya Niseko:** If money is no object, you can't go wrong by staying at one of these private apartments next to Niseko's slopes (page 563).

★ **Daisetsuzan Shirakaba-sō:** This large wooden lodge with open-air onsen puts you smack in the middle of Hokkaido's wild interior (page 579).

★ **ARtINn:** This unique art hotel is near the verdant shores of Kussharo-ko (page 585).

★ **Hotel Kifu Club Shiretoko:** This chic property on the remote Shiretoko Peninsula offers rooms that face the windswept coast of the Sea of Okhotsk (page 590).

★ **Maruzen Pension Rera Mosir:** An adventurous mountain guide runs this clean, modern inn sitting at the edge of Rishiri Island's wild interior (page 593).

the island boasts **Akan National Park;** here, the fading Ainu culture has survived the longest. Roughly 50 kilometers (31 mi) south of the Akan area, the **Kushiro Wetlands** (part of Kushiro-Shitsugen National Park) are famous for their thriving population of red-crested cranes.

The remotest region of them all is **Northern Hokkaido,** where towns are few and far between. More than 200 kilometers (124 mi) northeast of Daisetsuzan, **Shiretoko National Park** is a UNESCO World Natural Heritage Site, a veritable showcase of biodiversity. Moving to the far northern reaches of the island, the Sea of Japan lies to the west, while the Okhotsk Sea spreads eastward. The main town here is Wakkanai. The beautiful islands of **Rishiri** and **Rebun,** gorgeous hiking spots in the warmer months for those who *really* want to get away from it all, lie about 60 kilometers (37 mi) west of this town, from where they can be reached by ferry. The northernmost point of Japan is at Cape Sōya, about 40 minutes' drive northeast of downtown Wakkanai. North of here looms the southern tip of the Russian island of Sakhalin.

PLANNING YOUR TIME

Given its far-flung position, Hokkaido is best visited either as a stand-alone destination or as an outdoorsy counterbalance to the vast sprawl of urban Japan. The vast distances between most of the island's main attractions means that there are few day-trip destinations. Most places call for an **overnight stay,** or at the very least, a well-planned stop before the next leg of your journey.

Another big factor in planning a trip to Hokkaido is season. Spring stretches from mid-March through early June, while mid-June through August accounts for the island's relatively mild summer. Autumn starts around early September and runs through November, while winter sets in and remains firmly in place from December through early March. Be aware that all seasons on Hokkaido see lower temperatures than elsewhere across the archipelago.

Hokkaido's ample ski slopes, from **Niseko** to **Rusutsu** and **Furano,** are among the best in the world, which means they can become alarmingly crowded during the height of **winter.** Book accommodations to any ski or onsen resorts several months—or better yet, a year—in advance. In **summer,** the island's climate is pleasantly mild and dodges the typhoons that sweep across the rest of the country. The more remote national parks, tricky to reach during winter, become a paradise for hikers during the warmer months. As an added bonus, they are among Japan's least crowded outdoor zones. Though it's cooler than the rest of Japan, weather in Hokkaido is also pleasant in the relative low seasons of **spring** and **fall.**

Beginning at the far south of the island, the port city of **Hakodate** is a good entry point to Hokkaido if you're traveling by train, connected to Aomori via the undersea Seikan Tunnel (54 km/33 mi). If you're flying into Hokkaido, **Sapporo** will most likely be your entry point. Plan to spend a night or two here before heading elsewhere. To the west, **Otaru** is a good day trip from Sapporo. To the south, the surprisingly accessible **Shikotsu-Tōya National Park** and nearby **Noboribetsu Onsen** both work well as either a day trip or an overnight stay.

Driving in Hokkaido

Public transportation in Hokkaido can be tedious due to infrequent bus departures, sporadic train schedules, and large parts of the island inaccessible by rail. Beyond the urban centers (Hakodate, Sapporo, Otaru, etc.), consider **renting a car** before striking off to remote locales, such as Daisetsuzan National Park or Shiretoko National Park. Hokkaido's country roads are refreshingly spacious, often straight for long stretches with sparse traffic. Driving will make exploring the island more enjoyable and will free you up to experience its natural splendor on your own terms.

A few **caveats:** Gas stations and convenience stores—ubiquitous in urban Japan—are scant in many parts of the island, and cell phone reception is often weak or nonexistent once you get away from it all. So be sure to fill your gas tank to the max and don't waste an opportunity to refuel or stock up on food or drinks. In addition, it's not advisable to drive in winter, when the roads are almost universally iced over and whiteouts can occur when sudden blizzards strike. It's best to stick to public transport during the island's long winters. Finally, wildlife is profuse in the rugged interior. Resist the urge to speed on the open road, even if there are no other cars in sight, lest a fox or deer suddenly crosses your path.

Itinerary Ideas

SAPPORO AND OTARU

Day One

1 Begin the day in Sapporo with a morning visit to **Hokkaido Jingū,** west of downtown (take Tōzai subway line to Maruyama-kōen Station, exit 3). Although quite young by Shinto standards, this grand shrine is perhaps the island's most significant religious structure.

2 Head back downtown for lunch to try one of Sapporo's renowned dishes, miso ramen, at **Shingen** (take Nanboku subway line to Susukino Station, exit 5). Aim to arrive a bit ahead of opening time to avoid a queue.

3 To walk off your lunch, amble about 15 minutes north toward the city's expansive central park, **Ōdōri-kōen,** a good place to people-watch and get a view of Sapporo TV Tower.

4 Walk north about 7 minutes until you reach the **Former Hokkaido Government Office** and the history museum now housed there. This red-brick building is a classic example of the structures that popped up during Hokkaido's development in the 19th century, the start of the modern era.

5 After the history lesson, walk about 10 minutes west to the **Hokkaido University**

Botanical Garden, a 14-hectare (34-acre) green expanse, lined with hiking trails and plenty of places to sit.

6 Before sunset, make your way to **Mount Moiwa** in the southwest of town. From Susukino, take the streetcar to Ropeway Iriguchi station (25 minutes), then walk 5 minutes to the Mount Moiwa Ropeway. Take the ropeway and cable car to the top of the peak and watch as the city lights twinkle.

7 Return downtown for dinner. **Daruma** is a good pick for Genghis Khan (Mongolian barbecue), a hearty option that's pure Sapporo.

8 If you've got the energy, explore the sprawling nightlife district of **Susukino.** Whether you want jazz, cocktails, or a club, there's a venue that will fit the bill; try Bossa for a jazz bar.

Day Two

Start your day by taking the train 40 minutes west to the port town of **Otaru.** If you had a big night out in Susukino, it's fine to start in the mid- to late morning. Atmospheric Otaru lends itself to leisurely exploration.

1 Upon arriving in town, walk about 10 minutes east down its long main central boulevard toward the ocean. Your first stop is the Otaru Canal and its row of atmospheric 19th-century warehouses. The **Otaru City Museum,** which sits beside the canal, gives a sense of Otaru's past as an important fishing hub.

2 Walk a few minutes west of the canal's south end and you'll find yourself on Nichigin-dōri, once known as the Wall Street of northern Japan. Admire the stately facades of the stone buildings, particularly the old Bank of Japan building. For lunch, **Sushiya Kōdai** is tucked down a small alley of eateries toward the western end of Nichigin-dōri. Amid stiff competition, this casual, standing sushi shop is known for its quality.

3 For dessert, walk about 15 minutes southeast to the **Kitakarō Otaru Honkan,** set in a handsome brick building. This sweets mecca is known for its German roll cakes, cream puffs, soft cream, and more.

4 Walk 2 minutes south toward the **Otaru Music Box Museum.** If a music box catches your fancy, you can likely buy it (if you've got the yen to spare).

5 End your day trip canal-side at **Otaru Beer,** a distinctive local brewery housed in a classic warehouse next to the water. If you stay until sunset, enjoy a stroll and take photos along the water's edge as the light softens before returning to Sapporo.

ONE DAY IN HAKODATE

1 Begin your exploration of Hakodate at the city's lively **morning market.** If you're feeling hungry, some of the stalls whip up a good seafood breakfast.

2 Hop on the tram and ride until the Goryōkaku-kōen-mae stop (from Hakodate-eki-mae tram stop, 17 minutes; ¥230). From here, walk 15 minutes north to the star-shaped **Fort Goryōkaku.** To fully admire this mighty fortress and its park, go to the top of the Goryōkaku Tower at the southwest corner of the park.

3 For lunch, make your way to the other side of town, backtracking by tram to the Suehiro-chō stop (from Goryōkaku-kōen-mae stop, 24 minutes; ¥250). Then walk 5 minutes southeast to the main shop of **Lucky Pierrot,** a local institution known across Japan for its Chinese-influenced chicken burger.

Sapporo and Otaru Itinerary Ideas

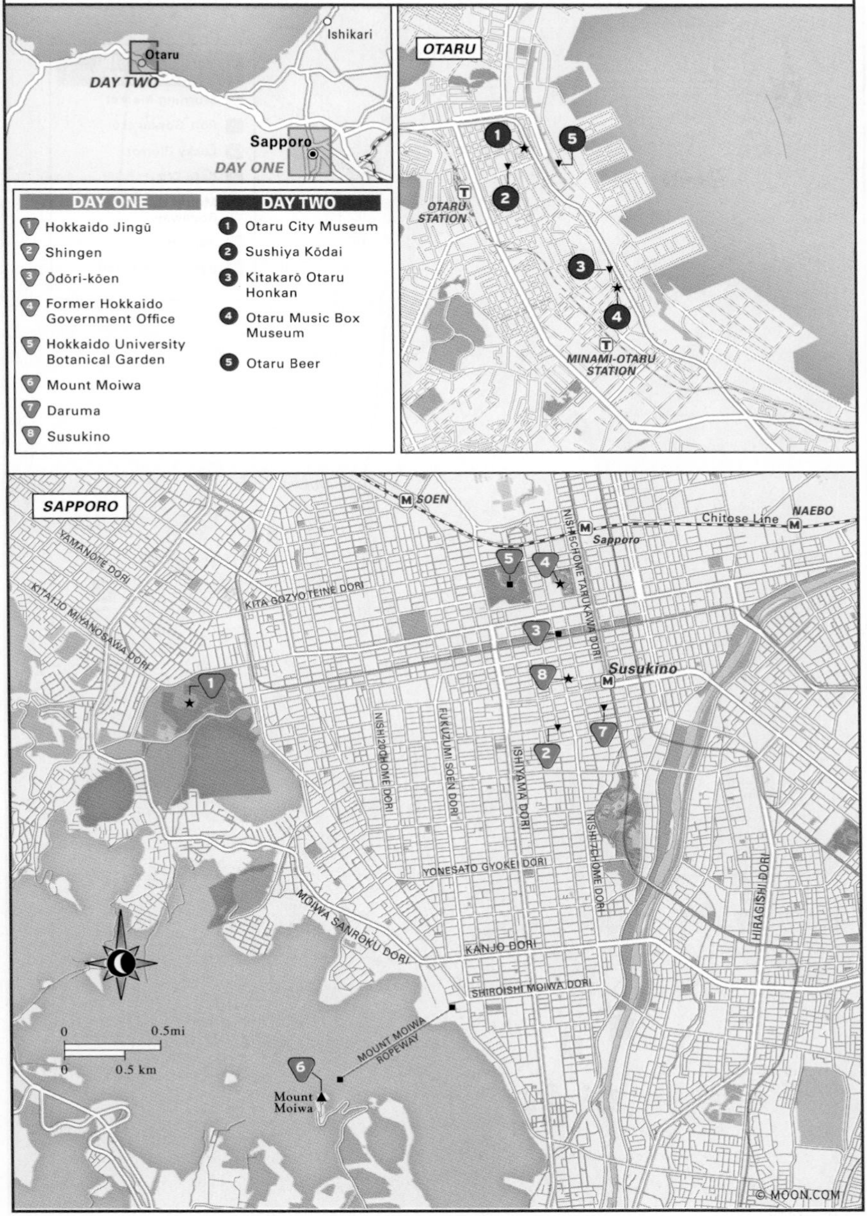

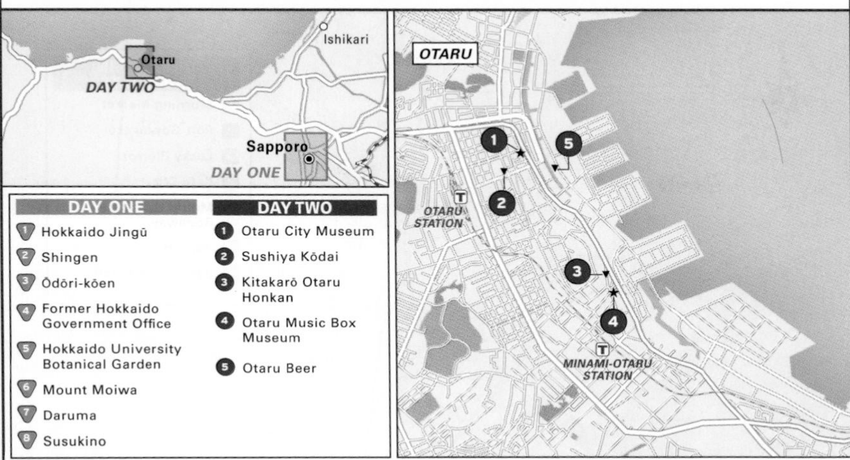

Ishikari
Otaru
DAY TWO
Sapporo
DAY ONE
DAY ONE
1 Hokkaido Jingū
2 Shingen
3 Ōdōri-kōen
4 Former Hokkaido Government Office
5 Hokkaido University Botanical Garden
6 Mount Moiwa
7 Daruma
8 Susukino
DAY TWO
1 Otaru City Museum
2 Sushiya Kōdai
3 Kitakarō Otaru Honkan
4 Otaru Music Box Museum
5 Otaru Beer
OTARU
OTARU STATION
MINAMI-OTARU STATION
SAPPORO
SOEN
NAEBO
Chitose Line
Sapporo
Susukino
YAMANOTE DORI
KITA1JO MIYANOSAWA DORI
KITA GOZYO TEINE DORI
NISHI5CHOME TARUKAWA DORI
NISHI20CHOME DORI
FUKUZUMI SOEN DORI
ISHIYAMA DORI
NISHI7CHOME DORI
YONESATO GYOKEI DORI
MOIWA SANROKU DORI
KANJO DORI
SHIROISHI MOIWA DORI
HIRAGISHI DORI
MOUNT MOIWA ROPEWAY
Mount Moiwa
0
0.5mi
0
0.5 km
© MOON.COM

One Day in Hakodate

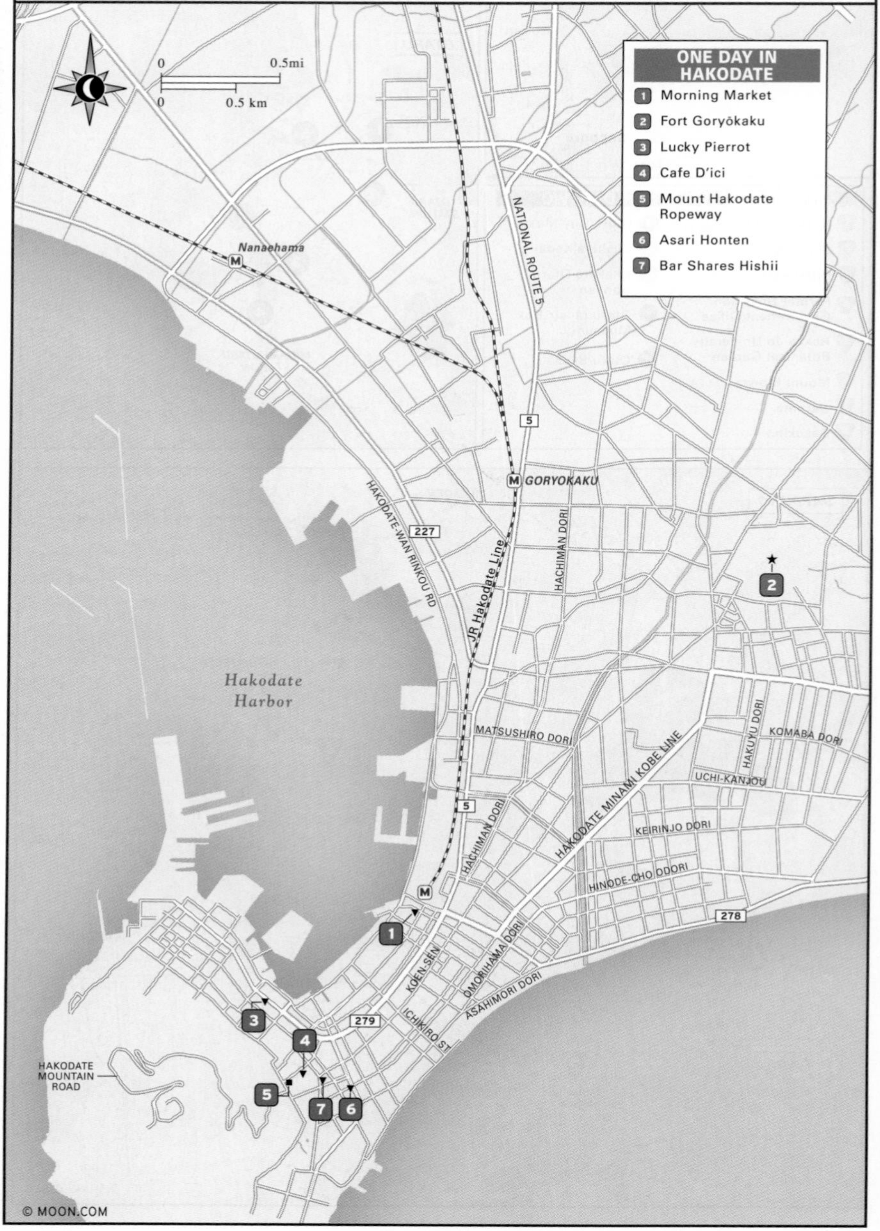

ONE DAY IN HAKODATE

1. Morning Market
2. Fort Goryōkaku
3. Lucky Pierrot
4. Cafe D'ici
5. Mount Hakodate Ropeway
6. Asari Honten
7. Bar Shares Hishii

0 0.5mi
0 0.5 km

Nanaehama
NATIONAL ROUTE 5
5
GORYOKAKU
HAKODATE-WAN RINKOU RD
227
JR Hakodate Line
HACHIMAN DORI
Hakodate Harbor
MATSUSHIRO DORI
HAKUYU DORI
KOMABA DORI
UCHI-KANJOU
HAKODATE MINAMI KOBE LINE
KEIRINJO DORI
HACHIMAN DORI
HINODE-CHO ODORI
278
KOEN-SEN
OMORIHAMA DORI
ASAHIMORI DORI
279
ICHIKIRO ST
HAKODATE MOUNTAIN ROAD

4 After fueling up, walk about 10 minutes south to the nearby historic district of Motomachi, spread across the foot of Mount Hakodate, its hilly streets lined with well-preserved 19th-century architecture. Make a pit stop at **Cafe D'ici** for some great coffee and cakes.

5 Before the sun sets, make your way to the **Mount Hakodate Ropeway,** just a few minutes' walk from Cafe D'ici. Ride to the top and wait for the city's lights to flicker on; this is widely considered one of Japan's most beautiful nighttime views.

6 For dinner, try yakiniku (Korean barbecue) at **Asari Honten,** which sits near the foot of Mount Hakodate.

7 After dinner, grab a few drinks at **Bar Shares Hishii,** less than 5 minutes west of Asari Honten.

Sapporo 札幌

The capital of Hokkaido and Japan's fifth-largest metropolis, Sapporo is the gateway to Japan's vast northern wilderness and a lively city in its own right. One thing that distinguishes this northern hub is its relative youth. As recently as 1857, a meager seven adventurous souls populated the place.

This all changed when the Meiji period (1868-1912) government hired a group of Americans to advise on the best way to develop this new frontier town. The legacy of this request for Western expertise can be seen in its abundance of green spaces, and at the street level, with the city's thoroughfares laid out in a classic grid pattern, in contrast to the zigzagging streets of old castle towns or more chaotic Tokyo.

Sapporo became a household name when it hosted the 1972 Winter Olympics, but it's also known for its snow festival. Attracting some 2 million visitors every February, the city creates impressively sculpted works of art in ice and snow—some of them the size of buildings. The climate has also played a significant role in the development of Sapporo's culinary heritage, mostly comprising hearty dishes such as heavy miso-based ramen, the local invention of soup curry, and "Genghis Khan" grilled lamb and seafood. And, of course, there's Sapporo beer. You'll find lots of it in sprawling Susukino, the country's largest nightlife district north of Tokyo.

Whether you make an overnight stop on your way to Hokkaido's pristine backcountry or explore the city on its own, plan to spend a day or two enjoying Sapporo's varied offerings.

ORIENTATION

Sapporo is the easiest city to navigate in Japan, thanks to its grid layout and numbered blocks. **Ōdōri-kōen,** which separates the city roughly into **northern** and **southern** halves, is the point from which every address is numbered. For example, the Old Hokkaido Government Office is located at "3 Kita 6 jō Nishi," with "Kita" being north and "jō Nishi" being "block 6." This means it is located three blocks north and six blocks west from the eastern edge of Ōdōri-kōen.

With this general note about addresses in mind, in simple terms, **Sapporo Station** is at the north end of downtown; Ōdōri-kōen, which runs east-west, is about 10 minutes' walk south of there; and the rambling nightlife zone of **Susukino** begins around a 10-minute walk south of Ōdōri-kōen. A handful of sites are scattered around the outskirts of town, such as **Mount Moiwa** in the southwest corner of town and **Moerenuma Park** northeast of downtown.

Sapporo

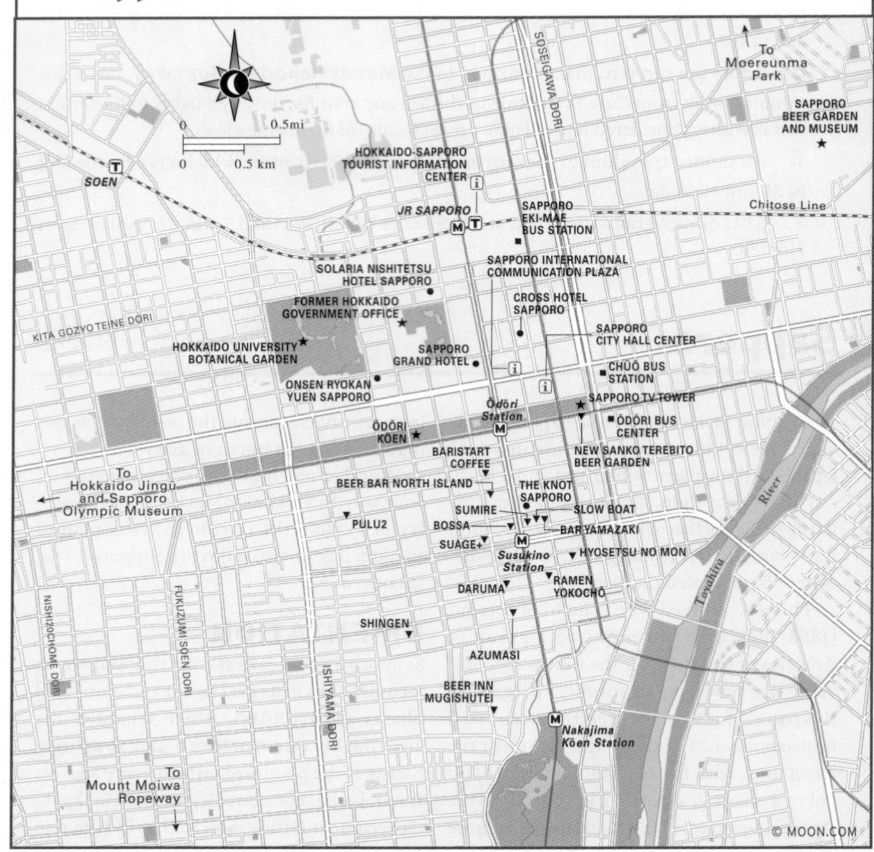

SIGHTS

Ōdōri-kōen and Around

大通公園

This stretch of centrally located green is a good place to orient yourself in Sapporo. Well-groomed lawns, benches, flowers, and fountains create a bubble of calm in the middle of downtown. Dividing the city into north and south, the park is a block wide and runs east to west for 1.5 kilometers (1 mi), spanning 13 blocks. In summer, it's a pleasant place to rendezvous or have a picnic; in winter, it's the primary site of the famed Sapporo Snow Festival.

SAPPORO TV TOWER

さっぽろテレビ塔

Ōdōri-nishi 1-chōme, Chūō-ku; tel. 011/241-1131; www.tv-tower.co.jp; 9am-10pm daily; ¥720 adults, ¥600 high school students, ¥400 junior high school students, ¥300 elementary school students, ¥100 children ages 3-5; take any of Sapporo's 3 subway lines to Ōdōri Station

At the eastern side of the park is Sapporo TV Tower. The hulking red structure rises almost 150 meters (492 feet) above the park below and is similar in appearance, and spirit, to Tokyo Tower, which some consider a blot on the landscape. Aesthetics aside, the tower does offer good views of the cityscape and surrounding mountains from its 90-meter-high (295-ft-high) observation deck. With Sapporo Station to the north and the dining, culinary, and nightlife hub of Susukino to the south, the city radiates from here.

North of Ōdōri-kōen

FORMER HOKKAIDO GOVERNMENT OFFICE

北海道庁

Kita 3 Jō Nishi 6-chōme, Chūō-ku; tel. 011/204-5019; www.pref.hokkaido.lg.jp/fs/2/3/9/5/6/7/8/_/akarengapanhuenglish.pdf; 8:45am-6pm daily; free; take any of Sapporo's 3 subway lines to Sapporo Station, exit 10, or walk 7 minutes north of Ōdōri-kōen

The Former Hokkaido Government Office building is worth a quick stop. Its stunning red-brick edifice is a prime example of the American neo-baroque style popular in the late 19th century; it includes a museum exploring Hokkaido's history.

HOKKAIDO UNIVERSITY BOTANICAL GARDEN

北海道大学植物園

Kita 3 Jō Nishi 8-chōme, Chūō-ku; tel. 011/221-0066; www.hokudai.ac.jp/fsc/bg; 9am-4:30pm Tue.-Sun. Apr. 29-Sept. 30, 9am-4pm Tue.-Sun. Oct. 1-Nov. 3, 10am-3:30pm Mon.-Fri. and 10am-12:30pm Sat. Nov. 4-Apr. 28, last entry 30 minutes before closing; ¥420 ages 16 and older, ¥300 ages 7-15, free for ages 6 and under in summer, ¥120 ages 7 and older, free for ages 6 and under in winter; take JR line to Sapporo Station, west exit (10-minute walk), or take Tōzai subway line to Nishi-Juitchome Station, exit 4 (7-minute walk)

Just west of the Former Hokkaido Government Office, the Hokkaido University Botanical Garden offers a 14-hectare (34-acre) leafy escape from the city with a network of hiking trails that weave through the remnants of the forest that once blanketed the wild plain that Sapporo now occupies. It's pleasantly devoid of crowds on most weekdays. This is a great place for a relaxing yet informative amble.

Sapporo Outskirts

HOKKAIDO JINGŪ

北海道神宮

474 Miyagaoka, Chūō-ku; tel. 011/611-0261; www.hokkaidojingu.or.jp; open 24/7; free; take Tōzai subway line to Maruyama-kōen Station, exit 3

Japanese religion crept onto the island relatively recently. Hokkaido Jingū, found in a heavily wooded area within the city limits, about 4 kilometers (2.5 mi) west of the city center, is one of the most prominent shrines in the prefecture. Feel the noise of the city fade as you walk deeper into the sylvan space. The cobblestone paths, dragon-shaped water spouts, imperial insignia, and hefty timber beams comprising the handsome inner sanctum may look stately and old. But compared with similar structures to the south, in the Shinto heartlands, this shrine is young, having been built in only 1869.

SAPPORO OLYMPIC MUSEUM

札幌オリンピックミュージアム

1274 Miyano-mori, Chūō-ku; tel. 011/641-8585; https://sapporo-olympicmuseum.jp; 9am-6pm (last entry 5:30pm) daily May-Oct., 9:30am-5pm (last entry 4:30pm) daily Nov.-Apr.; ¥600 high school students and older, free for junior high school students and younger; take Tōzai line to Maruyama-kōen Station, exit 2; then take bus no. 14 (twice hourly) to Ōkurayama-kyōgijō-iriguchi bus stop and walk 2 minutes northwest to the stadium on the hill

With a rundown of Japan's triumphs in winter Olympic history, the Sapporo Winter Sports Museum turns out to be surprisingly fun. Housed west of downtown in the stadium where the ski jump competition was held during the 1972 Winter Olympics, this highly interactive, slightly zany museum allows you to simulate an Olympic ski jump on screen. After testing your skills on the computerized slopes, pay an additional fee to ride the adjacent **Okurayama Observation Lounge Lift** (https://okurayama-jump.jp/en/; 8:30am-9pm, last entry 8:45pm, daily Apr. 29-Oct., 9am-5pm, last entry 4:45pm, daily Nov.-Apr. 28; round-trip ¥1,000 age 13 and older,

1

2

3

¥500 elementary school students and younger, round-trip and museum combination ticket ¥1,200 high school students and older) to the top of the jump where Olympians really did risk life and limb while the world watched. This museum is roughly 2.5 kilometers (1.6 mi) west of Hokkaido Jingū and 6 kilometers (3.7 mi) west of downtown.

Mount Moiwa Ropeway
藻岩山ロープウェイ

5-3-7 Fushimi, Chūō-ku; tel. 011/561-8177; https://mt-moiwa.jp; 10:30am-10pm (last entry 9:30pm) daily Apr.-Nov., 11am-10pm (last entry 9:30pm) daily Dec.-Mar.; round-trip for ropeway and cable car ¥1,800 adults, ¥900 age 12 and younger, round-trip for ropeway only ¥1,200 adults, ¥600 age 12 and younger, round-trip for mini cable car only ¥600 adults, ¥300 age 12 and younger; from Susukino, take the streetcar to Ropeway Iriguchi station (25 minutes), then walk 5 minutes to the Mount Moiwa Ropeway

The Sapporo TV Tower may provide a good vista of Sapporo's downtown from up close, but for a more sweeping glimpse of the cityscape, head to Mount Moiwa at the southwestern corner of town. Ride the Mount Moiwa Ropeway over the gentle verdant slope of this mountain within the metropolis. The ropeway transports you three-quarters of the way up, where you transfer to a miniature cable car that takes you to an observation deck with stunning views of the city, particularly at dusk when the lights flicker.

Sapporo Beer Garden and Museum
サッポロビール博物館

Kita 7 Jō Higashi, 9-1-1, Higashi-ku; tel. 011/748-1876; www.sapporobeer.jp/brewery/s_museum/; museum 11am-6pm Tue.-Sun., closed Tue. if Mon. is holiday; free entry; take Tōhō subway line to Higashi-Kuyakusho-mae station exit 4, then walk 10 minutes south

Sapporo is synonymous with beer. See where this association all began at the Sapporo Beer Garden and Museum, located east of Sapporo Station, or about 2 kilometers (1.2 mi) northeast of the city center, in a historic brick building with ivy creeping up its sides. The museum depicts the beer-making process and the history of Sapporo beer's rise within the country's brewed ranks. A free one-hour tour—English-language headsets available—caps off with a reasonably priced tasting, a few hundred yen per beer. The **beer garden** next to the museum has four restaurants. Opt for the classic: "Genghis Khan" grilled lamb, washed down with the hometown tipple.

1: Hokkaido Jingū 2: flight at the Sapporo Beer Garden and Museum 3: Sapporo Beer Garden and Museum

Moerenuma Park
モエレ沼公園

1-1 Moerenuma-kōen, Higashi-ku; tel. 011/790-1231; http://moerenumapark.jp; 7am-10pm (last entry 9pm) daily; free; take Tōhō subway line to Kanjodōri-higashi Station, then local bus number 69 or 79 to the Moernuma Kōen Higashi-guchi bus stop (the only park exit open year-round) (25 minutes, ¥210, 2 buses hourly)

Moerenuma Park is on the outskirts of town, but if you've got time it's worth the trip. Roughly 5 kilometers (3 miles) around, the park's wide open green spaces are dotted by hulking geometric sculptures imagined by the brilliant late Japanese-American sculptor, artist, and landscape architect Isamu Noguchi. The Sapporo government asked Noguchi to dream up a park on the grounds, which were formerly a landfill. Strolling through the park is like stepping into Noguchi's mindscape. Noguchi died in 1988 before the park could be completed, but his vision was still actualized and the park opened in 2005.

FESTIVALS

★ SAPPORO SNOW FESTIVAL
さっぽろ雪まつり

www.snowfes.com; early Feb.; free

During the Sapporo Snow Festival, intricate, sometimes towering sculptures made from snow and ice populate Sapporo's Ōdōri-kōen, the streets of Susukino, and Tsudome (885-1 Sakae-machi, Higashi-ku; tel. 011/784-2106;

www.sapporo-sport.jp/tsudome; 10am-8pm Mon.-Sat., 8:30am-9pm Sun.), a large event space on the outskirts of the city. Teams from around the globe come to try their hands at creating elemental effigies of characters and entities ranging from outsized anime characters and fish to dragons and mermaids. If you show up during the first week of the festival, before the Susukino and Ōdōri-kōen sites open, you can watch artists dressed like construction workers wield industrial-grade saws, hammers, and chisels, which they use to chip away ice and hammer out minute details in nimbly poised mermaids and skulking tigers.

Pop idols perform for massive crowds on stages made of piled-up snow. Vendors sell roast corn, potatoes drenched in butter, sausages, beer, and hot cocoa, as well as a sampling of regional specialties from around Japan. Crowds gleefully mill about the city or sit under large outdoor heaters, contentedly nursing hot wine in routinely below-freezing temperatures. Snowboarders do competitive jumps from a massive snow ramp built in the center of Ōdōri-kōen. There are snow slides with rentable sleds and small ice skating rinks too. Given the large crowds—a few million come each year—nightlife gets rowdy, which is a good or bad thing depending on your perspective.

Given the festival's wild popularity, it's wise to book accommodations at least three or more months in advance.

FOOD

The majority of restaurants in Sapporo recommended here are concentrated south of Ōdōri-kōen.

Ramen

RAMEN YOKOCHŌ

Minami 5 Jō Nishi 3-6, Chūō-ku; www.ganso-yokocho.com; 11am-3am (hours vary by store); ¥1,000; take Nanboku subway line to Susukino Station, exit 5

In a city as obsessed with ramen as Sapporo, it's hard to know where to begin. For an introduction, make your way to Ramen Yokochō. This narrow, covered alleyway is brimming with options, from noodles tossed in a heavy miso-based soup to lighter salt-based broths. It's hard to go wrong with any shop here. If photos don't pull you into a particular one, just opt for one with a healthy number of customers and step in. When searching for the alley, look for the sign over the entrance emblazoned with red and green neon Japanese characters.

SUMIRE

Pixis Bldg. 2F, Minami 3 Jō Nishi 3-9-2, Chūō-ku; tel. 011/200-4567; www.sumireya.com; 5pm-1am Mon.-Sat., 5pm-midnight Sun.; ¥1,000; take Nanboku subway line to Susukino Station, exit 5

A great stand-alone ramen shop just a few blocks north (4 minutes' walk) from Ramen Yokochō, this second-floor shop feels slightly more spruced up inside than the old-school shops of Ramen Yokochō. Along with your noodles, expect perfectly boiled eggs and thick strips of pork floating in an incredibly fragrant soup. It's a great choice after a night out drinking in Susukino. Be forewarned that the soup is quite salty—calling it rich is an understatement.

★ SHINGEN

Minami 6 Jō Nishi 8-8-2, Chūō-ku; tel. 011/530-5002; 11am-midnight daily; ¥1,000; take Nanboku subway line to Susukino Station, exit 5

An excellent ramen joint in the Susukino area frequented by locals is Shingen. Around a dozen seats line the countertop at this greasy spoon, which is a wonderful place to get a real taste of Sapporo. Shingen excels in delivering rich creamy soup that manages to retain subtle flavors without being overwhelmed by salt or oil—a tricky balance for miso ramen. The waits here can be a little daunting at peak times; try to come mid-afternoon or late at night. If there's a queue, don't fret too much. It tends to move quickly.

Soup Curry

PULU2

B1F Kentaku Bldg. 29, Minami 2 Jō Nishi 9-chōme, Chūō-ku; tel. 011/272-1190; http://www5d.biglobe.ne.jp/~pulu2-cr/; 11am-8pm Mon.-Sat.; ¥1,000; take Tōzai subway line to Nishi Juitchome Station, exit 2

If you want your soup curry with a side of reggae, head for Pulu2. Set in a basement with reggae piped through a solid sound system, Jamaican flags and Peter Tosh posters adorn the walls, while in the open kitchen the master and owner can be seen at work whipping up a mean curry. Dishes have large chunks of vegetables, chicken, or lamb, and spiciness levels range from 0 to 100. After eating a 20, I shudder to think what anything above 50 would taste like. It's a little out of the way, but is well off the tourist trail.

★ SUAGE+

2F Miyako Shimatsu Bldg., Minami 4 Jō Nishi 5-chōme, Chūō-ku; tel. 011/233-2911; https://suage.info/ja/; 11:30am-10:30pm (last order 9:30pm) daily; ¥1,200; take Nanboku subway line to Susukino Station, exit 5

Along with ramen, soup curry, served with a side of rice, is another classic Sapporo dish. Suage+ is a popular spot with an interior reminiscent of a wine bar more than a soup curry shop. In Susukino, the shop uses great ingredients such as huge maitake mushrooms, chicken, and lavender pork. You can choose your spice level. Try cheese as a topping for your rice.

Genghis Khan

NEW SANKO TEREBITO BEER GARDEN

Ōdōri-nishi 1-chōme, Chūō-ku; tel. 011/252-1800; https://sapporoclassic-beergarden.gorp.jp; noon-9:30pm (last order 9pm) daily; ¥1,800; take any of Sapporo's 3 subway lines to Ōdōri Station

If your goal is to eat delicious, reasonably priced Genghis Khan and swill beer on tap like the locals, this no-frills open-air spot, also known simply as Sapporo Classic Beer Garden, is a great pick. Ensconced directly under Sapporo TV Tower, with seating for up to 500, the atmosphere can get buzzing on weekends. With occasional musical performances, it's a fun place to make new friends too. An English menu is available.

★ DARUMA

Minami 5 Jō Nishi 4-chōme, Chūō-ku; tel. 011/552-6013; https://sapporo-jingisukan.info/main/; 5pm-3am daily; ¥4,000; take Nanboku subway line to Susukino Station, exit 5

Although slightly touristy and crowded, Daruma is the quintessential Genghis Khan (Mongolian barbecue) restaurant. Thin cuts of lamb and copious onions sizzle and splatter from atop the dome-shaped skillets arrayed around the counter, where about 15 diners sit enveloped in cooking smoke. A small menu of side items includes kimchi, seaweed, and rice.

Seafood

AZUMASI

Minami 6 Jō Nishi 4-4-1, Chūō-ku; tel. 011/513-7800; https://azumasi.owst.jp; 5pm-9pm (last order 8:25pm) Sun.-Thurs., 5pm-1am (last order 12:30am) Fri.-Sat.; ¥3,000; take Nanboku subway line to Susukino Station, exit 5

Azumasi is a cozy oyster bar with a trendy interior with both counter and floor seating. Friendly owners and stylish patrons help make this a good place for oysters and sake in the heart of Susukino.

HYOSETSU NO MON

Minami 5 Jō Nishi 2-chōme, Chūō-ku; tel. 011/521-3046; www.hyousetsu.co.jp.e.em.hp.transer.com; 11am-11pm daily; ¥3,000 lunch, ¥8,000 dinner; take Nanboku subway line to Susukino Station, exit 5

Hyosetsu no Mon is a fantastic choice for sampling some excellent Hokkaido crab. Established in 1964, the shop serves a wide range of crab dishes: sashimi, sushi, tempura, chawanmushi (savory egg custard), and more. Try the king crab shabu shabu (hot pot), packed with vegetables. As the pot boils, the broth is infused with rich flavors of the meat.

1
2
3
4
docomo
Asahi
生
SUPER
"DRY"
アイフル
docomo
マルハン
すすきのビル
Coca-Cola
NIKKA

Café

BARISTART COFFEE

Minami 1 Jō Nishi 4-8, Chūō-ku; tel. 011/215-1775; www.baristartcoffee.com; 10am-5pm daily; ¥500; take Tōzai or Nanboku subway line to Ōdōri Station, exit 2

The artistes at Baristart Coffee not only make great artisan brew, they use incredibly rich milk sourced from Hokkaido farms in all of their dairy-infused options. Try their excellent latte.

★ BARS AND NIGHTLIFE

As if Sapporo's deep connection with beer brewing wasn't already enough party cred, its **Susukino** district is the nation's largest nightlife zone north of Tokyo. All told, some 4,000 bars, dance clubs, jazz joints, and host and hostess clubs vie for the attention of sometimes raucous clientele. Aside from a copious amount of beer on tap, there are also world-class cocktail lounges and a handful of underground clubs with top-notch sound systems. The center of Susukino is about 0.6 km (0.4 mi) south of Ōdōri-kōen. The nexus of the area is Susukino Crossing, from where the district spreads outward for many blocks in all directions.

Beer Bars

BEER BAR NORTH ISLAND

Large Country Bldg. 10F, Nishi 4-chōme, Minami 2 jo, Chūō-ku; tel. 011/251-8820; https://northislandbeer.jp/beeabar/; 5:30pm-11:30pm Mon.-Sat., 3pm-10pm Sun. and holidays, open until 11:30pm on days before public holidays; take tram to Tanuki-koji tram stop, then walk 2 minutes west, or take Namboku subway line to Susukino Station, exit 2, then walk 6 minutes northwest

A good place to start a night out in Sapporo, this cozy brewpub is tucked away on the tenth floor of a building. With exposed brick, wooden tables, and great views of the cityscape below, the bar has a nice selection of locally brewed IPAs, stouts, and more on tap. You can pair your suds with a menu of good, simple grub.

BEER INN MUGISHUTEI

Minami 9 Jō Nishi 5-chōme, Chūō-ku; tel. 011/512-4774; http://www.ezo-beer.com/mugishutei.htm; 7pm-3am daily; take Nanboku subway line to Nakajima Kōen Station, exit 2

If your idea of a good night is drinking your way through as many obscure varieties of beer as you can in a mellow setting, Beer Inn Mugishutei just might blow your mind. Located in a quiet corner of southern Susukino, this underground beer mecca offers more than 300 types of beer from all around the globe. Rows upon rows of vintage cans line the walls. The atmosphere is no-frills—darts, foosball, and some old wooden tables. One caveat: There's a ¥900 "charm charge." If this doesn't put you off, you'll be hard-pressed to find another spot offering this many types of beer.

Cocktail Bars

BAR YAMAZAKI

4F Katsumi Bldg., Minami 3 Jō Nishi 3-chōme, Chūō-ku; tel. 011/221-7363; www.bar-yamazaki.com; 6pm-12:30am (last order midnight) Mon.-Sat.; take Nanboku subway line to Susukino Station, exit 1

Bar Yamazaki is a classic cocktail lounge with a famously innovative former master, Tatsuro Yamazaki, who sadly passed in November 2016 at the ripe old age of 96. The bar has an appealing dark wood interior, softly lit by elegant old-fashioned lamps. Plush chairs line the bar and there are comfortable private booths. The menu features some 200 cocktails, among them an array of award-winning original concoctions, including the "Sapporo," which snagged a prize at the Amaretto Di Saronna Cocktail Competition in Italy. The quality cocktails and service do come at a price, however: There's a ¥1,000 seating charge and a 10 percent service charge.

1: Sapporo Snow Festival 2: soup curry at Suage+ 3: Genghis Khan Mongolian barbecue 4: Susukino district at night

Live Music

BOSSA

2F Silver Bldg., Minami 3 Jō Nishi 4-chōme, Chūō-ku; tel. 011/271-5410; www.bossa.tv; 11am-1am; take Nanboku subway line to Susukino Station

For a bar with a classy yet vivacious atmosphere, try Bossa. Café by day and lively bar by night, this excellent jazz joint opened in 1971 and boasts a seriously good sound system. The owner has some 9,000 vinyl records and 6,000 CDs. Posters of jazz greats adorn the walls, and potted plants give the all-wood interior a relaxed, cozy vibe. Customers chat and laugh freely with an excellent jazz soundtrack. Check out the "Milky Way" section of the menu, which includes a number of dairy-based cocktails that use locally sourced milk. There's also an all-you-can-drink option for ¥1,850.

SLOW BOAT

4F Morini Bldg., Minami 3 Jō Nishi 3-chōme 1-4, Chūō-ku; tel. 011/210-5144; www.jazz-slowboat.jp; 7:30pm-1am daily; cover from ¥3,000; take Nanboku subway line to Susukino Station

If you like your jazz jammed live, make your way to Slow Boat, a stone's throw from Bossa. This stalwart of Sapporo's jazz scene is a known quantity among aficionados, but remains off the radar for most. Founded by late jazz pianist Ryo Fukui in 1995, the club is a cozy place to enjoy a broad spectrum of the art, from big-name acts like Barry Harris, who made the pilgrimage numerous times, to talented local amateurs. Two sets are played nightly (8:30pm, 10:30pm), with hours varying for special big-ticket events. Check the schedule before making the trip to be sure you catch the main gig. Note that the club closes on irregular days.

ACCOMMODATIONS

¥10,000-20,000

SOLARIA NISHITETSU HOTEL SAPPORO

Kita 4 Jō Nishi 5-chōme 1-2, Chūō-ku; tel. 011/208-5555; https://nnr-h.com/solaria/sapporo/; ¥11,400 d; take JR lines to Sapporo Station, exit 10

Conveniently located near Sapporo Station, this hotel has spotless modern rooms with Japanese-style accents. Bathrooms are well-appointed and spacious, and the friendly staff speak English. Breakfast, Western or buffet, is available for an additional ¥2,300. There's also a bar and spa on site.

THE KNOT SAPPORO

Minami 3 Jō Nishi 3-chōme 16-2, Chūō-ku; tel. 011/200-5545; https://hotel-the-knot.jp/sapporo/en/; ¥12,400 d; take Nanboku subway line to Susukino Statio, exit 1

In the center of things near Ōdōri-kōen, this new property has reasonably priced, bright, and comfortable (if somewhat petite) rooms, with minimalist design and amply appointed bathrooms. There's a French restaurant and bar on-site, and Japanese-style breakfast made with seasonal ingredients is available for an extra ¥2,500. The helpful staff speak English.

CROSS HOTEL SAPPORO

Kita 2 Jō Nishi 2-23, Chūō-ku; tel. 011/272-0010; www.crosshotel.com/sapporo/; ¥15,000 d; take JR lines to Sapporo Station

The Cross Hotel Sapporo is a great hotel in an excellent location that offers a lot for its price tag. The clean, modern rooms are furnished with a designer's touch—with choices of natural, urban, and hip decor—and are generously sized. There's a large public bath on the top floor with great views of the city below. A filling set meal is provided at breakfast. The friendly staff speak English.

¥20,000-40,000

ONSEN RYOKAN YUEN SAPPORO

Kita 1 Jō Nishi 7-chōme 6, Chūō-ku; tel. 011/271-1126; www.uds-hotels.com/yuen/sapporo/; ¥20,900 d; take JR lines to Sapporo Station

On a corner near Hokkaido University Botanical Garden, this chic property has stylish, comfortable rooms with modern Japanese aesthetics—tatami floors, futons, and low-standing tables with floor cushions. Besides well-appointed en suite baths, there's a hot spring and sauna on-site free for guests to use. Japanese-style breakfast is available for an extra ¥2,200.

SAPPORO GRAND HOTEL

Kita 5 Jō Nishi 2-5, Chūō-ku; tel. 011/251-2222; www.jrhotels.co.jp/tower/english; ¥34,000 d; take JR lines to Sapporo Station

The Sapporo Grand Hotel has been welcoming guests since 1934; it was the city's first European-style hotel. Today, attendants in white gloves and attentive staff make all guests feel as if they're visiting dignitaries. There are swanky bars and a range of restaurant options, and smart, understated elegance infuses the rooms. If you've got a little extra to spend, this is a great choice.

INFORMATION AND SERVICES

- **Hokkaido-Sapporo Tourist Information Center** (JR Sapporo West Concourse, Kita 6 jō Nishi 4, Kita-ku; tel. 011/213-5088; www.sapporo.travel/info/about/tourist-information-center/; 10am-5:30pm daily)
- **Sapporo International Communication Plaza** (3F MN Building, Kita 1 jō Nishi 3, Chūō-ku; tel. 011/211-3670; www.plaza-sapporo.or.jp; 9am-5:30pm Mon.-Fri.)
- **Sapporo City Call Center** (tel. 011/222-4894; 8am-9pm daily)

GETTING THERE

Air

There are dozens of flights daily to and from Tokyo and Sapporo. Both major Japanese carriers and smaller budget airlines cover the route between Haneda Airport and Narita Airport in Tokyo, and Sapporo's **New Chitose Airport** (www.new-chitose-airpot.jp). You can also fly to Sapporo from Nagoya, Osaka, and Hiroshima, among others. The journey takes about an hour and a half from Tokyo, with one-way flights ranging from less than ¥10,000 to upwards of ¥40,000.

Rapid trains run regularly to Sapporo from New Chitose Airport (30 minutes; ¥1,500). There's a second airport in the city, **Okadama,** but flights to this smaller hub are limited. From there, you can reach downtown via a **shuttle bus** that runs between the airport and **Sakaemachi** subway station (5 minutes; ¥210), from which the rest of the city is within easy reach.

Cross Hotel Sapporo

Train

It's also possible to take the train to Sapporo from Tokyo. Board the **Tohoku/Hokkaido** shinkansen in Tokyo and ride until Shin-Hakodate-Hokuto (6 hours; ¥23,630). From there, transfer to the **Hokuto limited express train** to Sapporo (3.5 hours; ¥9,440). Although hardly economical or efficient, this journey can still make sense if you have a JR Pass, which covers the whole trip. It also makes sense if you're traveling through Tohoku en route to Hokkaido. Note that a seat reservation is required for the Hayabusa shinkansen running from Tokyo to Shin-Hakodate-Hokuto. **JR Sapporo Station,** the city's shinkansen hub, is located in the northern part of downtown, 0.6 kilometers (0.4 mi) north of Ōdōri-kōen and 1.2 kilometers (0.8 mi) north of Susukino.

Bus

If you're coming to Sapporo from within Hokkaido, chances are there's a bus route that will work just as well as taking a train. There are a number of expressway bus operators on the island, running routes to Sapporo's main bus hubs: **Sapporo Ekimae Bus Station,** the busiest terminal in the city near JR Sapporo Station; **Chūō Bus Station,** northeast of Sapporo TV Tower; and to the southeast of Sapporo TV Tower, **Ōdōri Bus Center.** Some of the destinations in Hokkaido with bus routes linking to Sapporo include **Niseko** (3 hours; ¥2,650), **Noboribetsu Onsen** (2 hours; ¥2,420), **Tōya-ko Onsen** (3 hours; ¥2,830), **Furano** (2.5-3 hours; ¥2,500), **Asahikawa** (2 hours; ¥2,480), and **Wakkanai** (6 hours; ¥6,200).

GETTING AROUND

Thanks to its grid layout and numbered blocks, Sapporo is very easy to navigate. The city's address system is based on where places are in relation to the eastern edge of Ōdōri-kōen, numbered by city block. As an example, Ramen Yokochō's address (Minami 5 Jō Nishi 3-6, Chūō-ku) breaks down to mean 5 blocks south (Minami) from the eastern edge of Ōdōri-kōen park and 3 blocks west (Nishi) from the eastern border of the park. The other aspects of the address (-6, Chūō-ku) indicate the specific place within that given block (-6) and the fact that this part of the city is the Central (Chūō) Ward.

There's a trusty **subway** system with three lines (from ¥210), buses run by **JR Hokkaido Bus** (covered by the JR Pass) and a few other operators not covered by the pass, a **tram** that does a loop around the Ōdōri-kōen area and Susukino in the south (¥200 fare for all destinations; enter from the rear of the tram and pay upon leaving through the front), and of course, **taxis,** which are similar to Tokyo in price, although fares vary based on the size of the vehicle and the operator. Typically, taxis start around ¥670, plus ¥265 for each additional kilometer.

When getting around the core of downtown, between roughly Ōdōri-kōen and Susukino, you will likely enjoy traveling on foot. Hopping on the subway, tram, or a local bus makes sense when heading north to the Sapporo Station area, out west to Hokkaido Jingū, Mount Moiwa, and around, or to points farther out like Moerenuma Park.

Public transport around the island leaves a bit to be desired the more remote you go. If you plan to venture far beyond civilization but start your journey in Sapporo, consider renting a car. **Toyota Rent-a-Car** (Kita 5 Jō Higashi 1-2-4, Chūō-ku; tel. 011/281-0100; https://rent.toyota.co.jp/; 8am-8pm daily), **Times Car Rental** (Kita 4 Jō Nishi 6-3-4, Chūō-ku; tel. 011/223-5656; https://rental.timescar.jp/hokkaido/shop/0151/; 8:30am-7pm daily), and **Nippon Rent-a-Car** (Minami 1 Jō Nishi 10-4-165; Chūō-ku; tel. 011/233-0919; www.nipponrentacar.co.jp; 8am-8pm daily) are good options.

Transportation Passes

There are a variety of one-day transportation passes for traversing the city. The **subway card,** which allows unlimited use of the city's three subway lines for one calendar day (¥830 adults, ¥420 children), can be purchased at ticket machines. The **Sapica IC card,** also purchased at ticket machines in subway stations, allows you to top it up and use it interchangeably on the subway, and on some (but not all) city buses and trams. It's unique in that each swipe allows you to gain 10 percent points that are applied toward future trips. Note that this card cannot be used beyond the Sapporo area. To travel further, you'll need a **Kitaca card.** To read more on all the various passes and on transportation in the Sapporo region, see www.sapporo.travel/learn/transportation/sapporo.

Around Sapporo

OTARU
小樽

Otaru is a town on the ocean with a picturesque harbor, nostalgic pockets of history, and loads of charm. Located 30-45 minutes west of Sapporo by train, the former herring center makes for a great day trip or a worthwhile stop between Niseko and Sapporo. Old-fashioned lanterns line its streets, with chic new restaurants, bars, cafés, and shops selling beautifully blown glassware set in stately brick buildings and ivy-covered warehouses.

Otaru's history is deeply associated with fishing, as seen in the cluster of large warehouses along its scenic canal, and in its old herring mansions where the city's rich fishing merchants once lived and worked. It's no surprise that the town's port was the terminus of Hokkaido's first railway, linking it to Sapporo. Its mercantile history is also displayed in the elegant brick façades gracing old structures around Nichigin-dōri, dubbed "Wall Street of the North" in its heyday from the late Taisho to early Showa periods (1920s-1930s).

Otaru Station is at the western edge of downtown, while the town's romantic **canal** is to the east of there, about 10 minutes' walk down the main thoroughfare of **Chūō-dōri.** Most sights and restaurants are found between the station and canal district.

Sights

OTARU CANAL
小樽運河

Along this famed stretch of water, lined by gas streetlamps, you'll find a row of alluring stone warehouses where a number of companies once did brisk business in shipping and trade. Finished in 1923, the canal fell into disuse when the city upgraded its docks so that ships could directly unload their cargo. In the 1970s, citizens turned the much-romanticized waterway into a road. Thankfully, the canal was saved. Since then, beer halls, eateries, dessert shops, and museums have opened in these charming buildings, evocative reminders of Otaru's past.

OTARU CITY MUSEUM
小樽市総合博物館

2-1-20 Iornai; tel. 0134/22-1258; 9:30am-5pm Wed.-Mon.; ¥400; from JR Otaru Station, walk 10 minutes down Chūō-dōri

Next to the canal is the Otaru City Museum, set in a renovated late-19th-century warehouse. This museum explores the natural and cultural history of Hokkaido and Otaru: the crucial role that herring fishing once played for the town, Ainu artifacts, and literary depictions of the city. An English-language guide is available at the front desk. There is another branch of this museum, highlighting the city's railways, but it's a bit out of the way.

NICHIGIN-DŌRI
日銀道り

From JR Otaru Station, walk 10 minutes

As you walk southeast along Otaru Canal, turn right on Nichigin-dōri, once known as northern Japan's Wall Street. Otaru was also a financial hub in its prime. The graceful facades of many buildings along the street recall that legacy, but none more so than the brick architectural gem that once housed Otaru's original branch of the **Bank of Japan** (1-11-16 Ironai; tel. 0134/21-1111; 9:30am-5pm Thurs.-Tues. Apr.-Nov., 10am-5pm Thurs.-Tues. Dec.-Mar.; free).

Built in 1912, the impressive office block also features owl cornerstones, a nod to Ainu tradition, which considers the bird a divine guardian. Inside, you'll find a free museum that explores Otaru's history as a crucial financial node.

MUSIC BOX MUSEUM
小樽オルゴール堂本館

4-1 Sumiyoshi-chō; tel. 0134/21-3101; www.otaru-orgel.co.jp; 9am-6pm daily; free; from JR Minami-Otaru Station, walk 7 minutes, or from the canal it's a 15-minute walk

One more museum worth visiting in Otaru is the Music Box Museum. Located at Marchen Crossroads, a historic intersection reached by walking 15 minutes southeast of the canal along Sakaimachi-dōri, the Music Box Museum is housed in an enchanting stone building, finished in 1912 and fronted by a Victorian-style steam clock, a gift from the city of Vancouver. Inside, you'll be bowled over by thousands of music boxes dating from the Renaissance onward. The museum also has three other locations dotting the area with a whopping 25,000 music boxes on display.

This is a shop as much as a museum. Be prepared to part with some yen if you see a box you like. If you'd like to try your hand at designing one of your own, workshops are offered too.

Festivals

OTARU SNOW LIGHT PATH FESTIVAL
小樽雪あかりの路

Otaru canal, various other locations around town; http://yukiakarinomichi.org; 5pm-9pm daily for 10 days in mid-Feb.; free

Similar to Sapporo, the town has a magic of its own in winter, when candles softly flicker within lanterns made from snow, lining the town's famed canal and tucked into various nooks and crannies around the city. All told, some 100,000 candles are lit in Otaru during this festival. It's an intimate, laid-back alternative to Sapporo's jam-packed snow festival.

★ Food

SANKAKU MARKET

3-10-16 Inaho; tel. 0134/23-2446; http://otaru-sankaku.com/access.html; 8am-5pm daily

historic warehouse on Otaru's canal

While Otaru's herring days may have faded, the city is still renowned for its fresh catch. To see where the town's sushi chefs source ingredients, head to Sankaku Market, located just northeast of JR Otaru Station in a roofed alleyway. You'll find stalls with squid arrayed on ice, massive king crabs in tanks, and salmon roe ready to be placed atop bowls of rice.

OTARU BEER

5-4 Minatomachi; tel. 0134/21-2323; https://otarubeer.com/jp; 11am-11pm daily

While strolling along Otaru's canal, pick the door to Otaru warehouse No. 1, or Otaru Beer Sōko No. 1, the first warehouse you'll come to after approaching the canal from JR Otaru Station via Chūō-dōri, where Otaru Beer is brewed on-site. The founder of this craft beer operation is one of Otaru's few German residents, Braumeister Johannes Braun, who follows the centuries-old German Beer Purity Law, which strictly regulates the ingredients used to brew. Appropriately, the menu also includes a range of German fare, and good pizza too. Smoking is allowed inside, so if you can put up with that, this is a great spot for either pre-dinner drinks or a dinner complemented by this good local craft brew.

KITAKARŌ OTARU HONKAN

7-22 Sakaimachi; tel. 0134/31-3464; www.kitakaro.com/ext/tenpo/otaru.html; 10am-5pm daily; from ¥100

This well-loved sweets shop, set in a historic brick building just south of the canal near the Music Box Museum, will certainly have something to satisfy your sweet tooth. It's best known for its German roll cakes (baumkuchen), beloved across Japan and made with local ingredients, but also sells apple cakes, cream puffs, velvety soft cream, and much more. The seating area is tiny, but everything sold can be comfortably eaten on the go.

KITA NO DONBURI TAKINAMI SHOKUDŌ

3-10-16 Inaho; tel. 0134/23-1426; www2.enekoshop.jp/shop/takinami/; 8am-5pm daily; from ¥2,000

Amid the stalls of Sankaku Market, this eatery stands out, known for its seafood donburi, or rice bowl topped with a generous portion of fresh catch—sea urchin, crab, jumbo shrimp, salmon, roe, and more. Meals come with a wonderful bowl of miso soup liberally infused with crab meat and rice. Grilled fish and more are also served. It's not cheap per se, but compared with seafood spreads at larger fish markets, given the quality and portions, this is a steal. It's a known quantity, so queues do form, but tend to move quickly thanks to ample seating. Look for the white sign with red script over the door, around which the options on the menu are shown in full-color photos.

SUSHIYA KŌDAI

1-4-15 Inaho; tel. 080/6073-6635; 6pm until close Thurs.-Mon.; ¥4,000

A different kind of seafood experience awaits at Sushiya Kōdai. Here, you stand while you eat. The chef here studied under a master at Isezushi, another Otaru sushi mecca. Sushiya Kōdai is down a small alley of 13 restaurants called **Otaru Yataimaura Renga Yokochō,** located 7 minutes' walk from JR Otaru Station. The ikura (salmon roe) is worthy of note.

★ ISEZUSHI

3-15-3 Inaho; tel. 0134/23-1425; www.isezushi.com; 11:30am-3pm (last order 2:30pm) and 5pm-9:30pm (last order 9pm) Thurs.-Tues.; courses from ¥6,500

This renowned sushi spot with a nod from Michelin is at the heart of Otaru's dining scene. The atmosphere is casual, and seating extends to tables, some in private rooms, and along the counter where the master works. English-speaking staff are happy to explain each dish, with an English menu available too. Lunch, served at counter-only seating, is a good value (from ¥2,800), if somewhat briskly paced. At dinner, more elaborate courses are rolled out at a more leisurely pace, and paired with a well-rounded drinks menu. The omakase (chef's choice) course is recommended: 16 seasonally chosen items, from snow crab and

Nikka Whisky Yoichi Distillery

Kurokawa-chō 7-6, Yoichi-chō; tel. 0135/23-3131; www.nikka.com/eng/distilleries/yoichi/; 9am-4pm daily Jan. 8-Dec. 24; from Otaru Station, take JR Hakodate line to Yoichi (26 minutes; ¥440), or from Sapporo, take JR Hakodate to Otaru, then transfer to JR Hakodate line train bound for Kutchan (1 hour 15 minutes; ¥1,290)

In the town of Yoichi, 20 kilometers (12.4 mi) west of Otaru, stands this distillery built in 1934 by Nikka Whisky founder Masataka Taketsuru. The son of a nihonshū brewer in Hiroshima, Taketsuru got his start in whisky-making after apprenticing for two years as a whisky maker in Scotland. Completing his education, he returned home with his Scottish wife Rita (a taboo then), and helped found the country's first whisky brand, Suntory. After 13 years at Suntory, Taketsuru moved with Rita to Japan's far north, where he used the island's cold climate (similar in ways to the Scottish Highlands), golden fields of wheat, fresh air, and pristine water to create Nikka, a whisky brand of international renown today. Visitors to the distillery can do self-guided tours for free (English audio tour available for smartphone download; also includes some English signage), complete with free tasting sample. Tastings of higher-shelf bottles are available for ¥1,000. Japan-language guided tours are also available (reservation required).

sea urchin to snapper, squid, and salmon. In the evening, by reservation only, there's also a full-course feast (¥12,000) with appetizers, sashimi, and various simmered, roasted, and steamed dishes. Whether for lunch or dinner, reservations—three months in advance recommended—are essential.

Information and Services

- **Otaru Station Tourist Information Center** (2-22-15 Inaho; tel. 0134/29-1333; 9am-6pm daily)
- **Canal Plaza Tourist Information Center** (2-1-20 Ironai; 9am-6pm daily; tel. 0134/33-1661)

Getting There

From **Sapporo,** take the **JR Hakodate** (50 minutes; ¥750), departing once hourly. Coming from **Niseko,** the JR Hakodate line also runs to Otaru in just under two hours (¥1,680).

A number of ferries operated by **Shin Nihonkai Ferry** (Otaru terminal; tel. 0134/22-6191; www.snf.jp) run between Otaru and cities on Honshu, including **Akita, Niigata, Tsuruga** (Fukui Prefecture), and **Maizuru** (Kyoto-fu). Check the website for details on route and fares. Reservations must be made between two months and 10 days before embarking.

TOP EXPERIENCE

NISEKO

ニセコ

With an average snowfall of 15 meters (49 feet) annually, just under 50 kilometers (31 mi) of ski runs weaving through 800 hectares (1,977 acres) of powdery terrain, and four interlinked resorts occupying the eastern slopes of Mount Niseko Annupuri, it's no surprise that Niseko is the most high-profile place for powder hounds in Japan. And with snow-capped Fuji look-alike Yotei-zan looming in the foreground, the views from the slopes are spectacularly dramatic.

Another point that sets Niseko apart is that it's the most foreign-friendly of Japan's major resorts. English is readily spoken, menus are easy to navigate, and the shelves at local shops are lined with a bounty of goods from overseas. Moreover, the foreign snowboarders and skiers have developed a community around the mountain, giving Niseko vibrant nightlife and excellent dining options.

Runs include well-groomed courses for beginners and intermediates, as well as off-piste and backcountry runs for the more experienced. It's possible to buy a pass for individual resorts or to access them all. And after a long day on the slopes, there are some 25 onsen in the area to soothe your aching muscles. The area is crowded December-February, but discount hotel rates and less crowded slopes await anyone who comes toward the end of the season in March-April.

★ Skiing

Moving clockwise southward around the mountain, Niseko's four resort areas include:

- **Grand Hirafu** (www.grand-hirafu.jp), by far the biggest and most popular, with extensive food and nightlife options and English readily spoken
- **Niseko Village** (www.niseko-village.com/en/), slightly upscale and the second largest, with a few large resort hotels and some of the steepest runs, but only a smattering of restaurants and bars
- **Niseko Annupuri** (https://annupuri.info), low-key, with less-crowded (and less-steep) runs and only a handful of guesthouses for accommodation
- **Niseko Niseko** (https://hanazononiseko.com/en), an extension of Hirafu on the east side of the mountain.

There is another, fifth resort west of Annupuri called **Moiwa** (https://niseko-moiwa.jp), which is much less crowded because it is not covered by the United Niseko pass. It's an attractive option for beginners, as its runs are much less intense.

Individual resort passes range from around ¥4,000 for a half day to around ¥5,000 for a full day, so shelling out a few thousand yen more for the **Niseko United All Mountain Pass** (www.niseko.ne.jp; 8am-8:30pm daily late-Nov.-early May.; ¥8,100 ages 16 and older, ¥6,500 ages 13-15, ¥4,900 ages 7-12 one-day mid-Dec.-mid-Mar., ¥5,700 ages 16 and older, ¥4,600 ages 13-15, ¥3,500 ages 7-12 one-day late Mar.-early Apr., ¥4,100 ages 16 and older, ¥4,100 ages 13-15, ¥3,500 ages 7-12 early Apr.-early May) is well worth it. This pass, which allows you to access the runs connected to four resorts at the foot of the mountain, can be purchased for a single day or multiple days. It gives you access to 18 lifts and 60 runs, and to shuttle buses between the resorts, which comes in handy, considering they are 5-10 kilometers (3-6 mi) apart.

Equipment rental shops are ubiquitous at all four resorts, as are English-speaking staff; top-notch gear rented at reasonable prices (skis from around ¥4,000 per day, snowboards

Niseko ski village

from around ¥4,500 per day, full equipment, clothing, boots sets from around ¥8,000) is the norm.

Onsen

Onsen options are plentiful in Niseko; many hotels have onsen on their premises, and the list below barely scratches the surface. If you'd like to find a hot-spring bath and your hotel doesn't have one, there are plenty of other options, most of which charge ¥500-1,000 per person. Your hotel's front desk will likely have no shortage of recommendations for a great one nearby.

NISEKO PRINCE HOTEL HIRAFU-TEI

204 Yamada, Kutchan-chō; tel. 0136/23-2239; http://hirafutei.info/hotspring/; 7am-10:30am and 1:30pm-11pm; ¥1,200 adults, ¥600 children ages 4-12

In Hirafu, a good option is the Niseko Prince Hotel Hirafu-tei, a huge complex with gender-separated bathing areas. A selling point is its views of Mount Yotei and Mount Annupuri.

HILTON NISEKO VILLAGE

Abuta-gun, Niseko-chō; tel. 0136/44-1111; https://nisekovillage.hiltonjapan.co.jp/plans/hotspring/143; noon-9pm; ¥1,200 adults, ¥700 children ages 6-12, ¥100 towel rental

In the Niseko Village area, try the Hilton Niseko Village. The facilities here are luxurious and include a stone outdoor tub facing a koi pond, with Mount Yotei gleaming in the distance.

IKOI NO YUYADO IROHA

477 Niseko, Abuta-gun; tel. 0136/58-3111; www.niseko-iroha.com/spa/index.html; 12:30pm-9pm (last entry 8pm); ¥800 adults, ¥400 children ages 6-12, ¥320 towel set

In the Annupuri area, Ikoi no Yuyado Iroha is a good option. The water here is said to be great for the skin.

Accommodations

Niseko is insanely popular. You'll want to book hotels six months or more in advance; even a year in advance is too late for many properties. If all the suggestions below are booked, visit https://book.nisekotourism.com/search?loc=niseko to see what else is still available.

Please also note that staying in Niseko is expensive, and it can be hard to give accurate prices here, as they fluctuate wildly by season. The prices below reflect realistic peak season rates.

NISEKO NORTHERN RESORT ANNUPURI

480-1 Aza Niseko; tel. 0136/58-3311; www.niseko-northern.com; ¥30,000 d

Niseko Northern Resort Annupuri is located on the quieter side of the mountain from Grand Hirafu in Annupuri. There is an indoor and outdoor onsen, a sauna, and even a library stocked with books in both English and Japanese. For both breakfast and dinner, there's an excellent buffet, and for the evenings, a supremely cozy bar with Scandinavian design accents where you can unwind.

HOTEL NISEKO ALPEN

204 Yamada, Kutchan-chō; tel. 0136/22-1105; www.hotel-nisekoalpen.jp/en; ¥40,000 d

Hotel Niseko Alpen is situated conveniently near the lifts for the slopes of Grand Hirafu. You'll find well-appointed, bright Western-style and Japanese-style rooms, an onsen, an indoor pool, and a sumptuous buffet prepared with local ingredients. Bilingual staff are ready to help with anything that may arise during your stay.

HILTON NISEKO VILLAGE

Onsen Higashiyama; tel. 0136/44-1111; www.niseko-village.com/en/stay/hilton-niseko-village.html; ¥40,000 d

The Hilton Niseko Village is another great choice for convenience. The cable car actually emerges from the hotel, which is ski-in, ski-out in the truest sense. There are indoor and outdoor onsen baths, stunning views of Yotei-zan looming in the distance, and excellent buffets for both breakfast and dinner.

★ AYA NISEKO

195-1 Yamada, Kutchan-chō; tel. 0136/23-1280; www.ayaniseko.com; from ¥65,000 for studio apartments

One of Niseki's best-located properties, these private apartments are roomy, stylish (contemporary Japanese aesthetic), and well-appointed (full bath, laundry facilities, etc.). The bilingual staff extend a warm welcome and are ready to help. The property is near the base of the Hirafu ski slopes and close to extensive restaurant options. The condominiums have 1.5-3 bedrooms, making them a great choice for large groups or families. If price is truly no object, there are full detached residences and a decadent penthouse with stratospheric nightly rates. For those traveling on a tighter budget, there are two "atelier"-style hotel rooms (which don't come cheap either). There are also onsen on-site (both private and sex-separated shared baths), and even a gym and gallery.

Information and Services

Online, the **Niseko Tourism** portal (https://nisekotourism.com) gives an extensive rundown in English on year-round activities, accommodations, food, nightlife, transportation information, and much more.

- **Explore Niseko** (190-13 Yamada, Kutchan-chō; tel. 050/5309-6905; www.explore-niseko.com; 9am-6pm daily)
- **Niseko Hiraifu Welcome Center** (Grand Hiraifu, 204 Yamada, Kutchan-chō; tel. 0136/22-0109; www.grand-hirafu.jp; 8:30am-9pm daily)
- **Michi no Eki Niseko View Plaza** (77-10 Motomachi, Abuta-gun, near Kutchan Station; tel. 0136/44-2420; www.hokkaido-michinoeki.jp; 9am-6pm daily)

Getting There

Niseko is sprawled out around the small town of **Kutchan,** 2.5-4 hours' drive from **Sapporo** and **New Chitose Airport.** During the ski season (Dec.-Mar.), several daily buses operated by **Chūō Bus** (tel. 011/231-0500; www.chuo-bus.co.jp) run between both Sapporo and the airport, and the three main resorts that comprise Niseko: Hirafu, Niseko Village, and Annupuri, from the morning hours until the early afternoon (from ¥2,650 one-way, from ¥4,500 round-trip). **Hokkaido Resort Liner** also links both New Chitose Airport and downtown Sapporo to Niseko (www.access-n.jp; ¥4,500 adults, ¥3,500 children) after passing through nearby ski resort Rusutsu on the way (¥4,000 adults, ¥3,000 children).

There are also local and rapid trains on the **JR Hakodate** line that run every hour and a half or so between JR Sapporo Station and **Kutchan Station** (2 hours; ¥2,100), the Niseko area's main hub. Note that in Otaru you'll have to transfer to the JR Hakodate line bound for Niseko. This ride is covered by the JR Pass. From Kutchan Station, buses depart every few hours to **Hirafu** (15 minutes) and less frequently to **Niseko Village** (30 minutes) and **Annupuri** (45 minutes). Many hotels offer to pick up guests at the closest of these stations. If you don't have a hotel pickup arranged, continue on to **JR Niseko Station** by transferring at Kutchan Station to the JR Hakodate line train bound for Oshamambe, another 15 minutes beyond Kutchan. You'll have better luck here catching a **taxi** at JR Niseko Station than you would at JR Hirafu Station. Weighing all factors, it's easier to reach any of Niseko's resorts by bus from Sapporo or New Chitose Airport. Plan ahead accordingly and reserve a seat well in advance, as skiers flock to the resort in winter.

Outside of the ski season, public transport in Niseko is very limited. You'll want to have your own wheels to reach the region via Route 5, which loops from Sapporo around the coast near Otaru, before turning toward the mountains to the south and inland where Niseko is located.

Getting Around

With a **Niseko United pass,** you'll not only

TOP EXPERIENCE

Beyond Niseko: More Skiing in Hokkaido

Though Niseko is Hokkaido's crown jewel for skiers, there are several other less crowded options, along with one practically within Sapporo's city limits.

RUSUTSU
留寿都

13 Izumi-kawa, Rusutsu; tel. 0136/46-3111; https://rusutsu.com/en/; 9am-4pm day, 4pm-8pm night, late Nov.-early Apr.; ¥6,500 adults, ¥3,500 children ages 4-12

Located 30 kilometers (18.6 mi) southeast of Niseko, Rusutsu Resort is a much less crowded alternative. There are fewer options for restaurants or nightlife, but the slopes are notably less packed.

You can either approach Rusutsu as a day trip from Niseko or stay at the family-friendly **Rusutsu Resort Hotel** (13 Izumi-kawa, Rusutsu; tel. 0136/46-3111; www.hokkaido-rusutsu.com; from ¥55,000 d with two meals). This sprawling complex is directly attached to Rusutsu Resort and has all the amenities you'll need, including restaurants, under one roof. For something independently owned, the **Villa Rusutsu** (55 Izumi-kawa, Rusutsu; tel. 0136/46-2830; www.villarusutsu.com; from ¥52,000 d with breakfast, 4-night minimum stay required during much of peak season) is a classic ski lodge with brilliant rooms, a hot tub, sauna, restaurant, and more.

To reach Rusutsu from Niseko, drive along **Route 230** toward Tōya-ko (30 minutes). A free shuttle bus runs between Sapporo and Rusutsu (2 hours; https://rusutsu.com/en/shuttle-bus-winter/; late Nov.-early Mar.). From December-early April, **Donan Bus** links Sapporo and Rusutsu (www.donanbus.co.jp/en/; ¥2,140). **Hokkaido Resort Liner** runs from downtown Sapporo and New Chitose Airport to Rusutsu (www.access-n.jp; ¥4,000 adults, ¥3,000 children) and Niseko beyond (¥4,500 adults, ¥3,500 children). Donan Bus operates a local bus every two hours daily during winter from Kutchan Station (near Niseko) to Rusutsu (www.donanbus.co.jp/map/toyako_makkari2/?hp_lang=en; 1 hour; ¥1,030). For all these routes, advanced booking is required; aim to do so at least a week in advance to be safe.

be able to access the slopes at the four resorts covered, you'll also be able to ride between them freely aboard a **shuttle bus.**

SHIKOTSU-TŌYA NATIONAL PARK
支笏洞爺国立公園

A few hours' drive south of Sapporo, Shikotsu-Tōya National Park is one of the more accessible of Hokkaido's outdoor escapes, a good pick if your time is limited. The park has five distinct areas, but its two focal points are the lakes it is named after: Tōya-ko and Shikotsu-ko. Hiking trails weave through the densely forested mountains surrounding this pair of sparkling caldera lakes. Elsewhere, volcanoes and onsen add a geothermal element.

Shikotsu-ko, due south of Sapporo, is set in a rugged volcanic landscape, flanked by the peaks of Eniwa-dake, Fuppushi-dake, and Tarumae-zan on the lake's southern shore, where excellent hiking awaits. It is the second-deepest lake in the country at 265 meters (869 feet) deep. If you're keen to camp, you're in luck—Shikotsu-ko has a number of well-appointed campsites. More civilized digs are found at ryokan around the lake's northern and eastern shores.

Tōya-ko has the added benefit of more infrastructure. Ascend to the summit of

FURANO

富良野

www.snowfurano.com; 8:30-sunset day, 4:30pm-7:30pm night, late Nov.-Apr.; ¥5,200 half day (1pm-7:30pm), ¥6,000 full day, ¥2,200 night

Another less crowded option is Furano Ski Area, one of Hokkaido's best. With 11 lifts, the runs are geared primarily toward newbies and intermediates, but there's enough to keep more advanced skiers and snowboarders happy, too.

For accommodations, **Furano Fresh Powder** (14-26 Kitanomine-chō; tel. 0167/23-4738; www.freshpowder.com; studio from ¥26,250) offers six well-appointed private apartments, from a studio up to a five-bedroom chalet, each with private, self-contained kitchens, bathroom facilities, and more. For a fuller list of accommodation options, and an online booking platform, visit https://www.allaboutfuranoholiday.com.

To reach Furano from Sapporo, take the limited express Kamui or Lilac train to Asahikawa, then transfer to the JR Furano line (2.5-3 hours; ¥6,430). **Hokkaido Chūō Bus** (tel. 011/231-0500, www.chuo-bus.co.jp) also operates several daily buses between Sapporo Station Bus Terminal and Furano (2.5-3 hours, ¥2,500 one-way, ¥4,720 round-trip). Seats cannot be reserved for these buses.

SAPPORO TEINE

サッポロテイネ

593 Teinehon-chō, Teine-ku; tel. 011/682-6000; https://sapporo-teine.com/snow/lang/en/; one-day pass ¥5,400 adults, ¥4,400 children ages 13-18, ¥2,800 children ages 4-12

For sheer convenience, Sapporo Teine right outside Sapporo is unbeatable. Only about 15 kilometers (9.3 mi) west of the city, this fully equipped ski resort has a beginner-friendly area (Olympia Zone) and the more advanced Highland Zone.

The easiest way to access the slopes is by taking the train on the JR Hakodate line from Sapporo Station to **Teine Station** (15 minutes; ¥340), then transferring to a shuttle bus (15 minutes, ¥380 for Olympia Zone; 30 minutes, ¥400 for Highland Zone). There are a variety of special combo tickets covering transport from downtown by bus and lift fare and more. Check the English-language website to suss out all possible options.

Usu-zan on the lake's southern side either on foot or via ropeway to survey the gorgeous surroundings. Nearby is Japan's youngest volcano, Shōwa-shinzan, which literally popped out of the farmland in 1944 and has been hiccupping fumes since. While it's quieted down in recent years, Usu-zan is also active. It last spewed ash across the area in 2000.

Yotei-zan, the mountain between the ski areas of Niseko and Rusutsu, is another one of the park's five main areas, as are the onsen towns of Jozankei and Hokkaido's most celebrated hot-springs resort, **Noboribetsu.**

If you plan to hike in the park, eat a meal and stock up on snacks before reaching the area. In the region, Tōya-ko has the most options for restaurants and shops.

Sights

VOLCANO SCIENCE MUSEUM

洞爺湖ビジターセンター 火山科学館

142-5 Tōya-ko Onsen; tel. 0142/75-2555; www.toyako-vc.jp/en/volcano; 9am-5pm daily; ¥600 adults, ¥300 children under 15; from the Tōya-ko bus terminal, walk 5 minutes west

At the Volcano Science Museum, you can experience a simulated eruption from the comfort of a theater and peruse educational displays on how volcanoes form, what causes them to erupt, and what kind of damage

MSR
1
2
3

they're capable of doing. The museum is housed in the same building as the **Tōya-ko Visitor Center.**

USU-ZAN WEST CRATERS

7am-6pm mid-Apr.-Sept., 7am-5pm Oct.-early Nov.; free

Around Tōya-ko, the Usu-zan West Craters (729 meters/2,391 feet) make for a great hike. Usu-zan erupted twice in 2000, creating some 60 new craters on its western slopes. Smoke billowed skyward, and nearby buildings and infrastructure were destroyed by the explosion. The ruins that still dot the devastated area can be explored on foot through a series of **hiking trails.**

Hiking

USU-ZAN ROPEWAY

有珠山ロープウェイ

184-5 Aza Showa Shinzan, Sobetsu-chō; tel. 0142/75-2401; www.wakasaresort.com; 9am-4pm daily, longer in summer; ¥1,800 adults round-trip, ¥900 elementary school students round-trip; from Tōya-ko Onsen, drive 10 minutes, take a taxi (about ¥2,000 one-way), or catch a bus (15 minutes, ¥340 one-way) to the village of Kazan-mura near the base of Shōwa-shinzan where the ropeway starts

After your education at the Volcano Science Museum, it's time to see volcanic activity in the real world. Make your way to the Usu-zan Ropeway, roughly 12 minutes' drive southeast of the museum. Usu-zan has erupted four times over the past century, most recently in 2000.

If you're willing to proceed with that slightly disconcerting information in mind, the ropeway will whisk you to a viewing platform near the summit of the volcano, with stunning views of Tōya-ko and the neighboring mountain Shōwa-shinzan. Walk to a neighboring platform to peer into a crater that formed in an eruption in 1977. Note that the ropeway is open later in summer and closes for a few weeks in winter for maintenance. Given the seasonal variations in operating hours, it's best to check the official schedule on the website (http://usuzan.hokkaido.jp/en/#SCHEDULE) before making the trip. Also, the bus from Tōya-ko Onsen only departs once every two hours and does not run from early November to late April. Check the website before making the trip.

TARUMAE-ZAN HIKE

Distance: *6.8-km (4.2-mi) loop*

Time: *2.5-3 hours*

Trailhead: *Seventh station (elevation of 650 meters; 2,132 feet), reached by gravel road linking northeast side of mountain to Route 141*

Information and maps: *Shikotsu-ko Visitor Center; https://hokkaidowilds.org/hiking/mt-tarumae*

Of the myriad mountains surrounding Shikotsu-ko, Tarumae-zan (1,041 meters/3,415 feet) stands out. One of the most active volcanoes in the country, it erupted as recently as 1981. It's a relatively easy ascent from the seventh station. Each station is essentially a waypoint. Depending on the popularity of a given route, these spots will sometimes provide basic amenities. Just as often, there will be a few primitive benches and a signpost indicating the elevation and distance to go until the end of the trail. Good views await of Shikotsu-ko, the barren landscape within the crater, and the Hidaka range and dormant volcano Yotei-san looming in the distance. You can then walk around the crater in about an hour, although entering it is not possible due to the presence of poisonous gases.

As for reaching the mountain, it's really not feasible without a rental car. If you have one, about 70 percent of the peak will be within reach. From the small town of Shikotsu Kohan on the lake's eastern shore, it's roughly a 45-minute drive on Route 141 to the trailhead at Nango-mae.

FUPPUSHI-DAKE HIKE

Distance: *8 km (5 mi) round-trip*

Time: *5-6 hours (from Tarumae-zan trailhead) round-trip*

1: camping at Shikotsu-ko **2:** walking trail near Noboribetsu Onsen **3:** Shikotsu-Tōya National Park

Trailhead: *Seventh Station (same as Tarumae-zan)*
Information and maps: *Shikotsu-ko Visitor Center; https://hokkaidowilds.org/hiking/fuppushi-dake-and-tarumae-zan-loop-hike*

Note that the trailhead for Tarumae-zan is also the starting point for a longer, more grueling hike up neighboring peak Fuppushi-dake (1,102 meters/3,615 feet), a good challenge for intermediate to advanced hikers. This hike is extremely steep in parts and can become treacherous in winter when there is a real risk of avalanche. It takes about six hours up and back, and is known to be an area where bear activity is notable. Exercise caution by wearing a bear bell. Pick up a map and get information about reaching the trailhead at the Shikotsu-ko Visitor Center.

KOMPIRAYAMA WALKING TRAIL

Distance: *2.8 km (1.4 mi) one-way*
Time: *1 hour 15 minutes one-way*
Trailhead: *Tōya-ko Visitor Center*
Information and maps: *Tōya-ko Visitor Center; www.toya-usu-geopark.org/english/trails/konpira*

The easiest hike to access to explore the Uzu-zan West Craters starts from the Tōya-ko Visitor Center in Tōya-ko Onsen. The 40-minute walk leads through a post-apocalyptic scene of apartment buildings, bridges, roads, and a public bath house laid waste by the blast. It's a sobering illustration of nature's destructive power.

Onsen

登別温泉

Noboribetsu Onsen, located near the coast at the southern edge of Shikotsu-Tōya National Park, is by far Hokkaido's most famed hot-spring retreat. The waters coursing beneath this onsen village, a known quantity since it was promoted as a place for injured troops to recover after the Russo-Japanese War (1904-1905), emerge from the colorfully named **Jigoku-dani,** or Hell Valley, located just above town. This valley does indeed invoke images of a barren inferno, minus the flames. Steam wafts from vents, streams are laced with heavy concentrations of sulfur (which permeates the air with its stench), and hissing sounds escape with each blast of heat.

The onsen options are extensive. Most hotels allow day-guests to use the baths during select hours for ¥700-2,000.

DAIICHI TAKIMOTOKAN

55 Noboribetsu Onsen-chō; tel. 0120/940-489; www.takimotokan.co.jp; 9am-6pm daily; ¥2,250 adults, ¥1,100 children (9am-4pm entry), ¥1,700 adults, ¥825 children (4pm-6pm entry) for non-staying guests

The highly curative waters in the numerous baths at this resort come from seven different springs, each with its own minerals and level of acidity. With bright, airy facilities, these are some of the best modern-style onsen baths in Japan.

SAGIRIYU PUBLIC BATH

60 Noboribetsu Onsen-chō; tel. 0143/84-2050; http://sagiriyu-noboribetsu.com; 7am-9pm (last entry 8:30pm) daily; ¥450 adults, ¥180 children

If you want to take a dip without spending too much, the Sagiriyu Public Bath does the trick. This is Noboribetsu's only public bath house, and unsurprisingly, it's offerings aren't as luxurious as what you'll find in the hotels around town. But the baths are still bright and nicely designed. Three pools are filled with two types of water, and there's a sauna too.

Accommodations

HANAYURA

100 Noboribetsu Onsen-chō; tel. 0143/84-2322; www.hanayura.com; ¥30,000 d with 2 meals, ¥33,500 d with private onsen bath and 2 meals

This luxury ryokan has spacious Japanese-style rooms, with some Japanese-Western hybrids too, some of which have private onsen tubs. There are also shared indoor and outdoor pools (sex-separated). Seafood-heavy kaiseki meals made with highly seasonal ingredients are served in private dining rooms in the on-site restaurant for both breakfast and dinner. It's located about 8 minutes north of the main Noboribetsu Onsen bus terminal next to the Kusurisanbetsu River.

KASHOUTEI HANAYA

134 Noboribetsu Onsen-chō; tel. 0143/84-2521; www.kashoutei-hanaya.co.jp; ¥45,300 d with 2 meals

This friendly, modern ryokan has ample Japanese- and Western-style rooms overlooking the Oyunuma River. The kaiseki meals are excellent, and the shared, sex-separated baths (both indoor and open-air) are inviting. It's well-located about 7 minutes' walk south of the Noboribetsu Onsen bus station.

Information and Services

- **Shikotsu-ko Visitor Center** (Shikotsu-ko Onsen; tel. 0123/25-2404; http://shikotsu-kovc.sakura.ne.jp; 9am-4:30pm Wed.-Mon. Dec.-Mar., 9am-5:30pm daily Apr.-Nov.)
- **Tōya-ko Visitor Center** (142-5 Tōya-ko Onsen; tel. 0142/75-2555; 9am-5pm daily)
- **Tōya-ko Tourist Information Center** (Tōya-ko bus terminal, 142 Tōya-ko Onsen; tel. 0142/75-2446; www.toyako-vc.jp; 9am-5pm daily)
- **Noboribetsu Park Service Center** (Noboribetsu Onsen-chō; tel. 0143/84-3141; www.bes.or.jp/nobori/; 9am-6pm daily)

Getting There

Having a **car** is all but essential for making a trip to Shikotsu-Tōya National Park worthwhile. Aside from a dearth of public transport servicing the park, there are no public transport links between Shikotsu-ko and Tōya-ko.

Starting with Shikotsu-ko, the lake is about 40 minutes' drive from **Shin-Chitose Airport,** 80 minutes' drive from **Sapporo,** and roughly an hour east of **Tōya-ko.** That said, there are 4-6 daily **buses** departing from Shin-Chitose Airport to the small town of Shikotsu Kohan on the eastern shore of the lake (1 hour; ¥1,050 one-way), or from Chitose Station to Shikotsu Kohan (45 minutes; ¥950 one-way). The problem with taking a bus to the lake is that many of the activities and sights around the lake, such as the trailhead to Tarumae-zan, are only accessible by private transport.

The best entry point to Tōya-ko is Tōya-ko Onsen, a small town on the southwest corner of the lake. The **Tōya-ko Onsen bus terminal** is linked to **JR Tōya Station** on the JR Muroran line, which in turn connects to **Hakodate** to the south (2 hours; ¥5,920), **Sapporo** to the north (2 hours; ¥6,360), and **Noboribetsu** (40 minutes; ¥2,970). To go from JR Tōya Station to Tōya-ko Onsen, take the local bus (20 minutes; ¥340), which stops close to Usu-zan West Crater en route.

Noboribetsu Onsen is about 15 minutes' bus ride (¥340) from JR Noboribetsu Station, located on the coast just south of the hot-spring village on the JR Muroran line. This train line also links JR Noboribetsu Station to Hakodate (2.5 hours; ¥7,460), Sapporo (1 hour 15 minutes; ¥4,780), and JR Tōya Station (35 minutes; ¥2,970). Note that buses run between Noboribetsu Onsen and JR Noboribetsu Station once or twice an hour. In a pinch, a **taxi** ride from JR Noboribetsu Station to Noboribetsu Onsen costs up to about ¥2,500.

Hakodate 函館

Located at Hokkaido's southern tip, Hakodate is the third-largest city in the prefecture and represents a spectacular fusion of what the island has to offer. The harbor was one of the first in Japan to welcome foreign trade after the 1854 signing of the Treaty of Kanagawa, which ended Japan's centuries-long policy of self-isolation. Once the city flung open its doors in the mid-to-late 1800s, a flood of Western influences poured in, from Europe, Russia, and beyond. This is most evident in the city's hilly Motomachi district, where

Hakodate

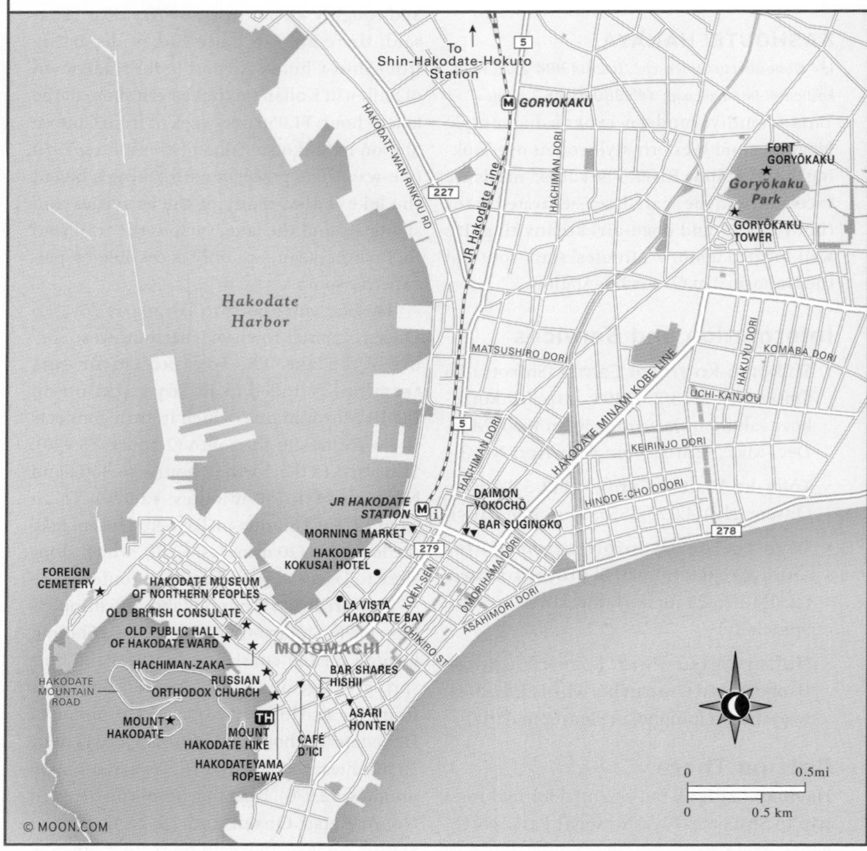

you'll find a Russian orthodox church, elegant brick facades, Western-style mansions, and, northeast of downtown, a star-shaped citadel with an Occidental touch that is now a fabulous cherry blossom viewing spot. There are also bustling markets, some of the country's best fresh-caught seafood, and one of the most twinkling nightscapes, seen from atop Mount Hakodate, of any city in Japan.

Hakodate is an ideal entry or exit point to the island if you're traveling by rail, thanks to the opening of the Seikan Tunnel in 2016, linking Hokkaido and Honshu. If you plan on passing through the city, make it an overnight stop. You'll be glad you have the time to soak up what this charming, historic, and visually appealing gateway town has to offer.

ORIENTATION

Hakodate Station sits roughly in the center of Hakodate, which sprawls across a narrow finger of land protruding in a southwestward direction into the Tsugaru Straits from Hokkaido's southeastern tip. Fronting the north side of town is **Hakodate Harbor** and the **Port of Hakodate.** Moving southwest from Hakodate Station, you'll pass through the core of downtown, culminating in **Motomachi,** one of the prime sightseeing districts. Just west of there, **Mount Hakodate** hovers at the southwestern tip of the peninsula, giving views in all directions of this scene spreading northeast from there. The bulk of Hakodate's sights, restaurants, and hotels are found within the stretch between Hakodate Station and Motomachi, and around the base of Mount Hakodate. Two notable exceptions are **Goryōkaku Park,** roughly 3 kilometers (1.8 mi) northeast of Hakodate Station, and **Shin-Hakodate-Hokuto Station,** 15 kilometers (9.3 mi) north of downtown Hakodate, where you'll arrive if you make the trip by shinkansen.

SIGHTS

Hakodate Museum of Northern Peoples

函館市北方民族資料館

21-7 Suehirō-chō; tel. 0138/22-4128; www.zaidan-hakodate.com/hoppominzoku; 9am-7pm daily; ¥300 adults, ¥150 students and children; from JR Hakodate Station, take city tram no. 5 to Suehirō-chō

Focused primarily on Hokkaido's indigenous Ainu, as well as the Oroks of Sakhalin Island, among others, the Hakodate Museum of Northern Peoples is a good place to get an introduction to this fascinating group and their sadly dwindling cultures. Housed in an old bank building, the relics on display include clothing, jewelry, tools, and housing, with Japanese and English signage.

Motomachi

元町

at foot of Mount Hakodate, bordered on the west by Motoi-zaka slope and Nijukken-zaka slope on the east; www.hakodate.travel/en/wp-content/themes/thakodate/th_top7/pdf/recommended_routes.pdf; from JR Hakodate Station, take tram no. 5 to Suehirō-chō, then walk up the hill

During the mid-1800s, foreign traders flooded into Hakodate, and the Motomachi district near the foot of Mount Hakodate is where they congregated. In many ways, this hilly area is strikingly similar to the neighborhood of the same name in Yokohama and Kobe's Kitano-chō, both of which were also hubs of foreign activity in the decades after Japan opened itself to foreign trade in 1854. Today, Motomachi is strewn with the architectural legacy of this tumultuous period of change. The entire neighborhood is a time capsule, with narrow cobblestone lanes and Western-style mansions, and beautiful views of the bay. The most prominent street in the area is the **Hachiman-zaka slope,** roughly in the center of the Motomachi area and perhaps Hakodate's most visually famous street.

Some of the highlights include the **Old British Consulate** (33-14 Motomachi; www.hakodate-kankou.com/british; 9am-7pm daily; ¥300), **Old Public Hall of Hakodate Ward** (11-13 Motomachi; www.zaidan-hakodate.com/koukaido; 9am-7pm daily; ¥300) and a **Russian Orthodox Church** (3-13 Motomachi; http://orthodox-hakodate.jp; 10am-5pm Mon.-Fri., 10am-4pm Sat., 1pm-4pm Sun.; ¥200 donation). There's also a **Foreign Cemetery** (23 Funamichō; dawn-dusk), dotted with gravestones that mark the final resting places of American sailors and preachers, a Russian surgeon, and other early pioneers from overseas.

Mount Hakodate

函館山

https://334.co.jp/eng; to reach the ropeway, take tram no. 5 from JR Hakodate Station to Jujigai tram stop (5 minutes) and walk 10 minutes southwest, or take the Hakodate Bus from JR Hakodate Station (10 minutes) to the ropeway terminal

The view from 334-meter-high (1,095-ft-high) Mount Hakodate, particularly at nighttime with the city's twinkling lights clearly delineating the outline of the peninsula where it stands, is one of the most recognizable nightscapes in all of Japan. To make your way to the top, you have the option of riding a gondola via the **Hakodateyama Ropeway** (19-7 Motomachi; tel. 0138/23-3105; www.334.co.jp; 10am-10pm late Apr.-mid-Oct., 10am-9pm mid-Oct.-late Apr.; one-way ¥1,000 adults, ¥500 children, round-trip ¥1,500 adults, ¥700 children), which departs from the Motomachi

1

2

3

district; taking a bus for 30 minutes from JR Hakodate Station (twice hourly during evening hours, late Apr.-mid-Nov.; ¥400), weaving and stopping on the way up the mountain at various lookout points; or even hiking in the warmer months of May through October. From the top, enjoy the views from the free observation decks.

Goryōkaku Park
五稜郭

44 Goryōkaku-chō; tel. 0138/21-3456; www.hakodate.travel/en/sightseeing_spots/view/goryokaku-park; 5am-7pm daily Apr.-Oct., 5am-6pm daily Nov.-Mar.; free; take tram to Goryōkaku-kōen-mae stop, then walk 10 minutes north

Northeast of JR Hakodate Station lies a massive geometric spectacle with an interesting backstory. **Fort Goryōkaku** was the first citadel constructed in Japan that mimics military strongholds found in the West. Built in 1864 in the shape of a star, the fort was meant to defend Hakodate from potential encroachment from abroad, specifically Russia. Its five-sided design was made to create a deadly gauntlet for an invading army that would be fired at from both sides. Rather than defending from a foreign enemy, the fort instead became the site of a civil war when Meiji imperial forces fought troops loyal to the shogunate, then in its death throes.

When its martial relevance faded, the site was instead turned into a free public park in the 1910s. The fort is gone, but its uniquely shaped moat, brimming with lily pads, remains. The beautifully landscaped grounds are dotted by some 1,600 cherry trees, making for an excellent spot for a stroll or picnic, especially in early to mid-May when the pink petals are in full bloom. This is easily one of the best hanami spots (places to welcome spring and enjoy cherry blossoms) in Hokkaido.

To glimpse the fort site from above, head to the nearby **Goryōkaku Tower** (五稜郭タワー; 43-9 Goryōkaku-chō; tel. 0138/51-4785; www.goryokaku-tower.co.jp; 9am-6pm daily; ¥900 adults, ¥680 junior high and high school students, ¥450 elementary school students; from JR Hakodate Station, take the tram to the Goryōkaku-kōen-mae stop, then walk 10 minutes north). This nearly 100-meter-tall (328-foot-tall) tower stands just outside the moat at the southwest corner of the park.

1: Hakodate waterfront 2: crabs and sea urchins for sale at Hakodate Morning Market 3: cable car ropeway to Mount Hakodate

HIKING

MOUNT HAKODATE HIKE

Distance: *2.9 km (1.8 mi) one-way*
Time: *1 hour one-way*
Trailhead: *Mount Hakodate Fureai Center*
Information and Maps: *Mount Hakodate Fureai Center; www.hakodate.travel/en/information/mt-hakodate.html; www.hakodate.travel/en/wp-content/themes/thakodate/information/mt-hakodate/img/mt_hakodate_trail_guide_map_img02.jpg*

Starting from Mount Hakodate Fureai Center (6-12 Aoyagi-chō, Hakodate; 0138/22-6799; 8:45am-5pm daily), five minutes' walk southwest of the lower station of the Hakodateyama Ropeway, the well-kept, clearly marked **Kyutozandō trail** leads to the top of the mountain. This is the easiest route to access and undertake, but a series of other trails can also be followed. A map showing the entire network of paths can be found online (www.hakodate.travel/en/wp-content/themes/thakodate/information/mt-hakodate/img/mt_hakodate_trail_guide_map_img01.pdf). Be sure to wear comfortable walking shoes in the warmer months, or boots appropriate for snow in winter.

FOOD

MORNING MARKET

Next to JR Hakodate Station; www.hakodate-asaichi.com; 5am-2pm daily, from 6am in winter; walk 1 minute south of the station

Held next to JR Hakodate Station every morning, the Morning Market, or Asaichi, is a bustling bazaar of seafood, produce, and sundry dry goods. It's a fun way to start your day and a good introduction to Hakodate. Walk among endless rows of stalls hawking squid, urchin, salmon roe, crabs, melons, and more, operated by earthy fishermen and kind aunties. Some of the stalls sell seafood breakfasts. If you show up before 8am, you may even catch a bit of auctioneering.

DAIMON YOKOCHŌ

7-5 Matsukaze-chō; tel. 0138/24-0033; www.hakodate-yatai.com; hours and prices vary by shop; walk 7 minutes east of Hakodate Station

Enter this network of alleyways festooned with glowing paper lanterns in the evening and you'll find about 25 eateries. The offerings range from seafood and okonomiyaki to yakitori. Follow your inspiration and you won't go wrong.

LUCKY PIERROT BAY AREA MAIN SHOP

23-18 Suehiro-chō; tel. 0138/26-2099; http://luckypierrot.jp/shop/bayarea; 10am-10pm daily; burgers from ¥350; walk 4 minutes southeast of Suehiro-chō tram stop (line 5)

This eclectic local burger shop is an institution. Look past the quirky decor reminiscent of an old carnival—clown mascot, antique merry-go-round horse—and you'll find a menu of cheap, tasty burgers and sides. Its Chinese chicken burger has been voted Japan's best burger.

CAFÉ D'ICI

22-9 Motomachi; tel. 0138/76-7476; 10:30am-7pm Fri.-Wed., closed 1st and 3rd Wed. every month; ¥1,100; walk 6 minutes southwest of Jujigai tram stop (lines 2, 5)

This small, inviting café, run by a charming local woman, serves great coffee and small nibbles (baked goods, desserts, small soup/salad sets). It's a great spot for a small bite or caffeine pit stop while strolling through Motomachi.

ASARI HONTEN

10-11 Horai-chō; tel. 0138/23-0421; 11am-8:30pm Thurs.-Tues.; courses ¥2,200-5,200; walk 1 minute west of Horai-chō tram stop (line 2)

This old-school wooden building with private dining rooms where guests sit on tatami floors serves great sukiyaki (beef hot pot). A fantastic place for an intimate meal with plenty of small-town charm. Reserve at least a few days in advance if you plan to go—the restaurant has a reputation and is often full. An English menu is available.

BARS AND NIGHTLIFE

BAR SUGINOKO

8-5 Matsukaze-chō; tel. 0138/23-4577; www5d.biglobe.ne.jp/~suginoko; 6:30pm-11pm Tues.-Sat.; walk 7 minutes east of Hakodate Station

Located right next to the eastern edge of the culinary alleyways of Daimon Yokochō, this storied bar is known for its friendly masters and signature rum highball, along with various cocktails meant to evoke the colors of Hokkaido (plenty of greens and blues). Seating spreads across two floors and includes comfy sofas and a line of swivel chairs at the bar.

BAR SHARES HISHII

27-1 Motomachi; tel. 0138/22-5584; www.bar-shares-hishii.info; 7:30pm-1am (last order 12:30am) Mon.-Sat.; cover charge ¥500; walk 5 minutes west of Horai-chō tram stop (line 2)

This dimly lit bar near the Mount Hakodate Ropeway in Motomachi has an impressive whisky and cocktail menu. The atmosphere exudes class, and the masters, in vest and tie, really know their way around the bar.

ACCOMMODATIONS

¥10,000-20,000

HAKODATE KOKUSAI HOTEL

5-10 Ōtemachi; tel. 0138/23-0591; www.hakodate-kokusai.jp; ¥15,000 d; from JR Hakodate Station, take Hakodate City Tram to Shiyakusho-mae stop

Hakodate Kokusai Hotel is elegant and sprawling, with more than 300 rooms occupying three buildings set near the bay. Its restaurants serve Chinese, Western, and Japanese fare, and it has a lounge with great nighttime views. Its central location, seven minutes' walk from JR Hakodate Station, makes it a convenient home base while you're exploring the city. A 20-minute walk to the southwest leads to the Mount Hakodate Ropeway station, and a 20-minute ride aboard the Hakodate city tram leads to Goryōkaku.

¥20,000-30,000

LA VISTA HAKODATE BAY

12-6 Toyokawa-chō; tel. 0138/23-6111; www.hotespa.net/hotels/lahakodate; ¥22,000 d; from JR Hakodate Station, take Hakodate City Tram to Uoichibadori stop

La Vista Hakodate Bay also sits on a prime spot, overlooking the bay. The atmospheric hotel has mood lighting, stylish dark wood furniture, Western-style rooms with Japanese accents, and a wonderful onsen on the roof. Restaurants on-site whip up Chinese and Spanish cuisine, making heavy use of seafood brought in from the waters just offshore.

INFORMATION AND SERVICES

- **Tourist Information Center** (JR Hakodate Station, 12-13 Wakamatsu-chō; tel. 0138/23-5440; www.hakodate.travel; 9am-7pm daily)

GETTING THERE

From Sapporo, take the **limited express train** (Super Hokuto) south on the **JR Hakodate line,** (3.5 hours; ¥9,440) to **Hakodate Station.** Take the same line from **Niseko** (3.5 hours; ¥5,990), changing trains at Oshamambe.

Coming from **Shin-Aomori,** take the **JR Hokkaido** shinkansen (reservation required) until Shin-Hakodate-Hokuto (1 hour), then transfer to the Hakodate line for the remaining 15 minutes of the trip to JR Hakodate Station, for a total cost of ¥8,360. If you're coming from points farther south, take the shinkansen all the way to Shin-Hakodate-Hokuto Station (from Tokyo 4 hours 10 minutes, ¥23,230; from Sendai 2 hours 30 minutes, ¥17,750), then take the local line to JR Hakodate Station from there.

Hakodate also has an international **airport,** with flights to cities such as Taipei and Seoul, and a number of airports within Japan. The flight from Tokyo takes about 1 hour 30 minutes and is relatively cheap (¥7,500-15,000). Buses run between the airport and JR Hakodate Station (25 minutes; ¥450).

GETTING AROUND

Hakodate is easily navigable **on foot.** That said, the **streetcars** are easy to catch and make for a fun ride (¥210-260). City **buses** are similarly priced (¥210-260). Tram lines 2 and 5 are useful; both of these run along the same route through downtown until Jujigai tram stop. From there, tram line 5 veers northward, tracing the eastern base of Mount Hakodate. Go to the tourist information center in JR Hakodate Station to pick up a one-day bus pass (¥800), a one-day streetcar pass (¥600), or a combination pass that covers them both (¥1,000).

If you plan to drive through Hokkaido and are arriving via Hakodate, note that rental cars are easy to pick up in the city. Try **Nippon Rent-a-Car** (22-5 Wakamatsu-chō; tel. 0138/22-0919; www.nrh.co.jp; 8am-7pm daily) just outside JR Hakodate Station, **Toyota Rent-a-Car** (19-2 Ōtemachi; tel. 0138/26-0100; https://rent.toyota.co.jp; 8am-7pm daily) five minutes' walk southwest of JR Hakodate Station, and **Times Car Rental** (22-7 Wakamatsu-chō; tel. 0138/27-4547; www.timescar-rental.com; 9am-6pm daily) 4 minutes' walk southwest of the station.

★ Daisetsuzan National Park 大雪山国立公園

At the geographical core of the island, Hokkaido is brimming with the very elements the island is known for. In summer, trekkers flock to the alpine vastness of Daisetsuzan National Park, which is rugged enough to please ambitious hikers and has rustic onsen towns for post-hike R&R.

Daisetsuzan is the biggest national park in all of Japan. This swath of untamed wilderness at the heart of the island covers 2,267 square kilometers (875 square mi), an area larger than Tokyo. The park is the first place in the country to see its leaves turn fiery red, golden yellow, and earthy brown in autumn, and it's the first to be dusted with snow. It's home to a host of wildlife, from the indigenous Ezo deer to brown bears and the rabbit-like Japanese pika.

This vast unspoiled kingdom is a paradise for hikers, with a smattering of excellent day-hikes, such as Asahi-dake, and the grueling week-long affair known as the Daisetsuzan Grand Traverse, stretching from Asahi-dake in the north to the peak of Tokachi-dake in the south. A network of huts and places to camp facilitate your journey. If roughing it is not your style, there are also a few onsen resort towns home to cozy ryokan with steamy baths, such as **Asahi-dake Onsen** in the northwest, **Sōunkyō Onsen** in the northeast, and bare-bones **Tokachi-dake Onsen** in the southwest. Note that of these three transit points, only Sōunkyō Onsen has an ATM and a few restaurants. Asahidake Onsen and Tokachidake Onsen don't even have a convenience store. So, pick up all your supplies before arriving in the park.

If traipsing through a landscape of steaming volcano craters, summer wildflowers, dense forests, and murmuring streams far from the hubbub of modern Japan appeals to you, Daisetsuzan has what you seek.

HIKING

June-September, Daisetsuzan is a hiker's paradise. The most popular area to begin any exploration of the park on foot is around the small hot-springs village of Asahidake Onsen, in the park's northwest. Here, you'll be at the base of the park's highest mountain, **Asahidake** (2,291 meters/7,516 feet), which makes for a great day hike. To see a map of the extensive trails snaking through the park at a glance, visit http://sounkyovc.net/data/pdfs/maps/route_all_en.pdf.

In truth, the list here merely scratches the surface of the multitude of hiking options in the park, ranging from a few hours on foot to the epic trek known as the **Daisetsuzan Grand Traverse,** a 5-7 day journey beginning either from Asahidake Onsen or Sōunkyō Onsen and running north-south through most of the length of the park, ending at the remote hot-spring village of Tokachidake Onsen.

If you're hankering for something more demanding, seek out more recommendations at one of the helpful information centers in Asahikawa Onsen or Sōunkyō Onsen, or contact **Hokkaido Nature Tours** (2-6 7-83 Ishiyama, Minami-ku; tel. 011/592-3959; www.hokkaidonaturetours.com). They offer excellent tours in English, including the extremely grueling but equally rewarding Daisetsuzan Grand Traverse. A fantastic online resource for Daisetsuzan and Hokkaido as a whole is the website **Hokkaido Wilds** (https://hokkaidowilds.org). For a certified bilingual guide with deep Hokkaido expertise, consider contacting **Jun Ishiguro** (www.explore-share.com/trip/

1: hikers ascending the Asahidake volcano in Daisetsuzan National Park **2:** Daisetsuzan Grand Traverse

1

2

hiking-hakuundake-kurodake-daisetsuzan), director of the Hokkaido Mountain Guides Association.

ASAHIDAKE ROPEWAY

Asahidake Onsen, Higashikawa-chō; tel. 0166/68-9111; http://asahidake.hokkaido.jp; 6am-5:30pm daily Jul.-mid-Oct., 9am-4pm daily mid-Oct.-Jun.; ¥3,200 round-trip or ¥2,000 one-way Jun.-Oct. 20; ¥2,200 round-trip or ¥1,500-one way Oct. 21-May

To hike up Asahidake, first take the Asahidake Ropeway, located in the heart of the hot-spring village of Asahidake Onsen, to Sugatami (1,600 m/5,249 ft). From here the ascent on foot begins. Arriving at the top of the ropeway, you'll be in a tundra zone, free of trees, with mountain flowers blooming in summer.

SUGATAMI-DAIRA

Distance: *2 km (1.2 mi) round-trip*
Time: *1 hour round-trip*
Trailhead: *Sugatami (via Daisetsuzan Asahidake Ropeway)*
Information and maps: *Asahidake Visitor Center*

From Sugatami, you have a few options. One is to walk the loop around Sugatami-daira, where you'll discover small bodies of water and vents releasing sulfur from the bowels of the earth.

ASAHIDAKE

Distance: *5.8 km (3.6 mi) round-trip*
Time: *4-5 hours round-trip*
Trailhead: *Sugatami (via Daisetsuzan Asahidake Ropeway)*
Information and maps: *Asahidake Visitor Center; https://hokkaidowilds.org/hiking/asahidake-ropeway-to-asahidake-summit*

For something more challenging, after exiting the ropeway car at Sugatami, follow the trail sign indicating the path to the summit of Asahidake, which is roughly a five-hour return hike. This trail weaves through snowfields, flowery meadows, and boggy marshland. Views from the top of Asahidake, one of Japan's "100 famous mountains," are spectacular.

KURODAKE

Distance: *12 km (7.5 mi) from Asahidake Ropeway to Kurodake Ropeway*
Time: *8 hours*
Trailhead: *Sugatami (if approaching from Asashidake side)*
Information and maps: *Asahidake Visitor Center, Sōunkyō Visitor Center*

For a more involved hike that lasts 1-2 days—only recommended for more experienced hikers—rather than returning from the summit of Asahidake, forge on to the neighboring summit of Kurodake (1,984 meters/6,509 feet). From there, you'll begin your descent toward the hot-spring town of Sōunkyō Onsen below (670 meters/2,198 feet). Begin this journey by walking to the seventh station of the mountain (1,520 meters/4,986 feet), where you'll find the upper station of a chair lift. This first jaunt takes 60-90 minutes. Take the chair lift (¥400 one-way, ¥600 round-trip), which descends to the fifth station (1,300 meters/4,265 feet), where you'll find the upper station of the **Kurodake Ropeway** (tel. 0165/85-3031; www.rinyu.co.jp/modules/pico01; 6am-6pm daily Jun.-Sept., 6am-5pm daily Oct. 1-15, 8am-4:30pm daily Oct. 16-Nov., 8am-4pm daily Dec.-Jan. 3; ¥1,900 one-way, ¥3,000 round-trip junior high school students and older, ¥950 one-way, ¥1,500 round-trip elementary school students). Hop aboard this ropeway and ride down to Sōunkyō Onsen below.

In total, trekking from Asahidake Ropeway to the Kurodake Ropeway can take up to 8 hours, so prepare accordingly. This includes reviewing the timetable for each ropeway. If you plan to extend this to an overnight journey, there's a mountain hut about 10 minutes' hike from the summit of Kurodake, which you can stay in without a reservation (though it can get packed during high season). The hike can also be completed in reverse order.

ONSEN

Hot-spring options in Daisetsuzan are plentiful, with the bulk of them being at hotels in the main entry points of Asahidake Onsen and Sōunkyō Onsen, including Daisetsuzan Shirakaba-sō. These hot-spring villages, in the northwest and northeast of the park, respectively, have plenty of hotels offering bathing options for non-staying guests for about ¥1,000.

KURODAKE-NO-YU

Sōunkyō Onsen, Kamikawa-chō; tel. 01658/5-3333; www.sounkyo.com/kurodakenoyu.html; 10am-9pm daily May-Oct., 10am-9pm Wed. Nov.-Apr.; ¥600 adults, ¥300 children

In Sōunkyō Onsen, Kurodake-no-yu is a gender-separated public bath on the main drag in the middle of this slightly more developed town about 6 minutes' walk south of the Asahidake Ropeway. Alongside gender-separated indoor pools, there's an open-air bath on the third floor. The views in this bath aren't anything spectacular, but after a long day of hiking, its waters can't be beat.

ACCOMMODATIONS

★ DAISETSUZAN SHIRAKABA-SŌ

Asahidake Onsen; tel. 0166/97-2246; http://shirakabasou.com; dorms with 2 meals ¥7,890 pp, private rooms with 2 meals ¥8,940 pp

This outdoorsy wooden lodge about 6 minutes' walk southeast of the Asahidake Ropeway contains private tatami-mat rooms and one Western-style room, as well as dorms with bunk beds—all using shared bathrooms. There's also a shared lounge and kitchen, a dining room, and a shop stocked with basics, from snacks to insect repellent and bear bells (8am-10pm daily). There's an open-air shared bath, which is free for guests. Be sure to check out the viewing deck, reached via a lofty spiral staircase. The **onsen** (1pm-8pm daily; ¥800 day guests; towel rental ¥200) is a good bathing option. A great base for exploring the park from the Asahidake Onsen side.

SŌUNKYŌ YOUTH HOSTEL

39 Sōunkyō; tel. 080/2862-4080; www.sounkyo-hostel.com; dorms (sex-separated) ¥3,500 pp, private doubles ¥9,000

Located about 10 minutes' walk (uphill) southeast from Sōunkyō bus stop and 7 minutes east of the lower station of the Kurodake Ropeway, this medium-size hostel has a mix of dorms with bunk beds and a few private tatami-mat rooms, all of which share a bathroom. There's a communal lounge area and kitchen amply stocked with utensils and seasoning that can be freely used, but no meals are served. A convenient base in Sōunkyō.

INFORMATION AND SERVICES

- **Asahidake Visitor Center** (Asahidake Onsen, Higashikawa-chō; tel. 0166/97-2153; www.asahidake-vc-2291.jp; 9am-5pm daily)
- **Sōunkyō Visitor Center** (Sōunkyō, Kamikawa-chō; tel. 01658/9-4400; http://sounkyovc.net; 8am-5:30pm daily Jun.-Oct., 9am-5pm Tues.-Sun. Nov.-May)

GETTING THERE AND AROUND

Starting from **Sapporo,** head northeast on the Hokkaido Expressway, then take Hokkaido Expressway 116, National Highway 452, Route 135, and Route 291 to the western edge of the park (2 hours 30 minutes; 136 km/84.5 mi). It's also possible to drive to **Asahidake Onsen** from **Asahikawa** (1 hour; 45 km/28 mi; via Route 1160) or **Biei** (40 minutes; 37.5 km/23.3 mi; via Route 213, then Route 1160). It's a slightly longer trip to **Sōunkyō Onsen** from Biei (1 hour 30 minutes; 81 km/50.3 mi; via Route 39) and Asahikawa (1 hour 15 minutes; 63.8 km/39.6 mi; via Asahikawa Monbetsu Expressway, National Highway 450, and National Highway 39).

The easiest way to reach Asahidake Onsen in the park's northwest by public transportation is via bus from **JR Asahikawa Station** (1.5 hours; ¥1,430), departing once every hour or two. To reach JR Asahikawa Station from JR Sapporo Station, take the limited express train (85 minutes; ¥5,220).

To enter the park via Sōunkyō Onsen, take a bus from JR Asahikawa Station (2 hours; ¥2,100). Or, take the JR Sekihoku line

Summer Wildflowers

Wildflowers of all hues blanket meadows and fields across Hokkaido in summer, causing a frenzy similar to the cherry blossom craze that sweeps across the whole of Japan every spring. Among Hokkaido's best spots to see wildflowers in summer are the fields around **Furano** (富良野) and **Bei** (美瑛), and on **Rebun Island** (page 591).

Here at Japan's northern edge, flowers bloom a bit later than in the south. Fields are awash in color from May-October. Lavender blankets the region in violet from late June-mid-August, and a host of other colorful flowers cover entire fields from June-September. Among them are poppies, lupines, and rape blossoms in June; lilies in July; and salvias, sunflowers, and cosmos from August-September. The heavy flow of travelers to the area—a million per year by some estimates—attests to their beauty. Given the distance from Sapporo, you'll get the most of a trip to see the wildflowers if you combine it with a trip deeper into the island's rugged center to Daisetsuzan National Park. That said, a day trip is possible from Sapporo if you get an early start.

FURANO

Farm Tomita (tel. 0167/39-3939; www.farm-tomita.co.jp; 9am-4:30pm daily Oct.-late Apr., 8:30am-6pm daily late Apr.-Sept.; free) is known for the striking contrast of its purple fields with the Toakchi mountains in the background; **Lavender East** (www.farm-tomita.co.jp/en/east; 9am-4:30pm daily in July only; free) boasts 14 hectares (35 acres) of lavender—the largest field in the area; and **Flower Land Kamifurano** (tel. 0167/45-9480; http://flower-land.co.jp; 9am-6pm daily Jul.-Aug., 9am-5pm daily May-Jun. and Sept.-Oct., 9am-4pm daily Mar.-Apr. and Nov.; free) has a plethora of blossoms, and a bus tractor (¥500 adults, ¥300 children) to take you on a tour of the fields.

Food and Accommodations

If you're hankering for a meal after surveying the nearby fields, **Cafe Nokka** (15 Go Nakafurano-Nishi 1 Sen-kita; tel. 0167/44-2578; https://r.goope.jp/nokka; 11am-4pm Fri.-Tues. May-Oct.; average ¥1,000) is a cozy spot about 25 minutes' walk west of Farm Tomita that serves light meals—sandwiches, soups, salads—and good desserts and coffee when it opens during the warmer months. If your schedule allows you to slow down and savor the scene for a night, there are some cozy pensions near Furano's fields. **Northern Star Lodge** (14 Go Nakafurano-Nishi 1 Sen-Kita; tel. 0167/44-2081; http://northernstarlodge.info; ¥12,600 pp with two meals), near Farm Tomita, and **Furano Hostel** (3-20 Oka-machi, Nakafurano; tel. 0167/44-4441; www.furanohostel.sakura.ne.jp; ¥3,700 dorms with two meals), conveniently close to Naka-Furano Station, are both good picks. For more extensive dining and accommodation options in English, visit www.furanotourism.com/sp/en/.

Getting There and Around

To reach Furano from **Sapporo,** take the limited express **Kamui** or **Lilac** train to Asahikawa, then transfer to the **JR Furano** line, which runs first to Biei, then reaches Furano (3 hours; ¥6,430). If you've got a rental car, take the **Doo Expressway** between Sapporo and Mikasa to Furano (2 hours; ¥1,500 in tolls). **Hokkaido Chūō Bus** (tel. 011/231-0500; www.chuo-bus.co.jp) also operates several daily buses between Sapporo and Furano (3 hours; ¥2,500). Seats cannot be reserved for these buses.

In town, the best way to get around is by bicycle, which you can rent at **Furano-Biei Tourism Center** (1-30 Hinode-machi in JR Furano Station; tel. 0167/23-3388; www.furanotourism.com; 9am-6pm daily).

You can shuttle between Furano and Biei on the **Furano-Biei Norokko train** (early to mid-June and late Aug.-late Sept. on weekends, and daily late June-mid-Aug.). Starting from Furano,

flower fields in Furano

catch the train at a station called **Lavender Farm Station,** 7 minutes' walk from Farm Tomita. The 35-minute journey from there to Biei is made through a scene of pastoral bliss (www.farm-tomita.co.jp/en/access/station.asp; ¥450). If you've got your own wheels, you can drive between Furano and Biei on Route 237 (33.7 km/20.9 mi; 45 minutes).

BIEI

Shikisai Hill (tel. 0166/95-2758; www.shikisainooka.jp; 9am-5pm daily Apr.-May and Oct., 8:30am-6pm daily Jun.-Sept., 9am-4pm daily Dec.-Feb., 9am-4:30pm daily Mar. and Nov.; free) is a lovely slope that is blanketed in flowers and lined with trails, while **Patchwork Road** is a splendid area about 3.5 kilometers (2.2 mi) northwest of town named for the way that it appears from above—like an earth-tone quilt.

Food and Accommodations

Sitting amidst the splendor near Patchwork Road, **Kitchen Hitosaji** (Okubo Kyōsei, Biei-chō; tel. 0166/74-8307; https://cafebiei.com; 11am-2:30pm Fri.-Mon. May-Oct.; ¥1,200) is a great lunch stop offering tasty soups, curries, and freshly baked bread. **Villa e Pizzeria iL coVo** (Ōmura Murayama, Biei-chō; tel. 0166/92-5489; www.ilcovo.jp; ¥20,000 pp for couples, ¥18,000 pp for groups of three with breakfast) is a friendly area inn that, as its name suggests, doubles as a pizzeria (pizzas ¥1,200). To peruse fuller restaurant and lodging options in English, check out www.biei-hokkaido.jp/en/.

Getting There and Around

To reach Biei from **Sapporo,** take the limited express **Kamui** or **Lilac** train to Asahikawa, then transfer to the **JR Furano** (2 hours 15 minutes; ¥5,990). If you've got a rental car, take the **Doo Expressway** that runs between Sapporo and Asahikawa to reach Biei (2.5 hours; ¥3,500 in tolls).

In Biei, the **Biei Tourist Information Center** (1-2-14 Motomachi, Biei-chō Honcho, next to Biei Station; tel. 0166/92-4378; www.biei-hokkaido.jp; 8:30am-7pm daily May-Oct.; 8:30am-5pm daily Nov.-Apr.; ¥200 per hour) offers information as well as bike rentals.

from JR Asahikawa Station to **JR Kamikawa Station** (local train 1 hour 15 minutes, ¥1,290; express train 40 minutes, ¥2,450), then take a bus departing once every hour or two to go the rest of the way to Sōunkyō Onsen (30 minutes; ¥890). If you're staying in Sōunkyō Onsen, ask if your hotel provides shuttle bus services to guests. Many of them offer pickup from Asahikawa. A few even go as far as Sapporo.

Eastern Hokkaido

Far from the more civilized towns and cities of southwestern Hokkaido, the eastern part of the island is a vast natural sanctuary. Akan National Park bears witness to the region's volcanic past with its three gorgeous caldera lakes: Akan-ko, Mashū-ko, and Kussharo-ko. Trails lining the region draw hikers in summer. Meanwhile, red-crowned cranes, representatives of longevity for the Japanese, congregate in the nearby Kushiro Wetlands, which can be explored by canoe. The region is also one of the best places to experience the culture of the Ainu, Japan's original inhabitants.

On the region's northern coast, UNESCO-listed Shiretoko National Park is home to hundreds of lumbering brown bears and the site of the southernmost drift ice floes in the world.

KUSHIRO WETLANDS
釧路湿原

Near the southeastern corner of Hokkaido lies Japan's most extensive marshlands, the Kushiro Wetlands National Park. The main appeal of Kushiro, which comprises 60 percent of Japan's marshland (269 square km/104 square mi), is the chance to explore it from the water level in a canoe, and to see the red-crested white cranes that were narrowly saved from extinction over the past 90-plus years, largely thanks to efforts to preserve their habitat in this small corner of Hokkaido's vast wilderness. Given the remoteness of the wetlands, it makes sense to combine your trip with Akan National Park.

Canoeing

While there are several observation platforms around the Kushiro wetlands, a far more powerful experience is seeing them while floating in a canoe down the Kushiro River. A number of canoe rental shops can be found at lake **Toro-ko** on the eastern side of the park, accessed by taking the JR Senmo line train from JR Kushiro Station to JR Toro Station (30 minutes; ¥540).

TŌRŌ NATURE CENTER

86-17 Toro Kita, Shibecha; tel. 015/487-3100; www.dotoinfo.com/naturecenter; 8am-5pm daily Mar.-mid-Dec.; from ¥9,500 per person

Tōrō Nature Center is a good starting point for your canoe trip through the wetlands. They offer a vast range of options for canoe tours, from an hour and a half to nine hours.

Getting There

If you're driving from Sapporo, take the Hokkaido Crossing Expressway to the Dōtō Expressway to Kushiro (4 hours 30 minutes; 300 km/186 mi). By public transport, the Kushiro Wetlands are best accessed via the port town of Kushiro, to the south. If you're coming from Sapporo, take the limited express train from JR Sapporo Station to **JR Kushiro Station** (4.5 hours; ¥9,990). From here, the JR Senmo line runs along the eastern edges of the park as it makes its way north to Abashiri, passing through **Kushiro Shitsugen Station** (20 minutes; ¥440) at the eastern side of the park on the way. Making it into the park's interior or western side requires a car.

Alternatively, you can make the trip by air from Sapporo's **New Chitose Airport** to **Kushiro Airport** (40 minutes; ¥13,000), then

Red-Crowned Cranes

In Japan, the Japanese crane has long been regarded a potent symbol of longevity and happiness. According to legend, the red-crowned crane can live for as long as a millennium. Yet, by the early 20th century, this graceful, powerful motif in Japanese culture was thought to be extinct due to heavy hunting.

A small population of these long-legged birds, with slender bills and white bodies trimmed with black and a tuft of red feathers atop the head, was thankfully discovered in the Kushiro Wetlands in 1924, after which the species was brought back from the brink through a heroic conservation effort. Today, more than 1,200 of the dignified birds breed, feed, squawk, dance, jump, and groom in the vast marshes around Kushiro. Hyperbole about their lifespan aside, they have been known to live up to 80 years in captivity. Besides having a long lifespan, the birds pair for life, making them a common allusion at weddings in Japan.

red-crowned cranes

CRANE SPOTTING

Visiting the Kushiro Wetlands November-March offers the best chance to see the red-crowned crane. If you're in Kushiro during that period and have a rental car, drive to the **Tsurui-Ito Red-Crowned Crane Sanctuary** (Nakasetsuri Minami, Tsurui-mura; tel. 0154/64-2620; www.wbsj.org/en/tsurui; 9am-4pm Thurs.-Mon. Oct.-Mar., open Tues.-Wed. on national holidays; free), which offers one of the least obstructed views of the birds in their natural habitat. There is also a Nature Center run by the **Japan Wild Bird Association** (www.wbsj.org) next to the sanctuary.

If you're relying on public transport and/or you're not visiting in winter, the **Kushiro City Red-Crowned Crane Natural Park** (112 Tsuruoka, Kushiro; tel. 0154/56-2219; www.kushiro-park.com/publics/index/72/; 9am-6pm daily Apr. 10-Oct. 14, 9am-4pm daily Oct. 15-Apr. 9.; ¥480 high school students and older, ¥110 junior high school and elementary school students) also allows you to observe the birds coming and going as they please at this sanctuary that has played a crucial role in their return to health. Perhaps the most direct views of all are to be had from a canoe. The **Tōrō Nature Center** offers canoe tours down the Kushiro-gawa, a river that winds through the wetlands where cranes often gather.

rent a car at one of the outlets with desks at the airport. The journey from Kushiro Airport into the heart of the wetlands takes about 45 minutes to 1 hour to drive (50 km/31 mi northeast from the airport; via Kushiro Shitsugen Road and National Highway 391).

Akan Bus Co. (tel. 0154/37-8651; www.akanbus.co.jp) offers guided tours from JR Kushiro Station to Kushiro Wetlands from mid-July through October.

Getting Around

The only way to get around the Kushiro Wetlands easily is with a **rental car.** There are a cluster of car rental shops around the southern side of **JR Kushiro Station.**

AKAN NATIONAL PARK
阿寒国立公園

Due north from Kushiro Wetlands lies the lake-studded mountainous region of Akan National Park. Spread over 905 square kilometers (349 square mi), it's chock-full of volcanoes and timberlands, penetrated by hiking trails and rustic onsen to soak weary muscles. Three caldera lakes, **Mashū-ko,**

Kussharo-ko, and **Akan-ko,** are the park's focal points. The town of **Akanko Onsen** on the lake's south shore is also a great place to see a traditional Ainu village and learn about the fascinating, sadly vanishing culture of Japan's first settlers.

Sights

AKAN KOHAN ECO-MUSEUM CENTER

1-1-1 Akan-ko Onsen, Akan-chō; tel. 0154/67-4100; http://en.kushiro-lakeakan.com; 9am-5pm daily Aug. 21-July 31, 9am-6pm daily Aug. 1-20; free

Marimo, the singular spherical species of algae that forms within Akan-ko, can be seen at the Akan Kohan Eco-Museum Center, located in the eastern side of Akan-ko Onsen.

AINU KOTAN

4-7-19 Akan-ko Onsen, Akan-chō; tel. 0154/67-2727; www.akanainu.jp

The Ainu Kotan is a village where Ainu crafts, a museum, a restaurant, and a performance space are clustered together on one street at the western end of Akan-ko Onsen. Enter through a gate watched over by an imposing owl, the guardian spirit of the Ainu. Admittedly, the development is geared toward tourists, but it still offers a glimpse of real Ainu culture if you look past the souvenirs.

Aside from a variety of shops selling handmade accessories, folk art, leather goods, and woodcrafts, there is a notable theater called **Ikor** ("Treasure," 4-7-84 Akan-ko Onsen, Akan-chō; tel. 0154/67-2727; www.akanainu.jp/en/about/ikoro; ¥1,500 and up for most performances), where traditional music, dance, puppet shows, and fire rituals are performed. The folklore museum **Ainu Living Memorial Hall Poncise** (4-7-20 Akan-ko Onsen, Akan-chō; tel. 0154/67-2727; www.akanainu.jp/en/about/hall; 10am-9pm daily; free) sits atop the hill at the end of the village's sole street, and gives a historical glimpse of daily life of the Ainu, including reconstructed traditional buildings recalling the old days. Fair warning: There are unfortunately a few pitiful displays of animals in cages—dogs and bears—in the village. This is sadly a common feature of many Ainu villages, meant to draw tourists.

Boat Cruises

AKAN SIGHTSEEING CRUISE

4-5-8 Akan-ko Onsen, Akan-chō; tel. 0154/67-2511; www.akankisen.com; ¥2,000 adults, ¥1,040 children

The Akan-ko Sightseeing Cruise departs from Akan-ko Onsen, plying the waters of Akan-ko in an 18-kilometer (11-mi) loop in 85 minutes. Along the way, the boat stops at a small research center on an island in the lake's north where balls of green algae, called marimo, bob in tanks. If it's sunny, the mossy orbs often come to the surface to bask in the light (photosynthesis). If it's cloudy or cold, they retreat. Akan-ko is one of the only places in the world where these little plants are known to form. It can take up to five centuries for one the size of a soccer ball to take shape.

Hiking

Before setting out on a hike, pick up an English-language map at one of the park's information centers.

ME-AKANDAKE

Distance: *7.5 km (4.7 mi) round-trip*
Time: *4-5 hours round-trip*
Trailhead: *Me-Akan Onsen, about 15 minutes' drive southwest of Akan-ko Onsen via Route 241*
Information and maps: *Akan Kohan Eco-Museum Center; www.mountainsofhokkaido.com/hikes/meakan-dake*

There are some great hikes around Akan-ko, with the trail leading to the summit of Me-Akandake (1,499 meters/4,917 feet) atop the list. This active volcano is the park's highest peak and is another member of Japan's "100 famous mountains" club. The trail is suitably volcanic in nature, with sparse vegetation sprouting from loose soil, including alpine blossoms like rhododendrons and carnations. The vista from the top of the lake-studded landscape is stunning.

The best way to approach the hike is first to drive to **Me-Akan Onsen** (720 meters/2,362 feet). Once you've reached Me-Akan Onsen, the trailhead begins in a spruce forest where you'll begin your ascent to the summit before returning to Me-Akan Onsen via the Onneto Nature Trail. A caveat: Be safe and pick up a map at the Akan Kohan Eco-Museum Center before setting out. Moreover, check on the current trail conditions. Me-Akandake acts up sometimes, prompting temporary trail closure due to falling rocks.

MASHŪDAKE

Distance: *14.4 km (8.9 mi) round-trip*
Time: *4-6 hours round-trip*
Trailhead: *Next to observation Deck Number 1 parking lot*
Information and maps: *Kawayu Eco-Museum Center; www.kawayu-eco-museum.com/english/wp-content/uploads/2017/03/mashu_english.pdf; https://japanhike.wordpress.com/2012/02/06/mt-mashu*

If you want to take in epic views of the pristine lake of Mashū-ko, the best way is to ascend to the top of Mashūdake (857 meters/2,811 feet). The trailhead for this wonderful hike is found near **Observation Deck Number 1,** just off Route 52 beside the southwestern edge of the lake. The trail curls around roughly one-third of the lake until it reaches the summit of the peak looming over the western rim of the caldera. It's just over 7 kilometers (4 mi) one-way, passing through grassland and forest. On a cautionary note, the area is known for being home to a large number of higuma (brown bears). Be safe and carry a bear bell to keep the lumbering creatures at bay.

Food and Accommodations

★ PORONNO

4-7-8 Akan-ko Onsen, Akan-chō; tel. 0154/67-2159; www.poronno.com; 12pm-9:30pm (last order 8:30pm) daily May-Oct., 12:30pm-8:30pm (last order 8pm) daily Nov.-Apr.; ¥1,500 lunch, ¥5,000 dinner

Be sure to have a meal at Poronno, located in the Ainu Kontan in Akan-ko Onsen. The eatery serves Ainu cuisine and eschews additives; instead, locally sourced items like venison set meals and ramen loaded with leeks pulled from local mountainsides are served.

★ ARTINN

3-2-40 Kawayu Onsen, Teshikaga-chō; tel. 015/486-7773; www.artinn.asia; ¥18,000 d

This artist-run hotel, about 2.3 kilometers (1.4 mi) east of Kussharo-ko in the town of Kawayu Onsen, ensures a quirky stay. There are three basic rooms with futons that guests can roll out as they please, and three galleries featuring left-field works by local artists. There's an open-air bath (private rental ¥3,000) available for each room. Some rooms have spacious balconies overlooking a river. All rooms have private restrooms. There's no food on-site, but the friendly staff speak limited English and can recommend eateries nearby.

FAMILY CAMP HANAFURARI

181 Kussharo, Teshikaga-chō; tel. 090/9753-4704; www.hanafurari.jp; from ¥6,000 tent rental with breakfast and dinner, from ¥5,000 pp private room (meals not included)

This unique setup includes a campsite for up to eight groups (tent rental is available) and a pension with four private rooms, sleeping from two to six guests, each with an en suite bath. There's a shared bathroom and toilet inside the pension for those who camp, and a space they can flee to should the weather take an intemperate turn. All guests have access to an unconventional breakfast of curry and a filling BBQ dinner for an additional sum (¥3,000 pp regular, ¥5,000 pp premium for those who stay in the pension). For those opting to camp, meals are automatically included in the price.

Information and Services

- **Akan Kohan Eco-Museum Center** (1-1-1 Akan-ko Onsen, Akan-chō; tel. 0154/67-4100; http://en.kushiro-lakeakan.com; 9am-5pm daily Aug. 21-July 31, 9am-6pm daily Aug. 1-20; free)
- **Kawayu Eco-Museum Center** (2-2-6

The Ainu

Japan's indigenous people, the Ainu, have maintained a culture of woodcraft, song and dance, and elaborate fire rituals for about seven centuries. Today, they have largely assimilated into modern Japan, but the historical journey has been less than smooth.

Ainu tribal handcrafted bracelet

AINU CULTURE AND SPIRITUALITY

Of Caucasian descent with mysterious roots somewhere in Siberia, Ainu men traditionally grow long beards, while the women once tattooed designs on their hands and at the corners of their mouths. They wore clothes made of feathers and fibers derived from trees in an array of complex geometric patterns, vaguely evocative of Polynesian art. They once dwelled in rectangular huts topped by roofs of rush and reeds.

Ainu spirituality is deeply rooted in the natural world, with rivers, rocks, mountains, and animals ascribed divine essence. Even today, many place names connected to nature reveal Ainu roots, particularly in Hokkaido. Some theories suggest that even the Japanese name of Mount Fuji (Fuji-san) is derived from the Ainu word for "fire," combined with san, or "mountain" in Japanese. The Ainu hold the bear in particular esteem as nature's highest spirit, and see the owl as a guardian.

HISTORY OF DISCRIMINATION

Before the onset of modernity, they lived off the land as hunter-gatherers and fishers, gradually pushed northward by the encroachment of the Japanese. Things took a turn for the worse in 1899 with the passing of the Hokkaido Former Aborigines Protection Act, which outlawed their language and their right to hunt and fish, essentially banning all aspects of their culture.

Given small barren parcels of land, the Ainu were instructed to become farmers. Many hid their ancestry and sought to blend in. Throughout the mid-20th century, tourism to Hokkaido began to grow, which gave new income avenues to those who were content to perform cultural rituals for tourists, although many found this trend demeaning. Following significant social activism from the 1960s on, the Ainu received recognition of their right to practice their own culture in 1997, when the Hokkaido Former Aborigines Protection Act was repealed. The Ainu were officially recognized as Japan's indigenous people in 2019.

Despite these welcome changes, the fact remains that only about 24,000 Ainu survive, only a few of whom have four Ainu grandparents.

VISIT AND LEARN MORE

If you're interested enough in Ainu ways to make a detour to explore their world more deeply, the **Nibutani Ainu Culture Museum** (55 Biratori-chō, Nibutani, Saru-gun; tel. 01457/2-2892; www.town.biratori.hokkaido.jp/biratori/nibutani; 9am-4:30pm daily, ¥400 adults, ¥150 ages 7-15) may be the best living representation in Japan of their dwindling ways. Located in the district of Nibutani in the town of **Biratori,** about 110 km/68 mi (1 hour 40 minutes' drive) southeast of Sapporo, 80 percent of the town's inhabitants are of Ainu heritage. English-language information at this museum is profuse, and amiable researchers are on staff to answer any questions you may have.

Kawayu Onsen; tel. 015/483-4100; www.kawayu-eco-museum.com; 8am-5pm Thurs.-Tues. Apr.-mid-July and Sept.-Oct., 8am-5pm daily 3rd week of July-Aug., 9am-4pm Thurs.-Tues. Nov.-Mar.)

Getting There

For minimal hassle, if you enjoy long drives under open skies, the best way to reach Akan National Park from Sapporo is by **rental car.** The drive to the western side of the park from Sapporo, via the Dōtō Expressway and National Route 241, is about four hours long (282 km/175 mi). As with any long drive in Japan, using your car's trusty inbuilt GPS (in English) is recommended.

Reaching Akan National Park via public transportation is tricky given its remoteness, but possible. The best option by public transport is to ride the limited express train from **JR Sapporo Station** to **JR Kushiro Station** (4.5 hours; ¥9,990). **Akan Bus Co.** (tel. 0154/37-8651; www.akanbus.co.jp) offers guided tours from JR Kushiro Station to Akan-ko and Mashū-ko from mid-July through October. The tours run from Kushiro to Abashiri, passing through Kawayu Onsen, Mashū-ko, and Akan-ko onsen along the way. Inquire for details. Reservations are required. Buses also run between Akan-ko Onsen and Asahikawa, en route passing through Sōunkyō Onsen in Daisetsuzan National Park, for a journey of 5 hours (¥4,800).

Another option is flying from Sapporo's **New Chitose Airport** to **Kushiro Airport** (40 minutes; ¥13,000). From Kushiro Airport, three to four daily public **buses** run to Akan-ko (2 hours; ¥2,190). There are also plenty of car rental outlets at the airport. Having your own wheels removes a lot of headache associated with getting around the region. From Kushiro, it's 1 hour 30 minutes' drive northwest via Highway 666 and Marimo National Highway (National Highway 240) to Akan-ko Onsen (71 km/44 mi), the closest gateway to Akan National Park.

If you're going directly to Kawayu Onsen, near Mashū-ko, it's possible to take the JR Senmo line from JR Kushiro Station, south of the park, to JR Kawayu Onsen Station (1.5 hours; ¥1,840). The JR Senmo line also runs from the northern port town of Abashiri to the west of Shiretoko National Park to JR Kawayu Onsen Station (1.5 hours; ¥1,640), or from Shiretoko-Shari, near the southwestern corner of Shiretoko National Park (1 hour, ¥930).

Getting Around

When it comes to getting around Akan National Park, the only feasible option is having your own **car.** Drive between Akan-ko Onsen, located on **Route 240,** and Mashū-ko via **Route 241,** stopping in Sokodai to take in some gorgeous scenery as you go.

★ SHIRETOKO NATIONAL PARK

知床国立公園

The Shiretoko Peninsula, which juts more than 60 kilometers (37 mi) into the Sea of Okhotsk in the island's faraway northeast, was once considered the edge of the earth by the Ainu. The very name Shiretoko National Park is adapted from the Ainu word "Sir etok," which means just that. The far-flung region is beautiful and untamed even by Hokkaido standards. So remote is Shiretoko that you can't even drive to its tip at Shiretoko Cape—roads stop roughly three-fourths of the way. One vista that can be seen by car is the **Shiretoko Pass** along Route 334, with views of **Rausu-dake** (1,661 meters/5,449 feet) from the small village of **Utoro** in the west, or **Rausu** in the east. Your only options from here are to hike vast distances or hop aboard one of the sightseeing boats that ply the peninsula's western coast.

The park is home to large populations of deer, foxes, and formidable brown bears that are a real and present danger for those venturing into its backcountry, with mountains blanketed in dense forest. During winter, some of the southernmost drift ice in the northern hemisphere forms off the peninsula's rugged western shore. The peninsula was named a UNESCO World Heritage Site in 2005 for its extraordinary wealth of biodiversity and the unique ways that its natural worlds interact on land and at sea.

It goes without saying that reaching and navigating this far-flung wonderland is a challenge. But those who make the journey reap ample rewards. If you want to see Hokkaido—and Japan—at its most wild, there is no better place.

Boat Cruises

Sightseeing cruise boats depart from Utoro and Rausu from mid-April to mid-November. A ride aboard one of these boats is the best way to see the rugged, otherwise inaccessible coastline of weather-beaten cliffs, punctuated by cascading waterfalls, lounging sea lions, deer, foxes, and foraging brown bear mothers with their cubs. Alongside stunning views of the dramatic Shiretoko coast, these cruises also get up close and personal with the diverse marine life of the area, including orcas, whales, and dolphins. Keep your eyes on the skies too. In winter, Steller's sea eagles and white-tailed eagles soar overhead. In the warmer months, shearwaters, skuas, and horn-billed puffins descend to the water to feed, and the occasional black-footed albatross appears.

SHIRETOKO NATURE CRUISE

27-1 Hon-chō, Rausu-chō; tel. 0153/87-4001; www.e-shiretoko.com; 7am-6pm daily; 1 hour ¥4,400 pp or 2.5 hours ¥11,000 pp in winter, 2.5 hours ¥8,800 pp in summer

Operating out of Rausu on the east coast, Shiretoko Nature Cruise offers excursions on smaller ships with open observation decks through the Nemuro Strait.

AURORA CRUISES

107 Utoro Higashi; tel. 0152/24-2146; https://ms-aurora.com/shiretoko/en; 9am-5pm daily late Apr.-Oct.; prices vary with season and route

On the west coast, Aurora offers cruises aboard larger ships with all the extras you'd expect—snack bar, indoor seating—from Utoro to Kamuiwakka Falls from late April to late October (1.5 hours; ¥3,100 adults, ¥1,550 elementary school students) and from Utoro to Cape Shiretoko (3 hours 45 minutes; ¥6,800 adults, ¥3,300 elementary school students). Aurora also offers hour-long cruises from late January through early April through drift ice floes aboard an icebreaker, departing from the port of Abashiri (tel. 0152/43-5000;

wooden boardwalk at Shiretoko Goko Lakes

https://ms-aurora.com/abashiri/en; 9am-5pm daily; ¥3,500 adults, ¥1,750 elementary school students).

Hiking

Before doing any hiking, stop by the helpful **Shiretoko Nature Center.** Stock up on English-language maps and pamphlets, and ask any questions here before setting off on any wilderness journeys.

More seasoned mountaineers should look into the **Shiretoko Traverse.** This 25-kilometer (15-mi) trek requires at least two full days; it starts at Rausu-dake in the south, heads north over the top of Io-zan, and ends at the warm cascade of Kamuiwakkayu Falls. There are four campsites along the way. The terrain is tough and the risks, including bears, are real. Stop by the Nature Center to inform staff of your plans and gather maps before striking out.

FUREPE WATERFALL

Distance: *2 km (1.2 mi) one-way*
Time: *20 minutes one-way*
Trailhead: *Shiretoko Nature Center*
Information and maps: *Shiretoko Nature Center; http://center.shiretoko.or.jp/guide/furepe*

If you don't intend to take longer hikes but would like to at least stroll through the landscape, weaving through fields that lead to dramatic cliffs, the walk to Furepe Waterfall begins from the Shiretoko Nature Center. It's a good addition to a short itinerary focused on nature cruises or driving through the park. Don't expect booming falls. At about 100 meters (328 feet) high, Furepe is fed by ground water and at times only trickles into the Sea of Okhotsk. The trail's main selling points are the scenery that surrounds it on the way to the falls, and its accessibility.

SHIRETOKO GOKO LAKES

Distance: *0.8 km (0.5 mi) for elevated boardwalk; 3 km (1.9 mi) for hike around all five lakes*
Time: *40 minutes for elevated boardwalk; 1.5 hours around all five lakes*
Trailhead: *Shiretoko Go-ko Lakes Field House*
Information and maps: *Shiretoko Go-ko Field House; www.goko.go.jp/multilingual_eng*

This cluster of five petite alpine lakes formed by the eruption of neighboring Io-zan (Sulphur Mountain) is set in a primordial forest, with the snow-streaked Shiretoko mountain range towering in the background. This region of the park's relative ease of access means that it can be inundated by hikers in the peak summer months. But crowds aside, this area boasts breathtaking scenery and a lush ecosystem.

You have the option to hike along a free, 800-meter (0.5-mi) elevated wooden platform that leads to the blandly named Lake 1 (open late Apr.-Nov.). The purpose of having this elevated path is to protect the delicate ecosystem. Or, you can also stay on the ground and walk a longer 3-kilometer (2-mi) path that winds around all five lakes.

To hike the longer trail late April-May 9 or August 1-October 20, you'll have to first register at the **Shiretoko Go-ko Lakes Field House** (tel. 0152/24-3323; www.goko.go.jp; 8am-4:30pm daily late Apr.-Jul., 7:30am-6:30pm Aug.-Sept. 15, 7:30am-6pm Sept. 16-30, 7:30am-5:30pm Oct. 1-20, 8:30am-5pm Oct. 21-31, 8:30am-4:30pm Nov. 1-8), purchase a ticket (¥250), and patiently sit through a lecture on bear safety. For perspective, some 600 higuma (brown bears) roam the forests, mountains, and coasts of Shiretoko alone.

This process becomes more involved during peak bear season, May 10-July 31. During this period, hikers are only allowed to take the longer trail as members of a tour group led by a licensed guide. It costs around ¥5,000 per person to join one of these tours, which accommodate up to 10 people. Tours last around three hours and depart from the field house roughly every 10 minutes. It's possible to join one of the tours on the same day if space allows, but register in advance online to be safe (www.goko.go.jp/fivelakes).

To reach the Shiretoko Go-ko Field House, drive about 5 kilometers (3.1 mi) north of Utoro, following the main road that leads into the park, then veer left at the Shiretoko

Nature Center. The Shiretoko Go-ko Lakes Field House will be at the end of the road. Parking costs ¥500 per car.

RAUSU-DAKE

Distance: *12 km (7.5 mi) round-trip*
Time: *7-9 hours round-trip*
Trailhead: *Hotel Chinohate (near Iwaobetsu Hot Spring)*
Information and maps: *Rausu Visitor Center; https://japanhike.wordpress.com/tag/shiretoko*

Another great hike at the southern edge of the park, smack in the middle of the peninsula, is Rausu-dake. The 1,660-meter (5,446-foot) peak stands amid the park's central north-south spine. Much of the snowcap melts from June-September, making it possible to walk to the summit in four to five hours. As elsewhere in Shiretoko, carry a bear bell on this hike. Brown bears are abundant in the Rausu-dake area.

Begin your ascent at the trailhead behind the now-closed Hotel Chinohate, located near Iwaobetsu Onsen, accessible from Route 93. From the top, you can simply return to Iwaobetsu Onsen. Alternatively, when you reach the three-way junction on your way back, follow the trail that leads down the opposite face toward Rausu, for roughly a three-hour descent. If you follow this trail, be sure to stop by **Kuma-no-yu**, a fantastically primitive, sex-separated outdoor onsen beside a sweltering river near the Rausu-side trailhead. Note that there is also a campsite near this ideal post-hike bath.

To access the trailhead with any reasonable level of convenience, you'll want to have a car. The trailhead is 4 kilometers (2.5 mi) from the nearest bus stop (Iwaobetsu), which adds a significant leg to the journey if you're walking the whole way. Also, think twice before taking a taxi from Utoro, as fares for the drive to the trailhead can climb to ¥7,000.

Onsen

KUMA-NO-YU

Yunosawa-chō, Rausu; tel. 0153/87-2126; 24 hours; free

Kuma-no-yu is an excellent outdoor onsen, with two pools separated by gender with a privacy fence. The pools sit beside a boiling river a few minutes' walk south of Rausu Onsen Campground (Yunosawa-chō, Rausu; tel. 0153/87-2126; https://kanko.rausu-town.jp/spots/view/29), and near the trailhead to Rausu-dake on the Rausu side of the mountain. The bare-bones baths are the ideal place to submerge yourself in Shiretoko's back woods. Stop by the Rausu Visitor Center for information on reaching these rustic pools.

Accommodations

SHIRETOKO SERAI

41-5 Rebuncho, Rausu-chō; tel. 0153/85-8800; www.shiretokoserai.com; ¥11,400 pp d with 2 meals

On the Rausu (eastern) side of the peninsula, this mid-size hotel has smart, well-appointed rooms with small but clean private baths and toilets. A Western-style breakfast buffet is served in the shared lounge, which functions as a bar in the evening. Lunch and dinner are also served from an a la carte menu to staying guests and visitors. The hotel arranges a number of tours around the park with English-speaking guides (www.shiretokoserai.com/en/tour; prices vary by tour).

★ HOTEL KIFU CLUB SHIRETOKO

318 Utoro-higashi, Shari; tel. 0152/24-3541; www.kifuu.com; ¥13,200 pp with 2 meals

With a mix of Japanese- and Western-style rooms, as well as a private cabin—all facing the Sea of Okhotsk—this property is a stylish and comfortable place to stay on the western coast of the peninsula near Utoro. There's a shared indoor onsen bath (sex-separated) and a private open-air onsen pool looking out to sea. Japanese-style breakfast and dinner are served in a dining area next to a communal lounge with a fireplace and a large wooden balcony facing the ocean.

Information and Services

- **Shiretoko Nature Center** (531 Iwaubetsu, Shari-chō; tel. 0152/24-2114; http://center.shiretoko.or.jp; 8am-5:30pm daily Apr.

20-Oct. 20, 9am-4pm daily Oct. 21-Apr. 19; 5 km/3 mi north of Utoro)

- **Rausu Visitor Center** (6-27 Yunosawa, Rausu; tel. 0153/87-2828; http://rausu-vc.jp; 9am-5pm Tues.-Sun. May-Oct., 10am-4pm Tues.-Sun. Nov.-Apr.)

Getting There and Around

It's possible to reach the park via public transport, but if you like scenic drives and aren't in a rush, driving a **rental car** across the island is an enjoyable option. Striking out from Sapporo, the roughly 450-kilometer (280-mi) drive is about 6-7 hours long, and goes through Asahikawa en route.

Via public transport, if you're approaching the park from the west, take the **JR Senmo** line from Abashiri Station, roughly 50 km (31 mi) north of Lake Kussharo on the northern coastline of Hokkaido's remote east, to **Shiretoko-Shari Station** (45 minutes; ¥970), located roughly 40 kilometers (25 mi) southwest of the park. To reach Abashiri Station from Sapporo, take Limited Express Lilac 13 to Asahikawa, then transfer to Limited Express Taisetsu 1 for the remainder of the trip (4 hours 30 minutes), which costs ¥10,540 from Sapporo and ¥8,560 from Asahikawa. Coming from the south, Shiretoko-Shari can be reached via the JR Senmo line from Kushiro (2.5 hours; ¥3,190). If you come all the way from Sapporo, via Kushiro, the entire journey takes about 6-7 hours (¥11,970). Note that if you prefer to drive for the second half of the journey, rental car outlets can be found around Abashiri Station and Kushiro Station.

Once in the park, infrequent **buses** or a rental car are the only means of transport in Shiretoko. Trains and buses running to and from the park are sporadic, so be prepared to exercise great patience if you plan to rely on public transport. From Shiretoko-Shari, public buses run to Utoro at the park's southwest edge (1 hour; ¥1,800). Buses continue on from Utoro to Shiretoko Go-ko (25 minutes; ¥700). From there, other buses run to Kamuiwakkayu Falls (30 minutes; ¥1,300). Other buses run between Utoro and Rausu (55 minutes; ¥1,380), and from Rausu down to Kushiro (3.5-4 hours; ¥4,940). Generally speaking, none of the buses linking to the park operates outside of the months of May-October.

Note that the road leading from Shiretoko Go-ko to Kamuiwakkayu Falls is only open for buses running between these two points August 1-25 and September 15-24. Otherwise, having your own car is by far the best way to make it around the park. Given how much effort is involved in making the journey to Shiretoko, it pays to combine a trip here with a jaunt to Akan National Park and the Kushiro Wetlands to the south.

Rishiri-Rebun-Sarobetsu National Park
利尻礼文サロベツ国立公園

Located off the far northern coast of Hokkaido, near the rough-and-ready port town of Wakkanai, the islands of Rebun and Rishiri are the focus of Rishiri-Rebun-Sarobetsu National Park. In summer they are awash in wildflowers and travelers. Rebun is focused on meadows of wildflowers, while Rishiri, a giant volcano, draws those hungry for a challenge.

Located about 80 kilometers (50 mi) west of Hokkaido's northernmost tip, **Rebun** (礼文島) is a long sliver of land defined by a rugged coastline of craggy cliffs and waterfalls, fishing hamlets, and a plethora of alpine flowers in summer. Gazing east from Rebun's shores, you'll see **Rishiri** (利尻島) about 10 kilometers (6 mi) to the south, towering like a scaled-down Mount Fuji, seeming to float on the ocean's surface. The round, lofty counterpart to flat Rebun, Rishiri's interior is dominated by Mount Rishiri, a dormant volcano.

HIKING

For more information on the Rebun's hikes, visit www.rebun-island.jp/en/rebunnavienglish.pdf.

Unlike Rebun, with a range of difficulty levels, hiking on Rishiri revolves around summiting Rishiri-zan (10 hours round-trip), a grueling ascent of 1,500 meters (5,000 feet) to the peak. Climbing season is limited (June-Sept.) and the slog to the top is easy to underestimate. For guided hikes on Rishiri (from around ¥5,000), visit www.explore-share.com/hiking-trips/japan/rishiri-island.

HIKING TO REBUN-DAKE

Distance: *4.5 km (2.8 mi) one-way*
Time: *4 hours round-trip*
Trailhead: *Nairo (eastern shore)*
Information and maps: *www.rebun-island.jp/en/trekking/index.html; https://mountainsofhokkaido.com/hikes/rebun-dake*

Of the many trails winding around Rebun, the one that affords the best vistas of the island's topography leads to the top of Rebun-dake (490 meters/1,607 feet). To reach the trailhead, take the bus from Kafuka to Nairo. From the top, the island's gently rolling contours come into focus.

HIKING TO SHIRETOKO

Distance: *5.3 km (3.3 mi) one-way*
Time: *5 hours round-trip*
Trailhead: *Kafuka (eastern shore)*
Information and maps: *www.rebun-island.jp/en/trekking/index.html*

Another worthwhile hike takes you over the rounded southern end of the island, through meadows of wildflowers during summer, to **Momoiwa** ("Peach Rock"). From this rock at an elevation of 250 meters (820 feet), continue on to **Shiretoko,** at the island's far southern edge, marveling at the flowers blanketing the hills. From Shiretoko, sporadic buses run to **Kafuka,** where you can take the ferry back to **Wakkanai** on the main island. Check the bus schedule before starting the hike. Luckily, you can kill time at **Usuyuki-no-yu** (961-1 Kafuka-mura; tel. 0163/86-2345; www.usuyuki.jp; noon-10pm daily; ¥600), where you can soak your tired muscles in an onsen overlooking the ocean, a stone's throw from the ferry station in Kafuka.

HIKING RISHIRI-ZAN

Distance: *12.9 km (8 mi) round-trip*
Time: *9-10 hours round-trip*
Trailhead: *Behind Rishiri Hokuroku Campsite*

view from a hike on Rebun Island

(about 4 km/2.5 mi south from Oshidomari Port, from which it's 40 minutes' walk or 10 minutes by taxi)

Information and maps: *Rishirifuji Tourist Information Center; https://mountainsofhokkaido.com/hikes/rishiri-yama/; www.halfwayanywhere.com/trails/japan-hikes/hiking-mount-rishiri-rishizan-guide/; https://hikesinjapan.yamakei-online.com/course/79.php*

Should you want to climb the whole peak of Rishiri-zan, the main trailhead for the island's most popular and accessible **Oshidomari Trail** is located about 5 kilometers (3.1 mi) inland from Oshidomari, the island's main ferry port. Ask about bus times and pick up a map at the island's tourist information center in Oshidomari. Should you need to take shelter for the night or during inclement weather, there's a no-frills **mountain hut** (no reservation needed), without running water, a bit above the eighth station (about 1,200 meters/4,000 feet).

Seen from neighboring Rebun Island, Rishiri resembles a floating peak, often cloaked in mist, emerging straight from the ocean's surface. From the trailhead (220 m/722 ft), elevation rises a significant 1,511 meters (939 ft), ensuring stellar views of Rebun Island and, farther still, Sakhalin on clear days. As you begin to ascend through the lower section of the trail, the path runs through a verdant forest of pine and beech trees. As you ascend the precipitous path, trees are replaced by vivid meadows of wildflowers that reach their peak in July-August. Note that there are actually two peaks, of which the taller (south) summit (1,721 m/5,646 ft) is closed to hikers, due to dangerous levels of erosion. Once you've reached the north summit, retrace your path back down.

Be sure to start early in the morning—6am is a good target—so you can return during daylight hours. Most accommodations on the island offer shuttle services to the trailhead and back for guests, most of whom make the trip solely to trek to the top of the peak. You'll also need to pick up a portable toilet kit at the tourist information center in Oshidomari Ferry Port Terminal (¥400). Some accommodations on the island provide them, too. There are no toilet facilities along the trail. Bring layers and rain gear, as well as plenty of water (2 liters/0.5 gallons or more) and some snacks from Oshidomari Port area.

To rest your feet after your hike, the steamy pools of **Rishiri Fuji Onsen** (227-7 Minato-machi, Oshidomari; tel. 0163/82-2388; 11am-9pm June-Aug., noon-9pm Sept.-May) are located on the main road that leads from Oshidomari to the Rishiri-zan trailhead.

ACCOMMODATIONS

★ MARUZEN PENSION RERA MOSIR

227-5 Sakaemachi, Oshidomari; tel. 0163/82-2295; www.maruzen.com/tic/oyado; ¥11,000 pp with 2 meals

The best place to stay overnight on Rishiri, this thoroughly modern B&B is surrounded by natural splendor, albeit slightly removed from the ferry terminal (a 20-minute walk). Contact the front desk ahead of your arrival to arrange a free pickup. The biggest draw of the inn, however, is the owner: a mountaineer who knows the island's trails intimately, who is ready to answer questions and is happy to whisk guests to the trailhead for Rishiri-zan. Dinners and Japanese-style breakfasts are served in the dining room.

PENSION U-NI-

Tonnai, Kaduka-mura; tel. 0163/86-1541; www.p-uni.burari.biz; ¥12,650 pp with 2 meals

For a spot to sleep on Rebun, Pension U-ni- is a very welcoming, family-owned inn that exudes a heavy dose of charm. Inform the desk ahead of time and they will pick you up at the ferry terminal for free.

INFORMATION AND SERVICES

- **Rebun Information Center** (Kafuka ferry terminal; tel. 0163/86-2655; www.rebun-island.jp; 9am-5pm daily mid-Apr.-mid-Oct.)
- **Rishirifuji Tourist Information Center** (Oshidomari Port Ferry Terminal; tel. 0163/82-2201; 8am-5:30pm daily mid-Apr.-mid-Oct.)

GETTING THERE

Driving from Sapporo, take Hokkaido Expressway to National Highway No. 232 and then Route 106 the rest of the way to Wakkanai (5 hours; 328 km/204 mi).

Coming from Sapporo by train, take the **limited express** to Asahikawa, then transfer to a separate limited express train bound for Wakkanai (5.5 hours; ¥11,090), a port town on the northern tip of Hokkaido. It's also possible to **fly** from Sapporo to **Wakkanai** (¥12,000-25,000); the airport is linked downtown by bus (35 minutes; ¥700). From Wakkanai, **Heart Land Ferry** (tel. 011/233-8010; www.heartlandferry.jp) runs to both Rishiri's Oshidomari port (1 hour 40 minutes; from ¥2,550) 2-4 times daily and Rebun's Kafuka port (1 hour 55 minutes; from ¥2,850) 2-3 times daily.

GETTING AROUND

On Rishiri, buses run in a loop around the island (¥2,250). The trip from **Kutsugata** on the west shore to Oshidomari, the site of the main ferry terminal, takes about 45 minutes (¥760). On Rebun, buses run from the main port at **Kafuka** on the eastern coast, north to **Sukoton-misaki** (70 minutes; ¥1,250). They also run between Kafuka and **Shiretoko** in the south (15 minutes; ¥300). Inquire about bus schedules and routes at the ferry terminal on each island. If you plan to **drive** or **cycle,** rental shops abound near the ferry terminals. Rebun's hilly terrain is best explored by car, while the relatively flat road around Rishiri begs to be explored by bicycle.

Kyushu 九州

Japan's third-largest island, Kyushu is an appealing alternative to the usual Kantō and Kansai circuits on most travelers' itineraries. The subtropical, southernmost of Japan's four main islands, Kyushu presents immense variety, from the ramen stalls and rowdy nightlife of cosmopolitan Fukuoka to the pottery kilns of Saga. Phoenix-like Nagasaki, rebuilt from the ashes of its tragic past, hums with joie de vivre today, and volcanic peaks and fertile valleys swathed in cedar beckon hikers to the heart of the island. And in the far south, Sakurajima (Japan's Vesuvius) smolders imposingly across the bay from the laid-back city of Kagoshima.

Indeed, throughout the island—Japan's most intensely volcanic and home to one of the world's largest calderas (Aso-san)—smoking

Itinerary Ideas 600
Fukuoka 605
Nagasaki...............624
Central Kyushu.........639
Miyazaki Prefecture 653
Kagoshima 660

Highlights

Look for ★ to find recommended sights, activities, dining, and lodging.

★ **Fukuoka's Street Food Stalls:** Squeeze in beside locals at one of Fukuoka's hundred-plus food stalls to gorge on tonkotsu ramen or grilled meat on sticks, washed down with beer (page 614).

★ **Saga's Pottery Towns:** Pore over stunning pieces of porcelain and finely sculpted clay in the ceramics centers of Karatsu, Imari, and Arita (page 620).

★ **Aso-san:** Marvel at the vast expanse that is one of the world's largest calderas, epitomizing Kyushu's volcanic terrain (page 643).

★ **Onsen:** Submerge yourself to the shoulders in some of Japan's best hot springs (page 650).

★ **Takachiho:** Delve deep into Shinto's roots at this remote sacred power spot, centered on a mossy gorge and a smattering of ancient shrines (page 653).

★ **Ibusuki's Hot-Sand Baths:** For a different take on warmth-induced R&R, bury yourself up to the neck in geothermally heated sand on Ibusuki's coast (page 669).

Kyushu

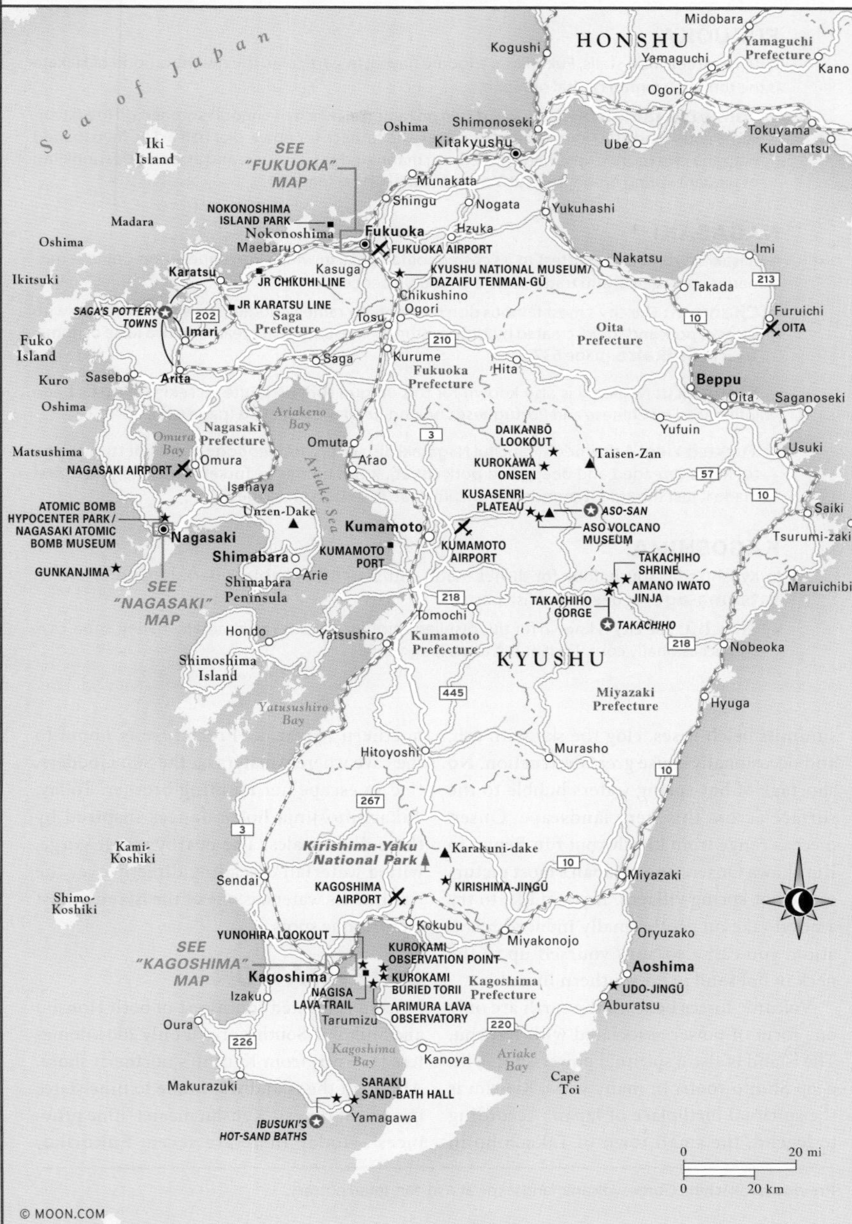
HONSHU
Sea of Japan
Midobara
Kogushi
Yamaguchi Prefecture
Yamaguchi
Kano
Ogori
Shimonoseki
Oshima
Tokuyama
Kitakyushu
Ube
Kudamatsu
Iki Island
SEE "FUKUOKA" MAP
Munakata
Shingu
Nogata
Yukuhashi
NOKONOSHIMA ISLAND PARK
Nokonoshima
Madara
Fukuoka
Hzuka
Oshima
Maebaru
FUKUOKA AIRPORT
Imi
Nakatsu
Kasuga
KYUSHU NATIONAL MUSEUM/ DAZAIFU TENMAN-GŪ
Karatsu
Ikitsuki
JR CHIKUHI LINE
Takada
213
Chikushino
SAGA'S POTTERY TOWNS
JR KARATSU LINE
Furuichi
202
Ogori
Saga Prefecture
Tosu
10
OITA
Imari
Oita Prefecture
Fuko Island
210
Kurume
Saga
Hita
Fukuoka Prefecture
Kuro
Sasebo
Arita
Beppu
Oita
Saganoseki
Oshima
Ariakeno Bay
Nagasaki Prefecture
Yufuin
Omura Bay
Omuta
3
DAIKANBŌ LOOKOUT
Usuki
Matsushima
Taisen-Zan
Omura
Arao
KUROKAWA ONSEN
NAGASAKI AIRPORT
Ariake Sea
57
Isahaya
10
KUSASENRI PLATEAU
ATOMIC BOMB HYPOCENTER PARK / NAGASAKI ATOMIC BOMB MUSEUM
Unzen-Dake
ASO-SAN
Saiki
Kumamoto
ASO VOLCANO MUSEUM
Nagasaki
Tsurumi-zaki
KUMAMOTO PORT
KUMAMOTO AIRPORT
Shimabara
TAKACHIHO SHRINE
GUNKANJIMA
Arie
AMANO IWATO JINJA
SEE "NAGASAKI" MAP
Shimabara Peninsula
Maruichibi
218
TAKACHIHO GORGE
Tomochi
TAKACHIHO
Hondo
Yatsushiro
Kumamoto Prefecture
218
Nobeoka
KYUSHU
Shimoshima Island
445
Miyazaki Prefecture
Hyuga
Yatusushiro Bay
Hitoyoshi
Murasho
10
267
3
Kirishima-Yaku National Park
Karakuni-dake
Kami-Koshiki
10
Sendai
KIRISHIMA-JINGŪ
Miyazaki
Shimo-Koshiki
KAGOSHIMA AIRPORT
Kokubu
Miyakonojo
Oryuzako
YUNOHIRA LOOKOUT
SEE "KAGOSHIMA" MAP
KUROKAMI OBSERVATION POINT
Kagoshima
KUROKAMI BURIED TORII
Aoshima
Kagoshima Prefecture
Izaku
NAGISA LAVA TRAIL
UDO-JINGŪ
ARIMURA LAVA OBSERVATORY
Aburatsu
Oura
Tarumizu
220
226
Kagoshima Bay
Kanoya
Ariake Bay
Cape Toi
Makurazuki
SARAKU SAND-BATH HALL
IBUSUKI'S HOT-SAND BATHS
Yamagawa
0
20 mi
0
20 km
© MOON.COM

Regional Food Specialties

FUKUOKA

With its street-food stalls, Fukuoka is a foodie haven. In particular, the neighborhood of Hakata is the tonkotsu ramen capital of Japan.

- **Tonkotsu ramen:** A widely loved spin on ramen in which the noodles are served in a flavorsome soup made by simmering pork bones and fatback for upward of half a day, then loaded with cha-shu (pork strips), hard-boiled egg marinated in soy sauce, and a generous sprinkling of piquant spring onion. Try it at **Yatai Mami-chan** (page 613).

NAGASAKI

Nagasaki's hybrid dishes attest to its cosmopolitan past, in which Portuguese and Chinese missionaries, merchants, and traders had a strong presence.

- **Chanpon:** The city's most famous dish is essentially ramen noodles served in salty soup with slices of pork and squid, created by 19th-century Chinese students yearning for a taste of home. Try it at **Shikairō** (page 637).
- **Shippoku:** Nagasaki is also known for this unique spin on haute kaiseki fare that's been influenced by Chinese and Portuguese cooking. Try it at **Kagetsu** (page 635).
- **Turkish rice:** A downright fanciful Nagasaki dish is this hodgepodge of spaghetti, rice, and tonkatsu (breaded and deep-fried pork cutlet). It has no ties to Turkey—the chefs who first made it just thought it sounded exotic. Try it at **Tsuruchan** (page 636).

KAGOSHIMA

In Kyushu's far south, look for dishes made with **kurobuta** (black Berkshire pork) and its **satsuma-age,** or deep-fried fish paste.

- **Shōchū:** The city is known for this distilled spirit made with sweet potato, barley, soba, rice, and occasionally corn. Try it at **Ishizue** (page 665).

summits belch gases, clog the sky with ash, and occasionally cause great destruction. No shortage of hot-spring waters bubble to the surface across this fiery landscape. Onsen meccas range from kitschy but fun Beppu to Kurokawa Onsen, one of Japan's most picturesque hot-spring villages. If you'd like to try a novel take on geothermally induced relaxation, you can also bury yourself up to the neck in hot sand in far southern Ibusuki.

Volcanic forces beneath the earth are only one form of power associated with Kyushu. The island is also a spiritual power-spot, with deep Shinto roots. In many ways, Kyushu is the spiritual birthplace of Japan. According to legend, the small town of Takachiho in northern Miyazaki Prefecture is home to the cave where Amaterasu, the Sun Goddess, fled to escape her taunting brother. Today, Takachiho-jinja hosts dances inspired by these divine tales. The nearby scenic gorge, with a waterfall cascading directly over the rim into its waters, is one of the island's most picturesque spots.

ORIENTATION

Kyushu is located southwest of both Honshu and Shikoku. South Korea is only 200 kilometers (125 mi) from Kyushu's northern shore. Although the island was home to nine states in ancient times—Kyushu means "nine provinces"—today there are seven: **Fukuoka,**

Previous: Takachiho Gorge; volcanic landscape at Aso-san; Imari pottery.

Saga, Nagasaki, Kumamoto, Oita, Miyazaki, and **Kagoshima.** It's easiest to divide these prefectures into three distinct regions: **northern Kyushu, central Kyushu,** and **southern Kyushu.**

Trains are the best way to get around Kyushu, though buses are good for reaching some more remote parts. It's possible to come to the island by ferry from western Shikoku too. Having a car is a godsend in the vast central region around **Aso-san,** some of the remote onsen villages like **Kurokawa,** and the spiritual hot spot of **Takachiho.**

Northern Kyushu

The entry point for most visitors to the island, Northern Kyushu is composed of **Fukuoka Prefecture** in the north-central part of the island, bordered by **Saga Prefecture** to the west, with **Nagasaki Prefecture** accounting for the island's northwest corner.

Fukuoka is the island's biggest city and Japan's eighth most populous, with shinkansen (bullet train) links and an international airport. In neighboring Saga Prefecture, you'll find a number of pottery villages and historic towns. The city of **Nagasaki,** capital of the prefecture of the same name, is the island's second largest metropolis.

Central Kyushu

Alternating between volcanic cones and verdant valleys, Central Kyushu offers stunning vistas, historic towns, and hot springs in the prefectures of **Kumamoto** and **Oita.** The region is among the most geothermally active on earth. East of Nagasaki, across the Ariake Sea, the castle town of Kumamoto is the capital of the prefecture of the same name, which accounts for a large section of the island's heartland including **Aso-san** and its surrounding plateaus and charming **Kurokawa Onsen** to the east. Northeast of Kumamoto lies **Oita Prefecture,** where you'll find the fashionable hot-spring town of **Yufuin** and the geothermal amusement park of **Beppu.**

Southern Kyushu

Kyushu's south includes **Miyazaki Prefecture** in the east and **Kagoshima Prefecture** in the west. This is the southernmost point of Japan's four main islands, and the vibe is laid-back, low-key, and uncrowded.

PLANNING YOUR TIME

By Japanese standards, Kyushu is vast. You could spend weeks slowly discovering its beauty, much of it hidden deep within its volcanic landscape and along its rugged coastline. To make it worth your while, aim to spend a minimum of **five days** on the island, or better yet, a **week.** Kyushu is best approached as a stand-alone destination, or in combination with neighboring Shikoku or Western Honshu. If you have the luxury of time, it's also possible to combine it with a trip into either Tokyo or Kyoto and Kansai.

The best time to visit Kyushu is either **spring** (mid-March-early May) or **autumn** (mid-October-November) when cherry blossoms pop and the leaves blaze red and orange. That said, there's really no time of year when the island cannot be visited, so long as you're prepared to deal with **rainy season** (tsuyu) from late May-June, hot and sticky days July-August, and the potential for **typhoons** September-October. **Winter** is a touch milder on most of the island than in the regions to the north, and snow is rare.

To make the most of your time, **Fukuoka** is the best base for the north of the island. From there, you can make day trips around **Fukuoka Prefecture,** as well as **Saga Prefecture** and even **Nagasaki,** which itself is worth spending a few days exploring. East of Nagasaki, the city of **Kumamoto** is a good jumping-off point for venturing into the island's rugged, volcanic heartland. The city of **Kagoshima** is a great base for maneuvering in the island's south, from **Ibusuki** to **Kirishima-Yaku National Park.**

Best Accommodations

★ **Sakamoto-ya:** You can expect top-notch service and plenty of historic ambience at Nagasaki's oldest ryokan (page 638).

★ **Yamada Bessō:** This family-run inn in the heart of Beppu is an authentic ryokan with an atmosphere that is rich in antique charm (page 649).

★ **Sansou Murata:** This rambling onsen resort artistically made of wood and stone is one of the top places to stay in the stylish hot-spring town of Yufuin (page 651).

★ **Ibusuki Syusui-en:** If you've got the funds, this upscale ryokan is an ideal place to crash after reaching a state of peak relaxation at Ibusuki's nearby hot-sand baths (page 669).

Itinerary Ideas

ONE DAY IN FUKUOKA

1 Start your day walking 10 minutes (about 0.5 km/0.3 mi) north from Hakata Station to **Tōchō-ji,** which houses a massive wooden Buddha statue.

2 Next, walk 5 minutes (0.5 km/0.3 mi) southwest to **Kushida-jinja,** the city's most significant shrine.

3 Swing by the **Fukuoka Asian Art Museum** (a 6-minute, 0.5-km/0.3-mi walk), which spans more than 3,000 works from 23 Asian countries.

4 After that, go for lunch at **Toriden Hakata Honten,** a chicken hot-pot restaurant just around the corner from the museum.

5 After lunch, hop on the Kūkō line at Nakasukawabata Station (4 minutes; 2 stops; ¥210) and head west to Akasaka Station. Go for a tea tasting at **Yorozu,** a chic space 9 minutes (700 m/0.4 mi) from the station where you can get a sense of the depth of Japan's tea tradition, which has deep roots in Kyushu.

6 Next walk 10 minutes (1 km/0.6 mi) west to the sprawling park of **Ōhori-kōen.** Explore the Japanese garden and Fukuoka Castle ruins.

7 As dinnertime approaches, make your way to Nakasu Island (35-minute walk; 2.7 km/1.6 mi to the east), known for its collection of yatai, facing the waterfront of the Nakagawa river. The food at **Tsukasa** is famous.

8 After you've filled up, explore the lively nightlife center of Tenjin, starting with a bawdy show at **Anmitsu Hime Revue,** a 20-minute (1.5-km/0.9-mi) walk from Nakasu Island. The bars here often don't start hopping until around midnight.

ONE DAY IN NAGASAKI

1 Begin your day by paying your respects at **Peace Park** on the northeast side of town. Aim to arrive around 9am.

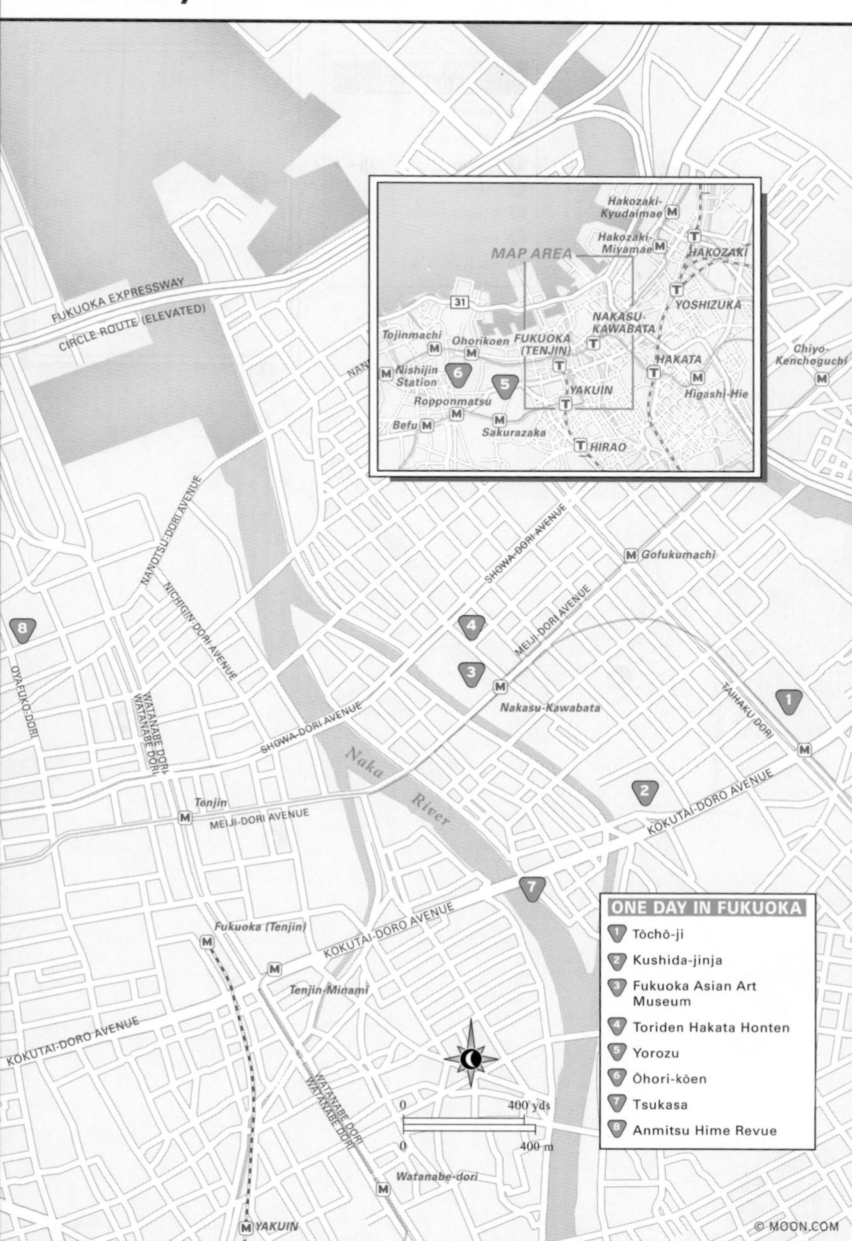

One Day in Fukuoka
FUKUOKA EXPRESSWAY
CIRCLE ROUTE (ELEVATED)
NANOTSU-DORI AVENUE
NICHIGIN-DORI AVENUE
SHOWA-DORI AVENUE
MEIJI-DORI AVENUE
TAIHAKU DORI
KOKUTAI-DORO AVENUE
OYAFUKO-DORI
WATANABE DORI
Naka River
Gofukumachi
Nakasu-Kawabata
Tenjin
Fukuoka (Tenjin)
Tenjin-Minami
Watanabe-dori
YAKUIN
Hakozaki-Kyudaimae
Hakozaki-Miyamae
HAKOZAKI
MAP AREA
YOSHIZUKA
NAKASU-KAWABATA
Tojinmachi
Ohorikoen
FUKUOKA (TENJIN)
HAKATA
Chiyo-Kenchoguchi
Nishijin Station
YAKUIN
Higashi-Hie
Ropponmatsu
Befu
Sakurazaka
HIRAO
31
0
400 yds
400 m
ONE DAY IN FUKUOKA
1 Tōchō-ji
2 Kushida-jinja
3 Fukuoka Asian Art Museum
4 Toriden Hakata Honten
5 Yorozu
6 Ōhori-kōen
7 Tsukasa
8 Anmitsu Hime Revue
© MOON.COM

One Day in Nagasaki

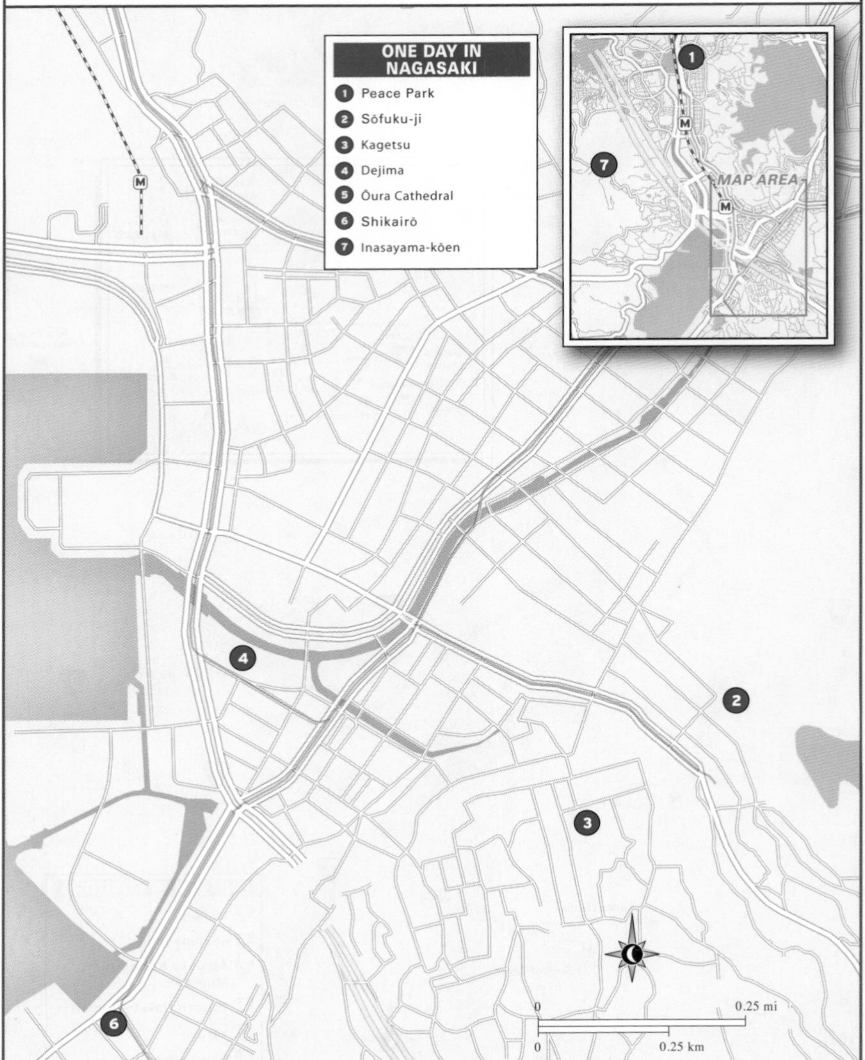

ONE DAY IN NAGASAKI

1. Peace Park
2. Sōfuku-ji
3. Kagetsu
4. Dejima
5. Ōura Cathedral
6. Shikairō
7. Inasayama-kōen

MAP AREA

0 0.25 mi

0 0.25 km

2 Board the tram (line 3) at Peace Park (Heiwa-kōen) tram stop and ride 10 stops south to Civic Hall tram stop (17 minutes; ¥140), then walk 4 minutes south to Meganebashi Bridge. Cross Meganebashi, also known as Spectacles Bridge, to Tera-machi ("Temple Town"). Stop by **Sōfuku-ji,** a temple whose design is heavily influenced by Chinese aesthetics, reflecting the city's deep historical ties to China.

3 For lunch, try Nagasaki's uniquely eclectic spin on kaiseki ryōri known as shippoku. **Kagetsu,** a 6-minute (0.5-km/0.3-mi) walk west from Sōfuku-ji, is one of the best choices.

4 Make your way to **Dejima** (a 10-minute, 700-m/0.4-mi walk northwest), the artificial island built in the 17th century to contain increasingly disruptive foreign traders, principally from Portugal and Holland.

5 Walk 20 minutes (1.5 km/0.9 mi) south and up Dutch Slope, stopping by **Ōura Cathedral.** This district and these specific sights serve as reminders of Nagasaki's long history of engagement with the West.

6 Make your way to Japan's oldest Chinatown (Shinchi), a 5-minute (0.5-km/0.3-mi) walk back down the hill, for dinner. Try **Shikairō,** where Nagasaki's famed chanpon dish originated.

7 Walk 2 minutes east to Ōura Cathedral tram stop and take tram line 5 to Shinchi Chinatown tram stop (3 stops; 6 minutes), then switch to line 1 and ride another 12 minutes north to Takara-machi tram stop (¥140 total). From Takara-machi, walk 15 minutes west, over the Uragami-gawa River, to the lower station of Nagasaki Ropeway to be lifted to the park above. Take in nighttime views of the city from atop **Inasayama-kōen,** considered one of Japan's most beautiful nighttime panoramas.

ONE DAY IN KAGOSHIMA

1 Begin your day at **Sengan-en.** Explore the lovely gardens, admiring the dramatic views of the smoldering cone of Sakurajima looming across the bay.

2 From Sengan-en, take the Machi Meguri Bus (35 minutes; ¥170) or City View Bus (1 hour; ¥190) to Suizokukanguchi bus stop, then walk 8 minutes southeast to the ferry

Ōura Cathedral

One Day in Kagoshima

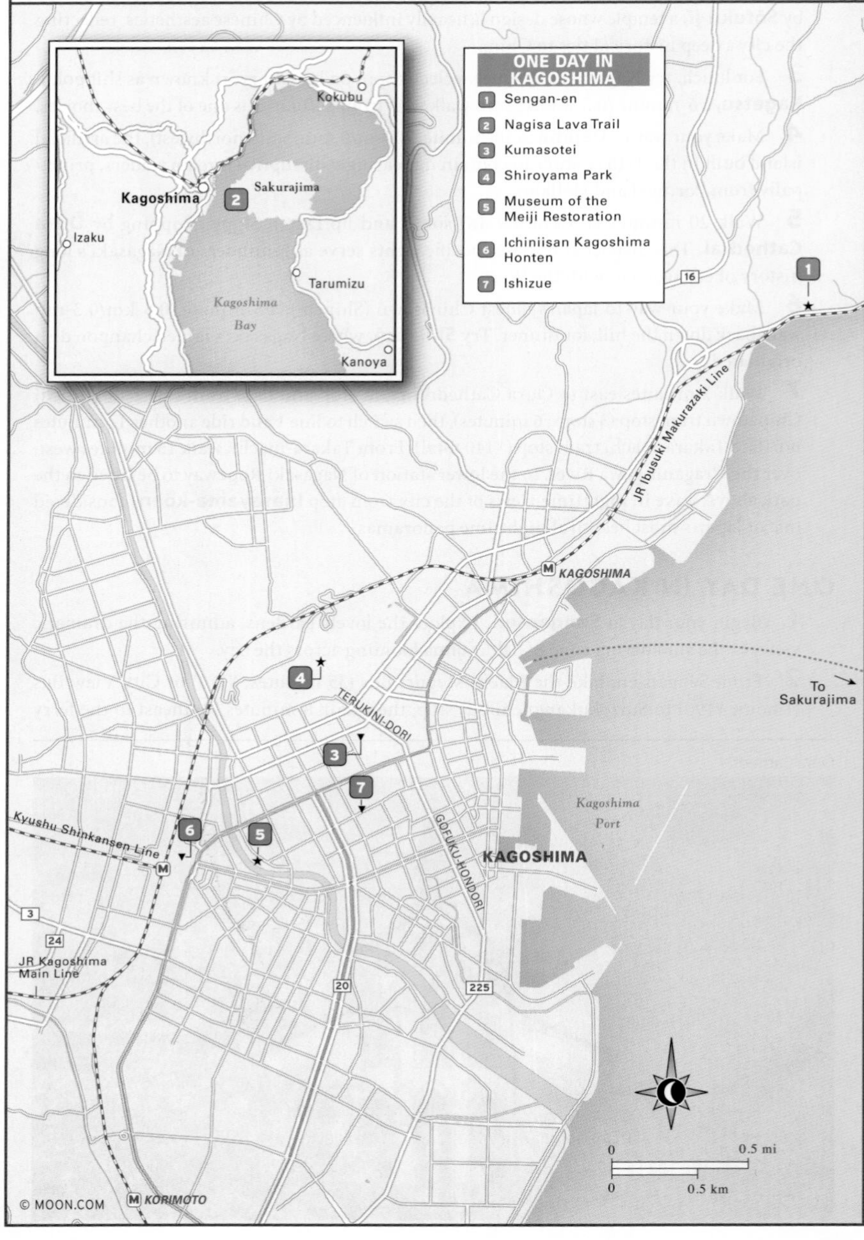

terminal. Board one of the ferries that depart regularly for the 15-minute journey across the bay to the foot of Sakurajima, Japan's answer to Mount Vesuvius. Walk along the **Nagisa Lava Trail** and try out the free footbath.

3 Return to downtown for lunch: **Kumasotei,** a 20-minute (1.5-km/0.9-mi) walk from the ferry terminal, is an eatery near Shiroyama Park that serves Kagoshima classics.

4 Make a trip up to **Shiroyama Park**'s observatory, a 15-minute (1-km/0.6-mi) walk. Admire the views over the city with Sakurajima dominating the horizon from afar.

5 Next, head 30 minutes (2 km/1.2 mi) southwest to the **Museum of the Meiji Restoration** for a quick fix on the city's history.

6 Eat dinner at **Ichiniisan Kagoshima Honten,** a 5-minute (0.5-km/0.3-mi) walk to the west, famed for its kurobuta (black pork) shabu-shabu (hot pot). Be sure to reserve a day or two in advance.

7 End your day by getting schooled on shōchū, Kagoshima's booze of choice, at the stellar bar **Ishizue,** a 20-minute (1.4-m/0.8-mi) walk to the east.

Fukuoka 福岡

Located closer to Seoul than Tokyo, with Shanghai not much farther, Fukuoka's engagement with the rest of Asia stretches back more than two millennia. Its harbor—as economically vital today as it has been for centuries—was the site of the ill-fated invasion attempted by the Mongols in the 13th century. Today, international freight ships and ferries running to Seoul and Shanghai ply the harbor's waters, domestic and international flights transit at the city's international airport, and bullet trains arrive from Honshu at its main railway station.

Divided by the Nakagawa river, this lively hub of commerce was formed through the amalgamation of two cities in 1889: the castle town of Fukuoka on the west side of the river and the mercantile port town of **Hakata** on the east side. The city is generally called Fukuoka now, but you'll sometimes still hear Hakata referenced. For example: the famed Hakata ramen, served in a pork-bone infused broth, or Hakata Station, the city's main railway hub.

Fukuoka has undergone something of a facelift in recent years. Formerly viewed as little more than an industrial city and transit point, today it is lauded for its quality of life and forward-looking mindset. As with most well-rounded modern cities, there's a sprinkling of museums and interesting buildings, as well as a good range of shopping and food. The main draw is the nightlife and street food, served from food stalls known as yatai, clustered in outdoor dining spaces arrayed throughout the city. The best place to experience this in action is either in the **Tenjin** district on the west side of town or the island of **Nakasu,** which sits about 15 minutes' walk east of Tenjin in the middle of the Nakagawa river.

Orientation

Most sights of interest are clustered in the eastern district of **Hakata** and the city's coastal area of **Momochi.** Cross to the west side of Nakagawa and you're in **Tenjin,** crossing **Nakasu,** an island in the river. Between Tenjin and the eastern Momochi area, **Ōhori Park** spreads its greenery. Southeast of the city the city lies **Dazaifu,** once a political hub, but now a sleepy, temple-studded town.

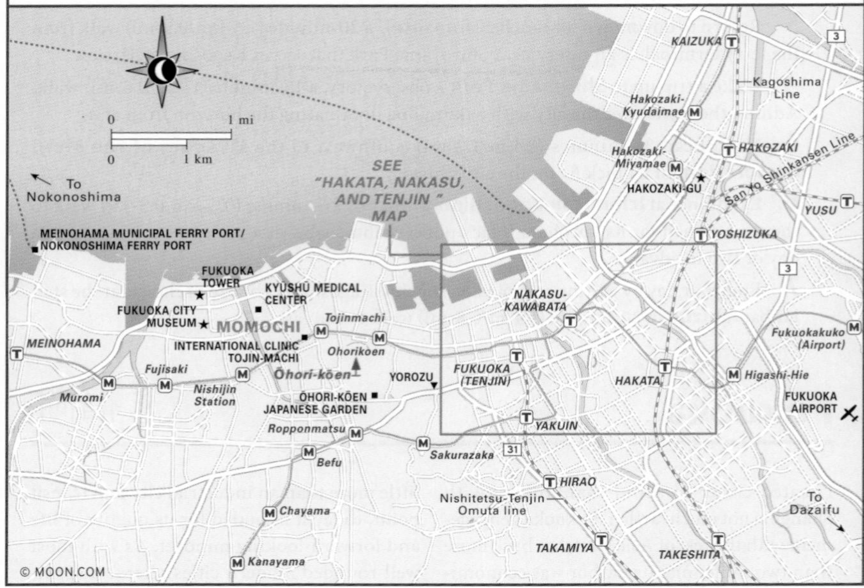

SIGHTS

Hakata

SHOFUKU-JI

聖福寺

6-1 Gokusho-machi, Hakata-ku; tel. 092/291-0775; http://shofukuji.or.jp; 24/7; free

Founded in 1195 by Eisai, the monk who introduced tea and the Rinzai sect of Buddhism from China, this was the first Zen temple in Japan. The buildings, razed and rebuilt numerous times throughout the ages, cannot be entered. Visitors can, however, freely roam through the leafy grounds, believed to be the place where tea plants were first cultivated in Japan.

TŌCHŌ-JI

東長寺

2-4 Gokusho-machi, Hakata-ku; tel. 092/291-4459; 24/7; free

It doesn't quite claim the heft of Nara's Daibutsu (Great Buddha) statue, but Fukuoka's very own wooden daibutsu is housed here. It's no lightweight either, clocking in at 10.8 meters (35 ft) high and weighing 27 tonnes (30 tons), making it the largest wooden figure of the enlightened one in Japan.

The temple's founding stretches far back into antiquity in 806, founded by Shingon sect founder Kūkai (aka Kōbō Daishi) just after his return from studying in China, making it the first Shingon temple in Japan. The mammoth wooden effigy was carved very recently, however, in 1992.

Be sure to pass through the Pilgrimage of Heaven and Hell, a pitch-black path accessed from beneath the left side of the wooden figure. As you enter the corridor, you'll see macabre paintings of various kinds of suffering, but don't let them faze you; pass through the inky darkness while gripping a handrail and continue until you emerge into the brightness on the other side and see a visual depiction of heaven, bathed in soft light. This imaginary

1: Shofuku-ji **2:** Tōchō-ji

1

2

Hakata, Nakasu, and Tenjin

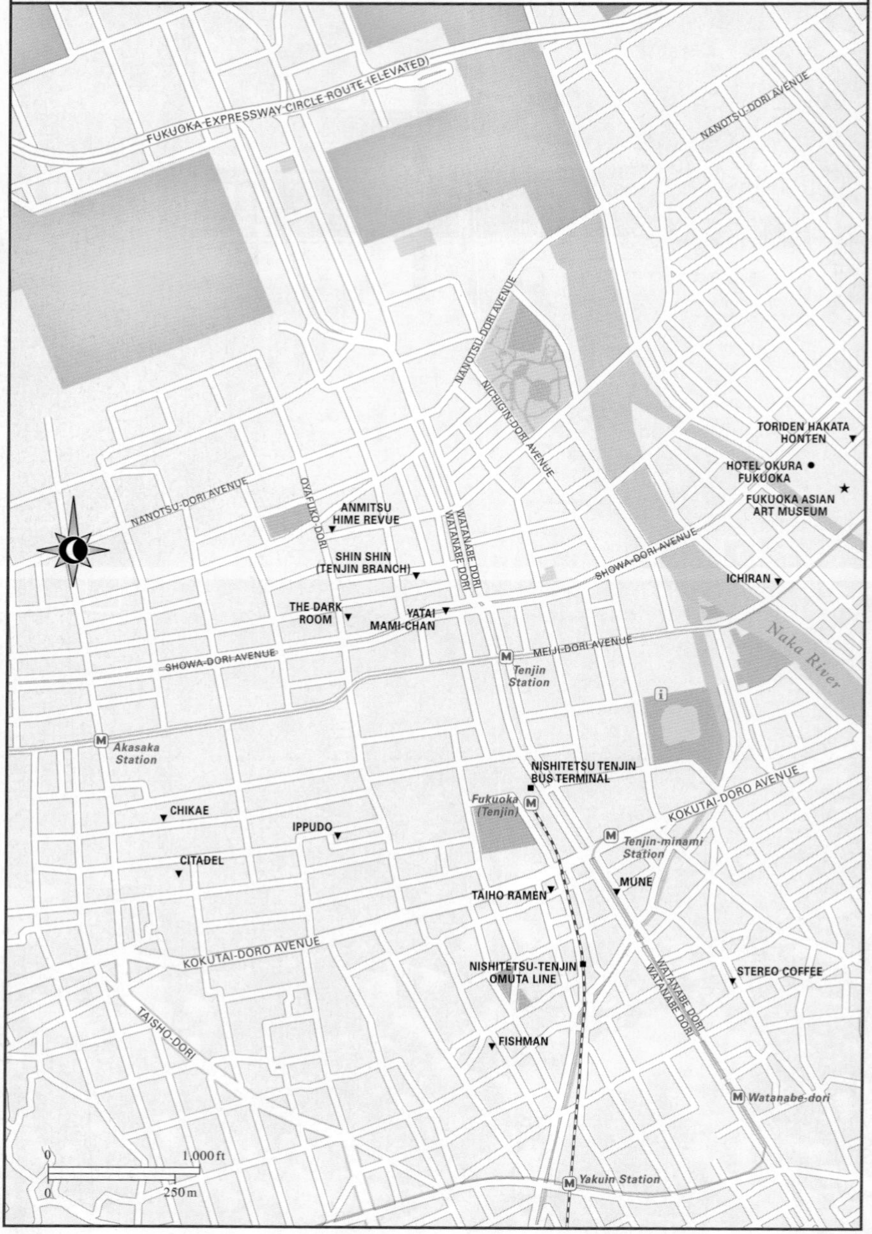
FUKUOKA EXPRESSWAY CIRCLE ROUTE (ELEVATED)
NANOTSU-DORI AVENUE
NANOTSU-DORI AVENUE
NICHIGIN-DORI AVENUE
NANOTSU-DORI AVENUE
OYAFUKO-DORI
WATANABE DORI
WATANABE DORI
ANMITSU HIME REVUE
SHIN SHIN (TENJIN BRANCH)
THE DARK ROOM
YATAI MAMI-CHAN
SHOWA-DORI AVENUE
SHOWA-DORI AVENUE
MEIJI-DORI AVENUE
Tenjin Station
TORIDEN HAKATA HONTEN
HOTEL OKURA FUKUOKA
FUKUOKA ASIAN ART MUSEUM
ICHIRAN
Naka River
Akasaka Station
NISHITETSU TENJIN BUS TERMINAL
Fukuoka (Tenjin)
KOKUTAI-DORO AVENUE
Tenjin-minami Station
CHIKAE
IPPUDO
CITADEL
TAIHO RAMEN
MUNE
KOKUTAI-DORO AVENUE
NISHITETSU-TENJIN OMUTA LINE
STEREO COFFEE
WATANABE DORI
WATANABE DORI
TAISHO-DORI
FISHMAN
Watanabe-dori
0
1,000 ft
0
250 m
Yakuin Station

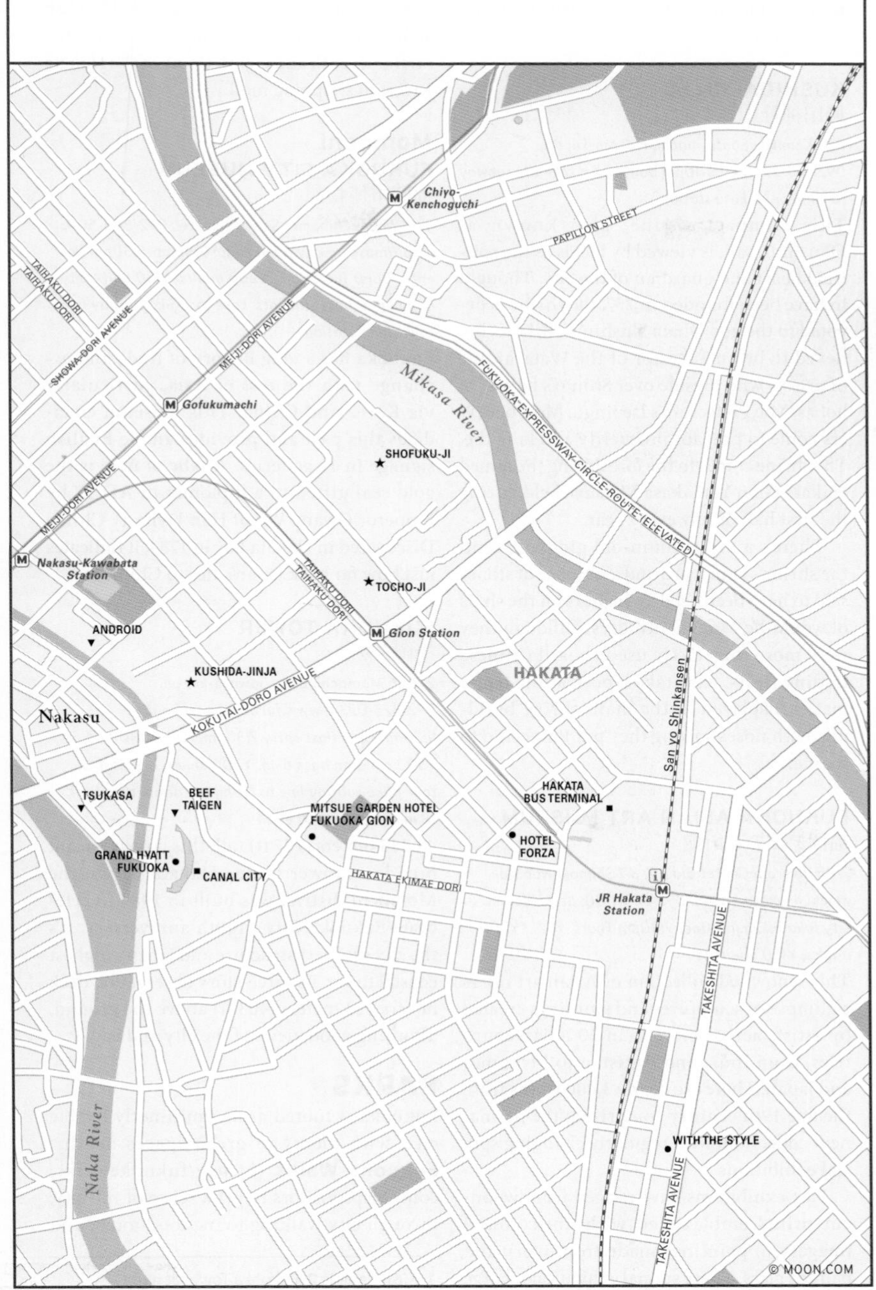

Chiyo-Kenchoguchi
PAPILLON STREET
TAIHAKU DORI
SHOWA-DORI AVENUE
MEIJI-DORI AVENUE
Mikasa River
FUKUOKA EXPRESSWAY CIRCLE ROUTE (ELEVATED)
Gofukumachi
SHOFUKU-JI
Nakasu-Kawabata Station
TOCHO-JI
ANDROID
Gion Station
KUSHIDA-JINJA
HAKATA
KOKUTAI-DORO AVENUE
Nakasu
San yo Shinkansen
TSUKASA
BEEF TAIGEN
MITSUE GARDEN HOTEL FUKUOKA GION
HAKATA BUS TERMINAL
HOTEL FORZA
GRAND HYATT FUKUOKA
CANAL CITY
HAKATA EKIMAE DORI
JR Hakata Station
TAKESHITA AVENUE
Naka River
WITH THE STYLE
© MOON.COM

journey into the Buddhist underworld is unexpectedly stirring.

KUSHIDA-JINJA
櫛田神社

1-41 Kamikawabata-machi, Hakata-ku; tel. 092/291-2951; 4am-10pm daily; free; take the subway to Gion or Nakasu station

This compact shrine, also known as Okushida-san, is viewed by locals as the spiritual heart and guardian of the city. Thought to have been founded in 757, the shrine is devoted to the god Ohata Nushima-Mikoto, believed to be an ancestor of the Watarai line of priests who preside over Shinto's holiest of holies, Mie Prefecture's Ise Jingu. Most believers come to pray for prosperity and long life. The shrine comes to the fore during the famed Hakata Gion Yamakasa Matsuri, held during the first half of July every year.

There's a millennium-old gingko tree in the shrine's courtyard and a number of stones said to have been used as anchors on the ships of would-be Mongol invaders, although they were more than likely used aboard Chinese trading fleets. Also take a peek at the tengu masks displayed in the main shrine building, with noses so long they put Pinocchio to shame.

FUKUOKA ASIAN ART MUSEUM
福岡アジア美術館

7-8F Riverain Center Bldg. 7, 3-1 Shimokawabata-machi, Hakata-ku; tel. 092/263-1100; http://faam.city.fukuoka.lg.jp; 10am-7:30pm Thurs.-Tues.; ¥200 adults, ¥150 students

This renowned collection of Asian art offers a glimpse of sculptures and paintings created by artists across more than 20 Asian countries, from India and Pakistan to Myanmar and Japan. There are nearly 3,000 works from the late 19th century comprising the permanent collection, with regularly changing special exhibitions.

Past exhibitions have ranged from woodcut prints emblazoned with anticolonial imagery to paintings made from ivory and painted glass. These special exhibitions charge a separate admission fee. There's good English signage throughout. The museum is located on the seventh and eighth floors of the Hakata Riverain shopping mall.

Momochi

FUKUOKA CITY MUSEUM
福岡市博物館

3-1-1 Momochihama, Sawara-ku; tel. 092/845-5011; http://museum.city.fukuoka.jp; 9:30am-5:30pm (last entry 5pm) Tues.-Sun.; ¥200 adults, ¥150 university and high school students; take the Kuku subway line to Nishijin Station

Fukuoka has a long history of trade and exchange with the rest of Asia, particularly via Korea and China. This museum elucidates this past and provides ample English signage in 11 galleries. A relic of note is the gold seal gifted to a diplomat in AD 57 by Emperor Gwang Wu of Han Dynasty China. Discovered in Hakata Bay in 1784, it indicates just how far back Japan's ties to China go.

FUKUOKA TOWER
福岡タワ

2-3-26 Momochihama, Sawara-ku; tel. 092/823-0234; www.fukuokatower.co.jp; 9:30am-8pm (last entry 7:30pm) daily; ¥800 adults, ¥500 children ages 6-15, ¥200 children ages 4-5; take Kūkō subway line to Nishijin Station, then walk 18 minutes north of exit 1

At 243 meters (797 ft) tall, this largely vacant broadcast tower beside Hakata Bay in the Momochi district was built in 1989 to celebrate Fukuoka City's 100th anniversary. It's the city's loftiest structure and Japan's highest coastal tower. Its three-story observation deck hovers 123 meters (403 ft) above the ground, affording good views of the city and bay.

PARKS

Fukuoka is touted as an emininetly livable city, with plenty of green spaces nearby. **Fukuoka Walks** (https://fukuokawalks.com) helps visitors to get a sense of the city, through city walking tours, food tours, and

1: Kushida-jinja **2:** Fukuoka Tower at night

1

2

everything in between, offered by friendly English-speaking guides.

ŌHORI-KŌEN

1-2 Ohorikōen, Chūō-ku; tel. 092/741-2004; www.ohorikouen.jp; open 24/7; free; take Kūkō subway line to Ōhori-kōen Station, then walk 5 minutes southwest

Essentially Fukuoka's Central Park, this expansive green zone, built from 1926 to 1929, in the heart of downtown wraps around a large central pond that once served as the moat to Fukuoka Castle. The park took its design cues from Hangzhou, China's West Lake. Three islands in the pond are linked to the rest of the park by tastefully hewn stone bridges.

Located within the park is the expansive **Ōhori-kōen Japanese Garden** (1-7 Ōhori-kōen; tel. 092/741-8377; 9am-6pm daily Tues.-Sun. Jun.-Aug., 9am-5pm daily Sept.-May; ¥240 adults, ¥120 children), which sits within a walled-in space of 12,000 square meters (129,166 square ft). Behind the white-plaster walls, streams, a waterfall, a sizable pond, teahouses, a dry garden, and more set the scene, which was created by Nakane Kinsaku, the famed garden architect who also conjured the beautiful gardens of Shimane Prefecture's Adachi Museum and Kyoto's Nijo-jō. Across the street, roughly 150 meters (492 ft) southeast of the garden sits Gokoku-jinja, a golden shrine approached via a path that leads you through a mammoth torii gate.

NOKONOSHIMA

https://yokanavi.com/en/spot/26970/; take Kūkō subway line to Meinohama Station, then ride Nishitetsu bus from Meinohama-eki Kitaguchi (in front of station's north exit) to Meinohama ferry terminal (15 minutes; ¥240 adults, ¥120 children); or take bus 300 or 301 from Nishitetsu Tenjin bus terminal to Meinohama ferry terminal (15 minutes; ¥360); from Meihnohama, take ferry to island (10 minutes; ¥230 adults, ¥120 children)

For a breather from the city, this lovely island is about 10 minutes away by ferry. Its 12-kilometer (7.5-mi) circumference is lined with walking paths that offer lovely sea and skyline views. On the north side, **Nokonoshima Island Park** (1624 Noko, Nishi, Nishi-ku; tel. 092/881-2494; http://nokonoshima.com/en; 9am-5:30pm Mon.-Sat. year-round, 9am-6:30pm Sun. and holidays Mar.-Nov.; ¥1,200 adults, ¥600 elementary and junior high school students, ¥400 children ages 3 and older) is swathed in flowers.

Next to the ferry terminal on Nokonoshima, **Noko Market** rents bicycles (tel. 092/881-2494; 9:30am-5pm daily; from ¥400 per hour, ¥1,300 per day). You can also pick up an English map here.

FESTIVALS AND EVENTS

HAKATA YAMAKASA GION MATSURI
博多祇園山笠

www.hakatayamakasa.com; July 1-15; free

Fukuoka's biggest festival centers around **Kushida-jinja,** also known as Okushida-san, viewed by locals as the spiritual heart and guardian of the city. A festive atmosphere builds July 10-14, with parades and practice runs taking place, until 4:59am on July 15, when seven teams of men—one for each of Hakata's seven districts—clad in loincloth-like fundoshi transport multi-level floats known as yamakasa, which depict figures and scenes from the city's past, on their shoulders in a procession starting from Kushida-jinja. The smaller-sized floats stand 5 meters (16 ft) tall and weigh a ton; the larger ones stand twice as high and weigh a whopping two tons.

Up to around 30 team members hoist these massive floats at any given time, while three or four team members ride up top, directing the changing of team members when they spot specific members starting to flag. The festival is said to have been inspired by the story of Shoichi Kokushi, a 13th-century Buddhist priest, who was said to have been carried through town on a platform so that he could pray and toss holy water onto the populace, which was suffering from a plague. Today, the raucous proceedings involve a lot of noise and a lot of water being doused onto the profusely sweating teams as they move through the streets.

The viewing areas near Kushida-jinja fill up many hours early, but it's possible to see the event elsewhere along the route, including the intersection of Meiji-dōri and Higashi-machi-suji, which affords views of the oncoming teams at a distance, and Showa-dōri and Taihaku-dōri, where it's possible to glimpse each float pass by twice, running along parallel lanes.

HOJŌYA
放生会

1-22-1 Hakozaki, Higashi-ku; tel. 092/641-7431; www.hakozakigu.or.jp/omatsuri/houjoya; 10am-10pm Sept. 12-18; free

Another of Fukuoka's great festivals, Hojoya takes place September 12-18 every year. More than a million people flock to the grounds of **Hakozaki-gu** (1-22-1 Hakozaki, Higashi-ku; tel. 092/641-7431; www.hakozakigu.or.jp; 6am-7pm daily; free) to thank the gods for nature's blessings, and to pray for success in business and safety for family members. Some 500 food, drink, and game stalls line the path leading up to the shrine, and a lively atmosphere pervades for the duration of the event. To experience the festival in full swing, aim to arrive in the evening, especially on the weekend days.

KYUSHU BASHŌ SUMO TOURNAMENT

Fukuoka Kokusai Center; 2-2 Chikko Hon-machi, Hakata-ku; tel. 092/272-1111; www.marinemesse.or.jp/kokusai, www.sumo.or.jp; mid-Nov.; seats ¥3,500-15,000

Every year in mid-November, a sumo bash takes place at the Fukuoka Kokusai Center. Tickets can be reserved online from early October (https://www.sumo.or.jp/EnTicket/) or bought same-day, with fans lining up at the complex around daybreak to snag them.

SHOPPING

All the big-name depaato (department stores) line a three-block stretch of busy thoroughfare **Watanabe-dōri** in the Tenjin neighborhood. True to the Japanese depaato tradition, the basement food courts are also a revelation.

Hakata
CANAL CITY

1-2 Sumiyoshi, Hakata-ku; tel. 092/282-2525; https://canalcity.co.jp; 10am-9pm daily

This sprawling mecca of commerce—the city's largest mall—was created by Jon Jerde, who also designed Tokyo's mammoth urban renewal project, Roppongi Hills. Like its Tokyo counterpart, Canal City has everything you could imagine under one roof: a multiplex cinema with capacity for more than 2,500, hotels, eateries, bars, some 250 name-brand shops, and, as the name suggests, a manmade canal in its inner courtyard. Here, fountains of water spray skyward every 30 minutes and there's a light show every evening.

FOOD

No other city in Japan is more closely associated with street food than Fukuoka. Yatai spill into byways across town from evening into the booze-fueled wee hours, with many only closing on Sunday. As evening falls, locals pile in, elbow to elbow, dipping chopsticks into bowls of offal stew and plucking grilled chunks of meat and vegetables from skewers.

Appropriately, given its reputation as the **tonkatsu ramen** capital, Fukuoka is home to the main shops of nationwide chains **Ichiran** (5-3-2 Nakasu; tel. 092/262-0433; www.ichiran.co.jp; 9am-8pm daily; from ¥890), widely considered the first tonkotsu ramen-dedicated shop in Japan; and **Ippudo** (1-13-14 Daimyō, Chūō-ku; tel. 092/771-0880; https://stores.ippudo.com/en/1001; 11am-3pm and 6pm-8pm Mon.-Fri., 11am-8pm Sat.-Sun.; from ¥1,000), a wildly popular chain in business since 1985.

Tenjin
★ YATAI MAMI-CHAN

2-13-1 Tenjin, Chūō-ku; tel. 090/1921-0389; http://yataimamichan.daa.jp; 6pm-1am Mon.-Sat., closed Mon. instead if Mon. falls on national holiday

Situated right on Shōwa-dōri on the backside

☆ Fukuoka's Street Food Stalls

The lively street food scene in Fukuoka adds to the city's inviting atmosphere. Some 150 of these makeshift dining rooms, called yatai, dot the city, each one generally seating anywhere from six to nine patrons at a time. Each is fronted by a red lantern indicating its specialty, whether it's ramen, yakitori, or any other food creation that lends itself well to a quick bite and an accompanying beer. For most of the year they are open to the elements. Thin plastic sheets in place of walls soften the bite of the cold during winter. Most are concentrated around the crossing of **Tenjin Shishi-dōri** and **Shōwa-dōri,** west of the Nakagawa, as well as the southwestern bank of **Nakasu Island.** For a full list of the city's yatai, visit https://yokanavi.com/en/yatai/.

Picking a yatai is usually about where you are, what you feel like, or what smells good; here are a few excellent stalls to get you started:

- **Yatai Mami-chan** (Tenjin, page 613)
- **Mune** (Tenjin, page 614)
- **Tsukasa** (Nakasu, page 615)

street food stall

of Fukuoka Honten Bank, this welcoming street food stall is run by the amiable Mami-chan herself. She loves to welcome foreign travelers and even has a website and an English menu. Good picks include roast pork, tonkotsu ramen, and the spicy Chinese favorite, mabo tofu.

MUNE

4 Watanabe-dōri, Chūō-ku; tel. 090/8665-1692; https://yokanavi.com/en/yatai/122493/; 7pm-2am Mon.-Sat.

Another good food stall choice in the Tenjin area is Mune, about 8 minutes' walk south of Yatai Mami-chan. It's located on the yatai stronghold of Watanabe-dōri. Try the mentai tamagoyaki (rolled omelet stuffed with pollack roe), followed by fried rice or a piping bowl of rich Hakata ramen topped with pickled ginger, sesame seeds, and pork.

SHIN SHIN (TENJIN BRANCH)

3-2-19 Tenjin, Chūō-ku; tel. 092/732-4006; www.hakata-shinshin.com; 11am-8am (last order 7:30pm) daily; from ¥700; take the Kūkō subway line to Tenjin Station, then walk 3 minutes, or take the Nishitetsu-Tenjin Omuta line to Nishitetsu Fukuoka (Tenjin) Station and walk 5 minutes

This is one of Fukuoka locals' favorite Hakata (tonkotsu) ramen joints, as indicated by the occasionally long lines and flurry of celebrity autographs adorning the walls. The soup, somewhat tame by Fukuoka standards, is complemented nicely by well-seasoned slabs of soft pork. There's an English menu, which also includes other delicious dishes like the miso chanpon, in which noodles are boiled directly in the miso-based soup.

TAIHO RAMEN

1-23-8 Imaizumi, Chūō-ku; tel. 092/738-3277; www.taiho.net; 10:30am-8pm daily; from ¥680; take the Nanakuma subway line to Tenjin-minami, then walk 4 minutes

For an even stronger broth, head to this Taiho Ramen outpost in Tenjin-imaizumi. The original shop is located south of the city in the suburb of Kurume, but the noodles and creamy soup are legit here, too. The soup is milky, even frothy. This is another great bowl and a good option about 10 minutes' walk south of Shin Shin in case the latter has a long queue.

STEREO COFFEE

3-8-3 Watanabe-dōri, Chūō-ku; tel. 092/231-8854; http://stereo.jpn.com; 8am-10pm Thurs.-Tues.; drinks from ¥350, dishes from ¥600

This indie standing-only coffee shop is a great spot for a caffeine hit. The coffee menu includes an impressive range of beans, which are all freshly ground. There's also a great sound system, and DJ and part-owner Yusuke Watanabe provides a steady stream of smooth tunes. The second floor serves as an art gallery, exhibiting work by budding artists. They also serve hot sandwiches.

FISHMAN

1-4-23 Imaizumi, Chūō-ku; tel. 080/4358-3875; https://sakanaotoko.com; 11am-2:30pm and 5:30pm-11:30pm (last order 10:30pm) Mon.-Fri., 11am-3pm, 5:30pm-11:30pm (last order 10:30pm) Sat.-Sun. and holidays; average lunch ¥1,500, average dinner ¥3,500; take the Nanakuma line or Nishitetsu-Tenjin Omuta line to Yakuin Station, then walk 6 minutes

Another great seafood option, this shop is stylish and inviting, with its interior of warm wood and minimal industrial lighting. The chefs in the open kitchen whip up dishes with an innovative spin, and creatively present them too, as seen in the spiral wooden staircase-like platters of sashimi. Staff speak some English and can help with the menu.

★ CHIKAE

2-2-17 Daimyō; tel. 092/721-4624; https://chikae.co.jp; 5pm-10pm Mon.-Fri., 11:30am-10pm Sat.-Sun. and public holidays for counter seating, 11:30am-8pm daily for private rooms (reservation only); lunch sets ¥3,000, dinner courses ¥5,000-20,000; take the Kūkō subway line to Akasaka Station, then walk 5 minutes

This local institution has been doing brisk business since 1961, with 200 seats surrounding a central counter of gingko wood on the first floor. Fish are plucked straight from rows of tanks in the center of the main counter, as kimono-clad servers attend to customers and an army of cooks assemble slap-up seafood feasts in the kitchen beyond. Order various items a la carte, from sashimi to hot pot, or try one of the good-value lunch sets. Expect to wait in line, especially at lunchtime. Private rooms are available by reservation.

Nakasu Island

TSUKASA

1-8 Nakasu, Hakata-ku; tel. 092/413-9248; www.yatai-tsukasa.com; 5:30pm-1am daily; dishes from ¥500

In the Nakasu Island area, Tsukasa is a wonderful food stall that sits beside the waterfront along the southwestern bank. Admittedly, it's known to occasionally attract a queue of tourists, and is a bit pricy, but the pull of its setting on the waterfront and its classic yatai ambience cannot be denied. The menu has everything from grilled asparagus and pork to fantastic cod-roe tempura. For ambience alone, this stretch of riverfront is the best place to go for full yatai immersion. Pick any stall that draws your attention, order some food with your booze of choice, and enjoy the friendly chatter with curious locals. You won't go wrong.

Hakata

BEEF TAIGEN

Canal City Hakata North Bldg. B1F, 1-2 Sumiyoshi, Hakata-ku; tel. 092/283-4389; www.taigen.jp; 11:30am-11pm (last order 10pm) daily; dishes from ¥1,700; take the Kūkō subway line to Gion Station, then walk 10 minutes

This stylish yakiniku (barbecue) joint serves only high-grade beef from Kagoshima Prefecture, along with side salads, miso soup, rice, and various vegetable dishes. It gets crowded at lunchtime, when its much-loved sets—including beef sausage, breaded and deep-fried beef cutlets, and more—are sold for ¥1,200 each, but it's a bit less crowded at dinnertime.

1

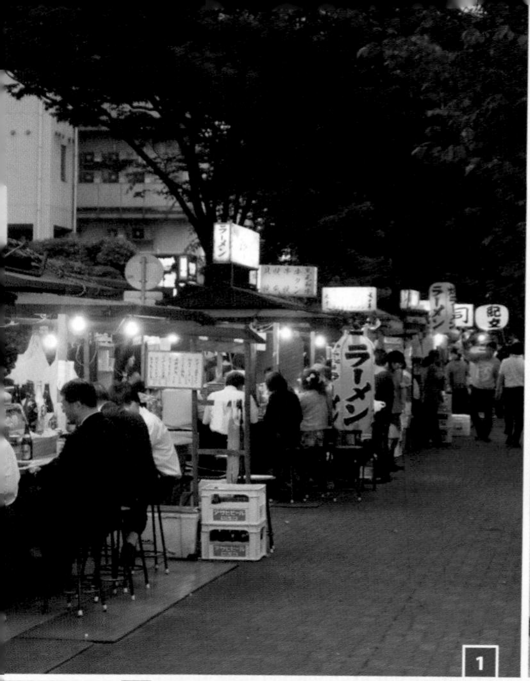

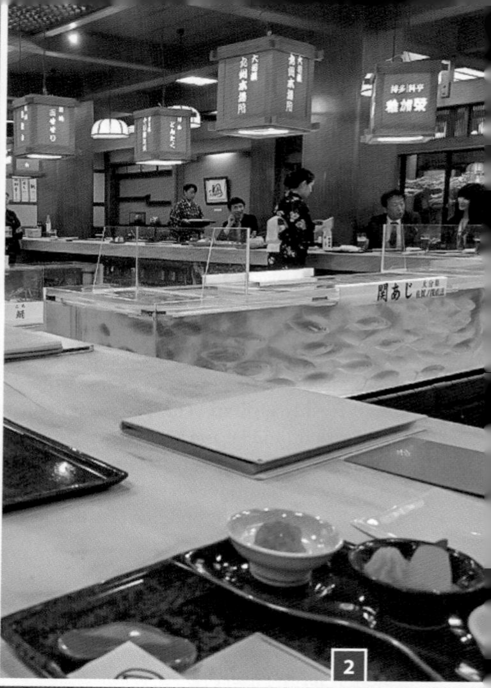

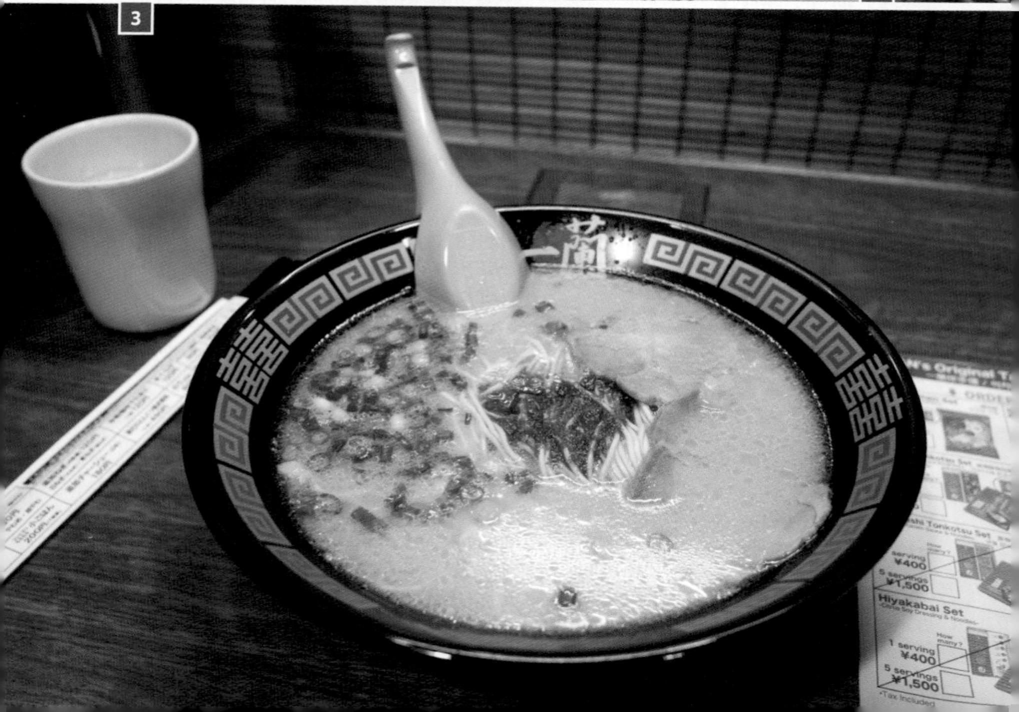

2

3

TORIDEN HAKATA HONTEN

10-5 Shimokawabata-machi, Hakata-ku; tel. 092/272-0920; https://toriden.com/#sec1; 11:30am-11pm (last order 10pm) daily; courses from ¥3,200; take the Hakozaki or Kūkō subway line to Nakasu-Kawabata Station, then walk 3 minutes

It takes six hours to make the creamy soup used in the excellent mizutaki (chicken hot pot) at this Kyushu-centric restaurant, which sources all ingredients from the island. First, eat vegetables and chicken cooked in the delicious broth at your table. Finish with either zosui (rice porridge) or ramen noodles. The portions are generous, too. Recommended.

Ōhori-kōen

YOROZU

2-3-32 Akasaka, Chūō-ku; tel. 092/724-7880; www.yorozu-tea.jp; noon-midnight Mon.-Sat.; tea and sweets sets ¥1,500-3,000

Yorozu does tea-tasting courses with traditional Japanese sweets, elevating tea preparation to an art. This is a chic space that has a nice wabi-sabi (Japan's traditional answer to shabby-chic) vibe to it.

BARS AND NIGHTLIFE

A thick concentration of bars, clubs, and unsavory establishments aimed at tipsy businessmen with stratospheric expense accounts clog the island of Nakasu, along with cheap, friendly food stalls. It's an interesting place to wander at night in urban-anthropologist fashion, but many of the bars on the island are exorbitantly priced and discriminate against foreign travelers without batting an eyelid. Friendlier, more reasonably priced bars and clubs line the streets of Tenjin, about 15 minutes' walk west of Nakasu, where depending on your stamina, you can party all night—things usually don't get hopping until around midnight. The thoroughfare of **Oyafukō-dōri** and the streets to its east are the heart of the action. That said, fun awaits in all corners of the city if you know where to look.

BPC Fukuoka (www.facebook.com/bpc-fukuoka) is a fun way to explore Fukuoka's pub scene (BPC stands for "British Pub Crawl"), run by a friendly Brit living in the city.

Tenjin

CITADEL

2F 1-8-40 Daimyō, Chūō-ku; tel. 092/688-4190; www.facebook.com/citadelfukuoka; 5pm-3am Tues.-Sat.

This watering hole in the trendy, youth-centric neighborhood of Daimyō is renowned for its coffee-based cocktails. Barman and master mixologist Yoshi incorporates everything from citrus accents to melon rum with coffee, and manages to balance all the elements perfectly.

THE DARK ROOM

3-4-15 Tenjin, Chūō-ku; tel. 092/725-2989; 8pm-3am daily

This industrial-chic bar is a good spot for fans of alternative and indie rock, with an impressive music library of about 50,000 songs. It's owned by an American who brings his kitchen chops to the fore from Thursday to Saturday, whipping up a menu from scratch. It gets hopping on Friday and Saturday nights.

ANMITSU HIME REVUE

2F TM-20 Bldg., 3-7-13 Tenjin, Chūō-ku; tel. 092/725-2550; www.okama.com; hours vary by event; ¥4,500

Audience participation is a big part of the show at this revue. High-energy performers in glittery, frilly, flamboyant costumes dance, croon, and act out slapstick routines amid a cacophony of playfully exaggerated Japanese motifs. Although it's often billed as a drag queen show, both men and women perform, and while some of the humor is a touch bawdy, nothing is overtly inappropriate for kids. You won't understand anything spoken, but it won't matter. The show will mesmerize you, and the performers will charm you and leave you beaming. It's tucked away on the second floor of a

1: street stalls in Fukuoka **2:** Chikae **3:** tonkotsu ramen building on Oyafukō Street in the heart of Tenjin. Recommended.

Hakata

ANDROID

B1F Shin-Kawabata Bldg., 11-1 Kamikawabata-machi, Hakata-ku; tel. 092/291-2760; 6pm-1:30am Mon.-Fri., 7pm-1:30am Sat., 7pm-11:30pm Sun.

Sip cocktails or throw back a few shots to a thoughtfully curated electronic soundtrack at this subterranean hideout east of the Naka-gawa. Soft lighting illuminates the space, which has a subtly sci-fi aesthetic. Comfy seating includes sofas and soft chairs.

ACCOMMODATIONS

Hakata

HOTEL FORZA

2-1-15 Hakata Ekimae, Hakata-ku; tel. 092/473-7113; www.hotelforza.jp/hakataguchi/; ¥8,000 d; walk 2 minutes from JR Hakata Station

This modern hotel just west of Hakata Station has clean, well-appointed rooms. Sitting on a quiet street, yet close to the action, this hotel is extremely convenient for exploring the city. The rooms are spacious and all are non-smoking. There's a good breakfast on offer, which includes both Japanese and Western fare.

MITSUI GARDEN HOTEL FUKUOKA GION

2-8-15 Hakata Ekimae, Hakata-ku; tel. 092/414-3131; www.gardenhotels.co.jp/fukuoka-gion/; ¥12,000 d with breakfast; walk 7 minutes west of JR Hakata Station

The hushed, elegant rooms in this conveniently located modern hotel are well-appointed, spic-and-span, and expansive (by Japanese standards). Facilities include a shared rooftop bath, a standing bar, and a restaurant that serves food made with regional and seasonal ingredients. Staff are friendly and speak English. The price includes either a Japanese breakfast buffet or Western breakfast a la carte.

HOTEL OKURA FUKUOKA

3-2 Shimokawabata-machi, Hakata-ku; tel. 092/262-1111; www.fuk.hotelokura.co.jp; ¥17,500 d; take the Kūkō subway line to Nakasu-Kawabata Station, then walk 5 minutes

This elegant hotel sits just east of the Naka-gawa, near Canal City. Genial staff, including a very helpful concierge, are ready to help. Rooms are petite but well-appointed. On-site restaurants include Japanese and Chinese fare, a patisserie, and craft beer, and there's a health club with a pool (¥2,000 for a swim).

GRAND HYATT FUKUOKA

2-81-1 Sumiyoshi, Hakata-ku; tel. 092/282-1234; https://fukuoka.grand.hyatt.com/en/hotel/home.html; from ¥27,000 d; take the Hakozaki or Kūkō subway line to Nakasu-Kawabata Station, then walk 10 minutes south

Connected to Canal City, with chic, modern Japanese decor, this luxury hotel is a cut above most properties in the city. Its stylish, open rooms are relaxing and packed with amenities, including a range of dining options and a fitness center with indoor pool. To avoid paying out of pocket for breakfast and access to the fitness center (¥2,000 per person for each amenity), book a club room for around an extra ¥10,000. With a club room, you'll also get afternoon tea and cocktails in the rooftop lounge in the evening.

WITH THE STYLE

1-9-18 Hakataeki-minami, Hakata-ku; tel. 092/433-3900; www.withthestyle.com; ¥40,000 d; walk 8 minutes southeast of JR Hakata Station

This is hands-down the city's most modish hotel. Step into the soothing lobby and feel the city fade away. Bathrooms are stocked with carefully chosen products. Each of the 16 suites has stylish, mid-20th-century American furniture, quirky artwork, and a complimentary minibar. All rooms have a space to chill, as well as a leafy balcony or terrace. The Penthouse serves complimentary breakfast and brunch (7am-1pm daily) and complimentary welcome drinks (4pm-midnight daily).

There's also a guests-only rooftop spa-jacuzzi, available 24/7 by reservation only.

INFORMATION AND SERVICES

Visitor Information

There are tourist information offices on the main concourse of **Hakata Station** (tel. 092/431-3003; 8am-9pm daily), on the ground floor of **Lion Plaza** in Tenjin (2-1-1 Tenjin, Chūō-ku; tel. 092/751-6904; https://yokanavi.com/tourist-information/27483/; 9:30am-7pm daily).

Fukuoka Now (www.fukuoka-now.com) is a great city-focused website, featuring extensive listings and activities for Fukuoka and around. Also helpful is the English-language website **Visit Fukuoka** (https://visit-fukuoka-japan.com/), produced by the Fukuoka Prefecture Tourist Association. This portal offers plenty of ideas for things to do, places to stay and eat, itineraries, and more for the whole prefecture.

- **JR Kyushu Travel Agency** (1-1-1 Hakataekichūō-gai; tel. 092/431-6215; 10:30am-7:30pm Mon.-Sat., 10am-6pm Sun.)

Health and Safetey

- **International Clinic Tojin-machi** (1-4-6 Jigyo, Chūō-ku; tel. 092/717-1000; www.internationalclinic.org; 9am-1pm and 2:30pm-5:30pm Mon.-Tues. and Thurs.-Fri., 9am-1pm Sat.)
- **Kyushu Medical Center** (1-8-1 Jigyohama; tel. 092/852-0700; www.kyumed.jp)

GETTING THERE

Train

A slightly confounding fact: Fukuoka has no main station called Fukuoka. Instead, the main terminal is found slightly east of the heart of town at **JR Hakata Station,** named after the former city of Hakata on the eastern banks of the Naka-gawa. JR Hakata Station is served by the shinkansen, meaning that it's possible to travel all the way to the city by bullet train from the hubs of Kansai—**Kyoto** (2 hours 45 minutes; ¥16,160), **Osaka** (2.5 hours; ¥15,400), and beyond—**Tokyo** (5 hours; ¥23,190), or even farther north.

JR Hakata Station is also where the Kyushu shinkansen line starts, which, along with various limited express trains, links the city to hubs deeper into the island, from **Saga** (limited express train; 40 minutes; ¥2,500) and **Nagasaki** (limited express; 2 hours; ¥4,800) to **Kumamoto** (shinkansen; 40 minutes; ¥5,030) and **Kagoshima** (shinkansen; 1.5 hours; ¥10,440).

From Fukuoka's **Nishitetsu-Fukuoka Station** in Tenjin, on the west side of the Naka-gawa, you can access many smaller towns on the island, including **Dazaifu** (30 minutes; ¥410), via Nishitetsu-Futsukaichi Station.

Air

Given its position in the south of Japan, flying into Fukuoka may be a good option, depending on where you're coming from. **Fukuoka Airport** (www.fukuoka-airport.jp/en/)—split into a domestic wing (tel. 092/621-6059) and an international wing (tel. 092/621-0303)—is surprisingly close to downtown, too. The domestic terminal is served by flights from all over the country, while the international terminal is covered by airlines around East and Southeast Asia.

You can access downtown from the domestic terminal by simply hopping on the **subway,** which is a mere 5 minutes' ride from Hakata Station (¥260) and just over 10 minutes to Tenjin (¥260). Free **shuttle buses** link the international terminal to the domestic one (15 minutes). Alternatively, you can take a **bus** from the international terminal to JR Hakata Station (15 minutes; ¥260) or Nishitetsu-Fukuoka Station (30 minutes; ¥320).

Bus

Highway buses service the **Nishitetsu Tenjin Bus Terminal** (2-1-1 Tenjin, Chūō-ku; tel. 0570/001-010), near

☆ Saga's Pottery Towns

A rural patchwork of charming villages and terraced rice fields leading down to the sea, the Saga Prefecture's good clay makes renowned pottery, from exquisite porcelain tea cups to earth-tone jars. The prefecture's famous ceramics come predominantly from historic kilns in the towns of Karatsu, Imari, and perhaps most famous of all, Arita, where the first porcelain was produced in Japan.

KARATSU

Collectively, Karatsu's ceramics are known as Karatsu-yaki (Karatsu ware). From humble earthen vases to showpieces by renowned potters that cost as much as a car, the exquisite wares produced in Karatsu are fired at 1,000°C (1,832°F), then coated in heavy glaze with earthy brown or black coloration. Other pieces are covered with white glaze with a cracked finish and adorned with floral patterns.

Stop by **Nakazato Tarōemon Shop and Kiln** (3-6-29 Chōda; tel. 0955/72-8171; www.nakazato-tarouemon.com; 9am-5:30pm Thurs.-Tues., closed 1st, 3rd, and 5th Thurs. of month). Although master potter Nakazato Tarōemon (1923-2009) has passed, the Nakazato family's shop, which doubles as a gallery and museum, is the most accessible of the 30 or so studios and kilns dotting Karatsu. There are plenty of antique pieces dating to the early days of Karatsu's exquisite pottery tradition. After taking in the visual feast of the shop, cross the street and check out the kiln.

To reach Karatsu from Fukuoka, hop on the Kūkō (Airport) subway line at either Tenjin or Hakata station and ride for about 15 minutes to Meinohama. Here, you'll either transfer to the JR Chikuhi line or simply stay put on the train you started on— it varies by train—and ride the rest of the way to JR Karatsu Station (total trip: 1 hour 20 minutes; ¥1,140).

IMARI

Tiles form blue and white motifs of dragons, flowers, and geometric patterns on Inari's signs, walls, and bridges. The town is known for its more delicate approach to porcelain: situated next to the sea, Imari was the port from which finished pieces crafted in Saga Prefecture were sent for distribution throughout Japan and the world beyond. Among collectors, porcelain that reached the outside world via Imari that dates to the Edo period (1603-1868) is now referred to as Koimari (Old Imari).

The first floor of the **Imari City Ceramic Merchant's Museum** (555-1 Imari-chō Kō; tel. 095/522-7934; www.city.imari.saga.jp/2943.htm; 10am-5pm Tues.-Sun.; free) exhibits a precious collection of antique Koimari dating to the 18th and 19th centuries. For a fuller appreciation of Imariware's refined beauty, leave downtown and head to **Ōkawachiyama Village** (www.

Nishitetsu-Fukuoka Station, and the **Hakata Bus Terminal** (aka Hakata Kōtsū Center; 2 Hakataekichūō-gai, Hakata-ku; tel. 0120/489-939), adjacent to JR Hakata Station. Given the length of the journey and relatively modest monetary savings, taking the train or even flying is a more appealing option if you're coming from other regions of Japan. That said, traveling to or from Fukuoka by highway bus may be an option worth considering for trips within Kyushu. For detailed timetables and routes, visit www.nishitetsu.jp/en/highway_bus.

GETTING AROUND

Fukuoka is easily navigable by subway and **on foot.** The easy-to-use **subway** has three lines, the most convenient being the **Kūkō line,** running from the airport's domestic terminal through the heart of the city with stops at Hakata and Tenjin (http://subway.city.fukuoka.lg.jp; single rides from ¥210, one-day pass ¥640).

There's also a **bus network** (www.nishitetsu.jp/en/bus) running through town (¥100 flat rate for single rides within city center, including Hakata and Tenjin; one-day

imari-ookawachiyama.com), one of the region's two major production sites, and stroll streets lined with some 30 galleries and workshops, as well as cafés and eateries.

Buses run from Imari Station to Ōkawachiyama roughly once every two hours (15 minutes; ¥170). If there's a long wait until the next bus, taking a taxi will set you back about ¥1,800. Or, if you feel like exploring the area on your own two feet, it's roughly a 1-hour walk southeast of Imari Station. Imari is easily reached from Karatsu via the JR Chikuhi line (50 minutes; ¥650). If you're coming from Arita, take the Matsūra-tetsudō line (25 minutes; ¥460). Note that this private line isn't covered by the JR pass. Once you've arrived at Imari, either take a bus (¥170), which shuttles to and from the station about five times daily, or a taxi (one-way about ¥2,000) to the Ōkawachiyama pottery district.

vase from Kakiemon Kiln

ARITA

The region's relationship with the clay arts began here in 1615, when a Korean potter named Ri Sampei uncovered kaolin clay, a necessary mineral for making porcelain, in the mountains just outside town. Lee's discovery was followed by an influx of Koreans who also set up shop. Early porcelain produced in the town was mostly blue and white, often with floral motifs. The style evolved into the more vividly colorful Kakiemon style, which caught the eye of European traders by the mid-17th century.

The **Kyushu Ceramic Museum** (3100-1 Toshaku-ōtsu; tel. 0955/43-3681; http://saga-museum.jp/ceramic; 9am-5pm Tues.-Sun.; free) is the best overall introduction to Kyushu's illustrious history with the clay arts. **Kakiemon Kiln** (352 Nanzan Tei; tel. 0955/43-2267; http://kakiemon.co.jp; 9am-5pm daily; free), **Kouraku Kiln** (2512 Maruno-hei; tel. 0955/42-4121; http://kouraku-kiln.com; 8am-5pm Mon.-Fri., 9am-5pm Sat.-Sun.; free) and **Imaemon Gallery** (2-1-15 Akae-machi; tel. 0955/42-3101; www.imaemon.co.jp; 8am-5pm daily, closed first Sun. of month; free) are all excellent places to see porcelain as a living art.

Coming from Imari, take the Matsūra-tetsudō line to Arita Station (25 minutes; ¥460). Starting in Fukuoka, hop on the limited express train, bound for Sasebo, at Hakata Station (about 1 hour 15 minutes; ¥3,270).

pass ¥900). Convenient stops include the **Hakata Bus Terminal** (aka Hakata Kōtsū Center; 2 Hakataekichūō-gai, Hakata-ku; tel. 0120/489-939), next to JR Hakata Station, and **Nishitetsu Tenjin Bus Terminal** (2-1-1 Tenjin, Chūō-ku; tel. 0570/001-010), near Nishitetsu-Fukuoka Station.

The **Fukuoka Tourist City Pass** (https://yokanavi.com/en/tourist-city-pass/) gives access for one day to almost all buses and trains in Fukuoka, from the subway to the JR and Nishitetsu lines, with one for Fukuoka city only (¥1,500) and another covering both Fukuoka city and Dazaifu (¥1,820). Pick up this pass at any tourist information counter or ticket window throughout the city's train and bus networks.

DAZAIFU
太宰府

For a dose of history close to the city of Fukuoka, head to Dazaifu, an ancient town set against a backdrop of sylvan slopes. Dazaifu was once the locus of administrative affairs for Kyushu, and today its legacy is seen in the handful of important religious complexes strewn throughout the town. Founded in the late 7th century, the town was the island's administrative hub for more than five centuries, with the port of Hakata to the north serving as an important point of contact with the rest of Asia.

Chief among the town's sacred sites is Dazaifu Tenmangu, a shrine honoring the exalted scholar-poet Sugawara Michizane, famed for its plum blossoms in early spring. The other main attraction is the excellent Kyushu National Museum, which offers an insightful glimpse into the island's history and heritage. The town makes for a pleasant day trip from Fukuoka or a stop en route to Nagasaki.

Sights

DAZAIFU TENMAN-GŪ
太宰府天満宮

4-7-1 Saifu; tel. 092/922-8225; www.dazaifutenmangu.or.jp; 6:30am-7pm daily Apr.-May and Sept.-Nov., 6:30am-7:30pm daily Jun.-Aug., 6:30am-6:30pm Dec.-Mar.; free; take the Nishitetsu line to Dazaifu Station, then walk 5 minutes east

If you're studying for an exam, you'd be wise to visit this shrine, dedicated to Tenman-Tenjin, the god of scholarship. Tenjin is actually the deified form of poet, politician, and scholar Sugawara no Michizane (845-903), the first person in Japan's history to be elevated to divinity after dying in exile in Dazaifu, where he was banished after his great gifts began to create tensions with the ruling Fujiwara clan in Kyoto. Soon after the great scholar's death, Japan suffered a series of natural calamities, which people began to suspect were being inflicted by Michinaze's angry spirit. People began to make offerings to his spirit in an effort to appease him. Thus, the practice of worshipping at Tenmangū shrines was born.

This sprawling shrine complex, built at the location of Michinaze's grave, is the most important Tenmangū shrine, along with Kyoto's Kitano Tenmangū. A long walkway lined with shops hawking mochi (rice cake) dumplings, soft-serve ice cream, and gimmicky souvenirs leads to the shrine's torii gate entrance. You'll see three bridges that reach across a small carp-filled lake that is shaped like the character for "heart" and edged by plum trees, which erupt with pink blossoms from late-February to mid-March. One famous tree named Tobiume, to the right of the main hall, is more than 1,000 years old. Plum trees are common at Tenmangū shrines nationwide.

The main hall, built in 1591, is continuously packed with visitors, especially university applicants who have come to buy amulets designed to boost their chances of scholastic success. On

Dazaifu Tenman-gū

the grounds, the **Kankō Historical Museum** illustrates the life story of Tenjin, while the **Dazaifu Tenman-gū Museum** presents relics from his bookish human life.

KYUSHU NATIONAL MUSEUM

九州国立博物館

4-7-2 Ishizaka; tel. 092/918-2807; www.kyuhaku.jp; 9:30am-5pm Tues.-Sun.; ¥430 adults, ¥130 students

Looming in the hills east of Dazaifu Station, this enormous complex resembles an international airport or basketball stadium more than a history museum. It opened to major fanfare in sleepy Dazaifu in 2005. It's only one of four national museums in Japan, the others being in Tokyo, Kyoto, and Nara. Each of these four museums has its own spin on Japanese history; Dazaifu's explores Japanese history through its interactions with the rest of Asia, many of which were made in Kyushu.

A series of elevators shooting through futuristic tunnels bring you to the fourth floor of the sprawling complex, where a large collection of relics from across Asia is displayed with Japanese and English signage. If you're making the trip to Dazaifu, be sure to visit this unlikely museum, notable both for its form and content.

KOMYOZEN-JI

光明禅寺

2-16-1 Saifu; tel. 092/922-4053; 9:30am-4:30pm daily; ¥500

Two phenomenal rock gardens, one of them also incorporating moss and maple trees, lie hidden within the grounds of this low-profile Zen temple. Located a short walk south of Tenmangū and about 5 minutes' walk east of Dazaifu Station on the way to Kyushu National Museum, this tranquil temple and its stunning grounds offers a bit of respite. The temple's open hours are unpredictable, so it's wise to call before making the trip.

Food

KASANOYA

2-7-24 Saifu; tel. 092/922-1010; www.kasanoya.com; 9am-6pm daily; set meals ¥750-1,950; 4-minute walk east of JR Dazaifu Station on the way to Tenman-gū

This is the place to try Dazaifu's local sweet of renown, umegaemochi, a mochi (rice cake) dumpling filled with sweet red bean paste. You can buy it outside and nibble it on the go—just look for the queue in front of the shop—or sit inside and have it with a cup of tea. Lunch sets including things like udon and soba noodles are also on offer.

UME-NO-HANA VILLA NATURE AN

4-4-41 Saifu; tel. 092/928-7787; https://umenohana-restaurant.co.jp/shop-list/info.php?id=1116; 11am-9pm (last order 8pm) daily; lunch ¥3,800, dinner ¥3,300-5,500; 3-minute walk from the side streets east of Kōmyōzen-ji

Come here for a delicious tofu lunch in picturesque surroundings. Seating is in elegant tatami rooms overlooking a garden. Prices aren't exactly cheap, although the quality speaks for itself and lunch sets are a good value. The variety of items is a revelation: smoked tofu cheese, steamed buns stuffed with tofu, and tofu skin to name a few. Reserve a day ahead for dinner. For lunch, aim to arrive by noon. Otherwise, be prepared to potentially wait for a bit.

Information and Services

- **Dazaifu Tourist Information Center** (Nishitetsu Dazaifu Station; tel. 092/925-1880; 9am-5pm daily)

Getting There and Around

Dazaifu is easily reached from Fukuoka. From **Nishitetsu Fukuoka Station,** situated in Tenjin, take the **Nishitetsu line** to **Nishitetsu Futsukaichi Station,** and switch to the train bound for **Dazaifu Station** (30 minutes; ¥410). Inquire at Nishitetsu Dazaifu Station about **bicycle rentals** (¥500 per day).

If you're making your way directly to Dazaifu from **Fukuoka Airport,** you can also hop on a **bus** directly from the latter (30 minutes; ¥510).

Nagasaki 長崎

Situated at the northwestern corner of Kyushu is Nagasaki Prefecture. This area's history is steeped in interactions with the outside world, but the prefecture's capital city of Nagasaki is sadly known more for its tragic past than its dynamic present. Exploring the remnants of the city that were ravaged by the A-bomb is understandably at the top of most visitors' itineraries to the city. Venture beyond the monuments and museums dedicated to this destructive act, however, and you'll find yourself in a vibrant, cosmopolitan city, often loosely compared to San Francisco. Trams glide through downtown, an attractive harbor lies to one side, and streets climb the hills behind the city, which looks spectacular from atop the peak of Inasayama.

There are many reminders of the city's long engagement with Christianity, including Ōura Cathedral, one of Japan's oldest. The legacy of the foreign traders who once thrived in the city are concentrated around a hilly neighborhood replete with European architecture known as the Dutch Slope. The city's burgeoning Chinese community has also made its mark in Chinatown, which includes one of the only Chinese-built Confucian shrines outside the motherland. Given this mélange of cultures, it's no surprise that culinary offerings in the city are eclectic.

To take all of this in properly, plan to spend a few days in Nagasaki, a city that is likely to surprise you.

SIGHTS

Peace Park and Around

The heart of the mellow suburb of **Urakami,** north of downtown, is where you'll find the hypocenter, where the atomic bomb landed and changed the city forever. The tragic event is commemorated at a number of sights in the area, which can easily be explored on foot. From Nagasaki Station, hop on tram line 1 or 3 and ride 10 minutes to the Peace Park (Heiwa-kōen) tram stop. From here, everything is a short walk away.

NAGASAKI ATOMIC BOMB MUSEUM 長崎原爆資料館

7-8 Hirano-machi; tel. 095/844-9923; https://nagasakipeace.jp/english/abm.html; 8:30am-6:30pm daily May-Aug., 8:30am-5:30pm daily Sept.-Apr.; ¥200 adults, ¥100 students and schoolchildren

This harrowing museum documents the city's past leading up to August 9, 1945, its unthinkable annihilation by the bomb, and its reconstruction. It also tells the sobering history of the development of nuclear weapons.

Upon entering the museum, the first section gives a glimpse of what Nagasaki was like before the bombing. This leads to the second section, which gives some sense of the catastrophic event.

Items and photographs documenting the carnage left by the blast are displayed in heart-wrenching exhibits: a water tank with twisted legs from a middle school that stood near the hypocenter, rosaries left by churchgoers at Urakami Cathedral when the bomb went off, singed clothing, contorted rocks and trees, warped glass, melted coins, and a clock with the hands frozen at 11:02, the time of the blast. The aftermath, including radiation damage and accounts from survivors, is also explored in detail. Note that some of the photographs and items displayed can be very disturbing, particularly for children.

The museum invites visitors to consider deeper questions related to the existence of nuclear weapons in the present. It explores the surge in antinuclear activism across the globe, and closes with an unsettling matter-of-fact list of the nations that currently have nuclear arsenals.

NAGASAKI NATIONAL PEACE MEMORIAL HALL FOR THE ATOMIC BOMB VICTIMS
国立長崎原爆死没者追悼平和祈念館

7-8 Hirano-machi; tel. 095/814-0055; www.peace-nagasaki.go.jp/en; 8:30am-5:30pm daily Apr., 8:30am-6:30pm daily May-Aug. (until 8pm Aug. 7-9), 8:30am-5:30pm daily Sept.-Mar.; free

This deeply stirring memorial, designed by architect Kuryū Akira, opened in 2003. Enter the outdoor space that houses the memorial, encircled by trees, and take in the expansive pool of water. This basin signifies the harrowing ordeal experienced by survivors left without water in the wake of the blast. As dusk falls, lights beneath the water's surface flicker briefly in honor of the 70,000 people who died in the blast.

After reading the inscriptions around this basin, descend into the first basement level. Here, you'll discover memoirs penned by survivors. Also on the first basement floor are 12 columns with books bearing the names of all victims. On the second basement floor, you'll encounter pictures of victims, audio and video related to the bombing, and harrowing accounts from victims about their experiences receiving medical care after the blast.

While the atmosphere at this memorial is undeniably somber, the combination of light, water, and serenity inspire a glimmer of hope for a future that is free of nuclear weapons.

ATOMIC BOMB HYPOCENTER PARK
原爆落下中心地公園

Matsuyama-machi; www.discover-nagasaki.com/en/sightseeing/124; free

Leaving the memorial, walk about four minutes north to this park. Steps arranged in concentric circles lead down to a central black column made of polished stone, which marks the spot just below where the bomb detonated. Near this pillar, a remnant of a wall that once belonged to the original Urakami Cathedral still stands.

PEACE PARK
平和公園

Matsuyama-machi; free

After visiting the hypocenter, walk north about five minutes to Peace Park. Every August 9, there's a memorial ceremony held here to honor the victims of the tragic blast, as well as a vocal antinuclear protest. There's a fountain shaped like a dove and a sculpture garden graced by peace-themed works made by artists from around the world.

The centerpiece of the park is the

statue in Nagasaki Peace Park; sculpture by Seibo Kitamura

Nagasaki

INASAYAMA-KOEN
NAGASAKI ROPEWAY

PEACE PARK
Nagasaki Baseball Stadium
PEACE PARK
Peace Park Station
M T Peace Park
ATOMIC BOMB HYPOCENTER PARK
NAGASAKI ATOMIC BOMB MUSEUM
NAGASAKI NATIONAL PEACE MEMORIAL HALL FOR THE ATOMIC BOMB VICTIMS
To Nagasaki
T Atomic Bomb Museum

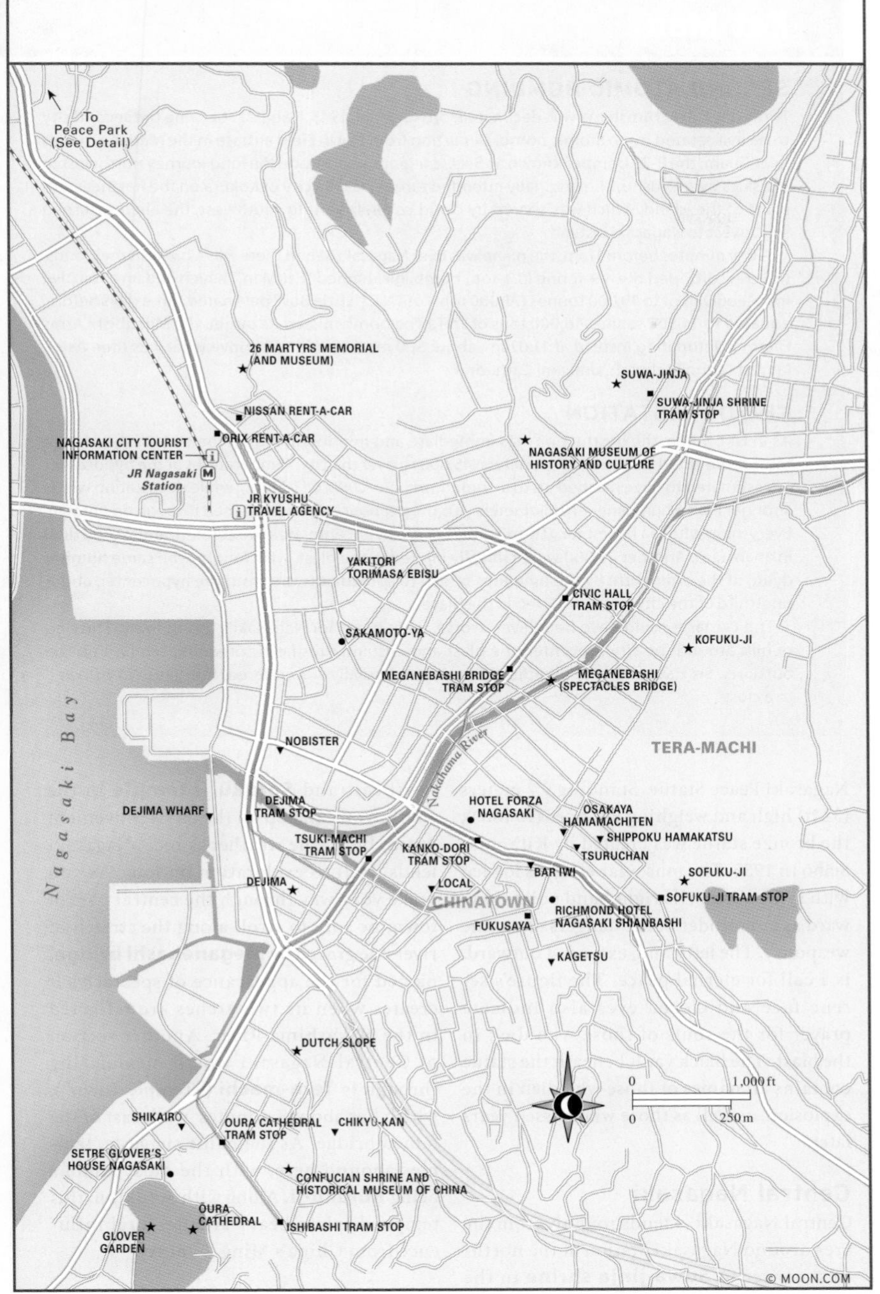
To
Peace Park
(See Detail)
26 MARTYRS MEMORIAL
(AND MUSEUM)
SUWA-JINJA
SUWA-JINJA SHRINE
TRAM STOP
NISSAN RENT-A-CAR
ORIX RENT-A-CAR
NAGASAKI CITY TOURIST
INFORMATION CENTER
JR Nagasaki
Station
NAGASAKI MUSEUM OF
HISTORY AND CULTURE
JR KYUSHU
TRAVEL AGENCY
YAKITORI
TORIMASA EBISU
CIVIC HALL
TRAM STOP
SAKAMOTO-YA
KOFUKU-JI
MEGANEBASHI BRIDGE
TRAM STOP
MEGANEBASHI
(SPECTACLES BRIDGE)
Nagasaki Bay
NOBISTER
Nakashima River
TERA-MACHI
DEJIMA WHARF
DEJIMA
TRAM STOP
HOTEL FORZA
NAGASAKI
OSAKAYA
HAMAMACHITEN
SHIPPOKU HAMAKATSU
TSUKI-MACHI
TRAM STOP
KANKO-DORI
TRAM STOP
TSURUCHAN
BAR IWI
SOFUKU-JI
DEJIMA
LOCAL
CHINATOWN
SOFUKU-JI TRAM STOP
RICHMOND HOTEL
NAGASAKI SHIANBASHI
FUKUSAYA
KAGETSU
DUTCH SLOPE
0
1,000 ft
0
250 m
SHIKAIRO
OURA CATHEDRAL
TRAM STOP
CHIKYU-KAN
SETRE GLOVER'S
HOUSE NAGASAKI
CONFUCIAN SHRINE AND
HISTORICAL MUSEUM OF CHINA
OURA
CATHEDRAL
ISHIBASHI TRAM STOP
GLOVER
GARDEN
© MOON.COM

Fat Man

SECOND ATOMIC BOMBING

Three days after Hiroshima was decimated, on August 9, 1945, Nagasaki became the second city to be eviscerated by an atomic bomb. Departing from North Field airbase in the Mariana Islands near Guam, the B-29 bomber known as *Bockscar (Bock's Car)* made the long journey northwest to the skies over Kyushu. The originally intended target was the city of Kokura on the northeastern coast of the island, which was spared by cloud cover. Diverting southwest, the aircrew turned southwest to Nagasaki instead.

A few minutes before 11am, the plane was over Nagasaki. When there was a break in the clouds, the crew dropped the 4.9-tonne (5.4-ton) bomb, nicknamed "Fat Man," which had an explosive force equivalent to 19,000 tonnes (21,000 tons) of TNT. ("Little Boy" detonated three days before, equated to 14,500 tonnes/16,000 tons of TNT.) The bomb missed its target, the Mitsubishi Arms Factory, detonating instead at 11:02am, about 500 meters (1,640 ft) above what was then Asia's largest Catholic church, Urakami Cathedral.

THE DEVASTATION

As in Hiroshima, the destruction was immediate and mindboggling. At the time of the blast, a mushroom cloud climbed 13,716 meters (45,000 ft) over the city. Temperatures at the hypocenter are estimated to have reached up to an unfathomable 4,000°C (7,232°F), while devastating winds stronger than a hurricane—70 kilometers (105 mi) per hour—furiously lashed through downtown. Everything within a kilometer (0.6-mi) radius of the hypocenter was eviscerated, and 74,000 died in an instant. Another 75,000 were critically injured in the blast, with roughly the same number dying in the aftermath. By the time fires began to spread outward from the hypocenter, about one-third of the city was subsumed in the blaze.

The carnage could have been even worse, were it not for Nagasaki's topography. The ring of hills around the city prevented the blast and ensuing fires from spreading too far into the outskirts. Six days after the dreadful blast, Japan formally surrendered, bringing World War II to a close.

Nagasaki Peace Statue. Standing 9.7 meters (32 ft) high and weighing 9 tonnes (10 tons), the bronze statue was created by Kitamura Seibō in 1955. The muscular effigy is loaded with symbolism: His right hand points skyward as a reminder of the dangers of atomic weaponry. The left hand, extended outward, is a call for eternal peace. The figure's serene face and closed eyes also indicate prayer for the souls of those who died in the blast. The black vault beneath the statue contains all names of those who died in the explosion, as well as those who passed years later.

Central Nagasaki

Central Nagasaki extends roughly from the area around Nagasaki Station at the northwest corner to **Suwa-jinja shrine** in the northeast and **Sōfuku-ji temple** in the south. You can hop on the city's convenient **tram,** but if the weather is nice, Nagasaki lends itself to exploration on foot. As you make your way through the central part of town, be sure to stroll along the stretch of riverside graced by **Meganebashi bridge,** named for the appearance of spectacles it creates when its two arches are reflected in the Nakashima River. Another section of Central Nagasaki worth meandering through is **Tera-machi** ("Temple Town"), which lies about 8 minutes' walk east of the famed bridge. As the name suggests, temples abound here, with the most famous being **Kōfuku-ji.** Along with Sofuku-ji, this temple displays heavy architectural influence from China's Ming Dynasty.

26 MARTYRS MEMORIAL (AND MUSEUM)

日本二十六聖人記念館

7-8 Nishizaka-machi; tel. 095/822-6000; www.26martyrs.com; 9am-5pm daily; memorial free, museum ¥500 adults, ¥300 high school students, ¥150 elementary school students; walk 7 minutes northeast of JR Nagasaki Station

From this wall protrude 26 reliefs commemorating a haunting incident in Nagasaki's history. It was at this post that 20 Japanese Christians (including a few boys aged 12 and 13) and six Spanish friars were crucified in 1597. It is said that one of the martyrs, Paulo Miki, delivered a final sermon as he hung on the cross and even forgave those who executed him. The museum explores the history of Christianity in Nagasaki and the brutal crackdown on the religion that was in full swing from the late 16th century.

NAGASAKI MUSEUM OF HISTORY AND CULTURE

長崎歴史文化博物館

1-1-1 Tateyama; tel. 095/818-8366; www.nmhc.jp; 8:30am-7pm (last entry 6:30pm) daily, closes third Mon. every month, closed Tues. if Mon. is holiday; ¥630 adults, ¥310 high school, junior high, and elementary school students; take tram line 3 to Sakura-machi, then walk 6 minutes northeast

This smart museum illuminates Nagasaki's storied, cosmopolitan past. A permanent exhibition spread across two floors explores the city's long history of engagement with the outside world, even at a time when the rest of Japan was sealed shut. Relics, art, documents, and various tools and visual illustrations are used to convey the city's storied exchange with powers from abroad.

There's also a section showing off Nagasaki's influence on refined crafts like porcelain and lacquerware, and another offering a glimpse into daily life in the city's heyday. Perhaps the most impressive section of the museum is its reproduction of the Nagasaki Magistrate's Office, where dignitaries were entertained in an elegant, expansive tatami room and smugglers were dealt with in a (reproduced) interrogation room. If you want to visit one museum during your time in the city, make it this one.

SUWA-JINJA

諏訪神社

18-15 Kaminishiyama-machi; tel. 095/824-0445; www.osuwasan.jp; open 24/7; free; take tram line 3 to Suwa-jinja Shrine tram stop, then walk a 10 minutes northwest

Beloved by locals, who sometimes refer to it as "O-suwa san," this Shinto shrine was founded in 1625. The deities enshrined here are the god of divine favor (Suwa no Okami), the god of matchmaking (Morisaki Okami), and the god of safe sea travel (Sumiyoshi no Okami). To reach the sprawling shrine, you'll need to plod up a series of stairways (almost 200 steps) to the top of a leafy hillock where the grounds are situated.

A variety of stone watchdogs stand guard around the grounds. The faithful sprinkle water into impressions on their heads. The particularly stout "turntable guardian dog" statue was once the object of choice for prostitutes who would pray to it to conjure storms that would delay sailors from coming to shore just a bit longer. The shrine is at its most lively every October 7-9, when it hosts the city's massive Kunchi festival.

SŌFUKU-JI

崇福寺

7-5 Kajiya-machi; tel. 095/823-2645; 8am-5pm daily; ¥300; take tram line 1 to Sōfukuji Temple tram stop, then walk 3 minutes north

This blazing-red temple, built in 1629, stands on the side of a hill. This temple belongs to the Zen sect known as Ōbaku, and like many of the temples in Nagasaki, a Chinese monk oversaw its building. Entering the temple grounds, you may be struck by the palpably different atmosphere here from what you have experienced in the vast majority of temples in Japan.

The imposing Ryugumon (Gate of the Dragon Palace) entrance gate is a prime example of such Ming dynasty flourishes.

This bright red entryway stands two stories high and is flanked by two stone guardians. Although the gate was first built in 1673, it succumbed to the elements numerous times, and the current iteration dates to 1849. After passing through the gate and walking up the hill to the temple main grounds, you'll see a number of halls housing a host of statues, including the Chinese goddess of the sea, Mazu ("Maso" in Chinese).

Elsewhere in the temple's inner sanctum, you'll find a temple bell made in 1647 and a massive cauldron in which food was made by resident priest Qianhai to feed starving residents during a famine in 1681. The Buddha Hall was designed in China and constructed with Chinese wood, transported to Nagasaki, and assembled in 1646, making it one of the city's oldest buildings.

Ample English signage elucidates all of this and more throughout the complex. Overall, this temple is the best example of a Chinese-constructed place of worship in the city.

Southern Nagasaki

Think of southern Nagasaki as starting near the mouth of the Nakashima River with **Dejima,** a manmade island, and **Chinatown** at the northern edge. While the tram network can save you a bit of time and energy, it only takes about half an hour to walk between the following sights, and walking is recommended if the weather cooperates.

Much of this area has been shaped by the city's historic Dutch presence. The cobblestone streets of the **Dutch Slope,** 10 minutes south of Dejima, or Oranda-zaka (Oranda being the Japanized pronunciation for Holland) evoke the bygone era when Holland was all the rage in Nagasaki. It's a picturesque streetscape to ramble along as you make your way through the south side of the city.

DEJIMA
出島

6-1 Dejima-machi; tel. 095/821-7200; http://nagasakidejima.jp; 8am-9pm (last entry 8:40pm) daily; ¥520 adults, ¥200 high school students, ¥100 junior high and elementary school students; take tram line 1 to Dejima tram stop, then walk 5 minutes south

Dejima was originally a manmade island built in 1636 to house the Portuguese and contain their evangelical activity. Soon after the construction of the district, the Portuguese were booted out of Japan for their persistent missionary efforts. From that point on, a small contingent of resolutely secular Dutch traders was then allowed to move its base of operations to Dejima. Although it's no longer an island, the whiff of its historic Dutch presence remains: Reconstructed warehouses, merchants' homes, walls, and gates line the streets, all in a seamless integration of Japanese and Western styles, which would have been the only window onto the outside Western world for nearly two centuries.

Plan to spend a few hours ambling through the area, easily navigable thanks to abundant English signage and free maps.

CONFUCIAN SHRINE AND HISTORICAL MUSEUM OF CHINA
長崎孔子廟中国歴代博物館

10-36 Ōura-machi; tel. 095/824-4022; http://nagasaki-koushibyou.com; 9:30am-6pm (last entry 5:30pm) daily; ¥660 adults, ¥440 high school students, ¥330 junior high and elementary school students for both shrine and museum; take tram line 1 to the Ishibashi tram stop, then walk 2 minutes

Given China's deep ties to Nagasaki, it's fitting that it's home to one of only a handful of shrines in Japan dedicated to the great Chinese sage Confucius. It's said to be the only one built with Chinese labor outside the motherland. Originally built in 1893, the Confucian Shrine (Kōshi-byō) was ravaged by fire that rippled across the city following the dropping of the A-bomb. Although it's a reconstruction, the shrine still packs a strong atmospheric punch.

As you enter, pass through a garden, crossing a bridge over a pond as the opulent

1: Confucian Shrine and Historical Museum of China **2:** Glover Garden **3:** Dejima Wharf

孔子廟
1
2 
3

buildings topped by yellow sweeping roofs come into view. The quad that fronts the complex is lined by 72 statues of the disciples of Confucius. The centerpiece of the main hall is a statue of the great sage himself, seated in repose. Beyond the shrine there's a small museum displaying a number of Chinese relics—archaeological discoveries, statues, porcelain, and more—as well as exhibits about the shrine.

ŌURA CATHEDRAL
大浦天主堂

5-3 Minamiyamate-machi; tel. 095/823-2628; https://nagasaki-oura-church.jp; 8:30am-6pm (last entry 5:30pm) daily; ¥1,000 adults, ¥400 high school and junior high school students, ¥300 elementary school students; take tram line 1 to Ōura Cathedral Station tram stop, then walk 6 minutes

About 10 minutes' walk southwest of the Confucian shrine is Ōura Church. Serving as yet another reminder of just how diverse Nagasaki was by Edo-period standards, this Catholic cathedral was completed in 1864, just before the Meiji Restoration led to the opening of Japan to the outside world. Its construction was overseen by two French priests, who catered to the growing community of foreign traders living in the city. Within the church's old seminary and bishop's living quarters, there's a small museum on Christianity's history in Japan, including the period in which "hidden Christians" were forced to live in self-exile to preserve their lives. If you don't have a strong interest in the religion's history in Japan, you can simply appreciate the structure from outside.

The first Western-style structure to be deemed a national treasure, the church is still actively used today. In 2018, the cathedral and a smattering of other sites related to the history of Christianity in Nagasaki were also added to UNESCO's World Heritage list.

GLOVER GARDEN
グラバー園

8-1 Minamiyamate-machi; tel. 095/822-8223; www.glover-garden.jp; 8am-6pm daily Oct. 10-Apr. 22, 8am-8:30pm daily Apr. 23-May 4, 8am-6pm daily May 5-Jul. 15, 8am-9:30pm daily Jul. 16-Oct. 9; ¥620 adults, ¥310 high school students, ¥180 junior high and elementary students; take tram line 1 to the Ōura Cathedral Station tram stop, then walk 6 minutes

Located next to Ōura Cathedral, this open-air museum is a great place to imagine how the well-heeled foreign business community lived in the 19th century. Several mansions and other buildings with arches and porticoes done in Greco-Roman style, and spacious wooden verandas, dot this lovely garden. Notice that some of the buildings have Japanese-style roofs. As the gardens sprawl across a hilltop, accessible by escalators, it also provides great views of the city and harbor.

The main residence once belonged to Thomas Glover (1838-1911), an influential Scottish trader who helped bring what were then cutting-edge technologies to Japan, such as industrialized coal mining, modern shipbuilding techniques, and even the steam locomotive. He also helped usher in the Meiji Restoration, which finally brought Japan's Edo period to an end.

Inasayama-kōen
稲佐山公園

www.inasayama.com/; 9am-10pm daily; free

If you're not going to Glover Garden, which offers excellent views of the city from the south side, head to this park, perched on a 333-meter-high (1,092-ft-high) hill overlooking downtown from the west. To reach the park, take tram line 3 to the Takara-machi tram station, then walk about 15 minutes to the lower station of **Nagasaki Ropeway** (tel. 095/861-3640; www.inasayama.com/ropeway/; 9am-10pm daily, closed first 10 days of Dec.; ¥730 adults, ¥520 high school and junior high school students, ¥410 elementary school students one-way, ¥1,250 adults, ¥940 high school and junior high school students, ¥620 elementary school students round-trip), which goes to the top of the hill. Alternatively, take city bus no. 3 or 4 from in front of JR Nagasaki Station to the Ropeway-mae bus

Gunkanjima: Battleship Island

Formally called Hashima, this island with a peculiar history lies about 20 kilometers (12.4 mi) south of Nagasaki Harbor, once home to a bustling coal mine that shut down in 1974. The nickname Gunkanjima ("Battleship Island," 軍艦島) comes from its resemblance to a warship floating on water, and you might recognize it from its appearance in the James Bond flick *Skyfall*.

HISTORY

The lord of Saga found the island's coal deposits in 1810, spurring the creation of a full-scale mining operation by the late-19th century, after which the Mitsubishi Corporation snapped up the property. Some of the island's history is a bit dark, particularly that of the Korean and Japanese enslaved people who worked there in the 1930s and '40s.

As the island's population swelled, buildings were squeezed into the already cramped quarters. At its peak in the 1950s, the community grew to around 6,000 people, making this tiny island—at 150 meters (492 ft) wide by 480 meters (1,575 ft) long—one of the most densely populated places in human history. Gunkanjima's coal mines abruptly shut down in April 1974, and today, all that's left are the remains of dilapidated housing blocks, crumbling schools, restaurants, a hospital, a public bath, and of course, mining operations—essentially, what is known in Japanese as haikyo (modern ruins).

HOW TO VISIT

Access to the island was blocked, and its concrete ruins were left to weather the elements until 2009, when a newly built boat dock opened for **guided tours,** which now usher visitors to three observation decks to gaze across the concrete wasteland (access to the structures is forbidden due to danger of collapse). Tours typically cost about ¥3,500-4,500 per person and last about three hours, including the time it takes to travel to and from the island (1 hour, one-way; departing multiple times per day). Check out **Gunkanjima Concierge** (www.gunkanjima-concierge.com), **Yamasa Kaiun** (www.gunkan-jima.net/en/), and **Gunkanjima Cruise** (www.gunkanjima-cruise.jp).

It's a surprisingly common occurrence for the tour boats to be unable to moor at the island's dock, even on sunny days. Further, the tours themselves feature a lot of Japanese language over loudspeakers and the boats can be crowded. If you're keen to make the trip anyway, reserve a seat ahead of time, and be sure to take sunscreen and use the bathroom before stepping off the ship, as no facilities are present on the island.

stop, then ascend the steps in the grounds of the nearby shrine. You'll find the lower ropeway station nearby.

FESTIVALS AND EVENTS

CHINESE NEW YEAR

Late-Jan. to mid-Feb.; free

Dragon dances and acrobatic performers fill the streets, and lanterns are festooned throughout Chinatown every lunar new year. Visit the neighborhood if you're here at the right time to feel the deep cultural influence of the city's Chinese community.

PEIRON (DRAGON-BOAT RACES) ペイロン（竜船競漕）

www.minatomatsuri.com; late July; free

Boats measuring 14 meters (46 ft) long are rowed with great speed by 26-man teams for two days in late July (starting 9am). This tradition was introduced in the mid-17th century by the city's Chinese community, who took to the harbor to race in efforts to placate the wrath of the sea god. Both nights also feature massive displays of fireworks, lasers, and music, with the first night being slightly more epic than the second.

Shimabara Peninsula

Lying east of the city of Nagasaki, the Shimabara Peninsula's main draws are the undulating volcanic landscape in **Unzen Amakusa National Park** (www.unzen-geopark.jp) and the historic seaside town of **Shimabara.**

UNZEN-DAKE

The main volcanic peak in Unzen Amakusa National Park is Unzen-dake (1,483 m/4,865 ft). As recently as 1991, the temperamental cone erupted, killing dozens of scientists and journalists who lingered too long near the peak attempting to document the blast, and forcing thousands to flee from surrounding towns. A visit to this peak makes for a good day trip from Nagasaki if you want to engage in some hiking and onsen R&R.

Once in the village of **Unzen Onsen,** stop by the **Mount Unzen Visitor Center** (320 Unzen; tel. 0957/73-3636; http://unzenvc.com; 9am-5pm Fri.-Wed., closed on Fri. if Thurs. is a holiday), which stocks a variety of English-language information and can store your luggage (10am-4:30pm; ¥300 pp). You can also get information at the **Mount Unzen Visitor Center** (320 Unzen; tel. 0957/73-3434; www.unzen.org; 9am-5pm daily).

About 5 minutes' walk northeast of the Mount Unzen Visitor Center, you'll discover a series of **jigoku,** or sulfurous boiling "hell" pools and seething steam vents. It's possible to walk among these gurgling pools, which conjur an otherworldly scene (24/7; free). You can also take a dip in one of the village's onsen pools; try **Kojigoku Onsen** (500-1 Unzen; tel. 0957/73-3273; https://seiunso.jp; 9am-9pm daily; ¥420 adults, ¥210 children).

Head to the **Unzen Ropeway** (551 Unzen; tel. 0957/73-3572; http://unzen-ropeway.com; 8:30am-5:20pm daily; ¥630 one-way), from where a number of hiking trails begin; one threads along a ridge to the nearby peak of **Fugen-dake** (1,359 m/4,458 ft; hike 2.1 km/1.3 mi one-way, 2 hours round-trip).

SHIMABARA

A little over 20 kilometers (12 mi) east of the Unzen area lies the town of Shimabara. Here, you'll find the reconstructed white-walled **Shimabara Castle** (1-1183-1 Jonai; tel. 0957/62-4766;

SHŌRŌ-NAGASHI (SPIRIT-BOAT PROCESSION)

精霊流し

Aug. 15; free

On the last night of the Obon festival, locals parade floats, impressively made from wood, bamboo, and other natural materials, through the city, before releasing them into the harbor. These glowing barges are said to carry the spirits of the ancestors, symbolized by the lanterns they are topped with. As they drift farther offshore, they are naturally subsumed by the waves.

NAGASAKI KUNCHI

長崎くんち (長崎伝統芸能振興会)

http://nagasaki-kunchi.com; Oct. 7-9; free

With roots that stretch back more than four centuries, this syncretic festival draws on the city's Dutch and Chinese ties with colorful aplomb. Dance groups kitted out in ostentatious attire represent the city's neighborhoods, as serpentine dragon puppets and floats in the shapes of lions, dragons, and ships from both China and Holland are dragged through the streets, to the beating of drums and clanging of cymbals.

The bulk of the action takes place around Suwa-jinja, but spills into Chūō Park, a few minutes' walk west of Meganebashi in the center of town, and the plaza at JR Nagasaki Station. For a good viewing spot, aim to arrive as early as possible (around 7am or even earlier). Don't fret if you don't snag a perfect seat, though. The revelry spills into the streets around town as the days drag on and a buzz fills the air throughout. English-language

https://shimabarajou.com; 9am-5:30pm daily; ¥550 adults, ¥270 high school, junior high, and elementary school students), located 10 minutes' walk west of Shimabara Station. There's also a **samurai district** (Teppō-machi area) set on a street lined with mostly inhabited samurai homes—some can be entered for free (9am-5pm daily). A neighborhood known as the **City of Swimming Carp** is famous for its canals filled with crystal-clear spring water teeming with multihued koi (carp). And stop by the **Shimeisō tea house** (2 Shin-machi; tel. 095/763-1121; www.city.shimabara.lg.jp/page943.html; 9am-6pm daily; ¥310 adults, ¥150 children), which stands above a lovely pond of spring water.

South of town, the **Mount Unzen Disaster Museum** (1-1 Heisei-chō; tel. 0957/65-5555; www.udmh.or.jp; 9am-6pm daily, last entry 5pm; ¥1,050 adults, ¥740 high school and junior high school students, ¥530 elementary school students) commemorates the 1991 eruption of Unzen-dake.

GETTING THERE AND AROUND

To reach **Shimabara Station** from Nagasaki Station, you must first travel to Isahaya Station. To do this you can either take the **JR local train** (about 30 minutes; ¥480) or the **limited express train** (20 minutes; ¥1,320). From Isahaya Station, transfer to the local Shimabara Railway to Shimabara Station (1 hour 10 minutes; ¥1,460). From Nagasaki Station, **buses** run three times daily to **Unzen Onsen** (1 hour 40 minutes; from ¥1,800). Hourly buses run from Shimabara Station to Unzen Onsen (50 minutes; ¥850).

The best way to get around the peninsula, however, is with your own wheels. There are plenty of rental outlets near Nagasaki Station, Isahaya Station, and Shimabara-gaikō Station. From Shimabara Port, accessible by bus from Shimabara Station (¥170), you can also catch a ferry across the Ariake Bay to Kumamoto. Ferry operators servicing this route include **Kyūshō Ferry** (tel. 096/329-6111; www.kyusho-ferry.co.jp; 1 hour; ¥890, ¥2,750 with economy-size car) and hydrofoil company **Kumamoto Ferry** (tel. 096/311-4100; www.kumamotoferry.co.jp; 30 minutes; ¥1,100). Once in Kumamoto, buses run from Kumamoto port to Kumamoto Kōtsū Center (40 minutes; ¥560).

festival information is readily available at the tourist information center.

FOOD

Shippoku

SHIPPOKU HAMAKATSU

6-50 Kajiya-machi; tel. 095/826-8321; www.sippoku.jp; 11am-9:30pm (last order 8pm) daily; lunch (11:30-3pm, last order 1:30pm) from ¥2,970, afternoon tea sets (1:30pm-5pm, last order 4pm) from ¥2,800, dinner courses from ¥6,500; take tram no. 1 or 4 from the Shianbashi tram stop, then walk 3 minutes

This sleek, modern restaurant is a less exorbitant place to sample shippoku (Japanese cuisine infused with Chinese and Portuguese flavors—though it's still not cheap. Lunch and dinner courses are prepared in several tiers. At the higher end, courses can cost upwards of ¥13,800. Book a table at least a few days in advance to be safe. At least two people are required to order a full course.

★ KAGETSU

2-1 Maruyama-machi; tel. 095/822-0191; www.ryoutei-kagetsu.co.jp; noon-3pm (last order 2pm) and 6pm-10pm (last order 8pm) Wed.-Mon.; lunch boxes ¥5,400 (Mon.-Fri.), lunch courses from ¥8,000, dinner courses from ¥15,000; take tram no. 1 or 4 from Sōfuku-ji tram stop, then walk 5 minutes

Occupying a 17th-century wooden structure that once served as a geisha house, this shippoku restaurant looks like the archetypal set for a samurai flick. You'll find tatami floors with low tables, windows looking out onto a dreamy garden, and servers shuffling about in kimono, deftly balancing trays loaded with lacquer bowls filled with delicacies. There are even gashes in a few wooden beams left by katana blades. This is the spot to go all out and experience Nagasaki's unique shippoku tradition, which imbues haute Japanese cuisine with accents from Chinese and Portuguese cooking—that said, you'll appreciate it much more if you're with someone who speaks Japanese to help make sense of the meal. At least two people are required to order a full shippoku course. If you can afford it, it will be an experience you'll not soon forget. Reserve as far in advance as possible.

Barbecue

OSAKAYA HAMAMACHITEN

11-11 Hama-machi; tel. 095/820-9198; www.facebook.com/osakayaq/; 5pm-midnight Sun.-Thurs., 5pm-2am Fri.-Sat.; courses from ¥5,000; take tram no. 1 or 4 from the Shianbashi tram stop, then walk 2 minutes

Come here if you're in the mood for a carnivorous feast. Excellent beef and pork platters, vegetable medleys, and a robust assortment of sake fill the menu. You'll barbecue the meat and added trimmings at your table. Making matters easier, there's an English menu and some staff speak English. Reserve a day or more in advance to ensure a seat. Recommended.

Yakitori

YAKITORI TORIMASA EBISU

6-18 Ebisu-machi; tel. 095/895-7227; https://akr0977110302.owst.jp; 5:30pm-midnight (last order 11:30pm) daily; average ¥3,000; walk 7 minutes southeast of JR Nagasaki Station, or take tram line 3 to the Sakura-machi tram stop, then walk 3 minutes

For char-broiled goodness, come to this excellent yakitori shop east of JR Nagasaki Station. The menu extends to beef, pork, seafood, and lamb, with a range of vegetables too. Staff and diners alike are friendly and open, and there's an English menu. A great place for a fun, hearty meal washed down with cold beer or hot sake.

Cafés and Light Bites

FUKUSAYA

3-1 Funadaiku-machi; tel. 095/821-2938; www.fukusaya.co.jp; 8:30am-8pm; take tram no. 1 or 4 to the Shianbashi tram stop, then walk 3 minutes

Overseas culinary influence can be tasted in Nagasaki's signature dessert and favored souvenir, the Castella sponge cake. Made with flour, eggs, sugar, and syrup, this dessert first arrived with Portuguese traders in the 16th century. This shop has been making the block-shaped sweet since 1624.

NOBISTER

1-3 Edo-machi; tel. 095/829-0831; http://nobister.com; 11am-2:30pm and 7pm-11pm Mon.-Sat.; lunch from ¥800; take tram line 1 or 2 to the Ōhato tram stop, then walk 1 minute

This friendly café serves vegetable-packed curries, sandwiches with lean cuts of meat, freshly baked bread, healthy lunch sets, delicious smoothies, and a range of vegan fare. There's an English menu. Takeout is also available.

TSURUCHAN

2-47 Aburaya-machi; tel. 095/824-2679; 9am-9pm daily; Turkish rice from ¥1,200

This café claims to have whipped up the first plate of Turkish rice in 1925. While the traditional variety includes a tonkatsu cutlet (breaded, fried pork), the menu here extends to beef and chicken, and offers a cream sauce in place of the customary curry-based gravy. If you're the type who wants to try Nagasaki's most peculiar dish once just to say you did it, you may as well go to the source.

International

DEJIMA WHARF

1-1-109 Dejima-machi; tel. 095/828-3939; http://dejimawharf.com; hours vary by shop; prices vary; take tram line 1 to the Dejima tram stop, then walk 3 minutes

This is a good place to go if you're feeling hungry and spontaneous. Seafood, steak, Italian, Chinese dishes, and more are served at this assortment of harbor-facing restaurants, housed in a two-story wooden building. It's an especially appealing spot to dine at lunchtime during the warmer months, given the great al fresco seating areas.

SHIKAIRŌ

4-5 Matsugae-machi; tel. 095/822-1296; http://shikairou.com; 11:30am-3pm and 5pm-9pm (last order 8:30pm) daily; ¥1,100 (signature dish, chanpon); take tram line 5 to the Ōura Cathedral tram stop, then walk 2 minutes

This cavernous Chinese joint with sweeping views of the harbor is admittedly on the tourist track, but as the originator of Nagasaki's beloved chanpon dish, it's worth a visit. The menu extends to gyoza (fried pork dumplings), fried spring rolls, and other Sino fare. Keep an eye out for the complex with massive red pillars and an entrance topped with a Chinese-style roof. It's a short walk from Glover Garden (5 minutes) or Ōura Cathedral (8 minutes).

BARS AND NIGHTLIFE

Nightlife in Nagasaki, some of it salacious, is concentrated in the neighboring quarters of Shianbashi and Dōza-machi. To reach the eastern side of this district, tightly packed with narrow lanes draped with lanterns and neon signs, take tram lines 1 or 4 to Shianbashi or Kankō-dōri tram stops, from where Shianbashi spreads to the south and west. You can also enter from the west by taking tram lines 1, 2, or 5 to Shinchi Chinatown or Nishi-Hamano-machi, from where the action starts in the Dozamachi area just east of either tram stop.

BAR IWI

1-7 Motoshikkui-machi; tel. 080/8887-9514; 7pm-2am Mon.-Thurs., 7pm-4am Fri.-Sat., 8pm-4am Sun.; take tram no. 1 or 4 to the Shianbashi tram stop, then walk 1 minute

With its all-black interior—drawing in those rugby fans—and an abundance of Ultraman figurines, this bar is a friendly spot to mingle with locals and expats over reasonably priced drinks.

LOCAL

7-8 Dōza-machi; tel. 095/823-0022; 5pm-2am Mon.-Fri., 3pm-3am Sat., 3pm-midnight Sun.; take tram no. 1 or 4 to the Kanko-dōri tram stop, then walk 1 minute

This cheery bar has a good range of imported beers on tap and a smattering of craft brews in the bottle. The first floor is standing only, while the second floor has limited seating.

ACCOMMODATIONS

¥10,000-20,000

RICHMOND HOTEL NAGASAKI SHIANBASHI

6-38 Motoshikkui-machi; tel. 095/832-2525; https://richmondhotel.jp/nagasaki; ¥13,000 d; take tram line 1 or 4 to the Shianbashi tram stop, then walk 1 minute

Conveniently located near a lively entertainment area with lots of restaurants and shops. Rooms are slightly above average in size and are well-appointed, with each one including a smart phone that can be used around town during your stay (calls and data). The breakfast buffet includes local dishes and Western staples, and is good for the price. This is a very good mid-range choice in the heart of the action.

HOTEL FORZA NAGASAKI

4-11 Hama-machi; tel. 095/816-2111; www.hotelforza.jp/nagasaki; ¥14,000 d; take tram line 1 or 4 to the Kanko-dōri tram stop, then walk 1 minute

This well-located modern hotel sits at the end of a shopping arcade. Modern rooms with a stylish touch and helpful staff at the front desk make it a great choice. A restaurant serves Japanese- and Western-style breakfast, and there's a shared lounge with free coffee. There's a small sofa and table squeezed into most rooms for a little chill-out space. All rooms are non-smoking.

¥20,000-30,000

SETRE GLOVER'S HOUSE NAGASAKI

2-28 Minami Yamate-machi; tel. 095/827-7777; www.hotelsetre.com/nagasaki/; from ¥20,000 d; take tram line 5 to the Ōura Cathedral tram stop, then walk 5 minutes

Housed in a handsome Western-style building

with antique furniture and romantic vibes, this classy hotel oozes European charm. It's a short walk from Glover House and Ōura Cathedral. Rooms are spacious and well-appointed. A swanky on-site restaurant serves Nagasaki's three core cuisines—Japanese, Chinese, and Western—and all guests have access to a plush lounge with complimentary drinks, comfy seating, and soft lighting. Staff are friendly and eager to help. Easily one of the city's best accommodations.

★ SAKAMOTO-YA

2-13 Kanaya-machi; tel. 0120/26-8210; www.sakamotoya.co.jp; from ¥30,000 d; take tram line 1 or 2 to Goto-machi Station, then walk 5 minutes

In business since 1894, the heritage of the city's oldest hotel shows in the wooden structure, tatami floors, sliding fusuma doors, and alcoves containing calligraphy and flower arrangements in ceramics fired in the island's kilns. There are only 11 rooms, each with a private bathroom with a cypress tub, and private gardens for those on the first floor. Service is highly personalized. Japanese meals are served, with the city's signature shippoku spreads available upon request. This is a great choice for the classic ryokan experience.

INFORMATION AND SERVICES

For information on the city and surrounding prefecture, your best luck is to go online. Nagasaki Prefecture's website (https://travel.at-nagasaki.jp/en/) provides extensive information on things to see and do not only in the city, but around the prefecture. If you'd like to join a guided walk in English, led by a local volunteer, check out **Nagasaki Walks** (www.keirinkai.or.jp/nagasaki-walks; 2-4 hours; from ¥1,600 pp).

- **Nagasaki City Tourist Information Center** (first floor of Nagasaki Station; tel. 095/823-3631; 8am-8pm daily)
- **JR Kyushu Travel Agency** (1-60 Onoue-machi; tel. 095/822-4813; www.jrkyushu.co.jp/ryoko/; 10:30am-6:30pm Mon.-Fri., 10:30am-6pm Sat.-Sun.)

GETTING THERE

Train

JR Nagasaki Station sits at the northwestern edge of the heart of downtown. It's serviced by local train lines that run to various parts of the island. The **Kamome limited express** runs to **Hakata** (Fukuoka) (2 hours; ¥4,800) and to Shin-tosu, from which you can continue to **Kumamoto** by shinkansen (2 hours 15 minutes; ¥7,940).

Air

Nagasaki Airport (tel. 095/752-5555; www.nagasaki-airport.jp) is a fair distance from the city center, about 40 kilometers (25 mi) north of town on an artificial island in Ōmura Bay. Along with servicing flights to and from a variety of domestic hubs—Tokyo, Osaka (Itami and Kansai International), Kobe, Okinawa, Nagoya—a smattering of international flights link the city to Seoul and Shanghai. Buses run between the airport and the **Kenei bus terminal,** located adjacent to JR Nagasaki Station (40 minutes to 1 hour; ¥1,000).

Bus

Highway buses serving routes throughout Kyushu come and go from the **Kenei Bus Terminal** (3-1 Daikoku-machi; tel. 095/826-6155), located across the street from JR Nagasaki Station. Destinations include Fukuoka, Kumamoto, Miyazaki, Kagoshima, and beyond. See the **Kenei Bus** (www.kenei-bus.jp) website for timetables and fares.

GETTING AROUND

Tram

Although Nagasaki is pretty spread out, it's blessed with a brilliant tram network that drastically simplifies getting around town (until around 11pm; single ride ¥130, one-day pass ¥500). There are **five color-coded lines,** of which no. 2 is only used for occasional events. Aside from being a handy means of transport, many of the tram cars are period pieces straight out of the early 20th century.

If you want to transfer to another line, which requires a noritsugi (transfer pass), **Tsuki-machi** is the only stop where you can do it for free. If you're taking a single ride on the tram network, simply drop your fare into the box beside the driver's seat as you exit the tram. Pick up a day pass at the tourist information center in **JR Nagasaki Station** or from a number of hotels.

Car

If you're looking to venture from Nagasaki to other regions of the island, having your own wheels is a good idea. There are a number of car-rental options around JR Nagasaki Station, including reliable chains like **Nissan Rent-a-Car** (2-9 Daikoku-machi; tel. 095/825-1988; https://nissan-rentacar.com) and **Orix Rent-a-Car** (14-5 Daikoku-machi; tel. 095/827-8694; https://car.orix.co.jp).

Central Kyushu

The central region of the island is dominated by the large prefectures of Kumamoto on the western side and Oita in the east. Fukuoka Prefecture borders both Kumamoto and Oita to the north, while Kagoshima Prefecture lies to the southwest of Kumamoto, and Miyazaki Prefecture is southeast of Kumamoto and south of Oita.

Kumamoto's capital city of the same name lies about 10 kilometers (6.2 mi) inland from Ariake Bay. The Shimabara Peninsula and Nagasaki Prefecture are on the other side of the water to the west. The massive caldera of Aso-san lies about 50 kilometers (31 mi) east of the city of Kumamoto, while the remote hot-spring village of Kurokawa Onsen is roughly 30 kilometers (18.6 mi) north of there.

From Kurokawa Onsen, crossing the border into Oita Prefecture, the quaint onsen town of Yufuin is about 50 kilometers (31 mi) to the northeast. The kitschy onsen mecca of Beppu, with its theme-park ambience, is another 25 kilometers (15.5 mi) east of there on Oita's coast.

KUMAMOTO

熊本

The largest city in Central Kyushu, Kumamoto is the island's most centrally located hub. Most of Kumamoto's action takes place in the northeast of town. Its main attraction is its castle, a scaled-down replica of the original 17th-century fortress. It serves well as a base for exploring the island's craggy interior, including the smoking cone of Aso-san.

Note that a series of earthquakes, topping out at 7.0 magnitude, struck Kumamoto in April 2016, dealing significant damage to the city and surrounding region. Train lines were ravaged; schools, office blocks, and homes collapsed; and more than 200 fatalities occurred. Historic and spiritual sights as far away as Aso-jinja were badly damaged, with some even toppling over. The rebuilding is ongoing and is expected to continue for decades to come.

Sights

KUMAMOTO-JŌ

熊本城

1-1 Honmaru, Chūō-ku; tel. 096/352-5900; https://castle.kumamoto-guide.jp; 9am-5pm (last entry 4:30pm) daily; ¥800 high school students and older, ¥300 junior high and elementary school students; from JR Kumamoto Station, take tram line A or B to the Kumamoto Castle/City Hall tram stop

Considered one of Japan's top three citadels, Kumamoto-jō cuts a striking profile. Its looming black keep is topped by a gently curving roofline accented by white-fronted eaves. Its imposing stone wall wraps 5.3 kilometers (3.3 mi) around it, and gaping moats bisect the grounds. It was, in many ways, the perfect citadel, which was exactly its intended purpose.

Originally built by local lord Katō Kiyomasa (1562-1611) over a seven-year period that culminated in 1607, the Kato clan's time in the fortress was short-lived. The castle was transferred to the Hosokawa clan 50 years after the complex was built. The Hosokawa clan ruled the region from the great black castle for the next two centuries.

Today, all but a few structures, such as the **Uto Turret,** are reproductions. The originals were wiped out in the battle that saw Saigō Takamori, the legendary "last samurai," lead his rebel forces against the newly ensconced Meiji imperial army, which fought from within the castle. Although the imperial troops prevailed and Saigō's men were forced to retreat after a two-month onslaught, the fighting dealt a heavy blow to the castle. Further, regardless of the imperial victory, the keep had burned down prior to the siege.

A museum within the reconstructed keep tells the illustrious history of the castle and the brutally elegant trappings of the samurai way. Along with the keep, there are a variety of structures that are likewise reproductions, including dozens of turrets and gates, the atmospheric **Former Hosokawa Residence**—closed due to earthquake damage at the time of writing—located in the northwest part of the grounds, and the stunning reproduction of the **Honmaru Goten Palace.**

Sadly, the castle took another serious blow in 2016 when a 7.0-magnitude earthquake struck Kumamoto. The main keep's interior reopened to the public in June 2021, but it could take another 20 years to completely repair all the damage done.

The good news is that you can still admire the sprawling fortress from a distance. A good walking route begins at **Sakuranobaba-Josaien,** where you'll also find the castle's tourist information center, and walk uphill to the **Ninomaru turret.** Walking a loop around the castle takes around an hour, two if you're walking at a leisurely pace. In late March and early April, some 800 cherry trees fill the grounds with an ocean of pink blossoms—understandably a popular time to visit.

Food

Kumamoto is best known for its basashi (horsemeat sashimi). While this may sound off-putting, if you're willing to entertain the thought, it's surprisingly tasty, especially when liberally seasoned with garlic, ginger, and a dipping sauce. Another local favorite is karashi-renkon (slices of deep-fried lotus root, stuffed with miso paste and hot mustard).

Kumamoto-jō

AND COFFEE ROASTERS

11-22 Kamitōri-chō; tel. 096/273-6178; www.andcoffeeroasters.com; 9am-6pm Wed.-Mon.; ¥450; from JR Kumamoto Station, take tram line A or B to the Suidō-chō tram stop, then walk 7 minutes

This hip, local café makes artisan coffee in a minimal, laid-back space. The friendly staff take their craft seriously. Upstairs, there's a small seating area. It's a great place for a caffeine hit.

SRI LANKA KUMAMOTO

2F Kumamoto Bldg., 1-4-3 Shimotōri, Chūō-ku; tel. 096/326-8085; www.facebook.com/srilankakumamoto/; 11:30am-5pm and 6pm-11pm daily; lunch ¥1,000, dinner ¥2,000; from JR Kumamoto Station, take tram line A or B to the Kumamoto Castle/City Hall tram stop, then walk 3 minutes

As the name suggests, this cozy restaurant serves authentic, mouthwatering Sir Lankan food. Keep an eye out for the Sri Lankan flag flapping on the sidewalk outside, then follow your nose.

★ YOKOBACHI

11-40 Kamitōri-chō, Chūō-ku; tel. 096/351-4581; www.yokobachi.com; 5pm-midnight daily; dishes from ¥600, courses from ¥2,500; from JR Kumamoto Station, take tram line A or B to the Suidō-chō tram stop, then walk 7 minutes

With its verdant inner courtyard, tatami rooms, al fresco seating in warmer months, and creative menu, this izakaya serves karashi-renkon—skewers of Higo beef, as the local form of wagyu (high-grade Japanese beef) is known; or try a Caesar salad topped with lotus-root chips, sweet potato, parmesan, and pancetta. There's an extensive alcohol menu, with a nice range of shōchū and a nomihōdai (all-you-can-drink) plan (90 minutes; ¥1,500). Reserve a table a few days early to be safe. Recommended.

Nightlife and Entertainment

It may lack the buzz of bigger cities, but meander through some of the side streets branching off from the Shimotōri shōten-gai (covered arcade), south of Kumamoto-jōm, and you're bound to discover a few unlikely gems.

GOOD TIME CHARLIE

5F, 1-7-24 Shimotōri, Chūō-ku; tel. 096/324-1619; 8pm-2am Thurs.-Tues.; take tram line A or B to Hanabata-chō Station, then walk 2 minutes

One of Kumamoto's favorite sons, Charlie Nagatani is a goateed Japanese gentleman known for his trademark black cowboy hat, aviator sunglasses, and jeans, and for strumming a guitar and singing with a distinctly country twang. Charlie singlehandedly brought country music to his homeland, and this bar in Kumamoto is his home base. Plastered to the hilt with photos of country greats and trimmings of Americana, it's clear where Charlie derives his inspiration. Whether you're into country music or not, visiting this bar, which hosts regular gigs, is an enjoyable, slightly surreal experience.

GLOCAL BAR VIBES

3F Arita Bldg., 1-5-6 Shimotōri, Chūō-ku; tel. 080/8350-9624; https://vibes222.wixsite.com/glocalvibes; 8pm-11:30pm Mon.-Sat., closes second Sat. of every month; take tram line A or B to Hanabata-chō Station, then walk 4 minutes

With barman Nori-san as your guide, this is an excellent spot to dive into the wonders of shōchū. Kumamoto has a reputation for producing a slightly sweet, rice-based variant of the distilled spirit so closely associated with Kyushu. The huge range of shōchū is reason enough to visit the bar, but enthusiastic, English-speaking Nori-san makes it unforgettable. Highly recommended.

Accommodations

KUMAMOTO HOTEL CASTLE

4-2 Jōtō-machi; tel. 096/326-3311; www.hotel-castle.co.jp; ¥16,000 d; take tram line A or B to the Kumamoto Castle/City Hall tram stop, then walk 5 minutes

This upscale hotel is well-located, only a short walk from the city's prime attraction after which it is named. Amiable staff provide great service, and the rooms are tastefully decorated, with many boasting castle views. Head to the elegant restaurant and bar on the 11th floor for arresting views of the fortress at night. Given its prime location and high standard of service, the rooms are a bargain.

HOTEL NIKKO KUMAMOTO

2-1 Kamitōri-chō; tel. 096/211-1111; https://nikko-kumamoto.co.jp; from ¥23,000 d; take tram line A or B to the Suidō-chō tram stop, then walk 2 minutes

This chic property is right in the center, walkable from the castle and a glut of dining options. Rooms, some with castle views, are expansive, and the in-house bathrooms are roomy and well-appointed. Smart, uniformed staff are eager to meet guests' needs.

Information and Services

Online, visit www.kumanago.jp and https://kumamoto.guide/en/ to glean more about the city and prefecture.

- **Tourist information center** (JR Kumamoto Station; tel. 096/327-9500; https://kumamoto-guide.jp/tourist-information/; 9am-5:30pm daily)
- **Jōsaien Complex Tourist Information Center** (1-1-3 Ninomaru, Chūō-ku; tel. 096/322-5060; https://kumamoto-guide.jp/tourist-information/; 9am-5:30pm daily)

Getting There

TRAIN

JR Kumamoto Station sits a few kilometers (just under 2 mi) south of the heart of town. It's serviced by the shinkansen and local lines, to and from JR Hakata Station in **Fukuoka** (shinkansen; 40 minutes; ¥5,030), Kagoshima-Chūō Station (shinkansen; 45 minutes; ¥6,870) in the southern hub of **Kagoshima,** and **Nagasaki** (take the Kamome Limited Express train to Shin-Tosu, then transfer to the shinkansen; 2.5 hours; ¥7,940).

AIR

Aso Kumamoto Airport (tel. 096/232-2311; www.kumamoto-airport.co.jp/en/), situated east of downtown, services domestic flights from Tokyo, Osaka, Nagoya, and Naha. Buses make the roughly 20-kilometer (12-mi) trip to JR Kumamoto Station (1 hour; ¥800), making stops at the main bus station of **Sakura-machi Bus Terminal** (3-10 Sakura-machi, Chūō-ku; tel. 096/354-1111; https://sakuramachi-kumamoto.jp/bus; 10am-8pm daily) on the way. If you don't mind spending the money, a taxi ride to the city center takes around 45 minutes and costs about ¥6,000.

BUS

The **Sakura-machi Bus Terminal** (3-10 Sakura-machi, Chūō-ku; tel. 096/325-0100; https://sakuramachi-kumamoto.jp/bus; 10am-8pm daily) is housed in the first floor of the **Sakura Machi Kumamoto** (https://sakuramachi-kumamoto.jp/) shopping mall, servicing long-distance routes around Kyushu and beyond (**Kyoto,** 10 hours, ¥8,000-11,700 depending on day, stopping at Osaka and Kobe en route). For detailed routes and fares to and from Kumamoto, and elsewhere in Kyushu, visit the website of **Kyushu Booking** (https://kyushubusbooking.com).

BOAT

It's possible to travel by regular ferry, operated by **Kyūshō Ferry** (tel. 096/329-6111; www.kyusho-ferry.co.jp; 1 hour; ¥890), or a snappy hydrofoil, run by **Kumamoto Ferry** (tel. 096/311-4100; www.kumamotoferry.co.jp; 30 minutes; ¥1,100) to and from the **Shimabara Peninsula,** which lies west of Kumamoto across the Ariake Bay, en route to **Nagasaki.** Buses run between Sakura-machi Bus Terminal and Kumamoto port (40 minutes; ¥560).

CAR

If you plan to venture into the heart of the island, to Aso-san and beyond, a car will prove indispensable. There are a number of rental agencies scattered around both the east and west sides of JR Kumamoto Station. On the road running just in front of the station's east side, **Nissan Rent-a-Car** (1-14-1 Kasuga,

Nishi-ku; tel. 096/356-4123; https://nissan-rentacar.com; 8am-8pm daily) and **Toyota Rent-a-Car** (1-14-28 Kasuga, Nishi-ku; tel. 096/311-0100; https://rent.toyota.co.jp; 8am-7pm daily) are both trusty options.

Getting Around

TRAM

While Kumamoto's main train station is admittedly a little out of the way, thankfully its tram system (6:30am-11pm daily; single ride ¥170; one-day pass ¥500) makes it easy to get into and around downtown. The network is simple, with two lines that begin east of the city and move toward downtown. These lines branch out when they reach the Karashima-chō tram stop, with **line A** moving southward toward JR Kumamoto Station and **line B** running north and doing a circuit around Kumamoto-jō. Pay for either single rides or day passes on the tram. If you plan to transfer between the lines, you must do so at the Karashima-chō tram stop. Request a norikae-kippu (transfer ticket) to change trams for free.

LOOP BUS

Roughly every 30 minutes, a loop bus departs from **JR Kumamoto Station** or the **Sakura-machi Bus Terminal** and makes a loop around the castle (www.shiromegurin.com; 9am-5pm daily; single ride ¥160, one-day pass ¥400). This is a convenient way to access the city's major sights.

★ ASO-SAN

阿蘇山

Traveling east from Kumamoto, the road dips, curves, and ultimately rises up the side of the formidable Aso Caldera, a very ancient and still active volcano that is, to put it mildly, massive. From east to west, its caldera spans 18 kilometers (11 mi); from north to south, 24 kilometers (15 mi). Its circumference is more than 120 kilometers (75 mi) around. The spread is so vast, entire villages and swaths of farmland exist within its basin. The main crater formed some 90,000 years ago after a mega-volcano imploded. A lake's worth of water then accumulated, and a number of diminutive additional cones rose as the moody volcano continued to gush. This cluster of five cones is known as Aso-san, one of the world's largest calderas.

The most heavily trafficked road into Aso-san's vast interior is the **Aso Kankō Toll Road.** Starting from **JR Aso Station,** take the road southward and the perfectly symmetrical cone of **Komezuka,** which literally means "Hill of Rice," comes into view. Legend holds that the peak was once a large mound of rice owned by the local god Takeiwatatsu-no-mikoto. When the townspeople in the area were struck with hunger, they pleaded with the god for food. He generously agreed to give a portion of his mountain-sized stockpile to the starving villagers. The divine scoop of sustenance resulted in the crater seen atop the mountain today.

As the road bends eastward, the **Kusasenri Plateau** unfolds as a calm scene of marshes and fields of grazing cows and horses, with **Naka-dake** (1,506 m/4,940 ft) looming beyond. This peak, accessed by ropeway, is Aso-san's only active cone. Note that gas levels near Naka-dake can become dangerously high, a particular problem if you have any kind of respiratory condition.

While it's generally safe to visit if you take proper precautions, Aso-san erupted as recently as October 2016, causing significant damage to the area around the peak. Also note that the earthquake that struck Kumamoto in April of the same year dealt a major blow to some of the area's sights. Among them, the ancient shrine **Aso-jinja** was sadly all but flattened.

Sights

DAIKANBŌ LOOKOUT

大観峰展望所

24/7; free

Located on the caldera's northern rim, this scenic viewpoint sits on one of seven promontories (aka "noses") that extend into the basin from its edge. While this used to be a strategic place for the Aso clan to gaze long distances in ancient times, today it serves as a lookout for buses full of tourists. The 360-degree views of the entire caldera are splendid. The five main peaks of Aso-san—all visible here—are said to resemble the outline of Buddha sleeping ("Nehanzo") on the basin floor. When clouds occasionally roll into the valley at just the right elevation, the enlightened one appears to be floating supine on them.

This is the best place to see Aso-san in all its majesty from a distance. It's a particularly good option if you're driving your own car and want to see the mountain in passing without spending too much time. To reach the viewpoint, from JR Aso Station on the JR Houhi Main Line, take the Kyushu Sanko bus heading northward toward Tsuetate. Get off at the Daikanbo Iriguchi bus stop. From there, follow the walking path to the left of the toilets in the parking area. You can either return the same way you came (10 minutes each way), or walk a longer loop that takes about 40 minutes total. It's wise to bring a jacket any time of year as it can get quite windy. Also, check the weather before making the trip. Sometimes fog rolls in and totally obscures the view.

MOUNT NAKA-DAKE
中岳

www.aso.ne.jp/~volcano/info; to reach the bottom cable car station, take the Kyushu Sanko bus (¥650 one-way) to Asosan-nishieki bus stop or drive (¥800 toll road) south from JR Aso Station for about 40 minutes

If conditions are right, Naka-dake is the most awe-inspiring sight at Aso-san. However, conditions could include dangerous levels of poisonous gases or the potential for an eruption. If the volcano is cooperating on the day of your visit, quite a scene awaits. Inside the crater, a lake infused with a heavy layer of gray ash gurgles as sulfurous steam wafts in the air.

You can reach the top of the crater and gaze upon this unearthly landscape by walking 30 minutes uphill from the Asosan-nishieki bus stop at the bottom station of the **Mount Aso Ropeway** line (808-5 Kurokawa; tel. 0967/34-0411; www.kyusanko.co.jp/aso/lang_en). At the time of writing, the ropeway itself was closed. It's uncertain when or if it will be operational again. It is, however, possible to board a shuttle bus in lieu of the ropeway and travel by road to the top of the crater (www.kyusanko.co.jp/aso/pdf/alsinfo_en.pdf; 9am-5pm daily; ¥750 one-way, ¥1,200 return adults; ¥370 one-way, ¥600 return children).

hiking around Aso-san

You can also make this same journey yourself via a toll road (¥800) if you've got your own wheels. Once on top, you can walk along a stretch of the crater's edge, but access to its north side is forbidden due to the deaths of two tourists in 1997 who were struck by a sudden blast of lethal fumes.

Although the odds of a full-scale eruption while you stand atop the peak are slim, eruptions did lead to loss of life in 1958 and 1979. Other sizable discharges happened in 1989, 1990, 1993, and 2016. If the earth starts to wobble or ominous clouds of ash begin to spew, keep your eyes peeled for the emergency bunkers arrayed around the mountain and take cover in one of them.

Be sure to check on daily conditions before making the trip to Naka-dake. It's not uncommon for the peak to be closed. And if you happen to have a respiratory ailment of any kind, don't go regardless of how the volcano is behaving that day.

Hiking

KUSASENRI PLATEAU

草千里高原

Distance: *5.5 km (3.4 mi)*

Time: *1.5 hours round-trip (Kijima-dake), 3 hours round-trip (Naka-dake)*

Information and maps: *Aso Volcano Museum information desk; www.explore-kumamoto.com/kusasenri-plateau*

Trailhead: *Aso Volcano Museum*

Taking the Kyushu Sanko bus (¥650 one-way) or driving your own car (¥800 for toll road) southward from JR Aso Station for about 40 minutes, you'll arrive at this grassy plain. Horses and cattle graze and drink from shallow crater lakes, while Mount Naka-dake looms just beyond. This is a great place to get up close and personal with this otherworldly landscape.

The **Aso Volcano Museum** (tel. 0967/34-2111; www.asomuse.jp; 9am-5pm daily, 4:30pm last entry; ¥880 junior high school students and older, ¥440 ages 7-12, age 6 and younger free) is across the street from the parking lot for the Kusasenri area. Although you wouldn't be missing much to skip it, there is a live feed of the happenings of the volcano's interior supplied by two heat-resistant cameras installed in the most active spot inside the volcano.

More significantly, this is a good starting point for exploring the unearthly terrain on foot. A 5.5-kilometer (3.4-mi) path that takes you to the top of **Kijima-dake** starts from behind the museum (30 minutes one-way).

Once you've reached the top and have gazed into the crater of this now extinct volcano, you can either return the way you came or descend into the belly of Kijima-dake, before trundling down a ski slope that merges with a path running beside the road to nearby **Naka-dake.** The one-way hike, from the Kusasenri parking lot to Kijima-dake and on to Naka-dake, totals about 1.5 hours. This is a good option if you want to explore the area on foot.

If you plan to also take the ropeway, or shuttle bus, to the top of Naka-dake to peer into its steamy vent, you can do so from this point. You can return via the ropeway (or bus), then make the return hike along the same trail. Alternatively, if you're relying on public transport, you can take a bus to Asosan-nishieki bus stop, in front of the ropeway's lower station, ride the ropeway (or bus) to the summit, then return via the ropeway (or bus) and starting from Asosan-nishieki bus stop, even walk down the trail to Kusaneri and catch a bus from the Aso Volcano Museum.

Food and Accommodations

★ TAKAMORI DENGAKU-NO-SATO

2685-2 Ōaza-Takamori; tel. 0967/62-1899; www.dengakunosato.com/index.html; 11am-8:30pm (last order 7:30pm) Mon.-Fri., 10am-8:30pm (last order 7:30pm) Sat.-Sun. and holidays Mar.-Nov., 11am-5pm Mon.-Fri., 10am-6:30pm Sat.-Sun. and holidays early Jan.-Feb.; sets from ¥1,980; take the Minamiaso Tetsudo local railway line to Takamori Station, then take a taxi (10 minutes; less than ¥1,000 one way)

Set within an atmospheric grove, this repurposed thatched-roof farmhouse is fitted with irori (floor hearths), around which diners sit on floor cushions. Fish, meat, vegetables, and tofu are deliciously glazed in miso paste and speared on skewers, then slowly grilled in the pit. This is an ancient form of rural cooking. A local spin includes the use of the taro root, which proliferates in the region. It's an experience as much as it is a meal.

ASO BASE BACKPACKERS

1498 Kurokawa, Aso-shi; tel. 0967/34-0408; www.aso-backpackers.com; dorms ¥2,800, twins ¥6,000, ¥6,600 d; walk 3 minutes south of JR Station

This spotless, cedar-scented hostel is a great base for exploring the region, and to meet fellow travelers. There are dorms (mixed and female-only) and private rooms, all of which share a bathroom. There's a shared lounge, kitchen, and balcony. The atmosphere is more akin to a cabin—including a wood-burning stove and mountain views—than a backpacker hub. The friendly staff speak English and are happy to help. It shuts down during the coldest part of the winter (check the website for dates). Recommended.

Information and Services

Online, to learn more about the wide range of activities on offer around Aso-san, from riding horses to paragliding, check out the region's tourism portal at www.asocity-kanko.jp.

- **Michi-no-Eki Aso Tourist Information Center** (1440-1 Kurokawa; tel. 096/735-5077; www.aso-denku.jp/denku; 9am-6pm daily; a one-minute walk east of JR Aso Station)

Getting There and Around

The train line that once linked Kumamoto city and Aso is operational again after it was put out of commission by the large quake that struck the region in 2016. The best way to reach Aso-san from Kumamoto city is by **limited express train** from JR Kumamoto Station to JR Aso Station (1 hour 10 minutes; ¥2,290), which depart once every two hours. If you're coming to Aso-san from Beppu, to the east, take the Aso Boy limited express train straight to **JR Aso Station** (2 hours; ¥3,950). Once you've arrived, buses shuttle from JR Aso Station to as far as the Kusasenri Plateau (¥570), but renting a car is a better option.

If you prefer to drive—a good option, given the area's limited public transportation options—there are numerous car rental outlets around JR Kumamoto Station, and **Toyota Rent-a-Car** (1478-1 Kurokawa; tel. 0967/35-5511; https://rent.toyota.co.jp; 9am-6pm daily) has an outlet just east of JR Aso Station. Given the popularity of exploring the region by car, try to reserve your car online at least a week or two before you plan to arrive.

It's also possible to arrive in front of JR Aso Station by **bus.** Destinations served by bus to and from Aso include Beppu, Kurokawa Onsen, Yufuin, and Kumamoto Airport.

BEPPU
別府

Beppu is brash, kitschy, and fun. Think of it as geothermal Disneyland. Beyond the aging hotel facades, the earth tells its own story through the cloud of steam, wafting from 2,500 springheads and hanging above the hilly town at all times.

The variety of baths in Beppu is daunting. This sprawling onsen resort is blessed with more hot water than any other in Japan: A whopping 100 million liters gurgles to the surface here every day, second only to Yellowstone National Park in volume of hot-spring water. It's possible to immerse yourself in hot muddy pools, bury yourself up to the neck in steaming sand, and sweat it out sauna-style. And, of course, practically every ryokan in town has its own private baths, from en suite tubs to shared outdoor pools. While Beppu is known to draw a crowd, you'll find a few secret baths outside downtown with more elbow room.

Beyond bathing, the town is also famous for its array of "hells," akin to some of the boiling pools seen, for example, at Yellowstone National Park. These seething cauldrons are purely for observation. The town's excess steam is even put to use in food preparation:

It's possible to steam-cook a meal with heat rising directly from the earth.

Sights

BEPPU CITY TRADITIONAL BAMBOO CRAFTS CENTER

別府市竹細工伝統産業会館

8-3 Higashi-sōen; tel. 0977/23-1072; https://takezaikudensankaikan.jp; 8:30am-5pm Tues.-Sun.; ¥310 high school students and older, ¥100 junior high and elementary school students; from JR Beppu Station, take bus 22 or 25 to the Takezaiku-densankan-mae bus stop

One of the simple pleasures of any trip to Japan is deeply immersing yourself in a bamboo grove. The area around Beppu is awash in bamboo. This sturdy plant, the fastest grower of all perennials, symbolizes prosperity and purity of mind in Japan. Moreover, the Japanese have learned to use the shoots in a multitude of ways, from eating it to employing it as a raw material for crafts (toys, baskets) and construction (fences, ladders).

To get a sense of how deep Japan's mastery of this versatile plant goes, pay a visit to this museum. From woven baskets to delicate works of art, the displays here will leave you with a new appreciation for this amazing plant and just how creatively Japan has learned to use it. You can also try your hand at making something from bamboo in one of the workshops held on the second floor. Reserve more than a week ahead, because the classes are popular.

HELL CIRCUIT (JIGOKU MEGURI)

地獄めぐり

tel. 0977/66-1577; www.beppu-jigoku.com; 8am-5pm daily; ¥400 all ages for single "hell" entry, ¥2,000 high school students and older and ¥1,000 junior high and elementary school students for combination ticket; both single and combination tickets can be purchased at any given "hell"

This is where Beppu brandishes its kitsch credentials. If you aren't put off by tacky motifs and assorted schlock, these infernal pools can be a bit of fun to see. There's a combination ticket that allows you to move freely between seven boiling pools, each with its own quirks. Of the seven hells covered by the combination ticket, five dot the Kannawa area, about 4 kilometers (2.5 miles) northwest of JR Beppu Station, while the other two are located in the more secluded district of Shibaseki, around 2.5 kilometers (1.6 mi) north of Kannawa. If you're keen to roll around in the kitsch, by all means, dutifully visit each hell. But if you'd rather just get a

Umi Jigoku

taste and avoid the cheesier displays, Umi Jigoku and Oniishibozu Jigoku in Kannawa should suffice.

To reach the Kannawa and Shibaseki districts, note that the closest train stations are Beppudaigaku (from Beppu Station, 4 minutes; ¥210) and Kamegawa (from Beppu Station, 7 minutes, ¥210) on the Nippo line. Buses run to the respective neighborhoods from both stations. Once in the Kannawa or Shibaseki area, it's possible to walk between each district's respective pools.

Onsen

TAKEGAWARA ONSEN

16-23 Moto-machi; tel. 0977/23-1585; www.gokuraku-jigoku-beppu.com/entries/takegawara-onsen; 6:30am-10:30pm daily; ¥300 onsen, ¥1,500 sand bath; walk 10 minutes east of JR Beppu Station

This nostalgic wooden bath house is Beppu's most famous. Built in 1879, the complex stands in the heart of a red-light district. Immerse yourself in the piping hot water filling its timeworn pools. Or, rent a yukata and get buried in steamy black sand, followed by a soak in the pool. Whether you opt for water or sand, you'll be sure to get a strong dose of retro charm.

BEPPU BEACH SAND BATH (AKA KAIHIN SAND BATH)

9 Shoningahama-chō; tel. 0977/66-5737; www.gokuraku-jigoku-beppu.com/entries/kamegawa-hamada-onsen; 8:30am-6pm (last entry 5pm) daily Mar.-Nov., 9am-5pm (last entry 4pm) daily Dec.-Feb.; ¥1,500; from JR Beppu Station, take the Nippo line to Beppudaigaku Station (4 minutes, ¥210) and walk 7 minutes east

In northern Beppu, this river-beachside sand bath is another local icon. It can get very crowded, so plan on going earlier in the day. The system is simple: suit up in a yukata and lay on your appointed beach plot, beneath a multicolor parasol. A staff member will then cover you with hot black sand up to your neck. Sit there for 15-20 minutes, then emerge refreshed.

ONSEN HOYŌLAND

5 Myōban; tel. 0977/66-2221; http://hoyoland.webcrow.jp; 9am-8pm daily; ¥1,100 junior high school students and older, ¥600 elementary school students, ¥350 age 5 and younger; from JR Beppu Station, take taxi about 25 minutes, or 15-minute walk west of Umi Jigoku in the "hell circuit"

About 5 kilometers (3 mi) west of the sand baths of Shōnin-ga-hama, this tumbledown complex is showing signs of age. Knowing its deeper history, this shabbiness only adds to the appeal: Bathing in these large vats of steamy mud is thought to stretch back as far as the 8th century. There are gender-separated changing rooms, but the mud baths themselves are mixed. While the mud obscures anything from view in the pools, a modesty towel is advised in the other areas. Nearby, there are also traditional, gender-separated baths of hot water, as well as steam baths. Local buses run to this onsen, a good one to visit before or after observing the Kannawa district's group of five "hells."

SHIBASEKI ONSEN

4 Noda; tel. 0977/67-4100; www.gokuraku-jigoku-beppu.com/entries/shibaseki-onsen; 7am-8pm, closed second Wed. of month; ¥300 adults, ¥100 children, ¥2,000 private rental for up to 4 people for 1 hour; take bus 26 or 26A from JR Beppu Station to Shibaseki Onsen Entrance (30 minutes), then walk 5 minutes, or take taxi 20 minutes from JR Beppu Station

Set beside a stream and surrounded by nature, this tranquil onsen in the hills outside of town feels a world apart from the crowded pools elsewhere in Beppu. In use since the Kamakura Period (1192-1333), there's a steam bath and two pools. One of the pools is deemed lukewarm (nuruyu), despite being pretty toasty. The second is labeled as hot (atsuyu), although it may feel borderline scalding for some. To be safe, enter slowly. It's possible to rent a private pool, intended for families (kazoku-buro), for up to four people (¥1,620 per hour). As an aside, this onsen is notable for its lax policy toward bathers with tattoos.

Local buses run to this onsen, and it is

within easy reach of the two hells of the residential Shibaseki district, Chinoike Jigoku and Tatsumaki Jigoku, which are both about 12 minutes' walk to the east.

Food

GYŌZA KOGETSU

1-9-4 Kitahama; tel. 0977/21-0226; 2pm-8pm Fri.-Sun.; ¥600 per plate; walk 5 minutes east of JR Beppu Station

Gyoza (fried dumplings) and beer—that's the entire menu. The former is cooked to crisp perfection; the latter is sold by the ice-cold bottle. The shop is tucked down a sidestreet behind a shopping arcade. A menagerie of maneki-neko (lucky cat) figurines stands poised in the window. This place has an ardent fan base, so be prepared to wait in line.

HAJIME ZUSHI

1-4-13 Kitahama; tel. 0977/25-8421; 11am-2pm and 6pm-11pm Mon.-Sat.; courses ¥1,500-3,000; walk 6 minutes east of JR Beppu Station

This welcoming sushi spot with a gregarious staff is routinely packed thanks to its reputation for sourcing only top-notch fish. Be sure to try the renowned anago (conger eel). The price-to-quality ratio is fantastic. Reserve a day or more in advance to snag a seat.

JIGOKU MUSHI KŌBŌ

5-Kumi Furomoto; tel. 0977/66-3775; http://jigokumushi.com; from ¥2,000; walk 15 minutes east of Umi Jigoku, or take taxi 20 minutes from JR Beppu Station

Come here to cook your own food in vats, using steam from onsen waters below. Tickets for chicken, pork, seafood, and vegetable sets can be purchased from a vending machine. Alternatively, bring your own ingredients and pay to use the vats. While Kannawa's hells are admittedly tacky, this DIY culinary experience in the same area is fun. Plan on working it into your tour of the area's hells.

TOYOTSUNE HONTEN

2-12-24 Kitahama; tel. 0977/22-3274; www.toyotsune.com; 11am-2pm and 5pm-10pm daily; lunch from ¥880, dinner courses from ¥2,350; walk 10 minutes east of JR Beppu Station

This down-to-earth restaurant serves Beppu's culinary fortes: fugu (blowfish), toriten (chicken tempura), Bungō beef (the local wagyu variant), and the fresh catch of the day. Check out the shōchū list too if you feel like sampling some of the local firewater.

Accommodations

★ YAMADA BESSŌ

3-2-18 Kitahama; tel. 0977/24-2121; http://yamadabessou.jp; from ¥15,500 d with breakfast; walk 7 minutes from JR Beppu Station

This family-owned gem is showing signs of wear, but it only adds to the charm. In business more than eight decades, the ryokan is set in a garden and housed in a quaint wooden building with inviting tatami rooms. Its rich tapestry of antique items conjures an early Shōwa-Period dream. Most of the rooms don't have their own bath, but the inn does have atmospheric shared pools (gender-separated). Some plans include a Japanese breakfast served on tableware made at one of the island's kilns.

SHINKI-YA

2-kumi; tel. 0977/66-0962; www.shinkiya.com; ¥23,000 d with two meals

There are seven cozy tatami rooms at this charming, family-owned ryokan hidden away in a quiet corner of Kannawa, north of Beppu's tourist fray. Most of the rooms have a toilet and sink, but hot-spring bathing is communal (gender-separated). Meals akin to feasts, including food cooked with onsen steam, are optional at an elevated rate. Recommended.

HOTEL UMINE

3-8-3 Kitahama; tel. 0977/26-0002; http://umine.jp; ¥34,560 d with breakfast; walk 15 minutes east of JR Beppu Station

This is one of Beppu's top luxury properties, right on the beach. Each room is bright and airy and features elegant furniture made of wood and leather, a living room area, and its own wooden onsen tub. There are views of the

TOP EXPERIENCE

☆ Kyushu's Best Onsen

There's no denying Beppu's kitschy geothermal amusement park is tons of fun, but it may leave something to be desired in terms of relaxation. Luckily, Kyushu is chock full of alternatives; here are two of the best.

KUROKAWA ONSEN

黒川温泉

Kurokawa Onsen is an understated mountaintop gem, easily ranking among Japan's most atmospheric hot-spring towns. All told, 24 rotemburo (open-air public baths) dot the town, which has a number of rustic public bath houses as well (8:30am-9pm daily for day visitors). Some highlights, all of which double as exquisitely traditional ryokan serving kaiseki meals, include:

- **Kurokawa-sō** (6755-1 Manganji; tel. 0967/44-0211; www.kurokawaso.com; ¥22,000 pp with 2 meals)
- **Shinmei-kan** (6608 Manganji; tel. 0967/44-0916; www.sinmeikan.jp; ¥35,200 d with 2 meals)
- **Fujiya** (6541 Manganji; tel. 0967/48-8117; www.ryokan-fujiya.jp; ¥46,200 d with 2 meals)

Information and Services

A **nyūto tegata** (wooden onsen pass) gives you access to the rotenboro (open-air baths) of any three of 24 participating onsen ryokan. You can pick up one of these passes for ¥1,300 (¥700 children) at the **Kurokawa Onsen Ryokan Association Information Center** (Kurokawa Sakura-dōri; tel. 0967/44-0076; 9am-6pm daily) or at the reception desk of any of participating ryokan. Without this pass, the cost is ¥600 per bath. Before you set off, be sure to ask which onsen are open that day, as some will sporadically be closed. Check out www.kurokawaonsen.or.jp/eng_new for more information.

Getting There

Buses link Kurokawa Onsen to many spots around the island, with the closest being **Aso** (50 minutes; ¥1,200) and **Beppu** (2.5 hours; ¥3,000), passing **Yufuin** on the way (1.5 hours; ¥2,000). Visit the website of **Kyushu Bus Booking** (https://kyushubusbooking.com) to book seats and peruse fares and timetables.

If you have a **car**, you'll be able to reach the remote town and explore the surrounding region more easily. Coming from Beppu, to make the drive without any tolls, you'll need to take a series of prefectural roads (2 hours 10 minutes; 87 km/ 54 mi). From Aso-san, the drive is 35 minutes (17 km/10.5 mi), and from Kumamoto, it's 1 hour 35 minutes (45 km/28 mi).

YUFUIN

湯布院

Yufuin is a slightly hipper onsen resort with chic cafés, restaurants, and fashionable shops selling artfully made Japanese crafts. Though the town's other public baths are reserved for local residents, two excellent ryokan with onsen are open to guests:

- **Tsuka no Ma** (444-3 Yufuin-chō Kawakami; tel. 0977/85-3105; https://tsukanoma.club;

pool in Kurokawa Onsen

9:30am-6:30pm Tues.-Mon., last entry 6pm; ¥800 adults, ¥500 junior high and elementary school students, ¥100 towel rental; from ¥36,000 d with 2 meals)

- **Musouen** (1243 Yufuinchō Kawaminami; tel. 0977/84-2171; www.musouen.co.jp; 10am-2:30pm daily, 2pm last entry, cleaning days Wed. for women, Fri. for men; ¥900 ages 13 and older, ¥700 ages 5-12, towel rental ¥1,000; from ¥38,000 d with 2 meals)

Food

For a snack with a view, try **Café la Ruche** (1592-1 Yufuin-chō Kawakami; tel. 0977/28-8500; https://cafelaruche.jp; 9am-5:30pm Thurs.-Sat. and Mon.-Tues., last order 5pm, 8am-5:30pm Sun., last order 5pm; average ¥1,200). And if you decide to stay the night in Yufuin, you have two very different options: **Country Road Youth Hostel** (441-29 Yufuinchō Kawakami; tel. 0977/84-3734; http://countryroadyh.com; dorms ¥3,900, private single ¥8,000, ¥9,600 d); and ★ **Sansou Murata** (1264-2 Yufuin-chō Kawakami; tel. 0977/84-5000; www.sansou-murata.com; from around ¥110,000 d with 2 meals), a truly luxurious onsen retreat.

Information and Services

For a fuller picture of what's on offer in Yufuin, stop at the **tourist information center** inside JR Yufuin Station (tel. 0977/84-2446; https://yufu-tic.jp; 9am-5:30pm daily). Pick up a copy of the English-language map showing the town's prime galleries and onsen pools.

Getting There

From **Beppu,** take the Sonic limited express train to Ōita, then transfer to the local JR Kyudai line to **Yufuin Station** (about 1.5 hours; ¥1,970).

ocean just beyond the property too. Meals are terrific, and service is just as personalized as you'd expect. Arrange ahead for pickup from JR Beppu Station East exit.

KANNAWA-EN

6-kumi Miyuki; tel. 0977/66-2111; www.kannawaen.jp; ¥40,000 d with meals

This high-end property offers plush rooms with private onsen tubs, exquisite kaiseki and teppanyaki meals, impeccable service, and alluring shared pools. It has a fantastic garden with an artificial waterfall, a central pond, teahouses, a swimming pool, and even an on-site Noh theater. Stay here if you can afford to splurge. It's an oasis of calm in the middle of Kannawa's "hells."

Information and Services

- **Beppu International Plaza Tourist Information Center** (12-13 Ekimae-chō; tel. 0977/21-6220; 8:30am-5pm daily; located in JR Beppu Station near the central east exit)
- **Kannawa Tourist Information Center** (306-1 Kannawa; tel. 0977/66-3855; 9am-4pm daily)
- **Beppu Medical Center** (1473 Uchikamado; tel. 0977/67-1111; https://beppu.hosp.go.jp; 20-minute walk west of Kamegawa Station, two stations north from Beppu Station on the JR Nippō line)

Getting There

TRAIN

JR Beppu Station, located in the heart of town, is well-connected: Coming from **Hakata,** the easiest route is to take the shinkansen train to Kokura, where you'll transfer to the Sonic limited express train on the JR Nippō line, which runs to JR Beppu Station (1 hour 40 minutes; ¥7,670). You can also take the Sonic limited express train directly to and from Hakata from Beppu (2 hours; ¥5,680).

Coming from JR Miyazaki Station in the south, take the Nichirin limited express to **Ōita Station,** then transfer to the Sonic limited express until Beppu (3 hours 40 minutes; ¥6,120). Farther south in Kagoshima, hop on the *shinkansen* from Kagoshima-Chūō Station to Hakata on the other end of the island, then follow the same route from Hakata described above to reach Beppu from there (3 hours 50 minutes; ¥15,110). Alternatively, take the shinkansen from Kagoshima-Chūō Station straight to Kokura, then ride the Sonic limited express to Beppu from there (3 hours 15 minutes; ¥15,940).

Coming from Aso in the west, take the limited express (2 hours; ¥3,950) straight to Beppu. Note that only three of these trains run each day. If you're coming from Nagasaki, first take the Kamome limited express to Hakata, then transfer to the Sonic limited express and ride until Beppu (4 hours; ¥10,370). From Kumamoto, the previously more direct route has been suspended since 2016 due to the large quake that struck the region. For the time being, you'll need to take the shinkansen north to Kokura, then hop on the Sonic limited express that runs directly to Beppu (2 hours 25 minutes; ¥11,660).

AIR

Ōita Airport (tel. 0978/67-1174; www.oita-airport.jp) services flights from Tokyo, Osaka, Nagoya, and Seoul. **Buses** shuttle between the airport and the beachside area of Kitahama (48 minutes; ¥1,500), terminating at JR Beppu Station (51 minutes; ¥1,500).

BUS

Long-distance buses run mainly to the **bus terminal** beside JR Beppu Station and to the Kamenoni bus terminal (2-10-4 Kitahama; tel. 0977/23-5170; www.kamenoibus.com), located near the Kitahama beach area. Taking a highway bus is particularly a good option if you're traveling from JR Kumamoto Station (5 hours; ¥3,960), which is currently only reachable by train via a circuitous route due to the blow dealt to the region's railway network in the large 2016 earthquake.

BOAT

Ferries operated by **Ferry Sunflower** (tel. 0977/22-2181; www.ferry-sunflower.co.jp) travel between Beppu and Osaka. On Shikoku, **Uwajima Unyu Ferry** (tel. 0977/21-2364; www.uwajimaunyu.co.jp) runs ferries to Beppu from Yawatahama, which is reachable from Uwajima on the Uwakai limited express (30 minutes; ¥1,960). Check the websites of both ferry operators for more details.

Getting Around

BUS

Downtown Beppu is navigable **on foot,** but you may want to make use of the town's efficient bus network if you plan to visit the various hells dotting Kannawa on the north side of town. There are a number of bus routes, most of which depart from outside **JR Beppu Station.** To be sure you're catching the correct bus, and that you're clear on the correct stop to wait for the bus, check with the staff of the **Beppu International Plaza** housed in the station.

There are a few bus passes worth knowing about. The **"mini" pass** (from ¥900) allows unlimited travel within Beppu's city limits for a day. The **"wide" pass** (from ¥1,600) covers all buses within Beppu, as well as the bus to the nearby onsen hub of Yufuin. You can purchase one of these passes at the Beppu International Plaza or ferry terminal.

CAR

If you plan to venture farther afield, renting a car is a good option. Situated inside JR Beppu Station, **Eki Rent-a-Car** (tel. 097/724-4428; www.ekiren.co.jp) is a good bet.

Miyazaki Prefecture 宮崎県

Bordering Oita to the north and Kumamoto to the west, sun-drenched Miyazaki comprises the beautiful southeastern corner of Kyushu. Thanks to its latitude, Miyazaki is blessed with a mild climate. This makes it a nice destination year-round and a place where tropical fruit can grow—mangoes, anyone?

Misty mountains in the north buzz with mystic significance due to their ties to Japan's creation myths. The fetching coast invites unplugging. Catch rays, or waves, and if you have a car, trundle down the gorgeous Nichinan Coast, renowned as a magnet for surfers. This laid-back enclave serves as an escape for stressed urbanites—a rare corner of Japan that seems designed for sun worship, beach bumming, and unleashing one's inner flower child.

★ TAKACHIHO

高千穂

Not far from Aso-San, but actually in the northern mountains of northern Miyazaki Prefecture, the Takachiho region is the backdrop to some of Japan's core mythology, said to be where the gods beamed down and created the whole archipelago from there.

Takachiho is also one of two contested spots, along with Kirishima National Park's Mount Takachiho-no-mine, where the sun goddess Amaterasu's grandson Ninigi no Mikoto is said to have descended to earth to establish Japan's imperial line.

To fully appreciate the magical atmosphere of Takachiho, plan to spend a night in the area. This makes the effort to reach the remote region more worthwhile. It also gives you a chance to slow down and savor the atmosphere of the place where Japan's most core myths were born.

Sights

TAKACHIHO SHRINE

高千穂神社

1037 Mitai, Takachiho; tel. 0982/73-1213; 24 hours; free

Set in a dense grove of cedars, some several hundred years old, this tranquil shrine is

1

2

Divine Dirty Dancing

Takachiho's deep Shinto roots are vibrantly alive today, as seen in the area's sacred dances known as **kagura.** The dances are performed across the villages and valleys of Takachiho, and the locals who keep them alive enact Shinto myths involving Amaterasu Omikami (the Sun Goddess), her brother Susano'o (the Storm God), and a host of other deities.

THE MYTH

Tired of her brother's shenanigans—trashing her palace and ravaging her rice fields—Amaterasu fled to a cave. She blocked the entrance with a large stone, thus depriving the world of her light. **Amano Iwato Jinja,** set in a grotto, marks the spot where Amaterasu is said to have gone into hiding. Dismayed, a throng of deities convened to formulate an ingenious (and rather cheeky) plan to coax her out. In short, the goddess Ame-no-Uzume (appropriately, the Goddess of Mirth and Revelry) cavorted in a manner so provocative it sent the other gods into a resounding fit of laughter. Hearing the commotion, the Sun Goddess couldn't help but take a peek outside the cave. Tajikarao (the God of Power) stood nearby and hauled away the boulder. And thus, her light returned to the world.

HOW TO SEE KAGURA

This tale is reenacted—sometimes in snippets, other times in full—throughout the year. For a glimpse, a drastically condensed one-hour performance depicts a few scenes of the story at **Takachiho Shrine** every evening. Aim to arrive at least 30 minutes, or even an hour, early for seats offering good views of these yokagura (night kagura) dances.

If you're keen and timing is right, the full divine saga is acted out by more than 20 troupes of local dancers, from kids to grannies, in 33 parts during winter weekends (Sat. nights, mid-Nov. to mid-Feb.). These epic performances test the endurance of the audience as well as the dancers, taking place through the night and into the next morning. These satokagura (village kagura) performances are held at shrines, public halls, and in private farmhouses to the accompaniment of flutes and drums. The atmosphere is light and laid-back, and a sense of humor pervades. Contact the **Takachiho Tourism Association** a few months in advance if possible to learn more or reserve a place.

unassuming. As dusk falls each day, the sacred space comes alive as professional dancers don masks (8pm-9pm; ¥1,000 junior high school students and older, free for elementary school students and younger) to do a condensed re-enactment of what is perhaps the most famous episode in all Shinto myth. Takachiho is also said to be the site of the cave where the sun goddess Amaterasu hid her light from the world for a time when she grew weary of her brother's pranks.

To reach the shrine, walk south along Route 50 for 10-15 minutes from the Takachiho Bus Center. It's recommended to combine a trip to the shrine with a visit to Takachiho Gorge, located just a bit farther south along Route 50.

1: Takachiho Shrine **2:** Takachiho Gorge

Once there, it's possible to either admire the gorge from above or to see it while gliding over the surface of the water in a rowboat (https://takachiho-kanko.info/en/boat_kagura/; 8:30am-5pm daily, 4:30pm last entry; ¥3,000 for 30-minute boat rental, ¥1,000 adults, ¥600 ages 6 and younger for boarding fee).

TAKACHIHO GORGE

Mukoyama, Takachiho; tel. 0982/73-1213; boat rentals 8am-5pm daily, reception until 4:30pm; boat rentals ¥3,000, plus ¥1,000 adults and ¥500 ages 0-6 boarding fee

This stunning gorge is the most impressive sight in Takachiho. The rock walls have been chiseled and smoothed by the steady flow of water over the ages by the Gokase River and waterfalls cascading endlessly over the gorge's edge. The tallest cascade, Manaitaki, drops 17 meters (56 ft). Vines and a blanket of emerald moss have crept in, contrasting dramatically with the gray rock, and heavier foliage clings to the top. You can hike along the edge of the gorge and take in this scene from above, or row a boat down the lazy river and see it from below (https://takachiho-kanko.info/en/boat_kagura).

AMANO IWATO JINJA
天岩戸神社

1073-1 Iwato, Takachiho; tel. 0982/74-8239; http://amanoiwato-jinja.jp; open 24/7; free; buses run once every 1 or 2 hours from Takachiho Bus Center (15 minutes, ¥200 one-way), or you can take a taxi (10 minutes; ¥2,500 one-way)

This shrine, located next to the Iwato-gawa river about 10 kilometers (6.2 mi) northeast of Takachiho's town center in the village of Iwato, is situated near the cave where Amaterasu went into hiding. Set among towering cedar trees, the shrine complex sits across the Iwato-gawa from the cave, which cannot be entered. If you ask the priest at the entrance to the shrine, it's possible to get a brief tour in Japanese of the precincts, including a stop at a viewing platform behind the shrine that looks across the Iwato-gawa toward the cave.

For the full impact of this holy site, don't stop here. Walk briefly north along the road that brought you to Amano Iwato Jinja, and descend along the walkway that leads to the river below. You'll know you're on the right path when you begin to see small piles of rocks on either side of the trail. With bigger stones at the bottom and increasingly smaller ones toward the top, these delicately made stacks are left by pilgrims to commemorate their sojourn to this spiritually charged spot. The deeper you push into this forest, the more of these markers appear.

This footpath ends at **Amano Yasukawara,** a shrine dramatically set inside the grotto said to be the place where the gods plotted their scheme to draw out the sun goddess. The air in the cave and the path leading to it is charged with a sense of the sacred, making it well worth the slight detour.

Food

CAFÉ MERCHEN

1101-12 Mitai, Takachiho; tel. 0982/72-2439; http://takachiho-kanko.info/gourmet/detail.php?log=1428993708; 11am-4pm and 6pm-9pm Mon.-Sat.; ¥1,000; walk 3 minutes from Takachiho Shrine

Pizza, pasta, salad, curry rice: these simple kissaten (old-school café) classics are served in this tiny space with one woman running the shop. Prepared to wait for your food if you're in a large group or if the restaurant is busy. Good food at very reasonable prices.

NAGOMI

1099-1 Mitai, Takachiho; tel. 0982/73-1109; http://takachiho.ja-miyazaki.jp/nagomi.php; 11am-2:30pm (last order 1:30pm) and 7pm-9pm (last order 8pm) Thurs.-Tues.; lunch ¥1,700-3,500, dinner ¥2,000-4,300; walk 6 minutes from Takachiho Shrine

Set in the **Gamadase Ichiba** complex, which houses a number of markets hawking local produce, this restaurant serves beef hot-plate set meals prepared by chefs in the kitchen, and yakiniku (Korean barbecue), which you grill yourself at the table. Beef comes straight from the butcher next door and is reasonably priced according to grade.

Accommodations

B&B UKIGUMO

983-7 Mitai, Takachiho; tel. 0982/82-2703; www.takachiho-ukigumo.com; from ¥3,700 d pp; walk 5 minutes from Takachiho Shrine

This cozy inn has clean, simple tatami rooms with en suite bathrooms. The helpful owner speaks English, and a simple, hearty Western-style breakfast is included. As a bonus, its location offers great views of the gorge. Recommended as a budget option.

SOLEST TAKACHIHO HOTEL

1261-1 Mitai, Takachiho; tel. 0982/83-0001; www.solest-takachiho.jp; from ¥11,880 d pp with 2 meals

Opened in spring 2018, this chic hotel has sleek, spacious rooms with contemporary decor. There's a well-rounded breakfast spread, including both Western- and Japanese-style dishes, and sumptuous dinner options. Staff don't speak much English, but they're amiable and keen to help where they can. It's located right in the middle of town, making it a good base for exploring the area.

Information and Services

Online, the town's English-language tourism portal (http://takachiho-kanko.info/en) is a helpful resource. Note that there's a notable dearth of ATMs in Takachiho. If you need to pull out money in town, there's an ATM at the **post office** (27-2 Mitai, Takachiho; tel. 0982/72-2615; ATM hours 8:45am-7pm Mon.-Fri., 9am-5pm Sat.-Sun. and holidays).

- **Takachiho Tourism Association** (809-1 Mitai, Takachiho; tel. 0982/73-1213; 8:30am-5pm daily; across the street from Takachiho Bus Center)

Getting There

Takachiho isn't the easiest place to reach. This is largely due to the extensive damage done to infrastructure in the surrounding area by the quake that hit Kumamoto in 2016. **Driving** or taking a **bus** is necessary at the time of writing.

If you're traveling from **Kumamoto,** the easiest way to reach the outpost is by driving. Otherwise, two daily buses, operated by **Kyushu Sanko Bus** (https://kyushu-busbooking.com) and **Miyazaki Kotsu (Miyakoh;** https://www.miyakoh.co.jp) depart from the bus terminal in front of Kumamoto Station and travel to **Takachiho Bus Center** (3 hours; ¥2,410 one-way, ¥4,110 round-trip), stopping at Kumamoto Airport (2 hours; ¥2,200) on the way. Coming from **Aso,** you'll need to take a bus to **Kumamoto Airport** (7 daily; about 1 hour), then change to one of the two buses that travel from the airport to Takachiho each day.

Coming from the east, the best starting point is **Nobeoka,** which can be be reached from **Beppu** by taking the **Sonic limited express** to **Oita**, then transferring to the **Nichirin limited express** (2 hours 25 minutes; ¥4,310), and Miyazaki (1 hour 20 minutes; ¥2,630), from where it's a straight-shot on the **Hyuga limited express**. At Nobeoka, transfer to one of the hourly buses that run to Takachiho Bus Center (1.5 hours; ¥1,820).

It's also possible to travel directly to Takachiho from **Fukuoka.** Buses travel from the bus terminal near Hakata Station to Takachiho Bus Center four times each day (3.5 hours; ¥4,100). You can either buy your ticket on the spot or make a reservation online via https://global.atbus-de.com/route_lists/?locale=en.

Getting Around

Once you've arrived in Takachiho, if you're only planning to visit the sights situated near the heart of town and the gorge, you can do it **on foot** if you're willing to walk a bit (the gorge is about 40 minutes' walk one-way from the heart of town). Amano Iwato Jinja is far enough to warrant hailing a **taxi** or hopping on one of the sporadic public **buses** that depart from **Takachiho Bus Center.**

If you'd prefer to get around on two wheels, you can rent a **bicycle** at the Takachiho Tourism Association (¥500 per hour).

Having a **rental car** is another great way to get around. Note that you'll need to rent a car elsewhere, such as Kumamoto, Aso, or Miyazaki, before making your way to remote Takachiho.

AOSHIMA

青島

Miyazaki's coast evokes the Mediterranean or Baja California more so than it does the bulk of Japan: palm trees, surf towns, pounding waves, and a pervading hippy ethos. As you make your way down the prefecture's lovely coast—a car is all but essential—the small island of Aoshima is worth a stop. Located just south of Miyazaki City, this small spit of land is connected to the shore by a footbridge. It's a tranquil place, fringed by sandy beaches with a dense crop of jungle at its center. The main draw is Aoshima-jinja, a shrine said to bestow good fortune on married couples. The walk to the shrine, alone on silent sandy beaches, is entrancing. With more than 5,000 trees and a few hundred subtropical plants, the island has a distinct "not-in-Japan" atmosphere.

As you walk around the island's 1.5-kilometer (0.9-mi) circumference, look out to the ocean just off the beach and take note of the peculiar basalt rock formations known as oni-no-sentaku-ita ("devil's washboard"), which emerge at low tide. This peculiar phenomenon, sculpted by waves, looks as if an intelligence shaped it. South of Aoshima, on the lush shoreline of the Nichinan Coast, you'll feel as if you've arrived in Hawaii. It's a gorgeous place to take a scenic drive.

Sights

AOSHIMA-JINJA
青島神社

2-13-1 Aoshima; tel. 0985/65-1262; https://aoshima-jinja.jp; shrine 8am-5pm daily, museum 8am-5pm daily Sept.-Jun. and 8am-6pm Jul.-Aug.; shrine free, museum ¥600

Walk through the gauntlet of souvenir vendors on the approach to this lovely island, pass under the torii gate, and make your way to this shrine. In many ways the nerve center of this island, which is considered a spiritual "power spot," this shrine draws a steady stream of couples and those in search of love. Even Emperor Akihito visited with Empress Michiko when they were still Crown Prince and Princess, spurring couples nationwide to flock to the sacred site for luck in matters of the heart.

At the main shrine, amulets are sold at the shrine both for those already partnered, as well as singles seeking love. Follow a side path that leads to the right of the main shrine, and you'll discover an inner shrine beyond. Here, you can purchase small clay disks. Lob them at the target nearby in the hopes of attracting good luck.

Also on the shrine grounds is a small museum called the **Legend of Hyūga Hall.** Offering a different spin on Shinto myth from the dances of Takachiho, this museum uses wax effigies to illustrate stories surrounding some of Shinto's most important characters, from the sun goddess to Japan's first legendary leader, Emperor Jimmu. English signage included.

UDO-JINGŪ

3232 Miyaura; tel. 0987/29-1001; www.udojingu.com; 6am-7pm daily Apr.-Sept., 7am-6pm daily Oct.-Mar.; free

Thirty minutes south of Aoshima by car is Udo-jingū, a unique shrine ensconced in a grotto carved into cliff above the crash of ocean waves. After descending down a stone staircase set into the side of the cliff, you'll come to the main shrine, set in a cave. En route to the shrine, about 4 kilometers (2.5 mi) south of Aoshima, you'll reach **Horikiri Pass,** known for the same "devil's washboard" striated rock formations seen at low tide around Aoshima, visible at the base of cliffs that drop beside the road.

Beaches and Surfing

AOSHIMA BEACH

2-2-233 Aoshima; tel. 0985/65-1055; www.aoshimabeachpark.com; 9am-6pm daily late Apr.-late Oct.

A white strand of oceanfront spreads 1.5 kilometers (0.9 mi) northwestward from the mainland side of the bridge that leads to Aoshima Shrine, which sits at the heart of a small island swathed in subtropical jungle. During the warmer months, shops and beach shacks hawk souvenirs and snacks to beachgoers, while surfers catch mellow, yet consistent waves. Beginner surfers will appreciate the relatively calmer swells at Aoshima Beach just west of Aoshima. If you'd like to try to catch some waves at Aoshima Beach, **Surf City** (2-1-11 Aoshima; tel. 050/3571-3238; http://surfcity-miyazaki.jp; 9am-10pm Tues.-Fri., 7am-6pm Sat.-Sun. and holidays, closed Tues. if Mon. falls on holiday; walk 8 minutes north of Aoshima Station), with

English-speaking staff, is a good surf shop in the area.

Food

FUJIYAMA PUDDING

2-11-1 Aoshima; tel. 070/5502-5670; https://so1320.wixsite.com/fujipurimiyazaki; 11:30am-4pm Wed. and Sat.-Mon.; dessert ¥300, curry ¥1,200; walk 3 minutes east from JR Aoshima Station

This café, housed in an all-white building, makes a mean curry with rice. Coffee is also great, as are the homemade puddings, with flavors including Uji green tea and Okinawa black sugar, and various baked sweets. The relaxing interior is all warm wood, down to the coasters. This is a good spot for lunch or a mid-afternoon break.

AOSHIMA BEACH PARK

2-2-233 Aoshima; tel. 0985/65-1055; www.aoshimabeachpark.com; 11am-6pm Thurs.-Tues. early Jul.-late Sept.; ¥1,000

From spring through autumn, a collection of transient beachside bistros pop up in the form of shipping containers a stone's throw from the entrance to Aoshima. They may not be permanent, but the shopfronts are thoughtfully designed. The restaurants serve a range of foods, from burgers and tacos to Thai cuisine. It's a great laid-back option when the weather is conducive.

GIN KHAAO

2-2-7 Aoshima; tel. 090/8639-5614; 11:30am-2:30pm and 6pm-8pm Wed.-Mon.; ¥1,000; walk 5 minutes from the bridge to Aoshima

At a stylish new location near the beach, this Thai eatery is a great spot for a meal in the heart of Aoshima. Its interior is bright, with seating along a wooden counter and a few private tables. The menu features deliciously sweet, sour, and spicy dishes (curries, spicy salads, Thai-style fried chicken), and of course, cold Singha Beer.

COAST LIFE

4710-13 Kaeda; tel. 0985/75-0673; www.coastlife.jp; lunch 11am-3pm (last order 2pm), café time 2pm-5pm, and dinner 6pm-10pm Fri.-Wed., Wed. lunch only; ¥1,500; take the JR Nichinan line from Aoshima Station to Sosanji Station, then walk 10 minutes toward the coast

"Coffee Wine Oyster and Beef" is the restaurant's stated credo, and this pretty much sums it up. It does all four, along with a good range of other items, very well, including sandwiches, risotto, and steak. Then there's the sterling beachside setting and calm-inducing vibes of the leafy, wood-paneled interior. It's a 25-minute walk north of Aoshima.

Accommodations

B&B PIER

7450-4 Kaeda; tel. 0985/65-2061; from ¥7,000 d; walk 1 minute from Kodomonokuni Station, 1 stop from Aoshima Station on the JR Nichinan line

This crisp white bed-and-breakfast houses clean, bright rooms, and a shared lounge and kitchen. All rooms share a bathroom. Breakfast is provided for all guests, as are free loaner bicycles. The affable owner is happy to advise on local attractions, and when available, to help you get around.

THE LITTLE GARDEN

7688-14 Uchiumi; tel. 080/1761-3302; www.facebook.com/thelittlegarden.miyazaki/; ¥2,750 mixed dorm, ¥8,800 room with two twin beds; walk 20 minutes from Ko-Uchiumi Station, 3 stops from Aoshima Station on the JR Nichinan line

This hilltop inn has a spacious common area with sweeping ocean views, a shared kitchen, clean and well-appointed rooms (some with kitchenettes and vistas of the sea), and, as the name suggests, a discreet garden-like space with picnic tables and outdoor furniture that invites lounging. Guests come here for access to good waves or just to unwind in this beautiful place. The affable staff are also ready at hand to help with activities around the area and more. Given its slight distance from Aoshima, it's a particularly good pick if you plan to explore the Nichinan Coast by car.

Getting There and Around

You can travel by train from Miyazaki Station,

on the JR Nichinan line to **Aoshima Station** (30 minutes; ¥380). The island itself is a bit over 10 minutes' walk east of the station. There's also an hourly **bus** that departs from near the west exit of Miyazaki Station and travels to the west side of a botanical garden that sits a few minutes' walk from the bridge that leads to the island.

Finally, if you want to roam more freely, with your own wheels, **Trip Base Aoshima** (2-2-7 Aoshima; tel. 0985/77-6858; www.aoshima.tripbase.jp; 7am-9pm daily; ¥13,200 for 6 hours, ¥26,400 overnight) rents camper vans for both day trips and overnight. There's also a glut of car rental shops scattered around Miyazaki Station, a straight-shot north on the JR Nichinan line from Aoshima.

Kagoshima 鹿児島

Entering Kagoshima Prefecture feels like arriving in the Mediterranean, or somewhere in Southeast Asia, perhaps. There's a subtropical vibe to this sun-drenched place, where more palms grow than pines. In the north, you can traipse among lush volcanic peaks in Kirishima-Yaku National Park, a dramatic landscape that spills across the border with neighboring Miyazaki. In the south, bury yourself to the neck in hot sand on the beach in Ibusuki. And in the balmy capital city of Kagoshima, southern Kyushu's largest metropolis, you can sip shōchū in the shadow of "Japan's Vesuvius" (Sakurajima).

The parallels between Kagoshima and Naples are notable. Both are sunny cities in warm climes and both sit beside looming volcanos. Sakurajima, Kagoshima's Vesuvius, hasn't wiped out a city Pompeii-style, but that doesn't stop the very active cone from occasionally clogging the skies with black ash, obscuring the sun, and coating everything in its path—umbrella recommended.

Occasional haze aside, the city is renowned for its gregarious disposition. Its denizens are widely considered to be some of the friendliest in Japan. As for sights, there are a few good museums focused on local history, and Sengan-en, a lovely garden with the dramatically borrowed scenery of Sakurajima in the background. Kagoshima also boasts a connection to fabled 19th-century warrior Saigō Takamori, who inspired the film *The Last Samurai*. Last but not least, the city presents an array of dining options, complemented by a seriously good shōchū scene. This is the best place in Japan to imbibe the spirit.

SIGHTS

Central Kagoshima

MUSEUM OF THE MEIJI RESTORATION
維新ふるさと館

23-1 Kajiya-chō; tel. 099/239-7700; http://ishinfurusatokan.info; 9am-5pm daily; ¥300 high school students and older, ¥150 junior high and elementary school students

Kagoshima has had an outsize influence on Japan's history, particularly in the Meiji Restoration of 1868, when the feudal age ended and power returned to the emperor. This museum explores Kagoshima's pivotal role in that tumultuous period. The displays reveal episodes from this exciting period of the nation's history, such as the ill-fated Satsuma Rebellion, led by Saigō, and the decision to send Satsuma's best and brightest young minds to study in the West.

Not all of the exhibits have English signage. For deeper understanding, download the museum's English audio guide or take the English headsets available at the reception

Kagoshima

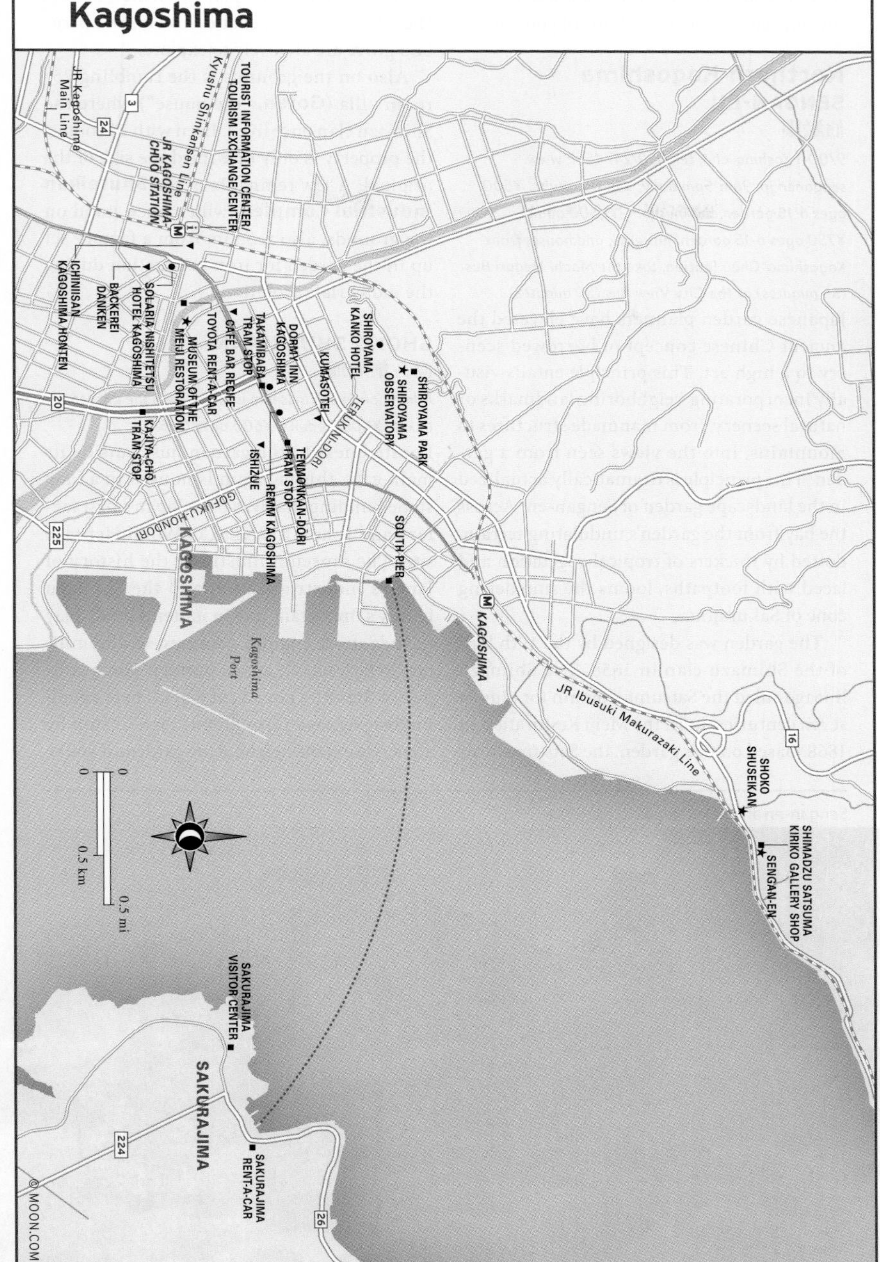
JR Kagoshima Main Line
Kyushu Shinkansen Line
TOURIST INFORMATION CENTER/ TOURISM EXCHANGE CENTER
JR KAGOSHIMA-CHŪŌ STATION
ICHINIISAN KAGOSHIMA HONTEN
BACKEREI DANKEN
SOLARIA NISHITETSU HOTEL KAGOSHIMA
TOYOTA RENT-A-CAR
MUSEUM OF THE MEIJI RESTORATION
CAFÉ BAR RECIFE
TAKAMIBABA TRAM STOP
DORMY INN KAGOSHIMA
SHIROYAMA KANKO HOTEL
KUMASOTEI
SHIROYAMA PARK
SHIROYAMA OBSERVATORY
TERUKUNI-DORI
KAJIYACHŌ TRAM STOP
TENMONKAN-DŌRI TRAM STOP
ISHIZUE
REMM KAGOSHIMA
GOFUKU-HONDORI
SOUTH PIER
KAGOSHIMA
Kagoshima Port
JR Ibusuki Makurazaki Line
SHOKO SHUSEIKAN
SHIMADZU SATSUMA KIRIKO GALLERY SHOP
SENGAN-EN
SAKURAJIMA VISITOR CENTER
SAKURAJIMA
SAKURAJIMA RENT-A-CAR
3
24
20
225
16
224
26
0
0.5 mi
0.5 km
© MOON.COM

desk. If you're interested in Japanese history, this museum is worth an hour of your time.

Northern Kagoshima

SENGAN-EN

仙巌園

9700-1 Yoshino-chō; tel. 099/247-1551; www.senganen.jp; 9am-5pm daily; ¥1,000 adults, ¥500 ages 6-15 garden and museum, ¥1,500 adults, ¥750 ages 6-15 garden, museum, and house; from Kagoshima-Chūō Station, take the Machi Meguri Bus (35 minutes) or the City View Bus (50 minutes)

Japanese garden planners have elevated the ancient Chinese concept of borrowed scenery to a high art. This principle entails visually incorporating neighboring landmarks or natural scenery, from manmade structures to mountains, into the views seen from a garden. This principle is dramatically actualized in the landscape garden of Sengan-en. Across the bay from the garden's undulating terrain, dotted by thickets of tropical vegetation and laced with footpaths, looms the smoldering cone of Sakurajima.

The garden was designed by the 19th lord of the Shimazu clan in 1658. The Shimazu lineage ruled the Satsuma domain for almost seven centuries, until the Meiji Restoration in 1868. Based on this garden, the Satsuma lords knew how to live: the ponds, shrines, butterflies flitting among exotic flowers, and bamboo grove are all lovely to explore.

Also on the grounds is the rambling 25-room villa (**Goten,** "the house") where the Shimazu clan once lived. Even with 25 rooms, the property is only one-third the size of the original. A few remnants of the **Shuseikan Industrial Complex,** which once stood on the grounds, also remain, from a factory set up in the garden for iron production during the industrial revolution.

SHOKO SHUSEIKAN

尚古集成館

Admission to the museum is included in the garden ticket (¥1,000 adults, ¥600 ages 6-15)

Located next to the garden, just outside its main gate, this museum is housed in a long stone building that was once Japan's first factory and is now a UNESCO World Heritage site. The museum illustrates the history of Japan's industrialization and the Shimazu family's important role in it. Items on display include steam engines, cannons, scrolls, military relics, locally made pottery, and examples of the city's famed cut glass. There's good English signage throughout. Plan to stop by after visiting the neighboring gardens if you're

Sengan-en and Sakurajima

keen to dig deeper into the Shimazu clan's part in Japan's journey toward becoming an industrial juggernaut.

Sakurajima

桜島

Across Kinko Bay from Kagoshima, the hyperactive volcano of Sakurajima hovers imposingly on the horizon, rising 1,117 meters (3,665 ft) skyward at its highest point, with two lower craters, and commanding a circumference of about 50 kilometers (31 mi). Since Sakurajima's first recorded eruption in 708, the peak has been continuously temperamental. It was an island until a major blast in 1914 created a land bridge to the Osumi Peninsula to the east. The last major eruption was in 1955, with several smaller eruptions taking place in 1994, 1995, and 2013. On average, the back of the crater spews ash 100-200 times a year, amounting to 100 millimeters (4 inches) annually. This dust-fall often turns the sky red at night and blocks out the sun.

While this may all sound quite ominous, this volcano is, in fact, a popular sight, just a cheap, 15-minute ferry ride from downtown. Once there, the best way to explore this rather large volcano (77 square km/30 square mi) is by renting a car.

ARIMURA LAVA OBSERVATORY

952 Arimura; tel. 099/298-5111; www.sakurajima.gr.jp/tourism/000351.html; open 24/7; free

Although no actual observatory awaits, this sheltered area has several vantage points from which to view fields where lava flowed relatively recently. This area is located about 15 minutes' drive southeast of the ferry terminal along Route 224.

KUROKAMI BURIED TORII

647 Kurokami-chō; tel. 099/298-5111; www.sakurajima.gr.jp/tourism/000352.html; open 24/7; free

This gate once stood 3 meters (9.8 ft) tall in front of Kurokami Shrine. Today, only its top portion protrudes from the ground, the remainder having been buried by volcanic ash in the 1914 eruption. While you're in the area, walk south from the buried shrine gate for about 10 minutes (1-minute drive) along Route 26 to the **Kurokami Observation Point,** with good views of the volcano's Showa Crater. To reach the gate, drive about 10 minutes northeast from the Arimura Lava Observatory, on Route 224 and Route 26.

YUNOHIRA LOOKOUT

1025 Koike-chō; tel. 099/298-5111; www.sakurajima.gr.jp/tourism/000350.html; 9am-5pm daily; free

Drive 10 minutes east of the ferry terminal to this high perch, offering stellar views of the volcano and the city across the bay.

Parks

SHIROYAMA PARK

城山公園

22 Shiroyamachō; tel. 099/216-1366; www.pref.kagoshima.jp/suisuinavi/22991.html; open 24/7; free; take the City View Bus (25 minutes) or walk (35 minutes) from Kagochima-Chūō Station

Atop Mount Shiroyama (107 m/351 ft) near the heart of downtown, this park is located on the site where the Satsuma Rebellion came to an end with the Battle of Shiroyama. It's crisscrossed with trails and is home to the **Shiroyama Observatory** (22-13 Shiroyamachō; tel. 099/298-5111; www.kagoshima-kankou.com/guide/10525; open 24/7; free). This lookout is a great place to snap a photo of the city from above, with the bay and Sakurajima hovering in the distance.

Hiking

NAGISA LAVA TRAIL AND FOOT BATH

Distance: *6 km (3.7 miles) round-trip*

Time: *1 hour round-trip*

Trailhead: *Behind Sakurajima Visitor Center*

This 3-kilometer (1.7-mi) trail runs along the waterfront, extending to the west of the ferry terminal, then crossing over a lava field created by an eruption in 1914 that has since been slowly reclaimed by vegetation, culminating at the Karasujima Observatory. The free **Nagisa Park Foot Bath** (1722-3

Shōchū: Kagoshima's Drink of Choice

When it comes to booze made in Japan, most think of rice wine, or nihonshu—often referred to incorrectly as sake (alcohol) overseas. Kagoshima breaks that stereotype with its own variety of firewater known as shōchū. The denizens of the balmy city not only consume the spirit more than those of any other locale in Japan, but the city also produces more of the stuff, with around 800 types, than anywhere else.

HOW IT'S MADE

This distilled spirit is made with **sweet potato** (Kagoshima's preferred base), **barley, soba, rice,** or, rarely, **corn.** It packs a punch with an alcohol content of 15-25 percent alcohol by volume, with some heavyweight varieties creeping toward 40 percent. Kagoshima's favorite tipple was long plagued by a somewhat tawdry image, but this has changed: Today shōchū has slowly garnered its own rightful following. It's often compared to vodka, but smoother, whether ordered neat, on the rocks, with warm water (oyuwari), mixed with soda water (chūhai), or fruit-infused in the form of a sawā (sour).

WHAT TO EXPECT

A few things to note: rice-based shōchū is a bit milder than the full-bodied sweet potato variety, while the rare corn-based variety can reach 35 percent or more. One of the city's best-loved lines is **Shiranami.** Good, reasonably priced, and widely available varieties include **Kaidō, Kuro,** and **Kojika.** For something higher-end, try **Maō** and **Mori Izō.** When in doubt, just ask the bartender "O-susume wa nan desu ka?" ("What's your recommendation?").

WHERE TO TRY IT

Kyushu brims with purveyors of the beverage, but Kagoshima is the best place for a deep dive. Hands down, **Ishizue** (page 665) is the place to go for this. If you're keen to hunt down a distillery, the owner can point the way. The added bonus of going to a place that takes its quality seriously is that the pricier varieties are less likely to leave you in agony the next morning.

Yokoyama-chō; tel. 099/298-5111; www.sakurajima.gr.jp/tourism/000677.html; 9am-sunset daily; free), about 10 minutes' walk west of the ferry terminal, is a great place to rest your feet and enjoy the view after the walk.

Shopping

SHIMADZU SATSUMA KIRIKO GALLERY SHOP

9700-1 Yoshino-chō; tel. 099/247-1551; www.senganen.jp/en/food-shopping/shimadzu-satsuma-kiriko-gallery-shop; 8:30am-5:30pm daily

The Shimadzu Satsuma Kiriko Gallery, situated in the Sengan-en grounds adjacent to the Shoko Shuseikan museum, is a great place to buy pieces of kiriko (cut glass), an art form with a long history in Kagoshima. The exquisite pieces are crafted at Satsuma Kiriko Glassworks, which sits behind the Shoko Shuseikan.

FOOD AND BARS

Japanese

ICHINIISAN KAGOSHIMA HONTEN

1-21-24 Shimoarata; tel. 099/285-8123; https://ichiniisan.jp/access/kagoshima/; 11am-10pm (last order 9pm) Mon.-Sat., 11am-9:30pm (last order 8:30pm) Sun. and holidays; lunch sets from ¥880, dinner courses from ¥3,500; walk 5 minutes east of Takenohashi tram stop

It's all about the pork at this local favorite—in particular, Kagoshima's renowned kurobuta ("black pork"), which refers to the color of the pig's skin. The juicy, tender meat is fantastic when eaten as shabu-shabu (hot pot made at the table with thin slices of pork, vegetables, and sometimes noodles). There are some great-value lunch sets as well, with thinly sliced boiled pork, rice, greens, and soup. Reserve ahead a day in advance for dinner if you can.

KUMASOTEI

6-10 Higashisengoku-chō; tel. 099/222-6356; www.kumasotei.com; 11am-2pm and 5pm-10pm daily; average lunch course ¥2,000, average dinner course ¥4,000; walk 4 minutes north of Tenmokan-dōri tram stop

With its dark wood interior and plenty of shōchū bottles on display, this restaurant sets the scene for a Satsuma-themed feast. Regional dishes include kurobuta shabushabu (hotpot with black pork), kurobuta tonkotsu (Satsuma black pork stewed in raw sugar, miso, and shōchū), satsuma-age (deep-fried fish paste), kibinago sashimi (sashimi served with vinegared miso dipping sauce), and of course, lots of shōchū. The spreads are quite diverse and filling, with numerous small dishes. An English menu is available.

Seafood

KAGOSHIMA FISH MARKET TOUR

tel. 099/226-8188; http://k-fishmarket-tour.com/english/; 6:45am-8am Sat. Mar.-Nov.; ¥2,000 adults, ¥1,000 children

Tokyo's grand seafood bazaar at Toyosu (formerly Tsukiji) can feel overwhelming. Kagoshima's much smaller-scale market is a great alternative. These tours, held on Saturday mornings from March to November, are collectively organized by a group of hotels and ryokan around town, many of which provide pickup on the morning of the tour. After exploring the market, the guides will be happy to direct you to some of the best shops for a breakfast sushi spread. Sushi may not seem like a logical breakfast choice, but when in Rome . . .

Reserve your spot as early as possible to give the tour company time to arrange an English interpreter. Very young children are not permitted, but kids from elementary school age and up are welcome. Tours have been on indefinite hold since March 2020, so check the website to see if tours are back on.

Cafés

BACKEREI DANKEN

16-5 Chūōchō; tel. 099/214-9550; https://backereidanken.jp; 8am-6pm Tues.-Sun.; baked goods from ¥180; walk 6 minutes southeast of JR Kagoshima Chūō Station, on Konan-dōri

This bakery serves excellent pastries packed with raisins, cinnamon, and chocolate, as well as savory items like sandwiches and calzones. It's a great spot to grab something on the go if you want to eat by the bay or in a park. They serve good coffee, too.

CAFÉ BAR RECIFE

1-3 Kajiyachō; tel. 099/213-9787; http://recife-wine.com; noon-midnight Thurs.-Mon.; lunch ¥1,000, dinner from ¥2,000; take tram line 2 to the Kajiya-chō tram stop, then walk 2 minutes

This bar and restaurant has a laid-back Brazilian vibe, oozing effortless charm. It serves good food—Latin American fare, salads, chicken dishes, taco rice—and has a solid but not pretentious wine list. There are occasional DJ events, with the space functioning more as a bar at night. When it's warm, the rooftop terrace is an inviting place to while away an evening.

Bars

ISHIZUE

6-1 Sennichichō; tel. 099/227-0125; www.honkakushochu-bar-ishizue.com; 8pm-3am daily; take tram line 1 or 2 to the Temmonkan-dōri tram stop, then walk 2 minutes

This intimate, wood-paneled bar is the best place to drink shōchū on home turf. Having once worked in a distillery himself, the bar's owner is a master of the spirit, which exhibits an impressive range of qualities across the 1,500 bottled varieties behind the counter. Look for a sign at street level that reads "Bar 4F." Highly recommended. Ishizue has been closed throughout much of the pandemic, so check the website before making the trip.

ACCOMMODATIONS

Under ¥10,000

DORMY INN KAGOSHIMA

17-30 Nishisengokuchō; tel. 099/216-5489; www.hotespa.net/hotels/kagoshima; from ¥9,000 d; walk 2 minutes from Takamibaba Station (accessible on tram lines 1 and 2), or walk 5 miutes from Tenmonkan Airport Shuttle Bus Stop

Clean, modern (if petite) rooms with the essentials are offered at a reasonable price at this centrally located hotel. There are shared hot-spring baths both inside and out, as well as en suite facilities. It's good value for the money, if you just want a clean, convenient place to sleep. The breakfast buffet is optional. Front desk staff speak English and are happy to help. Complimentary shuttle pickup from JR Kagoshima Chūō Station is available with reservation.

¥10,000-20,000

SOLARIA NISHITETSU HOTEL KAGOSHIMA

11 Chūōchō; tel. 099/210-5555; https://nnr-h.com/solaria/kagoshima/; from ¥11,400 d; in front of JR Kagoshima Chūō Station

Some of the rooms at this modern hotel offer sweeping views of the city and Sakurajima looming beyond. Smartly decorated rooms are compact, with en suite bathtubs. There's a French restaurant onsite that serves a breakfast buffet of Japanese and Western food, as well as French fare during lunch and dinner hours. Coin laundry facilities are onsite. Request a room facing the bay.

REMM KAGOSHIMA

1-32 Higashisengokuchō; tel. 099/224-0606; www.hankyu-hotel.com/hotel/remm/kagoshima; ¥12,100 s, ¥16,500 d; walk 2 minutes from Takamibaba Station (accessible on tram lines 1 and 2), or walk 2 minutes from Tenmonkan Airport Shuttle Bus Stop

Another good, modern hotel in the heart of town, Remm has slightly more spacious rooms and a stylish onsite restaurant serving breakfast. Helpful staff speak English at the 24-hour front desk. There are shops, cafés, and restaurants aplenty in the area.

¥20,000-30,000

SHIROYAMA HOTEL KAGOSHIMA

41-1 Shinshoinchō; tel. 099/224-2211; www.shiroyama-g.co.jp; from ¥25,000 d; use complimentary shuttle service

One of the city's best places to stay, this hotel on the slopes of Mount Shiroyama boasts arguably better views than those had from Shiroyama Park. There are vistas of the smoldering cone of Sakurajima throughout the property, including from an open-air onsen onsite. There's also a spa with a mist sauna, flower bath, and masseuses on staff. A good breakfast buffet with Western and Japanese dishes is served in one of seven restaurants on site, and the Sky Lounge offers gorgeous views of the volcano across the bay. A helpful English-speaking concierge service is happy to assist with reservations. Complimentary shuttles run between the inn and the airport as well as other places around town. Recommended.

INFORMATION AND SERVICES

Online, visit the **Kagoshima Visitor's Guide** website run by the **Kagoshima Internationalization Council** (http://kic-update.com) for a rundown on things to see and do, as well as dining and events listings around town and beyond. The prefectural website gives a broad view of activities and experiences on offer in the prefecture (www.kagoshima-kankou.com).

- **Kagoshima Tourist Information Center** (second floor of JR Kagoshima-Chūō Station's Sakurajima exit; tel. 099/253-2500; www.kagoshima-kankou.com/for/attractions/52457; 8am-7pm daily)
- **Tourism Exchange Center** (Kankōkoryū Center, 1-1 Uenosono-chō; tel. 099/298-5911; www.kagoshima-kankou.com/for/attractions/52888; 9am-7pm daily; walk 6 minutes east of JR Kagoshima-Chūō Station)
- **Sakurajima Visitor Center** (1722-29 Yokoyama-chō, Sakurajima; tel.

099/293-2443; www.sakurajima.gr.jp/svc/english; 9am-5pm daily)

GETTING THERE

Train

If you're arriving in Kagoshima by shinkansen, your terminus will be **Kagoshima-Chūō Station,** located on the west side of town. It's possible to arrive by shinkansen from Kumamoto (50 minutes; ¥6,870) and Hakata (1.5 hours; ¥10,440), or farther afield, from Hiroshima (2 hours 50 minutes; ¥17,800) and Shin-Osaka (4 hours 40 minutes; ¥22,110).

As for local trains, the JR Nippō line's southern terminus is **JR Kagoshima Station,** situated on the north side of town. This line terminates in Kagoshima after traveling south all the way from Kokura in northeastern Kyushu, hugging the east coast of the island, with stops at other key hubs such as Beppu and Miyazaki. If you're coming from Beppu, you can travel using limited express or local trains all the way down the eastern coast if you're happy to move at a snail's pace. For example, you can take the Sonic Limited Express from Beppu to Oita, then transfer to the Nichirin Limited Express to Miyazaki, where you'll then hop aboard the Kirishima Limited Express and ride the rest of the way to Kagoshima for a total trip-time of more than 6 hours (¥10,320). Sticking only to local trains can extend that journey to upwards of 8 hours.

If you have a JR pass or don't mind absorbing the shock of a higher fare, a faster option for traveling to Kagoshima from Beppu is to first head north to Kokura on the Sonic Limited Express, then transfer to the shinkansen and travel directly to Kagoshima-Chūō Station from there (3 hours; ¥15,950). Coming from Miyazaki is thankfully a much simpler (and quicker) affair. Just hop on the Kirishima Limited Express and ride directly to JR Kagoshima Station (2 hours 20 minutes; ¥4,310).

Air

Kagoshima Airport (www.koj-ab.co.jp) has links to Asian hubs Seoul, Shanghai, Taipei, and Hong Kong, though these were paused during COVID, as well as domestic connections to Tokyo, Nagoya, Osaka, and Okinawa. Until around 9pm, buses shuttle from the airport to downtown, about 30 kilometers (19 mi) to the south, stopping at Kagoshima-Chūō Station (45 minutes; ¥1,300) and the central Tenmonkan shopping district (1 hour; ¥1,300). Select buses continue on to Kagoshima's ferry ports.

Bus

Highway buses operated by **JR Kyushu Bus** (www.jrkbus.co.jp) and **Nishitetsu** (www.nishitetsu.jp/en/highway_bus/) serve the bus terminal near the east exit of Kagoshima-Chūō Station and from the bus stops (1 Sennichi-chō) in front of Tenmonkan's **Takashima Plaza** and next to the Tenmonkan-dōri tram stop. Destinations include the island's main hubs, such as Miyazaki, Nagasaki, and Fukuoka. Although timetables and fares are detailed on the JR Kyushu Bus website, the lack of even basic English functionality makes booking a challenge. Inquire at the Tourism Exchange Center for assistance. Nishitetsu, meanwhile, has an English-language help line (tel. 0120/489-939).

Boat

Kagoshima is a prime jumping-off point for traveling to Japan's southwest islands, starting with Yakushima, and Okinawa beyond. If you're bound for lush Yakushima, head to **South Pier** (Minami-futō), located next to **Water Front Park** (5-4 Honkōshin-machi; tel. 099/805-7413; www.pref.kagoshima.jp/su-isuinavi/22966.html). From there, both daily regular ferries (1 daily, 4 hours; ¥4,900) and jetfoils (6 or 7 daily; 2-3 hours; ¥9,200 one-way, ¥16,600 round-trip) travel to and from Yakushima's Miyanoura and Anbo ports. Tickets can be booked at www.directferries.com. To reach the South Pier, hop on the tram directly in front of Kagoshima-Chūō Station and ride to Izuro-dōri tram stop (10 minutes; ¥170). Disembark, then walk about 15 minutes eastward towards the sea, with the

Sakurajima's smoldering cone in the backdrop serving as your beacon.

GETTING AROUND

Tram

Kagoshima is served by a convenient tram network (6:30am-10:30pm; single journey ¥170, one-day pass ¥600). Two lines start from **JR Kagoshima Station** and trundle toward the central **Tenmonkan** shopping district. At Takamibaba, **line 1** forges southward into the burbs, while the better situated **line 2** stops at **JR Kagoshima-Chūō Station** and other places in the heart of town. Pay for a single trip as you exit the tram. Buy a one-day pass at the tourist information center. Note that the one-day pass can also be used on the City View Bus (see below).

Bus

Don't bother with Kagoshima's arcane city bus system, but the clearly marked **City View Bus** (every 30 minutes; 9am-6:20pm; single journey ¥190, one-day pass ¥600) is a convenient way to take in the city's main sights. Beginning from the **E-4 bus terminal** outside JR Kagoshima-Chūō Station's east exit, these buses follow three routes around the city. To learn more about the routes, visit www.kotsu-city-kagoshima.jp/en/e-tourism/e-sakurajima-tabi. Note that the one-day pass, which can be purchased at the tourist information center, is also valid on the tram network.

Ferry

Ferries run between a **pier** in Kagoshima (4-1 Honkōshin-machi; tel. 099/223-7271; www.city.kagoshima.lg.jp/sakurajima-ferry) and **Sakurajima Port** (61-4 Yokoyama-chō; tel. 099/293-2525) on the west side of the island. The journey across is quick and cheap (15 minutes; ¥160), and ferries are plentiful, running 24/7. Pay the fare on the Sakurajima side. To reach the ferry terminal, ride tram line 1 or 2 to Suizokukanguchi tram stop, then walk about 7 minutes southeast.

Car

Car rental outlets abound near JR Kagoshima-Chūō Station. Good options include **Toyota Rent-a-Car** (5-46 Chūō-chō; tel. 099/250-0100; https://rent.toyota.co.jp; 7am-9pm daily), about 8 minutes' walk east of the station, and **Nissan Rent-a-Car** (4-43 Chūō-chō; tel. 099/250-2123; https://nissan-rentacar.com; 8am-9pm daily), 5 minutes' walk northeast of the station.

By far, the best way to explore Sakurajima is by car. This allows you to travel quicker to the more picturesque north shore of the island and to do a full loop, which generally takes about one hour, if you're keen. You can rent one at **Sakurajima Rent-a-Car** (60 Yokoyama-chō, Sakurajima; tel. 099/293-2162; 8am-6pm daily; ¥4,800 2 hours, ¥11,000 1 day), located about 10 minutes' walk east of the island's ferry terminal.

KIRISHIMA-YAKU NATIONAL PARK

霧島錦江湾国立公園

This region's otherworldly terrain, which has more than a hint of lunar quality, was the first to be designated a national park in Japan. The volcanically active Kirishima range straddles the prefectural border of Miyazaki and Kagoshima. A second far-removed section of the park—accounting for the "Yaku" portion of its name—is located to the south on the island of Yakushima, an emerald, sylvan wonderland reached by ferry from Kagoshima.

Given their otherworldly appearance, it's no surprise that the peaks of the Kirishima region serve as the backdrop to many Japanese myths. While it's disputed with the Takachiho region, the Kirishima range is also said to be the place where Ninigi no Mikoto, the sun goddess Amaterasu's grandson, descended to earth and founded the Japanese imperial line.

In this mystical landscape, trails weave through grassy plateaus, around calderas and electric-blue lakes set in craters, and down hillsides laden with a thick layer of red dust. After rambling through the otherworldly landscape, recuperate with a soak in an onsen

☆ Ibusuki's Hot Sand Baths

Ibusuki (指宿) is an onsen town in the far south of the Satsuma Peninsula where you can do something you probably never knew was possible: bury yourself up to the neck in beach sand that's heated by onsen water running just below the ground. It's said to relax, detox, and soften the skin. The singular experience alone justifies a day trip from Kagoshima, about an hour away on the train.

hot sand bath

SARAKU SAND-BATH HALL

5-25-18 Yunohama, Ibusuki; tel. 0993/23-3900; http://sa-raku.sakura.ne.jp; 8:30am-8:30pm daily; sand bath and onsen ¥1,100; walk 20 minutes from Ibusuki Station or take a taxi (5 minutes)

Here's how it works: First, buy a ticket at the Saraku Sand-Bath Hall, located about 1 kilometer (0.6 mi) from Ibusuki Station. Head to the locker room to suit up in a rental yukata and pick up a towel to bundle your head, to keep your hair clean as you lay directly on the beach.

Next, go outside to find a comfy-looking plot along Surigahama Beach. Finally, wrap your head and lay down for one of the staff to cover you in the beach's hot gray sand, which puts off a slightly sulfurous odor. While this may sound unpleasant, the soft embrace of the sand and feeling of heat emanating from underneath is more akin to curling up in a cocoon.

After a few minutes, the staff offer to shovel more warm sand over you, sucking you further into the womb-like state. The choice is yours. Most sand-bathers stay put for up to 15 or 20 minutes. After that, arise like Lazarus, shake off the sand, and go hop in the shower. You'll have to return the yukata, but you can keep the commemorative towel used to cover your head (¥120) as a souvenir. Note that larger bath towels are rented separately (¥200).

★ IBUSUKI SYUSUI-EN

5-27-27 Yunohama; tel. 0993/23-4141; www.syusuien.co.jp; from ¥27,500 pp with meals

If you want to linger longer near the rejuvenating hot sand, this luxury property has all the makings of a premium ryokan experience: expansive tatami rooms with en suite bathrooms, antique furniture, scroll paintings hanging in alcoves, incredible service by staff clad in kimono, and fantastic kaiseki meals. There's also a public onsen onsite. Admittedly, it's pricey. But it's an ideal place to idle in a kimono, dine on lavish seafood spreads, and sip matcha (powdered green tea) while gazing onto a landscape garden. It's only a few minutes' walk south of the town's famed sand baths, or about 20 minutes' walk southeast of JR Ibusuki Station. Recommended.

GETTING THERE

From JR Kagoshima-Chūō Station, both local and limited express trains run directly to Ibusuki Station. You can either take the local **JR Ibusuki Makurazaki** line (1-2 trains hourly; 1 hour 20 minutes; ¥1,020) or the **Ibusuki-no-Tamatebako** limited express train (50 minutes; ¥2,180). Note that seats must be reserved for this particularly stylish limited express, which runs three times daily. Its interior is fitted with pine paneling and is furnished with special seats that face the ocean. Once you're in Ibusuki, the "My Plan" bus deal allows you unlimited rides around town for one day (¥1,100 adults, ¥550 children). Another alternative is renting an **electric bicycle** from the tourist information desk in Ibusuki Station (¥500 for 2 hours).

For more information on your hot sand bath outing, there's a **tourist information desk** in JR Ibusuki Station (tel. 0993/22-4114; www.ibusuki.or.jp; 9am-5pm daily), or visit the **Ibusuki Sightseeing Information Center** (2-5-33 Minato; tel. 0993/22-3252; www.ibusuki.or.jp; 9am-5pm daily), about 6 minutes' walk east of JR Ibusuki Station.

pool. One of the cones in the park, Shinmoe-dake, spewed ash and smoke thousands of feet skyward as recently as March 2018. Increased volcanic activity, including Shinmoe-dake's recent belch, has caused some of the hiking trails to close indefinitely.

Be sure to check conditions before setting off for any forays into the park. Besides noxious gases and ash, the region also receives its fair share of storms, especially during the rainy season from mid-May through June. Temperatures also plummet in the dead of winter. While it's certainly possible to take a day hike here, to fully enjoy the park, it would be better to stay at least one night, or even longer—a particularly appealing prospect if you book a room at one of Kirishima Onsen's attractive ryokan.

Sights

KIRISHIMA-JINGŪ
霧島神社

2608-5 Kirishimataguchi; tel. 0995/57-0001; www.kirishimajingu.or.jp; open 24/7; free

Dedicated to Ninigi-no-mikoto, the god who touched down on nearby Takachiho-no-mine, this shrine stretches back into the 6th century. The current complex was constructed with the backing of the Shimazu clan in 1715. The backdrop of surrounding peaks, with a view all the way to Sakurajima on clear days, is a phenomenal sight. From JR Kirishima-Jingū Station, take the Iwasaki bus bound for Kirishima-Iwasaki Hotel, and get off at Kirishima-Jingū Mae bus stop (15 minutes; ¥250; one bus every 1-2 hours).

Hiking

Due to recent Shinmoe-dake volcanic activity, many of Kirishima-Yaku's scenic trails remain closed to the public. Standout hikes include the **Ebino-Kōgen Circuit** (5.2 km/3.2 mi; 2 hours), a leisurely walk through crater lakes; **Karakuni-Dake** and **Onami-Ike Crater Lake** (9.7 km/6 mi; 6.5 hours), which traces the rim of a caldera and circles around a crater lake; and **Takachiho-no-mine** (6.8 km/4.2mi; 3 hours), a mountain ascent, but almost all of these hikes have recently been closed due to unsafe conditions.

The best strategy is to start out at one of Kirishima-Yaku's excellent visitor centers—the **Ebino-kōgen Eco Museum Center** or the **Kirishima City Tourism Information Center**—to see what hikes are available. Staff will be able to provide maps and advise you on the best routes. For a good rundown online, visit www.env.go.jp/en/nature/nps/park/guide/kirishima/recommend/index.html.

Food and Accommodations

Lodging and food options are clustered around the park's peaks in **Ebino-kōgen,** and in the area leading up to **Kirishima-jingū.** Perhaps the most important thing to keep in mind in these areas is that restaurants close early. If you're not staying in a ryokan that provides meals, aim to buy all the food you'll need for the evening before setting off for a day of hiking. If you're staying at one of the area's many ryokan, meals are provided.

EBINO PLATEAU CAMP VILLAGE

1470 Suenaga, Ebino; tel. 0984/33-0800; www.city.ebino.lg.jp/display.php?cont=210609131433; Apr.-Oct.; campsite ¥830, tent rental ¥1,440, cabin ¥1,650 pp

This is a wonderful base for exploring the park. You'll have the option of pitching your own tent, renting a tent, or staying in a cabin. It's situated about 10 minutes' walk south of the Ebino-kōgen Eco Museum Center, amid pines and bisected by a murmuring stream. There's an onsen onsite (2pm-8pm daily). Restrooms are clean by campground standards. The price spikes a bit in mid-summer and the campground closes for a time in winter. Cooking utensils, blankets, and more are available for rent. Online reservations are unavailable at the time of writing; have a Japanese speaker call ahead to reserve a tent or cabin.

KIRISHIMA HOTEL

3948 Makizono-chō, Takachiho; tel. 0995/78-2121; www.kirishima-hotel.jp; from ¥35,000 d with meals

Situated on the Kirishima-jingū side of the park, this onsen hotel has clean, though somewhat dated, rooms with en suite baths. The staff are helpful, and the restaurant serves decent Japanese fare. But most enticing are the singular onsen baths. The pools here are neither the standard open-air type nor the indoor variety. Instead, a large central pool sits within a cavernous hall, with a number of smaller baths dotting the periphery. Many of the baths are mixed-gender, but there's a corner reserved for women only. Further, only women are allowed to enter 7:30pm-10pm every day. Although the rates are a bit on the high side, finding good deals online is not uncommon.

Information and Services

The Kirishima City Tourism Association maintains a website (http://kirishimakankou.com) and operates an English-language help hotline (tel. 0995/78-2115).

- **Ebino-kōgen Eco Museum Center** (1495-5 Suenaga, Ebino; tel. 0984/33-3002; www.ebino-ecomuseum.go.jp; 9am-5pm daily)
- **Kirishima City Tourism Information Center** (2459-6 Taguchi, Kirishima; tel. 0995/57-1588; 9am-6pm daily Apr.-Sept., 9am-5pm daily Oct.-Mar.)

Getting There

Given the remoteness of the region, the best way to reach Kirishima is with your own wheels. That said, it's possible to arrive via **rail.** If you're approaching the park from the east, from JR Miyazaki Station, take the JR Nippō line to Miyakonojo, then transfer to the JR Kitto line bound for Hayato and ride until **Kobayashi Station** (2 hours 20 minutes; ¥1,680). To slightly shorten the ride, simply take the Kirishima limited express train from Miyazaki to Miyakonojo, then finish the rest of the journey to Kobayashi as just described (1 hour 50 minutes; ¥2,840). This will put you on the northeast side of the park.

Coming from the south, take the Kirishima limited express train from Kagoshima-Chūō Station directly to **Kirishima-jingū Station** (55 minutes; ¥950), situated on the south side of the park. The station is located about 7 kilometers (4 mi) south of the village that sits near the southern edge of the sprawling shrine complex after which the station is named. Regular buses shuttle (1-2 hourly) to and from Kirishima-jingū Station and the small village near the shrine's grand southern gate (15 minutes; ¥260).

Getting Around

Having a **car** to get around Kirishima is all but essential. That said, a few daily buses run between **JR Kirishima-jingū Station** in the south to **Maruo** (30 minutes; ¥490). From Maruo, infrequent buses trundle on to **Ebino-kōgen** in the park's northwest (2-3 buses daily; 30 minutes; ¥430). The likelihood of missing a connection or waiting ages for the next bus to arrive makes driving a significantly more appealing option.

Okinawa and the Southwest Islands

Itinerary Ideas 679
Yakushima..............682
Okinawa-Hontō........687
Kerama Islands..........701
Miyako Islands..........705
Yaeyama Islands 711

At Japan's southwestern edge, a cluster of island chains stretches some 1,000 kilometers (621 mi) into the East China Sea. Laid-back, with a climate that alternates between subtropical and tropical, these islands—about 160 in all—show a side of Japan that many outsiders don't know exists, with tangled jungles, azure waters, coral reefs, white-sand beaches, and mangrove swamps. Most of these islands are located at roughly the same latitude as Miami.

They begin in the north with lush, mountainous Yakushima, a UNESCO World Heritage Site, and extend to the far-flung Yaeyama Islands off the eastern coast of Taiwan. In between, the prefecture's main and largest island of Okinawa-Hontō buzzes with life, the nearby Keramas draw divers to deep emerald waters, and the sands

Highlights

Look for ★ to find recommended sights, activities, dining, and lodging.

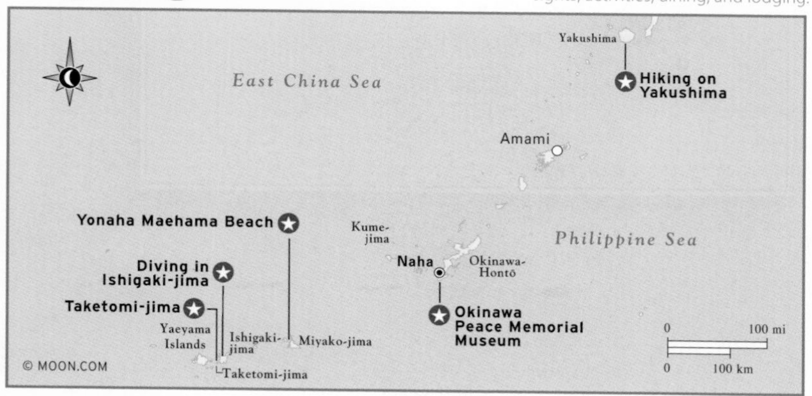

★ **Hiking on Yakushima:** Covered in dense cedar forest, this mossy, subtropical island makes for lovely hikes (page 683).

★ **Okinawa Peace Memorial Museum:** This museum offers a sobering reminder of the horrors of combat on an island where one of World War II's bloodiest battles took place (page 697).

★ **Yonaha Maehama Beach:** Maehama's white sands continue for miles and gently descend into warm, crystal-clear waters that are great for swimming and water sports (page 705).

★ **Diving in Ishigaki-jima:** This island refuge is considered by many to be the best place to scuba dive in the country (page 712).

★ **Taketomi-jima:** Cycling or walking through the villages of this island offers a chance to experience Okinawa's living traditional culture (page 715).

Okinawa and the Southwest Islands

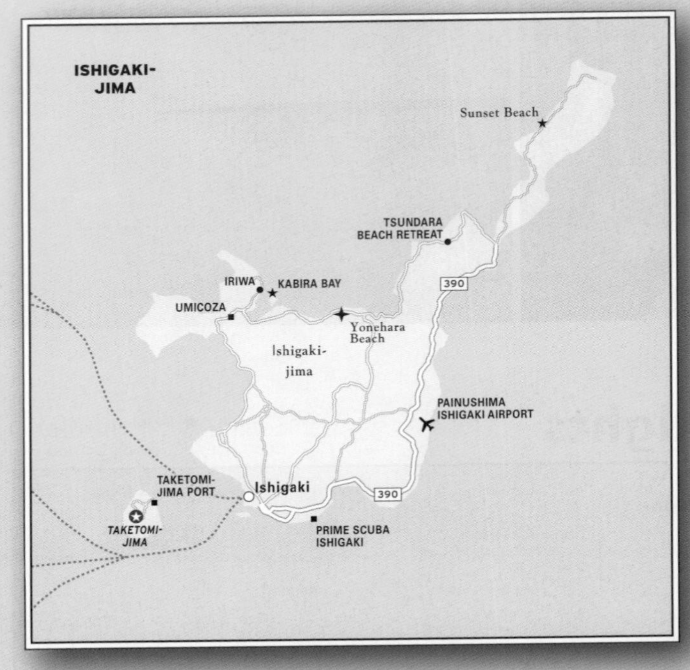

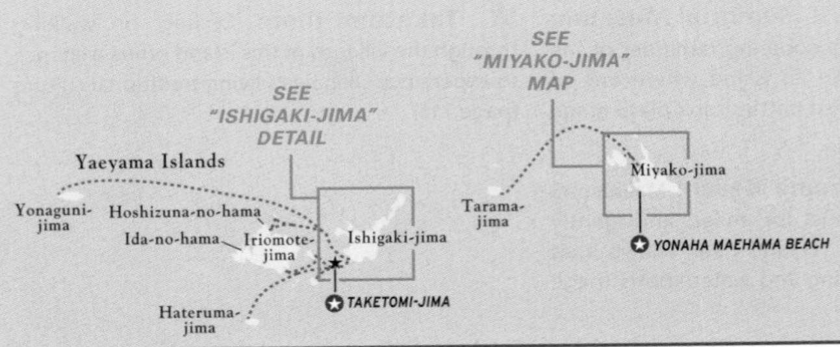

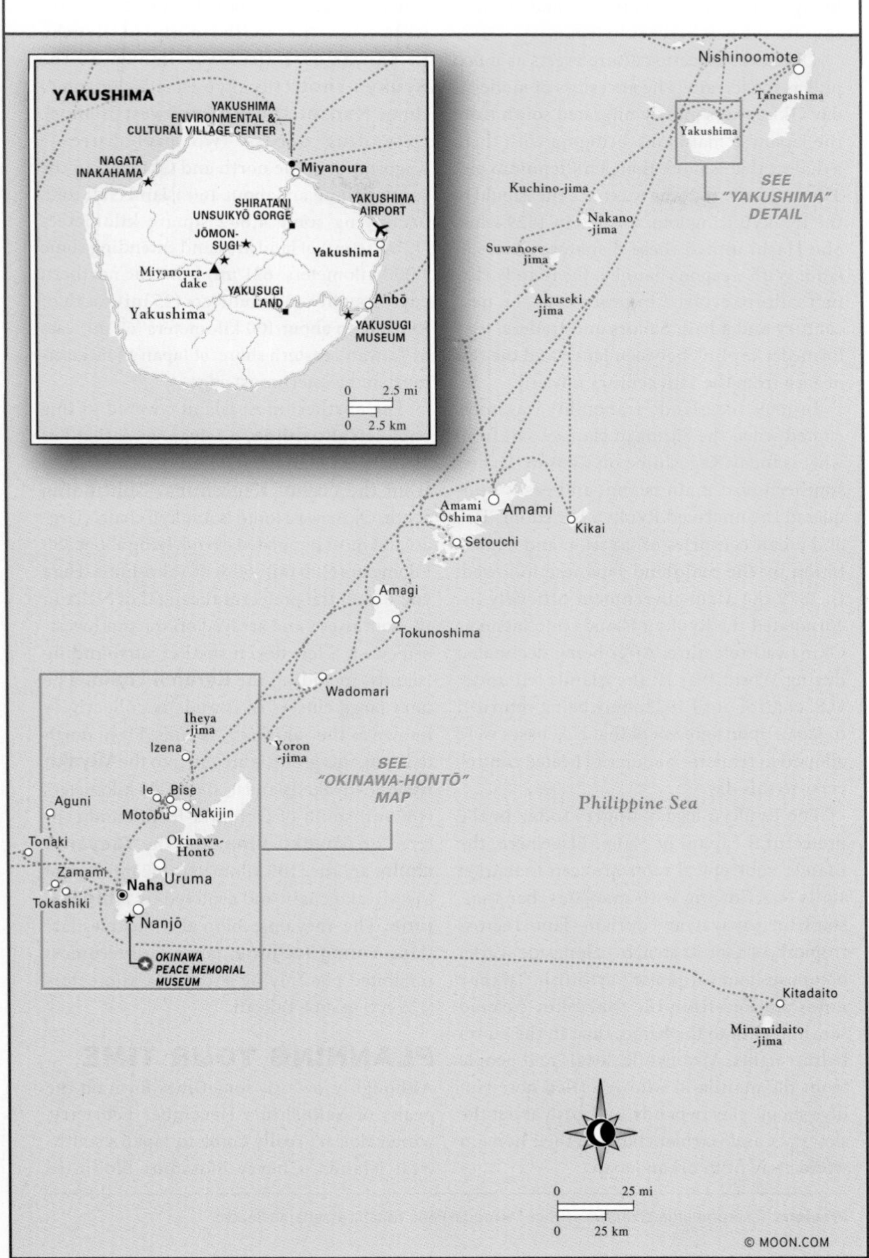

YAKUSHIMA
YAKUSHIMA ENVIRONMENTAL & CULTURAL VILLAGE CENTER
NAGATA INAKAHAMA
Miyanoura
YAKUSHIMA AIRPORT
SHIRATANI UNSUIKYŌ GORGE
JŌMON-SUGI
Yakushima
Miyanoura-dake
YAKUSUGI LAND
Anbō
Yakushima
YAKUSUGI MUSEUM
0 2.5 mi
0 2.5 km
Nishinoomote
Tanegashima
Yakushima
SEE "YAKUSHIMA" DETAIL
Kuchino-jima
Nakano -jima
Suwanose-jima
Akuseki -jima
Amami Ōshima
Amami
Kikai
Setouchi
Amagi
Tokunoshima
Wadomari
Iheya -jima
Izena
Yoron -jima
SEE "OKINAWA-HONTŌ" MAP
Ie
Bise
Aguni
Motobu
Nakijin
Tonaki
Okinawa-Hontō
Zamami
Uruma
Naha
Tokashiki
Nanjō
OKINAWA PEACE MEMORIAL MUSEUM
Philippine Sea
Kitadaito
Minamidaito -jima
0 25 mi
0 25 km
© MOON.COM

of the sun-splashed Miyako chain summon loungers, swimmers, snorkelers, and divers to some of the best beaches in Japan.

Okinawa's eclectic culture exerts as much pull as the terrain. The ancestors of modern-day Okinawans mostly migrated south from the Japanese mainland, bringing with them a dialect that is more than a millennium old. The main city of Naha was once the capital of the Ryūkyū Kingdom, formed in 1429 when Sho Hashi united these disparate slivers of land. With weapons banned, the islands' disinct culture evolved in peace over the next century and a half. Sailors and traders, they formed a key link between Japan and the rest of Asia from the 14th century onward.

In 1609, the islands' tranquility was interrupted when the Shimazu clan set sail from what is today Kagoshima on Kyushu, Japan's southernmost main island, and easily conquered the unarmed Ryūkyū Kingdom. Two and a half centuries of taxation and exploitation by the mainland Japanese followed. In 1879 the Meiji government officially incorpotated the Ryūkyū Islands into Japan as Okinawa Prefecture. After being decimated during World War II, the islands fell under U.S. control until 1972, only being returned to Japan upon agreement that U.S. bases were allowed to remain—a source of heated controversy to this day.

The Ryūkyū legacy lingers today in the prefectural capital of Naha. Elsewhere, the islands' subtropical roots are seen in market stalls overflowing with mangoes, bananas, star fruit, papayas, and durian—famed across tropical Asia for its stench—alongside scarlet octopuses and turquoise parrotfish. Twangy notes plucked from the snakeskin-covered sanshin, akin to the banjo, float in the air on balmy nights. Meanwhile, locals and people from the mainland who resettled here run dive shops, play in bands, and gush about the slow pace and warmer climes of their home, a world away from urban Japan.

ORIENTATION

The entire arc of islands that extends southwest from the southern tip of Kyushu to Taiwan is collectively known as the **Ryūkyū-shotō** (Ryūkyū Islands), or sometimes **Nansei-shotō** (Southwest Islands). Extending across two prefectures—Kagoshima in the north and Okinawa in the south—there are about 160 islands, all told, occupying some 4,642 square kilometers (1,792 sq mi) of land area and extending some 1,000 kilometers (621 mi) from the northern edge, roughly 40 kilometers (25 mi) south of Kyushu, to about 100 kilometers (62 mi) east of Taiwan's eastern shore, at Japan's southernmost and westernmost edge.

The northernmost island covered in this book is **Yakushima,** a sylvan jewel that lies about 150 kilometers (93 mi) south by ferry from the city of Kagoshima. Continuing south, Okinawa-Hontō is Ryukyū chain's largest and most populated island, lying about 480 kilometers (300 mi) south of Yakushima. Here you'll find the prefectural capital of Naha in the southwest, and arrayed off the southwestern coast, a few dozen smaller surrounding islands, including the **Kerama chain.** The next large cluster of islands is collectively known as the Sakishima Islands. From north to south, this group is broken into the **Miyako Retto** (Miyako Islands), about 300 kilometers (186 mi) south of Okinawa-Hontō and centered on **Miyako-jima,** and the **Yaeyama chain,** another 100 kilometers (62 mi) west of the Miyako chain and centered on **Ishigaki-jima.** The Yaeyama chain also includes far-flung **Yonaguni-jima,** Japan's westernmost inhabited place, lying about 224 kilometers (139 mi) east of Taiwan.

PLANNING YOUR TIME

Although snowcaps sometimes form on the peaks of Yakushima December-February, winter doesn't really come to Japan's southwest islands. Cherry blossoms bloom as

Previous: Taketomi-jima; Okinawa's Peace Memorial Park; Yonaha Maehama Beach.

Regional Food Specialties

Okinawan cuisine differs markedly from food on the mainland. Dispense with ideas of elaborate creations on lacquer trays—instead, think soul food that is healthy despite the fact that much of it is whipped up in a frying pan. The cuisine is simple and homegrown, with a plethora of unique ingredients not found elsewhere—thanks to this nutritious intake, the people of the Ryūkyū Islands are among the longest-living in the world.

If Okinawan cuisine has piqued your curiosity and you'd like to learn how to whip up a few classics at home, it's relatively simple: In the main town of Naha, **Taste of Okinawa** (1-6-21 Tsuboya, Naha; tel. 098/943-6313; https://tasteof.okinawa) is a craft beer bar and restaurant that offers one-off cooking classes (3:30pm-6:30pm Tues.-Sun.; ¥6,500 adults, ¥3,500 children).

KEY INGREDIENTS

The Okinawan diet is rich in soy, ginger, and turmeric. For protein, pork is the meat of choice. Unique ingredients include:

- tofu-like **fu,** or wheat gluten made by rinsing the starch out of wheat flour dough, served either raw or dried
- bitter **goya** (melon), renowned for its cancer-fighting properties and for being nearly unpalatable
- **umibudo** (sea grapes), a form of seaweed with green, transluscent bubbles, often dipped in a light ponzu (citrusy soy) sauce and eaten raw
- **mozuku** seaweed, served in thick, nutrient-dense, sticky strands, both raw and cooked
- the deep-purple sweet potato known as **beni-imo,** packed with vitamins A and C, fiber, folic acid, and beta carotene
- slivers of the salty, canned pork product **SPAM,** which have been a staple in the islands' pantries since World War II

TYPICAL DISHES

- **Champuru:** A number of Okinawan classics are stir-fries, referred to locally as champuru, which usually include a mix of fu, eggs, pork—or Spam—and bitter goya. Try it at **Usagi-ya Honten** (page 712).
- **Okinawan soba:** The noodles in this popular dish are made from wheat (rather than buckwheat), served in a warm, light, pork-based broth topped with green onions and hunks of boiled pork, and tossed with red ginger. Try it at **Shuri Horikawa** (page 693).
- **Taco rice:** This famed fusion dish is a reasonably priced Tex-Mex spin-off: a bed of rice topped with the main ingredients of a taco. This dish was created on the island but is now widespread throughout Japan. Try it at **Borrachos** (page 693).

LOCAL BREWS

- **Awamori:** Okinawa's own local alcoholic brew can be as high as 120-proof. Try it at **Yūnangī** (page 694).
- **Bukubuku cha:** This cold tea is made from a combination of brown rice and white rice with crushed peanuts sprinkled on top. Try it at **Nuchigafu** (page 693).

Best Accommodations

★ **Sankara Hotel & Spa:** This luxury resort and spa on the southeastern coast of the lush isle of Yakushima has Balinese vibes (page 686).

★ **The Naha Terrace:** Put yourself in the center of Naha's action at this smart hotel with a bar featuring live jazz shows every night and upper-floor rooms with sweeping views (page 695).

★ **Private Resort Hotel Renn:** A stone's throw from one of Japan's best beaches, this chic B&B has a rooftop balcony and lovely ocean views (page 710).

★ **Iriwa:** This guesthouse near Ishigaki-jima's Kabira Bay has all the markings of a beach house—surfboards, tropical plants—and hosts who relish introducing their island to guests (page 714).

★ **Tsundara Beach Retreat:** If your aim is to have a stretch of beachfront all to yourself, you won't go wrong with this private beach house in Ishigaki-jima's remote north (page 714).

early as December or January, while the prefecture's official red deigo flower and other beautiful blooms color the islands all year. Typhoons occasionally sweep through from June-October, with regular cloudbursts occurring during the **rainy season** from late May-June, sometimes disrupting transport networks. The best time to dive in Okinawa is from **April-June,** before typhoons whip through the archipelago; in winter, the water temperature dips to as low as 15°C (59°F).

Domestic tourists swarm the islands' beaches during the **Golden Week holidays** in late April and early May, as well as during the peak **summer** months (June-August). The best time to visit—both for weather and crowds—is from March through the first three weeks of April, and the latter three weeks of May, before the rainy season begins.

Jumping between the various chains is relatively straightforward thanks to extensive flight and ferry networks. The islands are all relatively small and don't require a huge amount of time to see, so plan to spend somewhere between **three days** and **a week** in the southwestern islands. If your only aim is to soak up rays on a beach, a weekend should suffice. If you plan to island hop, hike, or dive, consider spending five days or longer. Note that reaching many of the smaller islands requires first traveling into a bigger hub, usually Naha, before hopping aboard a ferry.

The best place to base yourself depends on which islands you plan to visit. To visit Okinawa-Hontō with an optional side trip to the Keramas, stay in Naha; on Miyako-jima, Hara has the most restaurants, while the area near Yonaha Maehama is best for beach access; Ishigaki-jima is a good base for exploring the island itself, as well as nearby Taketomi-jima; Iriomote-jim and Yonaguni-jima are remote bases unto themselves.

Okinawa is a good standalone destination. That said, given the effort it takes to reach it from most places in the world, it makes the most sense to go there as part of a longer trip to somewhere on mainland Japan, such as Tokyo, Kansai (Kyoto, Osaka), or Kyushu, from where direct flights are available. If it's beach season—May-October—it's a great addition to any trip to Japan's core if you want some beach time and to see the country at its most relaxed and least Japanese.

Itinerary Ideas

TWO DAYS ON OKINAWA-HONTŌ AND THE KERAMA ISLANDS

Day One: Naha and the Okinawa Peace Memorial

1 Start your morning a 30-minute drive southwest of Naha at the **Okinawa Peace Memorial Museum,** doing your best to grasp the pivotal, brutal battles that took place on the island.

2 Back in Naha, change the mood a bit with an Okinawan-style lunch at **Shuri Horikawa,** a local noodle shop near Shuri Castle with a loyal following.

3 Head over to **Shuri Ryusen,** a shop 10 minutes' walk away selling bingata (colorful Okinawan textiles). The friendly staff will be happy to show you upstairs, where the pros craft exquisite patterns.

4 Hop on the monorail at nearby Gibo Station (15 minutes' walk northeast) and ride to Makishi Station (9 minutes; ¥270). From here, walk 10 minutes south to the **Tsuboya Pottery Street.** Enjoy popping in and out of the street's many shops.

5 End your stroll down Tsuboya Pottery Street with a cup of specialty local tea bukubuku cha at **Nuchigafu,** set in a historic house on a quiet corner.

6 Head out for dinner at the popular izakaya **Yūnangī,** 20 minutes' walk west, for more Okinawan dishes.

7 Walk 15 minutes east to enjoy live performances on the sanshin (three-stringed instrument resembling a banjo) over cheap drinks (with optional nibbles) at down-and-dirty **Showamura.**

Day Two: The Beaches of the Kerama Islands

You can book your ferry ticket to Zamami-jima the day you plan to travel, although reserving a day ahead doesn't hurt during high season (Apr.-Oct.), but be sure to note all return ferry times before setting out.

1 At 9am, hop on a jet foil at Tomari Port bound for the nearby Kerama Islands (1 hour 10 minutes; ¥3,200). Aim to arrive by 8:30am to snag a seat. Your destination: the idyllic isle of Zamami-jima, accessible from Naha in just over an hour by normal ferry. Upon arriving at the island's main village, which sits beside the port, rent an electrically assisted bike, then pedal up and over the steep incline that stands between the village and the island's finest piece of oceanfront property, **Furuzamami Beach.** Spend the balance of the morning swimming and lounging to your heart's content.

2 Come lunchtime, there's a snack bar on the south side of the promenade at Furuzamami Beach if you get hungry. But if you'd like a change of scenery and something heartier, pedal back into town and have a surprisingly tasty burger and fries at **Zamami Burger.**

3 After fueling up, spend the remainder of your afternoon back at Furuzamami Beach, perhaps snorkeling. Return your bicycle around 4:30pm and take a jet foil directly back to Naha from Zamami-jima just after 5pm. After all that sun, you may want some time at your hotel to cool off. Then join the locals at rowdy **Sakaemachi Arcade,** sampling street food and wandering in and out of the bars.

Itinerary Ideas

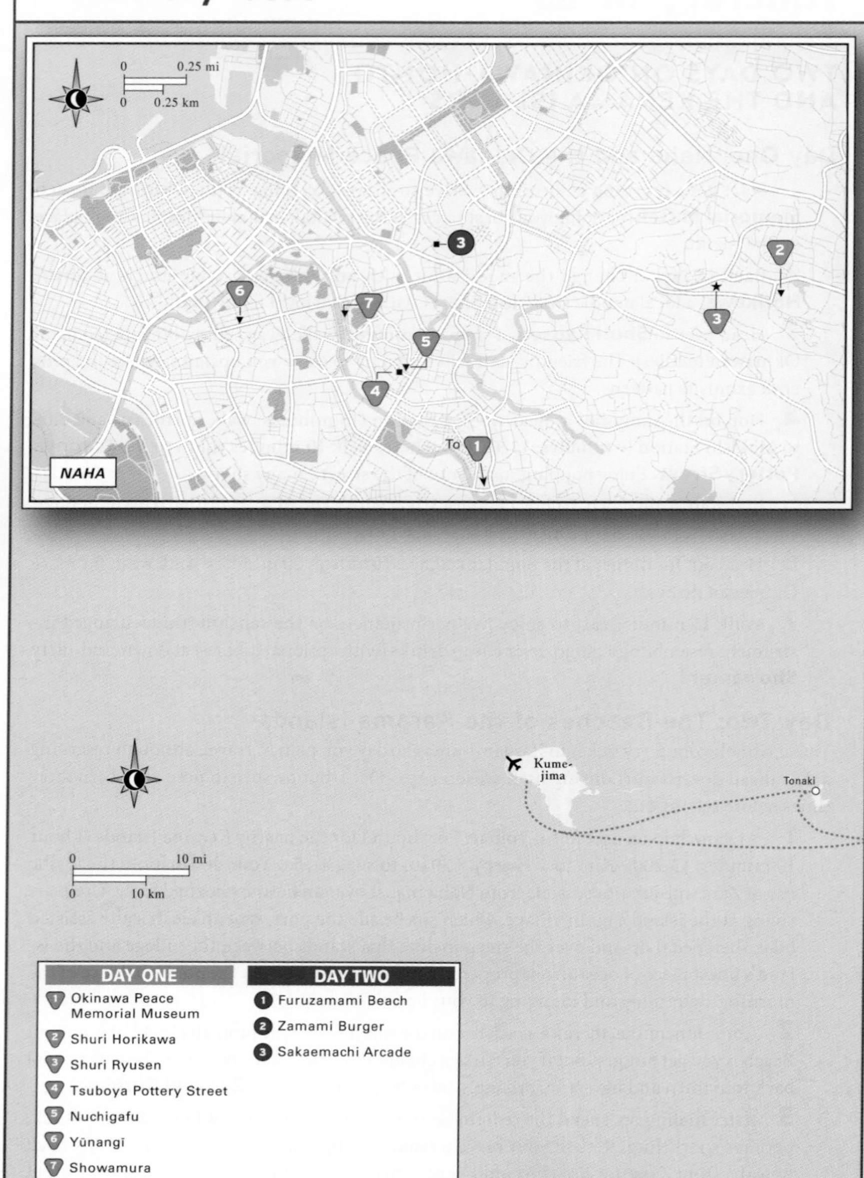

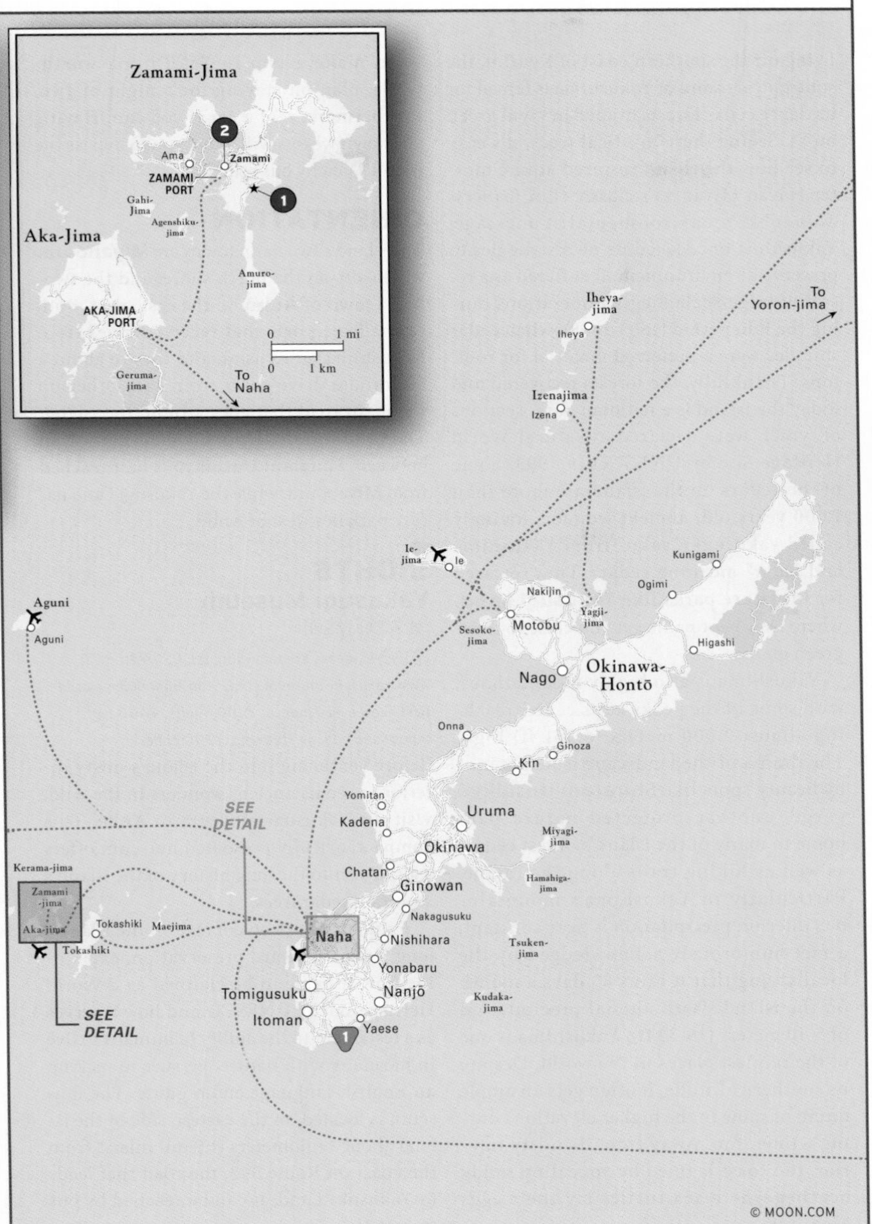
Zamami-Jima
Ama
Zamami
ZAMAMI PORT
Gahi-Jima
Agenshiku-jima
Aka-Jima
Amuro-jima
AKA-JIMA PORT
Geruma-jima
To Naha
0 1 mi
0 1 km
Iheya-jima
Iheya
To Yoron-jima
Izenajima
Izena
Ie-jima
Ie
Kunigami
Ogimi
Nakijin
Yagji-jima
Aguni
Motobu
Sesoko-jima
Higashi
Nago
Okinawa-Hontō
Onna
Ginoza
Kin
Yomitan
Uruma
SEE DETAIL
Kadena
Okinawa
Miyagi-jima
Kerama-jima
Chatan
Hamahiga-jima
Zamami-jima
Ginowan
Aka-jima
Tokashiki
Maejima
Nakagusuku
Naha
Tsuken-jima
Nishihara
Yonabaru
Tomigusuku
Nanjō
Kudaka-jima
Itoman
Yaese
© MOON.COM

Yakushima 屋久島

Lying off the southern coast of Kyushu, the subtropical island of Yakushima is famed for its dense cedar forests draped in vivid green moss. Seeing these mystical trees, it's easy to see how the island inspired anime master Hayao Miyazaki's classic film *Princess Mononoke*'s environmentalist message. Yakushima once faced its own struggles to preserve its environment: It suffered as a result of large-scale logging operations during the Edo period (1603-1868), when cedar shingles were a preferred material for rooftops. Thankfully, the forests recovered and today the island is a national park, sections of which were declared a Natural World Heritage Site by UNESCO in 1993. Some of the cedars on the island are more than 7,000 years old, ancient wonders lovingly called yakusugi ("yaku" from Yakushima and "sugi" meaning cedar). They're cared for in nature parks like **Yakusugi Land,** where well-kept paths get you close to these green giants.

Yakushima is also highly mountainous, with some of the peaks at its center reaching almost 2,000 meters (6,561 ft) high. The drama of the landscape is heightened by beauty spots like **Shiratani Unsuikyō** gorge, another protected nature park home to many of the island's oldest cedars as well as hiking trails along the ravine. Particularly in Yakushima's mountainous interior, precipitation is near constant, a fact humorously acknowledged by the local saying that it rains 35 days a month on the island. With annual precipitation of 5-10 meters (16-32 ft), Yakushima is one of the rainiest places in the world. Despite its southern altitude, it often gets an ample dump of snow in the higher elevations during winter, too. Away from its misty interior, the coast is lined by appealing sandy beaches where sea turtles lay their eggs May-July.

To make a trip to Yakushima worthwhile, plan on staying for a night or two. Furthermore, rent a car if you can. Having your own wheels will allow you to bypass the island's patchy bus schedule.

ORIENTATION

The island's two main towns are **Miyanoura,** which sits on the north shore, and the two-horse town of **Anbō** on the east coast. Both towns have ports that receive ferries from Kagoshima on Kyushu, and they're about a 30-minute drive apart from each other on the main road that goes around the island. The **Yakushima Airport** is about halfway in between. Shiratani Unsuikyō is best reached from Miyanoura, while the Yakusugi Land nature park lies west of Anbō.

SIGHTS

Yakusugi Museum

屋久杉自然館

2739-343 Anbō, Kumage-gun; tel. 0997/46-3113; www.yakusugi-museum.com; 9am-5pm daily, closed first Tues. every month; ¥600 adults, ¥400 high school and college students, ¥300 children

Before venturing into the island's misty interior to see its ancient wonders in the wild, visit the Yakusugi Museum in Anbō. This compact, artfully presented museum offers a glimpse into the long history of the island's stunning cedar trees.

Exhibits give deep context on the island's long journey toward preservation, explaining how it came to be claimed as a World Heritage site by UNESCO and how it serves as a testament to the ability of humans to live in harmony with nature. Be sure to pick up an English-language audio guide. The museum is located on the eastern side of the island about 3 kilometers (1.9 mi) inland from the coast on Route 592, the road that leads to Yakusuki Land. It can be reached by bus from Anbō.

Yakushima's Sea Turtles

The island's famous flora isn't its only draw. The coasts of Japan are the part of the northern Pacific where loggerhead sea turtles come to lay their eggs. Nearly half of the loggerhead turtles who give birth in Japan do so on Yakushima. Along the lovely stretch of beach known as **Nagata Inakahama** (永田いなか浜), in the island's northwest, the bulk of these sea turtles lay their eggs starting from May and nest through July, until the beach fills with hatchlings in August.

To see the turtles in action, make a visit with the **Nagata Sea Turtles Association** (tel. 0997/45-2280; http://nagata-umigame.com; 1pm-5pm daily Apr. 1-Aug. 31; ¥1,500 adults, children free for nighttime tour), a nonprofit group that leads tours to the beach at night from April-August. Note that the main purpose of these tours is to protect the turtles and their babies. Resist the urge to walk through the sand without a tour group during turtle season, lest you disturb the creatures' delicate habitat.

Jōmon-sugi

Miyanoura; open 24/7; free

Jōmon-sugi is the granddaddy of all the island's yakusugi trees. The giant Cryptomeria is something like the island's mascot. It was luckily spared the saw during the Edo period logging days due to its asymmetrical shape. It's not particularly tall, at about 25 meters (82 ft), but it makes up for it with its exceptionally rotund trunk measuring 5 meters (16 ft) around, with gnarled vertical ridges and limbs sprouting from its top in random directions. Its fabled look is in keeping with the fantastical surroundings, swathed in moss and veiled in mist. Aged somewhere between 2,000 and 7,200 years, this tree dates to the Jōmon period (14,000-300 BCE), after which it is named. The only way to reach this near-mythical tree is on foot along a trail that begins from a trailhead at Arakawa-tozanguchi and that takes 10 hours round-trip.

★ HIKING

Yakushima's prime attraction is its dense primeval forests, ideally explored on foot: The forest zones covered in this book merely scratch the surface of the island's vast hiking options. If you're keen to go deeper into the island's interior, **Yakumonkey** (www.yakumonkey.com), an excellent resource about the island, sells a popular guidebook chock-full of information on sights, hiking trails, and sundry practicalities.

If you plan to summit any of the island's drizzly peaks, such as its highest point **Miyanoura-dake** (1,935 m/6,348 ft), bear in mind that the temperature difference between sea level and the highest points inland is about 11°C (19.8°F). Wear waterproof footwear and fast-drying clothes, and carry a change of clothing. Be sure to tell the reception desk at your hotel, register at the nearest Tourist Information Center, or jot the details of your intended hike at the trailhead on a form called a tōzan todokede before striking out on any long-distance hike.

Guides and Supplies

If you'd like to explore alongside a locally knowledgable guide, there are several English-speaking tour providers that lead treks on the island, from custom hikes to overnight journeys:

- **Yakushima Life** (www.yakushimalife.com)
- **Yakushima Experience** (www.yakushimaexperience.com)
- **Yes! Yakushima** (www.yesyakushima.com)
- **Yakushima Geographic Tour** (http://yaku-geo.com)

Further, if you're in need of apparel to protect you from Yakushima's oftentimes relentless rain, stop by **Nakagawa Sports**

(421-6 Miyanoura; tel. 0997/42-0341; http://yakushima-sp.com; 9am-7pm daily, closed every second Wed.).

Transportation

During prime hiking season, from March to November, private cars are not permitted to make the 30-minute journey from Anbō to the popular Aarakawa Trailhead, from where hikes to the ancient Jomon-sugi cedar tree depart. This is meant to prevent traffic jams caused by the rush of hikers. You must instead take a **shuttle bus,** which departs from the Yakusugi Museum (35 minutes; ¥1,380 round-trip, ¥1,000 for conservation efforts) in the early morning (5am-6am) and returns between 3pm-6pm. Many hotels provide their guests with transport to the Yakusugi Museum for this purpose.

Purchase a bus ticket at least a day before you plan to go on the hike. **Tickets** are available at the airport or the tourist centers in Miyanoura and Anbō (page 686).

Yakusugi Land

tel. 0997/42-3508; http://y-rekumori.com; 9am-5pm daily; ¥300

A wonderful introduction to the island's forest magic, Yakusugi Land's network of trails leads to some of the island's most accessible ancient trees. This is a good choice if your time is limited and ease of access is your main priority, with well-maintained trails (1-4.5 km/0.6-3 mi) suitable for beginners and children. **Four hiking courses,** ranging in length from 30 minutes to 2.5 hours, allow you to tailor the length of your walk. They all follow the same basic route, with each looping back to the trailhead. English signage is found throughout, and English pamphlets can be picked up at the trailhead.

The easiest section of the trail is made of a wooden boardwalk. As you progress farther into the woods, the trail and the terrain slowly change. The longest hike ends atop the peak of **Tachudake** (1,457 m/4,780 ft). As you venture into these woods, you'll cross a suspension bridge that takes you over a river set in a mossy gorge. Deeper in the woodlands, you'll find the area is populated with trees more than 1,000 years old.

There are two daily round-trip **bus services** between Anbō and Yakusugi Land (40 minutes; ¥740 one way). A **taxi** ride from Anbō will take about 30 minutes and costs about ¥4,000.

hiking on Yakushima

Shiratani Unsuikyō Gorge

Miyanoura; tel. 0997/42-3508; http://y-rekumori.com; open 24/7; ¥300

Another pristine area of the island to marvel at its wondrous trees is Shiratani Unsuikyō Gorge. This park is lined with trails—Edo-period footpaths, wooden walkways, trails of stone—ranging from one to five hours in length.

SHIRATANI UNSUIKYŌ GORGE LOOP

Distance: *10 km (6.2 mi) round-trip*
Time: *4 hours round-trip*
Trailhead: *Shiratani Unsuikyō Gorge bus stop*
Information and maps: *Miyanoura Tourist Information Center*

The full loop is a popular way to see yakusugi trees without being forced to walk any overly strenuous trails. The sylvan scenes found along the paths that run along the gorge are so archetypal they almost look unreal. From a lookout rock called Taiko-iwa, the woodlands of the island stretch out like an endless green carpet. To access the trailhead, take a bus from Miyanoura to Shiratani Unsuikyō Gorge bus stop (30 minutes; ¥550). There are upward of five round-trip journeys per day.

Arakawa-Tozanguchi Hike

Distance: *19.5 km (12.1 mi) round-trip*
Time: *about 10 hours round-trip*
Trailhead: *Arakawa-tozanguchi*
Information and maps: *Anbō Tourist Information Center*

This lengthy but moderate hike brings you close to Jomon-sugi, perhaps the island's most beloved cedar tree. You'll follow an old railroad track before switching to a mix of dirt, wooden boardwalks, and steps. If you're in good physical condition and feel confident about your ability to keep a solid pace, it's possible to make the journey in a long day trip. To pull this off, leave before dawn to ensure you finish by sunset.

If you'd rather not push too hard, the unstaffed **Takatsuka Hut** is about 200 meters (656 ft) beyond the tree. Pack your own food, toiletries, and water if you plan to stay at this bare-bones lodging. Mercifully, the trail is well marked in English.

To reach the hike from March-November, when private cars are prohibited on the road up to the trailhead, you must first take the **shuttle bus** (35 minutes; ¥1,380, plus ¥2,000 for conservation efforts) from the Yakusugi Museum in the town of Anbō, roughly 15 kilometers (9.3 mi) to the southeast. It's possible to drive yourself to the trailhead from December-February.

FOOD

While there isn't a surfeit of eateries on Yakushima, there are decent options in the two port towns of Miyanoura in the north and Anbō on the eastern shore. You can also stock up on goods, like snacks and camping supplies, in these two towns. For a rundown on some of the items you'll see on the island's menus, from tobiuo (flying fish), served raw, minced, and deep-fried, to homegrown oranges and tea, along with more extensive restaurant listings, visit www.yakushimatourism.com/food-and-drink.

★ PANORAMA

60-1 Miyanoura; tel. 0997/42-0400; http://panoramayakushima.com; 6pm-11pm (last order 10:30pm) Thurs.-Tues.; plates ¥300-900; walk 5 minutes south of Miyanoura Port

Set in a nicely madeover former hardware store with long picnic-style tables and bar seats in front of an open kitchen, this stylish neighborhood izakaya in Miyanoura serves a menu of dishes made with locally sourced produce and seafood caught just offshore. Dishes are diverse, from pizza and chicken liver pâté with baguette to braised pork belly over rice, fried flying fish, poke (Hawaiian-style marinated sashimi), and more. The atmosphere is casual and friendly, and the drinks menu includes craft beer and shōchū brewed on the island and fruit-infused sodas made in-house. An English menu is available.

WARUNG KARANG

103-2 2F Anbō; tel. 070/4416-4567; https://warung-karang.com; lunch 11:30am-5pm (last order 4:30pm) Mon.-Tues. and Fri., 11:30am-3pm (last order 2:30pm) Sat.-Sun., dinner 7pm-11pm Fri.-Tues.; lunch ¥1,500, dinner ¥3,000; walk 10 minutes south from Anbō Port

This stylish second-floor eatery, café, and bar whips up a nutritious, Indonesian-inspired menu. Choose deli items a la carte or set meals (rice, salad, assorted entrees) during lunch hours, or tuck into a set course of six fixed dishes at dinnertime. The bright, minimal space is graced by plants and has good views of the fishing port and Anbō River flowing just outside. Reservations at least a day prior are required for dinner. Good dessert and drinks are on offer too.

ACCOMMODATIONS

For a map of more extensive accommodation options across the island, check out www.yakushimatourism.com/accommodation.

SŌYŌTEI

521-4 Nagata; tel. 0997/45-2819; http://soyotei.net; ¥15,000 pp with 2 meals; walk 3 minutes west of Nagata Inakahama bus stop

This family-owned ryokan is about 40 minutes' drive west of Miyanoura Port near the lovely beach of Nagata Inakahama. There are 11 semidetached Japanese-style rooms, each with a veranda facing the ocean. Each room has its own toilet but shares a number of baths, both indoor and open-air, supplied with onsen water. There's a communal dining hall looking out to the ocean where seafood-heavy meals are served twice daily.

★ SANKARA HOTEL & SPA

553 Haginoue, Mugio; tel. 0997/47-3488; https://sankarahotel-spa.com; from ¥47,300 pp with 2 meals; drive 20 minutes (10 km/6.2 mi) southwest of Anbō Port

On the island's southeast coast, overlooking the ocean, this world-class accommodation offers plush villas decked out in Balinese-style decor, with plenty of teak and all the bells and whistles you'd expect at a luxury property. There are two onsite restaurants—the casual Ayana and more formal Okas—where the chefs adroitly concoct exquisite French fare using locally sourced ingredients, as well as a pool, spa, and library. The staff are incredibly attentive, freely sharing knowledge about the island's hidden gems, and exhibit the same level of omotenashi (hospitality) you'd expect at one of Kyoto's most exclusive ryokan. It's possible for guests to rent a car from the hotel with an advanced reservation (¥1,500 per hour). Highly recommended.

INFORMATION AND SERVICES

Online, a wealth of free English-language information, from hotel and restaurant listings to maps and bus timetables, can be downloaded from http://yakukan.jp/doc/index.html.

- **Tourist Information Center, Miyanoura Ferry Terminal** (tel. 0997/42-1019; 9am-5pm daily)
- **Tourist Information Center, Anbō** (187-1 Anbō; tel. 0997/46-2333; 8:30am-6pm daily, 4-minute walk north of MOS Burger, near Anbō Bridge)
- **Yakushima Environmental & Cultural Village Center** (823-1 Miyanoura; tel. 0997/42-2911; 9am-5pm Tues.-Sun., closed Tues. if Mon. is national holiday; ¥520 adults, ¥360 high school students, ¥260 elementary and junior high students)

ATMs are hard to come by on the island. Plan to handle any banking matters before arriving in Yakushima—or make any withdrawals at one of the eight post office ATMs around the island (8:45am-6pm Mon.-Fri., 9am-5pm Sat.-Sun. and national holidays).

GETTING THERE

Daily flights are available from Kagoshima (35 minutes; discount fares from ¥10,000 one-way), Osaka (1 hour 40 minutes; discount fares from ¥26,000), and Fukuoka (1 hour; discount fares from ¥18,000) to **Yakushima**

Airport (501 Koseda; tel. 0997/42-1200), located between Anbō and Miyanoura on the island's northern coast.

If you prefer to go by boat, jet foils from Kagoshima's high-speed ferry terminal (south of Minamifutō pier) run by **Tane Yaku Jetfoil** (tel. 099/226-0128 in Kagoshima, tel. 0997/42-2003 in Miyanoura; www.tykousoku.jp; ¥8,300 one-way, ¥15,000 round-trip) head to **Miyanoura Port** (1 hour 50 minutes) five times daily (less during winter), and twice daily to the town of **Anbō** (2 hours). Book tickets in advance by asking for assistance from your accommodation or filling in a ticket request form on the website of English-speaking agent Yakushima Travel (www.yakushimatravel.com/ticket-english.html). Or, do it the old fashioned way: Go to the jetfoil terminal window and purchase a ticket in person.

Slower car ferries operated by **Ferry Yakushima 2** (http://ferryyakusima2.com) bound for Miyanoura also depart from Kagoshima New Port once every morning and return in the afternoon (4 hours; ¥4,900 one-way, ¥8,900 round-trip).

GETTING AROUND

The easiest way to navigate Yakushima is by **rental car,** with rental shops at Miyanoura port and at Yakushima Airport.

If you're not planning to have your own car, buses also move about once per hour around the main road that runs around Yakushima's coast. There are two bus operators: **Tanegashima-Yakushima Kotsu** and **Matsubanda Kotsu** (www.yakushima.co.jp/index-5.php). You buy a pass for one day (¥2,000), two or three days (¥3,000), or four days (¥4,000) for buses operated by Tanegashima-Yakushima Kotsu. Inquire at either Miyanoura or Anbō bus terminal for details. Limited buses also run into the island's interior from Miyanoura and Anbō. Check the timetable at either bus terminal before making any journeys inland, as buses are often infrequent.

Okinawa-Hontō 沖縄本島

The biggest and most populated (1.3 million) island in the extensive Ryūkyū chain, Okinawa-Hontō was once the beating political heart of the Ryūkyū Kingdom. The island's elongated shape—120 kilometers (70 mi) from north to south with 476 kilometers (295 mi) of jagged coastline—inspired the name Okinawa, which literally translates as "offshore rope." The original inhabitants pictured it as a rope floating on the sea. Today the island is the main entry point for those traveling to the Ryūkyū Islands, with the capital city of Naha, on the southwest coast, being the main urban center.

South of Naha, memorials commemorate the horrific Battle of Okinawa and the island's pivotal role in World War II. In the central section of the island you'll find good beaches, particularly around the Motobu peninsula. And in the Yambaru region in the north, rustic fishing hamlets on the coast and farming villages in the verdant hills are home to some of the world's longest living people, with more than 30 centenarians per 100,000.

Controversially, the island is nearly 20 percent covered by U.S. military installations. Tokyo pays Washington $1.8 billion annually for the 27,000 service personnel currently based on the island. On one hand, this means ample access to overseas goods and a bit more widespread use of English than elsewhere in Japan. On the other hand, these bases are a constant reminder of ghosts of the island's past: American fighter jets and helicopters routinely whoosh through the otherwise calm skies over the island. An air crash in 2016 and a series of high-profile sexual and

Okinawa-Hontō

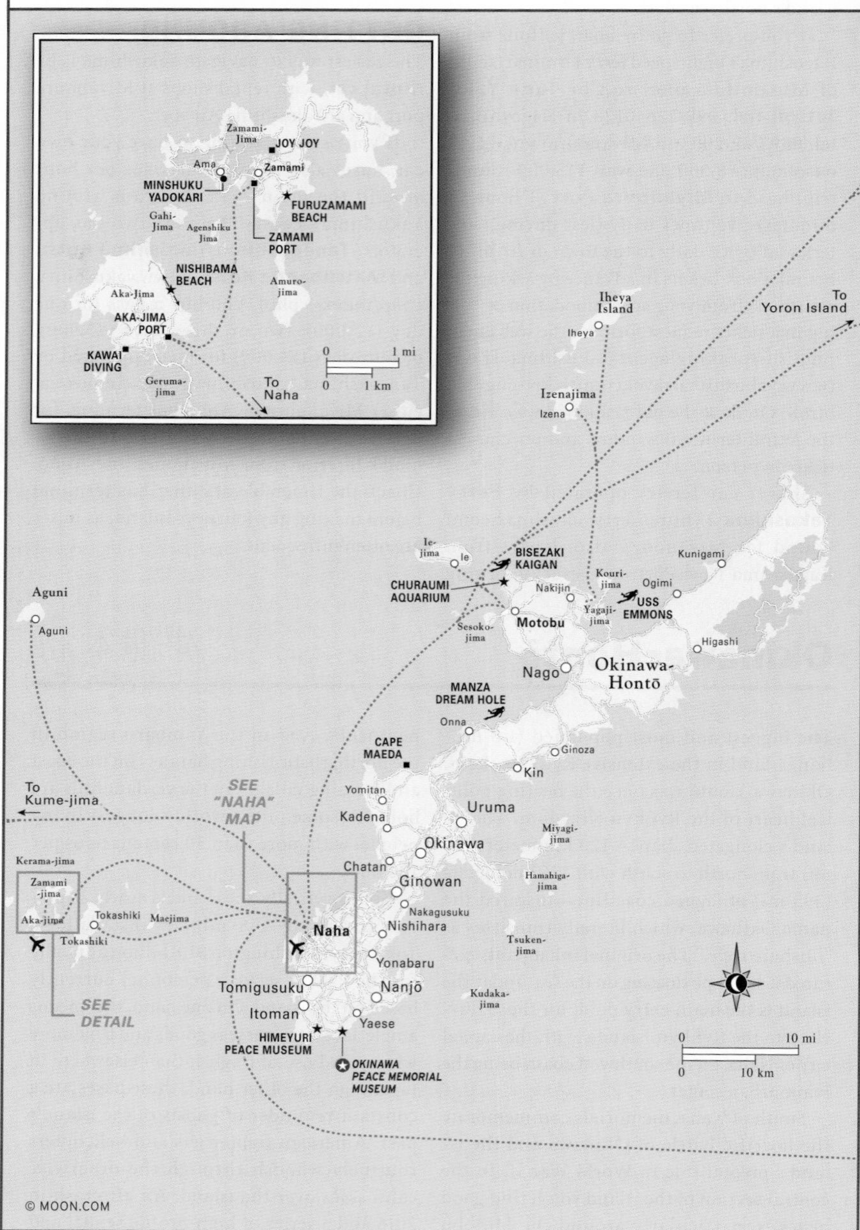

violent crimes committed by service personnel have exacerbated the tension, with the public pushing to remove the bases entirely. Aside from a handful of sites of cultural and historical significance, Okinawa-Hontō is best used as a base for traveling by boat or plane to other less intensely developed islands where old ways and pristine stretches of sand are in abundance.

NAHA

那覇

Naha, Okinawa's prefectural capital and its largest metropolis with a population of more than 300,000, is a thoroughly modern city, laid out on a grid after being rebuilt because of the city's utter destruction during World War II. Today, the concrete sprawl is defined at its western edge by Naha Ariport, with the bulk of downtown, centered on monorail stops such as Miebashi, Makishi, and Asato, roughly in the geographic heart of Naha proper, northeast of the airport. Within the city's heart are Makishi Public Market and Tsuboya Pottery Street, as well as Tomari Port. Okinawa Prefectural Museum sits at the northeastern edge of downtown, while Shuri Castle overlooks Naha from a hilltop east of downtown. The city's main thoroughfare is **Kokusai-dōri,** a lively if garish strip lined with restaurants, bars, clubs, and kitsch souvenir shops that cuts east to west through downtown. But veer off the main drag and you'll discover pockets of local color where Okinawan culture survives.

South of Kokusai-dōri are the bustling bazaars of **Ichiba-dōri** and **Heiwa-dōri,** as well as the raucous Makishi Public Market, overflowing with tropical seafood, fruits, and vegetables. You'll find a more homegrown side of the city wandering these rambling arcades and visiting the Tsuboya pottery district. At night, head to the charming if slightly run-down Sakaemachi Arcade and the surrounding streets lined with tumble-down bars and restaurants full of friendly locals.

Sights

SHURI-JŌ

首里城

1-2 Kinjō-chō; tel. 098/886-2020; http://oki-park.jp/shurijo; 8:30am-6pm daily free areas, 9am-5:30pm (last entry 5pm) paid areas; ¥400 adults, ¥300 high school students, ¥160 elementary and junior high school students, free for children under 6; take Okinawa Monorail to Shuri or Gibo station

Shuri Castle was wrecked in World War II, when it served as the Japanese military's headquarters, and then was rebuilt in 1992 and designated a UNESCO World Heritage Site. Unfortunately, Shuri Castle was very badly damaged by a devastating fire in October 2019. Efforts to rebuild this precious cultural landmark are ongoing, with the reconstruction expected to be completed in 2026.

Today, the outer walls, some gates, and the surrounding park can be visited for free. As you approach the inner sanctum, however, parts of which require an entrance fee, you'll be met with views of rubble and building materials where the majestic main keep, now a shell of its former self, once stood. The choice whether to visit or not depends largely on your interest in history. If you are coming mainly for an awe-inspiring sight, you'll likely be disappointed. But for a lesson on the history of the Ryūkyū Kingdom, the museum in the paid area gives a good rundown. For a free, suggested walking course through the castle ground as it stands, visit https://oki-park.jp/shurijo/en/info/4860.

Until the fire, this was one of the few visual reminders of the Ryūkyū Kingdom left in Okinawa. Overlooking Naha's urban sprawl from a hilltop, the original structure was constructed in the late 14th century during the rise of the Ryūkyū kings, who maintained it as their base of power until Okinawa was formally annexed by Japan in the 19th century.

To reach Shuri Castle, take the Okinawa Monorail to Shuri station. Exit on the west side and descend the staircase to street level. Walk straight ahead from here, crossing first a busy thoroughfare and then a second street. Turn right here and walk along the

Naha

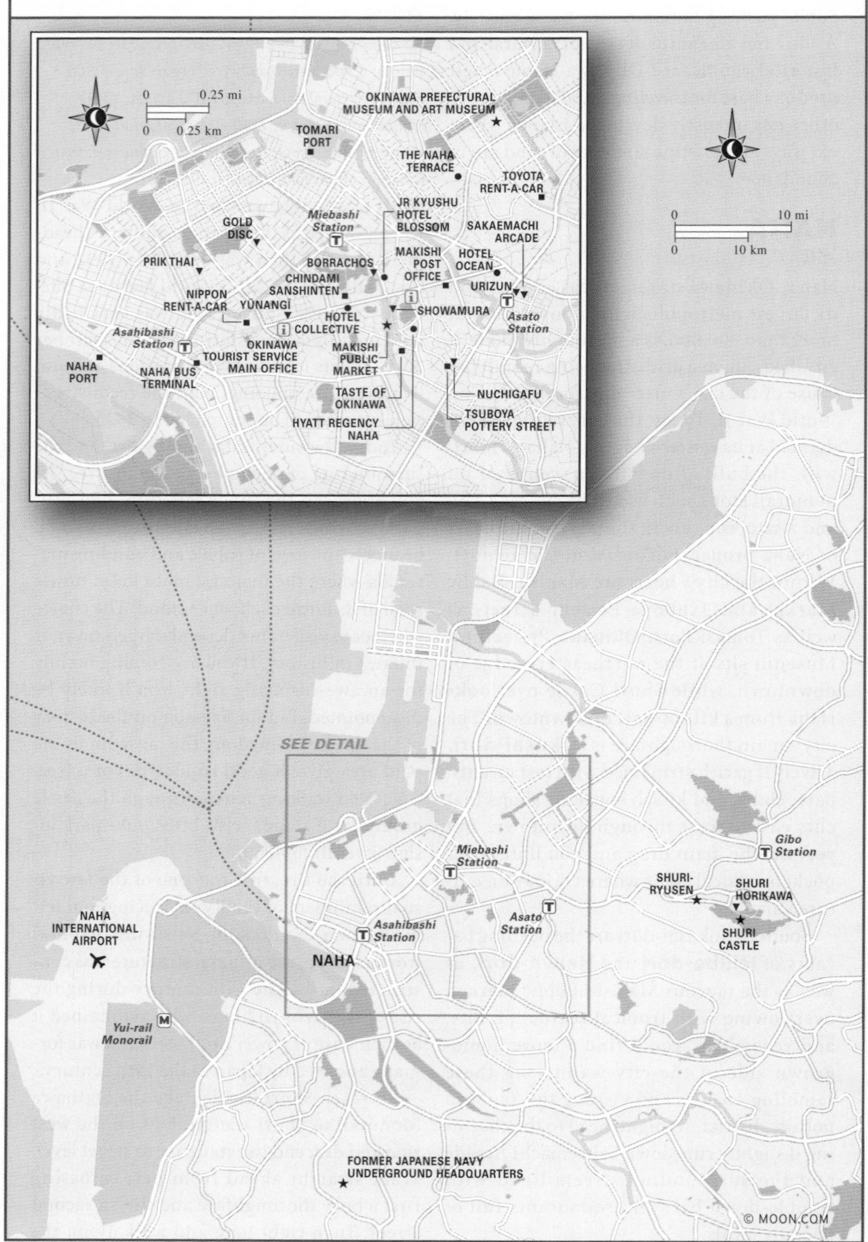
0 0.25 mi
0 0.25 km
OKINAWA PREFECTURAL MUSEUM AND ART MUSEUM
TOMARI PORT
THE NAHA TERRACE
TOYOTA RENT-A-CAR
JR KYUSHU HOTEL BLOSSOM
GOLD DISC
Miebashi Station
SAKAEMACHI ARCADE
PRIK THAI
BORRACHOS
MAKISHI POST OFFICE
HOTEL OCEAN
CHINDAMI SANSHINTEN
URIZUN
NIPPON RENT-A-CAR
YŪNANGĪ
SHOWAMURA
HOTEL COLLECTIVE
Asato Station
Asahibashi Station
OKINAWA TOURIST SERVICE MAIN OFFICE
MAKISHI PUBLIC MARKET
NAHA PORT
NAHA BUS TERMINAL
TASTE OF OKINAWA
NUCHIGAFU
HYATT REGENCY NAHA
TSUBOYA POTTERY STREET
0 10 mi
0 10 km
SEE DETAIL
Miebashi Station
Gibo Station
SHURI-RYUSEN
SHURI HORIKAWA
Asato Station
Asahibashi Station
SHURI CASTLE
NAHA INTERNATIONAL AIRPORT
NAHA
Yui-rail Monorail
FORMER JAPANESE NAVY UNDERGROUND HEADQUARTERS
© MOON.COM

left side of this second smaller street until you see signs pointing the way to Shuri Castle, which is on the hillside to the left of this street. The walk should take about 15 minutes. Alternatively, take the monorail to Gibo Station, from where it's about 10 minutes' walk south.

OKINAWA PREFECTURAL MUSEUM AND ART MUSEUM
沖縄県博物館・美術館

3-1-1 Omoromachi, Naha; tel. 098/941-8200; http://okimu.jp; 9am-6pm Tues.-Thurs. and Sun., 9am-8pm Fri.-Sat.; museum ¥410 adults, ¥260 high school and college students, ¥150 elementary and junior high students; art museum ¥310 adults, ¥210 high school and college students, ¥100 elementary and junior high students; ride monorail to Omoromachi station, then walk 10 minutes northwest

These museums provide a fantastic introduction to Okinawa's rich, varied history and culture. There's a history section and a wing dedicated to Okinawa's unique cultural and artistic heritage in this complex, which opened in 2007. Included are English-language explanations beside the Japanese.

The historical side begins in pre-Ryūkyū times and traces the natural and archaeological records up to the modern age, taking in traditional crafts and folklore along the way. The slightly smaller art museum has a more contemporary edge, displaying paintings, sculptures, and video pieces throughout a number of galleries. Alongside its permanent collection, special exhibits with additional entrance fees are occasionally held.

FORMER JAPANESE NAVY UNDERGROUND HEADQUARTERS
旧海軍司令部壕

236 Aza Tomishiro, Tomigusuku; tel. 098/850-4055; http://kaigungou.ocvb.or.jp; 8:30am-5pm daily Oct.-Jun., 8:30am-5:30pm daily Jul.-Sept.; ¥440 adults, ¥220 children; take bus no. 55 or 98 to Tomigusuku Minami bus stop (20 minutes, ¥260), then walk 5 minutes

These underground tunnels south of Naha give a dismal glimpse into the dank space—dug entirely with hand tools—where the Japanese navy ran their operations in the final days of the war. Displays of naval documents, weapons (including a crudely handmade spear), uniforms, and soldiers' letters to their families tell the story of Admiral Ota and his 174 men, all of whom met their demise in this cold, bleak labyrinth of tunnels

Shuri-jō

in June 1945, as the war's end drew close. Ota and his commanding officers committed suicide, while some 400 sailors were either killed by grenade blasts or took their own lives toward the final days of the war. It's a sobering testament to the horrors of war. Outside the museum, a monument at the top of a hill overlooking Naha and the ocean beyond commemorates the men whose lives were lost at this site.

Sports and Recreation

OKINAWAN SUP

http://okinawansup.com/; tours start from around ¥5,000

If you're not going to make it to the Kerama Islands but would like to do something active closer to Naha, reach out to gregarious, deeply knowledgable local guide Shion, who runs a Naha-based private tour service called Okinawan SUP. He primarily focuses on stand-up paddling (SUP), but also leads waterfall hikes and has led literally thousands of snorkeling and diving trips around the archipelago. He speaks basic English and has explored every nook and cranny of the island. Inquire directly for tour availability and pricing.

Shopping

TSUBOYA POTTERY STREET

1-21-14 Tsuboya; take Okinawa Monorail to Makishi station, then walk 10 minutes south

Tsuboya Pottery Street is an atmospheric thoroughfare that has been at the center of Naha's thriving ceramics trade since 1682. Today, the shops along this historic street hawk decorative objects, thimble-sized awamori cups, and pairs of leonine shisa guardian figurines: The one with its mouth agape welcomes good fortune, while the one with mouth closed keeps it from escaping. **Kiyomasa Toki** (1-16-7 Tsuboya; tel. 098/862-3654; 10am-7pm daily), a shop with 320 years of history, stands out. Whether you're shopping or not, it's worth strolling down this street to soak up the atmosphere.

CHINDAMI SANSHINTEN

1-2-18 Makishi; tel. 098/869-2055; http://chindami.com; 11am-8pm daily; take Okinawa Monorail to Miebashi station, then walk 7 minutes south

After a few days in Okinawa, if the haunting sound of the three-stringed sanshin has seeped sufficiently into your brain that you are intrigued by the possibility of learning to play the instrument yourself, you're not alone. Chinadami Sanshinten, situated down a side street about 10 minutes' walk south of Miebashi monorail station, is the best place in Naha to peruse models of this lacquer-necked banjo-like instrument covered in python skin. Owner Higa-san is a sanshin-maker renowned for his craft. He doesn't speak English, but happily offers a basic lesson to anyone with a hankering to learn.

SHURI-RYUSEN

1-54 Shuri Yamagawa-chō; tel. 098/886-1131; www.shuri-ryusen.com; 9am-6pm daily; walk 15 minutes south of Gibo station

Shuri Ryusen is a wonderful, family-owned shop that sells Okinawa's hand-painted, batik-like variety of textile known as bingata. The first floor of this handsome building is overflowing with vivid handbags, pillows, handkerchiefs, scrolls, and much more. DIY workshops are held on the second floor, while the masters can be seen at work on the third floor. It's a 10-minute walk west of Shuri Castle.

Food

MAKISHI PUBLIC MARKET
第一牧志公設市場

2-10-1 Matsuo; https://kosetsu-ichiba.com; 10am-8pm daily; take Okinawa Monorail to Makishi station, then walk 12 minutes southwest

For a look into Okinawa's collective kitchen, be sure to stroll through Makishi Public Market. This bustling bazaar branches off south of the covered shopping arcade known as Ichibahon-dōri that runs south of Kokusai-dōri. Fishmongers hawk lobsters, scarlet octopus, and parrotfish, while produce merchants offload local vegetables, mangoes, papaya, and pineapples. Upstairs, hole-in-the-wall eateries will prepare fish you've just bought downstairs. All told, some 400 shops fill the rowdy marketplace, which has an atmosphere more akin to Bangkok than anywhere in mainland Japan. Though the market has become mostly geared toward tourists in recent years, it's still worth passing through as you explore the area.

SHURI HORIKAWA

1-27 Shuri Mawashi-chō; tel. 098/886-3032; 11am-4pm or until sold out Fri.-Wed.; ¥1,000; walk 12 minutes south of Gibo Station

This reasonably priced local favorite serves hot bowls of homemade Okinawan soba noodles in a mild broth with all the fixings (spring onion, fresh ginger). Tucked away in a residential area, the cozy wooden interior is an appealing place to sample this quintessential soul food before or after visiting Shuri Castle.

PRIK THAI

2-20-21 Kume; tel. 098/800-2227; www.facebook.com/prikthaicollab/; noon-2:30pm and 6pm-11pm Thurs.-Tues.; ¥1,000 lunch, ¥2,500 dinner; take Okinawa Monorail to Prefectural Office station, then walk 9 minutes northwest

The Thai-born chef at the helm of this cozy eatery rustles up excellent Thai cuisine, from soups and curries to sticky rice, pork-herb-spice medleys, and deep-fried spring rolls. The flavors—salty, bitter, sour, sweet, and spicy—are well-balanced, and everything is made with the right touch. On the drinks menu, you'll find a decent selection of Southeast Asian beers, lassis, and more. Recommended.

BORRACHOS

1F Taihei Bldg., 1-3-31 Makishi; tel. 098/800-2227; 11am-2:30pm and 5pm-2:30am Mon.-Thurs., 11am-2:30pm and 5pm-4:30am Fri.-Sat., 11am-2:30pm and 5pm-1:30am Sun.; http://borrachos.jp; ¥1,100-2,600; take Okinawa Monorail to Miebashi station, then walk 5 minutes southeast

This chic, atmospheric Mexican restaurant serves a savory range of appetizers and main dishes: jalapeño poppers, nachos, quesadillas, tacos (hard and soft shell), burritos, enchiladas, and more. Some of the dishes have an Okinawan touch, like local mainstay taco rice. The extensive drinks menu has a varied tequila list and a pleasing mix of Mexican and Latin American cocktails. Everything is made with garden-fresh ingredients—guacamole is mashed with mortar and pestle at the table—and liberal dollops of refried beans, cheese, and sour cream. Staff are hip and friendly. Reservations are recommended.

★ NUCHIGAFU

1-28-3 Tsuboya; tel. 098/861-2952; https://bukubuku.okinawa/; 11:30am-5pm and 5:30pm-10pm Wed.-Mon.; ¥1,200 tea set, ¥3,000 dinner; take Okinawa Monorail to Makishi station, the walk 10 minutes south

For something more refined, head to Nuchigafu, a restaurant and teahouse located down an alley at the southeastern edge of the atmospheric Tsuboya Pottery Street. Set in a beautiful historic building, the restaurant, which serves tasty Okinawan set meals, is primarily known for its bukubuku cha. This local specialty drink is a tea made of polished white rice (occasionally substituted with brown rice) with an unlikely top layer of mashed peanuts. The cold beverage is served in a lacquer bowl and stirred with a bamboo whisk that produces a layer of foam on top; it's refreshing and unique. Combine a stop here with your visit to the nearby pottery street.

URIZUN

388-5 Asato; tel. 098/885-2178; http://urizun.okinawa/index.html; 5:30pm-midnight daily; ¥3,000; walk 3 minutes northeast of Asato monorail station

Urizun is a great down-home izakaya (pub) serving up Okinawan classics in the heart of Naha. Dark wood tables and walls, jars of awamori lined up on shelves, and tatami floors create a cozy vibe. Anything on the menu (which has pictures, but is not in English), will be good. Try the rafute (soft pork belly left to stew in brown sugar and soy sauce) or any one of the chanpuru dishes.

Have your hotel front desk reserve a table for you a day or more beforehand to be safe.

★ YŪNANGĪ

3-3-3 Kumoji; tel. 098/867-3765; 12pm-3pm and 5:30pm-10:30pm Mon.-Sat.; lunch ¥1,000, dinner ¥4,000; take Okinawa Monorail to Prefectural Office station, then walk 5 minutes east

At Yūnangī, diners seated at tables, on tatami mats, and along the open-kitchen bar are treated to some of Naha's tastiest local eats. Bitter gourd stir-fries, soba noodles, pork ribs, fried fish, seaweed, peanut tofu, and much more can be washed down with selections from their veritible stash of awamori. The friendly staff are eager to help and the menu has basic English translations. Be ready to wait for a seat, as this spot has made a name for itself. Reservations are unfortunately not taken. The prices are slightly higher than some local spots, but portion sizes are fair and the quality justifies it.

Nightlife

SHOWAMURA

3-1-20 Makishi; tel. 098/866-0106; 5pm-1am Mon.-Fri., 5pm-3am Sat.-Sun.; take Okinawa Monorail to Makishi station, then walk 8 minutes west

A highlight of any trip to Okinawa should include a night out at a bar or restaurant with a live band playing Ryūkyū minyo, as the islands' folk music is called. Showamura is a boisterous, down-and-dirty izakaya, beloved by travelers from the Japanese mainland. Performances last 30 minutes and take place on the hour at 8pm, 9pm, and 10pm. Ascend the stairs to the third floor where you'll find a large tatami space full of low tables, and a platform in back with horigotatsu seating (low tables with recessed floor underneath). There's a food menu of the islands' classics and an extensive awamori menu. Don't expect gourmet fare, but feel free to try a few casual nibbles if you're hungry. Otherwise, go for booze, which goes down well with the spirited music, including a nomihōdai (all you can drink) deal for ¥1,000. With the right crowd, the restaurant will be on its feet by the end of the night.

GOLD DISC

B1 Matsu-machi Peatsuti Bldg., 1-14-19 Matsuyama; tel. 098/868-1268; 6pm-1am Mon.-Thurs., 6pm-2am Fri.-Sat., 6pm-midnight Sun.; ¥1,500 cover; take Okinawa Monorail to Miebashi station, then walk 10 minutes west

Gold Disc is an institution. Situated in a somewhat sordid area, this bouncing music club hosts nightly bands that rock out hits from the 1950s and 1960s, from Elvis to Ray Charles and the Supremes. Think guitarists with ducktails and dancers in polka-dotted circle skirts.

SAKAEMACHI ARCADE

381 Asato; tel. 098/886-3979; walk 2 minutes northeast of Asato monorail station

If you feel like having a little urban adventure, head to the Sakaemachi Arcade. The area is a marketplace by day, but from 6pm on, izakaya, ramshackle bars, and hazy yakitori joints fill with a diverse crowd. Mom-and-pop shops, tucked down covered lanes snaking around the market area, give glimpses of another side of Naha. Rather than go to a specific bar, just wander the lanes and enter any place that draws you in.

Accommodations

JR KYUSHU HOTEL BLOSSOM

2-16-1 Makishi; tel. 098/861-8700; www.jrk-hotels.co.jp/Naha/; ¥12,000 d with breakfast; take Okinawa Monorail to Miebashi station, then walk 5 minutes southeast

This elegant, affordable property is right in the heart of the action downtown, just a five-minute walk south of Miebashi Station and one minute on foot from Kokusai-dōri. Decor is chic with traditional elements, and amenities include an inviting lounge with a terrace, a relaxation salon, and a restaurant.

HOTEL COLLECTIVE

2-5-7 Matsuo; tel. 098/860-8382; https://hotelcollective.jp; twin rooms from ¥15,000 (breakfast included); take Okinawa Monorail to Miebashi station, then walk 9 minutes south

This new boutique hotel is a refined spot to

Awamori, Okinawan Firewater

Okinawa's local firewater, awamori, is a distant cousin of vodka, whisky, and rum that packs a serious punch: It's typically in the range of 60-80 proof. (Some of the fiercest labels sport a proof as high as 120.) There are many takes on the liquor, which is infused with ingredients from spices to honey. The liquor is based on Thai Indica rice, highlighting Okinawa's proximity to Southeast Asia. The rice is fermented in a yeast extract called **koji** before being single-distilled. A high-end bottle of awamori is aged in a clay jar in the dark, cool recesses of a cave for upwards of three years. One of these prized bottles can set you back tens of thousands of yen (hundreds of dollars). Whatever variety of awamori you order, drink it on the rocks, neat, or **mizu-wari** (its bite softened with water).

And if you ever enter a bar in the southwest islands and spot a jar with a coiled pit viper inside, beware. This is **habushu,** named after the habu pit viper and a dramatic variety of awamori. If you do take the habushu plunge, know that you'll be rewarded for your courage. This serpentine spirit is believed to bestow physical healing or—ahem—stamina.

Pro tip: when saying "cheers" in Okinawa, "kampai" works just fine. But if you want to impress your drinking companions by using the local tongue, raise your glass and offer a hearty "kari!" (kah-ree).

stay right on Kokusai-dōri. Located 10 minutes' walk from both Miebashi Station and Makishi Station, the sleek rooms are spacious by Japanese standards, with well-appointed bathrooms (some graced by whirlpool tubs). There's also an outdoor pool, a fitness room, a sauna, a spa, four eateries, and a cocktail lounge.

HOTEL OCEAN

2-4-8 Asato; tel. 098/863-2288; www.hotelocean.okinawa; ¥15,000; take Okinawa Monorail to Makishi station, then walk 4 minutes east

Hotel Ocean is a sound choice for a mid-range place to bunk down in the center of Naha. Only four minutes' walk from Makishi monorail station, the hotel has both Japanese- (tatami) and Western-style rooms. The Makishi Public Market is only seven minutes away on foot. Staff are friendly and the environment is family-friendly, with a children's play space on the first floor. Okinawan-style breakfast is served.

★ THE NAHA TERRACE

2-14-1 Omoromachi; tel. 098/864-1111; www.terrace.co.jp/en/naha; ¥18,000 twin; take Okinawa Monorail to Makishi station, then walk 11 minutes north

The Naha Terrace is a great hotel that's within walking distance of basically everywhere you'll want to go within the city, yet it is just far enough from the bustle to feel private, even quiet. It offers Western- and Japanese-style breakfasts, a bar with live jazz every night, and staff who are chipper and eager to help. There are small decorative touches throughout, like tropical flowers in the lobby and large windows overlooking the city in the upper-level rooms, many of which have large soaking tubs.

HYATT REGENCY NAHA

3-6-20 Makishi; tel. 098/866-8888; https://naha.regency.hyatt.com; ¥25,000 twin; take Okinawa Monorail to Makishi station, then walk 8 minutes southwest

Hyatt Regency Naha offers luxury at a relatively low price. Only open since 2015, this new hotel is in a good location between Makishi monorail station (eight minutes' walk) and Tsuboya Pottery Street (three minutes' walk), and is less than five minutes' stroll from Kokusai-dōri too. The hotel is not quite as luxe as some locations in the Hyatt chain, but the price tag isn't as high either.

Information and Services

- **Okinawa Tourist Service Main Office** (1-2-3 Matsuo; tel. 098/862-1111; www.otsinfo.co.jp/branch/honten.html; 9:30am-7:30pm Mon.-Fri.; 9:30am-4:30pm Sat., three-minute walk from Prefectural Office monorail station)
- **Tourist Information Office** (3-2-10 Makishi; tel. 098/868-4887; 9am-8pm daily)
- **Makishi Post Office** (3-13-19 Makishi; tel. 098/863-3880; 9am-5pm Mon.-Fri., just outside Makishi monorail station on Kokusai-dōri)

Getting There

Naha is easily accessed by plane, with daily flights coming into its **Naha International Airport** from Tokyo, Osaka, Nagoya, Fukuoka, Kagoshima, and more. Domestic flights can be quite cheap if booked more than a month in advance (e.g., as little as ¥10,000 or less one-way on discount airlines such as Vanilla Air, Jetstar Japan, and Skymark). Coming from abroad, direct flights also make the journey from Taipei, Hong Kong, Shanghai, and Seoul. There's a tourist information counter (tel. 098/857-6884; 9am-9pm daily) in the first-floor arrivals terminal. The airport is located west of downtown, accessible via Naha Airport Station on the monorail, an easy ride of about 15-20 minutes to most major stations.

It's far less convenient, but you can travel to Naha by ferry, arriving in **Naha Port** (10-minute walk south of Asahibashi monorail station) from Kagoshima. Operated by **A Line Ferry** (tel. 099/226-4141; www.aline-ferry.com) and **Marix Line** (tel. 099/225-1551; www.marix-line.co.jp), these ferries depart from Kagoshima New Port every other day and make the 25-hour journey to Naha. Fares range from about ¥15,000 for second class and from about ¥29,000 for first class. On the ferry, there are sleeping quarters and a restaurant that serves no-frills meals, as well as vending machines and a small shop. Note that Naha Port is different from **Tomari Port**, which is eight minutes' walk north of Miebashi Station on the monorail and is the one used to access the neighboring Kerama Islands.

Getting Around

Naha's Yui-rail **monorail** is the only form of public transport beyond buses in Okinawa-Hontō. Most of the city's attractions are easily accessed by the monorail, which is cheap and runs right through the center of downtown. The monorail line begins at Naha International Airport in the city's south and ends at Shuri, near Shuri Castle, in the north. Single journeys range in cost from ¥150 to ¥330, and an unlimited pass can be purchased for one day (¥800 adults, ¥400 children) or two days (¥1,400 adults, ¥700 children). Ask for details at any monorail station.

Besides the monorail, Naha also has a city **bus** network, but navigating it can be confusing; stick to the monorail when possible. Of course, **taxis** are available too, which can be a decent option when you're in a hurry, given that distances between most places aren't too prohibitive—quick trips around Naha can be made for ¥1,000-1,500. Better yet, **walking** from Prefectural Office Station on the west side of downtown to Asato Station in the east takes only about 25 minutes. Besides the Shuri Castle area, most sights, restaurants, shops, and nightlife are a stroll away.

Though regional buses do travel around the island, leaving from **Naha Bus Terminal** (1-chōme-20 Izumizaki), just south of Asahibashi monorail station, the easiest way to get around the island by far is to simply rent a car. Pick one up in the arrivals hall at Naha Airport. If you're already in Naha and haven't rented one yet, head to **Nippon Rent-a-Car** (1-1-1 Kumoji; tel. 098/867-4554; www.nrgroup-global.com; 8am-8pm daily) just outside the Prefectural Office monorail station. Another option is a branch of **Toyota Rent-a-Car** (4-1 Omoromachi; tel. 098/860-1530; https://rent.toyota.co.jp; 9am-8pm daily) just outside Omoromachi monorail station.

SOUTH OF NAHA

The area south of Naha, colloquially known as Nanbu, was the setting where the bloody Battle of Okinawa, which lasted from April-June 1945, saw its last days play out. Japanese troops held out as long as they could, as U.S. forces invaded and overtook the island. The death toll was stratospheric, with some 200,000 people, including more than 100,000 civilians and 12,500 U.S. troops, dying in the battle.

Museums and monuments dot the area south of Naha, providing a somber reminder of the horrific battle and paying tribute to those who died in the fighting, from soldiers committing mass suicide to civilians trapped in the crossfire. For a sense of the profound scar left on Okinawa's psyche by the war, make time for a half-day or day trip to the island's deep south, where some of the bloodiest combat took place.

Sights

War memorials are spread across the town of **Itoman,** occupying the southern tip of the island, centered on **Peace Memorial Park** (444 Mabuni, Itoman; tel. 098/997-2765; https://heiwa-irei-okinawa.jp; 24 hours; free). This park sprawls over Mabuni Hill, where the horrific Battle of Okinawa came to an end. Within this immense park, which offers spectacular views of the Pacific, you'll find a 12-meter-tall (39-ft-tall) lacquer Buddha statue, seated in repose on a giant lotus, in the **Okinawa Peace Hall** (448 Mabuni, Itoman; tel. 098/997-3011; www.okinawakyoukai.jp; 9am-5pm daily; ¥450 adults, ¥350 high school and junior high school students, free for elementary school students and younger); a meditative forest; the moving Peace Memorial Museum; and just south of the Peace Memorial Museum, the **Cornerstone of Peace** (614-1 Mabuni, Itoman; tel. 098/997-3738; dawn-dusk daily; free). Here, rows upon rows of granite slabs bear the names of all who died in the horrific battle, from Japanese civilians and soldiers to American, British, Taiwanese, and Korean civilians and service personnel.

★ OKINAWA PREFECTURAL PEACE MEMORIAL MUSEUM
沖縄県平和祈念資料館

614-1 Mabuni; tel. 098/997-3844; www.peace-museum.okinawa.jp/index.html; 9am-5pm daily; ¥300 adults, ¥150 children

On the eastern edge of Peace Memorial Park, facing the Pacific Ocean, this complex gives you a moving look at the days leading up to the bloody three-month Battle of Okinawa (a "typhoon of steel"), which was the largest fought in the Asia-Pacific theater during World War II; the horrors experienced by those who were caught in the battle itself (civilians and troops on both sides); and the long slog to rebuild Okinawa from rubble after the war. The museum's displays may feel one-sided on some points, but the overarching message of its exhibits is one that all can agree on: War is terrible and should be avoided at all cost. Clear English-language signage is available throughout the museum.

The harrowing material on display in its five main sections contrasts starkly with the lovely setting of the area today. The museum itself is a sprawling, bright complex with traditional Okinawan red roof tiles, neatly landscaped expansive grounds, and beautiful ocean views from its floor-to-ceiling windows. Some of the most moving exhibits in the museum are those that emotively reveal the human cost among civilians, who were not only under attack by U.S. forces but also brutalized by Japanese Imperial troops. Real objects from the war, photos, and film footage show just how much the island was marred by the "typhoon of steel" that bombarded it, even changing the very landscape itself in places. Personal testimonies from those who surivived the horror are also on display, providing a harrowing account of what was experienced by those who survived. The museum also effectively tells the story of the postwar refugee camps and the transformation of Okinawa into an immense base for the U.S.

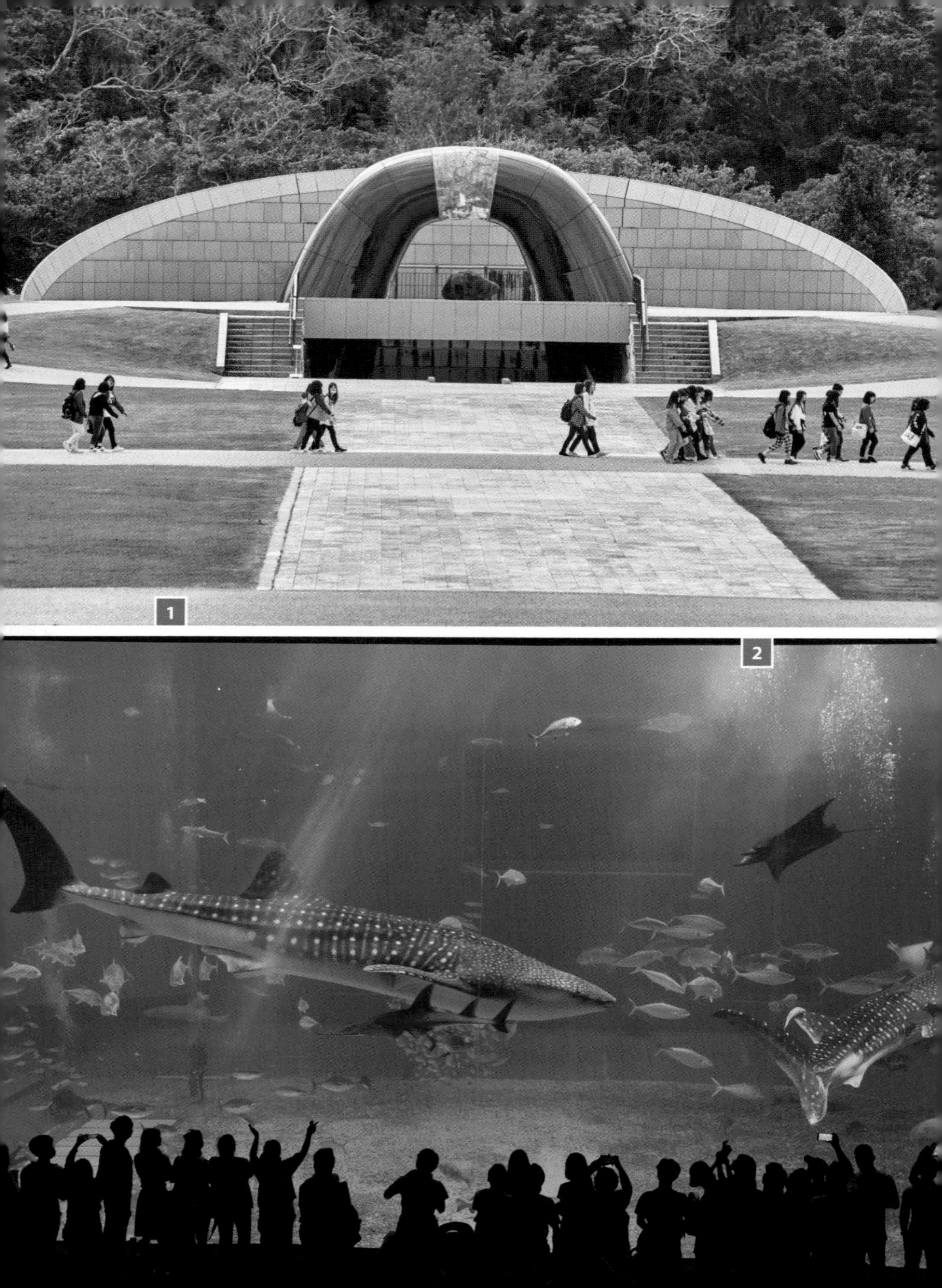
1
2

military as tensions ratcheted up during the Cold War era. Akin to the peace memorials and exhibits of Hiroshima and Nagasaki, it's a lot to take in, but there's no doubt it will move you and deepen your understanding.

To reach the museum, take bus no. 89 from Naha Bus Terminal outside Asahibashi monorail station to Itoman Bus Terminal (1 hour, departs several times hourly; ¥580). At Itoman, take bus no. 82 until Heiwakinendo Iriguchi bus stop (20 minutes, departs once or twice hourly; ¥470). By car, it's about a 35-minute drive (about 20 km/12 mi) south of central Naha on Prefectural Route 15.

HIMEYURI PEACE MUSEUM
ひめゆり平和祈念資料館

671-1 Ihara; tel. 098/997-2100; www.himeyuri.or.jp; 9am-5:30pm daily; ¥310 adults, ¥210 high school students, ¥110 elementary and junior high school students; take bus no. 89 from Naha Bus Terminal to Itoman Bus Terminal (1 hour, ¥580), then transfer to bus number 82, 107, or 108 and ride to Himeyuri-no-to bus stop (20 minutes, once or twice hourly, ¥320)

The Himeyuri Peace Museum commemorates the tragic experience of 240 high school-age girls who were forced to serve as nurses in the last months of the war, nursing maimed Japanese troops in hidden caves dotting the area around Itoman. The museum displays artifacts including some of the girls' pre-war diaries, with journal entries written during their time working under horrendous conditions as the battle raged on. A photographic portrait of each girl is also on display in the museum. The vast majority of the girls did not make it through the battle alive.

Getting There and Around

If you plan to venture south of Naha, there are regional **buses** running throughout the island. That said, the easiest way to get around the island by far is simply to rent a car. Given that the bulk of the sights in the island's south are found in Peace Memorial Park, the easiest way to access the area is by driving about 18 kilometers (11 mi) south of Naha on Prefectural Route 15 for a total trip time of about 35 minutes.

1: Okinawa Prefectural Peace Memorial Museum
2: Churaumi Aquarium

NORTH OF NAHA

A few hours' drive to the north of Naha, the Motobu Peninsula offers a very different set of attractions. In the heart of the peninsula is Ocean Expo Park, where you'll find the fantastic, if crowded, **Churaumi Aquarium.** And off the coast of the small neighboring island of Kōri-jima, divers can explore underwater wreckage from World War II.

Sights

CHURAUMI AQUARIUM
美ら海水族館

424 Ishikawa, Motobu; tel. 0980/48-3748; http://oki-churaumi.jp; 8:30am-8pm daily Mar.-Sept., 8:30am-6:30pm daily Oct.-Feb.; ¥1,850 adults, ¥1,230 high school students, ¥610 elementary and junior high school students; after 4pm ¥1,290 adults, ¥860 high school students, ¥430 elementary and junior high school students

This truly massive aquarium on the Motobu Peninsula is an awe-inspiring collection of marine life. Part of **Ocean Expo Park** (424 Ishikawa, Motobu; https://oki-park.jp/kaiyohaku/; 8am-6pm daily; fees vary by attraction), which also includes a tropical arboretum, a reproduced traditional Okinawan village, the Oceanic Cultural Museum, a beach, and more, Churaumi is the undisputed champion of Japanese aquariums. The Kuroshio Tank is among the world's biggest, with gigantic whale sharks swimming inside along with majestic manta rays and small schools of multihued tropical fish.

To access the aquarium by car—about two hours' drive one-way—take the Okinawa Expressway (¥1,020 one-way) to Nago at its northern end. From there, take local roads running through the Motobu Peninsula to Ocean Expo Park. If you don't have your own wheels, take the Yanbaru Express Bus (http://yanbaru-expressbus.com; ¥2,000 one-way), which goes directly to the aquarium from Kenchō Kitaguchi (Okinawa Prefectural Office) bus stop, a few minutes' walk south of the Prefectural Office monorail station (2 hours; 1-2 buses hourly). Alternatively, take Expressway bus no. 117 from Naha Bus Terminal just outside Asahibashi monorail station (1-2 buses hourly; 2 hours; ¥2,550 one-way), which runs all the way to Kinen Kōen Mae bus stop in front of Ocean Expo Park.

BISE FUKUGI TREE ROAD

389 Bise; tel. 0980/47-3641; www.motobu-ka.com/tourist_info/tourist_info-post-687/; open 24 hours; free

If you make the trip to the aquarium, you should take time to walk about 15 minutes north to the small hamlet of Bise. This little slice of traditional Okinawa has a famous, 1-kilometer-long (0.6-mi-long) path, Bise Fukugi Tree Road, lined with fukugi trees (evergreens found throughout East and Southeast Asia). More than 200 red-tile-roof homes dot the area. To reach this little pocket of residential bliss, walk north from the aquarium on Route 114 for about 10 minutes, following the signs pointing the way to Bise Fukugi Tree Road and veering left at the fork in the road in front of Hotel Orion Motobu Resort and Spa Galaxy. Passing by the hotel on your left, continue along this road for another five minutes or so until you reach the tunnel of shrubbery. Here, wander and soak up the ambience. This is what Okinawa was before concrete crept in.

Beaches

EMERALD BEACH

424 Ishikawa, Motobu; tel. 0980/48-2741; open 24 hours; free

Another beautiful spot about 15 minutes' walk (1 km/0.6 mi) from the aquarium, also accessed through Ocean Expo Park, is Emerald Beach. Occupying the park's northern fringe, this pristine white-sand beach is nestled in a lagoon, with crystal-clear azure waters. It routinely gets mentioned among Japan's best swimming beaches. There are free showers, lockers (¥100-500), parasols (¥515), and folding beach beds (¥515) available for rent.

Diving and Snorkeling

There are some excellent diving opportunities north of Naha, along the western coast of Okinawa-Hontō. About 50 minutes' drive north of Naha, **Cape Maeda** is one of the island's most popular diving spots, known for its underwater Blue Cave and colorful schools of fish. Note that this popular spot is beginner-friendly.

Farther up the island's west coast, a fantastic dive of intermediate difficulty is the **Manza Dream Hole.** Descend about 6 meters (20 ft) and enter an expansive chamber teeming with thousands of marine creatures. Exit through a wall of fish, past fan corals and garden eels poking their heads out of the sand below. For something even more challenging, advanced divers can consider going farther north to the final resting place of the sunken American warship the ***USS Emmons,*** off the coast of Kōri-jima, a speck of land near the northeastern coast of the Motobu Peninsula. The ship is 100 meters (328 ft) long and remains largely intact.

Finally, not far from Bise Fukugi Tree road (about 0.9 km/0.5 mi, 11 minutes on foot or a 4-minute drive), you'll come to **Bisezaki Kaigan,** a great snorkeling spot teeming with colorful tropical fish (damselfish, butterfly fish, and more). But be sure to bring your own snorkeling equipment, and note there is no lifeguard on duty (life jackets should be worn at high tide). You should also wear marine shoes as the rocky, coral-blanketed seafloor in the area is quite rough. There are basic facilities onsite, including free parking and bathrooms, and showers that can be used for a small fee.

English-speaking dive outfits operating in the region include:

- **Piranha Divers** (tel. 098/967-8487; www.piranha-divers.jp)
- **Reef Encounters** (tel. 098/995-9414; www.reefencounters.org)

- **Natural Blue Diving Company** (tel. 090/9497-7374; www.natural-blue.net/jp)

Getting There and Around

You can hop on one of the regional buses (Yanbaru Express and bus line 117) running throughout the island to head north, usually departing from Naha Bus Terminal or in front of Naha Prefectural Office, but the easiest way to get around the island is renting a car. With your own wheels, follow the Okinawa Expressway from Naha north to Nago (¥1,040 tolls). From there, local roads spread across the Motobo Peninsula and lead to Churaumi Aquarium and beyond. The total trip time is around two hours, give or take, depending on traffic.

Kerama Islands 慶良間諸島

TOP EXPERIENCE

Only 35 kilometers (22 mi) west of Okinawa-Hontō, the Kerama Islands are the first port of call for those venturing to Okinawa's sakishima (outer islands). These islands—some 20 in all—are renowned for their crystal-clear waters, teeming with manta rays, sea turtles, and tropical fish that beckon divers and snorkelers. Start your exploration of the Keramas on Zamami-jima. This is the island with the most businesses, including diving outfits, mom-and-pop restaurants, and a smattering of B&Bs, as well as Zamami Beach, which has the best amenities in the island chain. This island is already relatively unspoiled, but if you go just a bit farther, to the small spit of land known as Aka-jima, you'll discover some of the most pristine, uncrowded beaches and best waters for diving in all of Japan.

ZAMAMI-JIMA
座間味島

Zamami-jima, the most developed of the lovely Kerama Islands, is less than an hour from Naha by jet foil or about two hours by normal ferry. Scattered around its 24-kilometer (14.9-mi) circumference (16.74 sq km/6.5 sq mi), the curvy island's beaches are excellent places to swim or relax under a parasol in the sand, which is why most people come to the island. If you want to stay overnight on one of the Kereama islands, it has the most B&Bs, some of which offer snorkeling and diving tours. The island's best beach is Furuzamami Beach, located about 1.3 kilometers (0.8 mi), or about 25 minutes' walk, southeast of the port and main village of the island. Bicycle rentals and all other businesses you'll need to access are conveniently clustered in the main village beside the port, in the island's south, where you'll find a well-stocked tourist information center with maps and more.

Beaches

FURUZAMAMI BEACH

20-minute walk southeast of the port and main village on the island

The island's prime sweep of oceanfront is Furuzamami Beach. This pristine expanse of white sand goes on for about 700 meters (2,300 ft). Showers, toilets, food vendors, and snorkel rentals (¥1,000) make it a convenient choice for a day at the beach for those coming from Naha. Note that the beach is on the other side of a sizable hill when coming from the port. Buses make the trip once hourly (5 minutes; ¥300), but a more enjoyable option is renting an electrically assisted bicycle in the village and getting there on two wheels. Bring a towel, but otherwise, you'll find a well-stocked beach house with a nice elevated wooden deck and all the needed amenities for a full day at the beach.

GAHI-JIMA AND AGENASHIKU-JIMA

While Furuzamami Beach is by no means thronged with crowds throughout most of the year, it can become slightly crowded in summer. If you yearn for a bit more isolation, board a boat at Zamami-jima's port and ride about five minutes (¥1,500 round-trip) south to the two tiny neighboring islands of Gahi-jima and Agenashiku-jima. The beaches on these smaller islands lack the amenities of Furuzamami Beach, but crowds are thinner and the crystal-clear water is home to abundant coral.

Diving and Whale-Watching

The turquoise waters of Zamami-jima and the small, neighboring islets of **Gahi-jima** and **Agenashiku-jima** are great for snorkeling and diving. The simplest option is to rent snorkeling gear at Furuzamami Beach, which has a decent range of coral not far offshore, but the following outfits offer more extensive options. Many of them are also guesthouses with lodging for divers.

- **Dive Center No-Y** (878 Zamami; tel. 098/987-3262; http://kerama-zamami.com; single boat dives from ¥5,400 plus equipment rental, two-hour whale-watching tour ¥5,400)
- **Dive-Inn-Hama** (97 Zamami; tel. 098/987-2013; http://diveinnhama.jp; boat dives from ¥6,000 plus equipment rental)
- **Joy Joy** (434-2 Zamami; tel. 098/987-2445; http://keramajoyjoy.com/eg/index.html; boat dives from ¥7,000 plus equipment rental)

Food

Zamami-jima, like most of Okinawa's farther-flung islands, becomes very sleepy at night. If you plan to spend the night, either confirm that your accommodation will be serving meals (most do), or be sure to visit one of the few restaurants offering dinner listed here. That said, if you're returning to Naha the same day, it's better to hop on a return ferry around 4-5pm and have dinner back on the main island, where you'll have significantly more options.

MARUMIYA

432-2 Zamami; tel. 098/987-3166; www.vill.zamami.okinawa.jp/guidemap/detail/138; 11am-2:30pm and 6pm-10:30pm Thurs.-Tues.; lunch specials from ¥800; walk 6 miles north of Zamami Port

This mom-and-pop shop serves up greasy spoon Okinawan classics like gōya champurū (bitter gourd stir-fry) and Okinawan-style soba, as well as otherwise standard Japanese fare (sashimi, tonkatsu, and more). Think home cooking. The staff are very welcoming,

Furuzamami Beach

too. It fills up fast with locals during lunch hours. An English menu is available.

ZAMAMI BURGER

126 Zamami; tel. 098/987-3626; noon-8pm daily; average ¥1,000; walk 4 minutes' north from Zamami Port

This foreign-owned burger joint is located in the Zamamia International Guesthouse. The eatery serves straightforward, delicious burgers, fries, and more through both lunch and dinner hours. A good spot for a casual, filling meal.

Accommodations

For a more extensive list of accommodations on the island, check out https://zamamitouristinfo.wordpress.com/stay/hotel-list/.

ZAMAMIA INTERNATIONAL GUESTHOUSE

126 Zamami; tel. 098/987-3626; http://zamamia-guesthouse.com; private twins ¥3,500 pp, mixed dorms ¥3,000 pp, female-only dorms ¥3,000 pp

This bare-bones, budget guesthouse is clean, cheerful, and run by helpful foreign and English-speaking local staff. The rooms are a mix of female-only and mixed dorms, as well as private twin rooms. All bathrooms and toilets are shared. Zamami Burger is housed onsite. There's also a large communal lounge.

MINSHUKU YADOKARI

142 Ama, Zamami; tel. 098/987-2231; https://zamamiyadokari.com; private tatami rooms ¥5,500 pp

Five minutes' drive west of the port, this quiet guesthouse has clean, basic Japanese-style rooms with tatami-mat floors and futons. Staff are cheerful and willing to assist with options on the island. Breakfast is served for an additional ¥550, while dinner (hard to come by on the island) is ¥1,650.

Information and Services

Online, the **Zamami English Guide** (www.zamamienglishguide.com/zamami) gives the lowdown on logistics, outdoor activities, and more on the island.

- **Tourism Information Center** (1-1 Zamami; tel. 098/987-2277; 9am-5pm daily, next to Zamami Port)

Getting There and Around

From Naha's Tomari Port, the **Queen Zamami** operates two high-speed ferries most of the year and three during peak season (Apr.-Sept., 1 hour 10 minutes; ¥3,200 adults, ¥1,600 children). There's also one normal ferry run by **Ferry Zamami** (2 hours; ¥2,150 adults, ¥1,090 children) that goes to Zamami Port every day, making a stop by the neighboring island of Aka-jima on the way. The port is located in the south-central part of the island, next to its main village. To book either one of these ferries, arrive at Naha's Tomari Port a half hour or more before the ferry you intend to catch and go to the ticket counter. It is possible to book a ferry in advance (recommended May-Oct.), but this isn't necessary at other times of year. Learn more about reserving a seat at www.zamamienglishguide.com/ferries, where you'll find ferry timetables, and https://zamamitouristinfo.wordpress.com/getting-here, which provides a link to a reservation page.

Getting around the island **on foot** is entirely possible, although **bicycles** and **motor scooters** can be rented at a few shops near the port. (An electrically assisted bike is recommended for the steep climb that leads to Furuzamami Beach.) The friendly staff at the tourist information center near the port are happy to point the way to rental shops that are open on any given day. There's also a **bus** that runs once hourly from the port to Furuzamami Beach (5 minutes; ¥300).

AKA-JIMA

阿嘉島

This tiny island, 15 minutes by boat from Zamami-jima, embodies a laid-back island vibe. Time flows slowly here, even compared to sleepy Zamami-jima. Graceful Kerama deer—petite, skillfully swimming descendents of the deer imported by conquerors from the Japanese mainland during the early 17th century—poke around this little slice of paradise, where the pristine beaches seem designed for whiling away long, lazy days in the sun. If you feel like exploring, just strike off and wander; the island is easy to negotiate on foot, although a bicycle will save you time, and is bordered by soft sand at almost every turn.

Compared to Zamami-jima's main village, **Aka Village** is pretty bare-bones. Besides a few clearly marked bicycle rental shops that double as cafés, there's not much to do. Your best plan here is to rent a bicycle, pedal to Nishibama Beach 1.5 kilometers (0.9 mi) north, and spend your day there. The sole restaurant that sits at the entrance to the beach doubles as a snorkel rental shop. Aim to board a ferry back to Naha by late afternoon (around 4-5pm is a good target), so you can be back in time for dinner.

Beaches

NISHIBAMA BEACH

Aka, Zamami

If your aim is to chill out and gaze at the azure seas surrounding the island on all sides, head for the main stretch of sand, Nishibama Beach. Furuzamami Beach's soft sands and nestled position make it well-suited for swimming and sunbathing. But the waters at Nishibama have more fish and are better for snorkeling. Like Furuzamami Beach, you can rent snorkeling equipment at Nishibama Beach, but there's no beach house here. Instead, pick up your gear at the beach shack next to the entrance of the beach, which serves as a restaurant and also rents essentials.

Diving

If you feel like exploring the island's underwater seascape, teeming with small tropical fish, a few dive operators also run guesthouses within a few minutes' walk of each other in Aka Village, near the island's south coast.

- **Marine House Seasir** (tel. 098/987-2973; www.seasir.com; single beginner dives from ¥12,000, double dives from ¥19,100 for certified divers, plus equipment rental)
- **Kawai Diving** (153 Aka; tel. 098/987-2219; www.kawaidiving.com/; single dives from ¥7,000, plus equipment rental)

Information and Services

- **Aka-jima Tourist Information Center** (936-2 Aka, Zamami; tel. 098/987-3535; www.facebook.com/sangoyuntakuvc/; 9am-4pm daily)

Getting There and Around

Queen Zamami (tel. 098/868-4567; www.zamamienglishguide.com/ferries) runs jet foils directly from Naha to Aka-jima twice a day (50 minutes; ¥3,200 adults, ¥1,600 children), and one daily standard ferry (1.5 hours; ¥2,150 adults, ¥1,090 children). Boats also run four times daily between Zamami Port and Aka-jima (15 minutes; ¥300 one-way).

Once on the island, a few shops rent **bicycles** in the village next to the port. To locate them, stop by the tourist information center next to the port to arm yourself with an English-language map marked with businesses.

Miyako Islands

The main island of the Miyako chain, sitting roughly 300 kilometers (186 mi) southwest of Okinawa-Hontō and the neighboring Keramas and 120 kilometers (75 mi) northeast of Ishigaki-jima, is Miyako-jima (宮古列島). The island, about 15 kilometers (9.3 mi) across from east to west and 25 kilometers (15.5 mi) north to south, is home to some of not only Japan's, but East Asia's best beaches, centered on Yonaha Maehama Beach in the island's southwest. If you're an advanced diver, take note of the tiny islands of **Irabu-jima** and **Shimoji-jima,** which are slightly farther out to sea but accessible by bridge from Miyako-jima. Each of these islands is a cave-diving mecca. There are also extensive coral reefs around the island, drawing snorkelers.

Miyako-jima's mostly flat terrain is swathed in fields of sugarcane, making its roads pleasant to explore by electrically assisted bicycle. There are a glut of hotels, pensions, and resorts scattered around the island, making it a good pick if you'd like to stay for a few nights and slow down. The main hub is **Hirara** (pop. 33,000), a laid-back town on the west coast, full of weather-beaten concrete blocks slowly being claimed by lush climbing plants, adding to the island's far-flung tropical appeal and reminding you that you're not on the mainland anymore.

BEACHES

Note that the waters around the Miyako Islands teem with box jellyfish from June-October, although stings are very rare. If you unfortunately suffer one, remove the tentacles, put vinegar on the wound, and seek prompt medical attention. Lifeguards are on duty at Yonaha Maehama to help.

SUNAYAMA BEACH
砂山ビーチ

Sunayama Beach (Sand Mountain) is about 4 kilometers (2.5 mi) north of Hirara. The beach is known for its picturesque rock formations, including an iconic arch carved out by waves crashing against a giant block of coral. Amenities include toilets and showers, but little else. The beach is easily accessible from Hirara by bicycle, making it a good choice if you don't have a car to get around the island's remoter beaches. Buses run to the beach very sporadically, so it's best to drive, pedal, or take a taxi to the parking lot beside the large sand dune looming behind the beach. Descend on foot to the waterfront from there.

★ YONAHA MAEHAMA BEACH
与那覇前浜ビーチ

This 7-kilometer-long (4.3-mi-long) tract of silky white sand at the southwest corner of the island is easily one of Japan's best beaches. The water is warm and clear, making it ideal for water sports. It's also an idyllic vantage point to watch the sun dip below the horizon. It's the archetypal beach: perfect sand—no need for protective footwear here; spacious, with several clusters of parasols spread over a long expanse; pristine water; almost no rocks or coral on the seafloor, which descends gradually—no sudden drop-offs; and minimal waves (save those made by the occasional Jet Ski). The water temperature is almost perfect, hovering around 25°C (77°F) or more from April-October. And the view, looking out across emerald waters to neighborhing Kurima-jima, is gorgeous. This is not a beach for snorkeling or diving, but is perfect for whiling away a day in the water or snoozing under a parasol.

There are ample facilities on the beach: showers, toilets, a beach house selling basic food, rental shops offering beach chairs, parasols, banana boats, and Jet Skis (which *can* get a little noisy during peak season). Access the beach either by local bus, bicycle, or rental car. It's located about 20 minutes' drive or 45 minutes' e-bike ride south of Hirara, just north

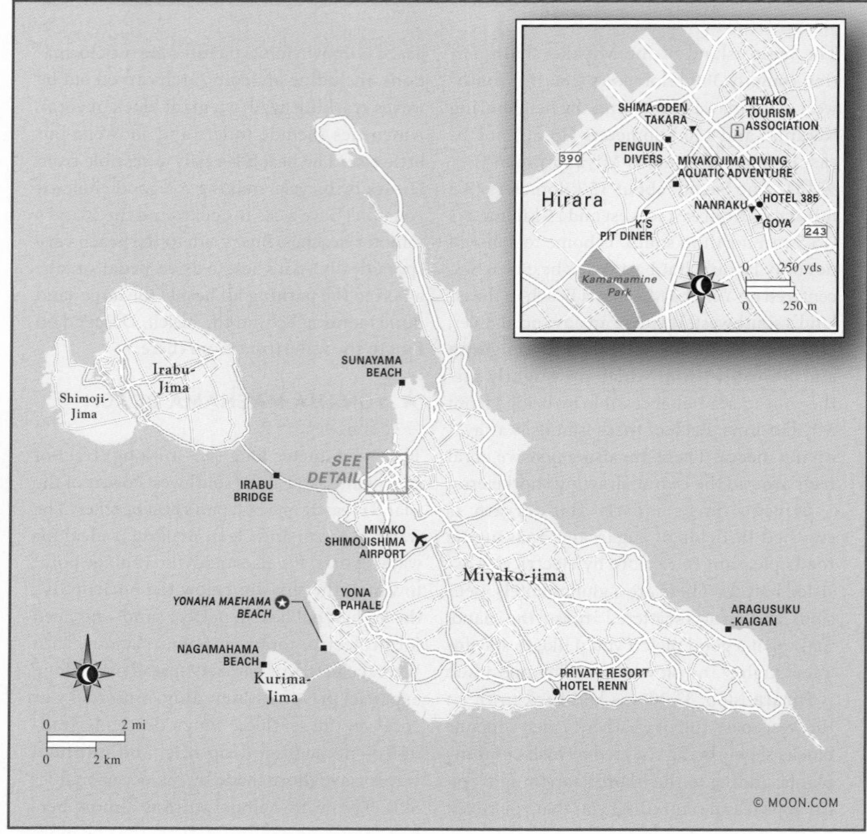

of the bridge that links Miayko-jima to the neighboring island Kurima-jima.

NAGAMAHAMA BEACH

長間浜

During peak season, the sands of Yonaha Maehama can sometimes be thronged with holidaymakers. Thankfully, there's an alternative not far away with a fraction of the crowds. Across the bridge just north of Yonaha Maehama, the small island of **Kurima-jima** is home to the excellent Nagamahama Beach on its northwest shore. If you choose to go to this hidden gem of a beach, be sure to bring everything with you that you'll need, including a snorkel and goggles, as coral is abundant just offshore. There are no rental shops, Jet Skis, or banana boats here. At night, it's also a known quantity among stargazing fans. At 5.3 kilometers (3.3 mi) away from Yonaha Maehama, across a long sun-drenched bridge, walking (1 hour) isn't recommended. But it's definitely worth visiting if you have an e-bike and enjoy exploring.

1: Sunayama Beach **2:** Yonaha Maehama Beach

Okinawa's Best Beaches

Virtually every island in Okinawa has a pleasant stretch of beach on it. They range from isolated and empy, fit for a castaway, to conveniently packaged for tourists in need of a summertime escape from the urban jungles of the mainland. Okinawa's most famous beaches tend to be popular for a reason: soft white sand, clear calm water, swimming-friendly. They also tend to have a beach house that offers various rentals (snorkeling gear, parasols, etc.), a beach shack or two selling basic food and drinks, as well as showers, bathrooms, and usually, a lifeguard on duty. That said, even Okinawa's most crowded beaches are never so crowded as to detract from the experience. There are also more off-the-beaten-path beaches, often requiring a ferry ride, or perhaps a bus, bicycle trip, or drive to the backside of an island, to access.

Here are some of the best places to swim and soak up golden rays around these islands:

- **Furuzamami Beach:** This beach is ideal for those who plan to stay based in Naha, from where it's less than an hour away by high-speed ferry. White sand and clear waters washing over extensive coral reefs make an ideal setting for swimming and snorkeling (page 701).
- **Yonaha Maehama Beach:** This 7-kilometer (4.3-mi) stretch of white sand on Miyako-jima is bordered by water that's emerald in the shallows and morphs into cobalt blue as it moves away from land. It's also known for its gorgeous sunsets. This beach is routinely cited as being one of the best in all of East Asia (page 705).
- **Yonehara Beach:** On Ishigaki-jima, renowned for diving, it's no surprise this beach is a great snorkeling spot, with coral reefs just offshore. Besides snorkeling, it's a great beach for lounging and swimming as well, with smooth sand and all needed amenities in place (page 712).
- **Kondoi Beach:** On the west side of the sleepy isle of Taketomi-jima, this beach is blessed with soft sand and calm water ideal for swimming, and is the stomping ground of a gang of local cats. Combined with the folk charms of the island's interior, this beach is an excellent choice for a day trip from nearby Ishigaki-jima (page 715).
- **Ida-no-hama:** With the slightly challenging access—ferry required—to reach this remote beach on already remote Iriomote-jima's isolated western shore, this beach has all the elements of a desert island. Fish with all the colors of the rainbow dart through the waters, and a jungle stands just beyond. Word has gotten out about this hidden jewel, but you might just have the place (nearly) to yourself (page 718).

ARAGUSUKU-KAIGAN
新城海岸

This fine stretch of beach on Miyako-jima is a good snorkeling spot, found along the southern portion of the island's eastern shore. The shallow water here teems with tropical fish. There are toilets and showers on the beach, and during the summer months a rental shop offers beach supplies. The beach is about 30 minutes' drive from Hirara.

DIVING

Just off the western coast of Miyako-jima, the tiny islets of **Irabu-jima** and **Shimoji-jima,** connected to each other by a bridge, are a beloved haunt of cave divers. **W-Arch,** off the coast of small neighboring islet Irabu-jima, is a great choice for beginners. The menacingly named **Satan's Palace,** off the tiny nearby island of Shimoji-jima, is for advanced divers only. Also off the coast of Shimoji-jima is the **"Antonio Gaudi" cave system,** replete with submarine archways reminiscent of the Spanish architect's surreal signature style.

A slew of other colorfully named formations lie submersed around these two islands. To learn more about the fantastic diving opportunities in the waters of Irabu-jima and Shimoji-jima, check out the following dive centers, both located in Hirara on Miyako-jima. Both dive shops have English-speaking staff.

- **Miyakojima Diving Aquatic Adventure** (543-1 Shimozato, Hirara; tel. 0980/79-5009; www.miyako-aquaticadventure.com; one boat dive ¥7,500 plus equipment rental)
- **Penguin Divers** (40 Shimozato, Hirara; tel. 0980/79-5433; www.diving-penguin.com; two cave dives ¥13,000 plus equipment rental)

FOOD

K'S PIT DINER

517 Shimozato; tel. 090/1821-1098; www.instagram.com/kspit.miyako/; 11:30am-3pm and 6pm-11pm Tues.-Sun.; ¥1,200

Sometimes you just want a burger and fries. When you do, head to this old-school American-themed diner—down to the red, white, and blue checkered plates—in the middle of Hirara.

★ NANRAKU

568 Nishizato; tel. 0980/73-1855; 6pm-midnight daily; ¥2,500

This restaurant is an institution, as attested to by the celebrities' signatures adorning the walls. The key word here is local: Ingredients—from vegetables to beef to fish—all come from Miyako, as does the chef. Be sure to try some umibudō (literally "sea grapes," a kind of edible seaweed), pulled from the waters just offshore, or beef sashimi sourced from Miyako farms.

SHIMA-ODEN TAKARA

172 Nishizato; tel. 0980/72-0671; 7pm-late Mon.-Sat.; ¥2,500

An izakaya with a menu focused on oden, a style of cooking that involves stewing a variety of things—from boiled eggs and deep-fried tofu to radish and pigs' feet—in a soy-based broth, often eaten with a dab of hot mustard. The restaurant has a classic island feel, with counter seats and tatami-mat-floor seating in private booths separated by bamboo curtains. Reserve a day in advance or plan to come after 9pm to ensure a seat.

GOYA

570-2 Nishizato; tel. 0980/74-2358; https://zumi-goya.com; 5:30pm-midnight Fri.-Wed.; ¥3,000

At Goya you'll find solid izakaya fare: sashimi, benimo (purple sweet potato) croquettes, various grilled meats, and more. The main draw is its spirited musical performances. Diners share long tables, and a live band jams every night (¥320 cover charge). Dancing is encouraged, and facilitated by the Orion beer on tap and the wide range of awamori on offer.

ACCOMMODATIONS

YONA PAHALE

777-1 Shimoji, Yonaha; tel. 0980/76-2241; www.yona-pahale.com; ¥7,000 d with private bath

Set amid sugarcane fields just north of the dreamy stretch of sand that is Yonaha Maehama, this inviting bed-and-breakfast is a real find. Run by a friendly couple (and their cat), the inn has three private rooms (one Japanese, one Western, one a fusion) and shared shower and washrooms, which are well-stocked and clean. Delicious home-cooked breakfast and dinner are served. The couple doesn't speak English, but are gracious hosts and eager to help—Google translate and a smile go a long way. Reserve via email on the website or on Rakuten Travel (https://travel.rakuten.com/hotel/info/78147/); aim to book several months in advance. Cash only.

HOTEL 385

561 Nishizato; tel. 0980/79-0998; www.hotel-385.com; ¥12,000 d

This bright, clean, and new hotel in the middle of Hirara makes for a convenient base from which to explore the island, even more so if you have your own wheels or take advantage of the pair of electrically assisted bicycles available for rent. It's about 15 minutes' cycle (or 5 minutes' drive) from Sunayama Beach and 45 minutes' cycle (or 20 minutes' drive) from Yonaha Maehama. The rooms and en suite bathrooms are spacious and well stocked. On the first floor, there's also a reasonably priced restaurant that serves good pasta and Asian dishes for lunch (from

¥1,000), although the takeaway breakfast bento boxes can be skipped. A recommended mid-range pick.

★ PRIVATE RESORT HOTEL RENN

422-2 Gurikubetomori; tel. 0980/77-7859; www.resort-renn.jp; ¥42,000

Offering charm, privacy, peace and quiet, and a helpful host, Mr. Renn, this intimate, elegant bed-and-breakfast is smack in the middle of the southern coast of the island, with easy access to both Yoneha Maehama Beach to the west and Nishi Henna-zaki to the east. The three rooms are big and clean with balconies. There's also a shared rooftop lounge with stellar ocean views. Continental breakfast is provided, courtesy of Mr. Renn's mother. If you have a rental car and want to splash out on digs a cut above the rest in town, this is a very good pick.

INFORMATION AND SERVICES

The island's handful of Family Mart convenience stores have ATMs, which should accept most foreign cards.

- **Miyako Tourism Association** (187 Nishizato, Hirara; tel. 0980/73-1881; https://miyako-guide.net; 9am-6pm daily; 20-minute walk southeast of the port on the second floor, across the street from town hall)
- **Hirara-Nishizato Post Office** (142 Nishizato, Hirara; tel. 0980/72-1617; https://map.japanpost.jp/p/search/dtl/300170311000/; 9am-5pm Mon.-Fri.)
- **Bank of The Ryukyus** (240-2 Nishizato, Hirara; tel. 098/72-2251; www.ryugin.co.jp/tenpo/atm_search/shop-5056/; 7am-10pm Mon.-Fri., 8am-9pm Sat.-Sun. and holidays for ATM, 9am-3pm daily for service counter)

GETTING THERE

Miyako-jima is one of the easier islands to reach. Direct flights to and from **Miyako Airport** (https://miyakoap.co.jp) run from Tokyo's Haneda Airport (3 hours), Osaka's Kansai Airport (2 hours), Naha Airport (45 minutes), and Ishigaki Airport (35 minutes). Miyako Airport is located in the island's center, roughly 8 kilometers (5 mi) south of Hirara (15 minutes' drive) and about the same distance and driving time from Yonaha Maehama, to the south. There's a tourist information desk in the airport (tel. 0980/73-1881; 7:30am-8pm daily). Limited flights also go between Haneda Airport and the newly renovated **Miyako Shimojishima Airport Terminal** (https://shimojishima.jp), located on Shimoji-shima, next to Irabu-jima, about 20 minutes' drive from Hirara. Once you've arrived at either airport, your best bet for getting to your accommodation will be renting a car—rental outlets are profuse in both airports—taking a taxi, or simply having your hotel pick you up (many offer free shuttle services to and from the airport for guests). Buses do exist, but they run very seldom, making them a potentially frustrating option at best.

GETTING AROUND

Renting a **car** will give you the most freedom to explore the beaches that are scattered around the Miyako-jima, and to visit neighboring islands that are accessible by bridge. Thanks to the completion of the Irabu Bridge in 2015, a boat is no longer needed to cross from Miyako-jima to Irabu-jima and closely neighboring Shimoji-jima (also accessible from Irabu-jima by bridge). The 3,540-meter (2.2-mi) bridge is the longest toll-free bridge in Japan. Make your way across by local **bus** or **rental car.** Renting a car is easy at Miyako Airport or in Hirara.

The next best way to get around is actually by **bicycle.** An electrically assisted bicycle is recommended for longer journeys. Simply ask at your accommodation's front desk, as most inns around Hirara offer bicycle rentals. The island is remarkably flat, which makes cycling a pleasurable way to explore.

Given the short distances between most points of interest, taxis are another option if you don't might spending a bit more. Even relatively longer trips you'll be likely to take on the island (say, up to 12 km/7 mi) shouldn't cost more than ¥2,000-3,000, give or take.

There is a local **bus** network, but connections are very infrequent. That said, if you have no other option, buses do shuttle between the airport and Hirara (10 minutes; ¥210), and from Hirara to Yoneha-Maehama Beach and the neighboring island of Kurima-jima (30 minutes; ¥390).

Yaeyama Islands 八重山諸島

Of all the southwest isles, the Yaeyama Islands offer the broadest and deepest experience of Okinawa. In Japan's far southern frontier, these remote islands feel like they belong in Southeast Asia. Life here moves at a laid-back pace; even the rhythms of relatively chilled-out Naha seem frantic by comparison.

The main island and gateway to the chain is Ishigaki-jima, where relaxed, friendly locals, excellent diving, and beaches abound. From Ishigaki, ferries shuttle back and forth daily to tiny Taketomi-jima, which offers the best possible glimpse of living Okinawan culture. Saunter or cycle through its rustic car-free villages on streets made of crushed coral and admire the cultural hybrid of architectural styles in its old homes, adorned with red-tiled roofs and dog-lion shisa guardians. Beyond Taketomi-jima, the landscape of Iriomote-jima, also reached by ferry, befits an *Indiana Jones* film set, with its dense mangrove swamps and jungles that almost call for a machete.

And at Japan's farthest southwestern corner, the far-flung Yonagumi-jima is home to the Atlas moth, the world's largest. This island is a magnet for divers, who come to witness the multitude of hammerheads that swarm through its waters during winter, and, more famously, to glimpse enigmatic underwater formations off the island's coast that appear manmade, although the jury is out.

ISHIGAKI-JIMA

石垣島

Ishigaki-jima is the gateway to the wondrous nature and distinct culture of the Yaeyama Islands, which include Japan's southernmost and westernmost bodies of land. At 222 square kilometers (86 sq mi), Ishigaki is the most populated and developed island in the Yaeyama group. The island has a peculiar, oblong shape, with a rotund base at the south and a long handle-like protrusion of land extending northward from its northeastern corner.

Ishigaki boasts great beaches and is rich in coral, making it a diving mecca in its own right, as well as a key transport hub for the Yaeyama chain with a lively dining and social scene, concentrated mostly in the small main town in the island's far south. Both the region's major airport, located along the southeastern coast, and ferry terminal, found in Ishigaki City, the main town in the far south, are located on the island. There's a glut of resorts around the diver's paradise of Kabira Bay and Yonehara Beach, roughly 20 kilometers (12 mi), or 30 minutes' drive north, of Ishigaki City. Elsewhere, trusty B&Bs are found at nearly every open stretch of beachfront, including the far northern reaches of the roughly 30-kilometer-long (19-mi-long) peninsula that juts into the remote northeast.

Ishigaki is relatively hilly and has the highest mountain in Okinawa Prefecture (Mount Omoto, 526 m/1,726 ft), located in the north-central region. While not as untamed as Iriomote-jima, the jungly interior does evoke wilderness. But the beaches and coral reefs are by far its main draws.

Sights

KABIRA BAY

川平湾

The waters of Kabira Bay are reserved for very

rare black pearl cultivation, so it's forbidden to swim. It's a lovely view, though, with some small rocks dotting the seascape. The **beach** fronting this picturesque scene is white sand. If you are hankering to get out on the water, it's possible to take a ride through the bay in a glass-bottomed boat, which departs from near the premises of the tour operator **Kabira Marine Service** (934 Kabira; tel. 0980/88-2335; www.kabiramarine.jp; 9am-5pm daily; 30 minutes; ¥1,030 adults, ¥520 children). Look down and you'll see a host of tropical fish at play. A caveat: Beware that habu box jellyfish occasionally inhabit the waters, especially June-October. If you are unfortunate enough to be inflicted with a sting—it's rare—promptly exit the water, remove the tentacles, douse the wound with vinegar, and seek medical assistance (dial 119 and request English).

Beaches

YONEHARA BEACH

米原海岸

Yonehara Beach is Ishigaki's prime stretch of sand. Located on the island's north coast, east of Kabira Bay, it has all the amenities of a major beach—showers, toilets, snorkel rentals—and allows camping. There are good sections of coral reef, but the current is strong, so don't go out too far if you're not a skilled swimmer.

SUNSET BEACH

Sunset Beach is a tranquil spot on the western side of the finger of land extending from the north of the island. It's a great place to snorkel and to watch the sun dip below the horizon. Showers and toilets are available, and parasols and beach chairs can be rented.

★ Diving

Ishigaki is one of the best places to dive in Okinawa, which makes it a strong contender for best dive spot in Japan. Coral reefs are found near Kabira Bay, Yonehara Beach, and beyond. But the island's most famous spot of all is known as the **Manta Scramble,** a natural occurrence that takes place each autumn near Kabira Bay: Manta rays congregate to be cleaned by a proliferation of plankton that builds up in the area. Divers come to the site en masse every autumn to dive below the rays and watch them circle and feed on the plankton, which also scrub them down. Among the island's many other stellar dive spots, **Osaki Hanagoi Reef** stands out. This reef is like a multihued coral jungle teeming with ocean life.

There are so many dive spots around the island that it pays to consult local pros, including:

- **Prime Scuba Ishigaki** (345-9 Maezato; tel. 0980/87-5980; www.primescuba-ishigaki.com/; 8:30am-6pm daily)
- **Umicoza** (1287-97 Kabira; tel. 0980/88-2434; https://umicoza.com; 8:30am-6pm daily)

Food

Ishigaki-jima is home to loads of charming izakaya serving up Ryūkyū classics like goya chanpuru (bitter melon stir-fried with tofu, eggs, and pork), mozoku seaweed tempura, locally caught fish served raw or grilled, and more.

SHIMANO TABEMONOYA PAIKAJI

219 Ōkawa; tel. 0980/82-6027; 5pm-midnight daily; ¥3,500

A homey, lively, and well-lit space with friendly staff, this is a great choice for dinner. Book a day in advance to ensure a seat. One caveat: The restaurant can get pretty smoky as the evening wears on.

★ USAGI-YA HONTEN

Nakamura Heights 102, 1-1 Ishigaki; tel. 0980/88-5014; http://usagiya-ishigaki.com; 5pm-11:45pm (last order 10:45pm) daily; dishes ¥380-3,580

Usagi-ya is more than a meal; it's an experience. The friendly staff, dressed in

1: Kabira Bay, Ishigaki-jima **2:** diving in the waters off Ishigaki-jima

1
2

Okinawan-style yukata, double as drummers and dancers for the nightly performances. An acoustic guitarist and a sanshin strummer jam 7pm-9pm nightly. The offerings are filling and delicious: green papaya salad, teppanyaki hot plate with locally sourced beef and vegetables (green and yellow bell peppers, potato wedges, bean sprouts, and a citrus-based dipping sauce). There are ample awamori options from distilleries around the Southwest Islands, and of course cold Orion is on tap. By the end of the evening, don't be surprised if the entire restaurant is on its feet dancing.

Accommodations

★ IRIWA

599 Kabira; tel. 0980/88-2563; iriwa.org; ¥2,500 dorm, ¥7,600 d

A rooftop terrace with ocean views, a shared living room and kitchen, and welcoming English-speaking hosts who want to introduce guests to the underwater wonders of Ishigaki-jima (with snorkel) are just a few of this guesthouse's selling points. If you enjoy communal living, it doesn't get much better than Iriwa, an island-chic guesthouse—surfboards and potted plants in the lounge—that sits near Kabira Bay. All rooms but one share bathroom facilities. Book far (months) in advance, because Iriwa has developed a name for itself.

★ TSUNDARA BEACH RETREAT

895-2 Nosoko; tel. 090/7587-2029; www.tsundarabeach.com; 2 adults ¥40,000 per night for 2-night minimum (¥10,000 per additional adult, ¥4,000 per night for children under 12), plus ¥10,000 cleaning fee

Located on the peninsula in Ishigaki-jima's far north, this amply sized detached cottage (100 sq m/1,076 sq ft) is fully private and only hosts single visitors or a group of up to four at any given time. It has direct access to the beach and sits on a lush plot of land awash in green. There's one bedroom, with extra hideaway beds in the living room, a full kitchen, and laundry facilities. Outside, there's a patio where you can barbecue or lounge in beach chairs. Walk down to the private beach to swim, go stand-up paddleboarding, snorkel, or sunbathe, as you please. It's owned by an American couple who also lives on the grounds in a separate house. They speak flawless Japanese and are happy to help guests maximize their stay on the island. A great place to go for a peaceful escape.

beef hotplate at Usagi-ya Honten

Information and Services

To pick up English-language information on the island, your best bet is to stop by the information desk (7:30am-9pm daily) at the airport upon arrival. The ferry terminal also has a smattering of English-language material on hand. Head to the **Yaeyama Post Office** to withdraw cash (12 Ōkawa; 8am-9pm daily; ATM in operation).

Getting There

It's possible to fly direct to **Painushima Ishigaki Airport** (tel. 0980/87-0468, www.ishigaki-airport.co.jp; 7:30am-9pm) from both Narita Airport and Haneda Airport in Tokyo, Kansai International Airport in Osaka, as well as from Naha, Miyako, and Yonaguni-jima. The airport is located in the southwestern corner of the island, about 10 kilometers (6 mi) northeast of Ishigaki City.

Ishigaki-jima can also be reached by direct ferry from other islands within the Yaeyama chain, including Iriomote-jima and Taketomi-jima. The port is located in the island's far south, where its main town spreads around it. The ferry operators servicing these routes are **Anei Kankō** (tel. 0980/83-0055; www.aneikankou.co.jp), **Yaeyama Kankō Ferry** (tel. 0980/82-5010; www.yaeyama.co.jp), and **Ishigaki Dream Kankō** (tel. 0980/84-3178; www.ishigaki-dream.co.jp).

★ TAKETOMI-JIMA

竹富島

A 15-minute ferry ride from Ishigaki Port brings you to Taketomi-jima, the island with perhaps the best sense of cultural identity in all Okinawa. The sole settlement has a population hovering around 300. There are no supermarkets or convenience stores, nor are there any stop lights. At only 5 square kilometers (2 sq mi), it's a tiny fleck of land, but it's big on local atmosphere.

As you exit the island's sole dock, fluttering butterflies hover around you and flowers line the roads, which are made from ground-up coral stones. Cars do exist on the island, but they are rarely seen or heard. The traditional homes are fenced in by walls made from coral and lined by fukugi trees, meant to protect them from being battered by typhoons. They are also elevated by stones to ward off dampness and invading insects. The exaggerated eaves of the roofs are meant to increase shade and keep cool air flowing indoors. Shisa guardians—lion-dog-hybrid talisman figures, cultural artifacts of the mingling of Chinese and Ryūkyū culture—stand atop gates, on roofs, and at entranceways to schools and banks across the whole Ryūkyū realm; they are meant to ward off evil spirits.

Just meandering through these streets and enjoying the peace and quiet is a highlight. In the town, sanshin-strumming bards drive tourists in **water buffalo carts** and regale them with ballads written on these islands. It's possible to ride in one of these carts (30 minutes; ¥1,200), but the drivers typically don't speak any English. There are a few nooks and crannies of this picturesque little island in the antipodes of Japan—a bike is perfect if you really want to explore. Trails weave through the fields of flowers, leading to beaches without another soul on them. Butterflies flit across the paths as you ride along. Elsewhere, graveyards and rustic shrines lie enshrouded by groves of trees. Simply rent a bicycle (¥300 per hour; ¥1,500 for a day) at one of the many clearly marked **bicycle rental shops** in the town center and explore. Look for staff members from these rental shops who come to greet travelers on ferries arriving at the port.

Beaches

KONDOI BEACH

コンドイ浜

Kondoi Beach is the best waterfront on the island. It's less a swimming or snorkeling spot and more a place just to chill out; there are ample tables for picnics, as well as an army of local cats. Basic facilities such as toilets and showers are onsite. The beach is relatively shallow, which makes it a good choice for families traveling with children. Another selling point: It's rarely crowded. The beach is located

1

2

3

Yonaguni-Jima: A Diver's Paradise

Far-flung Yonaguni-jima is the westernmost inhabited island in Japan. At the edges of this 28.5-square-kilometer (11-square-mi) chunk of land, foamy seas crash into soaring cliffs. The main draw for most visitors to the island is the chance to dive off its coast.

DIVE SPOTS

There are two main points of interest to divers who make the journey to Yonaguni:

- **Irizaki Point,** where hammerheads are known to congregate.
- **Kaitei Iseiki,** a mysterious underwater structure that looks like it could be the remnants of a civilization lost to the deep, Atlantean-style.

DIVE OPERATORS

- **Sou-Wes Diving** (59-6 Yonaguni; tel. 0980/87-2311, http://www.yonaguni.jp/en/index.html; ¥12,000 two boat dives, plus equipment rental)
- **Yonaguni Diving Service** (3984-3 Yonaguni; tel. 0980/87-2658; https://yonaguniyds.com/; ¥12,500 two boat dives, plus equipment rental)

Note that the proprietors of Yonaguni Diving Service also run an inn called **Minshuku Yoshimaru-sō** (3984-3 Yonaguni; tel. 0980/87-2658; www.yonaguniyds.com/yoshimaru; dorm with 2 meals ¥6,000, private room with 2 meals ¥7,050).

GETTING THERE

Three daily **flights** go between Ishigaki and Yonaguni (30 minutes; ¥7,500-13,000 one-way), while one daily flight operates between Naha and Yonaguni (95 minutes, ¥17,000-33,000 one-way). The airport sits at the center of the island's northern shore. On the island, public bus transport is so infrequent, it's best to **rent a car** at the airport upon arrival.

about 1.5 kilometers (1 mi) from the village at the island's core.

Getting There

Reaching Taketomi-jima from Ishigaki-jima is a cinch. Three **ferry** operators run boats dozens of times daily from Ishigaki Port, departing every 30 minutes between 7:30am and 5:30pm (¥600 one-way, ¥1,330 round-trip). Located on the northeast coast of the island, it's about 10-15 minutes by ferry from the port in the far south of Ishigaki-jima, a one-hour flight from Naha. Go to the ticket counter inside Ishigaki Port and purchase a ticket there. The process is straightforward. Just be sure to catch the last ferry for the day if you're planning on returning to Ishigaki-jima.

1: sidewalk tiles in Ishigaki-jima **2:** biking Taketomi-jima's sandy streets **3:** traditional Okinawan homes

IRIOMOTE-JIMA
西表島

The second-largest island in all of Okinawa, at 289 square kilometers (112 sq mi), Iriomote-jima has a mere couple of thousand residents. Away from its minimally developed northern, eastern, and southeastern coast, its landscape is even more wild, untamed, and fundamentally different from the rest of Japan. Nearly 90 percent of this subtropical island is covered in mangrove forests, with rivers coursing through it (the largest of which being the Urauchi-gawa, which empties into the ocean near Uehara Port in the island's northwest). Waterfalls crash over its precipitous interior, which is home to a rare breed of wildcat, the Iriomote lynx, a housecat-size subspecies of leopard, only 100 of which are thought to exist. In many ways, it is the southern subtropical complement to Shiretoko National Park in the far northern frontier of Hokkaido.

Broadly speaking, the island is split into east and west. Its only road threads around the perimeter of its eastern half, from the main southeastern town of Ōhara, through Uehara, continuing to its end in the western town of Shirahama. The most popular beach within direct reach of this road is Hoshizuna-no-hama, near Uehara Port in the northwest. The more remote, secretive slice of waterfront at Ida-no-hama in the deep west is beyond the reach of this road, however, and can only be accessed by ferry (from Shirahama). The island has three main ports: one in the village of Ōhara in the island's southeast, another in the northwestern town of Uehara, and a third in Shirahama, the gateway to the island's remote west.

Beaches

IDA-NO-HAMA

イダの浜

Ida-no-hama is a spectacular beach on the west coast of Iriomote. The beach sits on a quiet, isolated bay that can be reached by taking a boat from Shirahama Port to the isolated village of Funauki, and walking about 10 minutes from there. Only 4-5 ferries (10 minutes; ¥500) make this trip daily, but the journey is worth it. Behind the beach, the wild jungle of the island looms, while turquoise water laps against the sand. The spot is stunning. And under the water, coral and tropical fish are in abundance. There are no amenities here, so come prepared with whatever you need. And be aware that the sand is a bit rough, strewn with dead coral, so flip-flops or marine footwear are recommended.

HOSHIZUNA-NO-HAMA

星砂の浜

Hoshizuna-no-hama (Star Sand Beach) is at the northern edge of Iriomote, roughly 3.3 kilometers (2 mi), or six minutes' drive, northwest of Uehara Port, and is composed of star-shaped grains of sand that are, in fact, skeletons of miniscule one-celled organisms that dwell in sea grass (marine footwear recommended). Moving past these protozoa, proceed to the waters with a snorkel and goggles to explore what's happening beneath the water. An impressive array of colorful fish can be seen darting in and out of the coral seascape off this beach. Note that there are no public toilets or showers. The sand is rough, so marine footwear is recommended.

diving boat off Iriomote-jima

Water Sports

Iriomote has a dramatic landscape that is 90 percent covered by jungle and lined by rivers and waterfalls. Taking a cruise down the **Urauchi-gawa,** a river that flows amid dense mangrove swamps, from the wild heart of the island toward the northwest where its mouth opens near the port in Uehara, is one of the most popular ways to get a taste of the island's wild natural beauty.

URAUCHI-GAWA KANKŌ

tel. 0980/85-6154; www.urauchigawa.com

The most well-known provider of boat tours through this unique ecosystem is Urauchi-gawa Kankō. The tour starts at the river's mouth, and journeys 8 kilometers (5 mi) inland (1 hour; ¥1,800 round-trip) to a point where it's possible to walk an additional 2 kilometers (1.2 mi) to the waterfall **Mariyudō-no-taki,** which leads to a second waterfall, **Kanpire-no-taki.** Beyond boat tours, the outfit also leads tours of several other activities, from snorkeling to SUP. A detailed English-language flier can be seen online at www.urauchigawa.com/urauchigawa-dm(eng)2.pdf. They give full instructions on preparing for a given tour, including the meeting time and place, when you make a booking.

IRIOMOTE OSANPO KIBUN

tel. 0980/84-8178; www.iriomote-osanpo.com; ¥6,000 half day, ¥10,000 full day

Kayaking makes it possible to see the Urauchi-gawa from closer to the water. A great outdoor tour provider on the island that offers kayaking trips is Iriomote Osanpo Kibun. Moving out to the coast, Iriomote Osanpo Kibun also offers snorkeling tours on the reefs that ring the island.

Hiking

SIMAMARIASIBI TREKKING ACTIVITIES

984-1 Taketomi-chō; tel. 0980/84-8408; www.simamariasibi.com; excursions range from 5-10 hours; ¥10,000-34,000 depending on length of time and number of participants

Iriomote is also a fantastic place to trek. It's essentially a large expanse of jungle punctuated by rivers and waterfalls. That said, it's tricky terrain that can be notoriously disorienting. It's unwise to venture into the interior without a paid guide. If you're keen to hike on this wild island, get in touch with Simamariasibi Trekking Activities. This Iriomote-based outfit leads people on excursions from canyoning and caving to summiting mountains in the rugged interior. Iriomote Osanpo Kibun also provides trekking tours to gorgeous spots like the waterfall **Pinaisāra-no-taki.**

Food

LAUGH LA GARDEN

550-1 Uehara, Taketomi; tel. 0980/85-7088; https://lalagarden.ti-da.net; 11:30am-2pm and 6pm-9pm Fri.-Wed.; ¥600-900; walk 3 minutes west of Uehara Port

Across the road from the pier at Uehara Port in the island's northwest, with a veranda that looks out to sea, this casual eatery serves reasonably priced lunch and dinner sets. Choices range from hamburgers and hot dogs to Okinawan classics like pork cutlets sourced from neighboring islands and gōya champurū (bitter gourd stir-fry). There's a robust alcohol menu, too.

KITCHEN INABA

742-6 Uehara; tel. 0980/84-8164; 11:30am-2pm and 6pm-10:30pm Tues.-Sun.; ¥350-1,800; drive 7 minutes west from Uehara Port, or drive 4 minutes south of Hoshizuna-no-hama

For island food with a slightly more refined touch, this restaurant on the west side of Uehara does the trick. They serve local dishes like inushishi-sashimi (wild boar sashimi) and crab soup, as well as items with a subtropical twist like papaya salad. Reserve ahead if you plan to go for dinner. A good choice if you're on the west side of the island.

Accommodations

IRUMOTE-SŌ

870-95 Uehara; tel. 0980/85-6255; www.ishigaki.com/irumote; dorm with dinner from ¥5,300, private room for one with shared toilet/bath and dinner from ¥6,000, private twin room with en suite bath/shower and dinner from ¥14,500; walk 20 minutes southeast of Uehara Port, or arrange free pickup at port

Friendly staff who are eager to help with arranging logistics for activities around the island, clean rooms, lush palm-studded grounds, and seaside views make this a great budget option in Uehara. The rooms are Japanese-style with tatami floors and futons, some with private bath/shower and some shared. Arrange ahead for pickup at Uehara Port to avoid the slightly long uphill walk to the inn. Given the meager increase in price from dorm to private room, it pays to go with the latter. The amiable hostess serves tasty, optional home-cooked dinners. Opting out of them will cut the rate by ¥1,200.

IRIOMOTE NEST

10-189 Uehara; tel. 0980/84-8178; https://english.iriomote-nest.com; ¥27,000 d, ¥30,000 d with breakfast; take free shuttle bus from Uehara Port (10 minutes)

Surrounded by lush vegetation and with well-manicured lawns, this smart boutique hotel has just three rooms with semi-private terraces that open directly onto a swimming pool. There's a shared lounge and sun terrace, as well as a restaurant, café, and bar on-site. All en suite bathrooms are roomy and well-equipped. A great pick if you feel like a few creature comforts after a day spent traipsing through the jungle. Request a free shuttle bus ticket when you buy your ferry ticket from Ishigaki-jima. Upon arriving at Uehara Port, simply tell the bus driver your destination is Nest.

Getting There and Around

High-speed ferries run to and from Ishigaki and two ports on Iriomote, namely **Ōhara Port** (40 minutes, up to 27 daily; ¥1,570) in the island's southeast and **Uehara Port** (1 hour, up to 20 daily; ¥2,060) in the northwest. Tickets can be purchased directly from Ishigaki Port on the day of travel.

Five-times-daily **buses** run between Ōhara Port and the town of Shirahama in the island's northwest, passing Uehara Port on the way (1.5 hours; ¥1,410). You can catch the bus anywhere along this road, which wraps halfway around the island, by simply flagging down a bus. You can buy a bus pass for unlimited rides (¥1,050 one day, ¥1,570 three days) at the ferry terminals. The ferry companies also operate shuttle buses into the few main towns dotting the island. That said, by far the easiest way to get around the island is to rent a car. There are plenty of rental outlets at both ferry terminals.

Background

The Landscape

The Landscape.........721
Plants and Animals.....725
History 729
Government and Economy 737
People and Culture 740

GEOGRAPHY

Despite the insistence of many Japanese people, their country is not a small place. At 377,915 square kilometers (145,914 square mi), it's a bit larger than Germany and slightly smaller than California. From the northeastern tip of Hokkaido to far southwestern Okinawa, the bow of islands extends 3,008 kilometers (1,869 mi), or roughly the same length, north to south, as the continental United States. This gives the country a wide range of climates and landscapes, and a vast coastline.

With so much natural splendor, it's no surprise that Japan is home

to 33 **national parks.** The first was created in 1934, following the birth of mountaineering among Japanese in the early 20th century.

Oceans and Coastline

Perhaps the most constant feature is the ocean. The Sea of Japan lies to the west, with the Korean peninsula and China on the other side. The Pacific stretches eastward, with the United States mainland lying more than 8,000 kilometers (about 5,000 mi) to the east. The lack of land borders has allowed Japan to develop its unique cultural universe.

Thousands of islands comprise Japan, but four make up the bulk of the landmass: the main island of Honshu; Hokkaido in the north, which is roughly the size of Ireland; and bordering the Inland Sea with Western Honshu in the nation's southwest: rustic Shikoku and volcanic Kyushu. All told, some 27,000 kilometers (16,777 mi) of coastline encircle these islands.

Mountains

Inland, the landscape is roughly 70-80 percent mountainous, pushing people and agriculture to the coastal fringes, comprising 20-30 percent of the land. Jagged peaks and foothills swathed in dense forest dot the sparsely populated natural wonderland of Hokkaido in the north. Honshu's geographic heart is in the Japan Alps (North, Central, and Southern), where you'll find most of the nation's tallest peaks, some of which top 3,000 meters (9,800 feet). Elsewhere on Honshu are the Hida and Kiso ranges, as well as Japan's tallest and one of the world's most recognizable peaks, the sublime Mount Fuji (3,776 meters/12,388 feet). As you move southwest or northeast of Honshu, the mountains dip to rolling foothills. Down south, Shikoku is shot through with more modest peaks, while craggy Kyushu is awash in volcanic activity.

Geothermal Activity and Volcanoes

Geothermal activity is rife in the country. Part of the Ring of Fire, Japan is located directly on the Pacific Plate ridgeline. The country's share of volcanic eruptions and earthquakes attest to that fact. Even Fuji itself is a volcano, which last erupted in 1707. All told, about 70 volcanoes dot Japan, including the famed cones of Aso-san and Sakurajima on Kyushu.

Cataclysmic eruptions are rare, but even minor flare-ups have caused deaths, such as the unexpected eruption of Mount Ontake on September 27, 2014. Eruptions are but a sidenote for most Japanese, however, who take advantage of the country's intense geothermal activity by periodically plunging into the waters of a hot onsen bath.

Rivers and Lakes

Japan's longest river is the Shinano River (Shinano-gawa) of Niigata (370 km/230 mi). Other notable rivers include the Tehio-gawa (Hokkaido); the Tone-gawa, which runs from Niigata to Chiba east of Tokyo and serves as a major source of freshwater for the capital region; Tokyo's Sumida-gawa, running through the old part of downtown (Shitamachi); Osaka's concrete-embanked Yodo-gawa, a key historic lane of commerce; and Kyoto's pleasant Kamo-gawa, lined with paths well suited for a summer evening stroll. Especially in the mountains, many rivers are short and fierce, whipping through narrow canyons on their way from mountains to the sea, with many dropping as much as 1,000 meters (3,280 feet) in elevation in the course of traveling less than 50 kilometers (31 mi). Some of these waterways are meccas for white water rafting, particularly in Shikoku and in the mountains of central Honshu. To the chagrin of many environmental activists, a major proportion of the country's waterways have been dammed for electricity, water storage, irrigation, or other traditional industries.

Previous: gardens at the Kyoto Imperial Palace.

Lakes are strewn across the archipelago, many fed by natural springs found upriver or placidly occupying extinct volcanic craters. The largest is Lake Biwa (Biwa-ko), which lies northeast of Kyoto. Other prominent lakes include the Fuji Five Lakes (Lake Kawaguchi and Lake Yamanaka being most famous), which frame the iconic peak; Hokkaido's Lake Akan; and the Tohoku region's Tazawa-ko, Japan's deepest, and Towada-ko, Honshu's largest crater lake.

CLIMATE

The vast majority of Japan has four neatly delineated seasons, but there are variations. The northern extremities of the country, particularly Hokkaido, fall into the Northern Temperate Zone, producing conditions similar to those of New England. Meanwhile, Okinawa and much of the far southwest enjoy subtropical warmth most of the year.

Several distinct climatic zones are delineated by mountain ranges and ocean straits. From northern Kyushu to Shikoku and up the eastern half of Honshu, the climate is defined by mild springs; hot, sticky summers; cool autumns; and chilly, crisp winters with the occasional dusting of snow or (even more rare) heavy snowfall.

Northern Honshu

Along the western side of the country, the differences between the four seasons are dramatic. Although the western side of the country may see less rain, this is compensated for with a heavy dump of snow in winter. In some places, up to 3 meters (9.8 feet) of powder accumulate during the colder months. Some parts of northwestern Tohoku—Yamagata, Akita, Aomori Prefectures—see some of the heaviest snowfalls on earth. Winds from Siberia and Mongolia howl over the Sea of Japan and make landfall on these snowy realms.

Central Honshu

In the mountainous interior of Central Honshu, a highland climate prevails. Snow piles up in the Japan Alps and surrounding ranges during winter, producing excellent winter sports conditions. Summers are warm, but less intensely humid than the coastal population centers. As a general rule of thumb, the temperature dips about 5°C (9°F) for every 1,000-meter increase in altitude.

Hokkaido

The far northern island of Hokkaido experiences long, bitter winters with heavy snowfall and pleasant summers that lack the oppressively sweltering humidity felt throughout much of the country. The northern island also sees less rain. The warmer seasons are shorter than in the rest of Japan, with spring coming late (around early May) and autumn coming early (around late September or early October).

Inland Sea

Moving south, the Inland Sea region, which includes northern Shikoku and the southern San'yo coast of Western Honshu, has a distinct climate of its own. This idyllic section of the country is largely sunny, but droughts can occur in the region. Moreover, the overwhelming floods that ravaged this mostly sun-drenched region in 2018 are a reminder that it's not immune to inclement weather.

Southern Islands

Farther south, from southern Kyushu to Okinawa, winters, spring, and autumn are significantly milder than elsewhere in the country, while summers are hot, though many of the islands are slightly cooled by a year-round sea breeze.

Tsuyu

From late May or early June, tsuyu (rainy season) descends on much of the country. Showers vary from heavy to nonexistent during this period. Then, from July through September, typhoons that begin farther south in the tropical Pacific begin to work their way across Japan, starting in Okinawa and moving north. These storms often batter the southern half of the country, before gradually tapering off as they reach Tohoku. Hokkaido, separated from Honshu by the Straits of Tsugaru, is generally spared. These midsummer squalls can be unpleasant and can occasionally turn dangerous. Take any forecasted typhoon into consideration when planning a trip, but not to the extent of avoiding the country altogether.

Extreme Weather Events

In recent years, in line with broader climate change sweeping the globe, Japan has had record-high temperatures in summer and winters that are either short and mild, or in some cases bitterly cold. Extreme rainfall, including floods and landslides, has also become more common. Most notably, in the summer of 2018 floods devastated large swaths of western Japan, killing nearly 200 people, leaving thousands without water and electricity, and forcing millions to evacuate.

ENVIRONMENTAL ISSUES

At a glance, Japan is stunning, with craggy spines blanketed in forest, pristine rivers coursing through steep ravines, and sweeping seaside cliffs plummeting into unspoiled bays. Look closer, however, and blemishes reveal a harsh truth: The postwar development rush has not been kind to the environment. The country's environmental issues are many, afflicting both land and sea.

Construction and consumer waste have blighted the landscape, and sustainable forestry has been supplanted by boundless sugi (cedar) plantations. Offshore, the oceans have been severely depleted by overfishing, Japanese ships sustain a highly contentious whaling industry, and smaller boats execute a deplorable dolphin hunt. Meanwhile, the nuclear catastrophe flowing out from Fukushima has seeped into the surrounding earth and spread to all corners of the planet, carried by ocean currents.

Overfishing

Japan's dietary dependence on seafood is taxing on the world's fish stocks. To lessen your own footprint, keep an eye on your consumption of the hardest hit species, such as uni (sea urchin) and hon-maguro (bluefin tuna). Japan agreed to halve its quota for southern bluefin tuna to 3,000 tonnes (3.3 tons) per year from 2005 to 2012, after overshooting the former quota of 6,000 tonnes (6.6 tons) by a whopping 1,800 tonnes (1.1 tons) in 2005.

Waste and Pollution

The proliferation of plastic and staggering levels of consumption of every kind make waste management a perennial challenge. All told, 41.1 tonnes (45.4 tons) of municipal solid waste are generated annually in Japan, the eighth-highest worldwide, with 20.8 percent of that being recycled.

Disposable wooden chopsticks (waribashi), which are dispensed freely by restaurants and convenience stores, further contribute to the excess of waste. About 130 million pairs of chopsticks are discarded daily; to avoid wasting wood and adding to the landfill, consider picking up a pair of "my hashi" (my chopsticks), which are stored in a case and reused. These chopsticks kits are sold in lifestyle shops like Tokyu Hands and Loft, and in some convenience stores. For perspective, some estimates place the toll for the production of these throwaway chopsticks at 400,000 cubic meters of forest annually.

Fukushima and Nuclear Power

The ongoing nuclear crisis in Fukushima is the most pressing environmental issue facing Japan today. When the mega-quake struck off the coast of Tohoku on March 11, 2011, six reactors melted down. Since then, radioactive fuel has been leaking from the complex, into which up to 150 tons of groundwater leaks daily. And this is an improvement. The figure once stood at 400 tons before TEPCO installed pumps and its $300 million ice wall.

Aside from the region immediately surrounding Fukushima's reactors, the country is officially deemed safe for visitors and citizens.

Nonetheless, groups of concerned citizens, scientists, and activists have taken radiation monitoring into their own hands. To find current radiation levels (from non-government sources), visit Safecast (https://blog.safecast.org) or the Citizens' Nuclear Information Center (www.cnic.jp) online.

Meanwhile, there are signs of hope that a deeper environmental consciousness is slowly taking hold. Civil consciousness surrounding nuclear energy has taken off significantly in the years following Fukushima. Protestors routinely gather in Tokyo's public squares and in front of government offices to voice their opposition to the use of nuclear power. Under former Prime Minister Shinzō Abe, who resigned in September 2020, the government pushed to keep nuclear power. It's hard to say what will happen under the new PM, Yoshihide Suga.

Plants and Animals

When it comes to flora and fauna, it helps to think of Japan as being divided into three broad regions: temperate in the center (Honshu, Shikoku, and Kyushu), subarctic in the north (Hokkaido), and subtropical in the far southwest (Okinawa and the other southwestern island chains).

Within these three zones, remarkable variations exist in plant life. To delve deep into the archipelago's natural world, **Japan Nature Guides** (www.japannatureguides.com) offers a range of services to help with birdwatching tours and other excursions, as well as in-depth guidebooks about wildlife of the islands.

TREES

Roughly two-thirds of Japan is forested, even after the post-World War II construction boom. While forests envelop much of Japan today, around half of this cover is comprised of matsu (pine) and sugi (cedar) plantations.

These cookie-cutter forests once served the lumber industry, falling into disuse in the 1970s when the nation began to import timber from its tropical neighbors at an eyebrow-raising rate. Historically, the Kiso Valley of Nagano Prefecture has been famous for its prized timber. The imperial seal of approval has meant that the wood from this region has long been used in the construction of key structures, with Tokyo's most venerable shrine, Meiji Jingū, among them.

Beyond the ubiquitous pines and cedars, other common species include hinoki (Japanese cypress), a smattering of bamboo varieties, and a host of deciduous trees, from oaks to maples that blaze with color every autumn, and, of course, the beloved cherry tree, famed for vivid pink petals that dazzle every corner of the nation every spring.

As you travel south, you'll also notice an increase in palm trees: Miyazaki Prefecture's Nichinan Coast resembles southern California more than it does most of Honshu's coast. In the far south, some of Okinawa's islands are swathed in forest that resembles jungle. Iriomote-jima's dense mangrove swamps are a prime example.

FLOWERS

Japan has a reverence for flowers. Plum blossoms, which bring winter to a close, are soon followed by waves of pink sakura (cherry blossoms): nature's way of announcing the arrival of spring. These beloved blossoms erupt northward, first popping in Okinawa in February, and finishing their journey in Hokkaido in May. The unofficial national flower of Japan, sakura has an outsize presence in the nation's psyche.

Meanwhile, violet wisterias bloom around the end of April; hydrangeas and irises flourish in June; and lotus blossoms, sunflowers, and lavender cover fields like patches of a quilt in July and August. These waves of summer blooms draw enthusiasts to wildflower hot

The Art of the Japanese Garden

Evolving over more than a millennium, Japanese gardens have a distinct way of mimicking nature in miniaturized, idealized form. Their elements are diverse—moss, trees, shrubs, stones, lanterns, water—and are often symbolic: raked sand embodies waves, ponds become vast lakes, moss-encrusted boulders evoke mountains in mythic landscapes from Chinese lore or Buddhist scripture.

GARDEN TYPES

Changing with the times, gardens in Japan have ranged from places of spiritual contemplation to aristocratic playgrounds. The earliest examples were the pebble-strewn promenades seen around Shinto shrines. As Chinese culture began to exert its pull in the 6th century, garden design followed the lead of the Middle Kingdom, with large ponds, stone bridges high enough for boats to pass underneath, and gravel areas for parties.

- The latter part of the Heian period (794-1185) saw the emergence of **Pure Land Gardens,** named after the eponymous school of Buddhism. These lofty creations were modeled after the paradise that followers were said to reach after a lifetime of devotion.
- With the ascent of Zen Buddhism and the warrior class during the Kamakura period (1185-1333), up through the Muromachi period (1333-1568), spare, pragmatic **kare-sansui (dry landscape) gardens** proliferated. The focus of these gardens is on gravel and sand raked into symmetrical patterns, punctuated by carefully placed large shards of stone. These stark spaces are maintained by contemplative monks.
- The next leap for garden design came in the Azuchi-Momoyama period (1573-1603), with the emergence of the classic **tea garden.** These spaces evolved alongside the development of the tea ceremony and sit beside rustic teahouses flanked by stone lanterns and surrounded by trees and shrubs.
- Tea gardens were largely subsumed into the next trend: **shūyū (stroll gardens),** elaborate Edo period (1603-1867) creations that are what you likely see in your mind's eye when you envision a Japanese garden. Paths lead through a fastidiously created landscape, often set beside castles and nobles' estates, with ponds teeming with koi, stone bridges, bamboo groves, teahouses, and open-air pavilions.

To dig deeper, good books include *Zen Gardens and Temples of Kyoto,* by John Dougill and John Einarsen; *Japanese Gardens: Tranquility, Simplicity, Harmony,* by Geeta Mehta, Kimie Tada, and Noboru Murata; and *The Art of the Japanese Garden,* by David and Michiko Young.

spots, while hikers marvel at similar displays in mountain meadows nationwide.

Heading into autumn, spider lilies unfold their spindly arms in September and October, while the chrysanthemum, Japan's official national flower, blooms from September to November.

MAMMALS

A vast range of mammals inhabit Japan. Kyushu, Shikoku, Honshu, and Hokkaido fall into the Palaearctic region, home to temperate and subarctic mammals, many of which have links to East Asia. Kyushu and the Okinawa Prefecture fall into the Oriental region, a balmier zone inhabited by subtropical and tropical animals linked to Southeast Asia.

Starting with Hokkaido in the far north, we find a subarctic menagerie: Ussuri brown bears (black grizzly) live here, along with arctic hares, Eurasian red squirrels, Siberian flying squirrels, and the cute northern pika, to name but a few. Sadly, the Hokkaido (Ezo) wolf, which once stalked the island, is now extinct.

Moving south, the iconic Japanese macaque (also referred to as a "snow monkey"), which is endemic to Japan, is perhaps the most recognizable mammal of all. These ornery primates live in an area that stretches from the northern periphery of Honshu to the emerald island of Yakushima, off the southern coast of Kyushu. Atop Honshu's food chain is the Asiatic black bear, smaller than its cousins in Hokkaido. Some 15,000 of these bears are believed to roam the forests and mountains of Honshu.

Other land-dwelling mammals include the endemic Japanese serow, which looks like a cross between a goat and an antelope, and lives in mountains and forests from northern Honshu to Shikoku and northern Kyushu; the wild boar (inushishi); Japanese sika deer; the tanuki, or raccoon dog; and red foxes, which feature heavily in Shinto myth. Note that the "fox villages" found in some parts of Honshu are sad affairs with cooped-up foxes and are not worth visiting. Honshu's coastal mammals include sea lions and fur seals, while endangered otters flit through some of Shikoku's remote rivers. Like the Ezo wolf, the Japanese wolf that once prowled the woodlands of Honshu is extinct.

In the subtropical southwest, a few interesting mammalian species include the large Ryūkyū flying fox (Ryūkyū fruit bat), the severely endangered Iriomote lynx, and on the Amami Islands just north of Okinawa, the endangered dark-furred Amami rabbit and the endangered Amami spiny mouse, a sexually flexible rodent that lacks Y chromosomes.

It's also worth noting that Japan has a few native dog breeds, namely the medium-size Shiba Inu and the larger Akita, which are both spitz types (pointed ears, thick fur). Cats are ubiquitous and beloved across Japan as well. In a few cases, they have proliferated to such a degree that they have come to occupy their own islands, such as Aoshima, off the coast of Shikoku in the Inland Sea, where felines outnumber humans.

SEA LIFE

All told, some 3,000 species of aquatic life inhabit Japan. This remarkable diversity of marine life is partly due to a few distinct ocean currents. Warm water flows from Taiwan to Okinawa and the southwest islands, branching off into two separate currents when it hits Kyushu. Meanwhile, coming from the north, the cold waters move toward northeastern Hokkaido, veering south toward northeastern Honshu.

Japan's most colorful sea life is found in the subtropical waters of Okinawa and the Southwest Islands, where anemone, butterfly fish, parrotfish, sea turtles, and many species of shark dart among vibrant coral reefs in the deep-blue waters. From January through March, humpback whales flock to the waters of Okinawa, escaping the frigid waters of Alaska's Aleutian Islands, 5,100 kilometers (3,169 mi) to the north.

In the Pacific south of Shikoku and Honshu swim loggerhead turtles, dugongs, and dolphins. The frigid waters off Hokkaido teem with humpback whales, gray whales, blue whales, orcas, and giant crabs. And elsewhere, a range of marine life teems in the oceans surrounding Japan, from dolphins and flying squid to sea bream, surgeonfish, tuna, seabass, sting rays, sharks, jellyfish, and snappers, to name but a few.

Freshwater fish living in the nation's rivers, lakes, and streams include carp, ayu (sweet fish), eel, and more.

BIRDS

Perhaps the most recognizable of Japan's numerous avian species is the red-crowned crane of Hokkaido, a lithe creature with a red crop of feathers atop its head. Throughout the country, there are many types of ducks, geese, swans, herons, kingfishers, pheasants, black kites, hazel grouses (Hokkaido), and cormorants. The Blakiston's fish owl, which lives only on Hokkaido, is one of the world's largest owls. The crested serpent eagle lives and hunts on some of the subtropical southwest islands, while the Steller's sea eagle, an imposing bird of prey, soars over northern Hokkaido.

REPTILES

Turtles and small lizards such as geckos are found throughout much of Japan, but make their strongest showing in the subtropical islands of Okinawa. In addition, some 50 species of snake live in Japan. As one of the Chinese zodiac's 12 animals, snakes have a potent symbolic significance in Japan, and elsewhere in East Asia, where they are traditionally thought to serve as divine messengers. While most of them are harmless, there are a few poisonous species on the islands extending southward from Kyushu. Of particular note, the thick habu (pit viper), which can grow to 2 meters (6.6 feet) in length or more, as well as coral snakes, slither through Okinawa's balmy forests.

INSECTS AND ARACHNIDS

To the chagrin of many residents in Japan's urban centers, gokiburi (cockroaches) are common any time of year in humid parts of the country, and most common during summer in drier climes. Another insect that sometimes finds its way into homes is the gejigeji (house centipede), which looks positively terrifying, though it's harmless and is only interested in eating other insects.

Outdoors, the hum of cicadas peaks at around 120 decibels during summer, making a walk through a forest or park as loud as a rock concert. Mosquitoes can be a nuisance in the warmer months and near any freshwater source.

Generally speaking, Japan's insects are relatively harmless and few are poisonous, but there are some insects to avoid. The vividly colored, spiked caterpillar known as the denkimushi (electric bug) secretes poisonous chemicals from small prickly stingers when touched. Leeches are common in the mountains, both on land and in water. Measuring up to 38 centimeters (15 inches), the mukade (giant centipede) has a highly poisonous bite. The most dangerous of all is the Japanese Giant Hornet, a subspecies of the Asian giant hornet, the world's largest. They can be aggressive if provoked, and their sting is extremely painful and may require a trip to the hospital.

Most of Japan's spiders are also harmless. Although the Huntsman spider is as wide as a dinner plate, it is harmless to humans. The Jorō spider, on the other hand—with black and yellow legs and a vividly colored body—is poisonous; its bite isn't deadly, but it is serious. The most dangerous spider found in Japan is the redback spider, whose bite can occasionally be deadly. Unfortunately, these spiders have been seen in more than 20 of Japan's prefectures, largely in the west.

AMPHIBIANS

Around 40 frog species live in Japan, including the Japanese rain frog, Japanese tree frog, and American bullfrog, which is common in ponds. A number of toad species are also found across the country. An amphibian of particular note is the Japanese giant salamander, the second-largest salamander in the world. Endemic to the rocky bottoms of swiftly flowing streams in southwestern Japan, the giant salamander reaches up to 1.5 meters (5 feet). In folklore, they are referred to as hanzaki, a name that suggests they remain alive even if they've been chopped in half (han). They are also popularly known as ōsanshōuo (giant pepper fish), a name that stems from the white, sticky mucus that smells like peppers, which they secrete when provoked by a predator.

History

ANCIENT CIVILIZATION

For a period of time around 18,000 BC, there was a land bridge linking Japan to the Asian continent. Japan's first inhabitants traveled over this bridge from the mainland. This overland link to the rest of Asia vanished when sea levels rose around 10,000 BC. Architectural touches and some facial features of the Japanese population today suggest that Polynesian seafarers may also have made the long journey north to the islands in the ancient past. In truth, the origins of Japanese people are highly complex and debated, with genetic input believed to originate in groups all around Asia, from Tibetans and Koreans to Han Chinese.

Jōmon Period

The earliest civilization emerged in Japan during the Jōmon period (14,000-300 BC), a hunter-gatherer culture known for its "cord-marked" pottery made by pressing cords onto wet clay. This pottery tradition is thought to be among the oldest not only in East Asia, but the whole world.

Yayoi Period

During the following Yayoi period (300 BC-AD 300), rice cultivation techniques and metalworking arrived from mainland Asia. An intriguing semi-mythical figure from this period was Queen Himiko (AD 183-248), who reigned over the realm of Yamatai. The name Himiko (Sun Child) hints at her divine descent from the sun goddess Amaterasu. She was an unmarried priestess purporting to wield significant shamanic power. Although Himiko does not appear in any of Japan's ancient records, she was mentioned in those of China, where she established diplomatic ties.

Scholars debate who Himiko really was and where Yamatai was located (the region around Nara has been proposed). Around 100 kingdoms were arrayed throughout the islands during Himiko's reign, of which she may have overseen a loose grouping of about 30. Her ruling over this small federation led the Chinese to view her as the leader of all Japan.

EARLY HISTORY

Yamato Period (250-710)

KOFUN PERIOD (250-538)

The first section of the Yamato period, the Kofun period was named after a type of burial mound used for the period's elite. These megalithic tombs ranged from relatively modest square-shaped mounds to massive mounds hundreds of meters long, surrounded by moats and laden with sometimes thousands of artifacts. All told, more than 160,000 Kofun have been discovered around Japan, with a heavy concentration around modern-day Kansai and Western Honshu.

During this period, the Shinto religion began to take shape, its principles and practices growing from older beliefs from the Yayoi period. During the Kofun period, a plethora of small kingdoms existed in Japan. The Yamato clan, which would eventually become the imperial family, rose to the top of that power structure. Contact with China and Korea also grew, with Japan taking on a more formal political identity of its own.

ASUKA PERIOD (538-710)

As the Kofun period drew to a close, the Yamato clan had fully established itself as the imperial family of Japan. The key features of the Asuka period were the introduction of Buddhism in the mid-6th century and the adoption and adaptation of Chinese characters to form Japan's own written script. Coinage, in the form of the Wado kaiho, was also introduced. Japan began to borrow heavily from China, perceived as a highly civilized role model. The period is named after Asuka, the capital during the period, today in the northern Nara Prefecture.

The first bona fide historical emperor rose to power during this period, Emperor Kimmei (509-571). Empress Suiko (554-628) and Prince Shōtoku (574-622) were by far the period's most prominent leaders. As Suiko's regent, Shōtoku initiated government reforms, stamped out corruption and entrenched nepotism, and established embassies with the Chinese Sui Dynasty around 607.

Shōtoku is believed to have drawn up Japan's first constitution, the Jushichijo-kenpo (Seventeen Article Constitution) in 604. This document centralized Japan's government and emphasized the Confucian principle of wa (harmony).

Shōtoku heavily promoted Buddhism, erecting 46 monasteries and temples, including Hōryū-ji in modern-day Nara, the only monastery still standing that was originally built in the Asuka period. This initial push to adopt Buddhism would significantly alter Japan's spiritual development over the longer term and signal to its more powerful neighbors that the country had "arrived." In addition to an increasingly sophisticated system of government and a deeper spiritual life, the Asuka period also saw a creative boom as music and literature flourished in and around the imperial court.

Within this milieu, the upstart Fujiwara clan rose to prominence through a coup in AD 645, wresting power from the Soga clan, which had controlled the government since 587. Inspired by China, Emperor Kōtoku reshaped the new government through the Taika Reform of 645, shortly after the death of Shōtoku. The sweeping changes of these reforms included introducing a codified system of law, nationalizing land, replacing forced labor with a tax system, reshuffling social classes, introducing an examination-based recruitment system for the civil service, and establishing the emperor's absolute authority. With the elevation of Emperor Tenjin (626-672), along with his senior minister Nakatomi no Kamatari (614-669), who was granted the surname Fujiwara, the Fujiwara clan ascended to a position of great power, where they would remain for centuries to come.

Nara Period (710-794)

During the brief Nara period, the capital relocated to Nara during 710-784. Until this time, the capital moved every time an emperor or empress died. Tōdai-ji, the world's largest wooden building which houses the towering Great Buddha, was built during this time. By the end of the Nara period, the capital's population swelled to around 200,000.

Two seminal texts were penned during the Nara period, placing the nation's mythical founding in the ancient past. According to the legends recorded in the 8th century, the Kojiki, Japan's oldest written chronicle, and the Nihon Shoki (aka Nihon-gi), the second oldest, say that the mythical first emperor, Jimmu Tenno, established the nation of Japan on February 11, 660 BC. This is why the National Foundation Day holiday is held on February 11 each year. Others put his actual existence, if he existed at all, closer to AD 100.

In many ways, the Nara period saw a continuation of trends that began in the Kofun and Asuka period. The city itself, then known as Heijokyō, was modeled after the Tang Dynasty's capital of Chang-an and was laid out on a Chinese grid pattern. Its architecture was similarly Chinese in appearance. A Confucian university was built and the government became increasingly bureaucratic, mimicking the mandarins of the Tang court.

Smallpox outbreaks (735-737) killed 25-35 percent of the population. Faced with widespread poverty, and occasionally struck with famine, the remaining citizens became resentful of the increased meddling of the Yamato court in Japan's outlying areas, and the largely agrarian provinces grew restless. The government in Nara responded by establishing military outposts in the provinces. Fujiwara no Hirotsugu raised an army in Dazaifu, Kyushu, then led a rebellion in 740 that was quashed by a 17,000-strong army sent by Emperor Shomu (724-749 CE).

It's worth noting that three empresses

ruled during the Nara period: Gemmei ruled 707-715; Gensho ruled 715-724; and Koken ruled 749-758 and again as Shōtoku 764-770. This would be the last empress for 800 years. Women were also able to own land during this time.

Heian Period (794-1185)

As the Nara period drew to a close, Emperor Kammu (736-806) moved the capital in 794 to Heiankyō (modern-day Kyoto), where the imperial court remained for more than a millennium, marking the start of a pivotal stage in Japan's history.

During this time, Japan began to wean itself off Chinese influence, taking on an isolationist stance that would greatly intensify in the ensuing centuries. Although the flow of cultural and commercial exchange did continue, Japan became less politically engaged with China. Exchanges between Japanese and Chinese scholars, monks, and creatives gradually wound down, however, and Japanese civilization began to take on its own distinct characteristics.

During this time, Shinto and Buddhism began to fuse, becoming both the state religion as well as the faith of commoners. Buddhism flourished, with Shingon Buddhism being founded by Kūkai (774-835), or Kobo Daishi. The Tendai sect was also founded during this era by Saicho (767-822).

It was during this period that Japan began to hone its own artistic style. Courtiers in elaborate silk costumes and poets engaged in trysts and intrigue, leading to a remarkable leap forward in the literary arts, with the penning of classic works of literature in the early 11th century such as *The Tale of Genji,* by Lady Murasaki Shikibu, and *The Pillow Book,* by Sei Shōnagon. Beyond literature, court artists actively developed the arts of screen paintings, scrolls, calligraphy, and music, and enjoyed teasing their intellects with the complex strategy board game known as go.

Politically, the period was marked by significant influence exerted by the Fujiwara clan, who eventually fell into a feud with lesser nobles, including the Taira (aka Heike) and Minamoto (aka Genji) families. Under the helm of Taira no Kiyomori (1118-1181), the Taira clan challenged the Fujiwara and Minamoto, and emerged victorious in 1160, ruling for 20 years. Taira rulers succumbed to corruption and vice and were supplanted by the victorious Minamoto clan, led by Yoritomo Minamoto (1147-1199), in the Genpei War (1180-1185), waged for control of the imperial throne.

Following the war's final conflict, the Battle of Dannoura, Tomomori, who led the Taira forces, and Antoku, the would-be young Taira emperor, committed suicide. Yoritomo then granted himself the title of Shōgun (Generalissimo) upon the death of Emperor Go-Shirakawa in 1192, an honor normally only granted to a general. With this bold move, the illustrious Heian period came to an end, ushering in the beginning of Japan's military-dominated feudal age.

FEUDAL JAPAN

Kamakura Period (1185-1333)

Japan's long, tumultuous feudal era would last seven centuries, beginning with the Kamakura period. Major political change came with this new era, including control of the government falling under the newly declared shogunate and military ruler, Yoritomo Minamoto.

Although Yoritomo officially operated under the distant emperor, in truth, he was the new de facto head of government. While the emperor remained in Heiankyō (Kyoto), Yoritomo set up his new bakufu (tent government) in Kamakura. A lord-vassal system emerged, and the age of the samurai was born. Staunch loyalty was a hallmark of the new cultural ethos, which was markedly militaristic in tone.

When Yoritomo died under suspicious circumstances in 1199, his widow, Masako, began to lay the foundation for the Hōjō Shogunate, under her own family. By the late Kamakura period, the state was tried by invasion attempts by Kublai Khan, who led forces from Mongolia across the Sea of Japan in 1274. He tried again in 1281, bringing with him a 100,000-strong armada. This time Japan was spared by a kamikaze (divine wind) that sunk half of the mighty fleet, while spirited warriors in Kyushu finished the job.

Still, Japan began to unravel internally due to increased regional infighting. Emperor Go-Daigo and his court made efforts to bring full control of the government under the throne, hatching a plot to do away with the bakufu. When the conspiracy was discovered, Go-Daigo was exiled to far-flung Oki Island off the coast of modern-day Shimane Prefecture.

Meanwhile, local chieftains in the Kinai area (modern Kyoto and Nara) assembled an army and took the Kamakura bakufu by storm. Two vassals of the ruling Hōjō clan, Ashikaga Takauji and Nitta Yoshisada, helped clinch the victory for the imperial forces, wiping out the majority of Hōjō elites. This effectively brought the Kamakura period to a close.

Muromachi Period (1333-1568)

Following the overthrow of the Kamakura bakufu, Emperor Go-Daigo returned from exile to Kyoto and swiftly instituted reforms aimed at restoring imperial rule, sending family members to serve as administrators in the outlying provinces.

Many warriors felt that Go-Daigo unfairly rewarded his own family, while neglecting the men who fought on his behalf. In response, Ashikaga turned on Go-Daigo and forced the emperor to the Yoshino Mountains outside Nara in 1336. Go-Daigo then established the Southern Court near Nara, while Ashikaga appointed a puppet emperor in Kyoto. These two rival courts were engaged in an ongoing feud for the next six decades, until Takauji's grandson Yoshimitsu finally settled the score in 1392, after which the imperial line descended through the Northern Court of Kyoto.

When Go-Daigo fled to Yoshino, Ashikaga Takauji established a bakufu of his own in Kyoto. From Kyoto, Takauji's grandson Yoshimitsu neutralized all rivals and was declared prime minister. He resuscitated trade and diplomatic relations with China, then in the Ming Dynasty.

Despite these advancements, the era was largely characterized by an ongoing state of civil war between regional lords (daimyo) and their loyal armies of bushi (samurai warriors). There was also widespread economic instability, famine, and disagreement over who would become the next shogun.

Combined, these developments created the perfect conditions for the breakout of the Onin War (1467-1477), which erupted around the midway point of the Muromachi period, marking the beginning of the Sengoku (Warring States) period (1467-1600). The eastern Hosokawa faction, backed by the shogun and emperor, clashed with the western Yamana faction, supported by the powerful Ōuchi family. Fires raged in the capital, decimating temples and grand homes. Fighting gradually bled into the provinces, where local samurai led defensive uprisings against shugo (military governors) who oversaw large swaths of land. Amid the chaos, some of these samurai ended up establishing themselves as local lords.

The warrior class set the cultural tone during this period. The ideals of Zen Buddhism, such as austerity, simplicity, and self-discipline, meshed well with the samurai class. This led to the rise of refined arts such as ikebana (flower arrangement), Noh theater, renga (linked verse) poetry, and the painstaking social ritual that is the tea ceremony. Many priests and aristocrats fled the volatile capital to surrounding towns, spreading Kyoto's rarefied culture to the outlying provinces.

In 1543, a Portuguese ship was blown ashore on the small island of Tanega-shima, off the southern coast of Kyushu. The exotic foreigners, who were the first Europeans to arrive in Japan's history, came bearing guns and Christianity. This disruptive foreign faith took off. Many daimyo adopted the new faith in hopes of facilitating commerce with European merchants and accessing the revolutionary weapons the Europeans brought with them.

True to the violent times, the arcane art of musket construction became prized knowledge among daimyo, who clamored to get their hands on the new military technology. A warlord with a particular affinity for firearms was the ruthless Oda Nobunaga (1534-1582). Although he never became shogun, he did manage to topple Kyoto and seize control of it in 1568, deposing Ashikaga Yoshiaki in 1573 and effectively bringing the Ashikaga shogunate to a close. This made Nobunaga Japan's de facto supreme leader.

Azuchi-Momoyama Period (1568-1600)

During this short period, Nobunaga and his brilliant successor, Toyotomi Hideyoshi (1537-1598), brought order to the chaos. Hideyoshi, one of Nobunaga's favorite, most brilliant generals, swiftly consolidated power and started the practice of requiring daimyo families to reside in Kyoto, effectively as hostages. Castles, built and refortified by regional daimyo, mushroomed around Honshu and Kyushu during this turbulent period.

Hideyoshi's main rival was Tokugawa Ieyasu (1543-1616), a local lord originally from a domain near modern-day Nagoya. Ieyasu decided to pledge his fealty to Hideyoshi, who allowed Ieyasu to remain in charge of his own domain. Meanwhile, Ieyasu diligently built up and strengthened his domain. In 1586, he moved his base farther east, away from Hideyoshi, where he laid in wait for his time to pounce.

Toward the end of his life, Hideyoshi became feverish with expansionist dreams. He launched two invasions of Korea, with the hopes of going on to topple China and control Asia. This had long been the dream of his predecessor Nobunaga. The attempted invasions failed miserably, however, and severely damaged ties between Japan and Korea.

Following Hideyoshi's death, his young son Hideyori was placed behind the protective walls of Osaka Castle until he was old enough to rule. This, however, was not to be. Ieyasu seized power in the Battle of Sekigahara (1600), widely considered one of the most epic battles in Japanese history.

Edo Period (1603-1868)

In 1603, Tokugawa Ieyasu became shogun, and established his base in Edo, which would one day become Tokyo. Under the Tokugawa Shogunate, Japan enjoyed relative peace for more than 250 years. A policy called sankin kotai forced daimyo and their families to alternate between the new capital Edo and their home state, controlling the daimyo and keeping any hidden ambitions in check.

During this time, Japan strictly enforced the sakoku (closed country) policy, spurred by meddling by foreign missionaries. Christianity was flat-out banned following the Shimabara Rebellion (1637-1638). In 1638, all foreigners were kicked out of the country, save for a cadre of Dutch traders who swore allegiance to commerce above religion. As a result, all Western medical and scientific knowledge came via the Dutch during this age of intense isolation.

By the early 18th century, Edo had a population of more than 1 million—the world's largest city at the time, as it is today. Osaka became a mighty mercantile center, while Kyoto became a hub of leisure and luxury. Four social classes emerged: the samurai, farmers, artisans, and merchants, based on the ancient Chinese ideal of the "four occupations," derived from Confucian thought. Existing above these classes were the emperor, imperial court, shogun, and daimyos.

The merchants, at the bottom of the hierarchy, were viewed as self-serving and less crucial than farmers and artisans, but this didn't stop them from carving out a vibrant place in society. Increasingly rich merchants indulged in the arts, entertainment, and culinary pursuits. Woodblock prints known as ukiyo-e depict many of the favored pastimes from this ukiyo (floating world), including sumo tournaments, kabuki, and sprawling pleasure quarters.

By the early 19th century, the shogunate's power had begun to wane, just as the merchant class saw its influence rise. Moreover, foreigners began trying to make contact. Commodore Perry's Black Ships sailed into Edo Bay on July 8, 1853, gunboat-diplomacy style. After firing blank shots from 73 cannons—which Perry claimed was in celebration of American Independence Day—Perry sent a letter to the shogunate threatening to destroy them if they didn't comply, promising to return again a year later.

Only six months later, Perry returned with a crew of 1,600 men aboard 10 ships. They sailed into Kanagawa, and negotiated the Convention of Kanagawa on March 31, 1854. The treaty granted access to the ports of Shimoda, Shizuoka Prefecture, and Hakodate on Hokkaido. Soon after, Townsend Harris was appointed the first American diplomat to Japan. Other countries and ports followed.

From the time of Perry's arrival until the Meiji Restoration, sentiment against foreign powers and the shogunate grew. The public increasingly yearned for the emperor to be put atop the government again. On the other hand, there was also a growing sense that adopting Western science and military technology was the only hope for Japan in the new age. The tension between these two contradictory impulses set the stage for the next major sea change in Japan's history.

MODERN HISTORY

Meiji Period (1868-1912) and the Lead-Up to World War II

By 1867, the Tokugawa shogunate was crumbling under internal politics and anti-shogunate sentiment. Emperor Mutsuhito (1852-1912), posthumously renamed Emperor Meiji, was reinstalled as the head of state in the Meiji Restoration of 1868. With this monumental gesture, the feudal age came to a close and the radically transformative Meiji period began.

In the early Meiji years, real power was wielded by oligarchs from Edo, freshly made the capital and renamed Tokyo (which literally means Eastern Capital). There was a sense that Japan desperately needed to play technological, economic, and political catch-up with the West to resist colonization. Japanese scholars were sent West, and Western scholars were invited to Japan.

The ensuing changes were swift and dramatic. The first railway was built, linking Yokohama to Tokyo. A new constitution was drafted, based on Prussian and English models, and nationalized industries were formed, then sold to chosen entrepreneurs. This led to the rise of conglomerates known as zaibatsu, many of which still exist today, such as Mitsubishi, Sumitomo, and Mitsui.

Amid these developments, State Shinto replaced the Shinto-Buddhist mix that had been in favor for centuries, a symbolic return to a "purer" Japanese state, with the emperor at the top. The ban on Christianity was lifted and the rigid four-tier class system was disbanded. This led to massive upheaval for a few years, but ultimately all, save for the imperial class, were equal under the law, though women were neglected.

Japan also became militarily expansionist, annexing Korea after the Sino-Japanese War (1894-1895). Next came the Russo-Japanese War (1904-1905), which Japan also won. This victory elevated Japan's reputation as a force to be reckoned with, and won Taiwan and Liaoning peninsula as colonies.

By historical standards, the Meiji period ended with the death of the emperor on July 30, 1912. The decades that followed, leading up to the outbreak of World War II (1939-1945), were defined by Japan's increasing military and economic confidence, solidifying Japan's newfound status as the preeminent power in modern East Asia.

When World War I (1914-1918) broke out, Japan sided with the Allies. In 1914, Japan gave Germany an ultimatum: Remove all ships from the waters of Japan and China and let go of the port city of Tsingtao in China's northeast. Germany agreed, and by extension Japan was able to gain control over China, laying the groundwork for Japan to exploit China's vast pool of labor and natural resources.

In 1923, the Great Kanto Earthquake led to immense loss of life in the region surrounding the capital, with around 100,000 killed. Highlighting deeply entrenched discrimination, Japan's ethnic Korean community were falsely blamed for widespread looting and additional loss of life following the disaster. Tragically, many ethnic Koreans were hunted down and lynched by angry mobs.

World War II (1939-1945)

In the years leading up to the outbreak of World War II, Japanese forces became embroiled in a growing number of skirmishes in Manchuria. By 1937, Japan was engaged in all-out war with China, with imperial troops sacking Shanghai and advancing on Nanjing. Over several months, a staggering number of people were raped and murdered in what would become known as the Rape of Nanking. The total number of victims in the atrocity perpetuated by Japanese troops in Nanking is still debated by scholars, with some estimates as high as 400,000.

As war officially broke out in Europe, and France was defeated in 1939, Japan swooped in and overtook French Indo-China. When Japan came to blows with the U.S. over demands that Japan stop its advance, the U.S. halted oil exports to Japan, leading to Japan's devastating attack on Pearl Harbor on December 7, 1941.

In 1942, an emboldened Japan proceeded to occupy a number of other countries in the region, including the Philippines, Dutch East Indies, Burma, Malaya, Hong Kong, and Guam, among others.

The turning point came in June 1942 at the Battle of Midway, in which the Allied forces managed to wipe out most of Japan's carrier fleet. After Midway, U.S. forces proceeded to route Japan's lines of support, advancing toward the Japanese archipelago itself. By 1944, U.S. planes were bombing Japanese cities, including devastating firebombing over Tokyo.

The war came to a dramatic, decisive end when the U.S. dropped atomic bombs on Hiroshima (August 6, 1945), and then Nagasaki (August 9, 1945). Both bombs killed tens of thousands in an instant, and hundreds of thousands more through subsequent fires and radioactive fallout. Faced with utter ruin, Emperor Hirohito formally surrendered on August 15, 1945, via radio. This was the first time that the Japanese people had ever heard the voice of the emperor, who until then had been believed to be a god. Along with surrendering, the emperor renounced his divine status.

Emperor Hirohito was loathed across Asia until his passing in 1989. To this day, the barbaric Battle of Nanking is a source of intense friction between the governments of Japan and China. In Korea, Japan's wartime use of Korean "comfort women," who were forced to serve as sex slaves, is still a source of ire.

Post-War Japan

After the war, the U.S. military occupied Japan and the imperial military and navy were completely disbanded. Under General Douglas MacArthur, a new postwar constitution was written and came into effect in 1947. The constitution created a parliamentary system that gave adults age 20 and over the right to vote. The document included a pacifism clause, under which Japan was forced to pledge not to have a military with the intent or capability of waging war. The emperor's status was brought down to that of a ceremonial figurehead. In 1951, Japan inked a peace treaty with the U.S. and other former foes. Japan was finally given independence and the U.S. withdrew, although a handful of U.S. military bases remain.

From the late 1940s to the early 1950s, Japan was heavily engaged in nation building and rebuilding. From the nuclear bombing of Hiroshima and Nagasaki to firebombing raids across the nation, much of urban Japan was in shambles. Many citizens were on the verge of starving.

American influence began to creep into everything from pop culture to the nation's diet—most notably, bread and wheat products—which led to an explosion of cheap, homegrown dishes like ramen, and the take-off of Japan's own music and pop cultural sensibility. The 1950s were also the dawn of what would become known as an "economic miracle," with Japan's industry and economy astonishingly ascending to become the world's second-largest after the U.S. by the 1960s. Economic growth roared through the 1970s and early 1980s. At the peak of Japan's growth, people were splashing around ¥10,000 bills in the way most would spend a ¥1,000 note today.

The 1950s also saw major realignment in international relations, with Japan joining the United Nations in 1956. It went on to hold the 1964 summer Olympics in a radically transformed Tokyo and unveiled the first shinkansen (bullet train) that same year. In 1972, the Japanese prime minister went to China, normalizing relations, and Japan closed its embassy in Taiwan. A decade later, in 1982, Honda opened its first factory in the United States.

Emperor Hirohito was never tried for war crimes; he passed away on January 7, 1989, marking the end of the Shōwa Era, which was the longest of any in Japan's long history.

CONTEMPORARY HISTORY

Rule passed on to Hirohito's son Akihito, giving birth to the Heisei (Peace Everywhere) Era. To the shock of diehard traditionalists, the emperor married a commoner. To top it off, there was no male heir for a long stretch, spurring talks of a female ascending to the throne for the first time in millennia.

From around 1986 the economy reached "bubble" proportions, fueled by inflated real estate and stock prices, until it popped in 1992. Stagnation stretched from 1991 until 2010, a period that is often called the "lost decades."

Underscoring the downturn were a series of calamities, starting with the 6.9-magnitude Great Hanshin Earthquake that struck Kobe on January 17, 1995. This natural disaster was followed two months later by the heinous sarin nerve gas attack on the Tokyo subway, carried out by members of the Aum Shinrikyo doomsday cult on March 20, 1995. Another major disaster rocked the nation 16 years later on March 11, 2011, when the 9.0-magnitude Great Tohoku earthquake and tsunami not only killed an estimated 18,000, but also triggered the ongoing meltdown at Fukushima's nuclear plants.

Japan's relations with its neighbors, namely Korea and China, began to improve in the early 2000s, beginning with Prime Minister Koizumi Junichiro's visits to Seoul in 2001 and Pyongyang in 2002. Then Chinese Prime Minister Wen Jiabao addressed Japan's parliament and touted the two nations' strengthening ties in April 2007, by which point Shinzō Abe had succeeded Koizumi as Prime Minister.

To the dismay of peaceniks, the government approved a reinterpretation of the pacifist Article 9 of the postwar constitution in July 2014. This reinterpretation calls for allowing Japan to come to the aid of allies if attacked. This controversial shift in tone has ignited furious debates. Former Prime Minister Abe declared that 2020 would be a deadline to finalize the revision of the article, but at the time of writing, the revision was still not yet finalized. Abe's decision to step down from power in September 2020 left the agenda hanging, although his replacement, Prime Minister Yoshihide Suga, expressed his intention to clarify the status and existence of Japan's Self-Defense Forces.

Emperor Akihito shocked the nation in August 2016 when he expressed his desire to abdicate: the first time this had been done in about two centuries. The Heisei era finally ended on April 30, 2019, when Crown Prince Naruhito officially ascended to the throne to become the 126th emperor of Japan, the beginning of the Reiwa period.

Naruhito has broken with tradition in a number of ways, having studied overseas at Oxford, married a commoner, and been surprisingly candid about the struggles that he and his wife, Empress Masako (nee Owada), have had with their attempts to have a male heir. Soul-searching about the legacy of the turbulent Heisei era is ongoing; only time will tell what the tone of the new era will be.

Government and Economy

ORGANIZATION

Japan is a constitutional monarchy with a parliamentary system. According to the postwar constitution, the emperor is head of state, but is expressly restricted from participating in politics. Pacifism is a key element of the constitution. Japan is banned from having atomic weaponry or maintaining a standing army, although it does maintain self-defense forces, which in recent years have gone on missions abroad but never engaged in combat.

The government is led by a prime minister who is elected from a majority ruling party of the government, known as the National Diet (legislative), plus Cabinet members (executive). The Diet is split between two parts, the House of Representatives, which is more powerful in practice, and the House of Councillors. Together, both houses draft and ratify all bills. The judiciary is headed by the Supreme Court, with three levels of lesser courts under it. A majority vote is needed to elect an official or pass a bill.

POLITICAL PARTIES

In theory, a range of parties occupy Japan's political spectrum. In practice, the Liberal Democratic Party (LDP), which leans conservative, has ruled the roost more or less from the time it formed in 1955, with only brief interludes. At the time of writing, the Prime Minister is Fumio Kishida, who took the place of Yoshihide Suga in October 2021. Another party that wields significant influence is the Komeito. This small fringe party is a stalwart coalition party of the LDP, as well as the political arm of the mainstream religious group Soka Gakkai, to which many ascribe cultish undertones.

The main opposition party was once the Democratic Party (DP), which was virtually wiped out in the 2017 general elections, and splintered into two factions: the Constitutional Democratic Party of Japan (CDP) and the Democratic Party for the People (DPP). Further toward the fringe are the Japanese Communist Party (JCP) and the Social Democratic Party of Japan (SDPJ).

Scandals have swirled around former Prime Minister Abe; among them was his alleged donation to a nationalist elementary school, which was able to buy government land for a fraction of its price. Abe's image took another hit when his friend and former Administrative Vice Finance Minister Junichi Fukuda was accused of committing sexual harassment in 2018. Abe has also been revealed to be a member of Nippon Kaigi (Japan Conference), a right-wing group of lobbyists intent on restoring Japan to the supposed glory of its pre-World War II imperial days; that would mean trashing the postwar constitution as well as human rights, doing away with sexual equality, and booting out foreigners.

ELECTIONS

Japan holds three types of elections: a general election for the House of Representatives (supposed to occur every four years, but snap elections are common); an election for the House of Councillors, held every three years; and local government elections held every four years.

Recent voter turnout has been lackluster. In the 2017 election for the House of Representatives, election turnout was around 54 percent, just above the nearly 53 percent turnout of 2014, which was the lowest in postwar Japanese history. Since 2018, citizens aged

18 and over have a legal right to vote. Despite the drops in voting age, young people remain largely unengaged, except for short-lived examples like the Students Emergency Action for Liberal Democracy (SEALDs), which led anti-LDP protests in 2015 and 2016.

In September 2020, Yoshihide Suga, the former prime minister Shinzō Abe's cabinet secretary, became Japan's 99th prime minister. PM Suga faced a daunting host of issues across the social, political, and economic spectrum, all exacerbated by the coronavirus pandemic. Amid criticism for his handling of the pandemic, Suga was replaced in October 2021 by Fumio Kishida, a hereditary politician with strong LDP ties who formerly served as Foreign Minister in Shinzō Abe's cabinet. Time will tell how his tenure shapes up.

AGRICULTURE

Japan conjures images of rice fields and rolling tea plantations. Yet, very little of Japan's land is actually suitable for cultivation, and it's shrinking—from 15.4 percent of the country in 1961 to 11.5 percent in 2015. Terrace farming allows for maximum use of limited space. Japan has one of the highest levels of crop yield per area of any country in the world.

Due to a decline in rice consumption, and wheat production facing a setback due to typhoon damage, the nation's food self-sufficiency dropped to 38 percent in 2016, the lowest in 23 years. The government has set an ambitious target of raising that figure to 45 percent by 2025.

Japan's agriculture sector is highly subsidized, even coddled, and sheltered from outside influences. Japanese farmers always take precedence, even if it means consumers paying top yen. This is particularly true for rice, by far Japan's most protected crop, with tariffs of up to 778 percent. Quotas have at least expanded through recent trade deals under the Trans-Pacific Partnership (TPP) and with the European Union.

INDUSTRY

Toyota. Honda. Sony. Nintendo. Nikon. Canon. Fuji. Toshiba. Panasonic. Softbank. Nippon Steel. Shiseido. Uniqlo. Muji. The list goes on. Japan is known globally as a juggernaut of industry and commerce, producing vehicles, electronics, ships, (bio)chemicals, machine components, tools, and increasingly softer items like snacks, cosmetics, fashion, lifestyle goods, and so much more. By far, Japan's main exports are vehicles, followed by machinery. As of 2012, Toyota was the largest vehicle producer in the world.

From the Meiji period through WWII, a cluster of zaibatsu exerted an outsized influence on the Japanese economy. The four biggest zaibatsu were still-surviving Mitsubishi, Mitsui, Sumitomo, and the disbanded Yasuda group. Sumitomo is the oldest of the lot, having been founded during the Edo period in 1615.

Following World War II, the keiretsu ("system" or "grouping of enterprises"), a new form of business grouping that is arranged horizontally and vertically, emerged. The members of these newer business groupings all own shares in each other's stock and are served by the same bank at the center, the idea being to reduce the risk of stock market turbulence and any potential takeover attempts. Former zaibatsu Mitsubishi, Mitsui, and Sumitomo have lived on as members of the "Big Six" keiretsu, along with Fuyo, Sanwa, and the Mizuho Financial Group.

When Sony released its Walkman in 1979, the product represented a major turning point for personal gadgets, ultimately leading to the ubiquitous MP3 player. While Japan has been knocked off its pedestal somewhat by electronics brands in South Korea and China, it remains a giant in the field.

DISTRIBUTION OF WEALTH

Japan has a robust middle class, with GDP per capita at $34,428.10 in 2017, making it 23rd globally. On paper, it is among the most equal economies in the world, but poverty does exist. Generally speaking, there is a widespread attitude among Japanese that it is virtually immoral for company executives to receive the kinds of exorbitant salaries that are commonplace in the West.

Under current laws, part-time workers do not have the same access to nationalized healthcare or to the pension system, leaving those not adequately plugged into the system in a precarious position. For those who do pay into the pension system, the returns are miniscule. For this reason, some elderly people can't afford to stop working, and many of them reside in rural areas, where resources are dwindling due to depopulation.

TOURISM

Before the COVID-19 pandemic, tourism had been a bright spot in Japan's otherwise sluggish economy in recent years. When the 2011 Tohoku earthquake and tsunami battered the country's economy and morale, inbound tourist numbers dipped to 6.2 million. When Tokyo won the bid to host the 2020 Summer Olympics, the government set about to change that trend, aiming to attract 20 million annual visitors by 2020. By 2015, the number of overseas visitors positively exploded, shooting up to 19.7 million. The figure just kept climbing, hitting 31.2 million in 2018 and 31.9 million in 2019.

With the initial target already long surpassed, the government had set its sights on a target of 40 million inbound visitors by 2020. This, unsurprisingly, has been completely derailed by the COVID-19 pandemic, with tourism numbers plummeting to essentially zero from the spring of 2020. At the time of writing, the government has made efforts to incentivize domestic travel in 2020 to try to breathe some life into the ravaged industry, although successive states of emergency, declared throughout 2020-2021, have dampened any potentially positive impact. The rescheduled 2021 Olympics, moreover, turned out to be the first in Olympic games in history to go ahead completely devoid of spectators, due to the COVID-19 pandemic. At the time of writing, there is hopeful talk of Japan reopening to foreign tourists in perhaps spring of 2022, although nothing is final.

The devastating blow dealt by COVID-19 to tourism aside, there's been a corresponding flood of positive press about Japan as a travel destination. It's appropriate that Mount Fuji itself, primordial symbol of the nation, and washoku (Japanese cuisine) as a whole were both bestowed heritage status by UNESCO in 2013.

The downside to this massive boost in soft power is that some places are now routinely clogged with camera-toters. Kyoto, which is visited by 25.9 percent of international visitors to Japan, is a prime example. From 2013 to 2017, Kyoto saw international tourist numbers surge by 279 percent. Tokyo (visited by 46.2 percent of inbound travelers) and Osaka (38.7 percent) have also been flooded by international tourists. With this surge comes a shortage of accommodations, especially during high season, and a high likelihood that you'll be gazing upon the more famous sights with a multitude of others. Prominent restaurants and shops are often overrun, too.

People and Culture

DEMOGRAPHY AND DIVERSITY

Japanese society is exceptionally homogenous, with less than 2 percent being foreign-born. The refrain of ware ware Nihonjin (we Japanese) is commonly heard, though the tone might be humble or proud. At the far-right end of the spectrum, it's downright xenophobic, underlying a pervasive belief that being 100 percent ethnically Japanese is a thing to be desired.

Zainichi

Chinese and Koreans have a long history of living on the fringes of Japanese society. The Zainichi Korean community took shape after World War II, when Koreans living on Japanese soil were stripped of their nationality, becoming essentially stateless. Many of these unfortunates caught up in geopolitical chaos were thrown out with the bathwater when Korea was divided into North and South, forcing people to choose sides. Even today, members of the Zainichi community are often treated as outcasts and second-class citizens. Until the 1980s, they were forced to relinquish their Korean names and adopt Japanese names to become Japanese. Although the majority have naturalized, discrimination remains entrenched.

Burakumin

The community that's faced, perhaps, the most discrimination in Japan, however, is the burakumin (hamlet people). Akin to India's "untouchables," this class comprises people employed in professions deemed "unclean," from sanitation staff, to slaughterhouse workers, undertakers, and even executioners (the death penalty is still enforced in Japan). Today, those of burakumin descent still face discrimination in everything from marriage to employment prospects, often being pushed into unskilled labor and low-income jobs. The government passed a law in 2016 that was meant to discourage discrimination against burakumin. Many have criticized the bill, however, saying it lacks teeth, because violators cannot be fined or imprisoned.

Immigration

Demographics and economics are forcing things to change. Japan's complex relationship with gaikokujin ("foreigners"; sometimes called by the more colloquial, slightly derogatory gaijin) is gradually evolving. A recent influx of Asian immigrants, hesitantly encouraged by the government due to labor shortages, is coming from Nepal, Vietnam, the Philippines, and beyond. This new wave of immigrants, which is often forced to speak Japanese at a higher level than many Westerners who come to work in Japan, is visible in the service industry, and many attend Japanese universities.

One trend indicating a change in Japan's makeup is the rise of mixed-race and mixed nationality marriages. The growing number of haafu ("half" or mixed) people has become a hot topic in the media. At best, mixed Japanese are put on a pedestal for their "exotic" looks. At worst, mixed-birth Japanese are treated like foreigners in their own country. To put a human face on this social problem, check out the documentary *Hafu—The Mixed-Race Experience of Japan,* directed by Megumi Nishikura, a filmmaker born to a Japanese mother and American father.

Population Decline

Recent immigration trends may be the tip of a much larger iceberg. For the first time in recorded history, Japan's population began to decline in 2016, when the census counted 127.1 million, down 0.7 percent from 2010. Estimates vary, but some numbers peg Japan's projected population in 2060 at around 87 million. At that point, 40 percent of the population will be 65 and up. This has myriad implications, from a smaller workforce to increased reliance on imports, which will in turn limit the growth of GDP.

The rise in retirees will also strain the government's pension system. Japan has the second-largest debt load—and growing—of any nation. One government response has been to raise the retirement age from 60 to 65 for employees in the private sector. While there's still time to find solutions, these trends paint an unsettling picture.

INDIGENOUS CULTURES

Ainu

A group known as the Ainu is the indigenous population of Hokkaido, or Ezo as it was once known. Ainu settlements could also be found in Tohoku, or northeastern Honshu, as well as some of the Russian Far East, such as the vast Kamchatka Peninsula and Sakhalin Island.

The Ainu are of mysterious origin, with possible links to the Jomon people of ancient Japan. They also have strong genes from the Okhotsk region of the Russian Far East. Under the Hokkaido Former Aborigines Protection Act of 1899, the Japanese government tried to assimilate the Ainu into mainstream society, banning the teaching of their own language and customs in schools until the act was finally repealed in 1997. There are only a handful of native Ainu speakers left, but some youngsters are trying to learn and revive the ancient tongue with no ties to Japanese.

As an indicator of their status in modern Japan, consider the fact that the Ainu were only officially recognized as the nation's indigenous culture in early 2019. Today, there are a mere 20,000 people who self-identify as Ainu, although the actual number of those who are unaware of their Ainu heritage is likely higher.

Ryūkyūan People

On the opposite side of the country, in the far south, the Ryūkyūan people are the indigenous inhabitants of Okinawa. From the 15th to the 19th centuries, the Ryūkyū Kingdom served as a tributary state to China. The kingdom was a key player in maritime trade and diplomacy, with a peace-loving reputation.

Genetically, they have strong ties to the ancient Jomon and Yamato people, as well as Chinese and Korean blood. The Ryūkyū Islands were first occupied by Japan via the Satsuma domain in southern Kyūshū in the early 17th century. The Ryūkyū Kingdom remained semi-autonomous for a time, but was gradually forced to serve as a tributary state to both China and the Satsuma domain.

Mirroring the experience of the Ainu in Hokkaido, the government banned the Ryūkyū language, customs, and more, stirring widespread resentment. Despite this treatment, many Ryūkyūans fought as imperial troops in World War II, which brought devastating battles to Okinawan shores.

Today, some 1.3 million Ryūkyūans live in Okinawa Prefecture, with about 600,000 abroad, mostly in Hawaii. The independence movement in Okinawa is largely fueled by the heavy presence of U.S. military bases on the islands.

RELIGION

There's a saying that most Japanese are born Shinto, are (sometimes) married Christian (aesthetically, anyway), and die Buddhist. In many ways, this truism is a good summary of the nation's spiritual life, which is highly pragmatic and involves a lot of mixing. From a Judeo-Christian or Western perspective, religion is a slippery concept in Japan.

Today, ask someone in Japan if they're religious and chances are they'll say they're not. Many will go as far as saying that Japan as a whole is not a very religious country. Yet, you won't have to look far to see throngs at Buddhist temples where they wave holy incense smoke around their heads and bodies, or at Shinto shrines where they toss coins into wooden boxes, ring bells to summon the resident kami (god), bow, clap their hands, and pray.

In the distant past, Shinto and Buddhism, Japan's two key faiths, mingled freely. Shrines and temples were often combined into single complexes until the late 19th century when they were crudely ripped apart. This government action set the stage for what would eventually become the creation of State Shinto. During the years leading up to World War II, the state labeled Buddhism and Christianity, among others, as religions, but conspicuously left Shinto off the list, classifying the Japanese system of nature worship as more of a proto-philosophy than a religion. This status was nullified after the end of the second world war, when the emperor publicly broadcasted that he relinquished claims to divinity. From that point on, Shinto was classified as a religion like any other. Nonetheless, the notion that Shinto is the spiritual fabric of the Japanese nation, beyond any kind of religious faith, persists.

Shinto

Of the two primary religions that color life for the vast majority of Japanese—Buddhism and Shinto—Shinto can claim to be the indigenous faith. Literally translated as "way of the kami," Shinto is predicated on the belief that kami (deity, gods, or divine beings) live in all things. Kami are believed to inhabit natural objects, from rocks to mountains to trees.

Today, shrines remain busy as ever, due to the widely held belief that kami can be called upon for help through prayer, or through specific rituals that often involve music and dance. Before beseeching a kami, purification is key. You'll notice water basins with bamboo scoops near the entrance to any shrine. All visitors to shrines are expected to carry out a simple purification ritual at these temizuya (water ablution pavilions).

Known as jinja, jingū, or sometimes simply bearing the suffix -gū, shrines are usually open-air, save for an inner sanctum or main hall, which can only be entered directly by priests. Shrines at the more elaborate end are approached via expansive paths lined by imposing torii gates. Meanwhile, small roadside structures are often fronted by a single, humble torii gate.

Famous shrines include Ise Jingū, Shinto's holiest spot; Izumo Taisha, the grand shrine in Shimane Prefecture; Miyajima's Itsukushima-jinja, famed for its "floating" torii gate; Tokyo's Meiji Jingū, and Nikko's opulent Tōshō-gū. Most ordinary Japanese visit shrines for births, to celebrate various rites of passage, sometimes for traditional weddings, for purification rites, or to receive blessings for things ranging from new homes to business ventures and new cars.

Buddhism

By far the foreign faith with the most lasting impact on Japan, Buddhism, specifically the Mahayana ("Great Vehicle"), was first brought to the country from Korea in the 6th century. It saw major leaps in sophistication from the 7th through 9th centuries, largely benefiting from its deepening in China. It was essentially combined with Shinto for centuries, until the two were split in the late 19th century. Even today, many Japanese may scratch their heads if you ask them to explain the difference between a temple and a shrine.

Contrasting with Shinto's here-and-now focus on life—births, blessings, rites of passage, matsuri (festivals)—Buddhist temples are associated with the hereafter. Most Japanese ultimately have Buddhist funeral rites. Graveyards are often situated next to temples. It's also common, especially in rural Japan, to see a small Buddhist altar, known as a butsudan, prominently displayed in a family's living space. These miniature altars, which often contain statues of the Buddha or various deities and scrolls inscribed with sacred text, are meant to honor deceased loved ones.

Known as ōtera or simply having the suffix -ji, temples range from towering wooden edifices housing giant bronze bells to small structures akin to local chapels in the West. Famous temples include Nara's massive Tōdai-ji; Kinkaku-ji, Kyoto's postcard-perfect gilt icon, as well as Kyoto's hillside complex Kiyomizu-dera; the mesmerizing cluster of temples and adjacent cemetery atop the mountain sanctuary of Kōya-san; and

Hase-dera, known for its towering wooden statue of Kannon (goddess or bodhisattva of mercy) in Kamakura, a town littered with majestic temples.

The main Buddhist sects include Tendai, the nation's oldest, founded at Hiei-zan in Kyoto; the more esoteric Shingon, founded at Kōya-san; Jodo, or Pure Land, which emphasizes faith in the Buddha over ritual; Nichiren, named for its founder, the monk Nichiren, centered on habitually reciting sections of the Lotus Sutra; and the austere school of Zen, heavily weighted toward strict meditation and asceticism, and once prized by the samurai class.

Christianity

Christianity received a tepid greeting upon reaching Japanese shores. Arriving with Portuguese merchants and missionaries in Kyushu in 1542, it was initially tolerated, but in 1587, Toyotomi Hideyoshi banned missionary activity and had 26 people executed in Nagasaki. The faith was outright banned by Tokugawa Ieyasu following the Shimabara Rebellion (1637-1638), after which thousands of Christians went into hiding for more than two centuries until the arrival of Commodore Perry's fleets in 1853-1854. With the Meiji Restoration of 1868, freedom of religion was declared.

Today, Christianity has only a minor presence in Japan, representing about one percent of the population. Faith aside, Christian wedding ceremonies are big business even among unbelieving Japanese. Held at mock wedding chapels, these ceremonies are often officiated by token foreigners playing the role of priest or pastor. Moreover, Christian holidays like Christmas and Valentine's Day have gained a purely secular, commercial foothold.

New Religious Movements

Alongside the mainstays of Shinto and Buddhism, a number of shinshukyō (new religions) have mushroomed in Japan since the mid-19th century. These new faiths are often centered around a charismatic leader, and range from bona fide religions to downright cults. Given this reputation, shinshukyō have an unsavory reputation among much of the public.

The most famous new religion is Soka Gakkai, a strain of Nichiren Buddhism with a major presence overseas. The influential group has claimed celebrity members such as rock star Courtney Love, actor Orlando Bloom, and jazz legend Herbie Hancock. Many who have left the group have brought attention to its cultish tendencies, as well as the right-leaning agenda being pushed by its political arm, the Komeito party.

The most infamous is Aum Shinrikyō ("supreme truth," often shortened as "Aum"), formed in 1984 by Shoko Asahara (birth name: Chizuo Matsumoto), who was born into a poor family of tatami mat makers. Asahara, who was blind since childhood, claimed divinity. The doomsday cult he founded combines teachings from Buddhism, Hinduism, and apocalyptic Christian prophecies. Aum made global headlines on March 20, 1995, when a group of its members carried out the worst terrorist attack in Japanese history, using sarin nerve gas during morning rush hour on the Tokyo subway. The chemical attack killed 12 commuters and forced some 6,000 others to seek medical help.

Asahara and six followers were executed by hanging in July 2018. Six other members remain on death row at the time of writing. At its peak, Aum had tens of thousands of members around the globe. Today, under the new name of Aleph, it still operates at the fringes, underground, with some estimates claiming its membership numbers at 1,500 and growing.

LANGUAGE

As far as linguists can tell, Japanese is related to the Altaic language family, but is not officially included in it. Together with the Ryūkyū languages, Japanese falls under the standalone Japonic language family. It is grammatically similar to Korean, but has no other clear links. The Japanese language has a reputation as being difficult to learn. In truth, it's not too hard to get the hang of the highly systematic Japanese pronunciation system.

Although the Tokyo dialect is the official version of Japanese, dialects known as ben maintain a strong hold on many parts of the country. Moving to the margins—rural Tohoku or southern Kyushu, for example—the chance that something may be lost in translation, even among two Japanese, is very real.

The written language is a convoluted affair, requiring much more effort to master. In any selection of Japanese text, you'll likely see a combination of three scripts: kanji, hiragana, and katakana. The most complicated aspect of learning to read and write Japanese is coming to grips with thousands of kanji, derived from Chinese characters that were adapted to fit the Japanese pronunciation system. Although there are around 50,000 kanji in use, Japanese are supposed to learn about 2,100 by the time they graduate from secondary school.

Making matters more complex, there is also hiragana, originally called onnade (women's script), a cursive script derived from Chinese characters originally created so that women could have the ability to write. By the 10th century, it was ubiquitous throughout Japanese society. The other syllabary, katakana, is also derived from Chinese characters. These boxy, angular characters are now primarily used to write foreign loanwords, onomatopoeia, and scientific terms, or to emphasize a given word or phrase.

LITERATURE

Traditional

With roots stretching back more than a millennium, Japan is rightly proud of its literary tradition. In the 8th century, a collection of orally transmitted ancient myths known as the *Kojiki* was written down, as well as a chronological account of Japan's origins, the *Nihonshiki*.

Some of Japan's earliest literature was written in verse. In the Asuka period (538-710), much of the poetry was being penned that would later be compiled in the *Manyoshu (Collection of 10,000 Leaves)*. This poetry anthology, which actually contains about 4,500 (not 10,000) poems, was put together around 760 CE, the first anthology in Japanese literature.

By the Heian period, women of the imperial court were writing groundbreaking works that would form the foundation of the novel. Specifically, *Genji Monogatari* (*The Tale of Genji*), considered the world's first novel, was penned by Lady Murasaki Shikibu, the pen name of an unidentified courtesan who lived in the late 10th and early 11th centuries. Another notable example, *The Pillow Book*, was written by courtesan Sei Shōnagon (966-1017 or 1025). Essentially a diary, the book offers an intimate glimpse of the intricacies and indulgences of Heian court life.

In the 13th century, the dramatic recounting of the battles between the Heike and Genji clans was put down in written form in Heike Monogatari (The Tale of the Heike). The saga tells the story of the Heike losing to the Genji clan in 1185. This classic story forms the basis of many theatrical performances.

By the Edo period, starting from 1682, writer Iharu Saikaku began scrawling the comedic tome *The Life of an Amorous Man*, based loosely on *The Tale of Genji*. Equally renowned for his poetic prowess, Saikaku worked in what was known as haikai renga (or hokku), or linked-verse, which laid the groundwork for haiku.

Although the name "haiku" didn't stick until the 19th century, the form emerged in the 17th century, composed of three unrhymed lines, split into five, seven, and five syllables, respectively. More than anyone else, the wandering poet Matsuo Bashō immortalized Japan through his masterful haiku in the later 17th century, exploring themes related to nature and the transient beauty of life. Later haiku masters include Buson (1716-1784), Kobayashi Issa (1763-1828), Masaoka Shiki (1867-1902), Kawahigashi Hekigotō (1873-1937), and Takahama Kyoshi (1874-1959).

Modern

In the late 19th and early 20th centuries, forward-thinking scribes began to write short, naturalistic stories with noticeable Western influence. Among the first authors of "I-novels," as first-person accounts were called in Japan, was Natsume Sōseki (1867-1916). His most famous works include *Wagahai wa Neko de Aru* (*I Am a Cat*), *Botchan*, and *Kokoro*.

The end of the 19th century and start of the 20th also saw the first reports by Western scribes who were eager to mystify their compatriots back home with tales and musings from the newly opened country. Writer Lafcadio Hearn (1850-1904), who was born to a Greek mother and an Irish father, was the first great Western interpreter of things Japanese. Moving from the United States, where he worked as a journalist, to Japan in the final decade of the 19th century, he lived in Matsue for 15 months before moving to Kumamoto and finally Tokyo, where he lived out the remainder of his life. After marrying a woman from a local samurai family in Matsue, he went on to write classics such as *Glimpses of Unfamiliar Japan*. For an introduction, check out *Lafcadio Hearn's Japan: An Anthology of his Writings on the Country and Its People*.

Moving into the early 20th century, other giants from the early modern period include Jun'ichirō Tanizaki (*The Makioka Sisters*) and Ryunosuke Akutagawa (*In a Grove*). Yasunari Kawabata (*The Izu Dancer, The Scarlet Gang of Asakusa, Snow Country*) became the first Japanese writer to win the Nobel Prize in Literature in 1968.

Writers who were working in the mid- to late 20th century include the controversial Yukio Mishima (*Confessions of a Mask, The Sound of Waves, The Sailor Who Fell from Grace*), a raging nationalist who visited the Tokyo headquarters of the Japan Self-Defense Forces calling for them to restore the emperor to power and overturn the pacifist constitution. He summarily committed seppuku—ritual suicide samurai-style—on a balcony as shocked troops watched from below.

A singular writer who came to prominence in the 1960s was Abe Kōbō (*Woman in the Dunes*), a surrealist master who often draws comparisons to Franz Kafka. Ōe Kenzaburō, whose work is interwoven with a deep strain of humanism, won the Nobel Prize in Literature in 1994.

Contemporary

Contemporary literature in Japan is dominated by the postmodern juggernaut Haruki Murakami (*The Wind-Up Bird Chronicle, Norwegian Wood*, the *1Q84* trilogy, and *Kafka on the Shore*). His whimsical world of talking frogs, psychic prostitutes, dancing gnomes, and scenarios wherein the supernatural and strange intrude onto the workaday world in bizarre, often comical and even erotic ways has amassed a giant cult following worldwide. A contemporary giant with a much darker gaze is Ryū Murakami (*Almost Transparent Blue* and *Coin Locker Babies*).

There are also a number of influential female writers making their mark in Japanese literature today. Some of the biggest include Yoko Ogawa (*The Diving Pool*); Banana Yoshimoto (*Kitchen*); Risa Wataya, who became the youngest author ever to win the Akutagawa Prize in 2003 for her novel *Keritai senaka;* Hitomi Kanehara (*Snakes and Earrings*), who shared the Akutagawa Prize in 2003 with Wataya; Sayaka Murata (*Convenience Store Woman*); and the novelist Mieko Kawakami (*Breasts and Eggs, Ms. Ice Sanwich*), a writer's writer whom Haruki Murakami has praised for her work, which spans many genres and is often written in her native Osaka dialect.

To dig deeper into contemporary literature, seeking out recent winners of the semi-annual Akutagawa Prize for up-and-coming writers is a good starting point. *Monkey Business* is an excellent anthology of short stories published annually.

Manga

Manga ("whimsical pictures"), as graphic novels or comics are known, accounts for nearly a quarter of all book sales in Japan. The popularity of this form of storytelling can loosely be traced back to the country's long history of caricature, seen in the woodblock prints known as kiboyoshi. The transition to manga came with the introduction of American comic books during the postwar occupation. In the ensuing decades, the form took on a life of its own. Topics range from high school antics to the psychedelically grotesque creations of visionary artists like Shintaro Kago to infamously graphic porn involving gigantic octopi.

Popular manga series, some running for many years, can be collected in massive volumes known as tankobon. The sprawling, violent, cyberpunk masterpiece *Akira,* which explores dystopian themes in a post-apocalyptic future, was serialized from 1982 to 1990. *Ghost in the Shell,* a brilliant post-cyberpunk sci-fi franchise that explored the nature of consciousness through a counter-cyberterrorist organization active in the mid-21st century, ran from 1989 to 1990.

VISUAL ARTS

Japan has a vibrant arts tradition, ranging from ancient Buddhist sculptures and landscape paintings of austere beauty to cheeky postmodern sculpture. Among Japan's most notable arts are painting, calligraphy, woodblock prints (ukiyo-e), ceramics, lacquerware, ikebana (flower arrangement), and a bleeding-edge contemporary scene.

Concepts

WABI-SABI

Of the many concepts to be aware of when viewing traditional Japanese art, a recurring aesthetic ideal is wabi-sabi. A remarkably deep principle, it is the appreciation of things that are blemished, rustic, earthy, asymmetrical, incomplete, transient, authentic, and, in a word, imperfect. This sensibility is deeply Buddhist, in its positing that there is no inherent eternal essence to things, and further, that life is impermanent. Wabi-sabi took root in Japan in the 15th century, when tea ceremony founder Sen no Rikyū and others sought to rebel against the extravagant tastes of the time.

MA

Another key element that runs through much of Japanese art is the spatial concept of ma (negative space). This idea highlights the importance of the empty space or gap between objects in a scene. You'll notice a preponderance of blank space in many landscape paintings and calligraphy scrolls, evoking the scene at hand all the more dramatically. This sensibility also accounts for the visual power that a simple flower arrangement or scroll exudes in an otherwise spare tatami-mat room.

Traditional Art Forms

PAINTING

Painting in Japan began with ink or black paint landscapes on washi paper, with deep influence from China. From the Heian period on, paintings that would later be known as yamato-e tended to depict court life. Starting in the Muromachi period, the ruling class began to patronize the arts, and the Tosa and Kano schools took shape.

The Tosa school shared characteristics with the older yamato-e tradition, with fine brushwork depicting elegant historic scenes. The Kano school, meanwhile, set the scene for marvelous sliding doors, folding screens, temple ceilings, and more, splashed with paintings of nature, and mythological creatures such as dragons and phoenixes.

Following the Edo period, contact with the West shook up Japanese painting, which split into the schools of yōga (Western-style painting) and nihonga (Japanese-style painting). Nihonga is distinct from older styles with its Western techniques such as shading.

CALLIGRAPHY

Originally imported from China, shodo (calligraphy) is deeply entrenched in the Japanese psyche. Throughout Japan's history it's been prized by the upper classes and is essentially the first art form taught to elementary school students today, along with learning kanji and kana characters. There are a variety of styles, from the blocky, clear-cut kaisho to gyosho (running hand, informal, semi-cursive) to sosho (fully cursive, formal, illegible to all but the initiated).

UKIYO-E (WOODBLOCK PRINTS)

Ukiyo-e (pictures of the floating world) evoke the fleeting pleasures and realm of the senses. These paintings became synonymous with the pleasure quarters of the Edo period. As such, they depict almost crude scenes in vivid colors. Kabuki, sumo, geisha, as well as landscape scenes all figure prominently in ukiyo-e. This style inspired the Japonisme movement in the West, which attracted such luminaries as Van Gogh and Manet.

CERAMICS

Jomon-era pottery is some of the oldest fired clay in human history. What began as functional over time took on added layers of complexity and beauty starting with the advent of the tea ceremony in the 16th century. Potters often worked in the mountains, where ideal clay was readily available, and Koreans leant their superior techniques in the early days.

LACQUERWARE

Shikki (lacquerware), also referred to sometimes as nurimono, is a delicate art form done by applying layer upon layer of sap from the lacquer tree to an object, from Buddhist statues and painted panels to teapots and bento lunchboxes. Once an object is lacquered, pigments are added—often black and red—and then the object is sometimes spruced up with inlays of silver, gold, or pearls. Aside from being beautiful, lacquerware is durable; lacquered wood is known to endure millennia.

IKEBANA

Likely introduced along with Buddhism, the art of ikebana (flower arrangement) involves the careful placement of flowers, usually in a vase, in a way that uses the flowers as well as the empty space around them to elicit a certain aesthetic response. An arrangement can also carry symbolic meaning. Several distinct schools have evolved, each with its own philosophy.

Contemporary Artists

Much of contemporary Japanese art has a pop touch. Perhaps the biggest name overseas from Japan's contemporary scene is Yayoi Kusama. Active since the 1950s, Kusama has created a singular body of colorful, polka-dotted tentacle-like sculptures; geometric, dot-infused abstract paintings; and immersive installations. Takashi Murakami, whose work is heavily influenced by manga and anime, is another heavyweight. He launched a postmodern artistic movement known as Superflat, which seeks to "flatten" a range of artistic forms, from graphic art and animation to pop culture and the fine arts. For something uplifting, check out the color-drenched photographs of Ninagawa Mika. Also worth noting is provocateur Aida Makoto, who works in a variety of mediums and tackles the dark facets of the nation's psyche.

Plenty of biennales and triennales (art festivals held every other year, or every third year, respectively) highlight Japan's buzzing contemporary art scene. Some of the most prominent ones are the Echigo-Tsumari Art Triennale (www.echigo-tsumari.jp), the Setouchi Triennale (https://setouchi-artfest.jp), and the Yokohama Triennale (www.yokohamatriennale.jp).

MUSIC

Traditional

Japan's musical heritage can be traced back to a troupe of Korean musicians who made the journey to Japan in the mid-5th century, and the arrival of Buddhism a century later. With the religion came a range of instruments, including the three-stringed shamisen, akin to a banjo; the biwa, a four-stringed lute shaped like a pear with a short neck often played by wandering monks; the koto, a 13-stringed zither; a variety of wind instruments, from the shakuhachi (five-holed bamboo flute) to panpipes to the oboe; and a range of percussion instruments from gongs to taiko drums of various sizes. (If you enjoy a good percussion show, check out the infectious beats of Kodō, a Sado Island-based taiko troupe of world renown.)

Contemporary

Japan is a country of audiophiles and deeply informed connoisseurs. Today, Tokyo is one of the best cities in the world to listen to music, with its deep network of dedicated DJ bars, jazz joints, classical music cafés, and thumping techno clubs. Likewise, record stores overflowing with rare vinyl of all genres dot the city. This isn't limited to the capital, however, with thriving music scenes found in Osaka, Kyoto, Kobe (known for jazz), and Sapporo.

ENKA

More than a century ago, trailblazing Japanese singers began to blend Western and Japanese music into a new genre that would become enka (roughly meaning "speech song" or "performance song"). Still immensely popular even today, enka, particularly from the postwar years, is the go-to genre for drunk salarymen at hostess bars where mama-sans know and can skillfully croon all the classics. The nostalgic themes of enka songs cover the usual range of topics that were routinely touched upon in Western music in the early to mid-20th century, such as heartbreak, homesickness, and loneliness.

Some of enka's leading lights include early pioneer Koga Masao, who composed a staggering 5,000 songs in his lifetime, and Misora Hibari, a legendary songstress who began performing from age nine. The younger cadre of enka stars includes "prince" Hikawa Kiyoshi and Jerome Charles White, Jr. (aka Jero), a young singer from Pittsburgh of Japanese and African American ancestry, known for performing in a hip-hop getup.

J-POP

Meanwhile, youth culture hatched J-Pop (Japanese pop), a juggernaut popularized by Hamasaki Ayumi, the queen, and boy-band SMAP, helmed by all-purpose celebrity Kimura Takuya. Pamyu Pamyu is a recent J-Pop singer whose saccharine hit songs and colorful fashion sense helped popularize Harajuku's kawaii aesthetic.

Another spin on the J-Pop shtick is the idol group genre, with acts like AKB48, comprising nearly 140 young female members; and Arashi (Storm), a five-member boy band, atop the heap. Meanwhile, the irresistibly catchy kawaii metal group Babymetal is composed of three young female members clad in goth-Lolita-style outfits, singing bubbly tunes to a metal soundtrack, energetically dancing and beaming lots of smiles.

DJS

Digging a bit deeper, DJ Krush is a renowned spinner of jazz, soul, and hip-hop instrumentals, while DJs like Ken Ishii and Satoshi Tomiie, and deeper still, Nobu, Wata Igarashi, So, Hiyoshi, Haruka, Takaaki Itoh, and so many more, provide the soundtrack of Japan's burgeoning techno, house, and underground music scenes.

THEATER

Noh

With elaborate wooden masks and enigmatic music, Noh is a highly refined and regimented form of theater that is downright baffling to the uninitiated. Truth be told, the arcane language (even for Japanese), long periods of inaction, and rarefied atmosphere of Noh are not everyone's cup of tea. But with patience, the world of Noh proves fascinating.

Noh plays take place on a beautiful yet austere stage, traditionally made of hinoki (cypress) and backed by the painted image of a single pine tree. Much of the story in a Noh play is told through an arcane system of gestures, movements, and subtle expressions. There are two main characters in a play: a shite (pronounced "she-te"), which is often a restless ghost; and a waki, which steers the shite to the climax of the play. The roots of Noh, Japan's oldest form of theater, are found in ancient Shinto dances. It is traditionally a male-dominated art, although women are gradually making headway in the modern age. Traditionally, female and otherworldly roles are depicted with the masks that Noh is known for, while male roles are done without masks. There are prominent families of Noh actors in Japan, well ensconced in society's upper rung.

There's an accompanying form of theater known as kyōgen, performed during the intermission of a Noh play. Kyōgen actors perform short humorous skits meant to both add context or comment on the happenings of the ongoing Noh play, but also to serve up a bit of comedic relief.

Kabuki

What began with former shrine maidens dancing would eventually become the theatrical art form known as kabuki (song-dance-skill). The pivotal moment came in 1603, when former shrine maiden Izu no Okuni and a number of other female dancers arrived in Kyoto and invoked the ire of the authorities with their suggestive performances.

After several crackdowns, the government decreed that only adult men could play roles in kabuki. Hence the creation of the onnagata (men who play women's roles), a mainstay in the kabuki world to the present day. Typical kabuki stories revolve around betrayal, samurai clashes, and dramatic suicides. Kabuki reached its apex in popularity during the Edo period, when it was voraciously patronized by the moneyed merchant class. Today, the style of theater is by far Japan's most recognizable overseas, thanks to its elaborate attire; heavily made-up actors; intense music known as nagauta (long song), played on shamisen, taiko drums, and flutes; and dramatic style of acting.

Bunraku

Bunraku is a style of theater that emerged in Osaka in the early part of the 17th century, employing puppets that are up to half the size of a grown adult. Rather than being manipulated by strings, a single bunraku puppet is controlled by three puppeteers. Bunraku grew out of the older tradition known as jōruri, in which minstrels told legends accompanied by a shamisen or biwa. The story being told, typically involving heroic feats and legends, is chanted by a narrator with exceptional vocal range who is separate from the puppeteers. Many of these tales were penned by Chikamatsu Monzaemon (1653-1724), regarded as Japan's very own Shakespeare.

The puppeteers, meanwhile, move the puppets to reflect the story as it unfolds with a shamisen being strummed in the background. The result is a surprisingly lifelike performance with theatrical precision and flair that most would never imagine possible with puppets.

Contemporary Theater

Starting in the 1960s, coinciding with the countercultural explosion taking place globally, new currents reached the theater scene, spawning the angura (underground) scene and, soon after, the "fringe theater" movement. Playwrights and thespians with an eye on creative revolution staged performances in public places, basements—anywhere they could.

Alongside those who favored overturning convention, there were some artists who connected with Japan's well of tradition. Director and playwright Kara Jūrō, for one, noted how kabuki was initially performed in the open-air. Noh was also. Other playwrights who were central to the angura period included Shūji Terayama; Abe Kōbō, the novelist of *Woman in the Dunes* fame; Shimizu Kunio; and Minoru Betsuyaku, famous for advancing "theater of the absurd" in Japan.

CINEMA

Japan's film history is peppered with illustrious names. As early as the 1930s, Japan was pumping out around 500 feature films annually.

Notable Directors

One of the earliest masters to emerge was Mizoguchi Kenji, who had been active since the 1930s but is best known for his 1954 samurai drama *Ugetsu Monogatari.*

The golden age of Japanese cinema was the 1950s. Akira Kurosawa (*Rashōmon, The Seven Samurai, Yōjimbō, Ran*) would cement his universally revered reputation during this time, along with Ozu Yasujirō (*Tokyo Story, An Autumn Afternoon*). The 1950s also saw the release of the original *Gojira* (*Godzilla*).

The 1960s saw the birth of a new genre of yakuza (mafia) flicks, many of which were directed by Suzuki Seijun, whose unflappable depiction of slick violence would later inform directors from Quentin Tarantino to compatriot Kitano Takeshi. The classic Tora-san series of films, among Japan's highest grossing of all time, debuted in 1969 with *Otoko wa Tsurai yo* (*It's Tough Being a Man*). The series ran until 1996, when the actor who played Kuruma Torajirō (Tora-san) passed away.

Kitano Takeshi (aka Beat Takeshi), a man of many talents from standup comedy to acting, made his first big directorial splash with Hana-bi (*Fireworks*) in 1997. Also gaining stature around this time were Japanese horror directors like Nakata Hideo (*Ring*) and Takashi Shimizu, who directed the Ju-on (*The Grudge*) series.

Takashi Miike, a director with a cult following whose splatter quotient would put Quentin Tarantino's most violent work to shame, also came to prominence in the mid-1990s and early 2000s, with films like the horror romance *Audition,* adapted from Ryū Murakami's novel of the same name; yakuza tale *Dead or Alive;* and hyper-violent *Ichi the Killer,* for which vomit bags were distributed ahead of its screening at film festivals in Toronto and Stockholm.

New voices have since emerged such as Kiyoshi Kurosawa, whose film *Tokyo Sonata* garnered praise at the Cannes Film Festival in 2008. Takita Yōjirō's *Departures* won the Oscar for best foreign-language film in 2009. And in 2013, Hirokazu Kore-eda snagged the 2013 Jury Prize in Cannes for his excellent *Like Father Like Son.*

Anime

Like manga, anime is geared toward all age groups and social classes in Japan. It covers everything from history to love stories, to surreal fantasy, sci-fi, and entertainment for kids. In many ways, anime achieved liftoff in the 1960s with the legendary Tezuka Osamu's *Astro Boy* television series. Sharing the airwaves with *Astro Boy,* a host of other hit shows with names like *Space Battleship Yamato* and *Battle of the Planets* were beginning to cast a spell over Japan's youth.

Other developments in the early days of anime included some of Toei's big releases, beginning with *Hakujaden* (*Tale of the White Panda*) in 1958. The Toei animated flick *Little Norse Prince* was directed by the late Takahata Isao (1935-2018), who would form Studio Ghibli with the genius director Hayao Miyazaki in 1985.

The anime film adaptations of *Akira,* directed by Ōtomo Katsuhiro, and *Ghost in the Shell,* directed by Oshii Mamoru, are both mind-expanding explorations of metaphysical and post-apocalyptic themes, interlaced with plenty of bizarre characters, psychedelic imagery, and philosophical speculation. The late anime master Kon Satoshi (1963-2010) also produced a challenging and unique body of work in his short life.

Looming above all these names, however, is anime maestro Hayao Miyazaki, the oft-grinning, bespectacled genius and cofounder of Studio Ghibli. Although he'd been churning out brilliant films since the 1980s, Miyazaki finally broke onto the international stage by winning the Oscar for best animated feature in 2001 for his masterpiece *Spirited Away.* From his deep oeuvre, some of the other standouts include *Princess Mononoke, My Neighbor Totoro,* and more recently, *The Wind Rises,* which has stoked controversy over the implications of its antiwar tone.

A director who has achieved wild success in recent years and who has been touted as "the new Hayao Miyazaki" is Makoto Shinkai, whose smash-hit romantic fantasy *Your Name* remains the third-highest grossing anime film of all time.

DANCE

Traditional

Buyō is the umbrella term for all forms of traditional Japanese dance. It extends from the dances performed by geisha to the theatrical movements of kabuki and Noh. All forms of buyō ultimately stem from ancient folk and Shinto dances. The movements of traditional Japanese dance tend to be slow, graceful, and contained. This is largely due to the fact that they were traditionally performed while wearing a kimono, which restricts movement. All told, there are a few hundred different varieties of buyō today.

Contemporary

Japan's contemporary dance scene exists on a spectrum between the gleeful, all-female musical extravaganza known as the Takarazuka Revue and the evocative, grotesque form of dance known as butō, which emerged from the urge to discard the stringent rules found in most forms of traditional Japanese dance, while tapping into something more ancient and primal. Visionary dancer Hijikata Tatsumi performed the first butō dance in 1959. A butō dancer is in an intensely vulnerable state, usually naked or close to it. Unsurprisingly, butō has been considered scandalous by many. This has only inspired many dancers to push even harder against boundaries and discover more cracks in the edifice of society.

Essentials

Transportation 752
Visas and Officialdom . . 761
Festivals and Events 762
Recreation 765
Food and Drink 768
Accommodations 771
Conduct and Customs 774
Health and Safety 775
Practical Details 776
Traveler Advice 781

Transportation

GETTING THERE

From North America

Tokyo's Narita International (NRT) and Haneda (HND) airports are linked by direct flights to several North American cities. Some carriers also fly direct to Osaka's Kansai International Airport (KIX) and Nagoya's Chubu Centrair International Airport (NGO).

Generally speaking, prices vary widely, with flights from the West Coast of North America being slightly cheaper than those from the East. Although less convenient in terms of access to Tokyo proper,

Getting to Japan from North America

Departure Airport	Arrival Airport	Carriers
New York City (JFK)	Tokyo (NRT)	Delta Air Lines
Detroit (DTW)	Tokyo (HND)	United Airlines
Chicago (ORD)		American Airlines
Los Angeles (LAX)		Air Canada
San Francisco (SFO)		All Nippon Airways
Honolulu (HNL)		Japan Airlines
Vancouver (YVR)		
Toronto (YYZ)		
Detroit (DTW)	Nagoya (NGO)	Delta Air Lines
Honolulu (HNL)		Japan Airlines

Narita is usually cheaper than Haneda. Deals can be found if you're willing to endure layovers. Moreover, avoiding peak season and buying as far in advance as possible (aim for three months or more) will naturally drive fares down. To fly economy from anywhere in North America, have a rough budget in mind of about US$1,000, give or take. A stopover can bring prices down to as low as US$500 during off-season from some airports.

From Europe

Carriers offering direct flights from London Heathrow (LHR) include British Airways (to NRT and HND), All Nippon Airways (to HND), and Japan Airlines (to HND). British Airways now flies direct to Osaka's KIX, too. It's generally cheaper to transfer en route.

Various carriers provide direct flights to Japan (mostly NRT and HND, but also sometimes KIX and NGO) from many European cities, including: Amsterdam (AMS), Brussels (BRU), Paris (CDG), Munich (MUC), Frankfurt (FRA), Zurich (ZRH), Vienna (VIE), Copenhagen (CPH), Helsinki (HEL), Madrid (MAD), Rome (FCO), Milan (MXP), Warsaw (WAW), and Moscow (SVO and DME).

Broadly speaking, if you're flying from Europe the budget is in the same ballpark as what it is from North America. Plan on spending roughly €850 (£750) for an economy class seat. A stopover will bring that figure down, and if you book several months in advance—three months or more is a good benchmark—you may land a bargain.

From Australia and New Zealand

It's possible to fly direct to Tokyo from Sydney, Melbourne, Perth, Brisbane, and Cairns in Australia, while most (but not all) flights from New Zealand first route through Australia, usually Sydney. Most of these flights land in NRT, although some do service HND. Carriers servicing these routes include Japan Airlines, All Nippon Airways, Qantas, and budget Japanese airline Jetstar, in addition to Air New Zealand from Auckland. There are limited direct flights to Osaka's KIX from Sydney, Cairns, and Auckland.

A stopover in another Asian city will likely make a flight significantly cheaper, but will tack on quite a bit of travel time. Rock-bottom prices can occasionally be snagged through budget carriers like Jetstar or AirAsia, but don't expect a plush ride. Again, try to book

Previous: the Keifuku line (aka Randen line), a sightseeing train in Kyoto.

Coronavirus in Japan

At the time of writing in November 2021, Japan was moderately impacted by the effects of the coronavirus, but the situation was constantly evolving. The country had so far been relatively lucky, compared to many harder-hit countries, with a comparatively low death rate; as of early November 2021, coronavirus deaths to date were just over 18,000 in Japan.

Japan never implemented a true lockdown. Rather, a series of emergency states have been declared at different times in Tokyo, Kyoto, Osaka, and a number of other prefectures with higher populations or with small populations but high popularity among domestic tourists (e.g., Hokkaido and Okinawa), with the government "requesting" citizens to minimize trips outside and for bars and restaurants to close early and limit alcohol sales, among other measures. The government has also encouraged avoiding the "three Cs": closed, poorly ventilated spaces; crowded public places; and close contact when people cough, sneeze, or speak. Businesses that may have closed or operated at limited capacity have largely reopened, with some voluntarily implementing a policy of social distancing. Masks, already a regular feature in Japan during cold and flu season, remain ubiquitous, and products like hand sanitizer are often placed at shop entrances. Some restaurants check customers' temperatures at the entrance too. At present, there are no vaccination requirements for sites such as museums or restaurants.

At the time of writing, traveling within Japan was freely permitted. Starting September 1, 2020, legal foreign residents were allowed to re-enter the country after controversially being stuck for months if they happened to be outside Japan when the border closed. Starting October 1, 2020, the government lowered entry restrictions for business travelers and those with visas of more than three months. Travelers with exceptional circumstances are required to take a coronavirus test within 72 hours of departure and again upon landing, and then quarantine for 14 days (if unvaccinated) or 10 days (if vaccinated) in a designated location.

These conditions and rules will inevitably have changed as the situation evolves. When planning your own trip, check the JNTO's coronavirus page (www.japan.travel/en/coronavirus) for an up-to-date breakdown on travel restrictions and entry requirements by country. If anything feels unclear, inquire with your local embassy or consulate, as well as the airline you plan to fly with. Better safe than sorry.

Now more than ever, Moon encourages its readers to be courteous and ethical in their travel. We ask travelers to be respectful to residents, and mindful of the evolving situation in their chosen destination when planning their trip.

BEFORE YOU GO

- Check websites and resources (listed below) for **local restrictions** and the **overall health status** of the destination and your point of origin. If you're traveling to or from a COVID-19 hotspot, you may want to reconsider your trip.
- Get **vaccinated** if your health status allows. At the time of writing, travelers who could enter Japan were required to receive a negative **coronavirus test** within 72 hours of their departure.
- Check with your airline and the Japanese Ministry of Health, Labour and Welfare (tel.

tickets three or more months in advance to avoid paying top dollar.

Given that Japan is about the same distance from Australia and New Zealand as it is from North America or Europe, the budget is similar. Plan on paying about A$1,400 (NZ$1,500) for an economy class seat.

South Africa

There are no direct flights between South Africa and Japan. Major Middle Eastern carriers do fly to Tokyo from South Africa's major airports, Johannesburg (JNB) and, to a lesser extent, Cape Town (CPT). These carriers include Emirates, requiring an interchange in

03/5253-1111; www.mhlw.go.jp/english) for updated **travel requirements.** Some airlines may be taking more safety precautions than others, such as limited occupancy; check their websites for more information before buying your ticket, and consider a very early or very late flight, to limit exposure. Flights may be more infrequent, with increased cancellations.

- Check the website of any museums and other venues you wish to patronize to confirm that they're open, if their hours have been adjusted, and to learn about any specific visitation requirements, such as **mandatory reservations** or **limited occupancy.**
- Pack **hand sanitizer,** a **thermometer,** and plenty of **face masks.**
- **Assess the risk** of entering crowded spaces, joining tours, and taking public transit.
- Expect **general disruptions.** Events may be postponed or canceled, and some tours and venues may require reservations, enforce limits on the number of guests, be operating during different hours than the ones listed, or be closed entirely.

RESOURCES

- Japan's **Cabinet Secretariat** (https://corona.go.jp/en) supplies daily case numbers, breakdowns of policies and recommended safety measures, and coronavirus-related links.
- The **Japan National Tourism Organization** (JNTO; www.japan.travel/en/coronavirus) has provided an extensive breakdown of case numbers, travel and safety tips, information on getting 24/7 medical assistance in foreign languages, and an up-to-date breakdown of screening and quarantine procedures. The JNTO also runs a 24/7 coronavirus-related hotline in English (tel. 050/3816-2787).
- The **Japan Times** (www.japantimes.co.jp/liveblogs/news/coronavirus-outbreak-updates) provides a continuously updated roundup of coronavirus-related news stories.
- The **Tokyo Metropolitan Government** has created a chart (https://japan2.usembassy.gov/pdfs/covid19-what-to-do-e.pdf) that shows just what to do if you think you may have contracted coronavirus.
- **Time Out Tokyo** provides a useful online guide to staying safe in Tokyo (www.timeout.com/tokyo/things-to-do/how-to-go-out-safely-in-tokyo-plus-social-distancing-rules-explained). They also maintain an archive of articles on COVID-related news (www.timeout.com/tokyo/things-to-do/live-updates-the-covid-19-coronavirus-situation-in-tokyo-and-japan-right-now), as well as a continuously updated list of businesses that were temporarily closed, but have since reopened (www.timeout.com/tokyo/things-to-do/attractions-in-tokyo-and-japan-that-are-closed-due-to-covid-19-coronavirus).
- **Osaka Prefecture** (www.pref.osaka.lg.jp.e.agb.hp.transer.com/iryo/osakakansensho/corona.html), **Kobe City** (www.city.kobe.lg.jp/a97852/kenko/health/infection/protection/english/corona.html), and **Kyoto Prefecture** (www.pref.kyoto.jp/kokusai/coronavirus_update.html) all maintain a coronavirus page.

Dubai; Etihad, with a layover in Abu Dhabi; and Qatar Airways, with a transfer at Doha. It's also possible to fly from South Africa to Tokyo on Singapore Airlines via Singapore, Cathay Pacific via Hong Kong, or British Airways via London.

As with booking flights from other regions, try to buy tickets three or more months in advance to avoid price gouging. Expect to pay similar to the other regions described above: R150,000 for an economy seat. Tickets from Cape Town tend to be slightly more expensive than from Johannesburg.

Addresses in Japan

Addresses in Japan can be baffling to the uninitiated. General elements include the **postal symbol** (〒) and **postal code, prefecture, municipality, subarea,** and three numbers separated by dashes, with the name of the business, name of the resident, and so on underneath all of that. The piece that's notably missing is a street name. Though some major thoroughfares do have names, such as Tokyo's Meiji and Yasukuni-dōri, most streets are unnamed.

Instead, when written in Japanese, addresses are organized by **district, block,** and **building,** indicated by the three numbers following the prefecture and municipality. Compounding the confusion, districts and blocks tend to be numbered in a relatively logical geographic progression, while the buildings that make up the blocks aren't numbered according to their physical placement in the block but rather according to when they were built, with the oldest building on a given block being numbered 1, and so on.

As an example, take the Nezu Museum's address: 6-5-1 Minami-Aoyama, Minato-ku, Tokyo. Minato-ku is the ward that Minami-Aoyama is a part of, and Tokyo is the prefecture. The "6" refers to district number 6 of the area known as Minami-Aoyama, the "5" refers to the block number within that district, and the "1" is the building number.

If you're a bit confused, you're not alone. Even taxi drivers end up scratching their heads and doing a few extra laps around an area before finding some destinations—mercifully often stopping the taxi meter at the point where they lose their way so as not to hike up the fare. It helps immensely to have a **printed map** of where you're going, a clear set of directions based on **landmarks,** or best yet, a data-only SIM card so you can simply punch an address into **Google Maps,** which will get you where you're trying to go.

GETTING AROUND

At the time of writing, in November 2021, public transportation across the country was mostly unaffected by coronavirus-related restrictions.

Train

Japan's rail network is world-famous for its cleanliness, safety, and punctuality. It's extensive, linking northernmost Hokkaido to far-flung southern Kyushu. It can be daunting to get the hang of all the transfers and ticket deals, but thankfully, it's possible to catch on fast.

The main train operator nationwide is **Japan Railways** (JR), which has numerous regional branches. There is also a slew of private operators—**Odakyu, Tokyū, Hankyū, Kintetsu,** and more—each with their own fare and ticketing system. Regardless of the train network you're on, larger stations will have their own ticket office. Buying tickets at these offices is often the way to go if the machines feel too daunting (though most ticketing machines can be switched to English). The staff at ticket counters are generally experienced with helping overseas travelers. However you buy it, once you've got your ticket in hand, simply put it in the slot at the ticket gate, and then pick it back up after passing through. Hold on to your ticket for the duration of the trip, as you'll need to insert it again at the ticket gate of your destination. If you happen to lose a ticket, there's a chance you may have to pay for your journey again on arrival.

Another factor of train travel in Japan is speed: some routes are local, and others are express or limited express train (slightly faster), while the shinkansen (bullet trains that reach up to 30 kmph/199 mph) is the way to go for long-haul trips. To save on fare, the **Japan Rail Pass** is a good idea if you plan to travel extensively over long distances. A number of regional passes are also sold.

If all this sounds intimidating, don't fret. Staff at train stations are happy to help and are comfortable with overseas travelers. Just be ready to bridge the communication gap with a smile and a sense of humor.

SHINKANSEN

Shinkansen run on an altogether different rail network than regular trains. There are two classes: **ordinary** (already a pleasant experience) and the pricier **Green Car,** akin to first class. Most of the cars of a shinkansen have reserved seats, which can be secured either at a ticket office or a ticket vending machine. Even if you have a Japan Rail Pass, you'll still need to stop by the ticket office if you want to sit in a reserved seat. For an unreserved car, you can simply queue and board with the JR pass in hand. Reserved seats are recommended as unreserved cars often fill up completely.

Note that shinkansen often depart from and arrive at entirely different areas within a station and sometimes from altogether separate stations. If shinkansen trains run through the same station also serviced by local trains, you'll likely have to go through another set of gates to enter the shinkansen area. Allow at least 10 minutes to get to the correct platform and find the correct car.

One more point to be aware of is that the ticketing system for shinkansen, as well as for limited express (see below), means that you will have two tickets instead of one. There's a joshaken (base fare ticket), which covers the journey itself, and the tokkyūken (special fare ticket), which allows you to travel aboard one of the more expensive, high-speed trains. Counterintuitively, you'll need to simultaneously put both tickets into the ticket machine as you enter the gate.

LOCAL, RAPID, EXPRESS, AND LIMITED EXPRESS TRAINS

There are several different categories of local trains. Local (普通, futsū/kaku-eki-teisha) trains are the most common, but are the slowest and make the most stops. Rapid (快速, kaisoku) trains skip some stations, while express (急行, kyūkō) trains generally skip even more, thus speeding up the journey. There's no extra expense to hop on either a rapid or express train.

To ride a limited express (特急, tokkyū) train, fares do jump. Moreover, these trains often have both unreserved and reserved seating, akin to the shinkansen, and carry a surcharge that can be bought on board or at the ticket office in advance. Like the shinkansen, limited express trains also require an additional ticket—one to cover the journey, the other to cover the added expense of riding in an extra-speedy train. Insert both into the machine at the ticket gate as you enter, and hold on to both tickets for the duration of your journey.

JAPAN RAIL PASS

The Japan Rail Pass (JR Pass, www.japanrailpass.net) can be purchased for either one, two, or three weeks, during which pass holders are able to travel freely on all JR lines, including shinkansen, as well as local buses in the JR network nationwide and the JR-West ferry that runs to Miyajima. Simply flash the pass to the staff each time you pass through the ticket gates at any JR station, bus station, or ferry terminal in the case of Miyajima, and hop aboard.

There are two grades available for the pass: regular and Green Car (first class). For the ordinary seat level, one week costs ¥29,650 per pass, two weeks costs ¥47,250, and three weeks will set you back ¥60,450. Upgrading to the Green Car will cost ¥39,600 for one week, ¥64,120 for two weeks, and ¥83,390 for three weeks. For children ages 6-11, rates are lower, while children under six can ride for free as long as they are accompanied by an adult with a JR Pass and no other passenger needs their seat.

Note that the fastest categories of shinkansen, known as Nozomi and Mizuho, are not covered by the pass. Another thing to be aware of is that even with the JR Pass, you'll still need to go to the ticket office to get a ticket for the reserved seat.

For many travelers, the pass is a no-brainer. Even a Tokyo-Kyoto round-trip on

The Almighty IC Card

Your first order of business on entering a Japanese train station for the first time should be to get a rechargeable smart card, known as an IC card in Japanese. These touch-cards are available from select vending machines at a station's ticketing counter. If you have an IC card, you can recharge it any time you are running low on funds at one of the IC card vending machines at any station.

Each region has its own, with **Suica** and **PASMO** being the variety sold in the JR East network, which includes Tokyo. The JR West network, including the Kansai region, issues the **ICOCA** card, but the cards are largely swappable, no matter where in Japan they are purchased. The **Suica** card, available at stations in the JR East network, is perhaps the most flexible.

IC cards will allow you to travel on local, rapid, and express trains, as well as subway networks in most cities. For shinkansen (bullet train) or limited express train journeys, you'll need to buy a ticket in advance or have the **JR Rail Pass.** The added bonus of having an IC card is that you can use it at vending machines inside stations and to make purchases at many convenience stores, whether inside a station or deep in a residential area.

the shinkansen will justify the seven-day pass for most travelers after taking into account the additional travel done on JR lines within either city. That said, the JR Pass isn't for everyone. Consider whether you will be doing enough travel to justify the cost of the pass. If you're traveling on a lavish budget, it's doubtful that the savings made with a JR Pass will feel worthwhile in exchange for the hassle of having to take on the limitations of the pass. If money is no object, you'll likely be happier booking transportation when and in what form you desire it.

If you'd like to book a JR Pass, you must be a **foreign traveler** entering Japan on a "temporary visitor" tourist visa. After you've bought a pass online and chosen a starting date for the pass, you'll receive a voucher at your home address, which can be exchanged for a proper pass at selected train station offices once you've arrived in Japan.

The JR Pass can only be purchased **outside Japan**—you cannot purchase it once you are in country. Also, you have to exchange the purchase voucher for the actual pass within three months of purchasing the voucher, so don't buy it too early.

INTERNET RESOURCES

There are some very useful sites to be aware of when it comes to train travel in Japan. **HyperDia** (www.hyperdia.com) provides step-by-step route information. All you do need to do is input the station you're leaving from and where you're going. You can also adjust the date and time, selected for either departure or arrival. **Jorudan** (https://world.jorudan.co.jp/mln/en) does the same thing. When all else fails, **Google Maps** is not only a trusty way to navigate a city street by street, but also allows you to compare how long it would take to make a journey by train, by taxi, or on foot.

Bus

Traveling by bus is less comfortable and slower than train or plane, but it scores points for value, and sometimes it's the only option for reaching remote areas. Most towns and cities have their own local bus networks, which can come in handy in some places, but in others, it's quicker to simply walk or pay a bit more and take a taxi.

For longer journeys, highway buses operate during both daytime and nighttime, often arriving and departing near major train stations. Main bus terminals are sometimes set apart in slightly inconvenient spots, so be sure you know where your bus terminal is before a major journey.

There are eight regional variants of **JR Bus.** Some JR Bus routes can be booked at the website of **Japan Expressway Bus Net** (www.kousokubus.net/JpnBus/en). **Willer Express** (http://willerexpress.com/en) is another major highway bus operator, which offers some good deals. It's one of the few highway bus operators in Japan that allows for relatively easy online reservations in English. Willer also offers the **Japan Bus Pass** (http://willerexpress.com/st/3/en/pc/buspass), which covers all long-distance journeys for either three days (¥10,200 Mon.-Thurs., ¥12,800 all days), five days (¥12,800 Mon.-Thurs., ¥15,300 all days), or seven days (¥15,300 Mon.-Thurs.).

A number of other regional discount bus passes are available, including: the **Hokkaido Budget Bus Pass** (www.budget-buspass.com/purchase), the **Tohoku Highway Bus Ticket** (www.tohokukanko.jp/en/transport/detail_1001089.html), the **Shoryudo Highway Bus Ticket** (www.meitetsu.co.jp/eng/ticket-info/shoryudo.html), covering much of Central Honshu, and the Kyushu-centric **SunQ Pass** (www.sunqpass.jp).

It's recommended to reserve seats ahead for any long journey, particularly if it's on a popular route. Unfortunately, many bus reservation websites are only usable in Japanese. A few exceptions to this rule include the website of Willer (see above), and the websites of **Japan Bus Lines** (http://japanbuslines.com/en).

For more information on the various types of buses and how to make them work for you, visit the website of the **Nihon Bus Association** (www.bus.or.jp/en).

Car

Given Japan's fantastic rail network, renting a car can be downright inconvenient in urban areas, where you'll be contending with traffic, lots of narrow one-way streets, and extortionate rates for parking, which is often hard to find.

If you're traveling in a part of the country where having your own wheels makes sense, roads are well-paved and maintained, and most drivers are conscientious and follow traffic laws, speed limits aside. Driving is on the **left** side of the road like it is in the UK, which may be challenging for drivers from the United States and Canada. Traffic laws are essentially the same as what you'd expect anywhere else. If you're on a motorcycle, you'll need a helmet.

Drivers from most countries need an **International Driving Permit** (IDP). Apply for it in advance in your home country or the country of your driver's license.

SPEED LIMITS

The average speed limit hovers around 30 kilometers (19 mi) per hour on smaller streets, 40 kilometers (25 mi) per hour on medium-size streets in cities, 80-100 kilometers (50-62 mi) per hour on expressways, and 50-60 kilometers (31-37 mi) per hour elsewhere. Signage is usually in Japanese and romaji (Roman alphabet). This comes in handy when navigating the country's extensive expressway network. Tolls are often hefty.

GAS

Gas stations, known as gasorin sutando ("gasoline stands"), are plentiful in most towns and at service areas (rest stops), dotting all expressways. They are often full-service, although self-service is increasingly common, and they may close at night. Gas prices have ebbed and flowed in recent years, but tend to hover around ¥140 per liter (0.26 gallon). Credit cards (kurejitto kaado) and cash (genkin) are both accepted. To keep matters simple, just request mantan ("full tank") when pulling into a full-service station. Note that rental car companies require all cars to be brought back with the tank full.

CAR RENTALS

Typically, car rentals start from ¥5,000 per day, plus daily insurance fees. Some car rental agencies give discounts for multiday rentals. Many rental cars from major agencies have navigation systems with English-language functionality. Having this set up before you hit the road will drastically simplify the task of navigating. Politely ask the car rental staff to switch the GPS system to English before you leave the agency—you'll be grateful you did later. If there's no English option for a given car's GPS, don't panic. The easiest solution is to punch in the phone number of your destination.

Japan's biggest car rental outlets include **Toyota Rent-A-Car** (https://rent.toyota.co.jp), **Nippon Rentacar** (www.nipponrentacar.co.jp), **Nissan Rent-A-Car** (https://nissan-rentacar.com), **Orix Rent-A-Car** (https://car.orix.co.jp), **Ekiren** (www.ekiren.co.jp), and **Times Car Rental** (https://rental.timescar.jp).

Although most of these agencies have some kind of English-language reservation system, **Japan Experience** (www.japan-experience.com/car-rental-japan) assists foreign travelers with making car rental reservations. **Rental Cars** (www.rentalcars.com) and **ToCoo! Travel** (www2.tocoo.jp/en) also offer English support with car rentals.

Plane

Japan's far-reaching flight network is best used if you're traveling a long distance domestically (e.g., from Sapporo to Osaka, Tokyo to Fukuoka, Hokkaido, or Okinawa).

Carriers flying domestically include Japan's big major airlines, such as **Japan Airlines** (www.jal.co.jp), or JAL, and **All Nippon Airways** (www.ana.co.jp), or ANA, as well as a host of low-cost carriers like **Jetstar** (www.jetstar.com), **Peach** (www.flypeach.com), **Vanilla Air** (www.vanilla-air.com), and **Skymark Airlines** (www.skymark.co.jp). While some of these domestic carriers offer one-way deals as low as ¥2,000, excluding taxes, there's always a catch. Often, baggage weight limits are unrealistically strict, seating is spartan, and add-on fees accumulate for a number of minor reasons.

JAL and ANA often cut fares significantly for flights purchased at least a month early, so book as far ahead as you can. Both carriers also offer air passes with flat fees for tourists on domestic flights. Check out ANA's **Experience Japan Fare** (www.ana.co.jp/en/ph/promotions/share/experience_jp; ¥10,800 per leg). If you're planning to specifically visit Okinawa, JAL subsidiary Japan Transocean Air (JTA) offers the **Okinawa Island Pass** (www.churashima.net/jta/company/island-pass_en.html). This pass, which must be purchased overseas, gives travelers the ability to hop between Okinawa Hontō, Miyako-jima, and Ishigaki-jima (up to five flights total) at discounted rates.

Here are a few destinations with airports that make sense to fly into to cut time on your journey.

- Travel to remote, northern **Hokkaido** is made easier with Sapporo's **New Chitose Airport** (www.new-chitose-airport.jp), **Hakodate Airport** (www.airport.ne.jp), and **Asahikawa Airport** (www.aapb.co.jp) for travelers interested in visiting Daisetsuzan National Park.
- If you're beginning a trip in **Kyoto** or **Kansai,** it may make sense to fly into Osaka's **Kansai International Airport** (Osaka, KIX; www.kansai-airport.or.jp) or **Osaka International Airport.**
- **Shikoku's** airports are also worth considering if you're starting from Greater Tokyo or anywhere north of there; key flight hubs include **Takamatsu Airport** (www.takamatsu-airport.com), **Tokushima Airport** (www.tokushima-airport.co.jp), **Kōchi Ryōma Airport** (www.kochiap.co.jp), and **Matsuyama Airport** (www.matsuyama-airport.co.jp).
- It can also make sense in some cases to reach **Kyushu** by air; though there are other airports on the island, **Fukuoka International Airport** (www.fuk-ab.co.jp) is your best bet.
- **Okinawa** can only be reached by ferry or plane, plane being more efficient. **Naha Airport** (www.naha-airport.com), on the main island of Okinawa-Hontō, is by far the region's major flight hub. Flights, or ferries, to other more far-flung islands can be caught from there.

Ferry

Although Japan's main islands are linked by bridges and undersea tunnels, ferry is the only option for reaching many islands in the Inland Sea, Yakushima off the coast of Kagoshima, and Okinawa's constellation of small islands.

You can usually buy tickets through individual ferry companies or through major travel agencies. Note that the water on some ferry routes can be notoriously choppy, so it pays to ask about this if you're prone to sea sickness.

Visas and Officialdom

PASSPORTS AND VISAS

Travelers from 68 countries, including the United States, Canada, UK, Australia, and New Zealand, as well as most European nations, receive short-term visas on arrival in Japan. The majority of these visas are for 90 days, with extensions of up to 90 days possible for a handful of countries, including the UK, Germany, and Switzerland, with a trip to the immigration office required. For a full list of visa-exempt nations, visit www.mofa.go.jp/j_info/visit/visa/short/novisa.html. Note that South African nationals must apply for a tourist visa at their nearest embassy or consulate.

Before traveling to Japan, check your passport's expiration date. It must be valid for at least six months from the date of your flight and entry into the country. Further, an onward ticket is required to enter the country.

Customs

Upon arriving in Japan, you'll be asked to fill out a customs declaration form. For this, have the address and phone number of where you plan to stay ready at hand. Simply writing the name of a city where you'll be staying won't be accepted.

A few official limitations to be aware of at customs: up to three 760-mililiter bottles of alcoholic beverages; 400 cigarettes, regardless of origin; all goods meant for personal use besides these two items may not exceed ¥200,000 in total value; a maximum amount of cash or travelers checks on hand no higher than ¥1 million; no more than 1 kilogram (2.2 pounds) of gold.

VACCINATIONS

Japan has an advanced medical system and is extremely safe from the perspective of communicable illnesses. No immunizations are required. At the time of writing in November 2021, the national government had provided coronavirus vaccinations for nearly all members of the public who wanted to be vaccinated in Japan for free, with over 70 percent of the population being fully vaccinated. There are currently no regulations yet in place related to coronavirus vaccinations for overseas visitors. At the time of writing, the Japanese government had begun to issue COVID-19 vaccine passports to citizens and residents for overseas travel and was seeking to make reciprocal agreements with foreign governments with the aim of reviving international travel. Check the various official coronavirus-related resources available online (page 754) for any updates to this continuously evolving situation.

Festivals and Events

TWICE-YEARLY

TAKAYAMA MATSURI

Takayama's old town, Apr. 14-15, Oct. 9-10

Considered one of Japan's three most visually stunning festivals, the Takayama Matsuri is held twice yearly, in spring and autumn. Throngs gather in the heart of the old town to witness a dozen towering floats strutted through the streets. The spring half of the event is known as the Sannō Matsuri and the autumn edition is known as the Hachiman Matsuri. The biggest thrill comes in the evenings, when the colorfully decked-out floats roll through town ridden by mechanical dolls.

FUJIWARA FESTIVAL

Hiraizumi; May 1-5, Nov. 1-3

Once in spring and again in fall, various games, dances, and a memorial service to honor the Fujiwara clan also take place during the festival. In autumn, the Fujiwara lords are again honored. There's also a parade of children in kimono, a Noh play on the stage at Chūson-ji, and various traditional dances.

SPRING

KANDA MATSURI

Tokyo, weekend closest to May 15

This is one of Tokyo's three biggest festivals, with hundreds of floats and omikoshi (portable shrines) carried by sweaty participants to the great shrine of Kanda Myōjin. It's a spectacle to behold.

SANJA MATSURI

Tokyo, third weekend of May

The largest festival in Tokyo celebrates the three founders of Tokyo's most famous Buddhist temple, Sensō-ji in Asakusa. The most visually stunning aspect is about 100 elaborate mikoshi (portable shrines), which symbolically house deities. The neighborhood around Sensō-ji overflows with yatai (food stalls), games, and plenty of locals beating drums, playing bamboo flutes, and milling around in yukata (lightweight kimono).

SUMMER

HYAKUMANGOKU MATSURI

Kanazawa, early June

The city's biggest festival, spanning three days in early June each year, commemorates Kanazawa's founding by Lord Maeda Toshiie on June 14, 1583. A procession of locals in 16th-century attire marches through the streets, a special tea ceremony is held in a variety of styles, Noh is performed in the ethereal glow of torch light, 1,500 floating lanterns drift down the lazy Asano-gawa, and thousands of youngsters advance through the streets bearing red lanterns and beating taiko drums.

GION MATSURI

Kyoto, throughout July

One of Japan's most iconic festivals, Kyoto's Gion Matsuri takes place during the sweltering month of July each year. It is rounded off with a parade of truly astounding floats pushed through the streets of Gion by revelers in traditional garb. The festival culminates July 14-17, when Kyoto's city center is blocked off to traffic and residents mill about in yukata, drinking beer and nibbling on grub from food stalls.

HAKATA YAMAKASA GION MATSURI

Fukuoka, July 1-15

During Fukuoka's biggest festival, a festive atmosphere builds July 10-14, with parades and practice runs taking place, until 4:59am on July 15, when seven teams of men—one for each of Hakata's seven districts—clad in loincloth-like fundoshi transport multilevel floats known as yamakasa, which depict figures and scenes from the city's past, on their shoulders.

TENJIN MATSURI

Osaka, July 24-25

Regarded as one of Japan's three blowout festivals, practically all of the city participates in this massive festival. Following a ritual and prayers on the first day, the festival reaches a crescendo on the second day when (starting from around 3:30pm) locals wearing traditional garb pull opulent portable shrines the size of cars, known as mikoshi, from Tenmangū through the surrounding streets, then proceed to glide through the Ō River in swarms of boats. The evening ends with a huge fireworks show along the Ō River.

MATSUMOTO-JŌ TAIKO MATSURI

Matsumoto, last weekend of July

During the last weekend of July every year, some of Japan's best taiko, or traditional drum, troupes converge on Matsumoto to beat hearty rhythms with hefty batons. Their high-energy performances against the stunning backdrop of one of Japan's most pristine original castles make for an impressive introduction to Japan's rich tradition of percussion.

AOMORI NEBUTA MATSURI

Aomori, Aug. 2-7

Every August in Aomori city, reaching a crescendo the night of August 5, locals parade large, luminous papier-mâché lanterns through heaving streets. The ornate floats depict samurai warriors, mythical figures, animals, and more. Revelers fill the streets wearing colorful, lightweight summer kimonos (yukata), nibbling on summer fare—yakitori, grilled corn—and downing beers.

KANTŌ MATSURI

Akita City, Aug. 3-6

The Kantō ("pole lantern") festival is among Japan's most visually impressive summertime spectacles. Daytime events are held around town, but the real buzz surrounds the nighttime performances that take place as dusk falls. Some 230 bamboo poles are hoisted aloft by Akita citizens, young and old, to the sound of flutes, shouts, and taiko drums. The poles are topped with up to 46 lanterns warmly lit by candles within and sacred offerings of intricately cut white paper known as gohei that flap in the breeze.

TANABATA MATSURI

Sendai, Aug. 6-8

It's all about love at the Tanabata Matsuri (Star Festival), one of Tohoku's biggest summer festivals. Kicking off the festivities on the evening of August 5 (from 7pm), upward of 15,000 fireworks are launched in Nishi-kōen, next to the bank of the Hirose River on the west side of town. The streets fill with sentimental revelers who are encouraged to (literally) wish upon a star by writing out their desires on paper strips known as tanzaku, which are then affixed to bamboo strewn throughout the city, and to freely reveal their bottled-up feelings.

YOSAKOI ODORI MATSURI

Kōchi, Aug. 9-12

Kōchi's flamboyant, kinetic Yosakoi Matsuri is one of the 10 largest festivals in Japan, and the energy level doesn't disappoint. Consecutive waves of dance troupes dressed in colorful costumes jump, shout, and groove through the city's downtown streets, fill covered shopping arcades, and perform in parks, on stages next to the castle, and in various other locations.

AWA ODORI MATSURI

Tokushima, Aug. 12-15

The Awa Odori Matsuri takes place during Obon, Japan's festival of the dead, when everyone traditionally returns to their hometown to honor their ancestors; it's as much a remembrance of those who have passed. The formula is simple: don geta (wooden sandals) along with a vivid yukata, and follow the lead of those around you, dancing in unison.

SHŌRŌ-NAGASHI (SPIRIT-BOAT PROCESSION)

Nagasaki, Aug. 15

On the last night of the Obon festival, locals

parade floats, impressively made from wood, bamboo, and other natural materials, through the city, before releasing them into the harbor. These glowing barges are said to carry the spirits of the ancestors, symbolized by the lanterns they are topped with. As they drift farther offshore, they are naturally subsumed by the waves.

DAIMON-JI GOZAN OKURIBI

Kyoto, Aug. 16

Another iconic Kyoto summer festival, this is an occasion to bid farewell to deceased spirits believed to visit the living during the holiday of Obon, celebrated in mid-August in Kyoto. Blazing fires in the shape of Chinese characters are lit and left to burn for about 40 minutes on the slopes of five mountains surrounding the city.

KŌENJI AWA ODORI

Tokyo, last weekend of Aug.

Kōenji Awa Odori is a pulsating, fun, and rowdy festival, by far Tokyo's best awa-odori dance festival. Although not quite as large as the one in Tokushima, more than 1 million people flock to the suburb of Kōenji to watch as troupes of drummers, flutists, shamisen players, and dancers weave through the neighborhood's streets. This is one of my personal favorites.

FALL

TOKYO JAZZ FESTIVAL

Tokyo, Sept.

Tokyo Jazz Festival brings together a world-class lineup of jazz stars from Japan and abroad for Japan's biggest jazz event. It's definitely recommended for serious devotees of the art.

JOZENJI STREETJAZZ FESTIVAL

Sendai, second weekend of Sept.

Buskers from across Japan jam in Sendai's downtown, drawing hundreds of thousands to the city center for this impressively free festival. Performances take place in the downtown area in parks, shopping arcades, and beyond, rain or shine. If jazz isn't your thing, there are also performances of other musical genres, from Latin and pop to rock and gospel.

WINTER

DŌSOJIN MATSURI (NOZAWA FIRE FESTIVAL)

Nozawa Onsen, Jan. 15

Considered one of Japan's top three fire festivals, 25- and 42-year-old men of the town fight with the rest of the village men in a literal flame battle. First, some 100 villagers build a towering wooden shrine, which, after being blessed by a Shinto priest, is defended at its base by the 25-year-olds, while the 42-year-olds guard the top. Encroaching hordes wielding torches descend on the structure with the goal of burning it to the ground. Throughout the event, participants and spectators alike are primed with a continuous flow of sake by—no joke—the local fire department.

SAPPORO SNOW FESTIVAL

Sapporo, early Feb.

During the Sapporo Snow Festival, intricate, sometimes towering sculptures are made from snow and ice by teams from around the globe. Vendors sell roast corn, potatoes drenched in butter, sausages, beer, and hot cocoa, as well as a sampling of regional specialties from around Japan. Crowds gleefully mill about the city or sit under large outdoor heaters, contentedly nursing hot wine in routinely below-freezing temperatures.

Recreation

BIKING

Japan's relatively tame streets make exploring by bicycle an attractive option. Rental outfits and tour operators are plentiful in many places, from Tokyo to Kyoto and Osaka. If you'd like to undertake a longer journey, consider the gorgeous **Shimanami Kaidō.** This 70-kilometer (43-mi) succession of bridges and roads allows cyclists to pedal their way across the Inland Sea, via six scenic islands, starting from the port of Onomichi on Honshu and ending in the town of Imabari in northwestern Shikoku.

For a good introduction to some of Japan's more popular cycling routes, visit the websites of **Japan Cycling Navigator** (www.japancycling.org/v2/) and Kansai-centric **KANCycling** (www.kancycling.com). Note that bicycle frames in Japan are often on the petite side for taller foreign travelers. If you're over 180 centimeters (5'11") tall, you may need to seek out a rental or tour outfit with larger frames available.

HIKING

While heavy-duty expeditions fall outside the scope of this book's terrain—for that, look to the loftier peaks of the Japan Alps, the wilds of Hokkaido, or volcanic Kyushu, to name a few—there are still some great hikes in the regions surrounding Tokyo and Kyoto, often somewhat urban and involving a decent amount of temple-hopping. The most strenuous hike in the region surrounding Tokyo, Kyoto, and Hiroshima is undoubtedly also Japan's most iconic: **Mount Fuji.**

SPECTATOR SPORTS

Though soccer and sumo each exert their own pull among the Japanese, baseball is by far Japan's favorite sport.

Soccer

Soccer—sakkaa ("soccer") or futtobōru ("football")—has gained traction over the past few decades. Since 1993, there's been a professional **J-League** (www.jleague.jp/sp/en), or J1 League, with 18 teams and a season that runs March-October. Japan has also been sending its **Samurai Blue** to the World Cup since 1998. After a rough entry, the team has since battled their way into the quarterfinals three times (2002, 2010, 2018). Japan's stellar women's team, **Nadeshiko Japan,** were the 2011 Women's World Cup champions and came in second place in 2015. Soccer matches are televised on various sports channels, which are sometimes only available on cable. There's also the **Emperor's Cup,** held between September and New Year's Day, in which literally any team, including ambitious high schoolers, can suit up.

Sumo

The most quintessentially Japanese of all sports, sumo is a singular spectacle. Huge men known as rikishi (professional sumo wrestlers), sporting impeccably styled hairdos and donning mawashi (padded loincloths), slam their bodies against each other with tremendous force in the center of a circular dōyo (ring) as an elaborately attired gyōji (referee) wielding a wooden war-fan known as a gunbai looks on.

The rules are relatively simple: Whoever gets pushed out of the ring or touches the ground with anything but their feet first loses. Grand tournaments known as bashō are held six times per year in different locations. In January, May, and September, Tokyo is where the clash occurs, while Osaka hosts in March, Nagoya in July, and Fukuoka does the honors in November. Attending one of these tournaments is a highlight and a rare glimpse into something deeply Japanese.

Martial Arts

Japan has a rich budō (martial way) tradition.

Baseball in Japan

Japan may be the most baseball-crazed country on the planet. Known in Japanese as yakyū ("field ball"), baseball was first introduced to the country in 1873 by Horace Wilson, an American English lecturer in Tokyo. The sport began to take feverish hold of the country during the first half of the 20th century, when a few exhibition games starred the likes of Babe Ruth, Lou Gehrig, and Joe DiMaggio. Throw in the vigorous endorsement of American GIs in the postwar years, which inspired Japanese corporations to begin funding teams, and you had all factors needed for the sport to enthrall the nation.

JAPANESE VERSUS AMERICAN BASEBALL

While the game in Japan stays mostly true to its American roots, there are a few differences. For one, the ball used is slightly smaller and more tightly wound. And in terms of play, there's less emphasis on thwacking home runs. In Japan, strategic strikes by the batter—just enough to keep teammates moving around the bases—are revered.

In terms of the viewing experience, watching fans can be as interesting as the game itself, joining in elaborate, choreographed cheers that vary by team and player. Rally towels are waved in synchrony, while balloons, umbrellas, and more dance rhythmically in the air, as cheerleaders prance around the field. For sustenance, "beer girls" patrol the stands bearing beer kegs weighing as much as 35 pounds, while food stands sell the classics (think: hot dogs, peanuts), alongside local options like yaki-soba and ramen.

SEASONS, LEAGUES, AND TEAMS

Nippon Professional Baseball (http://npb.jp) is split into the Central and Pacific leagues, with six teams on each. The season runs from late March-October, when the Nippon Series (Japan's World Series) has the nation glued to its television sets for the final showdown between the top team from each league. By far, the most popular teams are Tokyo's **Yomiuri Giants** and their main rivals, Kansai's **Hanshin Tigers,** whose home base is 55,000-seat Koshien Stadium, between Kobe and Osaka. Other teams with healthy followings include the **Hokkaido Nippon-Ham Fighters,** Tokyo's **Yakult Swallows,** and Fukuoka's **SoftBank Hawks.** Although the Giants have the strongest record in Japan's pro-baseball history, with 45 titles to date (combined Central and Japan Series wins), the Tigers undoubtedly have the most ferocious fans.

HOW TO CATCH A GAME

If you're keen to watch the pros play, your best bet is trying to catch a game either in Tokyo (Yomiuri Giants, Yakult Swallows) or outside Osaka (Hanshin Tigers) at Koshien Stadium. Tickets start from as low as around ¥1,000 for the standing section and up to ¥6,000 or more for prized seats near the field. And for a fascinating, in-depth look at the quirks of the game as it's played in Japan, with a generous helping of humor, check out Robert Whiting's classic book *You Gotta Have Wa.*

Perhaps the most recognizable of all Japan's martial arts is **karate.** Literally meaning "empty hand," karate originated in Okinawa, a fusion of Okinawan and Chinese techniques. Various styles have splintered off the original, and today many flock to Japan to study the iconic fighting art on its home turf.

Among the other schools, **aikidō's** aim is to use the opponent's own force and strength against them. The name of this fighting school translates to "way of harmonious spirit." Founded relatively recently in the early 20th century by Morihei Ueshiba, it combines elements of karate, judō, and kendō. **Jujitsu,** which focuses on combat in close quarters and involves lots of on-the-mat tussles, first emerged during the Warring States period (1467-1600). **Judō** is a gentler spinoff of jujitsu. Derived from sword fighting, **kendō** sees participants kitted out in bōgu (armor) use bamboo swords known as shinai lunge, strike, and roar spirited shouts known as kiai as they land blows.

While these varied styles of fighting are more a participatory than spectator sport for many, **tournaments** occasionally draw large audiences. Large tournaments are occasionally held at **Nippon Budōkan** (2-3 Kitanomaru-kōen, Chiyoda-ku; tel. 03/3216-5100; www.nipponbudokan.or.jp), a huge indoor arena near Tokyo's Imperial Palace.

ONSEN

Of all quintessential experiences in Japan, submerging yourself to the shoulders in water heated by magma in the earth may be the most revelatory. Iceland may have given us the word "geyser," but the ritual of soaking in hot water has arguably seeped more deeply into Japan's collective psyche than anywhere else on earth. Hot springs, or onsen ("hot water spring"), are found in every region of this exceedingly volcanic country, with the sulfuric resort town of Hakone atop the list within the scope of this book.

Technically speaking, the water gurgling up into the pools of an onsen must be at least 25°C (77°F), although it usually hits around 39-42°C (102-107.5°F) or even more scalding levels. It must also contain at least one of the naturally occurring chemical elements on a list of 19—many of which are believed to possess healing powers to smooth skin, boost circulation, and more.

These pools, often made with marble, granite, or cypress wood, are found in a range of settings: indoors (often attached to ryokan), outdoors (aka rotenburo), next to rivers, on mountainsides, in steamy valleys, and next to the ocean. They are typically segregated by gender—though not always!—and must be entered in the buff. Unsurprisingly, as with many things in Japan, a complex code of etiquette governs bathing in an onsen; here are a few of the basics:

- Upon entering, **slip off your shoes** and deposit them at lockers or shelves near the door.
- **Enter the appropriate changing room** (men: 男; women: 女).
- **Bathe and rinse off before getting in the pool** in the separate area for washing.
- Most onsen will provide or rent **towels,** though simple ones will not (in which case you will need to bring your own). You may use a small modesty towel to cover up on your way to the bath, but this is not necessary, and should not be brought into the water.
- **Never put your head underwater;** if you have long hair, wrap it up in a towel or tie it up in a hairband.
- **Don't be rowdy;** alcohol is frowned upon, though pleasant in moderation if you have access to private baths.
- When you exit the bath, **wipe off excess water** before returning to the changing room.
- Many onsen have a strict policy against **tattoos.** Cover up small ones with band-aids or medical tape, or visit https://blog.gaijinpot.com/how-to-onsen-if-you-have-tattoos for a list of tattoo-friendly hot springs.

If this all sounds intimidating, many ryokan and onsen resorts have private tubs available for rent. Whatever type of onsen pool you choose, you'll be greatly rewarded if you take the plunge. As an aside, public bathhouses called sento are also ubiquitous across Japan, typically in more urban settings. The difference is that the water in a sento tub is artificially heated.

Food and Drink

EATING OUT

The sheer range of restaurant offerings in Japan can be daunting. Many restaurants in Japan specialize in only one type of dish. Many meals that leave a lasting impression will likely be from a chef who embodies the traits of a shokunin, someone who brings a sense of pride to their work. Another thing to note is an emphasis on seasonality.

Some general restaurant types include:

- **"Family restaurants"** (think: Denny's and similar), where a range of set meals and items can be ordered a la carte.
- **Shokudo canteens,** which are essentially cafeterias that serve simple set meals of home-cooked Japanese fare.
- **Cafés,** in the modern sense, and their antecedents, **kissaten,** which are nostalgic coffeehouses preserved with their old brewing methods and atmosphere intact since the postwar years.
- **Izakaya,** or pub-cum-restaurants with sometimes quite extensive food offerings, featuring lots of small dishes that are typically shared by the whole table (think grilled meat on sticks and various dishes that pair well with booze).
- The humble **yatai,** or street stall, commonly seen at traditional festivals and arrayed throughout the city of Fukuoka.
- The **yokochō,** or culinary alleyway, is another phenomenon abundant throughout Japan.

If you follow basic etiquette, your experience dining out in Japan will be smooth. First things first, when entering a restaurant, you'll be greeted with "Irasshaimase" ("Welcome, come in"). A server will likely come to you and ask "Nan mei sama desu ka?" ("How many are in your party?"). While answering in Japanese may feel like an achievement, it's perfectly fine to just hold up the number of fingers to indicate how many you'll be dining with. Now is the time to either request a smoking seat (kitsuen seki) or non-smoking (kin-en seki). Note that many restaurants permit smoking anywhere, so you may have to endure a bit of secondhand smoke.

A vast range of seating styles are found at restaurants in Japan. Besides tables (or counters) and chairs, some restaurants have tables that sit close to the ground with seating that ranges from thin cushions on a tatami floor, known as zashiki style, to sunken spaces in the floor beneath the table where diners put their legs. As with tatami floors in any environment, always remove your shoes before stepping on the tatami mats.

A common feature of a restaurant meal is being presented with a wet towel known as an oshibori, which is often either chilled or heated (depending on season). Use this to clean your hands before eating; resist the urge to wipe your face or neck with it.

If dining with a group, once everyone has placed their order, it's considered good manners to wait until everyone's food has arrived to begin eating. When it comes time to call for the check, call over a server again with a polite sumimasen ("excuse me"), then say "o-kaikei onegaishimasu" ("check please"). Japan is still very much a cash-based society. Unless you're at a high-end restaurant, plan on paying with cash. **Tips** are simply not accepted in Japan. If you do try to give a tip, you'll likely be chased down by the staff to return your "forgotten change." Be aware, however, that some upscale restaurants may add a 10 percent service charge or a seating charge ranging from ¥200 to upward of ¥1,000 at swankier establishments.

Unless you're going to a 24-hour chain restaurant or convenience store, you're unlikely to find good food outside typical opening times. Breakfast is usually eaten at home, but cafés will often serve "morning sets" from around 8am until 10am or 11am. Lunch is typically served from 11:30am to 2pm or 3pm, while dinner hours are usually from 5pm or 6pm until 10pm or 11pm.

To make a reservation, language barrier can be a real challenge. Your best bet is to ask the staff at your accommodations to call on your behalf.

EATING IN

Eating a meal at someone's home in Japan is a great pleasure and a revelatory cultural experience. Most Japanese don't expect foreigners to have expert command of the multitude of nuanced table manners, but mastering a handful of small things will make a first-rate impression on your hosts. Note that most of the following also holds true for eating at restaurants.

First things first, if alcohol is being served, the meal will normally begin with a toast. In a Japanese home, more often than not, meals consist of many shared dishes, clustered in the center of the table. In this situation, turn your chopsticks around and use the opposite ends to take food from the individual shared dishes. Alternatively, some dishes may have chopsticks, or other utensils, solely used for serving. Use these instead of your own chopsticks if they are available.

A few pointers on chopsticks. Try to practice using them before making your trip. You'll feel more confident and will enjoy dining situations more. Western utensils will often simply not be available. Don't use your chopsticks to point or gesticulate. It's also considered rude to spear any form of food with chopsticks.

While you'll want to use your chopsticks to lift the food to your mouth from each small dish, when eating from a small bowl of rice in particular, it's customary to lift the bowl close to your mouth and take the rice from there with your chopsticks. In the case of miso soup, sip it directly from the small bowl. But don't lift other bowls in this manner, especially larger ones. Another point: Put soy sauce or any other kind of dipping sauce into a small dish that will be provided with the rest of the dishes, rather than pouring sauce directly onto your food, especially white rice.

When drinking, it's considered good manners to refill the glass of anyone sitting next to you. They will likely offer to do the same. Try not to leave food uneaten—as much as you can manage. Perhaps counterintuitively, slurping noodles is encouraged, especially when served in soup. Finally, at the end of a meal try to put all your dishes back in their original places. Then, give your compliments to the host with a hearty "gochisōsama deshita" ("It was a feast!").

A final word on coming prepared for a meal at someone's home: Bring a bottle of booze (wine, nihonshū, etc.), some nicely packaged tea, or a dessert that everyone can share. If you'd like to experience a meal at someone's home during your trip, **Nagomi Visit** (www.nagomivisit.com) matches travelers and English-speaking locals living across Japan for a home-cooked meal.

REGIONAL SPECIALTIES

On the casual end of the spectrum, popular options when dining out include **donburi** (rice bowls topped with various types of meat or fish) and a glut of noodles, from **ramen** (typically thin noodles), to **udon** (thick noodles made of wheat flour), to **soba** (thin noodles made from buckwheat). It's worth noting that ramen alone is said to have 26 varieties, served in a range of soups (tonkotsu, or pork bone-based, miso-based, soy sauce-based, etc.). Udon and soba can also be served in broth, or separately and dipped in a side bowl of broth or sauce. Another heartier casual option is **tonkatsu,** or breaded and deep-fried pork cutlet often served with rice, shredded cabbage, and various condiments and sauces. Another great casual mainstay is the **yakitori** shop. Here you'll find most parts of a chicken (and many vegetables) slow-grilled on skewers over charcoal.

While most of the above will be prepared by a chef and served to you at a table or counter, you'll also prepare some types of meals at your table. Common examples include **okonomiyaki,** a savory pancake stuffed with vegetables, seafood, meat, cheese, and more, cooked on a griddle built into your tabletop, then dabbed in a sweet, savory sauce; **sukiyaki,** a hotpot dish containing choice thin cuts of beef and vegetables, thoroughly boiled in a pot then dipped in a dish of raw egg (it's safe!); **shabu-shabu,** which is similar to sukiyaki, but the meat (and sometimes fish) is merely parboiled then dipped in sauce infused with sesame or citrusy ponzu. Another DIY classic is **yakiniku** (Korean barbecue), which consists of meat, vegetables, and more, brought to your table where you'll cook them at a grill that is either built into the table or on a brazier that will be brought to you by the staff.

At the haute end of the spectrum, **kaiseki ryōri,** which grew out of the traditional tea ceremony, is essentially a multicourse banquet, often served at a plush ryokan or exclusive restaurant. Kaiseki dishes are highly seasonal and include a range of often inventive concoctions made with all manner of ingredients that are only limited by the imagination of the chef. Tempura, a style of cooking in which vegetables, seafood, and more are battered and deep-fried, can also get pricey at the higher end of the spectrum. And of course, the price of an upmarket sushi or sashimi spread can be exorbitant.

DRINKS AND ALCOHOLIC BEVERAGES

The legal drinking age in Japan is 20. It's worth saying a few words about Japan's most famous alcoholic beverage, **nihonshū** (rice wine; literally, "drink of Japan"). Although nihonshū is widely referred to overseas as sake, this word literally just means "alcohol." Breweries across the islands make nihonshū every winter using a mix of water, a special type of polished rice, and a yeast extract known as koji.

While a sommelier approaches nihonshū with the same level of nuance you'd expect of wine in the West, at the most basic level, nihonshū is usually described as being either kara-kuchi (dry) or ama-kuchi (sweet). Typical ways of drinking it include jō-on (room temperature), reishu (chilled), or nurukan (heated). It's often poured from a small ceramic flask known as a tokkuri into drinking cups known as o-choko. When it comes to choosing nihonshū, as well as how to drink it, your best bet will be to simply ask for a recommendation from the staff at a bar or restaurant. It's easy to get carried away when drinking nihonshū, which can be deceptively smooth, but be careful: It ranges in strength from 15 to 22 percent.

O-cha is the general term for tea, and the default is green tea, or **matcha.** Roasted matcha is known as hōjicha, which is a darker brown color and less caffeinated. Warm hōjicha is often served for free at restaurants. A refreshing tea that tastes great chilled is mugicha, made with roasted barley. Sometimes you'll come across kōcha (black tea) too, although the aforementioned types of the beverage are more common.

DIETARY RESTRICTIONS

Eating out in Japan can admittedly be tricky if you've got dietary restrictions, from being vegetarians or vegan, to dealing with gluten intolerance or other allergies, to having religious commitments that forbid certain products (halal, kosher). To smooth things, consider carrying cards that explain in Japanese exactly what you can't eat. **Just Hungry** provides free, printable cards that do just that (www.justhungry.com/japan-dining-out-cards). In a pinch, simply saying you have an allergy to a specific ingredient will ensure that the restaurant staff does due diligence to confirm whether it's present in a specific dish or not.

A good option for vegetarians is shōjin-ryōri, served at Buddhist temples. Kaiten-zushi (conveyor belt sushi) provides a surprising number of veggie sushi (cucumber roll, pickled vegetable sushi, etc.), as well as some side dishes and desserts. Convenience stores are another unlikely option, selling a range of salads, pickled vegetables, tofu dishes, egg sandwiches, and more.

A few other good resources for finding food options with dietary limitations include the website **Happy Cow** (www.happycow.net), a global database of vegan restaurants, and the online, Japan-specific restaurant guide **Bento** (https://bento.com), which allows you to apply vegan or vegetarian filters to search results. **Halal Gourmet** (www.halalgourmet.jp) is a good source for Muslim-friendly dining options. If you must avoid gluten, be aware that some types of soy sauce may contain wheat. The **Legal Nomads** website has compiled a good guide to eating gluten-free in Japan (www.legalnomads.com/gluten-free/japan).

Accommodations

Japan has an eclectic range of accommodations, ranging from hyper-modern to traditional, with all types available for every budget. Even modest accommodations are usually well-maintained. Moreover, travelers are routinely wowed by Japan's justifiably famous hospitality (omotenashi).

That said, room rates in Japan can run quite high, and the rooms quite small. To avoid being charged sky-high rates, plan and book as far in advance as possible, especially during peak season (hanami, or cherry blossom season, in late March or early April; Golden Week holidays in late April and early May; or the Obon holidays in August).

The following websites tend to be particularly helpful for reserving accommodations in Japan, particularly ryokan and minshuku:

- **Travel Rakuten** (https://travel.rakuten.com)
- **Japanese Guest Houses** (www.japaneseguesthouses.com)
- **Japan Ryokan and Hotel Association** (www.ryokan.or.jp/english/)
- **Ryokan Collection** (www.ryokancollection.com)
- **Japanese Inn Group** (www.japaneseinngroup.com)
- **Jalan** (www.jalan.net)
- **Japan Hotel Association** (www.j-hotel.or.jp)
- **JAPANiCAN**, run by travel agency giant JTB Group (www.japanican.com/en)
- **Japan Hotel & Ryokan Search**, run by Japan National Tourism Organization (www.jnto.go.jp/ja-search/eng/index.php)

HOTELS

There is a plethora of different types of Western-style hotels. At the cheaper end of the spectrum, **business hotels** are compact, no-frills options that are normally located near transport hubs. What they lack in soul, they make up for in reasonable rates. Singles tend to go from around ¥8,000, while doubles usually go for about ¥12,000 per night. There's often an optional breakfast buffet on offer.

Mid-range options are readily available in Tokyo and Kyoto, where hotels with a truly boutique touch are only recently gaining more traction. At the higher end, the sky is the limit to how much you could spend on a luxury room.

RYOKAN

A ryokan is the most quintessentially Japanese accommodation: tatami-mat floors, futons instead of beds, and meals served to your room, all within the walls of a creaky, old wooden building. A deep sense of hospitality is something that respected ryokan are known for. A ryokan is much more than just a place to sleep. Most offer the option of an elaborate dinner and breakfast, often served to your room, where you eat while lounging in a yukata (lightweight kimono).

Ryokan are often located in onsen towns; many have a private, in-house onsen (hot spring), which can typically be rented hourly for ¥2,000-4,000, or a shared, gender-separated onsen that can be used by guests and sometimes visitors during specific hours only.

Both cheap and expensive ryokan exist. For the full experience, expect to spend in the range of ¥15,000-25,000 per person.

Ryokan Etiquette

Upon entering, slip off your shoes and ease into the slippers provided. In your room, be sure to take off your slippers before entering any tatami-mat area, where only socks or barefoot are acceptable etiquette. Ditch your day clothes in favor of a much more comfortable yukata.

Although it's by no means necessary or expected, upon leaving, nudge an envelope with a **cash tip** to the staff if their service impresses you. Tipping isn't customary in Japan, but ryokan are an exception due to the stellar hospitality they often provide.

BED-AND-BREAKFASTS

A traditional Japanese bed and breakfast, or minshuku, is typically family-owned and often set in a private home that's been converted into a lodging. They're similar to ryokan but tend to charge more affordable rates, and are often clustered around ski resorts, mountain towns, and hot-spring areas. More often than not, guests share toilet and bathroom facilities. Expect to pay in the range of ¥5,000-12,000 per person.

HOSTELS

If you don't mind sharing bathroom facilities and potentially even the room itself, there are a growing number of hostels in Japan, particularly in larger cities. Most hostels are either part of the **Japan Youth Hostel** (JYH) network (www.jyh.or.jp/e) or operate independently or as part of a small chain. Bedding will be included in the price. Room types include both dormitory and private, with a private room in an independent hostel costing around the same or more than a private room in a business hotel. This is worth considering if you're keen to have privacy, as a business hotel room has the added benefit of a private bathroom.

JYH membership gives you a discount on prices of member hostels (usually starting around ¥3,300 for members, from ¥4,000 for non-members). JYH-member hostels often offer food (breakfast and dinner) for a small fee, but the kitchen can't be used freely by guests. They may also have a curfew. Check the JYH website to see what properties are available. Make sure you've read the fine print so that you're not surprised by strict conditions around points like the timing for check-in and check-out or whether there's a curfew.

At independently run hostels, dorm beds tend to start from around ¥2,000 at the low end, although a more realistic starting figure is ¥3,000. Normally, private hostels will have a shared kitchen and lounge. Curfews will be less common, too. Chains include **J-Hoppers** (https://j-hoppers.com), **K's House** (https://kshouse.jp/index_e.html), and **Khaosan** (http://khaosan-tokyo.com/en).

CAPSULE HOTELS

A night spent in a capsule hotel could be either a matter of urban survival for a drunk salaryman or a one-off novelty for the experience-seeking traveler. A capsule hotel is literally what its name suggests: a capsule or pod in which you can bed down for a night, with lockers outside for your luggage. You'll likely have just enough room to crawl in and lay down.

Naturally, you'll be using a shared toilet and bath. Most capsules have air-conditioning, a power outlet, and a small television. Don't expect much in the way of privacy, and note that not all chains accept female guests. If a chain does accept female guests, the floors are usually segregated by gender.

Given their nature, a capsule hotel isn't a practical choice for more than an overnight

Love Hotels

Another "only-in-Japan" accommodation is the ubiquitous love hotel. As the euphemistic name suggests, these establishments are geared toward those engaged in the pursuit of "love." Let's face it—space and privacy are hard to come by in many Japanese homes, hence the explosion of this novel form of accommodation. Appropriately, they tend to be clustered around entertainment districts or near highway exits.

These hotels have increasingly snuck onto mainstream booking websites. The easiest way to tell if you've stumbled upon a love hotel listing will be if it happens to say "adults only" or something to that effect in the description. These rooms will usually contain an array of condoms and sex toys (handcuffs, blindfolds, whips), and are often decked out in lavish (if dated) bathing facilities. Don't worry—the cleaning crews are said to do a legendarily thorough job.

On the street, the easiest way to spot a love hotel is by its placard out front containing by-the-hour rates. More often than not, rather than dealing with a receptionist (the shame!) you'll be selecting your room from an electronic board that shows vacancies. Note that same-sex couples aren't always admitted, and multi-night stays usually aren't allowed. Prices can differ wildly depending on the area and rise dramatically on the weekends or for overnight stays. Generally speaking, renting a room to "rest in" for a few hours usually costs from around ¥3,000, while overnight stays start from about ¥6,000.

Despite the overtly risqué nature of love hotels, they can actually make for a fun experience. Rooms are often decked out in wacky themes and offer a firsthand glimpse into Japan's collective private life.

stay. If you plan to stay in one of these cubes for more than a night, you'll have to actually check out each morning and then check back in. Prices hover around ¥3,500-6,000 or a bit higher for more stylish options.

TEMPLE STAY (SHUKUBO)

The shukubo (temple stay) phenomenon allows travelers to sleep in a temple. This highly recommended experience is a great way to see inside a Buddhist temple and offers guests a chance to potentially join in morning meditation or some form of ritual, such as prayers or fire ceremonies.

Two meals will be served of the Buddhist vegetarian variety known as shōjin-ryōri, and rooms tend to be traditional (tatami mat, futon, with yukata for guests to wear). Depending on the temple, both shared and private rooms can be chosen, of which some have private bath and toilet facilities, while others are shared. While there are temples around the country that offer shukubo lodgings, the best place to experience a temple stay is in one of the dozens of temples that offer lodgings in the sacred hermitage of Kōya-san.

AIRBNB

Despite making massive inroads to so many tourism hot spots around the globe, Airbnb's footprint in Japan is notably small. This is largely due to new accommodation laws that came into effect in 2018, which imposed more stringent laws for shared accommodations, from making it mandatory for all rented rooms to have clearly marked emergency exits to requiring those running Airbnb rooms to have a license number. This doesn't mean that Airbnb isn't an option. Have a look on the website and peruse rooms if you're a fan of the service. Just be aware that the company's reach isn't as deep in Japan as it is in most places around the world.

Conduct and Customs

Japanese people have a reputation for being a bit buttoned-up. There is some truth to this, as seen in the complex etiquette that governs social interactions. While foreigners are granted quite a bit of leeway, if you observe basic customs it will be reciprocated with friendliness and appreciation. Keeping things as simple as possible, here are some fundamentals.

GENERAL TRAVEL ETIQUETTE

One important area of etiquette in Japan revolves around footwear. **Remove your shoes** in the genkan (entryway) of anyone's home you visit, without fail. Some restaurants will also require patrons to remove their footwear at the entrance, and castles or old-school ryokan also require you to slip out of your shoes at the door.

On the subject of floors, be sure to carefully handle **luggage** indoors. Try not to roll, let alone drag, any luggage across wooden or tatami floors. In fact, try to avoid putting luggage on tatami floors altogether, whether at someone's home or in an old ryokan.

In public, use common sense when it comes to **noise** levels. Keep your voice down on public transit, especially if you get onto a train or bus and no one around you is talking.

It's also worth noting that eating and drinking when walking around in public or riding on public transportation is considered impolite. This doesn't apply to high-speed trains such as shinkansen or any others with reserved seating, due to the more private nature of each given seat.

If you'd like to have a guide to etiquette that accounts for any situation you'll likely encounter, the playfully illustrated book *Amy's Guide to Best Behavior in Japan: Do It Right and Be Polite!* is a great resource that doesn't overwhelm.

Greetings

When greeting someone in Japan, lightly bow and offer a friendly "yoroshiku onegaishimasu." Or, simply use English if your new acquaintance seems comfortable with it. If you happen to be in a business situation, extend a business card with two hands as you bow, ensuring that the text is facing the recipient's direction so they can read it when they receive it. Don't be shocked if you are simply met with a handshake, which is commonly offered to foreign guests. The one thing you want to avoid doing is embracing or kissing on the cheek Mediterranean-style. Doing so would only cause awkwardness and discomfort.

HOUSES OF WORSHIP

When visiting shrines (Shinto) and temples (Buddhist), the etiquette is quite similar. At a **shrine,** bow before walking through the torii gate that marks the entrance. After passing through the torii, walk along either side, but not the center, of the path that leads to the shrine. It's believed that the kami (gods) proceed down the center of the path. After walking farther into a shrine's ground, you'll come to a water basin, where it's customary to fill the ladle resting on the basin, pour a small amount of water on your left hand, followed by your right, and rinse your mouth with it. Finally, tilt the ladle upright so the small remaining bit of water runs down the handle, thus cleansing the ladle itself. If you want to say a prayer, toss in a coin (¥5 is standard), then ring the bell hanging over the offering box, deeply bow twice, clap your hands two times, pray silently, then bow once more and walk away.

When visiting a **temple,** you can essentially follow these same guidelines, minus clapping your hands. Note that not all temples have purification basins. Some have large incense burners where you can purchase incense as an offering for a small fee (usually around

¥100). If you choose to do so, light the incense from the other incense already protruding upright from within the ash that fills the burner, wave it around your head and body, then stick the bundle of incense sticks into the burner along with the others.

Photography can be limited at shrines and temples. Watch out for signs and heed them.

ATTIRE

On the subject of attire, aim to dress slightly more formally than you may be used to. On average, Japanese people are quite dapper and, cutting-edge trendsters aside, modest. You'll notice that many men wear suits, especially while working, while women tend to dress in classic cuts.

SMOKING

Be aware that smoking is still considered very normal in Japan. That said, smoking on the street isn't permitted, except in designated areas. Frustratingly for many, smoking is often permitted indoors, including in restaurants and bars. Some restaurants will have smoking (kitsuen) and non-smoking (kinen) sections.

PHOTOGRAPHY

Ask before taking photos of people. Not only is it courteous, it's also the law. Taking photos in which people in public spaces are visibly recognizable and publishing them without their permission is illegal.

Also, watch out for places, especially at religious structures and museums, where photography is forbidden.

Health and Safety

Japan sets a high benchmark for cleanliness and safety. Your chances of encountering any serious physical danger in the country are very low. Nonetheless, arm yourself with basic knowledge on a few things to be aware of during your trip.

MEDICAL EMERGENCIES

If you need emergency medical assistance, dial 119. Most operators only speak Japanese, but they will transfer your call to someone who speaks English. Japanese hospitals and clinics only accept Japanese medical insurance. Foreigners will generally be asked to pay upfront and claim it back after returning home. Just be sure to get medical/travel insurance before your trip. If you do find yourself in need of medical assistance, the standard of care is high, but little English is spoken. Large university-affiliated hospitals, typically in major cities, tend to have more English-speaking doctors on staff, as do pricey international clinics, which are also usually in urban centers.

CRIME

Alongside being a very clean, safe place in terms of health, Japan is also blessed with some of the lowest crime rates in the world. Still, resist the temptation to lull yourself into a false sense of security. To call the police about a crime or accident, dial 110. For English-language help with emergency services assistance, available 24/7, dial 0120/461-997 (www.jhelp.com/en/jhlp.html). Alternatively, contact your embassy if you're not in immediate danger. On the flipside, if stopped by police, be polite and cooperative. If they ask to see your ID, you are legally obligated to show them. Sometimes foreigners are stopped in this manner. The more cooperative you are, the quicker you'll likely be on your way.

Petty theft is thankfully a rarity. If you've lost something, or suspect if may have been stolen, go to the closest kōban (police box). Chances are someone has handed it in. Likewise, if you lose something on a train, go report the matter to the station staff when you get off the train. Tales of kindly train attendants recovering wallets and high-end cameras are commonplace.

One common crime is drink spiking, which occurs routinely in small, dodgy corners of select nightlife zones such as parts of Tokyo's Roppongi and Kabukicho districts. If you happen to go out in one of these two areas, keep an eye on your drink to be safe. Also, never follow a tout into any establishment in either neighborhood.

ILLICIT DRUGS

When it comes to drugs, be aware that Japan has a zero-tolerance policy, with even first-time offenders usually charged (and jailed) or deported. In the event of arrest, try to contact your local embassy. They won't provide legal aid but may be able to recommend a lawyer or translator. You may not be given this option, however, with Japanese detention laws being rather severe, with police having the right to detain anyone without charges for up to 23 days. Japan's controversial detention practices were dramatically revealed in the high-profile detention saga of Brazilian-born French ex-chairman and CEO of Nissan, Carlos Ghosn, in 2018.

NATURAL DISASTERS

Being caught up in a natural disaster is more likely than falling victim to a crime in Japan. Foremost, there are regular earthquakes, which are usually small, but the "big one" always looms. If you happen to be unlucky enough to be in the country when the next big one strikes, drop close to the ground, cover your head and neck—either under a table or under your backpack; whatever is at hand—and hold onto something to keep your footing steady.

While rare, devastating tsunamis do sometimes strike after significant tremors. Typhoons, which sweep through the country from July through early October, as well as occasional landslides, volcanic eruptions, extreme heat waves at the peak of summer, and occasional snowstorms in the depths of Tohoku and Hokkaido during winter are other potential natural dangers.

Information on weather, earthquakes, and more is available in English on the website of the Japan Meteorological Agency (www.jma.go.jp/jma/indexe.html). The same information is also disseminated by the national broadcaster, NHK, in up to 18 different languages on their NHK World website (www3.nhk.or.jp/nhkworld).

Practical Details

WHAT TO PACK

First things first, note that storage on public transport is often limited, so you should opt for a small bag if possible. Also, before packing anything else, be sure to take a small **gift**—something linked to where you're from is best—for anyone whose home you may be visiting. This little gesture goes a long way in Japan.

When it comes to attire, everyday dress tends to be a bit more **formal** than you may be used to. For perspective, many salarymen go to work in a suit every day. For dinner in an upscale restaurant, men should pack a dress shirt; for women, a smart-casual dress or blouse should do the trick. And, of course, be sure to pack for the season. Depending on where you're going and when, you may need proper winter attire or only loose, breathable clothing. Layers that you can add or remove are almost always a good bet.

Bring a **plug adapter** from home if you're traveling from a country with a different system. (Outlets in Japan are two-prong, like in the United States.) You can check if you'll need an adapter at https://world-power-plugs.com/japan. Most electronic stores will sell them, but may only have the Japan to international version if not in a tourist hot spot/large city.

To be on the safe side, bring all **medicines** with you that you may need during your trip, preferably in the original packaging. Pharmacies (yakyoku) are plentiful—simply look for the internationally recognizable red cross symbol out front—but there are fewer over-the-counter medicines in Japan than overseas. In a pinch, most pharmacists can usually speak limited English and will likely be able to read and write some, too. On that subject, certain antidepressants and painkillers, which are mostly legal overseas, are illegal in Japan unless they're under a certain strength. To learn more, read the information on classes of drugs and how to bring those that are legal into the country, as explained by the **Ministry of Health, Labour and Welfare** (www.mhlw.go.jp/english/policy/health-medical/pharmaceuticals/01.html), which has also provided a helpful Q&A page on the matter (www.mhlw.go.jp/english/policy/health-medical/pharmaceuticals/dl/qa1.pdf).

Another item that you may want to consider bringing is a handkerchief or hand towel. Particularly in summer, you'll spot people of all ages occasionally wiping their brow, but beyond this, some restrooms in shops, restaurants, or train stations will not have any means of drying your hands. This trend has increased during the coronavirus pandemic, as many air dryers have been sealed shut to prevent the spread of germs. If you forget to pack one, don't fret. Once you're in Japan, you'll see no shortage of colorfully designed tenugui (all-purpose traditional hand towels) at souvenir or lifestyle shops, or the plain cotton variety on convenience store shelves.

BUDGETING

Japan isn't the cheapest country, but it also isn't prohibitively expensive. Your main costs will come from transportation and accommodation. **Book in advance** to increase your chances of landing a deal. Further, if you'll be traveling long distances in a short period of time, it will likely pay to get a **rail pass.** Otherwise, budget quite a bit more (at least ¥10,000 per leg) for transportation—shinkansen in particular are pricey, and it doesn't take long for a taxi meter to top ¥2,000. Food, drink, and entertainment costs can be as high or low or as you like, as the proliferation of Michelin stars going to affordable ramen restaurants attests.

A good baseline daily budget would be around ¥8,000. This will typically get you a hostel bed (¥3,000), three cheap meals a day (¥500-1,000 each), basic transportation, and perhaps one splurge such as a café pit stop or a moderate entry fee. A good mid-range daily budget would be around ¥10,000-25,000 (business hotel or private room in guesthouse from ¥8,000, dinner ¥3,000 per person at an izakaya or restaurant, and extra funds of roughly ¥6,000-9,000 for miscellaneous things like admission fees or local tours). For a bit more luxury, the prices jump quite a bit. A night in a good hotel will likely start from around ¥25,000, while an upmarket dinner will likely cost at least ¥10,000 per person.

To trim food costs, try to eat a big lunch. Many good restaurants offer ¥1,000-2,000 lunch sets that can be surprisingly satisfying. Alternatively, see what surprisingly substantial food items convenience stores sell, or go to a supermarket or department store food hall around 30 minutes to an hour before closing time to hunt for discounted bento (boxed meals).

- **Sandwich:** ¥300-500
- **Cup of coffee:** ¥300-500
- **Beer:** ¥500 for draft beer at local izakaya
- **Lunch:** ¥1,000 for a rice bowl topped with meat or fish
- **Dinner:** ¥1,500 for mid-range meal without drinks; ¥3,000 for a meal at an izakaya with drinks
- **Train ticket (local):** from around ¥180 if traveling only a few stops
- **Train ticket (regional):** ¥3,000-8,000 for journeys on limited express trains; ¥8,000-25,000 for longer shinkansen trips

- **Hostel bed:** ¥3,000
- **Business hotel or private guesthouse:** ¥8,000
- **Small ryokan (often with 2 meals):** ¥12,000

MONEY

Japan's currency is known as the yen (pronounced "en"). Its symbol is ¥, and its abbreviation is JPY. Banknotes come in denominations of ¥1,000, ¥5,000, and ¥10,000. Coins include the small, lightweight silver ¥1, the copper ¥5 (with a hole in the center), the copper ¥10, the nickel ¥50 (with a hole in the center), the nickel ¥100, and the hefty copper-nickel blend worth ¥500. Vending and ticketing machines will often take ¥10, ¥50, ¥100, and ¥500 coins, but not ¥1 or ¥5. Generally, shops do not let you break bills without purchasing something. But, when paying, most shops will have change for a ¥10,000 note, unless you're at a flea market or street stall.

At the time of writing, the exchange rate was as follows for a range of currencies: US$1 = ¥107, £1 = ¥132, €1 = ¥117, AU$1 = ¥72. Check for latest rates at www.xe.com or www.oanda.com. Note that ATM exchange rates are often better than those offered by money changers, especially those at the airport. Reputable but smaller exchange offices in big cities, close to train stations, will often have better rates. For U.S. travelers, thinking of ¥100 as US$1 makes the conversion easier—just think of the last two digits of any price as cents, and you have a U.S. dollar estimate: ¥1,750 is roughly $17.50.

ATMs are on nearly every corner in the downtown of most big cities. Give a pre-trip travel notice to your card provider, and you'll likely not have an issue using your card at select ATMs. Be aware that making a withdrawal may incur a small fee (¥216). A good rule of thumb is to look out for 7-Eleven ATMs (Seven Bank), which tend to be the most accessible for those with overseas cards. Beyond the cities, ATMs are a bit harder to find. If you're heading into the countryside, withdraw enough cash to cover you until you plan to be back in a larger town.

Japan is quite slow to the credit card game. A surprising number of businesses still only accept cash. To be safe, plan on paying for the bulk of your trip with cash.

COMMUNICATIONS

Cell Phones

To dial a number in Japan from overseas, first dial your country's exit code (00, 011, 0011, depending on country), then Japan's country code (81), followed by the number. If the number you're trying to dial begins with a 0, drop that digit, then dial it from the second digit on. To dial direct to an overseas line from Japan, follow the same procedures you would if calling Japan from overseas. First, dial the international dialing access code (010), followed by the country code where you're calling (e.g., 1 for dialing to the U.S.), then the number. To dial a domestic number from within Japan, just dial it as is.

Japan's largest players in the mobile market are **NTT Docomo** (www.nttdocomo.co.jp/english), **Softbank** (formerly Vodafone; www.softbank.jp/en/mobile), and **au** (owned by KDDI; www.au.com/english).

Assuming you have a cell phone that is both unlocked and works on a Japanese network, you can also buy a **prepaid Japan SIM card** for it. Note that SIM cards on offer for foreign travelers often only allow for data usage. This means you'd only be able to make voice calls on internet-based apps like Skype and WhatsApp. If your phone has Wi-Fi connectivity, of course you'll be able to access the internet anytime you have Wi-Fi access.

The best prepaid card on offer right now is available through **Mobal** (www.mobal.com). You'll get unlimited cellular data, English-language support, and the ability to make and receive voice calls—a rarity among the main prepaid SIM card options—for any plan above the 30-day option (¥7,500). They send their SIM cards worldwide, so you can place your order and receive it before ever setting foot on a plane. Alternatively, you can reserve in advance, then fetch it on arrival at the airport.

For something a bit less expensive, but without voice calls and with limits on data usage, vending machines stocked with **U-Mobile SIM cards** (for one or two weeks) are found scattered around Narita Airport. You can also just walk into a major electronics shop (Bic Camera, Yodobashi Camera, Labi) and pick up a store-branded prepaid SIM card with limited data and no voice calls. These cards tend to run around ¥4,000 for a week or so of use.

Internet Access

Despite its high-tech reputation, finding Wi-Fi in Japan can be a challenge. It's often available in cafés, at some restaurants, and even in some public spaces (at train stations, etc.), but it tends to be slow or require an inconvenient amount of hoop-jumping to get what is often only 30 minutes to 1 hour of very patchy access. As a saving grace, most accommodations do offer some form of internet, whether Wi-Fi in the rooms or (bare minimum) a shared computer for emails and basic web surfing in a shared lounge.

The best way around this is to rent a pocket Wi-Fi router for internet access when you're on the go. The best pocket Wi-Fi provider is **Ninja WiFi** (https://ninjawifi.com), which offers up to 10GB of daily data use from ¥900 per day. Conveniently, it's possible to rent a Ninja WiFi pocket router along with a JR Pass, allowing you to pick up both of them at once at the airport or have them delivered to your accommodation. You can read more about this option at www.jrpass.com/pocket-wifi.

Shipping and Postal Service

Post offices are widespread throughout Japan, as are red post boxes often seen sitting beside the road. Post offices and post boxes alike are marked with a 〒 symbol. **Japan Post** (www.post.japanpost.jp/index_en.html) runs a useful English-language website where you can search for the nearest post office. It's easy to send letters, postcards, and packages anywhere on the globe for reasonable rates from any Japan Post branch. You'll have the option of attaching a tracking number to your shipment and more.

When you're on the ground, Japan's well-oiled luggage forwarding service, known as takkyūbin, is a major boon. This service eliminates the need for you to lug your baggage up steep staircases or through crowded train stations. Most service desks providing this service can be found at airports and train stations. Be aware that you'll need to fill a day-pack with your necessities if using one of these services, as you'll likely be waiting for your bag the day after you've sent it. To learn more about this handy service, check out the helpful **Luggage-Free Travel** website (www.luggage-free-travel.com). Rates tend to be around ¥2,000, give or take, per item.

OPENING HOURS

All offices are closed on **public holidays,** but many businesses (shops, museums, restaurants, cafés) will often be open but closed on the day after the public holiday. Department stores and many shops often operate from around 10am-8pm daily. Museums and galleries likely stay open 9am-5pm, with last entry around 4:30pm or even 4pm. They are often closed on Monday, unless Monday is a public holiday, in which case they close on Tuesday.

Bars tend to open from 5pm at the earliest, but more often start serving from around 6pm or later, then stay open until midnight or in some cases, much later. **Restaurants** normally open for lunch from 11:30am-2pm or 3pm, then again for dinner from 6pm-10pm or 11pm (last orders tend to be taken 30 minutes or even 1 hour before closing time). Later opening hours tend to be more common in cities or for chains.

Banks tend to be open from 9am-3pm (counter can be until 5pm as well) Monday-Friday and are closed on public holidays. Some banks may be closed on Sunday and only open until 5pm or earlier on other days. Meanwhile, **post offices** are usually open

9am-5pm Monday-Friday, with some large branches maintaining longer hours and offering services on Saturdays and sometimes even Sundays (limited hours). Truly large ones will have pickup points for mail that are open 24/7.

Public Holidays

Restaurants, shops, and most tourist attractions are still open on national holidays, with the exception of New Year, when almost everything closes down. Another point to be aware of: holidays are moved to the following Monday if they happen to fall on a Sunday. Further, if there are two national holidays within two days apart, the day between them also becomes a holiday. This sometimes happens during **Golden Week** in late April to early May, when a handful of holidays are clustered close to each other.

- Jan. 1: **New Year**
- Jan. (second Mon): **Coming of Age Day**
- Feb. 11: **National Foundation Day**
- Feb. 23: **The Emperor's Birthday**
- Mar. 20 or 21: **Spring Equinox Day**
- Apr. 29: **Shōwa Day**
- May 3: **Constitution Day**
- May 4: **Greenery Day**
- May 5: **Children's Day**
- Jul. (third Mon): **Ocean Day**
- Aug. 11: **Mountain Day**
- Sept. (third Mon): **Respect for the Aged Day**
- Sept. 22 or 23: **Autumnal Equinox Day**
- Oct. (second Mon): **Health and Sports Day**
- Nov. 3: **Culture Day**
- Nov. 23: **Labor Thanksgiving Day**

OBON

Ancestors who have passed on are believed to return to the land of the living during this important Buddhist holiday. Lanterns are festooned in front of homes and around towns intended to guide the spirits to their destination, dances are performed at local festivals by everyone from children to the elderly, and people tend to the graves of their ancestors and leave offerings of food at temples and home altars. The festival is brought to a close by releasing floating lanterns into rivers, lakes, and the ocean to light the way back to the spirit world for the ancestors who have visited.

This day was traditionally celebrated from the 13-15 on the seventh month of the year on the lunar calendar (August). Today, however, many regions follow the solar calendar, which makes it fall in July (July 13-15). Semi-officially, August is the month that is treated like a holiday, with August 10-17 being one of the busiest tourist seasons in Japan, as companies nationwide let their staff take off. It's best to either avoid traveling during this peak time, or to book accommodations, flights, and more *well* in advance.

WEIGHTS AND MEASURES

Japan is on the **metric system.** All weights, measures, and distances on road signs will be in metric units.

When it comes to voltage, **100V** is the norm, unlike the 110-120V standard for the U.S. or Europe's 220-230V. That said, the plugs are the same type as those used in the U.S., with two flat prongs.

TOURIST INFORMATION

More often than not, you'll find a little tourist information center inside or near main train stations or close to popular tourist spots. Staff tend to be more proficient in English on average in bigger cities, but English-language help becomes hit or miss in the countryside. Thankfully, there are usually a healthy number of English-language leaflets.

While you can't expect every tourist office to handle all of your logistical needs, many helpful members of staff will be willing to assist with things like booking onward travel, booking tickets, reserving accommodations, and more.

Traveler Advice

ACCESS FOR TRAVELERS WITH DISABILITIES

The keyword for accessibility when traveling with a disability is baria-furii ("barrier free"). Accessibility in Japan is improving in cities, mostly due to an aging population and the Olympics, but the issues remain in rural areas.

On the street, traffic lights are synced up with different songs that indicate when it's safe to cross. And train platforms have raised dots and lines worked into the pavement as tangible guidance. A good rule of thumb for wheelchair users would be to contact any tourist sites or restaurants ahead of time to ask about access such as a separate entrance with a ramp. Many sites marked as "accessible" will unfortunately still have gravel pathways or sharply inclined slopes.

Most train lines will have a car or several cars for wheelchair users, while the priority seats at each end of the carriage, near the doors, are reserved for elderly, pregnant, and disabled people. Also note that most trains have a gap between train and platform. To board, the best thing to do is inform a staff member. They will then bring a portable ramp to lay down and help you on. They will also call ahead to the station you're getting off at, where another member of staff will be there at your car with a ramp to help you get off. Buses usually have priority seats, too, which are sometimes stowaway seats that are often marked with a different color of upholstering.

The multilingual **Japan Accessible Tourism Center** website (www.japan-accessible.com) has extensive information about wheelchair accessibility. It also includes good information about hotels and more for a number of cities. For accommodations that do have barrier-free rooms, book as far in advance as you can to secure them.

WOMEN TRAVELERS

Japan is a very safe country, including for women travelers. There are incidences of groping or unwanted contact on crowded trains, but they are not common. In cities, trains and metros often have dedicated women-only cars to decrease the possibility of inappropriate behavior from men. Open harassment, such as catcalls and gestures, is practically nonexistent.

Although sexism is in many ways still rooted in Japanese society, it primarily affects women living in Japan. Some capsule hotels don't allow women guests, but otherwise, there are few ways in which women travelers are limited in their experience of the country.

TRAVELING WITH CHILDREN

There's plenty of kid-friendly stuff to do in Japan, from beaches and attraction parks to arcades, pop culture sites, outdoor activities, and more.

Be aware that you'll likely end up walking significant distances in big cities. Further, there are often elevators in train stations, but few ramps exist near many tourist sites. Children ages 6-11 receive half-price train fare (including for the shinkansen), while those under 6 are free. There is priority seating on trains and city buses for pregnant women and those with small children.

When dining out, note that picky eaters can be placated with Western-style foods like sandwiches at convenience stores, cafés, and more. There are plenty of bakeries and family restaurants with kids' menus in Japanese towns, too. Note that highchairs aren't ubiquitous in Japan.

When choosing accommodation, be aware that hotels can usually provide cots, assuming there's space. Even double rooms can be quite small in Japanese hotels. Quad rooms or two double beds are rare, although triple rooms are occasionally available. For these reasons, staying in a traditional accommodation such as a ryokan or minshuku might be easier if you want everyone to be in one room. A room in one of these traditional digs will probably be one large tatami room with several futons.

If you're traveling with an infant or a toddler, when it comes time to change a diaper, changing stations are usually found in the women's bathrooms in (large) train stations, department stores, larger shops, and malls. You can pick up diapers and other basics at larger pharmacies and at some larger supermarkets. Breastfeeding in public isn't common and is somewhat frowned upon. It will likely go unnoticed if you find a corner and cover up.

SENIOR TRAVELERS

With its aging population, Japan has relatively good infrastructure for senior travelers. Be aware, though, that there are still lots of steps and little ledges (often unmarked) that you'll have to navigate. There are priority seats for seniors on trains and buses. Some tourist attractions offer discounts (even some domestic travel tickets), but are often either unmarked or only explained in Japanese.

LGBTQ TRAVELERS

LGBTQ travelers are unlikely to encounter any discrimination, especially in urban areas like Tokyo and Osaka. If anything, Japan is relatively accepting, although prejudice does still exist. Homosexuality is legal, but gay marriage isn't. Foreign marriages aren't recognized in Japan, but partnership certificates are available in several cities or districts.

Same-sex couples should not have a problem getting reservations or staying in a hotel. Regardless of sexual orientation, overt displays of affection are not very welcome in public. For trans people, the main issue may be onsen and bathrooms, as you'll be expected to go to one that matches your physical sex. The best solution is to rent a private onsen.

By far, Tokyo is Japan's main LGBTQ hub. The city's LGBTQ community throws the large **Tokyo Rainbow Pride** (https://tokyo-rainbowpride.com) parade in May each year as part of a multiday celebration.

For up-to-date information on what's happening in Japan's LGBTQ community, particularly in Tokyo, check out the website of **Utopia Asia** (www.utopia-asia.com). LGBTQ groups on Meetup.com are active in Tokyo, too.

TRAVELERS OF COLOR

Only about 2 percent of Japan's population is foreign-born. There's not a whole lot in the way of diversity, especially of those who look significantly different. People are mostly polite to foreigners, although the occasional microaggression and even overtly racist behavior do occur. Those with East Asian features will be assumed to speak Japanese. Expect some confusion if you don't. In general, this can make visiting Japan more of an "invisible tourist" experience for those of East Asian descent. Sadly, those perceived to have Korean features report having been the victims of derogatory comments from older Japanese.

Some travelers report that if you're black or brown, some people may appear to avoid sitting next to you on trains—this may happen to foreigners of other ethnicities too, and in some cases, small children may stare.

Unfortunately, blackface makes an occasional appearance on primetime television. The situation is changing, though, and social discourse around diversity is on the rise. Good references for black travelers are the ***Black Eye*** column in *The Japan Times*, written by American expat Baye McNeil; **The Black Experience Japan** (www.blackexjp.com), where you'll find videos, interviews, and more, as well as Facebook groups and pages such as **Black in Japan** (www.facebook.com/groups/BlackinJapan).

TOUR GUIDES AND OPERATORS

For a service that connects you with various professional tour guides who can also serve as interpreters on the go, there is the **Japan Guide Association** (tel. 03/3863-2895; www.jga21c.or.jp; fee varies by tour). Its website allows you to search for licensed guides nationwide. The Japan National Tourism Organization (JNTO) also offers a system of goodwill guides who work on a volunteer basis around the country. If you employ their services, just be aware that you will need to cover their transportation, admission to any sites or events, and meals eaten during the tour. For a nationwide list of goodwill guide groups, visit www.japan.travel/en/plan/list-of-volunteer-guides.

For a more tailored experience, there are a number of stellar tour bespoke trip outfits:

Boutique Japan (https://boutiquejapan.com) excels in this area. This small Japan-focused tour operator specializes in immersive private itineraries throughout the country. They offer high-end trips, especially for travelers deeply interested in off-the-beaten-path cultural and culinary experiences. Each trip is completely unique.

Be Here (http://behere.asia) operates with a similar philosophy, albeit with less of a focus on high-end accommodation and food (although these things can be part of a tour, too!). These tours tend to put travelers in touch (literally) with local arts and crafts, and put a premium on learning in a hands-on way by taking a cultural deep dive into out-of-the way corners of the country.

Shikoku Tours (https://shikokutours.com) provide a wide range of reasonably priced tours around all corners of Shikoku. They offer single-day and multiday tours to the remotest parts of the island, from white-water rafting and exploring rustic onsen to doing legs of the 88-temple pilgrimage route by taxi. The staff are friendly, good-humored, and really know their stuff.

Hokkaido Wilds (https://hokkaidowilds.org) is not a tour provider per se, but is the work of an adventure sports-loving collective based on the northern island that has created an excellent online resource. On their website, you'll find loads of free, self-guided bicycle, skiing, hiking, and canoeing tours, and various other practical information on the island's deep wilderness.

As its name suggests, **Walk Japan** (https://walkjapan.com) offers a variety of trips through the country, undertaken on your own two feet. Self-guided and custom tours are possible.

If you'd prefer to get around by bicycle, there are a number of tour providers. **Cycle Japan** (https://cyclingtoursjapan.com) and **Bike Tour Japan** (https://biketourjapan.com) both offer enticing rural journeys, including both led and self-guided. If you prefer to design your own tour, check out **Japan Cycling** (www.japancycling.org).

Resources

Glossary

annaijo (案内所): information desk
bijutsukan (美術館): art museum
cha (茶): tea; often *o-cha*
chūi (注意): caution
dōzo: please, go ahead
eki (駅): train station
futsū (普通): regular; for trains, *futsū* means local, making all stops
-gai (街): district
gaijin: shortening of *gaikokujin;* although often casually used, it is an impolite term for foreigner
gaikokujin: foreigner
genkin: cash
geta: traditional Japanese wooden sandals; shoe storage closets are called *getabako* (*geta* box)
gohan: rice
goran kudasai: please look around; often heard in shopping areas
goyukkuri: please take your time (often used with dōzo)
hakubutsukan (博物館): museum
hashi (橋): bridge, sometimes changes to *-bashi* when part of a name
hashi (箸): chopsticks, often *o-hashi*
hiragana: Japanese phonetic alphabet used for Japanese words
irrashaimase: Welcome! Often heard when entering an establishment
izakaya: Japanese pub with bar bites but not full meals
jiyūseki (自由席): open seating, as opposed to reserved (e.g., on trains)
kaikei: bill, check (at restaurant)
kaiseki ryōri: traditional Japanese multi-course meal
kaisoku (快速): rapid (for trains)
kaku-eki-teisha: local train; literally, stopping at all stations
kami: god
kanji: Chinese character-based Japanese writing system
katakana: Japanese phonetic alphabet used to write foreign words
kawa (川): river, sometimes changes to *-gawa* when part of a name
kawaii: cute
kin-en (禁煙): no smoking
kissaten: café
kitsu-en (喫煙): smoking
kōban (交番): neighborhood police booth
kōen (公園): park
koto: Japanese zither
kushikatsu: deep-fried pork skewers
kyūkō (急行): express (for trains)
madoguchi (窓口): ticket window
maiko: geisha in training
maki: form of sushi with items rolled into the center of a tube of rice and seaweed
manga: comic book
masuku (マスク): mask
matsuri: festival
-meisama: party of [number], e.g., *nimeisama* is party of two; this is only used by restaurant employees when confirming the number of customers in a party, not the other way around—use *futariseki* to ask for a table of two
minasan: everyone (often heard when ad-

dressing, or trying to get attention from, a group)

misoshiru: miso soup

mochi: sweet rice cake, often *o-mochi*

nigiri: form of sushi with an oblong ball of rice topped with a piece of fish

okonomiyaki: Japanese savory pancake

okyakusan/okyakusama: customer

otsumami: snacks

otsuri: change (when making a purchase)

rotenburo: open-air onsen

ryokan: traditional Japanese inn

ryokō/ryokōsha: travel/traveler

sakura: cherry blossom

shakuhachi: traditional Japanese flute-like instrument

shamisen: traditional Japanese guitar-like instrument

shima (島): island; *shima* sometimes changes to *-jima* when paired with the name of the island

shinkansen: bullet train

shiteiseki (指定席): reserved seating (e.g., on trains)

shosho omachikudasai: please wait a moment

shōjin-ryōri: Buddhist vegetarian food

shokuji: meal

shukubo: temple lodging

takoyaki: octopus dumpling

tera: temple; often *o-tera*; *tera* sometimes changes to *-dera* when paired with the name of the temple

tokkyū (特急): limited express (for trains)

tomare (止まれ): stop

tonkatsu: pork cutlet

torii: gate at Shinto shrines

uketsuke (受付): reception desk

washiki: Japanese-style (e.g., toilet)

yakiniku: grilled meat

yakitori: grilled chicken on skewers

yama (山): mountain; 山 is also read *san* and sometimes *zan* when paired with the name of the mountain

yakuza: Japanese mafia

yokochō: culinary alleys; side streets lined with food stands

yōshiki: Western-style (e.g., toilet)

yukata: lightweight kimono worn in the summer or as loungewear at ryokan

Japanese Phrasebook

ALPHABETS AND WRITING

The phonetic alphabets used in Japanese (hiragana and katakana) are made up of five vowels, same as English (*a, i, u, e, o*), 39 consonant-noun pairs (*ka, ki, ku, ke, ko, sa, shi su, se, so*, etc.), plus one single consonant (*n*) and one single particle (*o*). The consonants *k, s, t, n, h, m,* and *r* are paired with each of the five vowels, with a few exceptions: there's *shi* instead of si; *chi* instead of ti; *tsu* instead of tu; *fu* instead of hu. *Y* is only paired with *a, u,* and *o* (*ya, yu, yo*); and *w* is only paired with a (*wa*).

This base 46-letter alphabet is extended with symbols that look like straight quotes (") on the k set to make the g sound (so, *ka* becomes *ga, ki* becomes *gi*, etc.); the *s* set to make the *z* sound (except for *shi,* which becomes *ji*), the *t* set to make the *d* sound (except for *chi,* which becomes *ji,* and *tsu,* which becomes *zu*), and the *h* set to make the *b* sound. A symbol that looks like the degree symbol (°) also can appear with the *h* set to make the *p* sound.

Kanji is the writing system that uses Chinese characters and is not phonetic. Kanji is what makes reading even the most basic signs and notices, let alone newspapers, a bit intimidating. (For reference, 2,136 characters are listed as jōyō kanji, or commonly used kanji.) Latin characters are called romaji in Japanese, and many signs are also written in romaji, especially in cities.

Hiragana and Katakana

English	wa	ra	ya	ma	ha	na	ta	sa	ka	a
hiragana	わ	ら	や	ま	は	な	た	さ	か	あ
katakana	ワ	ラ	ヤ	マ	ハ	ナ	タ	サ	カ	ア
English		ri		mi	hi	ni	chi	shi	ki	i
hiragana		り		み	ひ	に	ち	し	き	い
katakana		リ		ミ	ヒ	ニ	チ	シ	キ	イ
English		ru	yu	mu	fu	nu	tsu	su	ku	u
hiragana		る	ゆ	む	ふ	ぬ	つ	す	く	う
katakana		ル	ユ	ム	フ	ヌ	ツ	ス	ク	ウ
English	-n	re		me	he	ne	te	se	ke	e
hiragana	ん	れ		め	へ	ね	て	せ	け	え
katakana	ン	レ		メ	ヘ	ネ	テ	セ	ケ	エ
English	o	ro	yo	mo	ho	no	to	so	ko	o
hiragana	を	ろ	よ	も	ほ	の	と	そ	こ	お
katakana	ヲ	ロ	ヨ	モ	ホ	ノ	ト	ソ	コ	オ
English					ba/pa		da	za	ga	
hiragana					は″/は°		た″	さ″	か″	
katakana					ハ″/ハ°		タ″	サ″	カ″	
English					bi/pi		ji	ji	gi	
hiragana					ひ″/ひ°		ち″	し″	き″	
katakana					ヒ″/ヒ°		チ″	シ″	キ″	
English					bu/pu		dzu	zu	gu	
hiragana					ふ″/ふ°		つ″	す″	く″	
katakana					フ″/フ°		ツ″	ス″	ク″	
English					be/pe		de	ze	ge	
hiragana					へ″/へ°		て″	せ″	け″	
katakana					へ″/へ°		テ″	セ″	ケ″	
English					bo/po		do	zo	go	
hiragana					ほ″/ほ°		と″	そ″	こ″	
katakana					ホ″/ホ°		ト″	ソ″	コ″	

PRONUNCIATION

Despite the difficult-looking characters, Japanese words are pronounced phonetically, so try saying them the way they look, and you won't be as far off as you might think. Following the pronunciation tips below, especially for the vowels, will increase your success.

Vowels

Speakers of Spanish will have no problem pronouncing the vowels in Japanese, as they are pronounced the same way. Japanese puts vowels in a different order than in English, and we've used the Japanese order.

SHORT VOWELS

a pronounced *ah*, like ta-da

i pronounced *ee*, like saying the vowel "e" in English

u pronounced *oo*, like food; sometimes reduced or silent when at the end of a word (e.g., *desu* often sounds like *des*)

e pronounced *eh*, like educate

o pronounced somewhat like *oh* but with a lighter touch; words like "go" and "no" in

English end with a slight "u" sound—the same words/syllables with a short "o" in Japanese are pronounced without that "u" at the end

LONG VOWELS

Long vowels in Japanese are indicated by a macron over the vowel (ō) or by a repeated letter (aa, ii, uu, ee). When a macron hasn't been used, the long o is spelled either *oo* or *ou,* depending on its hiragana spelling. Long vowels are pronounced by simply holding the sound of the short vowel for longer. (There is a slight pronunciation difference between *oo* and *ou*, but not one beginners should worry about.)

VOWEL COMBINATIONS

Vowel combinations are essentially pronounced as each vowel would be individually, although a few are more distinct.

ai pronounced like a long *i* in English, e.g., *tai* is pronounced tie

ao pronounced somewhat like *ow,* like in renown

ei pronounced like a long *a* in English, like in ace

Consonants and Consonant-Vowel Combinations

Consonants in Japanese are generally pronounced as they are in English, keeping the following notes in mind. Note that the Japanese alphabet does not use the consonant c by itself (although ch is used), l, q, v, or x. Nor is the sound "th" used.

g at the beginning of a word, always hard, as in *game*, no matter what vowel follows it; in the middle of a word, often pronounced like the g in *song*, but pronouncing it as a hard g in all cases is fine

r somewhere between the English r and l, but just pronouncing it as an English r is fine

tsu this combination is rare in English, but there is a Japanese word commonly used in English that includes it: tsunami

When two consonants are together, there is usually a slight pause between them.

In some cases, when preceded by a certain sound, words that would normally be said/written with a *k* are pronounced/written with a *g*, an *s* with a *z*, a *t* with a *d*, and an *h* with a *b* or a *p*. An example of this is *hyaku* (100) changing to *-byaku* in some cases (as in *sanbyaku* or 300) or *-pyaku* in others (as in *roppyaku* or 600).

Intonation

Japanese is not a tonal language, and stresses on syllables are subtle. Beginners should try to speak without putting too much emphasis on any particular syllable.

PHRASES

Although macrons are used in the rest of the book, long vowels in this phrasebook are depicted with repeated letters (or ou when relevant) to help with pronunciation. The particle *o* (を in hiragana) is spelled "wo" in romaji, but in this phrasebook "o" is used since that is how it is pronounced. Similarly, the particle は is spelled with the *ha* hiragana, but in this phrasebook, it's spelled "wa" to reflect the pronunciation.

Many Japanese nouns below start with "o," although if you were to look them up in an English-Japanese dictionary, the word without the "o" would appear. The "o" prefix makes the word more polite.

General

Excuse me Sumimasen

Do you speak English? Eigo o hanasemasu ka?

Hello (during the day) Konnichiwa

Hello (after dark) Konbanwa

Good morning Ohayougozaimasu (only said first thing in the morning)

Good night Oyasuminasai (literally, get rest; only said when turning in for the night)

Good-bye Sayounara

Thank you Arigatou (casual)/arigato gozaimasu (polite)

please onegaishimasu (literally, "I wish for this")

I'm sorry Gomennasai

yes hai
no iie
I don't understand Wakarimasen
I don't speak Japanese. Nihongo o hanasemasen.
Could you write that down? Sore o kaitekuremasen ka?
Where is/where are...? ...wa doko desu ka?
Where are the restrooms? Otearai wa doko desu ka?
Do you have this in Latin characters/ English? Romaji/Eigo de kaitearu no arimasu ka?
I would like.../may I have... ... kudasai (literally, "please give me") or ....onegaishimasu (e.g., miso ramen kudasai is "I would like/may I have the miso ramen")
I'm looking for... ...o sagashite imasu (e.g., deguchi o sagashite imasu—"I'm looking for the exit.")
How much is this? Ikura desu ka?
Can you take our picture? Shashin o totte kuremasenka?

Note: "How are you" is a useful phrase in English, but it is not as ubiquitous in Japanese conversation and does not have an easy Japanese equivalent. The closest is *genki desu ka?*, which translates to "are you healthy?" and would be odd to say to someone upon entering a shop, for example.

Terms of Address

In Japanese, the terms "I," "me," and "you" are generally omitted from sentences. "You," in particular, should be avoided. When you are being addressed by a salesperson or someone in the service industry, most likely you will be called okyakusama (customer) or, if your name is known, by your last name with -san or -sama.

Mr./Mrs./Ms. ... ...-san (regular), -sama (very polite, used for people in a higher station than the speaker); for example, Ms. Suzuki is Suzuki-san or Suzuki-sama
I/me watashi
My name is ... ...to moushimasu (Note: Japanese people go by their last names, and first names are generally only used with friends and family. Foreigners can use either to introduce themselves—use whichever name they would like to be called by.)
adult otona
child kodomo

Directions and Transportation

(travel) information desk	(ryokou) annaijo	(旅行) 案内所
map	chizu	地図
here	koko	
there	soko	
over there	asoko	
left	hidari	左
right	migi	右
up	ue	上
down	shita	下
straight	massugu	
north	kita	北
south	minami	南
east	higashi	東
west	nishi	西
entrance	iriguchi	入口
exit	deguchi	出口
in front of	mae	
behind	ushiro, ura	
next to	tonari	
road	douro/-douri (as part of a name)	道路/通り
street	michi	道
signal	shingou	
bridge	hashi/-bashi	橋
address	juusho	住所
bicycle	jitensha	自転車
car	kuruma	車
taxi	takushii	タクシー
subway	chikatetsu	地下鉄
train	ddensha	電車
train station	eki	駅

train platform	hoomu	ホーム
[Number] track number	[number]-ban sen	[number character]番線
[Number] train car	[number]-gousha	[number character]号車
What track number/ train car?	Nan ban sen/ nan gousha desu ka?	
plane	hikouki	飛行機
airport	kuukou	空港
bus	basu	バス
bus stop/ station	basu tei	
ticket window	madoguchi	窓口
How do I get to…?	Douyatte… ni ikimasuka?	
How far is it to…	…wa dono gurai desu ka?	
Is it close/far?	Chikai/toi desu ka?	
I want to go to…	…ni ikitai desu.	
kilometer	kiro (also used for kilogram)	キロ
I would like [one, two, etc.] (tickets)	(Kippu) [ichi, ni, etc.]-mai kudasai. Note that including kippu is optional since what you are requesting would be clear from the context.	
one-way	katamichi	片道
roundtrip	oufuku	往復
luggage	nimotsu	荷物

Accommodations

hotel	hoteru	ホテル
traditional inn	ryokan	旅館
key	kagi	鍵
room	heya	部屋
single room	hitoribeya	
double room	futaribeya	
western-style rooms (i.e., beds not futons)/ Japanese-style rooms	youshitsu/ washitsu	
I want to check in.	Cheku in onegaishimasu.	
I want to check out.	Cheku aoto shimasu.	
Can I get another key?	Kagi mou hitotsu onegaishimasu. (If asking for more than one, change "hitotsu" to the counter number you want.)	
Can I get another towel/ blanket?	Taoru/Moufu mou ichimai onegaishimasu. (If asking for more than one, change "ichi" to the number you want.)	
I can't get into my room.	Heya ni hairemasen.	
Is breakfast/ are meals included?	Asagohan/ shokuji tsuki desu ka?	
What time does breakfast start/end?	Asagohan wa nanji kara/ made desu ka?	
hotel	hoteru	ホテル
traditional inn	ryokan	旅館

Food and Drink

breakfast	asagohan	朝ご飯
lunch	hirugohan	昼ご飯
dinner	bangohan	晩ご飯
restaurant	resutoran	レストラン

A table for one/two, please.	Hitori/futari seki onegaishimasu (if asking for more than two people, change hitori-/ futari seki to [number]-nin seki)	
chopsticks	ohashi	
fork	fooku	
spoon	supuun	
knife	naifu	
napkin	napukin	
menu	mennyu	
water	omizu	お水
coffee	koohii	コーヒー
tea	ocha	お茶
cream	kuriimu	
beer	biiru	ビール
sake	osake	酒
wine	wain	
milk	gyuunyuu/ miruku	
bread	pan	
egg	tamago	卵
fish	sakana	魚
shrimp	ebi	海老
Meat	niku	
pork	buta	豚肉
beef	gyuuniku/biifu	牛肉
chicken	toriniku/chikin	鶏肉
ramen	ramen	ラーメン
sushi	sushi	寿司
sugar	sato	
I would like to order.	Chuumon onegaishimasu	
I would like the check.	Okaikei onegaishimasu	
to eat	taberu	食べる
to drink	nomu	飲む
I cannot eat…	…o taberaremasen.	
I cannot drink…	o nomemasen.	
vegetarian/ vegan	bejitarian/ biigan	
breakfast	asagohan	朝ご飯

Money and Shopping

money	okane	お金
bank	ginkou	銀行
post office	yuubinkyoku	郵便局 (Note: Post offices in Japan perform banking functions and are a reliable place to find an ATM.)
shop	mise	店
How much is this?	Ikura desu ka?	
Can I pay by credit card?	Kaado de harattemo ii desu ka?	
Can I try this on?	Shichaku shitemo ii desu ka?	
postcard	hagaki	
souvenir	omiyage	
money	okane	お金

Problems and Health

Help me! (emergency)	Tasuketekudasai!
I lost…	…o nakushimashita
My…was stolen.	…ga nusumaremashita.
wallet	saifu
phone/cell phone	denwa/keitai denwa
passport	pasupouto
I don't feel well.	Guai warui desu.
I feel sick to my stomach.	Onaka ga itai desu.

(I need to go to the) hospital/doctor.	Byouin/isha (ni ikanakereba narimasen).	病院/医者
It/that hurts.	Itai desu.	
mask	masuku	マスク
fever	netsu	熱
drugstore	yakkyoku	薬局
medicine	kusuri	薬
earthquake	jishin	地震
typhoon	taifuu	台風
embassy	taishikan	大使館
police	keisatsu	警察

Numbers

1	ichi	一
2	ni	二
3	san	三
4	yon/shi	四
5	go	五
6	roku	六
7	nana/shichi	七
8	hachi	八
9	kyuu/ku	九
10	juu/too	十
14	juuyon (not juushi)	十四
17	juushichi/juunana (both okay)	十七
20	nijuu	二十
30	sanjuu	三十
40	yonjuu	四十
50	gojuu	五十
60	rokujuu	六十
70	nanajuu	七十
80	hachijuu	八十
90	kyuujuu	九十
100	hyaku	百
300	sanbyaku	三百
400	yonhyaku (not shihyaku)	四百
600	roppyaku	六百
700	nanahyaku (not shichihyaku)	七百
800	happyaku	八百
1,000	sen	千
10,000	man	万

For numbers greater than 10, just combine the words for each digit. For example, 14 is juuyon: juu for the 10s digit and yon for the 1s digit. Similarly, for three-digit numbers, combine the various units: 256 is nihyaku gojuu roku.

Counting

Counting is complicated in Japanese because how you count depends on what you are counting. For example, the counter for small items (e.g., small fruits) is -ko (ikko, niko, sanko, etc.), the counter for flat items is -mai (e.g., tickets, postcards, shirts, etc.), for long narrow items (e.g., bottles of beer) is -hon (which changes to -pon for three and six), and the list goes on. A good default is -tsu, which is also meant for small items but only goes up to nine items. Beyond nine items, just try using the number with no counter.

1	hitotsu
2	futatsu
3	mittsu
4	yottsu
5	itsutsu
6	mutsu
7	nanatsu
8	yattsu
9	kokonotsu

Time

day	nichi	日
today	kyou	今日
yesterday	kinou	昨日
tomorrow	ashita	明日
morning	asa	朝
before noon/am	gozen	午前
noon	hiru	昼
afternoon/pm	gogo	午後
evening	ban	晩
night	yoru	夜
[number] o'clock	[number] ji (e.g., goji)	[number] 時
What time is it?	Nanji desu ka?	
What time are we leaving?	Nanji ni shuppatsu shimasuka?	

Days of the Week

Monday	getsuyoubi	月曜日
Tuesday	kayoubi	火曜日
Wednesday	suiyoubi	水曜日
Thursday	mokuyoubi	木曜日
Friday	kinyoubi	金曜日
Saturday	doyoubi	土曜日
Sunday	nichiyoubi	日曜日

Months

January	ichigatsu	一月
February	nigatsu	二月
March	sangatsu	三月
April	shigatsu (not yongatsu)	四月
May	gogatsu	五月
June	rokugatsu	六月
July	shichigatsu (not nanagatsu)	七月
August	hachigatsu	八月
September	kugatsu	九月
October	juugatsu	十月
November	juuichigatsu	十一月
December	juunigatsu	十二月

Dates

To express dates, the first part of the month doesn't follow the same pattern as the rest of the month. After the 10th, the dates follow the pattern [number] + nichi. There are a few exceptions, which are listed below. Also, except for tsuitachi, the dates also double as the counter for the number of days.

1st	tsuitachi	一日
2nd	futsuka	二日
3rd	mikka	三日
4th	yokka	四日
5th	itsuka	五日
6th	muika	六日
7th	nanoka	七日
8th	youka	八日
9th	kokonoka	九日
10th	tooka	十日
14th	juu-yokka	十四日
17th	juu-shichinichi	十七日
20th	hatsuka	二十日
21st	nijuu-ichinichi	二十一日
24th	nijuu-yokka	二十四日
27th	nijuu-shichinichi	二十七日

Suggested Reading

HISTORY

Embracing Defeat: Japan in the Aftermath of World War II (John W. Dower, 1999). This engaging tome explores Japan's rough road to recovery through the prism of the years after World War II. The book draws on numerous first-person accounts, documentary photographs from the period, and piercing historical analysis. This book, which won both the Pulitzer and the National Book Award for Nonfiction, is a powerfully focused lens onto the ways that World War II altered Japan's psyche and destiny forever.

CULTURE

A Geek in Japan: Discovering the Land of Manga, Anime, Zen, and the Tea Ceremony (Hector Garcia, 2019). Just released in revised and expanded form, this hit explores Japanese pop culture from A to Z. It also unravels many arcane social constructs and rituals, and elucidates topics ranging from architecture to video games. It's beautifully illustrated with hundreds of photos, too, making it a great visual primer on contemporary Japan as a whole.

Yokai Attack! (Hiroko Yoda and Matt Alt, 2012). This fun, light series consists of three books: *Yokai Attack: The Japanese Monster Survival Guide, Ninja Attack: True Tales of Assassins, Samurai, and Outlaws,* and *Yurei Attack: The Japanese Ghost Survival Guide.* Each volume explores a different aspect of Japan's rich lore, ranging from the supernatural (*Yokai Attack* and *Yurei Attack*) to historical figures (*Ninja Attack*) with serious battlefield cred. Playful illustrations breathe life into the outlandish tales contained in the books.

Zen and Japanese Culture (D.T. Suzuki, 1938). Originally published in 1938, this scholarly masterwork is a deep dive into the evolution of Zen Buddhism and its profound influence on Japan's traditional culture and arts. Samurai swordsmanship, haiku poetry, tea ceremony, painting, calligraphy, architecture—it's all there. It's been refreshed numerous times over the decades and no version will disappoint. For an up-to-date version, the edition published in the Princeton Classics series (2019) is a good pick.

Tokyo Vice: An American Reporter on the Police Beat in Japan (Jake Adelstein, 2010). In this colorful memoir, American investigative journalist Adelstein tells all about his 12 years of reporting on Tokyo's underworld, from murder and corruption to human trafficking and plenty of yakuza (mafia). As he goes deeper and deeper, he encounters more danger than he bargained for.

FOOD AND DRINK

Rice, Noodle, Fish: Deep Travels Through Japan's Food Culture (Matt Goulding, 2015). This lauded book is written in a literary voice and comes with a visual feast of images from across Japan's exceptional culinary world. Goulding explores the food culture of Japan's great cities—Tokyo, Osaka, and Kyoto—but also ventures farther afield to Hiroshima, Fukuoka, Hokkaido, and the remote Noto Peninsula.

Food, Sake, Tokyo (Yukari Sakamoto, 2010). This book follows chef, sommelier, and writer Yukari Sakamoto through Japan's vast capital, exploring its department store food halls, sake bars, izakaya, markets, and more. The book brilliantly decodes arcane dishes, explains a range of exotic ingredients, gives the lowdown on which fish are in season at various times of year, gives a sake primer, and introduces Tokyo's brilliant food culture.

TRAVEL WRITING

The Inland Sea (Donald Richie, 1971). This timeless book, written by Japan's foremost interpreter of the 20th century, is an elegiac hymn to the joys of traveling in "old Japan"—specifically, the dazzling Inland Sea. Part memoir, part travel narrative, Richie muses on what was then—and only more so now—a vanishing way of life. He describes the seascape, the tiny island towns, and his encounters with a host of characters with great humanity, humor, and warmth. The result is a dreamlike travelogue on Japan that remains unsurpassed.

The Roads to Sata: A 2,000-Mile Walk Through Japan (Alan Booth, 1997). This insightful, often hilarious travelogue recounts the author's walk from the northern tip of Hokkaido to Kyushu's far south, along backcountry lanes. His poignant descriptions of rural Japan, and the people he met along the way—from fishermen to bar owners—reveal a salty side of Japan that remains hidden to the vast majority of foreign visitors.

Another Kyoto (Alex Kerr with Kathy Arlyn Sokol, 2018). If you're keen to delve beneath Kyoto's surface, this "spoken book" contains decades of insight, spoken by Kerr and then transcribed by Kathy Arlyn Sokol, into the overlooked details of the ancient capital, from its gardens to its architecture and customs, gleaned from the city's priests, monks, art dealers, and intellectuals.

MEMOIR

Lost Japan: Last Glimpse of Beautiful Japan (Alex Kerr, 1993). This beautifully written and award-winning book—impressively first written in Japanese, then translated into English—weaves together three decades of the author's rich life experience in Japan. Kerr takes readers deep into the kabuki theater scene, Tokyo's boardrooms during the heady 1980s (before the bubble had popped), Kyoto's rarefied traditional arts, and the remote Iya Valley of Shikoku, where he would ultimately make a home. Juxtaposing all this beauty is a sense that Japan's ancient traditions and natural splendor have been blemished by the country's race to modernize.

The Lady and the Monk: Four Seasons in Kyoto (Pico Iyer, 1992). This book recounts the year that celebrated travel writer Pico Iyer first came to Japan to study Zen Buddhism at a monastery—a goal that didn't last long—and ultimately fell in love with a woman who would eventually become his wife. The book is very much a love letter penned by a besotted young Iyer. He followed up this work recently with *Autumn Light* (2019), a deeply mature, meditative book on the passage of time, ageing, and how decades living in Japan have informed his outlook on life.

Internet Resources and Apps

TRAVEL

www.japan.travel/en

The Japan National Tourism Organization (JNTO) promotes travel to Japan and provides a good deal of English-language information on its website. It's a good place to go for trip ideas and suggested itineraries, and to download maps (www.japan.travel/en/things-to-do).

www.outdoorjapan.com

Outdoor Japan's website and full-color, seasonal print magazine cover Japan's wild side. It's a great resource for discovering outdoor adventure opportunities in off-the-radar areas.

NEWS AND MEDIA

www.japantimes.co.jp

The Japan Times is Japan's largest English-language newspaper. It's a good resource for keeping up on news, learning about local happenings, and checking out event listings.

https://gaijinpot.com

GaijinPot is a portal for the foreign community in Japan that runs great content on everything from culture and travel to what it takes to set up a life in Japan. Its Japan 101 section is packed with practical information on topics ranging from banking to doctors. Its sister site **Japan Today** (https://japantoday.com) is a good source for news.

www.kansaiscene.com

In addition to the website, Kansai Scene free print zines are found at more than 300 pickup points in Kyoto, Osaka, Nara, Hyogo, Shiga, and Wakayama prefectures. It's a great portal into the Kansai region, including features about culture and happenings in the region, food and nightlife options, and event listings.

FOOD

https://tabelog.com/en

Tabelog's national restaurant database is comprehensive, including information like business hours, average prices, and more. You can search restaurants by location and cuisine type, as well as make informed decisions on where to eat based on user rankings. Anything with a rating above 3.5 stars tends to be dependably good.

https://gurunavi.com

Gurunavi is a good supplement to Tabelog, which scores points for its user rating system (allowing for discernment), but is more limited in its English-language coverage. Gurunavi, however, lacks Tabelog's useful user rating system. If you use both websites creatively, you'll usually be able to find a good choice for a meal anywhere you go.

TICKET RESERVATION SERVICES

www.ticketsgalorejapan.com

Tickets Galore Japan, a ticket proxy service, is a godsend. Basically, you contact the service about ticket(s) for an event you'd like to attend. The service then buys the ticket(s) on your behalf, charging a reasonable service fee. This saves massive hassle and potentially losing out on great events, as buying tickets for events in Japan—let alone from overseas—can be quite convoluted at the best of times.

TRANSPORTATION

www.hyperdia.com/en

While in Japan, Hyperdia, a user-friendly train trip-planning website, will quickly become your new friend. The website allows you to input your starting point and destination, then gives you a full itinerary for a train journey, accurate to the minute. There are many other search options, such as boxes where you can select what categories of train (local, express, etc.) you'd like to include in the search results. Note that it is available as a smartphone app for both Android and iOS.

ONLINE LANGUAGE SERVICES

https://jisho.org

Denshi Jisho, an easy-to-use online dictionary, has a mercifully simple user interface. It'll come in handy when you're searching for the name of a dish or asking for medicine at a pharmacy.

https://translate.google.com

It may seem too obvious to mention, but Google Translate also does a great job with translating on the fly.

MONEY

www.xe.com

XE is a user-friendly, up-to-date currency conversion website that also has an app for both Android and iOS. Download it so you can convert prices in yen on the fly.

HEALTH

Japan Hospital Guide

In case you need to find a hospital on the road, this app draws on data from Google Maps to provide information on hospitals and clinics. All pertinent details—opening hours, phone numbers, and more—are given. Be aware that you'll have to allow your smartphone to know your location for the app to work.

CHAT APPS

https://line.me/en

If you plan to make any new friends in Japan, forget WhatsApp. The chat app of choice here, hands down, is Line. It's available on both iOS and Android, and has an English option, so downloading it and setting it up is pretty self-explanatory.

Index

A

Abeno Harukas: 355
accessibility: 781
accommodations: 771–773; Kyoto 332–336; Osaka 366–367; Tokyo 134–138; *see also specific place*
Adachi Museum of Art: 444–445
Adashino Nenbutsu-ji: 32, 310
addresses: 756; Kyoto 282
advance reservations: 27; around Tokyo 152; Tokyo 49
Agenashiku-jima: 701–702
Ainokura: 31, 258–259
Ainu Kotan: 584
Ainu people: 586, 741
Airbnb: 773
air travel: 29, 752–755, 760; Kyoto 337; Osaka 368; Tokyo 141–143; *see also specific place*
Aka-jima: 703–704
Akan Kohan Eco-Museum Center: 584
Akan National Park: 583–587
Akihabara and Ueno: 31, 48, 80–81; accommodations 137–138; entertainment/events 91; food 119–120; map 78; shopping 105–107; sights 77–81; sports/recreation 99
Akita Prefecture: 520–535
alphabet, Japanese: 785–786
Alps, Japan: 21, 31, 234–244
Amano Iwato Jinja: 656
Amerika-mura: 351, 364
Ameya Yokochō: 120–121
Andō Jozo Miso: 527
animal cafés: 116
animals: *see* plants/animals
anime: 750
Anmitsu Hime Revue: 617–618
Aoba Castle: 499–500
Aomori Nebuta Matsuri: 17, 532–533, 763
Aoshima: 657–660
Aoyama: *see* Harajuku and Aoyama
Aragusuku-kaigan: 708
Araiya: 164
Arashiyama: 283; crowds, tips for avoiding 310; food 328–329; sights 309–312
Arashiyama Bamboo Grove: 32, 311
Arashiyama Yoshimura: 329
Arimura Lava Observatory: 663
Arita: 621
Art Fair Tokyo: 91
Art House Project: 433, 435
Art Islands: 16, 432–443
Asahidake Hike: 578
Asakusa and Ryōgoku: 31, 48; accommodations 138; food 120–122; map 82; shopping 107–108; sights 81–84
Asakusa Samba Carnival: 92
Asari Honten: 574
Aso-san: 40, 643–646
Atomic Bomb Hypocenter Park: 625
Atsuta Jingū: 223
autumn foliage: *see* kōyō (autumn foliage)
Awa Jūrobe Yashiki: 465–466
awamori: 695
Awa Odori: 17, 22, 465
Awa Odori Kaikan: 463, 465
Awa Odori Matsuri: 763

B

Bar Cordon Noir: 331
Bar Nayuta: 365
Bar Rocking Chair: 331
Bar Shares Hishii: 574
bars/nightlife: Kyoto 329–332; Osaka 363–366; Shinjuku 12; Tokyo 123–134; Yokohama 164–165; *see also specific place*
Bar Tram: 126
baseball: 766; Hiroshima 409–410; Tokyo 98
Bashamichi: 156, 164
Battleship Island: 633
bay cruises (Tokyo): 98
beaches: 708; Aka-jima 704; Aoshima 658–659; Iriomote-jima 718; Ishigaki-jima 712; Kamakura 173–174; Kerama Islands 19; Miyako Islands 705–708; Okinawa-Hontō 700; Taketomi-jima 715, 717; Zamami-jima 701–702
bed-and-breakfasts: 772
Bei: 580–581
Benesse House Museum: 435
Beppu: 646–653
Beppu City Traditional Bamboo Crafts Center: 647
biking: *see* cycling
Bise Fukugi Tree Road: 700
Blue Sky Coffee: 123
boat tours: 466, 506, 584, 588–589, 719
boat travel: 29, 761; *see also specific place*
Bodai-ji: 531–532
bombing of Hiroshima: 408
bombing of Nagasaki: 628
British House: 162

Buddhism: 742–743
budgeting: 777–778
Buke Yashiki: 527
bunraku: 355, 357, 749
burakumin community: 740
bus travel: 29, 758–759; Kyoto 337, 339, 340; Osaka 368–369; Tokyo 143–144, 147; *see also specific place*

C

Café Bibliotic Hello!: 328
Cafe D'ici: 574
Café du Lièvre (Bunny House): 123
Cafe Lente: 418
canoeing: 582
capsule hotels: 772–773
Caraway Curry House: 174
car rentals: 759–760
car travel: 29, 759–760; Kyoto 339; Tokyo 144, 147; *see also specific place*
castles: 230; *see also specific castle*
cell phones: 778–779
Center Gai: 67
ceramics: 747
Chatei Hatou: 115
cherry blossoms: *see* hanami (flower viewing)
Chichū Art Museum: 435
Chidorigafuchi: 94–95
Chikurin-ji: 488
children, traveling with: 781–782
Chinatown (Yokohama): 160, 162, 163
Chinese New Year (Nagasaki): 633
Chion-in: 32, 296
Chōkoku-no-mori: 190
Christianity: 743
Chubu Centrair International Airport: 226–227
Chūō-kōen: 465
Churaumi Aquarium: 699–700
Chūson-ji: 35, 514–515
cinema: 749–751
climate: 723–724
Comiket: 94
Confucian Shrine and Historical Museum of China: 630, 632
convenience stores: 26
cooking classes: 317
cormorant fishing: 485
COVID-19: 21, 754–755
crime: 775–776
crowds, tips for avoiding: 26; Inland Sea 443; Kyoto 284, 303, 308, 310; Tokyo 49–50
culinary alleys: 120–121
culture: 740–751
Cupnoodles Museum: 159–160
customs (at the border): 761
customs (cultural): 774–775
cycling: 765; Inland Sea 424–425; Kamakura 176; Kyoto 315–316, 340–341; Tokyo 97

D

Daibutsu Hiking Course: 172–173
Daikanbō Lookout: 643–644
Daikanyama: 47, 64, 100
Daimon-ji Gozan Okuribi: 314, 764
Daimon Yokōcho: 36
Daisetsuzan National Park: 38, 576–582
Daishō-in: 416–417
Daitoku-ji: 309
dance: 751
Danjō Garan: 387
Daruma: 551
Dazaifu: 621–623
Dazaifu Tenman-gū: 622–623
Dejima: 39, 630
Denshōen: 517
depato (department store): 110
Design Festa: 91–92
Dewa Sanzan: 510–511
disabilities, advice for travelers with: 781
diving/snorkeling: 700–701, 702, 704, 708–709, 712, 717
Dōgo-kōen: 479
Dōgo Onsen: 21, 477–478
donburi: 769
Dōsojin Matsuri (Nozawa Fire Festival): 236–237, 764
Dōtombori: 33, 351, 364–365
Downtown and Central Kyoto: 282–283; accommodations 334–336; bars/nightlife 330–332; food 323–328; map 292–293; shopping 318–321; sights 304–305
Dragon Burger: 321
drinks: 12, 125, 127, 330, 560, 664, 695, 770
drugs: 776

E

earthquake, 2011: 504
Ebisu: 31, 47; bars/nightlife 126, 128; food 112–113; map 65; shopping 100–101; sights 63–66
Ebisu-bashi: 353
Ebisu Yokochō: 113, 120
economy: *see* government/economy
Edo period: 733–734
Edo-Tokyo Museum: 84
88-Temple Pilgrimage: 17, 22, 464, 467, 480, 489
Eikan-dō: 302
embassies/consulates: Osaka 368; Tokyo 140
Emerald Beach: 700
Engaku-ji: 167–169
enka: 748
Enoshima: 171–172

Enoshima Iwaya Caves: 172
Enoshima-jinja: 172
Enoshima Samuel Cocking Garden and Sea Candle: 172
entertainment/events: Kyoto 313–314; Osaka 355–357; Tokyo 87–94; *see also specific place*
Entsū-in: 506
environmental issues: 724–725

F

fashion: 103, 104–105
festivals: 17, 762–764; Aomori 532–533; Kyoto 313–314; Osaka 357; Sapporo 549–550; Tokushima 465–466; Tokyo 91–94; *see also specific festival; specific place*
fishing: 485
flowers: 580–581, 725–726; *see also* hanami (flower viewing)
folk villages: 16, 258, 517
food: 768–771; Hiroshima 398; Kyoto 320–329; Osaka 16, 359–363; Tokyo 46, 108–123; *see also* regional specialties; *specific place*
Former Hokkaido Government Office: 38, 547
Former Japanese Navy Underground Headquarters: 691–692
Fort Goryōkaku: 36, 573
Fuji Five Lakes: 207–211; map 201
Fuji-Hakone-Izu National Park: 189, 200
Fujiwara Festival: 515–516, 762
Fukuoka: 22, 39, 605–623; itinerary ideas 600; maps 601, 606, 608–609
Fukuoka Airport: 619
Fukuoka Asian Art Museum: 39, 610
Fukuoka Castle Ruins: 39, 612
Fukuoka City Museum: 39, 610
Fukuoka Tower: 610
Fukusen-ji: 517
Fukushima: 724–725
Fuppushi-dake Hike: 567–568
Furano: 580
Furano Ski Area: 564–565
Furepe Waterfall Hike: 589
Furuzamami Beach: 40, 701
Fushimi Inari-Taisha: 11, 35, 290, 294
Futarasan-jinja: 181

G

Gahi-jima: 701–702
Ganso Kushikatsu Daruma: 361
gardens: 12, 265, 726; *see also specific garden; specific place*
Garyū Sansō: 485
gay travelers: 782
Geibi-kei (Geibi Gorge): 35, 515
geisha: 298–299
geography: 721–723
Ghibli Museum: 31, 84, 86–87
Ginkaku-ji: 32, 302
Ginza and Marunouchi: 47; accommodations 134–135; bars/nightlife 124; entertainment/events 87–89, 90; food 108–111; map 58–59; shopping 99–100; sights 54–56; sports/recreation 94–95
Giō-ji: 32, 310
Gion: 32, 278, 282; accommodations 332–334; food 321–322; map 292–293; shopping 317; sights 297
Gion Matsuri: 313–314, 762
glossary: 784–785
Glover Garden: 39, 632
Godai-dō: 506
Godai-san: 487–488
Gokayama: 16, 31, 259
Golden Gai: 31, 133
Good Mellows: 175
Gōra: 191
Goryōkaku Park: 573
government/economy: 737–739
Great Buddha at Kōtoku-in: 171
Great Japan Beer Festival Yokohama: 162
Grill Jūjiya: 380, 382
Gunkanjima: 633

H

Hakata Yamakasa Gion Matsuri: 612–613, 762
Hakkōda-san Hike: 521–522
Hakodate: 20, 36, 569–575; itinerary ideas 542–545; maps 544, 570
Hakodate Museum of Northern Peoples: 571
Hakone: 31, 189–199; map 190
Hakone-jinja: 193
Hakone Museum of Art: 191
Hakone Open-Air Museum: 191
Hakone Yuryō Onsen: 193
Hakuba: 239–244; map 240
Hakuba Valley: 237
Hama-rikyū Onshi-teien: 57, 60
hanami (flower viewing): 24–25, 26
Hanazono-jinja: 76
Haneda Airport: 141, 142–143, 752
Hantei: 119
Happo-en: 64, 66
Harajuku and Aoyama: 30, 48; bars/nightlife 131; entertainment/events 89–90, 90; food 117–118; map 71; shopping 102–104; sights 70, 72
Harbor View Park: 162
Harmonica Yokochō: 121
Hase-dera: 171
health/safety: 775–776; *see also* medical services
Heian-jingū: 298–299
Hell Circuit (Jigoku Meguri): 647–648

Hida-no-Sato Folk Village: 258–259
Higashi Chaya-gai: 266–267
Higashi Hongan-ji: 289
high season: 26; Tokyo 49
hiking: 765; Akan National Park 584–585; Aso-san 645; Daisetsuzan National Park 576, 578; Fuji Five Lakes 207, 209; Hakuba 239, 241–242; Iriomote-jima 719; Ishizuchi-san 485–486; Iya Valley 472–473; Kagoshima 663–664; Kamakura 172–173; Kamikōchi 246, 248; Kirishima-Yaku National Park 670; Kyoto 316–317; Minakami 185–186; Miyajima 417–418; Mount Fuji 200, 203–205; Rishiri-Rebun-Sarobetsu National Park 592–593; Shikotsu-Tōya National Park 567–568; Shiretoko National Park 589–590; Towada-Hachimantai National Park 521–523; Yakushima 683–685
Himeji: 21; itinerary ideas 347; map 350
Himeji-jō: 35, 381
Himeyuri Peace Museum: 699
Hiraizumi: 514–517
Hirauchi Kaichu Onsen: 40
Hirosaki: 528–531
Hirosaki Castle: 529
Hirosaki Neputa Matsuri: 529–530
Hiroshima: 21, 34, 402–414; maps 400, 404–405
Hiroshima Castle: 408–409
history: 729–737
hōjicha: 326–327, 770
Hojōya: 613
Hokkaido Jingū: 37, 547
Hokkaido University Botanical Garden: 38, 547
Hōkoku-ji: 169
holidays: 780
Hōnen-in: 33, 302, 304
Hōryū-ji: 373
Hoshizuna-no-hama: 718
hostels: 772
hotels: 771; *see also* accommodations
Hōzen-ji: 353
Hyakumangoku Matsuri: 268, 762

I

Ibusuki: 669
IC card: 758
Ichiniisan Kagoshima Honten: 664–665
Ida-no-hama: 718
ikebana (flower arrangement): 747
Ikuta Jinja: 379
Imari: 620–621
immigration: 740
Imperial Palace: 55–56
Inasayama-kōen: 39, 632–633
information/services: Kyoto 336; Osaka 367–368; Tokyo 139–141; *see also specific place*
Inland Sea: 424–425
Inokashira-kōen: 31, 95–96
internet: 779; Tokyo 140
Inujima: 441–442
Inujima Art House Project: 442
Iriomote-jima: 717–720
Isaniwa-jinja: 478–479
Ise: 389–392
Ise-jingū: 389
Ishigaki-jima: 711–715
Ishite-ji: 479
Ishizuchi-san: 485–486
Ishizue: 665
Isui-en: 373
Itami Airport: 368
Itchiku Kubota Art Museum: 207
itinerary ideas: 30–40; Kyoto 285–288; Tokyo 50–54; *see also specific place*
Itsukushima-jinja: 34, 415–416
Iwate Prefecture: 514–520
Iya Valley: 22, 470–475
Izumo: 448–451
Izumo Taisha: 21, 448–449

J

Japanese Sword Museum: 84
Japan Rail Pass: 27, 756, 757–758
Jōchi-ji: 172
Jodogahama Beach: 518
Jōjakkō-ji: 32, 310
Jōken-ji: 517
Jōmon-sugi: 683
Jozenji Streetjazz Festival: 502, 764
J-Pop: 748

K

Kabira Bay: 711–712
kabuki: 89, 749
Kabukichō: 124, 130
Kabuki-za: 87–88
Kagatobi Dezomeshiki: 268
Kagetsu: 635–636
Kagoshima: 22, 40, 660–671; itinerary ideas 603–605; maps 604, 661
kagura: 655
kaiseki ryōri: 14, 277, 320, 770
Kakiya: 418
Kakunodate: 36, 526–528
Kamakura: 20, 167–176; itinerary ideas 153; maps 154, 168
Kameyama-kōen: 315
Kamiari-sai: 449
Kamihaga Residence: 483
Kamikōchi: 244–249; map 245
Kamikōchi to Shin-Hotaka Hike: 248

Kanazawa: 21, 260–273; map 261
Kanazawa-jō Kōen: 262
Kanda Matsuri: 92, 762
Kanda Myōjin: 77
Kanmangafuchi Abyss: 182
Kansai International Airport: 337, 368, 752
Kantei-byō: 160, 162
Kantō Matsuri: 763
Kappa-bashi to Taishō-ike Hike: 246
Kappa-bashi to Tokusawa Hike: 246
kappō-ryōri: 360
Karatsu: 620
Kasaoka Islands: 443
Kasuga Taisha: 372
Katase Higashihama Beach: 173–174
Katsura Rikyū (Imperial Villa): 312
Kazura-bashi: 470, 472
Kenchō-ji: 169
Kenroku-en: 12, 21, 262, 263
Kenzo's Bar: 133
Kerama Islands: 19, 40, 701–704; itinerary ideas 679; map 680–681
Kichijōji: 31; map 86
Kii Peninsula: 385–392
Kiji: 359
Kikunoi Honten: 321
Kinkaku-ji: 32, 307–308
Kirishima-jingū: 670
Kirishima-Yaku National Park: 668–671
Kishiwada Danjiri Matsuri: 357
Kita: 351, 358, 359, 364, 366
Kitakarō Otaru Honkan: 559
Kitano-chō: 377
Kitayamazaki: 518–519
Kiyomizu-dera 32, 295–296
Kobe: 21, 35, 377–385; itinerary ideas 347; maps 350, 378
Kobe beef: 383
Kobe City Museum: 379–380
Kobe Jazz Street Festival: 380
Kōbō Daishi: 464
Kochi: 487–493; map 488
Kochi-jō: 487
Kōdai-ji: 297
Kōenji: 48
Kōenji Awa Odori: 94, 764
Kōfuku-ji: 370, 372
Koishikawa Korakuen: 79
Kompirayama Walking Trail: 37, 568
Komyozen-ji: 623
Kondoi Beach: 715, 717
Kongōbu-ji: 387
Konkai-kōmyō-ji: 303
Konpira-san: 462–463
Kōraku-en: 429
Kotoku-in: 167, 171
Kowakidani: 190
Kōya-san: 21, 34, 385–389
kōyō (autumn foliage): 24–25, 26
Kūkai: 464
Kumamoto: 639–643
Kumamoto-jō: 21, 639–640
Kumano Kodō: 21, 390–391
Kumasotei: 665
Kura: 375
Kurama to Kibune Hike: 316–317
Kurashiki: 426–428
Kurodake Hike: 578
Kurodake Ropeway: 38
Kurokami Buried Torii: 663
Kurokawa Onsen: 39–40, 650
Kusama's *Yellow Pumpkin*: 435
Kusasenri Plateau Hike: 645
Kushida-jinja: 39, 610
kushikatsu: 360
Kushiro Wetlands: 39, 582–583
Kyoto: 21, 32, 35, 274–341; accommodations 332–336; bars/nightlife 329–332; entertainment/events 313–314; food 320–329; information/services 336; itinerary ideas 285–288; maps 275, 279, 280–281, 286–287; planning tips 283–284; sports/recreation 315–317; transportation 337–341
Kyoto Gyōen: 315
Kyoto Imperial Palace: 304
Kyoto International Manga Museum: 305
Kyoto Museum of Crafts and Design: 298
Kyoto National Museum: 295
Kyoto Railway Museum: 289
Kyoto Samurai and Ninja Museum with Experience: 305
Kyoto Station Area: 276; accommodations 332; food 320-321; map 290; shopping 317; sights 289–290
Kyoto Tower: 289
Kyushu Bashō Sumo Tournament: 613
Kyushu National Museum: 623

L

lacquerware: 747
Lake Kawaguchi: 207
Lake Motosu: 207
Lake Sai: 207
Lake Shōji: 207
Lake Yamanaka: 207
Landmark Tower: 157
landscape: 721–725
language: 743–744
Le Case: 375
Les Archives Du Cœur: 440
LGBTQ travelers: 782
Lilo Coffee Roasters: 361

literature: 744–746
love hotels: 773
low season: 26; Tokyo 49
Lucky Pierrot: 574

M

Magome: 228–229
Maisen: 117
Makino Botanical Garden: 488–489
Manabe-shima: 433, 443
Manchinro Honten: 163
Mandarake: 106
manga: 745–746
martial arts: 765–767
Marunouchi: *see* Ginza and Marunouchi
Maruyama-kōen: 315
Mashūdake Hike: 585
matcha: 770
Matsue: 21, 444–448
Matsue-jō: 444
Matsumoto: 21, 227–233
Matsumoto City Museum of Art: 229, 231
Matsumoto-jō: 227–229
Matsumoto-jō Taiko Matsuri: 231, 763
Matsushima Bay: 35, 504–507
Matsuyama: 476–483; map 477
Matsuyama-jō: 476–477
Mausoleum of Kūkai: 387
Me-Akandake Hike: 584–585
medical services: 775; Kyoto 336; Osaka 367–368; Tokyo 140; *see also specific place*
Meiji Jingū: 11, 30, 70, 72
Meiji period: 734–735
Meriken Park: 380
Minakami: 185–189; sports/recreation 185–188
Minami: 351, 353–355, 358–359, 360–363, 366–367; map 354; nightlife 364–365
Minato Mirai: 156, 157–160
Miraikan (National Museum of Emerging Science and Innovation): 60
Miyagi Prefecture: 499–507
Miyajima: 21, 34, 415–419; maps 401, 416
Miyajima Ropeway: 417
Miyajima Water Fireworks Festival: 418
Miyako Islands: 705–711; map 706
Miyanoshita: 190
Miyazaki Prefecture: 653–660
Moerenuma Park: 549
Momijidani-kōen: 417
Momotarō: 431
money: 778
Monkey Park Iwatayama: 315
Mori Art Museum: 62
Motomachi: 36, 571
Mōtsū-ji: 515
mountains: 722
Mount Dread: *see* Osore-zan
Mount Fuji: 13, 20, 199–206; hiking 200, 203–205; map 201; views 202
Mount Fuji Panoramic Ropeway: 207
Mount Hakodate: 36, 571, 573
Mount Hakone: 190
Mount Kurodake: 38
Mount Misen: 34, 417–418
Mount Moiwa Ropeway: 549
Mount Naka-dake: 644–645
Mount Tanigawa: 186
Museum of the Meiji Restoration: 660, 662
music: 747–748
Music Box Museum: 558
Myōryū-ji (Ninja-dera): 266
Myōshin-ji: 308–309

N

Nagamachi: 264
Nagamahama Beach: 706
Nagano: 234–235
Nagasaki: 22, 39, 624–639; itinerary ideas 600–603; maps 602, 626–627
Nagasaki Atomic Bomb Museum: 624
Nagasaki Kunchi: 634
Nagasaki Museum of History and Culture: 629
Nagasaki National Peace Memorial Hall for the Atomic Bomb Victims: 625
Nagisa Lava Trail and Foot Bath: 663–664
Nagoro Scarecrow Village: 472
Nagoya: 31, 217–227; accommodations 224–226; food 223–224; information/services 226; map 218–219; transportation 226–227
Nagoya-jō: 220, 222
Naha: 23, 40, 689–696; itinerary ideas 679; maps 680–681, 690
Nakameguro: 64
Nakano Broadway: 87
Nakasendo: 228–229
Nakasu Island: 39, 605, 614; map 608–609
Namba: 33, 351, 365
Nansei-shotō: 676
Nanzen-ji: 32, 299, 301
Naoshima: 432–438
Nara: 21, 369–377; itinerary ideas 347; maps 348–349, 370
Nara-kōen: 369
Naramachi: 369
Nara National Museum: 372
Narita Airport: 141, 752
Naruto whirlpools: 469
National Art Center, Tokyo: 63
National Museum of Modern Art (MOMAT): 56
National Museum of Nature and Science: 79–80
Neputa Mura: 529
Nezu-jinja: 80–81

Nezu Museum: 30, 72
Nichigin-dōri: 38, 557–558
nightlife: *see* bars/nightlife
Nihonbashi Bridge: 54
Nihon-ōdōri: 156, 160, 163
nihonshū: 770
Nijō-jō: 32, 304–305
Nikka Whisky Yoichi Distillery: 560
Nikko: 20, 177–185; map 178
Ninna-ji: 308
Niseko: 560–564
Nishibama Beach: 704
Nison-in: 32, 310
Noboribetsu Onsen: 37, 568
Noh: 89, 748–749
Nokonoshima: 612
Nombei Yokochō: 120
Noritake no Mori: 220
Northern Higashiyama: 282; accommodations 334; bars/nightlife 329; crowds, tips for avoiding 303; food 322–323; shopping 317–318; sights 298–304
Northwest Kyoto: 283; crowds, tips for avoiding 308; food 328; sights 305–309
Noto Peninsula: 269
Nozawa Onsen: 235–239
Nozawa Onsen Snow Resort: 236–237
Nuchigafu: 693
nuclear power: 724–725
Nunobiki Herb Gardens and Ropeway: 378–379
NYK Hikawa Maru: 160
Nyūtō Onsen: 36, 524

O

Obon: 26, 780
Ochudo Trail: 204–205
Odaiba Kaihin-kōen: 95
Odawara: 190
Ōdōri-kōen: 38, 545
Ogimachi: 31, 258–259
Ōhara Museum of Art: 427
Ōhori-kōen: 612
Oirase-Keiryū Gorge: 522–523
Okada Museum of Art: 191
Okama Crater Hike: 510–511
Okayama: 428–432
Okinawa-Hontō: 23, 687–701; map 688
Okinawa Prefectural Museum and Art Museum: 691
Okinawa Prefectural Peace Memorial Museum: 697, 699
Okkundo: 410
Ōkōchi Sansō: 32, 311–312
okonomiyaki: 360, 398, 411, 770
Okonomiyaki Lopez: 410
Ōkonotaki waterfall: 40
Oku Iya Nijū Kazura-bashi: 472
Okuno-in: 34
omamori: 318
Omen: 322-323
Omi-chō Market: 262
Omoide Yokochō: 118–119, 120
omotenashi: 28
Omotesandō: 30
Onomichi: 420–426; map 421; maps 422
onsen: 18, 37, 650–651, 767; Beppu 648–649; Daisetsuzan National Park 578–579; Hakone 193–194; Hakuba 242; Iya Valley 473; Minakami 185; Niseko 562; Nozawa Onsen 235–239; Shikotsu-Tōya National Park 568; Shin-Hotaka Onsen 249–250; Shiretoko National Park 590; Tokyo 99; Towada-Hachimantai National Park 523–524; Zaō-san 512
opening hours: 779–780; Tokyo 49
Origami Kaikan: 77, 79
Osaka: 21, 32–33, 351–369; accommodations 366–367; bars/nightlife 363–366; entertainment/events 355–357; food 16, 359–363; information/services 367–368; itinerary ideas 346; maps 348–349, 352, 354; shopping 358–359; sports/recreation 357–358; transportation 368–369
Osaka Aquarium Kaiyūkan: 355
Osaka-jō: 353
Osore-zan: 531–535
Ōsu Kannon: 222–223
otaku: 80–81
Ota Memorial Museum of Art: 72
Otaru: 38, 557–560; itinerary ideas 541–542; map 543
Otaru Beer: 559
Otaru Canal: 557
Otaru City Museum: 38, 557
Otaru Snow Light Path Festival: 558
Ōura Cathedral: 39, 632
Ōwakudani: 193
Ōzu: 484–485
Ōzu-jō: 484

P

pachinko: 225
packing tips: 26, 776–777
Panorama Dai Hiking Trail: 207, 209
parks: Fukuoka 610, 612; Kagoshima 663; Kyoto 315; Matsuyama 479; Miyajima 417; Tokyo 94–96; Yokohama 163
PASMO card: 49, 144, 146, 758
passports/visas: 26, 761
Peace Memorial and Peace Message Lantern Floating Ceremonies: 409
Peace Memorial Museum (Hiroshima): 406, 408
Peace Memorial Park (Hiroshima): 34, 406

Peace Park (Nagasaki): 39, 625, 628
Peiron (Dragon-Boat Races): 633
people of color, travel advice for: 782
Philosopher's Path: 33, 301–302
phrasebook: 785–792
pilgrimages: 17, 390–391, 464, 510–511
planning tips: 20–29, 776–780; Kyoto 283–284; Tokyo 49–50; *see also specific place*
plants/animals: 725–728
Pola Museum of Art: 191, 193
pollution: 724
Ponto-chō: 32, 303
Port of Kobe Earthquake Memorial Park: 380
postal services: 779; Hiroshima 413; Kyoto 336; Tokyo 139–140
pottery: 620–621
pronunciation: 786–787
public transportation: Kyoto 339–340; Osaka 369; Sapporo 556–557; Tokyo 49, 144–147; *see also specific place*
Purikura: 101

R

rafting and canyoning: 186, 188
ramen: 769
Rausu: 39, 587
Rausu-dake Hike: 590
reading, suggested: 793–794
Rebun-dake Hike: 592
Rebun Island: 580
recreation: *see* sports/recreation
red-crowned cranes: 583
regional specialties: 46, 151, 214, 345, 398, 454, 497, 539, 598, 677, 769–770
religion: 741–743
Rinnō-ji: 177, 179
Rishiri-Rebun-Sarobetsu National Park: 591–594
Rishiri-zan Hike: 593
Risshaku-ji: 35
Ritsurin-kōen: 459–460
Roppongi: 47; accommodations 135; bars/nightlife 125–126; entertainment/events 90; food 111–112; map 61; sights 60–63
Roppongi Art Night: 92
Roppongi Hills: 60
Running Man billboard: 353
Rusutsu Resort: 564–565
Ryōan-ji: 32, 307
Ryōgoku: *see* Asakusa and Ryōgoku
ryokan: 15, 28, 771–772
Ryūkyūan people: 741
Ryūkyū-shotō: 676

S

safety: *see* health/safety
Saga Prefecture: 620–621
Saihō-ji: 312
Sakaemachi Arcade: 694
sake: 125, 770
Sakurai Japanese Tea Experience: 117–118
Sakurajima: 40, 663
sand baths: 669
Sanja Matsuri: 92, 762
Sanjūsangen-dō: 295
Sanmachi Suji: 31, 251–252
Sannomiya: 377
Sanriku Coast: 518–519
Sapporo: 22, 37–38, 545–557; accommodations 554–555; bars/nightlife 553–554; festivals 549–550; food 550–553; information/services 555; itinerary ideas 541–542; maps 543, 546; transportation 555–557
Sapporo Beer Garden and Museum: 549
Sapporo Olympic Museum: 547, 549
Sapporo Snow Festival: 549–550, 764
Sapporo Teine: 564–565
Sapporo TV Tower: 546–547
Saraku Sand-Bath Hall: 669
seasons: 23–26
sea turtles: 683
Seirensho Art Museum: 441–442
Sendai: 35, 499–504; map 500
Sendai City Museum: 500–501
Sengan-en: 40, 662
Sengūkan: 389–390
senior travelers: 782
Sennyū-ji: 294
Sensō-ji: 31, 83
shabu-shabu: 770
Shelter: 130
Shibuya: 31, 48; accommodations 136; bars/nightlife 128–130; food 113–117; map 68–69; shopping 101–102; sights 66–70; sports/recreation 95
Shibuya Crossing: 66–67
Shibuya Sky: 31, 67, 70
Shiga Kōgen: 236
Shikairō: 637
Shikoku Mura: 460
Shikotsu-Tōya National Park: 564–569
Shima: 267
Shimabara: 634–635
Shimanami Kaidō: 424–425; map 421
Shimane Museum of Ancient Izumo: 449
Shimokitazawa: 31, 66, 124
Shingen: 550

Shin-Hotaka Onsen: 249–251; map 245
Shin-Hotaka Ropeway: 250
Shinjuku: 31, 48; accommodations 136–137; bars/nightlife 12, 131–134; food 118–119; map 74–75; shopping 104–105; sights 72, 76–77; sports/recreation 99
Shinjuku Gyōen: 76
Shinjuku Ni-chōme: 124
shinkansen: 29, 757
Shin-kyo (Sacred Bridge): 177
Shinnyo-dō: 303
Shinsaibashi: 33, 351, 364
Shin-Sekai: 365
Shinto: 742
Shiraishi-jima: 433, 443
Shirakawa-gō: 16, 31, 258–259
Shiratani Unsuikyō Gorge: 685
Shiretoko Goko Lakes Hike: 589–590
Shiretoko Hike: 592–593
Shiretoko National Park: 39, 587–591
Shirouma-dake: 241–242
Shiroyama Park: 663
Shirubee: 113, 115
shōchū: 664
Shōdo-shima: 433, 443
Shofuku-ji: 606
shōjin-ryōri: 320
Shoko Shuseikan: 40, 662–663
shopping: Kyoto 317–320; Osaka 358–359; Tokyo 99–108; *see also specific place*
Shōren-in: 296–297
Shōrō-nagashi (Spirit-Boat Procession): 634, 763–764
Showamura: 694
shrines: *see* temples/shrines
Shukkei-en: 409
shukubo (temple stay): 773
Shuni-e: 374
Shuri Horikawa: 693
Shuri-jō: 21, 689, 691
Shuri Ryusen: 692
skiing: Hokkaido 564–565; Minakami 188; Nagano Prefecture 236–237; Niseko 18, 561–562; Towada-Hachimantai National Park 523; Zaō-san 512
smoking: 775
snorkeling: *see* diving/snorkeling
soba: 769
soccer: 765
Sōfuku-ji: 39, 629–630
Sone: 382–383
Sōun-zan: 191
Southeast Kyoto: 276, 278; food 321; sights 290–294
Southern Higashiyama: 278; accommodations 332; bars/nightlife 329; sights 294–297
souvenirs: 101, 106, 318
sports/recreation: 765–767; Kyoto 315–317; Minakami 185–188; Osaka 357–358; Tokyo 94–99; *see also specific place*
stand-up paddling: 692
Steak Aoyama: 382
street food: Fukuoka 614; Osaka 16, 345, 360; Tokyo 113, 118–119, 120–121, 123
Subashiri Trail: 204
subway: Kyoto 339; Tokyo 43, 46–47, 146–147; *see also specific place*
Suganuma: 31, 258–259
Sugatami-daira hike: 578
Suica card: 49, 146, 758
sukiyaki: 770
Sumidagawa Fireworks: 92
sumo: 96–97, 765
Sunayama Beach: 705
Sunset Beach: 712
Suntory Museum of Art: 62–63
Suntory Yamazaki Distillery: 330
surfing: 658–659
Sushiya Kōdai: 559
Susukino: 38, 545, 553
Suwa-jinja: 629

T

Taiyūinbyō Temple: 181–182
Takachiho: 653–657
Takachiho Gorge: 655–656
Takachiho Shrine: 653, 655
Takamatsu: 458–463
Takanawa Gateway: 21
Takayama: 21, 31, 251–260; map 252
Takayama Jinya: 253
Takayama Matsuri: 253, 762
Takayama Shōwa Museum: 252–253
Takenaka Carpentry Tools Museum: 379
Taketomi-jima: 715, 717
Takigi Noh Matsuri: 231
takoyaki: 360
Tamamo-kōen: 458–459
Tanabata Matsuri: 501, 763
Tanigawa-dake Ropeway: 186
Tarumae-zan Hike: 567
tattoos: 159
taxis: 29; Kyoto 341; Tokyo 147; *see also specific place*
tea: 326–327, 770
temples/shrines: 11, 33, 774–775; *see also specific place; specific temple/shrine*

Temple Walk: 420, 422
Tempura Tsunahachi: 119
Tenen Hiking Course: 173
Tenjin Matsuri: 357, 763
Tennō-ji: 365
Tenryū-ji: 32, 309–311
Teramachi: 39, 266
Teshima: 438–441
Teshima Art Museum: 439
Teshima Yokoo House: 439
theater: 89, 748–749; Kanazawa 267; Kyoto 313; Tokyo 87–90
theme parks: 98–99
Tōchō-ji: 39, 606, 610
Tōdai-ji: 21, 372–373
Tōfuku-ji: 294
Tō-ji: 289–290
Tōji-in: 308
Tōkasan Yukata Festival: 409
Tokugawa Art Museum: 222
Tokushima: 463–469
Tokyo: 20, 30–31, 41–147; accommodations 47, 134–138; bars/nightlife 123–134; entertainment/events 87–94; food 46, 108–123; information/services 139–141; itinerary ideas 50–54; maps 42, 44–45, 52–53, 58–59, 61, 65, 68–69, 71, 74–75, 78, 82, 86; planning tips 49–50; shopping 99–108; sports/recreation 94–99; transportation 141–147
Tokyo Bay Area: 47; bars/nightlife 125; food 111; sights 56–60; sports/recreation 95
Tokyo City View and Sky Deck: 61
Tokyo Jazz Festival: 94, 764
Tokyo Metropolitan Government Building: 72, 76
Tokyo Metropolitan Teien Art Museum: 64
Tokyo Midtown: 60
Tokyo National Museum: 31, 79
Tokyo Photographic Art Museum: 64
Tokyo Rainbow Pride: 91
Tokyo Skytree: 83–84
Tokyo Station: 54
Tokyo Towe:r 63
tonkatsu: 769
Tōno: 517–520
Toriden Hakata Honten: 617
Tōshōdai-ji: 374
Tōshō-gū: 179, 181
Tōsuirō: 325
Tottori Sand Dunes: 451
tourism: 739
tours: 782–783; Kyoto 329; Osaka 360; Takayama 253, 254; Tokyo 96–97, 108, 124
Towada-Hachimantai National Park: 520–526
Towada-ko: 521
Tōya-ko: 37
Toyosu Market: 57
Toyota Commemorative Museum of Industry and Technology: 220
train travel: 29, 756–758; Kyoto 337, 339; Osaka 368; Tokyo 143, 144–146; *see also* shinkansen; *specific place*
transportation: 29, 752–761; Kyoto 337–341; Osaka 368–369; Tokyo 141–147; *see also specific place*
trees: 725
Triangle Park: 364
Tsuboya Pottery Street: 692
Tsugaike Nature Park: 239, 241
Tsukasa: 615
Tsukiji Outer Market: 57
Tsumago: 228–229
tsunami, 2011: 504
Tsurugaoka Hachiman-gū: 169
Tsurugi-san: 472–473
Tsūten-kaku: 353, 355
21st-Century Museum of Contemporary Art, Kanazawa: 264
26 Martyrs Memorial (and Museum): 629

UV

Uchiko: 483–484
Uchiko-za: 483
Udo-jingū: 658
udon: 769
Ueno: *see* Akihabara and Ueno
Ueno-kōen: 95
Uji: 326–327
ukiyo-e (woodblock prints): 747
Umeda Sky Building: 351, 353
Unicorn Gundam Statue: 57
Unzen-dake: 634
Usu-zan Ropeway: 567
Usu-zan West Craters: 567
vaccinations: 754–755, 761
visas: *see* passports/visas
volcanoes: 722
Volcano Science Museum: 37, 565, 567

W

wabi-sabi: 746
Wakakusayama Yamayaki: 374
water sports: 719
weather: 724; *see also* seasons
Western Tokyo: 48; food 122–123; sights 84–87
whale-watching: 702
whisky: 12, 127, 330, 560
white water rafting: 473
winter sports: *see* skiing
women travelers: 781
World War II: 735

Y

Yaeyama Islands: 711–720
yakiniku: 770
yakitori: 769
Yakushi-ji: 373–374
Yakushima: 23, 40, 682–687
Yakusugi Land: 40, 684
Yakusugi Museum: 682
Yamadera: 17, 35, 507–508
Yamagata Prefecture: 507–513
Yamashita-kōen: 163
Yamate: 156, 162
Yasaka-jinja: 297
Yasukuni-jinja: 56
Yayoi Kusama Museum: 76–77
Yokohama: 20, 156–167; bars/nightlife 164–165; itinerary ideas 153; maps 155, 158
Yokohama Archives of History: 160
Yokohama Bay Brewing Kannai: 165
Yokohama Cosmoworld: 157, 159
Yokohama Foreign General Cemetery: 162
Yokohama Jazz Promenade: 162–163
Yokohama Museum of Art: 157
Yokohama Port Museum and Nippon Maru: 157
Yokohama Tattoo Museum: 159
Yonaguni-jima: 717
Yonaha Maehama Beach: 705–706
Yonehara Beach: 712
Yorozu: 617
Yosakoi Odori Matsuri: 489–490, 763
Yoshida-jinja: 303
Yoshida Trail: 203–204
Yoshiki-en: 373
Yoyogi-kōen: 95
Yufuin: 650–651
Yuigahama Beach: 173
Yūnangī: 694
Yunohira Lookout: 663

Z

Zainichi community: 740
Zamami Burger: 703
Zamami-jima: 40, 701–703
Zaō Onsen Ski Resort: 512
Zaō Ropeway: 508, 510
Zaō-san: 508–513
Zenkō-ji: 234–235
Zuigan-ji: 35, 505–506
Zuihōden: 501

List of Maps

Front Map
Japan: 2-3

Discover Japan
chapter divisions map: 20

Tokyo
Tokyo: 44–45
Itinerary Ideas: 52–53
Ginza and Marunouchi: 58–59
Roppongi and Around: 61
Ebisu and Around: 65
Shibuya and Around: 68–69
Harajuku and Aoyama: 71
Shinjuku and Around: 74–75
Akihabara and Ueno: 78
Asakusa and Ryogoku: 82
Kichijōji: 86

Around Tokyo
Around Tokyo: 150
Itinerary Ideas: 154–155
Yokohama: 158
Kamakura: 168
Nikko: 178
Hakone: 190
Mount Fuji and the Five Lakes: 201

Central Honshu
Central Honshu: 216
Nagoya: 218–219
Hakuba: 240
Kamikōchi and Shin-Hotaka Onsen: 245
Takayama: 252
Kanazawa: 261

Kyoto
Kyoto Area: 279
Kyoto: 280–281
Itinerary Ideas: 286–287
Kyoto Station Area: 290
Gion and Downtown and Central Kyoto: 292–293

Kansai
Kansai: 344
Osaka and Nara Itinerary Ideas: 348–349
Himeji and Kobe Itinerary Ideas: 350
Osaka: 352
Minami: 354
Nara: 370
Kobe: 378

Western Honshu
Western Honshu: 396–397
Hiroshima Itinerary Ideas: 400
Miyajima Itinerary Ideas: 401
Hiroshima: 404–405
Miyajima: 416
Onomichi and the Shimanami Kaidō: 421
Onomichi: 422

Shikoku
Shikoku: 456–457
Matsuyama: 477
Kochi: 488

Tohoku
Tohoku: 496
Sendai: 500

Hokkaido
Hokkaido: 538
Sapporo and Otaru Itinerary Ideas: 543
One Day in Hakodate: 544
Sapporo: 546
Hakodate: 570

Kyushu
Kyushu: 597
One Day in Fukuoka: 601
One Day in Nagasaki: 602
One Day in Kagoshima: 604
Fukuoka: 606
Hakata, Nakasu, and Tenjin: 608–609
Nagasaki: 626–627
Kagoshima: 661

Okinawa and the Southwest Islands
Okinawa and the Southwest Islands: 674–675
Itinerary Ideas: 680–681
Okinawa-Hontō: 688
Naha: 690
Miyako-jima: 706

Photo Credits

All images © Jonathan DeHart except: title page photo: JNTO; page 5 © bady abbas | Unsplash.com; page 6 © (top left) Samuel Berner | Unsplash.com; (top right) courtesy Hakone Yuryo Onsen; (bottom) Alisali | Dreamstime.com; page 7 © (top) Kirsty Bouwers; (bottom left) Imron Muhammad | Dreamstime.com; (bottom right) Sepavo | Dreamstime.com; page 8 © JNTO; page 9 © (top) Roméo A. | Unsplash.com; (bottom left) Cowardlion | Dreamstime.com; page 10-11 © Bennymarty | Dreamstime.com; page 12 © (bottom) Shirota Yuri | Unsplash.com; page 13 © Karn2608 | Dreamstime.com; page 14 © Kyoto Convention & Visitors Bureau (KCVB); page 15 © JNTO; page 16 © (top) Apichartthan | Dreamstime.com; (middle) Sepavo | Dreamstime.com; (bottom) Kaori Chin | Unsplash.com; page 17 © (top) Sepavo | Dreamstime.com; page 18 © (top) JNTO; (bottom) Videowokart | Dreamstime.com; page 19 © Photos7384 | Dreamstime.com; page 22 © (top) Dominiquebonnet | Dreamstime.com; page 23 © (left) KCVB; (right)Tohoku Tourism; page 27 © Blanscape | Dreamstime.com; page 28 © JNTO; page 30 © (right) Ryoji Iwata | Unsplash.com; page 32 © (right) KCVB; page 34 © (right) Smithore | Dreamstime.com; page 36 © (left) Leung Cho Pan | Dreamstime.com; page 37 © JNTO; page 38 © (left) Niels Vos | Dreamstime.com; (right) Andreas Zeitler | Dreamstime.com; page 41 © Sepavo | Dreamstime.com; page 42 © (top left) Sepavo | Dreamstime.com; (top right) Daboost | Dreamstime.com; page 55 © Blanscape | Dreamstime.com; page 62 © Bennymarty | Dreamstime.com; page 73 © (top) Niphon Subsri | Dreamstime.com; (bottom) Sanga Park | Dreamstime.com; page 85 © (top) Cowardlion | Dreamstime.com; (left middle) Cowardlion | Dreamstime.com; (right middle) Mosaymay | Dreamstime.com; (bottom) Cowardlion | Dreamstime.com; page 93 © (top left) Erik Lattwein | Dreamstime.com; page 106 © JNTO; page 114 © (top left) Watcharapong Thawornwichian | Dreamstime.com; (bottom right) Sakurai Japanese Tea Experience; page 127 © Eudaemon | Dreamstime.com; page 132 © Nataliya Hora | Dreamstime.com; page 133 © Fukamiyoga | Dreamstime.com; page 137 © Park Hyatt Tokyo; page 148 © JNTO; page 149 © (top left) Electropower | Dreamstime.com; (top right) Kanagawa Prefecture; page 161 © (top) CUPNOODLES MUSEUM; (bottom) JNTO; page 170 © (top) Bennymarty | Dreamstime.com; (left middle) Tupungato | Dreamstime.com; (right middle) Sergio Torres Baus | Dreamstime.com; (bottom) Giemgiem | Dreamstime.com; page 180 © (top) JNTO; (left middle) Maria Vazquez | Dreamstime.com; (right middle) Cowardlion | Dreamstime.com; (bottom) Pablo Hidalgo | Dreamstime.com; page 187 © (top) Gypsygraphy | Dreamstime.com; (bottom) Navapon Plodprong | Dreamstime.com; page 192 © (top left) Milezaway | Dreamstime.com; (top right) Retina2020 | Dreamstime.com; (bottom) courtesy Hakone Open Air Museum; page 196 (top) courtesy Hakone Yuryo Onsen;(left middle) courtesy Hakone Yuryo Onsen; (right middle) courtesy Hakone Yuryo Onsen; (bottom) courtesy Hakone Yuryo Onsen; page 202 © Luciano Mortula | Dreamstime.com; page 204 © Nattama Dechangamjamras | Dreamstime.com; page 208 © (top) Worldwidestock | Dreamstime.com; (bottom) Phurinee Chinakathum | Dreamstime.com; page 213 © (top right) Anujak Jaimook | Dreamstime.com; page 221 © (top left) Khuntapol | Dreamstime.com; (top right) Vodickap | Dreamstime.com; (bottom) Cowardlion | Dreamstime.com; page 229 © Ollerana | Dreamstime.com; page 230 © Umarin Nakamura | Dreamstime.com; page 237 © Umarin Nakamura | Dreamstime.com; page 241 © Navapon Plodprong | Dreamstime.com; page 247 © (top) Hgl428 | Dreamstime.com; (bottom) Tobyhoward | Dreamstime.com; page 254 © (top left) Nuvisage | Dreamstime.com; (top right) Katinka2014 | Dreamstime.com; (bottom) Katinka2014 | Dreamstime.com; page 258 © Phurinee Chinakathum | Dreamstime.com; page 263 © (top right) Pipa100 | Dreamstime.com; page 265 © JNTO; page 269 © Juite Wen | Dreamstime.com; page 274 © Pablo Fierro | Unsplash.com; page 275 © (top left) Joymsk | Dreamstime.com; (top right) Finallast | Dreamstime.com; page 277 © KCVB; page 291 © (top) David Evison | Dreamstime.com; (bottom) Noppakun | Dreamstime.com; page 295 © KCVB; page 299 © KCVB; page 300 © (top) KCVB; (right middle) Cebas1 | Dreamstime.com; (bottom) Sepavo | Dreamstime.com; page 303 © Seaonweb | Dreamstime.com; page 306 © (top left) Sergio Torres Baus |

Dreamstime.com; (top right) Rolf52 | Dreamstime.com; (bottom) Umarin Nakamura | Dreamstime.com; page 311 © Nicholashan | Dreamstime.com; page 314 © Kuruneko | Dreamstime.com; page 319 © KCVB; page 327 © KCVB; page 330 courtesy Beam Suntory; page 343 © (top right) Cowardlion | Dreamstime.com; page 356 © (top) Tapiocatong | Dreamstime.com; (left middle) JNTO; (right middle) Cowardlion | Dreamstime.com; (bottom) Edmond Leung | Dreamstime.com; page 360 © Mroz | Dreamstime.com; page 362 © (bottom right) Juliana Barquero | Unsplash.com; page 371 © (top) Dreamstime Agency | Dreamstime.com; (bottom) Vadim Lerner | Dreamstime.com; page 381 © Sepavo | Dreamstime.com; page 386 © (top left) JNTO; (bottom right) Cowardlion | Dreamstime.com; page 391 © JNTO; page 393 © JNTO; page 394 © (top left) Mikekwok | Dreamstime.com; page 403 © (top) Sepavo | Dreamstime.com; (bottom) Audrey Foo; page 407 © (top left) F11photo | Dreamstime.com; (top right) Cowardlion | Dreamstime.com; (bottom left) Jlobo211 | Dreamstime.com; (bottom right) Pipa100 | Dreamstime.com; page 417 © Phuongphoto | Dreamstime.com; page 425 © JNTO; page 434 © (top) Tadasu Yamamoto, courtesy Benesse Art Museum; (left middle)(right middle) Ken'ichi Suzuki, courtesy Benesse Art Museum; (bottom) CHUN-CHANG WU | Dreamstime.com; page 439 © Christophorushasto | Dreamstime.com; page 446 © (top) Sepavo | Dreamstime.com; (bottom) Gnohz | Dreamstime.com; page 451 © Kazutakadream | Dreamstime.com; page 453 © (top left) Aagje De Jong | Dreamstime.com; page 459 © JNTO; page 471 © (top) Contrail1 | Dreamstime.com; (left middle) JNTO; (right middle) JNTO; (bottom) JNTO; page 478 © Sepavo | Dreamstime.com; page 489 © Katinka2014 | Dreamstime.com; page 491 © (top) Mrnovel | Dreamstime.com; (left middle) JNTO; (right middle) JNTO; page 495 © (top right) Feng570423 | Dreamstime.com; page 501 © Phillip Maguire | Dreamstime.com; page 505 © Leung Cho Pan | Dreamstime.com; page 509 © (right middle) JNTO; page 511 © Tohoku Tourism; page 525 © (top) Tohoku Tourism; (left middle) Anucha Pongpatimeth | Dreamstime.com; (right middle) Tohoku Tourism; (bottom) Ssizzcraft | Dreamstime.com; page 527 © Tohoku Tourism; page 530 © Piti Sirisriro | Dreamstime.com; page 534 © Motive56 | Dreamstime.com; page 536 © HokkaidoWilds.org; page 537 © (top right) Rangsiroj Akrachaka | Dreamstime.com; page 548 © (top left) Artitwpd | Dreamstime.com; (top right) Keechuan | Dreamstime.com; (bottom) Simone Matteo Giuseppe Manzoni | Dreamstime.com; page 552 © (bottom) Sepavo | Dreamstime.com; page 555 © Cross Hotel Sapporo; page 561 © Chung Jin Mac | Dreamstime.com; page 566 © (top left) Hokkaido Wilds; (top right) JNTO; (bottom) Sepavo | Dreamstime.com; page 572 © (top left) Sepavo | Dreamstime.com; (top right) Niradj | Dreamstime.com; (bottom) Blanscape | Dreamstime.com; page 577 © (top) Jens Tobiska | Dreamstime.com; (bottom) Hokkaido Wilds / Rob Thomson; page 581 © Wangyining | Dreamstime.com; page 583 © Andreas Zeitler | Dreamstime.com; page 586 © Nuvisage | Dreamstime.com; page 588 © Kaedeenari | Dreamstime.com; page 592 © FaerOut | Dreamstime.com; page 595 © JNTO; page 596 © (top left) JNTO; (top right) ColBase, colbase.nich.go.jp; page 603 © Sepavo | Dreamstime.com; page 607 © (top) Ixuskmitl | Dreamstime.com; (bottom) Raúl Rodríguez Arias | Dreamstime.com; page 611 © (top) Ixuskmitl | Dreamstime.com; (bottom) Julia Burlachenko | Dreamstime.com; page 614 © Bestforlater91 | Dreamstime.com; page 616 © (top left) Kirsty Bouwers; (top right) Audrey Foo; (bottom) Bankoo | Dreamstime.com; page 621 courtesy Kakiemon; page 622 © Cowardlion | Dreamstime.com; page 625 © Thitichot Katawutpoonpun | Dreamstime.com; page 631 © (top left) Motive56 | Dreamstime.com; (top right) Galinasavina | Dreamstime.com; (bottom) Sanga Park | Dreamstime.com; page 640 © Sepavo | Dreamstime.com; page 644 © JNTO; page 647 © Pipa100 | Dreamstime.com; page 651 © JNTO; page 654 © (top) Chun Kit Ho | Dreamstime.com; (bottom) JNTO; page 662 © Victormwli | Dreamstime.com; page 669 © Jefwod | Dreamstime.com; page 672 © Hiroko Yoshii | Unsplash.com; page 673 © (top left) Harismoyo | Dreamstime.com; (top right) Eyeblink | Dreamstime.com; page 684 © Violetyellow | Dreamstime.com; page 698 © (top) Kuzmire | Dreamstime.com; (bottom) erik | Unsplash.com; page 702 © Photos7384 | Dreamstime.com; page 713 © (top) Vladimir Haltakov | Unsplash.com; (bottom) Hiroko Yoshii | Unsplash.com; page 716 © (top right) Nuvisage | Dreamstime.com; page 718 © Hiroko Yoshii | Unsplash.com; page 721 © Crisfotolux | Dreamstime.com; page 752 © KCVB

Caribbean

Europe, Middle East & Africa

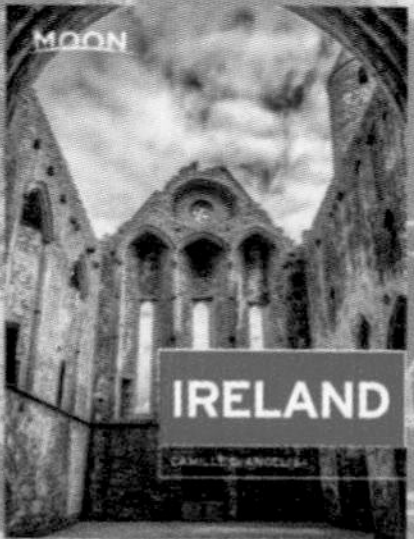

Craft a personalized journey through the top national parks in the U.S. and Canada with Moon Travel Guides.

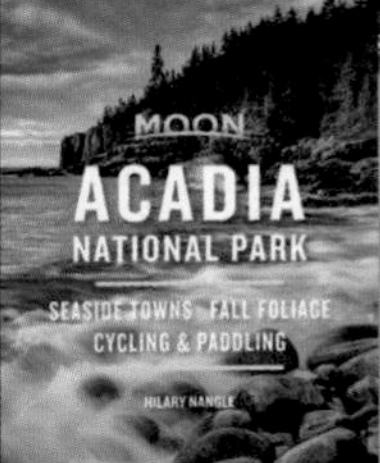
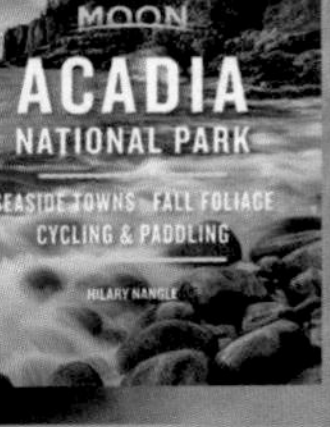

MAP SYMBOLS

- Expressway
- Primary Road
- Secondary Road
- Unpaved Road
- Trail
- Ferry
- Railroad
- Pedestrian Walkway
- Stairs
- City/Town
- State Capital
- National Capital
- Highlight
- Point of Interest
- Accommodation
- Restaurant/Bar
- Other Location
- Information Center
- Parking Area
- Church
- Winery/Vineyard
- Trailhead
- Train Station
- Airport
- Airfield
- Park
- Golf Course
- Unique Feature
- Waterfall
- Camping
- Mountain
- Ski Area
- Glacier

CONVERSION TABLES

°C = (°F - 32) / 1.8
°F = (°C x 1.8) + 32
1 inch = 2.54 centimeters (cm)
1 foot = 0.304 meters (m)
1 yard = 0.914 meters
1 mile = 1.6093 kilometers (km)
1 km = 0.6214 miles
1 fathom = 1.8288 m
1 chain = 20.1168 m
1 furlong = 201.168 m
1 acre = 0.4047 hectares
1 sq km = 100 hectares
1 sq mile = 2.59 square km
1 ounce = 28.35 grams
1 pound = 0.4536 kilograms
1 short ton = 0.90718 metric ton
1 short ton = 2,000 pounds
1 long ton = 1.016 metric tons
1 long ton = 2,240 pounds
1 metric ton = 1,000 kilograms
1 quart = 0.94635 liters
1 US gallon = 3.7854 liters
1 Imperial gallon = 4.5459 liters
1 nautical mile = 1.852 km

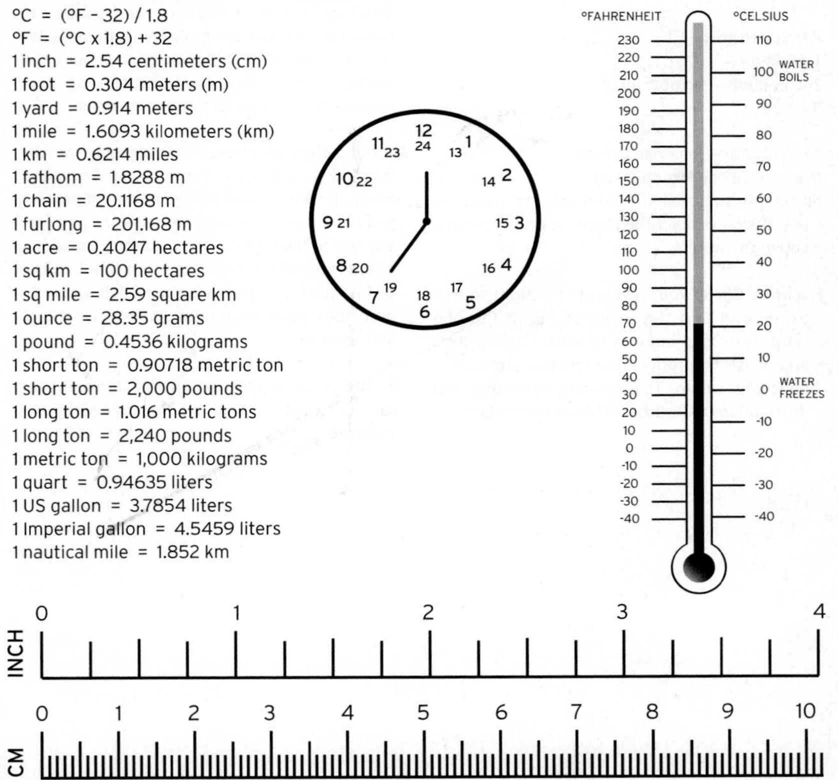

MOON JAPAN
Avalon Travel
Hachette Book Group
1700 Fourth Street
Berkeley, CA 94710, USA
www.moon.com

Editor: Megan Anderluh
Managing Editor: Hannah Brezack
Copy Editor: Jessica Gould
Graphics Coordinator: Ravina Schneider
Production Coordinator: Ravina Schneider
Cover Design: Toni Tajima
Interior Design: Domini Dragoone
Map Editor: Albert Angulo
Cartographers: Mark Stroud - Moon Street Cartography (Durango, Co), Karin Dahl, and Albert Angulo
Proofreader: Lina Carmona

ISBN-13: 978-1-64049-645-3

Printing History
1st Edition — 2020
2nd Edition — October 2022
5 4 3 2 1

Front cover photo: Yamadera Temple. © Biosphoto | Alamy.com
Back cover photo: Kenroku-en garden. © Jonathan DeHart

Printed in Malaysia for Imago.